THE BAKER
ILLUSTRATED
BIBLE
HANDBOOK

THE BAKER
ILLUSTRATED
BIBLE
HANDBOOK

Edited by

J. Daniel Hays and J. Scott Duvall

BakerBooks

a division of Baker Publishing Group
Grand Rapids, Michigan

© 2011 by J. Daniel Hays and J. Scott Duvall

Published by Baker Books
a division of Baker Publishing Group
P.O. Box 6287, Grand Rapids, MI 49516-6287
www.bakerbooks.com

Printed in the United States of America

Library of Congress Cataloging-in-Publication Data

The Baker illustrated Bible handbook / edited by J. Daniel Hays and J. Scott Duvall.
   p. cm.
Includes bibliographical references.
ISBN 978-0-8010-1296-9 (cloth)
   1. Bible—Handbooks, manuals, etc. I. Hays, J. Daniel, 1953– II. Duvall, J. Scott. III. Title: Illustrated Bible handbook.
BS417.B34 2011
220.6′1—dc22   2011005211

11   12   13   14   15   16   17   7   6   5   4   3   2   1

Interior design by Brian Brunsting

We dedicate this book to our parents,
Jim and Carolyn Hays,
Bob Duvall, and Peggy Duvall Scheler,
who first taught us to love and listen to God's Word.
We will always be deeply grateful
for your godly influence on our lives.

Contents

Acknowledgments

First of all, we wish to thank Jack Kuhatschek at Baker for his friendship and for entrusting us with this project. Likewise we are grateful to Brian Vos, Robert Hand, and Brian Brunsting, the talented and hard-working editorial and layout team at Baker that worked in close partnership with us to produce this book. In addition, kudos to Cheryl Van Andel for the great cover design. We also thank our many friends and colleagues in seminaries and universities around the world who contributed articles. They represent the very best of biblical scholarship in the world today. Jim Martin and John Walton assisted us with the pictures; we are most appreciative. Several Ouachita Baptist University students helped us by proofreading early drafts and organizing pictures. Thus we want to thank Reneé Adams, Leasha May, and Darlene Seal for their hard work. Finally we want to thank our wives, Donna Hays and Judy Duvall, for their input, encouragement, and loving patience.

Contributors

Dr. Richard Schultz (Wheaton College): *The Servant Songs of Isaiah*

Dr. Boyd Seevers (Northwestern College): *Old Testament Fortifications*

Dr. Joe M. Sprinkle (Crossroads College): *Hittite Treaties and the Structure of Deuteronomy*

Dr. W. Dennis Tucker Jr. (George W. Truett Theological Seminary): *Music in the Old Testament*

Dr. John H. Walton (Wheaton College): *Other Flood Accounts in the Ancient Near East*

New Testament Contributors

Dr. Kenneth A. Berding (Talbot School of Theology): *Spiritual Gifts*

Dr. Darrell L. Bock (Dallas Theological Seminary): *The Resurrection of Jesus; Jesus's Postresurrection Appearances*

Dr. Jeannine K. Brown (Bethel Seminary): *The Strong and the Weak; Contextualizing the Message*

Dr. David B. Capes (Houston Baptist University): *Paul's Co-workers; Honor and Shame; Early Christian Hymns*

Dr. Robbie Fox Castleman (John Brown University): *The City of Corinth; Women in Ancient Corinth*

Dr. Jeff Cate (California Baptist University): *The Synagogue; Slavery in the New Testament*

Dr. Lynn H. Cohick (Wheaton College): *Roman Citizenship; The City of Rome*

Dr. Bruce Corley (B. H. Carroll Theological Institute): *The Trial(s) of Jesus*

Dr. Joseph R. Dodson (Ouachita Baptist University): *Discipleship in the New Testament; Jesus the Teacher; Teachers of the Law (Scribes); Christ (Messiah); Pharisees in the New Testament; Roman Soldiers*

Dr. George H. Guthrie (Union University): *Triumphal Procession; God's Power in Weakness; Warning Passages in Hebrews; The Jewish High Priest*

Dr. Justin K. Hardin (Wycliffe Hall, Oxford University): *The Sign of Circumcision*

Dr. Larry R. Helyer (Taylor University): *The House of Herod; The Sanhedrin*

Dr. Douglas S. Huffman (Talbot School of Theology): *Martyrdom in the New Testament; Persecution in the Early Church*

Dr. Paul Jackson (Union University): *The Destruction of Jerusalem in AD 70; The Jerusalem Council*

Dr. Scott Jackson (Ouachita Baptist University): *Luke's Use of Koinonia; The House Church*

Dr. Karen H. Jobes (Wheaton College): *Household Codes*

Dr. Craig S. Keener (Palmer Theological Seminary): *Jewish Marriage and Wedding Customs; The Holy Spirit in the New Testament*

Dr. Bobby Kelly (Oklahoma Baptist University): *The Family of Jesus; Women Followers of Jesus*

Dr. William W. Klein (Denver Seminary): *Stoicheia (Elements) in the New Testament; Angels and Demons*

Dr. Jonathan M. Lunde (Talbot School of Theology): *Herod's Temple; The Samaritans*

Dr. Thomas H. McCall (Trinity Evangelical Divinity School): *Deity and Humanity of Christ*

Dr. Grant R. Osborne (Trinity Evangelical Divinity School): *The Setting for the New Testament*

Dr. C. Marvin Pate (Ouachita Baptist University): *The Relationship between Israel and the Church*

Dr. Nicholas Perrin (Wheaton College): *Eternal Life; Jerusalem in the Time of Jesus*

Dr. Brian M. Rapske (Northwest Baptist Seminary): *Roman Prisons; Shipping in the Ancient World*

Dr. Rodney Reeves (Southwest Baptist University): *Son of Man; Jesus the Servant*

Dr. E. Randolph Richards (Palm Beach Atlantic University): *Roman Names; Paul the Letter Writer; Jerusalem Offering*

Dr. Mark A. Seifrid (The Southern Baptist Theological Seminary): *Justification by Faith; Law and Grace in Paul's Letters*

Dr. Todd Still (George W. Truett Theological Seminary): *The Restrainer?; Work and the Thessalonian Christians*

Dr. Mark L. Strauss (Bethel Seminary): *An Overview of the Life of Christ; What Is a Gospel? And Why Are There Four Gospels?; The Twelve Disciples of Jesus; Jewish Sabbath Observances*

Dr. Preben Vang (Palm Beach Atlantic University): *John the Baptist; The Virgin Birth; Jesus and the Kingdom of God; Incarnation; Pentecost*

Dr. Ray Van Neste (Union University): *False Teachers; Church Leaders*

Dr. Joel Williams (Columbia International University): *God as Light and Love; Hospitality*

Dr. Matthew C. Williams (Talbot School of Theology): *The Synoptic Problem; Seven Signs in John's Gospel; "I Am" Sayings of Jesus; Mary, Martha, and Lazarus*

Dr. Dan Wilson (California Baptist University): *The Crucifixion of Jesus*

Dr. Mark W. Wilson (Asia Minor Research Center): *The Cult of Artemis; The City of Ephesus; Numbers in Revelation; The Imperial Cult*

Part II: How the Bible Came to Be

Dr. Stephen Dempster (Atlantic Baptist University): *The Production and Shaping of the Old Testament Canon*

Dr. Bryan Harmelink (SIL International): *Translations for the World*

Dr. Karen H. Jobes (Wheaton College): *The Septuagint*

Dr. C. Marvin Pate (Ouachita Baptist University): *The Dead Sea Scrolls*

Dr. M. James Sawyer (Western Seminary): *The Canon of the New Testament*

Dr. Mark L. Strauss (Bethel Seminary): *The Inspiration of the Bible*

Dr. Daniel B. Wallace (Dallas Theological Seminary): *Writing, Copying, and Transmitting the New Testament Text*

Part III: Digging Deeper into the Bible

Dr. Darrell L. Bock (Dallas Theological Seminary): *Responding to Contemporary Challenges to the Gospels*

Dr. Gary Manning (Pacific Rim Christian College): *The Use of the Old Testament in the New Testament*

Dr. Steven M. Ortiz (Southwestern Baptist Theological Seminary): *Archaeology and the Bible*

Dr. D. Brent Sandy (Grace College): *Literary Features in the Bible*

Meet the Primary Authors and Editors

of The Baker Illustrated Bible Handbook

Dr. J. Daniel Hays is a professor of Old Testament at Ouachita Baptist University. In Part I Danny wrote all the articles on the individual Old Testament books of the Bible. Also, within the Old Testament section, he wrote the short articles that are not attributed to one of our contributors. In Part III he wrote *The Unity and Diversity of the Bible; How to Interpret and Apply the Old Testament Law; How to Interpret and Enjoy Figures of Speech;* and *Are There Hidden Codes in the Bible?*

Dr. J. Scott Duvall is a professor of New Testament at Ouachita Baptist University. Scott is the author of the introductory articles *The Grand Story of the Bible; How Is the Bible Organized?;* and *The Beginning and the End.* He also wrote all the articles on the individual New Testament books in Part I, as well as articles in the New Testament section that are not attributed to other contributors. In Part II he wrote *Bible Translations and the English Bible,* and in Part III he wrote *How to Read, Interpret, and Apply the Bible* and *How to Interpret Parables.*

A word from the authors (Danny and Scott) to the reader: One of the great passions of our lives is teaching the Word of God to people who hunger to know it. There are few things in this life that are more important than listening to God's Word and following our Lord in obedience! Likewise, there are few things that get us as excited as when we are able to help God's people to grow closer to the Lord through a better grasp of his Word. One of our basic goals for this book was to help people in the church to understand the Bible better. As we wrote each article, we tried to keep a visual picture of you (the reader) in mind, and we endeavored to write as if we were talking to you and teaching you in person. Thus the tone of this book is somewhat informal (especially in Part I). We hope you read it as if we were chatting with you. Along those same lines, one of the things we really enjoy when teaching the Bible is helping our students and readers (you) make connections between the different parts of the Bible. That is, one of our goals is to help you see how the Bible fits together and interconnects. Thus throughout the Old Testament and New Testament sections in Part I we frequently add a note at the bottom of the page (marked with a ✛ symbol) that emphasizes special connections between different passages in the Bible. We hope you enjoy these "connection" notes as you read through the main text. Although our tone is informal, we also want to bring you the very best of biblical scholarship. Thus throughout the book our twofold goal is to present the most up-to-date evangelical biblical scholarship in a manner that is readable and easy to understand, so that God's people in the church can understand the Word of God and apply it to their lives. We pray that you find it helpful.

God's Story

(and Your Story)

The Grand Story
of the Bible

Everyone has a story to live by. Questions we must ask ourselves include, "Which story tells the true story about God, our world, and life?" and "Does my story line up with the true story?" What constitutes a basic story line is much the same in novels, TV shows, movies, and plays. The story opens with things going well. The characters are introduced, and we get essential background information. Everything is good (or at least stable) to start with. Then a problem or crisis arises that threatens the characters and their future. Much of the story is taken up with solving this problem (i.e., conflict resolution). Usually during this period of resolution, there is a climax where the tension builds to a critical point. Here the heart of the problem is solved. Finally (and this may take a while), the resolution is worked out so that things are not just good but great. When there is no happy ending, we call this a tragedy. The phases of a grand story are summarized as follows:

- Opening—setting provided and characters introduced
- Problem—conflict threatens the well-being of the characters
- Resolution—solution to the problem
- Climax within resolution phase—most intense conflict followed by solution to heart of problem
- Closing—resolution worked out for the characters

The Bible claims to be God's story for the whole world. In the Bible we find the one grand story (or metanarrative) that best explains reality. Here is how the Bible breaks down into a grand story:

- Opening—Genesis 1–2
- Problem—Genesis 3–11
- Resolution—Genesis 12–Revelation 18
- Climax within resolution phase—life, death, and resurrection of Jesus Christ
- Closing—Revelation 19–22

To put the grand story of the Bible into a memorable format, consider the outline below that uses "c" sounds:

Creation—The story begins with the creation of the world and human beings.

Crisis—When tempted by Satan, humans choose to satisfy self and rebel (or sin) against God. They do this repeatedly. Sin brings disastrous and deadly consequences: pain, suffering, death, and separation from God.

Covenant—God begins to solve this problem of sin by choosing Abraham and establishing a covenant with him so that he might become the father of a people who will worship God. God wants to make Abraham into a great nation and to give him a land along with many descendants and blessings. Then God wants to bless all the nations of the world through Abraham, and to use this one nation to bring the rest of the world into a relationship with himself.

Calling Out—Genesis tells the story of the patriarchs: Abraham, Isaac, Jacob (Israel), Joseph. Through a series of events they move to Egypt where this small group grows into a nation and experiences slavery. God uses Moses to deliver his people from slavery through the exodus event. God's miraculous deliverance of his people from bondage in Egypt becomes a pattern that foreshadows God's ultimate deliverance of his people from spiritual slavery.

Commandments—After God rescues his people, he enters into a covenant with them (the Mosaic covenant). He gives them the law (summed up in the Ten Commandments) and calls his people to holiness. God's expectations for his covenant people are spelled out in the book of Deuteronomy.

Conquest—God uses Joshua to help his people take the Promised Land (Canaan).

Kingdom—God's people acquire a king. Samuel becomes the link between the judges and the kings of Israel: Saul (the first king), David, Solomon.

Kingdom Divided—After Solomon there is a civil war that leads to the division of the kingdom: Israel = northern kingdom, Judah = southern kingdom. There are many kings, some good but most bad.

Captivity—Because God's people have failed to worship him alone, they face terrible judgments, including the loss of the Promised Land. Their enemies take them captive. Israel is conquered by the Assyrians in 722 BC, while Judah is conquered and taken captive by the Babylonians in about 586 BC.

Coming Home—The people finally return from exile under Ezra and Nehemiah.

Christ (Climax to the Story)—About four hundred years later God sends his Son, Jesus the Christ, to save his people from their sins. Jesus announces the coming of God's kingdom through his teachings and miracles. His death and resurrection forms the climax to the biblical story.

Church—Those who accept Jesus become part of the church—the people of God—comprising both Jews and gentiles. God continues to use his people to extend his offer of salvation to a sinful world.

Consummation—God closes history with a final victory over evil. Those who have rejected God will suffer judgment, while those who have accepted him will live with him in a new heaven and new earth. God's promises are now fulfilled (see Rev. 21:1–4).

Because it is true, the grand story of the Bible provides the best answers to the basic questions of life:*

1. Where are we? What kind of world do we live in? The grand story of Scripture says we are in a world created and sustained by God. There is more to this world than science or technology or progress or our own imaginations.
2. Who are we? What does it mean to be a human being? The Bible says that we are human beings created in God's image for the purpose of being in a loving relationship with God and with other human beings. We are not just autonomous selves in control of our own destiny or multiple selves depending on our environment.
3. What's wrong? What is the essential problem with us and the world? Scripture says that the problem is sin. We have chosen to rebel against

---

* See Brian J. Walsh and J. Richard Middleton, *The Transforming Vision: Shaping a Christian World View* (Downers Grove, IL: InterVarsity, 1984); N. T. Wright, *Jesus and the Victory of God* (Minneapolis: Fortress, 1997); and Craig Bartholomew and Michael Goheen, *The Drama of Scripture: Finding Our Place in the Biblical Story* (Grand Rapids: Baker Academic, 2004).

our Creator, and sin has damaged our relationships. We can't just blame outside circumstances.

4. What's the solution? What can fix the problem? The Bible says that only God can fix the problem. We do need saving and we can't save ourselves, but God has come to our rescue in Jesus Christ, whose life, death, and resurrection provides a way to God.

5. Where are we in the story? Where do we belong and how does the story affect our lives right now? What role do we play in the story? Each of us must answer these questions personally.

As you read and study specific sections of Scripture, keep in mind the larger picture. The Bible is a collection (a minilibrary) of sixty-six books, but it also functions as a single book. The grand story of the Bible answers the basic questions of life better than any other story. It's true. You can count on it. When people come to faith in Christ, they are basically saying, "I want God's story to become my story." That's what conversion is—embracing the grand story of Scripture as our personal story to make sense of life.

How Is the Bible Organized?

The English word "Bible" comes from the Greek word for books or scrolls: *biblia* (plural). In 2 Timothy 4:13, Paul asks Timothy to bring his "books" (*biblia*) when he comes to visit him in prison. Our word "Bible" is singular because it refers to the entire collection of sixty-six books: thirty-nine in the Old Testament and twenty-seven in the New Testament. (Roman Catholic and Eastern Orthodox Bibles contain a few extra books in the Old Testament.)

Pentateuch	Historical Books	Psalms	Wisdom Books	The Prophets
Genesis	Joshua	Psalms	Job	**Major Prophets:**
Exodus	Judges		Proverbs	Isaiah
Leviticus	Ruth		Ecclesiastes	Jeremiah
Numbers	1–2 Samuel		Song of Songs	Lamentations
Deuteronomy	1–2 Kings			Ezekiel
	1–2 Chronicles			Daniel
	Ezra			**Minor Prophets:**
	Nehemiah			Hosea
	Esther			Joel
				Amos
				Obadiah
				Jonah
				Micah
				Nahum
				Habakkuk
				Zephaniah
				Haggai
				Zechariah
				Malachi

Gospels	Acts	Letters of Paul	General Letters	Revelation
Matthew	Acts	Romans	Hebrews	Revelation
Mark		1–2 Corinthians	James	
Luke		Galatians	1–2 Peter	
John		Ephesians	1–3 John	
		Philippians	Jude	
		Colossians		
		1–2 Thessalonians		
		1–2 Timothy		
		Titus		
		Philemon		

The word "testament" comes from the word *testamentum*, the Latin translation of the Hebrew and Greek words for "covenant." The English word "testament" refers to a covenant. Christians accept both the Old Testament and the New Testament, while Jews reject the new covenant that confesses Jesus as the Messiah. In the biblical sense, a covenant refers to what God has done to establish a relationship with human beings. Over time, the term "testament" came to refer to the writings that describe the covenant.

The Old Testament

The Old Testament was originally written in Hebrew (with a small portion in Aramaic), the language used by the Jewish people. The Old Testament is divided into five parts: the Pentateuch, the Historical Books, the Psalms, the Wisdom Books, and the Prophets.

The Pentateuch

The first five books of the Bible (Genesis, Exodus, Leviticus, Numbers, and Deuteronomy) are often referred to as the "Pentateuch" (the "five scrolls" or "five-scroll collection"). In the Hebrew Scriptures, these books are referred to as the "Torah," meaning the "teaching" or "instruction." These books tell the story of God's creation of the world, of human sin and rebellion against God, of God's covenant with Abraham, of God's deliverance of his people from slavery in Egypt, of God's covenant with Moses, of God's laws for his people, and of their journey to the Promised Land. The last book, Deuteronomy, spells out the blessings and penalties for keeping or rejecting the Mosaic covenant.

The Historical Books

The Old Testament books from Joshua to Esther are known as the "Historical Books." The first group of books (Joshua through 2 Kings) is closely connected to the book of Deuteronomy, and it continues the story of the Pentateuch. Deuteronomy closes with the important question, "Will Israel be faithful to the Lord and his laws [the Mosaic covenant]?" The tragic answer is, "No, they will not remain faithful," and 2 Kings ends with the destruction of Jerusalem and the exile of Israel from the Promised Land. The second group of historical books (1 Chronicles through Esther) is written from a different perspective. These books focus on those who have returned to the Promised Land after the exile, encouraging them to remain faithful to the Lord.

The Psalms

The book of Psalms is unique and cannot be placed in any of the other Old Testament categories. It stands alone as a book of praises, testimonies, and laments. The Psalms were to be used both in public worship and private meditation.

The Wisdom Books

The Wisdom Books (Job, Proverbs, Ecclesiastes, and Song of Songs) remind God's people of the importance of listening, thinking, considering, and reflecting. Their purpose is to encourage the development of godly character and the ability to make wise decisions in a variety of circumstances. Proverbs presents basic principles of life, things that are normally or usually true, while the three other books treat exceptions to these rules: Job (when the righteous suffer), Ecclesiastes (when the rational approach to life doesn't have all the answers), and Song of Songs (the "irrationality" of romantic love).

The Prophets

After entering the Promised Land, Israel turns a deaf ear to God's instructions and follows other gods. As the nation spirals downward, God sends the prophets with a final message for his people: (1) you have broken the Mosaic covenant through idolatry, social injustice, and religious ritualism, and you need to turn back to a true worship of God; (2) if you fail to repent, then you will face judgment; and (3) there is still hope beyond judgment for a glorious, future restoration for God's people and for the nations. The people continue to rebel and face judgment, which comes in the form of two invasions: the Assyrians in 722 BC to destroy the northern kingdom of Israel, and the Babylonians in 587/586 BC to destroy the southern kingdom of Judah and the city of Jerusalem. The prophets also promise a time of future restoration that includes a new covenant, involving all the nations of the world. This fulfills God's original promise to Abraham in Genesis 12:3.

The New Testament

The New Testament was originally written in Greek, the common language of much of the Roman Empire during the first century AD. The main topic of the New Testament is the covenant established by the life, death, and resurrection of Jesus Christ, and the people who embrace that covenant, the church. The entire New Testament period covers less than one hundred years. The New Testament includes the Gospels, the book of Acts, the Letters of Paul, the General Letters, and the book of Revelation.

The Four Gospels

The four Gospels—Matthew, Mark, Luke, and John—tell the story of Jesus Christ. The English word "gospel" comes from the Greek word *euangelion*, which means "good news." These four books tell the good news of salvation God has provided in Jesus Christ through his powerful ministry, his atoning death, and his miraculous resurrection. While the term "gospel" refers to the message about Jesus, it came to be used of the written accounts of this message—the four "Gospels." The first three Gospels are known as the "Synoptic" Gospels because they can be placed side by side and "seen together" (syn-optic), while John follows a slightly different chronology and style in presenting the story of Jesus.

The Book of Acts

We have four versions of the life of Jesus (the Gospels), but only one account of the life of the early church—the book of Acts. The term "Acts" refers to the book as "The Acts of the Apostles," but is perhaps more accurately described as "The Acts of the Holy Spirit through the Apostles and other Christians." The book of Acts tells the story of the birth and growth of the early church from about AD 30 to the early 60s.

The Letters of Paul

Traditionally, the apostle Paul is credited with writing thirteen letters that are included in the Bible. Those letters may be organized into four groups: early (Galatians, 1–2 Thessalonians), major (Romans, 1–2 Corinthians), prison (Ephesians, Philippians, Colossians, Philemon), and pastoral (1–2 Timothy, Titus). In the Bible, Paul's letters are arranged according to length, from the longest (Romans) to the shortest (Philemon).

The General Letters

James, 1–2 Peter, 1–3 John, and Jude (and sometimes Hebrews) are often called the "General" or "Catholic" Letters (meaning "universal") for one simple reason: they take their title not from the people receiving the letter but from the author. In contrast to Paul's letters, which are addressed to more specific groups (e.g., to the Philippians or to the Colossians), the General Letters are addressed to more general audiences. Often 1–3 John are referred to as the Johannine Letters.

Because Hebrews does take its name from the audience rather than the author (like Paul's letters), some do not include Hebrews with the General Letters.

Revelation

The final book of the New Testament depicts God's ultimate victory over the forces of evil. The title "Revelation" comes from the Greek word *apocalypsis*, meaning "revelation" or "unveiling." The book is a "revelation of Jesus Christ" (Rev. 1:1), suggesting the book reveals something about Jesus, or Jesus reveals something about God's plan, or perhaps both. Revelation differs from the other New Testament books in that it integrates three different literary types: letter, prophecy, and apocalyptic literature.

2100–1800 +/-	Patriarchs (Abraham, Isaac, Jacob) and Joseph
1446 or 1270	Moses and the exodus
1000–962	Reign of David
962–922	Reign of Solomon and construction of temple
722	Israel (northern kingdom) and the city of Samaria destroyed by Assyrians
586	Judah (southern kingdom) and city of Jerusalem destroyed by Babylonians; people go into exile
538–445	People return from exile; reconstruction of Jerusalem and temple
6–4	Jesus born

AD

5–10	Paul born
28	Jesus's public ministry begins
	Jesus's death and resurrection, and Pentecost
	Paul converted
	Jerusalem Council
	Paul martyred
70	Jerusalem destroyed by Romans

The Beginning
and the End

The final chapter in the grand story of Scripture (Revelation 19–22) offers a beautiful picture of how God will reverse the curse of sin and restore his creation in a way that even surpasses Genesis 1–2. If the opening chapters of Genesis could be described as "good," the closing chapters of Revelation should be characterized as "great." Believers who become familiar with the beginning and the end of the biblical story can expect encouragement, perspective, and hope as a reward for their labor.

The introduction to the book of Revelation (1:4–8) concludes with a bold pronouncement that God is "the Alpha and the Omega." In the Greek alphabet, the first letter is *alpha* and the last letter is *omega*. In Revelation, the "Alpha and Omega" (and similar designations) are used for both God and Christ:

- God—"I am the Alpha and the Omega" (1:8)
- Christ—"I am the First and the Last" (1:17)
- Christ—"the First and the Last" (2:8)
- God—"I am the Alpha and the Omega, the Beginning and the End" (21:6)
- Christ—"I am the Alpha and the Omega, the First and the Last, the Beginning and the End" (22:13)

Along with affirming the deity of Christ and his oneness with the Father, these descriptions also assert the Triune God's complete control of history. He is the origin and goal of history, the first and last word. As the Sovereign

Lord of all creation, God plans to bring his story to a victorious and beautiful conclusion.

Our place in the story is between the climax of Jesus's death and resurrection and the final outworking of God's perfect plan. God has won the ultimate war, but we still struggle with sin and Satan in a fallen world. In the final chapters of Revelation we see how things will ultimately work out in the future as sin's curse is reversed and God's new creation is ushered in. All this is consistent with God's character as the Alpha and the Omega.

Perhaps the best way to see the depth and richness of the victorious conclusion to the story of Scripture is to set the beginning elements in Genesis side by side with the concluding elements in Revelation. In this way we see that Genesis 1–11 and Revelation 19–22 serve as bookends to the entire biblical library.

The Beginning	Genesis	The End	Revelation
"In the beginning, God . . ."	1:1	"I am the Alpha and the Omega, the Beginning and the End"	21:6
God creates the first heaven and earth, eventually cursed by sin	1:1	God creates a new heaven and earth where sin is nowhere to be found	21:1
Water symbolizes unordered chaos	1:2	There is no longer any sea	21:1
God creates light and separates it from darkness	1:3–5	No more night or natural light; God himself is the source of light	21:23; 22:5
God gives humans dominion over the earth	1:26–30	God's people will reign with him forever	20:4, 6; 22:5
"Marriage" of Adam and Eve	1:27–28; 2:7, 18–25	Marriage of Last Adam and his bride, the church	19:7; 21:2, 9
Satan introduces sin into world	3:1–7	Satan and sin are judged	19:11–21; 20:7–10
The serpent deceives humanity	3:1–7, 13–15	The ancient serpent is bound "to keep him from deceiving the nations"	20:2–3
Death enters the world	3:3; 4:6–8; 6:3	Death is put to death	20:14; 21:4
Sin enters the world	3:6	Sin is banished from God's city	21:8, 27; 22:15
Sinful people refuse to serve/obey God	3:6–7; 4:6–8; 6:5	God's people serve him	22:3
Community forfeited	3:8; 4:8	Genuine community experienced	21:3, 7
God abandoned by sinful people	3:8–10; 6:5	God's people (New Jerusalem, bride of Christ) made ready for God; marriage of Lamb	19:7–8; 21:2, 9–21
Sinful people ashamed in God's presence	3:8–11	God's people will "see his face"	22:4
People rebel against the true God, resulting in physical and spiritual death	3:8–19	God's people risk death to worship the true God and thus experience life	20:4–6

The Beginning	Genesis	The End	Revelation
Sin brings pain and tears	3:16–17; 6:5–6	God comforts his people and removes crying and pain	21:4
Sinful people cursed	3:16–19	The curse removed from redeemed humanity and they become a blessing	22:3
Sinful people forbidden to eat from tree of life	3:22–24	God's people may eat freely from the tree of life	22:2, 14
Sinful people sent away from life	3:22–24	God's people are given life and have their names written in the book of life	20:4–6, 15; 21:6, 27
Exclusion from bounty of Eden	3:23	Invitation to marriage supper of Lamb	19:9
Sinful humanity separated from presence of holy God	3:23–24	God's people experience God's holiness (cubed city = holy of holies)	21:15–21
Sinful people sent away from garden	3:23–24	New heaven/earth includes a garden	22:2
Sinful people are banished from presence of God	3:24	God lives among his people	21:3, 7, 22; 22:4
Sinful humanity cursed with wandering (exile)	4:10–14	God's people given a permanent home	21:3
Sinful humanity suffers a wandering exile in the land	4:11–14	God gives his children an inheritance	21:7
Creation begins to grow old and die	5:6, 8, 14, 17, 20, 27, 31; 6:3	All things are made new	21:5
Sin results in spiritual sickness	6:5	God heals the nations	22:2
Water used to destroy wicked humanity	6:1–7:24	God quenches thirst with water from spring of life	21:6; 22:1
Sinful people scattered	11:3–9	God's people unite to sing his praises	19:6–7
Languages of sinful humanity confused	11:8–9	God's people are a multicultural people	21:24, 26; 22:2

We certainly anticipate many things that God will do at the end of the story, such as destroying his enemies—Satan, sin, demons, and death. We also expect him to reverse many of the effects of sin and the fall, such as taking away pain and suffering. We can easily imagine getting rid of many of the horrible things people experience now. Perhaps we can even envision some of the good things we experience now being made perfect (e.g., serving God or experiencing a true multicultural community or receiving a lasting inheritance). What is harder to imagine is the sheer magnitude of the beauty and goodness of the new creation, where the physical creation functions in perfect harmony with the Lord and his people. What may be most difficult of all to grasp is the level of intimacy we will experience with the Lord himself. We were made for God. We are his bride. We will see his glorious face. He will wipe away all our tears. We will experience his perfect holiness and his complete love. We will reign with him and sing praises to him alongside the angels. And best of all, he will live with us forever.

For Christians, there is more to the story than just being saved and going to heaven when we die. We often underestimate the end of the story because we forget that God is both the Alpha (Genesis 1–2) and the Omega (Revelation 19–22). His very character assures us that he will finish what he began, with more beauty, goodness, holiness, glory, and love than we can possibly imagine.

The Old Testament

The Pentateuch

What Is the Pentateuch About?

The first five books of the Bible (Genesis, Exodus, Leviticus, Numbers, and Deuteronomy) are often referred to as the "Pentateuch." The word "pentateuch" comes from combining two Greek words, *pente*, which means "five," and *teuchos*, which means "scroll" or "book." Thus the term "pentateuch" refers to a five-scroll or five-book collection. The math is accurate, but this title doesn't really give us much information regarding what these books are about.

The term for these five books in the Hebrew Bible is "Torah." In Hebrew, Torah means "teaching" or "instruction." This title gives us a little more insight into the content of the first five books, for they are definitely filled with divine teaching and instruction.

Also, within the Pentateuch/Torah we find the laws that God gave to Israel as part of the covenant he mediated through Moses (the Mosaic covenant). Portions of Exodus and Numbers, as well as practically all of Leviticus and Deuteronomy, are filled with the laws that, taken together, define the Mosaic covenant. Because of the many laws in the Pentateuch, these first five books have also been called "the Law," "the Books of the Law," "the Book of the Law," or "the Law of Moses."

Yet these first five books of the Bible also present a story. It is the unfolding of this story that ties the books of the Pentateuch together, and it is the story that connects the books of the Pentateuch to the rest of the Bible. The laws in the Pentateuch did not just randomly drop down out of heaven; God gave them to Israel at a particular point in the story for a particular purpose. That is, the laws in the Pentateuch are embedded into the narrative story that flows throughout these first five books and into the books that follow.

So to understand each of the five books in the Pentateuch, we need always to be aware of the overarching story that ties them together. Likewise, our best approach to understanding the laws in the Pentateuch is to study them as they function within the story, striving to grasp the "teaching" or "instruction" that comes from the interaction between story and law.

Genesis 1–2 starts the story off with God's creation. He creates a wonderful garden and places humankind into the garden where they can have close fellowship with him. How do humans react to this wonderful blessing? Genesis 3–11 narrates a series of tragic events illustrating how people sin repeatedly and rebel continuously against God. This separates them from God and ultimately results in death. By Genesis 11 the situation of the world is grim. What will happen? How will humankind ever be saved and restored again to close fellowship with God?

Genesis 12 introduces the answer and begins the exciting story of redemption and salvation. A continuous story runs from Genesis 12 all the way to 2 Kings 25, tying the Pentateuch very closely to the historical books that follow (Joshua, Judges, Ruth, 1–2 Samuel, 1–2 Kings; we call these books the Deuteronomy-based history). In Genesis 12–17 God makes a one-sided covenant with Abraham. This covenant drives much of the biblical story throughout the Old Testament and into the New Testament. The promises of this covenant are passed down throughout the rest of Genesis from Abraham to Isaac and to Jacob. Yet Genesis closes with Jacob and his twelve sons residing in Egypt, with most of the Abrahamic promises still unfulfilled.

Exodus comes next, picking up the story in Egypt with Abraham's descendants and moving it forward in fulfillment of God's promise to Abraham. In the first part of Exodus, God delivers Israel (Abraham's descendants) from Egyptian oppression and leads them to Mount Sinai. There God makes a covenant with them (the Mosaic covenant). A central part of that covenant is a promise that God will actually dwell among the people of Israel. If he is to dwell among them, he will need an appropriate place to stay, so the second half of Exodus describes the construction of the tabernacle, God's new dwelling place.

Leviticus picks up right here, for if the holy, awesome God is going to dwell right in their midst, then all aspects of life for the Israelites will change. Their entire worldview will now need to revolve around the concepts of holiness and what is clean and unclean. They will also need to know how to approach God and how to serve him. Thus Leviticus deals with how the Israelites were to live with the holy and awesome God dwelling right there among them.

In Numbers the Israelites continue on their journey to the Promised Land that they began back in Exodus. The land was part of God's promise to Abraham. Unbelievably, when the Israelites get there they reject the

Promised Land! So God sends that generation back into the wilderness to wander around until they all die off.

Then God takes the next generation back to the Promised Land. When they get close, right before they enter the land, God restates the terms of the Mosaic covenant to them. He presents Israel with the terms by which they can live in the Promised Land with God in their midst and enjoy wonderful blessings. This is the book of Deuteronomy. It delineates both the blessings and the penalties that will result based on whether Israel keeps the terms of Deuteronomy (the Mosaic covenant). In the next book (Joshua), Israel indeed enters the land. The question that now drives the story from Joshua all the way to 2 Kings 25 is, "Will Israel obey the book of Deuteronomy?"

The authorship of the five books of the Pentateuch has traditionally been attributed to Moses. It is possible, however, that God used a few other divinely inspired writers to put the final touches and flourishes on the "Books of Moses." The description of Moses's death, for example, was probably written by another inspired author (Deut. 34:1–12). Likewise some of the geographical names in the Pentateuch appear to have been updated with the terms used by later generations of Israelites (see, e.g., Gen. 14:14).

Genesis

Creation, Sin, and Covenant

God brings you and me into existence, blessing us with life itself, and then doubly blessing us by giving us a great world to live in and a chance to know him personally. But we mess it all up, sinning against God and doing stupid, selfish things—in essence rejecting him and his blessings. This action of ours separates us from God and ultimately results in death. God, however, takes a special initiative and provides a way of salvation, a way to regain our relationship with him and receive life. This is the story of Genesis, and indeed, the story of the Bible. It is also your story and my story.

What Is the Setting for Genesis?

In the Hebrew Bible, each of the first five books (the Torah) takes its name from the opening lines of the book. Thus the first book of the Hebrew Bible is titled "in the beginning." When the Hebrew Bible was translated into Greek (the Septuagint), the translators titled this book "Genesis," which in Greek means "beginnings." Our English Bibles derive the title we are familiar with (Genesis) from the Septuagint.

In this case, the title does reflect the setting of the book, for Genesis starts out "in the beginning." Genesis 1–2 deals with the creation of the world, and Genesis 3–11 covers what is called "primeval history." It is difficult to determine the actual dates for this period. Genesis 12 (the promise to Abraham) begins a story that runs chronologically and sequentially all the way to 2 Kings 25. Suggested dates for Abraham vary from about 2100 BC to about 1800 BC.

Quite a bit of geographical movement takes place in Genesis. After God creates the heavens and the earth (Genesis 1), the setting tends to move eastward. God plants "a garden in the east" (2:8); he apparently banishes Adam and Eve to the east, leaving cherubim to guard the gate to the garden on the east side (3:23–24); the murderer Cain is driven away, to the east (4:16); and people migrate "eastward" (or perhaps "from the east," 11:2).

When the story of Abraham begins (Genesis 12), he is in Mesopotamia, which is in the east. Abraham, however, obeys the Lord and migrates west to Canaan. He has a short stay down in Egypt (12:10–20), which does not go well, and then Abraham returns to the land of Canaan. Abraham's grandson Jacob will travel back to Mesopotamia and live there for a while, before returning to Canaan. Jacob's family will then move to Egypt, and Genesis ends with the family of Jacob (Abraham's descendants) all living in Egypt.

Traditionally, Christians have taken clues from the rest of the Bible and concluded that Moses wrote the book of Genesis. This would place the initial setting for the composition of the book during the exodus, as Israel entered into covenant relationship with God and moved toward the Promised Land (like the garden in Genesis 2). Keep in mind that these people are fairly new in their relationship with God. All the people around them worship pagan gods. Most of these religions had creation stories, and most of these gods were connected in some way to agricultural cycles and seasons. This cultural milieu would have had a very strong influence on the thinking of the Israelites regarding what God is like. Genesis 1 is underscoring that the Lord God of Israel is quite different from the pagan gods of Israel's neighbors. He did not struggle and fight to bring the world into ordered being as the pagan gods did; he just spoke and it was so. The agricultural cycles and seasons are not connected to the death and rebirth of pagan gods (as the Canaanites maintained, for example); they were determined by God's decree at creation. Furthermore, the creation of people is at the climax of the story, and God creates the man and woman in the image of God, giving a special and wonderful status to all people, a concept quite foreign to the pagan religions of the ancient world.

✝ The biblical story begins in a garden (Genesis 1–3) and ends in a garden (Revelation 22).

What Is at the Heart of Genesis?

Genesis plays an introductory role for the Pentateuch (Genesis, Exodus, Leviticus, Numbers, Deuteronomy), for the entire Old Testament, and for the entire Bible. The story of Genesis is paradigmatic (representative) for the story of Israel, as well as for the grand story of human existence. God creates a good place for people to live where they can have a close relationship with him. This is a fantastic blessing (Genesis 1–2). These human creatures (and we need to see ourselves here as well) repeatedly rebel and sin against God, resulting in separation and death (Genesis 3–11). This is the story of humanity. In God's great mercy he provides a way of salvation, and this salvation story starts in Genesis 12 with Abraham and culminates in the New Testament Gospels with Jesus Christ, reaching its final consummation in Revelation 21–22 with the re-creation of the new heavens and earth.

Genesis 1–11 is a cosmic story, dealing with all people of the earth. The initial blessings of God and the rebellion, sin, and rejection of God by humankind portrayed in Genesis 3–11 are universal and include all people of all nations. As the story of salvation begins in Genesis 12, however, the focus is on Abraham and his descendants, the people of Israel. But Genesis 12:3 sets the ultimate universal agenda: "all peoples on earth will be blessed through you." God is going to work through the descendants of Abraham to provide a way of salvation for all who will accept it.

God makes a covenant with Abraham in Genesis 12, 15, and 17. It is this Abrahamic covenant that will provide the framework for God's unfolding plan of salvation for everyone in the world who will believe. It is the fulfillment of the Abrahamic covenant that drives the story throughout the Old Testament and even into the New Testament. It is the fulfillment of the Abrahamic covenant that reunites the story of Israel (Genesis 12–2 Kings 25) with the story of humanity as declared in the Prophets and consummated in Jesus Christ.

Michelangelo's depiction of God creating Adam. *Creation of Adam*, Sistine Chapel, Vatican City.

The story in Genesis can be outlined as follows:

- Creation of the World, People, and the Garden (1:1–2:25)
- Paradise Lost: Sin, Death, and Separation from God (3:1–11:32)
  - Sin #1: Adam and Eve eat the forbidden fruit and are banished from the garden (3:1–24)
  - Sin #2: Cain kills his brother, Abel, and is driven away (4:1–26)
  - Sin #3 (and then some): Worldwide wickedness brings on the flood (5:1–9:29)
  - Sin #4: The tower of Babel results in scattering (10:1–11:32)

- God's Response to Human Sin: Deliverance through the Abrahamic Covenant (12:1–50:26)
  - Abraham: The promise and the obedience of faith (12:1–23:20)
  - Isaac: Continuing the patriarchal promise (24:1–25:18)
  - Jacob: Struggle and the beginning of the twelve tribes of Israel (25:19–36:43)
  - Joseph: Faithfulness and God's sovereign deliverance (37:1–50:26)

What Makes Genesis Interesting and Unique?

- Genesis answers the big questions of life: Why am I here? Who has brought me into being? What is life all about?
- Genesis tells the story of creation.
- God creates man and woman, and institutes marriage.
- A serpent talks to Eve and convinces the couple to disobey God.
- Genesis contains the fascinating stories of the flood and the tower of Babel.
- Genesis has a universal focus (1–11) and an Israelite focus (12–50).
- The phrase "these are the generations of" (KJV, or "this is the account of," NIV) occurs repeatedly throughout the book (2:4; 5:1; 6:9; 10:1; 11:10, 27; 25:12, 19; 36:1, 9; 37:2).
- Abraham is a remarkable man of faith (most of the time).
- God makes a covenant with Abraham that impacts the rest of the Bible and all of human history.
- God destroys the cities of Sodom and Gomorrah after arguing with Abraham about it.
- God tests Abraham by commanding him to sacrifice his son Isaac, but provides a substitute just in time.
- Jacob tricks his father, Isaac, in order to get his blessing.
- Jacob wrestles with God.
- Joseph is sold into slavery by his brothers but rises to the second most powerful position in the world, just in time to save his family.
- Joseph forgives his brothers who sold him into slavery.

What Is the Message of Genesis?

Creation of the World, People, and the Garden (1:1–2:25)

Genesis 1:1 is a summary statement for the entire process of creation. This single introductory verse also has profound implications for us. If we accept the truth of Genesis 1:1, then we can easily accept the many miraculous works of God throughout the Bible. Likewise, if we acknowledge Genesis 1:1, our basic relationship to God is defined: he is the creator and we are the created beings. Thus he has the right (and the power) to determine what life for us is all about.

✚ In Genesis 1 God *speaks* and the world obeys, taking on form and function. The *word of God* will continue to be a major theme throughout the Bible.

Genesis 1:2 is a background statement. The story of creation in the Bible does not start with "nothingness." That God creates matter out of nothing is implied, but the story in Genesis actually starts with a chaotic watery world. Thus the Genesis 1 creation account is not so much an account of creation out of nothing as it is an account of bringing order out of chaos, and life out of nonlife. Genesis 1:2 also mentions the "Spirit of God" hovering over the waters, underscoring the close connection between God's Spirit and creative power, a theme that will continue throughout the Old Testament.

The creation account in Genesis 1 is fascinating, for it is presented not mechanically or in a boring way, but colorfully, even poetically. It has structure and symmetry. Numerous things are repeated: "and God said," "evening and morning," "it was good," and so on. God is not following a step-by-step instruction manual. He is more like an artist creating a masterpiece, who can paint outside the lines if he wants to.

In addition, the account is not strictly linear, but is presented in two interrelated cycles. On days 1–3 God creates domains or regions. On days 4–6 he creates the inhabitants or occupants of those regions or domains.

Day 1 (vv. 3–5)	Day 4 (vv. 14–19)
Separates light from dark	Creates sun, moon, and stars
Day 2 (vv. 6–8)	Day 5 (vv. 20–23)
Separates the sea from the sky	Creates fish and birds
Day 3 (vv. 9–13)	Day 6 (vv. 24–31)
Separates water, dry ground, creates vegetation	Creates livestock, crawling things, wild animals, humankind

Throughout this creation account, God is not only bringing things into being, but he is also assigning functions to each thing and thus bringing order and purpose to the creation.

As the climax of creation, God creates man and woman in the image of God. The overview of this is presented in 1:26–31, and the details are presented in 2:4–25. God makes people "in the image of God," thus giving them a very special status. Furthermore, note that Adam and Eve are not associated with any tribe or race (they are not called Hebrews, for example). This implies that all people of all races and socioeconomic levels have this special status and value; they are created in the image of God. Although scholars are divided over the exact meaning of "the image of God," it probably includes several things: we are similar to God in several aspects (spiritual, emotional, relational) and we have been appointed as God's representatives to administer his creation.

✦ The Hebrew word *adam*, the proper name of the first created man, is also the Hebrew word used for "people" and humanity in general.

Genesis 1 is an overview of the entire creation process, while Genesis 2 "windows in" on the specific details involved in the creation of the man and the woman. The entire creation story concludes with the man and the woman brought together in the institution of marriage (2:18–25).

Paradise Lost: Sin, Death, and Separation from God (3:1–11:32)

Cain and Abel by Titian.

Genesis 3–11 chronicles the sad story of how humans respond to God's gracious blessings given to them in creation. Four sinful episodes are listed in a row; the human race is not off to a good start!

Sin #1: Adam and Eve eat the forbidden fruit and are banished from the garden (3:1–24)

We believe this to be a historical story, but it is also one that typifies human behavior and gives an accurate pessimistic foreshadowing of how people in general will stubbornly refuse to obey God, allowing temptation to lead them astray. Adam and Eve, tempted by the lies and half-truths of the serpent (i.e., Satan), eat from the one tree that God told them not to eat from, and then they each try to blame someone else. The consequences are serious. Sin disqualifies them from living the good life in the garden in close fellowship with God. Death will now be a reality for them (3:19), and immortality will come only through childbirth, accompanied by great pain. Since he rejected the rules of the good garden, the man is now destined to hard, hot, sweaty work in the fields. Finally, God banishes them from the garden.

Sin #2: Cain kills his brother, Abel, and is driven away (4:1–26)

Outside the garden, the human race does not behave any better. With only two brothers on the earth, it is rather ironic (and disturbing) that one would kill the other. This also is a sad picture of human behavior, for we are still killing one another with some regularity. Just read any newspaper headlines or listen to the evening news.

God, however, continues to work in the background, and this action quietly suggests hope for the future. Seth replaces the slain Abel and begins to call on the name of the Lord (4:26).

✝ The Hebrew word *adam* is also closely related to the Hebrew word for dust or dirt. Note that Adam was taken from the dirt, he worked the dirt, and then was buried in the dirt.

Sin #3 (and then some): Worldwide wickedness brings on the flood (5:1–9:29)

Time passes and generations go by. There are now lots of people in the world (5:1–32). As the population grows and spreads, sin seems to keep pace, as Genesis 6:5 declares, "The Lord saw how great man's wickedness on the earth had become, and that every inclination of his heart was only evil all the time." Fortunately, there are exceptions to this indictment, and a man named Noah finds grace in God's eyes.

The wickedness is so bad that God decides to destroy the creation and start over. Genesis 6–9 describes the flood that God sends on the earth. In general, the description of the flood uses the same terminology as was used of the creation in Genesis 1–2, only in reverse. In Genesis 1, "God saw that it was good" (1:4, 10, 12, 18, 21, 25, 31). Now in 6:5, "The Lord saw how great man's wickedness on the earth had become." Likewise, the separation of the waters above and the waters below (1:6–7) collapses into a great flood (7:11). Just as God commanded the dry ground to appear (1:9), now it all disappears back under the waters (7:17–20), destroying all life outside the ark, both humans and animals, created back in Genesis 1.

In essence, God does start over, and just as the Spirit of God was hovering over the waters in 1:2, so now God sends a wind (the Hebrew words for "spirit" and "wind" are the same) over the earth, and the "re-creation" begins as the waters recede and the animals emerge out of the ark (8:1–22).

In Genesis 9, God makes a covenant not to destroy the world again this way. He also makes a strong prohibition against murder. Noah's story ends rather curiously, however. His son Ham does something quite offensive (the text is not clear to us), and Noah then pronounces a curse on Ham's son Canaan (9:18–27), from whom the Canaanite people will develop.

The cuneiform tablet containing the flood account in the Epic of Gilgamesh.

Apparently Noah looks beyond his sons and grandsons to see the people who will develop from them. Thus he pronounces a fitting curse on Canaan. The Canaanites will become the prototypical "bad guys" in the Old Testament, worshiping Baal and causing all kinds of theological and moral problems for Israel in the future. None of the son's names (Ham, Shem, and Japheth) have anything to do with racial classifications, and the so-called curse of Ham has absolutely nothing to do with ethnicities.

Sin #4: The tower of Babel results in scattering (10:1–11:32)

The genealogy in Genesis 10 presents some challenging interpretive difficulties, for the list contains names of individuals, peoples, tribes, countries, and cities. The basis for the

✦ Several of the four terms *clans, languages, territories,* and *nations* used to define the scattering in Genesis 10 (vv. 5, 20, 31) resurface in other passages that reverse the scattering situation, particularly Genesis 12:1–3 and Revelation 5:9; 7:9; 10:11; 11:9; 13:7; 14:6; and 17:15.

Other Flood Accounts in the Ancient Near East

John H. Walton

The Israelites lived in an ancient world in which there was a common currency of ideas, traditions, customs, perceptions, and stories. As with any culture, they had their own versions of each of these that were tailored to suit their individual beliefs and culture. Unlike the rest of the ancient world, they received revelation from their God that, at critical points, drew them out of their cultural surrounding and endowed them with a distinct understanding. In most other ways they remained very similar to their cultural neighbors.

Given the nature of the tradition found commonly in the ancient Near East, that there was a flood of immense scope that virtually wiped out the ancient world, it is no surprise that accounts of this flood survive both in the Bible and in the larger culture. Even as the accounts mirror the culture in which they are found, they also reflect common elements that tie them to a central event that they record. The biblical account naturally understands the event as an act of judgment by a single, righteous deity who was disappointed with the sin of his creatures, but saved one righteous family from worldwide devastation. The picture of God and humanity is consistent with the biblical ideals.

In the ancient Near Eastern versions found in Sumerian texts, in the Atrahasis Epic, and in the Gilgamesh Epic, we likewise find accounts consistent with the ideas they had about the gods and humanity. Consequently we see a Divine Council that decides to send the flood with the intention that all humanity be destroyed. It is only by breach of the trust of the Council that one god arranges for a few humans to escape the judgment. The reasons for the action of the Council are rooted in views of deity current in Mesopotamia. There the gods could be viewed as petty or selfish, and they are understood to have needs that humans meet. In these ancient Near Eastern accounts, the humans that are spared offer a sacrifice to the gods to appease them, and the gods come to recognize their need of humanity.

Numerous other differences could be identified, and none of them is surprising. The similarities attest that a common world binds these people together. The distinctions testify to the basic differences in theology and the impact of revelation on the Israelites. There is no need to discuss the question of who borrowed from whom, for there was no need to borrow what was already ingrained in ancient memory. Of greater significance is the recognition that Israelites had been given a different form of the tradition that coincided with how God was known to them.

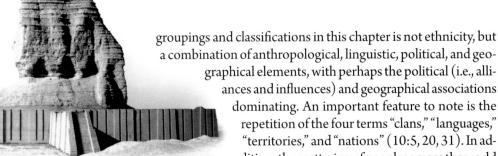

groupings and classifications in this chapter is not ethnicity, but a combination of anthropological, linguistic, political, and geographical elements, with perhaps the political (i.e., alliances and influences) and geographical associations dominating. An important feature to note is the repetition of the four terms "clans," "languages," "territories," and "nations" (10:5, 20, 31). In addition, the scattering of peoples across the world into clans, languages, territories, and nations is the result of the tower of Babel episode in Genesis 11. So it appears that the event of Genesis 11 actually takes place first and then leads to the situation described in Genesis 10.

The partially restored Ager Quf Ziggurat. Numerous temple-towers like this were built as worship sites throughout Mesopotamia. The tower of Babel was perhaps a forerunner of these ziggurats.

In Genesis 11 people gather in Babel and attempt to build a tower up to the heavens so that they can make a name for themselves. God, however, does not approve, and he confuses their language and scatters them across the land. A fun wordplay drives this story. Babel is the word from which Babylon comes, and to the Babylonians, the word Babel means "gate of the gods." In Hebrew, however, the word Babel sounds a lot like a Hebrew word meaning "to confuse." So the wordplay implies that this is not the "gate of the gods," but rather the place and the cause of confusion (and scattering). This story represents prideful and pretentious humanism. It reflects humanity's attempt to gain security and meaning apart from God through city-building. Throughout the Bible, the city of Babylon becomes the prototype of all prideful nations, cities, and empires that raise themselves against God (e.g., note the use of Babylon in Rev. 14:8; 16:19; 17:5; 18:2). Note that Genesis 9:25–27 pronounces a curse on Canaan while Genesis 11:1–9 implies judgment on Babylon. In the Old Testament, the Canaanites and the Babylonians are the major enemies of Israel, the Canaanites at the beginning during the conquest and the Babylonians at the end during the exile.

God's Response to Human Sin: Deliverance through the Abrahamic Covenant (12:1–50:26)

Abraham: The promise and the obedience of faith (12:1–23:20)

In Genesis 3–11 the human race has demonstrated its propensity to rebel against God and sin repeatedly. God's response to human sin is to provide a way of salvation. This story—the story of salvation—begins in Genesis 12 with God's covenant promises to Abraham, and culminates with the death and resurrection of Christ. Thus God's covenant with Abraham plays a critical role in tying the entire biblical story together.

✦ In Genesis 10–11 people are scattered across the world into nations and languages. In Acts 2 the Spirit unites God's people together again, removing the language barrier. Thus the event at Pentecost in Acts 2 reverses the situation created in Genesis 10–11.

God calls Abraham while he is still in Mesopotamia (11:27–12:1), instructing him to leave his country and his people (i.e., a separation for service to God, a common theme in the Pentateuch) and to go to the land God will show him. In 12:2–7 God promises Abraham several things. He will make Abraham into a great nation; he will bless Abraham and make his name great; he will bless all peoples on earth through Abraham; and he will give Abraham's descendants the land of Canaan. This is a big agenda, and fulfilling it will drive the rest of the biblical story.

In 12:10–20 Abraham makes some poor decisions, ending up in Egypt and almost losing his wife, Sarah. God, however, works behind the scenes to straighten things out and blesses Abraham anyway, demonstrating the tight connection between God's grace and the Abrahamic promises. In 13:1–14:24 God continues to bless Abraham, and these blessings spill over onto those who are associated with Abraham as well.

In Genesis 15 and 17 God appears to Abraham and formalizes his promises to Abraham into a covenant. Abraham is worried because he has no apparent heirs, but God tells him that he will have descendants as numerous as the stars in the sky (15:5). Abraham believes in God's promise, and God "credited it to him as righteousness" (15:6). Then God and Abraham participate in a formal covenant-making ceremony. Abraham cuts several animals in half. Normally in a covenant ceremony both parties would pass between the cut halves, signifying what would happen to each of them if they broke the covenant. Amazingly, in this ceremony

The Negev, one of the regions in which Abraham lived and traveled.

✦ In Genesis 12, at the beginning of the Abraham story, the patriarch is called Abram, which means "exalted father." In 17:4–5, as God formalizes his covenant with Abram, God changes his name to Abraham ("father of many").

Carchemish Haran Nineveh
Aleppo
Ugarit Ebla Asshur
Hamath
Byblos Mari
Hazor Damascus Babylon
Shechem Ramoth Gilead Nippur
Succoth
Hebron
Beersheba Ur of the
Chaldeans
LOWER
EGYPT
Memphis
Saqqara Sinai
Arabian
Desert
UPPER
EGYPT
Abydos
Thebes

Caspian Sea
MEDITERRANEAN SEA
Tigris R.
Euphrates R.
Persian Gulf
Red Sea

0   200   400 mi
0   200   400 km

only God passes between the cut animals. That is, God apparently pledges himself unilaterally to keep the Abrahamic covenant. This is what grace is about.

In Genesis 17 God expands the covenant, promising Abraham (and Sarah) that many nations and many kings will come from their descendants. God tells Abraham that circumcision will be the sign for Abraham and his descendants to indicate they are under this great covenant. In reference to Abraham's descendants, God also declares, "I will be their God" (17:8). Throughout the Old Testament God will define his relationship to his people with a three-part formula statement: I will be your God; you will be my people; I will dwell in your midst (or "I will be with you"). The relationship is introduced as part of the Abrahamic covenant.

Genesis 18–19 describes the destruction of the wicked cities of Sodom and Gomorrah. Remarkably, Abraham argues with God over this judgment, and God apparently listens patiently to Abraham's arguments (18:16–33). But Abraham cannot come up with even ten righteous people in these cities, and God destroys them. Only Abraham's nephew, Lot, and his daughters survive.

At long last, in their old age and just as God had promised back in 18:1–15, Abraham and Sarah have a son, Isaac (21:1–21). Their happiness, however, is rattled severely in Genesis 22 when God tells Abraham to offer Isaac as a sacrifice (22:1–2)! How can this be? Abraham painfully complies, but just before he actually kills Isaac, the Lord stops him and provides a substitute ram for the sacrifice (22:3–14). The Lord commends the strong, unquestioning faith of Abraham and then restates his covenant promises (22:15–19). Many people have been troubled by this passage. What kind of God would do this? The answer perhaps lies in observing the many (sometimes very specific) similarities between this event and the crucifixion of Christ. The

50

✛ In the New Testament, Paul stresses the implications that the Abrahamic covenant/ promise has for Christians, especially regarding grace, faith, and justification (Rom. 4:1–25; Gal. 3:6–14). Paul quotes Genesis 15:6 directly twice (Rom. 4:3; Gal. 3:6).

The Covenants of the Bible

A covenant is a binding, formal agreement made between two parties. Covenants play a very important role in the Bible because God is often one of the parties involved in the covenant. In fact, God is the one who usually initiates the covenant, thus binding himself to an agreement or to a set of promises.

God makes several covenants in the Old Testament. In Genesis 9 God makes a covenant with Noah (along with his descendants and all living animals) that he will never destroy all life on the earth again with a flood. God makes a covenant with Abraham in Genesis 12, 15, and 17, promising several things: God will make Abraham into a great nation; he will bless Abraham and make his name great; he will bless all peoples on earth through Abraham; and he will give Abraham's descendants the land of Canaan. An important feature of the Abrahamic covenant is that God appears to bind himself to this covenant unilaterally. That is, the Abrahamic covenant is a one-sided or "divine commitment" covenant. God puts stipulations on himself, but not on Abraham and his descendants. Thus in the New Testament Paul will associate the Abrahamic covenant with the concept of "grace." The Mosaic covenant, by contrast, is quite different, for it emphasized human obligation ("keeping the law"). The Mosaic covenant is defined by the laws of Exodus, Leviticus, Numbers, and Deuteronomy. This covenant defined the terms by which Israel could live in the Promised Land with God in their midst and receive spectacular blessings. In the New Testament Paul will associate the Mosaic covenant with "law." In 2 Samuel 7 God makes a covenant with David, promising to establish a Davidic dynasty ("house") that will last forever.

This covenant also appears to be one-sided, with God being the primary party that takes on obligations. Finally, in Jeremiah 31 God promises that in the future he will make a new covenant. This covenant will be very different from the old covenant (i.e., the Mosaic covenant), for in the new covenant God's laws will be written on people's hearts instead of on stone. This covenant will be characterized by forgiveness of sins and a much greater knowledge and understanding of God. Like the Abrahamic and Davidic covenants, the new covenant is a one-sided, divine-commitment type of covenant. In the New Testament Jesus establishes this covenant at the Last Supper when he declares, "This cup is the new covenant in my blood" (Luke 22:20).

The Abrahamic, Mosaic, Davidic, and New covenants play a critical role in the Old Testament story and in connecting the Old Testament to the New Testament. God's fulfillment of these covenants drives the story throughout the Old Testament and into the New Testament. Israel will fail miserably at keeping the terms of the Mosaic covenant, and thus they will experience the judgment promised in Deuteronomy (the exile). God, however, in his grace, continues to be faithful to his unilateral promises in the Abrahamic and Davidic covenants, so even as Israel shatters the Mosaic covenant, there is still hope for a future. The Old Testament prophets will proclaim judgment on Israel because they broke the Mosaic covenant, but the prophets will proclaim hope for a glorious future, based on God's promises in the Abrahamic and Davidic covenants, promises that find ultimate fulfillment in Jesus Christ as he inaugurates the promised new covenant.

events take place at very nearly the same location. In each, a father has to sacrifice his son. There is a hill, a donkey, and wood carried by the innocent son. The big difference is that Abraham does not have to go through with the sacrifice, while God the Father does. We suspect that Genesis 22 is a prophetic typology of the cross, showing the pain and difficulty of the crucifixion from the Father's perspective. Is this a horrible and painful story? "Absolutely!" God answers. This story drags you and me up that hill and forces us to try to come to grips with having to sacrifice one's son, something that our heavenly Father had to do.

Isaac: Continuing the patriarchal promise (24:1–25:18)

Abraham and Sarah eventually die, and the story moves to their son, Isaac. In general, Isaac plays a passive role in most of the episodes he is in (with his father, Abraham, or his sons, Jacob and Esau). He is important, however, for God does restate the covenant promises to him (26:1–5), and he is the link that passes the covenant from Abraham to Jacob and then to the twelve tribes.

Jacob: Struggle and the beginning of the twelve tribes of Israel (25:19–36:43)

In contrast to his father, Isaac, who is passive in the story, Jacob connives, struggles, and fights for his inheritance and the promises that go with it, not always recognizing that the covenant promises were a gift of grace. Jacob (whose name figuratively means "the deceiver") tricks his blind father, Isaac, into giving the family blessing (the inheritance) to him instead of his twin brother, Esau, who was a few moments older than he (27:1–40). The enraged Esau threatens to kill his deceiving brother, so Jacob flees to Paddan Aram, back in Mesopotamia, where the distant relatives of his mother, Rebekah, live. Jacob works for a relative named Laban, who tricks Jacob (who is the deceiver,

The Jabbok River. Jacob wrestles God near this river in Gen. 32:22–37.

remember) into marrying both of his daughters instead of just the younger and more beautiful, Rachel (29:1–30). These two wives, along with their maidservants (who become like concubines or secondary wives to Jacob), bear twelve sons to Jacob. From these twelve sons develop the twelve tribes of Israel. Jacob then returns to Canaan and makes amends with his brother, Esau. Along the way, he encounters and "wrestles" with God, who then renames him "Israel."

Thus Jacob's story is foundational for the formation of the nation Israel. Jacob takes on the name Israel and fathers the twelve sons that later develop into the twelve tribes (actually there

The Sacrifice of Isaac by Rembrandt.

are thirteen tribes, for Jacob's son Joseph produces two tribes, Manasseh and Ephraim). In accordance with the Abrahamic covenant, God blesses this family, even though they do not always behave properly, foreshadowing perhaps the later problems that the nation Israel will have.

Joseph: Faithfulness and God's sovereign deliverance (37:1–50:26)

Joseph is one of the few in this family who seem to trust in God and live a righteous life. His brothers are jealous of the young Joseph, so they sell him into slavery (37:1–36). Joseph ends up in Egypt, where he continues to trust God and to behave virtuously, in contrast to his brothers back at home (38:1–39:23). God blesses Joseph and empowers him to interpret dreams, leading to his promotion to the second-highest position in Egypt. Joseph actually implements a program that saves Egypt from an upcoming

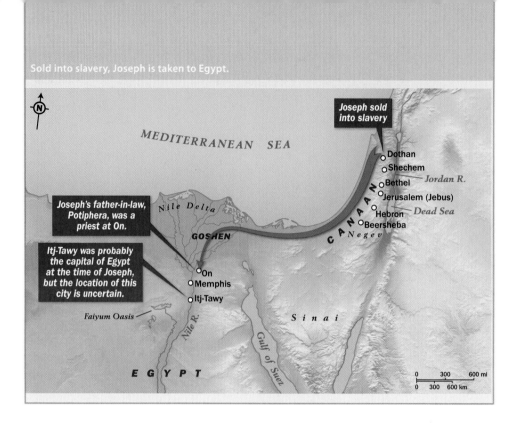

Joseph sold into slavery

MEDITERRANEAN SEA

Dothan
Shechem
Bethel — Jordan R.
Jerusalem (Jebus)
Hebron — Dead Sea
Beersheba
Negev

Nile Delta

Joseph's father-in-law, Potiphera, was a priest at On.

GOSHEN

Itj-Tawy was probably the capital of Egypt at the time of Joseph, but the location of this city is uncertain.

On
Memphis
Itj-Tawy

Faiyum Oasis

Sinai

Gulf of Suez

Nile R.

E G Y P T

| 0 | 300 | 600 mi |
| 0 | 300 | 600 km |

famine (40:1–41:57). This famine affects Canaan too, and eventually Joseph's family comes to Egypt for food. Instead of punishing his brothers for their treachery, Joseph forgives them and cares for his entire family in Egypt (42:1–47:31). Joseph's father, Jacob, grows old, but pronounces blessings on Joseph's two sons, Manasseh and Ephraim (48:1–22), as well as on his own eleven other sons (49:1–28). Joseph's family prospers in Egypt, but as he dies, he reminds the family that God promised their forefather Abraham a land and that God would one day take them to that land (50:1–26). So as the book of Genesis ends, the descendants of Abraham are in Egypt, waiting for God to fulfill his promise to their forefather. This fulfillment will be the story of Exodus.

So What? Applying Genesis to Our Lives Today

One of the most important lessons we can learn in life is that God is the creator and we are the created ones. This pretty well delineates our relationship with him and clarifies who has the authority to make the rules. We immediately get into trouble when we forget this order and try to act as though we were the ones who created the universe and thus have the right to determine right and wrong, true worship and false, and so on.

The story of Abraham teaches us about God's continuing grace. There is a straight line of grace that connects the creation to the Abrahamic covenant to Jesus Christ. Likewise, as the apostle Paul repeatedly points out, from Abraham we also learn the importance of faith. It is through faith and faith alone that righteousness is received.

Our Favorite Verse in Genesis

I am God Almighty; walk before me and be blameless. (17:1)

✚ As the story of Genesis comes to a close, the descendants of Abraham are in Egypt. Exodus, the next book, will pick up the story in Egypt.

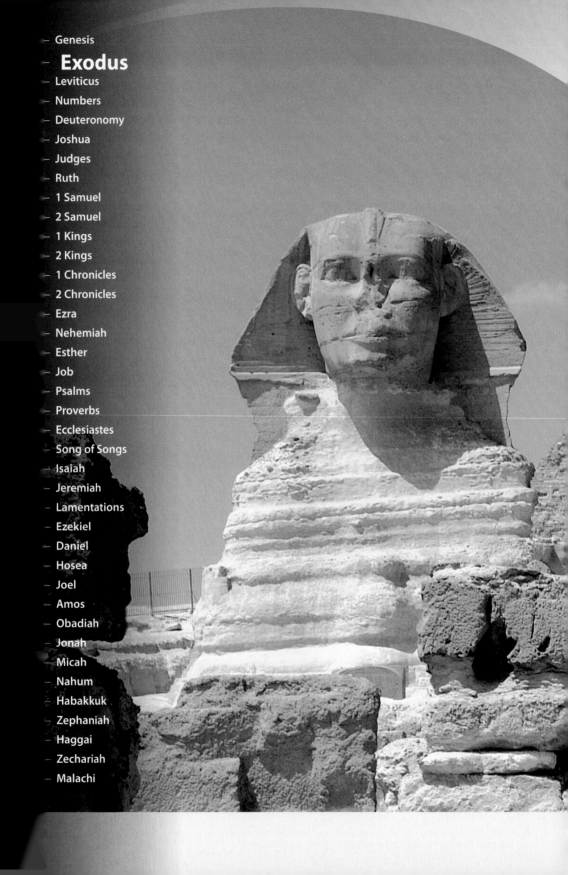

Exodus

Deliverance and the Presence of God

The book of Exodus is packed with powerful and exciting stories that have been told and retold throughout Jewish and Christian history. The story of Exodus is so fascinating that even Hollywood recognized the grip it has on people, producing *The Ten Commandments* and *The Prince of Egypt*, two great movies based on the story. The book is filled with strong, colorful characters like Moses and Pharaoh who play dramatic roles in a tense life-and-death drama. God himself is a major character, appearing often in this story and playing a major—one could say *the central*—role. Ultimately, the book of Exodus presents the story of salvation—how God crashes dramatically into human history to save his people. So while fascinating and dynamic people like Moses and Pharaoh are critical to the story of Exodus, the truth is that the book of Exodus is primarily about God.

The central themes of Exodus echo throughout the entire Bible and are tightly interwoven into our most basic Christian theology. In the Old Testament the exodus event becomes the paradigm, or model, of what salvation is all about. Thus the exodus event is to the Old Testament as the cross is to the New Testament. The story of God's

This painting from a tomb in Egypt (ca. 1450 BC) depicts brickmaking and construction.

deliverance in Exodus shapes the theo-logical thinking of the entire Old Testament in regard to the character of God and the nature of his gracious salvation. Throughout the rest of the Old Testament, God's favorite way to identify himself to his people is the repeated phrase, "I am the Lord, who brought you up out of Egypt." Likewise, Exodus stresses the importance of the Presence of God, a central biblical theme that runs from Genesis to Revelation.

What Is the Setting for Exodus?

Exodus continues the story that began in Genesis. Recall that Genesis 12–50 is about the three patriarchs Abraham, Isaac, and Jacob, ending with a focus on Jacob's twelve sons. The later chapters in Genesis (37–50) stress the story of Joseph (the boy with the special coat), one of the sons of Jacob. The other sons sell Joseph into slavery, and he ends up in Egypt. God, however, looks after him and enables him to prosper in Egypt, where Joseph becomes a top official, second in power only to Pharaoh. Joseph then plays a key role in saving Egypt from a terrible famine. The rest of his family later flees to Egypt to escape the famine in Canaan and is reunited with Joseph. The book of Genesis ends with this family in Egypt.

The book of Exodus picks up the story in Egypt and continues it. Exodus 1:1–8 reminds the readers of this connection. The opening verses in Exodus indicate that time has passed and a new pharaoh has come to the throne, a pharaoh who has no memory of how Joseph saved Egypt from the famine back in Genesis. Perhaps a dynastic change has taken place. In fulfillment of the Abrahamic promises (Genesis 12, 15) the sons of Jacob (Israel) have proliferated and are now so numerous that they frighten the Egyptians. However, in spite of this particular promise fulfillment, the Israelites still do not have their own land, and thus a critical aspect of God's promise to Abraham remains

✦ The title "Exodus" comes from a Greek word that means "to go out." The book was given this title when it was translated from Hebrew into Greek (the Septuagint). Our English Bibles have followed the Septuagint in using this title for the book.

Dating the Exodus

Peter Enns

Dating Israel's departure from Egypt is an exceedingly complex scholarly problem. This is partly due to ambiguity with the biblical data, but also to the extrabiblical (archaeological) data at our disposal.

The two general proposed dates are the fifteenth century (about 1446 BC) and the thirteenth century (about 1270–60 BC), also known as the early and late dates, respectively. The former date is arrived at by a literal reading of 1 Kings 6:1, where 480 years are given from the exodus to the fourth year of Solomon's reign (966 BC). That would yield a date of 1446 BC. Although one might think that this settles the issue, the matter is more complicated than it might first appear. First, if one adds up the dates given elsewhere in the Old Testament, from the wilderness period to Solomon, one arrives at a figure of about six hundred years. Hence, 480 is typically understood as a symbolic number, likely representing a completion of an "era" and described as 12 x 40 (twelve generations times either a typical length of a generation or perhaps twelve times the length of the wilderness wandering).

The early date is also problematic for archaeological reasons. First, Exodus 1:11 refers to the storehouses Rameses built. The scholarly consensus is that only Rameses II could be meant, who ruled from 1279 to 1213 BC. The storehouse known as Pi-Rameses, which is typically identified with the site mentioned in Exodus 1:11, was built in about 1270 BC. If this identification is correct, then the exodus could have happened only sometime after 1270 BC.

One important factor that lends some support for the late date is the archaeological evidence for the conquest of Canaan. Although not without its own set of scholarly problems, it generally holds that the date of the destruction of numerous Canaanite cities did not happen in the fourteenth century BC (which would be required by the early date), but later in the thirteenth century and afterward. This does not in any way prove a late date, but it does make an early date difficult to maintain on archaeological grounds.

Part of the scholarly difficulty is that there is actually very little extrabiblical evidence from which to argue, and the Bible itself is ambiguous on the matter. Nevertheless, for scholars who accept an exodus event more or less in keeping with the Bible's presentation, the late date is the most commonly accepted position.

unfulfilled. The fulfillment of the "land promise" aspect of the Abrahamic covenant will drive the story from Exodus to Joshua, where it is finally fulfilled.

What Is at the Heart of Exodus?

Three major themes dominate the book of Exodus:

1. God delivers his people and brings them up out of Egypt. The fundamental message of Exodus is that God saves and delivers his people. Throughout the rest of the Old Testament, the exodus event becomes the primary picture of what salvation is all about.

2. As God delivers Israel, he will act in such a way that everyone will "know" and recognize his power. Those who trust in him will "know" his salvation. Those who defy him will "know" his judgment. One way or the other, everyone will know him. There is no middle ground and no way to ignore him.

3. A critical aspect of the covenant relationship that God establishes with the sons of Israel after he rescues them from Egypt is that he will dwell in their midst. Thus the Presence of God is a major theme throughout the book. The second half of the book (Exodus 25–40) deals with the construction of the tabernacle, where the Presence of God will dwell.

Closely connected to the three central themes in Exodus are two frequently repeated phrases that occur throughout Exodus in various formulations. First is the statement, "I am the Lord, who brought you up out of Egypt." This occurs in several forms, all stating that God is the one who brought the Israelites up out of Egypt. This connects to the main themes of deliverance and knowing God. The second frequently repeated statement, occurring over seventy times in Exodus, is "that you might know that I am the Lord." As mentioned above, one of the central themes in Exodus is that God's spectacular demonstration of his power will be decisive and not ambiguous. Everyone will know that "he is the Lord," either in salvation or in judgment.

The story in Exodus is generally in chronological order. The major units are as follows:

- Deliverance from Egypt (1:1–15:27)
  - Pharaoh, women, and babies (1:1–2:10)
  - Holiness, presence, and power: The Lord calls Moses (2:11–4:17)
  - Who is the Lord? Initial encounters with Pharaoh and the people (4:18–7:5)
  - Pharaoh versus the Lord: The first nine plagues (7:6–10:29)
  - The Lord delivers Israel from Egypt (11:1–15:21)
- Inaugurating the Sinai Covenant (15:22–24:18)
  - The journey to Mount Sinai (15:22–18:27)
  - The revelation at Mount Sinai (19:1–25)
  - The Ten Commandments (20:1–21)
  - The book of the covenant (20:22–23:33)
  - Ratification of the covenant (24:1–18)

- "I Will Dwell in Your Midst": The Tabernacle and God's Presence (25:1–40:38)
  - Instructions for building the tabernacle (25:1–31:18)
  - An interruption: Rebellion and covenant renewal (32:1–34:35)
  - Completing the tabernacle (35:1–40:38)

What Makes Exodus Interesting and Unique?

- The story of Moses is one of the most fascinating and colorful stories in the Bible.
- God appears numerous times in Exodus as one of the main characters.
- The story of the confrontation between Pharaoh and God (with Moses as God's representative) is packed with drama and irony.
- Exodus contains a high concentration of miraculous actions and appearances by God.
- God gives the Ten Commandments in Exodus.
- The family of Abraham becomes the nation of Israel in the book of Exodus.
- The Passover is first described in Exodus.
- Ironically, Exodus contains one of the most tragic rebellious actions by Israel against God (the golden calf episode in Exodus 32).

Gigantic statue of Rameses II at the Temple at Memphis in Egypt. Many scholars think that Rameses II is the Pharaoh of Exodus 1, but the evidence is not conclusive.

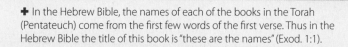

✝ In the Hebrew Bible, the names of each of the books in the Torah (Pentateuch) come from the first few words of the first verse. Thus in the Hebrew Bible the title of this book is "these are the names" (Exod. 1:1).

What Is the Message of Exodus?

Deliverance from Egypt (1:1–15:21)

Pharaoh, women, and babies (1:1–2:10)

Exodus opens by connecting back to the patriarchal story in Genesis. Jacob and his sons go into Egypt as a family; they will come out as a great nation. Recall that back in Genesis God renames Jacob as "Israel." In Exodus the phrase "sons of Israel" occurs 125 times. Many English translations translate this phrase as "the Israelites."

The opening verses of Exodus also connect back to the Abrahamic covenant (Genesis 12, 15, 17). The Israelites are now very numerous, as God had promised to Abraham. But they do not have a land yet. And soon Pharaoh will enslave them and treat them miserably. One of the promises God gave to Abraham was, "I will bless those who bless you, and whoever curses you I will curse" (Gen. 12:3). Pharaoh's horrible treatment of the Israelites puts him on a collision course with God's promise to Abraham.

Statue of an Egyptian overseer, with whip in hand.

Exodus 1:8 explains that a new pharaoh has come to power who has no memory of Joseph and how Joseph had saved Egypt. Thus this pharaoh sees the Israelites only as a threat and not as a possible blessing. It is interesting that the book of Exodus does not identify this pharaoh. Usually the Bible is quite clear in naming the kings throughout the region, especially if that particular king has direct dealings with Israel. Yet this king (i.e., pharaoh), even though he plays a huge role in the story of Israel, remains unnamed. We suspect that this is intentional and reflects a put-down of sorts. This arrogant pharaoh was the most powerful man in the world at the time and was considered by the Egyptians to be divine. The Bible, however, does not even leave us his name. In contrast, the names of two lowly midwives are given (1:15), suggesting perhaps that in the overall scheme of things, the midwives are more important to God than the hard-hearted pharaoh. An interesting side note is that scholars today do not agree on who the pharaoh of the Exodus actually was. So while everyone knows the name Moses, no one even knows for certain who the pharaoh was.

The blessing of Abraham through the proliferation of descendants is the very thing that sets the story in motion. Pharaoh becomes alarmed at the growing population of Israelites and tries to curb their population growth. He tries three successive, but unsuccessful, plans. First he tries simply to overwork them, decreeing that the Israelites work as slaves to build store cities for Egypt (1:11–14). The irony of this is rich, for remember that Joseph was the one who introduced the concept of store cities to Egypt (Genesis 41). When this plan doesn't work, Pharaoh takes a much more drastic step and orders the midwives to kill all newborn Hebrew boys at birth, a horrific command. The Hebrew midwives, however, fear God more than Pharaoh and defy his orders (1:15–21). So Pharaoh then enacts his third and most terrible plan to curb the population growth of the Israelites, ordering that all newborn Hebrew boys be thrown into the Nile River. This is a nightmarish order for the Israelites. But recall God's promise to Abraham ("whoever curses you I will curse"). Pharaoh has chosen to attack God's people in a most direct and terrifying manner, killing the most defenseless and innocent ones. Thus Pharaoh provokes the wrath of God. The image of Israelite babies dying in the Nile provides the background for several of the plagues God sends on Egypt (turning the Nile into blood, death of all the Egyptian firstborn, etc.). Likewise, note the irony

Moses's mother hides him in the reeds along the banks of the Nile River. Shown above is a tomb wall painting of an Egyptian hunting birds in the reeds along the Nile (1400 BC).

✝ The characters in the story of Exodus 1:1–2:10 are Pharaoh and five women who oppose his decrees: the two midwives, Moses's mother and sister, and Pharaoh's daughter.

and fitting poetic justice of the final judgment by God on Egypt in Exodus 14. God drowns the entire Egyptian army! In Exodus 1, Pharaoh attacks God and God's people by drowning the Israelite infant sons. In response, God systematically destroys Egypt economically and militarily, destroying all their agriculture, killing all their firstborn, and then drowning their entire army (Exodus 7–14).

Exodus 2:1–10 introduces Moses into the story in a most ironic way. Pharaoh has ordered that all the newborn Israelite boys be thrown into the Nile. Moses's mother, however, places him in a watertight basket and then places the basket among the reeds in the Nile, hiding the baby in the very place where the babies were supposed to die. Adding to the irony is that the daughter of Pharaoh finds the baby Moses and determines to keep the baby and raise him herself, in defiance of her father's decree. Thus the Egyptians will nurture and educate the very one who will lead in God's destruction of Egypt.

Holiness, presence, and power: The Lord calls Moses (2:11–4:17)

In Exodus 2:11–22, Moses is reintroduced into the story, now as a grown man. As the future leader of Israel, however, he doesn't really get off to a very good start. This opening episode probably illustrates how weak Moses really is and how poorly he performs when he works in his own power and understanding, without the empowering Presence of God. In 2:11–15 Moses kills an Egyptian for beating a Hebrew slave, but then flees into the desert of Midian, fearing Pharaoh's reprisal. He then marries into a Midianite family and settles down, apparently for good. Note the inner

The Nile River today.

✦ The Presence of God, the holiness of God, and the power of God are three central interrelated themes that frequently appear together in the Bible.

The Two Primary Names for God in the Old Testament

The Old Testament uses two primary Hebrew words for God. The first is *Elohim*, the name used in Genesis 1:1 ("In the beginning God [Elohim] created the heavens and the earth"). The word "Elohim" occurs 2,570 times in the Old Testament. It is a "generic" term and just means "god." It can be used of the true God of Israel or it can be used of false gods like Baal or Molech. Almost all Bible translations will translate this word as "God" (capitalized) if it refers to the true God of Israel, and as "god" or "gods" (without caps) if it refers to the pagan gods of Israel's neighbors. Technically Elohim is in a plural form, so when used of pagan deities it can be translated as "gods" (plural). Yet when used of the God of Israel, this plural form is always used with singular verbs and with singular pronouns (he and him, not they), so it clearly refers to a singular entity. In this case the plural form in Hebrew is used to stress majesty or intensification. Elohim is used especially in contexts of God relating to the entire world (his creation, his power over the nations, etc.).

The other central Hebrew word used for God in the Old Testament is *Yahweh*. This word occurs over 6,800 times and functions as the personal name of God. It is used in contexts of God's personal relationship with people, especially through the covenant. Thus throughout the Old Testament God will frequently say, "I am Yahweh, who brought you up out of Egypt" (or something similar to this), stressing the close connection between his name, Yahweh, and his strong action of deliverance as seen in the exodus. The character of God as revealed through the name Yahweh is best understood by seeing and grasping what he did in the Exodus story.

The name Yahweh is probably related to the Hebrew verb meaning "to be." Thus God's self-identification to Moses as "I am who I am" is a clear (yet complex) wordplay on the name Yahweh. In most English Bibles the name Yahweh is usually translated as "the LORD," with LORD all in caps. It doesn't really mean "Lord," as in the sense of "master" (Hebrew has another term, *adonai*, that actually means "master, lord"), although it certainly implies that relationship. In this handbook we will simply translate Yahweh as Lord.

The two terms (Elohim and Yahweh) are often used together or in the same context. Usually in this case the stress is that Yahweh is Israel's God (Elohim). Thus in the great Shema of Deuteronomy 6:4–5 (*Shema* is the Hebrew word for "hear"), Moses declares to Israel, "Hear O Israel, Yahweh our Elohim, Yahweh is one. Love Yahweh your Elohim with all your heart and with all your soul and with all your strength."

tension as to Moses's identity. In 2:11 he identifies with the Hebrews. In 2:19 the girls at the well (and his future wife) refer to him as an Egyptian. After marrying and settling down with the Midianites, he apparently becomes a Midianite. Note also that this family is a "priestly" Midianite family (2:16). Numbers 25 indicates that the Midianites worshiped Baal. What is Moses doing here?

Exodus 2:23–24 is a very important transition. God hears the Israelites crying out in their slavery, and he decides to act, based on his promise to Abraham. Note that the people of Israel haven't repented or turned back to

✛ Jesus declares, "Before Abraham was born, I am!" (John 8:58). Jesus is obviously identifying with the name of God revealed to Moses in the burning bush episode of Exodus 3.

God. They have merely cried out in their pain and misery. God hears this cry, remembers his covenant with Abraham, and decides to act (in Exodus 3 he will assign Moses to lead them).

In 3:1–4:17 Moses has an incredible encounter with God. Moses is frittering away his life in the outback of Midian. For all essential purposes he is a Midianite. God confronts him, reveals himself to him, and then sets him on an entirely new path in life: to lead the Israelites out of Egypt and to the Promised Land.

God appears to Moses from within a burning bush. As Moses draws near, God tells him to remove his shoes for the ground around God is holy. This appearance of God to Moses reveals the close interconnection between God's Presence, his holiness, and his enabling power.

God identifies himself to Moses as the same God whom Abraham worshiped (3:6). God explains that he has heard the cries of the Israelites, and thus he has come down to rescue them. Then, to Moses's surprise, God states that he is sending Moses to Pharaoh to deliver the Israelites.

Moses puts forth four feeble objections to God's plan, and God counters all four objections with reassuring words. First, Moses questions his ability and adequacy, and God promises him the power of God's presence (3:11–12). Furthermore, God offers a sign—after Moses has brought the people out of Egypt, he will lead them back to this very spot to worship God. But Moses objects, declaring that he doesn't even know exactly who God is, to which God explains, "I am who I am" (3:13–15). The Hebrew word for "I am" is related to the Hebrew name for God, which is usually translated into English as "the Lord."

In objection number three, Moses asks what he will do if the people of Israel don't believe him. God then gives him three dramatic miraculous signs: turning his staff into a snake, turning the skin on his hand into leprous skin, and turning water into blood. If they don't believe you, God states, then show them these miraculous signs (4:1–9). The signs carry symbolism

Possible locaton of Mount Sinai/Horeb.

as well. The symbol of Egyptian power, especially associated with the pharaoh, was the cobra. The pharaohs of Egypt often wore crowns with a golden cobra coiled on top. Moses is about to grab Pharaoh "by the tail," so to speak, and yet he will prevail; his staff commands more power than Pharaoh.

Finally, Moses objects regarding his speaking ability, and then begs God to send someone else (4:10, 13). God gets angry at this, but declares that Aaron, Moses's brother, will serve as his spokesman (4:14–16), along with his powerful miracle-working staff (4:17).

The cobra symbolized Lower Egypt. The Egyptian pharaohs often placed cobras on their crowns, signifying their rule over Lower Egypt.

Who is the Lord? Initial encounters with Pharaoh and the people (4:18–7:5)

Moses gathers his family and starts his return to Egypt. Along the way he has a very strange encounter with God (4:18–26). Apparently Moses had not yet circumcised his sons. Circumcision, remember, was the sign of being in the Abrahamic covenant. God seems to insist that Moses circumcise the boys in his family before he can take command of the Israelites.

Moses meets Aaron (4:27–28), and the two of them return to Egypt. They tell the Israelites all God has said to Moses, and they show them the miraculous signs. The Israelites believe and worship God (4:29–31). Things start out well for Moses.

Pharaoh, however, is a different matter. When Moses tells Pharaoh that the Lord demands he let the Israelites go, Pharaoh makes a fateful statement: "Who is the Lord, that I should obey him and let Israel go? I do not know the Lord and I will not let Israel go" (5:2). God answers this defiant challenge dramatically. By the end of Exodus 14, with Egypt destroyed, all their firstborn dead, and the entire army dead on the shores of the Red Sea, Pharaoh will know who the Lord is.

At the present time, however, Pharaoh responds to Moses's request by making life harder for the Israelites, requiring them to increase their output of bricks using less material (5:3–20). The Israelites, who had responded favorably to Moses at first, now speak against him (5:21). How fickle the Israelites are going to be throughout Exodus!

So Moses comes to God and whines a little about how things are going (5:22–23). God explains to Moses that he has something

✚ God wants the Israelites to *know* that he is the one who delivered them; likewise he wants the Egyptians to *know* that he is the one who destroyed them.

Exodus   67

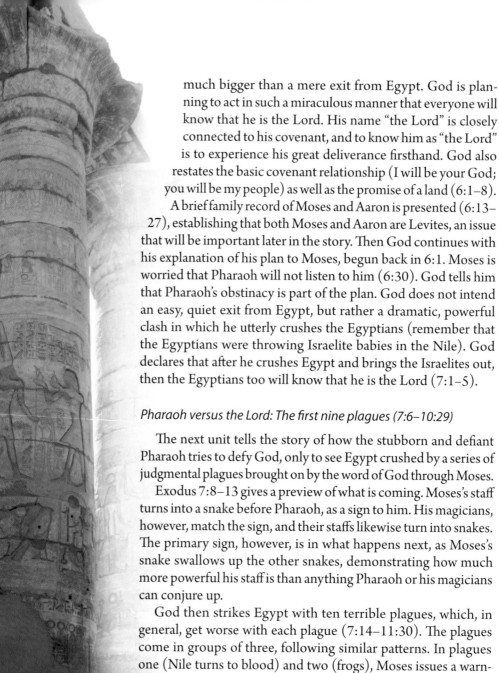

much bigger than a mere exit from Egypt. God is planning to act in such a miraculous manner that everyone will know that he is the Lord. His name "the Lord" is closely connected to his covenant, and to know him as "the Lord" is to experience his great deliverance firsthand. God also restates the basic covenant relationship (I will be your God; you will be my people) as well as the promise of a land (6:1–8).

A brief family record of Moses and Aaron is presented (6:13–27), establishing that both Moses and Aaron are Levites, an issue that will be important later in the story. Then God continues with his explanation of his plan to Moses, begun back in 6:1. Moses is worried that Pharaoh will not listen to him (6:30). God tells him that Pharaoh's obstinacy is part of the plan. God does not intend an easy, quiet exit from Egypt, but rather a dramatic, powerful clash in which he utterly crushes the Egyptians (remember that the Egyptians were throwing Israelite babies in the Nile). God declares that after he crushes Egypt and brings the Israelites out, then the Egyptians too will know that he is the Lord (7:1–5).

Pharaoh versus the Lord: The first nine plagues (7:6–10:29)

The next unit tells the story of how the stubborn and defiant Pharaoh tries to defy God, only to see Egypt crushed by a series of judgmental plagues brought on by the word of God through Moses.

Exodus 7:8–13 gives a preview of what is coming. Moses's staff turns into a snake before Pharaoh, as a sign to him. His magicians, however, match the sign, and their staffs likewise turn into snakes. The primary sign, however, is in what happens next, as Moses's snake swallows up the other snakes, demonstrating how much more powerful his staff is than anything Pharaoh or his magicians can conjure up.

God then strikes Egypt with ten terrible plagues, which, in general, get worse with each plague (7:14–11:30). The plagues come in groups of three, following similar patterns. In plagues one (Nile turns to blood) and two (frogs), Moses issues a warning to Pharaoh and demands that he let the Israelites go. Pharaoh refuses, and God then initiates the plague. Plague three (gnats), however, strikes Egypt without warning. The next cycle follows the same pattern. Plagues four (flies) and five (dead livestock) are preceded by warnings and the demand to let God's people go. Plague six (boils) comes without warning. The next cycle repeats in

Spectacular columns in the Temple of Amun Re, the Egyptian sun god.

The Plagues

Peter Enns

The plagues are ten acts that God inflicted on the Egyptians through Moses's leadership. The main narrative of the plagues begins in Exodus 7:14 with the waters of the Nile turned to blood, and ends in Exodus 11:1–13:16 with the death of the firstborn, the institution of the Passover, and Israel's release from Egyptian slavery. The plagues are also alluded to in Psalm 78:44–51, although the sequence is different and only six of the ten are mentioned. (See also Ps. 105:28–36.)

Descriptions of these are well-known, even in popular culture (e.g., river to blood, frogs, boils, darkness, death of firstborn), but the theological role the plagues play in the book of Exodus is not always appreciated. One question that immediately comes to mind is why there are ten. In fact, why are there plagues at all? Why did God not simply get the Israelites out without all the fanfare? The reason is stated in 9:15–16. God's purpose in the plagues was not to convince Pharaoh that his resistance was futile. Rather, God raised Pharaoh up so that, through a prolonged process, he might show his power to Pharaoh and have his name proclaimed throughout the earth.

It is important to understand that the plagues are not a process whereby God wore Pharaoh down so that he would eventually relent. By the time we get to the second (frogs) and fourth (flies) plagues, Pharaoh had already had enough (he begs Moses to make them stop). True, after the second plague is over, he hardens his heart (see also plagues three, four, six, and seven where Pharaoh either hardens his heart or it becomes hardened). But, beginning with plague six and continuing to plagues eight, nine, and ten, it is *God* who hardens Pharaoh's heart. Even though Pharaoh is ready to give in, God is not. He prolongs the process to make a point, namely, that he is not only the God of Hebrew slaves but also over Egypt and the other nations as well. Pharaoh was his tool to make that known.

The plagues also have some religious significance. At least some of the plagues seem to reflect elements of the Egyptian pantheon. For example, the Nile was personified and worshiped as a god (Hapi). To turn the Nile to blood was to overpower the god that brought life to Egypt. Likewise, the solar deity, Re, was very important to Egyptian religion. Pharaohs were sometimes referred to as the sons of Re. The plague of darkness (ninth) was not only an inconvenience, but also a statement of the superiority of Israel's God over those of Egypt.

The plagues also show that Israel's God can control the elements. Pharaoh's magicians could reproduce the first two plagues (as well as the staff turning into a snake), but no more. Also, only Israel's God could make them *stop*. God has at his disposal the created order to bring about Israel's salvation. Hence, through the plagues, he shows himself to be the true creator and deliverer.

Egyptian tomb relief of the form of the frog-goddess Heket, goddess-protector of pregnant women and childbirth.

the same manner. Moses declares warnings prior to plague seven (hail) and plague eight (locusts), but plague nine (darkness) comes without warning. The tenth and final plague (death of the firstborn) likewise comes after a serious warning.

Several of the plagues carry symbolic significance, connecting especially to the opening chapter of Exodus and Pharaoh's execution of the Israelite newborn boys. The first plague turns the Nile into blood (7:14–24). The Nile was the symbol of Egypt and represented Egyptian prosperity and power. Thus the red blood symbolized the death of Egypt itself. But keep in mind that Pharaoh had been killing the Hebrew babies by throwing them into the Nile. Thus when the Nile turns to blood, it reminds all of the terrible deaths that took place there. The magicians can duplicate the plague, but not reverse it or stop it. That is, they can use their power to bring more judgment on Egypt, but they can't do anything to repulse God's plague or to stop the judgment.

The second plague (frogs) also connects back to the death of the Hebrew babies. In the religion of the ancient Egyptians, the god and protector of pregnant women was a god called Heket, who was usually portrayed in the form of a frog. This was probably because in Egyptian thinking, the transition from tadpoles to frogs symbolized the growth and birth of human babies. When the Egyptians are overrun with frogs in this plague, it serves to remind them what a terrible crime against pregnant women and newborns had been committed. The magicians, probably to Pharaoh's chagrin, cannot stop the frogs, but can only bring more frogs (and thus more judgment).

As the plagues progress, all of Egypt's agricultural prosperity is systematically destroyed. Pharaoh and his officials, however, continue to harden their hearts and refuse to let the Israelites go. Plague nine (darkness) is also quite symbolic, for the major deity of Egypt was Re, the sun god, and Pharaoh was known as the "son of Re."

Exodus 12:38 states that large herds of cattle accompanied the Israelites as they left Egypt. Pictured is a fragment of a tomb wall painting that depicts Egyptian cattle being counted in order to be taxed (1400 BC).

The Lord delivers Israel from Egypt (11:1–15:21)

The final and climactic plague is the death of the firstborn (11:1–10), a fitting final and terrible judgment on

✚ Pharaoh drowns the Hebrew babies in Exodus 1; God drowns the entire Egyptian army in Exodus 12.

Egypt for executing the Israelite babies in Exodus 1. As the Israelites leave, God gives them two commemorative rituals (the Feast of Unleavened Bread and the Passover) so that they will always remember this special time of deliverance (12:1–28). The actual exodus takes place in 12:31–51 after the death of the Egyptian firstborn. The Egyptians totally capitulate, allowing the Israelites to leave as conquerors, carrying off the wealth of Egypt (12:36). The events surrounding this exodus were obviously well-known throughout Egypt, for numerous other peoples of various nationalities accompany the Israelites as they depart (12:38), fulfilling God's promise made to Abraham of blessing the gentiles (Gen. 12:3). In Exodus 12:43–51 God decrees that these foreigners can participate in the Passover if they have been circumcised, and 13:1–16 describes how to commemorate this special day, as well as how to consecrate Israel's future firstborn.

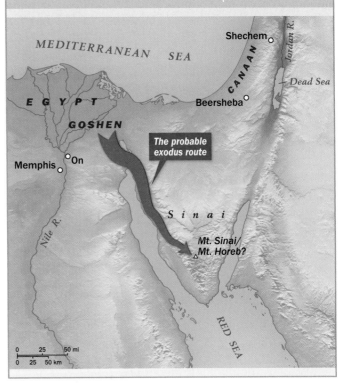

The probable exodus route

The route the Israelites traveled when they left Egypt. It is difficult to determine the exact route based only on the details of Exodus 12–19, and scholars differ on the route. Depicted above is the most probable route.

Next, the Israelites come to a significant body of water referred to in Hebrew as the *yom suph* ("sea of reeds"). Later in the biblical story, 1 Kings 9:26 states that Solomon sails ships on the *yom suph*. In 1 Kings 9:26 the reference is clearly to the modern body of water known today in English as the Red Sea, so probably the *yom suph* in Exodus is the same body of water. At any rate, it is a formidable obstacle, one that blocks the Israelites from escaping from the Egyptians, and one that ultimately drowns the entire Egyptian army.

The Presence of God plays a crucial role in the deliverance of the Israelites. God's Presence accompanies Israel as they travel, appearing in a pillar of cloud by day and a

✚ The Passover in Exodus 12 foreshadows the death of Jesus Christ in the New Testament.

pillar of fire by night (13:20–22), both to guide the Israelites and also to protect them (14:19–24). God miraculously parts the Red Sea, allowing Israel to safely cross over, and then closes the sea on the Egyptian chariots as they pursue Israel. The climax of Exodus 1–14 is expressed succinctly by 14:31: "And when the Israelites saw the great power the Lord displayed against the Egyptians, the people feared the Lord and put their trust in him and in Moses his servant."

Exodus 15 closes the first half of the Exodus story in a song of victory celebration. Moses and the Israelites (apparently the men) sing a victory song (15:1–18), followed by a similar song by Miriam, his sister, and the women (15:19–21).

Inaugurating the Sinai Covenant (15:22–24:18)

The journey to Mount Sinai (15:22–18:27)

Having delivered Israel through a spectacular display of power, God now guides his people to Mount Sinai, where he will enter into a covenant agreement with them. Incredibly, however, along the way Israel quickly loses faith, complaining and grumbling to Moses about water (15:22–27), food (16:1–36), and then water again (17:1–7). Each time God provides for them. In 17:7, however, they ask in doubt, "Is the Lord among us or not?" God answers in 17:8–16 by giving them a victory over the Amalekites. Jethro, Moses's father-in-law (or perhaps his wife's uncle), visits Moses in Exodus 18, interrupting the negative flow of Israelite grumbling, and gives Moses good solid advice about organizing a sound judicial system that could take some of the leadership load off Moses.

The revelation at Mount Sinai (19:1–25)

In the burning bush episode back in Exodus 3, God told Moses that after he delivered the people up out of Egypt, he would bring them right back to that very same spot (Mount Sinai) to worship God (3:12). Now, when they do arrive back at Mount Sinai, God gives the people a similar experience to what Moses encountered back in Exodus 3 at the burning bush. In Exodus 3, God spoke just to the one man Moses; in Exodus 19 he speaks

The Sinai desert.

to all the people. In Exodus 3, fire is concentrated in one solitary bush; in Exodus 19 the entire mountain is burning. In both encounters the ground is declared to be holy, due to the Presence of God. What is the point of this similarity? Just as God commissioned Moses, so now he commissions the entire nation, declaring them to be a "kingdom of priests and a holy nation" (19:6). Indeed, throughout Exodus 19 the people are treated like priests. The mountain becomes like a temple, the people consecrate themselves like priests (19:10–15), and then they meet with God himself (19:17)—an event that is typically reserved only for priests.

The Ten Commandments (20:1–21)

God has dramatically delivered Israel from slavery in Egypt and has brought them to Mount Sinai, where his glory and holiness is revealed to the people in terrifying thunder, lightning, smoke, and fire (19:17–19). God also declares that the entire nation will be like priests to him. In this context, God now enters into a special covenant relationship with the people of Israel, a spectacular opportunity for blessing and rich meaning in life brought about by the powerful Presence of God. Now that the Israelites are in this new relationship with God, they need to know how to live as his special people. In Exodus 20–24 God gives Israel the stipulations that define this new covenant relationship (often called the Mosaic covenant). At the heart of this covenant are the Ten Commandments, representing the essence or core elements of the new relationship the Israelites now have with God.

The Ten Commandments focus on relationship and faithfulness. The first four commandments define how the people are to relate to God. Idolatry is strictly forbidden; they are to worship the Lord and him alone. These first four commandments are (1) do not worship other gods, (2) do not make images of God or other gods, (3) do not take the Lord's name in vain, and (4) keep the Sabbath. The next six describe how the people are to relate to one another, within their families and within the broader community. These six family/community-oriented commandments are (5) honor parents, (6) do not commit murder, (7) do not commit adultery, (8) do not steal, (9) do not give false testimony, and (10) do not covet.

✚ In the New Testament Peter is drawing from Exodus 19:6 when he states, "You are . . . a royal priesthood, a holy nation" (1 Pet. 2:9).

The Ten Commandments

Michael Grisanti

HISTORICAL CONTEXT

When Moses led the Israelites out of Egypt and the people began their journey toward the land of promise, they were a people without a clear identity and purpose. They left behind an Egyptian sojourn of 430 years. At the Red Sea, the Lord orchestrated one of the most stupendous miracles of the Old Testament. The Israelites' crossing of this body of water on dry ground represented the Lord's commitment to bring to pass what he had promised to his people, and served as a paradigm for God's character and activity in the rest of the Old Testament. Once the people camped at the base of Mount Sinai, the Lord then led Israel to a greater depth in their relationship with him.

TEN COMMANDMENTS: CORE OF THE LAW (THE LORD'S COVENANT EXPECTATIONS)

Moses ascended Mount Sinai as Israel's representative to receive the law from the Lord. The Lord himself etched the words of the Ten Commandments (or "Ten Words," hence *Decalogue*) on two stone tablets (Exod. 20:1–17; Deut. 5:6–21). These ten far-reaching divine requirements represented the heart of what Yahweh expected of his people. The first four commandments focus on one's relationship with God (vertical) while the other six commandments give attention to one's relationship with fellow Israelites (horizontal).

It is important to notice that the Ten Commandments begin with a preface, something common in ancient Near Eastern treaties. This preface or prologue generally describes the past dealings of the parties of the treaty. In this passage, the prologue demonstrates that God did not deliver his covenant demands to Israel in a vacuum, but in the context of an intimate relationship, clearly evidenced by his surpassing character and abundant activity on Israel's

behalf. His gift of the law was preceded by an act of love and grace. He gave these covenant demands to a people with whom he had already established a relationship, not as a means to enter that relationship (which always was and is "by faith").

It is also essential to understand these commandments as requirements anchored in a covenant relationship. The Lord began that relationship with the descendants of Abraham (Genesis 12, 15, 17), but formalizes and deepens that relationship with the Ten Commandments and the rest of the law of Moses. These covenant demands give concrete direction to Israel's relationship with God. They were to obey these stipulations, not purely for the sake of obedience, but to demonstrate the character of the Lord to the surrounding nations (Exod. 19:4–6; Deut. 26:16–19).

DETAILED LEGISLATION: DELINEATION OF THE TEN COMMANDMENTS

The detailed rules and regulations that fill much of Exodus, Leviticus, and Deuteronomy are not a free-floating set of rules that have no connection with the Ten Commandments. Rather, they represent the detailed application of the character of God to every area of an Israelite's life. Furthermore, these regulations operate in two basic spheres: vertical and horizontal (cf. Christ's summary of the Mosaic law into two spheres—Luke 10:25–28). Some laws, primarily those concerning the worship ritual and requirements that do not directly impact fellow Israelites (dietary regulations, for example), focus on an Israelite's walk with God. They can be summed up as a call to live a life of total allegiance before the Lord. Other laws concern the way Israelites should treat their fellow citizens. In summary, God's chosen people are to treat one another with love, justice, and equity.

✛ The Ten Commandments appear twice in the Old Testament, once in Exodus 20:1–17 and again in Deuteronomy 5:6–21.

The book of the covenant (20:22–23:33)

This unit is often called "the book of the covenant," and it contains general principles flowing out of the Ten Commandments as well as applications of these principles. Again, keep in mind that God is explaining how his people are to live within this new covenant relationship they have with him. A variety of laws are presented in this unit, showing that God is concerned with all areas of life. For example, God wants his people to be honest and just (23:1–3, 6–8). He obligates them to be responsible for the well-being of others (23:4–5), especially foreigners, orphans, and widows (those who were socioeconomically weak in the culture; 22:21–27). Also included in this section are the guidelines for three annual festivals (the Feast of Unleavened Bread, the Feast of Harvest, and the Feast of Ingathering; 23:14–19). These festivals were the primary times when Israel gathered to worship God and celebrate their relationship with him.

Ratification of the covenant (24:1–18)

In Exodus 24 the new covenant relationship described in Exodus 19–23 is ratified. The terms of the agreement are repeated to the people twice, and twice they agree to obey these terms (the laws in Exodus 20–23). Then Moses sprinkles blood on them to formally put the covenant into effect, declaring, "This is the blood of the covenant" (24:8). Jesus will use similar words when he later inaugurates the new covenant (Matt. 26:28; Mark 14:24; Luke 22:20).

The elders of Israel next partake of a meal in the very Presence of God (24:11), demonstrating the close relationship they now have with him, and foreshadowing the future "messianic banquet" described in the Prophets and alluded to frequently in the New Testament.

"I Will Dwell in Your Midst": The Tabernacle and God's Presence (25:1–40:38)

Instructions for building the tabernacle (25:1–31:18)

At the heart of the covenant relationship between God and his people is the three-part formula statement: I will be your God; you will be my people; I will dwell in your midst. A highly significant (and very radical) new feature of this relationship is that God is

The gods of the ancient Near East were often portrayed as calves or bulls. Shown here is a bronze Apis bull from Egypt.

Moses Breaking the Tablets of the Law by Rembrandt.

actually coming to live among them. If the holy and awesome God is coming to dwell among them, then he will need an appropriate place to live—a place where the Israelites can enjoy the blessings of knowing and worshiping him without being consumed by the power of his holy Presence. Thus the central focus of Exodus 25–40 is the design and construction of the tabernacle, the place where God will dwell. Over one-third of the book of Exodus is dedicated to describing the tabernacle, indicating the critical importance of this theme—the Presence of God dwelling with his people. Exodus 25–31 describes the ark of the covenant, the table for the bread of the Presence, the lampstand, and the tabernacle itself. Priestly procedures are described, including the garments they are to wear and the utensils they are to use for the sacrifices and for burning incense.

An interruption: Rebellion and covenant renewal (32:1–34:35)

Exodus 32–34 is a dramatic and terrible interruption to the wonderful texts that describe how to build and operate the tabernacle (Exodus 25–40). Chronologically Exodus 32 connects to the story right after 24:12–18. While Moses is up on Mount Sinai receiving the Ten Commandments written by the very hand of God, the people become impatient and construct a golden calf idol, declaring, "These are your gods, O Israel, who brought you up out of Egypt." At this particular moment, nothing could have been more dishonoring or blasphemous to God. Filled with anger, the Lord tells Moses that he is going to destroy the people (32:9–10). Moses intercedes and talks God out of destroying Israel (32:11–14). But when Moses arrives back at the camp and actually sees the golden calf, he gets angry too. He shatters the tablets with the Ten Commandments on the ground, destroys the golden calf, and calls the people to renew their commitment to God, executing three thousand people who don't (32:19–29).

Exodus 33 focuses once again on God's Presence. Moses knows that if they lose God's Presence then all is lost, so he pleads with God to stay with them. God agrees, and in Exodus 34 new stone tablets are formed and the covenant is renewed.

✦ The Presence of God, lost in the Garden in Genesis 3, is restored (to some extent) as God comes to dwell among his people in the tabernacle (Exod. 25:8; 29:45–46).

Completing the tabernacle (35:1–40:38)

After the shocking interruption of the golden calf episode, the story now returns to finishing the construction of the tabernacle. The willing obedience of the people is now stressed, in contrast to the disobedience of the previous episode (Exodus 32). Many of the details from Exodus 25–31 are repeated. The climax of the second half of Exodus comes in 40:34–38 as the glory of the Lord comes and fills the tabernacle. God's Presence now dwells with his people!

So What? Applying Exodus to Our Lives Today

The book of Exodus is filled with numerous powerful principles that we can apply to our lives today. The example of the courageous midwives in Exodus 1, when they defied the pharaoh to obey God, challenges us to stand firm for what is right, regardless of the consequences.

We can also draw encouragement from watching God work behind the scenes to raise up Moses, who eventually brings about the spectacular deliverance of God's people. We are exhorted to avoid the doubt and fickleness that the people of Israel so often reflect throughout Exodus.

There is much in this book that we can learn about God. He is one who delights in saving his people, even if they do not always appear worthy of being saved. Along these lines, in the New Testament Paul will later declare, "But God demonstrates his own love for us in this: While we were still sinners, Christ died for us" (Rom. 5:8). Furthermore, Exodus 32 illustrates for us how powerful and effective intercessory prayer can be, due to the compassionate character of God.

Finally, the many aspects about the Presence of God that are revealed in Exodus can help us understand better how to walk in the power of the Spirit, the manifestation of God's Presence in our lives as believers today. Presence and power are always closely connected to holiness. Thus as we enjoy the power and Presence of God through the Holy Spirit, we realize that we are likewise called to lead holy lives.

Wood from the acacia tree, shown below, was used in the construction of the tabernacle.

Our Favorite Verse in Exodus

God said to Moses, "I am who I am. This is what you are to say to the Israelites: 'I am has sent me to you.'" (3:14)

✚ Throughout the rest of the Old Testament God will frequently describe himself as "the Lord who brought you up out of Egypt."

Leviticus

Be Holy for I Am Holy

When most people read through Leviticus they are struck that it contains some really strange verses. "Do not wear clothing woven of two kinds of material" (19:19). "When a man has lost his hair and is bald, he is clean" (13:40). "A woman who becomes pregnant and gives birth to a son will be ceremonially unclean for seven days" (12:2). We quickly realize that if we read Leviticus out of context, we will most likely end up with some rather bizarre theology. Yet when placed in the proper context, we find that Leviticus makes perfect sense (at least most of it does). The laws in Leviticus explained to the Israelites how they should live with the holy and awesome God residing among them in the tabernacle.

In the Hebrew Bible, the third book of the Torah (Pentateuch) has the title "And he called," reflecting the opening phrase of the book in 1:1. Our English title, Leviticus, comes from the Latin translation (called the Vulgate), which in turn derived its title from the Greek translation (called the Septuagint). The term "Leviticus" means "the Levitical book" or the "book of the Levites." The tribe of Levi, remember, was the tribe in Israel of which the priests were to be members. So the title is somewhat accurate in its description. The book of Leviticus is about priestly things—sacrifice, worship, festivals, holiness, priestly activities, and cleansing.

What Is the Setting for Leviticus?

The essence of God's covenant relationship with Israel is expressed in the three-part statement, repeated over and over in the Old Testament: I will be your God; you will be my people; I will dwell in your midst. In the book of Exodus, God delivered the Israelites in a spectacular manner, bringing them up out of Egypt. At Mount Sinai he then entered into a covenant agreement with them. A critical component of that covenant was the promise that God's Presence would dwell among them. Thus the final unit of Exodus (25–40) describes how to construct the tabernacle, that is, the place where God will live among them. Leviticus is a logical sequel to these latter chapters of Exodus, for Leviticus describes the procedures that will be used in the tabernacle.

Keep in mind that the Israelites were on their way to Canaan, where they were to settle and to employ the ritual practices delineated in Leviticus to define their religious practices (the way to approach God in their midst). In the process, they were to reject the common pagan beliefs and practices that were everywhere around them. The influence of pagan beliefs in the region was very strong and permeated into all aspects of life, especially agriculture and procreation. Much of Leviticus is concerned with countering these pagan beliefs and reorienting Israel's entire worldview toward the God of Abraham, who had just delivered them from Egypt.

A pagan temple vessel probably used in Canaanite fertility libation offerings.

What Is at the Heart of Leviticus?

If the holy, awesome God is coming to dwell among the Israelites in the tabernacle (Exodus 25–40), how will that change their lives? How can sinful people survive with the holy, awesome God living in their midst? How should they approach him? What is the appropriate way to praise God and thank him for his blessings? How can sin be covered so that the relationship is not severed? The book of Leviticus answers these questions. Leviticus stresses that *everything* in their lives will change; for now—with the holy Presence of God residing in their midst—all of their thinking and acting (their worldview) will revolve around what is holy and what is clean. Within this context, four primary themes run throughout the book: (1) the Presence of God, (2) holiness, (3) the role of sacrifice, and (4) how to worship and live within the covenant.

Structurally, the book of Leviticus can be organized into the following outline:

- Sacrifices for Individual Worship (1:1–7:38)
- The Institution and Limitations of the Priesthood (8:1–10:20)
- The Issue of Uncleanness and Its Treatment (11:1–15:33)
- The Day of Atonement (Sacrifice for the Nation) (16:1–34)
- Laws for Holy Living (17:1–25:55)
- Covenant Blessings and Curses (26:1–46)
- Dedication Offerings (27:1–34)

What Makes Leviticus Interesting and Unique?

- Leviticus illustrates the practice of sacrifice, essential for understanding the New Testament theology of the cross.
- Leviticus describes the Day of Atonement.
- Leviticus teaches us how serious God is about keeping holy things separate from profane things.
- Four times in Leviticus God repeats the phrase, "Be holy for I am holy" (11:44, 45; 19:2; 20:26).
- Leviticus contains the second great command, "Love your neighbor as yourself" (19:18).

What Is the Message of Leviticus?

Sacrifices for Individual Worship (1:1–7:38)

The first seven chapters of Leviticus deal with sacrifices made by individual people. Leviticus 1:1–6:7 covers sacrifices from the perspective of

✤ The Presence of the holy God dwelling among his people—this is the theme that connects Leviticus back to Exodus.

regular people (not priests) while Leviticus 6:8–7:38 focuses on the role of the priests in making the sacrifice.

Two major categories of sacrifices are described in these chapters: (1) voluntary fellowship/thanksgiving sacrifices, and (2) obligatory sin/guilt offerings. When the voluntary fellowship/thanksgiving offerings are burned, the smoke becomes "an aroma pleasing to the Lord" (1:9, 13, 17; 2:2, 9; 3:5, 16; 6:15, 21). There are three specific fellowship/thanksgiving offerings. Leviticus 1:1–17 and 6:8–13 describe the "burnt offering," made as one dedicates or devotes oneself completely to God. The "grain offering" (or "cereal offering") is presented next (2:1–16; 6:14–23), an offering of thanksgiving in recognition of God's goodness in meeting daily needs. The third offering in the fellowship/thanksgiving category is the "peace offering" (3:1–17; 7:11–36), which can be given for specific or general thankfulness, or as part of a vow.

In contrast, the sin/guilt offerings were not voluntary, but were mandatory whenever one sinned. The sin offering (4:1–5:13; 6:24–30) was made by one who had sinned unintentionally, by omission, or had become ceremonially unclean. The guilt offering (5:14–6:7; 7:1–6) covered inadvertent sin and intentional sin as well, including sins against other people, such as stealing, cheating, or lying.

The Institution and Limitations of the Priesthood (8:1–10:20)

The literary style of this section changes from instructions about how to do something to a narrative about what actually happened. Back in Exodus 29 God gave Moses instructions about how to consecrate the priests, and Leviticus 8 describes the actual event. Thus in Leviticus 8 Aaron (the brother of Moses) and his sons are ordained as the top priests, and in Leviticus 9 they begin ministering. In the next chapter, however, a shocking event interrupts the story, for Aaron's two sons Nadab

Replica of a "horned" altar at Beersheba.

The Sacrifices

Archie England

Sacrifice is often synonymous with offering, occurring frequently in the Old Testament in the context of worship. Though sacrifice in the Bible is primarily directed to the worship of the God of Israel, it also reflects the cultural practices of the neighboring ancient Near Eastern peoples. As such, sacrifice could be viewed positively, as the worship of God (Gen. 46:1; Exod. 3:18; 5:3; 8:8; 12:27; 20:24); negatively, as the worship of false gods (Exod. 22:20; 34:15; Num. 25:2; Judg. 16:23), demons (Lev. 17:7; Deut. 32:17; Ps. 106:37), or heavenly hosts (Jer. 19:13); or neutrally, as the common manner of transacting business in the ancient Near East.

The concept of sacrifice is introduced early in biblical history. In the opening chapters of Genesis God covered Adam and Eve's nakedness with animal skins, and Abel brought animal offerings to God. Both acts involved the shedding of blood, which is essential for some types of sacrifices. Though not proving that people then perceived sacrifice as redemption or reconciliation, it might suggest sacrifice was associated with relational commitment. Two nonworship examples of sacrifice reflect this assessment: (1) the cutting of animals to establish a covenant (cf. Gen. 15:9–12), and (2) the devoting of land, goods, animals, or persons to God (Leviticus 27). Both reinforce the "lord-subject" relationship, which indeed was common in ancient Near Eastern cultures.

The act of sacrifice typically involved the giving of something valuable (food, animals, or, among Israel's neighbors Moab and Ammon, even humans) to a being esteemed or feared as greater, such as a deity or sovereign. Beginning with the Passover lamb (Exodus 12), the law of Moses further instructed Israel to procure doves, sheep, goats, rams, and bulls for sacrifice. In severe times even a grain offering (Leviticus 2) would suffice. Various subcategories of sacrifices existed within the sacrificial system. These included burnt, peace, thanksgiving, drink, grain, and wave offerings. Closely associated with the annual festivals, the laws on meat and meal offerings also described what portions the participants could eat after God had received the most desired fatty portions and after the Levites had also taken their designated portions. In this way, corporate sacrifice stressed forgiveness, blessing, and fellowship. Along with the observance of Passover, the Day of Atonement (Leviticus 16) best demonstrates these aspects. Though the corporate worship of biblical festivals constitutes the major focus of the Old Testament, individuals (Gen. 31:54; Job 1:5) and small groups (family) could also make sacrifices.

During the time of the divided monarchy, however, the sacrificial system became especially corrupt. The kings and priests of Israel and Judah merged many of the pagan sacrificial practices of their neighbors with that prescribed in Leviticus, sometimes even abandoning the biblical practice altogether. These inadequate sacrifices, coupled with superficial religious practices and the horrendous practice of child sacrifice (Mic. 6:6–8), incurred the condemnation of the prophets.

and Abihu try to approach God in an unauthorized manner, "contrary to his command" (10:1). Fire comes out from the Presence of the Lord and consumes them both! This is a very serious reminder to Israel that God and God alone determines how he can be approached and worshiped. No one, not even special priests like Aaron's sons, can determine on their own how to approach God.

Leprosy in the Old Testament

Robert Bergen

"Leprosy" is a term used in many English Bibles to translate a Hebrew noun referring to various blemishes that may appear on skin, cloth, leather, and interior walls of houses. Common to each of the conditions labeled as "leprosy" (Heb. *tsara'at*) is that they appear on a surface, quickly increase in size, degrade the appearance of the surface on which they are found, and cause the afflicted person or object to be removed from the community of the Lord's people.

Eleven passages in the Old Testament make reference to leprosy: four describe this condition or provide guidelines associated with it (Lev. 13:2–14:57; 22:4; Num. 5:2; Deut. 24:8), six mention individuals afflicted with it (Exod. 4:6; Num. 12:10; 2 Kings 5:7–27; 7:3–10; 15:5; 2 Chron. 26:16–21), and one includes it in a curse (2 Sam. 3:29).

Descriptions of the condition as it affects a person's skin are provided in Leviticus 13:2–44. The affliction creates a whitish or reddish patch that expands noticeably within a week's time; the affected area may include a boil, raw skin, scab, or discolored hair. Medically, these symptoms are associated with favus, kwashiorkor, psoriasis, eczema, or seborrheic dermatitis. They do not seem to describe Hansen's disease, the more common name for what is today termed leprosy. Hansen's disease is a slow-developing bacterial infection that typically has a three- to five-year incubation period, produces large nodules on the skin, leads to nerve damage and weakness in the arms and legs, and may result in the loss of bodily extremities.

The leprosy that can affect cloth, leather, and dwellings produces a reddish or greenish discoloration that spreads within a week's time. This description fits well with mold infestations, which can grow on any of these surfaces in the presence of moisture.

Persons diagnosed with this condition in the Old Testament were to wear torn clothing, leave their hair hanging loose, cover their mouth, and live apart from the community of God's people. If their condition cleared up, a priest could authorize their reentry into the community following an eight-day ritual involving animal sacrifice, washing, shaving, and the presentation of an offering (see Lev. 14:1–32). Cloth, leather, and affected building materials were to be destroyed.

Because the afflicted person or object was removed from the community of God's people, leprosy was associated with divine judgment (see Num. 12:10; 2 Sam. 3:29; 2 Kings 5:27; 2 Chron. 26:19–21).

The Issue of Uncleanness and Its Treatment (11:1–15:33)

This section can be challenging for the modern reader to grasp, and there is no consensus among scholars on how to approach this section. It is perhaps best to view the unit within a larger context of holiness and cleansing. Within the Levitical system or worldview, "clean" was the normal state of most things and persons. If people come into contact with something "unclean," they themselves become unclean and must undergo a ceremonial cleansing to become clean again. From the clean status, one can then be ceremonially "sanctified" (or "set apart") to become "holy," in order to serve God or to come close into his Presence. Apparently God wanted the Israelites to be constantly thinking about his holiness and their holiness/cleanness. Thus just about everything that they would come in contact with was to be viewed in the categories of "clean" or "unclean." Leviticus 11–15 deals with the major categories of contact with animals, childbirth (probably due primarily to contact with blood), and diseases. These chapters describe how one who is made unclean by contact with something unclean could then be ceremonially cleansed.

The Day of Atonement (Sacrifice for the Nation) (16:1–34)

The Day of Atonement was at the very heart of the sacrificial system, for it was a sacrifice done on behalf of the entire nation. It covered the sin of the nation and served to maintain the covenant relationship between God and the nation of Israel. After sacrificing a bull to purify himself (16:1–14), Aaron, the high priest, would sacrifice a goat on behalf of the people, take some of the blood of the goat into the Most Holy Place of the tabernacle, and sprinkle the blood in front of the "atonement cover" (the cover on the ark of the covenant, also called the "mercy seat"). He would then place his hands on a live goat, confess the sins of the nation, and then send the goat away into the wilderness, symbolizing the removal of sin from the people (16:20–22). In essence, the Day of Atonement sacrifice validated the rest of the sacrificial system.

The hyssop plant was used especially in ceremonies for spreading blood (Exod. 12:22; Lev. 14:4–6, 49–52).

Laws for Holy Living (17:1–25:55)

Leviticus 17–25 contains numerous regulations dealing with a wide spectrum of life, grouped around the concept of holy living. This unit is sometimes called "the holiness code," due to the phrase "Be holy because I, the Lord your God, am holy" (19:2).

Leviticus 17 discusses blood and blood sacrifices. Blood was a

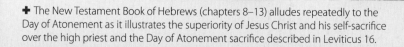

✝ The New Testament Book of Hebrews (chapters 8–13) alludes repeatedly to the Day of Atonement as it illustrates the superiority of Jesus Christ and his self-sacrifice over the high priest and the Day of Atonement sacrifice described in Leviticus 16.

symbol of life, and eating it was prohibited (a pagan practice). In Leviticus 18, God stresses that his "kingdom of priests," the people of his special covenant relationship, will live by very high standards regarding marriage and sexual relationships. Leviticus 19 focuses primarily on interpersonal relationships, echoing the Ten Commandments and stressing that holy living also involves caring for the poor (19:9–10) and the disadvantaged (19:14), treating workers fairly (19:13), practicing justice (19:15–16), caring for foreigners (19:33–34), and carrying out economic transactions with honesty (19:35–36). Leviticus 20 lists capital offenses, including the terrible pagan practice of sacrificing one's children. Chapters 21 and 22 stress special rules of holiness for the priests.

Terra-cotta lamp-stand/incense burning stand, 1850–1250 BC.

Most of the material in these chapters (especially the lists) is structured around the number seven (or multiples of seven, such as fourteen or twenty-one). Consider Leviticus 19, for example. The first unit (19:1–18) opens with "Be holy because I, the Lord your God, am holy." This unit repeats the phrase "I am the Lord" seven times (19:3, 4, 10, 12, 14, 16, 18) and contains twenty-one laws. The next unit (19:19–37) opens with "Keep my decrees." It also repeats "I am the Lord" seven times (19:25, 28, 30, 31, 32, 34, 36–37), and it also contains twenty-one laws. The unit then concludes wth a summary admonition ("Keep all my statutes") followed by a closing ("I am the Lord"). Thus one can see that this entire unit (Leviticus 17–25) is highly structured, with the number seven (symbolizing completion or perfection) playing an important role.*

Leviticus 23 lists the various holy days and festivals that Israel was to keep. These were special days of remembrance and celebration. This included the Sabbath, the Passover, the Feast of Unleavened Bread, the Firstfruits ceremony, the Feast of Weeks (which becomes Pentecost), the Feast of Trumpets, the Day of Atonement, and the Feast of Tabernacles. These special days and feasts were the major times that Israel gathered to worship God and remember corporately what he had done for them.

Leviticus 24:1–9 describes the maintenance of a lamp that was to burn continually before God, as well as the daily bread offerings. The next section (24:10–23) is a reminder of how serious the holiness and Presence of God really is, recounting the story of the stoning of one who blasphemed

---

* John Sailhamer, *The Pentateuch as Narrative* (Grand Rapids: Zondervan, 1995).

✚ The New Testament book of James draws heavily from Leviticus 19.

The Day of Atonement

Christine Jones

The Day of Atonement is a ritual involving (1) the sacrifice of animals by which the sanctuary is cleansed, and (2) the transference of sins onto a scapegoat whereby the sins of Israel are sent away. It is a day during which the people fast and deny themselves, stopping all labor as they would on the Sabbath day. Mentioned in both the Old and New Testaments, the Day of Atonement is a significant day for Israel.

IN THE OLD TESTAMENT

The most extensive explanation of the Day of Atonement is found in Leviticus 16 (also Lev. 23:26–32; Num. 29:7–11). In this passage, the Lord communicates the details of the ritual to Moses, who is to pass them along to Aaron, the high priest. The sanctuary is a holy place warranting special conduct for those who enter, especially those who enter the Holy of Holies, the area where the ark is kept and where God resides. Aaron and subsequent high priests are not free to enter the Holy of Holies at their own choosing; rather, they may enter only on a special day. The Day of Atonement is that special day, observed once a year on the tenth day of the seventh month (September–October).

In preparation for entering the sanctuary, the high priest must first prepare himself by cleansing his entire body and putting on special linen garments, the holy vestments.

On that day, a bull is brought by the high priest and offered as a sin offering for the atonement of the high priest and his family. After it is killed, the high priest enters the Holy of Holies with coals and incense, which he places on the fire before the Lord in order to produce smoke to shield him from God's Presence. He then sprinkles the mercy seat seven times with the blood of the bull.

At that point, the entire congregation brings two male goats to the high priest; one is used as a sin offering for all the people and the other as a scapegoat to be sent away into the wilderness. The casting of lots determines which is offered and which is sent away. The first goat is sacrificed, and its blood is also sprinkled in the Holy of Holies. Then the blood of the bull and the goat together are put on the horns of the altar outside the tent. This sprinkled blood cleanses the various parts of the sanctuary of all uncleanness.

The second goat serves a different purpose. The high priest places his hands on the live goat and confesses all the sin and rebellion of the nation, thus symbolically transferring the sins of the people onto this goat. Finally, a designated person leads the goat into the wilderness, thus carrying the sins of the people away.

IN THE NEW TESTAMENT

The Day of Atonement ceremony is mentioned in Hebrews 9:6–7. This text points out that this sacrifice had to be repeated every year, illustrating that it was not really effective at removing sin. In contrast, Christ has become the High Priest, entering heaven, the perfect sanctuary, and offering his own blood in a perfect sacrifice that satisfies the need for atonement forever.

God. Leviticus 25 declares that the land, like the people, needs rest; thus a sabbatical year was proclaimed. Likewise, every fifty years was to be a year of Jubilee, when indentured slaves were to be released, and purchased or forfeited land was to be returned to its original owners.

✚ Peter quotes from Leviticus 11:44–45; 19:2; and 20:26 when he writes, "But just as he who called you is holy, so be holy in all you do; for it is written: 'Be holy, because I am holy'" (1 Pet. 1:15–16).

Leviticus   87

Covenant Blessings and Curses (26:1–46)

When God delivers the Israelites out of Egypt, he enters into a covenant relationship with them. The terms of this relationship are spelled out in the books of Exodus, Leviticus, Numbers, and Deuteronomy. This particular covenant is called the Mosaic covenant. It differs from the covenant made back in Genesis with Abraham (Genesis 12, 15, 17) in that it carries specific conditions that the Israelites must fulfill. In essence, the Mosaic covenant defines the terms whereby Israel could live in the Promised Land with God in their midst and be blessed abundantly. Leviticus 26 presents the good news/bad news aspect of the Mosaic covenant. If the Israelites obey God's laws and stay faithful to him, then God will bless them richly in the Promised Land (26:1–13). If they don't obey God, however, the blessings will be replaced with curses, and terrible things will happen to them, including the loss of the Promised Land (26:14–39). As mentioned above, however, God's covenant with Abraham is different, and the continuation of this covenant and the blessing received from this covenant are not contingent on obedience to the law. Interestingly, in Leviticus 26:40–45 God states that after Israel has disobeyed, indeed, shattered, the Mosaic covenant, some of them will repent. Then God will remember his covenant with Abraham and restore them. This is the story that unfolds later in the Prophets. Israel will abandon the Mosaic covenant (the laws in Exodus, Leviticus, Numbers, and Deuteronomy) and turn to other gods. After pleading with them and warning them for centuries through the Prophets, the Lord will judge them for this, and they will actually lose the Promised Land (i.e., they are exiled to Babylonia). However, in accordance with Leviticus 26:40–45, God restores them and promises an ultimate, even greater restoration in the future, a restoration that includes the gentiles (part of the Abrahamic covenant; Gen. 12:3).

Dedication Offerings (27:1–34)

Leviticus closes with an entire chapter dealing with how one could dedicate things to God. This provides an appropriate conclusion to

Leviticus 26:1 forbids making or worshiping foreign gods. Pictured here is a Canaanite deity (1400–1200 BC).

✦ Leviticus 26 is very similar to Deuteronomy 28. In both passages Israel is presented with two options: obedience, resulting in blessings; or disobedience, resulting in curses.

the long discussion in Leviticus regarding holiness, for total dedication and devotion to God is the essence of holiness. The chapter stresses that the ritual declarations of dedication must be sincere and not hypocritical or just for show. Tied tightly into the discussion are specific financial guidelines. Apparently in the culture of ancient Israel, as in ours today, money was a critical issue. How one dealt with finances reflected the sincerity of one's devotion and dedication to God. Furthermore, Leviticus 27:26–33 points out that some things cannot be dedicated to God because he already owns them (the tithe and the firstborn)!

So What? Applying Leviticus to Our Lives Today

In John 1:29, when John the Baptist sees Jesus approaching, he declares, "Look, the Lamb of God, who takes away the sin of the world!" It is only because of Leviticus that we can understand what John was talking about. It is Leviticus that teaches us the concepts of substitutionary sacrifice and atonement, concepts that find ultimate application in the crucifixion of Christ.

In addition, the concept of clean/unclean and the issue of holiness are essential to mature Christian living. Jesus points out that there is a distinction between understanding the issue of clean and unclean as mere ritual behavior and understanding the true issue of being clean. He explains that "what goes into a man's mouth does not make him 'unclean,' but what comes out of his mouth, that is what makes him 'unclean.' . . . The things that come out of the mouth come from the heart" (Matt. 15:1–20; Mark 7:1–23). Likewise, although we are not saved by our works, we are, nonetheless, called to lead holy lives (1 Pet. 1:15–16). The rituals of Leviticus forced the Israelites to view all of life in terms of clean/unclean and holy/profane. We can learn from this, for modern Western Christians have a tendency to compartmentalize the "spiritual" and the "secular." Yet we have the holy, awesome God dwelling right within us, and not off in the tabernacle or temple. Thus we should be even more conscious of holiness and the need for us to be clean and holy than the ancient Israelites in Leviticus were. Wow, what a challenge!

This type of common lamp was popular throughout Palestine (fourteenth century BC).

Our Favorite Verse in Leviticus

Do not seek revenge or bear a grudge against one of your people, but love your neighbor as yourself. I am the Lord. (19:18)

Numbers

Taking the Long Way to the Promised Land

Have you ever had a major detour in your life . . . a time when you just couldn't seem to make progress toward your primary goal? Numbers is a book about detours. Israel has to learn the hard way about the most basic reality of life. When they trust in God and faithfully obey him, their journey goes well, filled with blessings. But when they rebel against God and refuse to follow him, they lose their way and wander around aimlessly in the wilderness.

In Numbers the Israelites come right up to the Promised Land. It is right there, waiting for them with rich blessings. The Israelites, however, refuse to obey God and thus squander the opportunity to enter into the land of promise. God, therefore, allows that entire generation to die off before he takes the next generation and tries again. The detour was quite unnecessary and tragic; an entire generation squanders their purpose in life.

The title of this book in Hebrew is "In the wilderness," taken from the first verse of the book. It is a very appropriate title, for the book explains why the generation saved in Exodus spends their life "in the wilderness" instead of in the Promised Land. When the Old Testament was translated into Greek (the Septuagint), the translators titled the book *Arithmoi*, apparently focusing on the importance that census data, with its many, many numbers, plays in the book. The Latin translation rendered the title as *Numeri*, and our English Bibles have followed this tradition, titling the book as Numbers.

What Is the Setting for Numbers?

In Exodus, God delivers Israel from slavery in Egypt and brings them to Mount Sinai, where he enters into a covenant relationship with them and gives them the law, as well as instructions on how to build the tabernacle. God's Presence then enters the tabernacle, and Leviticus, the following book, explains how Israel should live in light of having the holy, awesome God living right there among them. Numbers picks back up on the story from Exodus. When Numbers opens, Israel is still at Mount Sinai, in the second month of the second year of the exodus journey (1:1). The setting for the events in Numbers is the journey from Mount Sinai to the Promised Land, although the Israelites take the long, "detour" route.

What Is at the Heart of Numbers?

The region of Kadesh-Barnea (also called just Kadesh) (Num. 13:26; 20:1–22; 32:8; 33:36–37; 34:8).

The book of Exodus describes the rescue from slavery; Numbers describes the journey to the blessing. Incredibly, when God brings them to the Promised Land, they say they don't want it

✚ In 1 Corinthians 10:1–13 Paul refers directly to many of the negative events in Numbers, concluding, "These things happened to them as examples and were written down as warnings for us."

if they have to exert any effort and faith to actually occupy it. "We wish we had died in the desert!" they complain to God in exaggeration, as they reject the Promised Land. "Fine," God answers, in essence. "Go back into the desert and die." God then leads them back into the desert to allow that rebellious generation to die off. Then he takes the upcoming "more obedient" generation and offers the land to them. The contrast between the old, disobedient generation and the new, obedient generation is huge, and identifying the transition from disobedience to obedience helps us to understand the book better. This book contains two big census lists (filled with numbers), one in Numbers 1 and another in Numbers 26. These two census lists identify and introduce the two differing generations. Thus Numbers 1–25 describes the old, disobedient generation, characterized by grumbling, doubt, rebellion, and death. Numbers 26–36, however, is quite different, and the themes for this generation shift to faith, hope, and life.

A silver amulet from the seventh century BC inscribed with the Priestly Benediction of Numbers 6:24–26. It is the oldest known fragment of a biblical text.

Running throughout the book, however, is evidence that God still watches over his people and remains faithful to the ultimate fulfillment of the Abrahamic covenant. For example, when Balaam attempts to curse Israel, God intervenes and prohibits it (Numbers 22–25).

All the while, throughout the entire book, the people are also journeying and encountering hostile nations along the way. God also engages with the Israelites frequently, supplementing the laws of Exodus and Leviticus, and exhorting them to trust him to deliver them from the enemies that oppose them in their journey. Another related feature of Numbers incorporated into this journeying story is that a lot of text and effort is devoted just to getting the Israelites organized enough to move efficiently. The large numbers reflected in the census underscore the mammoth task of organizing the twelve chaotic tribes into one unified people with a smoothly functioning worship system and a just legal system, a people who could travel through the desert in an organized manner, maintaining their focus on the centrality of God's Presence in the tabernacle.

Numbers is composed of numerous different types of literature: narrative stories, poems, songs, census results, laws, letters, and travel itineraries. Yet all of it combines to tell the story of how God moves the rebellious Israelites from Mount Sinai to the Promised Land.

There is not a consensus among scholars regarding how to outline the book of Numbers, but the following outline is a helpful way to view the story:

- The Disobedient Generation (1:1–25:18)
  - A hopeful start: God gets Israel organized (1:1–10:10)
  - Israel does the unthinkable—they reject the Promised Land (10:11–14:45)
  - Israel wanders in the wilderness (15:1–22:1)
  - Encountering Balaam and Moab: God still protects his people (22:2–25:18)
- The Obedient Generation (26:1–36:13)
  - Generational transitions—the census, daughters, and leaders (26:1–27:23)
  - Reminders of worship, holiness, and faithfulness (28:1–30:16)
  - Conclusion to the Balaam challenge (31:1–54)
  - Preparing to enter the land (32:1–36:13)

What Makes Numbers Interesting and Unique?

- Numbers contains the famous blessing, "The Lord bless you and keep you; the Lord make his face shine upon you and be gracious to you" (6:24–26).
- Moses marries a woman from Cush, an African nation south of Egypt.
- The Israelites reject the Promised Land and so wander in the wilderness for forty years.
- Balaam's donkey talks to him.
- Moses completely destroys the Midianites (his former in-laws?).

Moses's new wife is a Cushite (Num. 12:1). An Egyptian wall painting from the time of Thutmose IV (1400–1390 BC) depicts Cushites bringing tribute to the Pharaoh.

What Is the Message of Numbers?

The Disobedient Generation (1:1–25:18)

A hopeful start: God gets Israel organized (1:1–10:10)

The book of Numbers starts out well. God organizes the tribes of Israel so that they can travel and be prepared to fight. In Numbers 1, God instructs Moses to take a census of all military-aged men. God then organizes the tribes around the tabernacle, locating three tribes on each side and the Levites in the middle (2:1–34). This is the way they are to travel and camp, being prepared for war but organized around the Presence of God in the tabernacle, which is to remain their focus. God next organizes the Levites (the priestly tribe), assigning to specific family clans within the Levite tribe the various tasks required for caring for, packing, and moving the sacred tabernacle (3:1–4:49). God is very concerned with the concepts of holiness and purity, and throughout Numbers (as well as in Leviticus) he gives Israel numerous regulations to assist in keeping themselves pure. Numbers 5 addresses the issue of adultery and how to determine whether one accused of adultery is guilty—faithfulness to intimate relationships like marriage is important to God. This chapter is ironic and perhaps a foreshadowing of things to come, for the prophets will later compare Israel's unfaithfulness to God with the adulterous behavior of an unfaithful spouse.

Numbers 6 describes how a man or a woman can take a special Nazirite vow to dedicate him or herself as an individual to the service of God. Thus it is not just the Levites who can serve God in a special way.

Recall that in Exodus 25–40 God gave instructions regarding how to construct the tabernacle. In Numbers 7:1 Moses completes the construction of the tabernacle, and the rest of the chapter describes how each tribe then

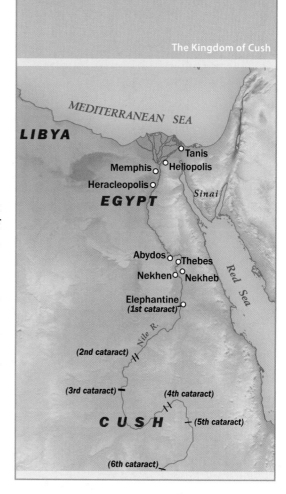

The Kingdom of Cush

MEDITERRANEAN SEA

LIBYA

Tanis
Memphis Heliopolis
Heracleopolis
EGYPT
Sinai

Abydos Thebes
Nekhen Nekheb
Elephantine
(1st cataract)

Nile R.

(2nd cataract)

(3rd cataract)   (4th cataract)

CUSH   (5th cataract)

(6th cataract)

✚ The guidelines for taking a Nazirite vow are explained in Numbers 6.
In Judges 13 God tells Samson's mother to raise him as a Nazirite,
implying that he should live according to these guidelines.

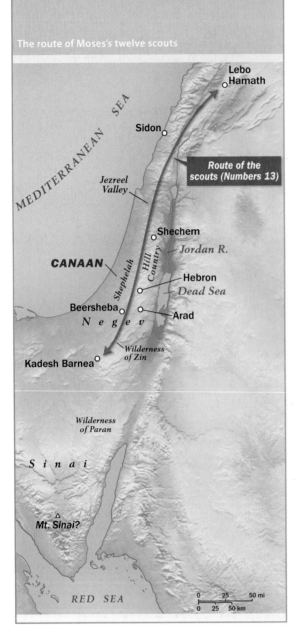

Lebo
Hamath

Sidon

MEDITERRANEAN SEA

Jezreel
Valley

Route of the
scouts (Numbers 13)

Shechem

Jordan R.

CANAAN

Shephelah

Hill Country

Hebron

Dead Sea

Beersheba

Arad

N e g e v

Wilderness
of Zin

Kadesh Barnea

Wilderness
of Paran

S i n a i

Mt. Sinai?

RED SEA

0   25   50 mi
0   25   50 km

comes to the tabernacle to offer a gift of dedication to God.

In Numbers 8 the priestly Levites are ceremonially purified and set apart for service in the tabernacle. God then instructs the Israelites to celebrate the Passover, in memory of his great deliverance of them from Egypt (9:1–14). As in Exodus 13–14, when God was leading and protecting them, a great presence covers the tabernacle, appearing as a cloud by day and as a fire by night, signifying the holy Presence of God. It is an exciting time for Israel. The tabernacle has been constructed and filled with the glorious Presence of God. Their worship system is well organized, with the Levites to lead them. In Numbers 10, they pack up and set out from Sinai toward the Promised Land!

Israel does the unthinkable— they reject the Promised Land (10:11–14:45)

Once on the road, however, things start to go bad. In Numbers 11 the people grumble and complain about the manna God gives them to eat (introduced in Exodus 16). God sends them quail to eat so that they can have the meat they crave, but their complaining and contempt toward his provision of manna has angered him. While Numbers 11 describes a rebellion against Moses by the people, in Numbers 12 the rebellion comes from his closest assistant leaders, Aaron and Miriam. Numbers 12:1 explains that Moses had married a Cushite woman (probably one who was part of the "many other people" who came out of Egypt with the Israelites; Exod. 12:38), and Aaron and Miriam speak against him because of it, apparently challenging

Who Are the Cushites?

Numbers 12:1 states that Moses married a Cushite woman. A helpful question to pursue is "Who are the Cushites?" Similarly, does his marriage to a Cushite have any special significance? Actually the Hebrew word *Cush* or *Cushite* shows up in the Old Testament fifty-four times, indicating that the Cushites were not an obscure group in the Old Testament era, but one that played an important role in the life of Israel.

English Bible translations vary in the way that they translate the Hebrew word *Cush*. The Greeks called everything south of Egypt by the name "Ethiopia," and so some English Bibles use the term "Ethiopia" to translate the Hebrew word *Cush*. This is a little misleading, because the modern country of Ethiopia is not the same place as the ancient kingdom of Cush, lying well to the southeast. Some translations use the term "Nubia," a later Latin term for the area.

The kingdom of Cush lay to the south of Egypt, along the "curvy" part of the Nile River in what is now the country of Sudan. It was an identifiable entity from before 2000 BC until AD 350. Cush was famous for gold mines and mercenary soldiers. Because of the gold mines, the Egyptians, throughout the Old Testament period, made it a top priority to keep Cush as part of their empire. Most of the time Egypt dominated the Cushites, but toward the end of the eighth century BC the Cushites overran Egypt and actually ruled Egypt for a while (see Isa. 37:9 and 2 Kings 19:9 for Cushite interaction with Israel/Judah during this period). After several engagements, eventually the Assyrians defeated the Cushites and ended their time of Egyptian domination (and their status as world power and major geopolitical player in the region). Ebed-Melech, the Cushite who rescued Jeremiah, was probably a mercenary in the Egyptian army.

At the time of Moses, the Egyptians controlled Cush, and there were probably thousands of Cushites in various occupations throughout Egypt. Probably the Cushite woman that Moses married was one of the "many other people" mentioned in Exodus 12:38 who left Egypt with the Israelites.

Because of their close relationship with the Egyptians, the Cushites appear numerous times in ancient Egyptian art (stone monuments and tomb paintings). These depictions of the Cushites portray them as black Africans. Thus there is little doubt that in Numbers 12:1 Moses marries a black African woman.

his leadership. God responds in anger, and Miriam is smitten with leprosy until Moses intervenes.

With these two negative episodes introducing the journey to the Promised Land, the reader is perhaps prepared for the rebellious behavior of the Israelites once they get there. Nonetheless, their reaction to the land is rather shocking. Moses sends twelve men into Canaan to spy out the land (13:1–20). They return and report that the land is indeed rich with "milk and honey," and filled with fruit. However, ten of the spies give a negative report and say the Canaanites are too strong and the Israelites cannot possibly defeat them (13:21–33). Only Caleb and Joshua urge the Israelites to trust God and attack the Canaanites. In Numbers 14 the unthinkable happens. The Israelites rebel against Moses and refuse to go into the Promised

Sorcery and Divination in the Ancient Near East

Numbers 22:1–7 indicates that Balaam was a "diviner" or "sorcerer" living in Mesopotamia. The words "sorcery" and "divination" are broad terms that refer to a wide range of magic-related practices that were common throughout the Near East during the biblical era. Usually this involved using various techniques to communicate with supernatural forces such as gods, demons, or other spiritual beings in order to determine the future, ward off evil, change something for the better (blessings), or change something for the worse (curses). Archaeologists have uncovered thousands of ancient literary texts from Egypt, Assyria, and Babylonia that contain accounts, recipes, or incantations that were used by these professional sorcerers/diviners. Numerous divination techniques were common throughout the region: astrology; observing the pattern made by drops of oil dripped into a bucket of water; observing the entrails of sacrificed animals, especially their liver; and observing the flight pattern of birds.

Educated, professional sorcerers/diviners were typically part of most royal courts in Mesopotamia and in Egypt (recall the magicians who confronted Moses in the court of Pharaoh). As in the case of Balaam, it appears they could also occasionally be hired by others. These individuals comprised a powerful class in most of the ancient Near Eastern societies.

In Deuteronomy, God strictly forbids this kind of divination and sorcery. Deuteronomy 18:9–14 gives an extensive list of those many related practices that were forbidden for the Israelites. These methods are described as "detestable to the Lord" (Deut. 18:12). In the very next passage (Deut. 18:15–22) God explains that he will not be contacted through divination, but through the true prophets that he himself will choose.

Divination and sorcery continued into the New Testament era. In Acts 8:9–25 Peter encounters a powerful sorcerer named Simon Magnus. At the beginning of Paul's missionary journeys he encounters a Jewish sorcerer on the isle of Cyprus (Acts 13:6–7). Other divination/sorcery/magic practices are mentioned in numerous places in the New Testament (Acts 16:16; 19:19; Rev. 9:21; 18:23; 21:8; 22:15).

Mesopotamian clay cuneiform tablet with astrological omens.

Land! This angers God, and, as in Exodus 32, only the intervention of Moses prevents God from destroying the nation. In the end, God decrees that the entire rebellious generation will return to the wilderness to die there; only Caleb and Joshua will actually be blessed with entering the Promised Land.

Israel wanders in the wilderness (15:1–22:1)

Ironically, as Israel returns to wander in the wilderness, God continues to give Moses directions for proper worship to be implemented when they finally get back to the Promised Land (15:1–41). In Numbers 16, however, a serious rebellion breaks out against Moses, and God quells it by killing 250 leaders of the opposition and then sending a plague on their followers, killing an additional 14,700. Numbers 17–21 describes several events that transpire as Israel travels in the desert. God continues to define the role of the Levitical priests (18:1–19:22). In Numbers 20 even Moses stumbles and gets reprimanded by God. Time passes and the years go by. In 20:28 Aaron dies, perhaps signaling the end of the rebellious generation. Moses heads the people toward Canaan, the Promised Land, and God enables the Israelites to defeat any enemies that try to stop them, including the powerful Amorites (21:1–35).

Encountering Balaam and Moab: God still protects his people (22:2–25:18)

The story of Balaam (Numbers 22–25, 31) is one of the most fascinating stories in the entire Bible. After the Israelites defeat the Amorites (Numbers 21), the Moabites and Midianites realize that they will probably be attacked next. Convinced that they cannot defeat Israel with regular military strength, the king of Moab offers a huge sum of money to a famous and powerful sorcerer named Balaam to put a curse on Israel.

In Numbers 21 the Israelites gain control of the eastern side of the Jordan by defeating King Sihon and King Og. The route of this campaign is shown here.

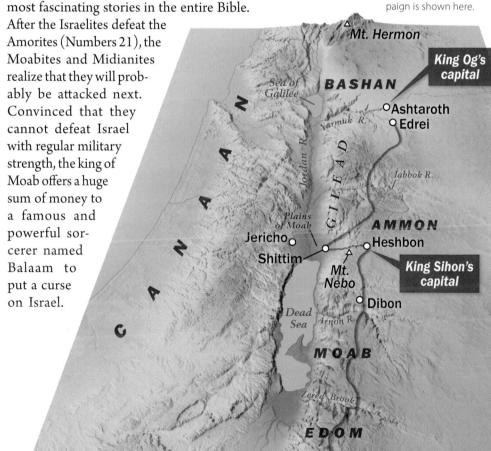

✛ The New Testament mentions Balaam in a very negative sense three times (2 Pet. 2:15; Jude 1:11; Rev. 2:14).

Numbers   99

Yet recall the promise God gave to Abraham back in Genesis 12:3: "I will bless those who bless you and whoever curses you I will curse." Balaam is about to set himself against this promise of God.

Although warned by God once that he cannot curse Israel, Balaam decides to go to Moab anyway. On his way (apparently to curse Israel; why else would he go?), Balaam is met by an angel of the Lord, armed with a sword, blocking Balaam's way. Balaam is unable to see the angel, but Balaam's donkey can, and three times the donkey tries to go another way. Each time Balaam beats his donkey, until finally the donkey turns and speaks to Balaam, asking what he has done to deserve a beating (22:23–30). Surprisingly, Balaam angrily rebukes and threatens the donkey! The angel then reveals himself to Balaam and explains that the donkey has actually saved his life. The angel allows Balaam to continue to Moab, but with the strict admonition to say only what the angel tells him to say (22:35). The irony of this humorous episode is that Balaam, the most famous and powerful "seer" or "spiritualist" in the ancient world, cannot see the dangerous angel in front of him, but his dumb donkey can. The donkey has enough sense and insight to know that this is not the right path to take. Balaam, however, probably secretly desiring the large reward offered to him by the king of Moab, continues on. This will eventually result in Balaam's death (31:8).

Balaam arrives at Moab, to the delight of Balak the king, and tries to curse Israel, but blesses the nation instead (23:1–12). At the urging of Balak, Balaam tries again to curse Israel, but once again only blessings come out (23:13–26). Finally, much to Balak's aggravation, Balaam abandons any attempt to curse Israel and simply blesses them instead (24:1–9), ending his oracle with a quote of Genesis 12:3, "May those who bless you be blessed and those who curse you be cursed" (24:9). Balaam then utters two more oracles that bless Israel (24:15–25).

Balaam, however, realizes that his clients, the Moabites and Midianites, cannot defeat Israel either militarily or through sorcery. So he concocts a scheme to corrupt them morally and theologically (see Num. 31:8, 16 for Balaam's part in this plan), so that their God would destroy them himself. Numbers 25 describes this attempt by the Moabites to use sexual immorality to lure Israel to participate in the worship of Baal. This god was a fertility god, and worship of Baal involved extensive sexual immorality. An Israelite priest named Phinehas, however, zealously intervenes and kills

A typical Middle Eastern donkey.

one of the Israelites who is openly participating in this immorality. God then sends a plague on the rest of the participants, killing 24,000 of them. Balaam is almost successful. He realizes that he cannot defeat Israel by directly attacking them or cursing them, so he tries instead to tempt them away from following God, and thus letting God destroy them. Fortunately, Balaam's plan fails.

The Obedient Generation (26:1–36:13)

Generational transitions—the census, daughters, and leaders (26:1–27:23)

In Numbers 26 the story shifts as a new generation comes of age. A new census is taken (26:1–65). Faithful daughters are recognized and awarded their inheritance (27:1–11), and Joshua is appointed to succeed Moses (27:12–23).

Reminders of worship, holiness, and faithfulness (28:1–30:16)

These chapters refocus Israel on worshiping God faithfully in the Promised Land. Important aspects of worship are revisited: the Sabbath offerings, the Passover, the various feasts, the Day of Atonement, and special vows.

The plains of Moab. Many of the events in Numbers 21–36 take place in Moab.

Conclusion to the Balaam challenge (31:1–54)

As the new generation comes of age, they clean up some earlier messes, and in 31:1–54 they destroy the Midianites/Moabites who had tried to seduce Israel away from God through sexual immorality and pagan worship of Baal. Balaam himself is killed (31:8). The Israelites capture a tremendous amount of plunder, including large numbers of livestock and large quantities of gold, which is brought to the tabernacle in dedication to God.

Preparing to enter the land (32:1–36:13)

The final chapters give a review of Israel's trip (33:1–56) and then describe the boundaries of the land. In Numbers 32 Moses allows the tribes of Gad and Reuben to remain on the east side of the Jordan, so long as they agree to send their soldiers across the Jordan with the rest of the Israelite army to help with the conquest. The boundaries of the Promised Land are delineated in Numbers 34. In 35:1–34 towns for the Levites (who serve God in the tabernacle and thus do not get a portion of the land) are designated, as well as cities of refuge, to which people who kill someone by accident can flee for safety. The final chapter picks back up on the daughters mentioned in 27:1–11. Their father (of the previous generation) had died without any sons to receive his inheritance. Numbers 36 reaffirms

Bashan, one of the regions given to the tribes who remained on the east side of the Jordan.

✚ In Numbers 31 Moses and the Israelites destroy the Midianites. Ironically, after fleeing from Pharaoh, Moses had settled among the Midianites and even married one of them (Exod. 2:15–22).

that these daughters shall receive their father's inheritance, but only if they marry within the tribe. The rule is intended to keep the land within the family.

Israel is on the east bank of the Jordan River, poised and ready to cross over and occupy the land. God, however, has a few more things to say and an agreement to work out with Israel regarding faithfulness. This will be the book of Deuteronomy, which God now delivers to Israel through Moses, delineating the terms by which Israel can live in the Promised Land and be blessed by God.

So What? Applying Numbers to Our Lives Today

Numbers provides one with a sobering picture of how rebellion against God can set a negative course for one's entire life. The consequences can be severe, and, without repentance, people can spend the rest of their life just spinning their wheels out in the wilderness and going nowhere. Fortunately, the Bible tells us that if we repent and turn to God, then he will restore us and bring us back into fellowship. But as Paul warns in 1 Corinthians 10:1–13, Christ calls us to obedience, not rebellion and disobedience.

Another application comes from the Balaam episode. It is hard to read the episode of Balaam's conversation with his donkey and not come away convinced that God has a sense of humor. One of our goals in studying the Old Testament is to know God better. In Exodus, Leviticus, and Numbers we have seen the holiness and power of God. We have also glimpsed his jealousy and his insistence that his people worship him and him alone. We get a fairly good look at his grace, as he repeatedly saves his people and gives them another chance. But the Balaam story also gives some insight into another aspect of God's character—his playful sense of humor and his delight in irony.

Our Favorite Verses in Numbers

The Lord bless you
  and keep you;
the Lord make his face shine upon you
  and be gracious to you;
the Lord turn his face toward you
  and give you peace. (6:24–26)

Deuteronomy

The Contract between God and Israel

W hen was the last time you signed a contract or entered into a formal agreement with someone? Perhaps you bought a house and signed a contract for the transfer of that property. Wow, do you remember that huge stack of papers that you signed? Or perhaps you recently got married. Your wedding ceremony and the vows you took formalized the relationship between you and your spouse and placed stipulations of faithfulness on each of you (to love and cherish, to honor and sustain, in sickness and in health, in poverty as in wealth, etc.).

In a nutshell, the book of Deuteronomy is a contract between God and Israel. It defines the terms by which Israel can live in the Promised Land with God in their midst and be blessed by him.

What Is the Setting for Deuteronomy?

In Deuteronomy 17:18 is a stipulation that every new king in Israel is to take a scroll and make a "copy of this law." In the Septuagint (the Greek translation of the Old Testament), this phrase was translated as *deuteronomion*, which literally means "the second law." The Septuagint then used this word as the title of the book, and our English translations have followed that tradition, transliterating the title as Deuteronomy.

The book of Deuteronomy is not literally a "second law," but is rather a formalized restatement of the law given to Moses at Mount Sinai. In fact, much of Exodus 20–23 is reproduced in Deuteronomy, often with more expansion and explanation.

In Exodus, God delivers his people from Egypt and moves them toward the land he had promised to their forefather Abraham. God also enters into a covenant relationship with them, defined by the three-part formula, "I will be your God; you will be my people; I will dwell in your midst." Most of the second half of Exodus deals with constructing the tabernacle, the place where God will dwell in their midst. The next book, Leviticus, describes how the Israelites should live with the holy awesome God in their midst (i.e., how to approach him, fellowship with him, deal with the sin that separates them from him, etc.). The book of Numbers follows next and relates the unthinkable story of how the Israelites reject the Promised Land. God, therefore, sends that generation back into the wilderness to wander for forty years until that entire generation dies off. Now, as Deuteronomy opens, the Israelites are back at the entryway to the Promised Land. They are camped on the plains of Moab, and are just about to cross over the Jordan and conquer the Promised Land. At this critical stage in Israel's history, God inspires Moses to deliver several speeches to the Israelites, in essence renewing their covenant relationship with God and defining the terms by which they can live in the Promised Land with God and be blessed by him. So Deuteronomy is presented to the new generation of Israelites who are poised and ready to enter into the Promised Land.

What Is at the Heart of Deuteronomy?

Deuteronomy is given just as Israel is about to enter the Promised Land, the land that was promised to their forefather Abraham. It is a gracious offer by God, based on his deep love for his people. Yet God is very specific about how his people will relate to him and receive these overwhelming blessings based on this relationship. He is crystal clear in stating that he (as creator, provider, and king) is the one who dictates the terms of the relationship. God is also unambiguous about how serious he is that they worship him alone. Likewise, he is also serious about how they relate to one another in their community. If they keep these terms (the laws in Deuteronomy), then tremendous blessings will come upon them. However, God warns seriously,

✚ Two central things driving the story in the Old Testament are the Abrahamic covenant (Genesis 12, 15, 17) and the book of Deuteronomy.

if they disregard and disobey Deuteronomy, thus abandoning the covenant relationship they have with him, terrible consequences will follow, including the loss of the Promised Land (Deuteronomy 28).

The format of Deuteronomy follows the treaty pattern used frequently in the ancient world (see the insert on Hittite Treaties on page 109). Thus God presents the book of Deuteronomy in a literary and legal format the Israelites would be familiar with. Yet this material is also presented as a series of three major speeches given by Moses to Israel, followed by a postscript about the death of Moses and the transition in leadership to Joshua. An introduction to each of the three major speeches marks the beginning of each (1:1; 4:44; 29:1). Incorporating the three-major-speeches format with the thematic elements of the formalized-covenant format (as in other ancient treaties) results in the following outline of Deuteronomy:

- The First Speech of Moses: A Review of the Recent Relationship between God and Israel (1:1–4:43)
    – Introduction (1:1–18)
    – The time in the wilderness—failures and victories (1:19–3:29)
    – Lessons to learn from this history (4:1–43)
- The Second Speech of Moses: The Terms of the Covenant (How Israel Is to Live in the Land) (4:44–28:68)
    – Introduction (4:44–49)
    – The basic principles of the covenant (5:1–11:32)

Portions of thirty manuscripts of Deuteronomy were found among the Dead Sea Scrolls.

✚ In the Hebrew Bible, the titles of each book of the Torah (the Pentateuch) are taken from the opening words in the book. Thus in the Hebrew Bible the book of Deuteronomy is entitled, "these are the words" (1:1).

– Specific principles and details of the covenant (12:1–26:19)
  – Blessings and curses (27:1–28:68)
- The Final Speech of Moses: Renewed Commitment to the Laws of the Covenant (29:1–30:20)
- The Postscript: Keeping the Covenant during the Leadership Transition from Moses to Joshua (31:1–34:12)

What Makes Deuteronomy Interesting and Unique?

- Deuteronomy is one of the Old Testament books most frequently quoted in the New Testament.
- Deuteronomy contains the Ten Commandments.
- Many refer to Deuteronomy as the "heartbeat of the Old Testament."
- The theology of Deuteronomy is a major driving force in the Old Testament story.
- The Prophets rely heavily on Deuteronomy.
- Deuteronomy stresses the importance of worshiping God alone.
- Deuteronomy demands that the people of God love and care for everyone in the community, especially those who can't care for themselves.
- The word "today" occurs over one hundred times in Deuteronomy.

The mountains of Gilead. This area on the east side of the Jordan River was given to the tribes of Manasseh and Gad. .

✛ Throughout much of the rest of the Old Testament, the central, underlying question driving the story is, "Will Israel obey the book of Deuteronomy and be blessed, or will she disobey and be cursed?"

Hittite Treaties and the Structure of Deuteronomy

Joe M. Sprinkle

George Mendenhall (in "Law and Covenant in Israel and the Ancient Near East," *The Biblical Archaeologist* 17.2 [May 1954]: 49–76) observed that God's covenant with Israel is very much like treaties made between suzerains (monarchs) and their vassals among the Hittites. Evangelical scholar Meredith Kline went on to argue that the book of Deuteronomy as a whole is structured after this pattern, showing how the book of Deuteronomy parallels major elements of the Hittite suzerain treaty pattern of the second millennium BC (M. Kline, *Treaty of the Great King* [Grand Rapids: Eerdmans, 1963]). In this analogy, "law" holds the same position as "stipulations" within a treaty.

These parallels with Hittite and other second-millennium treaties support the early date and authenticity of Deuteronomy. Although liberal scholarship has sought parallels in first-millennium treaties, the best parallels are with the second-millennium ones. Thus the structure of Deuteronomy is evidence for its early date and evidence against the

argument that seeks to date Deuteronomy to the seventh century.

The parallel between Hittite treaties and Deuteronomy gives insight into the relationship between law and covenant: God, like a suzerain, is the great King and initiator of the covenant. The Israelites, like the vassals of the Hittite treaties, are inferiors in the relationship and merely receive the offer of a relationship. Moreover, God's laws, like the stipulations of treaties, regulate a relationship only after it is established. Keeping stipulations of treaties did not establish a relationship between the Hittites and their vassals; instead, the relationship is established first by accepting the treaty, and then comes the obligation to keep the stipulations. Similarly, law keeping did not establish Israel's relationship with God; the covenant did. Thus covenant is more basic than law, since the covenant establishes a relationship, not the keeping of the laws. Even under the Mosaic covenant a relationship with God was based on God's gracious offer of a covenant relationship, not on Israel's keeping the law first.

Hittite Treaty Form	Parallel in Deuteronomy
PREAMBLE Identifies the parties of the treaty	*Deuteronomy 1:1–5*
HISTORICAL PROLOGUE Reviews events leading to the treaty	*Deuteronomy 1:6–3:29*
GENERAL STIPULATIONS States substance concerning the future relationship and summarizes the purpose of the specific stipulations	*Deuteronomy 4–11* This is a long exhortation of Moses for Israel to obey God.
SPECIFIC STIPULATIONS	*Deuteronomy 12–26* The sermon continues with a detailed exposition on what the law demands of Israel.
BLESSINGS AND CURSES	*Deuteronomy 27–28*
DOCUMENT CLAUSE Calls for storage and periodic reading of the treaty	*Deuteronomy 27:1–5*
DIVINE WITNESSES TO THE COVENANT Various deities are called on to witness the treaty	*Deuteronomy 29–33* Moses calls on heaven and earth as witnesses of the covenant between God and Israel (30:19; 31:28; 32:1–43).
[No parallel]	*Deuteronomy 34* Death of Moses

What Is the Message of Deuteronomy?

The First Speech of Moses: A Review of the Recent Relationship between God and Israel (1:1–4:43)

Introduction (1:1–18)

Deuteronomy 1:1–4 ties the book of Deuteronomy into a very specific historical context. The people of Israel are on the east side of the Jordan River preparing to enter the Promised Land. The date is also provided—forty years and eleven months after the Exodus. In 1:6–8 God restates that he has given them this land as he promised to their forefathers Abraham, Isaac, and Jacob. Therefore, God declares, it is time to go into the land and take possession of it. The time of wandering in the wilderness is over. Deuteronomy 1:9–18 describes the appointment of leaders over Israel, but the main point seems to be the prolific growth of the Israelite population ("you are as many as the stars in the sky"). Thus several connections to the Abrahamic covenant are made (the land, 1:8; numerous descendants, 1:10; blessing, 1:11), indicating once again that the gift of the Promised Land was a fulfillment of the gracious promise that God made to Abraham back in Genesis (12, 15, 17).

The time in the wilderness—failures and victories (1:19–3:29)

Moses now reminds the people of their recent time in the wilderness. First he describes the terrible rebellion when the Israelites refused to go in and take the Promised Land (originally described in Numbers 13–14). As a consequence, the Israelites were sent into the wilderness to wander for thirty-eight more years, or until that entire rebellious generation passed away (2:14–15). But God also gave them dramatic victories in the wilderness, especially in recent days as they started back toward the Promised Land. In 2:16–3:11 Moses draws attention to these fresh victories, especially the victory over Sihon the Amorite and Og, king of Bashon (described in Num. 21:21–35), which gave Israel total control of the area on the east side of the Jordan River. Moses's point is to remind Israel that God can enable them to be victorious over powerful enemies; thus they should not be afraid of entering Canaan and fighting the Canaanites. Moses then reviews the manner in which he distributed this land on the east side of the Jordan,

A Canaanite god, probably El. Idolatry was the most serious covenant violation.

✚ "The Land" is mentioned over 125 times in Deuteronomy, from 1:8 ("I have given you this land") to 34:4 ("This is the land I promised on oath to Abraham, Isaac, and Jacob").

giving it to the tribes of Reuben and Gad, but insisting that they still help their brothers conquer Canaan on the west side of the Jordan (3:12–20). Moses next mentions regretfully that while God has allowed him to see the Promised Land, he himself will not actually be able to enter it (due to an incident of disobedience in Num. 20:1–12; see also Deut. 32:48–52). Thus Joshua would be the one to lead them into the Promised Land (3:21–29).

Lessons to learn from this history (4:1–43)

Moses then stresses important principles that Israel should learn from its history. Follow these laws that God is giving you, Moses exhorts. Obey him and teach his commandments to your children (4:1–14). Never in our past, Moses warns, did God ever reveal himself in the form of an idol. Therefore, he tells Israel, be especially careful to avoid idolatry, for it strikes at the heart of the covenant (4:15–31). Moses then summarizes the central lessons that Israel should learn from their history: "Because he loved your forefathers and chose their descendants after them, he brought you out of Egypt by his Presence and his great strength, to drive out before you nations greater and stronger than you and to bring you into their land to give it to you for your inheritance, as it is today." Acknowledge God's power and worship him alone, Moses exhorts. Keep these commands he is giving to you (i.e., Deuteronomy), and you (and your children) will be blessed in the land (4:37–40).

The Second Speech of Moses: The Terms of the Covenant (How Israel Is to Live in the Land) (4:44–28:68)

Introduction (4:44–49)

These brief verses introduce the following larger section, referring to that section as "the stipulations, decrees and laws Moses gave them when they came out of Egypt." These verses also restate the context of the recent military

Deuteronomy repeatedly forbids the construction and worship of pagan idols. Shown below is a Canaanite goddess, probably Astarte. Hundreds of idols like these have been found in excavations in and around Jerusalem, underscoring the fact that Israel did not obey the commandment to avoid idolatry.

victories over the two kings Sihon and Og, who had controlled the area on the east side of the Jordan.

The basic principles of the covenant (5:1–11:32)

As Moses introduces the major laws of the covenant (the Ten Commandments), he stresses to the Israelites that this is not just a covenant with their forefathers, but a covenant with *them* (5:1–5).

Next God identifies himself as the God who has saved them ("I am the Lord your God, who brought you out of Egypt, out of the land of slavery"), clearly establishing his relationship with them. He reminds them of their encounter with him at Mount Sinai (Exodus 19–20), when they first received the Ten Commandments. Then God once again presents the Ten Commandments, laws that summarize the most basic elements of the covenant and how God expects them to live. The first commandment ("you shall have no other gods before me") is the critical starting point, for God insists on absolute faithfulness and loyalty to him. The Ten Commandments, as presented in Deuteronomy 5:6–21, are almost identical to the presentation of the Ten Commandments in Exodus 20:1–17. The first four commandments deal with how the people relate to God, and the remaining six commandments deal with how they relate to other people. The one difference between the two presentations of the Ten Commandments is in regard to the Sabbath law (the fourth commandment). In Exodus the Sabbath rest is tied to God's great act of creation, while in Deuteronomy the Sabbath rest is connected to God's great act of deliverance in the Exodus. Both presentations of the Ten Commandments stress faithfulness—to God, neighbors, spouses, parents, and people in general.

Moses reminds the people that God himself wrote the Ten Commandments and that the awesome encounter with him was accompanied by the fire and cloud that surround his Presence. Moses also reminds them that back at Mount Sinai the people swore to obey God and keep his commandments. God then expressed his wish that they would follow his commands so they could receive his blessings. So once again, the Lord calls on them to be faithful and to follow his commands so that they might be blessed in the new land (5:22–33).

Deuteronomy 6 follows up the Ten Commandments by underscoring the most basic commandment. The Lord their God is the only real God, and they are to worship him in total commitment with all they are and all they have (6:4–5). The other central thrust of Deuteronomy 6 is the emphasis

Deut. 6:9 instructs the Israelites to write God's commandments on the doorframes of their houses. Most Jews today place a small emblem (called a Mezuzah) on the doorframe of their houses with a reminder of Deut. 6:4 written on it.

✤ The Hebrew word for "hear" is *shema*. In the Jewish faith, Deuteronomy 6:4–5 ("Hear O Israel: The Lord our God, the Lord is one") is often called the "Great Shema" after the first word in 6:4 ("hear").

on passing on this tradition to their children. Don't forget the commandments, and be sure to tell these things to your children, God stresses (6:6–9). Likewise, God points out that as they move into the rich Promised Land, complete with fields and houses already built, they will be tempted to forget all that God has done for them. Be sure to explain to your children, God states once again, how he miraculously delivered them from Egypt and graciously brought them to this wonderful land, which they will enjoy if they stay faithful to God.

In Deuteronomy 7 Moses reminds the people that they are a special people to God, chosen and holy (7:6); thus when they conquer the Promised Land they are to stay separate from the corrupting influences of the pagan inhabitants. Drive them all out, God commands, and be especially careful not to intermarry with them, for that will bring pagan worship into the people of Israel (7:1–5).

Like a broken record, the theme of "do not forget what God has done for you" continues repeatedly throughout Deuteronomy, and is stressed once again in Deuteronomy 8. Another repeated theme is that Israel did nothing special to deserve being chosen by God; they are God's chosen people only because of his good grace, not because of their righteousness (9:1–6). In fact, God points out rather clearly, their actions have been quite to the contrary, for Israel has repeatedly been rebellious and stubborn, as the golden calf episode (recorded in Exodus 32) demonstrated. Fortunately for rebellious Israel, Moses interceded for them, and God graciously withheld his judgment on them (9:7–10:11).

Deuteronomy 10:12–11:32 calls on the people to love God and to

Deut. 6:8 instructs the Israelites to tie God's commandments on their hands and heads so that they will never forget them. Many Orthodox Jews today seek to fulfill this commandment literally by wearing leather pouches (called tefillin or phylacteries) that contain portions of the Torah on their hands and forehead.

✛ In the New Testament, when Satan tempts Jesus with food in the wilderness, the Lord quotes Deuteronomy 8:3, "Man does not live on bread alone but on every word that comes from the mouth of God" (Matt. 4:4; Luke 4:4).

obey him, understanding that the concepts of love and obedience are tightly interconnected. Likewise, since God himself loves all people, the Israelites are to do likewise, showing love especially to those who are in need—the poor, the widows, the orphans, and the foreigners living among them.

Specific principles and details of the covenant (12:1–26:19)

Having presented the most basic principles and stipulations of the covenant that will govern their life in the Promised Land, Moses now expands on these concepts, adding specific examples and details that relate to the covenant and the worship of God. In general, the arrangement of the topics discussed in this section follows the order of topics addressed in the Ten Commandments.

A table set for a modern Jewish Passover celebration (the seder meal). Deuteronomy 16 restates the importance of remembering the exodus by keeping the Passover celebration.

For example, Deuteronomy 12–13 reflects expansions and implications of the first three of the Ten Commandments, relating to who God is and how he alone is to be worshiped. Thus this section underscores that God himself determines the way he will be worshiped, and Israel is not to follow the ways of her pagan neighbors in worshiping her God. Idolatry is very, very serious, God declares, and advocates of idolatry must be removed, whether they are false prophets (13:1–5), close relatives (13:6–11), or an entire Israelite town (13:12–18). Related to this theme is the summary discussion in 14:1–21 regarding clean and unclean foods (in Leviticus). God, not the pagan neighboring nations, determines the clean/unclean system of dietary laws. As mentioned in Leviticus, this system forced the Israelites to be conscious at all times in all activities that the holy God lived in their midst and demanded they stay holy and separate from impure and unclean things.

The fourth commandment (Sabbath observance) is expanded in 14:22–16:17 as God explains that all of life is to be governed by similar "holy rhythms." This includes regular worship practices such as tithing (14:22–29); canceling debts and providing for the poor (15:1–18); sacrificing the

✦ God's commandments in Deuteronomy 16:18–18:22 regarding leadership in Israel will echo repeatedly throughout 1–2 Samuel, 1–2 Kings, and the Prophets, as Israel's leaders continually fall short of the standard presented in Deuteronomy.

firstborn animals (15:19–23); and celebrating the Passover, the Feast of Weeks, and the Feast of Tabernacles (16:1–17).

The fifth commandment (honoring one's parents) is expanded with discussions of other authority structures, including judges and courts (16:18–17:13); the king (17:14–20, still future at this time); priests and Levites (18:1–8); prohibited occultist professions (18:9–13); and prophets (18:14–22).

Deuteronomy 19–21 discusses issues spinning off the sixth commandment (prohibiting murder), addressing cities of refuge that protect those who commit accidental homicides (19:1–14); the importance of honest testimony in court (19:15–21, also related to the ninth commandment, false testimony); the rules of warfare (20:1–20); how to deal with unsolved murders (21:1–9); and how to execute guilty criminals (21:22–23). Also inserted in this section are several laws that seem to relate more closely to family issues (21:10–21), therefore reflecting the fifth commandment (honoring parents), the seventh commandment (prohibiting adultery), and the tenth commandment (coveting).

Deuteronomy 22:1–12 is similar to the "holiness code" of Leviticus 17–25, and contains several miscellaneous laws relating primarily to two issues: (1) everyone has responsibility for caring for the welfare of others, and (2) the concept of keeping clean and unclean things separate should permeate all aspects of life.

The seventh commandment condemns adultery, and thus various sexual offenses are discussed in Deuteronomy 22:13–30. The final unit in this section is Deuteronomy 23:1–26:19. This unit contains a wide variety of laws. Commandments eight (prohibiting stealing) and ten (prohibiting covetousness) imply the establishment of an unselfish community that

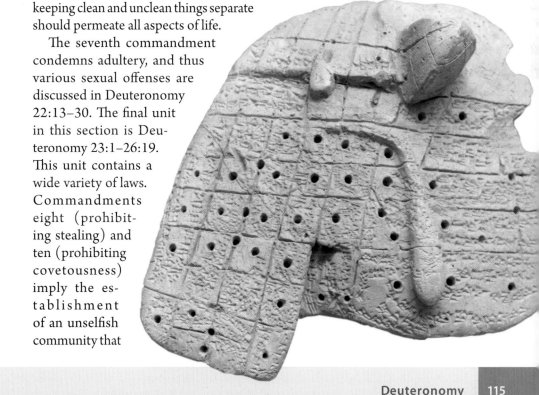

Clay model of a sheep's liver, used in pagan divination. From Mesopotamia (1900–1600 BC). Deut. 17:9–13 strictly forbade divination and sorcery in Israel.

cares for the well-being of everyone, and thus provides the starting point for many of the laws here. However, the list of laws in this section is quite diverse, and these laws relate to many of the other commandments as well, often in a repetitive manner. Some of the issues addressed are uncleanness (23:9–14); temple prostitution (23:17–18); charging interest on loans (23:19–20); divorce (24:1–4); care and justice for the poor and the foreigner (24:17–22); honesty in commercial transactions (25:13–16); and tithing (26:1–15). This section concludes with a call to obey all of these laws (26:16–19).

Blessings and curses (27:1–28:68)

Ancient treaty agreements usually had a section containing blessings and curses—blessings for keeping the treaty and curses for breaking it. Deuteronomy, in following this ancient treaty form, includes blessings and curses in Deuteronomy 27–28. Deuteronomy 27 describes a ceremony that is to take place once Israel is in the Promised Land. First they are to write all of the laws of Deuteronomy on two large plaster-covered stones. This stresses the ongoing permanence of the covenant. Then the Israelites are to have a solemn public ceremony involving the entire nation. Six of the tribes will stand on Mount Gerizim and six will stand on Mount Ebal (two mountains on either side of the city of Shechem). Then these tribes will call out twelve curses from the tops of these

Mount Gerizim and Mount Ebal, location for the covenant blessings/curses ceremony described in Deuteronomy 27.

✚ In discussing law and grace, Paul quotes from the twelfth and climactic curse of Deuteronomy 27 (from the Septuagint), "Cursed is everyone who does not continue to do everything written in the Book of the Law" (Gal. 3:10; Deut. 27:26).

mountains, curses on people who do not keep various laws given in Deuteronomy. This ceremony is later carried out in Joshua 8:30–35.

Deuteronomy 28 is even more explicit regarding blessings and curses, and plays a very important role in Israel's history. Moses lays out very clearly the two contrasting consequences of the covenant. On the one hand, if the people truly obey God, then they will be blessed abundantly (28:1–14). Rain will be plentiful and their crops will grow; their animals will be fruitful and reproduce; Israel will have victory over all its enemies; in short, the Israelites will prosper and do very well in the land. On the other hand, Moses warns, if they do not obey God, and instead ignore the stipulations of Deuteronomy, then terrible curses will come upon them. All the blessings will be reversed. It won't rain and thus their crops will die, their animals will not reproduce, and their enemies will be victorious over them. The curses section is much longer than the blessings section, and it continues on and on, describing a nightmarish situation of foreign invasion and exile from the Promised Land. Indeed, this chapter describes a reversal of the salvation history that has taken place in the life of Israel so far. The curses in 28:58–68 parallel the plagues that God brought on Egypt back in Exodus when he delivered Israel. If Israel turns away from God, then the plagues of Egypt will fall on them, and, indeed, they will find themselves back in slavery again. God is not fooling around. He is deadly serious about the gravity of this covenant agreement. Wonderful blessings will come from obedience, but terrible curses will come from disobedience.

✦ Later in history the prophets will rely heavily on Deuteronomy for their critique of Israel's sin. Isaiah opens his book with a call on the witnesses of Deuteronomy ("heavens and earth") to bear witness to Israel's serious covenant violation (Isa. 1:2).

Deuteronomy 28 sets the stage for the rest of the Old Testament. The driving question is, "Will Israel be faithful to Deuteronomy and receive blessing?" The tragic answer will be no. The prophets will rely heavily on Deuteronomy 28 as they come and announce judgment on Israel for disobeying the covenant laws of Deuteronomy.

The Final Speech of Moses: Renewed Commitment to the Laws of the Covenant (29:1–30:20)

Moses sums up the book of Deuteronomy and gives a synopsis in his final speech. He retells the story of the Exodus and stresses once again God's faithfulness to the people of Israel. Then he exhorts them to be faithful to God and to obey the laws of the covenant. Yet Moses also predicts prophetically that in the future the Israelites will break the covenant, turn to worshiping idols, and thus be banished from the land (29:19–29). But after that, Moses prophesies (much like Isaiah and Jeremiah will prophesy), God will restore them once again to the land and bless them (30:1–10). Moses ends his speech in dramatic fashion, declaring, "I set before you today life and prosperity, death and destruction" (30:15). The choice is theirs. They can obey and be blessed, or disobey and be cursed. This offer at the end of the Pentateuch (obey and be blessed in the Promised Land) parallels the offer made to Adam and Eve at the beginning of the Pentateuch (obey and be

Jordan River. God gives Israel the book of Deuteronomy just before they cross over the Jordan River to enter the Promised Land.

blessed in the garden). This is the question that is put before each generation of Israelites throughout Old Testament history.

The ancient treaty format also contained a section for witnesses. Usually, since these treaties were those of pagan nations, the witnesses would comprise their gods. Deuteronomy follows the ancient treaty format, but for witnesses God uses "heaven and earth" (30:19; 31:28; 32:1).

The Postscript: Keeping the Covenant during the Leadership Transition from Moses to Joshua (31:1–34:12)

Moses has played a central role in mediating the covenant from God to the people of Israel. God does not want the covenant relationship to die with Moses. Thus he provides for a smooth transition in leadership. First of all, Joshua is chosen to be the one who will lead Israel into the Promised Land, although God continually stresses that he is the one who will actually bring about the victory (31:1–8). Moses exhorts Joshua to "be strong and courageous," for God will be with him (31:7–8). This exhortation will be repeated numerous times in the opening chapter of Joshua.

While the transition in human leadership is important for maintaining the covenant, the most important element will be the written word. Several times in Deuteronomy God orders Israel to write down these laws for future generations to read. This is stressed again in 31:9–13. It is interesting to note that Joshua will not completely replace Moses. Joshua will become the military leader of Israel and will lead in the conquest of the Promised Land. But the role of mediator between Israel and God that Moses has played throughout Exodus, Leviticus, Numbers, and Deuteronomy, especially the mediation of the word of God to Israel, will be transferred from Moses to the written word. The written law of Moses will replace Moses as the mediator of the word of God.

To connect with the people on a popular level, God also gives Moses a song to be written down and taught to the Israelites so that they can sing it (31:19). This song proclaims God's faithfulness and, in contrast, Israel's unfaithfulness (32:1–43).

Throughout the portion of the Pentateuch that deals with the Mosaic covenant (Exodus, Leviticus, Numbers, and Deuteronomy), the people of Israel have repeatedly disobeyed God and broken his laws. Likewise here in the closing chapters of Deuteronomy, at the end of the Pentateuch, one would hope that such disobedient behavior was a thing of the past and not a pattern for the future. God, however, states very clearly that in the future Israel will not keep the laws of Deuteronomy and will not remain faithful to him: "They will forsake me and break the covenant I made with them. . . . They will

An Assyrian wall relief depicting the horrifying results of an Assyrian attack. Israel and Judah will disobey Deuteronomy and thus experience tragic and terrible invasions by the Assyrians and the Babylonians.

turn to other gods and worship them, rejecting me and breaking my covenant" (31:16, 20). Thus from the very inauguration of the Mosaic covenant, God declares that this covenant will not be successful because the people of Israel will not be able to obey its laws. So as the Pentateuch closes, the reader realizes that hope for the future lies with the Abrahamic covenant, which is characterized by God's promise and grace, rather than with the Mosaic covenant, which Israel will soon shatter and abandon. In this sense there is an interesting parallel between the beginning of the Pentateuch and the ending. Genesis 3–11 focuses on worldwide sin and the tendency of people in general to sin. The solution to this sin problem is presented in Genesis 12, the Abrahamic covenant. The ending of Deuteronomy reminds the reader that the nation Israel follows the same pattern as sinful humankind did in Genesis 3–11. Even with the Mosaic covenant and the great encounter with God at Mount Sinai, Israel will do no better than typical sinful humankind of Genesis 3–11. Hope for salvation in Deuteronomy lies in God's grace and his gracious promise to Abraham, just as it did in Genesis.

Finally, like a great patriarch blessing his children, Moses pronounces a blessing on each of the tribes of Israel (33:1–29). Then he climbs Mount Nebo and looks down on the Promised Land. God once again declares that this is the land he promised to Abraham, Isaac, and Jacob. God is now giving it to the Israelites in fulfillment of that promise (34:4). Thus even though most of Exodus, Leviticus, Numbers, and Deuteronomy has focused on the Mosaic covenant, here at the very end of the Pentateuch, the reader is once again reminded that it is God's promise to Abraham that continues to move the story forward, even after Israel has been disobedient (28:9–11; 29:13; 31:20; 34:4).

Moses then dies, and Joshua is filled with "the spirit of wisdom," completing the transfer of leadership (34:9). Deuteronomy ends with a eulogy for Moses, declaring that "since then, no prophet has risen in Israel like Moses, whom the Lord knew face to face" (34:10).

So What? Applying Deuteronomy to Our Lives Today

The book of Deuteronomy is filled with important theological principles that we should grasp and apply to our everyday lives. One of the central themes of Deuteronomy that has special relevance for people today is the repeated stress that God determines the way to approach him and the way to salvation; it is not left up to us to come up with a theological belief system that sounds good or resonates with our culture. In Deuteronomy (as throughout Scripture) God emphatically rejects the idea that his people can synthesize belief in him with other mystical beliefs. There are not multiple ways to "the divine," and other religions (like Buddhism and Islam) are not valid approaches to God. Other religions are not simply different expressions of faith in the same God. Deuteronomy (and the Pentateuch in general) demands that God's people worship him alone, he who is Creator of the heavens and earth, he who is the God of Abraham, he who brought up Israel from Egypt. No one can approach him except through the means that he determines.

Deuteronomy also teaches us that God loves all people, and that he also wants us to care for people. This is especially true for those who are down and out and cannot care for themselves.

Deuteronomy also turns our gaze forward to the Prophets and to the New Testament, for it presents us with the sobering reality that the Israelites (and we too) are simply unable to keep the law, and thus find themselves under God's judgment. Their only hope lies in his grace and his faithfulness to his promise to Abraham, and his promise of a new and better system in the future. In the New Testament, the apostle Paul will explain this to us very clearly, underscoring that Deuteronomy demonstrated the need for Jesus and his death and resurrection.

Our Favorite Verses in Deuteronomy

Hear, O Israel: The Lord our God, the Lord is one. Love the Lord your God with all your heart and with all your soul and with all your strength. (6:4–5)

Mount Nebo. Moses viewed the Promised Land from this mountain (Deut. 34:1).

The Historical Books

Introduction to the Historical Books

The typical general and generic term "Historical Books" can be applied to the books of Joshua, Judges, Ruth, 1–2 Samuel, 1–2 Kings, 1–2 Chronicles, Ezra, Nehemiah, and Esther. On closer analysis, however, this long list of books falls into two distinct groups, which we will call "the Deuteronomy-based history" (Joshua through 2 Kings) and "the Chronicler's history" (1 Chronicles through Esther).

The Deuteronomy-based history includes Joshua, Judges, Ruth, 1–2 Samuel, and 1–2 Kings. These books are generally in chronological order, and they continue the story of the Pentateuch. The books of Exodus, Leviticus, Numbers, and Deuteronomy present the Mosaic covenant, the terms by which Israel could live in the Promised Land and be blessed by the awesome God living in their midst. The question at the end of Deuteronomy, as the Israelites prepare to enter the Promised Land, is, "Will Israel be faithful to the Lord and the laws (the Mosaic covenant) he has given them and thus be blessed?" This question drives the plot of the story line throughout the Deuteronomy-based history (Joshua through 2 Kings). The tragic answer (already predicted by God in Deut. 31:14–21) is no. The books in the Deuteronomy-based history describe this tragic downfall of Israel, as the nation fails to obey God and follow him.

The beginning and the ending of the Deuteronomy-based historical books are in contrasting and ironic parallel. The book of Joshua opens with Israel destroying the city of Jericho and then moving in and possessing the Promised Land. Second Kings, in contrast, ends with the destruction of Jerusalem and the exile of Israel from the Promised Land. Just in case the reader missed this significant parallel, 2 Kings 25:1–5 describes a small detail that pulls it all together. As Jerusalem falls, the disobedient and rebellious King Zedekiah sneaks out of the city and flees for his life. The Babylonians, however, overtake him *in the plains of Jericho* (2 Kings 25:5), where the whole story of conquering the Promised Land started.

Thus the Deuteronomy-based history opens with Israel going into the Promised Land (Joshua) and it closes with Israel being expelled from the land (2 Kings). In between, Israel will have several ups and downs. The book of Joshua is "up," as Israel obediently conquers the land. Judges is definitely a "down," as Israel quickly spirals down and becomes as corrupt and defiled as the Canaanites they were supposed to dispossess. Who will save them from the mess they are in? The book of Ruth answers this very quietly, providing a transition to David, who will be the one to save them and get them back on track. First and Second Samuel is about David, his rise to power and his reign. David completes the conquest and gets Israel back on track as far as worshiping God goes. This is one of the "ups" in the story—indeed, perhaps the high point theologically. But David cannot sustain the role of savior. He is, after all, merely a great man. One night he looks down from his palace, sees the beautiful and naked Bathsheba, and his entire kingdom crumbles. So, while 1–2 Samuel starts out on an "up" beat, it ends with the story heading down. In 1–2 Kings, a few valiant, good kings try to stop the downward slide of Israel into idolatry and disregard of God's law. But the momentum is too great, and most of the leadership in Israel (kings, prophets, priests, nobles) is encouraging, even leading, the downward slide away from God's commands. The end is tragic, and just as God predicted in Deuteronomy, Israel loses the Presence of God and the right to live in the Promised Land.

✦ The "Deuteronomy-based history" (Joshua through 2 Kings) tells the story of how Israel turns away from God, refusing to obey Deuteronomy.

They are expelled from the land, carried off into exile in Babylon. Very little hope is expressed at the end of the Deuteronomy-based history, which is primarily concerned with explaining why the judgment of the exile occurred. For hope beyond the exile, we will have to listen to the prophets.

The Chronicler's history (1 Chronicles to Esther) is written from a slightly different perspective. It does not focus on explaining why the exile occurred, but rather speaks to those who have returned to the land after the exile and points to the way forward, focusing on the everlasting promises of the Davidic covenant, on establishing true and faithful worship in the temple, and on trusting in God even if they remain weak and under foreign political domination.

As mentioned in Part II, the Hebrew Bible is divided into three main sections: the Torah (what we call the Pentateuch), the Prophets, and the Writings. In the Hebrew canon the books of the Deuteronomy-based history (Joshua, Judges, Ruth, 1–2 Samuel, 1–2 Kings) are included in the Prophets, placed at the front of that group and labeled as "the Former Prophets." They also follow Deuteronomy and provide a tight historical and theological connection to the Torah (Pentateuch). The authorship of the books in the Deuteronomy-based history is not stated in each book, but probably they were written by unidentified court prophets, perhaps one of the reasons the Hebrew canon refers to them as part of the Prophets.

Likewise, in the Hebrew canon, the Chronicler's history (1 Chronicles through Esther) is located in the section called the Writings, which closes the Hebrew Bible. The order is slightly different as well, with 1–2 Chronicles falling at the very end and closing the Hebrew canon.

Joshua

Conquering the Promised Land

At last! After forty years of wandering in the wilderness, it is now time to cross the Jordan River and enter into the land that God has promised. Now the Israelites will live in houses instead of tents, and they will have luscious fruit trees right in their front yard. Instead of moving from oasis to oasis, always searching for water and grass, now will live by streams, springs, and wells, with plenty of grass for their livestock to eat. Furthermore, everybody is going to get an equal share. Those who were slaves in Egypt are now going to get their own farms, vineyards, houses, and wells. It was like winning the lottery! The wonderful promise of land (and rest) is about to be fulfilled.

The book of Joshua is a "good news" book, optimistic and upbeat. In contrast to the constant grumbling and disobedience of the Israelites that has characterized the story ever since God first sent Moses to deliver them from Egypt, now the Israelites generally obey and do what God (and his servant Joshua) tells them to do. Not surprising to the reader—for God and Moses have told them this repeatedly in Exodus, Numbers, and Deuteronomy—such obedience results in tremendous blessings: victory over the inhabitants of the land and other enemies, leading to the possession of a rich and bountiful land.

What Is the Setting for Joshua?

The book of Joshua is a continuation of the Pentateuch story. In Genesis 12 God makes a covenant with Abraham, promising him land, numerous descendants, and blessings. God also promises to make him into a great nation and that this nation would be a blessing to all peoples. This promise drives the Old Testament story. Genesis ends with Abraham's grandson Jacob, along with his twelve sons, residing in Egypt. They are only seventy in number, and they have no land. About four hundred years later, when the book of Exodus begins, the Israelite population has exploded, and they are so numerous that the Egyptians feel threatened. So part of the Abrahamic covenant has been fulfilled (numerous descendants), but not the promise of land. Likewise, since the Egyptians enslave them and mistreat them terribly, the promise of blessing does not seem to be fulfilled either. The story running from Exodus to Joshua is the story of God delivering the Israelites, blessing them with his powerful Presence and the Mosaic covenant, and then actually giving them the land promised to Abraham. In Numbers, the original generation of Israelites had rejected the Promised Land, so God sent them back into the wilderness to wander aimlessly around until all of that rebellious generation passed away. Then God led them back toward the Promised Land. When they got close to the land, God used Moses as the mediator to deliver the book of Deuteronomy to the Israelites. Deuteronomy restated and expanded on the Mosaic covenant and called on the people to renew their commitment to God and to the Mosaic covenant. The Mosaic covenant (the laws in Exodus, Leviticus, Numbers, and Deuteronomy) provided the terms by which Israel could live in the Promised Land with God right in their midst, and receive blessings from him. So the book of Joshua is an exciting and dramatic conclusion to a long and painful journey. Now, at last, the Israelites are actually going to enter the Promised Land, drive out the Canaanites, take possession of this wonderful place, and live peacefully at rest.

What Is at the Heart of Joshua?

The action story line of the book of Joshua is about conquering, distributing, and taking possession of the Promised Land. The theological story line is the same as that presented in Exodus, Numbers, and Deuteronomy: obedience and trust in God result in deliverance, victory, and blessing, while disobedience results in tragic defeat, judgment, and the onset of curses (i.e., the opposite of blessings). Also at the heart of this book is the proclamation that God is faithful to his promises. He gives Israel the land of Canaan, just as he promised their forefather Abraham.

Important subthemes run throughout the book as well. For example, closely related to the themes of "land" and "blessing" is the promise of "rest," a theme recurring frequently in Joshua (1:13, 15; 11:23; 14:15; 21:44; 22:4; 23:1). After wandering for years and waging war constantly, now they will soon be able to settle down on their own farms and raise their families quietly and peacefully. Another subtheme that emerges early in Joshua through the long episode dealing with Rahab (Joshua 2) and Achan (Joshua 7) is

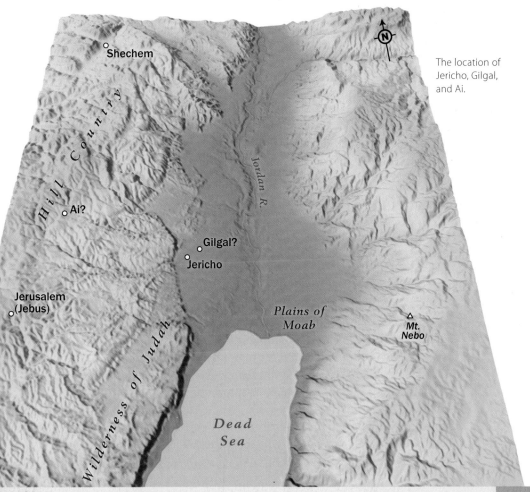

The location of Jericho, Gilgal, and Ai.

✦ Although it ends in tragedy, the "Deuteronomy-based history" (Joshua through 2 Kings) starts out well, for Joshua is a "good news" book, filled with victory and success.

The Morality of the Conquest of Canaan

Some aspects of the story in Joshua can be a little disquieting for us. For example, God orders the Israelites to kill all of the Canaanites, every man, woman, and child. This can seem harsh to us, perhaps even unjust. What about the love and grace of God? There are several points to consider as we grapple with this problem. First of all we need to place this story in its proper context within the Bible, and to read the texts carefully. Note that the order to destroy all the inhabitants of a conquered city was not a universal order applying to every city the Israelites conquered, but applied only to cities within the Promised Land, where the Israelites would settle. Second, remember the Canaanite society Israel is destroying has been portrayed regularly throughout the Pentateuch as one that is especially corrupt and immoral. Genesis 19 (the Sodom and Gomorrah episode) presents a paradigmatic representation of Canaanite society as incredibly immoral. Leviticus 18 echoes this sentiment, connecting perverse sexual behavior to the Canaanites. Back in Genesis 9:25 Noah proclaimed a "prophetic" curse on the Canaanites, a prophecy that finds fulfillment in the conquest. Third, we learn from Genesis 15:16 that God was apparently offended by the sin of the Canaanites as early as the time of Abraham, but in his grace and perseverance he waited four hundred years before actually judging them. So the Pentateuch stresses that the Canaanites were so corrupt and immoral that they deserved judgment long before Joshua and the Israelites arrive. God delays that judgment, apparently giving the Canaanites time to repent. God then uses the Israelites to carry out his judgment on the Canaanite society, just as he used fire and brimstone to destroy Sodom and Gomorrah. Finally, don't miss the huge irony of this discussion. In a book about annihilating the Canaanites, the first major story in the book is about Rahab, a Canaanite who is not destroyed, but rather is included into Israel, becoming a prominent and important woman in the lineage of David (and Christ!). This is an important episode in Joshua. It is placed prominently at the beginning of the book of Joshua, and a lot of text is devoted to the Rahab episode. Is this story presented as a pattern? Obviously Rahab is a huge exception to the annihilation command, but does her story imply that there were others? Her story (combined with the story of Achan, Joshua 7) qualifies the annihilation command, underscoring that it is those who trust in the Lord who will live, and it is those who don't trust in him who will die. Likewise, just as a woman (Rahab) and her family are spared and included into Israel in Joshua 2–6, so in Joshua 9 an entire city (the Gibeonites) dodges destruction. So the pattern of deliverance set by the individual Canaanite Rahab is repeated by an entire Canaanite city.

that ultimately inclusion into the people of God is based on trust and faith in God, and not on Hebrew ethnicity. This is another example of how God works behind the scenes of the story to fulfill the Abrahamic covenant ("all peoples on earth will be blessed through you"; Gen. 12:3).

Finally, another faint subtheme that nonetheless persists throughout the book is the quiet, subtle reminder that the Israelites are not quite successful in driving out all the Canaanites (13:1–5, 13; 15:63; 16:10; 17:12), something that will come back to haunt them in the book of Judges and in the years to follow.

✛ In a sense, the Promised Land parallels the garden back in Genesis 2. It is a wonderful, bountiful land filled with great things to eat, and it is a place where God's people can encounter him in fellowship and blessing.

The story in the book of Joshua can be outlined as follows:

- How to Successfully Conquer the Promised Land (1:1–18)
- A Test Case: Jericho (2:1–7:26)
  - Rahab the believer is saved (2:1–24)
  - Crossing the Jordan River into the Promised Land (3:1–5:12)
  - The siege and fall of Jericho (5:13–6:27)
  - Achan the unbeliever is destroyed (7:1–26)
- Back on Track: The Capture of Ai and Recommitment to the Covenant (8:1–35)
- Conquering the Rest of Canaan (9:1–12:24)
  - The southern campaign (9:1–10:43)
  - The northern campaign (11:1–15)
  - Summary of the conquest (11:16–12:24)
- Distributing the Promised Land (13:1–21:45)
- Resolving Conflict among the Tribes (22:1–34)
- Renewal of Covenant Commitment (23:1–24:33)

What Makes Joshua Interesting and Unique?

- In a book about annihilating all the Canaanites, the first major story is about the deliverance and salvation of the Canaanite prostitute, Rahab.
- There is a fascinating and ironic contrast between Rahab (Joshua 2) and Achan (Joshua 7).
- In a book filled with war, the thematic goal is "rest."
- Joshua has an encounter with "the Commander of the army of the Lord" (Josh. 5:14–15).
- The book of Joshua contains the fascinating story of the walls of Jericho falling down.
- In Joshua, God parts the Jordan River, allowing Israel to cross over on dry ground, just as he had parted the Red Sea back in the book of Exodus.

The water from the Jordan River and its tributaries is used for irrigation and drinking in several countries (Israel, Jordan, Palestine, Syria, and Lebanon). Thus today the Jordan River (what remains of it) is quite a bit smaller than the river that Joshua and the Israelites crossed.

What Is the Message of Joshua?

How to Successfully Conquer the Promised Land (1:1–18)

The story in Joshua 1 picks up immediately from the end of Deuteronomy. Moses has just died, Israel is on the east side of the Jordan River, preparing to cross over into the Promised Land, and God has just appointed Joshua as the new leader of Israel. Joshua 1 introduces several major themes of the book. First of all, Joshua is the new leader, providing continuity with Moses (1:1–9). God declares that he will be with Joshua as he was with Moses (1:5), thus providing the same power of his Presence that was experienced in the exodus. But Joshua's role is not quite the same as Moses's, and he will not carry out the "mediator" role that Moses played. As mentioned in our discussion in Deuteronomy, the mediation role of Moses now transfers not to Joshua, but to the written word (i.e., the "Book of the Law"). Note also that while Moses is frequently called "the servant of the Lord" (1:1, 2, 13, 15), Joshua is called "the servant [or aide] of Moses." He is not called "the servant of the Lord" until the end of his life, after the conquest is over (24:29). Another interesting observation is that Joshua is told to be "strong and courageous" numerous times. Moses tells him this (Deut. 31:6), the people tell him this (Josh. 1:18), and God repeatedly tells him this (Deut. 31:23; Josh. 1:6, 7, 9).

Another important theme that Joshua 1 picks up and continues from Deuteronomy is that the land is God's gracious gift to Israel. Several times and in various ways God refers to "the land I am about to give to you" (1:2, 3, 13, 15). Finally, Joshua 1 continues to echo what God has been saying to Israel ever since the exodus: if they remain faithful and obey God's law, they will be successful and will find blessing (1:8–9).

Some scholars have suggested that this woman is a Canaanite prostitute, but the exact significance of this ivory carving is unclear (ninth to eighth century BC).

A Test Case: Jericho (2:1–7:26)

Rahab the believer is saved (2:1–24)

The immediate challenge in conquering Canaan is the city of Jericho, a strong, well-defended city right across the Jordan River from the Israelites. Recall that the last time the Israelites were in this situation, Moses sent twelve men to spy out the land, and ten of them came back saying that the Israelites could not possibly

Comparisons and Contrasts between Rahab (Joshua 2) and Achan (Joshua 7)

Rahab	Achan
A woman	A man
She is a Canaanite, but fears the Lord	He is an Israelite, but doesn't fear the Lord
A prostitute (not respectable)	Respectable
Should have perished, but survives	Should have survived, but perishes
Her family survives	His family perishes
All that belongs to her survives	All that belongs to him perishes
Her nation (Jericho) perishes	His nation (Israel) prospers
She hides the spies from the king	He hides the loot from Joshua and the Lord
She hides the spies in her house	He hides the loot in his tent
She hides the spies on the roof	He hides the loot in the ground
Her house survives	His tent perishes
The cattle, sheep, and donkeys of her city (Jericho) perish	His cattle, sheep, and donkeys perish, like those in Jericho
She obeyed indirect revelation from the Lord	He disobeyed direct revelation from the Lord
She lives—like the Israelites	He dies—like the Canaanites

win (Numbers 13–14). This time Joshua sends two handpicked men. They sneak into Jericho and encounter a prostitute named Rahab, who hides them from her king, thus saving their lives. Rahab then makes a remarkable declaration to them of her strong faith in Israel's God, acknowledging that God has given them this land, and asking that the Israelites spare her and her family (2:8–13). The Israelite spies agree to spare Rahab and her family, even though she is a Canaanite. As mentioned below, the faith and trust of Rahab are in strong contrast to the disdain and disobedience of Achan (Joshua 7), illustrating that it is the people of faith who inherit the Promised Land and not just those who are ethnically related to Israel.

Crossing the Jordan River into the Promised Land (3:1–5:12)

Crossing the Jordan River officially ends the exodus event and is perhaps the climactic event in the book of Joshua. It has numerous parallels and contrasts with the crossing of the Red Sea in Exodus 14. In Exodus the Israelites are leaving Egypt, the land of slavery; in Joshua they are entering Canaan, the Promised Land of plenty. In Exodus they are fleeing from the pursuing Egyptian army; in Joshua they are advancing to attack Jericho. The Presence of God plays a huge role in both events. In Exodus God is in the fire and

✚ Rahab is listed in the genealogy of David and Jesus as the mother of Boaz (Ruth's husband) and the great-great grandmother of David (Matt. 1:5–6).

cloud that protects fleeing Israel. In Joshua the Presence of God is in the ark of the covenant, which is at the center of this significant event.

Apparently during the time of wandering in the wilderness, the Israelites had not been continuing the practice of circumcision, perhaps signifying a rupture in their covenant relationship with God. Now, after crossing the Jordan, the Israelites circumcise all of those who had been born in the wilderness, thus recommitting to the covenant (5:1–9). They then celebrate the Passover in the Promised Land and eat of the produce from the land. The daily provision of manna ceases (5:10–12). The exodus is officially over.

The siege and fall of Jericho (5:13–6:27)

As children, most of us learned the old song, "Joshua fought the battle of Jericho, Jericho, Jericho; Joshua fought the battle of Jericho, and the walls came tumbling down." Joshua 5:13–6:27 describes that event. One important thing to note is that the ark of the covenant plays the central role in the siege. The "siege" involves marching around Jericho with the ark—which is more like a religious festival procession than a military siege. God gives Israel an easy victory. The walls do tumble down, and Israel captures the strong Canaanite city that protected the entrance to the land of Canaan. Everyone in the city is killed, except Rahab and her family. In obedience to God, the Israelites do not keep any valuable materials captured in Jericho. All silver, gold, and bronze articles they place in the tabernacle of the Lord. Everything else is destroyed.

Immediately west of Jericho were the rugged hills that would later be known as the Judean wilderness.

Achan the unbeliever is destroyed (7:1–26)

There is one small glitch in the Jericho victory, however. One of the Israelites, Achan, disobeys God and keeps several valuable items that he found in Jericho. Thus when Israel undertakes its next campaign, a minor operation against a very small town called Ai, God no longer empowers the Israelites to win, and they are defeated (7:1–5). Joshua is devastated at this defeat and cries out to God (7:6–9). God informs Joshua that someone has stolen things that were supposed to be dedicated to the tabernacle, in serious violation of God's instructions. God then indicates to Joshua it was Achan who did this (7:10–18). Joshua and the Israelites then destroy Achan, his family, and all his possessions. In essence Achan becomes like a Canaanite, and he dies like the Canaanites in Jericho, perishing along with his family and all his possessions. His story is the bookend parallel to that of the Canaanite Rahab, who trusts in God and is saved, along with her family and her possessions, becoming, in essence, an Israelite.

Back on Track: The Capture of Ai and Recommitment to the Covenant (8:1–35)

With the Achan episode behind them, the Israelites then get the conquest back on track, quickly finishing off Ai (8:1–29). Joshua then builds an altar (8:30–31) and recommits the people to covenant obedience, carrying out a public covenant commitment ceremony ordered by God back in Deuteronomy 27:11–26.

Conquering the Rest of Canaan (9:1–12:24)

The southern campaign (9:1–10:43)

The rest of the conquest of Canaan takes place in two major phases, a southern campaign (9:1–10:43) and a northern campaign (11:1–15). The southern campaign opens with an unusual event, for an entire city (Gibeon) tricks Joshua and the Israelites into thinking they come from a far land, when in reality they live just over the hill and would be one of the very next cities to be attacked. Joshua enters into a treaty with the Gibeonites, and even after he realizes he has been duped, he pledges to stay faithful to his treaty with them (9:1–26). Thus, as in the case of Rahab, we find an opening story about Canaanites who are not destroyed because they acknowledge that God has given this land to the Israelites and he cannot be defeated.

Ironically, it is Joshua's treaty commitment to the Gibeonites that precipitates the commencement of the southern campaign. Gibeon is attacked

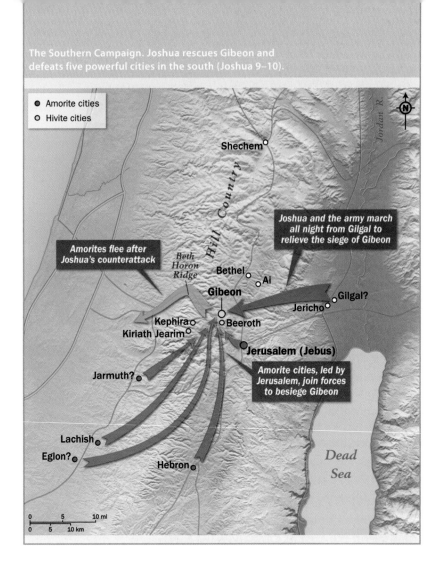

The Southern Campaign. Joshua rescues Gibeon and defeats five powerful cities in the south (Joshua 9–10).

- ● Amorite cities
- ○ Hivite cities

N

Jordan R.

Shechem○

Hill Country

Joshua and the army march all night from Gilgal to relieve the siege of Gibeon

Amorites flee after Joshua's counterattack

Beth Horon Ridge

Bethel○
○Ai
Gibeon○

Gilgal?○
Jericho○

Kephira○ ○Beeroth
Kiriath Jearim○

Jerusalem (Jebus)●

Jarmuth?●

Amorite cities, led by Jerusalem, join forces to besiege Gibeon

Lachish●
Eglon?●
Hebron●

Dead Sea

0 5 10 mi
0 5 10 km

by the other Canaanite cities in the region, and Joshua, as a faithful treaty partner, comes to its rescue. God steps in and miraculously defeats the Canaanite coalition army by "hurling large hailstones down on them" and then making the sun stand still, which gives the Israelite army more daylight by which to complete the annihilation of this major Canaanite coalition army (10:9–15). Joshua then proceeds to conquer the rest of the southern areas (10:16–42).

The northern campaign (11:1–15)

Next Joshua moves north and subdues the entire northern region as well. As he defeats these kings and cities, he follows the Lord's command and does not incorporate the enemy chariots into his army, but instead hamstrings the

✚ Deuteronomy 17:16 warned the future kings of Israel not to accumulate horses (probably chariot horses). Joshua (although not the king) obeys this command by hamstringing the captured enemy chariot horses (Josh. 11:9).

horses and burns the chariots (11:6, 9). This allows the horses to be used for domestic purposes, but not for pulling chariots. God wants Joshua to trust in him for military victory, not in chariot armies.

Summary of the conquest (11:16–12:24)

Joshua 11:16–12:24 provides a wrap-up or summary of the conquest. On the one hand, the summary states that "Joshua took the entire land, just as the Lord had directed Moses" (11:23), implying that the conquest was finished rather quickly. On the other hand, 11:18 indicates "Joshua waged war against all these kings for a long time." Likewise, throughout the rest of the book of Joshua, numerous verses indicate that several small areas remained to be subdued (13:1, 13; 15:63; 16:10, etc.). What Joshua 1–12 indicates is that Joshua has broken the back of any large-scale organized resistance and he has effective control of the region. Now he gives each tribe their portion of the land, and it becomes their responsibility to finish the conquest and crush any remaining resistance in their tribal region, a task many of the tribes fail to carry out. Likewise, many cities had been captured, and these victories needed to be followed up quickly with Israelite occupation, which did not always happen, allowing the original inhabitants to return.

Distributing the Promised Land (13:1–21:45)

Joshua 13–21 describes how the Promised Land was specifically distributed to each of the tribes of Israel. Thus this section gives boundaries for each tribal inheritance, something that is rather boring for us as modern readers, but which was rather important and very interesting to those who lived on this land and passed this inheritance on to their children.

Cities of refuge (defined in Numbers 35) are designated (20:1–9). Likewise specific cities for the Levites, who did not get any specific tribal area, are chosen and set aside, distributing the Levites (the priests responsible for instructing the people in the law) throughout the other twelve tribes (21:1–42).

As mentioned above, while Joshua is generally an upbeat "good news" book, there is a quiet disturbing subtheme that surfaces in this section. Joshua 13:1–5 indicates that in Joshua's old age, several regions had still not been subdued by the various Israelite tribes. Then as the boundary descriptions are given in Joshua 13–21, the text quietly mentions areas in each tribal region not yet conquered (13:13; 15:63; 16:10; 17:12). The individual tribes are not as conscientious about completing the conquest as Joshua is. Once he splits up the land and gives each tribe their respective areas, they

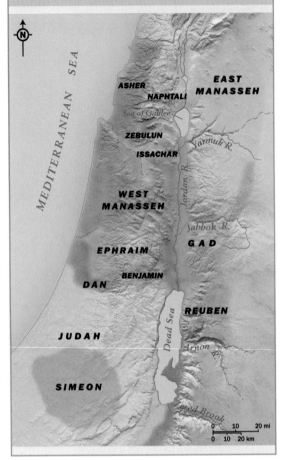

The tribal distribution of the Promised Land (Joshua 13–19)

lose their motivation and begin settling in, neglecting the command to drive out *all* the Canaanites and other inhabitants of the land. This will come back to haunt them in the book of Judges.

This unit concludes with an overall summary statement in 21:43–45, reiterating how God has given this Promised Land to Israel just as he promised their forefathers. He has also empowered them to conquer and possess the land, thus fulfilling all his promises to them.

Resolving Conflict among the Tribes (22:1–34)

One of the most basic problems Israel will face in the years to come is maintaining unity as the people of God. Almost immediately, conflict arises between those tribes who had settled on the eastern side of the Jordan (Reuben, Gad, Manasseh) and the rest of the nation. It is largely a misunderstanding, and Phinehas the priest intercedes and clears things up. This story ends on a good note, but it probably foreshadows negative things to come.

Renewal of Covenant Commitment (23:1–24:33)

Joshua has grown old, and in 23:1–16 he gives his farewell address. He repeats the main themes of Joshua 1, telling Israel to be strong and to obey everything written in the Book of Moses (23:6). He seems to acknowledge that the conquest is incomplete as he warns the Israelites against the influence of the remaining original pagan inhabitants (23:7). He restates how God has fulfilled every promise he made to their forefathers (in the Abrahamic covenant), and he warns them to stay faithful to God and his commandments, lest God reverse the wonderful blessings and bring his wrath on them, driving them back out of the land (23:12–16).

Not surprisingly, the book of Joshua concludes with a recommitment to the covenant. Joshua recounts the history of how God had repeatedly delivered them, given them victory, and blessed them (24:1–13). Now, Joshua exhorts the people, it is imperative that they continue to serve the Lord. Joshua declares that his family will serve God (24:15), and the people vow that they too will serve the Lord (24:16–18, 21). Joshua then writes all this down, confirming and validating this covenant commitment.

The postscript at the end of the book records the death of Joshua, finally referring to him as the "servant of the Lord" (24:29). Complimenting Joshua and the generation of Israelite leaders who had carried out the conquest, the book of Joshua ends on a high note, declaring, "Israel served the Lord throughout the lifetime of Joshua and of the elders who outlived him and who had experienced everything the Lord had done for Israel" (24:31).

So What? Applying Joshua to Our Lives Today

The repeated exhortation to Joshua to be strong and courageous is something we should apply in our lives today. If God calls us to be Christian leaders, he also exhorts us to be strong and courageous, for the task will not be easy. Yet God also tells Joshua to meditate on his Word and realize the power of God's Presence so that he can be successful in the task before him. These things (strength, courage, God's Word, God's empowering Presence) are precisely the things that will enable us as leaders to be successful in the tasks that God calls each of us to undertake.

View of Shiloh. Joshua places the tabernacle in this area (Josh. 18:1). The ark stays here at Shiloh until it is lost to the Philistines (1 Samuel 4).

Important truths are to be grasped from the story of Rahab as well. First of all, this story indicates that God saves some very unusual and unlikely people, something that Jesus also illustrates in his actions. This should affect how you and I look at people who do not know the Lord yet. There are no "likely to be saved" and "unlikely to be saved" categories. God seems to delight in saving the most unlikely and unusual people; we should delight in this too and try to follow his leading.

Our Favorite Verse in Joshua

But as for me and my household, we will serve the Lord. (24:15)

Judges

An Israelite Disaster:
They Become Like the Canaanites

Throughout the Bible, God calls on his people to be different from the unbelievers. He wants his people to be set apart to serve him. He wants them to be holy and to be faithful to him and him alone. Judges is one of the most tragic books in the Bible, for after God saves Israel out of Egypt and gives them the wonderful Promised Land, they stay faithful to him for only one brief generation. Then they collapse completely, embracing the idolatry and degenerate behavior of the Canaanites. The end of Judges is unbelievable—and rather disgusting—as Israel sinks to a new low and becomes just like the Canaanites they were supposed to drive out of the land.

What Is the Setting for Judges?

The story of Judges begins right where the book of Joshua ended. God delivered Israel from slavery in Egypt and entered a covenant relationship with them (Exodus, Leviticus, Numbers, and Deuteronomy), stating very clearly that if they remained faithful to him and kept his laws, then they could live in the wonderful Promised Land, with God dwelling in their midst and richly blessing them. However, throughout Exodus, Deuteronomy, and Joshua, God warns them that if they abandon him and turn to idols, embracing the corrupt behavior associated with idolatry, then he will punish them and even expel them from the land. In the book of Joshua, under Joshua's leadership, Israel moves into the Promised Land, defeating the major powers in the region and capturing most of the fortified cities. The book of Joshua ends by noting that the leaders of the generation that first entered the land remained faithful to God all their lives. Thus the book of Joshua is very positive, a "good news" book. Judges picks up the story just as this first generation is passing off the scene, and things are about to change drastically.

What Is at the Heart of Judges?

The purpose of Judges is to show the failure of Israel to keep the Mosaic covenant (Exodus, Leviticus, Numbers, and Deuteronomy) after God gives them the Promised Land. The book of Judges paints a dreadful picture of a rapid, downward decline, both theologically and morally. A terrible cycle is repeated over and over. The people will sin and turn away from God, and thus a foreign nation will overrun them and oppress them. God, in his mercy and grace, will send a judge to deliver them and re-establish peace and blessing. The people, however, will soon turn away from God again, only to be conquered and oppressed again. God will send another judge to deliver them, and the pattern will repeat. However, as the story moves along, things seem to get worse and worse. Most of the judges themselves are tainted in some way, and they do not quite measure up in their behavior. Along the way the reader begins to realize that not only have the Israelites failed to drive out the Canaanites, but they are quickly becoming just like the Canaanites themselves, serving Canaanite gods and embracing Canaanite morality. At the end of the book, things are absolutely disastrous. A Levite becomes a leader in idol worship, selling out to the highest bidder; the tribe of Dan leaves its inheritance and migrates north, also falling into idolatry; an Israelite city behaves just like Sodom and Gomorrah (the prototype for Canaanite immorality), attacking a visitor; and rather than driving out the Canaanites, the Israelites unite to destroy one of their own tribes (Benjamin).

It is also enlightening to note which people the Israelites are fighting in this book. At the beginning they are fighting the Canaanites, attempting to complete the conquest as God commanded them. But soon they find themselves oppressed by and at war with the Moabites, Midianites, and Ammonites, peoples from *outside* the land that Israel had soundly defeated back during the exodus. So things are going backward for them. In Judges

✦ The individuals referred to as "judges" in the book of Judges are primarily political/military leaders and not "judges" in a courtroom or other legal setting.

13–16 the Israelites are struggling against a new group, the Philistines, who, like the Israelites, have recently migrated into the region and are trying to take over Canaan. The Philistines threaten to drive Israel right out of the Promised Land. Then if this wasn't bad enough, at the end of the book, the Israelites are simply killing each other.

An outline of the book is as follows:

- The Cycle of Disobedience (1:1–3:6)
- The Downward Spiral of the Twelve Judges Who Deliver Israel (3:7–16:31)
  - Othniel (3:7–11)
  - Ehud (3:12–30)
  - Shamgar (3:31)
  - Deborah and "what's-his-name" (4:1–5:31)
  - Gideon and his boys (6:1–9:57)
  - Tola and Jair (10:1–5)
  - Jephthah (10:6–12:7)
  - Ibzan, Elon, and Abdon (12:8–15)
  - Samson (13:1–16:31)
- Israel Hits Rock Bottom (17:1–21:25)
  - The Levite, the Danites, and idols (17:1–18:31)
  - Sodom and Gomorrah revisited (19:1–30)
  - Killing one another (20:1–21:25)

A stand from a Canaanite temple used for pouring out offerings to a Canaanite god.

What Makes Judges Interesting and Unique?

- God gives victory over the Canaanites through two women (Deborah and Jael).
- Gideon defeats a huge Midianite army with only three hundred men.
- All the judges except Othniel and Deborah are tainted in some way.

- Judges contains the colorful and tragic story of Samson and Delilah.
- Although Judges is about battles and wars, women play critical roles throughout the book as judge, mother, daughter, sister, wife, and concubine.
- Judges 19–21 (the end of the book) contains what is perhaps the most disgusting story in the Bible.

What Is the Message of Judges?

The Cycle of Disobedience (1:1–3:6)

Judges continues the story from Joshua, and actually starts off well as Caleb and the tribe of Judah continue to fight and defeat the Canaanite inhabitants of the land (1:1–18). But starting in 1:19, the book of Judges lists the many peoples and cities that were not conquered or driven out of the land, underscoring the overall failure of the tribes to follow up on Joshua's victorious campaigns and to complete the conquest. Although the generation of Israelites who participated with Joshua in the initial conquest remained faithful to God throughout their lives (Josh. 24:31; Judg. 2:7), the generation that follows forgets all that the Lord had done for them and begins worshiping the Canaanite god Baal, abandoning the Lord (2:10–13). Judges 2:16–19 describes the cycle that characterizes the book. The people sin, committing idolatry, and therefore God hands them over to foreign enemies who raid and plunder them. Then God raises up a judge (leader) to deliver them and return them to a good situation. However, even after such deliverance, the people quickly return to their sin and the story repeats. The summary statement in 3:5–6 is grim: "The Israelites lived among the Canaanites, Hittites, Amorites, Perizzites, Hivites and Jebusites. They took their daughters in marriage and gave their own daughters to their sons, and served their gods."

The Downward Spiral of the Twelve Judges Who Deliver Israel (3:7–16:31)

Othniel (3:7–11)

After Israel begins worshiping Baal and Asherah, God allows the people of Aram to subjugate Israel. The Israelites cry out to God, and he raises up Othniel to deliver them. Othniel, already mentioned back in 1:13, is a good man. He delivers Israel and provides peace for them. So the book starts out fairly well; Othniel is a good judge.

Ehud (3:12–30)

Now the Israelites have been overrun by the Moabites, with help from the Ammonites and Amalekites. Ehud is the one who delivers Israel, but his tactics are a bit unusual. He comes to Eglon, the king of Moab, saying he has a private message "from God" for him. Once in private, Ehud pulls out a hidden short sword, stabs the Moabite king, and then slips away before anyone realizes what he has done. He then rallies Israel and defeats the Moabites.

Yet this is not exactly the behavior of a true hero. Yes, Ehud is brave for killing this king, but murdering him in private when he is unarmed is not exactly valiant. It is not the kind of thing that David (the future hero) would have done. So by the time of the second judge, the judges are reflecting a character that is a little bit questionable.

Shamgar (3:31)

Not much information is given about Shamgar, the third Judge, other than he killed six hundred Philistines (quite a feat!). Strangely, though, his father is named Anath, which is also the name of the violent, bloodthirsty, Canaanite goddess of war, often depicted as the consort of Baal. The name Shamgar is also unusual, for it is not an Israelite name either.

Deborah and "what's-his-name" (4:1–5:31)

Deborah is one of the few judges other than Othniel who does not seem to have some kind of character flaw, and she emerges from this story as a true hero (along with Jael). Israel has sinned again and God has handed them over to Jabin, a Canaanite king reigning from the

The Kishon River. Deborah and Barak defeat Sisera and his Canaanite army at the Kishon River (Judg. 4:7, 13; 5:21; Ps. 83:9).

✚ Deborah is the only one of the "judges" who does seem to function as a judge in the sense that she makes legal rulings (4:4–5).

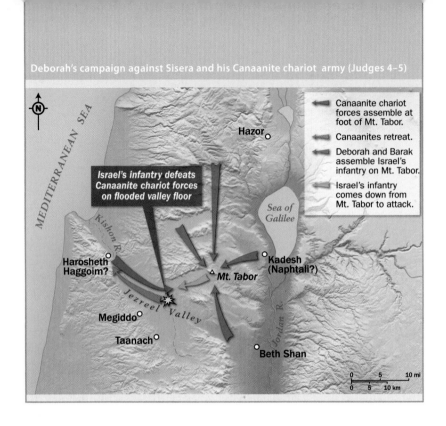

Canaanite chariot forces assemble at foot of Mt. Tabor.

Canaanites retreat.

Deborah and Barak assemble Israel's infantry on Mt. Tabor.

Israel's infantry comes down from Mt. Tabor to attack.

Israel's infantry defeats Canaanite chariot forces on flooded valley floor

city of Hazor. Deborah, a prophetess and judge, tries to get a man named Barak to rally Israel and attack Jabin's commander of the army, Sisera, and the Canaanites. In contrast to Deborah, the man Barak is timid and afraid; he won't fight unless Deborah goes with him. She agrees, but informs Barak that he won't get any of the glory for the victory, for the Lord will hand Sisera over to a woman (4:4–10). Deborah (with Barak tagging along) then leads Israel against Sisera and the Canaanites. God enables the Israelites to rout the Canaanite army, and Sisera flees. He stops to rest at the tent of an ally named Heber, and he is welcomed by Jael, Heber's wife. While Sisera is sleeping, Jael takes a hammer and drives a tent peg through his head, killing him (4:17–22). In Judges 5, Deborah (and Barak) sing a victory song, one that praises the women in the story and ridicules some of the Israelites.

So a great victory was achieved, although a most unusual one. The battle against the Canaanites was initiated and led by a woman (very unusual in the ancient world!) and, indeed, the foreign king's army commander was slain by another woman.

Gideon and his boys (6:1–9:57)

In many sermons and Bible study lessons Gideon is often portrayed as a valiant and brave warrior, a true model for us. Yet a close reading of this story suggests he is perhaps more complex than that and, like many of the other judges, has some serious flaws in his character.

The story opens by informing us that the Midianites are now raiding Israel whenever they please, stealing any livestock, food, or other valuable items they find. Note the irony of this, for the Israelites soundly defeated and plundered the Midianites back in Numbers 31 as they made their way from the wilderness toward the Promised Land. So for the Midianites to be plundering the Israelites signifies a serious reversal of the "exodus/salvation" story.

An angel of the Lord comes to Gideon and finds him threshing wheat, hidden down in a winepress in an attempt to hide from the Midianites. The Lord himself calls on Gideon to deliver Israel and promises that "I will be with you," the famous promise of God's empowering Presence (6:11–16). Gideon, however, is not convinced and asks for a sign (6:17), as if the conversation with the angel of the Lord is not evidence enough. As the story progresses, it takes repeated miraculous signs (four of them) to keep Gideon on board. In addition, as the story moves along, Gideon's fear is underscored in other ways (6:27; 7:10–11).

The angel of God delivers the first sign to Gideon by sending fire that miraculously consumes a small offering Gideon had prepared (6:20–22). Gideon is still rather timid and afraid (6:23–31), but God sends his Spirit on him, and he calls Israel together for war. But even after the conversation with the angel of the Lord and the miraculous sign of the fire, Gideon still wants more signs. He asks God for two more signs, specifically related to dew on a fleece and on the ground. God complies and gives him these two additional signs (6:36–40).

God, however, apparently has a sense of humor and, since Gideon has been testing him, now gives Gideon two "tests" to comply with. Gideon, already timid and afraid, is told he has too many men, and through two different exercises God has him trim down his army to only three hundred men (7:1–8), even though the Midianites are as thick as locusts, and their camels were like the sand on the seashore (7:12)! God wants the Israelites to know it is his powerful hand that will give them victory, and not their numbers.

Gideon, however, is still frightened (7:10–11), so God gives him one more sign, allowing him to overhear a dream of one of the Midianite soldiers that foretells an Israelite victory (led by Gideon). Finally, Gideon seems to "get it" and decides to attack (7:15–18),

Gold earrings. Gideon's soldiers each give him a gold earring they took from the slain Ishmaelites.

although he apparently wants to share the glory with the Lord, calling to his troops as they attack, "for the Lord and *for Gideon*" (7:18). God gives the Israelites a great victory, and as Gideon leads them, Israel thoroughly routs the Midianites (7:17–8:21).

The story, however, does not end yet, and the way in which a story ends is usually very important to its overall meaning. Unlike after the previous defeat of the Midianites (Num. 31:48–54) or after the capture of Jericho during the original conquest (Josh. 6:24), there is no mention in Gideon's victory of dedicating the captured gold and silver to the Lord by placing it in the tabernacle. Instead, Gideon collects a portion of the gold the Israelites captured and makes it into an "ephod," a garment that priests traditionally wore. Then, rather than placing this in the tabernacle, Gideon puts it in his own hometown, and "all Israel prostituted themselves by worshiping it [the golden ephod] there, and it became a snare to Gideon and his family" (8:23–27).

The remains of an ancient gate at Shechem. The city of Shechem and her citizens play a major role in Judges 9.

Furthermore, Gideon does not leave a good legacy, for as soon as he dies, Israel returns to worshiping Baal (8:33–35). In addition, Abimelech, one of Gideon's sons (the name Abimelech means "my father is the king"), murders his seventy brothers and has himself crowned king (9:1–6). His reign is short, however. After only three years he is killed in a siege by a woman who drops a millstone on his head (9:50–55). Thus like the Canaanite Sisera in the Deborah story, Abimelech is killed by a woman. He is not considered one of the judges.

Tola and Jair (10:1–5)

Not much information is given about the judges Tola and Jair, and they do not play a major role in the overall story. Perhaps they are briefly mentioned so the total number of judges discussed in the book would be twelve, a symbolic number in the Bible.

✛ In Joab's report to David in 2 Samuel 11:18–21, he references Abimelech's death in Judges 9. This is probably a subtle, yet ironic comparison of Abimelech's defeat by a woman to David's "defeat" by a woman (Bathsheba).

Jephthah (10:6–12:7)

The Jephthah story is introduced by stressing the many foreign gods Israel was now worshiping (10:6). The list of pagan gods is getting longer; apparently things are getting worse in Israel. God hands them over to the Philistines and the Ammonites (10:7–10). Israel then cries out to God, apparently repenting and putting away their foreign gods. Deliverance for them comes from an unlikely individual (Jephthah), but the text never states that God actually called him or raised him up. In addition, Jephthah's lineage is questionable, for his mother is a prostitute and his father is "Gilead" (the name of the region to the east of the Jordan). He becomes an outcast and a bandit, but he agrees to lead the Israelites in Gilead against the Ammonites, and the Spirit of the Lord comes upon him to empower him (11:29).

Jephthah, however, commits a huge mistake and makes a dumb vow to God. He promises that if God gives him victory, he will sacrifice whatever (or whoever) comes out of his house to greet him when he returns (11:30–31). Throughout the Bible, however, God responds to repentance and sincere worship, not to foolish vows. Ironically, it is the Ammonite and Moabite god Molech that is known for granting victory to warriors if they sacrifice their children to them. God gives Jephthah a great victory, yet when he returns to his home (11:34), it is his daughter (his only child) who comes out to greet him (who did he think would come out?). Jephthah goes through with his vow, even though God never once says that this is required. The sacrifice of children is an Ammonite and Moabite practice that God abhors, illustrating the continued slide of Israel and the "judges" that fight to deliver them.

As Jephthah rules, things deteriorate, and he ends his reign by leading the Gileadites (the Hebrews who settled in the east side of the Jordan) in a war against their brother tribe of Ephraim (12:1–7), another example of the Israelites fighting one another rather than driving out the foreign inhabitants of the land, as God had commanded them to do.

Ibzan, Elon, and Abdon (12:8–15)

Three more minor judges are mentioned in 12:8–15, but little information is provided. As mentioned above, including these three helps to bring the total number of judges up to twelve.

Samson (13:1–16:31)

Samson is the last judge mentioned in the book, and four entire chapters are devoted to his story, underscoring the important role the Samson episode plays in the book of Judges. The Philistines have now taken control of Israel. There is no mention of Israel crying out to God, but he raises up a deliverer anyway. God tells a childless woman from the tribe of Dan that she will conceive and that she is to dedicate that child to God as a Nazirite (13:1–5). A Nazirite is someone who takes a special vow and is thus set apart in special dedication for service to God. The requirements and restrictions for a Nazirite are spelled out in Numbers 6:1–21 and comprise three basic elements:

1. A Nazirite is not to have any contact with wine or anything from the vine.
2. A Nazirite is not to have any contact with anything that is dead.
3. A Nazirite is not to cut his or her hair.

The child is born and the woman names him Samson (13:24–25). Samson, however, does not seem to be the least bit interested in delivering Israel from the Philistines. In fact, he is not interested in anything but satisfying his own pleasure. In 14:1–2 he insists on marrying a Philistine woman. Intermarrying with the Philistines is a far cry from driving them out of the land! As the story unfolds, almost inadvertently Samson ends up fighting against the Philistines—fights that are usually precipitated by some squabble between Samson and the Philistines that makes him mad. God does give Samson great strength and power, so he is successful whenever he fights the Philistines. So in one sense, even though his motives are perverted, Samson begins to deliver Israel. However, along the way he repeatedly violates the restrictions of his Nazirite vow. He comes in contact with vineyards (and probably wine as well) at the town of Timnah (14:5, 10). Regarding contact with the dead, not only does Samson kill a lion, but he *eats* honey that was formed in the dead carcass and even gives some to

A decorated Philistine jug, probably used for serving beer.

his parents. How disgusting! (14:5–9). Likewise, later he kills a thousand Philistines with the jawbone of a dead donkey (15:14–17).

The only part of the Nazirite vow he appears to keep is the prohibition against cutting his hair. Yet even that requirement falls by the wayside as he tells Delilah that the secret of his great strength lies in his hair (16:1–20). After she cuts Samson's hair, he no longer fulfills any Nazirite requirement, and so God withdraws his power. Samson is then captured, blinded, and imprisoned. In the meantime, his hair grows back out. The Philistines bring him out to a big party to use him for entertainment. Samson, praying apparently for the first time, calls out to God, has his strength renewed, and pushes apart two pillars of the building, bringing the structure down on himself and the Philistines, destroying many of them (16:25–30). But even in this final act, Samson's motive is strictly one of personal revenge. Thus he dies a tragic death. The reader can only marvel at the squandered potential and wonder what might have happened if Samson had been virtuous and had actually led Israel against the Philistines.

What do we make of the Samson story, especially in its prominent position as the climactic ending of the list of judges? Although Samson is undoubtedly a real person, his story symbolically represents the parallel story of Israel itself. Called to be separate unto God, both Samson and Israel ignore God's commandments that set them apart. Samson chases after foreign women just as Israel chases after foreign gods. Israel, like Samson, was loaded with tremendous potential, due to God's empowering Presence. Yet, like Samson, the Israelites squander that potential, spit in the face of God, and find themselves enslaved by foreigners. Thus the Samson story is a fitting conclusion to Judges 1–16. He is the climactic worst of the judges, symbolizing the nation Israel as it spirals down theologically and morally.

Pottery used in an ancient pagan Canaanite temple.

Israel Hits Rock Bottom (17:1–21:25)

The Levite, the Danites, and idols (17:1–18:31)

As bad as the situation in Israel was by the time of the Samson story, it nonetheless continues to get worse until, here in the final chapters, Israel hits the bottom. In 17:1–13 Micah (not the same man as the prophet Micah), an Israelite from the tribe of Ephraim, receives some silver from his mother (silver he had stolen from her and then given back), with which he makes an idol, adding it to his shrine that contains other idols and an ephod. Along comes a young Levite, apparently with no means of support, and Micah persuades him to stay and become his priest to lead in worshiping his household idols.

Meanwhile, the tribe of Dan had been unable (or unwilling) to drive out the Amorites from their allotted territory (Judg. 1:34). So in Judges 18:1–31 they send scouts up north to find an easier area to possess, ignoring the tribal boundaries that Moses and Joshua had assigned. The scouts discover a city called Laish that looks prosperous and yet defenseless. So the tribe of Dan migrates north, out of their inherited portion of the Promised Land, to a new area that would be easier to conquer. Along the way they come across Micah and his pagan priest (from the tribe of Levi). They make a higher offer to the priest, and he decides to join the tribe of Dan to be their priest. He and the Danites steal the idols from Micah and take these pagan gods with them to their new home. Judges 18:30–31 notes that the tribe of Dan continued to serve these gods until they were exiled from the land.

So the theological situation portrayed in this story is grim. Israelites are worshiping idols instead of the Lord, and Levitical priests are assisting. One of the tribes of Israel abandons their inherited allotment from God and moves to a new area. A Levite priest sells out to the highest bidder and steals some idols from another Israelite, taking them along with him for his new tribe to worship. This is a long way from Deuteronomy and Joshua.

A Canaanite figurine of a bull, associated with the god Hadad.

Sodom and Gomorrah revisited (19:1–30)

Yet things continue to get even worse. Another Levite travels from Judah to recover his runaway concubine (a secondary wife) (19:1–3). After partying for several days with the woman's father, the Levite, getting a late start in the day, takes his concubine and heads for home. As it gets late in the evening he bypasses a city of Jebusites and pushes on to the city of Gibeah

The Valley of Sorek,
home of Delilah.

in Benjamin, in order to spend the night in an Israelite town (19:4–15). An old man from Ephraim puts him up for the night, but a crowd from the city surrounds the house and demands that the Levite visitor be given to them for sexual activities (19:16–22). Recall that this is very similar to the story of Sodom and Gomorrah in Genesis 19, except that Gibeah is an Israelite city and Sodom and Gomorrah were Canaanite cities. It was sinful behavior such as Sodom and Gomorrah illustrated that led to God's judgment on the Canaanites carried out in the conquest. So this story in Judges 19 demonstrates in vivid fashion that Israel has not only failed to drive out the Canaanites from the land, but they have become just like the Canaanites themselves.

The grim story continues. The callous Levite throws his newly recovered concubine out to the crowd, who abuses her throughout the night, dumping her back on the doorway in the morning after they are finished. Apparently she is now dead. The furious Levite cuts her up into twelve pieces and sends a piece to each tribe in Israel, calling for vengeance on the tribe of Benjamin (19:21–30).

Killing one another (20:1–21:25)

The other tribes of Israel descend on Benjamin and virtually destroy the entire tribe (just like they were supposed to do to the Canaanites, but didn't) (20:1–48). In Judges 21 the people of Israel then feel remorse for the loss of Benjamin, but since they have taken an oath (another dumb

✚ The obvious questions at the end of Judges are, "Is there any hope for Israel? Who will save them from this mess?" The answer is David, who is introduced next in the book of Ruth, and then takes center stage in 1–2 Samuel.

oath) not to intermarry with the Benjaminites, they do not see any way to help re-establish that decimated tribe. Eventually they concoct a way for the Benjaminites to steal wives from a worship festival in Shiloh (ironically a community that was apparently worshiping the Lord properly). The book of Judges then ends with the repeated phrase that points to the governing chaos: "In those days there was no king in Israel; all the people did what was right in their own eyes" (18:1; 19:1; 21:25 NRSV).

So the end of Judges is disastrous for Israel. By the end of the book they are violating God's law and their covenant with him (Deuteronomy) in ways unimaginable. They are worshiping idols, and the Levites are leading them in this. They have become corrupt morally, sinking to the despised depths of the wretched Canaanite cities of Sodom and Gomorrah. They have ceased struggling to drive out the Canaanites and instead are becoming like the Canaanites. Finally, the Israelites turn on one another and annihilate one of their own tribes.

So What? Applying Judges to Our Lives Today

Judges illustrates for us quite graphically the tragic consequences of sin. Once people abandon worshiping God they usually quickly embrace the corrupt morals of their surrounding culture and spiral down morally and theologically until they hit the bottom with a big splash. The most amazing thing about the book of Judges is that the Bible does not end here. That is, after reading Exodus, Deuteronomy, and Joshua, one is surprised that the terrible sin of Israel in Judges does not simply bring an end to the story—God should destroy them and that's that. We get a good picture of how deep God's grace and mercy really are as we read on and realize that in spite of their terrible sin, God will send them real deliverers (Samuel, David, and ultimately Christ).

Another lesson to be learned is from the tragic story of Samson. Here was a man given tremendous potential and tremendous opportunity to do great things. Yet Samson was selfish and self-centered, concerned only with fulfilling his personal pleasure. Thus he squandered his great potential and became a tragic figure (a bum, if we are honest). Thus Samson becomes a negative model for us, filled with character traits for us to avoid.

Our Favorite Verse in Judges

The Lord said to Gideon, "You have too many men for me to deliver Midian into their hands." (7:2)

Ruth

God at Work behind the Scenes

After reading about so many wars and battles in Joshua and Judges, the book of Ruth comes as a pleasant surprise. It is a quiet story about an unfortunate Israelite widow named Naomi and her foreign daughter-in-law Ruth, who is also widowed. There are no battles or military conquests. There are no burning bushes or partings of the Red Sea. In fact, God never speaks directly anywhere in the book. There is just a poignant, powerful story about two women struggling to survive during a very difficult time. Emerging out of this story of two simple peasant women is the realization that God is at work here, quietly directing things behind the scenes to bring about deliverance from the mess Israel created in the book of Judges.

What Is the Setting for Ruth?

After God delivers the people of Israel from Egypt (Exodus), he makes a covenant with them (the Mosaic covenant), defining the terms by which they could live in the Promised Land and be blessed by God (who lived in their midst). These terms are spelled out in the second half of

Exodus, as well as in Leviticus, parts of Numbers, and Deuteronomy. If they stay faithful to God and obey his law (especially as defined in Deuteronomy), they will be blessed; if they abandon God and turn to idols, they will be cursed (see Deuteronomy 28). In the book of Joshua the Israelites enter the land and get off to a very good start. The book of Judges, however, is a disaster, and in that book Israel disobeys God in unthinkable ways. By the end of Judges, the covenant as defined in Deuteronomy seems to be completely forgotten, and Israel is worshiping idols. The questions emerging at the end of Judges are, "Is there any hope for Israel? If so, who will deliver them from the mess they are in?" The answer, of course, is David. In 1–2 Samuel David will rise to power and straighten out the mess created in Judges. The book of Ruth, a quiet story off of the main history line of battles and wars, shows God at work behind the scenes to bring David into the story through two courageous women.

The opening lines of Ruth locate the story during the time of the Judges (1:1), thus connecting Ruth's story to the disaster recorded in the book of Judges. This setting also underscores that Ruth lived in a very dangerous time. Events portrayed in the book of Judges indicate that it would have been very risky and quite frightening for two women (one of them a foreigner) to travel alone across Israel.

What Is at the Heart of Ruth?

The book of Ruth illustrates how God is at work very quietly and behind the scenes to provide a solution (a deliverer, David) to the terrible situation Israel has created for itself in Judges. Thus Ruth bridges the story from Judges (disaster in Israel) to 1–2 Samuel (David the hero).

The book of Ruth is not about kings, generals, prostitutes, or priests. It is a story about three simple farming people (Naomi, Ruth, and Boaz) and how God brings them together. When Naomi's Israelite family leaves the land (the place of blessing), terrible things happen, and all the men in the family die. But when the widows make their way back to the land, blessings return. The book of Ruth also presents these three people (Naomi, Ruth, and Boaz) as virtuous people, even though they are real people expressing real sorrow over real problems. At its core, this is a love story, with a theologically significant genealogy added to the ending of the story. A brief outline of the story is as follows:

- Leaving the Promised Land Results in Tragedy (1:1–22)
- Boy Meets Girl (2:1–23)
- Proposal and Marriage (3:1–4:12)
- From Naomi and Ruth to David: A Genealogy (4:13–22)

✦ Like Rahab in Joshua 2, Ruth is a foreign woman who is brought into the people of God and included in the genealogy of David and Jesus (Matt. 1:5).

Where Should the Book of Ruth Be Placed?

In the Christian canon, the book of Ruth is located between Judges and 1–2 Samuel, thus providing a transition between them. The book of Ruth introduces David, who will be the solution to the terrible situation in Judges, as revealed in the story of 1–2 Samuel, which is primarily about David. In the Hebrew canon, however, Ruth is located right after Proverbs. This is probably due to the phrase "woman of noble character." In Proverbs 31:10 the question is posed, "A wife [or woman] of noble character who can find?" The rest of Proverbs 31 describes this woman/wife (the Hebrew word is the same) of noble character. In Ruth 3:11 Boaz tells Ruth that everyone knows she is a "woman of noble character," using the exact same Hebrew phrase as Proverbs 31:10. So in the Hebrew canon, Proverbs 31:10 asks, "A woman of noble character who can find?" and as one turns the page, behold! There she is! Ruth, the woman/wife of noble character. For more discussion on this topic, see "The Production and Shaping of the Old Testament Canon" in Part II.

What Makes Ruth Interesting and Unique?

- The book of Ruth is a story about two women, Naomi and Ruth.
- At the center of this book is a delightful "boy meets girl" love story.
- God works behind the scenes in this story.
- The story ends happily; Naomi and Ruth go from emptiness, tragedy, and despair to happy fulfillment.
- Unlike those in the book of Judges, the main characters in Ruth are all decent people.
- Ruth is called "a woman of noble character," the exact same Hebrew phrase that is used in Proverbs 31:10.
- The book of Ruth is filled with dialogue. More than half of the book is composed of direct speech.
- Of the three main characters (Ruth, Naomi, Boaz), the title character, Ruth, speaks the least.

What Is the Message of Ruth?

Leaving the Promised Land Results in Tragedy (1:1–22)

The opening phrase of Ruth, "In the days when the judges ruled," ties the book of Ruth directly to the terrible situation described in the book

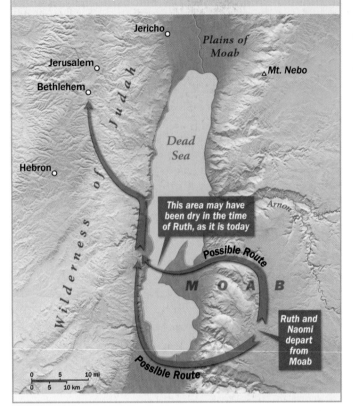

Jericho

Plains of Moab

Jerusalem

Bethlehem

Mt. Nebo

J u d a h

Dead Sea

Hebron

This area may have been dry in the time of Ruth, as it is today

Arnon R.

Possible Route

M O A B

W i l d e r n e s s   o f   J u d a h

Ruth and Naomi depart from Moab

Possible Route

0   5   10 mi
0   5   10 km

of Judges. Throughout Judges, Israel has been disobedient, abandoning the Lord and turning to pagan idols. Thus the next phrase in Ruth 1:1, "there was a famine in the land," comes as no surprise. Deuteronomy 28 had spelled out quite clearly the negative consequences that would come to the Israelites if they turned away from God and worshiped idols. Famine was one of the judgments mentioned.

As the story begins, a man from Bethlehem named Elimelech takes his wife, Naomi, and his two sons and moves from Bethlehem (in Israel) to the land of Moab. To modern Western readers this seems fairly harmless, for we move around with regularity. But in the ancient world it was rather unusual, and for Israelites living in the Promised Land it was not proper at all. God had given the Israelites the land, and they were not supposed to move away from it. Blessings for them were tied to the land. Thus as soon as this family moves away from the land, terrible things happen—the men in the family die.

The two sons had married Moabite women, so the wife, Naomi, is left with only two Moabite daughters-in-law. One of them returns to her Moabite family, but Ruth, the other Moabite daughter-in-law, refuses to leave Naomi, declaring resolutely: "Where you go I will go, and where you stay I will stay. Your people will be my people and your God my God" (1:16). Without any men in the family, Naomi and Ruth are destitute, so Naomi decides to return to her hometown in Bethlehem. She cries out, "I went away full, but the Lord has brought me back empty" (1:21). Once she is back in the land, however, her fortunes will change. Indeed, even as Naomi and Ruth arrive back in Bethlehem, the text states that the barley harvest was beginning;

✝ In Hebrew, the name "Bethlehem" means "house of bread." Thus the opening verse 1:1 is quite ironic, for there is a famine in the "house of bread."

apparently the famine was over (1:22).

Boy Meets Girl (2:1–23)

Even after Naomi and Ruth arrive in Bethlehem, their fate is uncertain, for there is no one to care for them and no easy way for them to earn a living. Ruth volunteers to go out to the fields and try to pick up off of the ground any grain the main harvesters dropped or missed. Deuteronomy 24:19 explicitly states that the Israelites are to allow destitute people (especially foreigners, orphans, and widows) to do this so that they can get food during the harvest time, but the book of Judges reveals quite clearly that very few people in Israel at this time cared anything about obeying Deuteronomy. Also, keep in mind these are violent times without any national law and order. It would be very dangerous and quite scary for this young foreign woman, without any man in her family to protect her, to venture out into the harvest fields alone.

This wall painting from an Egyptian tomb depicts the various aspects of harvesting grain in the time of Ruth.

"As it turned out," the text states in 2:3 (and we certainly see the hand of God working behind the scenes here), she ends up in the fields of Boaz, a fairly prosperous man and a distant relative of Elimelech's (Ruth's deceased father-in-law). As Boaz visits his fields, he notices Ruth (Can we not assume that she was attractive?) and asks about her (2:5–6). In 2:8–13 they meet and speak to each other for the first time. The dialogue is intriguing. Boaz encourages her to stay in his fields, so that she will be safe (2:8–9). Boaz tries to sound businesslike, but Ruth appears to be politely flirting as she answers, "Why have I found such favor in your eyes?" What kind of question is that to ask a guy? Her question seems to make him a bit uncomfortable (perhaps we are overreading this, but we don't think so). Things move along quickly, and in 2:14 they have their "first date" as Boaz invites her to share lunch with him. Then Boaz tells his workmen to leave lots of extra sheaves of grain on the ground so it will be easy for Ruth to gather. Are the workmen rolling their eyes and smiling at one another over their "smitten" boss?

Ruth returns to Naomi, loaded down with more grain than Naomi could have possibly expected. Ruth tells Naomi what happened in the fields, and Naomi gets to thinking—and planning (2:17–23), like a good mother (or mother-in-law).

Proposal and Marriage (3:1–4:12)

Even though things have gone well for Ruth, and Boaz apparently continues to look out for her during the harvest, the relationship seems to have stalled; Boaz (like some men) is apparently slow to move the relationship to the next level (marriage). So Naomi decides to give him a big nudge.

Boaz is celebrating the harvest. As was the tradition, after threshing wheat all day, he and his workers have a feast (eating and drinking) and then sleep right on the threshing floor. Naomi instructs Ruth to clean up, put on her best dress, and even add perfume (3:1–3). Following Naomi's instructions, Ruth waits until the men are asleep, and then sneaks into the threshing floor area, and lies down at the feet of the sleeping Boaz. Before long he wakes up, startled to find a woman there with him in the dark. Ruth identifies herself and states, "Spread the corner of your garment over me, since you are a kinsman-redeemer" (3:4–9). This is probably a very daring proposal of marriage, outside the normal practices but still legitimate. If Boaz lets her stay there for the night, then in the eyes of the community, they are married. If he sends her away, then he has rejected her and she will be humiliated.

Boaz, probably wide-awake by now, compliments her character, stating, "All my fellow townsmen know that you are a woman of noble character" (3:11). However, Boaz is in a quandary because there is another relative that legally has the first option to marry Ruth. Essentially he tells Ruth he will marry her if he can work things out legally with this other relative (3:12–13). The next day Boaz convenes a town court and obtains the legal right to buy all of Naomi's property (only the next of kin could do this), which would include the right (and obligation) to marry Ruth and care for Naomi. The town elders not only rule in his favor, but they also call on the Lord to bless Ruth, establishing their full acceptance of her into the community (4:11–12).

From Naomi and Ruth to David: A Genealogy (4:13–22)

The story ends happily. Boaz marries Ruth, and she gives birth to a son (a sign of blessing). Naomi, who had nothing at the beginning of the story, now has a family to care for her and a grandson for her to love (4:13–16). She has shifted from one who was outside of the land and destitute to one who lives in the land and is blessed by the Lord.

The blessing is even bigger than Ruth or Naomi imagine, for the text then tells us that Ruth's child would be the father of Jesse and the grandfather of David (4:17). As the reader knows, David will be the solution to the terrible situation in Israel that is described in Judges and alluded to in Ruth 1:1. So God has worked very quietly behind the scenes through two humble women

✦ In Deuteronomy, God frequently calls on Israel to care for the foreigner, the fatherless, and the widow (Deut. 10:18; 24:17–21; 26:12–13; 27:19). Ruth is a Moabite widow without a father to look after her, thus fulfilling all three categories.

(Naomi and Ruth) and one faithful man (Boaz) to start the process of raising up a mighty deliverer, David.

In 4:11–12 the elders bless Ruth by referring to Rachel and Leah, wives of the patriarch Jacob. But the elders also move to the next generation of patriarchs, stating, "May your family be like that of Perez, whom Tamar bore to Judah" (4:12). The significance of this blessing is that Tamar was a foreigner. Thus Perez, the son of Judah, had a foreigner for a mother, but is

Modern threshing scene from rural Egypt.

still considered a famous forefather. The book of Ruth then closes with a genealogy (4:18–22), which tracks the lineage of David from Perez (with the foreign mother Tamar) through Boaz (with the foreign wife Ruth) to Obed (Ruth's son) to Jesse to David, the hero of the next book (1–2 Samuel).

So What? Applying Ruth to Our Lives Today

There is much for us to learn from the character of Ruth. Faithfulness is a very important virtue in the Bible, and the Lord stresses it throughout the Old Testament. Ruth was concerned more about the welfare of her mother-in-law than she was about her own welfare or her own personal future. Yet in the end, God blessed Ruth tremendously. From this we learn to be faithful in all our relationships, trusting in God to see us through difficult times.

From Boaz we learn that God's people can live in faithful obedience to him even if the entire society is acting contrary to God's will. Boaz lived as an upright, compassionate man, faithful to the Lord and unwilling to cut any ethical corners. God blessed him as well.

From the big picture we learn that God often works quietly behind the scenes through regular people (like you) in ways we cannot recognize until we look back and see how he has marvelously directed things in order to bless us.

Our Favorite Verse in Ruth

All my fellow townsmen know that you are a woman of noble character.
(3:11)

1–2 Samuel

The Rise and Fall of David

Back in the late 1960s, when the United States was having an identity crisis and searching for heroes to latch on to, Paul Simon wrote a song that cried out, "Where have you gone, Joe Dimaggio? A nation turns its lonely eyes to you" (from "Mrs. Robinson"). We certainly like our heroes. David, the central character in 1–2 Samuel, is definitely a hero. While the man Samuel, as prophet and judge, is a good and likeable guy, it is David who captures our hearts as the hero. After the many flawed leaders in Judges and the total collapse of Israel because of their poor leadership, followed by the inept and timid rule of King Saul, we are more than ready for David, who comes crashing into the story as a fearless young man marching out to slay the obnoxious but fearsome warrior Goliath. All Israel loves him and so do we. After all, David is a man of integrity, a man after God's own heart. He is a musician, but he also fights bad guys and sweeps the girls right off their feet. What a guy!

But this is not a simple comic book story, and David is not a simple character. Like us, he is complex. And like us, he is both strong and weak. First and Second Samuel are about the rise to power of King David, Israel's great deliverer, perhaps as great a man as Moses. Yet our hero is only human. He has feet of clay, and much to our dismay, he gives in to temptation and crumbles. He is not the ultimate Messiah. For that we have to look beyond David—and wait for the son of David to arrive in the New Testament.

What Is the Setting for 1–2 Samuel?

Although scholars continue to be divided over the date of the Exodus (and thus the dates for the conquest of Canaan and the chronology of the Judges), the chronology of 1–2 Samuel is a little more certain. Working backward from firm historical dates in 1–2 Kings, we can determine that David reigned from 1011 BC until his death in 971 BC. Saul then would have reigned the forty years prior to David, so Saul's reign was from 1051 BC to 1011 BC. For the sake of memory it is perhaps good to associate David with the year 1000 BC.

As far as the story setting goes, 1 Samuel opens during the latter years of the Judges. Samuel himself can be considered the last judge and the first major prophet since Moses. Samuel is the bridge from the era of the Judges to the era of the monarchy.

Remember that at the end of the book of Judges the situation is extremely bad in Israel, both morally and theologically.

What Is at the Heart of 1–2 Samuel?

First and Second Samuel are primarily about David, the hero and the one who delivers Israel from the mess at the end of Judges. Samuel is an important character, but his role is transitional; he institutes the monarchy and anoints the first two kings. Likewise King Saul, the first king, is

It was common practice in the ancient Near East to capture the idols of a defeated city and carry them home as trophies of war. In the Assyrian wall relief here, the top panel depicts the Assyrians capturing a city, and the lower panel depicts them carrying away the city's idols.

The Book of Samuel?

First and Second Samuel were probably originally written as one book. All early Hebrew manuscripts (such as the Dead Sea Scrolls) present this material as one book (Samuel). Not until the fifteenth century AD did Hebrew Bibles split this story up into two books. It was the Septuagint (the Greek translation of the Old Testament) that in about 150 BC first divided Samuel into two books. This was because the Greek text of the Septuagint took up more space than the Hebrew text, and the Septuagint translators could not fit the entire book of Samuel (now in Greek) on one scroll (scrolls had a limited length).

but a foil for David, the main character and second king. Saul is a stumbling, fumbling bumpkin whose role in the story is to provide a contrast to David and to remind everyone what happens if people choose their leaders by looking at externals rather than at internal character. It is not Saul but David who gets the story back on track. David is a man after God's own heart. David is courageous and trusting in God. After he becomes king he completes the conquest, on hold since the death of Joshua. David establishes Jerusalem as the capital, he brings the ark of the covenant to Jerusalem, and he reestablishes the national worship of the Lord God of Abraham, Isaac, and Jacob. God even makes a special covenant with David himself.

Unfortunately, the story does not end on a high note. We discover that David is not a sinless Messiah; he is but a mere man. His affair with Bathsheba and his murder of Uriah (2 Samuel 11–12) are shocking and scandalous! After this serious sin, God forgives him personally, but no longer sustains his kingdom, which starts to fall apart rather quickly. Before the Bathsheba event, everything in David's life goes well, but after that event, everything goes bad, and his life in general unravels. We are left to look to the future for the real Messiah.

The story in 1–2 Samuel is fascinating, fun, and complex. The story can be placed into an overview outline as follows:

- From Corrupt Priests to Corrupt King: The Transition from Judges to Monarchy (1 Sam. 1:1–15:35)
  - Hannah and her son, Samuel, contrasted with Eli and his wicked sons (1:1–3:21)
  - The ark narrative: God defeats Philistia by himself (4:1–7:1)
  - Samuel anoints and establishes Saul as king (7:2–12:25)
  - Saul disqualifies himself by three boneheaded mistakes (13:1–15:35)

- Who Will Be King? The Contrast between Saul and David (1 Sam. 16:1–31:13)
  - David is anointed by Samuel and empowered by the Spirit of the Lord (16:1–23)
  - David slays Goliath, acting like a king empowered by the Spirit (17:1–58)
  - The decline of Saul (and his madness) versus the rise of David (and his greatness) (18:1–31:13)
- The Rise of David and the Restoration of Israel (2 Sam. 1:1–10:19)
  - David becomes king and reunites the kingdom politically (1:1–5:25)
  - Through David, Israel is restored to covenant relationship with God (6:1–7:29)
  - David completes the conquest and restores Israel to military prominence (8:1–10:19)
- Humpty Dumpty's Great Fall: The Bathsheba Affair (2 Sam. 11:1–12:31)
- The Consequences of Sin: The Unraveling of David's Kingdom (2 Sam. 13:1–20:26)
- The Good and the Bad: A Summary of David and His Kingdom (2 Sam. 21:1–24:25)

What Makes 1–2 Samuel Interesting and Unique?

- The young boy Samuel is called by God in the middle of the night.
- The ark of God moves by itself through Philistia as if on a military campaign.
- The young man David slays the huge warrior Goliath with a sling and a stone.

A church has been built over the site of ancient Mizpah. Samuel ruled over Israel primarily from the city of Mizpah (1 Sam. 7:5–6, 16).

✝ The man Samuel functions as priest, prophet, and the last of the judges. Thus he serves as a transition from the era of the judges to the era of the kings.

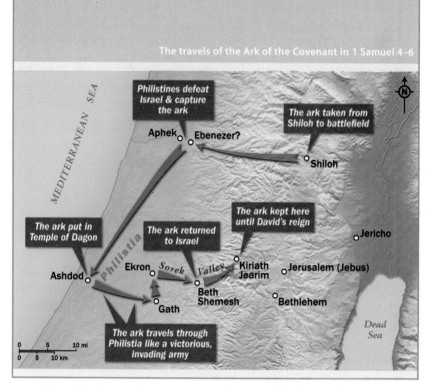

- King Saul consults a creepy medium and talks with the deceased Samuel.
- God makes a covenant with King David, promising to put one of his descendants on the throne forever.
- King David is portrayed as a real person, with both strengths and weaknesses. He is a valiant hero, but with flaws.
- King David has a steamy, adulterous affair with Bathsheba and has her husband, Uriah, murdered, much to our surprise and shock.

What Is the Message of 1–2 Samuel?

From Corrupt Priests to Corrupt King: The Transition from Judges to Monarchy (1 Sam. 1:1–15:35)

Hannah and her son, Samuel, contrasted with Eli and his wicked sons (1:1–3:21)

The opening story presents a contrast between a peasant woman, Hannah, and the high priest, Eli. She is barren but will have a son who will be righteous and serve God faithfully. Eli has two rotten sons who care nothing about serving God and instead live selfish, sinful lives. As we saw in the book of Judges, the worship of the Lord in Israel had been corrupted. In this opening episode, the righteous boy Samuel will become the new priest and mediator between God and the people, replacing the corrupt priesthood and worship system of Eli and his scandalous sons. Samuel's mother, Hannah, sums up the theological movement of this story in her song of 2:1–10:

> He [the Lord] humbles and he exalts.
> He raises the poor from the dust
> and lifts the needy from the ash heap. . . .
> It is not by strength that one prevails;
> those who oppose the Lord will be shattered. (2:7–10)

It is in this context that the familiar story of God's calling the boy Samuel in the middle of the night occurs (3:1–18). The point is not just that God is calling this boy, but that God is speaking to this boy instead of to the high priest, Eli. Indeed, God informs Samuel (like a prophet) that judgment is coming on Eli's corrupt household.

The ark narrative: God defeats Philistia by himself (4:1–7:1)

As this episode begins, the Israelites are at war with the Philistines, and losing badly. Since the ark of the covenant played such a prominent role in Israel's great victories back in the glory days of Joshua, the Israelites decide to bring the ark into the battle with them. They do not inquire of God, offer repentance, or make sacrifices. They assume they can manipulate the ark and that it is like a fetish they can employ to their benefit. Accompanying the ark as priests are Eli's two sons, Hophni and Phinehas (4:1–4).

Yet the Israelites lose anyway. Hophni and Phinehas are killed (as God had prophesied to the boy Samuel in 3:11–14), and the ark is captured by the Philistines. When Eli hears about it, he falls off of his chair, breaks his neck, and dies (4:12–22).

Losing the ark is highly significant, for it represents the Presence of God and is foundational to the covenant between God and Israel. In keeping with the terrible downward slide described in Judges, Israel now hits the climactic bottom as its immoral "priests" fritter away the ark of the covenant, the very Presence of God. Without the Presence of God there is no point to living in the land, and the Israelites certainly won't have any power to remain there!

In the ancient world, often the connection was made between a nation's victory and the power of its gods. Thus when Philistia defeats Israel in 4:10–11, some might suspect that Dagon, the god of the Philistines, had also defeated the Lord, the God of Israel. Obviously, this is an incorrect assumption, as God will dramatically demonstrate in the story that follows.

✦ Every time the story mentions Eli, he is either sitting or lying down (1:9; 3:2; 4:13). Never does the story portray Eli as effectively serving in the tabernacle.

The Philistines take the captured ark to the city of Ashdod and place it as a captured trophy before the statue of their god Dagon. When they return the next morning, however, Dagon has fallen on his face (i.e., bowing down to the ark). The Philistines pick up the fallen idol and prop him back up (someone probably got fired over this). Yet when they return the next day, Dagon has not only fallen down before the ark, but his head and hands have been cut off (5:1–5). In the ancient world, the victorious king would often cut off the hands and/or the head of the defeated king. So the Lord is making a strong statement about who won the battle. No doubt finding their god Dagon lying beheaded on the temple floor before the ark rattled the Philistines in Ashdod.

A Byzantine church in modern Kiriath Jearim. After returning from Philistia, the ark remains in Kiriath Jearim for twenty years.

God then strikes the city of Ashdod with a terrible plague. The people in Ashdod wisely decide to send the ark somewhere else, and they promptly donate it to their sister city of Gath. However, when the plague follows the ark to Gath and strikes the inhabitants there, the Philistines in Gath decide to send the ark to Ekron, another nearby Philistine city. The Philistines in Ekron, however, are not dummies. They strenuously object to housing the ark in their city. They request that this dangerous god be sent back to his home in Israel (5:6–12). The Philistine priests and diviners recommend a guilt offering be made to this god, so the Philistines make five golden models of rats and five golden models of "tumors" (we are

✝ In the ancient world, "hand" was often a symbolic reference to power. In the ark narrative (1 Samuel 4–6), the term "hand" is used repeatedly (5:4, 6, 7, 9, 11; 6:3, 5, 9).

Jonathan's rout
of the Philistines
takes place in this
vicinity, at the
cliffs of Michmash
(1 Sam. 14:1–14).

not sure what these were), both of which were associated with the plague (perhaps like the bubonic plague, which was spread by rats). They place this gold in a cart with the ark and hook it to two cows who had never pulled a cart before. Without any human drivers involved, this cart with the ark of the covenant on it, along with quite a bit of gold, makes its way by itself back to Israel (6:7–7:1).

Ironically, this story reads like a military campaign. God first goes to Ashdod, slays their god Dagon, and smites them with a plague. The people of Ashdod surrender, and God moves on to besiege the next city, Gath, which also quickly surrenders. Next the city of Ekron capitulates. The Philistines then pay expensive tribute (the golden rats and tumors), and God returns home alone, loaded with gold, just like a conquering king. The point is that while Israel may have been defeated by the Philistines, God most certainly was not defeated by Dagon. Quite to the contrary, the God of Israel defeats Dagon and the Philistines by himself, without any Israelite involvement, further demonstrating his supreme power.

Samuel anoints and establishes Saul as king (7:2–12:25)

As Samuel rises to power, he is able to convince Israel to turn away from their idols and worship the Lord God alone (7:2–4). When they do this, God enables them to defeat the Philistines and make peace with the Amorites. Thus Israel has peace, with Samuel serving as their judge (7:5–17).

Samuel, however, grows old. His sons, like Eli's sons, are corrupt and unjust. The people do not want his sons as their judges. So they appeal to Samuel to give them a king, like the other nations have. They want someone strong and bold, who can lead them into battle. Samuel tries to talk them out of this, pointing out that the establishment of a monarchy will bring centralized government and lots of taxes, as well as forced service in the army and at court. The people refuse to listen to Samuel. They want their king. God tells Samuel to go ahead and give them a king (8:1–22).

So Samuel anoints Saul as king of Israel. In Saul's introductory episode he appears to be a bit of a clod, searching somewhat aimlessly for his dad's lost donkeys (9:3–20). Furthermore, even after he is anointed, Saul is rather timid and shy, hiding out among the animals and the baggage (10:20–24). However, Saul has several things working in his favor to help him be a successful king. First of all, he is a foot taller than anyone else in Israel (9:2; 10:23), a true asset when the primary requirement of the people is that the king be a good fighter who can lead them in battle. More important, God gives Saul the Spirit to help him (10:6–10), as well as Samuel to advise him. Then to ensure he gets off to a good start, God's Spirit empowers Saul to begin his reign with a great military victory over the Ammonites (11:1–15).

So Saul's reign begins well, and Samuel transitions from being the main leader to being an adviser in semiretirement. In 1 Samuel 12:1–24 Samuel gives a long farewell speech, calling on Israel and her new king to remain faithful to God (very similar to the final speeches of Moses and Joshua in Deuteronomy 32 and Joshua 24). Samuel's final words are ominous and perhaps predictive: "Yet if you persist in doing evil, both you and your king will be swept away" (12:25).

Saul disqualifies himself by three boneheaded mistakes (13:1–15:35)

Even though God enables Saul to start off well, the new king just does not have the character required to be a good, righteous king. Soon Saul commits three boneheaded mistakes. First, in 1 Samuel 13 he disobeys Samuel's instructions, failing to wait for Samuel and instead offering the sacrifice himself. Second, in the midst of a battle in which Saul had done little to win, he makes a very foolish vow (like Jephthah in Judges 11). This vow does nothing to help with the battle, but it does indict with a death penalty Saul's own son Jonathan, who was the actual hero of the battle (1 Sam. 14:1–48). Unlike in the time of Jephthah, however, the army intervenes and stops Saul from carrying out his vow and executing his son Jonathan (14:41–45). In Saul's third and most critical mistake (1 Samuel 15), he flagrantly disobeys a direct command from God. The Lord gave Saul a great victory over the Amalekites, but in fulfillment of Deuteronomy 25:17–19 God had instructed Saul to totally destroy all the Amalekites and all their livestock. When Samuel comes to greet Saul after the battle, Saul declares, "I have carried out the Lord's instructions!" (15:13). Samuel points out the indicting evidence to the contrary: "What then is this bleating of sheep in my ears? What is this lowing of cattle that I hear?" (15:14). Saul tries to blame others (15:20–21,

---

✚ Saul is introduced as one looking aimlessly for his father's lost donkeys while David is introduced as one who is caring for his father's sheep. The contrasts between these two are many and are emphasized throughout the story.

24), but Samuel tells him that this violation is conclusive—God is now rejecting him as king. Furthermore, even though Saul begs and pleads, Samuel notes that God is not going to change his mind on this; it is over for Saul as far as God is concerned (15:24–35).

Who Will Be King? The Contrast between Saul and David (1 Sam. 16:1–31:13)

David is anointed by Samuel and empowered by the Spirit of the Lord (16:1–23)

So God moves on and leads Samuel to anoint the young man David as the next king. In contrast to Saul, David is not big (16:6–7). He is still a young man out tending his father's sheep. Samuel is a bit surprised, and God reminds him, "Do not consider his appearance or his height, for I have rejected him [David's big brother Eliab]. The Lord does not look at the things a man looks at. Man looks at the outward appearance, but the Lord looks at the heart" (16:7). Samuel then anoints David, and the Spirit of God comes upon David (16:12–13). Even though Saul is still king, it is David who has the empowering Spirit of God. The next episode (1 Sam. 16:14–23) illustrates how the power of the Spirit works in David's life in contrast to Saul, who is troubled by a spirit that torments him.

David slays Goliath, acting like a king empowered by the Spirit (17:1–58)

The victory over Goliath (1 Samuel 17) is a defining moment for David. Israel is at war with the Philistines again, and the Philistine champion, Goliath, is taunting the Israelite army, challenging them to send out their champion to fight him in one-on-one combat

This is perhaps the most detailed depiction of a harp from the time of David. In this painting from Egypt a harpist plays to the falcon-headed sun-god.

(17:1–10). Who would Israel's champion be?

Recall the whole reason the Israelites wanted a king in the first place was so that he would lead them in battles (1 Sam. 8:19–20). Also recall that Saul is the tallest Israelite in the land, a head taller than anyone else (9:2; 10:23). We also find out that, unlike everyone else in the Israelite army, Saul has a suit of armor (13:19–22; 17:38–39). In addition, based on our best ancient manuscripts, Saul may be almost as big as Goliath (see the discussion on page 173). So Goliath's challenge is probably directed at Saul, and King Saul is the obvious and only plausible candidate to fight Goliath. Saul, however, along with the rest of the army, is frightened by Goliath (17:11).

Egyptian relief of captured "sea people" warriors, probably Philistines.

David now comes on the scene. He is a shepherd boy bringing supplies to his older brothers in the army. David is not even part of the army. This is not his fight! Yet David is incensed at the insults from Goliath, and he volunteers to fight the loud-mouthed Philistine (especially when he hears that the one who kills Goliath will marry the king's daughter) (17:12–32). Saul doubts David will have much of a chance, but David confidently tells him he has often killed both bears and lions when they threatened his father's sheep (17:33–37). For the first time in the story we find out that David is no novice to dangerous mortal combat. If he has faced lions and bears all alone in the field and emerged victorious, then maybe he can handle Goliath.

David refuses to use Saul's armor (Saul will not be able to finagle any credit out of David's victory), and instead confronts Goliath solely with his staff and his sling, the weapons of a shepherd (17:38–40). After some trash talk from Goliath and David (and David wins the battle of words too), the battle begins, and David kills the Philistine champion and beheads him, leading to a total rout of the Philistine army (17:41–58).

So David, even though he is a young man, has acted like a king, empowered by the Spirit of God to deliver Israel from the Philistines. At this point he is indeed the true king of Israel, chosen by God, anointed by Samuel, and confirmed through a great victory. Unfortunately, Saul and the Israelites don't recognize it yet, or at least they don't admit it. In reality, humanly speaking, David could probably have taken the throne by force at this point. The army would probably have followed him. David, however, is a man of character and virtue; he will wait for God to remove Saul from the throne.

✚ Just as David the shepherd protected his human father's sheep and killed the lions that threatened them, so David (like a shepherd-king) will kill Goliath, the "lion" that threatens his divine father's sheep.

The decline of Saul (and his madness) versus the rise of David (and his greatness) (18:1–31:13)

The story in the rest of 1 Samuel revolves around the contrast between Saul and David. God has chosen David to replace Saul as king, but Saul refuses to give in. Throughout this unit David exemplifies good leadership just as Saul continues to demonstrate his incompetence. David will grow stronger and stronger throughout this unit, just as Saul grows weaker and more pathetic as he becomes paranoid about killing David.

In 1 Samuel 18–20 we see David in three relationships: (1) with Saul's son Jonathan and Saul's daughter Michal, who both love David; (2) with the people, who also love David; and (3) with Saul, who repeatedly tries to kill David. Indeed, in this section Saul makes numerous unsuccessful attempts to kill David (18:11, 17, 25; 19:1, 10, 11). In 1 Samuel 18 Saul is subtle in his attempt to kill David, but in 1 Samuel 19 he openly tries to kill him. First Samuel 20 stresses the close, but ironic, friendship between David and Saul's own son Jonathan, who clearly recognizes and supports David as king.

As the story moves along, Saul again demonstrates his unrighteous character by massacring the entire Israelite town of Nob, along with eighty-five priests, just for helping David. In contrast, David protects and provides for the one priest who survives (1 Samuel 21–23). Unlike Saul, David is able to inquire of God and receive answers (23:2). Furthermore, in the meantime David is fighting the Philistines, trying to deliver Israel. Saul, however, is exerting all his effort on finding and killing David, needlessly massacring a whole city of Israelites.

First Samuel 24–26 contains three related stories. In 1 Samuel 24 David has an opportunity to kill Saul, but spares him. Likewise, a similar event takes place in 1 Samuel 26, as David is provided another excellent opportunity to kill Saul, but instead spares him. Sandwiched in between these two events is the intriguing story of David and the beautiful woman Abigail. Nabal, Abigail's surly husband (Nabal means "fool"), foolishly insults David. As

The valley of Elah, where David fought Goliath (1 Sam. 17:1–3).

How Tall Was Goliath?

In the Hebrew text that most of our English Bibles are based on, the height of Goliath in 1 Samuel 17:4 is "*six* cubits and a span." In the ancient world, a cubit was about eighteen inches, and a span was about nine inches. Thus Goliath would have been about nine feet, nine inches tall. This is the way he has usually been portrayed in Christian tradition.

Surprisingly, in a scroll of Samuel found with the Dead Sea Scrolls, the height of Goliath is given as "*four* cubits and a span," or only about six feet, nine inches. Likewise, the Septuagint, the early translation of the Old Testament into Greek and the Bible of the early church, also lists the height of Goliath as "four cubits and a span."

The oldest Hebrew manuscript that has "six cubits and a span" dates to AD 935. No Hebrew manuscripts earlier than this list Goliath's height at "six cubits and a span." The Samuel scroll from the Dead Sea Scrolls, however (reading "four cubits and a span"), dates to about 50 BC, nearly one thousand years earlier. Likewise, we have Greek manuscripts of the Septuagint reading "four cubits and a span" that date to the fourth and fifth centuries AD.

Scholars are not quite sure what to make of this. In recent years, more and more scholars are acknowledging that the earlier manuscripts might contain a reading that is more likely to be original; thus perhaps Goliath was only six feet, nine inches.

Nothing else in the text requires Goliath to be nine feet, nine inches. He is never actually called a giant in the Bible. His armor (described in 17:5–7) is not something that a big, strong, six-foot-nine man could not carry, and besides, being taller does not imply being stronger.

This discussion is not a challenge to the accuracy or inerrancy of the Bible. It is just an attempt to get at what the original reading was.

How would the shorter height of Goliath affect our understanding of the story? It is important to note that in the ancient world, people in general were quite a bit shorter than they are now. At this time in Palestine (about 1000 BC) the average height of men was only about five feet, two inches. So Goliath at six feet, nine inches was still an unusually large man. But remember that King Saul was a head taller than anyone in Israel (9:2). So Saul is probably six-foot-five or so, not much shorter than Goliath. Saul also has armor. So Saul is the likely candidate who should go forward and fight against Goliath. Note when Saul counsels David in 17:33, Saul does not seem concerned with Goliath's size, but rather with Goliath's years of training and experience.

Of course this is just a possibility. Scholars remain divided over what to do with the two heights of Goliath in the ancient manuscripts. Most English Bible translations still follow the traditional reading and list Goliath as nine feet, nine inches or as "six cubits and a span," but this might change in the future.

An Egyptian cubit measuring rod made of wood.

David travels to massacre Nabal and his family, Abigail meets David, offering him her apologies as well as gifts and a strong argument against destroying her family. As a result of Abigail's persuasion, David spares Nabal, just as he spares Saul in the surrounding stories. God strikes Nabal dead ten days later, and David marries the beautiful and wise Abigail, illustrating to David that he should always wait on God's timing.

In the meantime, Saul is still after him (in spite of his oaths to the contrary), and David leaves Israel to live among the Philistines, of all peoples (1 Sam. 27:1–7)! Saul has certainly forced David into a topsy-turvy world! From there David tries to continue fighting against the other enemies of Israel, tricking the Philistines into thinking he is fighting Saul and the Israelites (27:8–12).

In 28:3, Samuel dies. Pathetic Saul once again has to worry about the Philistines, but he no longer has Samuel to guide him. He wants a word from God about how to fight the Philistines, but God refuses to answer Saul in any way. So in one of the more bizarre stories in the Bible, Saul seeks out a medium, a woman who can summon the dead. Saul asks her to call up Samuel from the dead (28:11), and apparently she does (but she seems shocked at seeing him; 28:12). Saul wants Samuel to tell him what to do in regard to the Philistines. Samuel, clearly annoyed at this disturbance, tells Saul that the Philistines will defeat Israel tomorrow, and that Saul, along with his sons, will be there in death with Samuel (28:15–19). Samuel's prediction comes true, and while David is fighting the Amalekites (Remember them? They were the beginning of Saul's troubles back in 1 Samuel 15), the Philistines defeat Israel and kill Saul along with Jonathan (1 Sam. 31:1–13).

The tel at Beth Shan. After killing Saul and his sons, the Philistines hang their corpses on the wall of Beth Shan (1 Sam. 31:8–13).

✛ The New Testament Gospels will clearly identify Jesus the Messiah as the one who fulfills God's promise to David for a descendant whose reign will last forever.

The Rise of David and the Restoration of Israel (2 Sam. 1:1–10:19)

David becomes king and reunites the kingdom politically (1:1–5:25)

David hears of Saul's death and honors both Saul and Jonathan with a lament (1:17–27). A civil war breaks out between those loyal to the house of Saul and those loyal to David. In contrast to how David had spared Saul, David's general, Joab, murders Saul's general, Abner, breaking the resistance. David now has complete control of Israel. All the tribes pledge loyalty to David (5:1–5), and after capturing Jerusalem he establishes that city as the capital (5:6–16). Then he crushes the Philistines (5:17–25).

Through David, Israel is restored to covenant relationship with God (6:1–7:29)

Now that his capital is established in Jerusalem, David wants to bring the ark of the covenant there. At first he attempts to move the ark incorrectly, as if it were a military trophy, and God strikes one of David's men dead. Even David cannot ignore the procedures given in the law for handling the ark, the Presence of God (Exod. 25:10–16; Num. 4:15; 7:9). David tries again, successfully this time because he follows the correct procedures (see 1 Chron. 15:11–15). David then expresses his desire to build God a permanent temple (literally, "house"). But God speaks to David through Nathan the prophet, making a covenant with David and promising to build David a "house" (i.e., a dynasty). In this covenant, God promises to raise up a special descendant of David whose kingdom will endure forever (7:1–17). David then humbly gives thanks to God in prayer (7:18–29).

David completes the conquest and restores Israel to military prominence (8:1–10:19)

The completion of the conquest (driving out the inhabitants of the Promised Land) had been on hold since the death of Joshua. David, now recommitted to obeying God and keeping the covenant, completes the conquest.

Humpty Dumpty's Great Fall: The Bathsheba Affair (2 Sam. 11:1–12:31)

Just as David reaches the height of his accomplishments, he crumbles and falls. From his rooftop, he sees the beautiful (and married) Bathsheba taking a bath, and he determines to have her. He brings her to his palace and sleeps with her (her feelings about all of this are not told) (11:1–5). She becomes pregnant and notifies David. The king brings her husband,

Uriah, back from the war and attempts to get him to go home to sleep with his wife in order to make him think that he is the father, but Uriah refuses. After several unsuccessful attempts at this, David then sends him back to the war with instructions for Joab, David's general (and "hatchet man"), to make sure that Uriah gets killed in action. In essence, David has Uriah murdered. David then marries Bathsheba.

Not surprisingly, God is quite upset about this (11:27), and he sends the prophet Nathan to rebuke David, who immediately repents (12:1–14). Nonetheless, the baby born to Bathsheba dies (12:15–19). Later, after Bathsheba marries David, she will give birth to Solomon (12:24–25).

God forgives David, even for such a horrendous sin as this, but the consequences of his sin continue to plague him for the rest of his life. Humpty Dumpty has indeed fallen off the wall, and no one is able to put him back together again.

The Consequences of Sin: The Unraveling of David's Kingdom (2 Sam. 13:1–20:26)

Just as the opening chapters of 2 Samuel describe how David strengthened and unified Israel, now, after the Bathsheba incident, everything goes in reverse as the strong, unified kingdom unravels. David has troubles both from within his own household

The capital cities of David and Saul. David establishes a new capital at Jerusalem (2 Samuel 5–6).

BENJAMIN

Saul's capital → ○ Gibeah

David moves capital from Hebron to Jerusalem (Jebus) → ○ Jerusalem (Jebus)

JUDAH

David's first capital for 7.5 years → ○ Hebron

Wilderness of Judah

Dead Sea

Jordan

✦ Psalm 51 describes David's repentance and his broken heart over the Bathsheba affair.

and from the outside. Amnon, David's oldest son, rapes his half sister, Tamar. Since David does nothing about it, another son, Absalom (Tamar's full brother), kills Amnon and then flees from David (13:1–38). Eventually Absalom returns to Jerusalem, only to plot a conspiracy to overthrow his father, David (14:1–15:12). David, the former hero and champion, now flees from Jerusalem, inept and unable to oppose the rebellious Absalom (15:13–37). Later in a battle, David's general, Joab (the hatchet man), kills Absalom, and David returns to Jerusalem (18:1–19:43). But things never return to the way they were. Second Samuel 20 describes a major rebellion of the ten northern tribes, foreshadowing the civil war that will split Israel apart after Solomon's death.

Uriah the Hittite, the husband of Bathsheba, is a soldier in David's army. Shown above is a Hittite soldier on a wall relief (tenth century BC).

The Good and the Bad: A Summary of David and His Kingdom (2 Sam. 21:1–24:25)

The final four chapters seem to be somewhat unrelated, but they are connected structurally in a parallel pattern (called a chiasm) that Hebrew authors love to use. The structure is as follows:

> A1. Narrative #1 (21:1–14): Saul's sin brings a famine; David's actions halt the famine.
> > B1. List of military exploits #1 (21:15–22)
> > > C1. David's song of praise #1 (22:1–51)
> > > C2. David's song of praise #2 (23:1–7)
> > B2. List of military exploits #2 (23:8–39)
> A2. Narrative #2 (24:1–25): David's sin brings a plague; David's actions halt the plague.

✝ Just as Eli was unable to control his sons at the beginning of 1–2 Samuel, so David is unable to control his sons at the end of 1–2 Samuel.

Ironically, this final unit summarizes the life and times of King David. He corrects Saul's mistakes, praises the Lord magnificently, and worships him sincerely, but his own troubles continue due to his own mistakes, and, in the end, only by his sacrifice and God's grace does he avert judgment.

So What? Applying 1–2 Samuel to Our Lives Today

We can learn and apply much from the faithful examples of Hannah and Samuel, who trusted in God. Likewise, we can learn from Eli, who let his immoral sons run free without correcting their sinful behavior. He becomes a negative example for us and a reminder that we are responsible to correct our children's behavior.

David has many, many virtues for us to try to inculcate into our own lives. He is a man after God's own heart, one who seeks to do what God wants more than fulfilling his own desires. David encourages us to be brave, to remember how God has empowered us in the past to do incredible things, and to act on that memory to undertake great (and often frightening) tasks. David is not concerned with what others think, but only with what God thinks. Developing this attitude in our lives will help us tremendously in our Christian walk.

Of course, we also have to come to grips with David's great sin with Bathsheba and Uriah. This should warn us that sexual affairs are always a great temptation, and even strong, committed people like David are vulnerable. So you and I should be quick to run from sexual temptation. When we encounter a "Bathsheba" temptation, we need to recall the rest of 2 Samuel and remember how David's life and kingdom crumbled. If we find someone tempting us toward an adulterous affair, we need to look into their eyes and *see our entire life in ruins.*

Finally, the great tragedy of David's life reminds us not to put our ultimate trust in people, but rather in the Lord, who will not fail us. David was one of the greatest individuals in the Bible, but ultimately he failed. He was not the Messiah. The Bible teaches us to put our hope and trust in Jesus, who is the Messiah and who did not fail and did not succumb to sin. People will always stumble and fall, but Jesus will not. He will deliver us.

Our Favorite Verse in 1–2 Samuel

You come against me with sword and spear and javelin, but I come against you in the name of the Lord Almighty, the God of the armies of Israel, whom you have defied. (1 Sam. 17:45)

The city of Rabbah (2 Sam. 11:1) was the capital of Ammon. The ruins of this city have been excavated in the center of the modern city of Amman, the capital of Jordan.

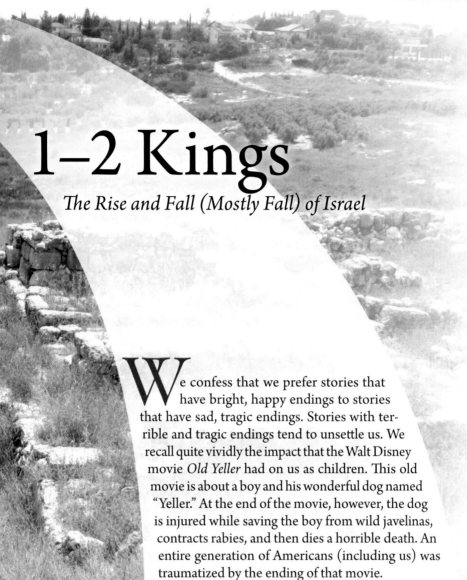

1–2 Kings

The Rise and Fall (Mostly Fall) of Israel

We confess that we prefer stories that have bright, happy endings to stories that have sad, tragic endings. Stories with terrible and tragic endings tend to unsettle us. We recall quite vividly the impact that the Walt Disney movie *Old Yeller* had on us as children. This old movie is about a boy and his wonderful dog named "Yeller." At the end of the movie, however, the dog is injured while saving the boy from wild javelinas, contracts rabies, and then dies a horrible death. An entire generation of Americans (including us) was traumatized by the ending of that movie.

First and Second Kings is even more tragic and traumatic than the fictional story of *Old Yeller*, for it tells the story of the numerous dumb decisions made by the Israelites that eventually led to the death of God's beloved nation of Israel.

What Is the Setting for 1–2 Kings?

Back in Exodus, God delivered the Israelites from Egypt and then led them into the Promised Land. Just prior to their entering the land, God gives them Deuteronomy, which contains the terms by which Israel could live in the Promised Land with God and be blessed. The driving question that runs throughout the story from Deuteronomy to the end of 2 Kings is, "Will Israel be obedient to the terms in Deuteronomy?" The simple and sad answer is no.

First and Second Kings is the concluding episode in the story of Israel that runs from Genesis 12 through 2 Kings 25. First Kings picks up the story immediately after the ending of 2 Samuel. Thus in 1 Kings 1, David (the central character in 1–2 Samuel) is old and about to die. In 1 Kings 2, David dies, and Solomon, his son, becomes king.

The dates and chronology of 1–2 Kings are interconnected quite firmly with documented ancient world history of this era. Thus we know fairly precise dates for most of the events in these two books. Solomon comes to the throne in 971 BC and reigns until 931 BC (1 Kings 1–11). After his death, a civil war ensues, and the nation splits into two parts: Israel in the north and Judah in the south. The northern kingdom, Israel, is destroyed by the Assyrians in 722 BC (2 Kings 17), and Judah is destroyed by the Babylonians in 587/586 BC (2 Kings 25).

What Is at the Heart of 1–2 Kings?

An Egyptian princess.

The original audience for 1–2 Kings was probably the Israelites who had been carried off into exile in Babylonia. With Jerusalem burned to the ground, these people no doubt struggled to make sense of it all and to maintain some kind of hope. Why did this happen? Is the Lord unfaithful? Or perhaps he is just weaker than the gods of Babylon? First and Second Kings provide a very clear and important answer to these questions. The exile came as a result of Israel's and Judah's repeated and continued obstinate disobedience to the Mosaic covenant (especially Deuteronomy). The great tragedy of this story is that they had only themselves to blame. There are several significant subthemes running throughout 1–2 Kings. One is the portrayal of the dismantling of the spectacular empire and temple that Solomon built. While the early chapters of 1 Kings describe how Solomon adds various valuable items to the temple, the later chapters describe how these same items are carried off by various foreign kings. Another theme in

✚ Many of the literary prophets live, preach, and write in Israel or Judah during the time period covered by 1–2 Kings. This includes Isaiah, Jeremiah, Hosea, Amos, Jonah, Micah, Nahum, Habakkuk, and Zephaniah.

How Do We Determine the Dates for the Events in the Old Testament?

Perhaps you have never pondered over it, but obviously the people in the ancient world did not use modern calendars and did not date events as we do now (AD or BC). In the histories and chronologies of the ancient Near East (including the Old Testament) most events were dated by relating them to the time that a certain king began ruling. For instance, we find statements like "in the fifth year of Joram son of Ahab king of Israel" (2 Kings 8:16) or "in the first year of Cyrus, king of Persia" (Ezra 1:1). But how do scholars know what year it was when Joram became king of Israel or Cyrus became king of Persia?

The Assyrians have inadvertently helped us out. There is an ancient document from Assyria called the Assyrian King List that lists the Assyrian kings in chronological order. The scribes who produced this document also assigned a unique name to each consecutive year, selected from the names of officials and called "eponyms." The Assyrians thus had a different eponym name for each year, and they used these eponyms to date the year of each king's accession to the throne in the King List. Likewise, Assyrian scribes dated other events in Assyrian history with these eponyms as well. Fortunately for those of us who are concerned with accurate dates, an Assyrian scribe mentioned that a solar eclipse occurred during one of these eponym years. Modern astronomers can calculate exactly when that solar eclipse occurred (June 15, 763 BC), letting us know that this particular ancient eponym corresponds to our date of 763 BC. Using that firm date, scholars can then use the eponym list and the Assyrian King List to determine the accurate dates for most of Assyrian history. The Babylonians have King Lists as well, and since these overlap with the Assyrian King List, scholars can also accurately date the kings and events of Babylonian history.

Several events in 1–2 Kings involve the Assyrians or the Babylonians and thus can be dated fairly accurately based on the correlations with the known dates of Assyrian and Babylonian history. Once a few firm dates are known in 1–2 Kings, then the dates for just about all of the events in 1–2 Kings and 1–2 Chronicles can be determined, since the Israelite and Judahite kings are linked together by accession to the throne and length of their reign. This also allows scholars to determine the dates for many of the events in the prophetic books as well. Thus we are fairly confident of our biblical dates from the time of Saul and David down to the time of Ezra, Nehemiah, and Esther.

1–2 Kings traces the reversal of the exodus and conquest (Israel's salvation history). Recall that as the conquest began, the Israelites entered the land and captured Jericho. At the end of 2 Kings, however, it is Jerusalem that is being captured, and the Israelites are being kicked out of the land. Ironically, the final king (Zedekiah) is captured by the Babylonians right outside Jericho (2 Kings 25:5), ending Israel's time in the land right where it began.

Another subtheme, introduced in the Elijah and Elisha stories, is that of a remnant. As the nation slides into apostasy and thus heads for national judgment, the Elijah and Elisha narratives illustrate that there is hope and deliverance for individuals who trust in God. A remnant will survive.

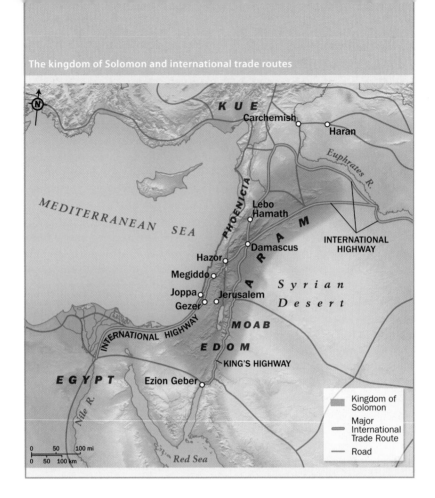

An outline summary of the story in 1–2 Kings is as follows:

- The Contradiction of Solomon: Splendor and Apostasy (1 Kings 1–11)
- Reversing the Conquest and Dismantling the Empire (1 Kings 12–16)
    - Stupidity, sin, and civil war (12:1–33)
    - God's disapproval of Bethel and Jeroboam (13:1–14:20)
    - Typical kings, good and bad (mostly bad) (14:21–16:34)
- God Sends Prophets to Confront the Corrupt Monarchy (1 Kings 17:1–2 Kings 8:15)
    - Elijah's ministry (1 Kings 17–19)
    - Judgment on Ahab, the prototypical bad king and enemy of the prophets (1 Kings 20–2 Kings 1)
    - Elisha's ministry (2 Kings 2:1–8:15)
- The Last Days of Israel (2 Kings 8:16–17:41)
    - Useless attempts at reform (8:16–12:21)

- Typical kings, good and bad (mostly bad) (13:1–16:20)
- The destruction and exile of Israel (17:1–41)
  - The Last Days of Judah (2 Kings 18:1–25:30)
    - Deliverance from Assyria (18:1–20:21)
    - Manasseh, the worst king ever (21:1–26)
    - The futile attempt of Josiah to reform Judah (22:1–23:30)
    - The destruction of Jerusalem and the exile of Judah (23:31–25:30)

What Makes 1–2 Kings Interesting and Unique?

- Solomon's spectacular building accomplishments are contrasted with his inexcusable apostasy.
- In 1 Kings we find the exciting story of Elijah's confrontation with hundreds of false prophets on Mount Carmel.
- The Elijah and Elisha stories contain more miracles by God than any other time in the Old Testament since Moses.
- God deals with the bad kings of Israel and Judah in different and unpredictable ways.

What Is the Message of 1–2 Kings?

The Contradiction of Solomon: Splendor and Apostasy (1 Kings 1–11)

Even though David stumbles through the latter years of his reign due to his affair with Bathsheba, his son Solomon still inherits a fairly strong kingdom. Solomon will then take this kingdom and develop it into a spectacular empire, indeed, a showplace other rulers visit just to see and marvel at.

First Kings 1–2 describes how Solomon (with help from his mother, Bathsheba) quickly consolidates power and establishes himself firmly as king after David dies. First Kings 3–4 then gives illustrations of Solomon's wisdom and his great organizational ability, as he greatly expands the royal administrative system. At the heart of the Solomon narratives is the description of the fantastic temple he builds for the Lord (1 Kings 5–9), along with his own palace and other important government buildings. The temple is overwhelmingly beautiful and opulent. God had blessed Solomon with great wealth, and Solomon uses this great wealth to finance a spectacular temple for God. Solomon also brings the ark to the temple, and the Presence of God

Hiram, king of Tyre, tells Solomon, "I have received the message you sent me and will do all you want in providing the cedar and pine logs. My men will haul them down from Lebanon to the sea, and I will float them in rafts by sea to the place you specify" (1 Kings 5:8–9). The Assyrians also obtained timber from Lebanon, and this wall panel from an Assyrian palace depicts the transportation of timber by sea from Lebanon.

fills the temple in dramatic fashion (8:1–13). Solomon dedicates the temple with a long prayer of dedication to the Lord (8:22–53) along with two shorter prayers of blessings on the people (8:14–21, 54–61). God's response is much briefer (9:1–9), acknowledging the temple but reminding Solomon to be faithful to him. First Kings 9:10–10:29 describes other spectacular aspects of Solomon's kingdom. Indeed, in 10:1–13 another monarch, the Queen of Sheba, visits Solomon and is overwhelmed at the splendor of his kingdom. The final verses in this section (10:14–29) stress the wealth of Solomon as well as his large powerful army (a large number of chariots and chariot horses).

On the surface, 1 Kings 1–10 appears to praise and glorify Solomon. However, if we read carefully, we notice that several things are just not right. As we dig into the text and place it in the context of Deuteronomy (which should be dictating how Solomon lives and rules), we see several contradictions; indeed, if we look closely, the story seems to be criticizing Solomon in the same breath

✦ Solomon does not have the same heart for God that David did.

as it praises him. The author of 1 Kings is apparently praising Solomon only on the surface in a sort of facetious or sarcastic manner. The author's true opinion of Solomon is mostly negative.

Remember that back in Deuteronomy 17:15–17, God provided guidelines for Israelite kings. This passage prohibits three things: the accumulation of chariot horses, especially from Egypt; the accumulation of silver and gold; and the accumulation of numerous wives. Ironically, 1 Kings 10:14–29 brags about Solomon's kingdom by stressing how much silver and gold he had, as well as how many chariots and chariot horses he had (imported from Egypt!), two of the things prohibited in Deuteronomy 17. Then 1 Kings 11:3 states that Solomon had seven hundred wives of royal birth (many of them foreign) as well as three hundred concubines. No matter how one interprets the prohibition of "numerous wives" in Deuteronomy 17:17, Solomon is well over the limit with one thousand.

As we look back over 1 Kings 1–10 with Deuteronomy and 1–2 Samuel in hand, we now realize that the author of 1 Kings 1–10 has been dropping subtle and not-too-subtle hints all along that things are not quite right in the house of Solomon. Even at the very beginning, as Solomon succeeds his father, David, the Lord does not say anything or do anything (at least overtly) to indicate his selection of Solomon. This silence of God regarding who the next king should be is in stark contrast to God's actions in 1–2 Samuel regarding Saul and David, and should alert us that something in the story of Solomon is not quite right. Also recall that Solomon's mother was Bathsheba, who came to be David's wife under questionable circumstances. It is rather unusual that her son should be the next king.

Numerous other comments in 1 Kings 1–10 should raise some eyebrows. In 3:1 the text states that Solomon marries "the daughter of Pharaoh," and she will be mentioned several times in the Solomon story. Throughout the Old Testament, Egypt almost always has negative connotations because it is so closely associated with the oppression of the early days of Exodus. Why is Solomon reconnecting Israel with Egypt?

In addition, 3:2–4 indicates that Solomon (and the rest of Israel) sacrificed at the high

Limestone bust of an Egyptian queen (ca. 1550 BC). Solomon marries an Egyptian princess (1 Kings 7:8; 9:24; 11:1).

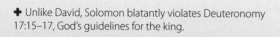
✚ Unlike David, Solomon blatantly violates Deuteronomy 17:15–17, God's guidelines for the king.

The Egyptians were famous for their chariots and chariot horses. Depicted above is Egyptian king Tutankhamen in his chariot defeating the Cushites, his enemies to the south. King Solomon of Israel had 12,000 horses for his army, many of which he imported from Egypt (1 Kings 10:26–29). Unfortunately, Deut. 17:16 forbids the king to accumulate horses, especially from Egypt!

places (pagan worship sites). Later in 1 Kings 11:7–8 the narrator will tell us Solomon even built these pagan "high place" altars for his many foreign wives, even for the gods Chemosh and Molech (gods known for requiring child sacrifice). Ironically, in 3:9 Solomon asks for, and receives from God, a "discerning heart," able to tell right from wrong. This gift to him from God is an indictment against him in 11:1–13, for it is precisely his heart (11:2, 4, 9) that is the root problem of his apostasy.

Likewise in 1 Kings 4, the text seems to be praising Solomon for the impressive administrative system he implemented, but remember that this is exactly what Samuel warned Israel about back in 1 Samuel 8 (taxes, forced labor, and drafted soldiers). First Kings 4:6 casually mentions that Adoniram was "in charge of forced labor." The issue of forced labor will be the flash point that sends the nation plunging into civil war after Solomon dies.

The account of the temple construction continues this subtle irony. In Exodus, the Lord gave very specific instructions for the construction of the tabernacle, and then the Spirit of God filled the craftsmen, empowering them to create the beautiful tabernacle. Thus God was intimately involved in the design and construction of the tabernacle. Nothing like that happens in 1 Kings 5–8. Solomon designs and constructs the temple.

Furthermore, the text states that it took seven years for Solomon to build the temple of the Lord, but that it took thirteen years for him to build his own house (6:37–7:1). What are the implications of spending more time on his own house than on the Lord's house? Solomon also builds an impressive

✚ The construction of Solomon's temple (1 Kings 5–9) contrasts dramatically with the construction of the tabernacle (Exod. 25–31; 35–40) in regard to direct input from God and the motivation of the workers and the people.

house for Pharaoh's daughter (7:8), who keeps showing up in the story in ironic situations.

God does not seem overly impressed with Solomon's great temple, and when God does respond to Solomon's dedication of the temple, the Lord focuses on the issue of faithfulness to the covenant. God notes that he is the one who makes the temple special by his Presence, not by the splendor of the construction materials (9:3). God then warns Solomon that he must keep the law and be obedient or else God will leave this temple and it will be destroyed (9:4–9), a very ominous foreshadowing of things to come in 2 Kings.

Finally, in 1 Kings 11:1–13 the author drops all subtlety and cuts to the chase. Solomon has allowed his foreign wives to lead him into idolatry on a huge scale (11:1–8). The Lord is very angry with Solomon, especially since God had appeared directly to him twice (11:9). The only thing that keeps God from tearing the kingdom out of Solomon's hands is the Lord's regard for David, Solomon's father (11:12–13). The irony is that even though Solomon builds a spectacular temple for the Lord, he totally reverses the theological progress that David had made in Israel's worship. Instead of driving all pagan idol worshipers right out of the Promised Land, Solomon embraces them and intermarries with a bunch of them. He even builds temples and worship sites for them! Thus in spite of all of his magnificent construction accomplishments, the "great" King Solomon leads Israel down the path of idolatry that will ultimately lead to destruction and loss of the Promised Land.

The final words about Solomon's reign (1 Kings 11:14–43) mention his three main political adversaries, foreshadowing the quick end of the peaceful "Solomonic Kingdom." One of these adversaries is Jeroboam. A prophet tells Jeroboam that God will soon tear ten tribes away from the house of Solomon and give them to Jeroboam. God promises to bless Jeroboam only if he obeys God's statutes and commandments (i.e., Deuteronomy).

Reversing the Conquest and Dismantling the Empire (1 Kings 12–16)

Stupidity, sin, and civil war (12:1–33)

After Solomon dies, his son Rehoboam comes to the throne. Remember that throughout his reign Solomon had carried out huge construction projects, often using Israelites for forced labor (like Pharaoh did back in Egypt). When Solomon dies, the

Calf idols were common throughout the ancient Near East.

✚ A civil war splits the kingdom into two. The ten tribes in the north form the nation of Israel, with their capital at Samaria. Judah and Benjamin in the south now take on the name of Judah, retaining their capital at Jerusalem.

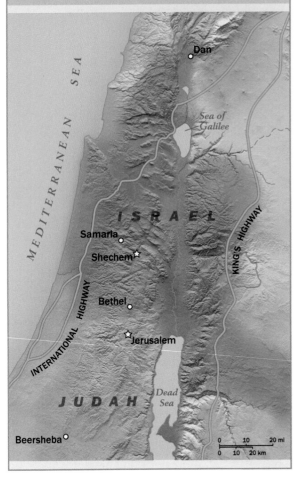

On the map: Dan, Sea of Galilee, MEDITERRANEAN SEA, ISRAEL, Samaria, Shechem, KING'S HIGHWAY, Bethel, INTERNATIONAL HIGHWAY, Jerusalem, Dead Sea, JUDAH, Beersheba, 0 10 20 mi, 0 10 20 km

A civil war divides the Promised Land into two different countries: Israel in the north and Judah in the south. The united country had often been described as extending from Dan to Beersheba (2 Sam. 3:10; 17:11; 24:2, 15; 1 Kings 4:25; 1 Chron. 21:2; 2 Chron. 30:5).

Israelites hope that the new king will give them some relief regarding the forced labor. The new king Rehoboam, however, declares that he will work the Israelites even harder than his father did. This angers most of the Israelites, for they have had enough of royal construction projects and forced labor. So all of the Israelite tribes except Judah and Benjamin rebel against King Rehoboam, plunging the kingdom into civil war (12:1–23).

These rebellious tribes call on Jeroboam to be their king. Remember God had predicted to Jeroboam that this would happen, and had promised blessings on Jeroboam if he remained faithful to Deuteronomy. Jeroboam, however, rejects the Lord and his laws from the beginning. Not wanting his new subjects to travel down to Jerusalem (now enemy territory) to worship God there, Jeroboam builds two new worship sites in his newly formed kingdom of Israel, placing one worship site at Bethel and one at Dan. Incredibly, Jeroboam constructs two golden calf idols at these two sites, declaring blasphemously, "Here are your gods, O Israel, who brought you up out of Egypt" (12:25–30). Thus he repeats—indeed, appears to celebrate—the great golden calf rebellion of Exodus 32. The northern kingdom, Israel, is off to a very bad start.

God's disapproval of Bethel and Jeroboam (13:1–14:20)

In 1 Kings 13, God sends a true prophet to prophesy judgment on the new idolatrous worship site at Bethel. Curiously, an old false prophet at Bethel convinces this new true prophet to ignore God's specific command and to disobey God. This results in the death of the true prophet. Through

✦ The construction of these two golden calves ("the sin of Jeroboam") will be referred to often in 1–2 Kings. This action immediately plunges the new northern kingdom of Israel into idolatry, from which they will never recover.

this story God is telling his people very clearly not to be enticed by the lies of false prophets, no matter how convincing they sound.

Since Jeroboam has blatantly disregarded God's word to him back in 11:29–39, choosing instead to lead Israel into worshiping golden calves, God now proclaims judgment on the house of Jeroboam instead of blessings (14:1–20).

Typical kings, good and bad (mostly bad) (14:21–16:34)

After the breakup of the Solomonic empire (i.e., the Promised Land), the northern kingdom, Israel, immediately slides into idol worship. The southern kingdom of Judah does not do much better, for King Rehoboam, with an Ammonite mother, also leads Judah into idolatry and other detestable Canaanite practices (14:21–24).

The rest of this unit recounts the largely negative reigns of various kings of Judah and Israel, setting the pattern that will continue until the Assyrians and Babylonians eventually destroy both kingdoms. Most of the kings are bad, "doing evil in the eyes of the Lord." A few kings in the south, like Asa (15:9–24), will try to reverse the trend and return Judah to faithful worship of the Lord. By and large they are unsuccessful.

One of the themes running throughout the rest of 1–2 Kings is the dismantling of the wealth and splendor of the Solomonic empire. Thus 14:25–28 and 15:18–19 describe the loss of gold and silver items from the temple that Solomon had accumulated.

This unit reaches its climax as Ahab comes to the throne of Israel. He is the prototypical "bad king." The text states he "did more evil in the eyes of the Lord than any of those before him" (16:30). Ahab is not just mixing pagan religions with worship of the Lord, a common syncretistic practice similar to what Jeroboam did (e.g., worshiping golden calves, but still connecting them to Israel's deliverance from Egypt). No, Ahab replaces the worship of the Lord God of Abraham with a thoroughgoing worship of Baal, the Canaanite god (16:31–33). Ahab also marries Jezebel, a wicked Canaanite woman from the city of Sidon. She will even try to stamp out all true worship of Israel's God, and she will kill all of the true prophets of God she can get her hands on. The monarchy of Israel is now openly hostile

A Phoenician (Canaanite) deity, probably Baal.

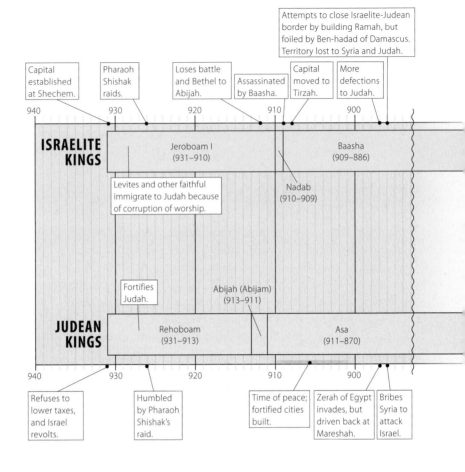

ISRAELITE KINGS

Capital established at Shechem.

Pharaoh Shishak raids.

Loses battle and Bethel to Abijah.

Assassinated by Baasha.

Capital moved to Tirzah.

More defections to Judah.

Attempts to close Israelite-Judean border by building Ramah, but foiled by Ben-hadad of Damascus. Territory lost to Syria and Judah.

940   930   920   910   900

Jeroboam I (931–910)   Baasha (909–886)

Levites and other faithful immigrate to Judah because of corruption of worship.

Nadab (910–909)

Fortifies Judah.

Abijah (Abijam) (913–911)

JUDEAN KINGS

Rehoboam (931–913)   Asa (911–870)

940   930   920   910   900

Refuses to lower taxes, and Israel revolts.

Humbled by Pharaoh Shishak's raid.

Time of peace; fortified cities built.

Zerah of Egypt invades, but driven back at Mareshah.

Bribes Syria to attack Israel.

to the God of Abraham, having completely adapted the pagan religion of the Canaanites. Unbelievable!

God Sends Prophets to Confront the Corrupt Monarchy (1 Kings 17:1–2 Kings 8:15)

Elijah's ministry (1 Kings 17–19)

The fascinating stories about the two prophets Elijah and Elisha come as a major interruption in the flow of 1–2 Kings, which has been focusing on the reign of various kings. Specifically, the stories of Elijah and Elisha interrupt the reign of Ahab, the worst of all the kings. The theology for us coming out of these stories now shifts to two levels. One level relates to the big, national story of Israel and continues to deal with the apostasy of the king and the nation. The other level is a personal one, as we now encounter numerous stories about individuals and their faith in God, in contrast to the national rejection of God and his covenant.

✚ The son of a Canaanite woman is raised from the dead in 1 Kings 17, contrasting sharply with the death of King Jeroboam's son in 1 Kings 14.

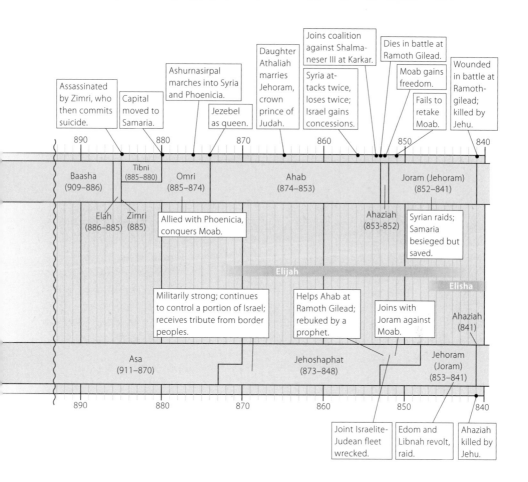

Assassinated by Zimri, who then commits suicide.	Capital moved to Samaria.	Ashurnasirpal marches into Syria and Phoenicia.	Jezebel as queen.	Daughter Athaliah marries Jehoram, crown prince of Judah.	Joins coalition against Shalmaneser III at Karkar.	Syria attacks twice, loses twice; Israel gains concessions.	Dies in battle at Ramoth Gilead.	Moab gains freedom.	Fails to retake Moab.	Wounded in battle at Ramoth-gilead; killed by Jehu.

890   880   870   860   850   840

Baasha (909–886)	Tibni (885–880)	Omri (885–874)	Ahab (874–853)	Joram (Jehoram) (852–841)

Elah (886–885)	Zimri (885)	Allied with Phoenicia, conquers Moab.		Ahaziah (853–852)	Syrian raids; Samaria besieged but saved.

Elijah

Elisha

Militarily strong; continues to control a portion of Israel; receives tribute from border peoples.	Helps Ahab at Ramoth Gilead; rebuked by a prophet.	Joins with Joram against Moab.	Ahaziah (841)

Asa (911–870)	Jehoshaphat (873–848)	Jehoram (Joram) (853–841)

890   880   870   860   850   840

Joint Israelite-Judean fleet wrecked.	Edom and Libnah revolt, raid.	Ahaziah killed by Jehu.

Under Ahab, the northern kingdom of Israel becomes a Baal-worshiping, "Canaanite-like" nation. God sends the prophet Elijah to counter this terrible situation. In 1 Kings 17, Elijah proclaims a drought and famine, a typical judgment from God coming right out of Deuteronomy 28. During this famine God miraculously works through a Canaanite widow from Sidon (note the irony of this, for Jezebel, Ahab's wicked wife, is from Sidon) to provide for Elijah. The son of this widow dies, but Elijah is able to bring the boy back to life! This story authenticates Elijah as a powerful prophet of God. It also underscores the faith of a gentile woman, in contrast to the apostasy of the Israelite nation. It also introduces the theme that in the midst of national apostasy and consequential judgment, God continues to provide for his own and to deliver them.

In 1 Kings 18 Elijah challenges Ahab's and Jezebel's prophets of Baal and Asherah (Baal's female consort) to a direct contest before the entire nation. Elijah, representing the Lord God of Israel, competes with 450 prophets of Baal and 400 prophets of Asherah. The contest involves

Traditional site of Elijah's confrontation with the prophets of Baal

Sea of Galilee

Kishon R.

MEDITERRANEAN SEA

Mt. Carmel Ridge

Jezreel Valley
Megiddo °Jezreel

I S R A E L

Tirzah

Samaria

Shechem

Major International Trade Route

Road

| 0 | 5 | 10 mi |
| 0 | 5 | 10 km |

Location of Mount Carmel, where Elijah defeated the prophets of Baal and Asherah.

building an altar and calling on one's god to send fire to consume the sacrifice on the altar. The prophets of Baal and Asherah go first. They energetically pray, dance, and plead with Baal, but nothing happens. Elijah ridicules them and their god. "Perhaps he is deep in thought," Elijah taunts, "or busy or traveling" (18:27). The Hebrew word translated as "busy" is a euphemism for relieving oneself, so Elijah is poking fun at Baal. When Elijah's turn comes, he soaks the wood of the altar and the sacrifice with water, and then calls on the Lord. Fire immediately comes down and consumes the stone altar, the wood, and the sacrifice. After this demonstration of power the people rally to Elijah, and he orders the execution of all of the prophets of Baal and Asherah. The drought ends, and it starts to rain.

Ahab and Jezebel, however, remain in power, and now Jezebel vows to kill Elijah. He flees into a remote area and becomes rather discouraged and disillusioned, feeling like he is the only true worshiper of God left (19:1–9). God, however, has not given up, and he orders Elijah back to

The Assyrian Empire

Doug Nykolaishen

The heartland of the Assyrian Empire was located in northern Mesopotamia, near the modern city of Mosul in northern Iraq. From there, the Assyrians developed an empire that at times reached southeast as far as the Persian Gulf and southwest through the Fertile Crescent as far as Egypt. The Assyrians' period of greatest power was approximately 911–609 BC, when they created an empire larger than any in the Near East up to that time.

In the early part of this period (911–745 BC), the Assyrians generally defended their empire against outside threats and took plunder and prisoners whenever they could. Sometimes their neighbors felt their presence strongly, as in the battle involving Ahab of Israel (1 Kings 22). At other times they didn't. Both Jeroboam II of Israel (2 Kings 14:23–29) and Uzziah of Judah (2 Chronicles 26) were able to expand their territory without interference from the Assyrians.

Tiglath-Pileser III (745–727 BC), however, also known as Pul, established a different pattern that became typical of subsequent Assyrian kings. During his reign, the large and powerful Assyrian army campaigned annually, extending the territory under the empire's control and putting down any rebellion that might flare up. Such continual warfare, waged either through direct combat or siege, was costly in terms of time and resources. Therefore, the Assyrians frequently attempted to persuade those resisting them to submit without a fight. For example, they might surround a walled city and have one of their officers call out to the city's inhabitants, urging them to end their resistance with the promise of lenient treatment (cf. 2 Kings 18). If this failed, they would attack or lay siege, depending on the situation. After defeating a city, the Assyrians would often cruelly mutilate many of the captured defenders, with flaying and impaling among their favorite techniques. Such tactics earned them a reputation for viciousness, often intimidating the other peoples of the ancient Near East.

Nevertheless, the peoples subjugated by the Assyrians did rebel from time to time. The northern kingdom of Israel rebelled several times. The Assyrians ultimately punished them by taking the population into exile in 722 BC, resettling some of them in cities in the central portion of the empire, and others farther east in the cities of Media (2 Kings 17). Forcing large groups of conquered people to move far away from their homes made it harder for such people to organize rebellion. It also provided labor for the cultivation of farmland and/or for major building projects in Assyrian cities such as Asshur, Nineveh, Calah, and Arbela.

But further rebellions, along with strife among the Assyrian elite, weakened the empire to the point where the Babylonians and Medes were able to capture Nineveh, the capital city, in 612 BC (see Nahum). By 609 BC the Babylonians had taken control of the empire once ruled by Assyria.

The Assyrian king Tiglath-Pileser III.

work. He tells Elijah he still has seven thousand people who worship him. This is part of the "remnant" theme that runs throughout the Old Testament. Even during times of national apostasy, God always has a small "remnant" of faithful believers. Furthermore, God informs Elijah, he still has several important tasks for Elijah to carry out. First, Elijah is to anoint Hazael as king of Aram (Syria) and Jehu as king of Israel. They are the ones who will carry out God's judgment on the house of Ahab. Second, Elijah is to anoint Elisha, who will succeed Elijah as God's prophet (19:15–18).

The Elijah narratives accomplish several important things. Elijah proclaims the prophetic indictment against the house of Ahab for covenant violation. These narratives also reveal a shift in the overall story from the national "big picture" to a focus on individuals. Even during national apostasy and judgment, faithful individuals are saved. Elijah demonstrates that salvation and deliverance, indeed life itself, are available through true worship of God, not through the monarchy and the king's royal religion.

Judgment on Ahab, the prototypical bad king and enemy of the prophets (1 Kings 20–2 Kings 1)

This section focuses on the evil activities of Ahab and the prophetic judgment that falls on him. In 1 Kings 21 Ahab, at the instigation of Jezebel, murders a man named Naboth because this man refused to sell Ahab a certain vineyard. Keep in mind that the land was a gift from God and was not to be sold. Naboth was being faithful to God when he refused to sell his inheritance to the king. Ahab, however, has him framed and then executed so that he can acquire Naboth's land. This story is appropriately surrounded by three episodes that all pronounce judgment on Ahab. These three episodes predict Ahab's death, Jezebel's death, and the death of all of Ahab's male descendants. These prophetic judgments come from an unnamed prophet (20:35–43); Elijah (21:17–24); and the prophet Micaiah (22:1–28). As prophesied, Ahab is killed in battle (22:29–40).

A typical Israelite house in the time of Elijah.

✚ There are many parallels between the miracles of Elijah/Elisha and the miracles of Jesus in the New Testament. Both heal people of leprosy, raise the dead, and feed large groups of people with a small amount of food.

The Babylonian Empire

Doug Nykolaishen

The region of Babylonia is referred to often in the Bible. It appears first in Genesis 10:10, although there and in a few other places it is called the land of Shinar. It is also sometimes called the land of the Chaldeans. In general, its geographic area extended from the vicinity of present-day Baghdad to the Persian Gulf, although from 605 to 539 BC the Babylonian Empire extended throughout most of the ancient Near East.

Even when Babylonians were not dominating the area politically, Babylonian ideas were very influential, and in a number of cases, it seems that biblical authors were intentionally correcting some of these notions. For example, the account of creation in Genesis 1–2 seems to have been presented partly as a corrective to the creation stories popular in Babylonia.

The role the Babylonian Empire would play in the latter parts of the Old Testament was foretold by the prophet Isaiah. When King Hezekiah of Judah (ruled 715–686 BC) received envoys from Babylon, he showed them all the valuables in his storehouses. After the envoys left, Isaiah prophesied that all the king's wealth, as well as Hezekiah's own descendants, would one day be taken away to Babylon (2 Kings 20:12–19).

This prophecy came true a century later. About eight years after the Babylonian king Nabopolassar defeated the Assyrians and took control of their empire, his son, Nebuchadnezzar, forced Judah to begin paying tribute to the new Babylonian Empire (597 BC). Eventually, in 586 BC, Nebuchadnezzar destroyed the city of Jerusalem, including the temple that Solomon had built, and took most of the prominent citizens into captivity, including those of the royal family who were not killed. Each of the books by Ezekiel and Daniel centers on one of these Judean exiles, true prophets who lived as exiles in Babylonia.

The prophets Jeremiah and Habakkuk foresaw that the coming Babylonian onslaught was part of God's judgment on Judah for unfaithfulness to his covenant. At the same time, these prophets, as well as Isaiah, made clear that the Babylonians were idolatrous and were in many ways regarded as the Lord's enemies. This is also how Babylon appears in Daniel 1–5. Each chapter features a power struggle of some kind between the Lord and the Babylonian king.

Under Nebuchadnezzar, Babylonia reached the height of its wealth and power. He carried out an impressive building program in his capital city of Babylon, funded largely by the tribute received from the subjugated peoples of his empire. Yet, only twenty-three years after his death, Babylon had become so weak that the Persians were able to capture the capital quite easily (539 BC) and assume control of the empire.

The reappearance of "Babylon" as the name of the prostitute in Revelation 17–18 seems connected to the pride, idolatry, greed, and ruthlessness characteristic of Babylon in the Old Testament.

Elisha's ministry (2 Kings 2:1–8:15)

In 2 Kings 2, Elijah passes the prophetic mantle to Elisha. This prophet's ministry is characterized by numerous powerful miracles that seem to stress the power and authority of God's prophet. Elisha's many miracles include: crossing the Jordan River (2:13–14); cleansing a town's water supply (2:19–22); striking dead those foolish enough to ridicule God's prophet (2:23–25); giving the Israelites and Judahites victory over the Moabites (3:1–27); making oil to provide for a prophet's widow (4:1–7); raising a boy from the dead (4:8–37); feeding a hundred men with twenty loaves of bread (4:42–44);

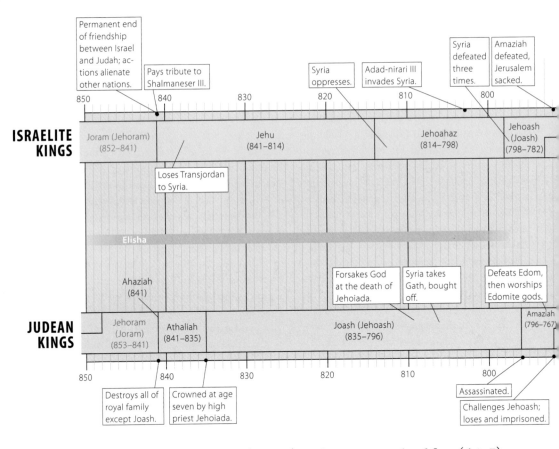

Permanent end of friendship between Israel and Judah; actions alienate other nations.

Pays tribute to Shalmaneser III.

Syria oppresses.

Adad-nirari III invades Syria.

Syria defeated three times.

Amaziah defeated, Jerusalem sacked.

850   840   830   820   810   800

ISRAELITE KINGS

Joram (Jehoram) (852–841)

Jehu (841–814)

Jehoahaz (814–798)

Jehoash (Joash) (798–782)

Loses Transjordan to Syria.

Elisha

Ahaziah (841)

Forsakes God at the death of Jehoiada.

Syria takes Gath, bought off.

Defeats Edom, then worships Edomite gods.

Amaziah (796–767)

JUDEAN KINGS

Jehoram (Joram) (853–841)

Athaliah (841–835)

Joash (Jehoash) (835–796)

850   840   830   820   810   800

Destroys all of royal family except Joash.

Crowned at age seven by high priest Jehoiada.

Assassinated.

Challenges Jehoash; loses and imprisoned.

healing a gentile of leprosy (5:1–27); making an iron axhead float (6:1–7); and defeating an enemy army by blinding them (6:8–23). Clearly it is not the kings who have power, but God's prophet. Remember also that back in Joshua 3–4 it was the ark of the covenant (God's Presence) that was so powerful and that stopped the waters of the Jordan so the people could cross over it. Now the water parts for the prophet Elisha. As in the Elijah stories, these miracles of Elisha show that in spite of national apostasy, God will still care for his faithful people. This unit also underscores that the only way to salvation or deliverance is by the way the Lord God provides. It must be according to his commands and his decrees. No other gods or religions can give life.

The Last Days of Israel (2 Kings 8:16–17:41)

Useless attempts at reform (8:16–12:21)

This section continues to chronicle the reigns of various kings of Israel and Judah, underscoring that both nations are seriously violating the Mosaic

✚ In contrast to Elisha, who feeds one hundred men with twenty loaves of bread (2 Kings 4:42–44), Jesus will feed five thousand men with five loaves and two fish (Mark 6:30–44).

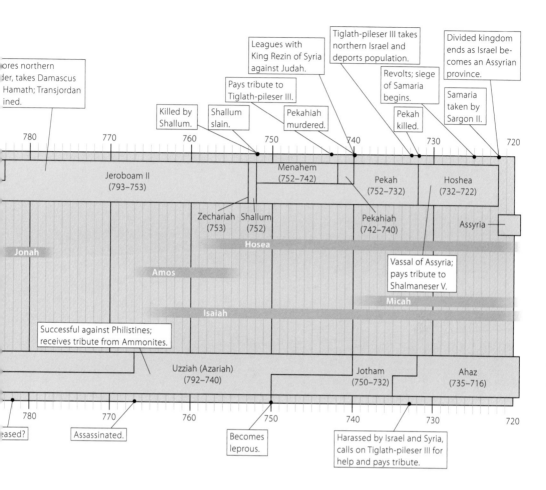

covenant and are not staying faithful to God. The judgment prophesied against the house of Ahab is carried out as Ahab's descendants, as well as Jezebel, are killed (9:30–10:17). Next there are two futile attempts at reforming each nation's pagan worship. Jehu, king of Israel, abolishes Baal worship, but retains the calf idols that Jeroboam had built back when Solomon died (2 Kings 10:18–29). By contrast, Joash, king of Judah, tries very hard to restore true worship of the Lord to Judah and Jerusalem. He works to repair the temple, which had fallen into ruin (12:4–16). The negative momentum, however, is just too great, and Joash's attempt at reform doesn't really stick. The people continue to offer sacrifices at the "high places" (12:3), and his reforms apparently generate quite a bit of opposition, for his officials assassinate him (12:20).

Typical kings, good and bad (mostly bad) (13:1–16:20)

This section tracks the reigns of numerous kings of Israel and Judah. A few of them in Judah are good kings, but the general trend is for the kings

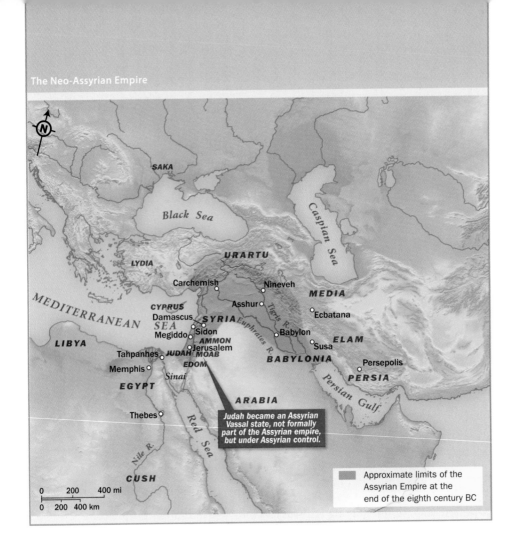

SAKA

Black Sea

Caspian Sea

URARTU

LYDIA

Carchemish

Nineveh

MEDIA

Asshur

Ecbatana

MEDITERRANEAN SEA

CYPRUS

Damascus SYRIA

Euphrates R.

Megiddo Sidon

AMMON

Babylon

ELAM

LIBYA

Tahpanhes JUDAH MOAB

Jerusalem

Susa

Memphis

EDOM

BABYLONIA

Persepolis

Sinai

PERSIA

EGYPT

ARABIA

Persian Gulf

Thebes

Red Sea

Nile R.

Judah became an Assyrian
Vassal state, not formally
part of the Assyrian empire,
but under Assyrian control.

CUSH

| 0 | 200 | 400 mi |
| 0 | 200 | 400 km |

Approximate limits of the
Assyrian Empire at the
end of the eighth century BC

to do "evil in the eyes of the Lord." The good kings are unable to halt the
national momentum of idolatry and pervasive social injustice in the land.

The destruction and exile of Israel (17:1–41)

Inevitably, the end comes for Israel. In 722 BC the Assyrians invade,
conquer Israel, and carry the Israelites off to Assyria in exile (17:1–23).
The king of Assyria then resettles this area with peoples of other nations the
Assyrians had conquered. This is a total reversal of the conquest, as Israel
loses the Promised Land and is replaced by other peoples. The reason for
this is clearly stated in 2 Kings 17: "All this took place because the Israelites
had sinned against the Lord their God, who had brought them up out of
Egypt. . . . They worshiped other gods and followed the practices of the
nations the Lord had driven out before them" (vv. 7–8).

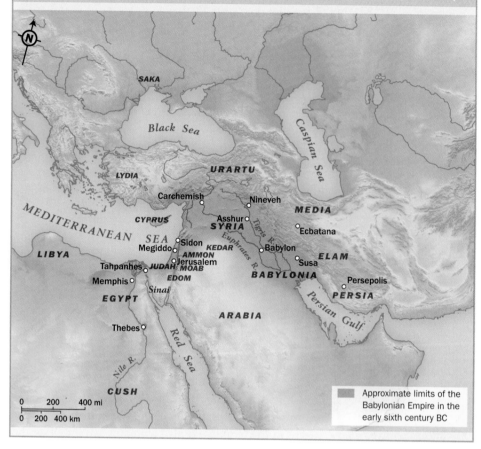

SAKA

Black Sea

Caspian Sea

URARTU

LYDIA

Carchemish

Nineveh

MEDIA

MEDITERRANEAN SEA

CYPRUS

Asshur
SYRIA

Ecbatana

Megiddo
Sidon
KEDAR

Euphrates R.

Tigris R.

Babylon

LIBYA

Tahpanhes
JUDAH
Jerusalem
AMMON
MOAB

ELAM

Susa

BABYLONIA

Persepolis

Memphis

EDOM

Sinai

PERSIA

EGYPT

ARABIA

Persian Gulf

Thebes

Red Sea

Nile R.

CUSH

```
0     200    400 mi
0   200  400 km
```

Approximate limits of the
Babylonian Empire in the
early sixth century BC

The Last Days of Judah (2 Kings 18:1–25:30)

Deliverance from Assyria (18:1–20:21)

Judah lasts for an additional 136 years, probably due to the influence of the few kings of Judah who tried to stay faithful to the Lord. After the Assyrians destroy the northern kingdom of Israel, a few years later they continue southward to attack Judah and Jerusalem as well. King Hezekiah, encouraged and strengthened by the prophet Isaiah, trusts in the Lord, and God miraculously defeats the Assyrian army, removing the Assyrian threat. This miraculous deliverance should be a positive model for Judah to remember in later years, but it appears to be soon forgotten.

A figurine of a Canaanite goddess,
probably Asherah, the consort of Baal.

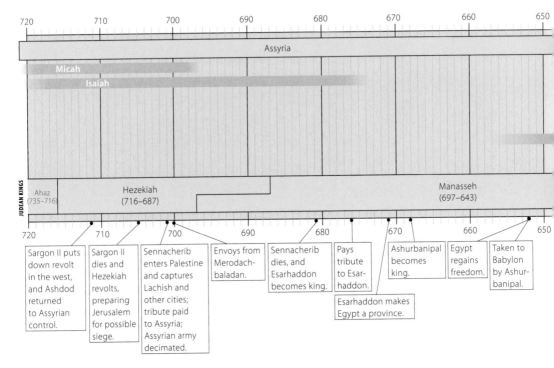

720	710	700	690	680	670	660	650

Assyria

Micah

Isaiah

JUDEAN KINGS

Ahaz (735–716) · Hezekiah (716–687) · Manasseh (697–643)

720	710	700	690	680	670	660	650

| Sargon II puts down revolt in the west, and Ashdod returned to Assyrian control. | Sargon II dies and Hezekiah revolts, preparing Jerusalem for possible siege. | Sennacherib enters Palestine and captures Lachish and other cities; tribute paid to Assyria; Assyrian army decimated. | Envoys from Merodach-baladan. | Sennacherib dies, and Esarhaddon becomes king. | Pays tribute to Esarhaddon. | Ashurbanipal becomes king. | Egypt regains freedom. | Taken to Babylon by Ashurbanipal. |

Esarhaddon makes Egypt a province.

Manasseh, the worst king ever (21:1–26)

Hezekiah is succeeded by his son Manasseh, who is the worst king in Judah's history. He leads the nation into worshiping Baal and Asherah (like Ahab did in the northern kingdom, Israel), even placing an Asherah pole right in the temple. He also worships astral deities and even sacrifices his own son (21:1–9). Judah sinks to new lows during the reign of Manasseh, and they are never able to recover.

The futile attempt of Josiah to reform Judah (22:1–23:30)

The last good king of Judah is Josiah, who tries valiantly to return Judah to a true worship of God. He orders that repairs be made to the temple, and in the process of repairing the temple, the book of Deuteronomy is discovered. Apparently it had been totally lost. Josiah reads it and realizes how serious their sin is. In response, he attempts to remove

This royal cuneiform prism describes the eight military campaigns of the Assyrian king Sennacherib (704–681 BC), including his campaign against Judah.

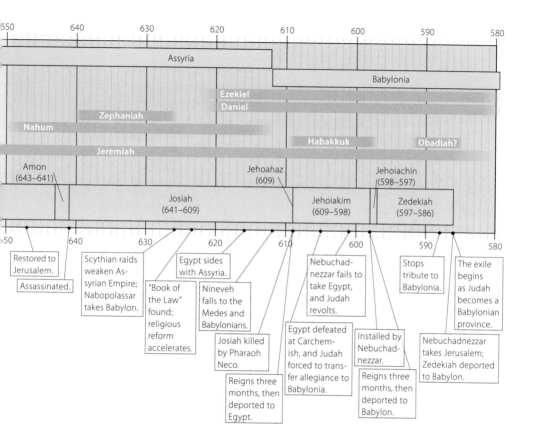

the pagan worship sites and to renew the covenant with the Lord (23:1–25). The negative momentum and the legacy left by Manasseh, however, are too great. Josiah is killed by the Egyptians as they march north to try to help the Assyrians stop the growing Babylonian juggernaut, and the nation of Judah slides right back into idolatry. The end is near.

The destruction of Jerusalem and the exile of Judah (23:31–25:30)

After the death of Josiah, Judah degenerates quickly as the few remaining kings all "did evil in the eyes of the Lord." Finally the end comes. The Babylonians overrun Judah and destroy Jerusalem completely. King Zedekiah, who tries to escape as Jerusalem falls, is captured near Jericho (2 Kings 25:5). The mention of Jericho is ironic, for the great victory at Jericho during the time of Joshua was the beginning of the conquest. Now the conquest is being reversed. It is not Jericho that is destroyed, but Jerusalem. The Israelites are not entering the Promised Land; they are being forced to leave.

The Babylonian army returns to Babylonia, forcing most of the defeated Israelites to go with them as exiles. The Babylonians leave behind a small group of Israelites and appoint a governor to administer Judah for them.

✛ The destruction of Jerusalem and the exile of Judah bring to a close the "Deuteronomy-based history" (Joshua–2 Kings). Israel and Judah have ignored Deuteronomy and thus suffered the dire consequences.

Some of the remaining Israelites, however, foolishly murder the governor and then flee to Egypt, fearing reprisals from the Babylonians. Thus the conquest reversal is complete, as this group actually returns to Egypt (25:22–26).

Another theme running throughout 1–2 Kings is the dismantling of the Solomonic empire. Second Kings 24:13 underscores the final stages of this, as the Babylonians carry off the remaining gold items Solomon had placed in the temple.

Throughout this final unit (23:31–25:30) the narrator of the story repeatedly informs the reader that this destruction and exile was because of Judah's great sin against God, especially the idolatry and child sacrifice initiated by King Manasseh (24:3–4, 20).

So What? Applying 1–2 Kings to Our Lives Today

First and Second Kings teach us a lot about sin and its consequences. On the one hand, if people repeatedly and continuously disobey God and haughtily refuse his calls for repentance, then they can expect to experience terrible judgment. On the other hand, everywhere throughout 1–2 Kings we see the grace and patience of God as he pleads and waits for the people to come around. Likewise, God pleads with his wayward people today to repent and return to him.

From Elijah and Elisha we learn that individuals can remain faithful to God even though the entire society becomes hostile to God and his call for righteous living.

The city of Megiddo guarded the Jezreel Valley and the route from Egypt to Syria. King Josiah is killed here by the Egyptian pharaoh Neco.

Our Favorite Verse in 1–2 Kings

But the Lord was gracious to them and had compassion and showed concern for them because of his covenant with Abraham, Isaac and Jacob. To this day he has been unwilling to destroy them or banish them from his presence. (2 Kings 13:23)

1–2 Chronicles

*Focusing on the Davidic Promise
and Worship in the Temple*

While it is important for us to acknowledge our sin, confess it, and receive forgiveness, it is also important to accept that forgiveness, put our past sin behind us, and move forward. First and Second Kings concludes the Deuteronomy-based history and looks back at the failure of Israel and Judah to obey Deuteronomy; it explains why the terrible judgment (exile) came. First and Second Chronicles opens the Chronicler's history and retells much of the same story but with a forward-looking orientation, in essence saying, "Let's move on."

What Is the Setting for 1–2 Chronicles?

In 539 BC the Persian king Cyrus decrees that the exiled Hebrews can return to their land. This is the final, concluding historical event mentioned in 1–2 Chronicles (2 Chron. 36:23). Yet the genealogies in 1–2 Chronicles extend beyond the decree of Cyrus. The last individual cited in the Davidic genealogy of 1 Chronicles is a man named Anani (1 Chron. 3:24), who was born in about 445 BC. Thus most scholars think that 1–2 Chronicles was written in about 400 BC. This places the setting for the composition of 1–2 Chronicles well after the terrible destruction of Jerusalem and the exile to Babylon in 587/586 BC described at the end of 2 Kings. By 400 BC several groups of exiles have returned to Jerusalem. The events in Ezra and Nehemiah have already taken place, and the rebuilt nation is struggling to move forward while still under Persian domination. Thus while 1–2 Chronicles retells Israel's history from Adam to the decree of Cyrus, the goal of the author seems to be to keep the people focused on two things: (1) the promises to David (regarding the coming future messianic king), giving hope for the future; and (2) proper worship in the temple (what to do in the meantime).

The author of 1–2 Chronicles is not known. Perhaps he was a priest like Ezra concerned with returning the Israelites to a true and proper worship of God centered on the rebuilt temple.

Like 1–2 Samuel and 1–2 Kings, 1–2 Chronicles was originally written as one book. It was split into two books when it was translated into Greek (the Septuagint) because Greek takes more space than Hebrew, and the entire book could no longer fit on one scroll. The original scroll appears to have been untitled. Interestingly, the Septuagint titled this work *Paraleipomena*, which means, "things left out," implying that the book contains additional information not included in 1–2 Samuel and 1–2 Kings. An ancient Hebrew tradition (but probably not original) called it "The book of the events of the days."

What Is at the Heart of 1–2 Chronicles?

First and Second Chronicles basically retell the same history of Israel that was covered in 1–2 Samuel and 1–2 Kings. Yet this is not simply a duplicate history. The author of 1–2 Chronicles seems to assume that the reader is quite familiar with 1–2 Samuel and 1–2 Kings. He is covering the same time period, but with a different emphasis and a different theological purpose. The Chronicler still acknowledges that Israel's sin and disobedience was what led to the exile, but he doesn't beat the reader over the head with this as does the Deuteronomy-based history (Joshua–2 Kings). The Chronicler is looking forward to the future and not back at the exile. Thus he zeroes in on two major themes. First he stresses God's divine covenant with

Bronze trumpet (1000–800 BC). When Solomon brings the ark to the temple, 120 priests blow on their trumpets in celebration. Trumpets play an important role in 1–2 Chronicles, where they are mentioned fifteen times.

An Egyptian wall relief containing a genealogy listing seventy-six Egyptian kings.

David (2 Samuel 7), which promised that a future descendant of David would sit on the throne and rule over Israel perpetually. The Chronicler ignores the many kings of the northern kingdom, Israel, for they are all non-Davidic. The promise and hope for the future, the Chronicler stresses, is tied to the line of David, the kings who ruled over Judah. Thus 1–2 Chronicles only tracks the kings of Judah (unlike 1–2 Kings, which goes back and forth from Judah to Israel). Since the Chronicler is looking forward and trying to focus on the positive aspects of the monarchy, he skips over many of the terrible sins and failures of the kings, especially the big sins of David (the Bathsheba affair) and Solomon (foreign wives and idol worship).

The second major theme of 1–2 Chronicles is worship in the temple. Much of the focus of 1–2 Chronicles is on the construction of the temple and on proper worship. Many of the kings in 1–2 Chronicles are evaluated on how they related to the temple (rather than how they related to Deuteronomy, as in 1–2 Kings).

A very broad outline of 1–2 Chronicles is as follows:

- A Genealogical History from Adam to the Return of the Exiles (1 Chronicles 1–9)
- The Reign (or Nonreign) of Saul (1 Chronicles 10)

✦ In the Hebrew Bible, 1–2 Chronicles comes at the end of the canon. Thus in Matthew 23:35 Jesus covers the entire Old Testament when he condemns Israel for spilling innocent blood from Abel (Genesis) to Zechariah (2 Chronicles).

1–2 Chronicles   213

- The Reign of David (1 Chronicles 11–29)
- The Reign of Solomon (2 Chronicles 1–9)
- The Reigns of the Rest of the Kings of Judah (2 Chronicles 10–36)

What Makes 1–2 Chronicles Interesting and Unique?

- The terrible sins of David and Solomon are not mentioned.
- A strong emphasis on the written word of God runs throughout 1–2 Chronicles.
- The focus of 1–2 Chronicles is positive, looking forward, in contrast to 1 Samuel through 2 Kings, which is negative, looking back.
- The stress on the lineage of David gives 1–2 Chronicles a messianic tone.
- First Chronicles 21:1 is one of the few Old Testament passages that mentions Satan.

What Is the Message of 1–2 Chronicles?

A Genealogical History from Adam to the Return of the Exiles (1 Chronicles 1–9)

Although it is somewhat foreign and strange to us, in 1 Chronicles 1–9 the Chronicler is telling a story through genealogies. In essence he is tracking the line of David from Adam down to the time of the exile. He is also tracking the genealogies of the people who returned to Judah after the exile ended. This is the focus of the concluding genealogies in 1 Chronicles 9:1–34.

Mount Gilboa, where Saul and his son Jonathan were slain (1 Chron. 10:1, 8).

The Role of the Genealogies in the Old Testament and the Ancient Near East

Richard S. Hess

A genealogy consists of a listing of parent-child (usually male) connections extending over more than one generation. In its simplest form this occurs frequently in the Bible and the ancient Near East as a means of identification, *x* son/daughter of *y*. However, the study of genealogies normally focuses on written and oral lists that extend over many generations. Genealogies can represent a single family, such as that of Achan in Joshua 7:1, or they can reflect a list of kings or rulers, such as the chiefs of Edom in Genesis 36. The latter may or may not be biologically related. Most genealogies name a single person in each generation, such as the line of Seth in Genesis 5, but some "segment" into several members of a given generation (cf. the Table of Nations in Genesis 10). Genealogies of many generations occur in the Bible primarily in Genesis and 1 Chronicles. There is also an implicit listing of kings of both the northern and southern kingdoms of Israel and Judah throughout the books of 1 and 2 Kings. Genealogies are found throughout the ancient Near East in Egypt, Assyria, Babylon, and Sumer, as well as elsewhere. Most of these genealogies are king lists.

The oldest king list is the Sumerian King List. It divides kings according to the city from which they reigned and according to those who lived before and after the flood. This may have served to legitimize the rule of Utu-hegel, who defeated the Gutians and established kingship in Sumer in about 2100 BC. It may have done the same for the Isin dynasty (about 2017–1794 BC) in what many believe to have been a later addition to the king list. By connecting a ruler or dynasty to earlier kings and ultimately to a line of divine or semidivine beings, a list such as this argued the same divine approval for the present sovereign.

This form (and its propagandistic purpose) seems to have been copied in later Assyrian, Babylonian, and Seleucid lists, with their own emendations and revisions to establish the legitimacy of other rulers. They may also have added a list of sages or counselors, one to each of the kings before and after the flood. These brought various aspects of culture and spirituality to the human race, much as do the notes attached to the line of Cain in Genesis 4:17–24 (and Enoch in 5:24). Similarities between a few names of these preflood figures and their corresponding kings have led some to note the same in Cain's genealogy and that of Seth (Genesis 5), for example, Enoch and Lamech. However, the Genesis lines are not presented as king lists; aspects of their form differ from that of all the known ancient Near Eastern king lists and other genealogies, and the common names are both identical in spelling (not found with the lists of sages and kings) and located in a different order in the sequence. Indeed, a figure such as Lamech appears to function so that his name is a literary "hinge" in both genealogies. The genealogies of Genesis are also embedded in and act as structuring devices for much larger narratives, unlike the extrabiblical king lists.

Egyptian priestly genealogies have been compared to those of priestly families in 1 Chronicles 6:1–15, 50–53; 9:11–13. The pseudo-Hesiodic Catalogue of Women has been compared to the Table of Nations, but the former's fragmentary nature and strong Greek bias give pause. Finally, some king lists (Ugarit, Hammurabi, and Egyptian mortuary) appear as part of rituals to honor the dead, something not found in biblical genealogies. The latter consistently represent the concerns of the biblical books of which they form a part.

1–2 Chronicles mentions numerous musical instruments. Depicted here are Egyptian women playing lutes and a double oboe.

The Reign (or Nonreign) of Saul (1 Chronicles 10)

This very short account of Saul skips over his life and only records his death. Interestingly, in this chapter he is never actually called a king or said to have reigned. To the Chronicler, apparently, the first real king is David.

The Reign of David (1 Chronicles 11–29)

First Chronicles 11 begins the story of David's reign, skipping over his struggle with Saul as well as David's colorful rise to power, but still stressing God's blessing and providence in his reign. The account of David's capturing Jerusalem is included (11:4–9), in keeping with the focus on the temple. The comments and lists in this section highlight the point that all Israel supported David as the king.

In 1 Chronicles 13–16 David brings the ark to Jerusalem and organizes the nation for worshiping and praising God. As in 2 Samuel 6:1–7, a man named Uzzah is killed for touching the ark in an attempt to steady it (1 Chron. 13:9–10). Here, however, the story explains that this was because David was not transporting the ark correctly. In 15:11–15 the Levites inform David of the correct procedure (they were required to carry the ark with poles). When David follows the proper Levitical procedure, then the

procession goes well. As part of the worship theme, this section also records a number of excerpts from the book of Psalms. First Chronicles 16:8–36 draws from Psalms 96:1–13; 105:1–15; and 106:1, 47–48. These Psalms stress the Lord's deliverance of Israel especially when Israel was small and weak. These words would have been very encouraging for the small, struggling postexilic audience of 1–2 Chronicles.

First Chronicles 17 recounts God's word to Nathan the prophet that establishes the Davidic covenant. In this covenant (also in 2 Samuel 7) God promises to build David a "house" (i.e., dynasty) and to establish a descendant of David on the throne forever. This promise gave hope to the postexilic audience of 1–2 Chronicles, which was under Persian rule, and it also provided the messianic expectation fulfilled by the coming of Jesus.

In 1 Chronicles 18–29 David defeats Israel's enemies (18:1–20:8) and then organizes his empire, focusing on extensive preparations for the building and operation of the temple (22:2–29:25). The strange story of David's census is retold (1 Chron. 21:1–22:1; cf. 2 Sam. 24:1–17), this time implicating Satan as the one who incited David to make the unfortunate census (21:1). The stress on the account in 1 Chronicles 21:1–22:1, however, is on the altar David builds on the threshing floor that he bought from a man named Arunah (21:14–30), for this is the site upon which the temple will be built.

The Reign of Solomon (2 Chronicles 1–9)

The description of Solomon's reign revolves around the two central themes of 1–2 Chronicles: worship in the temple and fulfillment of the Davidic covenant. This section reveals Solomon as an immediate (and yet partial) fulfillment of the Davidic covenant. This section also focuses on the spectacular temple Solomon built. As in 1 Kings 9, the Lord appears to Solomon after the dedication of the temple and calls on him to be obedient. But God seems to look into the future, acknowledge the future covenant violation by Israel, and yet in his grace promises that "if my people, who are called by my name, will humble themselves and pray and seek my face and turn from their wicked ways, then will I hear from heaven and will forgive their sin and will heal their land" (2 Chron. 7:14). This particular verse would have been extremely applicable to the original postexilic audience of 1–2 Chronicles.

The Reigns of the Rest of the Kings of Judah (2 Chronicles 10–36)

As mentioned above, this part of 2 Chronicles differs from the account in 2 Kings in that the Chronicler only tracks the reigns of the kings of Judah and omits the kings of Israel. Also, several of the kings are portrayed in a more favorable light in 2 Chronicles than in 2 Kings, for some even repent of their evil ways (Manasseh, for example; 2 Chron. 33:10–16). Another difference is that in keeping with the overall theme of 1–2 Chronicles, the kings in this unit are often evaluated in light of how they related to the temple. Finally, 2 Kings ends with the destruction of Jerusalem and the exile, while 2 Chronicles ends with the decree of Cyrus, which allowed the Hebrew exiles to return to Judah and rebuild the temple (2 Chron. 36:22–23).

✠ The edict of Cyrus cited at the very end of 2 Chronicles is cited again (more completely) at the beginning of Ezra, the very next book (Ezra 1:2–4), tying these two books together.

So What? Applying 1–2 Chronicles to Our Lives Today

First and Second Chronicles teaches us that even if we find ourselves in difficult circumstances, we should grasp God's promises and continue to worship him wholeheartedly. Likewise, if we mess up and sin, then we should humble ourselves and repent. We should then claim God's forgiveness and move on in life, putting our sinful past behind us.

Our Favorite Verse in 1–2 Chronicles

If my people, who are called by my name, will humble themselves and pray and seek my face and turn from their wicked ways, then will I hear from heaven and will forgive their sin and will heal their land. (2 Chron. 7:14)

The Siloam Inscription. In preparing for the Assyrian invasion, King Hezekiah of Judah constructed a tunnel that would supply his fortress in Jerusalem with water. Faintly inscribed on this stone (taken from the wall of the tunnel) is a description of the construction of the tunnel.

✦ Interestingly, 2 Chronicles 36:23 ends in the middle of a sentence, "Let him go up." In the opening verses of Ezra, the sentence is completed, "Let him go up *to Jerusalem in Judah and build the temple of the Lord, the God of Israel*" (Ezra 1:3).

Ezra

Rebuilding the Temple and the People of God

As we know by experience, it is easier to break things than to fix them, and easier to tear things down than to rebuild them. The book of Ezra is about fixing things—rebuilding the temple (destroyed by the Babylonians in 587/586 BC) and rebuilding the people of Israel (shattered emotionally and theologically, and exiled from the land by the Babylonians). Ezra is about the long and difficult road of reconstruction, and how God's hand is at work to bring about that restoration according to his plan.

What Is the Setting for Ezra?

The ending to the story that runs from Exodus to 2 Kings is sad, but clear. God had delivered Israel from Egypt and placed them in a wonderful Promised Land. He gave them the Mosaic covenant (Exodus–Deuteronomy) and told them if they stay faithful to him and keep his commandments, then they would live happily ever after in the Promised Land with God himself right in their midst. But if they didn't, God warned (Deuteronomy 28), they would be banished from the land and his blessings.

Starting in Judges and climaxing in 2 Kings, the tragic story of Israel is that they do not stay faithful to God and they do not even come close to keeping his commandments (especially Deuteronomy). Eventually, God's patience runs out and the judgment comes (as clearly predicted in Deuteronomy). Jerusalem is destroyed, and the people are exiled to Babylonia (587/586 BC). This is the sad ending of the story in 2 Kings.

The book of Ezra picks up the story in 538 BC. Cyrus, king of Persia, has overthrown the Babylonians and now controls the regions where the exiled Israelites currently live, as well as their devastated homeland. He promptly issues a decree allowing the Israelites to return to their homeland and rebuild their temple. Ezra 1–6 tells the story of the first wave of exiles to return to Jerusalem, led by a man named Zerubbabel, and their struggle to rebuild the temple. These events take place in 538–515 BC. Time passes, and in 458 BC Ezra shows up in the story, bringing the second wave of returned exiles with him (Ezra 7–10). The events in Nehemiah, closely related to the story in Ezra, begin in 445 BC and describe the third wave of Hebrew exiles to return to the land.

Throughout Ezra (and Nehemiah) the story clearly and repeatedly reminds the reader that Israel is under the domination of the Persians. This is a constant reminder that a Davidic king does not sit on the throne in Jerusalem. Thus the wonderful time of restoration promised by the prophets is still future.

The earliest manuscripts, both in Hebrew and Greek (the Septuagint), combine Ezra and Nehemiah into one book, indicating that it was probably originally composed as one book. Our English Bibles separate it into two separate books following the tradition set by the Latin Vulgate, followed by Wycliffe in the first English translation of the Bible. The

Clay tablet containing a list of the titles and conquests of Darius the Great (521–486 BC).

author of Ezra–Nehemiah is not stated, but Ezra himself is the most likely candidate.

Ezra and Nehemiah are included in the Historical Books, but are part of the subunit we have called the "Chronicler's history" (1–2 Chronicles, Ezra, Nehemiah, Esther). Thus Ezra–Nehemiah is closely connected to 1–2 Chronicles. In fact, the ending of 2 Chronicles (36:23) is a partial citation of the decree of Cyrus, and Ezra 1:2–4 cites the same decree with the exact same wording, but completes an important verse. In 2 Chronicles 36:23 the verse ends with "let him go up." Ezra 1:3 finishes the sentence, "let him go up to Jerusalem in Judah and build the temple of the Lord." Ezra thus picks up the end of the story in 2 Chronicles and quickly introduces one of the main themes of his book—returning to Jerusalem and rebuilding the temple.

What Is at the Heart of Ezra?

There are two central themes of Ezra: rebuilding the temple and reconstituting the people of God. Nehemiah will later add a third theme: rebuilding the walls of Jerusalem. After the destruction of Jerusalem and the exile, the return of the Jews back to Jerusalem and the reconstruction of the temple are nothing short of miraculous. Indeed, the prophets had proclaimed that after the judgment, there would be a glorious restoration of Israel to the land. Perhaps this is it!

Ezra, however, as well as Nehemiah and the postexilic prophets Haggai, Zechariah, and Malachi, gives the sobering answer, no. This return is not the wonderful, glorious restoration promised by the prophets. The very constant presence of Persian monarchial power throughout the story of Ezra and Nehemiah is a stark reminder that Israel very definitely does not have a Davidic king on the throne and does not rule over the gentile nations (as the prophets prophesied). Furthermore, conspicuously missing from Ezra's account of the temple reconstruction is the Presence of God. The Lord does not come to fill the temple with his Presence as he did in the case of the tabernacle in Exodus 40:34–38 and the Solomonic temple in 1 Kings 8:10–11, so the glorious restoration must still be in the future.

So what is happening in Ezra? God is setting the stage for the coming of the Messiah. For a Davidic king and deliverer to come from Israel, the nation must stay intact and maintain a national identity. So God preserves the nation, albeit in remnant form. In the meantime, while they wait for the great coming restoration, those Jews who are back in the Promised Land are to continue worshiping the God of their fathers. Only as they stay faithful

✚ Ezra 1:3 finishes the uncompleted sentence at the end of 2 Chronicles 36:23, thus tying the two books closely together.

Ezra   223

to the Lord in worship and in obedience to his commandments will they be able to keep focused on the coming messianic hope, the fulfillment of the Davidic and Abrahamic covenants. Finally, even though the re-establishment of Israel described in Ezra and Nehemiah falls short of the glorious restoration promised by the prophets, it is nonetheless a significant start. It is a reminder that God has not abandoned his people and that he is moving forward with his plan to fulfill his promises.

The outline of Ezra reflects the two time eras covered in the book as well as the two major themes:

- Rebuilding the Temple (1–6) (538–515 BC)
- Reconstituting the People of God (7–10) (445 BC)

What Makes Ezra Interesting and Unique?

- Ezra is a priest and a teacher of the law.
- Numerous Persian kings are mentioned in the book of Ezra.
- Curiously, the temple is rebuilt, but there is no mention of the Presence of God returning to the temple.
- The book of Ezra is connected tightly to both 1–2 Chronicles and Nehemiah.
- God can be seen working behind the scenes in the book of Ezra, but he does not do any spectacular, public miracles as in the days of Moses or Elijah and Elisha.
- One of the major problems that Ezra confronts is intermarriage between the Israelites and pagan worshipers.

What Is the Message of Ezra?

Rebuilding the Temple (1–6) (538–515 BC)

The book of Ezra opens with the reign of the Persian king Cyrus and his decree that allowed the Jews to return home (538 BC). Ezra stresses that this decree of Cyrus fulfilled the word spoken by the prophet Jeremiah. Ezra is probably referring to Jeremiah's prophecy that Israel would return after seventy years in exile (see Jer. 25:10–12; 29:10). Ezra also points out clearly that God moved the heart of Cyrus to make this decree. Ezra 1:5 states that God moved the hearts of the family leaders of Benjamin and Judah, along with the priests, to take advantage of Cyrus's decree and move back to their

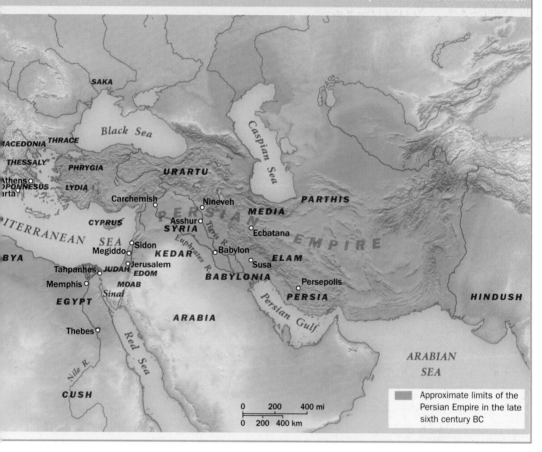

The Persian Empire in the time of Ezra/Nehemiah

Approximate limits of the Persian Empire in the late sixth century BC

homeland. Ezra 1:6–11 describes how they prepared for their task by taking up a collection of silver and gold that was to be used in rebuilding the temple. Ezra 2 is a registry of those who returned.

In Ezra 3 the Israelites return and obediently rebuild the altar, offering sacrifices on it in accordance with the law of Moses (and in contrast to the disobedience of the Israelites before the exile). A leader named Zerubbabel arrives, quickly organizes the Israelites, and begins the temple reconstruction, laying the foundations (3:7–11). This ragtag group of returned exiles, however, cannot possibly match the resources that Solomon poured into the temple, so their reconstructed temple is but a poor and shabby shadow of the Solomonic temple, evident already just from the size of the foundations. Thus reconstruction of the foundations brings a mixed reaction from the people—joy because they have actually started on the reconstruction of the temple, and sorrow because what they are able to build pales in comparison to the original temple Solomon built (3:11–13).

✚ Isaiah prophesied that King Cyrus of Persia would be the one who allows Israel to return to the land and rebuild Jerusalem and the temple (Isa. 44:28).

The Persian Kings

Doug Nykolaishen

When Cyrus II took control of the city of Babylon in 539 BC, the Babylonian Empire passed into the hands of the Persians. In many ways the Persians continued the practices of their predecessors, the Assyrians and Babylonians. They expanded their empire until it stretched from India to Greece, and they required their subjects to pay high taxes. Even the practice of allowing some of their exiled subjects to return to their homeland, which contributed to Cyrus's fame, had been used by the Assyrians and Babylonians before him.

The Persian kings were committed to doing anything that looked as though it would strengthen their power. For example, they wanted their subjects to believe that Persian rule was divinely appointed. In ancient times, whoever rebuilt a destroyed temple was thereby claiming to have been chosen by the god of that temple to rule over the people who worshiped that god. Cyrus does this in 2 Chronicles 36/Ezra 1. His aim is to assert that the Lord God of Israel had chosen him to rule over the Jews. Darius also takes similar action (Ezra 6). In addition, the strengthening of outlying areas was always an important military strategy, which is probably why Artaxerxes decides to allow Nehemiah to rebuild the walls around Jerusalem (Nehemiah 2). Of course, the kings were always on the lookout for individuals who could contribute to Persian well-being and increase the security of Persia. These motives play out in Daniel 6 and the book of Esther.

In contrast to the actions of the Assyrian and Babylonian kings recorded in the Old Testament, which usually bring hardship and destruction to Israel or Judah, the actions of the Persian kings usually seem to help them. This may give the impression that the biblical writers viewed the Persian monarchs as benevolent, and were perhaps even content to remain under their rule. The actions of these kings recorded in the Bible, however, were actually part of their attempt to consolidate political power and gain favor with their subjects. The Israelites were not the only people who benefited from their policies, and most of the Persian subjects understood their emperors' aims. In fact, it was not unusual for the kinds of favorable treatment extended to the Israelites and others to be reversed suddenly if the Persian king thought that such a course would be to his advantage. Therefore, the writers of Chronicles, Ezra, Nehemiah, Esther, Isaiah, and Daniel did not intend to portray the Persian kings as sincere worshipers of the Lord or as being especially friendly toward Israel, nor did they expect their readers to get such an impression. Rather, they marveled at how the sovereign Lord used the political strategies of these powerful kings to bring about the promised restoration of his people from exile.

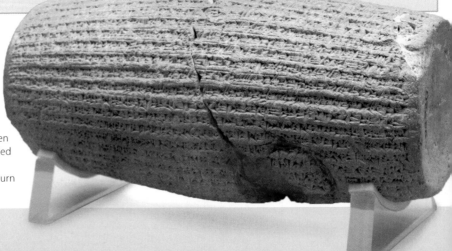

The Cyrus Cylinder describes how Cyrus captured Babylon and then allowed the exiled nationalities in Babylonia to return to their homes.

Opposition to the reconstruction of Jerusalem and Israel's temple begins in Ezra 4:1 and continues throughout Ezra and even until the end of Nehemiah. Political intrigue, deception, and maneuvering occur as local enemies try to convince the Persian kings to oppose any reconstitution of Jerusalem and the temple there. As mentioned above, Ezra 1–6 is a historical account of events that take place in 538–515 BC, but in Ezra 4:6–23 there is a parenthetical break as the narrative presents the correspondence between later enemies of the Jews and King Artaxerxes, who reigned much later (465–424 BC). The distressing situation that developed because of Artaxerxes' letter recorded in Ezra 4:18–23 is the setting for the opening of Nehemiah 1. Ezra apparently includes this story from a later time because it connects to the theme of opposition.

Ezra 5–6 returns back to 518 BC. A letter is sent to Darius, now the reigning monarch in Persia, questioning if the reconstruction of Jerusalem and the temple there is to be permitted. Darius searches the archives and recovers Cyrus's decree, thus allowing the Jews to finish the temple. In 6:14–15 the temple is completed, and a dedication service is held (6:16–18), followed by a Passover (6:19–22). On the one hand, God is clearly at work to move the hearts of the pagan Persian monarchs to allow the Jews to rebuild the temple. On the other hand, there is no mention of the Presence of God returning to this temple, a glaring and highly significant absence. The Jews are back in the land and the temple is rebuilt, but things are not back to the way they were. Things are quite different. The Presence of God has not come to dwell in the temple, there is no Davidic king on the throne, and the Persians rule over Jerusalem.

Reconstituting the People of God (7–10) (445 BC)

Ezra 6 concludes Ezra's historical account of the first wave of Jewish exiles who returned to Jerusalem and rebuilt the temple. These events took place in 538–515 BC. In Ezra 7 the story jumps ahead to the time of Ezra. The year is now 458 BC, and Ezra is one of the characters in the story.

Ezra travels from Babylon to Jerusalem accompanied by a significant group of Israelites (Levites, singers, temple servants, etc.). He is a priest, but his specialty is the law of Moses (7:1–10). He arrives with a letter of strong support from the Persian king Artaxerxes (7:11–26). The story makes it clear, however, that it is really God who is behind these events and who is supporting Ezra. There are numerous references in Ezra 7–8 to the "hand of the Lord" or similar phrases like "the good hand of my God," indicating God's active but behind-the-scenes involvement (7:6, 9, 28; 8:18, 22, 31).

A Persian king, either Darius the Great or Xerxes, seated on his throne, with the crown prince behind him.

Ezra 8 tells the story of their journey from Babylon to Jerusalem. They are carrying a lot of gold and silver, but Ezra does not want to ask the king for soldiers to protect them. Instead, they look to God for protection on their trip, and they arrive safely (8:21–32).

When Ezra arrives, the major problem he encounters is that many of the Jews back in Judah and Jerusalem have been intermarrying with foreign unbelievers. This is a serious problem and is the focus of Ezra 9–10, as well as Nehemiah 13:23–27. Keep in mind the important background for this issue. In the time of the conquest, when Israel was moving into the Promised Land, God told them specifically that they could not intermarry with the Canaanites and other inhabitants of the land because such intermarriages would lead them away from God and into idolatry. This had nothing to do with race or ethnicity. Interracial or interethnic marriages were allowed, but only with those who were from outside the land (Deut. 21:10–14; Num. 12:1). The issue is theological, not racial. After the Israelites move into Canaan, however, they repeatedly violate the prohibition against marrying Canaanites (Judg. 3:5–6). The theological problem of marrying those who worship idols is also explicitly stressed in the story of Solomon, whose wives led him away from the Lord and into the worship of idols (1 Kings 11:4–6). Both Ezra and Nehemiah know that the judgment on Jerusalem and the terrible exile to Babylonia were due to the apostasy of Israel as they forsook their God and turned to worshiping idols, and that one of the underlying causes for this was intermarriage with idol worshipers. Thus both vigorously oppose such marriages. When Ezra finds out about it, he tears his tunic, pulls hair from his head and beard, and sits down, appalled (9:3). He then prays a long prayer of intercessory confession on behalf of the Israelites (9:5–15), and then convinces the people to divorce these foreign, unbelieving wives and to confess their sin (10:1–17). The book of Ezra ends, somewhat awkwardly, with a list of those who had intermarried.

Recall that Ezra and Nehemiah were originally composed as one book. So the intermarriage issue of Ezra 9–10 is connected immediately to the

✚ The books of Ezra and Nehemiah are closely interconnected; they were originally combined together as one book.

situation that Nehemiah hears about in Nehemiah 1—things are on the decline in Jerusalem and not going well.

So What? Applying Ezra to Our Lives Today

The book of Ezra teaches us that God is sovereign and in control, even though we don't always see his direct hand in things. Often God works slowly (it seems to us) and behind the scenes, but he has his plans, and he moves his program along according to his timing and not ours. Our job is to trust in him and to continue worshiping him.

The book of Ezra resonates with us because God does not work directly through spectacular miracles in this book (as he did, say, in Exodus or in 1–2 Kings). Thus the way God works in Ezra is more similar to how he works in our lives (with some exceptions). In Exodus the people see God's glory demonstrated in spectacular miracles (the plagues, the parting of the Red Sea) and in his very Presence (the cloud, fire, and smoke on Mount Sinai). In Ezra the encounters are different. For example, in Ezra 1:5 the text states, "Everyone whose heart God had moved" returned to Jerusalem. This is very similar to the way in which God usually works in our lives today.

Related to this is the reality that carrying out God's will and furthering his kingdom on earth can be frustrating and challenging. This was true for Israel's leaders in the book of Ezra, and it is true for us today. Leaders must cling to God's Word and his promises. Indeed, Ezra reminds us how important the Word of God is and how important it is that we know and understand God's Word, especially when we undertake difficult and challenging tasks.

Our Favorite Verse in Ezra

The gracious hand of our God is on everyone who looks to him, but his great anger is against all who forsake him. (8:22)

Friezes of griffins (composite animals) decorated the walls of the Persian palace at Susa.

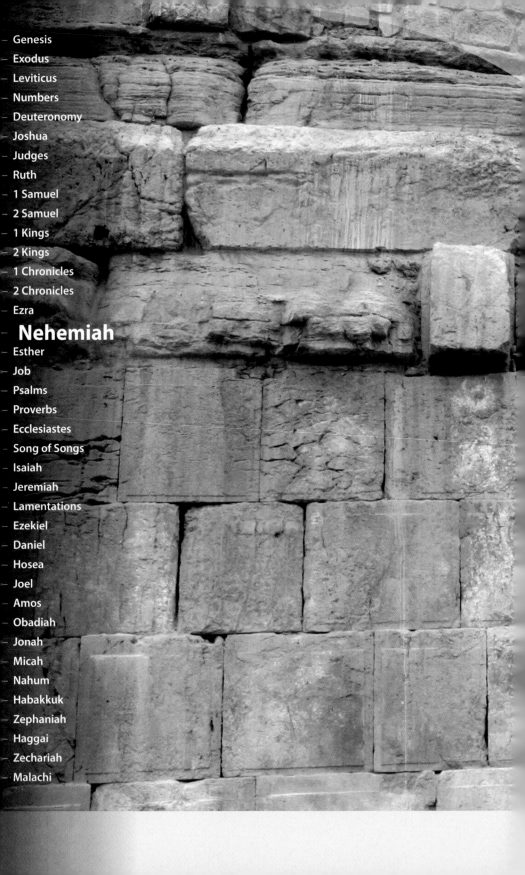

Nehemiah

Rebuilding the Walls and the People of Jerusalem

There is something exciting about construction projects, especially something big, like a new skyscraper or a new sports stadium. The process is really quite incredible. At first there is nothing but an empty field. Then the bulldozers show up and start pushing dirt around. Soon the concrete trucks come and start pouring concrete for the foundations. To this point things have moved slowly and there is not much to see. But then, once the concrete in the foundations has dried, the steel frames come up quickly, and we see the new building or stadium rise up miraculously right before our eyes. Eventually the project is completed, and often there is a dedication celebration or opening-day ceremony.

The book of Nehemiah is about a construction project—rebuilding the walls of Jerusalem. It is a story about how divine intervention and divine enablement combined with good leadership and hard work to complete a huge project in an impossibly short period of time, in spite of formidable opposition. Yet the walls of Jerusalem, while critically important, are only half of the story, for the book of Nehemiah is also about the reconstruction of the people of Jerusalem.

What Is the Setting for Nehemiah?

The Deuteronomy-based history (Joshua through 2 Kings) tells the sad story of how Israel repeatedly rebels against God and abandons him for idol worship. Eventually, as the prophets had continually warned, judgment comes, and Israel loses its right to live in the Promised Land. In 587/586 BC the Babylonians capture Jerusalem and destroy it. They also round up most of the inhabitants and force them to move to Babylonia. This is known as the exile. After seventy years in exile, in fulfillment of God's promise (Jer. 25:12–14), the Persians, who now control the region, allow the shattered Hebrews to return home. The books of Ezra and Nehemiah tell the story of that return.

The Jews return to Jerusalem in three waves. A leader named Zerubbabel leads the first group back in 538 BC. For the next twenty years or so they struggle to rebuild the temple, finally completing it in about 515 BC. This story is told in Ezra 1–6. In 458 BC Ezra, a priest and teacher of the law, leads another group of Jews from Persia

back to Jerusalem and then tries to get the Jews in Jerusalem reorganized so they can worship God properly (Ezra 7–10). Nehemiah, appointed by the Persians to be governor over Judah, brings a third group back in 445 BC with the primary goal of rebuilding the walls of Jerusalem (Nehemiah 1–7). Like Ezra, Nehemiah knows that obedience to God is the most crucial thing, and thus he also gets rather involved in trying to get the people to stay on track in their worship and in their day-to-day obedience to God. These two remarkable leaders, Ezra and Nehemiah, provide a one-two punch, working together to build Jerusalem and Judah back up from the ashes.

Originally the books of Ezra and Nehemiah were combined together as one book. All of the earliest Hebrew manuscripts and Greek translations (the Septuagint) have Ezra and Nehemiah as one book. Only later in Bible translation history were the two split into separate books. The author of Ezra/Nehemiah is not identified. Both books tell part of their story in first person (I, me, us, etc.), but the use of first-person pronouns in the Old Testament does not necessarily indicate autobiographical authorship. It is possible that Nehemiah wrote Ezra/Nehemiah, but it is perhaps more likely that Ezra wrote it (Ezra is described as a priest and scribe, skilled in reading and understanding the Law of Moses; Ezra 7:6, 10, 11; Neh. 8:1–3, 9, 13).

What Is at the Heart of Nehemiah?

The book of Nehemiah tells the miraculous story of how Jerusalem is re-established in the postexilic period. First of all, in spite of serious opposition from those who were enemies of the Jews, Nehemiah, the new governor, rebuilds the walls of Jerusalem, thus providing the city with a means to defend itself, re-establishing the city as a viable political entity. The book of Ezra focuses on rebuilding the temple. With a rebuilt temple (Ezra) and a rebuilt city wall (Nehemiah), the physical components are in place for a rebuilt people. Rebuilding the people around a true worship of God is probably the true ultimate goal of both Ezra and Nehemiah; the temple and the wall are just part of the means. Thus the latter half of Nehemiah focuses on his efforts to address internal problems and to get the Jews who are back in Judah to follow and obey God faithfully. The reality is that rebuilding the nation is perhaps more difficult than rebuilding the wall or the temple. Both Ezra and Nehemiah struggle with this, and as the book of Nehemiah ends, the jury is still out on whether the people are going to remain faithful to God without Nehemiah standing right over them watching.

Stone wall relief of Persian soldiers from the Persian palace at Susa.

The story of Nehemiah can be outlined as follows:

- Rebuilding the Walls of Jerusalem (1:1–7:3)
  - Prayer and preparation (1:1–2:9)
  - Construction begins in spite of regional opposition (2:10–3:32)
  - More opposition and response (4:1–23)
  - Internal problems (5:1–19)
  - Failed attempts to frighten Nehemiah (6:1–14)
  - The completion of the wall (6:15–7:3)
- Rebuilding the Nation of Israel (7:4–12:26)
  - A list of those who had returned (7:4–73)
  - Hearing and understanding the law (8:1–18)
  - Confession of sin (9:1–37)
  - The leaders and the people pledge to keep the law (9:38–10:39)
  - The new inhabitants of Jerusalem (11:1–12:26)
- Dedicating the Wall (12:27–47)
- Disobedience of the People: Is the Work of Nehemiah All in Vain? (13:1–31)

What Makes Nehemiah Interesting and Unique?

- The race to rebuild the wall before Israel's enemies can mobilize and attack is an exciting, suspenseful story.
- Nehemiah gives us a good model for leadership.
- The story connects the success of Nehemiah to his good leadership,

A wealthy but unknown Persian (or Median) man wearing what was perhaps typical formal dress for the Persian court.

Old Testament Fortifications

Boyd Seevers

Biblical texts and archaeological discoveries tell us about the fortifications that protected cities during the time of the Old Testament. Large fortified cities were typically built on *tels*—hills that provided natural defense and gradually rose higher as the city was destroyed and rebuilt multiple times. These cities usually had outer protective walls with one or more gates for people to enter or exit the city. Abraham sat at such a gate at Hebron when he purchased the cave to bury Sarah (Genesis 23). This probably occurred during the Middle Bronze period (2000–1550 BC) when many cities had massive fortifications that included a city wall, gate(s), glacis (a steep artificial earthen slope built below the city wall to protect it from attackers), and bastions or projections from the wall to help with its defense.

The subsequent Late Bronze period (1550–1200 BC) witnessed a general cultural decline that affected fortifications, so by the time the Israelites left Egypt and returned to Canaan, many cities were apparently rather vulnerable. Some still used the strong earlier defenses (see Deut. 1:28). Most had little to help ward off attackers other than building homes in a ring so that their connected, exterior walls formed a simple type of city wall. This general weakness probably helped Joshua's conquest (see Josh. 10:29–39) and continued through the time of the judges during Iron Age I (1200–1000 BC).

The cultural and population resurgence experienced in about 1000 BC was likewise reflected in city fortifications. Archaeologists have uncovered the corner of a fortified building, perhaps a palace/fortress for Saul at his home in Gibeah (1 Sam. 10:26), north of Jerusalem. No fortifications have definitively been connected to David, but Solomon's fortifications at the key sites of Gezer, Megiddo, and Hazor (1 Kings 9:15) are apparently reflected in the similar gates and walls found there. The gates all have six chambers, perhaps for storage or guards, and are connected to casemate walls, made of parallel walls a few yards apart with adjoining perpendicular walls that form rooms. These rooms were used as living space during peacetime (note Rahab in Jericho's wall—Josh. 2:15) and filled with rubble to form a solid wall during wartime.

Iron Age II (1000–586 BC) saw Israelite fortifications flourish. Major cities had strong, solid city walls up to twenty-three feet thick, with towers and bastions. A few cities like Jerusalem (2 Kings 20:20) and Megiddo also had impressive water systems hewed through bedrock that enabled residents to access water even during times of siege. But all these cities had fallen to conquerors by 586 BC, and those like Nehemiah who helped rebuild these fortifications in the postexilic period would have struggled with far fewer resources than in earlier days. Likewise, they would have been rebuilding smaller cities for smaller populations.

his hard work, his perseverance, and the providence of God—a very interesting mix.

- Nehemiah prays frequently throughout the story.
- Nehemiah's external challenge (the wall) is easier to deal with than his internal challenge (the faithfulness of the people).
- The dedication of the rebuilt wall is celebrated by men and women both with singing and great joy.

What Is the Message of Nehemiah?

Rebuilding the Walls of Jerusalem (1:1–7:3)

Prayer and preparation (1:1–2:9)

The background for the opening of Nehemiah is Ezra 4:7–23, in which Artaxerxes, king of Persia, sent a letter to the officials over the region of Judah and Jerusalem, forbidding any attempt to rebuild Jerusalem. Nehemiah, a Hebrew and a fairly high-ranking official in the service of King Artaxerxes, is living in Susa, one of the Persian capitals, and he receives a very negative report from Jerusalem of the consequences of this decree. Nehemiah takes this problem to the Lord, praying and fasting for days as he formulates a plan (1:1–11). After praying seriously for days, Nehemiah approaches King Artaxerxes and asks if he could return to his home and rebuild Jerusalem. Remember that Artaxerxes has already prohibited any rebuilding of Jerusalem (Ezra 4:18–23), so Nehemiah is quite bold in this request. The king, however, grants his daring request, and even adds things Nehemiah didn't have the nerve to ask for (like a military escort, 2:9; official Persian troops are going to come in handy for Nehemiah in the difficult days to come). Nehemiah attributes his spectacular success to "the hand of God."

Construction begins in spite of regional opposition (2:10–3:32)

Jerusalem, however, is a long way from Persia, and three powerful regional rulers (Sanballat of Samaria, Tobiah the Ammonite, and Geshem the Arab) ignore Nehemiah's letter of authority from Artaxerxes, opposing anyone who seeks to restore Jerusalem to power (2:10, 19). So far, Nehemiah has not told anyone that he plans to rebuild the walls. Secretly at night, he inspects the ruins of the walls (2:11–16). Pointing out that God is behind this project, Nehemiah calls on the Israelites in Jerusalem to join with him in rebuilding the walls, and the people agree (2:17–18).

The construction begins! Nehemiah 3 explains how the work is divided among the people. Various sections of the wall, as well as the critical gates, are assigned to specific families, guilds of workers, or people from certain towns. A very interesting and wide range of people participate, including priests, individual families, goldsmiths, merchants, perfume makers, and administrators. Interestingly, one man named Shallum repaired his section of the wall with the help of his daughters (3:12). The scope of this project is huge; the length of wall Nehemiah is trying to rebuild is one and a half miles long, including numerous gates.

More opposition and response (4:1–23)

When Nehemiah's enemies find out construction on Jerusalem's walls has actually started, their opposition grows stronger. They publicly ridicule the project, seeking to discourage the workers (4:1–3). In response, Nehemiah and his fellow workers pray and continue to make great progress on the wall (4:4–6). Unsuccessful with their strategy of public ridicule, Nehemiah's enemies now form a military coalition and conspire to attack Jerusalem before the walls can be completed. The threat of a military attack changes the stakes for those working on the wall in Jerusalem. Many of the builders, as well as those Jews living around Jerusalem, become frightened and discouraged

Wall frieze of Persian soldiers from the Persian palace at Susa. Nehemiah was probably grateful to have a unit of Persian soldiers with him

(4:10–12). Nehemiah, however, responds by calling on his people to trust in God. In addition, he prepares them for war, arming his workers and posting a guard. Nehemiah 4:16 mentions "my men," probably a reference to the professional Persian troops the king sent with Nehemiah when he made the trip from Persia. Nehemiah did not have the nerve to ask for these troops, but God had worked behind the scenes to move the king to provide them anyway. With an attack looming, these well-armed professional troops are a huge asset. The workers on the wall keep working, but they also keep their swords and spears nearby, thwarting any possibility of a surprise attack and an easy victory for their enemies.

Internal problems (5:1–19)

Having held off the military threat of his enemies, Nehemiah now has to deal with some internal problems, primarily economic ones. The wealthier and more powerful Jews in Judah and Jerusalem are exploiting and oppressing their poorer countrymen. This situation is hampering the construction of the wall, as well as any hopes of rebuilding the society (5:1–5). Nehemiah gets downright angry at this (5:6), and he rebukes the Israelite nobles and officials who are responsible, ordering them to give back the fields, produce,

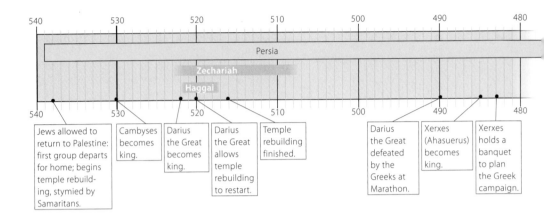

and money they had extorted unethically (5:7–13). Nehemiah then makes it very clear that he, personally, has not come to Jerusalem for the money, but to serve God (5:14–19). Nehemiah thus provides a good model for leadership among God's people, for he is not in it for the money.

Failed attempts to frighten Nehemiah (6:1–14)

As the wall nears completion, Nehemiah's enemies step up their efforts to stop him. They plot to assassinate him (6:1–4), and then they accuse him of treason against the king (6:5–7). They also try to persuade him to run and hide so they could then discredit him before the people (6:10–13). Nehemiah responds to these threats against him by praying and by continuing the work (6:9, 14).

The completion of the wall (6:15–7:3)

Nehemiah turns the tables on his enemies who were trying to frighten him in 6:1–14, for in 6:15 it states that Nehemiah and the Jews completed the wall in fifty-two days, which completely rattles and unnerves their enemies (6:16). Then Nehemiah finishes the gates, hangs the doors in place, and installs a man of integrity (who "feared God more than most men do") in charge of the gates and the defense of Jerusalem.

Rebuilding the Nation of Israel (7:4–12:26)

A list of those who had returned (7:4–73)

Now that Jerusalem is safe from attack, Nehemiah pushes on to repopulate the city and to ensure that the re-established population would be faithful to God. In 7:4–73 Nehemiah searches and locates proper genealogical records that establish clearly and legally who had the rights to the property in the city.

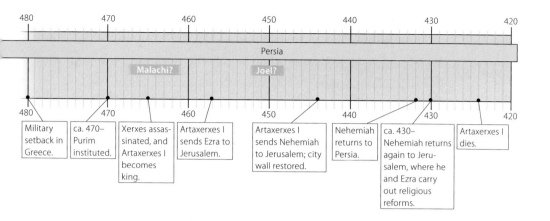

480		470		460		450		440		430		420
Military setback in Greece.	ca. 470– Purim instituted.	Xerxes assassinated, and Artaxerxes I becomes king.	Artaxerxes I sends Ezra to Jerusalem.	Artaxerxes I sends Nehemiah to Jerusalem; city wall restored.	Nehemiah returns to Persia.	ca. 430– Nehemiah returns again to Jerusalem, where he and Ezra carry out religious reforms.	Artaxerxes I dies.

Persia

Malachi?

Joel?

Hearing and understanding the law (8:1–18)

The walls are now complete but a major theological challenge still lies ahead. The people must remain faithful to God and must obey his law. In Nehemiah 8 the people are all assembled together, and Ezra, a priest and teacher of the law, reads the "book of the Law" (literally, "the book of the Torah") to all who could understand, both men and women (8:1–6). This was perhaps the book of Deuteronomy, but it could have been the entire Pentateuch. Ezra would read a section of the law to the entire assembly and then pause to allow the Levites to explain that unit to the people in smaller, "break-out" groups. Then in obedience to the law they had just heard, the returned exiles celebrate the Feast of Booths (8:13–18), as prescribed in Leviticus 23:37–40.

Confession of sin (9:1–37)

Realizing the exile had happened because of Israel's rebellion and sin against God, the people now confess their sins to God and worship him (9:1–37). They reaffirm that while Israel has repeatedly been unfaithful, God has been completely faithful to all of his promises, especially his covenant promises to Abraham.

The leaders and the people pledge to keep the law (9:38–10:39)

Both the leaders and the people now pledge to be faithful to God and to keep his law. They mention three specific areas in which they will be obedient: (1) they won't intermarry with pagans, (2) they will keep the Sabbath, and (3) they will support the temple financially. This is an ominous pledge, for all three of these promises will be broken in Nehemiah 13.

✚ Israel/Judah had been destroyed and exiled because they failed to obey the book of Deuteronomy. In Nehemiah 8 Ezra reads Deuteronomy to the people, calling them back to obedience.

The new inhabitants of Jerusalem (11:1–12:26)

Jerusalem was still underpopulated (and thus probably underdefended), so the people cast lots and choose one out of every ten people in Judah to come live in Jerusalem (11:1–36). Nehemiah 12 then lists the priests and Levites who had returned to live in Jerusalem and to work in the temple. Slowly but surely, Jerusalem is growing stronger.

Dedicating the Wall (12:27–47)

In what is probably the climax of the book of Nehemiah, the returned exiles of Israel now have a huge celebration as they dedicate the new wall. The dedication of the wall in Nehemiah 12 parallels the dedication of the temple back in Ezra 6. Also, in contrast to the weeping and mourning that resulted from the fall of Jerusalem and the destruction of the city (see especially Lamentations), now the focus is on joyful celebration.

Disobedience of the People: Is the Work of Nehemiah All in Vain? (13:1–31)

Nehemiah 13, however, is quite troubling. Nehemiah has been governing the exiles in Judah for twelve years. He has rebuilt the wall of Jerusalem in miraculous fashion and has reorganized the people so that they are now worshiping God faithfully. Nehemiah now has to return to Persia to report back to King Artaxerxes, a not-so-subtle reminder that the Persians still reign over Jerusalem, not a Davidic king as promised in the restoration. After a brief stay in Persia, Nehemiah comes back to Jerusalem, only to find that things in Jerusalem have gone downhill rapidly while he was away. All three of the specific acts of obedience to God promised by the people in Nehemiah 10:30–39 are being violated with some regularity. The people are not financially supporting the temple, which has caused the Levites to go back into farming in order to survive (13:10–11). Thus the worship in the temple is collapsing. The people are also violating the Sabbath (13:15–22) and intermarrying with idol-worshiping foreigners (13:23–28). Nehemiah jumps right on these problems, straightening them out as quickly as he can. Yet the readers are left wondering: Are the Israelites going

These magnificent stone bulls sat on top of huge columns and supported the roof beams for the Persian palace at Susa. The bulls also probably symbolized the power of the Persian king.

to be faithful to God only so long as someone like Nehemiah is hounding them? If the Israelites can't even keep the three specific laws they pledged to keep, how will they possibly keep God's other laws?

Thus the book of Nehemiah ends on a disturbing note. Although Nehemiah himself works heroically to rebuild Jerusalem and to reconstitute the people of God, the people themselves don't appear to be all that different from their ancestors, who had lost the land and gone into exile. Once Nehemiah leaves, they backslide immediately. We as readers are acutely aware, therefore, that the return of these exiles is not the glorious restoration of Israel the prophets promised. Furthermore, things are not back to the way they were before the exile. Israel is still unable to keep the law of God, and thus the hope for ultimate restoration must still look to the future when a true Davidic king will provide deliverance and a new covenant relationship.

So What? Applying Nehemiah to Our Lives Today

Nehemiah is clearly following God's will, drawing strength and power from God at several points in the story. Nonetheless, Nehemiah confronts numerous obstacles and enemies, both from without and from within. So even though he is doing God's will, his task is never easy or simple. This is a good lesson for us to grasp. Just because God leads us to do a task does not mean that the task will suddenly become easy. Likewise, just because a task becomes difficult or just because opposition arises, it does not necessarily mean that completing this task is not God's will. All too often, perhaps, we sit around waiting for God to show us "the open door," assuming that if the door is not easily opened then it must not be God's will for us to take that path. But in these situations, Nehemiah suggests to us that perhaps God wants us to kick in the door, or perhaps find a window to climb in. God wants us to follow his leading and trust in him for empowerment, but he also expects us to plan, lead well, work hard, and persevere in spite of opposition and so-called closed doors.

Our Favorite Verse in Nehemiah

O Lord, let your ear be attentive to the prayer of this your servant and to the prayer of your servants who delight in revering your name. (1:11)

✦ When Ezra discovered that the Israelites had intermarried with pagan foreigners, he tore his cloak and pulled out his hair (Ezra 9:3). When Nehemiah, however, encounters this problem, he beats the culprits and pulls out *their* hair (Neh. 13:25).

Esther

God Uses a Beautiful Young Woman to Save Israel

The story of Esther is an enchanting Cinderella-like story about an orphaned, peasant Jewish girl who, because of her great beauty and character, is selected to marry the powerful and wealthy Persian king. In some regards, her story is similar to Ruth's, another orphan who also meets a wealthy man and marries him. But the contrasts between Ruth/Naomi/Boaz and Esther/Mordecai/Xerxes are perhaps as interesting as the similarities. Ruth is a Moabite who marries an Israelite husband in the land of Israel. Esther, however, is an Israelite, and she marries a pagan Persian king in Persia. Ruth's marriage provides immediate security and happiness for her and her mother-in-law. In the long term her lineage leads to David, who delivers Israel from the terrible situation of the judges. The marriage of Esther has serious and immediate significance well beyond her limited family, for through her influence the entire Jewish people are delivered from annihilation. Esther plays the same game Ruth does (courtship and marriage), but the stakes are much higher for Esther, at least in the short term. For Esther, the immediate fate of the entire Jewish people hangs in the balance.

The tomb of Xerxes.

What Is the Setting for Esther?

The story of Esther takes place in the Persian capital city of Susa, the same city that Nehemiah is residing in at the beginning of the book of Nehemiah. The story of Esther, however, takes place earlier than the story of Nehemiah does. Her story occurs during the reign of the Persian king Xerxes (485–465 BC). Xerxes is referred to as Ahasuerus in the Hebrew text and thus in some English translations. Nehemiah's story takes place during the reign of the following king, Artaxerxes.

In the Hebrew Bible, the book of Esther is included in the third major division of the canon, the Writings. Within the Writings, Esther is part of a smaller unit called the Megilloth (scrolls), comprising Ruth, Song of Songs, Ecclesiastes, Lamentations, and Esther. Among other things, the book of Esther explains the origins of the Jewish festival of Purim. This is probably why it was located in the Megilloth, for each of the five books in this unit were read on special Jewish festival days.

Both in the Septuagint (Greek translation of the Old Testament) and in our English translations, Esther is placed at the end of the Historical Books, and more specifically, at the end of the Chronicler's history. The author of Esther is unknown, and while the exact date of composition is also unknown, it was most likely written in about 400 BC, near the time when Ezra/Nehemiah and 1–2 Chronicles were written.

What Is at the Heart of Esther?

The story of Esther is an entertaining one. Yet while the story is rather easy to read, it is not easy to interpret, and there is no consensus regarding the point of the story. Likewise there is disagreement over how to interpret the character of Esther. Of course, on the one hand, the purpose of the book was to explain the origins and the meaning of the Jewish Festival of Purim (9:18–28), which celebrated and remembered God's deliverance of the Jews from the gentile plot to eliminate them. On the other hand, as we probe the story to gather clues to help interpret the story, we discover some unusual features. First of all, the name of God is never mentioned in the entire book of Esther. None of the characters in the story ever pray or inquire of God.

Esther does partake of a three-day fast (4:16), and some interpreters assume this was an indication of her piety before God. Yet it is quite curious that she never actually mentions God or prays to him, asking for help and success (as Ezra and Nehemiah did). In fact, there doesn't seem to be much of a spiritual awareness at all in any of the characters in the book. One can perhaps read some faith into Mordecai's warning words to Esther in 4:12–14, especially in his ending comments, "Who knows but that you have come to royal position for such a time as this?" But this is a pretty fuzzy indication of faith, especially in the context of Ezra and Nehemiah, who clearly and repeatedly look to God for help and who also repeatedly acknowledge God for all of their successes. The characters in Esther do neither.

Likewise the names of the hero and the heroine are disturbing. Mordecai's name probably means "man of Marduk." Marduk was the primary god of the Babylonians, so this is an alarming name for an Israelite hero. Similarly, the name Esther is probably derived from Ishtar, the Mesopotamian goddess of love. The meaning of the names, of course, is not conclusive for determining the meaning of the story, but names often do play a role, and these particular names are especially disconcerting.

Thus while it is tempting to raise up Mordecai and the beautiful young Esther as heroes and models of faith like Ezra and Nehemiah, it is doubtful that the author of Esther intended the story to be understood that way.

What is the point, then? As predicted by the prophets, the salvation-history story line follows those Israelites who moved back to the land of Israel after the exile. This is the story that is tracked by Ezra/Nehemiah, as well as by the postexilic prophets (Haggai, Zechariah, and Malachi). Obedient Jews (like Ezra and Nehemiah) moved back to

From the Persian royal palace at Persepolis, a depiction of the King (probably Xerxes) entering the palace, accompanied by two attendants carrying a fan and an umbrella.

✚ The name of God is never mentioned in the entire book of Esther.

An alabaster vase inscribed with the name "Xeres the Great King."

the Promised Land. Yet not all the Jews did this; many stayed in Mesopotamia, refusing to return to the land of their forefathers. The book of Esther illustrates the fate of those who stayed in exile. None of the Jews in the book of Esther are portrayed as praying, sacrificing, worshiping, or acknowledging God in any way. A beautiful Jewish woman named after the goddess Ishtar marries a pagan, foreign king. This action has tremendous symbolic significance, especially in light of the very close connection throughout the Old Testament between idolatry and intermarrying with pagans. Such intermarriage is a huge issue in Ezra and Nehemiah, and Esther's marriage to Xerxes should probably be understood in that context.

The book of Esther teaches that even though the Jews who remained back in Persia were not strong in their faith, God worked powerfully behind the scenes to deliver them from total annihilation anyway. The reader knows that this is based on God's grace and on his covenants with Abraham and David. Yet this is something we learned from Ezra, Nehemiah, and the rest of the Old Testament, not from the characters in Esther. The characters of Mordecai and Esther are certainly bold and brave, but they do not seem to be faith-driven, and they probably symbolize those Jews who had remained in exile. God works behind the scenes through Mordecai and Esther, not because of their great faith (which is absent), but because of his great grace, and in spite of their lack of faith.

A brief outline of the story is as follows:

- The Fall of the Persian Queen Vashti (1:1–22)
- The Persian Beauty Contest (2:1–18)
- Haman's Plot to Destroy Mordecai and All the Jews (2:19–3:15)
- Esther Thwarts Haman's Plot and Turns the Tables on Him (4:1–7:10)
- The King's Decree and the Jews' Revenge (8:1–10:3)

What Makes Esther Interesting and Unique?

- The story of Esther is an enchanting rags-to-riches story.
- A brave and beautiful young woman is the main character of the story.
- The book of Esther also has an evil villain, a classic bad guy named Haman.

- Esther is selected as queen through a very interesting "beauty pageant."
- Nowhere in the book of Esther is the name of God mentioned. Likewise, no one in Esther prays or mentions any of the covenants, in strong contrast to Ezra/Nehemiah.
- In the book of Esther the entire Jewish population is about to be annihilated. Only the action of Esther (and God behind the scenes) prevents this total destruction of the Jewish people.
- Esther is never quoted in the New Testament.

What Is the Message of Esther?

The Fall of the Persian Queen Vashti (1:1–22)

King Xerxes of Persia rules over the entire ancient Near East, and is, undoubtedly, the most powerful man in the world. He throws a huge banquet and invites his wife, Vashti, to attend. Strangely, Vashti refuses, offending Xerxes greatly. Thus he deposes of Vashti as queen.

The Persian Beauty Contest (2:1–18)

The Persians conduct an empirewide "beauty contest" to find a beautiful woman to replace Vashti. The most beautiful young women from all over the Persian Empire are brought in, given beauty treatments, and then presumably added to Xerxes' harem as concubines and candidates for the position of queen. The young, Jewish woman Esther is one of these candidates. Following the orders of her relative Mordecai, she keeps her Jewish nationality a secret, which is a bit strange. Nonetheless, Esther pleases the king more than any other woman, and so he chooses her to become the new queen.

Haman's Plot to Destroy Mordecai and All the Jews (2:19–3:15)

In the meantime, two things happen. First, Mordecai uncovers a plot to assassinate King

These bottles held eye makeup, which was applied with a metal rod.

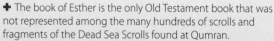

✛ The book of Esther is the only Old Testament book that was not represented among the many hundreds of scrolls and fragments of the Dead Sea Scrolls found at Qumran.

Xerxes and passes this information to Esther, who gives it to the king. Thus the plot is thwarted and the plotters executed (2:21–23). Second, for reasons not explained in the story, Mordecai refuses to bow down and show honor to one of the king's highest officials, a man named Haman. This infuriates Haman. Perhaps Mordecai has good reasons for his disrespectful behavior toward this important official, but on the surface it certainly looks like this was not a wise course of action. Haman, a very powerful man in the court of King Xerxes, now hates Mordecai and plots to kill him. Not content with killing just Mordecai, Haman decides to kill all of Mordecai's people, the Jews. Haman convinces Xerxes to give an official order that on a certain day, all the Jews in his empire would be executed and their property plundered. Xerxes is not aware that Esther, his queen, is a Jew.

Esther Thwarts Haman's Plot and Turns the Tables on Him (4:1–7:10)

When the Jews hear of this, they fast, weep, and wail (4:1–3), but, as mentioned above, there is no mention of prayer, confession, or sacrifice to God, a glaringly obvious omission. Mordecai tells Esther she must intervene with the king. She protests that it is dangerous to approach the king uninvited, but in the end, she agrees (4:4–17).

Esther does approach the king, even though he has not invited her to come to him. However, he seems happy to see her. Cleverly, she asks that the king and his high official Haman both come to a banquet she has planned, where she will make a request of the king. At the banquet she presents her request. She asks that she and her people be allowed to live, explaining how Haman has connived to kill her people, the Jews. This enrages the king, and he declares that Haman be hanged on the very gallows he had been building for the execution of Mordecai (5:1–7:10).

The King's Decree and the Jews' Revenge (8:1–10:3)

Xerxes now reverses his earlier order and issues a decree that allows the Jews to protect and defend themselves against all enemies (8:9–11), an important edict especially in the later story of Nehemiah, who does organize and defend the Jews from their local enemies. In Esther 9:1–17 the Jews throughout the empire embrace the new edict and turn on those who had plotted against them, killing thousands of their enemies. A complete reversal of fates takes place in this story. Haman, a powerful official at the beginning, is now hanged, and his estate is given to Esther. Mordecai, Haman's nemesis, is honored and placed in charge of Haman's old estate. The Jews, close to being annihilated, instead are able to destroy their enemies. Esther 9:18–32 describes how this great story was enshrined in the Feast of Purim and how this feast was established in Jewish custom. Finally, Esther 10:1–3 extols King Xerxes, as well as Esther's relative Mordecai, who, like Joseph in the court of Pharaoh in Egypt, now rises to the second-highest position in the land.

Gold signet ring from Egypt. The king's signet ring is mentioned four times in Esther (3:10; 8:2, 8, 10).

So What? Applying Esther to Our Lives Today

Esther was quite brave, and we can learn much about bravery from her. The primary lesson for us in the book of Esther, however, comes from the actions of God. In Esther we learn that God often works quietly behind the scenes to implement his plan. God rescues the Israelites, not because of Esther's piety, but because saving them is part of his character and his plan, even though at that moment the Jews in Persia are not living obediently. God often works in our lives even when we do not deserve it. God is faithful to his promises and to his plan in spite of us. This should give us great encouragement in difficult times.

Our Favorite Verse in Esther

And who knows but that you have come to royal position for such a time as this? (4:14)

Xerxes is famous for his war with Greece. On this painted water jar, two Greek soldiers fight against a mounted Persian.

The Wisdom Books and Psalms

What Are the Wisdom Books About?

One of the most important and most basic things that the Bible tells us is to "believe!" Faith in God is a critical starting point for the Christian life, and thus we find the imperative "Believe!" everywhere throughout the Bible. Likewise, close on the heels of "Believe!" we find the constant biblical imperative of "Obey!" Other important and closely associated imperatives are "Trust!" "Love!" and "Be faithful!" The Pentateuch, the Historical Books, and the Prophets stress these crucial imperatives.

The Wisdom Books, however, stress a different set of imperatives, for the Wisdom Books tell us to "Think!" "Consider!" and "Reflect!" It is not that the Wisdom Books don't want us to believe or obey. These things are assumed in the Wisdom Books and are viewed as foundational. Yet the focus of the Wisdom Books is to build on that foundation by exhorting the people of God to "Understand!"

The Wisdom Books are not engaging in mere intellectual exercise for those who are disconnected from the real world. Far from it. The Wisdom Books challenge us with the imperatives "think," "look," "listen," and "reflect" in order to build character in us. This is perhaps the overarching purpose of the Wisdom Books—to build character in the reader/student for life in this world. Thus "wisdom" in the Bible has a strong practical aspect. Real character in a person is only demonstrated when that person engages with the real world around him or her. The Wisdom Books give us guidance and develop character in us so that we can live wise and godly lives in the rough-and-tumble, everyday world in which we find ourselves.

The four Wisdom Books are Proverbs, Job, Ecclesiastes, and Song of Songs. These books do not contain collections of independent universal promises, but rather valuable, yet contextual, insight into wise and godly living. They provide guidance for how to build wise and godly character into our lives. Each book has a different focus, and taken together they balance one another. Proverbs presents the basic approach to life. It gives us the norms of life, things that are generally and normally true. For example, Proverbs teaches us that if people work hard, they will prosper. But if they are lazy, they will be poor. This is normally the case, but not necessarily universally so. Certainly not all prosperous people are hardworking, and not all poor people are lazy! Also in Proverbs life is calm, rational, and ordered. Everything makes sense and can be understood through a fairly simple system of cause and effect.

But life is not always like that. Frequently it is very complex and filled with unusual situations that do not follow a simple cause-and-effect relationship. The other three Wisdom Books interact with the exceptions and the abnormalities of life, thus balancing the norms of Proverbs. The first big exception to the norms of Proverbs is the suffering of the righteous. The book of Job grapples with this tough topic. The second exception is seen in Ecclesiastes, which deals with the big picture of life rather than the day-to-day details, the focus of Proverbs. Ecclesiastes struggles with the observation that the rational, ordered approach doesn't always have the answer and thus doesn't provide ultimate meaning to life. Finally, Song of Songs engages with what is perhaps the biggest irrationality of life—the wild, romantic love between a husband and wife.

Where Does the Book of Psalms Fit In?

In our Bibles the book of Psalms is located with the Wisdom Books, following right after Job and preceding Proverbs. In the traditional Hebrew canon, Psalms is placed at the beginning of the "Writings" section. Thus it follows Malachi and precedes Job and the rest of the Wisdom Books. So as far as location in the Bible goes, Psalms is associated closely with the Wisdom Books.

However, in regard to content and style, Psalms is very different from the Wisdom Books. Psalms is a collection of testimonies, laments, and praises that were used both in public worship and in private meditation. While most of the Bible contains God's word to us, the Psalms are somewhat unique in that they reflect the words of the psalmists as sung and spoken to God. They contain joyful praises offered up to God and testimonies to his great saving actions. They also contain cries of pain and agony over life's difficulties, followed by pleas to God for deliverance and statements of trust in God.

The point here is that the Psalms are simply unique, and they do not fit in neatly with any other biblical category. Yet Psalms is located among the

✚ The books of Job, Ecclesiastes, and Song of Songs probe into the perplexing exceptions to the general principles in Proverbs.

Wisdom in the Ancient Near East

Tremper Longman III

The Old Testament refers to wisdom traditions in the ancient Near East (1 Kings 4:30). Indeed, though here Solomon's wisdom is said to exceed that of Egypt and the people of the east, the compliment only makes sense if ancient Near Eastern wisdom had value.

Many ancient wisdom texts are available for study today. Egypt had a strong wisdom tradition represented by instructional texts and speculative works. In Egyptian, the instructional literature was known as *sbyt*, which is probably best translated as "teaching" or "enlightenment." These texts are like the book of Proverbs and appear as early as the Old Kingdom period (about 2715–2170 BC) down to the late Egyptian period. The *sbyt* were instructions of a father to a son. In some examples the father is the king. The father is old and experienced, about to step down from his high position in society, and his son is just starting. The best-known example is the Instruction of Amenemope (thought to have been composed a century before Solomon). Egyptian literature also attests a tradition of speculative wisdom literature that expresses a more pessimistic view of life, questioning the justice of this world. The Eloquent Peasant is a study of the exploitation of the poor by the powerful. The Dispute over Suicide expresses severe disappointment in this life in a manner comparable to the Teacher in Ecclesiastes.

Wisdom traditions also stretch back to some of the earliest writings of the Sumerians, inhabitants of Mesopotamia in the third millennium BC. Proverb collections are known from 2600–2550 BC. Besides these lists of proverbs, Sumerian literature also has an instructional text similar to Proverbs and the Egyptian *sbyt* literature called the Instructions of Shuruppak, named after the speaker of the teaching. Shuruppak advises his son Ziusudra, the famous hero who survived the flood. While Akkadian literature (the language of second- and first-millennium inhabitants of Mesopotamia, the Babylonians and Assyrians) has no significant proverb collection, it does attest a number of speculative wisdom texts. The Babylonian Theodicy may be the best known and is most like the book of Job. This text is a dialogue between two men who are friends and keep the conversation civil, but they disagree about the relationship between suffering and the gods.

Finally, mention should be made of an ancient wisdom text written in Aramaic titled Ahiqar after its main character. The story is set in the seventh century BC and begins with the story of a wise man who was betrayed by his nephew. He escaped execution and fled into exile. After his restoration, he instructed his nephew by proverbs that constitute the large end of the text.

Wisdom Books. Thus we have included the discussion of the book of Psalms in its canonical order (after Job), but in regard to classification, we have opted to treat the book of Psalms as a separate and unique category.

Thoth, the ibis-headed Egyptian god of knowledge, science, wisdom, and writing.

Job

When Life Just Isn't Fair

In Proverbs we learn that good things happen to good people and bad things happen to bad people. Most of us like this theology of Proverbs because it presents us with a world that makes sense, a world in which all events have logical causes, a world that runs by tight rules of fair play. And indeed, much of the time the world is that way. But occasionally we are slapped in the face with some great incongruity of life, something that is just not fair or just not right, something that contradicts Proverbs. A two-year-old child of godly parents is killed in a car wreck, or the most righteous and giving person we know comes down with terminal cancer. These events rattle our faith and leave us searching futilely for answers that make sense. Why do these things happen?

The story of Job grapples with this issue and provides us with insight on how to cope with these difficult questions of life.

What Is the Setting for Job?

There is nothing in the book of Job that tells us specifically who wrote the book or when it was written. On the one hand, there is no mention of anything from Israel's history that would assist us in determining a date for the book. The actual setting of the story appears to be quite ancient, perhaps during the patriarchal period, well before the settlement of Israel in the land. On the other hand, the book of Job appears to allude to other parts of Scripture (Genesis 1–3 and Psalm 8, for example), and the friends of Job seem to espouse a theology developed from Proverbs and Deuteronomy. This tends to point to a later date, at least for the composition of the book. A plausible setting for the composition of Job is during the reign of either Solomon (971–931 BC) or Hezekiah (716–687 BC), since both were very interested in wisdom literature. Yet no one really knows for sure.

What Is at the Heart of Job?

The book of Job is not a list of theological statements that can be taken individually as doctrinal statements. It is a story. This story has a few narrative sections, most notably at the beginning and at the end, but most of the story is told through dialogue. The context of each dialogue is important, and each statement must be placed in the overall context of the book. The point of the story, as with most stories, doesn't really emerge until the end of the book.

Assyrian wall relief depicting captured camels. A Chaldean raiding party captures all of Job's camels (1:17).

The book of Job deals with the difficult question of how we as wise, godly people are to handle great tragedies in our lives that seem to be unfair or without any logical explanation. There are four interrelated theological conclusions emerging from the book of Job: (1) God is sovereign and we are not; (2) God knows all about the world, while we actually know very little; (3) God is always just, but he does not always explain his justice to us; and (4) God expects us to trust in his character and his sovereignty when unexplained tragedy strikes us.

The story of Job unfolds according to the following outline:

- The Testing of Job: An Unexplained Tragedy (1:1–2:10)
- The Search for Answers and the Slide into Accusation (2:11–37:24)
  - Job curses the day he was born (3:1–26)
  - Job and his three friends search for answers (4:1–26:14)
  - Job accuses God of injustice (27:1–31:40)
  - Elihu's hot-air speeches (32:1–37:24)
- God's Verbal Response to Job (38:1–42:6)
- God's Restoration of Job (42:7–17)

What Makes Job Interesting and Unique?

- Job is one of the few Old Testament books in which Satan actually appears.
- Job deals with one of the most troubling questions of life: why do bad things happen to good people?
- God himself appears in this book, both at the beginning and at the end. Toward the end, God delivers two long speeches to Job.
- When God speaks to Job, he speaks in highly polished Hebrew poetry.
- Job challenges the way God runs the world; God rebukes him mildly and gently.
- God never actually tells Job what caused his time of affliction.

What Is the Message of Job?

The Testing of Job: An Unexplained Tragedy (1:1–2:10)

The story of Job has a very strange beginning. Job is introduced as a blameless and upright man who fears God. He is blessed with a large family and

✦ The book of Proverbs and the book of Job balance each other. They should be interpreted together.

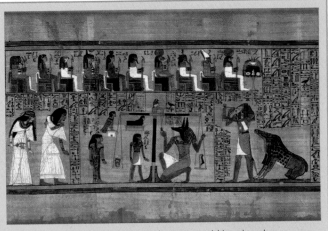
Job cries out that if his anguish and misery could be placed on the scales it would outweigh the sands of the sea (6:1–2). Shown above is a scene from the Egyptian Book of the Dead in which the jackal-headed god of the dead weighs the heart of the deceased on a scale against a feather.

great wealth. Satan, however, comes before God and challenges Job's true motives. Satan argues that Job would not worship God if all of his blessings were removed. So God gives Satan permission to remove all of Job's blessings (1:1–12). Satan brings on a series of disasters that decimates Job's family and destroys his wealth. Job, however, remains faithful and declares: "The Lord gave and the Lord has taken away; may the name of the Lord be praised" (1:13–22).

So Job's actions have proven Satan to be wrong. Satan, however, changes his position and now argues that if Job also lost his health, he would then curse God. So the Lord agrees to let Satan take away Job's health. Job is afflicted with terrible sores. Furthermore, his own wife turns against him, assuming that he must have done something terrible for all of this misfortune to have happened to him. Job remains faithful and somewhat stoic, stating: "Shall we accept good from God and not trouble?" (2:1–10).

So the story unfolds. The great blessings of Job's life, including his health, are removed. Job, at least at first, accepts it and is able to still praise the name of the Lord. In essence Satan has now been proved wrong and the story should end. But Job and his fellow thinkers now try to analyze these disastrous events in Job's life. Their attempts to find causation and meaning in Job's misfortune lead to forty more chapters of theological dialogue.

The Search for Answers and the Slide into Accusation (2:11–37:24)

Job curses the day he was born (3:1–26)

Apparently a period of time goes by. Job, who back in chapter 2 had accepted what happened to him, now grows bitter, saying that it would have been better not even to have been born. He curses the day of his birth and ends his speech by saying, "I have no peace" (3:1–26).

✦ The prophet Ezekiel mentions Job twice (Ezek. 14:14, 20), pointing to Job's righteousness.

Job and his three friends search for answers (4:1–26:14)

This long middle section of Job is composed of numerous speeches given by Job and his three educated friends. Three main cycles of speeches are presented, whereby each friend speaks, followed by Job's rebuttal (4:1–14:22; 15:1–21:34; 22:1–26:14). In essence they are all struggling to make sense of the events in Job's life. Yet Job and his friends have slightly different perspectives, and his friends are quick to judge him.

Job's friends begin with two major methodological assumptions. They assume that through the skills of human wisdom they can answer any problem, including this one. Second, they assume they have access to all of the information they need to understand the problem. Unfortunately, both assumptions are wrong.

Job's friends believe (correctly) that God is moral and just. In their thinking, Job is obviously being punished by God, so they conclude that Job obviously committed some great sin against God. What is needed, therefore, is for Job to repent. Notice that in essence this is the theology of Proverbs—people get what they deserve in this life. Their theology is not bad, just shallow, and their application of that theology to this situation is wrong. Furthermore, they do not really endeavor to comfort their friend Job. Rather, they seek to explain the tragedy. Explaining and comforting are two very different things. Finally, these friends with their nice, simple understanding of the world seem totally oblivious to the chaos and havoc Satan can cause in the world.

As his friends wax eloquent on justice and the character of God, Job seems to grow increasingly distraught over his dilemma. He knows he has not committed some great sin against God. Yet he is having trouble answering his friends' logic. Early in the story Job accepts what has happened, concluding stoically that God does what he pleases. In 9:14–21 Job praises the justice and power of God. "How then can I dispute with him?" Job asks in 9:14. "Even if I summoned him and he responded, . . . he would crush me with a

Job feels like an outcast, "a brother of jackals"—scavenger canines.

storm. . . . Even if I were innocent, my mouth would condemn me. . . . He is not a man like me that I might answer him" (9:16–20, 32). Job's words in chapter 9 foreshadow what will happen in chapters 38–42 when God does respond to Job's summons by coming in a storm.

Job continues to struggle, and by chapter 23 his tone has changed, and he starts to question God. In 23:1–24:25 Job declares his wish to have his day in court before God. In Job's mind there has been some kind of big-time foul-up made in the divine justice of the world, and if Job could be allowed to present his case, he is sure he could clear things up (23:1–7). But alas, Job mourns, the Almighty does not set office hours to hear such complaints (24:1).

Cast bronze mirror from Egypt. In Job 37:18 God mentions a "mirror of cast bronze."

Job accuses God of injustice (27:1–31:40)

As Job continues to suffer, his calm, stoic demeanor disappears, and he becomes more agitated and more direct in disagreeing with God's actions. In 27:2 Job states that God has denied him justice, a serious charge against God. Job proclaims his innocence (27:3–6), and reiterates his belief that it is the wicked who receive punishment (27:7–23). In 28:1–28 Job declares that wisdom is deep (like precious minerals and jewels that lie deep in mines) and that only God knows the way to it. He then reminisces about the old days, longing for those bygone days when he was healthy, blessed, and respected by all (29:1–25). Now, by contrast, Job complains, "They mock me, men younger than I, whose fathers I would have disdained to put with my sheep dogs" (30:1). Then in chapter 31 Job gets specific about his innocence. He lists his many virtuous actions and his overall moral integrity (31:1–34). Then Job declares dramatically, "Oh, that I had someone to hear me! I sign now my defense—let the Almighty answer me; let my accuser put his indictment in writing" (31:35). Job figuratively puts into writing his request for a hearing and the case for his innocence. He then throws it into the face of God and demands an answer.

Elihu's hot-air speeches (32:1–37:24)

Elihu is a new character who has not been mentioned before. He is younger than the other men, and so he had to wait until they finished for a chance to speak. He is angry at Job's profession of innocence and angry at the other men's inability to verbally refute Job (32:1–5). So now Elihu gets his chance to put in his two cents' worth. He really doesn't say anything new, but does develop in more detail some of the points made by Job's three friends. He rambles on for seven chapters! Then, in contrast to the speeches made by the other friends, neither Job nor the others answer Elihu or respond to him, which probably implies that no one takes him seriously. He is waved away without rebuttal. One wonders if he is to be included among the young men Job referred to in 30:1.

In Job 38:1 God speaks to Job out of a storm.

God's Verbal Response to Job (38:1–42:6)

Job has challenged God's justice repeatedly, declaring that if he only had his day in court, he could prove his innocence to God. Job calls on God to respond, confident in his case against the way that God has been running the world. God is about to show up, as Job has requested repeatedly, but things are going to go rather differently than Job expects.

God certainly has a sense of humor. In 9:16–17 Job declared poetically, "Even if I summoned him and he responded, . . . he would crush me with a storm." Then in the final flowery speech of Elihu, the young speaker describes the power of God by connecting God to the lightning, wind, clouds, and rain of a storm (37:1–24). So it is rather ironic that when God does appear, he comes blasting down out of a storm, demanding, "Who is this that darkens my counsel with words without knowledge? Brace yourself like a man; I will question you, and you shall answer me" (38:2–3). Job has been wanting his day in court when he could pepper God with questions and present his rational and reasoned defense. Now finally God is here, but God declares that he himself will be the one to ask the questions. God immediately fires off question after question at Job. "Where were you when I laid the earth's foundations? Tell me, if you understand. Who marked off its dimensions? Surely you know!" (38:4–5). All these initial questions deal with aspects of God's great creation. Job has challenged the way God runs the universe. Therefore, God is asking Job just how much he knows about the universe. "Surely you know," God states sarcastically, "for you were already born! You have lived so many years!" (38:21). God continues for two long chapters, poetically describing the wonders of creation and stopping to ask Job if he understands all of these things—the seas, the stars, light, the animal world.

Finally, in 40:1–2 God pauses and gives Job a chance to answer. After all, Job has been demanding an audience with God for chapters. Now, however, with God speaking from the storm and pointing out to Job how ridiculously little he really knows about the world, Job probably realizes he has made a big mistake in demanding an audience with God. He wisely covers his mouth and hushes (40:4–5).

God, however, is not finished. He has some more questions for Job. "Brace yourself like a man," God again warns Job from the storm. "I will question you and you shall answer me" (40:7). While in general God rebukes Job only mildly, probably scaring him half to death but not really hurting him, nonetheless God is rather upset about Job's accusations against his justice. Thus God asks Job pointedly: "Would you discredit my justice? Would you condemn me to justify yourself?" (40:8). God then continues to stress how powerful he is and how his power is demonstrated by his control over the powerful animals of the world.

It is rather interesting that God ends with a long section detailing his power over the sea monster "leviathan" (41:1–34). Although some scholars have attempted to equate leviathan with crocodiles or something similar, most scholars maintain that leviathan, along with Rahab (see 9:13 and 26:12), probably represents the chaotic forces in the sea that are associated with Satan (the serpent in Genesis 3 and the dragon in Revelation 12 are part of this association). Thus the book opens with a challenge by Satan, and it ends with God declaring his absolute power over the forces of Satan. God is also making an important point to Job. In essence, Job has challenged God's right to rule the world, implying that he (Job) has a better understanding of justice. God responds by informing Job that he (Job) does not know much about the world and that he does not have the power to run the world. Furthermore, God seems to be saying in Job 41, "How could you, Job, possibly deal with the powers of Satan?"

God pauses, and Job quickly acknowledges his mistake, declaring, "Surely I spoke of things I did not understand, things too wonderful for me to know" (42:3). Job then repents.

God's Restoration of Job (42:7–17)

The story is coming quickly to an end, but first God has a few loose ends to tie up. He rebukes Job's friends, pointing out to them that "you have not spoken of me what is right, as my servant Job has" (42:7). God tells them that Job will pray for them and that he (God) will accept Job's prayer. Job does pray for his friends (42:10), and after that God blesses Job with tremendous blessings for the rest of his life. Job is blessed again and restored, but it is interesting to note that God never did explain to Job about Satan's challenge and the real reason for Job's trials. It is enough that Job recognizes

✦ At the beginning of the book, Satan accuses Job (Job 1–2); at the end of the book, God declares his absolute power over Leviathan (Job 41), a creature associated with Satan.

God as the great and powerful creator of the world, one who rules with strength and justice.

So What? Applying Job to Our Lives Today

There is much we can apply from Job. First of all, if we want to comfort our friends who are suffering from some great tragedy in their lives, we do not want to be like Job's friends, who spend all their time trying to understand the "why" instead of simply sitting with Job and hurting with him.

Second, of course, we can apply Job to our lives when inexplicable tragedy strikes us. Even in such angry and confusing times, we can cling to the theological truths God teaches us through the story of Job. First of all, we need to remember that God is sovereign and we are not. Furthermore, God knows all about the world, while we actually know very little. Thus our view is very limited. We do not see all the causes and effects; nor do we always see spiritual battles. We also need to realize and reaffirm that God is always just, but he does not always explain his justice to us, thus sometimes we cannot see it or understand it. He never told Job about the cosmic issues involved and the challenge of Satan that precipitated Job's story. Finally, and most important, God expects us to trust in his character and his sovereignty when unexplained tragedy strikes us. When we are hurt and confused, even perhaps a little angry, we should cling to what we know is true about the character of God, and trust that he knows how to run the world.

Our Favorite Verse in Job

Where were you when I laid the earth's foundation?
Tell me, if you understand. (38:4)

"Does the eagle soar at your command?" (Job 39:27).

Psalms

Worshiping God

Most people love the book of Psalms, discovering Psalms early in their Christian walk and cherishing these ancient songs throughout their lives. You probably feel the same way, and the reasons are obvious. In the Psalms we find comfort and encouragement when we are discouraged. In the Psalms we find just the right words for praising our Lord and rejoicing over what he has done for us. The psalmist expresses our feelings and our emotions, but somehow he just seems to say it better than we can. So whether we are happy and rejoicing in the Lord, or struggling in despair and doubt, the Psalms enable us to talk to God about it. Usually after meditating on one of the psalms and praying to God with the psalm, we find ourselves encouraged, uplifted, and strengthened. What a wonderful and powerful collection of songs this book is!

What Is the Setting for Psalms?

The title "Psalms" in our English Bibles comes from the Septuagint, the Greek translation of the Old Testament. The word in Greek that we have transliterated as "psalms" implies a song that is sung to accompaniment. In the Hebrew Bible, the title of this book is a word that means "praises."

The book of Psalms is a collection of 150 individual psalms, grouped into five "books." This grouping into five probably is intended to parallel the five books of the Pentateuch (Torah). Each of these five books ends with a statement of praise to the Lord. The five books are as follows:

Book	Contents	Ending
Book 1	Psalms 1–41	"Praise be to the Lord. . . . Amen and Amen." (41:13)
Book 2	Psalms 42–72	"Praise be to his glorious name forever. . . . Amen and Amen." (72:19)
Book 3	Psalms 73–89	"Praise be to the Lord forever! Amen and Amen." (89:52)
Book 4	Psalms 90–106	"Praise be to the Lord. . . . Let all the people say, 'Amen!' Praise the Lord." (106:48)
Book 5	Psalms 107–150	"Let everything that has breath praise the Lord. Praise the Lord." (150:6)

The entire text of Psalm 150 is a praise to the Lord, so that psalm as a whole is the praise that concludes the overall collection of Psalms.

The individual psalms were probably written, collected, and organized into these five books over a long period of time. The order of the five books is probably due to the chronology of the collection process. Also, within the five books are indications of other smaller, earlier collections. Note the comment at the end of Psalm 72, "This concludes the prayers of David son of Jesse" (v. 20). Another apparent collection is associated with the "sons of Korah" (Psalms 42–49 and Psalms 84–88). Likewise Psalms 73–83 (the psalms of Asaph) probably circulated as an early collection. Perhaps Psalms 120–134 ("pilgrim Psalms" or "songs of ascent") were also collected together as a unit before being placed in book 5.

Psalms 1 and 2 function as an introduction to the entire book, and were perhaps added toward the end of the compilation process. Psalm 1 states that the way to find blessing (and meaning) in life is to meditate on and delight in the Torah (or Law; i.e., the Pentateuch). Some scholars have suggested that Psalm 1 is really directing the audience to meditate on and delight in

Twelve different psalms mention praising God on the harp. Shown below is a Mesopotamian harpist.

266

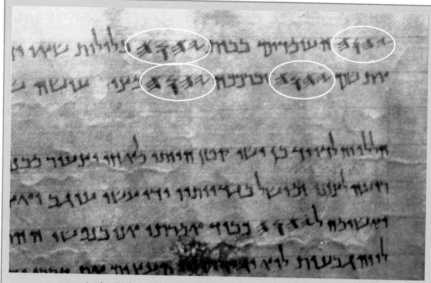

In this Psalms scroll from the Dead Sea Scrolls, the style of Hebrew letters used throughout the scroll is from the first century AD, but the name for the Lord (Yahweh) is always written in the centuries-old ancient paleo-Hebrew script.

the psalms that follow. While this is possible, it is not at all clear that this is the case. Psalm 2 is also introductory and directs the audience to look for the coming messianic king, implying that messianic nuances are present in those psalms that discuss the king or the reign of God.

Likewise, the final group of Psalms (146–150) stresses the praise of God and thus provides a fitting conclusion to the collection, with Psalm 150 providing the climactic ending, where the Lord is praised in every verse.

We do not know who actually finalized the Psalms collection into the final form we have today, or exactly when this occurred. Since some of the Psalms clearly refer to the time of exile in Babylonia ("By the waters of Babylon, there we sat down and wept, when we remembered Zion"; 137:1 ESV), we can probably conclude that the finalizing of the collection occurred after the exile, perhaps near or during the time of Ezra and Nehemiah (450–400 BC), but this is just an educated guess.

Many, but not all, of the Psalms have a superscription or heading at the very beginning. Usually our English translations place these headings above and separate from the actual text of the psalm, just prior to verse 1. For example, the superscription of Psalm 110 is "Of David. A psalm." Yet these superscriptions are part of the inspired text, and in Hebrew Bibles they make up verse 1, so we should not skip over them. These superscriptions provide a variety of information. They can indicate authorship (e.g., "of David," Psalm 143); historical setting ("When the prophet Nathan came to him after David had committed adultery with Bathsheba"; Psalm 51); a destination or perhaps

✚ Hebrew Bibles normally have 150 Psalms, as do our English translations. Interestingly, one of the Dead Sea Scrolls has another Psalm of David added to the end (i.e., Psalm 151).

a dedication ("For the director of music"; Psalm 31); purpose ("For the dedication of the temple"; Psalm 30); or music-related instructions ("To the tune of 'The Lily of the Covenant'"; Psalm 60).

Some scholars do not think that the Hebrew phrase usually translated "a psalm of David" indicates authorship, but perhaps a dedication ("a psalm to David") or a reflection ("a psalm related to David," or even "like David," etc.). However, there is strong evidence for understanding this phrase as an indication of authorship, and this has been the traditional understanding of the church throughout history.

David is not the only author mentioned in the superscriptions of the Psalms. The breakdown of authors who are cited in the superscriptions is as follows:

Author	Psalms attributed to him
David	73 psalms, concentrated in books 1 and 2, but also scattered throughout books 3, 4, and 5.
The sons of Korah	Psalms 42–49, 84–88
Asaph	Psalms 50, 73–83
Solomon	Psalms 72 and 127
Heman	Psalm 88
Ethan	Psalm 89
Moses	Psalm 90

Harp from ancient Egypt.

How were the Psalms originally used, and what was their purpose? We cannot be 100 percent sure, but probably the Psalms were originally used both in group worship and individual prayer. Some of the Psalms were obviously sung, accompanied by musical instruments. We do not know how they were performed, but probably there was interchange between the leader and the congregation.

Another important feature of the Psalms is that they are written in Hebrew poetry. Although many books of the Old Testament contain poetry, Psalms is the most thoroughgoing poetic book in the Bible. Thus Psalms is full of colorful figures of speech (see the discussion on figures of speech in Part III), including hyperbole. Also, a central feature of Hebrew poetry is called *parallelism*, a structural feature in which the author uses two lines of text to say one main point. Most of the verses in Psalms contain two lines of Hebrew text, and these two lines should be taken together. The first line makes the main statement, and the second line adds to that statement.

✚ In the Hebrew manuscripts of Psalms, the term *selah* appears in the margins occasionally (see, e.g., 66:4, 7, 15). Scholars do not know for certain what this term means, but suspect that it is some type of music or performance term.

The Psalms and the Messiah

The Psalms make numerous references to "the king." Much of the time these references are clearly referring to the current king who is ruling in Jerusalem at the time of the composition of that psalm. Sometimes the king is David. In many cases, however, the description or comments regarding the king seem to move in an idealized direction to foreshadow or perhaps even prophesy the coming messianic king. Both Psalm 2 and Psalm 110 clearly refer to the coming messianic king, and the New Testament verifies this connection (Ps. 2:7 is quoted in Heb. 1:5; Jesus identifies himself as "David's Lord" of Ps. 110:1 in Matt. 22:41–45; Mark 12:35–37; and Luke 20:41–44).

Another fascinating psalm that is connected to Jesus in the New Testament is Psalm 22, a personal lament. Jesus quotes Psalm 22:1 as he hangs from the cross: "My God, my God, why have you forsaken me?" (Matt. 27:46), indicating for us that Psalm 22 may be describing more than David's suffering. In fact, Psalm 22:15–18 appears to describe the crucifixion of Christ with remarkable accuracy: dried mouth, pierced hands and feet, garments divided, and lots cast. Apparently in Psalm 22 David is describing his own terrible suffering with figurative language that will also apply to Jesus literally.

The New Testament writers quote from Psalms more than any other Old Testament book. They connect many verses in Psalms with various aspects in the life of Christ. One of the most explicit examples of this is found in Acts 2:25–36, where the apostle Peter quotes Psalm 16:8–11 and Psalm 110:1, connecting both of these psalms to Jesus, particularly to his resurrection and exaltation.

What Is at the Heart of Psalms?

While the Psalms do inevitably address doctrine and moral behavior, their primary purpose is not focused on teaching doctrine and moral behavior. Their primary purpose is to give us divinely inspired models or patterns of how to pray to God, how to praise God, and how to meditate on God, in response to all God has done for us. Thus it is important to remember that most of the Psalms are addressed to God, not to us. They enable us to express to God our deepest emotions and needs, especially in the crisis times of life.

The Psalms can be grouped into two main categories relating to very different contexts of human life. First, there are times when we are doing well, and we simply want to praise God for all of the wonderful blessings he has given us. Or perhaps we simply want to praise God because he is so great and praiseworthy. As we reflect on God or meditate about God, our normal response should be to break out in praise. There are many psalms that lead us in this.

The second main category of Psalms is called "lament." A lament is a woeful cry of anguish and hurt, an ancient theologically shaped form of the blues. Sometimes life hits us so hard that we feel as if someone has punched us right in the stomach. Tragedy can strike without warning or without any rhyme or reason, devastating us and crippling us so that we can barely breathe or function. Pain and anguish, mixed with fear and doubt, can downright overwhelm even the strongest of God's people (like David, for example). The psalmists in general, and David in particular, are brutally honest with God in these situations, pouring out their heartfelt anguish, doubt, anger, fear, and pain to him in powerful, poetic laments. Usually the psalmists use their cry in the Psalms to work through their pain, often eventually ending up with resolve to trust, worship, and praise God, in spite of their difficulties. This too is a model for us, but it does not preempt the need to cry out in pain.

So the two central themes of Psalms are praise and lament, with the lament usually eventually ending up as praise.

What Makes Psalms Interesting and Unique?

- The Psalms connect with us emotionally perhaps more than any other book in the Bible.
- The psalmist is brutally honest about his emotions—his fear, his doubt, his discouragement, and also his joy, his comfort, and his encouragement.
- The book of Psalms is the longest book in the Bible.
- The New Testament quotes from Psalms more than any other Old Testament book.
- The Psalms contain numerous messianic references.
- The Psalms are written in highly structured Hebrew poetry, frequently employing vivid figures of speech.

A shofar being played.

Music in the Old Testament

W. Dennis Tucker Jr.

INTRODUCTION

Music was foundational to all cultures in the ancient Near East, and those cultures that dwelled in Israel/Palestine were no different. Nearly two millennia prior to the Davidic monarchy, music played a central role in the cultures located in the region of Palestine, and it remained an important part of the cultures in that region. Archaeological-iconographic evidence is extensive. Terra-cotta figurines playing a variety of musical instruments have been found, as well as actual clay rattles, cymbals, and flutes. Numerous drawings depict dancing and the playing of instruments. For example, archaeologists have unearthed floor stones in rooms adjacent to an altar in the city of Megiddo (3000 BC). Those stones depict warriors and hunters, but also dancers, a female harpist, and a drummer.

The Old Testament literature itself suggests something of the antiquity of music. The earliest mention of music appears in Genesis 4:21. There Jubal is mentioned as the ancestor of all those who played the lyre and pipe. The occupation of musician is mentioned alongside those of herdsman (4:20) and of metallurgist (4:22), suggesting that music was not considered an ancillary part of life, but rather central to the composition of society itself.

SOCIAL SETTINGS

War

The biblical text records the close connection between war and music or musical instruments. For example, Gideon's military assault on the Midianites included the blasting of horns (*sopar*) as war began (Judg. 7:19–20). When David and Saul returned from battle, women met them who were singing and dancing as well as playing the tambourine (*top*) and the sistrum (*salis*). A similar scene appears in Exodus 15, when Miriam and the other women sing and play the tambourine following the rout of the Egyptian army.

Royal Court

Musicians were part of the royal retinue. Saul lauded David's ability as a court musician (1 Sam. 16:23). Singing men and women are mentioned in 2 Samuel 19:35. Amos's social statement of the northern kingdom included a critique of the wealthy rulers who stretched out upon couches and sang songs to the sound of the harp (*nebal*).

Prophecy

Music was frequently associated with prophecy in the Old Testament. Biblical texts suggest music was used to induce a state of prophetic ecstasy. In 1 Samuel 10:5, Samuel tells Saul that he will encounter a band of prophets playing the harp (*nebal*), the tambourine (*top*), the flute (*halil*), and the lyre (*kinnor*). Upon hearing the music Saul will fall into a prophetic frenzy, and the spirit of the Lord will be upon him (cf. 2 Kings 3:15).

Temple

Music was central to worship in the temple, and the book of Psalms provides ample evidence for the use of singing and instrumental music in the temple. Numerous instruments are mentioned throughout the Psalter, as is the frequent command for the people to sing or lift up a song (cf. Ps. 81:3–4). The superscriptions contain what many believe are musical expressions such as "According to the Lilies" (Psalms 45 and 69), but the precise meaning of these directives has been lost to history.

Other Occasions

Music, singing, and dancing were a part of everyday life as well (Gen. 31:27; Judg. 21:20–21; Isa. 16:10–11).

✚ Saint Augustine, an influential church father from the fourth century AD, took the title for his famous book *The City of God* from Psalm 87:3, "Glorious things are said of you, O city of God!"

What Is the Message of Psalms?

The book of Psalms is so vast (150 psalms!) that space does not allow us to comment on each individual psalm. But the Psalms can be grouped into categories based on their theme and their structure, and we can get a good feel for the message of Psalms as a whole by looking at several of the categories. Keep in mind that the psalms are poetic, and poetry, almost by definition, resists categorizing. So the classic features we present below are basic generalizations. Exceptions abound.

As we stressed above, the two central themes in Psalms are lament and praise. The lament psalms can be broken down into two distinctive groups: personal or individual laments and national or community laments. Likewise, the praise psalms can be broken down into several subgroups: individual testimony psalms; descriptive praise psalms; enthronement psalms; royal psalms; and songs of Zion (often called pilgrim psalms). In addition, there are a handful of psalms that are unique and do not fit neatly into any of these specific categories.

A fascinating feature that occurs in several psalms is the use of the Hebrew alphabet to structure the psalm. These are called alphabetic psalms (sometimes called "acrostic psalms"). The alphabetic psalms are categorized by this peculiar alphabetic feature and not by content. Thus an alphabetic psalm can also fall in one of the other categories (e.g., Psalm 9 is both an alphabetic psalm and an individual lament).

In general there is a transition throughout the book of Psalms from lament (many of the psalms in book 1) to praise, which dominates the later books.

Individual Lament Psalms

The individual lament psalms are those psalms where an individual (often David, but not always) cries out to God about his specific personal problem. The individual lament psalms include the following: Psalms 3–5, 7, 9–10, 13–14, 17, 22, 25–28, 31, 35, 39–43, 52–57, 59, 61, 64, 69–71, 77, 86, 88–89, 109, 120, and 139–142. These psalms can be grouped together both by theme (lament) and by form. That is, they all share a similar structure in that the topics they cover follow the same general order.

The general structure of individual lament psalms

Address These psalms begin with an introductory cry for help and/or a statement of turning to God.

✚ Jesus quotes from Psalm 22:1 while on the cross, just prior to his death (Matt. 27:46; Mark 15:34).

Lament In either a brief or extended fashion the psalmist describes his state of suffering. Frequently this section has three subjects—You, O God; I; and my foes.

Confession of trust This section contains a statement of renewed trust or faith in God. Often it is placed in contrast with the lament section and is frequently introduced with "but" or "however."

Ancient musicians in Mesopotamia playing at a temple foundation ceremony (2100 BC).

Petition In this section the psalmist presents his petition to God; that is, what he is asking God to do. Frequently he presents two actual petitions—for God to be favorable to him and for God to intervene into his troubles.

Vow or declaration of praise The psalmist will go one of two directions here. Either he will make a vow, describing how he will praise God if God answers his petition (prayer), or he will go ahead and praise God in advance for answering his prayer, confident that God will indeed intervene and rescue him from his situation.

Psalm 142: An example of an individual lament psalm

Address (142:1–3a) "I cry aloud to the Lord; I lift up my voice. . . . I pour out my complaint before him."

Lament (142:3b–4) "Men have hidden a snare for me. . . . No one is concerned for me. . . . No one cares for my life."

Confession of trust (142:5) "I say, 'You are my refuge.'"

Petition (142:6–7a) "Rescue me from those who pursue me. . . . Set me free from my prison."

Vow or declaration of praise (142:7b) ". . . that I may praise your name."

National or Community Lament Psalms

The national or community lament psalms are those in which an entire community, often the entire nation of Israel, cries out to God and asks him to help them or deliver them. Often these psalms are in response to the terrible destruction of Jerusalem by the Babylonians and the consequential exile of Israel to Babylon. The national/community lament psalms include Psalms 12, 44, 58, 60, 74, 79–80, 83, 85, 90, 94, 123, 126, 129, and 137. The structure of these psalms is identical to the individual lament psalms (address, lament, confession of trust, petition, vow or declaration of praise) except that the pronouns are plural ("we" instead of "I"), and the point of view is the community or nation.

Psalm 74: An example of a national lament psalm

Address (74:1–2) "Why have you rejected us forever, O God? . . . Remember the people you purchased of old."

Lament (74:3–11) A description of the destroyed temple in Jerusalem.

Ancient trumpet player from western Anatolia (800–500 BC).

Confession of trust (74:12–17) "But you, O God . . . bring salvation upon the earth."

Petition (74:18–23) "Do not forget the lives of your afflicted people forever. Have regard for your covenant. . . . Rise up, O God, and defend your cause."

Vow or declaration of praise Psalm 74 does not contain a vow of praise. This is a reminder that there are variations from the pattern and not all psalms will follow the pattern in every detail (this is poetry, remember). However, some have suggested that Psalm 75 in its entirety functions as the "declaration of praise" for Psalm 74.

Individual Testimony Psalms

In these psalms, the psalmist praises God by proclaiming publicly what God has done for him. While the lament psalms look forward ("Save me! Rescue me!"), the individual testimony psalms look back at God's deliverance and proclaim, "He saved me; he rescued me." These psalms are similar to a modern "testimony" shared with a Christian community in which someone, out of gratitude to God, shares how God answered his or her prayers and worked in his or her life. Individual testimony psalms include Psalms 18, 21, 30, 32, 34, 40–41, 66, 116, and 138.

The general structure of individual testimony psalms

This type of psalm exhibits more variety than some of the other types, but typically it will conform to most of the following pattern:

Proclamation of praise to God These psalms open with a declaration of praise or adoration of God, such as "I will praise the Lord," "I will exalt you, O Lord," or "I love you, O Lord."

Introductory summary statement The psalmist often gives a one- or two-verse summary statement of what he has learned about God (and why he is praising him).

The story of deliverance In these verses the psalmist shares what actually happened. Often he will revisit the initial situation from which he cried out to God for help. Then he will describe how God intervened to deliver him.

Praise and teaching Here the psalmist either vows to praise God or just goes ahead and states his praise. Sometimes this turns into a "teaching" or "instruction" section as the psalmist proclaims to his audience truths about the Lord and his work, often exhorting them to join him in praising God.

Psalm 34: An example of an individual testimony psalm

Proclamation of praise to God (34:1–3) "I will extol the Lord at all times."

Introductory summary statement Psalm 34 does not have a summary statement, unless 34:4 serves as the summary and the introduction into the story of deliverance.

The story of deliverance (34:4–7) "I sought the Lord, and he answered me; he delivered me from all my fears. . . . This poor man called, and the Lord heard him; he saved him out of all his troubles."

Praise and teaching (34:8–22) Psalm 34 has mostly teaching in this section. "Taste and see that the Lord is good. . . . Come, my children, listen to me; I will teach you the fear of the Lord."

Descriptive Praise Psalms

These psalms exhort the audience to join in praising God because of his greatness (especially as seen in creation) or because of his grace (especially as revealed through his great acts in human history). Psalms in this category are perhaps the easiest to identify because they begin with the Hebrew word

✚ The New Testament quotes from Psalms more than any other Old Testament book.

Psalms   275

Assyrian wall relief showing a soldier and three prisoners, possibly Israelites, playing the lyre (seventh century BC).

hallelujah, which means "praise the Lord!" Included in this category are Psalms 33, 106, 111, 113, 117, 135, and 146–150.

The general structure of descriptive praise psalms

Prologue These psalms will start off with *Hallelujah* ("Praise the Lord!").

Call to praise The psalmist will usually call on others (servants of the Lord, people in general, the heavens, angels, his own "soul," etc.) to join him in praising the Lord.

Reason for praising God Often there is a summary statement followed by specific illustrations.

Concluding statement Here the psalmist usually gives an exhortation, petition, or a renewed call to praise as a concluding summary statement.

Epilogue Often the descriptive praise psalms also end with *Hallelujah* ("Praise the Lord!"), just as they began.

Psalm 113: An example of a descriptive praise psalm

Prologue (113:1a) "Praise the Lord."

Call to praise (113:1b–3) "Praise, O servants of the Lord. . . . From the rising of the sun to the place where it sets, the name of the Lord is to be praised."

Reason for praising God (113:4–9a) "The Lord is exalted over all the nations, . . . sits enthroned on high, . . . raises the poor from the dust[,] . . . settles the barren woman in her home as a happy mother of children."

Concluding statement Psalm 113 does not have a concluding statement.

Epilogue (113:9b) "Praise the Lord."

Enthronement Psalms

These psalms are classified by content and not by structure like those above. The enthronement psalms are indicated by the phrase "The Lord reigns" or a similar phrase. These psalms describe God as the King over all the earth. Often they have messianic implications. Included in the enthronement psalms are Psalms 47, 93, and 96–99.

Royal Psalms

The royal psalms usually deal with some event or aspect in the life of a current reigning king. In contrast to the enthronement psalms (which proclaim the Lord as King), these psalms seem to focus on the human king. Yet like the enthronement psalms, the royal psalms often have messianic nuances (see especially Psalm 110). The royal psalms include Psalms 2, 18, 20–21, 45, 72, 101, and 110.

Songs of Zion (Pilgrim Psalms and Songs of Ascent)

Technically Mount Zion was the bluff or ridge that the temple was built on. Eventually the term Zion was used to refer poetically to the entire city of Jerusalem, while still retaining a focus on the temple. These psalms were probably sung by pilgrims as they went up to Jerusalem to worship at the temple for one of Israel's festivals, thus they are sometimes called "pilgrim psalms" or "songs of ascent." Psalms that can be placed in this category include Psalms 84 and 120–134.

Alphabetic Psalms

Alphabetic psalms have a peculiar and fascinating structure that is noticeable only in the original Hebrew, for these psalms will follow the Hebrew alphabet in some manner. For example, consider Psalm 34. The first Hebrew letter of the first verse ("I will extol the Lord") is the letter *aleph*, which is the first letter in the Hebrew alphabet. The next verse (34:2) starts with *bet*, the second letter of the Hebrew alphabet, and so forth all the way through the alphabet.

There are other variations on how the psalms use the alphabet. Psalm 119 is a good example. The verses in this long psalm are organized into groups of eight. Each line of the first eight verses (119:1–8) starts with the Hebrew letter *aleph*, the first letter in the alphabet. Then the first lines of the next eight verses (119:9–16) all start with *bet*, the second letter of the alphabet, and so forth until 119:169–176, in which each line starts with *tav*, the last letter of the Hebrew alphabet.

The purpose of this alphabetic organization is not clear. Perhaps it aided in memorization. Perhaps it was merely written this way for aesthetic purposes (i.e., an artistic touch). Most likely it symbolized the completeness of the topic. For example, in English we can say "that's the truth from A to Z" meaning the complete truth. Thus the psalmist in 119 would be extolling and praising God's law "from A to Z" (Hebrew, *aleph* to *tav*).

So What? Applying Psalms to Our Lives Today

Most of you are probably already quite adept at applying the Psalms in your lives. You have used them to lead you in worshiping and praising God. You have used them to draw comfort and strength during trying times. You may have also used them to meditate on during your personal devotional time. These are valid applications of the Psalms. Keep using them that way.

But there is also another powerful application of the Psalms in our lives that is perhaps not quite as commonly appreciated. The Psalms tell us (indeed provide us with inspired models) that it is okay to cry out in pain and frustration to God. Sometimes in the church we convey to people that it is spiritually immature to express anything other than bright, upbeat optimism. This implies (incorrectly) that mature Christians always have it all together. The psalmist contradicts this, crying out, "How long, O Lord? Will you forget me forever? How long will you hide your face from me?" (13:1). Again in Psalm 22:2 we find the psalmist pouring out his heart in anguish because God won't answer his prayers: "O my God, I cry out by day, but you do not answer." If we prayed like this in church, no one would ever call on us to pray again. Yet these psalms (especially the laments) are very important because they give us divinely inspired models of how to cry out to God honestly when we are hurting. Psalms teaches us it is okay to hurt and to express that pain to God, even publicly (or especially publicly). Sometimes an entire church congregation can be devastated by a tragedy, and the entire church can suffer and hurt. The Psalms give us a way to publicly and corporately cry out in pain to God, a critical step on the way to healing.

Our Favorite Verse in Psalms

The Lord is my shepherd, I shall not be in want. (23:1)

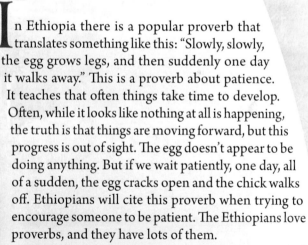

Proverbs

For Attaining Wisdom and Discipline

I n Ethiopia there is a popular proverb that
translates something like this: "Slowly, slowly,
the egg grows legs, and then suddenly one day
it walks away." This is a proverb about patience.
It teaches that often things take time to develop.
Often, while it looks like nothing at all is happening,
the truth is that things are moving forward, but this
progress is out of sight. The egg doesn't appear to be
doing anything. But if we wait patiently, one day, all
of a sudden, the egg cracks open and the chick walks
off. Ethiopians will cite this proverb when trying to
encourage someone to be patient. The Ethiopians love
proverbs, and they have lots of them.

Proverbs are embedded into North American culture as well. "Don't count your chickens before they're
hatched." "You can lead a horse to water, but you can't
make it drink." "If you can't stand the heat, get out of
the kitchen." These are some of our favorites. How many
other folksy proverbs can you think of? Which are your
favorites? If you are from another culture, can you think
of proverbs in your culture? Almost every culture and

language of the world uses short, pithy proverbial statements to try to pass on commonsense wisdom from generation to generation.

What Is the Setting for Proverbs?

Headings in the book of Proverbs indicate that the book is composed of four major collections, each with different authors or editors (collectors). Thus Proverbs 1–24 is attributed to Solomon; Proverbs 25–29 are additional proverbs of Solomon that are copied by King Hezekiah's scribes (probably collected and edited by them as well); Proverbs 30 is attributed to a man named Agur, unknown to us elsewhere, but perhaps a scribe; and Proverbs 31 is attributed to an unknown king named Lemuel (who learned this material from his mother).

Wisdom in the ancient world can be defined as rational guidelines for right living. No doubt peasants and farmers in the ancient world had folksy proverbs, similar to ours today. Yet even before the time of Solomon, across the ancient Near East there were kings, scribes, priests, and other educated individuals who were involved in the formal intellectual pursuit of practical wisdom. In extolling Solomon's great wisdom, 1 Kings 4:30 mentions the wisdom of the "East" (i.e., Mesopotamia) as well as the wisdom of Egypt. First Kings 4:29–34 implies that Solomon was familiar with the wisdom from these areas. He probably studied the wisdom literature from Mesopotamia and from Egypt. First Kings 4:32 says that Solomon "spoke" three thousand proverbs. The text is not clear about whether he composed these or just knew them and was able to recite them. Probably Solomon collected proverbs, both from within Israel and from the rest of the ancient Near East. He probably also created some of his own. Under the inspiration of God, during the reign of Solomon (971–931 BC) and later during

A sheet of papyrus from the Instruction of Ankhsheshonq, containing numerous one-line Egyptian proverbs.

Proverbs in the Ancient Near East

Tremper Longman III

The proverb was a popular genre in the ancient Near East. We find proverb collections and instructional literature that contains proverbs written in Egyptian, Sumerian, Akkadian, and Aramaic. Proverbs are among the earliest literature known, dating to the first half of the third millennium BC, and they persisted to the latest periods of ancient Near Eastern literature.

Ancient Near Eastern proverbs provide a background to the study of the book of Proverbs, and indeed there is strong evidence that the biblical writers were aware of other ancient Near Eastern texts and sometimes even drew inspiration from them as they wrote their proverbs in Hebrew.

Egyptian proverbs are the best known and most important for the study of Hebrew proverbs. These proverbs are found within instructions of a father to a son, one of the most popular Egyptian genres. The earliest examples (Hardjedef, Kagemni, Ptahhotep, and Merikare) come from the third millennium BC. The most famous example, though, is the Instruction of Amenemope from the end of the second millennium BC, which was first presented to the public in 1923. Immediately, scholars noted similarities between its structure and its content and the book of Proverbs, in particular the section subtitled "words of the wise" (22:17–24:22). Significance has been attached to how the Egyptian text has thirty chapters while the biblical text has thirty sayings (22:20). While Amenemope is the best-known example, many of the other Egyptian texts express similar teaching as the biblical book. Even so, the theological foundation of Proverbs radically separates that book from all ancient Near Eastern texts ("the fear of the Lord is the beginning of wisdom"; Prov. 1:7).

In Mesopotamia, the earliest Sumerian literature includes extensive collections of proverbs. Today more than twenty-five collections of proverbs are known from this early period. Some of the topics are similar to those treated in Proverbs, including family relationships, women, the liar, the court, and the good/righteous person. Sumerian also has an instructional text where the flood hero Ziusudra receives advice from his father, Shuruppak (Instructions of Shuruppak). The Babylonians and Assyrians did not produce original proverbs in their own language, though they continued the use of the Sumerian collections.

Finally, Ahiqar is an Aramaic text, set in the seventh century BC, that also provides background to the book of Proverbs. Ahiqar was an adviser to Assyrian kings. His nephew framed him so that he was to be executed, but he escaped and was eventually restored to his position. After beating his nephew, he then instructs him by means of proverbs. Some of these proverbs seem closely related to the teaching of Proverbs, perhaps most notably, "Spare not your son from the rod; otherwise, can you save him [from wickedness]?" (Saying 3, compare Prov. 13:24; 23:13–14).

the reign of Hezekiah (716–687 BC), a large number of these were collected, edited, and included in the Bible as Proverbs 1–29.

Throughout this process there was probably a constant interaction and mixing of folksy, homespun proverbial wisdom from the farms of Israel and intellectual, philosophical reflection from educated scholars (including Solomon) in the courts of Jerusalem.

What Is at the Heart of Proverbs?

The purpose of the book of Proverbs is expressed clearly in the opening verses: "for attaining wisdom and discipline[,] ... doing what is right and just and fair" (1:2–3), and for teaching both the simple or young as well as the wise and discerning (1:4–5). The book of Proverbs is tied theologically to the rest of the Old Testament by 1:7: "The fear of the Lord is the beginning of knowledge," thus underpinning the search for wise living to obedience before God.

Proverbs at its core is about building character. It provides guidelines for right and wise character development. It stresses that character produces behavior and that behavior produces serious consequences.

As mentioned above in our introduction to the Wisdom Books (Job, Proverbs, Ecclesiastes, Song of Songs), Proverbs presents the norms of life— things that are generally and normally true, things that one should build their character around. For example, Proverbs teaches that by working hard, one will prosper and do well. This is normally true, and a hard-work ethic is certainly a foundational virtue that will help one to live wisely. But this is not universally true; neither is it an unqualified promise from God. There are exceptions to this in life, as Job aptly illustrates. There are modern exceptions as well. For example, in the mid-1980s there was a terrible drought and famine in Ethiopia. Thousands of godly Christian farmers were affected by the drought and devastated by the famine. These people were not lazy; they were hardworking, as hardworking as any in the world. Hard work was still a good character virtue for them to embrace, but the consequences of that proverbial truth did not apply to them due to their unique situation. It is normally true, not universally true.

So Proverbs presents the norms of life, and the other books (Job, Ecclesiastes, Song of Songs) focus on the exceptions. All the Wisdom Books need to be taken together to balance one another. Proverbs without Job can lead to

A clay tablet containing Sumerian proverbs (2000–1800 BC).

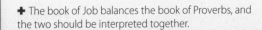
✚ The book of Job balances the book of Proverbs, and the two should be interpreted together.

incorrect practical theology, as Job's three friends illustrate. Part of becoming truly and biblically wise is learning how to apply the various proverbial teachings in the book of Proverbs to the differing contexts of life.

Because the maxims in Proverbs are normally true, most of the time we can apply the majority of them to our lives quite easily. The book of Proverbs deals with the most basic aspects of life: family, neighbors, work, speech, society, and so on. Out of this day-to-day "living in the real world" context, several central themes emerge from Proverbs: wisdom versus folly; improper aspects of speech (anger, gossip, etc.); spouses and families (including sexual immorality); laziness versus hard work; proper attitudes toward the poor; and the righteous versus the wicked.

One of the ways that Proverbs teaches wisdom is through its portrayal of four basic character types. First there is the *simple* (or *naive*). This person is not too smart and doesn't want to be. Second is the *fool*. He is not smart either, but thinks he is and has convinced the *simple/naive* one that he is. Third is the *scoffer* or *mocker*. He is actually very smart (in human terms), but he does not fear the Lord, thus his intelligence does not translate into true wisdom, and he becomes a bitter skeptic. The fourth character type portrayed in Proverbs is the *wise*, who is smart and discerning, but who also fears the Lord. The central teaching in Proverbs is the exhortation to us to strive to become like the *wise*, and not like the *simple*, the *fool*, or the *scoffer*.

A brief structural outline of Proverbs is as follows:

- The Proverbs of Solomon (1:1–24:34)
  - Introduction (1:1–7)
  - A father's wisdom for the young and gullible (1:8–9:18)
  - Short proverbs (10:1–22:16)
  - Sayings of the wise (22:17–24:34)
- The Proverbs of Solomon Collected by Hezekiah's Scribes (25:1–29:27)
- The Sayings of Agur and Lemuel (30:1–31:31)

What Makes Proverbs Interesting and Unique?

- Proverbs gives us help about how to deal with issues in our daily lives, relating to family, friends, and work.
- Many of the individual proverbs can be applied fairly easily.

✚ James 4:6 and 1 Peter 5:5 quote directly from the Greek Septuagint translation of Proverbs 3:34.

- Proverbs warns against sexual immorality.
- There are many proverbs that address speech problems (gossip, honesty, anger).
- Numerous proverbs speak of the importance of friends.
- Proverbs gives lots of advice about how to raise children.
- Proverbs opens with a focus on fathers and sons, and closes with a focus on a mother and wives.

What Is the Message of Proverbs?

The Proverbs of Solomon (1:1–24:34)

Introduction (1:1–7)

The opening verse associates the following proverbs with Solomon and then states the purpose of the book. Two goals are mentioned here. The first goal is attaining wisdom and understanding. The second goal is a result of the first and involves how one lives—doing what is right and just and fair (1:2–6). Proverbs 1:7 then reminds the reader that true knowledge cannot be obtained without a proper relationship with God.

A father's wisdom for the young and gullible (1:8–9:18)

The book of Proverbs does not start off with the typical short, pithy, two-lined proverbs, but rather with several long admonitions from a father to his son, interrupted twice as the voice of personified wisdom chimes in. The son stands on the verge of adulthood with two very different paths before him. On the one hand, he hears the voice of wisdom from his father. On the other hand, he feels the strong temptation of sexual immorality as well as peer pressure to run with a rowdy, less-than-virtuous gang who entices him to pursue easy money that doesn't require hard work. The two worldviews before him are wisdom versus folly, resulting in either life or death.

Thus in Proverbs 1:8–19 the father encourages the son to reject the gang and the lure of easy money acquired through violence. The personified voice of wisdom interrupts in 1:20–33, rebuking the naive (or simple) and the fool because they refuse to listen to her. In 2:1–22 the father speaks again, telling the son that true wisdom will protect him from wicked men (2:11–15) and wicked women (i.e., the adulteress; 2:16–19). Yet true wisdom can never be lived out without faith and trust in the Lord. Thus 3:1–35 directs the young man to God. Proverbs 3:5–6 summarizes the advice: "Trust in the Lord with all your heart and lean not on your own understanding; in all your ways acknowledge him, and he will make your paths straight." In 4:1–27 the father exhorts, almost pleads, with the son to learn from him and to embrace wisdom. Proverbs 5 tells the young man to stay faithful to his wife and to avoid adultery at all costs. In Proverbs 6 the father advises his son to work hard (6:1–11), watch out for scoundrels (6:12–19), and understand the severe consequences that result from adulterous affairs (6:20–35). Proverbs 7 continues to warn against the temptation of adultery, vividly describing how a simple/naive young man succumbed to this temptation, going in to the seductive adulteress "like an ox going to the slaughter" (7:22). In contrast to the seductive woman patrolling the streets and looking for gullible, naive young men (7:1–27), in Proverbs 8 it is wisdom who calls out to young men in the streets. Listening to the adulteress leads to death (7:27), while listening to wisdom leads to life and favor with the Lord (8:35). Proverbs 9 continues a similar analogy of contrasting women, this time between "lady wisdom" and "lady folly." Once again the son is informed that the "fear of the Lord is the beginning of wisdom," resulting in life (9:10–11), while "lady folly" leads those who are simple/naive (i.e., without wisdom) to death (9:18).

Proverbs 6:1–5 exhorts one to free oneself from debt "like a gazelle from the hand of the hunter." The scene below shows Assyrians hunting gazelles.

✚ Several proverbs are repeated twice. Sometimes the two forms are identical and sometimes they reflect slight variations. See, for example, 6:10–11=24:33–44; 10:1=15:20; 14:12=16:25; 16:2=21:2; 19:5=19:9; 20:10=20:23.

The Lord abhors dishonest scales (Prov. 11:1; 16:11; 20:23). Shown above is a set of ancient bronze scales.

Short proverbs (10:1–22:16)

This section contains 375 short, two-line proverbs. These proverbs are seemingly unrelated to one another; that is, there is little clear, discernable structural organization in each chapter. Proverbs 15:33 ("the fear of the Lord teaches a man wisdom"), however, does appear to break this section into two basic units (10:1–15:33; 16:1–22:16), and there are some commonalities that unite each unit.

The first unit (10:1–15:33) is dominated by "antithetical" proverbs, where the second line of the proverb gives an opposite and contrasting reality from that stated in the first line. For example, in Proverbs 15:1 the first line reads, "A gentle answer turns away wrath." The second line is the opposite, contrasting reality: "but a harsh word stirs up anger." The second unit (16:1–22:16) contains two-line proverbs as well, but it contains a high concentration of synonymous or "complementary" type proverbs in which the second line echoes or adds to the first. For example, in Proverbs 19:17 the first line states, "He who is kind to the poor lends to the Lord." The second line is not antithetical, but complementary (in this case consequential): "and he [the Lord] will reward him for what he has done." Two slight differences in the two units are that Proverbs 16:1–22:16 has a higher concentration of proverbs dealing with the king, and also has more proverbs that mention the Lord.

Yet there are numerous common themes that resurface repeatedly throughout both subunits of Proverbs 10:1–22:16. The most frequent theme is the contrast between the wise man and the fool. Closely related to this is the contrast between the righteous and the wicked. Other important themes include laziness versus hard work; the family (children, parents, wives); controlling the tongue (how one speaks); poverty and wealth; pride and humility; and anger. Thus this section gives wise advice across a wide gamut of practical living.

Sayings of the wise (22:17–24:34)

Interestingly much of the material in this section is very similar to an ancient Egyptian wisdom book titled *The Teachings of Amenemope*. This book predates Solomon, so apparently as Solomon gathered wisdom books from all over the known world, this was one of the books that he acquired and incorporated into his collection. One of the main topics of this collection is teaching young men how to interact with the wealthy (probably in the royal court) without being sucked into the vain pursuit of wealth.

The Proverbs of Solomon Collected by Hezekiah's Scribes (25:1–29:27)

This section is similar to Proverbs 10–22, and contains many of the same themes: the wise man and wisdom versus the fool and folly; righteousness versus wickedness; laziness versus hard work; and how to control one's speech. This unit also has numerous proverbs that speak of God, and proverbs dealing with the king. Especially prevalent in this section are proverbs that deal with the poor, especially in regard to the legal system.

The Sayings of Agur and Lemuel (30:1–31:31)

We do not know anything about the wise man Agur and King Lemuel outside of the references to them here in Proverbs 30–31. They are probably from the same country, but they are probably not Israelites, for neither name is a Hebrew name.

Agur's proverbs are different in structure from most of those in the rest of Proverbs. His collection is characterized by the literary structure of mentioning "three things" and then "four," followed by a list of four things that illustrate his point.

Proverbs 31, "the sayings of King Lemuel," is actually attributed to the king's mother. Thus just as the book of Proverbs opens with advice from a father to his son, it closes with the advice of a mother to her son (31:1–9), followed by the description of a wife of noble character (31:10–31). Lemuel's mother tells him to watch out for women and hard drinking. Instead, she exhorts, focus on helping the poor (31:1–9).

It is rather significant that Proverbs ends with a lengthy description of a "wife/woman of noble character." The book of Proverbs is filled with good advice about wise living, much of it aimed at young men. The ending seems to say that one of the wisest things a young man can do is to marry an outstanding woman like the one described in Proverbs 31:10–31. Likewise, the character of the woman described in this passage also provides a strong model for young women to aspire to.

"Reckless words pierce like a sword" (Prov. 12:18).

There are several interesting aspects of this closing section, in addition to its fascinating content. First of all, Proverbs 31:10–31 is an "acrostic," similar to the alphabetic psalms we encounter in the book of Psalms. In Hebrew, each line in Proverbs 31:10–31 begins with the next consecutive letter of the alphabet. Thus verse 10 begins with *aleph*, the first letter in the Hebrew alphabet, and verse 31 begins with *tav*, the final letter in the alphabet. This is kind of like saying, "Here is the ideal wife, described from A to Z."

Another interesting aspect of ending Proverbs with this "woman of noble character" is that in the Hebrew canon, the book of Ruth follows immediately after Proverbs. In Proverbs 31:10 the question is raised, "A wife of noble character, who can find?" In Hebrew, the same word is used both for "wife" and for "woman." In Ruth 3:11 Boaz tells Ruth that everyone knows she is a "woman of noble character." The phrases "wife of noble character" (Prov. 31:10) and "woman of noble character" (Ruth 3:11) are identical. The link between these two identical phrases probably provides the rationale for placing Ruth immediately after Proverbs, as found in the Hebrew canon. Proverbs 31:10 asks who can find a woman of noble character, and then, in the very next book, such a woman appears: Ruth!

✚ Proverbs opens with a focus on fathers and sons, but closes with a focus on mothers and wives.

So What? Applying Proverbs to Our Lives Today

The book of Proverbs is filled with teaching that is applicable and relevant to us today. Proverbs teaches us not to be boastful or proud. We learn here, as throughout the Bible, that God just does not like prideful people, and that we should strive to be humble and concerned about others. This is part of wise living.

A wall relief from the palace at Susa showing a wealthy woman (perhaps a queen or princess) seated with a spindle in hand (cf. Prov. 31:19).

Proverbs also has a lot to say about our attitude toward the poor. Proverbs 17:5 implies that if we ridicule or make fun of the poor, we ridicule and make fun of God, for he created them.

We also learn in Proverbs that if we are wise, we will be calm, even-tempered, and slow to anger. We will speak soothing words that calm crisis situations. We will also be listeners, cautious about spouting off our own opinions and always ready to learn more wisdom from others.

Our Favorite Verse in Proverbs

A friend loves at all times,
and a brother is born for adversity. (17:17)

"Where there are no oxen, the manger is empty [i.e., clean with no mess], but from the strength of an ox comes an abundant harvest" (Prov. 14:4). Shown is an Egyptian model of oxen plowing (2000–1650 BC).

Ecclesiastes

What Is the Meaning of Life?

cclesiastes is one of the strangest books in the
Bible, and it is very, very different from the
book of Proverbs. If we try to read Ecclesiastes like
Proverbs, treating individual verses as independent
of each other and pulling them out of context, we
can come up with some very "un-Bible-like" statements. Consider 10:19, for example: "A feast is made
for laughter, and wine makes life merry, but money is
the answer for everything." Wow! Is Ecclesiastes telling
us that wisdom involves seeking after parties, drinking,
and money?

The answer, of course, is no. Ecclesiastes must be read
as an entire unit. It is an intellectual search for meaning
in life, and it is brutally honest about observed realities
in life, especially incongruities and injustices. Ecclesiastes
is very similar to Job in the respect that the answer to the
search does not come until the end of the book, so we must
persevere to the final chapter before we can hope to grasp
what the author is truly saying to us about life.

What Is the Setting for Ecclesiastes?

The opening lines of Ecclesiastes identify the content of the book as "the words of the Teacher, son of David, king in Jerusalem" (1:1). The Hebrew word that is translated by the New International Version as "teacher" is *Qohelet*, a very interesting word. It refers to one who speaks in the "assembly," which probably implies both a legal and political setting. In the Hebrew Bible *Qohelet* is the name of the book. The Septuagint (the ancient Greek translation of the Old Testament) translated this term as Ecclesiastes, meaning "the one who sits/speaks in the assembly" (Greek, *ekklesia*). Most of Ecclesiastes is written in first person (I), but it opens and closes by identifying the speaker as the Teacher (*Qohelet*) (1:1, 12; 12:8, 9). Most English Bibles either translate this word as Teacher or as Preacher.

Any of the kings descended from David could be called a "son of David," so the identity of the actual author is not completely clear. Traditionally, Christians have understood the author to be Solomon. Thus the book would have been written in about 900 BC. Although numerous scholars have proposed that Ecclesiastes was written much later than Solomon, the evidence seems to suggest that Solomon is the most plausible author of the book.

A Hittite banquet scene (ninth century BC). Eccl. 2:1–3 probably refers to party-like banquets.

Meaningless! Meaningless! Everything Is Meaningless!

The Hebrew word *hebel* is a critically important word in Ecclesiastes, occurring thirty-eight times. The importance of this word is stressed from the very beginning. After the heading, Ecclesiastes 1:2 provides an opening synopsis for most of the book. In Hebrew this verse has eight words, and five of these eight words are *hebel*. The New International Version translates the verse as follows:

> "'Meaningless! Meaningless!' says the Teacher.
> 'Utterly meaningless! Everything is meaningless.'"

Hebel is a difficult word to translate into English. The King James Version, the English Standard Version, and the New Revised Standard Version render it as "vanity," while the New International Version and the New Living Translation opt for "meaningless." The Holman Christian Standard Bible translates it as "futile."

The root meaning of *hebel* is related to breath or vapor, and the word can also be used to describe a mist. In this sense it refers to something that looks like it is there, but really isn't. A low-lying cloud or mist looks like something firm from a distance, but as you draw close, it disappears, and you realize that it was just an illusion of sorts. The Teacher of Ecclesiastes tells us that, when viewed apart from God, the meaning of life is this way. You think you can see it and grasp it, but, like a cloud vapor, it disappears and leaves you with nothing.

A similar meaning is conveyed by the phrase "chasing after the wind." This phrase is often added alongside of the concept of *hebel* to further enhance the nuance of meaninglessness or futility (1:14, 17; 2:11, 17, 26; 4:4, 6; 6:9).

The prophet Jeremiah also likes the term *hebel*. He uses it to refer to the emptiness and worthlessness of idolatry—that is, it looks like something is there (the stone idol), but in reality there isn't really anything there (Jer. 2:5; 8:19; 10:3, 8, 15; 14:22; 16:19; 51:18). Thus Jeremiah proclaims that both the idol and the worshipers of idols are *hebel*.

What Is at the Heart of Ecclesiastes?

Ecclesiastes is one of the Wisdom Books (Proverbs, Job, Ecclesiastes, and Song of Songs) and should be interpreted in the context of Old Testament "wisdom." The book of Proverbs defines the normal function of wisdom—how to live wisely in the world. According to Proverbs the world is ordered and rational. It operates according to basic cause-and-effect relationships. If you are righteous, you will be blessed. If you are wicked, you will be cursed. If you work hard, you will prosper, and if you are lazy, you will be poor. In Proverbs life makes sense and is fairly straightforward.

Job, however, shatters the notion that the logical retribution-based world of Proverbs is universal, applying to all situations. Ecclesiastes is very similar to Job, underscoring that there are exceptions to the norms of Proverbs. Yet the Teacher in Ecclesiastes moves beyond Job in probing the philosophical implications of the incongruities that he sees in life, for the Teacher is

✚ Ecclesiastes discusses the apparent contradictions one discovers when trying to understand the world logically, an issue not covered in the wisdom of Proverbs. In this sense Ecclesiastes complements the book of Proverbs.

"I also owned more herds and flocks than anyone in Jerusalem before me" (Eccl. 2:7). Depicted on this ancient Egyptian wall painting are herds of cattle.

intellectually and spiritually rattled by things that he sees in life that don't match up to the ordered and logical world of Proverbs. He realizes that while the rational, ordered approach to life ("wisdom") is good and certainly to be preferred over folly and stupidity, nonetheless the "wisdom" approach does not give him a framework with which to grasp the meaning of life.

Ecclesiastes is a story about the Teacher's intellectual search for meaning in life using the tools of wisdom (observation, reflection, correlation). Unfortunately, wisdom does not give him any satisfactory answers for ultimate meaning. It merely provides good intellectual tools with which to see the problems and inconsistencies in life. The Teacher wants to understand life and be able to come up with an overarching framework from which he can understand all of life, even the incongruities. In this he fails, and this is one of the main subpoints of the book (as it was for Job).

The final theological conclusion to Ecclesiastes, however, and the main point of the book, is that one should "fear God and keep his commandments, for this is the whole duty of man" (12:13). Wisdom is a good approach to life, and it is infinitely better than folly, but one cannot find meaning apart from acknowledging God as the ultimate creator (12:1). In addition, humankind cannot understand and comprehend everything, nor can they explain all observed phenomenon through simple cause-and-effect analysis. For this they need to believe and trust in God. Just as Proverbs opens with this truth (Prov. 1:7), so Job and Ecclesiastes end with the same truth, establishing that rational thought (traditional wisdom) and vibrant faith in God must go hand in hand for one to be truly and biblically wise. In the meantime, Ecclesiastes suggests, we should view life not as a mystery to be solved and understood, but rather as a gift to be enjoyed.

An outline of Ecclesiastes follows the intellectual search of the Teacher:

- The Introduction to the Teacher and His Quest for the Meaning of Life (1:1–18)
- The Futility of Play and Hard Work, and the Common Fate of All (2:1–26)
- God Establishes Order and Purpose in the World (3:1–22)
- But There Are Significant Exceptions (4:1–6:9)
  - Oppression (4:1–16)
  - Unjust wealth (5:1–6:9)
- Wisdom Is Good, but Ultimately It Fails; Man Cannot Understand Life (6:10–8:17)
- The Common Fate of All (9:1–12)
- Wisdom Is Better Than Folly, but Still Futile (9:13–11:10)
- The Conclusion: Remember Your Creator and Fear God (12:1–14)

What Makes Ecclesiastes Interesting and Unique?

- Ecclesiastes asks numerous hard, penetrating questions about the purpose of life.
- This book explores various unsuccessful avenues by which people try to find meaning (wealth, hard work, pleasure, understanding, etc.).
- The tone throughout most of Ecclesiastes is cynical and pessimistic.

"A time to mourn" (Eccl. 3:4). In the ancient world, mourning was often a public activity. These Egyptian women are mourning the death of the Pharaoh (1319–1204 BC).

✚ Prior to chapter 12, the Teacher's approach is primarily secular, seemingly oblivious to any concept of afterlife. He discovers that without God the secular intellectual search for meaning leads only to cynicism and despair.

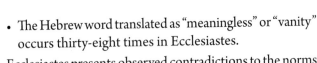

- The Hebrew word translated as "meaningless" or "vanity" occurs thirty-eight times in Ecclesiastes.
- Ecclesiastes presents observed contradictions to the norms of life described in Proverbs (e.g., Eccl. 7:15).

What Is the Message of Ecclesiastes?

The Introduction to the Teacher and His Quest for the Meaning of Life (1:1–18)

Ecclesiastes 1:1 and 1:12 introduce the Teacher (Hebrew, *Qohelet*). Ecclesiastes 1:2 then presents a clear summary of chapters 1–11. Thus we know from the beginning where this search will lead the Teacher. He has searched for meaning in life and come to the conclusion that life is utterly meaningless. This opening statement sets the pessimistic and cynical tone that will continue throughout the book until chapter 12.

In 1:12–18 the Teacher explains how he devoted himself to the study of wisdom. Likewise he wanted to understand madness and folly. But all this endeavor, he tells us here at the beginning of the book, is meaningless and a chasing after the wind.

The Futility of Play and Hard Work, and the Common Fate of All (2:1–26)

The Teacher tries to find meaning in life through some typical avenues. He tries physical pleasure (2:1–3, 10) as well as great building projects (2:4–9), but does not find meaning in either endeavor. He tries both folly and wisdom (2:3, 12). He recognizes wisdom as better than folly, but is terribly bothered by the observation that the same fate awaits both the wise man and the fool—they will both die (2:13–26). "So what's the point?" the Teacher asks.

God Establishes Order and Purpose in the World (3:1–22)

In the first part of this chapter the Teacher explains that God has established an ordered world—there is a proper time for everything.

"If the axe is dull and its edge unsharpened, more strength is needed" (Eccl. 10:10). Most axes in the ancient Near East at this time were made of bronze or copper alloy, thus needing frequent sharpening. Shown here is an axe from Mesopotamia.

Yet the Teacher continues by noting that people can't really understand what God has done. Paralleling the end of chapter 2, the Teacher then pessimistically notes the same fate awaits people that awaits the animals—they will both die (3:18–21). You might as well enjoy your work on earth, he concludes, for there is nothing else (3:22).

But There Are Significant Exceptions (4:1–6:9)

Oppression (4:1–16)

In Ecclesiastes 3:1–15 the Teacher declares that God established the cyclical times of life, giving order to our existence. Thus God seems to be in control of things. In the next section the Teacher points out several inconsistencies with that conclusion. How is one to understand terrible oppression? Those people are better off dead, he concludes (4:1–3). Then he revisits the futility of work (4:4–6), followed by the tragedy of being friendless (4:7–12), and the meaninglessness of political power (4:13–16).

Unjust Wealth (5:1–6:9)

The Teacher recognizes that working and striving for wealth lies at the heart of human existence (the ordered world as he sees it). Yet in reality, he notes, wealth is hardly a good motivator. Often it is acquired unjustly (5:8–9). Furthermore, one who desires wealth never seems to be satisfied with the wealth already acquired (5:10), and, among other problems, you can't take your wealth with you when you die (5:13–15). Finally, many wealthy people never actually get to enjoy their prosperity (6:1–9). Thus, the Teacher concludes, pursuing wealth as one of life's goals is meaningless and a chasing after the wind.

Wisdom Is Good, but Ultimately It Fails; Man Cannot Understand Life (6:10–8:17)

In this unit the Teacher explores wisdom as a way to understand life. Ultimately, he concludes, wisdom fails. His conclusion is stated in 8:17: "No one can comprehend what goes on under the sun. Despite all his efforts to search it out, man cannot discover its meaning. Even if a wise man claims he knows, he cannot really comprehend it."

"A live dog is better off than a dead lion!" (Eccl. 9:4). Dogs were common in the ancient Near East. Depicted here is a terra-cotta statue of a dog from Cyprus (750–500 BC).

The Common Fate of All (9:1–12)

Everyone is going to die, the Teacher points out, and how one fares in life has as much to do with chance as it does wisdom or righteousness.

Wisdom Is Better Than Folly, but Still Futile (9:13–11:10)

Wisdom is a good and even powerful thing, but it can be undermined so easily. Furthermore, even with wisdom one cannot understand what God is doing in the world.

The Conclusion: Remember Your Creator and Fear God (12:1–14)

The Teacher has tried to understand life through human wisdom alone, and this search has left him cynical and pessimistic about people, wisdom, and the meaning of life. It is all meaningless and a chasing after the wind. One cannot find meaning through human wisdom alone. This is the somber conclusion of Ecclesiastes 1–11.

Finally, in Ecclesiastes 12, the Teacher turns his search toward God. He introduces this section by calling on his audience to remember God, their creator, while they are young and still have their mental faculties. He then states the ultimate conclusion of his search: "Now all has been heard; here is the conclusion of the matter: Fear God and keep his commandments, for this is the whole duty of man" (12:13). The Teacher finally realizes that life is about serving God. It is in serving God that one finds ultimate meaning. Our goal in life, then, is not to understand life, but to serve God and enjoy life as a gift from him. The Teacher is not negative toward wisdom for day-to-day living. Certainly wisdom is to be preferred over folly. But he now realizes that human wisdom by itself falls short. Only when wisdom is built on "the fear of the Lord" is it truly profitable as a guide for life.

So What? Applying Ecclesiastes to Our Lives Today

As strange as Ecclesiastes is, when understood properly it resonates very well with many people today. Ecclesiastes tells us that we will not find meaning in life apart from serving God. As in

Ecclesiastes, many people today try to find meaning for their life through their work, their lifelong quest to accumulate wealth, or through the pursuit of pleasure and/or happiness. As the Teacher of Ecclesiastes tells us, a life lived only for these goals is meaningless, futile, and a chasing after the wind. Regardless of how smart we are or how hard we work, it is only as we serve God that life takes on significant meaning.

Our Favorite Verse in Ecclesiastes

Of making many books there is no end, and much study wearies the body. (12:12)

The Jewish cemetery just outside the walls of Jerusalem. "All share a common destiny— the righteous and the wicked" (Eccl. 9:2).

Song of Songs

Wild and Crazy Love Songs

Those who assume that the Bible is either boring or prudish are in for a real shock when they read the Song of Songs carefully. This book is a collection of mushy love songs in which a man and a woman sing joyfully and intimately to each other. This couple, who apparently marries in the middle of the book, also celebrates their sexuality, praising each other for the joy and pleasure each counterpart brings to the relationship. This is a steamy, R-rated book.

What Is the Setting for Song of Songs?

The opening verse in the book serves as a title, "Solomon's Song of Songs." Although some scholars argue that this book was probably written long after Solomon, the church and the synagogue have traditionally accepted Solomonic authorship. Yet while it is perhaps correct to see Solomon personally involved in developing this "song," it does not mean that this love story is necessarily autobiographical of Solomon. First Kings 4:32 declares that Solomon composed 1,005 songs. The title "song of songs" means "the best song," implying perhaps that this praise of sexuality in marriage was the high point of his song-writing endeavor.

But how was such a racy book to be used in the life and worship of Israel? Some scholars have suggested that Song of Songs was to be read at weddings as part of the wedding ceremony. This is possible, but there is no real conclusive evidence for this. Most likely it is best to understand this book as part of the wisdom literature, as indicated by its location in the canon. The Wisdom Books address how one is to live wisely, touching on topics such as work, family, friends, wealth, and misfortune, among others. Clearly the role of human sexuality is a very important component of living. One's intimate relationship with their spouse is one of the most foundational and critical relationships in their lives. To be truly wise, one needs to know how to love their spouse properly. The Song of Songs gives us guidance in this area of life.

What Is at the Heart of Song of Songs?

In Proverbs 1–9, remember, the father warns his son repeatedly to be on his guard against adultery and to avoid the temptations of loose women. Regarding marriage, the book of Proverbs gives some basic sound advice. First, on the negative side, it cautions us against marrying someone who nags or is quarrelsome (Prov. 19:13; 21:9, 19; 25:24; 27:15). Second, on the positive side, it advises us to marry someone of stellar character (Prov. 12:4; 31:10–31). This is good, sound, logical (wise) advice. But it is not enough. The quiet, reserved, prim and proper demeanor of Proverbs toward one's spouse is fine and appropriate for public life. Song of Songs, however, tells us that things need to change when the couple is home alone and the lights go out. Now a truly "wise" man is to be madly in love with his wife. Both he and his wife are to enjoy a rather wild and crazy love for each other. The rational, determined, and reflective philosophical approach to life (i.e., Proverbs) now gives way to sensuality. The calm, careful, and reserved speech of the wise one in Proverbs now gives way to mushy, sappy love whisperings in the ear of one's spouse.

At various times throughout history Christians have interpreted Song of Songs

Egyptian necklace (1330 BC). "You have stolen my heart with one glance of your eyes, with one jewel of your necklace" (Song 4:9).

304

as an allegory about Jesus Christ (the beloved) and his bride, the church. But this understanding is difficult to sustain if one reads carefully. Practically all scholars today concur that this is a book celebrating human sexuality.

The Song of Songs is really a series of short songs that a man and a woman (called the Shulamite in 6:13) sing to each other. Occasionally a group of friends chime in. This account is probably an idealized account of newly married lovers, written or collected by Solomon, but not necessarily autobiographical of Solomon, who had one thousand wives.

Pomegranate fruit. Pomegranates are mentioned several times in Song of Songs (4:13; 6:11; 7:12; 8:2).

These statements by the man and the woman (she does most of the talking) are extremely mushy and corny, but of course this is true only to us as outsiders. To those couples who are madly and wildly in love, corny and mushy intimacies are quite wonderful.

The Song of Songs can be roughly outlined as follows:

- The Courtship (1:1–3:5)
- The Wedding (3:6–5:1)
- The Honeymoon (5:2–8:14)

What Makes Song of Songs Interesting and Unique?

- The Song of Songs contains very colorful and fairly explicit poetic language about a husband's and wife's affection for each other.
- In contrast to Proverbs 1–9, which warns against illicit sexual activities, Song of Songs celebrates sexuality within marriage.
- Song of Songs has a courtship, a wedding, and a honeymoon.
- Song of Songs corrects the misnomer that in the Bible the purpose of the physical relationship in marriage was merely to produce children. Song of Songs does not mention children at all, but has lots to say about love.

What Is the Message of Song of Songs?

The Courtship (1:1–3:5)

The woman speaks first (1:2–4) and seems to take most of the initiative in the dialogue throughout the book. In 1:2–7 she longs for her lover's affection. In 1:8–2:7 the woman and the man exchange compliments to each other, expressing their affection for each other. In 2:8–17 the woman seems to

✚ The woman in Song of Songs calls herself "a rose of Sharon" (2:1). Sharon was a fertile plain to the south of Mount Carmel, often referred to symbolically (Isa. 33:9; 35:2; 65:10). Peter ministers in this region in the New Testament (Acts 9).

Wall relief of a gazelle from Carchemish. Song of Songs mentions gazelles five times (2:9, 17; 4:5; 7:3; 8:14).

reflect back on their courtship, while in 3:1–5 she dreams about him at night.

Throughout Song of Songs, the imagery will go back and forth from rustic settings in the vineyard and in the pasture (1:6–8) to urban settings in the city (3:6–11; 5:7–8).

The Wedding (3:6–5:1)

Song of Songs 3:6–11 describes a wedding procession, complete with a beautiful carriage. The implications are that 4:1–5:1 derive from the wedding night. Here the groom showers his lovely wife with multiple compliments about her beauty.

The Honeymoon (5:2–8:14)

In 5:2–8 the woman bemoans a time when her husband came and knocked on her door, but left because she couldn't respond in time. She then ran aimlessly out into the city looking for him. Probably this episode is also from a dream, but the text is not clear. She then talks with her friends about how handsome her man is, giving a lengthy and glowing description of him (5:9–6:3). For the rest of the book (6:4–8:14) the two lovers address each other intimately, occasionally interrupted by the chorus of friends. This section is dominated by the many, many compliments the man and the woman give to each other about how beautiful/handsome and desirable they are.

So What? Applying Song of Songs to Our Lives Today

This book is especially applicable to couples who have just married. In the early days of celebrating the marriage it can be fun to read this aloud to each other (i.e., let the new wife read the woman's part and the new husband read the man's part). This can be rather humorous, but nonetheless fun and instructive.

But the Song of Songs is also a book of wisdom for all married couples as well. We can apply this book by expressing our love to our spouse with lots of mushy, dopey, intimate compliments. The goal of wisdom is to develop character, so as we progress toward this goal we will embrace this model of

✦ Twice the man in Song of Songs compliments his beautiful young wife's teeth—white like sheep, each with its twin (4:2; 6:6); that is, she is not missing any teeth! In the ancient world that was remarkable indeed.

having an expressive intimate love relationship with our spouses. In public we will follow the model of Proverbs and be distinguished, respectable, and reserved. But at home when the lights go out, we should follow the pattern provided by these two young lovers in Song of Songs, and be a little goofy and crazy about each other.

On a humorous note, if you do try to apply Song of Songs to your marriage relationship, it would be wise to contextualize your mushy compliments to fit today's culture. We don't think it will go over too well, for example, if a husband tells his wife that her hair looks like a flock of goats (4:1) or that her nose looks like the tower of Lebanon (7:4).

Our Favorite Verses in Song of Songs

Place me like a seal over your heart,
*   like a seal on your arm;*
*   for love is as strong as death,*
*   its jealousy unyielding as the grave.*
It burns like a blazing fire,
*   like a mighty flame.*
Many waters cannot quench love;
*   rivers cannot wash it away. (8:6–7)*

Depicted below on an Assyrian wall relief is a royal chariot. "Look! It is Solomon's carriage" (Song of Songs 3:7).

The Prophets

Without doubt, the Old Testament prophetic books contain some of the most fascinating and colorful passages in the entire Bible. Many of our most favorite Bible verses are in the Prophets. What about you? Perhaps your favorite is Isaiah 40:31:

> But those who hope in the Lord
>   will renew their strength.
>   They will soar on wings like eagles;
>   they will run and not grow weary,
>   they will walk and not be faint.

Or maybe you have found Jeremiah 29:11 especially encouraging: "'For I know the plans I have for you,' declares the Lord, 'plans to prosper you and not to harm you, plans to give you hope and a future.'" Or perhaps you have been especially touched by the powerful messianic prophecies scattered throughout the Prophets, verses like Isaiah 53:6:

> We all, like sheep, have gone astray,
>   each of us has turned to his own way;
>   and the Lord has laid on him
>   the iniquity of us all.

Or perhaps you have found yourself skimming over most of the verses in the prophetic books, wondering how on earth any of these strange things have any relevance to you. Have you puzzled over the many grim texts of judgment in books like Amos and Jeremiah, or perhaps scratched your head at the bizarre images in Ezekiel, Daniel, and Zechariah? Our goal in the pages

✦ The Old Testament prophetic books are about the same size as the entire New Testament.

that follow is to provide you with some basic guidelines that will enable you to truly grasp what the Prophets are saying.

The Context for Understanding the Prophets

To make sense of the Prophets we must first place them into their proper context within the biblical story. Let's review the biblical story and revisit how the Prophets connect.

The Bible begins in Genesis 1–2 with the wonderful story of creation, but Genesis 3–11 recounts how the people God had created repeatedly sin against him, resulting in separation from him. God's solution to this problem is presented in Genesis 12–17, where God makes a covenant promise to Abraham. God promises to make Abraham into a great nation and to give him a land, millions of descendants, and wonderful blessings. God also promises that through Abraham all the nations of the world will be blessed (Gen. 12:1–3). Much of the Bible is concerned with the fulfillment of these early promises of God to Abraham.

In Exodus, God miraculously delivers his people Israel out of Egypt and enters into a covenant relationship with them (the Mosaic covenant). At the heart of this covenant was a threefold formula statement: I will be your God; you will be my people; I will dwell in your midst. Then, just prior to taking his people into the Promised Land (i.e., promised to Abraham), God presents the people with the book of Deuteronomy, which restates the Mosaic covenant relationship between God and Israel. The book of Deuteronomy states the terms whereby Israel can live in the Promised Land and be blessed by God, who will live in their midst. God makes the terms very clear in Deuteronomy 28. If they obey him and worship him alone, then they will be blessed tremendously. But if they don't—and Deuteronomy 28 is crystal clear on this—then terrible judgments will come upon them, including the loss of the Promised Land. At the end of Deuteronomy Israel repeatedly vows to keep this covenant agreement. In the story that follows (Joshua through 2 Kings), as Israel enters into the Promised Land, the central question that drives the story is, "Will the people of Israel be faithful to their agreement with God, primarily as defined in the book of Deuteronomy?" The unfortunate answer to that question is no, they won't.

Tragically, under peer pressure from the neighboring peoples, Israel abandons her God and turns to idol worship. At the same time Israel turns away from the ethical guidelines spelled out in Deuteronomy and the nation quickly deteriorates, not only theologically, but also morally.

After several hundred years of downward spiraling (Judges through 2 Kings), interrupted only briefly by the story of Samuel and David, God's patience finally runs out. He sends the prophets to deliver a final plea to his people: repent and turn back to a true worship of God as you agreed to do in Deuteronomy. If you don't, the prophets warn, the terrible judgments spelled out in Deuteronomy 28 will come upon you. In essence, the prophets function like God's prosecuting attorneys. They stand before his judgment throne with Deuteronomy in their hand, pointing out the many ways that Israel has violated this covenant agreement. Next they announce the judgment that will come if Israel does not repent immediately. That judgment comes in the form of two terrible invasions. The Assyrians will come in 722 BC and completely destroy the northern kingdom, Israel, and the Babylonians will come in 587/586 BC to destroy Jerusalem and the southern kingdom, Judah.

Yet, while the prophets announce judgment based on the broken Mosaic covenant (especially as defined in Deuteronomy), they will also reach back to the Abrahamic covenant (Genesis 12, 15, 17) and to the Davidic covenant (2 Samuel 7) and promise a wonderful

The Prophets warn of the terrible judgment that the Assyrians and Babylonians will bring if Israel and Judah do not turn back to God. Depicted in this wall relief is an Assyrian soldier executing an inhabitant of a captured city.

✦ The Prophets provide the theological bridge that connects the New Testament to the Old Testament.

future time of restoration, a time when God will make a new and better covenant with his people. Furthermore, as the description of this new and better coming time (i.e., the messianic era) unfolds, God reveals that this plan is bigger than just a plan to restore Israel. As the prophets describe this spectacular new covenant, they reveal that it also includes all the nations of the world. Indeed, in fulfillment of the Abrahamic promise in Genesis 12:3, God's plan of future restoration includes the solution to the global problem of sin described in Genesis 3–11. People of faith from all the nations of the world will unite together in true worship of God.

The Prophets in a Nutshell

So as you can see from the discussion above, the message of the Prophets can be boiled down to three basic points:

1. You (Judah/Israel) have broken the Mosaic covenant; you had better repent!

Defeated people being led into captivity by Assyrian soldiers. Israel and Judah do not listen to the Prophets, and they end up like these captives.

✝ In the New Testament Gospels, Jesus refers to the Old Testament prophets repeatedly because they are foundational for understanding his message.

2. No repentance? Then judgment!
3. Yet there is hope beyond the judgment for a glorious, future restoration, both for Israel/Judah and for the nations.

The prophetic books are very repetitive. Thus these three themes repeat over and over throughout the Prophets. The specific sins listed under Point 1 ("You [Judah/Israel] have broken the Mosaic covenant") are also repeated over and over throughout the Prophets. These sins, or covenant violations, can be grouped into three basic indictments against Israel: (1) idolatry, (2) social injustice, and (3) reliance on religious ritual to cover the idolatry and injustice. The prophets will accuse Israel of these three central sins throughout the prophetic books.

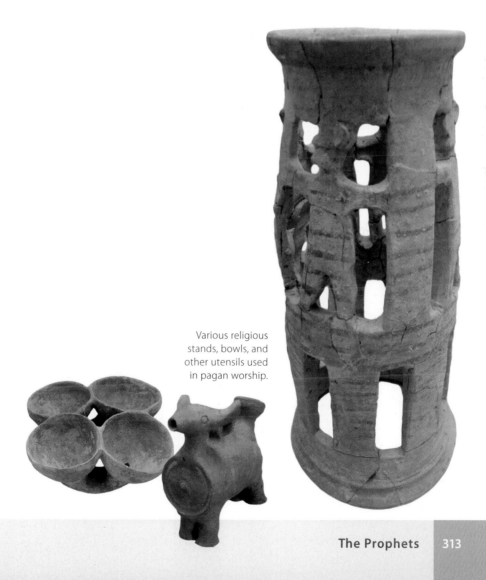

Various religious stands, bowls, and other utensils used in pagan worship.

Isaiah

*Judgment for Breaking the Covenant,
but Salvation through God's Coming Servant*

The book of Isaiah is one of the best known and best loved of the Prophets. One of our favorite songs is the famous chorus in Handel's *Messiah* from Isaiah 9:6,

> For unto us a child is born,
>   unto us a son is given:
>   and the government shall be upon his
>   shoulder;
>   and his name shall be called
>   Wonderful, Counsellor, The mighty God,
>   The everlasting Father, The Prince of Peace.
>   (KJV)

Likewise, as Christians we are moved by the powerful description of the suffering Messiah in Isaiah 53 and the clear statement by God that the Messiah's suffering was for *our* sin: "We all, like sheep, have gone astray, each of us has turned to his own way; and the Lord has laid on him the iniquity of us all" (v. 6).

Yet we cannot forget that Isaiah was a prophet and that the prophets speak powerfully about sin—breaking the covenant, rebelling against God, trusting in ourselves and our own power instead of in God, worshiping idols, ignoring justice for the weak, and relying on ritual to cover over and hide our sin. Isaiah's wonderful promise of the Messiah is not delivered in a vacuum. Nor is it presented as merely the icing on an already good cake. Isaiah, as well as the other prophets, points out clearly and repeatedly that the nations of Israel and Judah have failed miserably at obeying God and at keeping his law. They have sinned so terribly and repeatedly that judgment is now inevitable; in fact, it is about to descend on them quickly. It is in this context of total darkness and hopelessness for Israel that Isaiah lights the candle of hope. "The people walking in darkness have seen a great light.... For to us a child is born" (Isa. 9:2, 6).

Who Is Isaiah?

Isaiah was not a mythical character, but a real person dealing with real people and real problems. He lived in Jerusalem, the capital of the southern kingdom, Judah, during the latter part of the eighth century BC and into the seventh century BC. The book of Isaiah provides us with an extensive account of the prophet's direct encounter with God himself (Isaiah 6), in which God dramatically calls and appoints Isaiah as a prophet. Isaiah is one of the few prophets who is also mentioned in the Historical Books of the Old Testament. He is a main character in the story of 2 Kings 19 and 20, events that are similar to Isaiah 36–39. Likewise, he is mentioned a few times in 2 Chronicles (26:22; 32:20, 32).

Tiglath-Pileser III, pictured below, begins a period of brutal Assyrian expansion that dominates the geopolitical situation throughout the ministry of Isaiah.

✦ The New Testament book of Revelation has many allusions and references to Isaiah.

What Is the Setting for Isaiah?

Isaiah preached through some very tumultuous years. Isaiah 1:1 locates the prophet's ministry during the reigns of Uzziah, Jotham, Ahaz, and Hezekiah, all kings of Judah. Although these kings reigned from 792 until 687 BC, most of Isaiah's prophetic ministry was concentrated in the latter half of the eighth century BC (about 740 to 700 BC). During this time period the Assyrians are expanding their empire, brutally subduing nation after nation until they control most of the ancient Near East. Indeed, the Assyrians conquer and destroy the northern kingdom, Israel, in 722 BC and then lay siege to Jerusalem in 701 BC. With such geopolitical uncertainty, and with the five-hundred-pound Assyrian gorilla already in the backyard, the driving question for the kings of Judah is, "Whom will you trust for deliverance?" This is the context for Isaiah 1–39.

The message of Isaiah 40–66 is directed toward a later context, written to those Jews who were carried off in the Babylonian exile (after 586 BC). Although some scholars assume that Isaiah 40–66 was written later during the Babylonian or Persian era and then added on to Isaiah 1–39, it is probably best to see Isaiah proclaiming the material in 40–66 to those future exiles that he knows will be in Babylonia after Jerusalem inevitably falls.

A Hittite idol. Isaiah accuses Israel and Judah of worshiping idols.

What Is at the Heart of the Book of Isaiah?

The book of Isaiah plays an important role in the Bible, in essence connecting the history of Israel that culminated with the fall and destruction of Jerusalem (Genesis 12–2 Kings 25; i.e., sin, the problem) with the coming of Jesus the Messiah in the New Testament (i.e., the solution to the problem). Yet Isaiah goes beyond this by also addressing the worldwide (cosmic) problem of sin introduced back in Genesis 3–11. That is, the world has a problem with sin (Genesis 3–11), and Israel has a problem with sin (Genesis 12–2 Kings 25). Isaiah provides an answer for both problems. In his view of the messianic future deliverance, God regathers the scattered, alienated gentiles of Genesis 10–11 and unites them with the regathered, restored Israel.

Most of Isaiah's message is repeated throughout the Old Testament Prophets. This basic prophetic message can be synthesized to three basic themes:

1. You (Judah/Israel) have broken the Mosaic covenant; you had better repent!
2. No repentance? Then judgment!
3. Yet there is hope beyond the judgment for a glorious, future restoration, both for Israel/Judah and for the nations.

Throughout the book, Isaiah will stress justice and righteousness, both as a characteristic of God and the coming Messiah, but also as a standard for God's people. Isaiah also stresses the importance of trusting in God during difficult times. The Lord, Isaiah underscores, is sovereign and the one who controls history.

The major themes of Isaiah can be seen in the following outline:

- Judgment, with Glimpses of Deliverance (1:1–39:8)
  - The covenant lawsuit (1:1–4:1)
  - The branch, the vineyard, and justice (4:2–5:30)
  - The call of Isaiah (6:1–13)
  - A special child is coming (7:1–12:6)
  - Judgment on the nations (13:1–23:18)
  - Judgment on the world (24:1–27:13)
  - Judgment contrasted with joyful deliverance (28:1–35:10)
  - King Hezekiah and the Assyrian siege of Jerusalem (36:1–39:8)
- Deliverance, with Glimpses of Judgment (40:1–55:13)
  - Be comforted and soar (40:1–31)
  - Do not be afraid, for I am with you (41:1–44:23)
  - God controls history and even King Cyrus of Persia (44:24–48:22)
  - The Servant of God and the restoration of Zion (49:1–55:13)
- Righteous Living While Waiting on God (56:1–66:24)
  - Who will live righteously? (56:1–59:21)
  - Have hope! For God is bringing salvation (60:1–62:12)
  - While waiting for future deliverance, obey God and live righteously (63:1–66:24)

What Makes Isaiah Interesting and Unique?

- Isaiah encounters God himself seated on a throne with seraphs flying around him.

✦ Isaiah 1–12, a subunit of chapters 1–39, opens with somber judgment and ends with joyful restoration. Likewise, as bookends the two key terms "Holy One of Israel" and "Zion" open and close this unit (1:4, 8; 12:6).

- Isaiah prophesies about a coming child named Immanuel, "God is with us."
- Isaiah also prophesies about a special child called "Wonderful Counselor, Mighty God, Everlasting Father, Prince of Peace."
- Isaiah includes the gentiles in his picture of future restoration.
- Isaiah connects the coming Messiah to the Servant of the Lord, a servant who often suffers.
- Isaiah describes the coming messianic deliverance as a "New Exodus."
- Isaiah introduces the concept of "new heavens and a new earth."
- The New Testament (especially the Gospels and the book of Revelation) leans heavily on the prophecies of Isaiah for understanding Jesus.

What Is Isaiah's Message?

Judgment, with Glimpses of Deliverance (1:1–39:8)

The covenant lawsuit (1:1–4:1)

Israel and Judah have continually ignored God and the law (covenant) he gave them (especially as defined in the book of Deuteronomy). Isaiah skips over any nice, pleasant introductions and begins his book with an outcry against Israel's and Judah's covenant violations and sinful living. God is seated in court and ready to judge (3:13). In the opening chapters, Isaiah, the prosecuting attorney, presents fact after fact that indicts Israel/Judah for their blatant, "in your face" violation of their covenant with God. They have sinned both against God (the vertical relationship) and against people (the horizontal relationship). Thus they have forsaken God and his commandments, ignoring him and belittling him by worshiping idols instead, and they have accepted as normal a standard of social behavior that practiced social injustice upon social injustice. Therefore, Isaiah proclaims, judgment is coming.

Gold jewelry from Persia. Isa. 3:16–26 states that God will remove all the jewelry and finery from the women of Israel and send them into captivity.

The branch, the vineyard, and justice (4:2–5:30)

Isaiah 4:2–6 interrupts the theme of judgment with a promise of restoration. Isaiah calls the Messiah

the "Branch of the Lord," a branch that will provide fruit for the land. In contrast, Isaiah 5:1–7 compares the nation Israel to a vineyard that produced bad fruit instead of good fruit. Because the vineyard (Israel) produces only bad fruit (idolatry and injustice), it will be destroyed in justice (Isa. 5:8–30). Jesus clearly draws on Isaiah 5 when he tells the parable of the vineyard (Matt. 21:33–46; Mark 12:1–12; Luke 20:9–19).

The call of Isaiah (6:1–13)

In Isaiah 6 the prophet has a direct encounter with the awesome, holy God, seated on his throne. Direct encounters with God like this are rather rare in the Old Testament. Moses falls down before God at the burning bush (Exod. 3:1–2), and Ezekiel sees God on his "chariot" throne amid the spinning wheels and cherubs (Ezekiel 1). These encounters are always overwhelming for the people involved, and God's majestic holiness and glory usually send the person involved to the ground in reverence. Isaiah responds to this revelation of God's glory and holiness with fear, but God offers him cleansing and forgiveness. God has a task in mind, and he asks Isaiah, "Whom shall I send? Who will go for us?" Standing before the holy and awesome God exalted high on his throne, with the ground shaking and the fiery seraphs flying around thundering "Holy! Holy! Holy!" Isaiah gives the only logical response, "Here am I. Send me!" (6:8).

A special child is coming (7:1–12:6)

Isaiah 7, 8, and 9 are united around the common theme of an expected special child. In Isaiah 7, the foolish King Ahaz of Judah refuses to trust in God for deliverance from the powerful Israelite-Syrian alliance against him, even though God offered him a sign. God gives him a sign anyway—a young woman (NIV, "virgin") will give birth to a child called Immanuel ("God is with us"). Before the baby is very old, the alliance against Ahaz will be defeated. However, because of Ahaz's unbelief, this sign will also foreshadow judgment (7:10–25).

An actual child (the son of Isaiah) is born in Isaiah 8, in apparent partial fulfillment of the Isaiah 7 prophecy. Isaiah 9, however, indicates that there are spectacular characteristics about the coming child that will be fulfilled only in the future through the Messiah. In 9:6–7 the prophet connects the coming child to the messianic promise of a coming great Davidic king. Yet Isaiah's description of this child

Bronze tongs from Cyprus (1200–1050 BC). "Then one of the seraphs flew to me with a live coal in his hand, which he had taken with tongs from the altar" (Isa. 6:6).

✦ Isaiah 6:9–10 ("ever hearing, but never understanding") is quoted more times in the New Testament than any other Old Testament passage (Matt. 13:14–15; Mark 4:10–12; Luke 8:10; John 12:39–41; Acts 28:26–27; and Rom. 11:8).

Babylon in Prophecy

Isaiah and the other prophets spend a considerable amount of time pronouncing judgment on the Babylonians. In fact, judgment on Babylon is the primary theme of Isaiah 13, 14, 21, and 47. Likewise Jeremiah spends two entire chapters proclaiming judgment on the Babylonians (Jeremiah 50–51). Why do Isaiah and Jeremiah devote so much of their prophetic voice to proclaiming judgment on the Babylonians? It is the Babylonians who utterly destroy Jerusalem in 587/586 BC, killing thousands and hauling the survivors off to Babylonia as captives. Isaiah sees this prophetically, and Jeremiah lives through the actual event. No other enemy devastates Jerusalem and Judah to the extent that the Babylonians do. Thus the Babylonians come to epitomize the ultimate enemy, and both Jeremiah and Isaiah preach judgment against Babylon as the climax of judgment on the nations, since Babylon is the "archenemy" of God's people. The book of Revelation appears to use the term "Babylon" in this sense (Rev. 14:8; 16:19; 17:5; 18:2, 10, 21). Many scholars believe that John uses the term "Babylon" in the book of Revelation to represent Rome and the Roman Empire.

But what happened to Babylon? Cyrus the king of Persia conquered Babylon in 539 BC, but did not destroy it. Part of the city was later destroyed in 482 BC after the Babylonians rebelled against the Persians. Seleucus, one of Alexander the Great's generals, seized Babylon in 312 BC, and his successor, Antiochus I (281–261 BC), moved the capital of the region to a new city, thus abandoning Babylon.

When the Parthians conquered the region in 122 BC they found only ruins at Babylon. Likewise when the Roman emperor Trajan traveled through this area in AD 116, he also saw only destruction and ruins where the mighty and spectacular Babylon had been.

Some modern writers have argued that Babylon was never destroyed exactly in the literal manner described by the prophets Isaiah and Jeremiah. Thus they maintain that Babylon will be rebuilt in the last days and destroyed again, this time in the exact manner prophesied by the prophets. We find this thesis to be unlikely. Isaiah and Jeremiah are using highly figurative, poetic language to describe the end of Babylon. They predict the literal demise of Babylon (which happened), but they use highly figurative language to describe that demise.

moves even beyond that of a mere human king, for he calls him "Wonderful Counselor, Mighty God, Everlasting Father, Prince of Peace."

A colossal human-headed winged bull that guarded the entrance to the palace of the Assyrian king Sargon II, contemporary to Isaiah.

✝ Matthew 1:23 declares that Jesus fulfills Isaiah 7:14 by his virgin birth and his role as Immanuel ("God is with us").

Judgment on the nations (13:1–23:18)

Throughout Isaiah's lifetime, the geopolitics of the entire region were characterized by international political intrigue, invasions, alliances, and betrayals. Isaiah 13–23 is composed of judgment prophecies against the many nations surrounding Judah that were involved in this. This unit includes prophecies against the following nations:

Babylon (13:1–14:23)	Egypt (19:1–25)
Assyria (14:24–27)	Egypt/Cush (20:1–6)
Philistia (14:28–32)	Babylon (21:1–10)
Moab (15:1–16:14)	Edom (21:11–12)
Damascus (17:1–11)	Arabia (21:13–17)
Nations in general (17:12–14)	Jerusalem (22:1–25)
Cush (18:1–7)	Tyre (23:1–18)

Judgment on the world (24:1–27:13)

After proclaiming judgment on the nations in Isaiah 13–23, God widens the horizon and describes a time of ultimate judgment on all of creation. God rules over heaven and earth, and on that judgment day he will bring about judgment on "the powers in the heavens above and the kings on the earth below" (24:21).

Judgment contrasted with joyful deliverance (28:1–35:10)

Isaiah 28–34 focuses primarily on judgment, both on Israel/Judah and on selected nations (Edom, Assyria). Isaiah 28 refers to the northern kingdom, Israel, by the name Ephraim. Recall that Ephraim was one of the sons of Joseph and thus became one of the tribes of Israel. Since Ephraim was the largest tribe in the northern kingdom, sometimes the prophets will refer to Israel simply by the name Ephraim.

One of the serious problems in Judah was that the people thought that if they carried out their religious rituals then God would be pleased with them no matter how they lived day to day. The prophets categorically reject this notion, proclaiming that ritual observance did nothing to cover social injustice and idolatrous practices.

A Babylonian tablet containing a map of the known world at that time, with various nations labeled.

"Woe to those who go down to Egypt for help, who rely on horses, who trust in the multitude of their chariots . . . but do not seek help from the Lord" (Isa. 31:1). Depicted above is a replica of an Egyptian wall painting of Pharaoh Rameses II.

Isaiah 29:13 refers to this situation, declaring, "These people come near to me with their mouth and honor me with their lips, but their hearts are far from me. Their worship of me is made up only of rules taught by men." Jesus quotes this passage to the Jews of his day in Jerusalem, implying that the judgment foretold by Isaiah would likewise fall on them (Matt. 15:8–9; Mark 7:6–7).

Sprinkled throughout the judgment passages, however, are short encouraging prophecies of hope. In 28:16, for example, God states, "See, I lay a stone in Zion, a tested stone, a precious cornerstone for a sure foundation; the one who trusts will never be dismayed." Likewise, Isaiah 35, standing at the end of this unit, provides a strong contrast with the many sad and grim judgment prophecies in Isaiah 28–34. Isaiah 35 describes a future kingdom characterized by peace and joy, a time when the blind will see and the crippled will walk as God's regathered and redeemed people enter into Zion (Jerusalem) with singing and joy.

King Hezekiah and the Assyrian siege of Jerusalem (36:1–39:8)

Unlike most of the rest of the book of Isaiah, these four chapters (36–39) are narrative and in chronological order. The Assyrians destroyed the northern kingdom, Israel, in 722 BC. In 701 BC they advance against the southern kingdom, Judah, and lay siege to Jerusalem. Isaiah 36–39 chronicles these events (in parallel fashion, 2 Kings 18–20 describes these same events). In Isaiah 36–37 the powerful Assyrians advance against Jerusalem, but Isaiah promises victory over them. Trust in God! Isaiah exhorts King Hezekiah.

✦ 1 Peter 2:6 quotes directly from Isaiah 28:16, identifying Jesus as the "precious cornerstone."

The Destruction of Sennacherib

From *Hebrew Melodies* (AD 1815)

Lord Byron, George Gordon

The Assyrian came down like the wolf on the fold,
And his cohorts were gleaming in purple and gold;
And the sheen of their spears was like stars on the sea,
When the blue wave rolls nightly on the Galilee.

Like the leaves of the forest when summer is green,
That host with their banners at sunset were seen:
Like the leaves of the forest when autumn hath blown,
That host on the morrow lay withered and strown.

For the Angel of Death spread his wings on the blast,
And breathed in the face of the foe as he passed;
And the eyes of the sleepers waxed deadly and chill,
And their hearts but once heaved, and forever grew still!

And there lay the steed with his nostril all wide,
But through it there rolled not the breath of his pride;
And the foam of his gasping lay white on the turf,
And cold as the spray of the rock-beating surf.

And there lay the rider distorted and pale,
With the dew on his brow, and the rust on his mail:
And the tents were all silent, the banners alone,
The lances unlifted, the trumpets unblown.

And the widows of Ashur are loud in their wail,
And the idols are broke in the temple of Baal;
And the might of the Gentile, unsmote by the sword,
Hath melted like snow in the glance of the Lord!

Unlike so many other kings, Hezekiah listens to the prophets and cries out to God for deliverance. God then sends an angel to attack the enemy camp, and this angel sends the Assyrians fleeing back to Assyria.

It is interesting to recall that the book of Isaiah has been placed in the Hebrew canon right after 2 Kings, which ends with the fall and destruction of Jerusalem 114 years later. Hezekiah's story stands in stark contrast with the behavior of the kings in Jerusalem toward the end of the nation's life. If the kings at the end of 2 Kings and in the book of Jeremiah had only listened and obeyed like Hezekiah did . . .

In Isaiah 39, however, Hezekiah foolishly entertains an envoy from Babylon and shows them his treasures. Isaiah, knowing that the Babylonians will be the ones who actually destroy Jerusalem in the future and carry the people into

This clay prism is one of several that are inscribed with accounts of Sennacherib's military campaigns. In general these royal annals are propagandistic and full of political spin. Understandably Sennacherib does not mention the disastrous defeat at Jerusalem, but he does not claim to have captured Jerusalem either. He only mentions his victories over the surrounding cities, and then of Hezekiah in Jerusalem, the prism states, "Himself [Hezekiah] I made a prisoner in Jerusalem, his royal residence, like a bird in a cage."

exile, rebukes Hezekiah for his shortsightedness. Thus as Isaiah 1–39 ends, God has dramatically delivered Jerusalem from the Assyrians, but the Babylonians are looming on the horizon, a fitting introduction to Isaiah 40–66, which looks prophetically to the time of Babylonian domination.

Deliverance, with Glimpses of Judgment (40:1–55:13)

Recall that the message of the Prophets contains three basic points: (1) You've broken the covenant, so repent! (2) No repentance? Then judgment! (3) Yet there is hope for a glorious, future restoration. Isaiah 1–39 deals primarily with the first two points, while Isaiah 40–55 focuses on the third point, hope in a future restoration. Thus the message in Isaiah 40–55 is anchored firmly in God's great saving grace. At the center of Isaiah's message of hope in these chapters are numerous messianic promises. Many of these messianic prophecies are concentrated in the four "Servant Songs" (42:1–7; 49:1–6; 50:4–9; 52:13–53:12).

King Hezekiah constructed this water tunnel to strengthen the defenses of Jerusalem against the Assyrians.

Be comforted and soar (40:1–31)

Isaiah 40 parallels Isaiah 1 in many respects. Just as Isaiah 1 introduces chapters 1–39, so Isaiah 40 introduces chapters 40–66. Furthermore, many of the words and themes used for judgment in Isaiah 1 parallel similar words and themes of comfort and restoration in Isaiah 40.

Isaiah 40 not only introduces 40–66, but it also summarizes many of the major themes of the larger unit. Isaiah 40 opens with comfort (40:1–2). Preparations need to be made, for the glory of God is coming and will be seen by all (40:3–5). Although humankind is frail and perishes quickly like grass, the word of God stands firm forever. In Isaiah 40:9–11 the sovereign God comes with a mixture of mighty, victorious power and tender, loving care. As mere mortals we cannot grasp this, because God is beyond our understanding or comprehension (40:12–14). Before God, the nations, so frightening in Isaiah 1–39, are like mere drops in a bucket (40:15–17). In contrast, the all-powerful God is sovereign, ruling over all the earth. Pagan idols cannot compare to him, for they are nothing and they have no power (40:18–26). The conclusion of this introduction is stated poetically in 40:27–31. Those

✚ The New Testament Gospel writers identify John the Baptist with the preparatory "voice" of Isaiah 40:3 (Matt. 3:3; Mark 1:2–4; Luke 3:2–6).

Isaiah   325

The Servant Songs of Isaiah

Richard Schultz

Although some occurrences of the word "servant" (Heb., 'ebed) in Isaiah 40–53 clearly refer to Israel (e.g., 41:8), others appear to refer to an individual and are distinctive in content (e.g., 53:11). Suggestions regarding this latter servant's identity include (1) corporate Israel as represented by an individual—(a) the entire nation, (b) the faithful remnant, or (c) ideal Israel; and (2) a historical, future, or ideal individual—(a) prophetic, such as "Second" Isaiah or a second Moses; (b) royal, such as Hezekiah or the Messiah; or (c) priestly.

Bernhard Duhm (1892) first distinguished 42:1–4; 49:1–6; 50:4–9; and 52:13–53:12 as "Servant Songs," although "song" is a misleading label. The number and extent of these poems, however, continue to be disputed. For example, Isaiah 61:1–3 may function as a final servant text (cf. Luke 4:16–22). Duhm's approach, unfortunately, isolates these passages from their literary context and ignores the thematic use of "servant" in the book of Isaiah.

An unidentified servant is introduced in 42:1–4. Like the nation Israel (41:8–10), he is chosen and upheld by God. Like the "one from the north" (the Persian ruler Cyrus?), he is called in righteousness (41:2; 42:6) by name (45:4; 49:1) and grasped by the hand (42:6; 45:1), and will accomplish Yahweh's will (44:28; 53:10). This servant, however, is also contrasted with the collective servant, the blind nation Israel, which fails to carry out its appointed task (42:18–20) and thus itself requires redemption (43:1, 14). Furthermore, unlike the violent ways of the mighty conqueror (41:2, 25), this servant will establish justice without even breaking a "bruised reed" (42:2–3).

The servant's mission is twofold: (1) to restore Israel, being made a "covenant for the people" (i.e.,

the means to re-establish their relationship with God, 42:6; 49:8); and (2) to "bring [God's] salvation to the ends of the earth" (49:6) as "a light for the Gentiles" (42:6; 49:6), opening blind eyes, and freeing those imprisoned in darkness (42:7). In Isaiah 49–57, the coming spiritual deliverance through God's servant is announced. Three passages describing the servant's election (49:1–13), opposition (50:4–11), and vicarious suffering and exaltation (52:13–53:12) alternate with three extended passages describing Zion's current condition (49:14–50:3), coming comfort (51:1–52:12), and glorious future (54).

This individual servant thus carries out both prophetic (50:10) and priestly (52:15; 53:10) functions, and he also shares royal traits with the future Davidic king of Isaiah 1–39. Both possess the Spirit (11:2; 42:1), are associated with Davidic covenantal promises (9:7; 11:1; cf. 55:3; also 42:6; 49:8), and establish justice (11:4; 42:3–4), delivering others from darkness (8:22–9:2; 42:6–7). Not surprisingly, New Testament authors repeatedly cite these "Servant Songs" with reference to Jesus (e.g., Matt. 8:17; 12:17–21; Luke 22:37; John 12:38; Acts 8:32–33; Rom. 15:21; 1 Pet. 2:22–25).

The presentation of this individual in Isaiah 40–53 is understood best in light of the development of the "servant" theme within Isaiah 40–66. In Isaiah 40–53, the word "servant" occurs only in the singular. Following the climactic description of the substitutionary death of the righteous servant in Isaiah 53, a shift occurs: in Isaiah 54–66, "servant" occurs exclusively in the plural, designating an obedient group within Israel. In sum, in Isaiah the obedient work of the individual servant restores the national servant so that individuals within Israel once again will serve God.

✦ Matthew 12:18–21 identifies Jesus and his actions as a fulfillment of the "Servant" prophecy in Isaiah 42:1–4.

who believe this and who trust in the sovereign God will not despair. They will have their strength renewed, and they will soar on wings like eagles.

Do not be afraid, for I am with you (41:1–44:23)

The comfort of Isaiah 40 is followed by repeated encouraging exhortations by God to "Fear not!" Isaiah 41:10 is typical and epitomizes much of the message in this unit: "So do not fear, for I am with you; do not be dismayed, for I am your God. I will strengthen you and help you; I will uphold you with my righteous right hand." The theme of God's powerful and empowering Presence is a major theme in the Prophets, and indeed, throughout the entire Bible.

Isaiah 42:1–7 contains the first of the four messianic Servant Songs. Justice continues to be closely associated with the coming Messiah (42:1, 3, 4). Likewise, God promises to put his Spirit on this Servant (42:1). However, in contrast to other kings and conquerors, the Servant will be quiet and meek (42:2–3). God also declares that the Servant will be a covenant for the people (probably a reference to Jeremiah's "new covenant" in Jeremiah 31) and a light for the gentiles (42:6). Thus the Servant is identified as the one who plays the decisive role in bringing the gentiles into the people of God.

Isaiah 43:1–7 continues the words of comfort as God addresses his people with intimate terms (you are mine, I love you, sons, daughters). God also tells them repeatedly to "fear not" because of his empowering Presence. In 43:14–21 God promises deliverance and then describes the deliverance as paralleling the exodus from Egypt, only greater. The future deliverance that God is planning will overshadow the spectacular deliverances of the past, including the exodus, the prototypical and paradigmatic salvation event in the Old Testament. "Forget the former things," God declares. "See, I am doing a new thing!" (43:18–19).

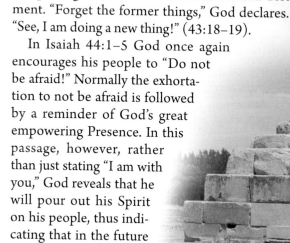

The tomb of the Persian king Cyrus.

In Isaiah 44:1–5 God once again encourages his people to "Do not be afraid!" Normally the exhortation to not be afraid is followed by a reminder of God's great empowering Presence. In this passage, however, rather than just stating "I am with you," God reveals that he will pour out his Spirit on his people, thus indicating that in the future

Light to the Gentiles

Light is a central theme running throughout the Bible. It can be used to symbolize the truth or the enlightenment that enables one to see the truth. In the Old Testament, light also carries some other nuances. Often light is connected to true justice or true righteousness. Light is often connected to God's powerful Presence and his creative activity (Genesis 1, for example). It also is often closely related to God's glory. Darkness, by contrast, is used in the Old Testament to represent not only foolishness and ignorance, but also judgment, particularly judgment that involves the loss of God's Presence, ultimately leading to death.

In Isaiah 9:2 the prophet Isaiah describes the coming of the wonderful Messiah as a time when light will replace darkness. In Isaiah 40–66 the prophet stresses that the Messiah (Servant of the Lord) will bring salvation both to Israel and to the gentiles (i.e., the nations). These two themes merge when God declares to the Servant, "I will also make you a light for the gentiles, that you may bring my salvation to the ends of the earth" (49:6; 42:6). So "light" in

this context includes enlightenment or knowledge (the gentiles will be able to understand), but it also provides an image of salvation itself—the "light to the gentiles" is the one who brings them salvation.

The New Testament continues to use this theme. John 1 connects Jesus to "light," ascribing to Christ many of the Old Testament nuances connected with light—the Presence of God, creative power, life, enlightenment. In John 8:12 Jesus makes a similar connection, declaring, "I am the light of the world." Likewise, as Paul shifts the focus of his work from the Jews to the gentiles, he quotes from Isaiah 49:6: "I have made you a light for the Gentiles" (Acts 13:47). This prophecy reaches its ultimate reality in the book of Revelation, for in the closing chapters, the climax of all human history is described as living in the light of God. Indeed, Revelation 21:23–24 pulls these strands together, proclaiming, "The city does not need the sun or the moon to shine on it, for the glory of God gives it light, and the Lamb is its lamp. The nations [gentiles] will walk by its light."

Copper "hanging" lamp from Babylon.

restoration God's Presence will be known in a new and more powerful way—through his Spirit.

Isaiah 44:6–20 wraps up this section with sarcastic ridicule of those who worship idols. Isaiah describes the ridiculous process of making an idol: a man cuts down a tree, using part of the wood in his fire to warm himself or to bake bread, and using the other part of the tree to make the idol, which he then bows down to and worships. Such foolishness! Worthless, powerless idols cannot be compared to the sovereign all-powerful God of Israel.

God controls history and even King Cyrus of Persia (44:24–48:22)

Keep in mind that Isaiah 40–66 is primarily directed at those Jewish exiles living in Babylonia. One of the comforting realities that Isaiah

✚ Isaiah 44:3 mentions the gift of God's Spirit, one of the spectacular features of the coming messianic era. Ezekiel 36:26–27 and Joel 2:28–29 add more detail to this prophecy, fulfilled in the New Testament on the Day of Pentecost (Acts 2:1–21).

shares with these distraught exiles is that God controls history, and, because he has sovereign control, he can (and will) bring them out of exile and restore them. The Babylonians will be defeated by King Cyrus of Persia in 539 BC. As a demonstration of God's control of history, he mentions Cyrus explicitly by name several times (44:28; 45:1, 13) and implicitly a few times (46:11; 48:14–15), stating that God himself will raise up Cyrus to judge Babylon, which will then enable the Israelites to return to their land. Isaiah 46 stresses that the idol gods, even those of Babylon, cannot do this and thus they are not to be compared with the Lord, the God of Israel. Isaiah 47 declares that Cyrus will bring about the end of Babylon. In Isaiah 48:20 God then tells the exiles, "Leave Babylon!" signaling the end of the exile.

The Servant of God and the restoration of Zion (49:1–55:13)

The previous section (Isaiah 44–48) identified Cyrus, king of Persia, as an individual God would use to bring about his plan. In this next unit, Cyrus fades away, and the focus is now placed on the Servant of the Lord as the main individual through whom God will inaugurate his new, fantastic plan of salvation. Part of this plan is the restoration of Zion (Jerusalem). These two themes of "the Servant" and "the restoration of Zion" interconnect and are intertwined throughout this section.

The second Servant Song (49:1–6) introduces this unit, placing all attention on the Servant, who actually speaks in this passage. Isaiah 49:1–4 describes the Servant's calling from God, and 49:5–6 lays out his twofold mission: restoration for Israel and salvation for the nations/gentiles (the same Hebrew word can be translated either "nations" or "gentiles"). The rest of the chapter describes elements of these two events and the joy that will result (49:13).

Isaiah 50:4–9 presents the third Servant Song. In this passage the Servant describes the persecution, ridicule, and suffering that he will endure, all the while trusting in God for strength and vindication. Isaiah 50:10–52:12 once again celebrates the restoration of Zion, repeating many of the themes we have already encountered in Isaiah: justice and righteousness, the new exodus, comfort, God the powerful creator, judgment on sinful oppressors, and joyful salvation.

The final—and most spectacular—Servant Song is presented in 52:13–53:12. This is perhaps the best-known passage in Isaiah. It contains numerous specific messianic prophecies, including a very detailed account of the suffering that the Servant will experience. Many of the details in this passage are fulfilled quite explicitly by the trial, beatings, and crucifixion of Jesus Christ. Likewise, the theme of substitutionary death (dying on our behalf, in our place, for our sin) is part of the song. Although suffering and

✦ The "former things" in Isaiah (41:22; 42:9; 43:9, 18; 46:9; 48:3; 65:17) usually refer to God's great acts of deliverance back in Exodus.

humiliation dominate the central portion of the song, it opens and closes with the exaltation of the Servant (52:13–15; 53:10–12). The contrasting themes of humiliation and exaltation bring a strong irony to the prophecy. The people do not recognize the Servant. Their negative misperception of him is contrasted with the reality of who he really is and how he will save them through his suffering. These same themes are characteristic of the life of Jesus Christ in the Gospels.

Isaiah 54 figuratively compares Jerusalem to a barren, abandoned woman who is now received warmly by her husband (God, who is also her maker and redeemer). She will now have a life characterized by joy and peace, filled with the blessing of many children. The prophets frequently use the marriage analogy to comment on the relationship between God (the husband or groom) and his people (the wife or bride).

Banquet and feasting images are also often used to depict the positive blessings of the glorious coming restoration. In Isaiah 55 the tired and thirsty exiles are invited to a free banquet feast. As part of the banquet God will inaugurate the fulfillment of the Davidic covenant (55:3), a promise he made to David in 2 Samuel 7 regarding the establishment of a descendant of David as the eternal king of Israel.

God then calls on sinners to repent and be saved (55:6–7). In light of the serious sin that Isaiah has been highlighting throughout the book, one might wonder how mercy and forgiveness can now be offered. Isaiah 55:8–9, however, reminds us that God's ways and his understanding are often above us and not easy for us to grasp. God declares that his word is powerful and will accomplish all that he sends it out to accomplish (55:11). Therefore his people—indeed, all creation—will be filled with joy due to this great deliverance (55:12–13).

"Zion" refers to the hill or ridge where the Temple was built. Today the El-Aksa Mosque and the Islamic shrine called the Dome of the Rock occupy much of that site.

Righteous Living While Waiting on God (56:1–66:24)

Isaiah 1–39 focuses on the coming judgment due to sin (the broken covenant) and Israel's refusal to repent and return to God.

Isaiah 40–55 then looks beyond the judgment to the bright hope for future restoration when God's Servant will bring salvation to both the shattered exiles and the gentiles (the nations). Isaiah 56–66, however, exhorts God's people to live righteously in the meantime, while they wait for the coming King. A major theme in this section is the condemnation of Israel's reliance on hypocritical, ritualistic worship.

The Assyrian king Sennacherib views the captured people from the city of Lachish. In contrast to arrogant kings such as Sennacherib, the Servant will be quiet and meek (Isa. 42:2–3).

Who will live righteously? (56:1–59:21)

Isaiah 56 opens with a call for justice, but then quickly moves to declare that typical "outsiders" (such as foreigners and eunuchs) who live faithfully will be included in the regathering of God's people (56:1–8). In contrast, the next passage highlights the hypocrisy of Israel's leaders who are lazy, greedy, and worshipers of idols (56:9–57:13). The chapter closes with a reaffirmation of God's willingness to mercifully accept the ones who come to him with a humble spirit of repentance.

As mentioned throughout our discussion, the Prophets highlight three basic sins that shattered the covenant: idolatry, social injustice, and reliance on hypocritical, religious ritual. Isaiah 58 unites the themes of social justice and religious ritual in a scathing critique of the hypocritical way the ritual of fasting was being practiced. If one is regularly practicing social injustice, God declares, then what good is fasting? God then sums up his attitude toward this ritual in 58:6–7: "Is not this the kind of fasting I have chosen: to loose the chains of injustice . . . to share your food with the hungry . . . to provide the poor wanderer with shelter?"

Isaiah 59 continues to describe sin in terms of injustice; indeed, the term "justice" is used throughout the chapter (59:4, 8, 9, 11, 14, 15). In the final section, however, the strong right arm of God will come in power and deliver his people. Throughout the earlier chapters of Isaiah (and throughout the Prophets), the traditional enemies of Israel have been the powerful nations in the region (Babylon, Assyria, Egypt, etc.). In Isaiah 59, however, the enemy

✦ Jesus quotes Isaiah 56:7 ("my house will be called a house of prayer for all nations") as he clears out the corrupt market set up in the temple area that was supposed to be reserved as a place where foreigners could pray.

Isaiah 331

that God crushes victoriously is "sin." A critical component of this victory over sin is God's new covenant and the role his Spirit will play (59:21).

Have hope! For God is bringing salvation (60:1–62:12)

Isaiah 60–62 continues to develop the promise of the great future restoration. Isaiah 60 stresses that the glory and light of God will dispel all darkness. In the messianic future "the sun will no more be your light by day . . . for the Lord will be your everlasting light" (60:19; cf. Rev. 21:23). Isaiah 61 proclaims good news to the poor and brokenhearted, once again stressing how important justice is to God (61:8). At the end of Isaiah 61, wedding imagery is once again used—a figure of speech that continues on into Isaiah 62 where the glorious restoration of Jerusalem and Israel is celebrated and culminates in the proclamation of a new name for the people, "the Holy People, the Redeemed of the Lord" (62:12).

While waiting for future deliverance, obey God and live righteously (63:1–66:24)

Isaiah 63 opens with the appearance of the divine warrior, who tramples his enemies like grapes in a winepress. This is followed by a prayer (63:7–64:12) offered up by Isaiah on behalf of the sinful people. God answers this prayer in the final section (Isaiah 65–66), highlighting the coming "new heavens and new earth" (65:17–20). Yet images of both judgment and hope alternate back and forth throughout this unit (as they have in many parts of Isaiah). God reminds his people that deliverance is not based on ethnicity, nor is it automatic. The glorious future restoration is coming, but in the meantime the people are called to live humble, faithful, and righteous lives before God.

Isaiah 66:15–24 draws the entire book to a conclusive ending by summarizing several prominent themes of the book. God's unfolding plan will bring about both judgment and salvation. On the one hand, some rebellious and sinful people (both gentiles and Israelites) will receive the consequential judgment of God. On the other hand, those who trust and obey God, both Israelites and gentiles, will be gathered together as God's people and brought into his glorious presence to worship him.

So What? Applying Isaiah to Our Lives Today

The book of Isaiah is overflowing with central biblical themes that apply directly to how you and I live each day. First of all, Isaiah tells us a lot about God, his character, and his heart. Isaiah emphasizes to us that God is sovereign

✦ At the beginning of his public ministry Jesus quotes Isaiah 61:1–2, identifying himself as the fulfillment of Isaiah's messianic prophecies (Luke 4:18–19).

and in control of history. We live in a sinful, fallen world, and thus terrible things can happen all around us. Nonetheless, God remains on the throne and in control. Eventually he will establish his kingdom, characterized by justice, righteousness, and peace. Thus even in difficult situations, we can claim the promise from Isaiah to "fear not."

Isaiah has a lot to say about sin. He tells us we should not trivialize God or assume God is somehow lackadaisical or indifferent to sin. Disobedience to God, especially if we abandon him or turn away from him, has serious consequences. God's holiness and righteousness demand judgment on sin. Yet, fortunately for us, Isaiah also prophesies that the wonderful Messiah (Jesus) who is coming will die in our place for our sin and restore us to God.

In the meantime, Isaiah calls you and me to live righteously day to day. He tells us to resist "idols" (those things that pull our devotion away from God) and instead to be totally faithful to God. Isaiah also tells us God cares deeply for those who are suffering, especially those at the low end of the socioeconomic strata who can't provide for themselves, and he expects us (his people) to have compassion on and actively care for those in the "underclass" who need help. Isaiah also tells us repeatedly that God wants us to walk closely with him in true ethical and spiritual obedience, instead of just mere ritual observance. If we do indeed trust in God completely—accepting the atoning sacrifice of his Servant Jesus, striving to know God's heart and act according to his great compassion, waiting on his great promised deliverance even in difficult times of suffering—then we can truly "soar on wings like eagles" (Isa. 40:31).

Our Favorite Verse in Isaiah

We all, like sheep, have gone astray,
each of us has turned to his own way;
and the Lord has laid on him
the iniquity of us all. (53:6)

Jeremiah

*Sin, Judgment, and Deliverance
through the New Covenant*

Often Jeremiah is called "the weeping prophet." This name is given because there are several passages in which Jeremiah pours out his soul to God, weeping (and maybe even "whining" a little) over the difficult persecution that he has encountered due to the scathing message of judgment he has delivered to the powerful people of Jerusalem. We prefer, however, to call him "the Dirty Harry of the Old Testament." In the old, classic Clint Eastwood movies, police officer Harry Callahan earned the name "Dirty Harry" because he was always given the toughest, most difficult, and most dangerous assignments. Jeremiah finds himself in a similar role as God sends him out to stand up against the entire nation of Judah (1:18–19) to proclaim publicly their sin and to call them to repentance—a call of futility, God informs him, for these people have hard hearts and will not repent.

Who Is Jeremiah?

Jeremiah is perhaps the most intriguing of the prophets, and he delivers a powerful, heart-wrenching message, both for ancient Judah and for audiences today. He was originally a priest from the town of Anathoth, not too far from Jerusalem. God calls him to be a prophet while he is still a young man (Jeremiah 1), and Jeremiah has a long prophetic ministry (over forty years). Jeremiah's job is tough, however, for the people of Judah and Jerusalem do not listen to him; indeed, they are downright hostile to him, occasionally arresting him and beating him. There are even plots against his life. From time to time Jeremiah gets discouraged, and he is quite honest in sharing his discouragement with his readers. God, however, exhorts him to stop whining and to get back to work.

What Is the Setting for Jeremiah?

During the previous several hundred years, the nation of Judah (with its capital Jerusalem) had become more and more enamored of foreign idols, and had thus become less and less faithful to God. King Josiah tries to reverse this disastrous trend, but on his death, the nation of Judah returns to their sinful ways and abandons following the law of God as spelled out in Deuteronomy. Not only do they fall into blatant idolatry, but their society also unravels morally as they disregard God's call to care for others and to be concerned with justice for all members of their society. Jeremiah lives and prophesies in Jerusalem during these tragic years leading up to the capture and terrible destruction of Jerusalem by the Babylonians. His ministry spans over forty years (627 BC to shortly after 586 BC), through the reigns of several kings in Judah: Josiah (the last good king of Judah), Jehoahaz, Jehoiakim, Jehoiachin, and Zedekiah, and then briefly into the period after the devastation of Jerusalem.

What Is at the Heart of the Book of Jeremiah?

Jeremiah's message is typical of the Old Testament prophets and can be synthesized down to the three basic themes of the prophetic message:

1. You (Judah) have broken the covenant; you had better repent!
2. No repentance? Then judgment!
3. Yet there is hope beyond the judgment for a glorious, future restoration, both for Israel/Judah and for the nations.

Much of Jeremiah 1–29 focuses on the many sins that characterize Judah and Jerusalem, underscoring how severely they had broken the covenant God

✠ Jeremiah is contemporary with the prophets Habakkuk, Zephaniah, Ezekiel, and the early years of Daniel. Additional historical background for Jeremiah is provided in 2 Kings 22–25 and in 2 Chronicles 34–36.

made with them in Exodus and Deuteronomy. These sins can be grouped into three major categories: idolatry, social injustice, and religious ritualism. Like a prosecuting attorney in a courtroom, Jeremiah accuses Jerusalem and its leaders of committing idolatry and social injustice. They are quite mistaken, Jeremiah declares, in thinking their religious rituals will cover their unethical behavior and make things all right with God. In fact, Jeremiah warns, a terrible time of judgment is coming.

Incense burner from nearby Arabia (the Sabaeans). Israel and Judah anger God by burning incense to Baal (11:17) as well as to other gods (19:13).

Jeremiah 30–33, by contrast, focuses on the coming glorious restoration after the judgment. At the center of this messianic message is the description of the coming "new covenant."

The remaining chapters, however, chronicle how the kings and people of Jerusalem refuse to listen and repent, thus sealing their fate. The Babylonians do indeed come, and the book of Jeremiah describes the terrible fall of Jerusalem. Also included in Jeremiah is an extensive section containing judgment on the surrounding nations for their sin.

Much of the book of Jeremiah does not follow chronological sequence; the structure of Jeremiah is based more on themes than on chronological order. The book is very much like an anthology, a collection of poetic oracles and proclamations, narrative events, and dialogues. The book of Jeremiah is very difficult, if not impossible, to outline in detail, and often the connection between the various episodes and prophecies is unclear. However, the overall message as discussed above is very clear, and Jeremiah repeats the three indictments (idolatry, social injustice, religious ritualism) and the three main points (broken covenant, judgment, restoration) over and over. Likewise, while tight logical connections between small sections are not always discernable, the book can be broken down into larger sections, unified by the following broad, general themes:

- Sin, Broken Relationship, and Judgment (1:1–29:32)
  - "Dirty Harry" is commissioned (1:1–19)
  - Idolatry—a betrayal of the relationship with God (2:1–37)
  - Repent! Repent! Repent! Please! (3:1–4:4)
  - The terrifying judgment will come quickly (4:5–6:30)
  - Lies and false religion (7:1–10:25)
  - The shattered covenant and God's prophet attacked (11:1–20:18)
  - Judgment on leaders and false prophets (21:1–29:32)

- Restoration and the New Covenant (30:1–33:26)
- The Terrible and Tragic Final Days of Jerusalem (34:1–45:5)
    - The unfaithful kings of Judah (34:1–36:32)
    - Jerusalem falls, but a remnant lives on (37:1–39:18)
    - The story of deliverance in reverse: The people return to Egypt (40:1–45:5)
- Judgment on the Nations (46:1–51:64)
- The Fall of Jerusalem Described Again (52:1–34)

What Makes Jeremiah Interesting and Unique?

- Jeremiah shares his personal fears and frustrations with us.
- Jeremiah is confronted numerous times with hostile "false prophets."
- Jeremiah clearly connects the new coming messianic era to a "new covenant."
- The marriage analogy of God's relationship with his people runs throughout the book.
- Jeremiah is perhaps the most colorful and yet the most scathing of all the prophets as he preaches against sin and announces judgment.
- The judgment imagery of 1–29 is reversed into salvation imagery in 30–33, using the exact same images (e.g., 1–29 speaks of incurable sickness; 30–33 speaks of healing, etc.).
- Many of Jesus's miracles and much of his teaching are connected to the book of Jeremiah.

What Is Jeremiah's Message?

Sin, Broken Relationship, and Judgment (1:1–29:32)

"Dirty Harry" is commissioned (1:1–19)

The book of Jeremiah starts with the prophet's divine call. Significant aspects of Jeremiah's call include the following:

1. God is the one who calls.
2. God chose him for this task before he was even born.
3. The call centers on the proclamation of the word of God.
4. God will empower the young Jeremiah to speak this word.

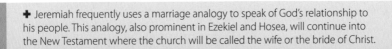

✦ Jeremiah frequently uses a marriage analogy to speak of God's relationship to his people. This analogy, also prominent in Ezekiel and Hosea, will continue into the New Testament where the church will be called the wife or the bride of Christ.

What Happened to the Ark of the Covenant?

The ark of the covenant was a wooden box, approximately 4 x 2½ x 2½ feet, covered inside and out with gold, capped with a golden mercy seat that was flanked by two golden cherubim. When God brought Israel up out of Egypt during the exodus, he gave Moses specific instructions on how to construct this ark (Exodus 25). Throughout the early history of Israel, the ark of the covenant played a critical role, for it represented the focal point of God's Presence among Israel, combining his holiness and his power with his desire to dwell among his people and relate to them.

In 3:16 Jeremiah makes a very radical prediction: in the future restoration the ark will be gone, and, more surprisingly, no one will even miss it. In accordance with Jeremiah's prophecy, the ark of the covenant disappears from biblical history after the Babylonians capture and destroy Jerusalem in 587/586 BC. What happened to it?

Numerous legends and theories that attempt to answer this question continue to circulate. One very questionable Jewish legend states that Jeremiah himself hid the ark beneath the Temple Mount just before the Babylonians captured the city. Some speculate that it is still there. A few people claim to have seen it. Most Old Testament scholars find this legend highly unlikely, without any verifiable evidence to support it.

Another legend about the ark comes from Ethiopia. The Ethiopian national "folk legend" states that the queen of Sheba was an Ethiopian queen. After she visited King Solomon in Jerusalem, she returned to Ethiopia and gave birth to Solomon's son, a boy named Menilek. Later, Menilek returned to Jerusalem to visit his father, but then stole the ark of the covenant, taking it with him back to Ethiopia, where it remains to this day. The Ethiopian Orthodox Church claims to have the original ark of the covenant in a church in the ancient city of Axum. Unfortunately, they will not let any scholars examine it.

The problem with this legend is that it doesn't square with history. King Solomon predates the Axumite kingdom of Menilek by nearly one thousand years. Thus it is highly unlikely that Solomon was Menilek's father. However, the Ethiopians have something very old and significant in that church that has produced this ancient legend, along with several church rituals relating to the ark. What do they actually have in that church?

One possibility relates to a Jewish colony that was built in ancient southern Egypt on the Isle of Elephantine on the Nile River. In the sixth century BC the Egyptians hired Jewish mercenaries to defend a fortress on this island. Archaeological excavations on this site indicate that these Jews apparently constructed a model of the temple in Jerusalem on their island, ostensibly to worship God. Did they also construct a model of the ark of the covenant to place in that temple? Perhaps. No one knows for certain what happened to these Jewish mercenaries who had settled in southern Egypt. Some suggest they migrated east into Ethiopia, taking their replica of the ark with them. If this scenario is true, then the Ethiopians might have this ark, a very old (and highly significant) replica of the ark of the covenant, but not the original.

Most scholars maintain that the most likely fate of the ark of the covenant is that the Babylonian army melted it down and carried the gold back to Babylonia. At any rate, Jeremiah was correct. The ark disappeared. God's people today experience God's Presence through the indwelling of the Holy Spirit; thus they do not miss the ark of the covenant.

Model of the ark of the covenant.

5. Opposition, even persecution, is promised. There is no "health and wealth" promise in Jeremiah's call.
6. God promises his empowering Presence ("I am with you").

Idolatry—a betrayal of the relationship with God (2:1–37)

Jeremiah lambastes the people of Judah, accusing them of idolatry and of abandoning God. Three times God declares they have "forsaken" him (2:13, 17, 19). In this chapter Jeremiah introduces one of his most powerful and emotional figurative images. Idolatry against God, Jeremiah proclaims vividly, is a betrayal of the relationship between God and his people (i.e., the covenant), much like the betrayal of a marriage that occurs in acts of adultery.

Repent! Repent! Repent! Please! (3:1–4:4)

Over and over God calls on his people to repent and turn back to him (3:12, 14, 22; 4:1). Israel, however, no longer even acknowledges her sin, much less returns back to God. Jeremiah moves the image beyond that of an adulterous wife to that of a harlot, for a harlot no longer even blushes in shame at her sin. Indeed, throughout the book Jeremiah frequently compares Judah/Jerusalem to a harlot; that is, the people are chasing after other gods just like a married harlot chases after lovers in a total abandonment of her marriage (and causing pain and embarrassment to the husband).

In 3:14–18, however, Jeremiah weaves a glimpse of the future restoration into his call for repentance. He paints a future picture of all the nations of the world coming to Jerusalem to worship God. At that time, Jeremiah proclaims, the ark of the covenant will no longer be with them in Jerusalem, but no one will even miss it. Since the time of Moses, the ark of the covenant had been the focal point of God's Presence as he dwelt among the Israelites. As the prophets look to the future restoration, however, they describe a new time when God's Presence will be enjoyed in a more intimate and more powerful way—through his Spirit. The prophets Joel and Ezekiel will develop this theme in some detail. Jeremiah just notes that the ark of the covenant, the current sign of God's Presence, will soon disappear, never to be replaced.

The terrifying judgment will come quickly (4:5–6:30)

In spite of Jeremiah's call to repentance, the people refuse to put away or even acknowledge their sin (idolatry, social injustice). Thus in 4:5–6:30 the prophet describes the terrible consequences. A horrific invasion by the Babylonians will take place, coming on Judah with unexpected lightning speed.

Several important themes are developed in this section. In contrast to the judgment, God states that he will not destroy everyone, but will deliver

✦ As he pronounces judgment on the temple, Jeremiah calls the place "a den of robbers" (7:11). In the New Testament Jesus likewise implies judgment as he quotes this verse to the market-sellers in the temple (Matt. 21:13; Mark 11:17; Luke 19:46).

The Laments of Jeremiah

One of the unique features of the book of Jeremiah is that the prophet provides us with a penetrating look into his personal thoughts and reactions. At several places in the book, Jeremiah cries out to God, complaining or lamenting about the difficult situation he faces. The passages that contain Jeremiah's "laments" are 11:18–20; 12:1–6; 15:10, 15–21; 17:14–18; 18:18–23; and 20:7–18. Sometimes Jeremiah laments about the sad state of affairs (morally and theologically) in Jerusalem. Often he cries out that everyone has rejected him and his message. He feels all alone, struggling futilely against the powerful leaders (king, prophets, priests, nobles) in Jerusalem. On the one hand, occasionally he seems to slide over into whining just a bit. On the other hand, the threats against Jeremiah's life are real. He is not imagining the danger. Thus sometimes in his lament to God he calls on God to deliver him and to smite those who plot to kill him. In general God seems to tolerate Jeremiah's complaints, and usually God answers with encouraging words. In 15:18, however, Jeremiah goes too far and accuses God of deceiving him. At this point God issues a mild rebuke: "If you repent, I will restore you that you may serve me; if you utter worthy, not worthless, words, you will be my spokesman. Let this people turn to you, but you must not turn to them" (15:19).

a "remnant" (5:10, 18). The focus of this unit also shifts from the sin of idolatry to the sin of social injustice, especially that of the wealthy leaders (5:26–31). Religious ritual will not cover the serious sin of social injustice (6:19–20). Another powerful image introduced in this unit is that of wounds/ sickness versus healing (6:7, 14). Jeremiah will use "wounds" and "sickness" as a figurative picture of sin and its consequences, in contrast to "healing," which he uses to portray forgiveness and restoration.

Lies and false religion (7:1–10:25)

In Jeremiah 7 God states repeatedly that the people have not listened to him nor obeyed him. In contrast, Jeremiah 8 focuses on what they have been listening to instead— the lies and deceit of their false prophets, priests, and other leaders.

This model of an Egyptian potter was discovered in an ancient Egyptian tomb.

In Jeremiah 10:1–16, God underscores the foolishness of believing in the lies of idolatry, ridiculing both the idols and those people who worship them. An idol, God declares, is "like a scarecrow in a melon patch." He can't walk or talk; thus he can't help you or hurt you either (10:1–5). In contrast, God is the all-powerful, all-wise Creator of heaven and earth (10:6–16). It is his judgment and his wrath that should be feared; not that of the man-made idols.

The shattered covenant and God's prophet attacked (11:1–20:18)

The central theme throughout Jeremiah 11–20 is that of conflict. On the one hand, Israel has shattered the Mosaic covenant made during the exodus, and now God's spokesman Jeremiah is under attack. In Jeremiah 11 God states that Israel and Judah have broken (i.e., ended) the Mosaic covenant. Thus God will no longer listen to their cries or allow Jeremiah to intercede for them (11:11–12, 14). On the other hand, the shattered Mosaic covenant points to the need for a "new" and better covenant (Jeremiah 31).

Jeremiah's words are unpopular, and in 11:18–23 men from his hometown plot to kill him. Jeremiah turns to God with a "complaint" or "lament" (12:1–4), imploring God to hurry with the judgment on these evil ones. God gently reminds Jeremiah not to give up so easily, for things are going to get much worse (12:5–6).

Jeremiah 13 contains an object lesson. God tells Jeremiah to bury a fine linen belt and then later to go back to dig it up. Of course by then the belt is ruined, symbolizing how the misplaced pride of Judah and Jerusalem will also be ruined.

Why doesn't Jeremiah intercede for the people and save them as Moses did (Exodus 32) and as Samuel did (1 Sam. 7:9)? In Jeremiah 14:1–15:9 God tells Jeremiah not to intercede as Moses or Samuel did, for now is the time for judgment, not intercession. Due to the coming judgment there is to be no rejoicing; thus in Jeremiah 16 God tells the prophet not to get married. Likewise, to symbolize that there will be little comfort during the coming time of judgment, God also tells Jeremiah not to attend any funerals. Jeremiah 17:5–13 is a psalm, reflecting the true wisdom of trusting in

The Mesha Stele, in which the Moabite king Mesha gives praise to his god Chemosh for giving him victory over Israel (ninth century BC). Chemosh is the god associated with child sacrifice.

✠ Deuteronomy 28 forms the critical covenant background for understanding Jeremiah 11.

God. Jeremiah then expresses his confident trust in God, in spite of all the difficulties he has faced (17:14).

Throughout Jeremiah we find the theme of inevitable judgment intermixed with the prophet's call to repentance in order to avert that judgment. Jeremiah 18 illustrates this through the analogy of a potter. Just as a potter can take a marred pot and reshape it as he sees fit, so God has the power to reshape people and nations based on their response to his call for repentance. In Jeremiah 19, however, the pot has hardened and thus cannot be reshaped. This time the pot is thrown down and smashed, appropriately in the Valley of Ben Hinnom, a site right outside the walls of Jerusalem where idol worship and even child sacrifice regularly took place.

A bronze sledgehammer head from Cyprus (1200–1050 BC). "Is not my word like fire," declares the Lord, "and like a hammer that breaks a rock in pieces?" (Jer. 23:29).

In Jeremiah 20:1–6 the prophet experiences persecution once again as a powerful priest named Pashhur orders Jeremiah to be beaten and placed in the "stocks" (probably a small dungeonlike cell rather than "stocks"). When released, Jeremiah proclaims judgment on Pashhur and then cries out to God in his final "lament," mixing both praise and trust with despair and discouragement (20:7–18). There is nothing superficial about Jeremiah. He lives in difficult times among dangerous people, but continues to deliver God's message, even if it is unpopular. And he continues to be honest with us about how tough his life and ministry are.

Judgment on leaders and false prophets (21:1–29:32)

In Jeremiah 21–22 the prophet proclaims judgment on the kings (Zedekiah in 21, Jehoiakim in 22) for their failure to carry out justice, especially in regard to the weak ones in the society (the poor, orphans, widows, and foreigners). In contrast, Jeremiah 23:1–8 looks to the time of future restoration when God himself will gather his people like a shepherd and then establish a Davidic king who will rule with justice and righteousness.

Jeremiah 23:9–40 returns to the theme of false prophets and the judgment awaiting them, but Jeremiah 24 speaks of a remnant that will return from the coming Babylonian captivity. Jeremiah 25 continues to discuss the captivity, specifying that it will last seventy years (a lifetime) and will be followed by judgment on Babylon and the nations allied with her.

Jeremiah 26–29 revisits the recurring topic of false prophets, who were apparently quite powerful in the royal court. Jeremiah 26 presents the results of the "temple sermon" that Jeremiah preached back in Jeremiah 7. He is

✚ Jeremiah prophesies that the exile will last seventy years (25:11; 29:10). This prophecy is cited in Daniel 9:2 and 2 Chronicles 36:21. Ezra 1:1 is also probably alluding to this same prophecy.

Jeremiah   343

False Prophecy in the Old Testament

Kevin Hall

False prophecy in the Old Testament is best understood against the backgrounds of the classic test of a genuine prophet outlined in Deuteronomy 18:14–22, the various clashes between genuine prophets and their rivals, and the nature and purpose of prophecy.

As the Deuteronomy text clearly states, if a prophet speaks in the name of the Lord and the thing he speaks does not materialize, the prophet is not a genuine spokesperson for the Lord (Deut. 18:22). Set in a context describing Moses as the premier model of a prophet, the test commands attention as an absolute, unconditional test. When examined in light of the overall nature and purpose of prophecy and the experiences of genuine prophets, however, the Deuteronomy test requires careful application.

In the prophet Jeremiah's vision at the potter's house, for example, Jeremiah is given to understand that the word of the Lord through a prophet does not, "strictly speaking," predict the future. Rather, the prophetic word provokes repentance as the condition for fulfillment of God's purposes among the nations (Jer. 18:5–11). Thus in a narrow sense the words of a true prophet may not come true. Jonah's seemingly unconditional prediction of Nineveh's destruction is the classic case in point.

It is in their role as a professional class and part of the leadership structure of the kingdoms of Israel and Judah that false prophets of the Old Testament are most clearly observed. The false prophets consistently throw their support behind those who

support them. Thus the genuine prophet Amos is compelled to bluntly state, "I was neither a prophet nor a prophet's son" (Amos 7:14), while his contemporary Micah decries the prophets who give oracles for money in collusion with those who build Jerusalem by violent corruption (Mic. 3:9–11). As Jeremiah's clash with Hananiah makes clear, a prophet may make statements that seem to magnify the power of the Lord, but which actually obscure the divine purpose (Jeremiah 28).

Particularly instructive concerning the phenomenon of false prophecy is the account of Micaiah, one of the court prophets of King Ahab of Israel (1 Kings 22:1–28). As the account unfolds, it becomes apparent that even a corrupt king like Ahab can tell the truth from a lie (v. 16). But given his investment in his idolatrous ambitions, including his support of hundreds of prophets who will tell him anything he wants to hear, Ahab finally succumbs to the lying spirit in the mouth of all his prophets (vv. 22–23). This strange account may seem troubling in that the Lord seems to actively engage lying spirits and use a true prophet to deceive Ahab. In the final analysis, however, false prophecy in the Old Testament is fueled by those who break faith with God's promises and purposes. As Jeremiah observes, "The prophets prophesy falsely ... and my people love to have it so" (Jer. 5:31 KJV).

seized by the priests, the prophets, and the people, who have every intention of executing him, only to be stopped by some of the elders of the land (i.e., people who are not from Jerusalem).

The next two chapters (Jeremiah 27–28) describe a run-in between Jeremiah and a false prophet named Hananiah. King Zedekiah forms an alliance of neighboring countries to fight against the Babylonian king Nebuchadnezzar. Jeremiah proclaims that such an alliance is futile and will end in defeat. Hananiah challenges Jeremiah's authority to speak for God, and announces victory instead. Jeremiah then pronounces judgment on Hananiah, a chilling prediction that comes true quite quickly: Hananiah dies two months later.

During the life of Jeremiah, the Babylonians conquer Jerusalem twice—a surrender in 598 BC and then a total destruction in 587/586 BC. When Jerusalem surrenders to the Babylonian army in 598 BC, the newly crowned young king Jehoiachin, as well as the rest of the nobility, is carried off to Babylonia (i.e., the first exile). Although the false prophets of Jeremiah's time predicted a quick return home for these exiles, Jeremiah sends the exiles a letter explaining that they will be in Babylon for seventy years, so they might as well settle down (29:4–23).

Restoration and the New Covenant (30:1–33:26)

In contrast to Jeremiah 1–29, which focuses on judgment (with glimpses of restoration), Jeremiah 30–33 focuses on restoration (but still has glimpses of judgment). It is within the promise of this future restoration that we find so many promises regarding the coming Messiah and his work—promises that are fulfilled by Christ.

In this encouraging unit, Jeremiah presents several themes relating to the coming messianic era. One prominent theme is that both Israel and Judah will be restored as a unified nation (Jer. 30:3, 10; 31:5–6, 8–9, 20, 27; 33:7). Likewise, this wonderful time of restoration will also be characterized by joy and joyful gatherings,

Assyrian wall relief depicting oxen yoked together and hitched to carts. Yokes play a major role in the story of Jeremiah 27–28 (27:2, 8, 11,12; 28:2, 4, 10–14).

✦ Jeremiah uses "sickness" as a symbol for sin and its judgment, pointing to the messianic age as a time of "healing." Jesus's healing ministry is both literal (a physical healing) and symbolic (restoration and forgiveness).

The Last Supper by DaVinci.

in contrast to the earlier judgments in Jeremiah, in which gatherings such as weddings are specifically excluded.

One of the most important contributions of Jeremiah is that he proclaims that God will make a "new covenant" with his people (Jer. 31:31–34), replacing the broken covenant of Jeremiah 11. This new covenant will be different from the old one, which the people broke, for it will be characterized by an internal change. That is, the new covenant will be written on their hearts rather than written on stone as the old covenant was (31:33–34). Furthermore, one of the central features of this new covenant is that it will be characterized by forgiveness.

Jeremiah 32 describes an incident that takes place during the Babylonian siege. Someone from Jeremiah's hometown offers to sell him some land, worthless now due to the presence of the Babylonians. God instructs Jeremiah to buy this property, a concrete expression of hope that in the future Israel would be restored to the land.

Jeremiah 33 continues the theme of restoration. In contrast to the earlier judgment passages in Jeremiah, in the future restoration there will be peace and healing (33:6). Likewise, there will be forgiveness (33:8), and the sound of joy will be heard again in Jerusalem and in Judah (33:11). This time of peace, justice, and righteousness will be brought about by the coming of a Davidic king (33:14–26). Once again, these prophecies are all fulfilled by the coming of Jesus Christ.

✚ Jesus inaugurates the new covenant of Jeremiah (Jer. 31:31–34) at the Last Supper (Matt. 26:28; Mark 14:24; Luke 22:20; 1 Cor. 11:23–26).

Jesus and the Reversal of Jeremiah's Curses

Jeremiah 1–29 contains numerous images of curses (wounds and sickness, no weddings or joy, etc.) that are reversed by Jesus Christ, as prophesied in Jeremiah 30–33. For example, as part of the judgment on Judah, Jeremiah proclaims the end of joyful celebrations, especially the joyful sound of weddings (16:8–9; 25:10). In the Book of Consolation (Jeremiah 30–33), however, God reverses the images of judgment as he describes the messianic future. The coming time of restoration will be one characterized by joyful singing and dancing, especially at weddings (30:19; 31:4, 7, 12, 13; 33:9–11). The messianic fulfillment is illustrated in John 2, when Jesus changes the water into wine. Jesus is at a wedding, and when the wine runs out, the joyful celebration is about to cease. Yet according to the prophets like Jeremiah, the Messiah will bring a time of joyful celebration, figuratively represented by weddings. Jesus creates the new wine in order to keep the joyful celebration going. Jeremiah's images (joyful weddings, healing, etc.) are primarily figurative. Jesus, however, fulfills them both in a literal sense (actual physical healing, creating literal wine) and in a figurative sense (spiritual restoration and salvation, true inner joy).

The Terrible and Tragic Final Days of Jerusalem (34:1–45:5)

The unfaithful kings of Judah (34:1–36:32)

Jeremiah 34–36 stresses how unfaithful the kings of Judah were. The first episode regarding unfaithfulness is recounted in Jeremiah 34:8–22. As part of the regular and persistent acts of social injustice being done by the king and other leaders of Judah, many Israelites had been enslaved. As the powerful Babylonian army approaches Jerusalem, King Zedekiah proclaims freedom for all the slaves in Jerusalem and makes a covenant with them, presumably so they would help fight against the Babylonians. A short time later, however, after the Babylonians apparently briefly withdraw to deal with another army, Zedekiah and his fellow nobles change their minds and re-enslave these people, thus breaking their promise. As a consequence, God proclaims "freedom" for Zedekiah and the other nobles, "'freedom' to fall by the sword, plague and famine" (34:17).

An Assyrian fisherman. In Jeremiah, fishermen catch people for judgment (Jer. 16:16). Jesus reverses this, sending fishermen to catch people for salvation (Matt. 4:19).

The story in Jeremiah 35 stands in strong contrast to this event in Jeremiah 34. Jeremiah 35 describes the Recabites, a group of people who remain faithful to the laws and traditions of their forefathers. They are presented as an example of faithfulness, in stark contrast to the people of Jerusalem, who had

✚ In the New Testament, the book of Hebrews explains the many ways in which Jeremiah's new covenant (as inaugurated and mediated by Jesus) is superior to the old (Mosaic) covenant (Hebrews 8–9).

abandoned the laws that God had given their forefathers. The faithfulness of the Recabites is an indictment on the king and the people of Jerusalem.

In Jeremiah 36 God tells Jeremiah to write his prophecies down on a scroll. Perhaps, God suggests, the people of Judah will listen to this written word. Baruch, Jeremiah's scribe, writes the words down as commanded, and then goes to the temple and reads the scroll aloud to all the people in the temple. The king's officials get wind of this and confiscate the scroll. They take it to the king and read it to him. Rather than tremble with fear at the words of judgment and repent of his sinful actions, the king defiantly cuts the scroll in pieces line by line as it is read and then burns each piece in a firepot. Thus even though the king held in his hand the actual written warnings from God, he chose to defy God and to attempt to destroy the unpleasant prophecies against him. He held the truth in his hands, but refused to believe it, thus sealing his fate. God reiterates the coming judgment on that king and orders Jeremiah to make another scroll.

Lachish, a Judahite fortress, was captured and destroyed by Nebuchadnezzar as he marched toward Jerusalem. Pictured below is one of the Lachish Letters, brief correspondances written on clay pot fragments from the commander at Lachish to the king in Jerusalem. In Lachish Letter 4, the commander writes that he can no longer see the fire signal from Azekah, indicating that Azekah has fallen.

Jerusalem falls, but a remnant lives on (37:1–39:18)

Unlike most of the rest of the book, Jeremiah 37–45 is in chronological order, dealing with the tragic final days of Jerusalem. The geopolitical situation was grave—the Babylonians were advancing toward Jerusalem. Jeremiah had preached and warned and pleaded, but to no avail. Jeremiah 37:2 sums up the tragic response of King Zedekiah and the people to Jeremiah's words: "Neither he [Zedekiah] nor his attendants nor the people of the land paid any attention to the words the Lord had spoken through Jeremiah the prophet." In fact, in Jeremiah 37, the prophet is arrested, beaten, and put in prison (vv. 11–16). Later he is released but confined to the courtyard where the king's bodyguard resides. Jeremiah, however, continues to proclaim the word of God, warning all who would listen that resistance to the Babylonians is futile. The only way to survive now, Jeremiah declares, is to surrender to them (38:1–3). This angers the officials and commanders of Jerusalem. After obtaining permission from King Zedekiah, they arrest Jeremiah again and place him in the bottom of a cistern, a large underground water storage cavern.

In all likelihood, Jeremiah would have died in this cistern, but a foreigner in Jerusalem, Ebed-melech the Cushite, confronts the king about Jeremiah's situation and then rescues Jeremiah (38:7–13). As Jeremiah has predicted, the Babylonians overrun Jerusalem, capturing and executing the officials who had opposed Jeremiah and plotted against him. The Babylonians gouge out King Zedekiah's eyes and then haul him to Babylon as a trophy. Likewise all the people in Judah, except for the very poorest and those who had escaped to the mountains, are taken into exile by the Babylonians, just as Jeremiah had prophesied.

Portrayal of a Cushite mercenary (or perhaps a warrior's attendant) from a Greek vase (540–530 BC).

One of the most significant events in the midst of this tragedy, however, is that God protects Ebed-melech the Cushite. Since this foreigner believed Jeremiah and defended him, God saves him and delivers him (39:15–18). Ebed-melech is contrasted with Zedekiah. King Zedekiah, because of his unbelieving defiance of God, is blinded and carried off to Babylon. Ebed-melech, however, is saved, because he believed the prophet and trusted in God. Thus Ebed-melech, a Cushite, becomes a symbol of those who will be saved—a gentile saved by his faith.

The story of deliverance in reverse: The people return to Egypt (40:1–45:5)

After capturing Jerusalem, the Babylonians release Jeremiah and allow him to choose where he wants to live. He opts to stay behind in Judah with the tattered remains of the nation. The Babylonians appoint Gedaliah as governor over Judah, and then they withdraw their army, leaving a small

✚ The New Testament story of the Ethiopian eunuch (Acts 8:26–40) has many parallels to the Ebed-melech story (Jer. 38:1–13; 39:15–18). In both stories a Cushite/ Ethiopian believes God's message precisely at the time that Israel rejects it.

garrison behind. At first, Jeremiah and the remaining people are doing well in the land (40:11–12), but then some army officers who had eluded capture by the Babylonians conspire and murder the Babylonian-appointed governor, Gedaliah, along with the small Babylonian garrison (41:1–3). The Babylonians are likely to retaliate with a vengeance, so these few remaining Israelites flee to Egypt, in spite of Jeremiah's strong opposition to that plan of action. They even force Jeremiah to accompany them (41:16–43:7). As this group of Israelites returns to the land of bondage, the great exodus story of deliverance that began in Exodus 1 is reversed. Jeremiah 44 is a tragic and sad postscript, describing how this group of Israelites in Egypt soon begins worshiping other pagan idols, even after all that has happened. Will they ever learn?

Jeremiah 45, in contrast, provides a brief description of the fate of Baruch, Jeremiah's faithful scribe. God states that even though the nation is under judgment, Baruch will survive (45:1–5).

Judgment on the Nations (46:1–51:64)

Most of the prophets in the Old Testament preach messages of judgment not only against Israel and Judah, but also against the surrounding nations. Jeremiah is no different, and in Jeremiah 46–51 he delivers prophecies of judgment on several foreign nations that played a hand in Judah's destruction—Egypt, Philistia, Moab, Ammon, Edom, Damascus, Kedar, Hazor (i.e., Arab tribes), Elam, and, especially, Babylon. However, sometimes Jeremiah prophesies judgment for other sins these nations have committed—idolatry, violence, arrogance, and so on. And sometimes no particular reason is stated—merely judgment. Apparently the reasons were clearly understood by his audience.

Jeremiah 46–51 ends with the statement, "The words of Jeremiah end here," indicating, perhaps, that Jeremiah 52 is an added postscript, still inspired Scripture but not preached or written by the prophet Jeremiah.

Amon was one of the primary gods of Egypt. In Jeremiah 46:25 the prophet proclaims judgment on Egypt and on the god Amon (Amun).

The Fall of Jerusalem Described Again (52:1–34)

Jeremiah 52 describes the terrible end of Jerusalem once again, repeating much of the material in Jeremiah 39 (as well as in 2 Kings 25). On the one hand, ending the book with a repeated description of the judgment on Jerusalem underscores the somber reality of judgment. On the other hand, this chapter ends with a brief mention of Jehoiachin, the young king who had surrendered to the Babylonians in 598 BC. Jehoiachin, who had not defied God's judgment but had accepted it, survives in Babylon, and thus provides a glimmer of hope for the exiles in Babylon.

So What? Applying Jeremiah to Our Lives Today

Jeremiah's message reverberates with us today on many levels. First of all, it may be instructive for us to recognize that Jeremiah was obedient to God but pretty much unsuccessful in actually reaching people. That is, no one really listened to him. If one measures success in ministry by counting heads, then Jeremiah was a flop. However, we surmise that Jeremiah was a successful prophet in that he obeyed God and did what God commanded him to do. Thus numerical success (or failure) in a ministry is not necessarily an indicator of obedience to God and/or of being in God's will.

Jeremiah also hammers away at the sins of idolatry, social injustice, and religious ritualism, sometimes hitting awfully close to home for us. What do we "idolize" and worship instead of God? Wealth? Success? Fame? Do we live for ourselves during the week, ignoring the call to stand for social justice, and then assume that attendance in church on Sunday will make it all okay? Have we let our rituals (how we do church) replace our relationship with God? Perhaps we need to listen carefully to the indictments of Jeremiah.

Fortunately, Jeremiah also preaches hope, and points those who will hear to the coming new covenant, the time of Christ, when the law will be written on hearts instead of on stone, a time characterized by forgiveness (Jer. 31:33). So just as Jeremiah slaps us in the face with the seriousness of sin, so he also offers us the solution, pointing us to Jesus, who forgives us of all our sin.

Our Favorite Verse in Jeremiah

I am the Lord, the God of all mankind. Is anything too hard for me? (32:27)

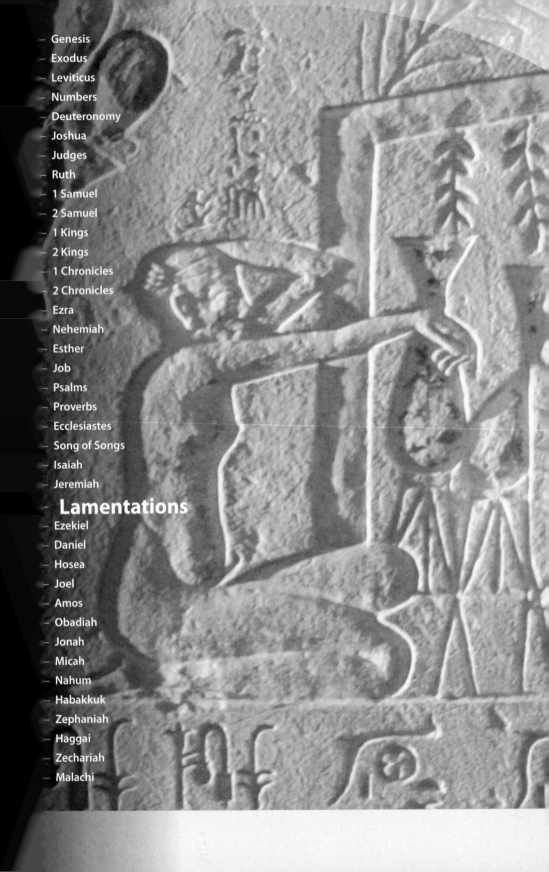

Lamentations

Mourning the Destruction of Jerusalem

Since the southern kingdom, Judah, persisted in its sins of idolatry and social injustice, refusing to listen to the word of God through the prophets, eventually the judgment came.

The book of Lamentations is a collection of five heartrending songs that sorrowfully describe the terrible destruction of Jerusalem carried out by the Babylonians after they captured Jerusalem in 587/586 BC. A "lament" is a mournful, "blues"-type song used in the ancient world to express grief and sorrow, often at funerals. In a manner of speaking, the book of Lamentations is a collection of songs to be sung at the "funeral" of Jerusalem. Acknowledging and expressing grief in such a manner also implies repentance.

Who Wrote Lamentations?

In the Hebrew Bible, no authorship of Lamentations is stated. The book is placed in a unit along with Song of Songs, Ruth, Ecclesiastes, and Esther. In Jewish tradition these books were each read on special festivals or religious holidays. Lamentations was to be read on the Ninth of Ab, a special religious day that commemorated the destruction of Jerusalem.

In the early Greek translation of the Old Testament (called the Septuagint), however, Jeremiah is identified as the author, and the book of Lamentations follows right after Jeremiah. In this location (followed by our English Bibles), Lamentations not only mourns over the destruction of Jerusalem (i.e., the consequences of sin), but it also vindicates Jeremiah's message, illustrating very clearly that the word of God delivered through Jeremiah was powerful and true.

The Poetic Structure of Lamentations

Lamentations is written in Hebrew poetry. Each chapter is a separate "lament" or sorrowful song. The first four laments (chapters 1, 2, 3, and 4) are also "acrostic" (alphabetic) songs. An acrostic is a literary technique that uses the order of the alphabet to structure its poetic lines. For example, in Lamentations 1, each verse has three lines of poetry. The first word of the first line in each verse starts with successive letters of the Hebrew alphabet. Thus the first word in 1:1 starts with *aleph*, the first letter of the Hebrew alphabet. The first word in 1:2 starts with *bet*, the second letter in the Hebrew alphabet, and so forth throughout the alphabet. Using the full range of the alphabet implies a complete expression of sorrow, grief, and repentance.

What Is the Message of Lamentations?

Lamentations 1 personifies Jerusalem and describes how the city weeps over what has happened to her. Amid the grief and weeping, the chapter contains confessions of her sin, but also stresses repeatedly that there is no one to comfort her in her grief (1:2, 9, 16, 17, 21), in contrast to Isaiah 40–66, for example, which promises that the coming Messiah will bring comfort. In Lamentations 1 the comfort is still future.

Lamentations 2 and most of chapter 3 poetically describe the wrath of God that fell on Jerusalem. Yet Lamentations 3 is not without hope beyond the

✦ Lamentations was a tragic reminder that unrepentant sin has its consequences, as Jeremiah had warned repeatedly.

judgment, for in 3:21–26 the song claims hope in God, due to his great love and compassion that are renewed every morning.

Lamentations 4 grimly returns to describing the terrible destruction of Jerusalem and the great suffering experienced in the aftermath. Lamentations 5 continues this theme, but the book ends with a humble prayer to God to remember them and to restore them to relationship with him.

So What? Applying Lamentations to Our Lives Today

Lamentations is a stark reminder to us of the serious consequences of sin and rebellion against God. Jeremiah preached and preached to Jerusalem, and no one listened. The people ignored God and hardened their hearts against God and his message. Thus, eventually, a terrible devastating judgment came. For us today this sobering reality is still true. Yes, we live in the era of the new covenant and wonderful forgiveness provided by Jesus Christ. But for those who reject this and who defy God and God's gospel message, there awaits judgment, as heartbreaking, sad, and terrible as that described in Lamentations.

Lamentations 3:21–33 also reminds us of God's great love and compassion on his people who trust in him. His "compassions never fail. They are new every morning; great is your faithfulness."

Our Favorite Verses in Lamentations

Because of the Lord's great love we are not consumed,
for his compassions never fail.
They are new every morning;
great is your faithfulness. (3:22–23)

Ancient clay tablet from Mesopotamia containing a poetic lament for the destruction of the city of Lagash.

Ezekiel

Sin and Salvation: Losing and Gaining the Presence of God

The book of Ezekiel contains some fascinating, yet sometimes strange, events. The prophet Ezekiel sees the throne of God surrounded by four "living creatures" that have four faces, four wings, and are covered completely with eyes. A little weird, isn't it? Later on, Ezekiel stands in a valley full of old bleached skeletons, the remnants of an old battle, and God then breathes on these skeletons, bringing them to life! Then there is the strange battle involving Gog and Magog, an event that modern prophecy buffs continually try to connect to contemporary events in the Middle East.

Yet all the unusual stories and prophecies in Ezekiel combine in harmony to focus on a simple truth that all the prophets likewise proclaim—repeated, unrepentant sin will bring separation from God's Presence (judgment), yet God in his grace will bring about a glorious restoration in the future, a salvation and deliverance characterized by close fellowship with his very Presence.

Who Is Ezekiel?

Ezekiel is from a priestly family, and as a young man he perhaps anticipated growing up and serving in the temple in Jerusalem. However, when Ezekiel is still a youth, the king in Jerusalem surrenders to the invading Babylonians, and these new conquerors carry off 10,000 or so people from Judah back to Babylon as "hostages." Ezekiel is included in this group of exiles. God calls him and commissions him as a prophet while he is living in Babylonia. Much of what God has to say in this book relates to the temple and to God's Presence; thus God determined that a priest, called to be a prophet, would be the appropriate one to deliver this message.

What Is the Setting for Ezekiel?

Ezekiel overlaps with the second half of Jeremiah's ministry. The kings and other leaders of Judah (priests and court prophets) disregard Jeremiah's warnings and continue to practice idolatry and social injustice, totally ignoring God's law in Deuteronomy and Leviticus. Thus, as Jeremiah predicted, the Babylonians invade—twice. The first invasion comes in 597 BC. Jerusalem surrenders, and the Babylonians carry off most of the leaders and other aristocracy of Judah into exile (including Ezekiel). Yet the new leaders in Jerusalem are just as rebellious (and dense) as the old ones were, and they continue to defy God. Likewise, against Jeremiah's advice, they rebel against the Babylonians, who respond by sending a huge army. In 587/586 BC they destroy Jerusalem and carry off most of the remaining population into exile. Ezekiel prophesies in the context of these two invasions and the consequential destruction of Jerusalem and the temple.

What Is at the Heart of the Book of Ezekiel?

Ezekiel is similar to the other prophets in proclaiming the standard prophetic message:

1. You (Judah) have broken the covenant; you had better repent!
2. No repentance? Then judgment!
3. Yet there is hope beyond the judgment for a glorious, future restoration, both for Israel/Judah and the nations.

About halfway through Ezekiel's ministry, the terrible destruction of Jerusalem actually occurs (judgment), so Ezekiel shifts from focusing on

✦ Ezekiel is contemporary with the latter years of Jeremiah's ministry, but Jeremiah prophesies in Jerusalem while Ezekiel prophesies in Babylonia.

warning and judgment to focusing on the future restoration. Within this context, two primary themes emerge out of the book of Ezekiel. One of the themes dominating the book is the sovereignty and glory of God. As Jerusalem and the spectacular Solomonic temple crumble into dust, Ezekiel proclaims that God is sovereign over all the nations and over all history, and thus God will ultimately be glorified. Connected to the sovereignty of God is the repeated phrase "I am the Lord." This phrase occurs seventy times in Ezekiel. God often says something or does something significant "so that you might know that I am the Lord."

The second primary theme of Ezekiel relates to the Presence of God. The most spectacular and wonderful benefit that Israel had from the old covenant was that God promised to actually dwell among the people. Under the covenant of Moses, God's Presence dwelt among the people, first in the tabernacle and then later in the temple. Due to repeated idolatry and other sin right in front of the Presence of God, his Presence is finally driven away from Jerusalem, a devastating loss. However, as Ezekiel looks to the future time of restoration, he describes it as a time when God's Presence will once again be a central element in his relationship with his people. This is stressed in the closing words of the book, as Ezekiel identifies the name of the new city as "The Lord is there."

Creatures composed of parts of different animals were not that unusual in the ancient Near East. Guarding an Assyrian palace entrance were two huge winged bulls with human heads.

The book of Ezekiel can be outlined as follows:

- Loss of God's Presence, and Judgment on Jerusalem (1:1–24:27)
  - The glory of the Lord and the call of Ezekiel (1:1–3:27)
  - Grim object lessons of judgment (4:1–7:27)
  - The glory of the Lord leaves the temple of Jerusalem (8:1–11:25)
  - The exile dramatized (12:1–28)
  - Ezekiel condemns the false prophets (13:1–23)
  - Judgment on Jerusalem announced (14:1–16:63)

What Makes Ezekiel Interesting and Unique?

- Ezekiel has a spectacular direct encounter with God, and he describes the wheels of God's "chariot" and the strange "living creatures" that hover around God's throne.
- Ezekiel describes the actual departure of God's glory (Presence) from the temple, a Presence that does not return to the temple until Jesus walks in through the gates.
- Ezekiel watches God breathe life back into people who are really, really dead (skeletons), demonstrating that there is always hope and life in God.
- Ezekiel declares that in the future God's Presence will be enjoyed in a fantastic new way; God will actually put his Spirit into his people.
- As the old temple smolders in ruins, Ezekiel gives an extensive description of the spectacular "new temple" of the future restoration.

Theophany: Direct Encounters with God

Although in one sense God is present everywhere throughout the world, there are times in the Old Testament when God appears to someone in a highly intensified Presence. These appearances, called theophanies, are fairly rare, and when they do occur, the event is extremely significant. Usually they occur at crucial times in the lives of God's people, and they provide new (or, at least, more clear) directions regarding the relationship between God and his people. The three most descriptive theophanies in the Old Testament are Moses's encounter with God at the burning bush (Exodus 3), Isaiah's encounter with God in the temple (Isaiah 6), and Ezekiel's encounter with God while in exile (Ezekiel 1). These appearances of God are usually frightening to the people involved, at least initially, but God moves quickly to calm their fear, for usually he has something very significant to reveal to that person—a promise or a call to a critical task. Such highly intense appearances of God (i.e., meeting "face-to-face") serve to underscore the importance of the event as well as to stress the personal relationship between God and the recipient. In addition, usually a theophany reveals important theological truth relating to the Presence of God—his holiness, his power, his relatedness, and the revelation of his word.

What Is Ezekiel's Message?

Loss of God's Presence, and Judgment on Jerusalem (1:1–24:27)

The glory of the Lord and the call of Ezekiel (1:1–3:27)

The book of Ezekiel opens with a description of a spectacular encounter the prophet has with "the glory of the Lord." Ezekiel sees the glory of God on a throne. This "throne" is apparently mounted on a four-wheeled chariot of sorts, each wheel able to go in any direction. Surrounding the vehicle are four living creatures (Ezekiel later identifies them as cherubim; Ezek. 10:1–22) with four wings and four faces, thus able to fly in any direction. God, the throne, the vehicle, and the creatures are apparently in the midst of a bright fire, accompanied by lightning. The point of the vision is that God is powerful and completely mobile. Even as his Presence prepares to depart from the temple in Jerusalem, God reveals his glory seated on a throne in Babylonia. God is not tied to the temple in Jerusalem, but he is free to roam and demonstrate his power anywhere at any time. His powerful Presence has come to Ezekiel to call him as a prophet and to empower him to speak God's word.

A Canaanite "high place" in Megiddo. In Ezek. 6:3 God announces judgment on the "high places" in Israel.

✛ Ezekiel's encounter with God (1:1–3:15) has numerous similarities to Isaiah's encounter with God (Isa. 6:1–13).

In Ezekiel 2 and 3 God appoints Ezekiel as a prophet, calling him a "watchman" and warning him that the rebellious Israelites will be hostile to him. Throughout the first three chapters, the phrase "glory of the Lord" is repeated, stressing the interconnected themes of Presence, glory, and empowerment.

Grim object lessons of judgment (4:1–7:27)

God does not rely solely on the preached word to get his message across to his people. In this section of Ezekiel, God orders the prophet to use two symbolic "object lessons" or "enacted dramas" to communicate the truth that Jerusalem would soon be attacked and destroyed. Ezekiel builds a model of Jerusalem and then lies down on the ground beside it for months, symbolizing the coming siege of the city. Next Ezekiel shaves his hair and his beard. He splits the cut hair into thirds. One third he burns, one third he strikes with the sword, and one third he lets the wind blow and scatter. This all symbolizes what will happen to the inhabitants of Jerusalem.

The glory of the Lord leaves the temple of Jerusalem (8:1–11:25)

These chapters describe one of the most significant events in the entire Old Testament. A critical component of God's covenant with his people was his promise to "dwell in their midst." The Presence of God dwelling in the temple in Jerusalem was a spectacular and powerful blessing. God's Presence blessed them and protected them. It allowed them to fellowship with him. In Ezekiel 8–11, however, God departs from the temple and does not return

A Babylonian stela with King Nabonidus and astrological religious symbols (the star of Ishtar-Venus, the winged disc of the sun god Shamash, and the crescent of the moon god Sin). Tammuz (Dumuzi) was the husband of Ishtar. Thus the Israelites in Ezek. 8:1–16 appear to be worshiping Mesopotamian gods.

until Christ walks in through the gates, over six hundred years later.

At the beginning of this section, God wants Ezekiel to see the extent of the horrendous idolatry being practiced in Jerusalem. So the Spirit of God takes Ezekiel back to the temple in Jerusalem and shows him four unthinkable things: a pagan idol near the altar in the entrance to the north gate (8:5–6); images of unclean animals and pagan gods painted on the inside walls of the temple (8:7–12);

Shamash the Syrian sun god. Ezekiel 14 continues the judgment on the Israelites for their idolatry. Shamash was apparently one of the gods they were worshiping (Ezek. 8:16).

women engaged in worshiping the Mesopotamian god Tammuz (8:13–15); and a large group of men in the inner court of the temple bowing down to the sun with their backs toward God (an insulting posture in the ancient world) (8:16). God has had enough. He declares that these things will drive him away from the temple (8:6).

Ezekiel 10 describes the actual departure of God from the temple. The glory of God is accompanied by the same creatures (here called cherubim) that were around his throne in the opening scene of Ezekiel 1. The continual sin of the people in Judah has become so great that it drives God right out of their midst. Many scholars believe this event signals the demise of the old (Mosaic) covenant. In the latter chapters of Ezekiel (33–48), however, the prophet will share prophecies that look to the future and speak of a new and powerful way the Presence of God will be enjoyed by his people.

The exile dramatized (12:1–28)

A part of Ezekiel's message is that the rebellious and disobedient people back in Jerusalem will soon be carried off into exile. In Ezekiel 12 God tells the prophet to act this out in a "skit" or drama. Acting as if he is in Jerusalem as it falls to the invading Babylonians, Ezekiel packs his things together and "escapes" through a hole he digs in the city wall.

Ezekiel condemns the false prophets (13:1–23)

During the time of Ezekiel and Jeremiah, numerous false prophets were in Israel who were making up prophecies and contradicting the message of God's true prophets. Such false prophecy brings on the wrath and anger of God, who proclaims, "Woe to the foolish prophets who follow their own spirit and have seen nothing" (Ezek. 13:3).

✝ Ezekiel 15 declares that Israel (the vine) was without fruit and thus useless and headed for judgment. In John 15 Jesus picks up this analogy, telling his disciples that if they abide in him (the true vine) they will produce much fruit.

Judgment on Jerusalem announced (14:1–16:63)

In Ezekiel 14 the prophet once again underscores the terrible sin of idolatry in Israel and the consequential judgment that was coming. In the following chapter God compares Jerusalem to a useless vine, one that does not produce any fruit. Ezekiel 16 returns to the analogy of the unfaithful wife. God declares that rejecting him for idols is like a woman rejecting her loving husband to become a prostitute. God reminds Israel that he delivered her and loved her as a devoted husband. Israel, however, rejects her husband's love and becomes a prostitute who sells herself to other men.

Judgment on Jerusalem arrives (17:1–24:27)

Ezekiel 17–23 repeats several prophetic themes—coming Babylonian judgment (Ezekiel 17); personal responsibility (Ezekiel 18); a sorrowful song (funeral dirge) over the coming destruction (Ezekiel 19); a recapping of the sad history of Israel's unfaithfulness to God (Ezekiel 20); the coming Babylonian invasion as the judging "sword of God" (Ezekiel 21); a review of the sins of Jerusalem, including social, moral, and economic sins (Ezekiel 22); and an extensive development of the unfaithful wife/prostitute analogy (Ezekiel 23). Ezekiel

An Egyptian temple at Karnak. Ezekiel 29–32 pronounces judgment on Egypt.

24 concludes the larger unit of 1–24 by proclaiming the actual fall of Jerusalem. Ezekiel's wife dies (24:15–18) as Jerusalem (symbolically God's wife) also dies (24:1–2, 25–27). The unit ends with God declaring, "And they will know that I am the Lord" (Ezek. 24:27), a theme that echoes throughout Ezekiel. Ultimately all people will know that God is "the Lord." People will know him either as a wonderful Savior or as a dangerous dispenser of justice and judgment. There is no middle ground.

The piles of dry bones Ezekiel sees are probably the remains of soldiers who died in a large battle. Depicted above is the Assyrian slaughter of the Elamites in the battle of Til-Tuba.

Judgment on the Nations (25:1–32:32)

The Old Testament prophets proclaim judgment on Israel for their sin and covenant disobedience, but they also proclaim judgment on the surrounding foreign nations for their sin. Ezekiel 25–32 proclaims God's judgment on Israel's neighbors—Ammon, Moab, Edom, Philistia, Tyre, Sidon, and Egypt. Ezekiel's judgment passages are brief for the smaller nations (Ammon, Moab, Edom, Philistia, and Sidon), but more extensive on the more powerful nations of Tyre (the naval power who controlled the Mediterranean) and Egypt. Some interpreters understand 28:11–19 as a reference to the fall of Satan. This understanding, however, does not fit the context of the passage at all, and most Old Testament scholars reject equating the city of Tyre with Satan.

God's Restored Presence and the New Temple (33:1–48:35)

From judgment to hope: God the shepherd will cleanse them and give them a new heart (33:1–36:38)

Ezekiel 33 transitions from judgment on Jerusalem to the hope centered on the coming shepherd. In Ezekiel 24:26–27 God tells the prophet to expect a messenger to arrive with the news of Jerusalem's fall. Next comes a parenthesis in the story, as Ezekiel 25–32 announces judgment on the

✦ Jesus identifies himself as the "Good Shepherd" (John 10), and thus fulfills the prophecy of the coming shepherd in Ezekiel 34.

Who Is Gog and Where Is Magog?

In Ezekiel 38:2 God tells Ezekiel to prophesy against someone named Gog from the land of Magog. Gog is called the "chief prince of Meshech and Tubal." The Hebrew word for "chief" or "head" is *rosh*, so a few translations read "Gog . . . the prince of Rosh, Meshech, and Tubal," but most Bible translations and most scholars translate the phrase as the "chief prince of Meshech and Tubal." The terms "Meshech" and "Tubal" show up in the literature of the ancient Assyrians and are identified with regions of what is now Turkey. Ezekiel 38:5–6 describes an alliance between Meshech/Tubal and five other nations. This alliance takes on a somewhat worldwide form, comprising seven nations from areas associated with north, south, east, and west. This "perfect coalition" attacks Israel but is defeated by God.

The book of Revelation mentions Gog and Magog again in a similar context. Revelation 20:7–8 reads: "When the thousand years are over, Satan will be released from his prison and will go out to deceive the nations in the four corners of the earth—Gog and Magog—to gather them for battle." Here in Revelation, Gog and Magog are used to represent nations from around the world. The terms are probably used similarly in Ezekiel 38.

Throughout history many Christian writers have tried to connect Gog to a people or person from their day and time. For example, in the fourth century AD some Christians claimed that Gog was the Goths. In the seventh century AD Gog was the Arabs, and in the thirteenth century AD it was the Mongols. Other writers then identified Gog as one of the popes or the Turks. In the twentieth century many popular writers claimed that Gog represented modern Russia, and that Meshech stood for Moscow. This identification is highly unlikely and is rejected almost universally by serious Old Testament scholars. Most Old Testament scholars do not believe that Ezekiel 38–39 has anything to do with Russia or specifically with the Muslims (a current popular understanding).

surrounding nations. Ezekiel 33 now continues the story, and in 33:21 the messenger predicted back in 24:26–27 actually arrives, announcing the fall of Jerusalem.

Ezekiel 34, however, moves beyond the judgment and introduces a large unit that focuses on hope, deliverance, and restoration. Using "shepherd" as an analogy for kings and leaders, Ezekiel 34 proclaims that in contrast to Israel's bad shepherds (the current kings and leaders), God himself will come and be their shepherd, caring dearly for them, ruling with justice, and establishing a new covenant relationship with them.

Ezekiel 35 and part of 36 return briefly to the theme of judgment, but starting in Ezekiel 36:24 God begins to unfold his spectacular plan for the future. God promises to regather his people from all over the world, to cleanse them, to create in them a "new heart," and then to place his Spirit in them (36:24–27), thus re-establishing his relationship and his Presence with them.

✛ The Presence of God is a central theme in Ezekiel. The Old Testament prophetic promise of God's indwelling Spirit is proclaimed in Ezekiel 36:24–27 and fulfilled in Acts 2:1–47.

God gives new life to those who are profoundly dead (37:1–28)

Many people will recall the famous song about "them bones, them bones, them dry bones." That song comes from Ezekiel 37. God takes the prophet to a valley filled with the dry, bleached bones of people who had died long ago, probably soldiers who fell in a great battle and were left unburied. God tells Ezekiel to prophesy to the bones, bones that then are filled with breath/wind/spirit (all the same word in Hebrew) and come alive! The point of this chapter is that these people are really, really dead, yet God brought them back to life. Thus there is always hope. If God can bring these bones back to life, he can restore fallen Israel, and he can bring anyone else back to life that he chooses. There is always hope when God is involved.

Another invasion? What will happen then? (38:1–39:29)

Ezekiel 37 describes a wonderful time of restoration for Israel beyond the terrible destruction brought about by the Babylonians. On the one hand, in Ezekiel 37:26 God speaks of a covenant of peace. Ezekiel 38–39, on the other hand, presents a strong contrast, for these two chapters are about another invasion and another (future) war. This attempted invasion of Israel appears to take place after the restoration, while Israel is at peace (38:11). Ezekiel 38:1–6 describes a coalition of seven nations from the north, south, east, and west (i.e., a sort of "perfect" coalition) and attacks peaceful Israel. Remember God had used foreign nations like Assyria and Babylonia to judge Israel. Ezekiel himself delivers these words to the exiles living in Babylonia. Yet, in contrast, the point of Ezekiel 38–39 is that when this powerful coalition attacks Israel in the future, things will be different, and this time God will intervene to destroy the invading enemies. Part

Assyrian wall relief showing the king's garden, filled with trees and watered by irrigation channels.

Measurements for the new temple are given throughout Ezekiel 40–48. Depicted above are Egyptian surveyors measuring a field.

of the picture of Israel's restoration is that their relationship with God will be restored, and he will once again be their strong defender and protector.

The glorious new temple and the restored Presence of God (40:1–48:35)

Throughout Israel's history the tabernacle, and then the temple, played a critical, important role because the tabernacle and the temple were where the Presence of God resided with his people. A properly functioning temple was filled with the powerful and holy Presence of God. This powerful Presence of God was a critical component in the special relationship that God had with his people in ancient Israel (as it is with his people today). As prophets like Isaiah, Jeremiah, and Ezekiel proclaimed, Israel's defiant and continuous sin, highlighted by their worship of idols, finally resulted in a broken covenant and a rupture in their relationship with God. Ezekiel 8–11 describes the terrible consequences—the glory and Presence of God actually leaves the temple (and Israel). Ezekiel 40–48, however, looks to the future and describes a wonderful time when God's Presence will once again be back among his people, dwelling again in a temple, but this time in a much better temple.

For several chapters (40–42) the prophet describes the details of the new future temple (rooms, altars, etc.). In 43:6–12 Ezekiel describes the exciting return of God, back to fill the temple with his holy and glorious Presence.

Ezekiel 47:1–12 contains a description of a river flowing out of the temple and down into the land, getting deeper as it flows and providing life to everything along the way. In the climactic closing chapter of the New Testament book of Revelation, the apostle John describes a scene in the New Jerusalem that is very similar to that described by Ezekiel (see Rev. 21:1–6), combining elements from Ezekiel's vision with aspects from the garden in Genesis 2–3. Scholars disagree over whether Ezekiel's vision of this future temple is to be interpreted literally (an actual temple like this will be built in future Israel) or symbolically (Christ is the new temple, etc.). Note that Ezekiel ends with a fitting climactic statement regarding this future city, "The Lord is there" (48:35). All scholars would agree that the Presence of God is a critical and central component of his relationship with his people, and his Presence will play a vital and spectacular role in the future, when God brings all things to completion.

So What? Applying Ezekiel to Our Lives Today

Ezekiel reminds us that God is sovereign, with complete control over human history, which he is moving toward his ultimate goal. This should encourage us and strengthen us from sliding into despair when we see evil temporarily flourishing in the world around us. God will ultimately triumph and establish his kingdom.

From Ezekiel we also learn how vital and important the Presence of God is. As Christians we recognize how wonderful it is and how privileged we are to know God's Presence through his indwelling Spirit, as Ezekiel prophesied. This allows us to encounter on a daily basis God's holiness and his power. This should, at the same time, thrill us, strengthen us, and perhaps frighten us. Accompanying the wonderful Presence of God we now enjoy are responsibilities—living according to God's holy desires for us.

Finally, Ezekiel 37 reminds us that there is always hope. If God can breathe life into those dry scattered bones, he can certainly restore you and me to fullness and to meaningful lives lived in close relationship to him. There is no situation that you might find yourself in that is so hopeless that God cannot deliver you. If he can bring those dry bones back to life, he can put your life back together as well.

Our Favorite Verse in Ezekiel

I will give you a new heart and put a new spirit in you. (36:26)

Broken fragment of an Egyptian measuring rod.

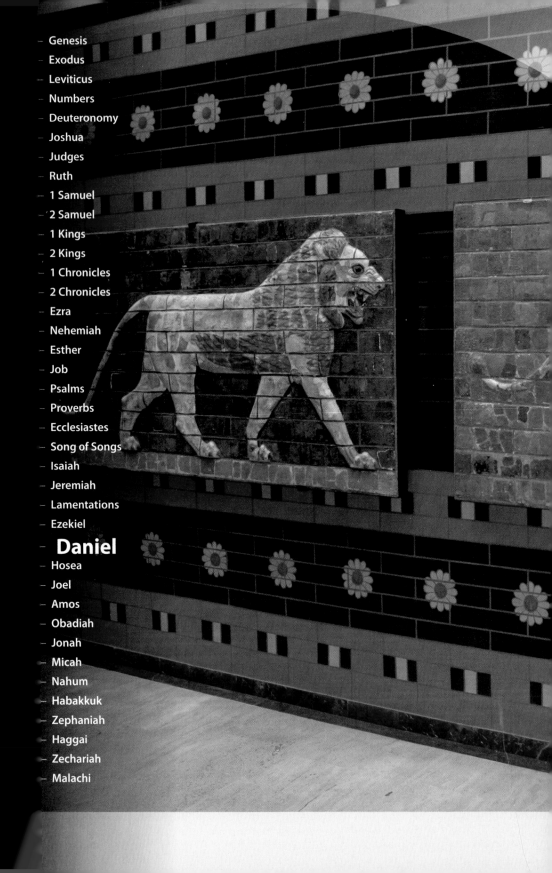

Daniel

God's Kingdom Will Not Be Destroyed,
and His Dominion Will Never End

We all love the story of Daniel in the lions' den. What courage and faith he had! What strong convictions he had! Likewise, we are moved by the powerful story about his friends Shadrach, Meshach, and Abednego, who are protected by God even though the Babylonian king Nebuchadnezzar angrily tries to kill them by throwing them into a fiery furnace. What a miraculous deliverance that was! This exciting book, however, is not really about the man Daniel, even though he was quite a remarkable individual. This book is about God. This book proclaims that no matter how bad things may appear on the surface, God is still sovereign and in control, carefully moving history forward to the culmination that he has planned and decreed.

Who Is Daniel?

Daniel is quite a bit different from the others who proclaimed and wrote the prophetic books, for he is neither a priest nor a professional prophet. Daniel is an administrator, and he has a long career as a successful administrator working in the Babylonian government.

While he was still a young man, Daniel was among the first group of exiles that the conquering Babylonians carried back to Babylonia. He was part of a smaller group of young men from Jerusalem and Judah that the Babylonians brought back to train in preparation for service in their rapidly growing empire.

What Is the Setting for Daniel?

Daniel 1:1 dates the beginning of his story to the third year of Jehoiakim (605 BC). The final date given in the book is tied to the third year of Cyrus, king of Persia (537 BC). Thus Daniel is a contemporary with Ezekiel and overlaps with the older Jeremiah by several years. Like Ezekiel, Daniel's prophetic ministry takes place in Babylon. He lives through the devastating and tumultuous times when the Babylonians destroy Jerusalem and carry off most of the surviving Israelites into captivity.

What Is at the Heart of the Book of Daniel?

The book of Daniel is composed of two major units. Chapters 1–6 contain stories about Daniel and his friends standing strong for their faith. The major theme in this unit, however, focuses on God, demonstrating that God is more powerful than the kings of Babylon and Persia. The second half of the book, Daniel 7–12, broadens the view to encompass God's great plan for the future, especially in regard to humanity's world empires in contrast to the establishment of God's world empire. The message of the book is that even in difficult times when it appears that forces hostile to God are dominating, God wants his people to live faithfully,

The ruins of Persepolis, one of the capitals of Persia.

✦ Along with Genesis, Psalms, Ezekiel, and Isaiah, Daniel is one of the Old Testament books most influential on the New Testament book of Revelation.

trusting in him and in his promise that he alone controls world history and that he will bring about his glorious kingdom, all in due time.

Thus the book of Daniel can be broken down into the following sections:

- God Is More Powerful than the Monarchs of Babylon and Persia (1:1–6:28)
  - Daniel and his friends in the Babylonian university (1:1–21)
  - King Nebuchadnezzar's dream about four world empires (2:1–49)
  - Can Nebuchadnezzar kill God's servants? The fiery furnace (3:1–30)
  - Nebuchadnezzar humbled by God (4:1–37)
  - Handwriting on the wall—Babylon falls to the Persians (5:1–31)
  - Daniel in the lions' den (6:1–28)
- World Kingdoms and God's Plan for the Future (7:1–12:13)
  - The Ancient of Days and the beast with ten horns (7:1–28)
  - Daniel's vision of a ram and a goat (8:1–27)
  - Daniel's prayer and the seventy "sevens" (9:1–27)
  - Daniel's final vision (10:1–12:13)

What Makes the Book of Daniel Interesting and Unique?

- This book contains several riveting stories (the fiery furnace, the lions' den) about how Daniel and his three friends remain faithful to God and thus are protected by God (Daniel 1–6).
- King Nebuchadnezzar (Daniel 2) and Daniel (Daniel 7) both have startling and symbolic visions portraying four world empires.
- Daniel sees a vision of the "Ancient of Days" (God) seated on his throne, holding court (7:9–10).
- Daniel sees a vision of "one like a son of man, coming with the clouds of heaven," an image that the New Testament connects to Christ (Matt. 24:30–31; Mark 13:26–27; Luke 21:27–28; Rev. 1:7, 12–18).
- Daniel's visions pertain to the near future (events that happen prior to Christ) as well as to the far future (events that apparently are yet to come).
- The book of Daniel is written in two languages. Daniel 1:1–2:4a is in Hebrew; 2:4b–7:28 is in Aramaic (the language of the Babylonians); and 8:1–12:13 is in Hebrew again.

Daniel 3 mentions the sound of "the horn, flute, zither, lyre, harp, pipes, and all kinds of music" several times (3:5, 7, 10, 15). The Assyrian wall relief above shows several different instruments.

What Is Daniel's Message?

God Is More Powerful than the Monarchs of Babylon and Persia (1:1–6:28)

Daniel and his friends in the Babylonian university (1:1–21)

Daniel and his three friends are taken from Judah to Babylonia, given new Babylonian names, and placed in a Babylonian educational institution to be trained for service in the Babylonian government. Although they are away from home and under strong pressure to abandon their religious identity, all four of these young men remain faithful to God, and even refuse to eat unclean foods (probably food that had been offered to idols). God honors their faith and gives them extraordinary knowledge and skill, thus allowing them to excel and prosper in Babylon.

King Nebuchadnezzar's dream about four world empires (2:1–49)

Nebuchadnezzar, king of the Babylonians, has a troubling dream that no one but Daniel is able to interpret. The dream is of a large statue comprising several different materials. The statue, Daniel explains, represents four world empires, starting with the current Babylonian Empire. In chapter 7 Daniel also has a vision representing four world empires (see the discussion below). The main point is that the powerful Babylonian Empire, overwhelming as it appears, will not last, but will be replaced with successive empires that diminish in glory, finally to be destroyed by God and replaced with his kingdom.

Can Nebuchadnezzar kill God's servants? The fiery furnace (3:1–30)

Many of us are familiar with this story, but perhaps we haven't stopped to ask what it really means within the context of Daniel. Nebuchadnezzar builds a huge new golden statue (compare this to the vision in chapter 2) and then orders everyone to bow down and worship the statue. Daniel's three friends refuse to obey. Infuriated by their obstinacy, the king throws them into a burning furnace (probably a kiln for manufacturing

✦ Daniel's experience in Babylon has many parallels to Joseph's in Egypt (Genesis 37, 39–45): exile as a young man, temptations, faithfulness to God, interpretation of a king's dream, and rise to power in a foreign government.

The Four Kingdoms of Daniel

In Daniel 2, King Nebuchadnezzar has a troubling dream about a large statue composed of different materials. Daniel describes and interprets the dream for him, explaining that the statue represents four kingdoms. In Daniel 7, Daniel himself is given a vision in a dream that involves four beasts. An angel explains to Daniel that "the four great beasts are four kingdoms that will rise from the earth" (7:17). Most scholars conclude that the two visions (Nebuchadnezzar's and Daniel's) describe the same four kingdoms. But which kingdoms are these? The first one is easy to identify because Daniel tells us it is the Babylonian kingdom. After that, things are trickier, and three different views of these kingdoms are possible. The following chart represents a comparison of the two most popular views.

A Comparison of the Two Major Traditional Views of Daniel 2 and 7

Man in Daniel 2	Beasts in Daniel 7	Traditional Evangelical View	Alternate View
Gold head	Lion	Babylon	Babylon/Assyria
Silver chest, arms	Bear	Medo-Persia	Media
Bronze belly, thighs	Leopard with four heads	Greece (Alexander the Great)	Persia
Clay and iron feet	Fourth beast	Rome/revived Roman Empire	Greece

A third option for understanding the statue and the beasts is to view all four kingdoms as symbolic, representing kingdoms of the world in general. In this view "four" represents north, south, east, and west, or all the kingdoms of the world. The point would be that evil human kingdoms will succeed one another throughout history until God intervenes at the climax of history to establish his ultimate kingdom.

In addition, there are numerous similarities between the "boastful horn" of Daniel's fourth beast in Daniel 7 and the beast/antichrist in Revelation 13, thus connecting the vision of Daniel 7 to the future events in Revelation 13. At the end of the twentieth century, some writers speculated that the European Union fulfilled the "ten-horned beast" prophecy as a revival of the Roman Empire, but since membership in the EU has swelled beyond ten members to include twenty-seven members, the likelihood that it represents a "ten-horned beast" seems remote. Likewise, attempts to connect the United Nations with Daniel's prophecy have not been convincing.

ceramic glazed bricks, for which Babylon was famous). Yet the fire does not kill the young men, and when the king looks into the fire he sees not three but four men walking around in the fire (the fourth is apparently either an angel or the Lord himself). This is not only a story about how God honors the faith of these young men, but it is also a statement to the Hebrew exiles. Nebuchadnezzar, the king who destroyed Jerusalem and who killed thousands of her inhabitants, is unable to kill these three Hebrew men, even though they are in Babylon, his own backyard! God is

✚ As the three young men are delivered from the fiery furnace (Dan. 3:1–30), perhaps they recall the words of the prophet Isaiah: "When you walk through the fire, you will not be burned . . . for I am the Lord, your God" (Isa. 43:2–3).

more powerful than Nebuchadnezzar and the Babylonians, even though Jerusalem lies in ruins.

Nebuchadnezzar humbled by God (4:1–37)

Nebuchadnezzar has a dream about a "tree" that is cut down. Daniel reluctantly informs the king that the vision refers to the king himself, who will be driven away from people and will live like an animal until he humbles himself and recognizes the power and sovereignty of God. The dream comes true, and Nebuchadnezzar lives like an animal until he humbly acknowledges the power of God, who then restores him to his throne.

Handwriting on the wall—Babylon falls to the Persians (5:1–31)

Time has passed. Nebuchadnezzar has died, and Daniel is an old man. The current Babylonian king, Nabonidus, has moved to Arabia, and his son and coregent, Belshazzar, now reigns over Babylon. During a banquet, while the king and the people are drinking wine from cups the Babylonians had looted from the temple in Jerusalem, a hand appears and writes on the wall. Once again, only Daniel is able to interpret this sign and decipher the writing, which announces the end of the Babylonian Empire. In fact, the Medes and the Persians capture Babylon that very night.

Daniel in the lions' den (6:1–28)

In Daniel 5, the Medes and the Persians overrun the Babylonians, and Daniel 6 then takes place during the time of Persian/Median rule. The king in this chapter is called Darius (a very common name among the Persians), and many scholars think that this is the same king as Cyrus the Great (or perhaps a general appointed by Cyrus). Once again, Daniel is pressured to compromise his faith in God, and because he refuses to cease praying to God, Daniel is sentenced to death and thrown into a den of lions. God, however, protects Daniel and keeps the lions from killing him. Just as the Babylonian kings had been forced to recognize the power of Daniel's God, so

This Babylonian clay tablet mentions Belshazzar, "son of the king."

Apocalyptic Literature

A literary style closely connected to Old Testament prophetic literature is called apocalyptic. While Old Testament prophecy typically uses colorful figures of speech and vivid imagery, apocalyptic uses highly symbolic, sometimes bizarre imagery (at least from our perspective) that goes beyond the normal figurative language of the prophets. For example, normal Old Testament prophecy compares God to a dangerous lion. That analogy is fairly easy to comprehend, for we are familiar with lions. Daniel, however, has a vision of a leopard with four heads and four wings, a creature we are not familiar with. Everything in this vision is highly symbolic (e.g., the four heads probably represent the four generals who split up Alexander the Great's empire). Other typical characteristics of apocalyptic literature include: (1) usually an angel gives an explanation of the vision; (2) the vision is often related to the unfolding of world history; and (3) the ultimate victory of God over his enemies in the future is stressed (i.e., final deliverance for God's people). This apocalyptic style occurs in the Old Testament books of Daniel, Ezekiel, and Zechariah, as well as in the New Testament book of Revelation. This style is also used in several nonbiblical ancient Jewish religious books (1–2 Enoch, 4 Ezra, 2–3 Baruch).

now the Persian king is forced to make the same acknowledgment. Indeed, the Persian king himself summarizes the point of Daniel 1–6 when he declares, "For he (the God of Daniel) is the living God and he endures forever; his kingdom will not be destroyed, his dominion will never end" (Dan. 6:26).

World Kingdoms and God's Plan for the Future (7:1–12:13)

The Ancient of Days and the beast with ten horns (7:1–28)

Back in chapter 2, Nebuchadnezzar had a dream of a statue made of different materials, which, as Daniel explained, represented four world kingdoms. Here in 7:1–8, Daniel, now a much older man, has a vision of "four great beasts," which also represent four world kingdoms (apparently the same four kingdoms). Daniel sees a lion with the wings of an eagle,

Mesopotamian courts often kept lions in cages so that the king could hunt them. The lions of Daniel 6 are probably lions kept for that purpose. Below is an Assyrian wall relief depicting the release of a lion for the hunt.

a bear with three ribs in his mouth, a leopard with four heads and four wings, and then a terrible fourth beast, which Daniel describes as being very different from the others, having iron teeth and ten horns, three of which are uprooted and replaced with a new little horn, characterized by boastfulness.

Next Daniel sees a vision of God himself coming to judge the terrible fourth beast (7:1–14). He describes God as the "Ancient of Days," clothed in white, seated on a fiery throne, attended by an uncountable multitude of attendants. The boastful horn is destroyed, and then "one like a son of man" comes with the clouds, and the "Ancient of Days" establishes his kingdom as an everlasting kingdom. In Daniel's vision the Son of Man is given "authority, glory and sovereign power," and "all peoples, nations and men of every language" worship him.

Daniel is then given an explanation of his vision (7:15–27). The four beasts represent kingdoms, with the fourth kingdom (the ten-horned beast) described as a very different kind of kingdom. The ten horns are ten kings, and the little horn is also a king (who replaces three of the ten). He will speak against God and oppress God's people, but God will judge him and then establish God's kingdom.

Daniel's vision of a ram and a goat (8:1–27)

Daniel sees a vision of a powerful ram that is then defeated by a goat. One of the horns of the goat breaks off and is replaced with four horns. Then the angel Gabriel explains the vision to Daniel, clearly identifying the ram as the Medes and the Persians, who ruled during the latter years of Daniel's life. The goat, Gabriel explains, represents Greece. Historically it is Alexander the Great who fulfills this prophecy by overrunning the Medo-Persian Empire and attempting to install Greek culture in every place he conquers. Alexander,

When Alexander dies, one of his generals establishes himself as king over Egypt and takes the name Ptolemy I Soter. In this wall relief, Ptolemy (on the left) is giving offerings to a god.

however, dies while still young, and his four generals divide his empire, thus fulfilling the "four horns" prophecy in Daniel 8.

Daniel's prayer and the seventy "sevens" (9:1–27)

Daniel recalls that the prophet Jeremiah had predicted that the "desolation of Jerusalem" would last seventy years. Daniel realizes the seventy-year period will end soon, and he prays to God about the restoration of Jerusalem, while also confessing Israel's sin and rebellion. Gabriel then comes to Daniel and gives him a complicated "apocalyptic" expansion on the seventy years mentioned by Jeremiah. Gabriel refers to seventy "sevens" (9:24), which probably

Pictured above is a drinking vessel (called a rhyton) from the Persian era. The ram in the vision of Daniel 8 represented the Medes and the Persians.

is a reference to 490 years, or perhaps a reference to a long, but complete period of time. Scholars are divided on how to understand 9:25–27. Some connect this prophecy to the terrible activities carried out by a king named Antiochus IV Epiphanes, who desecrated the temple in Jerusalem in 167 BC. Other scholars believe that Daniel 9:25–27 refers to the activities of the future antichrist described in the New Testament. Another possibility is that Antiochus Epiphanes fulfills the prophecy in a limited sense, with the antichrist fulfilling the prophecy in a final, ultimate sense.

Daniel's final vision (10:1–12:13)

Chapter 10 opens with Daniel mourning over a vision he saw about a terrible, great war. An angelic figure appears to Daniel and explains that he had attempted to come earlier, but was delayed by opposition from the "prince of the Persian kingdom" until Michael, "one of the chief princes" (i.e., an archangel), helped him. This interesting passage implies that there may be powerful territorial spiritual powers that oppose God and his people, a reality implied as well in other passages (Deut. 32:8; Psalm 82; Eph. 6:12; Rev. 12:7).

✚ The New Testament Gospels connect Daniel's vision of the "Son of Man" (Dan. 7:13) with the return of Jesus (Matt. 24:30; 26:64; Mark 13:26; 14:62; Luke 21:27). In addition, Jesus frequently calls himself "the Son of Man."

Throughout Daniel 11 the angel continues to explain to him about numerous wars and conflicts. Most of what the angel describes actually takes place in Palestine a few hundred years later, during the third and second centuries BC. However, some of the verses in Daniel 11, such as 11:31, seem to refer both to the desecration of the temple carried out by Antiochus IV Epiphanes (167 BC) as well as to a desecration carried out by a future antagonist (the antichrist of the New Testament), an identification made clear by Matthew 24:15. Some scholars also note that Luke 21 appears to connect Daniel 11 to the destruction of Jerusalem by the Romans in AD 70.

In the concluding chapter of the book, the angel who is explaining things to Daniel makes an amazing prediction—"everyone whose name is found written in the book will be delivered" (12:1). This climactic deliverance, however, is no mere restoration to the land, but involves resurrection from the dead, a resurrection to eternal life.

So What? Applying Daniel to Our Lives Today

The courage and faith of Shadrach, Meshach, and Abednego in the fiery furnace and the steadfast faithfulness of Daniel in the lions' den still stand as models for us today. All these men refused to waver in their commitment to God. They remained totally obedient to God, in spite of the unpleasant and seemingly overpowering circumstances that engulfed them. These stories encourage us to stand firm for

Alexander the Great fulfills the prophecy of Daniel 8.

our Lord regardless of the pressure exerted on us by our culture or by unfortunate circumstances. These men did not compromise their faith, even at the risk of losing their lives. They challenge us to do likewise.

Daniel's overall message has special relevance to us today as well. Daniel reminds us that God is sovereign and that his kingdom will ultimately triumph over all hostile world powers, a triumph that includes our resurrection from the dead.

Antiochus IV on a silver coin.

Our Favorite Verse in Daniel

Multitudes who sleep in the dust of the earth will awake: some to everlasting life, others to shame and everlasting contempt. (12:2)

Silver coin with the head of Alexander the Great.

✚ Daniel 12:2 is one of the few texts in the Old Testament that speaks clearly of the resurrection from the dead. The New Testament, however, will expand on this theme, placing it at the center of the Christian hope regarding the future.

Daniel   381

Hosea

God's Enduring Love of His People

Hosea is a rather shocking book. Quite frequently the other prophets (especially Jeremiah and Ezekiel) compare Israel to an unfaithful wife: one who is so promiscuous that she becomes a harlot. In the same way that this figurative woman abandons her loyal, loving husband to become a harlot, so Israel actually abandons the Lord her God and turns to worship other gods. This is a literary analogy that the other prophets use regularly. For poor Hosea, however, this "analogy" is played out in real life. God tells Hosea to marry a harlot. We are rather puzzled by God's request! However, Hosea obediently complies and marries a harlot. Soon, to no one's surprise, Hosea's wife abandons him to become a harlot again, only to eventually end up in slavery. Now the real shocker comes! God tells Hosea to buy her back, love her, and take her back *as his wife*, thus illustrating in his life the love and forgiveness that God has for his people, even after they have sinned against him. What a story! What a God we have!

Who Is Hosea?

Hosea was a prophet who lived and preached in Israel during much of the eighth century BC. During his early ministry he would have been contemporary with Amos and Jonah. Later in his life he would have overlapped with Isaiah and Micah. Hosea marries a harlot named Gomer; indeed, his marriage to this woman becomes a focal point of the book's theological message.

What Is the Setting for Hosea?

Hosea 1:1 indicates his ministry spanned much of the eighth century BC. During the early years of Hosea, Israel was strong politically and quite prosperous economically. The latter years of his ministry, however, placed him in a particularly tumultuous time for the northern kingdom of Israel. The Assyrians grow strong and eventually overrun and destroy the northern kingdom in 722 BC. In 701 BC the Assyrians unsuccessfully besiege Jerusalem. Thus Hosea lives and preaches in a very unsettled and dangerous time.

What Is at the Heart of the Book of Hosea?

The basic message of Hosea is similar to that of the other preexilic prophets. Thus Hosea proclaims:

The Assyrians besiege a city in Mesopotamia. During the later years of Hosea, the Assyrians grow strong and eventually overrun and destroy Israel.

✦ The prophets frequently use the marriage relationship as an analogy of the relationship between God and his people.

The Book of the Twelve

The prophetic books in the Old Testament comprise the four Major Prophets (Isaiah, Jeremiah, Ezekiel, and Daniel), followed by the twelve Minor Prophets (Hosea, Joel, Amos, Obadiah, Jonah, Micah, Nahum, Habakkuk, Zephaniah, Haggai, Zechariah, and Malachi). The terms "major" and "minor" have nothing to do with importance or emphasis, but rather with size—Isaiah, Jeremiah, Ezekiel, and Daniel are generally longer than the other twelve prophetic books.

Traditionally Christians have read and studied each of the twelve Minor Prophets separately. That is, interpreters usually assume that each book is a stand-alone unit with an independent message. Scholars today, however, are taking a second look at this approach. While they still believe that each Minor Prophet is quite coherent by itself and certainly can be understood in isolation from the others, more and more scholars are noting numerous connections among the twelve individual books called the Minor Prophets. So in recent years, numerous Old Testament scholars have suggested that Christians should read the twelve Minor Prophets not as individual books, but as a unit—one large book titled the Book of the Twelve.

What is the evidence for such an approach? Very early nonbiblical Jewish writers (approx. 200 BC to AD 100) refer to the prophets as Isaiah, Jeremiah, Ezekiel, and the Twelve Prophets (the ancient Jewish writers placed Daniel in a separate place in their Bible). Likewise, early Greek translations of the Minor Prophets placed all of them on one scroll. Also, keep in mind that the number twelve carries special symbolic significance.

What are the themes that connect the Book of the Twelve? The focus is on the character and actions of God. The "day of the Lord" is a frequent theme (Hosea 1:5; 2:16–18; Joel 2:31; Amos 5:18–20; Obadiah 15; Mic. 2:4; Hab. 3:16; Zeph. 1:7–16; Hag. 2:23; Zech. 14:1; and Mal. 4:1). Likewise the Book of the Twelve opens by stressing the love of God (Hosea 1–3) and ends by stressing the love of God (Mal. 1:2). Numerous smaller themes or "catchwords" often tie the books together. For example, Joel 3:16 declares "the Lord will roar from Zion," and the following book, Amos, opens with "the Lord roars from Zion" (1:2). Amos ends with judgment on Edom (9:12), and the following book, Obadiah, stresses the destruction of Edom.

1. You (Judah/Israel) have broken the covenant; you had better repent!
2. No repentance? Then judgment!
3. Yet there is hope beyond the judgment for a glorious, future restoration.

Like the other prophets, Hosea's indictments against Israel fall into three main categories: idolatry, social injustice, and religious ritualism. One of the major themes running throughout the book is the love God has for his people.

The book of Hosea breaks down into two major sections:

- The Marriage Analogy (1–3)
- The Broken Covenant and the Coming Judgment (4–14)

What Makes Hosea Interesting and Unique?

- Hosea marries the harlot, Gomer, and his relationship with her illustrates God's relationship with Israel.
- Hosea has three children, all with very significant, symbolic names.
- The deep love of God for his people is stressed.
- Not only does Hosea use the husband/wife analogy, but also the parent/child analogy.

What Is Hosea's Message?

The Marriage Analogy (1–3)

To illustrate God's relationship with Israel, God tells the prophet Hosea to marry a prostitute! Wow, this must have been tough for him. Yet Hosea obeys and marries a harlot named Gomer (1:2–3). She has three children, all of which are given significant names. The firstborn is named Jezreel, which is the name of the place where all of the members of the previous royal dynasty of Israel were slaughtered when the current ruling dynasty came to power. The child's name proclaims that God has not forgotten that event and will likewise judge the current ruling house of Israel (1:4–5). The second child is named Lo-Ruhamah, which means "not loved," and the third child is named Lo-Ammi, which means "not my people." These names proclaim that the covenant between God and Israel has been shattered. Throughout the Old Testament, at the heart of the covenant between God and Israel was the threefold formula statement: I will be your God; you will be my people; I will dwell in your midst. When God names Hosea's child "not my people," he is proclaiming the end of his covenant relationship with Israel. Thus the northern kingdom is overrun and destroyed by the Assyrians in 722 BC.

Yet in the very next passage, the book of Hosea moves past the judgment to proclaim restoration. In 1:10 God refers back to the Abrahamic covenant (Genesis 12, 15, 17) and promises that Israel will be like the sand on the seashore. Then in Hosea 2, a symbolic, poetic portrayal of God's marriage relationship with Israel, the Lord speaks of how his unfaithful wife (Israel) has turned away from him to other lovers (the idols). Incredibly, and reflecting the wonderful grace of God, he nonetheless takes her back and restores her as his wife! Thus God reverses the symbolic names of the people back to "my people" and "my loved one" (2:1, 23). This signifies the re-establishment of the covenant relationship. Then to illustrate this restoration in Hosea's life, God tells the prophet to take his unfaithful wife, Gomer, back and to love

✦ The northern kingdom, Israel, was composed of ten Israelite tribes, of which Ephraim was the largest and most powerful. Thus Hosea will often refer to the entire northern kingdom nation by the term "Ephraim."

her again (3:1–3). Apparently Gomer's promiscuity had led her into a tragic life that resulted in her becoming a slave. Hosea obeys God by buying her back and then taking her to be his wife again.

The Broken Covenant and the Coming Judgment (4–14)

In Hosea 4 God brings "courtroom-like" accusations against Israel, listing its many sins and underscoring how severely it has broken the covenant (especially as defined in Deuteronomy). God indicts the Israelites because they are unfaithful, without love or true knowledge of him (4:1). Indeed,

The ruins of Samaria, the capital of the northern kingdom, Israel. Hosea announces judgment on Samaria (Hosea 7:1; 8:5–6; 10:5, 7; 13:16).

✦ Twice Jesus quotes Hosea 6:6 ("I desire mercy, not sacrifice") to hypocritical Pharisees, indicting them for failing to grasp the meaning of this verse (Matt. 9:13; 12:7).

they are characterized by their many violations of the Ten Commandments (cursing, lying, stealing, adultery, murder) (4:2). Their priests, who should work to keep the people faithful, are the very ones who lead them into idolatry (4:6–19).

The next several chapters of Hosea (6–13) continue the theme of judgment. As in the other prophetic books, God declares he is not impressed with their meaningless rituals, stating, "I desire mercy [loyal love], not sacrifice, and acknowledgment of God rather than burnt offerings" (6:6). Throughout this section the theme of sinful behavior (idolatry, social injustice) is intertwined with the theme of judgment (invasion, destruction, and exile; i.e., loss of the Promised Land). In Hosea 11, God changes analogies from husband/wife to that of father/child. Like a loving father, God declares, he taught Ephraim (Israel) to walk as a toddler, caring for him. God agonizes over the judgment that is coming, crying out, "How can I give you up, Ephraim?" (11:8), and once again he looks to the future restoration beyond the coming judgment (11:9–11).

In Hosea 11–13 the Lord frequently refers back to the exodus, that spectacular event of salvation and deliverance that echoes throughout the Bible. As in many other places in the Bible, here in Hosea God defines himself and his relationship with Israel by saying, "I am the Lord your God, who brought you up out of Egypt" (12:9; 13:4).

The book of Hosea ends with a last-minute plea for repentance. If only Israel would repent and turn back to God, Hosea declares sorrowfully, God would restore them (14:1–8). But they don't repent, and judgment does indeed come upon Israel. The closing words of Hosea read like a proverbial warning, "Who is wise? He will realize these things. . . . The ways of the Lord are right; the righteous walk in them, but the rebellious stumble in them" (14:9).

"Throw out your calf idol, O Samaria!" (Hosea 8:5). Shown here is a limestone statue of an Egyptian Apis bull, the earthly representation of the god Ptah. Calves and bulls were worshiped throughout the ancient Near East.

✚ In Hosea 11:1 God reflects back on how he delivered Israel from the Egyptians, stating, "Out of Egypt I called my son." Matthew quotes this verse in Matthew 2:15.

So What? Applying Hosea to Our Lives Today

Romans 5:8 states that "God demonstrates his own love for us in this: While we were still sinners, Christ died for us." The story of Hosea paints a powerful picture of the depths of God's love. Even if we have been like an unfaithful and wayward spouse toward God, abandoning our relationship with him to pursue our own desires, oblivious to his constant love for us, he still loves us with a deep and abiding love that continually calls us to return to him. If we return to him, he forgives us and restores us to a wonderful, loving relationship that puts us under his powerful care.

Our Favorite Verse in Hosea

For I desire mercy, not sacrifice,
and acknowledgment of God rather than burnt offerings. (6:6)

An Egyptian temple in the city of Karnak. Often in the Old Testament God identifies himself as "the Lord your God, who brought you up out of Egypt" (Hosea 12:9; 13:4).

✚ Jesus quotes Hosea 10:8 in judgment on Jerusalem as he carries his cross to Calvary (Luke 23:30).

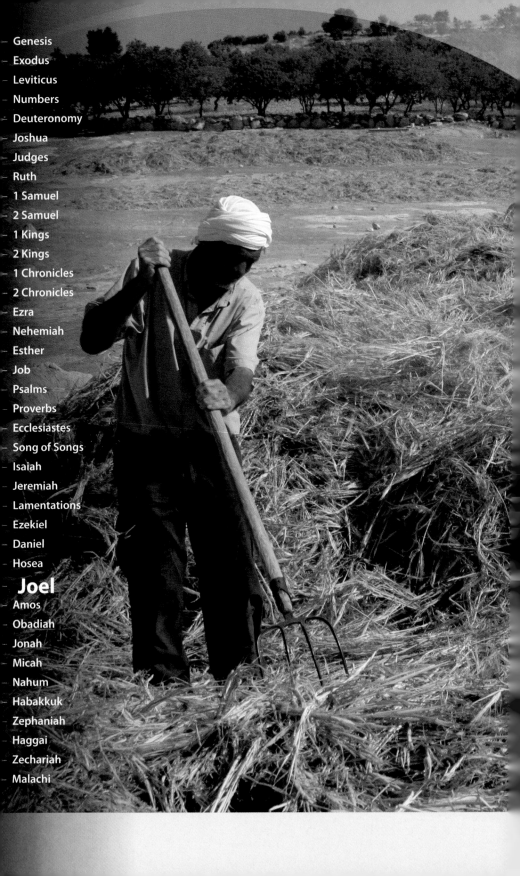

Joel

Locust Plagues and the Spirit of the Lord

The prophet Joel packs a lot into his small book of three chapters. He spends the entire first chapter and part of the second describing a horrendous locust plague. In chapters 2 and 3 he speaks of the "day of the Lord," a time filled with both judgment and deliverance. He also describes a marvelous future event when the "Spirit of the Lord" will be poured out on all God's people. Joel also calls for true repentance, telling God's people to rend their hearts and not just their garments. "Return to the Lord your God," Joel exhorts, "for he is gracious and compassionate, slow to anger and abounding in love" (2:13).

Who Is Joel?

We don't know much about the prophet Joel. He is not mentioned anywhere in the Bible except in the opening verse of the book that bears his name. While many of the other prophetic books like Jeremiah give us a wealth of information about the author, the book of Joel tells us nothing about him other than the word of the Lord came to him. However, this singular fact—that the word of the

Lord came to him—makes him important, and the other unknown aspects of his life we would like to know (where he was from, when he lived, etc.) would probably pale in comparison to what we do know.

What Is the Setting for Joel?

Unlike many of the other prophetic books, the book of Joel does not provide any historical heading. In Hosea 1:1, for example, the ministry of the prophet Hosea is tied directly to the reign of several known kings. Thus we can pinpoint the historical setting for Hosea very accurately. The life and message of Joel, however, are not tied to any king, and the book does not mention any specific historical event. But most scholars believe the locust plagues that Joel describes (especially the one in Joel 2:1–11) predict a foreign invasion, either the Assyrian invasion of Israel in 722 BC or the Babylonian invasion of Judah in 586/587 BC. Many scholars assume that Joel is prophesying just prior to one of these invasions.

What Is at the Heart of the Book of Joel?

The prophets preach to Israel and Judah with the book of Deuteronomy in their hand. That is, the prophets announce that the people of Israel have broken the covenant agreement as legally documented in Deuteronomy, and thus they will experience the terrible consequences clearly spelled out in Deuteronomy (especially in chapter 28). Unlike most of the other prophets, Joel skips over listing the specific covenant violation sins of Israel (idolatry, social injustice, reliance on religious ritualism), and in his opening two chapters he goes straight to judgment. Pulling from Deuteronomy 28:38 and 28:42, Joel describes a terrible locust plague that comes on the land as God's judgment for rejecting and abandoning the laws of Deuteronomy. Yet like the other prophets, Joel also moves beyond the judgment to describe the wonderful time of future restoration—a time when God would pour out his Spirit on all his people. The short book of Joel can be outlined as follows:

- Judgment and Calls for Repentance (1:1–2:17)
  - The coming locust invasion (literal?) and a call to repentance (1:1–20)
  - The coming locust invasion (figurative?) and a call to repentance (2:1–17)

Middle Eastern locust, similar to a grasshopper.

- God's Response (2:18–3:21)
  - Restoration and the giving of God's Spirit to all his people (2:18–32)
  - Judgment on the nations (3:1–21)

What Makes Joel Interesting and Unique?

- Joel presents an extensive and very graphic picture of a coming locust plague.
- Joel makes several references to "that day" or to "the day of the Lord."
- Joel prophesies that God will pour out his Spirit on all his people, an event that is fulfilled in the New Testament at Pentecost.

What Is Joel's Message?

Judgment and Calls for Repentance (1:1–2:17)

The coming locust invasion (literal?) and a call to repentance (1:1–20)

In Deuteronomy 28 God warned that if Israel abandoned him and disregarded his law, then God would send judgments on them, one of which would be a locust plague (Deut. 28:38, 42). Joel opens his book with a graphic description of the locust plague judgment. In Joel 1:1–20 the prophet describes a devastating locust plague that swarms over the land and destroys the crops, vineyards, and orchards. This is probably a literal locust plague that Joel warns Israel about. In Joel 1:13–14 the prophet calls on the priests, elders, and all the people to repent by fasting, wearing sackcloth, and crying out to God. Joel connects this terrible time of judgment to "the day of the Lord" (1:15), that future time when God will crash into human history both to judge those who reject and rebel against him, as well as to save those who trust and obey him.

The coming locust invasion (figurative?) and a call to repentance (2:1–17)

Joel 2:1–11 continues to describe a locust plague, but this time he is probably using it as a figurative representation of a real military invasion, either the Assyrian invasion in 722 BC or the Babylonian invasion in 587/586 BC. That is, Joel warns that a foreign army will swarm over the land like

✛ Plagues of locusts were a regularly recurring nightmare in the Old Testament world, similar to hurricanes today on the American Gulf Coast or tornadoes in the Midwestern states.

Joel   393

locusts, devouring and destroying everything in its path, just as the locusts did in Joel 1.

In 2:12–17 Joel calls on the people to repent with sincerity, turning to God truly with their heart, and not just externally ("rend your hearts and not your garments"). The reason why such repentance is effective, Joel then explains, is because of God's character. In Joel 2:13 the prophet gives us a wonderful description of the loving character of God: gracious, compassionate, slow to anger, and abounding in love, one who relents from sending calamity.

God's Response (2:18–3:21)

Restoration and the giving of God's Spirit to all his people (2:18–32)

In Joel 2:18–32 God looks beyond the judgment to the future time of restoration. A critical element of this time that the prophets discuss regularly is the Presence of God. Persistent and flagrant sin such as idolatry and social injustice will drive away the Presence of God from Israel, but in Joel 2:27–32 God promises a new era when his Presence will be experienced by his people much differently than in the past. Then in Joel 2:28–32 God makes the spectacular promise that he will put his Spirit within his people. This is a radically new and dramatic promise of a special new way people will experience the Presence of God. Joel and Ezekiel are the two prophets who predict this wonderful new arrangement between God and his people (see Ezek. 34:26–27). Yet even though God's people will be delivered and will know God's Presence in this very special way, this event is intertwined with the entire concept of the "day of the Lord" (2:31), a time that includes wonderful salvation for those who trust in God, but also terrible judgment on those who defy him (2:31–32).

Judgment on the nations (3:1–21)

The future ("day of the Lord") that the prophets describe is one that brings wonderful salvation to those who trust in God, whether Israelites or gentiles, and yet also a time of judgment on those who defy and oppose God, both Israelites and gentiles. Joel 3:1–21 describes the coming judgment on the gentile nations who have defied and opposed God.

So What? Applying Joel to Our Lives Today

On the one hand, Joel reminds you and me that sin is very serious and that God's wrath and judgment are a reality only a fool would ignore. On the

✚ In Acts 2:16–21 Peter quotes Joel 2:28–32 to explain the coming of the Spirit at Pentecost and to exhort the Jews in Jerusalem to believe in Christ in order to be saved from the coming judgment.

other hand, the good news of the Bible is that "everyone who calls on the name of the Lord will be saved" (Joel 2:32; Rom. 10:13). Turning to God and trusting in Jesus Christ will save us from the terrible coming judgment.

Joel also prophesies the wonderful indwelling of the Holy Spirit. One of the central promises of the Old Testament covenant is the promise of God's Presence ("I will dwell in your midst"). The people of the Old Testament experienced God's Presence primarily by his residence in the tabernacle and then in the temple. Because of their sin and disobedience, they lose the empowering and comforting Presence of God (Ezekiel 8–10). In the coming future days, Joel tells us, things will be different (and better!), for God's people (all of them—men, women, young, and old) will enjoy the power and comfort of God's Presence in a new and better way: through his indwelling Spirit! All New Testament believers, those who have believed in Jesus Christ, experience the power and comfort of the very Presence of God in our lives through this very privileged situation—the Spirit of God dwells within us.

Our Favorite Verse in Joel

And everyone who calls
on the name of the Lord will be saved. (2:32)

Comparing locusts to soldiers, Joel states, "They charge like warriors; they scale walls like soldiers. They all march in line, not swerving from their course" (2:7).

✝ Paul quotes Joel 2:32 ("everyone who calls on the name of the Lord will be saved") in Romans 10:13.

Amos

The Severe Consequences of Injustice

I f you want to stay complacent toward the
poor, and content with your current attitude
toward injustice, then it would be wise to skip
over the book of Amos. Likewise, if you are squea-
mish, or if you want to read only G-rated material,
then Amos may be too graphic for you. In the time
of Amos, Israel was experiencing a time of lavish
prosperity for the wealthy and devastating poverty
for the poor. Amos blasts the people responsible for
this terrible social inequity, which had developed
because Israel had abandoned any serious attempt
to keep the law of Deuteronomy. Amos is scathing,
even brutal in his critique, and he has no concern for
political correctness. He ruffles everybody's feathers.
Amos is, without doubt, one of the most graphic and
blunt of all the prophets. Read him at your own risk!

Who Is Amos?

Several of the other prophets come from priestly families
(e.g., Jeremiah and Ezekiel). Amos, by contrast, comes
from the farm. He is called a shepherd in 1:1 and 7:14,
a term that probably implies "a breeder of sheep"; that is,

Amos probably is the owner of a substantial flock of sheep. In addition to "shepherd," Amos says he is also a keeper of sycamore-fig trees. So Amos is probably a farmer/sheepherder who raises figs and sheep. He is from a village called Tekoa, which is located about ten miles south of Jerusalem. This is important, for it locates Amos in the southern kingdom of Judah. Ironically, he will deliver his scathing criticism and pronouncement of judgment to those in the northern kingdom of Israel.

What Is the Setting for Amos?

The ministry of Amos is dated to the reign of Uzziah, king of Judah (783–742 BC) and the reign of Jeroboam II of Israel (786–746 BC). The opening verse also dates his prophecy to "two years before the earthquake." Archaeological evidence suggests a major earthquake may have occurred in about 760 BC. Perhaps that is the earthquake to which Amos 1:1 is referring. At the time of Amos the northern kingdom of Israel was rather powerful and quite prosperous, but that prosperity was limited to the upper classes. The theological situation in Israel was terrible. Remember what had happened. After the death of Solomon, a civil war ensued, and the northern kingdom of Israel split from the southern kingdom of Judah. Israel then immediately turned away from God and built pagan altars with calf idols at worship centers such as Bethel, Dan, and Gilgal. (For more background information, reread the narrative description of these events in 1 Kings 11–12). By the time of Amos, the northern kingdom was well entrenched in idolatry and the corrupted moral behavior that went along with it.

What Is at the Heart of the Book of Amos?

In general, Amos delivers the same basic three-part message that the rest of the preexilic prophets proclaim:

1. You have broken the covenant; you had better repent!
2. No repentance? Then judgment!
3. Yet there is hope beyond the judgment for a glorious, future restoration, both for Israel/Judah and for the nations.

Yet Amos focuses primarily on the first and second points—the sins that have shattered the covenant and the consequential coming judgment. Amos also directs his message almost exclusively toward the northern kingdom, Israel. Another difference between Amos and some of the other prophets

✦ At the end of Joel is a reference to God's "roaring" like a lion (3:16). This connects Joel to Amos, for Amos presents God as a dangerous, roaring lion.

(e.g., Isaiah, Jeremiah, Hosea) is that the others tend to sprinkle passages of hope and restoration throughout their message, mixing these encouraging passages of hope in with the passages of doom and gloom. In Amos, however, one looks in vain for any hope: none in Amos 1, 2, and 3; still none in Amos 4, 5, and 6, only sin and judgment; and the same in Amos 7, 8, and the first half of 9. Finally, at last! At the very end of Amos, the rustic prophet gives his audience a few verses of hope regarding the coming Davidic Messiah (9:11–15). The theme that does occur repeatedly throughout Amos is God's concern for social justice. When Israel ignores the law of God and breaks away from an obedient relationship with him, they soon lose all sense of ethical concern and fall into a "the rich are getting richer and the poor are getting poorer" situation where exploitation by the rich and powerful runs unabated. Amos is unrelenting in his criticism of these people and the situation they have created.

The book of Amos is not structured around a clear outline, but the various aspects of Amos's message can be grouped loosely into the following units:

- Social Injustice and Judgment (1:2–9:10)
  - Multitudes of sins (1:2–2:16)
  - The wrath of God will come like a devouring lion (3:1–4:13)
  - God demands justice, not mere cold-hearted ritual (5:1–6:14)
  - Four visions of judgment and a confrontation (7:1–8:3)
  - Judgment on Israel (8:4–9:10)
- The Coming Davidic King and Restoration (9:11–15)

By the time of Amos, the northern kingdom, Israel, was well entrenched in idolatry. Pictured above is Asherah, the Canaanite goddess, venerated by many in Israel and Judah (eighth century BC).

What Makes Amos Interesting and Unique?

- Amos is a rustic farmer who blasts the rich and wealthy.
- Amos stresses the theme of social justice repeatedly ("Let justice roll on like a river"; 5:24).

- Amos uses colorful and yet scathing language (e.g., he compares the wealthy women in Israel to cows; 4:1).
- Amos uses graphic judgment language ("As a shepherd saves from the lion's mouth only two leg bones or a piece of an ear"; 3:12).
- Amos portrays God in his wrath as a hungry devouring lion.

What Is Amos's Message?

Social Injustice and Judgment (1:2–9:10)

Multitudes of sins (1:2–2:16)

The opening phrase of Amos 1:2 summarizes the book: "The Lord roars from Zion." The word "roars" is used especially in regard to lions. Thus Amos is comparing God to a dangerous and terrifying lion about to pounce on its prey. Indeed, most of the book of Amos focuses on the terrible judgment that is coming on Israel due to her continued sin and rejection of God. In 1:3–2:16 God announces judgment on six foreign but nearby nations: Damascus (i.e., Syria/Aram), Gaza and Ashdod (i.e., Philistia), Tyre, Edom, Ammon, and Moab. Each judgment oracle is introduced with the formula, "for three sins of x, even for four, I will not turn back my wrath." This "formula" is a poetic way to say that these nations are committing lots of sins. The nations listed for judgment circle Israel, including Judah to the south (2:4–5). Everyone in Amos's audience would have approved of God's bringing judgment on all these nations, for they are Israel's enemies. But then in 2:6–16 the tables are turned, and the climactic judgment of this poetic section zeroes in on Israel. Because of the horrendous sins of Israel (economic injustice and oppression of the poor, immorality, and idolatry), God is coming to judge it as well.

The wrath of God will come like a devouring lion (3:1–4:13)

This unit compares the coming wrath of God to the destruction and havoc that a rampaging lion can bring. "The lion has roared—who will not fear?" Amos asks in 3:8. In regard to how many Israelites

Israelite altars from Arad (tenth to seventh century BC). Amos declares that God wants social justice, not hypocritical ritual.

Old Testament Ethics

M. Daniel Carroll R.

The Old Testament is a wonderful resource for ethics. It begins where all ethical systems must begin: the value of human life and the care of the created order (Genesis 1–2). Human beings are made in the image of God. All people, therefore, have worth and potential as his representatives and are to steward the creation. The breadth of the Old Testament's concerns is impressive: it addresses personal issues (like sexuality, the use of money, and honesty in the workplace), as well as socioeconomic and political matters, such as oppression of the poor, corruption in government, and war. This wide purview of moral matters allows for different perspectives on many topics. One example is the treatment of the poor. Whereas Proverbs locates the blame for some misfortune in laziness or lasciviousness, the prophets denounce the systemic injustice that perpetuates the exploitation of the vulnerable, and the law legislates measures to alleviate the needs of the poor, widows and orphans, and the sojourner. Each view contributes to a fuller understanding of the problem and its treatment.

In the Old Testament, Israel, the chosen people of God, was to be an ethical light before the world. They were to be God's channel of blessing—both spiritual and material (Genesis 12)—and their society a model of what God would want of all nations (Deut. 4:5–8). The Historical Books chart the failure to live up to that role, and the prophetic literature is full of scathing denunciation for the ills of Israelite society. The prophets also emphasize that it is impossible to separate ethical life from worship of God, something Jesus and the New Testament writers echo.

The perennial challenge for those who embrace the Old Testament as Scripture is ascertaining the best way to appropriate the text for moral life today. On the one hand, it contains material many find objectionable. There are accounts of lying, political dishonesty, adultery, murder, and rape—even by some of the most respected leaders of the people of God. In these cases, it is important to distinguish the biblical portrayal of such acts from a prescription to emulate those behaviors and attitudes. Much of what is described is offered as negative examples to avoid. On the other hand, some Christian theological systems are reluctant to appeal to the Old Testament, because the theocracy that was Israel no longer exists.

The way forward is to appreciate that the Old Testament presents enduring values that transcend the centuries. The law is a paradigm. It establishes how an ancient people were to incarnate the ethical standards of God in every sphere of personal, social, and religious life. Those principles necessarily take a different shape in the modern world. The Old Testament also depicts the lives of godly and wise people in its narratives, proverbs, and prophetic books. It predicts as well a kingdom of worldwide abundance and peace. The Old Testament, in other words, is an ethical guide in the present and provides an ethical hope for the future.

will survive the coming judgment (the Assyrians), Amos again turns to the lion imagery, "As a shepherd saves from the lion's mouth only two leg bones or a piece of an ear, so will the Israelites be saved." Thus the destruction will be devastating.

Twice in this unit Amos mentions sins associated with the city of Bethel (3:14; 4:4). Remember that it was in Bethel that King Jeroboam set up golden calf idols for Israel to worship (1 Kings 12:28–29). Amos also lambastes the wealthy women as well as the men, calling them "cows of Bashan" and accusing them of oppressing the poor (4:1). In 4:6–11 God declares that he has tried to warn Israel to repent and turn back to him, but to no avail. The sobering consequence of Israel's defiant sin and stubborn rebellion? "Prepare to meet your God, O Israel!" (4:12).

God demands justice, not mere coldhearted ritual (5:1–6:14)

The theme of justice and righteousness runs throughout Amos, but is presented with particular focus in Amos 5. This chapter accuses Israel of numerous social injustices: trampling on the poor and extorting grain (their food) from them; paying bribes to judges in order to deprive the poor of justice; and corrupting the entire legal system in general (5:11–13). The terrible consequences are presented in the opening verses. Israel will fall (5:1–2) with only 10 percent surviving (5:3).

In this context of extensive social injustice, God states that he takes no pleasure at all in people's hypocritical worship of him; indeed, he "hates" their religious rituals (5:21–23). In contrast to meaningless religious ritual, what God demands is that "justice roll on like a river, righteousness like a never-failing stream" (5:24). Amos 6 continues by proclaiming judgment on the complacent wealthy individuals who party in luxury without concern for the fate of Israel.

Four visions of judgment and a confrontation (7:1–8:3)

In this unit God gives Amos four visions of the terrible judgment to come: a destructive locust plague (similar to Joel); a destroying fire; a weakened wall about to fall over (representing the weak defenses of Israel); and a basket of ripe fruit, indicating that the time is ripe for judgment. In the middle of these visions is an interruption. We are provided with a narrative story about Amos's confrontation with Amaziah, a priest at Bethel (an Israelite pagan worship site with a golden calf idol). Amaziah sends a report to the king, accusing Amos of conspiracy, and then orders Amos to cease his negative prophecies against Israel and to return home to Judah (7:10–13). Amos responds by saying that he is not really a prophet, but a farmer. Nonetheless, he continues, God has ordered him to prophesy against Israel. Amos concludes his defiance of Amaziah by proclaiming judgment on the pagan Israelite priest himself and then reiterating the certainty of the coming judgmental exile of Israel away from their land (7:14–17).

✦ The book of Amos ends with judgment on Edom (9:12), thus connecting it to the next book, Obadiah, which focuses on that very theme.

Judgment on Israel (8:4–9:10)

In this section Amos continues to chastise the Israelites for their economic dishonesty and their mistreatment of the poor (8:4–6). God then once again declares coming judgment on Israel (8:7–9:10).

The Coming Davidic King and Restoration (9:11–15)

At the very end of the book, just when we thought Amos would never get around to hope and restoration, we finally find a short passage that looks beyond the terrible judgment to prophesy a Davidic Messiah and the regathering of Israel back in the land.

So What? Applying Amos to Our Lives Today

The book of Amos is unrelenting in its challenge to us and all other readers regarding our concern for the poor and those who suffer. Throughout the book, God repeatedly reveals his heart in this matter. God is indignant and impatient with those who enjoy living in luxury while the poor all around them suffer in poverty. The truth that emerges for us is startling: God is very concerned for the poor and suffering, and he expects his people to have the same compassion. He desires his people to work hard to alleviate the suffering of others. He gets particularly upset with us when we separate ourselves from the plight of the poor and simply focus on enjoying our high standard of living. Likewise, if we disregard the suffering of others, God views our worship of him as hypocritical, and it does not please him. Many times we as Christians state our goal in life is to "know God." The book of Amos helps us with this goal, for it reveals much about God's heart and his desires for his people. What God wants from us is not hypocritical worship that is separated from everyday empathy and compassion. God wants us to care for people and to work to alleviate suffering. As we do this we can truly get to know him and worship him properly, for our hearts will then be in line with his.

An ancient pair of sandals. Twice Amos decries the fact that the needy were being bought and sold for a pair of sandals (Amos 2:6; 8:6).

Our Favorite Verse in Amos

But let justice roll on like a river,
righteousness like a never-failing stream! (5:24)

✚ Amos stresses that God's people have a responsibility to care for the poor. This theme is not restricted to the Old Testament, for in the Gospels Jesus makes this one of his major themes as well.

Obadiah

The End of Edom

Most of the prophets proclaim a similar three-part message, directed primarily at Israel/Judah: (1) You've broken the covenant, repent! (2) No repentance? Then judgment! and (3) Future hope and restoration. We call this the "standard prophetic message." Obadiah, by contrast, is quite different. He does not preach directly to Israel or Judah, but instead addresses the nation of Edom. Obadiah is short—only one brief chapter—and his message is that judgment is coming to Edom because of its sin.

Immediately before the book of Obadiah, Amos 9:12 mentions Edom. Obadiah is probably located right after Amos because of this connection. While Edom was a real nation that was indeed destroyed, there is a sense in which the Bible occasionally will use Edom as a symbol of all those who oppose God and his people (cf. Joel 3:19; Amos 1:11–12; 9:12). The book of Obadiah is perhaps using Edom in both senses.

Who Is Obadiah?

The name Obadiah means "servant of the Lord." It is a very common name in the Old Testament, used for thirteen people. The prophet Obadiah prophesies shortly after the fall of Jerusalem in 587/586 BC, so he is contemporary with Jeremiah and Zephaniah. Other than that, we know very little about him.

What Is the Setting for Obadiah?

The Nabateans displaced the Edomites and built the spectacular city of Petra, shown below.

The nation of Edom was adjacent to Judah, located to the southeast. Edom often conspired with Judah against the larger empires, but when the Babylonians invade Judah and Babylonian victory seems unstoppable, Edom switches sides and joins the Babylonians in plundering Judah. Obadiah prophesies that Edom will be destroyed for betraying and attacking Judah.

What Makes Obadiah Interesting and Unique?

- Obadiah is the shortest book in the Old Testament (only twenty-one verses).
- Obadiah applies the "day of the Lord" judgment to Edom.
- The colorful description of Edom in Obadiah 3–4 aptly describes the area occupied by the spectacular ruins of Petra, built by the people who destroyed and displaced the Edomites.

What Is Obadiah's Message?

Because the nation of Edom had betrayed Judah and assisted in plundering her, Obadiah prophesies the destruction of Edom. The prophets often declare judgment on the various nations, but usually those same nations are also mentioned in the prophetic picture of future restoration, when the gentiles are included as part of the people of God. The situation for Edom,

✚ Jeremiah prophesies against Edom at about the same time that Obadiah does. In fact, the short book of Obadiah and Jeremiah 49:7–22 are very similar.

however, appears to be different. Obadiah, along with several of the other prophets, proclaims the end of Edom. That is, Edom will be destroyed and will never be restored. Obadiah then proclaims that Israel, by contrast, will be restored in the future and will actually rule over the region once controlled by Edom (vv. 17–21).

So What? Applying Obadiah to Our Lives Today

The short book of Obadiah is a reminder to us that sin has consequences and that God will ultimately judge all those who oppose him and rebel against him. God's people, however, will be restored and ultimately vindicated. In this sense Obadiah's theme connects to the book of Revelation, which incorporates this same theme into the climactic end of human history, when God establishes his kingdom.

Our Favorite Verse in Obadiah

The day of the Lord is near for all nations.
(v. 15)

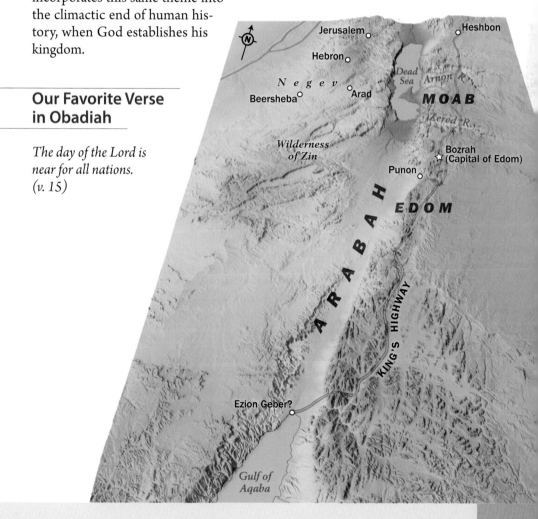

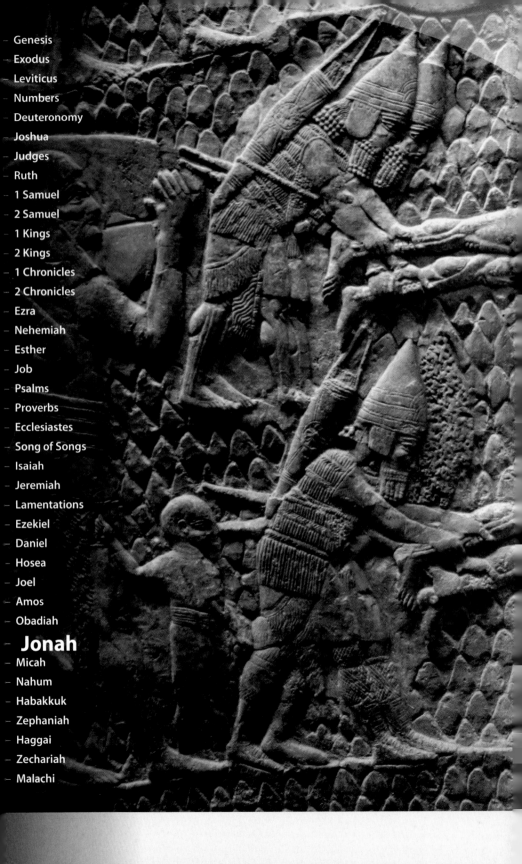

Jonah

Concern for the Salvation of the Gentiles

Most of us learn the story of Jonah and the whale while we are still very young. Indeed, the story of Jonah is fascinating, not only for youngsters but also for all ages. Jonah's story is full of irony and exciting events. Unlike Isaiah, Ezekiel, and Jeremiah, when Jonah is called by God to prophesy, at first he refuses to obey and instead flees from God. Only after he almost dies in the sea does he reconsider and obey. Furthermore, in general the people of Israel ignore the message of the prophets. The people don't repent, and thus judgment comes on them (the Assyrian invasion and then the Babylonian invasion). In the book of Jonah, by contrast, the audience (the pagan Ninevites!) responds to the prophetic message, repenting and asking God to spare them. So, in effect, Jonah is about the only prophet who is truly successful and who brings about a repentant attitude in his audience. Ironically, he doesn't like it, and he gets angry about it, only to be rebuked by God. In the end, besides being a book about salvation for all people, the book of Jonah stands as a foil for the rest of the prophetic books; what happens in pagan Nineveh is what should have happened in Jerusalem, but didn't.

The book of Jonah is also very different from the other prophetic books regarding literary style. Most of Jonah is composed of narrative, instead of preached poetic oracles as in the other prophetic books.

Who Is Jonah?

The book of Jonah does not tie the prophet's message to a specific king or historical setting. However, the book does identify the prophet as "Jonah, son of Amittai," a prophet who is also mentioned in 2 Kings 14:25. From the reference in 2 Kings 14 we can clearly date Jonah to the reign of Jeroboam II (786–746 BC), thus making him contemporary with Hosea and Amos. The reference in 2 Kings 14:25 also tells us Jonah was a prophet from Gath Hepher (a town on the eastern border of the territory of Zebulun) who had predicted that Jeroboam II would successfully expand the boundaries of Israel to include Syria (Aram) in the north and to extend down to the Red Sea in the south.

What Is the Setting for Jonah?

During the reign of Jeroboam II (786–746 BC) the nation of Israel was fairly strong and prosperous. As mentioned above, Israel had subdued Syria (Aram) to the north and Israelite hegemony extended right up to the borders of Assyria. In the generation following Jeroboam II, the Assyrians will rise to power and become the five-hundred-pound gorilla of the ancient Near East, subduing just about every city and nation in the region. During the time of Jonah, however, the Assyrians are somewhat unstable and relatively weak. Ironically they are probably no stronger than Israel, a nation they will totally crush later in the eighth century. Nineveh was the capital of Assyria. Even by the time of Jonah, the Assyrians had achieved a reputation of being brutal and vicious warriors. People feared the Assyrians, and no one liked them.

What Is at the Heart of the Book of Jonah?

Jonah is a book about obedience, illustrating how foolish it is to refuse to obey God or to try to flee from God and his calling. Jonah is also a book about compassion and concern for one's enemies or for those who are merely different. God had compassion on the Assyrians in Nineveh, and he rebukes Jonah for his lack of concern over their salvation. Jonah is also a book that

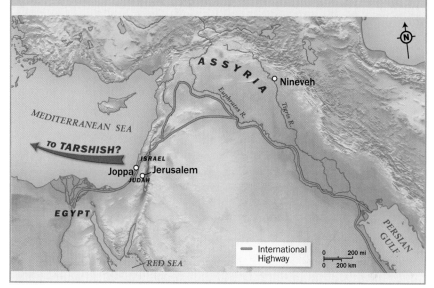

underscores how serious and unthinkable it was for the Israelites back in Jerusalem to ignore the prophetic call to repent and return to God. The repentant actions of the Assyrians in Nineveh, from the king down to the lowest peasant (and even the cows!), lead to their deliverance, in contrast to the obstinate, hostile, and unrepentant attitude of the kings and people back in Israel and Judah, which results in foreign invasion and judgment.

The book of Jonah breaks down neatly into two parallel episodes:

- Jonah, the Sailors, and Deliverance (1–2)
- Jonah, the Ninevites, and Deliverance (3–4)

What Makes Jonah Interesting and Unique?

- Jonah is very different from the other prophets (he disobeys God, his audience listens to him, he pouts when people are saved, etc.).
- Jonah is swallowed by a large fish (or perhaps a serpent?), which symbolizes both deliverance and judgment.
- The repentance of the city of Nineveh is so complete that even the cows fast and wear sackcloth. God mentions his concern for the cows in 4:11 (sarcastically?).
- The events of Jonah 1–2 are paralleled by the events of Jonah 3–4.
- Jonah's spoken message (only one verse long) is directed to the Ninevites, but the literary message is probably directed to Israel.

The Size of Nineveh

In Jonah 1:2 God refers to Nineveh as a "great city." Jonah 3:3 states that "Nineveh was a very large city; it took three days to go through it." Translating literally from the Hebrew, this verse reads, "Nineveh was a great city to God, a going of three days." Scholars and translators have been puzzled for years over how to translate the phrase, "a going of three days." In the past, many assumed this referred to how big Nineveh was; that is, it took someone three days to walk across it. The problem with this understanding is that none of the cities in the ancient Near East were big enough to require three days to walk across. Furthermore, ancient Nineveh has been excavated, and the time required to walk across the site is a few hours (at most) and not three days. Recently several scholars have argued that "a going of three days" has nothing to do with the physical size of the city, but rather refers to the status of the city in regard to the protocol required for official visits. That is, if a king sent an emissary to Nineveh, the status of the city required the emissary to stay there for three days.

What Is Jonah's Message?

Jonah, the Sailors, and Deliverance (1–2)

In the opening verses God tells the prophet Jonah to go and preach against the city of Nineveh. Surprisingly, instead of obeying, Jonah flees from God and takes a boat headed for Tarshish, in the opposite direction. Nineveh is located to the north and east of Israel, while Tarshish (probably a port city on the coast of Spain) is at the other end of the known world, as far away from Nineveh as one could get.

You probably know the story well. God hurls a tremendous storm against the boat. What was Jonah thinking? Was he going to run from God? Did he think the God of Israel was a regional deity with no power over the sea? Or that God would perhaps forget about him? The sailors try frantically, yet unsuccessfully, to row back to land. Eventually they confront Jonah and discover he is the cause of this fearsome storm. Reluctantly they throw Jonah into the sea, and the storm ceases immediately, causing the sailors to fear God and to offer sacrifices to him.

Meanwhile a "great fish" swallows Jonah. The Hebrew Bible calls this creature a "great fish," and we immediately assume it must be a whale. The early Greek translation of the Old Testament (the Septuagint), however, translates this with a Greek word that means "sea monster" or "sea serpent," and in the artwork of the early church this animal is regularly portrayed as

✦ When the Pharisees ask for a sign, Jesus tells them that the only sign they will get is "the sign of Jonah" (Matt. 12:38–41; Luke 11:29–32), a prediction of Jesus's resurrection as well as an indictment on the Pharisees' unbelief.

a huge sea serpent/monster. Jonah spends three days and three nights in this creature (either a whale or a sea monster). In Jonah 2 the prophet cries out to God from within the creature. In this regard Jonah 2 is very similar to some of the Psalms. God hears Jonah's cry, and the creature spits him up onto dry land.

Many people have tried to explain that this event could really have happened; that is, they try to demonstrate that it is possible to be swallowed by a whale and to survive. Some writers even cite a story of a modern (nineteenth century AD) sailor who supposedly did survive after being swallowed by a whale. Yet there is no evidence that the story of this sailor ever actually happened. Furthermore, we suspect that writers who cite that story are missing the point. This event—and other miraculous actions by God in the Bible—are by definition unusual, implausible, even impossible events. That is the nature of divine miracles. We miss the point of the miracle if we try to prove that "it really could have happened." No, without the divine intervention of God, it couldn't have happened. That's what miracles are.

Jonah, the Ninevites, and Deliverance (3–4)

After the storm and fish/creature experience, Jonah is now more obedient, and he finally goes to Nineveh and preaches a very brief message of coming judgment: "forty more days

The book of Jonah was popular among the early Christians and scenes from Jonah appear frequently in the tombs of early Christians who were buried in the catacombs near Rome. The sarcophagus below depicts several scenes from Jonah's life. Note, however, that since early Greek and Latin translations of Jonah used a word for "fish" that implied a "sea monster" or "serpent," portrayals such as this depict the "fish" as looking like a sea monster (see bottom of the sarcophagus).

and Nineveh will be destroyed." Incredibly, and in strong contrast to what did not happen back in Israel and Judah, the Ninevites, from the greatest to the least, believe God and repent. The king even calls for a national time of fasting and repenting for all his people (and even the animals!). When God sees that the Assyrians have truly repented (that is, their actions have changed), he has compassion on them, and he cancels the coming imminent judgment.

At this point Jonah gets angry and complains to God (with some irony) that he knew God was gracious and compassionate, and that was why he did not want to preach to the Ninevites (Jonah 4:1–2). Like a pouting child, Jonah then asks God to take his life. God, of course, does not take Jonah's life, and instead gives him a mild rebuke. Jonah then goes outside the city to sit and wait to see what would happen. Is he ignoring the "three-day stay" requirement? What does he think will happen? Is he still expecting God to destroy the city? Does he think that his pouting will change God's mind?

Surprisingly, God provides another miracle. This time he does not send a great fish/creature to deliver Jonah, but rather a plant, which grows up miraculously and provides Jonah with shade from the scorching sun. However, on the next day a worm eats the plant, and it dies. Jonah then complains again to God. At this point God seems to get a little impatient with Jonah, pointing out that Jonah was so concerned over the plant (i.e., his own well-being) but that he had no concern for the entire city of Nineveh, a city with 120,000 people (not to mention the cows!). God, however, is concerned with these people and will save them when they repent as they did.

Note the many parallels between the story in Jonah 1–2 and the story in Jonah 3–4. In the first story Jonah is disobedient, but ends up praising God for his own deliverance. In the second story Jonah is obedient, but ends up criticizing God for the deliverance of others. Likewise the boat, the sailors, the captain, and the

✦ When Nineveh repents, even the cows fast and are covered in sackcloth (3:7). In the last verse of the book, God states his concern for Nineveh, which has 120,000 people in it . . . and many cattle as well.

fish/creature of the first story parallel the city of Nineveh, the people, the king, and the plant of the second story.

So What? Applying Jonah to Our Lives Today

One of the obvious applications to make from the book of Jonah is that if God tells us to do something or to go somewhere, we should be obedient. If God calls us into a specific work or ministry, we are foolish if we think we can run away from him and the task he has called us to.

Another central lesson for us today is to realize that God's compassion is boundless, and that he loves everybody (even the cruel and violent Assyrians!). One of the major themes running throughout the Bible is that God saves the most unlikely people (the Canaanite Rahab, the Moabite Ruth, and the entire city of Assyrian Ninevites).

Likewise, the story of Jonah is an indictment against us if we are more concerned with our own well-being than with the plight of those who are lost. To use the plant analogy in Jonah 4, are we more concerned about our own lawn dying than our neighbors perishing?

Our Favorite Verse in Jonah

When God saw what they did and how they turned from their evil ways, he had compassion and did not bring upon them the destruction he had threatened. (3:10)

An ancient ship anchor.

Micah

Justice, Judgment, and Hope for the Future

Micah cries out for justice in the land. He is particularly critical of Israel's leaders and their lack of justice. Therefore, Micah declares, due to the lack of justice and due to the pervasive idolatry in Israel and Judah, the judgment of God is coming (the Assyrian invasions). However, Micah also looks into the future and declares a glorious time when God will send a deliverer and restore his people.

Who Is Micah?

The name Micah means "who is like the Lord?" He was a contemporary of Isaiah, Amos, and Hosea, prophesying during the tumultuous time when the Assyrians were expanding their empire and invading Israel and Judah (late eighth century BC). Apparently Micah's words became very well-known. Nearly one hundred years later, in 609 BC, as recorded in Jeremiah 26:17–19, the prophetic words of Micah (3:12) are quoted in defense of Jeremiah, who had preached judgment on Jerusalem.

What Is the Setting for Micah?

As mentioned above, Micah overlaps with Isaiah, Amos, and Hosea, prophesying during the reigns of Jotham, Ahaz, and Hezekiah (toward the latter years of the 700s, or eighth century BC). In 722 BC the Assyrians conquer the northern kingdom, Israel, and completely destroy the capital, Samaria. Then in 701 BC the Assyrians lay siege to Jerusalem, but the Lord intervenes for King Hezekiah and defeats them (2 Kings 17–20; Isaiah 36–39). Micah preaches in this context.

What Is at the Heart of the Book of Micah?

Micah is a typical preexilic prophet, and the essence of his message can be synthesized down to the three standard themes of the prophets:

1. You (Judah/Israel) have broken the covenant; you had better repent!
2. No repentance? Then judgment!
3. Yet there is hope beyond the judgment for a glorious, future restoration, both for Israel/Judah and for the nations.

Likewise, as in many of the other prophetic books, when Micah declares that Israel and Judah have broken the covenant, he focuses on three major sins: idolatry, social injustice, and religious ritualism. In similar fashion to the other prophetic books, the book of Deuteronomy provides the theological background for Micah's message. When Micah declares that Israel and Judah have broken the covenant, it is the covenant as formulated in Deuteronomy that he has in mind.

Like some of the other prophetic books, Micah is more of an anthology than an easily outlined essay. Nonetheless, the message in the book of Micah does seem to break down into the following three central units:

- Judgment, yet Promise for the Future (1–2)
- Justice, Leadership, and the Coming One (3–5)
- Life in the Present and Hope for the Future (6–7)

"They will beat their swords into plowshares" (Mic. 4:3). Pictured above is an ancient sword and an ancient plowshare.

✦ The book of Micah, although much shorter, is very similar to the book of Isaiah. In fact, Micah 4:1–3 is practically identical to Isaiah 2:1–4.

Dominating the historical background for Micah is the expanding Assyrian empire. Pictured above from a wall relief in Sennacherib's palace is a scene of captured people being deported.

What Makes Micah Interesting and Unique?

- Micah presents a very colorful wordplay on various cities.
- Micah prophesies that the future deliverer/shepherd will come from Bethlehem.
- Micah uses the powerful imagery of hammering swords into plowshares to symbolize the peace that the Messiah will bring.
- Micah 6:8 succinctly summarizes what the Lord wants from his people: to act justly, love mercy, and to walk humbly with God.

What Is Micah's Message?

Judgment, yet Promise for the Future (1–2)

Micah indicates in 1:1 that his prophecy concerns both Jerusalem and Samaria, the respective capitals of the southern kingdom, Judah, and the northern kingdom, Israel. In 1:2–7 Micah opens his prophecy by declaring that Judah and Israel are guilty of idolatry; God himself bears testimony against them and comes in judgment. The next unit (1:8–16) uses repeated wordplays to convey the message of coming judgment. Micah mentions

✚ Micah mentions numerous cities in 1:10–15, starting with Gath and ending with Adullam. Back in 1 Samuel 22:1, David flees from Saul, starting in Gath and ending up in Adullam.

numerous cities, using judgment words that either sound similar to the city or that play on the meaning of the city (like saying, "I will deal with Dallas, cleave Cleveland, and pound Little Rock into pebbles").

In 2:1–5 Micah proclaims colorfully that just as people are planning to extort and steal land from others (land was God's gift of inheritance, remember), so God is planning to send disaster on them. Appropriately the punishment is exile and loss of the land. In 2:6–11 Micah castigates the false prophets of his day, and then ends the chapter with a brief statement of restoration, using shepherd imagery.

Justice, Leadership, and the Coming One (3–5)

Micah 3 focuses on the corrupt leaders and on their failure to carry out justice in the land, a theme recurring throughout Micah (and the other prophetic books as well). The chapter ends with judgment on Jerusalem. Micah 4, by contrast, describes the future messianic restoration, when those weak and lame exiles will be regathered, peace will prevail ("beating swords into plowshares"), nations will stream to the Lord's temple to worship him, and a Davidic king will rule. In 5:1–5 Micah describes the coming Davidic king as a great shepherd. He will come from Bethlehem (the city of David), will shepherd his people like sheep, and will bring about peace for them.

Life in the Present and Hope for the Future (6–7)

Micah 6 opens with a "covenant lawsuit" charge against Israel (Isaiah 1 is very similar). In 6:6–8 the prophet addresses the common problem of religious ritual, whereby the people thought that if they participated in religious rituals (sacrifices, burning incense, etc.) then surely God would be pleased with them. In 6:6–7 Micah states that God is not necessarily pleased with sacrificial rituals, no matter how outrageous they may be (thousands of rams, a firstborn child). Micah 6:8 declares what the Lord really desires from his people: "To act justly and to love mercy and to walk humbly with your God." However, the people are not living in this manner, and Micah 6:9–7:6 underscores how angry God is at their continued social injustices (dishonest scales, violence, lying, bribes, etc.).

At the end of the book, Micah returns to the encouraging theme of hope for a future restoration. Micah's name, remember, means "who is like the Lord." In a probable wordplay on his own name, at the end of the book Micah asks, "Who is a God like you, who pardons sin and forgives the transgression of the remnant of his inheritance?" (7:18). Micah's closing verse connects

✦ Micah's prophecy in 5:2 not only identifies the city the Messiah will come from (Bethlehem), but also connects the Messiah to the Davidic covenant (2 Samuel 7), since Bethlehem was the city of David. Matthew quotes this verse in Matthew 2:3–6.

the future restoration to the fulfillment of God's promise to Abraham back in Genesis 12, 15, and 17, a theme that will be echoed by the New Testament.

So What? Applying Micah to Our Lives Today

Micah 6:6–8 is especially applicable to us today. What does God want from us? Does he want only ritual (like extensive church attendance)? Obviously not. God wants us to live lives that are characterized by justice and a deep zealous desire for love and mercy as we live day by day in close relationship with him, humbly recognizing him as our great Creator and Savior. It is only in this context that our rituals (how we do church) have meaning and reflect true worship and adoration of God.

Micah's clear identification of Bethlehem as the place where the coming Messiah will be born (5:2) illustrates the powerful predictive aspect of the Old Testament prophets, confirming that Jesus was indeed the fulfillment of the Old Testament. This should encourage us to trust in God, who clearly has control of history and is moving to bring about the fulfillment of his plan.

Our Favorite Verse in Micah

He has showed you, O man, what is good.
And what does the Lord require of you?
To act justly and to love mercy
and to walk humbly with your God. (6:8)

The Church of the Nativity in Bethlehem. Micah prophesies that the coming shepherd-deliverer will come from Bethlehem (5:2).

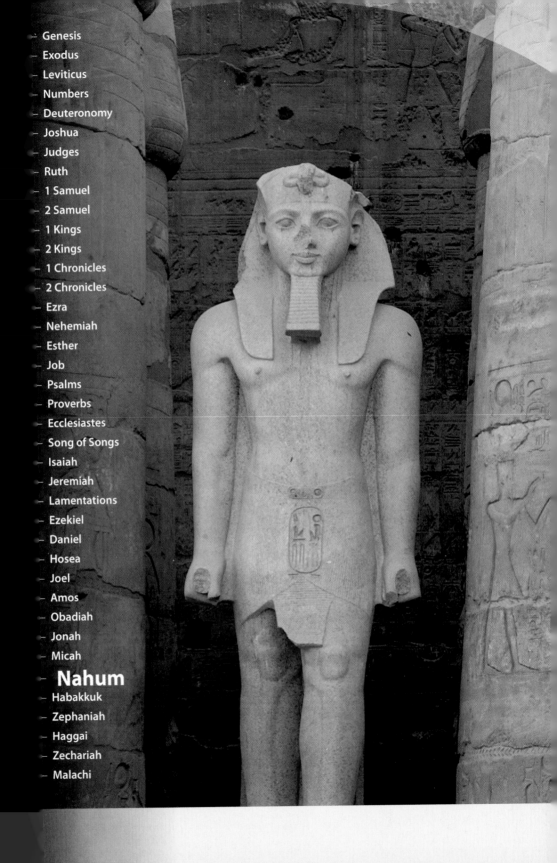

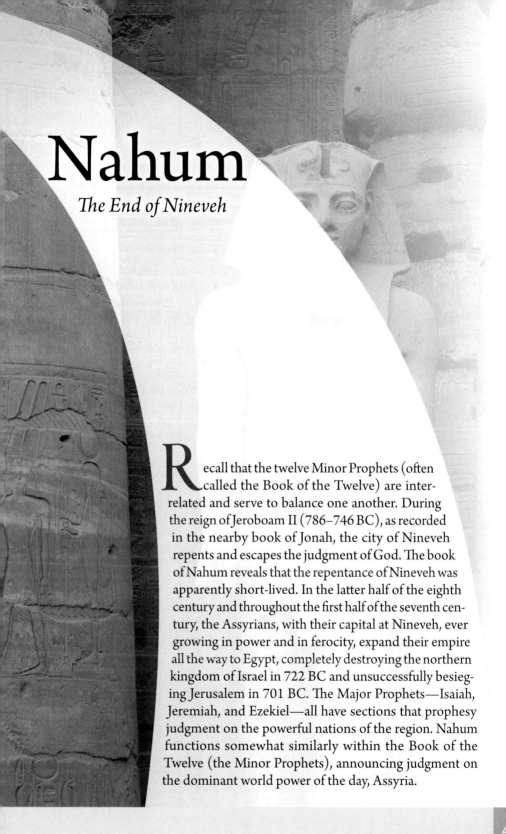

Nahum

The End of Nineveh

Recall that the twelve Minor Prophets (often called the Book of the Twelve) are interrelated and serve to balance one another. During the reign of Jeroboam II (786–746 BC), as recorded in the nearby book of Jonah, the city of Nineveh repents and escapes the judgment of God. The book of Nahum reveals that the repentance of Nineveh was apparently short-lived. In the latter half of the eighth century and throughout the first half of the seventh century, the Assyrians, with their capital at Nineveh, ever growing in power and in ferocity, expand their empire all the way to Egypt, completely destroying the northern kingdom of Israel in 722 BC and unsuccessfully besieging Jerusalem in 701 BC. The Major Prophets—Isaiah, Jeremiah, and Ezekiel—all have sections that prophesy judgment on the powerful nations of the region. Nahum functions somewhat similarly within the Book of the Twelve (the Minor Prophets), announcing judgment on the dominant world power of the day, Assyria.

Who Is Nahum?

Little is known about the prophet Nahum. He lives and prophesies around the middle of the seventh century BC (between 663 BC and 612 BC). Nahum's name means "consolation," but it does not appear anywhere else in the Old Testament outside of this book. In Nahum 1:1 the prophet is said to be an Elkoshite, but we know nothing about this tribe or town.

What Is the Setting for Nahum?

The temple-filled city of Thebes in Egypt was destroyed by the Assyrians in 663 BC. Nineveh, the capital of Assyria, was destroyed by the Babylonians in 612 BC. Nahum writes in between these two events—after the fall of Thebes but before the fall of Nineveh. At this time in history the brutal Assyrians dominate the ancient Near East.

Here is a pleasant scene from a wall relief of the Assyrian king Ashurbanipal. He and his wife are dining to music in the garden, but note the grisly head of one of his enemies hanging in the tree to the left.

What Is at the Heart of the Book of Nahum?

Nahum proclaims judgment on the Assyrians and the destruction of their capital city, Nineveh.

What Makes Nahum Interesting and Unique?

- Nahum taunts the king of Assyria with the coming judgment ("everyone who hears the news about you claps his hands at your fall"; 3:19).
- Nahum mentions the destruction of the Egyptian city Thebes, an important event in Egyptian history.
- Nahum balances out Jonah, where the Ninevites escape judgment by repenting.

What Is Nahum's Message?

In the opening verses Nahum declares that the Lord will bring about judgment on his enemies. Then throughout the book, Nahum describes the coming judgment on Nineveh, the Assyrian capital. He uses colorful and graphic language to describe the end of Nineveh. For example, in 2:11 he compares the destruction of Nineveh to the end of a lions' den, where the cubs and the lioness previously ate safely, but can no longer. Nahum ends the book by saying that everyone who hears about the fall of Assyria will clap their hands in joy because they have all felt the cruel hand of the Assyrian army.

So What? Applying Nahum to Our Lives Today

Nahum is a reminder that God does ultimately bring about judgment and punishment on those who oppose him and oppress his people. Back in the book of Jonah, God responded with compassion and forgiveness for the people of Nineveh when they humbled themselves, fasted, quit doing evil deeds, and cried out to God for deliverance. However, as time passed and as Assyria became a brutal, vicious, empire-building nation, God's wrath was aroused and, lacking any repentance on their part, he judged them, using the Babylonians to destroy Nineveh just as Nahum predicted.

Our Favorite Verse in Nahum

The Lord is good,
a refuge in times of trouble.
He cares for those who trust in him. (1:7)

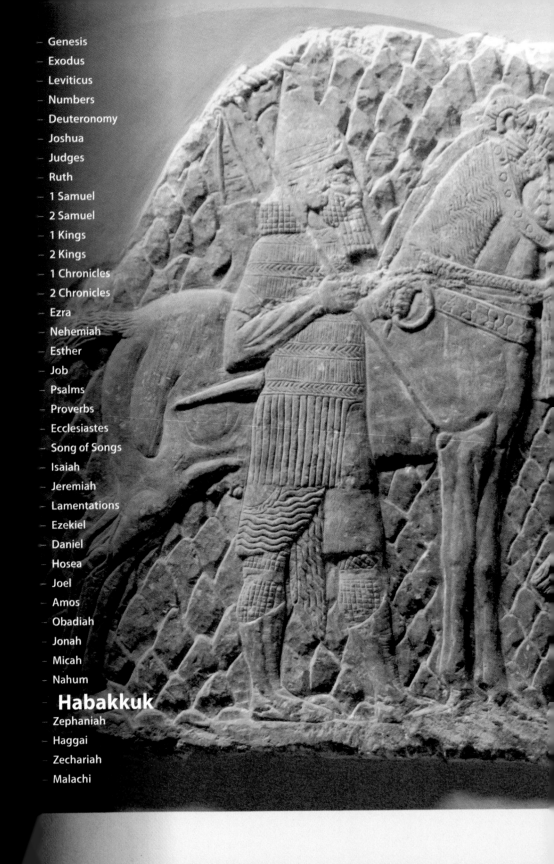

Habakkuk

Talking with God about Judgment

Sometimes we look at the evil and sin all around us and wonder why God doesn't do something about it. This is exactly what the prophet Habakkuk did. He saw such terrible things in his home country of Judah that he complained to God, "Why do you make me look at injustice? Why do you tolerate wrong?" (1:3). The book of Habakkuk deals with how God answered Habakkuk and how the prophet came to grips with that answer.

Who Is Habakkuk?

We know very little about Habakkuk other than that he was a prophet. God's statement to him in 1:6 allows us to place him in the time era just prior to one of the Babylonian invasions of Judah. Habakkuk 3 is a psalm, intended to be sung (3:1, 19). Thus a few scholars have suggested that Habakkuk might be a musician-prophet who works in the temple, as described in 1 Chronicles 25:1. The name Habakkuk comes from a Hebrew root word that means "to embrace."

What Is the Setting for Habakkuk?

The book of Habakkuk does not have an opening historical superscription tying the book to the reign of a certain king, but Habakkuk 1:6 indicates that the setting for Habakkuk is in the southern kingdom of Judah just prior to one of the Babylonian invasions (597 BC or 587/586 BC). This would make Habakkuk a contemporary with Jeremiah and Zephaniah. Josiah, the last good king of Judah, was killed by an Egyptian army in 609 BC, and the kings that succeeded him, along with the nobles and most of the priests and court prophets, quickly led the nation into a moral and theological decline. The book of Jeremiah provides us with a good picture of the blatant idolatry and social injustice that characterized Jerusalem in the time of Habakkuk. The prophet Habakkuk is one of the few people, along with the other true prophets, who react against this degeneration.

What Is at the Heart of the Book of Habakkuk?

In essence Habakkuk follows the standard three-part prophetic message:

1. You (Judah) have broken the covenant; you had better repent!
2. No repentance? Then judgment!
3. Yet there is hope beyond the judgment for a glorious, future restoration.

However, the style of Habakkuk is quite different from that of the other prophetic books, for the book of Habakkuk is structured as a dialogue between Habakkuk and God. Thus the book unfolds as follows:

- Habakkuk's Question to God: Why Don't You Do Something about All the Injustice in Judah? (1:1–4)
- God's Answer: I Am Doing Something—Raising Up the Babylonians (1:5–11)
- Habakkuk's Follow-Up Question: How Can That Be Right? They Are Worse Than We Are (1:12–2:1)
- God's Answer: Nonetheless, Wait, for This Judgment Is Certainly Coming (2:2–20)
- Habakkuk's Concluding Response: I Will Wait for the Judgment and Rejoice in God (3:1–19)

✚ Habakkuk and Jeremiah both lived in Judah at about the same time, so they probably knew each other, even though they never mention each other in their books.

What Makes Habakkuk Interesting and Unique?

- The book of Habakkuk is a dialogue between the prophet and God.
- Habakkuk struggles with why God allows injustice to occur in Judah.
- In the New Testament Paul uses Habakkuk 2:4 as a foundational verse for explaining justification by faith (Rom. 1:17; Gal. 3:11).
- Habakkuk learns to rejoice in God, even though judgment is coming on Judah, his home country.

What Is Habakkuk's Message?

Habakkuk's Question to God: Why Don't You Do Something about All the Injustice In Judah? (1:1–4)

Habakkuk cries out to God about the injustice and wrong that he sees all around him. He asks God how long he has to cry out before God will listen to him and do something about the terrible situation in Judah.

God's Answer: I Am Doing Something— Raising Up the Babylonians (1:5–11)

God tells Habakkuk that he is doing something about the situation in Judah. He is raising up the Babylonians (Chaldeans) to judge Judah for their sin. God then describes how the ruthless Babylonian army will sweep down across the land, easily overrunning Judah's fortified cities.

Habakkuk's Follow-Up Question: How Can That Be Right? They Are Worse Than We Are (1:12–2:1)

God's answer is not exactly what Habakkuk had hoped for. Apparently he wanted God to fix the problem from within, not destroy them via a Babylonian invasion. Thus Habakkuk objects, pointing out that the Babylonians are worse than

The book of Habakkuk takes place just prior to the Babylonians' rise to power. This clay tablet gives a description of the Babylonian capture of Nineveh, the Assyrian capital, a critical event in the shift in power from Assyria to Babylonia.

the Judahites (1:13). Then Habakkuk resolves to wait and see how God responds (2:1), apparently expecting God to revise his solution.

God's Answer: Nonetheless, Wait, for This Judgment Is Certainly Coming (2:2–20)

God soon answers Habakkuk, but he does not revise his plan to use the Babylonians to judge Judah. This judgment is so certain that God tells Habakkuk to write it down. Wait for it, God instructs Habakkuk, for it is most certainly coming. God then contrasts two people. One of these people represents the Babylonians—arrogant and greedy, taking numerous peoples into captivity (2:5). The other individual is a righteous person. Even though the Babylonians will bring death and destruction, this person will believe in God, remain faithful to God, and thus will live (2:4). Yet judgment will then come on the Babylonians. Habakkuk 2:6–20 contains five "woe" passages (like funeral dirges) that are to be sung over the fallen Babylonians. In contrast, God's plan moves forward, and God will be glorified (2:14). This section concludes by proclaiming that "the Lord is in his holy temple; let all the earth be silent before him" (2:20).

Habakkuk's Concluding Response: I Will Wait for the Judgment and Rejoice in God (3:1–19)

This final chapter of Habakkuk is different from the rest of the book. It is in the form of a psalm, and it has its own separate introductory superscription (3:1). Habakkuk accepts God's plan for judgment on Judah, but he asks God to remember mercy during the wrath (3:2). Habakkuk then describes God as a conquering warrior who comes in awesome power (3:3–7). Yet Habakkuk resolves to be like the one described in 2:4. He accepts the coming judgment of God, even though it terrifies him. He knows God is just and will eventually judge the

Rhytons, large cup-bowl vessels made for mixing and drinking wine, have been found in numerous archaeological sites. This one was found in Syria (fifth century BC). Habakkuk, as well as several other prophets, uses the image of drinking wine as one of judgment. Hab. 2:16 declares, "The cup from the Lord's right hand is coming around to you."

Babylonians as well. So because his trust and faith are in God, Habakkuk declares that he will rejoice and find strength in the Lord (3:16–19).

So What? Applying Habakkuk to Our Lives Today

Habakkuk teaches us that often we do not understand how God is working. Sometimes, like Habakkuk, we ask why God does not intervene and do something. This book tells us to trust in God's long-range plan and to wait patiently in the meantime, rejoicing in God's control of the outcome.

In addition, as Paul so eloquently explains in Romans and Galatians, faith in God is a critical component of a true relationship with God and should be a central feature in our day-to-day understanding of how God works in the world. Faith, life, and salvation are inextricably bound together.

Our Favorite Verse in Habakkuk

But the righteous will live by his faith. (2:4)

✚ The New Testament quotes Habakkuk 2:4 three times (Rom. 1:17; Gal. 3:11; Heb. 10:37–38). In Romans and Galatians, Paul uses Habakkuk 2:4 as a foundational verse for explaining justification by faith.

Habakkuk   431

Zephaniah

The Day of the Lord Is Near

Sometimes we as Christians want to talk only about the love of God and his great salvation. In one sense this is valid; love and salvation are major themes in the Bible and lie at the very heart of the gospel. But salvation is also related to justice—that is, we are saved for something (eternal life) and from something (the wrath of God). When Jesus returns he will gather his people together for salvation, but he will also bring judgment on those who have defied him and opposed him. The prophets in general, and Zephaniah in particular, describe a coming time when God will crash into human history and, according to his plan, bring about salvation and blessing for his people who trust him, as well as terrible wrath on those who have rejected him. Zephaniah calls this time in history "the day of the Lord."

Who Is Zephaniah?

Zephaniah 1:1 places the ministry of Zephaniah during the reign of Josiah, the last good king of Judah (640–609 BC) and one of the few kings of Judah who obeyed God and worshiped him alone. Thus Zephaniah's ministry overlaps the early years of Jeremiah. Zephaniah is called the "son of Cushi." "Cushi" means "the Cushite," a reference to people from the nation of Cush, a powerful African kingdom just to the south of Egypt that ruled over Egypt at the end of the eighth century and the first half of the seventh century BC. We are uncertain as to the implications of Zephaniah's father having the name "Cushi" (the Cushite). Perhaps he was a native Cushite, or perhaps he had dark skin and looked like a Cushite. Or perhaps his parents gave him this name to honor the Cushites, who had allied with Judah against the Assyrians at the close of the eighth century and into the early seventh century.

What Is the Setting for Zephaniah?

As mentioned above, the ministry of Zephaniah is tied tightly to the reign of King Josiah (640–609 BC). At the beginning of Josiah's reign, the Assyrians still dominate the region, having driven the Cushites out of Egypt and destroying Thebes, the center of Cushite religious domination of Egypt (see Nah. 3:8–10). But to the east of Assyria, the Babylonians are rising to power. By the end of Josiah's reign the Assyrians are in retreat, and the Babylonians are aggressively expanding.

What Is at the Heart of the Book of Zephaniah?

Like the other preexilic prophets, Zephaniah's basic message can be synthesized down to the three standard prophetic themes:

1. You (Judah) have broken the covenant; you had better repent!
2. No repentance? Then judgment!

An Egyptian portrayal of a Cushite.

3. Yet there is hope beyond the judgment for a glorious, future restoration, both for Israel/Judah and for the nations.

Likewise, Zephaniah accuses Judah of the same basic covenant violations that the other prophets rage against—idolatry, social injustice, and religious ritualism. The basic thought of Zephaniah can be organized into the following units:

- Judgment: The Day of the Lord (1:1–2:3)
- Judgment on the Nations (2:4–15)
- Judgment on Jerusalem (3:1–8)
- Restoration of Jerusalem and the Nations (3:9–13)
- Rejoicing in the Lord's Salvation (3:14–20)

What Makes Zephaniah Interesting and Unique?

- Zephaniah is called the "son of Cushi," implying some kind of connection to ancient Cush in Africa.
- The "day of the Lord" is a central theme of Zephaniah.
- Zephaniah preaches salvation for all peoples of the earth.
- Zephaniah declares that God sings when he rejoices over his people.

What Is Zephaniah's Message?

Judgment: The Day of the Lord (1:1–2:3)

Zephaniah does not ease into his message politely or dance around the heart of the matter. His message explodes in the opening verses with descriptions of the terrible judgment that is coming as part of the "day of the Lord." "I will sweep away everything," God declares (1:2), and "I will stretch out my hand against Judah" (1:4). Indeed, the wrath of God is coming, closely associated with the "day of the Lord," a phrase occurring seventeen times in 1:1–2:3. The judgment is coming on sinful Jerusalem and Judah, due to their terrible idolatry (1:4–6). This wrath will fall on the nobility (1:8), the corrupt priests (1:4, 6, 9), and the wealthy and complacent (1:10–13, 18). Finally, in 2:1–3, a call to repentance emerges, as Zephaniah calls on the people to seek God through humility and obedience.

✦ The call in Zephaniah 1:7 to "be silent before the Sovereign Lord" connects Zephaniah to Habakkuk by continuing the theme in Habakkuk 2:20, "The Lord is in his holy temple; let all the earth be silent before him."

The Day of the Lord

The prophets use the phrase "the day of the Lord" to refer to the time when God will intervene into human history in a dramatic and decisive way to bring about the fulfillment of his plan. In addition to the phrase "the day of the Lord," the prophets will also use similar terms such as "that day" and "the day" to convey the same concept. On the one hand, "the day of the Lord" is a time of judgment on God's enemies—those who oppose him, oppress his people, or rebel against him. It is also a time of judgment on Israel and Judah for their rejection of God and their terrible sins against the covenant (Isa. 3:18–4:1; Amos 5:18–20). On the other hand, for the true people of God who trust in him, "the day of the Lord" is a time of wonderful blessing and restoration. This applies both to restored Israel/Judah and to the nations. "The day of the Lord" is a major theme throughout the prophetic books. Among the Major Prophets, Isaiah employs this phrase the most frequently. It is also a central unifying theme in the Book of the Twelve (the Minor Prophets), playing a central role especially in Joel and here in Zephaniah.

The New Testament, closely linked to the Old Testament prophets, uses this term as well, likewise frequently employing close synonyms such as "those days," "that day," or "the great day." The New Testament writers will use the term to refer to that time in the future when God will dramatically enter into human history to bring about the fulfillment of his plan. In the New Testament, this usually refers to the second coming of Christ, a time of deliverance for his people but a time of judgment on the unbelievers (Mark 13:24; 1 Cor. 5:5; 1 Thess. 5:2; 2 Thess. 2:2; 2 Pet. 3:10, 12).

Judgment on the Nations (2:4–15)

In this unit Zephaniah moves beyond Judah and Jerusalem to proclaim that the "day of the Lord" includes judgment on all the nations. Zephaniah symbolically includes all the nations of the world as he mentions nations from each point of the compass: Philistia to the west (2:4–7), Moab and Ammon to the east (2:8–11), Cush to the south (2:12), and Assyria to the north (2:13–15).

Judgment on Jerusalem (3:1–8)

As demonstrated clearly in the book of Jeremiah, the people in Jerusalem do not listen at all to the prophetic warnings of Zephaniah or Jeremiah. Zephaniah 3:1–8 states that because of Jerusalem's rebellious and defiant attitude, God will bring judgment on the city.

Restoration of Jerusalem and the Nations (3:9–13)

Throughout the book, Zephaniah has been proclaiming judgment on Judah/Jerusalem and on all the nations. Now he moves beyond the judgment to describe the future time of restoration and deliverance, a time of salvation for both Judah/Jerusalem and all the nations. Included in this restoration is the African kingdom of Cush, used by Zephaniah to represent all the gentiles of the world.

Zephaniah preaches judgment on the cities of Philistia (2:4–7). Pictured are the ruins of the Philistine city of Ashkelon.

✚ Zephkaniah 3:9–10 contains numerous allusions back to the Tower of Babel story in Genesis 11, implying that the time of future salvation includes a reversal of the judgment at the tower of Babel (as is seen in Acts 2 as well).

Rejoicing in the Lord's Salvation (3:14–20)

The book of Zephaniah ends on a happy note. For God's people, the coming "day of the Lord" will bring a wonderful time of salvation and restoration, characterized by joy and celebration. "Sing, O daughter of Zion!" Zephaniah exhorts in 3:14. Even the Lord joins in this time of rejoicing by singing himself (3:17)! Have you ever thought that God gets so excited about the salvation of people that he starts singing?

So What? Applying Zephaniah to Our Lives Today

Like the other prophets, Zephaniah sweeps away all superficial piety and declares unambiguously that arrogant, defiant, and rebellious people who ignore God's call and reject his message can expect to experience severe judgment. The prophets are not fuzzy on this point. Sin is serious business; God does not merely look the other way or ignore it. However, Zephaniah proclaims a message that foreshadows the gospel. God provides a way of salvation for those who humbly and obediently seek him and listen to his message.

Clay cylinder with an inscription of Nebuchadnezzar recording how he repaired a temple to Shamash, the sun god.

Another interesting application from Zephaniah is that it can help us to know God better. Many people picture God as somber and cold, an old man with a beard sitting on a throne and scowling at everyone. Zephaniah pictures God as singing and rejoicing over those who are saved. Usually we anticipate that when we first see God in heaven he will be seated up on a high throne, perhaps looking at us sternly. Zephaniah introduces the idea that when we first see God he might be overflowing with excitement and joy to the extent that he breaks out in a joyful song!

Our Favorite Verse in Zephaniah

The Lord your God is with you,
   he is mighty to save.
   He will take great delight in you,
   he will quiet you with his love,
   he will rejoice over you with singing. (3:17)

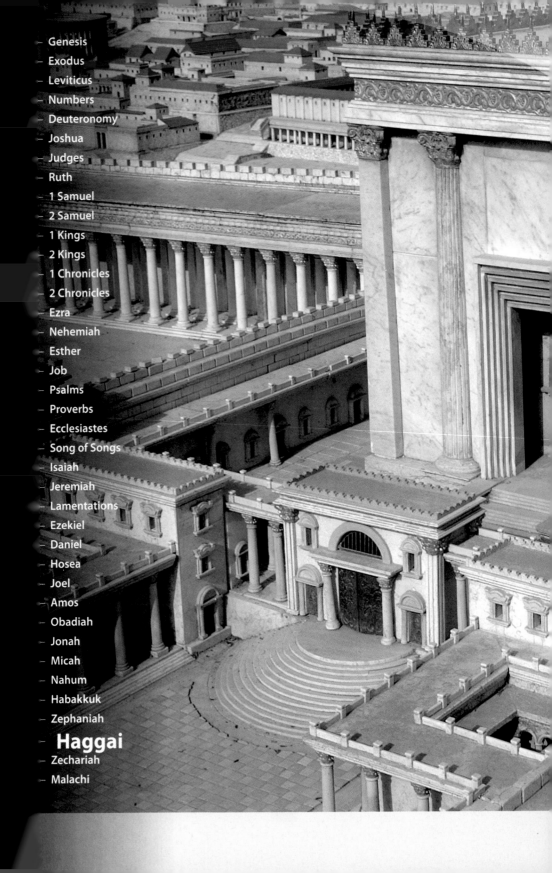

Haggai

Rebuilding the Temple

Many of the Israelite exiles did indeed return to Israel after the Persian king Cyrus decreed that such peoples could go back to their lands. But such a return is difficult. Resources are scarce, and these former exiles are not wealthy. Many of them resettle in Jerusalem and begin to rebuild the society and the commercial structure there. Yet the people become so focused on their own personal well-being that they neglect to keep their focus on God. They abandon any idea of rebuilding God's temple, thus relegating the worship of God to the fringes of their concerns. Haggai, however, confronts them over this marginalization of God, and convinces them once again to focus on worshiping God. Step 1, Haggai proclaims, is to rebuild the temple. This is the major theme of Haggai.

Who Is Haggai?

Haggai is a prophet living in Jerusalem during the postexilic time. He delivers the words of his prophecy in 520 BC.

Unlike audiences of many of the other prophets, the people actually listen to him and obey his words, rallying to rebuild the temple.

What Is the Setting for Haggai?

Haggai prophesies in the postexilic period. The Israelite exiles have returned from Babylon and begun rebuilding the city of Jerusalem. The continued reference throughout the book to the reign of Persian kings (1:1, 15; 2:10) reminds the reader that the Persians still dominate the area and that Davidic kings do not sit on the throne in Jerusalem.

What Is at the Heart of the Book of Haggai?

The central concern of Haggai is to rebuild the temple. When the exiles return to Jerusalem, the temple still lies in ruins. Haggai criticizes the people for building nice houses for themselves while neglecting to rebuild God's house. This, the prophet proclaims, reflects a distorted view of worship and service. Haggai encourages the people to rebuild the temple, and they obediently carry out this project. The theme in the book breaks down into four brief units:

- The Call to Rebuild the Temple (1:1–15)
- The Future Glory of the Temple (2:1–9)
- Moving from Defiled to Blessed (2:10–19)
- Restoration through the Lord's Ruler (2:20–23)

What Makes Haggai Interesting and Unique?

- The book of Haggai stresses the continued Persian domination.
- Haggai focuses on rebuilding the temple.
- Haggai speaks of the future glory (Christ) that will come to this temple.

What Is Haggai's Message?

The Call to Rebuild the Temple (1:1–15)

In this passage Haggai challenges the people in Jerusalem to rethink their priorities. The returned exiles in Jerusalem had been able to finish their

✚ Four times in Haggai God tells the people to "give careful thought to your ways" (1:5, 7; 2:15, 18).

The Postexilic Prophets

After the death of King Solomon, a civil war divides the nation into two countries: Israel (in the north) and Judah (in the south). The northern kingdom, Israel, falls into idol worship immediately, never again to return to a true worship of God. The southern kingdom, Judah, soon follows suit and slides into idolatry and social injustice. A few kings struggle against this slide, but without success. The preexilic prophets like Isaiah, Amos, and Jeremiah preach and preach, but to no avail; no one really listens to them. By the time of Jeremiah and Zephaniah, both the leaders and the people have completely abandoned God. Even though God pleads with them through his prophets, the people remain rebellious and hostile, refusing to repent and to return to God. Thus the judgment comes. The Assyrians destroy the northern kingdom of Israel in 722 BC, and the Babylonians later destroy the southern kingdom of Judah in 587/586 BC. The Presence of God departs from Jerusalem (Ezekiel 10–11), and the Babylonians raze Jerusalem to the ground, carrying most of the population into exile; thus the Israelites lose the Promised Land.

But then the Lord begins to unfold his plan of restoration. Cyrus, king of Persia, overruns the Babylonians, and in 538 BC he decrees that exiled people like the Israelites can return home. In several waves over the next one hundred years or so, the shattered Israelite exiles return back to the Promised Land. This is the context in which the postexilic prophets (Haggai, Zechariah, and Malachi) write.

With Israel back in the land, some people might have thought that the great time of restoration predicted so often by the preexilic prophets had begun.

Numerous things, however, point out that the great deliverance remained in the future. Yes, Israel is back in the land, but there is no Davidic king on the throne, and the Persians continue to dominate Israel politically (a fact stressed throughout the postexilic literature). Also important is that even after the Israelites rebuild the destroyed temple, the Presence of God does not return to the temple. In contrast to the spectacular entry of God's Presence into the Solomonic temple described in 1 Kings 8:10–11, nothing at all is mentioned about the Presence of God in the rebuilt temple during the time of the postexilic prophets. Indeed, the postexilic prophets proclaim that the situation created by the struggling group of Israelites back in the land does not represent the great time of restoration and deliverance predicted by the preexilic prophets, or a return to "the way things were" under the blessings of Deuteronomy. They also underscore that the terrible sins of their forefathers should be seen as lessons, exhorting the current community to follow God in serious obedience. Yet the postexilic prophets do proclaim that the time of restoration has "begun" to a limited extent. Haggai, Zechariah, and Malachi tell the ragtag nation of Israelites who have returned to the land that they live in between the beginning of the restoration and the ultimate consummation, which is still future. These prophets announce that the postexilic community is living in an interim time, and they should worship and serve the Lord faithfully as they await the coming of the Messiah who will actually bring about the glorious restoration prophesied by the preexilic prophets.

own personal houses, but had ignored rebuilding God's house. Through Haggai, God declares that this kind of self-centered behavior dishonors God; thus they were not receiving his blessings. Unlike the people in Jerusalem during the time of Jeremiah, these people listen to the prophet and do indeed reconstruct the temple. God then restates his central covenant promise with his people, "I am with you," a promise of comfort and power (1:13).

The Future Glory of the Temple (2:1–9)

The people work on the rebuilt temple energetically, but they simply do not have the resources to build an impressive building, much less a spectacular structure such as their forefather Solomon built. Thus they are disappointed in their new temple. God, however, does not seem to be bothered by this, and he exhorts them to be strong and continue the work, restating, "I am with you" (2:4). The Presence of God among them is more important than the splendor of the stones in the physical temple structure. Then in 2:9 the Lord declares, "The glory of this present house will be greater than the glory of the former house." This is a surprising statement, for the old Solomonic temple was spectacular, and the current rebuilt temple pales in comparison. This promise finds fulfillment, however, when Jesus Christ enters this temple 550 years later. When Christ arrives at this temple, he brings such glory with him that it overshadows the glory of the Solomonic temple, even with all of its gold and splendor.

"I will make you like my signet ring" (Hag. 2:23). Signet rings were used to authenticate and authenticate royal documents. Shown above is an Egyptian royal signet ring (575 BC).

Moving from Defiled to Blessed (2:10–19)

The earlier attitude of the people, when they had been preoccupied with their own comfort instead of God's glory, had in essence "defiled" them. In this passage God underscores that now, because of their obedience, they will move from being defiled to being blessed.

Restoration through the Lord's Ruler (2:20–23)

The current governor, Zerubbabel, is a descendant of David, and he obediently listens to and obeys the prophetic word. In essence he becomes a "foreshadowing" type of messianic ruler. God calls him his signet ring,

✛ The book of Ezra also describes the rebuilding of the temple. As in Haggai 2:3, the people in Ezra 3:12 express disappointment when they compare the modest rebuilt temple with their memory of the original Solomonic temple.

indicating that a time was coming when the one who ruled would not be a Persian king, but a Davidic king of God's choosing.

So What? Applying Haggai to Our Lives Today

For many of us in the church today, Haggai 1 nails us right between the eyes. Haggai points out that the people of Jerusalem have their priorities mixed up because they are more concerned with their own houses than with the worship of God. Does this apply to us today? Ouch! Most certainly. We spend more and more on ourselves, often giving to the Lord our meager leftovers, if any at all. Haggai tells us to make the Lord our top priority in everything, including our budgets.

Our Favorite Verse in Haggai

Is it a time for you yourselves to be living in your paneled houses, while this house remains a ruin? (1:4)

A modern church under construction. The application of Haggai challenges us in regard to setting our priorities.

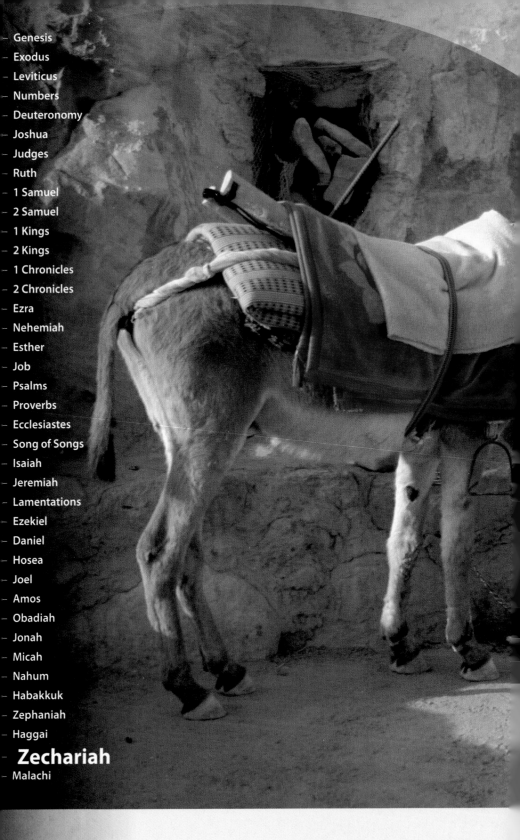

Zechariah

Looking to the Future

The book of Zechariah is a little different than the other prophetic books. While in some places Zechariah does use typical prophetic language, in other places he describes some very unusual, perhaps even weird, visions that he was shown. Furthermore, while most of the prophets stress covenant violation and judgment, Zechariah focuses on the future, the wonderful time when the Messiah will come and gloriously restore his people (and the nations) to relationship with him.

Who Is Zechariah?

Zechariah is a postexilic prophet, one who lived and preached to the Israelites who had returned to Jerusalem/Judah after the Babylonian exile. Zechariah 1:1 identifies his grandfather as a man named Iddo, a priest who returned to the land under Zerubbabel (Neh. 12:4, 16). Thus, like Ezekiel, Zechariah was probably a priest as well. His name means "the Lord remembers," a name that fits very well with the message of the book.

What Is the Setting for Zechariah?

Zechariah provides us with several precise dates for his ministry, all connected to the reign of Darius, the powerful king of Persia. These dates place Zechariah's ministry in the years 520–518 BC and make him contemporary with Haggai. Thus Zechariah speaks to the postexilic situation. The terrible judgment predicted by the preexilic prophets (the Babylonian invasion, the destruction of Jerusalem, and the exile) has come and gone. Now the Israelites—or at least some of them—are back in the Promised Land and are trying to re-establish the shattered nation. Zechariah's frequent mention of the Persian king Darius is a reminder that the postexilic situation is not the glorious restoration that was promised by Isaiah, Jeremiah, and the rest of the preexilic prophets, for that wonderful time of restoration will be characterized by a powerful Davidic king ruling over Israel with all other nations in subordination. This is a far cry from the situation in Zechariah's time, when Israel is a small, struggling, ragtag collection of returned exiles, still under the domination of the powerful Persian Empire.

What Is at the Heart of the Book of Zechariah?

Zechariah does mention the problem of sin and covenant violation, and he does issue a call to faithful and just living, but his stress is clearly on the coming future restoration. Like Haggai, Zechariah is concerned with the rebuilding of the temple, but like Ezekiel, he also points to something in the future that is bigger and more spectacular, that is beyond the temple they are building. Intertwined into this future vision is the Presence of God, a constant theme in the prophetic books.

Ancient oil lamp.

Like the other prophetic books, Zechariah also addresses the foreign nations. He proclaims judgment on them for their sinful actions, but he also includes them in his picture of the glorious future, when they will come streaming to Jerusalem to worship God.

✚ Portions of Zechariah, along with Daniel, Ezekiel, and Revelation, contain "apocalyptic" visions. Apocalyptic literature is characterized by unusual and highly symbolic visions that are often interpreted by angels.

Zechariah breaks down into two main units. The first eight chapters are in prose and are organized around historical superscriptions (dates). The final six chapters are composed of two "oracles" and contain primarily poetry. A suggested outline for Zechariah is as follows:

- Visions, Justice, and Restoration (1:1–8:23)
  - The introductory call to repentance (1:1–6)
  - Eight visions (1:7–6:8)
  - A symbolic crowning of the high priest (6:9–15)
  - A call to live by justice (7:1–14)
  - Future restoration (8:1–23)
- The Coming Messiah (9:1–14:21)
  - Oracle 1: The advent and rejection of the Coming One (9:1–11:17)
  - Oracle 2: The advent and acceptance of the Coming One (12:1–14:21)

What Makes Zechariah Interesting and Unique?

- Zechariah contains some very unusual visions (a flying scroll, a woman in a basket, etc.).
- Many of the visions and images in the book of Revelation are connected to Zechariah.
- Zechariah describes the Coming King as riding into Jerusalem on a donkey.
- Zechariah is told that God's Spirit will empower those who are carrying out his plan.

What Is Zechariah's Message?

Visions, Justice, and Restoration (1:1–8:23)

The introductory call to repentance (1:1–6)

Right at the beginning of the book, God speaks through Zechariah to remind the people how their forefathers had sinned against God (the preexilic prophetic message). God then calls on them to repent and turn to him. Unlike the people in the preexilic era (during the days of Isaiah and Jeremiah), the people do repent, acknowledging that the judgment of the exile had been what their forefathers deserved.

Eight visions (1:7–6:8)

Zechariah is then shown eight consecutive visions. In each vision an angel accompanies him and explains the vision to him. This type of imagery is called "apocalyptic" (see the discussion of apocalyptic literature on page 377).

In the first vision (1:7–17), Zechariah sees four horsemen (although the number is implied and not stated) who have been surveying the world and are now reporting back to God. The Lord then declares that he himself will return to Jerusalem with mercy, bring about the reconstruction of his house, and bless Jerusalem with prosperity. Thus this vision combines the restoration themes of Presence, temple, comfort, and well-being.

In the second vision Zechariah sees four horns, representing the powerful nations around Israel who had been responsible for destroying it. He then sees four craftsmen, who terrify the horns, apparently because they have the power to carve the horns and to throw them down. Thus judgment will come on those nations who conquered and dominated Israel and Judah.

Next (2:1–13), Zechariah sees a man who is surveying Jerusalem in preparation for reconstruction. An angel, however, tells him that there is no need to rebuild the walls, because the Presence of God will be the defense for the city. Revelation 21 presents a similar vision about the glorious future Jerusalem at the end of human history (an angel measuring the city, and gates that are always open—i.e., a city at total peace).

In the fourth vision (3:1–10), Zechariah sees a vision that symbolizes the cleansing and restoration of the priesthood, an institution that had become extremely corrupt during the preexilic period (see especially the book of Jeremiah). God then tells the priests that he is going to bring his Servant (recall the Servant Songs of Isaiah), whom he calls the Branch (Jer. 23:5 identifies the Branch as the coming Davidic king). This Servant and Branch is also a stone with seven eyes (compare this with Rev. 5:6), and at that time God will remove the sin of the land in one day, thus pointing prophetically to the atoning sacrifice of Jesus.

The fifth vision (4:1–14) contains a golden lampstand and two olive trees that provide the lampstand with oil. The lampstand appears to symbolize the temple, while the two olive trees symbolize God's anoninted leaders, including Zerubbabel. The golden olive oil aparently symbolizes the Spirit. The angel explains that the current ruler, Zerubbabel, will overcome huge obstacles and complete the temple. This will be accomplished, he continues, not by power or might, but by the Spirit of God (4:6).

Next Zechariah sees a huge flying scroll (5:1–4), pronouncing judgment on thieves and those who lie. Part of the postexilic message was a call to live obediently in conformance to the ethical demands of the law.

✦ Western culture probably derived its traditional portrayal of angels as women with wings from Zechariah 5:9, although this text does not explicitly identify these women as angels.

The seventh vision (5:5–11) is somewhat humorous. The Hebrew word for "iniquity, wickedness" is a feminine conjugated word, so this vision uses a woman to symbolize iniquity. She is stuffed into a basket and then flown to Babylon, symbolizing the cleansing of the land and the removal of iniquity.

Zechariah's final vision (6:1–8) is of four horse-drawn chariots (similar to the four horsemen of the opening vision), patrolling the world with power emanating from the Presence of God. This vision probably anticipates the coming day of the Lord, when justice will be established throughout the world.

Zechariah's Vision of the Four Chariots by Gustav Doré.

A symbolic crowning of the high priest (6:9–15)

Zechariah is instructed to crown the high priest, thus uniting the priesthood with the royal office for the task of rebuilding the temple. This probably also foreshadows the dual role of the coming Messiah (Jesus) as priest and king.

A call to live by justice (7:1–14)

In similar fashion to Jeremiah, Micah, and the other prophets, in this passage God tells his people he is much more concerned with true justice—especially to the weak ones in the society—than he is with meaningless rituals. Thus Zechariah continues to call people to do justice, a theme that has been consistent throughout the Prophets.

Future restoration (8:1–23)

This chapter is filled with the main prophetic themes about the future restoration: the return of the Presence of God (8:3) and the regathering of the people, accompanied by peace and prosperity (8:4–13) and the inclusion of the nations of the world into those who seek and worship God (8:20–23).

✚ In the New Testament (Rev. 6:1–8) the apostle John also sees a vision of four horsemen, but John's horsemen bring judgment while Zechariah's horsemen report peace.

The Coming Messiah (9:1–14:21)

Oracle 1: The advent and rejection of the Coming One (9:1–11:17)

While this unit starts off with judgment on the nations (9:1–8), it quickly shifts to a description of the Coming King, the one who will bring about the great restoration. This king comes in great power, establishing peace. Ironically, he also comes in great humility ("riding on a donkey"). Zechariah 10 continues with themes of regathering.

Yet in Zechariah 11:4–17 an unthinkable thing happens—the people reject this great glorious Shepherd that God has sent to save them, an event similar to the rejection of the Servant of the Lord in Isaiah 53. Fittingly, this section, which spoke so much of hope and restoration, ends instead in judgment (11:15–17).

Oracle 2: The advent and acceptance of the Coming One (12:1–14:21)

Picking up the central theme in the Book of the Twelve (the Minor Prophets), Zechariah's final unit focuses on the day of the Lord. God rescues Jerusalem and smites her enemies (12:1–9). The people respond with mourning and repentance (12:10–14). God then forgives them and cleanses them from their sin, also removing the last vestiges of idolatry and false prophecy (13:1–6). This restoration climaxes in the restatement of the covenant formula that has bound God's people to him throughout the Old Testament: "They will call on my name and I will answer them; I will say, 'They are my people,' and they will say, 'The Lord is our God'" (13:9). The final chapter of Zechariah continues describing the climactic day of the Lord, a time of deliverance for God's people but a time of judgment on God's enemies. The final verses focus on sanctifying ("making holy") everything in Jerusalem and Judah, probably a reference to the future sanctifying work of Jesus by which all people who are in him are made holy (sanctified).

So What? Applying Zechariah to Our Lives Today

Zechariah is filled with numerous prophetic references to the Messiah that were fulfilled by Jesus Christ. This should help to convince us, beyond a shadow of a doubt, that Jesus was indeed the Messiah promised by God through the Old Testament prophets. Zechariah also gives us numerous guidelines for our day-to-day lives. He points out that the important accomplishments of life are not done by human might or power, but by God's Spirit. Zechariah reminds us of the close association between God's holiness, his Presence, and his power made available to us. In addition, Zechariah

✦ In the New Testament Jesus enters Jerusalem on a donkey (Matt. 21:4–5; John 12:14–15), fulfilling the prophecy in Zechariah 9:9.

echoes the ever-present prophetic theme of social justice, admonishing us to "administer true justice; show mercy and compassion to one another. Do not oppress the widow or the fatherless, the alien or the poor. In your hearts do not think evil of each other" (7:9–10).

Our Favorite Verse in Zechariah

So he said to me, "This is the word of the Lord to Zerubbabel: 'Not by might nor by power, but by my Spirit,' says the Lord Almighty." (4:6)

In Zechariah 4 the prophet describes a vision involving two olive trees. Olive trees are still grown today throughout the Middle East.

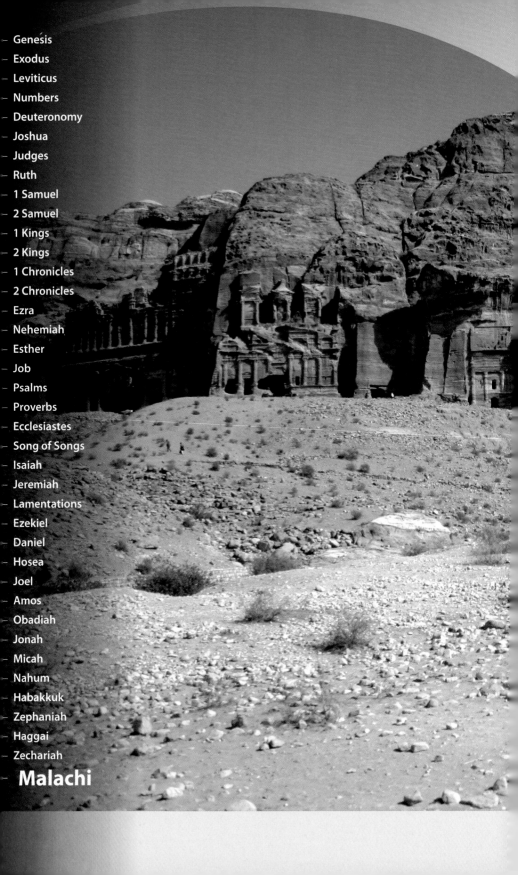

Malachi

Connecting the Old Testament to the New Testament

Malachi is the last book in the Old Testament, but it brings the Old Testament to a close only with a comma, and not a period. That is, Malachi points forward to the coming day of the Lord, and he declares that the prophet Elijah will signal the inauguration of that day. We then turn the page from Malachi to Matthew, and soon John the Baptist shows up, whom the New Testament associates with Elijah. Thus there is very little break between the Prophets (as concluded by Malachi) and the Gospels, which describe the fulfillment of the prophetic message.

Who Is Malachi?

The name Malachi means "my messenger." This word is used to mean "my messenger" in Malachi 3:1. Some scholars have suggested that the name of the book should be "My Messenger," but in light of the parallel with the other prophetic books, it is probably best to view Malachi as the proper name of the prophet—a proper name with a significant meaning.

What Is the Setting for Malachi?

Unlike Haggai, Malachi does not contain any historical superscriptions that tie his ministry to the reign of a certain king. Thus it is difficult to date Malachi with precision. However, the situation that Malachi appears to address in his book seems very similar to the situation that Nehemiah encountered. If Malachi was indeed a contemporary with Nehemiah, then the setting for his book is about 430 BC, or ninety years after Haggai and Zechariah.

What Is at the Heart of the Book of Malachi?

Malachi, along with Haggai and Zechariah, addresses the postexilic community—those Israelites who have returned to Jerusalem and the surrounding areas after the Babylonian captivity. Some may have thought that this return was the great and glorious restoration that the earlier prophets had predicted, but the postexilic prophets (Malachi, Haggai, Zechariah) disagree and remind everyone that the great day of the Lord still lay primarily in the future, even though the return of the exiles could be viewed as the early beginnings of God's unfolding plan of restoration.

Malachi is particularly concerned with how Israel will live and worship God in the meantime, while they await the coming day of the Lord. Thus Malachi speaks strongly against the corrupt forms of worship and living that were occurring in his time—unacceptable sacrifices, corrupt priests, refusal to tithe and support the temple, and social injustice. The book of Malachi is structured around six dialogues between God and the Israelites in Jerusalem. Thus the outline for Malachi can be viewed as follows:

- Dialogue 1: The Lord's Love for Israel (1:1–5)
- Dialogue 2: The Corruption of the Priesthood (1:6–2:9)
- Dialogue 3: Unfaithfulness—Divorce and Marrying Pagans (2:10–16)
- Dialogue 4: When Will God Bring Justice? (2:17–3:5)
- Dialogue 5: Will You Rob God? (3:6–12)
- Dialogue 6: Deliverance for the Righteous, Judgment for the Wicked (3:13–4:3)
- Conclusion: Obey and Wait (4:4–6)

✚ Like bookends, the theme of God's faithful love opens (Hosea 1–3) and closes (Mal. 1:2) the Minor Prophets (also called "the Book of the Twelve").

Ornate incense shovels like these were often used in temple worship to remove ash from incense burners. Malachi rebukes the priests of Jerusalem for corrupt, hypocritical, ritualistic worship.

What Makes Malachi Interesting and Unique?

- Malachi ends the Book of the Twelve with the same theme that began it—the love of God for his people.
- Malachi is structured around six dialogues or disagreements between God and his people.
- Malachi prophesies that Elijah will come again, signaling the inauguration of the day of the Lord.
- Malachi contains some of the strongest language against divorce in the Old Testament.
- In Malachi, God accuses Israel of "robbing God" because they did not tithe.

What Is Malachi's Message?

Dialogue 1: The Lord's Love for Israel (1:1–5)

The book of Malachi opens with a strong statement of God's love for his people. The people, however, having been through the exile, are skeptical,

✚ In Romans 9:13 Paul quotes Malachi 1:2–3 ("I have loved Jacob, but Esau I have hated") to prove that not everyone who has descended from Abraham physically is part of true Israel, but only those who are people of the promise.

and they ask for proof. God points out that Jacob and Esau were twins, but that the Edomites, the descendants of Esau, have totally disappeared, never to be restored, while Israel is back in the Promised Land, awaiting the wonderful future fulfillment of restoration.

Dialogue 2: The Corruption of the Priesthood (1:6–2:9)

One of Malachi's central concerns is for Israel to serve God faithfully and worship him correctly while they await the great coming restoration. Yet the priesthood has become corrupted, and worship practices have degenerated into sacrificing the poorest and weakest of animals, and then complaining about it. Thus even though Israel has put away idolatry and has reinstituted the worship of the Lord in the rebuilt temple, she quickly lost the point of worship and turned it into mere ritual, something she carried out reluctantly and without heart. In the second dialogue, God criticizes the priests and the people severely for this.

Dialogue 3: Unfaithfulness—Divorce and Marrying Pagans (2:10–16)

In this dialogue God addresses two practices related to marriage of which he does not approve. First of all, some of the Israelites were marrying outside the faith; that is, they were marrying the daughters of people who worshiped idols. God severely reprimands them for this. Intermarrying outside the faith, after all, is one of the things that led them into idolatry, resulting in the exile. The other practice that God objects to is divorce. Apparently among the Israelites divorce had become quite common. God speaks very strongly against this, declaring, "I hate divorce" (2:16).

Dialogue 4: When Will God Bring Justice? (2:17–3:5)

Since evil people continued to flourish, and the day of the Lord still had not come, some of the people grew cynical, asking sarcastically, "Where is the God of justice?" (2:17). God responds by saying that his messenger is indeed coming to prepare the way. But when "the day" comes, God declares, it will be a time of refining and purifying (3:1–4). It will also be a time of justice and judgment, but this judgment will be on sorcerers, adulterers, perjurers, and those who practice social injustice (not paying fair wages to workers, oppressing widows and orphans, depriving foreigners of justice, and not fearing God).

Elijah and John the Baptist

In Malachi 3:1 God promises to send his messenger to prepare the way before him. Then in 4:5 God declares that he will send Elijah just prior to the coming day of the Lord. The New Testament clearly associates John the Baptist with both of these prophecies, although there is a bit of confusion about the connection. Matthew, Mark, and Luke clearly associate the ministry of John the Baptist with the messenger of Malachi 3:1 (Matt. 11:10; Mark 1:2; Luke 7:27). In addition, Jesus appears to identify John the Baptist as the fulfillment of the Elijah prophecy of Malachi 4:5 (Matt. 11:11–14; Mark 9:11–13). John's connection to Elijah in Malachi 4:5 is so obvious that people ask him if he is Elijah (John 1:21), to which he replies in the negative, a truly puzzling response for us. Is he or isn't he Elijah? The answer to this problem may lie in Luke 1:17, where an angel of the Lord tells Zechariah that his son (John the Baptist) "will go on before the Lord, in the spirit and power of Elijah . . . to make ready a people prepared for the Lord." So John the Baptist apparently fulfills the Malachi 4:5 prophecy in that he embodies the "spirit and power" of Elijah. Therefore, Christ can identify him with the Elijah prophecy while John himself can deny that he is literally Elijah.

Dialogue 5: Will You Rob God? (3:6–12)

In this dialogue God accuses the postexilic community of robbing him. "How have we robbed you?" they ask (3:6–8). God declares that they have failed to bring their tithes to the temple, in violation of the Mosaic law. The operation of the temple and the very livelihood of the Levitical priesthood depended on the tithe of the people. Apparently they had abandoned this responsibility, probably assuming that this money was better spent if they spent it on themselves. God challenges them to test him by giving their tithe and seeing if he didn't bless them richly for it.

Dialogue 6: Deliverance for the Righteous, Judgment for the Wicked (3:13–4:3)

As seen throughout the book of Malachi, there were many people in Jerusalem who had turned away from God, cynically saying, "It is futile to serve God" (3:14). They just didn't see any immediate results, and they concluded that worshiping God was not worth their time or money. In this final dialogue God points out that the day of the Lord is definitely coming and will result in deliverance for those who revere his name, but will be a roaring fire of judgment on those arrogant ones who scoff at him.

Conclusion: Obey and Wait (4:4–6)

In this concluding short unit, Malachi tells the community to obey the laws given to Moses (Exodus, Leviticus, Numbers, Deuteronomy) and to wait expectantly for the coming of Elijah, who will signal the arrival of that great day of the Lord.

So What? Applying Malachi to Our Lives Today

Malachi offers us a lot of great applications. We can see how important it is to worship God truthfully, with a sincere heart, and not just ritually or hypocritically. Likewise, Malachi reminds us that failing to support the true worship of God is robbing from him. If we fail to tithe to our local churches, selfishly keeping this money for ourselves, it indicates that we are not worshiping God sincerely; indeed, we are stealing from him.

The book of Malachi also adds to the witness of the other biblical books that God's intention for marriage is that both man and wife stay

faithful to each other. Furthermore, Malachi also exhorts us to marry within the faith.

Finally, Malachi gives us encouragement to continue to look to the future expectantly. We should not be discouraged or become cynical just because the wicked are flourishing for a short while. We should trust in God's word through the prophets—he is working to bring about his kingdom and to establish justice throughout the world. The Lord will return and all things will be brought under his rule. Justice will be established, and God's people will be blessed beyond imagination.

Our Favorite Verse in Malachi

But for you who revere my name, the sun of righteousness will rise with healing in its wings. (4:2)

While Israel waits for the Messiah, they are to obey the laws and teaching (Torah) that God gave to Moses at Mount Horeb (Mount Sinai).

✚ The prophecy regarding Elijah in Malachi 4:5 at the very end of the Old Testament points to the ministry of John the Baptist at the beginning of the New Testament Gospels, thus forming a smooth connection from the Old Testament Prophets to the New Testament Gospels.

The History between the Old and New Testaments

The History of Palestine between the Old and New Testaments

James L. Johns

The Period in General

The interval between the Old and the New Testaments spans about four centuries, beginning in about 430 BC. During this period, the world's power center migrated from Asia to Europe. The Persian Empire collapsed under the attacks of the Macedonians, and over time the Greek Empire gave way to Roman rule.

The Persian Period

The Persian period extends from the end of the Old Testament story to 334 BC.

Due to a lack of Persian sources, much of our knowledge of events of the Persian Empire greatly depends on Greek historians. We have only scant references in external sources for the history of the Jews during this period.

In 539 BC Cyrus of Persia conquered Babylon and began to rule over its former territories. Cyrus's empire spread from Greece to India and from the Caucasus to Egypt. Cyrus allowed those Jews who so wished to return to Judea and rebuild their temple and capital city. Thereafter, Persian rule of Palestine was generally tolerant.

During the fourth century BC, Cyrus's Persian Empire began to crumble, and European power moved into Palestine for the first time.

The Greek Period

Alexander and the Diadochi

Philip II of Macedon began a new period in the history of Palestine after uniting the city-states of Greece and Macedonia. Philip's son, Alexander III ("the Great"), defeated Persia in battle, thus combining Egypt, Palestine, Syria, Asia Minor, Greece, and the Persian territory into an extensive empire. The expanded empire was administered following principles of the Greek *polis* (city-state), with Greece forming new cities and reshaping existing cities. This process of blending Greek culture with native cultures, "Hellenization," continued throughout the intertestamental period.

After Alexander's death in 323 BC, his empire was divided among his four generals, the Diadochi ("successors"). Most significant to Palestine were Ptolemy I, whose forces held Egypt and North Africa, and Seleucus Nicator (Seleucus I), whose armies secured Syria, Asia Minor, and Babylonia.

The Ptolemaic Period

The Ptolemaic kings governed Palestine from 323 to 198 BC, allowing the Jews to govern themselves and observe their religious customs. In 198 BC, however, Antiochus III, ruler of the Seleucids, defeated his Ptolemaic rival and annexed Palestine.

✦ Much of the history about Palestine during this period comes from 1–2 Maccabees. These books, written toward the end of the second century BC, are called deuterocanonical books (included in Catholic Bibles but not in Protestant Bibles).

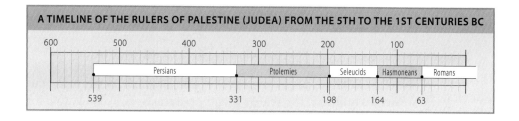

The Seleucid Period

Antiochus III continued the Ptolemies' policy of religious toleration. In 175 BC, however, Antiochus IV "Epiphanes" ("the manifest god") acceded to power, which began the most significant crisis of Second Temple Judaism before Pompey's invasion and the onset of Roman rule. Antiochus IV, along with others in Jerusalem, supported the radical Hellenization of Jerusalem. He outlawed Judaism, made pagan worship practices compulsory, and brought in foreign mercenaries to maintain order. An altar to the Syrian god, Zeus, was erected in the temple. By 167 BC, animals forbidden by Mosaic law were sacrificed on the altar, and prostitution was sanctioned in the temple precincts.

The Maccabean-Hasmonean Period

A priestly family named Hasmonean after one of its ancestors, consisting of a man named Mattathias and his five sons, raised a revolt that proved successful after a severe struggle. (This family was also called Maccabees—from the nickname "Maccabeus" ["the Hammer"] given to Judas, one of Mattathias's sons.)

Mattathias and his sons rallied a guerilla army, including at first the Hasideans (Hasidim), waging war against the Syrians and attacking Jews who had abandoned Torah observance. Antiochus IV revoked the prohibitions against Torah observance. Judas Maccabeus and his revolutionaries defeated the Syrians, recaptured the temple, and purged it of pagan trappings in 164 BC.

The Hasmonean dynasty degenerated through a series of unfit kings. The political aims of the Hasmoneans alienated many former supporters, including the Hasideans, who split into the Pharisees and the Essenes. The aristocratic supporters of the Hasmonean priest-kings became the Sadducees. Toward

Alexander the Great (AD 300).

the end of the Hasmonean dynasty the Pharisees basically dominated the country.

The Hasmonean dynasty ended in civil strife. In 67 BC, a war broke out between two brothers, Hyracanus II and Aristobulus II, each fighting for the title of high priest and king. Both appealed to Rome to settle the issue, effectively inviting the Roman general Pompey to conquer Jerusalem in 63 BC and bring Judea under direct Roman administration.

The Roman Period

Under its emperors, Roman culture remained Greek, with the distinctive Roman contributions of central administration and the promise of peace through superior force.

Antiochus III.

Pompey, the Roman general who seized control of Jerusalem and the surrounding area, delegated much of the former Hasmonean territory to the nearby Roman governor of Syria, and after conferring only the title of high priest on Hyracanus II, appointed an Idumean (a descendant of Esau) named Antipater and his sons, Phasel and Herod, as governors of Judea and Galilee. Hyracanus II's years of limited religious rule ended with defeat by the Parthians. In turn, Rome defeated the Parthians, and then confirmed Herod ("the Great") as ruler in 37 BC, even calling him king.

During these early years of Roman control, Rome was generally quite tolerant of Judaism. In addition, Roman power provided a period of relative peace for the region. However, throughout the period of Roman domination, sporadic Jewish resistance movements emerged.

Antiochus IV.

Herod was an efficient ruler and a clever politician. He kept Rome satisfied, thus providing stability against external forces. Among his many building projects, perhaps his greatest contribution to the Jews was the expansion and beautification of the temple in Jerusalem. Herod is also known for promoting Hellenistic (Greek) culture throughout his realm. Herod's reign was filled with internal political intrigue, plots, murders, wars, and brutality until his death in 4 BC. Lacking their father's ability and ambition, Herod's sons ruled over separate parts of Palestine into the New Testament period.

✚ Synagogues are not mentioned in the Old Testament, yet during the intertestamental period Sabbath worship in local synagogues becomes a central, defining feature of Judaism.

The New Testament

The Setting for the New Testament

Grant R. Osborne

The New Testament cannot be understood deeply without knowing the political, social, and religious world into which it was sent. Galatians 4:4 says, "When the time had fully come, God sent his Son." The purpose here is to describe "the fullness of times" God chose—the actual political, social, and religious setting in which the New Testament came into existence.

The Political Setting

The Jewish Political Setting

The Old Testament period ended with the Assyrian and Babylonian exiles and the return from exile in the sixth to the fifth centuries BC. The intertestamental period (see "The History between the Old and New Testaments" in this volume) changed Judaism from a temple-centered, hierarchical religion to a more democratic religion with synagogues for worship and teaching (developed during the Persian period to stand for the temple that had been destroyed). The synagogues had lay leaders who taught Torah and developed the "oral tradition," a set of rules meant to "build a fence around the law" and help the people to obey the Torah in the vastly different culture of 400 BC to AD 70. The primary leaders became the scribes and Pharisees (who developed from the Hasidim of the intertestamental period) and the Sadducees (who developed from the Hasmoneans or aristocrats of that period).

At the top of the political ladder under the Romans was the Herodian family. Herod the Great was the son of Antipater, an Idumean Arab made procurator by the Romans. Herod brought peace to the land and began rebuilding the incredible Jerusalem temple in 46 BC, but he also built Roman temples and entire Roman cities in Palestine (e.g., Caesarea Maritima) and brought a new level of Hellenistic culture to Palestine, a process that had begun under the Ptolemies in the third century BC. When King Herod died in 4 BC his kingdom was divided between three surviving sons: Archelaus (ethnarch of Judea, Samaria, Idumea), Antipas (tetrarch of Galilee, Perea), and Philip (tetrarch of Iturea, Trachonitis). Archelaus was a brutal ruler who was deposed and replaced by prefects (like Pilate). Antipas was a better ruler and is known for the execution of John the Baptist and for taking part in the trial of Jesus (Luke 23:7–12). Herod Agrippa II, a grandson, took part in Paul's trial before Festus in Acts 25–26.

The high priest by this time had become the religious and civic leader of the Jews. He presided over the Sanhedrin in Jerusalem, a council of seventy-one members that was both the congress and the supreme court of the people. The major groups were the Sadducees (among whom were the "chief priests" or priestly aristocracy), the scribes (trained experts in Torah, many of

✝ Many things that appear in the New Testament but not in the Old Testament developed during the intertestamental period (e.g., the Pharisees).

whom were Pharisees), and elders (the lay nobility). They decided religious, civic, and political issues that concerned the Jewish people (the Romans allowed them that authority). Legally, they had little authority in Galilee, a separate administrative region, but within Judaism they had influence even in diasporate lands (e.g., in Acts 9:1–2 when they authorized Paul to take the persecution of Christians into Syria).

At the local level the synagogues had great influence. The "ruler of the synagogue" was the head official, though he tended to be a patron given an honorary position. The presiding officer was the "attendant" who would do the administrative work and train the children. It was governed by three "elders" or lay leaders from the congregation. The synagogue was not only the center of instruction but was the core of the civic life of the community and the judicial center where discipline was ministered in civil affairs. Offenders were disciplined by flogging (Acts 5:40) and by excommunication (John 9:34).

The Greco-Roman Political Setting

While Rome dominated the first-century world politically, Greek ideas and mores dominated culturally. So we call this the Greco-Roman world. It dominated the region from Spain to the Euphrates and from Gaul (and Britain) to Northern Africa. Still, the *Pax Romana* (Roman peace) was guaranteed by the sword, and *ius gladii* (the law of the sword) controlled the lands. From the time of Augustus (Julius Caesar's nephew, Octavian, who destroyed the Roman Republic in honor of his assassinated uncle), Rome divided its lands into two kinds of provinces: senatorial (nonmilitary, ruled by a proconsul under the senate) and imperial (military, ruled by a procurator, answerable to the emperor). The emperor controlled the military and foreign policy; the Roman senate established the civic laws and had judicial authority.

Rome was the center of western government, Antioch the center of eastern rule. Each province was led by a governor of senatorial rank, with local officials in each small district responsible for taxation and civil affairs. Roman direct taxes were of two types—a land tax centered on the size and produce of the land (often with ten magistrates appointed to oversee its collection), and a poll tax of usually 1 percent for all subject peoples outside Italy. In addition, there were indirect taxes on transported goods, on goods sold, or on inheritances. As in the New Testament, they normally chose nationals who were called "publicans" for collecting taxes. These publicans would frequently misuse their authority to defraud people, and thus were extremely unpopular.

✚ The *Pax Romana* allowed Christian missionaries to travel freely and efficiently across the Roman Empire with the gospel.

The Social Setting

The Jewish Social Setting

There was not as much social stratification in the Jewish world as in the Roman world. At the top were the chief priests and their families, the aristocratic elders, and the wealthy landowners. There was no middle class in the Roman world, but still some were better off than others, such as merchants and even fishermen. The Sadducees mainly belonged to the upper class, the Pharisees either the upper portion of the lower class or (if there was one) the middle class. Most others—small farmers, tenant farmers, day laborers, freedmen—formed the lower class. There were actually more Jewish people outside Palestine (called the Diaspora) than inside the land. Jews had been deported at several different junctures—millions during the two exiles, many more conscripted into the armies of both the Ptolemies and the Saleucids during the Greek period of rule, thousands deported by Pompey the Great when Rome took over in 63 BC, and many others moving simply because of the poverty of Judea and the economic advantages elsewhere. In these foreign lands some Jews remained thoroughly Jewish, with little interaction outside their communities, but many others like Philo of Alexandria or Josephus participated in Hellenistic culture and wrote to commend Judaism to the Greco-Roman world. In those communities, the synagogues became the social as well as religious centers of Jewish life, and the laws of purity, food, and Sabbath kept most of the people thoroughly Jewish.

The Greco-Roman Social Setting

Roman society was stratified, but not totally rigid. A small amount of social mobility was possible, say within the military, through the amalgamation of huge fortunes, or through marriage. For the most part, however, it was a settled way of life. At the top, of course, was the emperor and his family, and under him there were three upper classes. First was the *senatorial* order, with six hundred families in the first century, with wealth determined primarily by ownership of land in the form of large estates outside Rome, worked by slaves. The Romans believed only agriculture was truly honorable; commerce/trade was disreputable (but so profitable that many took part on the sly). To be in this class, one's total property had to be worth at least two hundred and fifty thousand denarii (one denarius was a single day's wage for a laborer). People in this class formed the magistrates of the empire, were tribunes in the legions, and held the highest offices in the empire (praetors,

✝ Jesus definitely came from a lower-class family.

provincial governors, judges). Second, the *equestrian* order (so named originally because they could ride to war on a horse) was the knights who owned land worth at least one hundred thousand denarii. They mostly differed from the class above them in that they were wealthy but had not engaged directly in military or political office. For the most part their wealth was also centered in large estates, and they held smaller administrative posts. Third, *decurions* were the aristocrats of the provinces (worth twenty-five thousand denarii) who received their wealth from land, commerce, manufacturing, or also inheritance. They served as the highest magistrates under Roman governors and formed a council of leaders in a province. The lower classes were far below these three groups. It is agreed there was no middle class as we know it, although there was a fair distinction between small landowners, general merchants (e.g., bakers, butchers, clothiers, etc.), soldiers, or craftsmen (like Paul) and the truly poor. The freedmen (called "plebs" if they were Roman citizens) were the poorest of the lot because they had no money and had to work as day laborers. Slaves often had a more comfortable life than freedmen.

The Roman social setting was ruled by two major social constructions. First, it was a patron-client society, as noted by Jesus when he said those with authority call themselves "Benefactors" (Luke 22:25). Phoebe in Romans 16:2 may well have been a patroness of Paul (see also Pilate as "Caesar's friend" in John 19:12). The patron was an upper-class person who became a sponsor and performed favors for those under him or her, giving them assistance when they needed it. Their clients owed them loyalty and service, showing gratitude and respect in many small ways. Patrons' reputations would be somewhat based on how many clients they had, the status these clients held in society, and how many praised their names in public. Second, the first-century world was an honor-shame society, which was at all times tied to the public regard for a person's actions and status in society. From birth the child was led to seek in all things a reputation that embodied the cultural values held high within the Roman world. This was a major source of problems in the early church, due somewhat to the differing standards within the Jewish and Hellenistic worlds, but due even more to the Christian worldview. For instance, Paul was mocked by the Corinthian leaders because he lacked the rhetorical skill (sophistry) they thought honorable; Paul's rejoinder was that he preferred the "foolishness" of the cross to all the "wisdom" of this world (1 Cor. 1:20–25). This is a powerful reminder that the honor of the world is shame to God.

The Religious Setting

The Jewish Religious Setting

There are two distinguishing aspects that separated the Jewish religion from all other religions of the ancient world: they worshiped the one and only God (monotheism versus polytheism), and the God they worshiped was the covenant God who had chosen, called, and loved them out of all the other nations. Moreover, he had given them a Promised Land and had returned them to that land after punishing them in the exile for their idolatry. God's faithfulness in spite of their unfaithfulness had led to the first period of time in their history (the four hundred years after returning from exile) in which they as a people had remained faithful to the Torah regulations and refused to go after other gods. They had become a people of the written law, and God's supreme gift was his revealed Word. The scribes and the Pharisees devoted themselves to its study and to developing a set of principles (the oral Torah) that would allow the common person to keep it. The people worshiped God every Sabbath in the temple (if they could) or the synagogue, a rectangular building with scrolls in recesses in the front and stone benches (or chairs) for the congregation. Speakers stood to read from the scrolls and sat to preach, and services consisted of reciting the Shema, prayer, the singing of psalms, readings, the sermon, and the benediction. Christian worship tended

✚ Jesus probably agreed more with the Pharisees theologically compared to the other religious groups, but he criticizes them for hypocrisy—that is, for not living out that theology consistently.

to follow this pattern. In addition, there were the religious festivals, with the religious calendar starting in March-April with Passover/Unleavened Bread followed by Pentecost (Festival of Weeks) fifty days later. In the month of Tishri (September-October) there were three festivals—Trumpets, Day of Atonement (Yom Kippur), and Tabernacles. In December came the one nonbiblical festival, Lights (Hanukkah, on the rededication of the temple in 164 BC), and in February-March there was Purim. The three main pilgrim festivals (with people coming from many diasporate lands) were Passover, Pentecost, and Tabernacles.

There were four primary religious groups: The *Pharisees* descended from the Hasidim of Maccabean times and were the lay teachers ("rabbis") from before Jesus's era who developed the oral tradition. They were deeply concerned about Sabbath observance, the food laws, and ritual purity in general. They believed the "oral Torah" originated alongside the written Torah and was binding. The *Sadducees* descended from the Hasmonean (Maccabean) aristocrats and counted most of the high priestly families among their numbers. They considered only the Torah as truly canonical, and they denied angels and the afterlife (often debating the Pharisees, as in Acts 23:6–10). They did not survive the destruction of the temple in AD 70. The *Essenes* are best known for their community at Qumran in the Dead Sea area where they produced the Dead Sea Scrolls. This was a monastic sect (though some followers were allowed to live in the towns) who sought to follow the Torah perfectly and believed mainstream Judaism was an apostate movement. Adherents had a one-year novice period followed by two years of probation and were expected to surrender all their belongings and live in the community. They believed God had predestined them to be the sole depositors of truth; they were the "children of light" while the rest of Judaism and the gentiles were "the children of darkness." Finally, the *Zealots* existed as a movement only in the years leading up to the revolt in AD 66 but had roots much further back (e.g., Simon the Zealot, Mark 3:18). Their zeal to overthrow the Romans was part of their "zeal" for the law and to free the Jews from pagan influence.

The Greco-Roman Religious Setting

The Greco-Roman religion was in many ways animistic, with the gods representing natural forces (e.g., Jupiter, the heavens; Juno, women; Apollo, music or youth; Diana, woods and the hunt). At the same time, it was mainly communal and corporate, as the cultic rituals were intended to hold society together. Unlike American religion, the stress was not on individual choice but on group participation in the sacred rites. Religious participation brought together the family, the polis, and national identity. There was no separation between church and state; religion permeated and united every aspect of life. Religion was also a contract between the deity and the person, with obligations on both sides. The rules for cultic life (how to pray, how to perform the sacrifices, etc.) ensured that both sides would do their part. The purpose was to influence the gods to work on behalf of the people. In all things they sought peace with the gods, and whenever troubles came they thought that the harmony had been somehow broken. The system of vows, prayers, and sacrifices was to maintain that proper relationship or to re-establish it if disaster had taken place.

The Greek pantheon was numerous and diverse, with detailed mythology to support the pantheon of the gods. The Roman gods were not as complex as the Greek deities; they had no marriage or offspring, no set of genealogical relationships, and no developed mythology. Therefore, when the Romans conquered the Greeks, they simply took over the Greek gods and identified their gods directly with the Greek gods. At the head of the gods was a supreme council of twelve: Jupiter/Zeus, Juno/Hera, Vesta/Hestia, Minerva/Athena, Ceres/Demeter, Diana/Artemis, Venus/Aphrodite, Mars/Ares, Mercury/Hermes, Neptune/Poseidon, Vulcan/Hephaestus, and Apollo (in both). Then there were earth gods and heroes. Prayers and sacrifices were intended to maintain relationships with the gods, who acted similar to patrons with clients in Greco-Roman Society. The philosophers had long doubted the existence of the gods, but at the same time the sense of civic and familial duty kept the allegiances alive.

In addition, both families and trades would have patron deities, so there arose the Roman cults, where groups would worship a single deity who then became their sponsor in life. The Romans were also open to new deities and new religious ideas, for example, the number who became "God-fearers" and embraced the Jewish religion. Also influential were the growing number of "mystery religions" (e.g., the cults of Isis, Demeter, Cybele, Mithra), which began in the New Testament times and became huge by the third century. Central was the view that the cycle of growth in the harvest represented the cycle of life, death, and especially the afterlife. Secret initiation rites (= mysteries) allowed adherents to rise above the earthly, unite with the deity, and achieve immortality. Some scholars have considered Christianity one of the mystery religions, but the differences are greater than the similarities.

✝ It's encouraging to know that Christianity first thrived and grew in a pluralistic culture with its many gods.

An Overview
of the Life of Christ

Mark L. Strauss

The Gospels do not give us precise dates for Jesus's birth or ministry, but approximations can be made. We know Jesus was born in the closing years of Herod the Great's reign (Matt. 2:1; Luke 1:5), and so sometime around 6–4 BC. (Our present calendar—developed in the sixth century by Dionysius Exiguus—was miscalculated by several years.) John the Baptist began preaching in the fifteenth year of Tiberius Caesar (Luke 3:1), which, depending on how it is calculated, could be either AD 26 or 29. The length of Jesus's public ministry, which began shortly after John's, is also uncertain. The three Synoptic Gospels (Matthew, Mark, and Luke) present a linear view that could fit all of the events into a single year. Jesus begins his ministry in Galilee and gradually moves southward to Jerusalem, where he is crucified at Passover. John's Gospel, however, has Jesus visiting Jerusalem regularly during various Jewish festivals. At least three Passovers are noted (John 2:13; 6:4; 11:55) together with other festivals (5:1; 7:2; 10:22). Since it was normal for a Galilean Jew to take such trips, scholars tend to view John's chronology as more precise, and calculate the length of Jesus's ministry as between two and a half and three and a half years, either AD 27–30 or AD 30–33.

✚ When Jesus died, he was between thirty-four and thirty-nine years of age (from 6–4 BC to AD 30 or 33).

The Birth and Childhood of Jesus

Two of the four Gospels, Matthew and Luke, provide accounts of Jesus's birth (Matthew 1–2; Luke 1–2). There are many parallels between the two: in both an angel announces before Jesus's birth that he will be the promised Messiah from the line of David; Mary is still a virgin when she becomes pregnant by the Holy Spirit; Jesus is born in Bethlehem, the hometown of King David (Mic. 5:2), but raised in Nazareth in Galilee. There are also important differences. Matthew's story focuses on Joseph, while Luke's on Mary. Matthew recounts the star that prompts the coming of the Magi, the attempt by Herod to kill Jesus, and the family's escape to Egypt. Luke parallels the birth of Jesus with that of John the Baptist, and describes the census of Caesar Augustus that brought Joseph and Mary to Bethlehem, Jesus's birth in a lowly stable, and the visit by the shepherds.

Both Matthew and Luke provide genealogies that confirm Jesus's credentials as the Messiah (Matt. 1:1–17; Luke 3:23–38). Matthew, however, traces Jesus's ancestry from Abraham to Jesus via the line of David's son Solomon. Luke's genealogy moves in the other direction, descending from Jesus through the line of Nathan, another son of David, all the way back to Adam. Various explanations have been proposed to explain how Jesus could have two genealogies. The traditional and simplest is that Matthew's contains Joseph's ancestors, while Luke's are those of Mary. Others suggest that Luke records the physical ancestry of Joseph while Matthew gives a legal or royal genealogy, or that Jesus had two lines because of an earlier levirate marriage (see Deut. 25:5–10). All such suggestions remain speculative.

Little is known about Jesus's childhood except for one story from Luke of a Passover visit to Jerusalem when Jesus was twelve. Jesus here demonstrates a growing awareness that God is his Father (Luke 2:40–52). Jesus likely had a rather ordinary childhood as a Jewish boy growing up in a conservative Israelite household. His father was a craftsman (*tekton*), a worker in wood, stone, or metal, and Joseph's sons followed him in this trade (Matt. 13:55; Mark 6:3). Jesus had four brothers—James, Joseph, Judas, and Simon—and at least two sisters (Mark 6:3).

Preparation for Ministry

All four Gospels precede Jesus's public ministry with that of John the Baptist. John is the beginning of the gospel, the prophetic bridge between the old covenant and the new. John came on the scene dressed in clothing reminiscent of the prophet Elijah and calling for repentance in light of the imminent judgment of God. He denied he was the Messiah, pointing instead to Jesus, the "Lamb of God" who would take away the sins of the world (John 1:29, 36). John announced he was merely a messenger and herald, preparing the way for the Lord (Isa. 40:3; Mal. 3:1). He baptized with water, but the Messiah would baptize with the Holy Spirit and with fire.

Two key events prepared Jesus for his messianic role. First, he submitted to John's baptism, identifying with the repentant people of God. When he came out of the water, a voice from heaven declared him to be the Son of God (Matt. 3:13–17 and parallels). Second, the Holy Spirit led him into the wilderness, where Satan tempted him for forty days. By resisting Satan's temptation to act in his own power and for his own good, Jesus proved he was ready to accomplish God's plan (Matt. 4:1–11 and parallels).

The Galilean Ministry

When John the Baptist was arrested (and eventually executed) by Herod Antipas, Jesus launched his public ministry. His message was, "The time has come. . . . The kingdom of God is near. Repent and believe the good news!" (Mark 1:15). In Jesus's preaching, the "kingdom of God" was the dynamic reign of God, his rule and authority over all things. God was in the process of restoring his fallen creation and calling a rebellious people back to himself.

The early part of Jesus's ministry was centered in the towns and villages around the Sea of Galilee. There he called his disciples, preached the kingdom of God, cast out demons, and healed the sick. The exorcisms demonstrated that the kingdom of God was assaulting and overwhelming Satan's authority in the world. Healing the sick previewed the restoration of creation predicted by Isaiah and the prophets, when the lame would walk, the blind would see, and the deaf would hear (Isa. 35:5–6). From his many followers, Jesus chose twelve, designating them as *apostles* ("messengers") and sending them out to preach and to heal (Mark 3:13–19). The number twelve is analogous to the twelve tribes of Israel and confirms that Jesus viewed his ministry in some sense as the restoration and renewal of the nation Israel.

While Jesus's reputation as a teacher and healer made him enormously popular among the common people of Galilee, he faced growing opposition from the religious authorities. His claims to divine authority, association with sinners and tax collectors, and apparent violations of the Sabbath law infuriated the Jewish religious leaders, who challenged his authority and accused him of blasphemy. The climax of the Galilean ministry came when, on an excursion to Caesarea Philippi, Jesus asked his disciples what they believed about him. Simon Peter, the frequent representative and spokesperson of the Twelve, said, "You are the Messiah!" From that point on Jesus began to teach them that his messianic mission was to go to Jerusalem to suffer and die (Matt. 16:13–23 and parallels). Jesus subsequently took his three closest disciples—Peter, James, and John—onto a mountain, where his appearance was radically changed in front of them (a transfiguration), briefly revealing his divine glory (Matt. 17:1–13 and parallels).

Last Days in Jerusalem

Although John's Gospel reveals that Jesus traveled often between Galilee and Judea, the Synoptics focus on this final journey as the defining moment of his life. Jesus came to Jerusalem with a purpose. On Palm Sunday, he rode into Jerusalem on a donkey from the Mount of Olives in fulfillment of Zechariah 9:9, his first public revelation as the Messiah. Entering the temple, he took a whip and drove out the moneychangers and sellers of sacrificial animals. The action was a symbolic judgment against Israel for turning God's temple into a marketplace and failing to be God's light to the nations. It was also a preview of Jerusalem's coming destruction. Such provocative actions could not go unchallenged, and during this week the Jerusalem religious authorities repeatedly confronted Jesus, challenging his authority and attempting to trap him in his words. Jesus responded, defeating them in debate and frustrating them further (Matthew 22–23 and parallels). Jesus also continued to teach his disciples, predicting Jerusalem's destruction and instructing them concerning

✛ Jesus's Galilean ministry centered in Capernaum, a city on the northwest shore of the Sea of Galilee. It was located on the *Via Maris*, an international trade route.

the events leading to the end of the age and his own return as the Son of Man (Matthew 24–25 and parallels).

The Passion of the Messiah

On Thursday evening, the last night before his crucifixion, Jesus brought his disciples together for a final meal. There he transformed the Jewish Passover into a new celebration—the Lord's Supper—a ritual where his disciples would eat bread and drink wine in remembrance of his sacrificial death on the cross. Jesus next took his disciples to the Garden of Gethsemane, an olive grove near Jerusalem, for a time of prayer. Judas, who had earlier agreed to betray Jesus, showed up with the religious leaders and a group of soldiers who took Jesus into custody.

In the hours that followed, Jesus was taken before the Jewish high court—the Sanhedrin—where he was accused of seeking to destroy the temple, of blasphemy, and of falsely claiming to be the Messiah. The high priest declared him guilty and pronounced a death sentence. The next morning they took Jesus to Pilate, the Roman governor of Judea, since the Sanhedrin did not have authority in capital cases. Pilate questioned Jesus and had him whipped, but found no reason to execute him. Yet the religious leaders persisted in their demands. Pilate, being an unscrupulous and self-serving ruler and fearing their influence with his superiors in Rome, eventually acceded to their demands and ordered Jesus to be crucified. Like other victims of crucifixion,

✚ Jesus's humiliating death powerfully fulfilled the prophecy about the suffering of the Lord's Servant in Isaiah 53.

Jesus died a horrific death of exhaustion, blood loss, and asphyxiation. His body was taken from the cross before the Sabbath began (Friday evening) and was laid in a new tomb owned by Joseph of Arimathea, a member of the Jewish high council.

The Resurrection of the Messiah

On Sunday morning, a group of women came to the tomb to anoint Jesus's body with spices as part of the burial process. Instead they found the tomb empty, the body gone, and an angel announcing that Jesus had risen from the dead. Jesus subsequently appeared to them, to the eleven disciples (Judas had committed suicide), and many others. The New Testament describes at least ten different resurrection appearances, compelling evidence that Jesus indeed rose from the dead (Matthew 28; Mark 16; Luke 24; John 20–21; 1 Cor. 15:3–8). The resurrection of Jesus is an essential foundation for the Christian faith, confirming (1) Jesus's claims about himself were true—claims to be the Messiah and the divine Son of God; (2) Jesus's death was an atoning sacrifice providing forgiveness for sins (Mark 10:45); and (3) we, like Jesus, will be raised in an immortal and imperishable body (1 Cor. 15:35–49).

What Is a Gospel? And Why Are There Four Gospels?

Mark L. Strauss

One of the first things readers opening their Bibles will notice is there are four books at the beginning of the New Testament that tell the same basic story. These "Gospels"—Matthew, Mark, Luke, and John—all recount the life and ministry of Jesus, climaxing with his death and resurrection. The first three Gospels—Matthew, Mark, and Luke—are known as the "Synoptic" (meaning "viewed together") Gospels, because they contain many of the same stories and recount the same basic chronology of Jesus's life. The fourth Gospel—John—is very different, with its own distinct style and with mostly unique content about Jesus.

So what is a Gospel? The English word "gospel" is a translation of the Greek word *euangelion*, which means "good news." It was the term chosen by the early Christians to describe the good news of salvation available through Jesus the Messiah (cf. Isa. 52:7). Christians first used it to refer to the spoken message about Jesus. In one of his earliest letters, the apostle Paul writes to the young church at Thessalonica that "our gospel (*euangelion*) came to you not simply with words, but also with

✦ We use the term "gospel" to refer both to written documents in our New Testament (i.e., Matthew, Mark, Luke, and John) and to the message about Jesus's life, death, and resurrection.

485

power, with the Holy Spirit and with deep conviction" (1 Thess. 1:5). The gospel is the message of the salvation accomplished through the life, death, and resurrection of Jesus Christ. In this sense there is only one gospel, one message of God's salvation that is now available to all people everywhere. In time, the word *euangelion*, "gospel," came to be used not just of the oral preaching of this message, but for the written accounts of the story of Jesus—the four "Gospels." The term was appropriate since these are not merely history books or biographies of a great man. They are joyful announcements of the great news that God has intervened in human history to fix what is broken and to bring hope and reconciliation to his people.

The question, then, naturally rises, "Why are there four Gospels, instead of one?" The reasons are both historical and theological. Each of the Gospels was written to communicate certain truths about the life and ministry of Jesus. Some scholars think each Gospel was written to a particular Christian community to meet the needs of that community. Others claim that the Gospel writers wrote more generally to the whole church. Whichever view is correct (the answer is probably somewhere in between), there is no doubt that each Gospel tells the story of Jesus in its own way and focuses on unique aspects of his identity and mission. Matthew, for example, is the most Jewish of the Gospels, stressing Jesus's role as the Jewish Messiah who came to fulfill the Old Testament prophecies (Matt. 1:1). Mark stresses Jesus's role as the Suffering Servant, whose sacrificial death paid the ransom price for our sins (Mark 10:45). Jesus's disciples are called to take up their own cross and follow Jesus through suffering to victory (8:34). Luke stresses that Jesus is the Savior of the world, who through his death and resurrection brought salvation and reconciliation to all people everywhere, whatever their race, gender, or social status (Luke 3:6; 19:10). The Gospel of John presents Jesus as the divine Son of God, who came to reveal the Father and to provide eternal life to all who believe in him (John 1:18; 3:16).

Of course the four Gospels have many more commonalities than differences. All four present Jesus as the Messiah and Son of God, who fulfills the prophecies of the Old Testament. In all four he is the Savior of the world, whose death on the cross provides salvation and resurrection life for all who believe in him. Yet each Gospel's content, style, themes, and purpose provide a unique angle and perspective. Like the many facets of a beautiful diamond, the four Gospels fill out and enrich our knowledge of Jesus and the salvation available through him.

✝ Luke admits in the beginning of his Gospel that he used other written sources, such as Mark and possibly Matthew (see Luke 1:1–4).

The Synoptic Problem

MATTHEW C. WILLIAMS

The "Synoptic problem" is the phrase used to explain how Matthew, Mark, and Luke agree, yet disagree, in three main areas: content, wording, and order.

In terms of *content*, about 90 percent of Mark's material is found in Matthew, while about 50 percent is found in Luke. In addition, nearly 235 verses in Matthew and Luke are similar. When Jesus's three-year ministry is considered, it is surprising that Matthew, Mark, and Luke—the Synoptic ("seen together") Gospels—often narrate the same events. Compared to John, the Synoptic Gospels have much in common. Why do we not find more unique stories in each of the Synoptics, such as we find in John's Gospel?

In the places where there is agreement in content, there are sometimes incredible similarities in the precise *wording*, even down to the same tense and mood of Greek words. Since Jesus probably spoke in Aramaic, these similarities are even more astounding because the Gospels were written in Greek. These similarities are not only found in the words of Jesus, but in descriptions of events. The Gospel writers sometimes have identical parenthetical material, which was not spoken by Jesus ("let the reader understand" in Mark 13:14 = Matt. 24:15). Despite these similarities, each Gospel writer also has his favorite vocabulary, themes, and emphases. Some "parallel" passages have very little in common, with each Gospel writer choosing his own unique words to describe an event.

Alternating agreement and disagreement in *order* between the three Gospels is also surprising. Sometimes the Synoptics have many passages in the same order. This similarity is all the more striking because many passages are gathered together for thematic reasons and are not chronological. For instance, the flashback to the death of John the Baptist would probably not be located in the exact order in two Gospels on the basis of oral tradition because it interrupts the story's chronological flow (Mark 6:17–29 = Matt. 14:3–12). At other times, though, there is very little agreement on order.

Keeping in mind that any solution must do justice to both these similarities and differences, there are various explanations to this Synoptic problem. Many scholars feel that there is no viable solution to the Synoptic problem. We simply do not have enough information to decode how they relate to one another.

Others think that oral traditions can account for the similarities found in the Synoptics, and suggest that there are no literary relationships. But what is the probability that three different authors often chose the exact same words and word order to describe events from Jesus's life? Oral tradition would also struggle to explain phrases that seem to be parenthetical, such as "he said to the paralyzed man" (Luke 5:24) or "let the reader understand" (Mark 13:14).

As a result, the majority of scholars hold to some kind of a literary relationship between the Synoptics—thinking that the authors, under the inspiration of the Spirit, used the other Gospels as a written source when they wrote their own Gospel. Though the solutions are myriad, the main literary solutions can easily be summarized.

✦ The Jewish people were extremely careful about passing down their stories accurately.

Markan priority proposes that Mark wrote first, and that Matthew and Luke used Mark independently as a written source when they wrote their Gospels. Some of the Markan priority solutions posit a "Q" source to account for the occasional similarities between Matthew and Luke; thus receiving the name "Two-Source Hypothesis" (Mark and Q are the literary sources) or "Four-Source Hypothesis" (Mark, Q, M [Matthean material], L [Lucan material]). The main line of evidence for Markan priority is that it seems Matthew and Luke have improved upon Mark's grammar and vocabulary in many places.

Other Markan priority proponents have eliminated the need for a Q source by suggesting that Mark was written first, followed by Matthew and then Luke, who used both Mark and Matthew as literary sources.

The Two Gospel (or Griesbach) Hypothesis suggests that Matthew was written first, Luke then used Matthew, and Mark then used both Matthew and Luke. This theory easily accounts for the "minor agreements" between Matthew and Luke.

The relationship of the Gospels to one another is not trivial but quite relevant for matters of apologetics, exegesis, and the theology of the individual Gospels. Any of the views are viable; the main question is which is more probable.

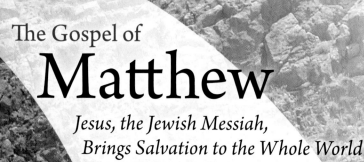

The Gospel of
Matthew

*Jesus, the Jewish Messiah,
Brings Salvation to the Whole World*

I f you had been a Christian living in the earliest years of the church, you probably would have learned about the life and teachings of Jesus through the Gospel of Matthew. This Gospel was the most widely read of all the Gospels during those early days, and it still speaks powerfully to us today. Matthew is a comprehensive Gospel, telling us first and foremost about Jesus Christ but also about God's master plan, about the new community of faith called the church, about how we are supposed to relate to one another, and about our mission in this world. Matthew touches on almost all of life. As you read and study Matthew, you can expect God to speak to you about many things from various angles.

Who Wrote Matthew?

Early church tradition unanimously connects this Gospel to Matthew/Levi, the tax collector who became a disciple of Jesus (Matt. 10:3; Mark 3:18; Luke 6:15; Acts 1:13). Early copies of this Gospel carry a title that attributes it to Matthew. In addition, the early Christian leader Papias

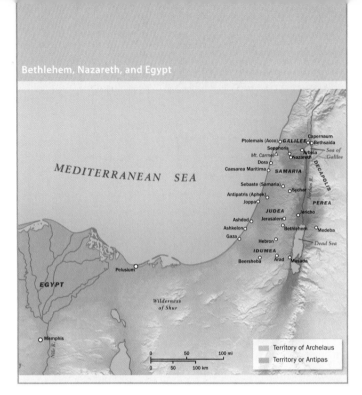

(bishop of Hieropolis in Asia Minor in the early second century) said that "Matthew composed (or compiled) the *logia* (oracles or sayings or even a gospel) in the Hebrew (or Aramic) language (or style) and everyone interpreted (or translated) them as best they could" (Eusebius, *Hist. eccl.* 3.39.16). Although the exact wording of Papias's statement is much debated by scholars (as you can tell by all the parentheses), it does attribute an important early Christian writing to Matthew.

The traditional conclusion that Matthew is the author of this Gospel makes sense of a lot of material within the book. The Gospel is the only one to refer to "Matthew the tax collector" (10:3), perhaps a subtle reference to God's redemptive grace in his life. The story of Matthew's call to follow Jesus is found in Matthew 9:9–13. Both Mark (2:14–17) and Luke (5:27–32) refer to him as Levi, suggesting that he was commonly known by two names (like Simon and Cephas or Peter). We find an emphasis on money themes in this Gospel (17:24–27; 18:23–25; 20:1–16; 26:15; 27:3–5; 28:11–15). For instance, this is the only Gospel to tell the story of Jesus paying the temple tax. The book is skillfully organized and structured as one might expect from a tax collector (like an accountant today?). It remains unlikely the early Christians would have ascribed this Gospel to a disciple with such a blemished background unless they had good reason for doing so.

Who Is Matthew's Audience?

Matthew is the most Jewish of the four Gospels. We read about Jewish customs without any explanation (e.g., 15:2; 17:24–27; 23:5, 27), and the book itself is organized into five major teaching sections (or discourses) reminding readers of the famous first five books of the Old Testament, the Pentateuch.

✤ Throughout his Gospel, Matthew uses expressions such as "this was to fulfill what was spoken through the prophet" (or something similar) to indicate how the story of Jesus fulfills the Old Testament story.

Interestingly, this Gospel shares much in common with the letter of James, another early Jewish-Christian document. For these and other reasons, most believe that Matthew is writing for a Jewish-Christian community (or at least a mixed community of Jewish and gentile Christians) that is in the process of breaking with Judaism. Matthew is very concerned to show that Jesus is the long-awaited Jewish Messiah who fulfills God's promises made to Israel. Many of Matthew's readers would have been involved in conflict with the larger Jewish community, and he wants to reassure them that God's true people follow Jesus the Messiah. Most evangelical scholars believe that Matthew relies on Mark's Gospel (the testimony of the apostle Peter) to some degree and that he wrote shortly after Mark (dated in the early to mid-60s).

What Is at the Heart of Matthew's Gospel?

Matthew's main concern is to show that Jesus is the true King and Messiah. From the very beginning Jesus is revealed as the "Christ (Messiah), the son of David, the son of Abraham" (Matt. 1:1). Matthew wants to show that this new movement within Judaism (eventually identified as Christianity) *is* authentic Judaism because these people are following the true Messiah— Jesus of Nazareth. Jesus is the Jewish Messiah, but he also fulfills God's plan to bring salvation to the nations, and the Gospel ends with a commission to "make disciples of all nations" (Matt. 28:19).

Matthew's first readers probably needed encouragement to endure persecution, to stay strong in their faith, and to take this good news of Jesus to the nations. No wonder the Gospel of Matthew was extremely popular in the early church.

The outline below shows how the book is arranged in five discourses or teaching units surrounded by teachings on who Jesus is and what it means to follow him.

- Introduction: The Birth and Childhood of the Messiah (1:1–2:23)
- Jesus's Preparation for Public Ministry (3:1–4:25)
- Discourse 1: Sermon on the Mount (5:1–7:29)
- Jesus's Messianic Authority Demonstrated (8:1–9:38)
- Discourse 2: The Mission of the Messiah (10:1–42)
- Opposition to Jesus the Messiah and His Mission (11:1–12:50)
- Discourse 3: Parables of the Kingdom (13:1–52)
- Jesus's Identity as the Messiah Is Revealed (13:53–16:20)
- Jesus, the Crucified and Risen Messiah (16:21–17:27)
- Discourse 4: The Community of the Messiah (18:1–35)

- Jesus Teaches on True Discipleship (19:1–20:34)
- Jesus Teaches on False Discipleship (21:1–23:39)
- Discourse 5: The Mount of Olives (or Olivet) Discourse (24:1–25:46)
- Jesus's Crucifixion, Resurrection, and Great Commission (26:1–28:20)

What Makes Matthew Interesting and Unique?

- Of the Synoptics (Matthew, Mark, Luke), Matthew was the most popular Gospel in the early centuries of the church because it had a direct connection to an apostle (Mark and Luke were not written by apostles, and John was written a few years later).
- The book of Matthew is recognized as the most Jewish of the four Gospels.
- Jesus is featured as the Teacher and organizes his teaching into five long teaching discourses: Sermon on the Mount (5–7), The Mission of the Messiah (10), Parables of the Kingdom (13), The Community of the Messiah (18), and the Mount of Olives (or Olivet) Discourse (24–25). The phrase "when Jesus had finished saying these things . . ." (or something very similar) comes at the end of all five discourses.
- This five-discourse structure may have reminded readers of the first five books of the Old Testament, depicting Jesus as the new Moses.
- The Sermon on the Mount (Matthew 5–7) includes many of Jesus's most famous teachings.
- Matthew emphasizes Jesus and his teachings as the true fulfillment of the Old Testament law and prophecies.

The remains of the Herodium, the fortress Herod built near Bethlehem.

✚ Matthew is more about Jesus's words while Mark is more about Jesus's actions.

- This Gospel stresses Jesus as the Son of David, King, the Christ (or Messiah), the Son of God, and Lord.
- Jesus strongly denounces the current Jewish religious leaders.
- Matthew uses the phrase "kingdom of heaven" more than the more common "kingdom of God" we find in the other Gospels, perhaps as a common Jewish way to avoid pronouncing the divine name.
- In spite of being considered the most Jewish Gospel, Matthew also emphasizes the Christian mission to the gentiles.
- The book concludes with a clear statement of the Great Commission (28:16–20).
- This is the only Gospel to mention the "church" directly (16:16–20; 18:15–20).

What Is Matthew's Message?

Introduction: The Birth and Childhood of the Messiah (1:1–2:23)

Matthew highlights how the birth and childhood of Jesus fulfill Scripture. Five times in chapters 1–2 he cites the Old Testament (1:22–23; 2:5, 15, 17–18, 23). He is presenting Jesus as the fulfillment of Israel's hope, the long-awaited Messiah.

Jesus is the Christ, son of David, son of Abraham (1:1–17)

See Luke 3:23–38. Matthew opens with an enormously important theological statement about Jesus. He is "the Christ" or Messiah, the one sent by God to restore Israel and establish God's kingdom. To clarify that Jesus is the Jewish Messiah, Matthew adds "son of David" (the greatest king of Israel) and "son of Abraham" (the father of the Jewish nation). Jesus's ancestry or genealogy is arranged in three groups of fourteen, perhaps because the numerical equivalent of the name "David" in Hebrew was fourteen. Matthew presents Jesus's legal genealogy through Joseph to show that Jesus has a right to David's throne. But biologically, Matthew makes it clear that only Mary was Jesus's human parent (the word "whom" following Mary in 1:16 is feminine). The purpose of a genealogy (or ancestry) in the ancient world was to show a person's social standing and status. Jesus's connection to this hall-of-fame list of Old Testament characters certainly conveys his importance. But Matthew also includes four women, and somewhat controversial women at that—Tamar, Rahab, Ruth, and Bathsheba. Perhaps he wants us to know that Jesus came to be the Savior of all kinds of people, including people with scandalous personal histories.

✦ Both Matthew's and Luke's genealogies help to show that Jesus is the long-awaited messianic king in the line of King David (cf. 2 Sam. 7:11–16; Isa. 9:1–7).

The virginal conception of Jesus (1:18–25)

See Luke 2:1–7. Mary and Joseph are pledged or betrothed, meaning they have entered a legally binding arrangement that would last about a year. Before they consummate their marriage, which would happen after the wedding ceremony, Mary becomes pregnant "through the Holy Spirit." This is a clear reference to the virginal conception of Jesus (see also Matt. 1:20). Joseph is a godly man and plans to balance compassion (love for Mary) with righteousness (the need to uphold his honor and reputation) by having a private divorce. God directly intervenes through a dream, something he will do again in 2:12, 13, 19, and 22. Joseph, the "son of David," is told to take Mary home as his wife since the child is a genuine work of God. Joseph is to name the son "Jesus," a Greek translation of the Hebrew name "Joshua," meaning "Yahweh saves." This event fulfills Isaiah 7:14 since Jesus is now Immanuel ("God with us"). Joseph responds by obeying God (always a good choice).

Jesus's birth and a visit from the magi (2:1–12)

It's hard to admit that our Christmas carols and nativity scenes depicting three wise men gathered around the manger have it wrong, but that seems to be the case. We are told in 2:11 that Mary and Joseph are now living in a house. And although the magi bring three gifts, we are never told there are three kings. Magi were probably Persian astrologers who studied the stars looking for signs of divine activity. What is most striking here is the contrast between pagan stargazers and King Herod. The outsiders are more in tune with what God is doing through Jesus than the Jewish insiders who are supposed to be looking for his coming. From the beginning Jesus is worshiped by those we least expect and rejected by his own. God outwits Herod and directly intervenes to save this special child and his family.

Jesus's escape to Egypt and return to Nazareth (2:13–23)

A winnowing fork.

See Luke 2:39–40. Soon after the magi leave, God intervenes again. Joseph is told in a dream to take Jesus and Mary to Egypt to escape from Herod. This sojourn into Egypt fulfills Scripture (Hosea 11:1) as Jesus's experience parallels (and fulfills) that of the nation of Israel. As God had earlier called Israel out of Egypt through the exodus, he now calls his Son out of Egypt. When Herod is outsmarted by the wise men, he goes on a rampage and murders all the boys two years old or younger in the vicinity of Bethlehem

✝ God's sovereign protection of the baby Jesus and his parents is evident throughout the Christmas story.

(probably around twenty children). This recalls the suffering mentioned by Jeremiah 31:15. After Herod's death, God intervenes again to instruct Joseph to return to Judea. In yet another dream Joseph is warned about the cruel ruler Archelaus, and he withdraws to Galilee and specifically to Nazareth. This also fulfills a scriptural theme (note the plural "the prophets" in 2:23) that Jesus "will be called a Nazarene." Since Galilee was generally disrespected and tiny Nazareth was viewed as a hick town (see John 1:46), we are reminded that God loves to use human weakness to accomplish his purposes.

Jesus's Preparation for Public Ministry (3:1–4:25)

Jesus's public ministry is preceded by the ministry of John the Baptizer, Jesus's submission to John's baptism of repentance, and Jesus's temptations in the wilderness. These not only prepare Jesus for the public ministry to follow, they also communicate to us the kind of ministry he would have.

John the Baptizer prepares the people for Jesus (3:1–12)

See Mark 1:2–8; Luke 3:1–18; John 1:19–28. In Matthew we learn that the coming of God's promised rule through the Messiah is near or at hand (3:2). As a result, people should prepare their hearts through repentance. Crowds from "the whole region of the Jordan" come to confess and be baptized by John (3:5–6). Jewish religious leaders come to inspect John's ministry. John sarcastically compares them to a bunch of snakes slithering away from a grass fire. Instead of relying on their religious heritage (Abraham is our father), they need to bear fruit that reveals a real change of heart (3:9). For those who do not produce good fruit as a result of repentance, judgment is looming, and this applies to the religious leaders as well (3:10). John's role is to prepare the people for the more powerful one (Jesus) who will baptize with the Holy Spirit and fire, a symbol of judgment (3:11). Matthew adds another note of warning when he describes Jesus with a "winnowing fork in his hand" ready to separate the precious wheat from the worthless chaff (3:12). Jesus's coming requires a decision about God's kingdom.

Jesus identifies with sinful humanity through baptism (3:13–17)

See Mark 1:9–11; Luke 3:21–22; John 1:29–34. Matthew includes an interesting conversation between John and Jesus (3:14–15). John tries to prevent Jesus from being baptized because Jesus doesn't need to repent. Jesus insists, however, and explains that his baptism is necessary "to fulfill all righteousness" (3:15). This ambiguous phrase probably refers to Jesus's identification with sinful humanity. He doesn't need to repent, but Israel does, and, in a way, he is repenting of Israel's sins. Later he will literally take on the sins of the world. (Luke 12:49–50 refers to Jesus's crucifixion as his "baptism.") When Jesus comes up out of the water, the heavens open, the Holy Spirit descends like a dove, and the Father proclaims from heaven, "This is my Son, whom I love; with him I am well pleased" (3:16–17). This is indeed a trinitarian event—the Son submits, the Spirit descends to empower, and the Father voices his approval. As in Mark's Gospel, three Old Testament texts come together to announce who Jesus is and what he came to do (3:17). He will be a royal king in the line of King David (Ps. 2:7), a willing sacrifice or Lamb of God (Gen. 22:2), and a servant (Isa. 42:1). We will hear these same three Old Testament texts again at Jesus's transfiguration.

Jesus the Messiah withstands temptation (4:1–11)

See Mark 1:12–13; Luke 4:1–13. As the newly anointed King, we might expect Jesus to march right into Jerusalem and set up his kingdom. Instead, the Spirit leads him into the wilderness to battle the devil. It does seem strange that the Spirit would empower Jesus for ministry one minute and lead him into the wilderness to be tempted the next. We too sometimes experience the very same situation in life as both a test from God (who wants to strengthen us) and a temptation from Satan (who wants to harm us). Temptation is not sin, but rather an invitation to sin. We know that Jesus was tempted, but we also know that he never sinned. After a forty-day fast, the tempter attacks. The introductory phrase "if you are the Son of God" is best understood to mean "since you are." Satan does not doubt Jesus is the Son of God, but rather tempts him to use his divine power in selfish ways. The first

The vast Judean wilderness.

✚ When tempted, Jesus responds by quoting Scripture from Deuteronomy 6–8, where Moses is challenging the Israelites to be faithful as they prepare to cross the Jordan River into the Promised Land.

Discipleship in the New Testament

Joseph R. Dodson

In the Great Commission, Jesus commands his disciples to make disciples. But what is discipleship? Christians weren't the only ones to make disciples in the ancient world. For instance, John the Baptist had disciples (e.g., Matt. 9:14; Luke 7:18–19; John 1:35–37; Acts 19:1–3) as did the Pharisees (e.g., Matt. 22:16; Mark 2:18; John 9:28–29). Moreover, in the New Testament world many philosophical schools, such as the Sophists and Stoics, had disciples. Within all of these groups, discipleship primarily involved imitation, following and adhering to the example of a god or master teachers or both.

Christian discipleship also called for imitation. According to Jesus, "A disciple is not above his teacher, but, once he has been fully trained, the disciple will be like his teacher" (Luke 6:40); indeed, as the teacher is, so should the disciple be also (Matt. 10:25). Jesus makes it clear that only his disciples will receive eternal life (e.g., Matt. 16:24–26; 19:21–23; John 10:27–28). Imitating him, however, calls for drastic measures—a willingness to deny self, to forsake possessions, to abandon loved ones, and to suffer persecution (Luke 14:26–27,

33; cf. John 6:60–66). Paul also called disciples to a life of imitation—"Imitate me as I imitate Christ" (1 Cor. 4:16; 11:1; Phil. 3:17; cf. 2 Cor. 3:18; Gal. 4:19; 1 Tim. 1:16); "for you yourselves know how you ought to follow our example" (2 Thess. 3:7–9); "be imitators of God" (Eph. 5:1; cf. 4:24); "set an example for the believers" (1 Tim. 4:12). According to Paul, discipleship requires imitation in attitude as well as in action, by cultivating moral virtues (such as humility and love) as well as enacting selfless service (Rom. 15:2–3; 2 Cor. 8:9; Phil. 2:1–11). Similarly, the author of Hebrews urged the disciples to emulate the exemplars of faithful endurance (Heb. 6:12; 11:1–12:1; 13:7).

The imitation motif especially occurs in contexts of suffering (1 Thess. 1:6–7; 2:14). For instance, Peter points believers to the example of Christ's suffering so they may follow "in his steps" (1 Pet. 2:21–23). In fact, even God acts as an agent in discipleship by using afflictions to disciple his children (Heb. 12:7–13) and by working suffering for good so the disciples of Christ may be conformed to his image (see Rom. 8:17–29).

temptation (4:3–4) entices Jesus to do the right thing (eating) at the wrong time (during his fast). People need more than bread to live; we need God's truth (John 4:13–14). Temporary hunger in the will of God is better than satisfaction outside of it. Timing is an important part of obedience.

The next temptation (Matt. 4:5–7) is for Jesus to test God rather than trust him. Satan even (mis)quotes Scripture (Psalm 91) to encourage Jesus to do something unusual, daring, and spectacular as a means of self-promotion. But the real question is, "Do we follow God or are we trying to make God follow us?" Jesus insists true faith doesn't try to manipulate God. Rather, genuine faith submits to God. Only when we lack true faith do we seek to control God.

The final encounter (4:8–10) tempts Jesus to make his mission for God greater than God himself. Jesus knows he will be a suffering-servant king, but

Satan now entices him to pursue his kingly rule apart from the suffering and death of a cross. He is being tempted to accomplish his life mission in a way that leaves God out of the picture. Jesus cuts through Satan's lie with the truth that any shortcut that omits the cross also omits the crown. If Jesus bows to Satan, he will no longer be king over all. Jesus answers all three temptations with Scripture—"it is written" (Matt. 4:4, 7, 10). Every time he quotes from Deuteronomy 6–8, where Moses challenges Israel to be faithful when they cross the Jordan River and enter the Promised Land. Jesus has just been baptized in that same river and is about to begin his public ministry. Where Israel had failed to obey God and bless the nations, Jesus, the obedient Son, would succeed. He responds to Satan with God's Word, quoted in context. After a long physical trial and a period of intense spiritual warfare, the angels bring him comfort and encouragement. He has won the initial battle in the cosmic war with evil. Jesus has resisted the devil, and the devil now leaves him. Our strategy should be the same (James 4:7; 1 Pet. 5:8–9).

Jesus relocates to Capernaum (4:12–17)

See Mark 1:14–15; Luke 4:14–15. After hearing that John has been imprisoned, Jesus returns to Galilee. He relocates from Nazareth to Capernaum, a town on the northwest shore of the Sea of Galilee. As is typical of Matthew, he points out that this move fulfills Scripture (Isa. 9:1–2). Ironically, the good news for Israel comes forth from an unexpected place ("Galilee of the Gentiles"), as the people living in darkness (probably referring to Israel) are about to see a great light. Of course, the light is Jesus, and his message is that people should turn their hearts to God because his kingdom is near (4:17).

Jesus calls his disciples (4:18–22)

See Mark 1:16–20; John 1:35–51.

Jesus begins his public ministry (4:23–25)

See Mark 1:39; 3:7–12; Luke 4:44; 6:17–19. Jesus travels throughout Galilee teaching in the Jewish synagogues, preaching the good news of the kingdom, and healing people. His popularity spreads beyond Galilee into places like Syria, the Decapolis, and beyond the Jordan—mostly non-Jewish places. Jesus heals people suffering from various diseases, from severe pain, from seizures (epilepsy), from paralysis,

✦ Jesus's favorite topic for teaching and preaching was the kingdom of God.

and from demon possession (carefully distinguished from diseases in the ancient world). The Sermon on the Mount that follows is presented to a mixed ethnic group, many of whom have been healed or delivered but who now need to be instructed in the ways of following Jesus.

Discourse 1: Sermon on the Mount (5:1–7:29)

Here we have what many say is history's most powerful sermon. Both Matthew (5–7) and Luke (6:17–49) record the sermon, although Matthew's version is much longer. It is likely that Jesus repeated his kingdom teachings many times, and we are blessed to have one of his typical "sermons."

The occasion of the sermon (5:1–2)

See Luke 6:20. The "crowds" of 5:1 are likely the same ones described in 4:25, but the primary audience is Jesus's disciples. Consequently, the sermon is not spelling out requirements for those who want to enter the kingdom, but is teaching those already committed to Jesus what it means to live as a community of genuine disciples. The location is a "mountainside" or in the hill country. The traditional location is on a hillside overlooking the northern shore of the Sea of Galilee.

The Beatitudes (5:3–12)

See Luke 6:20–23. We get the word "beatitude" from the Latin word for "blessing." The word "blessed" (*makarios*) means more than being happy; it's like receiving a congratulations or approval from God. We stand in God's favor and under his blessing because we are his followers. The blessings come to those who demonstrate the appropriate heart attitudes (poor, mourning, meek, hungering and thirsting for righteousness, merciful, pure in heart) and actions (peacemakers, persecuted, insulted, and accused). Some of the blessings can be experienced in the present, while many are reserved for the future age. Don't miss the fact that the context assumes Christ's followers will

Saint Peter's fish from the Sea of Galilee.

Jesus the Teacher

Joseph R. Dodson

It was his custom to teach. Day after day he taught—in synagogues and in the temple, on the sea and beside it, on plains and upon mountains, from his hometown to Jerusalem. Most were astonished at his teachings, so full of authority and wisdom; but many, including his own disciples, frequently failed to comprehend them. On one occasion, when his disciples did understand his teaching, the majority rejected it and simply walked away (John 6:60–66). Once, Peter even went so far as to rebuke Jesus for his teaching (Mark 8:31–32). While some glorified Jesus when they heard him (Luke 4:15), others accused him of being demon-possessed (John 7:20) and sought to kill him (Mark 11:18; Luke 23:4–5). Although there were exceptions (e.g., John 3:2), many of the Jewish leaders were vexed by such extraordinary teachings from such an "uneducated" man (John 7:15). In response, Jesus professed that his education came directly from God (John 7:16).

There are at least six methods Jesus used to teach. He taught (1) by using parables, (2) by asking and answering questions, (3) by commenting on Scripture, (4) by proclaiming beatitudes and leveling woes, (5) by contextualizing his messages, and (6) by performing miracles. Jesus taught many things through parables both to instruct and to condemn (see Mark 4:10–20). He based some parables on interpersonal relationships—such as the prodigal son and the good Samaritan—and others on agrarian and economic themes—such as the parable of the sower and of the talents. Jesus also educated others by asking and answering questions: "Which is lawful on the Sabbath: to do good or to do evil, to save life or to kill?" (Mark 3:4); "David calls him 'Lord.' How then can he be his son?" (Luke 20:44). When asked about taxes, Jesus answered, "Give to Caesar what is Caesar's" (Matt. 22:21). And when someone inquired about the greatest commandment, Jesus replied, "Love the Lord your God" (Mark 12:28–30). Jesus also instructed others by commenting on Scripture, for example, from Isaiah 61 (Luke 4:16–21) and the Pentateuch (Matt. 5:21–48). Furthermore, Jesus taught by declaring blessings and woes—"Blessed are you who are poor. . . . But woe to you who are rich" (Luke 6:20–26; see also Matt. 5:1–11; 23:1–39). Furthermore, Jesus taught with objects around him—be it Herod's temple (John 2:18–21), Jacob's well (John 4), or a barren fig tree (Matt. 21:19–22). Finally, Jesus used his miracles as lessons: he heals the paralytic to teach others that he has authority to forgive sins (Mark 2:10–11) and follows an exorcism with a lesson on the kingdom of God (Luke 11:14–20). The praise that Jesus gave to Mary may indicate his view of his teaching: she chose what is better, the only thing necessary, that which will not be taken from her—the opportunity to sit at his feet and listen to his teachings (Luke 10:42).

face opposition from the world. Most importantly, we see that kingdom spirituality is an "inside-out" spirituality, since the followers of Christ are to reflect the character of God.

A disciple's influence (5:13–16)

See Mark 4:21; 9:49–50; Luke 8:16–18; 11:33; 14:34–35. Disciples are described as "the salt of the earth" (5:13) and "the light of the world" (5:14). In a culture without electricity and refrigeration, salt and light become extremely important. Jesus is challenging his followers to use their influence as change agents in this world. Salt enhances and preserves, while light illumines and reveals. Rather than abandoning our influence and becoming useless, Jesus challenges us to "let our light shine" before people so they may see our good deeds and praise our Father.

Jesus fulfills the law and brings heart righteousness (5:17–20)

See Luke 16:16–17. Jesus did not come to "abolish the Law or the Prophets" but to "fulfill them" (5:17). He is not opposed to the Old Testament, but came to work out the spirit of it and bring it to completion. Jesus doesn't just interpret the Old Testament, but stresses its true purpose and intention as it is fulfilled in his life, ministry, and teaching. In this way, Jesus declares himself to be Lord of the Law and the Prophets! Jesus explains that kingdom righteousness doesn't merely relate to religious rules, but neither does it lack God's holy standards. On the contrary, as a heart righteousness it works from the inside out and far surpasses the sometimes hypocritical piety put forth by some religious leaders.

Jesus's righteousness illustrated in six scenarios (5:21–48)

See Mark 9:43–48; Luke 6:27–30, 32–36; 12:57–59; 16:18. The way Jesus fulfills the Law and the Prophets is now clearly illustrated in the six scenarios. In each case, we see (1) a statement attributed to the Old Testament or to

The Church of the Beatitudes in Tabgha on the Sea of Galilee.

✚ Jesus's righteousness surpasses that of the religious leaders because it flows from the heart; it is not merely religious practice. The new "law" has now been written on people's hearts (see Jer. 31:33).

Jewish tradition ("you have heard that it was said"), (2) Jesus's reinterpretation of the statement ("but I say to you"), and (3) the illustration and application of Jesus's teaching (except in 5:31–32). Jesus not only condemns murder, he warns against the anger that leads to murder. Disciples must seek reconciliation whenever possible (5:21–26). Along with condemning adultery, Jesus condemns adultery of the heart (or lust) as well, and disciples must take radical steps to separate themselves from situations that foster lust (5:27–30). Jesus warns against divorce except in the case of marital unfaithfulness (5:31–32). He condemns swearing oaths and instructs his followers to be people of integrity who keep their word (5:33–37). In place of retaliation, Jesus tells his disciples to respond to personal insult with kindness and generosity (5:38–42). Finally, Jesus calls us to love our enemies and pray for those who persecute us. In this way, we will maturely reflect the character of our heavenly Father (5:43–48).

Jesus's way of practicing authentic acts of piety (6:1–18)

See Mark 11:25; Luke 11:1–4. Kingdom righteousness manifests itself in authentic acts of piety such as giving (6:1–4), praying (6:5–15), and fasting (6:16–18). In all three cases, Jesus makes the same point—we are not to practice our piety for the purpose of impressing people. We are not to announce our giving. Rather, we should give discreetly with the motive of pleasing our Father. Our reward comes from God alone. We are to avoid praying in order to be seen by people. We forfeit our heavenly reward if that is our motive. Instead, we are to direct our prayer to the Father. The Lord's Prayer (better termed "The Disciples' Prayer" since our Lord didn't need to ask for forgiveness) gives us a helpful pattern for prayer—first focus on intimacy with and submission to God, then tell him of our need for physical provision, forgiveness, and spiritual protection. As with giving and praying, we are to fast only to be seen by our Father rather than to draw attention to ourselves.

A replica of an ancient scroll.

✝ Jesus came to fulfill the Old Testament rather than abolish or destroy it. The Old Testament remains extremely relevant for Christians.

Kingdom priorities related to wealth and worry (6:19–34)

See Luke 11:34–36; 12:22–34; 16:13. This section teaches disciples how to relate to money (and other material possessions) or lack thereof. Above all, we should trust God and seek first his kingdom and his righteousness (6:33). Jesus instructs us to pursue heavenly treasures, which are permanent and secure, rather than earthly treasures, which are temporary and fleeting. He knows our heart will always follow our treasure (6:19–21). Next he speaks of the eye as the "lamp of the body" (6:22–23). The eye functions here as an expression of our souls (i.e., our priorities or focus) rather than the entryway into our souls. If we make righteous decisions and set godly priorities, then what comes out of our lives will be light rather than darkness. We can either use money to love God and serve people, or we will love money and use people. Jesus boldly portrays God and material possessions as opposing gods (6:24). We can serve one or the other, but not both. In 6:25–34 Jesus comforts those who worry about daily necessities such as food, water, and clothing. People are more important to God than birds, grass, or flowers. If God cares for his creation, how much more will he care for his children? And Jesus reminds us that worry cannot add anything to our lives; it's totally counterproductive and useless. People who don't know God pour all their energy into meeting their own needs, but disciples should trust rather than worry. The needs are real, but God is good. (He often uses the community of disciples to meet his children's needs.) We should pursue God's concerns, abandon worry, and trust him to take care of us.

Kingdom relationships (7:1–12)

See Mark 4:24–25; Luke 6:31, 37–42; 11:9–13. Here we read about how we should relate to others and how God relates to us. We should not be judgmental of others, but we will sometimes have to make discerning judgments and decisions regarding others (7:5–6). Our standard of judgment is what God will apply to us, so we should judge wisely and sensitively only after having scrutinized our own lives. In our relationship with God, we should pray persistently and boldly to our loving Father. If sinful human parents know how to give good gifts to their children, how much more will a holy and loving God answer with good gifts for his children? The body of the sermon closes with the famous Golden Rule—"in everything, do to others what you would have them do to you" (7:12). Unlike other Jewish teachers who are credited with similar sayings, Jesus is the only one to state the rule positively. This closing rule represents the very heart of Jesus's relational teachings.

The conclusion to the sermon (7:13–27)

See Luke 6:43–49; 13:23–27. Jesus concludes his sermon with three illustrations that make a similar point: in the end we must either choose for Jesus or against him. The narrow gate leads to life, while the wide gate leads to destruction (7:13–14). A good tree produces good fruit, while a bad tree (those who profess to speak for God but are pretenders) cannot bear good fruit (7:15–23). A wise person builds upon solid rock by hearing and obeying Jesus's teachings, while a foolish person builds upon sand by failing to heed his words (7:24–27). The sermon closes with a solemn warning. There are only two ways or options, and not everyone who is associated with Jesus actually has a personal relationship with him. Knowing Jesus personally (or being known by him) is what matters most (7:21–23).

The reaction of the crowds (7:28–29)

Although the primary audience throughout has been Jesus's disciples, the surrounding crowds are amazed at his authoritative teaching. Unlike the religious teachers they are used to, Jesus's authority is not derived from others. Jesus's sermon calls the first audience (and us) to acknowledge God as the source and center of life and adjust our lives accordingly.

Jesus's Messianic Authority Demonstrated (8:1–9:38)

Jesus now confirms his powerful words with authoritative deeds. In Matthew 8–9 we find three groups of three miracles separated by short teachings on what it means to follow Jesus. Jesus's messianic authority is demonstrated through his ability to heal diseases, calm storms, cast out demons, and even raise the dead. His compassion for people moves him to minister to them. In sharp contrast, the Jewish leaders are more interested in sustaining their powerful religious positions than shepherding the people.

Jesus heals a man with leprosy (8:1–4)

See Mark 1:40–45; Luke 5:12–16. When Matthew and Mark share material, as is the case here, Matthew (although the longer Gospel) is normally more concise. For example, Matthew does not include the part found in both Mark and Luke about the news of the healing spreading throughout the region. Above all, what we shouldn't miss is that Jesus makes himself "unclean" by touching this leprous man in order to make the man clean.

✦ Following the Sermon on the Mount, Jesus now demonstrates his authority through actions such as healing and exorcism.

Jesus heals a centurion's servant (8:5–13)

See Luke 7:1–10. Along with touching an untouchable in the previous episode, Jesus now heals a Roman centurion's servant. Devout Jews despised gentile soldiers and viewed them as religiously unclean. But the centurion approaches Jesus with respect (calling him "Lord"), humility (a powerful gentile coming to a traveling Jewish teacher for help), and a great faith (unlike anything Jesus has yet seen in Israel). Consequently, Jesus boldly announces that at the great heavenly feast, many gentiles (those from "the east and the west") will dine beside the famous Jewish patriarchs, while some "subjects [or heirs] of the kingdom" will be excluded and banished into the darkness. Devout Jews never expected to be banned from the heavenly banquet. Jesus then heals the centurion's servant from a distance and sends the soldier home in peace (8:13). What matters most in Jesus's kingdom is not religious ancestry but humble faith in Jesus the Messiah.

Jesus heals Peter's mother-in-law and others (8:14–17)

See Mark 1:29–34; Luke 4:38–41. Having cured a leper and a gentile servant, Jesus now heals a woman—all three would have been disrespected by orthodox Jews. Jesus casts out the evil spirits "with a word" (8:16), indicating that it is his powerful speech alone that drives out the demons. Matthew also observes (as he often does) that Jesus's healing ministry fulfills Scripture, specifically Isaiah 53:4. This servant-song passage speaks of the Messiah taking on the people's infirmities and diseases in order to reverse the curse of sin.

Ancient anchors.

Following Jesus takes real commitment (8:18–22)

See Luke 9:57–62. After this first group of three miracles, Jesus encounters two people who are interested in following him. The first seems overzealous and boasts, a bit naively it appears, that he will follow Jesus wherever he goes. Jesus replies that while animals have homes, the "Son of Man" (the first time this important title is used in Matthew's Gospel) has "no place to lay his head" (8:20). Potential disciples should know up front that following Jesus brings the very real possibility of experiencing rejection and opposition. The second person wants to delay discipleship until his father has died. Following Jesus must take priority over even the most important human relationships. In the end, both men fail to realize the exacting demands of discipleship to Jesus.

Jesus stills the storm (8:23–27)

See Mark 4:35–41; Luke 8:22–25. Now we encounter three more miracles that demonstrate Jesus's authority over Satan and sin. Matthew calls this storm a *seismos* (literally "a violent shaking"), which may indicate that Satan causes the storm. Also, when Jesus calms the storm, he uses the same term (*epitimao*) he uses elsewhere when casting out demons (see Mark 1:25; 9:25; Luke 4:41). After rebuking his disciples for having too little faith and too much fear, Jesus stills the storm. The disciples are amazed and ask, "What kind of man is this? Even the winds and the waves obey him!" (8:27). People familiar with the Old Testament stories would know how to answer that question—God is able to calm the storms, just as he did in the time of Jonah. Interestingly, the "sign of Jonah" is mentioned just a few chapters later in another context of Satanic opposition to Jesus (Matt. 12:38–42).

Jesus casts out demons (8:28–34)

See Mark 5:1–20; Luke 8:26–39. Jesus now ventures into gentile territory and is met by demonized men who live in the local cemetery. The demons quickly acknowledge Jesus as the Son of God and beg for mercy. Jesus gives them permission to enter a nearby herd of pigs. Ironically, the unclean spirits destroy the unclean animals by running them into the sea, a common biblical symbol for evil. The whole town reacts negatively to Jesus's demonstration of power and urges him to leave. Matthew speaks of two demonized men while Mark and Luke only mention one (although they never say "only one," and characterize the demons as "Legion" or many). On a few other occasions Matthew includes two of something when the other Gospels speak of one (Matt. 9:27; 20:30). Craig Blomberg suggests this is because Matthew is sensitive to his Jewish audience and follows the principle of Deuteronomy 19:15, where a testimony needs to be confirmed by two or three witnesses.*

Jesus heals and forgives a paralyzed man (9:1–8)

See Mark 2:1–12; Luke 5:17–26. In the third miracle in the second set of three, Jesus returns to Capernaum where he forgives and heals a paralyzed man. Here Jesus again identifies himself as the "Son of Man" (see Dan. 7:13–14), who now has "authority on earth to forgive sins" (Matt. 9:6), a task only God can perform. In contrast to the Jewish leaders, the crowd responds with awe and praise to God.

The call of Matthew/Levi to become a disciple (9:9–13)

See Mark 2:13–17; Luke 5:27–32. After the second set of three miracles, we return again to what it means to follow Jesus. In this case, the response of Matthew to Jesus's call to discipleship is positive. As was common, Matthew likely had two names since he is named "Levi" in both Mark and Luke.

A question about fasting (9:14–17)

See Mark 2:18–22; Luke 5:33–39. With the coming of Jesus, the kingdom of God has drawn near. Now celebration is more appropriate for Jesus's disciples than fasting. Jesus, the bridegroom (a common metaphor for God in the Old Testament), has ushered in a whole new age. The new ways of the kingdom expressed in the teachings of Jesus cannot be restricted to the old ways of legalistic righteousness.

---

* Craig Blomberg, *Matthew*, New American Commentary (Nashville: Broadman, 1992), 151.

The Sea of Galilee.

✙ In Daniel 7:13 "one like a Son of Man" is a heavenly being who receives from God an eternal kingdom on earth.

The Gospel of Matthew   509

Jesus heals a bleeding woman and raises Jairus's daughter (9:18–26)

See Mark 5:21–43; Luke 8:40–56. This is the first miracle in the last group of miracles in Matthew 8–9. Here we actually find two healings combined into one episode, perhaps to compare and contrast the bleeding woman and Jairus's daughter more closely. Matthew concludes by saying that "news of this spread through all that region" (9:26).

Jesus heals two blind men (9:27–31)

We read about a similar miracle in Matthew 20:29–34, Mark 10:46–52, and Luke 18:35–43, but the locations are different from those described here. Jesus undoubtedly heals many blind people during his earthly ministry. In this case, the blind men demonstrate their unique awareness of who Jesus is by calling him "Son of David" and displaying strong faith (9:27–28). Their ability to see Jesus with spiritual eyes leads to their physical healing. Jesus warns them not to tell anyone about the healing, perhaps to avoid giving people the wrong idea about his larger mission. Nevertheless, the news spreads quickly, and Jesus's popularity grows (9:31).

Jesus heals a demon-possessed mute man (9:32–34)

See Mark 3:22; Luke 11:14–15. In this third miracle in the series, Jesus is presented with a demonized man who cannot talk. Jesus drives out the demon, the man speaks, and the crowd reacts with amazement—"nothing like this has ever been seen in Israel" (9:33). But the Jewish leaders are not jumping on the bandwagon. Instead of believing in Jesus, the Pharisees accuse him of performing miracles by the power of Satan. As Jesus's popularity grows, the reactions become more and more polarized: some enthusiastically welcome Jesus (9:33), while others viciously reject him (9:34).

The ministry of the Messiah continues (9:35–38)

See Mark 6:6, 34; Luke 8:1; 10:2. Jesus continues his ministry of teaching, preaching, and healing (see 4:23–25). He is motivated by "compassion" for the crowds because they were "harassed and helpless, like sheep without a shepherd" (9:36). This last phrase—"sheep without a shepherd"—may reflect Ezekiel's indictment of the leaders of his time (Ezekiel 34) and serve as a rebuke to the religious leaders of Jesus's day. Using this messianic image of a shepherd, Jesus indicates that God has sent him to properly lead and care for the people. One wonders if Jesus's compassion is not the main reason for the leaders' opposition. Jesus cares

✝ In the Old Testament, the Lord consistently presents himself as a good shepherd to his people (e.g., Isa. 40:11; Jer. 31:10; Ezekiel 34; Psalm 23).

Matthew 10:1-4	Mark 3:13–19	Luke 6:12-16
Simon (Peter)	Simon (Peter)	Simon (Peter)
his brother Andrew		his brother Andrew
James son of Zebedee	James son of Zebedee	James
his brother John	John (Sons of Thunder)	John
	Andrew[1]	
Philip	Philip	Philip
Bartholomew	Bartholomew	Bartholomew
Thomas	Matthew	Matthew
Matthew the tax collector[2]	Thomas	Thomas
James son of Alphaeus	James son of Alphaeus	James son of Alphaeus
Thaddaeus	Thaddaeus	
Simon the Cananaean	Simon the Cananaean	Simon the Zealot[3]
		Judas son of James[4]
Judas Iscariot	Judas Iscariot	Judas Iscariot

1. Mark prefers to keep the three most prominent disciples together in his list (i.e., Peter, James, and John) while Matthew and Luke prefer to keep the brothers Peter and Andrew together in their lists.

2. We might expect Matthew to mention his profession of tax collector.

3. Cananaean is the Aramaic word for "Zealot." Luke translates the Aramaic into Greek.

4. It seems that Thaddaeus (Mark and Matthew) and Judas son of James (Luke) are the same person. Five of the names in the list are qualified by additional names—e.g., James son of Zebedee. The name Judas Iscariot suggests that there was another Judas—Judas son of James. Perhaps Mark and Matthew referred to the other Judas as Thaddaeus because of the stigma associated with Judas. Why Luke did not do so is hard to tell.

more about people than he does building religious institutions or programs. The image then shifts from taking care of sheep to harvesting grain, and the "Lord of the harvest" is currently enlisting workers to labor in the fields. The mission Jesus has in mind becomes the topic of his second main discourse in Matthew 10.

Discourse 2: The Mission of the Messiah (10:1–42)

Jesus commissions twelve disciples as apostles, instructs them about their mission, and teaches them what to expect as a response. Some of Jesus's predictions are fulfilled in the immediate future with the Twelve, while others are fulfilled later as the church carries on Jesus's work (the book of Acts contains many examples of how these predictions are fulfilled).

The commissioning of the Twelve (10:1–16)

See Mark 3:13–19; 6:7–11; Luke 6:12–16; 9:1–6; 10:3. Jesus calls twelve disciples and empowers them for ministry (10:1). He designates these twelve

The Twelve Disciples of Jesus

Mark L. Strauss

Although Jesus had many followers, he selected twelve key disciples whom he appointed and designated apostles. "Apostle" (*apostolos*) means a "messenger" sent out with a commission. Jesus's choice of twelve is reminiscent of the twelve tribes of Israel and suggests that Jesus viewed his mission as the restoration or reconstitution of the people of God, with himself as its leader. Jesus says as much when he promises the Twelve that they will sit on thrones in his kingdom, "judging the twelve tribes of Israel" (Luke 22:30). Here is a brief description of the Twelve.

Simon Peter. Simon Peter is always named first in the lists of disciples, and often serves as their representative and spokesperson. Jesus called Simon to be a disciple and nicknamed him "Peter" (Greek: *Petros*; Aramaic: *Cephas*; John 1:42), meaning a "rock" or "stone." Known for his boldness and an impetuous spirit, it was Peter who first acknowledged that Jesus was the Messiah (Matt. 16:13–20 and parallels) but later denied that he even knew Jesus (Matt. 26:69–75 and parallels). After the resurrection, Jesus restored

Peter to a position of leadership (John 21:15–19), and in the book of Acts Peter appears as a key leader in the early church.

Andrew, Brother of Simon Peter. Andrew was originally a follower of John the Baptist, until John pointed Jesus (the "Lamb of God") out to him. Andrew brought his brother Simon to meet Jesus (John 1:40–42). He is known as the disciple who kept bringing others to Jesus: his own brother, the boy with the loaves and fishes (John 6:8–9), and, together with Philip, a group of Greeks who wanted to meet Jesus (John 12:20–22). Andrew and Peter were from Bethsaida (John 1:44) but operated their fishing business in Capernaum (Mark 1:29).

James, Son of Zebedee. Like Peter and Andrew, James and his brother John were fishermen who followed the call of Jesus (Matt. 4:21–22). Jesus nicknamed them *Boanerges*, meaning "sons of thunder" (Mark 3:17), perhaps because of their volatile personalities (Luke 9:54). James was arrested and executed by Herod Agrippa I; he was the first apostle to die as a martyr (Acts 12:1–2).

as "apostles," meaning one sent as an authorized representative or agent of another (10:2–4). Jesus first instructs the Twelve for their short-term mission to "the lost sheep of Israel" (10:5–6), which will later expand to include the entire world (10:18; 24:14; 28:18–20). The apostles are to preach the kingdom, heal the sick, raise the dead, and drive out demons (10:7–8), just as they had seen Jesus doing. They are to travel lightly, live simply, and rely on generous hospitality (10:9–13). Jesus prepares them for rejection (10:14–15), warns them about the dangers of the mission, and charges them to be both shrewd and innocent (10:16).

Disciples should expect persecution (10:17–25)

See Mark 13:9–13; Luke 6:40; 12:11–12; 21:12–19. Followers of Jesus should expect harsh treatment by governing authorities before whom they

✚ Jesus's apostles also serve as shepherds to his lost and scattered people.

John, Brother of James. John, James, and Peter make up the "inner circle," Jesus's closest disciples who accompanied him at key points in his ministry: the raising of Jairus's daughter (Mark 5:37), the transfiguration (Mark 9:2), and the Garden of Gethsemane (Mark 14:33). John is traditionally identified as the Beloved Disciple and the author of the fourth Gospel, the letters of 1–3 John, and the book of Revelation.

Philip. Philip, who was from Bethsaida, introduced Nathanael to Jesus (John 1:45). Outside of the lists of disciples, he appears only in a few scenes in John (John 6:5–7; 12:21–22; 14:8–9).

Bartholomew. Bartholomew means "son of Tolmai" and may be another name for Nathanael (John 1:45).

Matthew, the Tax Collector. The Gospel of Matthew identifies this disciple as the tax collector called "Levi" by Mark and Luke (Matt. 9:9; Mark 2:14; Luke 5:27). He is traditionally believed to be the author of the Gospel that bears his name.

Thomas. Also known as Didymus (meaning "the twin"), Thomas is best known as the disciple who doubted Jesus's resurrection until he saw and touched Jesus himself (John 20:24–29). Church tradition claims Thomas later evangelized eastward into India.

James the Son of Alphaeus. Sometimes identified as "James the Lesser" (or younger) of Mark 15:40, he may be the brother of Matthew/Levi since both of their fathers are named Alphaeus (Mark 2:14).

Thaddaeus, Lebbaeus, or Judas the Son of James. This name is the most disputed of the Twelve. Matthew and Mark refer to Thaddaeus (some manuscripts say "Lebbaeus"). Luke instead has Judas the son of James, which could be another name for the same person.

Simon the Zealot. In Luke, this disciple is called the "Zealot"; in Mark and Matthew, the "Cananaean," from an Aramaic term meaning "zealous one" (not a "Canaanite"!). It is unclear if Simon was zealous for the law of Judaism or whether he was a former member of the revolutionary movement known as the Zealots.

Judas Iscariot, Who Betrayed Jesus. "Iscariot" probably means "man from Kerioth" (a region of Judea) and was a family name (John 6:71). The fourth Gospel asserts that Judas, as treasurer, used to pilfer the group's money even before he betrayed Jesus (John 12:6).

will have the opportunity to bear witness to Jesus (10:17–18). When that happens, "the Spirit of your Father" will give them words to speak (10:19–20). Persecution comes because of their devotion to Jesus (10:18, 22). (When difficulties come for other reasons, such as an obnoxious personality, disciples have only themselves to blame.) If Jesus himself was hated and falsely accused, his followers should expect nothing less (10:22, 24–25). Persecution is to be expected but not sought out since avoiding it may at times be the wisest move (10:23). This hostility will be especially painful when it involves family members (10:21). In this original context people who experienced such family division were leaving one religious tradition for a different tradition, like a Muslim today converting to Christianity and facing rejection from his or her family. Jesus reminds us perseverance is needed, and he will return to vindicate his people (10:22–23).

Fearing God more than people (10:26–33)

See Luke 12:2–9. Disciples are not to fear rejection or persecution (10:26). God will hold the persecutors responsible, and one day all things will be revealed (10:26–27). Rather than fearing those who can only destroy the body, disciples should fear God, who is capable of destroying both soul and body in hell (10:28). Our Father responds to our fear (or respectful obedience) with love and care (10:29–31). Our job is to acknowledge Jesus publicly and be faithful in our witness rather than fearing people and being ashamed of Jesus. This challenge comes with both a promise and a warning (10:32–33).

Loyalty to Jesus above family (10:34–39)

See Luke 12:51–53; 14:25–27; 17:33; John 12:25. Jesus's mission doesn't automatically bring peace and harmony (10:34). Varied responses to Jesus stir up relational conflict even within families (10:35–36). Anyone who puts family loyalties above loyalty to Jesus is not worthy of being Jesus's disciple (10:37). Disciples must be willing to take up their cross (a symbol of hardship and rejection) and follow Jesus (10:38). Paradoxically, people who attempt to secure life apart from Jesus will lose life, while those who lose their lives for Jesus's sake will find life (10:39).

Receiving God's representatives (10:40–42)

See Mark 9:41; Luke 10:16; John 13:20. The way people respond to Jesus's messengers (prophets, righteous ones, and "little ones," or disciples) shows how they would respond to Jesus himself. This, in turn, shows how God will respond to them. Those who "receive" these followers of Jesus, perhaps protecting them from persecution in some way, will not go unrewarded. Even in the worst of times for God's people, some will respond to them with compassion.

Barley harvest.

✝ Those who follow God are often warned of the possibility of persecution and difficulty in this life. This has always been the case.

Opposition to Jesus the Messiah and His Mission (11:1–12:50)

In Matthew 11–12 the opposition to Jesus grows more intense. John doubts whether Jesus is the "one to come," the surrounding cities are rejecting his message, and the Jewish leaders bring accusations. He even faces a subtle rebuke from his own family. Through it all, however, Jesus is affirmed as God's Spirit-anointed Servant who has a unique relationship to the Father and promises soul rest for those who follow him.

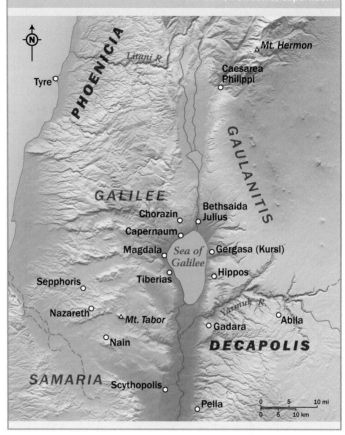

Chorazin, Bethsaida, Capernaum

John the Baptizer and Jesus (11:1–19)

See Luke 7:18–35; 16:16–17. Matthew 11:1 (like 7:28–29) serves as a conclusion to the previous discourse. Some disciples of John the Baptizer approach Jesus with a question, "Are you the one who was to come, or should we expect someone else?" (11:3; cf. Matt. 3:11). Jesus lets his messianic work of preaching and healing speak for itself (11:5). John and his followers will be blessed if they do not stumble over Jesus (11:6). When doubts arise for us, we should let Jesus's activity reveal his identity. Jesus then comments on John's role as the prophetic messenger who has come to prepare the way for the Messiah (11:7–15). Jesus then tells a story about a children's game to make the point that both John and Jesus are not meeting the people's expectations (11:15–19). John is too withdrawn and strange while Jesus celebrates too much. This generation, Jesus implies, is like a bunch of whining, spoiled children. But in the end "wisdom is proved

✢ The Old Testament predicted that the Messiah would bring healing and cleansing and life and forgiveness (e.g., Isa. 35:4–6; 61:1; Jer. 30:17; 33:6). Jesus's actions reveal his authenticity.

right by her actions" (11:19), and we will see that both John and Jesus are doing God's will.

Jesus rebukes those who reject him (11:20–24)

See Luke 10:12–15. The cities Jesus rebukes are in Galilee, the primary area of his ministry up to this point. He uses the Old Testament form of a "woe" to stress that greater revelation leads to greater accountability. God will judge these people more severely because they have clearly heard Jesus's message and seen his miraculous ministry and still rejected him.

Jesus praises the Father and offers rest to those who follow him (11:25–30)

See Luke 10:21–22. In spite of being misunderstood and rejected, Jesus praises the Father for outsmarting the self-reliant and revealing himself to the humble and trusting (11:25–26). Jesus has a unique and intimate relationship with the Father (11:27). Jesus invites the "weary and burdened" to come to him for "rest for your souls" (11:28–30). While the "yoke" was commonly understood to refer to the law, Jesus invites people to come to him and his teachings instead. Jesus doesn't welcome us into a passive life, but into a life of restful action in which our burdens are eased because we have someone to depend upon. What we find in Jesus is a whole new way of doing life.

Sabbath controversies (12:1–14)

See Mark 2:23–3:6; Luke 6:1–11. Jesus's opponents now confront him directly over two controversial Sabbath incidents. First, Jesus and his disciples pick and eat grain on the Sabbath and are accused of reaping, a forbidden activity

A wooden yoke used to harness animals for plowing.

✙ Jesus uses the Old Testament form of a "woe" to pronounce judgment on cities that have received clear and repeated revelation and have still failed to respond (see Num. 21:29; Isa. 3:9–11; Jer. 13:27; Ezek. 24:6–9).

Jewish Sabbath Observances

Mark L. Strauss

The word "Sabbath" comes from a Hebrew word meaning to "rest" or "cease" (from work). The principle of a Sabbath rest has its roots in the creation account. God created the heavens and the earth in six days and then rested on the seventh, blessing it and declaring it to be holy (Gen. 2:2). The command to rest on the Sabbath first appears in Scripture after the Exodus from Egypt, when the Israelites were forbidden to gather manna on the Sabbath (Exod. 16:21–30). The official enactment of the command came through Moses at Mount Sinai. The fourth of the Ten Commandments is to "remember the Sabbath day by keeping it holy" (Exod. 20:8–11; Deut. 5:12–15). No work was to be done on that day—either by human or animal. All were to rest. The penalty for work was death (Exod. 31:14; Num. 15:32–36).

During the intertestamental period and beyond, Jewish rabbis became ever more scrupulous with reference to the Sabbath, seeking to define the parameters of what constituted work. Two entire tractates in the Talmud are devoted to Sabbath observance (there are about sixty-three tractates in all). While the goal of applying God's law to everyday life was a noble one, the result was often legalism, where the letter of the law became more important than its spirit.

As a faithful Jew, Jesus kept the Sabbath and attended Sabbath synagogue services (Luke 4:16). Yet he came into frequent conflict with the religious leaders over legalism attached to its observance. When criticized because his disciples picked grain on the Sabbath, he pointed to David's example of eating consecrated bread when he and his men were in need (1 Sam. 21:1–6). The Sabbath, he said, was made for human beings and was intended for human benefit rather than burden (Matt. 12:1–14; Mark 2:23–3:6; Luke 6:1–11). Jesus also healed on the Sabbath, since the alleviation of human suffering took precedence over legalistic observances (Luke 13:10–17; 14:1–6; John 5:1–18; 9:1–41). Ultimately, he declared himself to be Lord of the Sabbath (Mark 2:28 and parallels), going so far as to assert that the Father worked on the Sabbath and so must he (John 5:17).

The apostle Paul maintained that the law has been fulfilled in Christ and that faith in Christ, rather than legalistic observance, makes one right with God (Rom. 3:28; Gal. 2:16; 3:1–3). Gentiles therefore need not be circumcised, keep Old Testament dietary laws, or observe the Sabbath day, since these are merely shadows of the reality—which is Christ himself (Col. 2:16–17; cf. Gal. 4:9–11). While the principle of Sabbath rest—setting aside special times for rest, worship, and reflection—remains an essential activity for those created in the image of God, for Paul the specific command to rest on the seventh day is no longer binding for believers. It is rather a matter of personal conviction. Paul writes, "Some consider one day more sacred than another; others consider every day alike. Everyone should be fully convinced in their own mind" (Rom. 14:5 TNIV).

(12:1–8). In response, Jesus reminds the leaders that God ranks mercy or compassion for people above religious ritual (Hosea 6:6; cf. Matt. 9:35–38) and that the "Son of Man is Lord of the Sabbath" (12:7–8). Second, Jesus heals a man with a shriveled hand on the Sabbath—another prohibited activity (12:9–14; see Mark 3:1–6). Jesus insists people are certainly more valuable than sheep, which according to the law may be rescued from a pit on the Sabbath. After Jesus heals the man, the Pharisees leave the synagogue and make plans to kill Jesus.

Jesus is God's Spirit-anointed servant (12:15–21)

See Mark 3:7–12; Luke 6:17–19. Aware of the Pharisees' evil intentions, Jesus withdraws from the conflict. He continues to compassionately heal people, asking them not to publicize his identity. In 12:18–21 Matthew notes that Jesus's response fulfills Isaiah's Suffering Servant prophecy (Isa. 42:1–4), the longest Old Testament quotation in Matthew's Gospel. The Servant is chosen and loved by God and anointed by the Spirit. He proclaims justice to the nations (or gentiles), and they respond by placing their hope in him. He fulfills his mission not through violence or coercion, but through gentle, faithful obedience.

Exorcism controversy (12:22–45)

See Mark 3:22–30; 8:11–12; Luke 6:43–45; 11:14–32; 12:10. Opposition to Jesus continues when he heals a demonized man who was blind and mute. The people are amazed and ask, "Could this be the Son of David?" (12:23), but the Pharisees accuse Jesus of casting out demons by "Beelzebub, the prince of demons" (12:24). Not only do they deny Jesus is divine; they insist that he is diabolical! After Jesus demonstrates the falseness of this claim (see 12:25–28), the only option left is that he casts out demons by the Spirit of God, whose activity is evidence the kingdom of God has arrived (12:28). Far from working for Satan, Jesus's exorcisms demonstrate he is the "stronger man" who binds or ties up the "strong man" (i.e., Satan; 12:29). Jesus is and will always be the "stronger man." Since people are either for Jesus or against him (12:30), attributing the work of God to Satan is a serious offense and constitutes blasphemy against the Holy Spirit (12:31–32). Rejecting the Spirit of God working through Jesus is an unforgivable sin because only Jesus can forgive. Words reveal the condition of a person's heart much like fruit reveals the condition of a tree (12:33). Good people speak good words, while evil people, like the Pharisees, speak evil (12:34–35). By those words we are either acquitted or condemned on judgment day (12:36–37). In response, the Jewish leaders ask for a miraculous sign (12:38), but Jesus refuses to play that game; the "sign of Jonah" has already been given, alluding to Jesus's coming death and resurrection (12:39–41). Even the gentile Ninevites repented at Jonah's preaching, and the gentile Queen of the South (Sheba) listened to Solomon. On judgment day, both will condemn this generation, who is not listening to one far greater than Jonah and Solomon (12:41–42). This entire controversy session begins with an exorcism, and Jesus closes it with a related warning (12:43–45). If God is not invited in to take the demon's place after the exorcism, it will return and establish an even greater hold. Similarly, unless this wicked generation follows Jesus (i.e.,

✦ Although the Ninevites listened to Jonah and the Queen of Sheba listened to Solomon, the religious leaders have rejected Jesus and will one day be condemned by these gentiles who responded to God.

fills their house with God), his work of liberating them from Satan will be for naught. They will be worse off than before.

Family controversies (12:46–50)

See Mark 3:31–35; Luke 8:19–21. Jesus's family now wants to speak with him (or perhaps prevent him from causing any more trouble). He takes the opportunity to redefine "family" in spiritual terms. His disciples are his family. We shouldn't miss Jesus's reference to God as "my Father in heaven" in 12:50. Although many are rejecting Jesus, whoever does God's will becomes part of Jesus's family. For many in our day whose biological families have disintegrated, becoming part of Jesus's family brings tremendous hope.

Discourse 3: Parables of the Kingdom (13:1–52)

In light of the increasing opposition, Jesus spends time teaching those who are interested in following him. Matthew 13, the third major discourse in this Gospel, contains eight parables that explain more about Jesus and his kingdom.

Parable of the sower (13:1–9)

See Mark 4:1–9; Luke 8:4–8. This parable teaches that many people will hear about the kingdom, and their responses will vary. The seed is sown in four types of soil: a dirt path, rocky places, among thorns, and on good soil. The parable emphasizes the many obstacles the kingdom message encounters, as well as its rich yield from the good soil.

Why Jesus teaches in parables (13:10–17)

See Mark 4:10–12; Luke 8:9–10; 10:23–24. Jesus now explains to his disciples why he teaches in parables. The secrets of the kingdom have "been given" (by God) to disciples, but not

The parable of the sower (rocky soil, thorns, path, good soil).

to others. God's sovereign plan to hide the kingdom from outsiders fulfills Isaiah 6:9–10. Interestingly, the outsiders' calloused hearts actually prevent their response to the message. In his explanation about the use of parables, Jesus appeals to both God's sovereign plan and to human responsibility. Those with hearts open to God are blessed. Specifically those walking with Jesus are especially blessed, since they are seeing many of the Old Testament promises fulfilled before their very eyes.

Interpretation of the parable of the sower (13:18–23)

See Mark 4:13–20; Luke 8:11–15. Jesus now interprets the parable of the sower for his listeners. The seed represents Jesus's message about the kingdom. The good soil represents people who hear, understand, and respond in obedience (i.e., true believers). The other three soils represent people who never were true believers since they failed to understand, endure hardship, or resist the worries and wealth of this world. The enemies of genuine disciples are apparent—the flesh, the world, and the devil. Only genuine believers go on to bear spiritual fruit.

Parable of the wheat and the weeds (13:24–30)

This parable indicates that wheat (the righteous) and weeds (the wicked) grow together for the time being. Again, the enemy (Satan) mixes bad seed with good seed during this age in an attempt to corrupt the entire crop. Only at the final judgment or harvest will God separate the wheat from the weeds. Jesus interprets this parable in 13:36–43.

Parables of the mustard seed and leaven (13:31–33)

See Mark 4:30–32; Luke 13:18–21. These parables make the point that something extremely small can grow into something very large and influential, just as Jesus and his followers would begin a world-changing movement.

Summary of Jesus's teaching in parables (13:34–35)

See Mark 4:33–34. Matthew notes that Jesus's parabolic teaching fulfills Psalm 78:2. Both passages reveal ways in which God is working.

Interpretation of the parable of the wheat and the weeds (13:36–43)

Jesus privately and straightforwardly explains for his disciples the earlier parable of the wheat and the weeds (see 13:24–30). Jesus as the Son of Man plays a crucial role in the coming judgment at the end of the age. Punishment awaits those who reject Jesus, while glory awaits those who follow him.

✦ The parables of Jesus have a dual effect: they both reveal truth to those whose hearts are receptive and they conceal truth from those whose hearts are hardened (see Isa. 6:9–10).

Parables of the hidden treasure and the costly pearl (13:44–46)

These two parables make the point that the kingdom is of such value that any price is worth paying.

Parable of the net (13:47–50)

This parable compares God's end-time judgment of all people to sorting out various kinds of fish after catching them in a dragnet—the righteous are saved and the wicked punished.

Parable of kingdom scribes (13:51–52)

Jesus concludes by asking his disciples if they understand better after the parables. He then compares them to scribes or teachers of the law who have been instructed about the kingdom. These kingdom scribes will be able to instruct others accurately in God's ways.

Jesus's Identity as the Messiah Is Revealed (13:53–16:20)

After concluding his third major discourse (see also 7:28–29; 11:1), the question of Jesus's identity takes center stage. The responses to Jesus continue to polarize those who misunderstand him completely and those who continue to follow him. Jesus continues to preach powerfully and perform miracles, but his disciples are still wrestling with his identity. Finally, the section climaxes with Peter's confession of Jesus as the Christ, the Son of the living God.

A mosaic of loaves
and fishes in the
church at Tabgha.

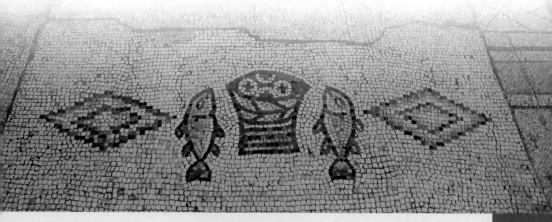

Jesus rejected by his hometown (13:53–58)

See Mark 6:1–6; Luke 4:16–30. After teaching through parables, Jesus returns home to Nazareth and teaches in the synagogue. Although initially impressed by his wisdom and miraculous powers, the hometown folk eventually take offense at him and dismiss him as no one important.

Herod murders John the Baptizer (14:1–12)

See Mark 6:14–29; Luke 3:19–20; 9:7–9. Another party to misunderstand Jesus is Herod Antipas. Having heard the reports about Jesus's miracles, Herod believes Jesus might be John the Baptizer raised from the dead. This prompts Matthew to retell the story of John's murder at the hands of Herod.

Feeding the five thousand—Israel (14:13–21)

See Mark 6:30–44; Luke 9:10–17; John 6:1–15. Here we see the only miracle aside from the resurrection present in all four Gospels. When Jesus hears of John's death, he withdraws to a solitary place. The crowds locate him, and Jesus has compassion on them, healing many and miraculously feeding the whole lot. Jesus also involves the disciples in this miracle to show them who he really is and perhaps to demonstrate how he will work in the future.

Jesus worshiped as the Son of God (14:22–36)

See Mark 6:45–56; John 6:16–21. In Matthew's Gospel the account of Jesus walking on the water leads the disciples to a deeper understanding of Jesus. The episode of Peter asking permission to walk out on the water to meet Jesus is unique to Matthew's Gospel (14:28–32). Peter becomes overwhelmed by the wind and waves and cries out for Jesus to save him. Jesus rescues him, reproves him for failing to have faith, and calms the sea as the two of them climb into the boat. At this point those in the boat confess, "Truly you are the Son of God" (14:33). When they arrive at Gennesaret, the people "recognize" Jesus and bring their sick for him to heal (14:34–36).

Coins of Herod Antipas.

Jesus as the true teacher of God's Word (15:1–20)

See Mark 7:1–23; Luke 11:37–41. Jesus is confronted by some Pharisees and teachers of law about his disciples' failure to keep the religious traditions related to ceremonial washing. Jesus asks in response why these leaders feel free to use religious loopholes to disobey the clear commands of God related to honoring their parents. They are nullifying God's Word for the sake of their tradition. He quotes Isaiah 29:13 in labeling them hypocrites who honor God with their talk but keep their hearts closed to him. Jesus then explains to the surrounding crowd that what really makes a person unclean is not failing to wash but having a wicked heart. When he hears from his disciples that he has offended the Pharisees, Jesus doesn't seem to care. "Leave them; they are blind guides," he says (15:14). As the true teacher of God's Word, Jesus explains to his dull disciples that it's not what goes into a person's mouth that defiles the person spiritually, but vices that come out from the heart. In 15:19 Jesus lists seven relational vices that can make a person spiritually unclean.

Jesus worshiped as the Son of David (15:21–28)

See Mark 7:24–30. As Jesus ventures further into Gentile country (Tyre and Sidon), he encounters a Canaanite woman who wants relief for her demon-possessed daughter. She cries out to Jesus as "Lord, Son of David" (15:22), revealing a special understanding that Jesus is the Jewish Messiah. The woman persists, and in spite of the fact that she is a gentile woman, Jesus finally heals her daughter. At first it might seem that Jesus is insensitive and unloving in his remarks to the woman, but he is demonstrating two things. First, his primary mission is to the Jews as God's chosen people. Second, he is testing her by asking her to demonstrate true faith and humility by trusting him (the kind of faith the Jews should have had but didn't). It's also helpful to note that Jesus's ministry in this and surrounding passages demonstrates his love and concern for gentiles.

Feeding the four thousand—gentiles (15:29–39)

See Mark 7:31–8:10. Jesus returns to the Sea of Galilee region (Mark has "the Decapolis") but remains in gentile country. There he continues to heal the lame, blind, crippled, mute, and many others. The predominantly gentile crowds are amazed and praise the God of Israel (15:31). This summary of Jesus's healing ministry (much like 14:13–14) is followed by another mass feeding (much like 14:15–21), but this one seems to be directed toward the gentiles. Again, it's Jesus's compassion that motivates him to minister to the multitudes (15:32), and again he works through his disciples to feed the crowds.

✦ While the hypocritical religious leaders fail to acknowledge Jesus, the gentile woman confesses him as Lord. God's plan all along has been to include the gentiles in his eternal family (Genesis 12).

The Jewish leaders reject Jesus (16:1–12)

See Mark 8:11–21; Luke 11:16, 29; 12:1, 54–56. Both the Pharisees and Sadducees, normally rivals, join forces to test Jesus. They demand a "sign from heaven" or some kind of proof that Jesus is God's Messiah. Jesus wonders how they can forecast the weather but as religious leaders can't interpret the spiritual realities of the times. How can they possibly miss the kingdom of God being ushered in by Jesus? He calls them a "wicked and adulterous generation" and refuses to give them any sign except the sign of Jonah, his coming death and resurrection (see Matt. 12:38–41). Later when in the boat with his disciples, Jesus warns them to beware of the "yeast" of the Jewish leaders. He is referring not only to their teachings (16:12) but also to their example of rejecting Jesus as Messiah (one of the few things they actually agreed upon). The disciples misunderstand Jesus, thinking he is reprimanding them for forgetting the bread. Jesus rebukes them for not "getting it" and clarifies that he is not talking about physical bread. Have they already forgotten he miraculously created bread for at least nine thousand people? Jesus can make bread! No, this is about the devilish influence and leadership of these religious leaders. The disciples should be on the alert. Sometimes we do well to warn others about devious, self-centered religious leadership.

The disciples identify Jesus as the Messiah, the Son of the living God (16:13–20)

See Mark 8:27–30; Luke 9:18–21; John 6:66–71. We come now to a major turning point in Jesus's ministry. At Caesarea Philippi, a city with a pagan reputation, Jesus asks the disciples, "Who do people say the Son of Man is?" (16:13). The crowds are saying he is a prophetic figure like John the Baptizer, Elijah, or Jeremiah. But Jesus is more than a prophet, and he wants to know what his own disciples think. So he asks the entire group (both words "you" are plural in v. 15)—"But what about you, . . . who do you say I am?" (16:15). Peter, the self-appointed spokesman, answers, "You are the Christ [Messiah], the Son of the living God" (16:16). Now that Peter has confessed Jesus, Jesus has something to say to Peter. First, he blesses Peter for receiving this divine revelation from the Father (16:17). Second, Jesus declares, "You are Peter" or *Petros* (this parallels Peter's confession of Jesus: "You are the Christ") and makes a wordplay on his name—"and on this rock (*petra*) I will build my church" (16:18). The word "rock" must refer to Peter in this context. Third, Jesus promises that Peter will serve as the foundation on which the church is built. This is the first use of the term "church" in the Gospels (see the other two uses in Matt. 18:17). The apostles, with Peter as the chief spokesman, serve as the foundation of the church (Eph. 2:20; Rev.

✚ The term "church" is only used in the Gospels in Matthew 16 and 18. After Pentecost (Acts 2), the term will be used much more extensively.

21:14). This new community Jesus is forming will prove to be indestructible and authoritative (16:18–19). Although Peter's confession of Jesus as the Christ is certainly a step in the right direction, Jesus is just now beginning to teach them that he will be the crucified Messiah.

Jesus, the Crucified and Risen Messiah (16:21–17:27)

After Peter's confession in the previous episode, Jesus begins to teach his disciples about his coming death and resurrection and what that means for them as his disciples.

The suffering Messiah and the cost of discipleship (16:21–28)

See Mark 8:31–9:1; Luke 9:22–27. Peter had recently confessed Jesus as "the Christ." Now Jesus explains that he came to be a crucified and risen Messiah (16:21). Peter, the very spokesman of the inspired confession, now starts to rebuke Jesus for saying such scandalous things. In return, Jesus quickly and forcefully rebukes Peter for thinking like Satan, who had earlier tempted Jesus to avoid the cross (see Matt. 4:1–11). Jesus then warns his disciples that they too should be prepared to walk this same road, since following him calls for self-denial and a willingness to suffer. The paradoxical choice is whether to entrust one's life to Jesus (and save it) or attempt to preserve one's life (and lose it). The choice is an eternal one that will be revealed when the Son of Man returns in glory and rewards people according to how they have lived (16:27). Some listening to Jesus can expect to catch a glimpse of his "second-coming" glory before they die, an obvious reference to the transfiguration soon to follow.

Jesus's transfiguration: A glimpse of future glory (17:1–9)

See Mark 9:2–10; Luke 9:28–36. About a week later Jesus takes Peter, James, and John up a high mountain (probably Mount Hermon) and is transfigured before them. The glory he will display at his second coming radiates out from his face and clothing. Moses and Elijah appear and talk with Jesus, which prompts Peter to suggest prolonging the experience by building three shelters. But the cloud of God's glory interrupts Peter's ramblings and descends on the group. The

Ancient keys.

People used silver
shekels like these to
pay their temple tax.

Father repeats what he had said at Jesus's baptism ("This is my Son, whom I love; with him I am well pleased") and adds, "Listen to him!" (Deut. 18:15). The disciples need to listen to what Jesus has been saying about suffering as the path to glory for both the Messiah and his followers. Jesus calms the disciples' fears and instructs them not to tell anyone about the experience until he has been raised from the dead.

The coming of Elijah (17:10–13)

See Mark 9:11–13. Elijah's presence on the mountain probably made the disciples wonder about the scribes' insistence that he must precede the Messiah. Jesus admits Elijah must come first and restore all things, but insists John the Baptizer has already fulfilled the role of Elijah (see 11:14). Just as John suffered at the hands of the Jewish religious leaders, so also the Son of Man will suffer.

Jesus heals a demonized boy (17:14–21)

See Mark 9:14–29; Luke 9:37–43; 17:5–6. Jesus and his inner circle come down from the mountain of glory to discover a demonized boy in misery but receiving no help from the remaining disciples. Jesus expresses frustration with his faithless disciples and their spiritual powerlessness and then proceeds to drive out the demon himself and restore the boy. When they ask why they couldn't drive out the demon, Jesus says it is because of their lack of faith. At the foot of the mountain of transfiguration, Jesus challenges his followers to have "mountain-moving" faith in God's power. Even a small faith can see God do great things.

✚ Moses too came down from a mountain to discover that the people below were struggling spiritually (Exodus 32).

Second prediction of the cross (17:22–23)

See Mark 9:30–32; Luke 9:43–45. For the second time Jesus predicts that he will be betrayed, killed, and raised to life. The disciples are "filled with grief" at the reminder (17:23).

Paying the temple tax (17:24–27)

Perhaps as a former tax collector, Matthew was interested in what Jesus had to say about taxes (he's the only Gospel writer to include this story). The tax collectors of Capernaum ask Peter whether Jesus pays the temple tax (worth about two days' wages). Peter says he does. Later in the house, Jesus asks Peter if earthly kings collect taxes from their own sons or from others, and Peter correctly says from others. Jesus concludes, "Then the sons are exempt" (17:26). The application for the disciples is probably that God's children (the "sons" rather than the "others") do not have to pay tax to God or to one another. Giving in the New Testament is voluntary. The disciples have also been set free from the obligation to keep the Jewish law, including paying a tax used to maintain the Jerusalem temple. But somewhat strangely, Jesus commands Peter to catch a fish that will provide a coin to pay the tax for both of them. By doing so, Jesus teaches another important application principle—disciples should also be cautious about causing offense unnecessarily.

Discourse 4: The Community of the Messiah (18:1–35)

In this fourth major discourse in Matthew's Gospel, Jesus teaches his followers what it means to live in community—having a humble attitude in our relationships, extending tough love on occasion, and offering forgiveness.

Disciples should be humble (18:1–5)

See Mark 9:33–37; Luke 9:46–48. The disciples want to know how to become the greatest person in the kingdom. Probably to their surprise, Jesus uses a little child to reveal humility as the quality that defines greatness in the kingdom. And humility is often demonstrated by how we treat other disciples of Jesus (the phrase "little child" of v. 5 refers to disciples—see Matt. 10:40–42).

Warning for those who cause disciples to stumble (18:6–9)

See Mark 9:42–50; Luke 17:1–2. As above, the expression "little ones" refers to disciples (18:6). Now Jesus warns of the danger of causing others to stumble and fall spiritually. Those who make a habit of causing others to sin will pay a heavy price. We should never underestimate our influence on others for good or bad, and Jesus reminds us to take drastic steps to reject anything that leads to sin (see Matt. 5:29–30).

The Father's care and protection of disciples (18:10–14)

See Luke 15:3–7. We are told not to despise or look down upon other disciples ("little ones"), perhaps especially those who fall into sin (see Gal. 6:1). God is extremely committed to restoring his struggling children. In fact, even angels keep watch over them. Jesus tells the parable of the one lost sheep. The shepherd who has one hundred sheep and loses one will most certainly seek to find and restore the one. Such is the heart of God (18:14), and we are called to imitate our heavenly Father.

Community discipline (18:15–20)

See Luke 17:3; John 20:23. Here Jesus outlines the process of dealing with someone who continues in sin and refuses to repent. Initially the offended person should speak directly and privately to the offender. If he doesn't listen, the offended person should take two or three others along as witnesses. If he still refuses to repent, then the church should be informed in order to practice community discipline. (The second and final uses of

A shepherd's field near Bethlehem.

the term "church" in Matthew's Gospel appear in 18:17.) Jesus assures the church that their "binding" or "loosing" (here withholding forgiveness or extending forgiveness) has God's authority behind it. This assumes, of course, they share Jesus's goal of restoration and follow his established guidelines. Matthew 18:19–20 is often quoted out of context and taken as a blanket promise for answered prayer as long as at least two people agree. In this context of church discipline, however, Jesus is repeating what he said in verse 18. He promises to be spiritually present with his church (no matter how small the fellowship) when they are working through the very difficult issue of disciplining an unrepentant disciple. The Spirit of Jesus will be with them during this tough-love process.

The need to forgive: Parable of the unmerciful servant (18:21–35)

See Luke 17:4. There is a balance in community life between maintaining standards of holiness on the one hand and forgiveness on the other. Having heard Jesus teach about tough love through church discipline, Peter now asks how many times he has to forgive a fellow disciple who sins against him. According to Jesus, we should forgive generously and do so without counting or keeping track (the point behind the number "seventy-seven times" in v. 22). This assumes that the fellow disciple repents and is in a place to receive forgiveness. Jesus then gives the parable of the unmerciful servant to drive home this point. Believers should have unlimited forgiveness for

✤ We see an example of church discipline at work in how the apostle Paul deals with an offender in the Corinthian church (see 1 Cor. 5:3–5; 2 Cor. 2:6–8).

other believers who ask for mercy and desire to change. In contrast, judgment awaits those who refuse to forgive (cf. Matt. 6:14–15).

Jesus Teaches on True Discipleship (19:1–20:34)

Jesus leaves Galilee for Judea, where (as he has been predicting) he will face a cruel cross. In the meantime, Jesus has much to say to his disciples. He has little time left to correct many of their misunderstandings about what it means to follow him. The topics come in rapid-fire succession as Jesus prepares them for what lies ahead.

Jesus's teachings on divorce (19:1–12)

See Mark 10:1–12; Luke 16:18. This passage on marriage, divorce, remarriage, and celibacy occurs in the context of a test from the Pharisees. Because of this controversy context, Jesus's teachings in this passage should not be expected to answer every contemporary question on the topic (e.g., abuse or neglect; see 1 Cor. 7:15). Some Jews felt divorce was permissible for minor reasons such as cooking a bad meal, while others permitted divorce only for something major such as immorality. Jesus points back to Genesis 1–2, where it is clear that God's original design for marriage is to be a permanent relationship between one man

Sycamore fig tree.

✚ Jesus bases his views of marriage and divorce on God's original blueprint for marriage found in Genesis 1–2.

and one woman. Moses permitted divorce, Jesus says, as a concession to sinful hearts, but that was not God's original plan. Jesus then concludes, "Anyone who divorces his wife, except for marital unfaithfulness (*porneia*), and marries another woman commits adultery" (19:9). The disciples wonder if it is better not to marry at all if the standards are so high. Jesus says that remaining single is a viable option, but only for those who believe God is leading them to accept that lifestyle.

The kingdom belongs to the childlike (19:13–15)

See Mark 10:13–16; Luke 18:15–17. Having rebuked the powerful Pharisees, Jesus now gathers the little children to bless them. The disciples are annoyed at the interruption, but Jesus uses the occasion as an object lesson about how a person enters the kingdom of God—in childlike faith.

What does it take to obtain eternal life? (19:16–26)

See Mark 10:17–27; Luke 18:18–27. A rich young man approaches Jesus wondering what good thing he must do to inherit eternal life (19:16). Jesus first shifts the focus from man's goodness to God's goodness. He then tells the man to obey the commandments, specifically the ones that relate to loving people (19:18–19). The young man insists he has kept all these commands and asks what else he needs to do. Jesus tells him to sell his possessions, give the money to the poor, and follow him. In this way Jesus moves the focus to a person's relationship to God, reminding us of the section in the Sermon on the Mount in which he describes material possessions as a rival god (6:19–34). The rich young man can't do what Jesus asks because of his allegiance to money, so he walks away dejected. When Jesus comments that it's practically impossible for rich people to choose God over money, the disciples wonder who can actually be saved. Because they assume rich people have been blessed by God, Jesus's statement confuses them. Jesus reassures them that what seems impossible to people is possible with God. As we see throughout the New Testament, even rich people by the grace of God are able to enter the kingdom.

Rewards for following Jesus (19:27–30)

See Mark 10:28–31; Luke 18:28–30. Peter is curious about what Jesus has in store for the Twelve since they have left everything to follow him. Jesus explains that at his glorious return and the "renewal of all things," his disciples will be given responsibilities to reign and judge with Christ (19:28). In addition, anyone who has left possessions and family in order to follow Jesus will receive "a hundred times as much and will inherit eternal life" (19:29). In contrast to the rich man who wanted eternal life, the reward for following

Jesus will be multiplied blessings now (although not necessarily material blessings because of all that has been left) and, in the future, eternal life.

The parable of the vineyard workers (20:1–16)

Following Jesus's discussion about gaining eternal life, this parable re-emphasizes God's grace. With God all things are possible! A vineyard owner hires five different groups of day laborers to work in his vineyard. Interestingly, the first group has the whole day to work, while the last group has only one hour before quitting time. At the end of the day, the owner pays all the workers the same amount. Those hired early complain that they deserve more, but the owner insists he has treated everyone justly or fairly by paying the agreed amount. While being fair to all, the owner has shown grace to those hired late in the day. While God is always just, he is often gracious to the least deserving. We shouldn't be envious because God is generous (20:15).

Third prediction of the cross (20:17–19)

See Mark 10:32–34; Luke 18:31–34.

Disciples should seek service over status (20:20–28)

See Mark 10:35–45; Luke 22:24–30. The two brothers James and John are seeking places of highest honor in the kingdom, and Matthew records that their mother actually makes this request for them (20:20–21). Jesus immediately connects glory with suffering ("can you drink the cup" of suffering in v. 22). They quickly and naively boast that they can suffer, and Jesus assures them they will; even so, only the Father may choose who occupies the seats of glory. The other ten disciples are furious at the two brothers for attempting to outmaneuver them for glory, so Jesus calls a timeout in order to address the issue. He talks about servant leadership in 20:25–28. Pagans use power to control and dominate, but disciples are to be totally different. Greatness in the kingdom relates to giving to others rather than taking from them. If James and John want to be great, they should prepare to be the lead slaves. In the kingdom, leaders are to be servants because we follow Jesus, the perfect servant leader. In fact, the main reason Jesus came to earth was to serve and "give his life as a ransom for many" (20:28). Here Jesus clearly teaches that he will die in our place as a sinless substitute for guilty sinners—the ultimate act of service!

The blind receive mercy and sight (20:29–34)

See Mark 10:46–52; Luke 18:35–43. We shouldn't miss the irony that the blind men see who Jesus really is, while the disciples are struggling to

✦ Jesus came to demonstrate that greatness is found in humble service (see Phil. 2:1–8).

grasp his mission (the previous episode) and the Jewish leaders are ready to kill him. They are traveling through Jericho, which is only about fifteen miles from Jerusalem. Only Matthew mentions that there were two blind men (see Matt. 8:28–34; 9:27–31). They cry out repeatedly for mercy from Jesus as "Lord" and "Son of David." Again, out of compassion, Jesus restores their sight, and they follow him.

Jesus Teaches on False Discipleship (21:1–23:39)

Jesus now enters Jerusalem and confronts the Jewish leadership in the temple. The leaders question Jesus's authority and test him repeatedly. He denounces their hypocrisy and challenges their authority to represent God to the people. After pronouncing a series of woes on these hypocritical spiritual leaders, the section closes with Jesus weeping over Jerusalem for continually rejecting God's messengers.

A vineyard.

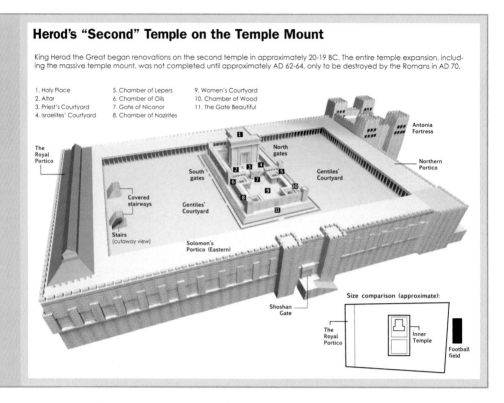

Herod's "Second" Temple on the Temple Mount

King Herod the Great began renovations on the second temple in approximately 20-19 BC. The entire temple expansion, including the massive temple mount, was not completed until approximately AD 62-64, only to be destroyed by the Romans in AD 70.

1. Holy Place
2. Altar
3. Priest's Courtyard
4. Israelites' Courtyard
5. Chamber of Lepers
6. Chamber of Oils
7. Gate of Nicanor
8. Chamber of Nazirites
9. Women's Courtyard
10. Chamber of Wood
11. The Gate Beautiful

Antonia Fortress

The Royal Portico

North gates

Northern Portico

South gates

Gentiles' Courtyard

Covered stairways

Gentiles' Courtyard

Stairs (cutaway view)

Solomon's Portico (Eastern)

Shoshan Gate

Size comparison (approximate):

The Royal Portico

Inner Temple

Football field

King Jesus enters Jerusalem (21:1–11)

See Mark 11:1–10; Luke 19:28–40; John 12:12–19. Jesus's journey to Jerusalem is now complete as the King descends into the city to the praise of the crowds. To show how Zechariah 9:9 is fulfilled, Matthew cites the prophecy (21:5). We also learn from Matthew that the people praise Jesus as the "Son of David" (21:9). Jesus enters the city as the promised King.

Jesus judges the temple (21:12–17)

See Mark 11:15–17; Luke 19:45–46. Jesus enters the temple area and begins disrupting the commercial activities. Since the court of the gentiles was a big place, Jesus wasn't trying to "cleanse" the temple by chasing out all the vendors as much as condemn it through a dramatic act. The temple authorities are converting the place of God's presence into a religious hideout for hypocrites (see Isa. 56:7; Jer. 7:11). Through this dramatic act, Jesus condemns the temple itself. He is not only condemning the actions of the opportunists but also the place itself for claiming to mediate God's presence. People should look to Jesus, rather than to the temple, to experience God's powerful presence. After Jesus welcomes and heals the blind and the lame (people typically deemed unworthy to enter the temple), children shout praises to the "Son of David" (21:15). Embarrassed and angry, the Jewish

✦ Jesus condemns the temple and presents himself as the only true mediator of God's presence (see Jeremiah 7).

leaders complain about the children's worship. Jesus responds with Psalm 8:2: "From the lips of children and infants you have ordained praise" (21:16). Jesus then leaves for nearby Bethany, his refuge during these final difficult days.

The cursing of the fig tree (21:18–22)

See Mark 11:12–14, 20–26. When Jesus finds no fruit on this leafy fig tree, he curses it. Through this second symbolic act, Jesus condemns the temple and its hypocritical leadership. He then exhorts the disciples to have a faith that could move "this mountain" into the sea. The specific phrase "this mountain" probably refers to the nearby Mount Zion on which the temple sat. Those trusting in Jesus will see the church as the true temple of the Spirit and the replacement for the Jerusalem temple with its privileged priesthood and exploitive sacrificial system. The way to God is through Jesus, not through the Jerusalem temple, which came to be destroyed in AD 70 by the Romans.

The religious leaders question Jesus's authority (21:23–27)

See Mark 11:27–33; Luke 20:1–8. This begins a series of controversies between Jesus and the Jewish leadership. Who has genuine authority to represent God—Jesus or the Jewish religious leaders? The authorities ask Jesus who gave him authority to do what he's been doing (e.g., condemning the temple, performing miracles, receiving praise). Jesus answers a question with a question about the authority behind John's baptism: was it from God or from men? If they say "from heaven," then the natural follow-up question is, "Why didn't you believe him?" If they say "from men," then the crowds will turn on them because John was a popular prophet. They're trapped and choose not to answer. As a result, Jesus refuses to answer their initial question. In all that follows, however, Jesus actually does answer their question—his authority comes from God himself.

The parable of the two sons (21:28–32)

Now Jesus tells three parables that answer the leaders' previous question (21:23) and reveal more about how people can respond to Jesus. In the first story, a father instructs his two sons to work in the vineyard. The father represents God, the rebellious son represents the current Jewish leadership, and the obedient son represents those who follow Jesus. The surprise in the story is that the "tax collectors and the prostitutes" are accepting Jesus and entering the kingdom ahead of the religious leaders, who rejected both John and Jesus.

The parable of the wicked tenants (21:33–46)

See Mark 12:1–12; Luke 20:9–19. This pivotal story clearly captures the heart of Jesus's relationship with the religious leaders. The landowner represents God, who has carefully cultivated his vineyard, Israel. The "farmers" represent the Jewish religious leadership to whom God has entrusted his people. God has sent various servants (e.g., the prophets) to collect the fruit, but they have all been mistreated and rejected (e.g., 1 Kings 18:4; 2 Chron. 24:20–21; Jer. 20:1–2; cf. Matt. 23:34). The landowner then sends his own son (representing Jesus as the Son of God), and the leaders kill him, previewing what will soon happen to Jesus. When the owner returns, he will avenge his son's murder and give the vineyard to other tenants who will produce fruit. Matthew cites Psalm 118:22–23 to point out how Jesus fulfills Scripture. The builders are the leaders of Israel who are rejecting Jesus. But God will highly exalt Jesus as the capstone, and it will indeed be a marvelous work! Jesus boldly concludes that the kingdom of God is being taken away from the Jewish leaders and given to a new people (*ethnos*), a new community that includes both Jews and gentiles. This new people of God will produce fruit. When Jesus (the stone) and hypocritical religious leaders collide, Jesus wins (see Isa. 8:14–15; Dan. 2:44–45).

The parable of the wedding banquet (22:1–14)

See Luke 14:15–24. The third parable compares the kingdom of heaven to a wedding banquet prepared by a king for his son. The king's servants tell the invited guests the banquet is ready, but they all make lame excuses, refuse to attend, and even kill his servants (22:3–6). The king is insulted and enraged. He sends his army to judge the murderers and destroy their city, a symbol of the coming judgment of the Jewish leadership and Jerusalem. The remaining servants are sent to gather "all the people they could find, both good and bad" to the wedding feast (22:10). When the king arrives he spots a man not wearing the proper wedding attire. Either the man fails to dress properly, or he rejects the wedding clothes provided by the king. The man is imprisoned and punished, representing the eternal punishment awaiting those rejected by the King. Jesus concludes, "For many are invited, but few are chosen" (22:14). The parable teaches that God invites all people to enter his kingdom, that those who reject the invitation will face judgment (e.g., the Jewish leaders), and that those who profess to know the King but don't truly have a relationship with him (e.g., Judas Iscariot) will also be condemned (see Matt. 7:21–23).

✦ God has always preferred faithfulness over heritage. Those who follow Christ are the true descendants of Abraham and heirs of the promises of God (Gal. 3:26–29).

A test related to paying taxes (22:15–22)

See Mark 12:13–17; Luke 20:20–26. This is the first of three traps the leaders lay for Jesus so they can put him to death. The Pharisees and Herodians, normally adversaries, now team up to test Jesus about the legality of paying taxes to Rome (Caesar). They represent different views on the issue and hope to trap Jesus no matter what his answer. He sees through their malicious motive and denounces them as hypocrites. He asks for a denarius with Caesar's image on it, which they just happened to have, and concludes that they should give some of their money to Rome *and* give their lives to God. They are stunned by his brilliant response.

A Jewish man wearing a phylactery.

A test related to marriage at the resurrection (22:23–33)

See Mark 12:18–27; Luke 20:27–40. This second test in the series comes from the Sadducees.

A test related to the greatest commandment (22:34–40)

See Mark 12:28–34; Luke 10:25–28. The final test comes from the Pharisees and scribes as one of them asks Jesus about the greatest commandment, a matter often debated in Judaism. Jesus first responds with Deuteronomy 6:5 on loving God and then adds Leviticus 19:18 on loving people. By including both of these commands, he shows the close connection between loving God and loving people.

Jesus questions the religious leaders (22:41–46)

See Mark 12:35–37; Luke 20:41–44. Having answered several of their antagonistic questions, Jesus has a question for the Jewish leaders. It relates to the true identity of the

✚ The Ten Commandments are summed up by Jesus in the two commands to love God and love people. The apostle Paul reduces it further to a single command—love (Gal. 5:14).

Messiah. "Whose son is he?" Jesus asks. They quickly reply with a good answer, "the son of David." Then Jesus asks how David (speaking by the Spirit) can call the Messiah (his son) "Lord." Jesus quotes Psalm 110:1 in support of his question. Jesus is really making the point that Messiah is "Lord" (the divine name for God in the Greek Old Testament). If David acknowledged Messiah as God and Jesus is the Messiah, why are the leaders rejecting Jesus? They had no answer and didn't dare ask him any more questions. This clearly answers the leaders' original question from Matthew 21:23 and cements their opposition to him.

Woe to the scribes and Pharisees (23:1–36)

See Mark 12:38–40; Luke 20:45–47. In this lengthy section dealing with judgment, Jesus warns the crowds and his disciples about the hypocrisy of the Jewish leaders. He recommends that people follow what these leaders say (when it lines up with Jesus's teachings) but avoid what they do. They do not practice what they preach (23:2–3). Instead, disciples are to relate to each other in humble authenticity (23:8–12). In 23:13–32 Jesus pronounces seven woes on the scribes and Pharisees. He condemns them for hypocrisy, for lack of genuine love for people, for their people-pleasing motives, for their unholy hearts, for loading people down with burdensome obligations, for focusing on minor issues and neglecting major ones, for persecuting God's faithful messengers, and for rejecting the kingdom of God being inaugurated by Jesus. They are, in Jesus's words, a bunch of snakes who will surely be condemned to hell (23:33).

The "seat of Moses" that Jesus mentions in Matt. 23:2 was the place in a synagogue reserved for a person of authority.

Teachers of the Law (Scribes)

Joseph R. Dodson

The teachers of the law (scribes) in the New Testament were the professional Torah teachers of the day, but in subsequent history they have been remembered more for their confrontations with Jesus and their partnership with the Pharisees. In fact, when the scribes encounter Jesus in Matthew's Gospel, they almost seem to be identical to the Pharisees (e.g., Matt. 5:20; 12:38; 23:2–31); however, Luke, who still closely associates the two groups, reveals more of a distinction (see Luke 11:39–46). It is probable, then, that the scribes were a subset of the Pharisees, scholarly experts among pious laypeople.

Since these teachers of Torah devoted themselves to understanding and applying the law's legislation to their contemporary setting, they were keen to hear how Jesus did the same. Therefore, the scribes often tested Jesus by besieging him with questions about his beliefs, lifestyle, and actions (Matt. 15:1–2; 21:15–16; Luke 11:53–54): "What is the most important commandment?" "Is it right to pay taxes to Caesar?" "Why do you eat with sinners?" "By what authority do you do these things?" On the whole, however, they strongly disagreed with his answers. In turn, Jesus asked questions that these "experts" could not—or *would* not—answer: "Is it lawful to heal on the Sabbath?" "John's baptism, was it from heaven or from men?" "If the Christ is the son of David, then why does David call him 'Lord'?"

Being rendered speechless before crowds by such questions undoubtedly embarrassed these teachers of the law (Mark 11:29–33; Luke 14:3–4; 20:26). So also, the people's praise for Jesus's authority over against their own teachings surely vexed them (e.g., Matt. 7:29; Mark 1:22; 11:18). Thus, with Jesus's blistering comments adding insult to injury (Matt. 23:1–32; Luke 11:45–51), the scribes' animosity toward him comes as no surprise. So great was their hatred for Jesus that it led them to join with the chief priests in their plan to kill him (Mark 11:18; 14:1; Luke 22:2). Finally, with Judas's betrayal of the Christ, the teachers got their wish: they arrested Jesus quickly, accused him vehemently, and mocked him mercilessly (Matt. 26:57–58; 27:41–42; Mark 14:43–53; 15:1, 31–32; Luke 23:10).

However, these actions smack of irony in that they validated Jesus's very prophecy about them: "The Son of Man will be betrayed to the chief priests and the teachers of the law. They will condemn him to death . . . [but] on the third day he will be raised to life!" (Matt. 20:18–19; cf. 16:21; Mark 10:33–34; Luke 9:22). This irony was not lost on the early church who interpreted Psalm 2 to refer to these specific events; indeed, the teachers of the law plotted in vain as they took their stand against the Lord and against his anointed one—only to do what God had already decided beforehand (Acts 4:24–28).

The King laments over Jerusalem (23:37–39)

See Luke 13:34–35. This section began in 21:1 with Jesus entering Jerusalem to the praise of the crowds. Now he grieves over the city. He mourns because the Jewish leaders have rejected God's Messiah. He takes no delight in pronouncing judgment because his heart is breaking. Jesus wishes he could gather the rebellious children under his wings like a mother hen gathers her chicks, but they will have none of it (23:37). What God wants and what the Jewish leaders want are two different things, and God highly respects human

The stone carvings inside the arch of Titus in Rome depict captives from Jerusalem following the destruction of the temple in AD 70.

freedom ("I have longed" vs. "you were not willing"). So Jesus, the Son of God, abandons the temple to desolation (Jer. 22:5). They will not see Jesus again until they declare, "Blessed is he who comes in the name of the Lord" (Ps. 118:26).

Discourse 5: The Mount of Olives (or Olivet) Discourse (24:1–25:46)

Jesus describes events (birth pains) that will occur throughout history but do not necessarily signal the very end. One especially "sharp pain" will be the destruction of Jerusalem in AD 70. Then he talks about the interim period of great distress—the entire period between Jesus's first coming and his second coming, or perhaps an especially intense time just prior to Christ's return. Jesus speaks of his return and reminds his disciples (including us) that they should always be prepared for this event, which is certain in spite of its timing remaining a mystery. The discourse closes with Jesus's depiction of the final judgment at the end of the age.

Jesus predicts the temple's destruction and the disciples ask questions (24:1–3)

See Mark 13:1–4. As Jesus and the disciples are walking out of the temple courts, the disciples comment on the magnificence of the temple itself (24:1). Jesus shocks them with the pronouncement that this amazing building will be destroyed (24:2). Later on the Mount of Olives, the disciples have two follow-up questions: (1) when will these things happen, and (2) what will be the sign of your coming and of the end of the age? Jesus's lengthy answer has been labeled by some as the "Olivet Discourse," while others call it the "Apocalyptic" or "Eschatological" discourse. In answering these two questions, Jesus speaks about two events—the destruction of Jerusalem in AD 70 and his second coming at the end of the age. He uses the first event in the near future to preview the second event in the distant future. The near future is intertwined with the far future. It's much like looking at a mountain range from a distance. All the mountains appear to be the same distance away, but in reality some mountains are much closer to where you

✦ Paul's teaching on the end times in 1 and 2 Thessalonians is based largely on Jesus's teaching in the Olivet Discourse.

are standing than others, perhaps miles closer. In the same way, some of what Jesus says in this discourse will be fulfilled in the first century (near future) and some will be fulfilled at the end of the age (far future). Thankfully, we don't have to understand all the details of the Olivet Discourse in order to grasp Jesus's main message.

Jesus answers the disciples' two questions (24:4–35)

BIRTH PAINS—EVENTS THAT OCCUR IN EVERY AGE (24:4–14)

See Mark 13:5–13; Luke 21:8–19. Jesus alerts the disciples to "birth pains" that will mark every age—deception, false messiahs, false prophets, wars and rumors of wars, famines, earthquakes, persecution for God's people, apostasy, betrayals, an increase of wickedness, a lessening of love, and the worldwide preaching of the gospel. Those who endure to the end will be saved.

THE DESTRUCTION OF JERUSALEM (24:15–20)

See Mark 13:14–18; Luke 21:20–24. Jesus warns his disciples about the imminent destruction of Jerusalem and its magnificent temple. When they see the "abomination that causes desolation" standing in the holy place, they should run to the mountains. The parallel passage in Luke clearly shows that this prediction relates to the Roman destruction of Jerusalem in AD 70. Luke says, "When you see Jerusalem being surrounded by armies, you will know that its desolation is near. Then let those who are in Judea flee to the mountains, let those in the city get out, and let those in the country not enter the city" (Luke 21:20–21). If possible, disciples should run away from this Roman destruction.

THE INTERIM PERIOD OF GREAT TRIBULATION (24:21–28)

See Mark 13:19–23; Luke 17:22–24. Jesus warns of a period of "great distress" or tribulation. This distress will certainly include the suffering associated with the destruction of the temple in AD 70, but it will also extend beyond that time. False messiahs and false prophets will appear and perform signs and wonders in an attempt to deceive God's people. We should not be duped by such religious trickery. When Jesus returns, his coming will be public, visible to all, and unmistakable. You won't miss it.

JESUS'S SECOND COMING (24:29–31)

See Mark 13:24–27; Luke 21:25–28. After the period of tribulation, Jesus the Son of Man will return with power and great glory amid cosmic anomalies (v. 29). Jesus's return will be seen and heard (but not welcomed) by all. He will send his angels to gather his people from everywhere to meet him.

✛ Jesus warns his disciples to expect tribulation and persecution (e.g., John 15:18–21; 16:33).

THE NEARNESS OF CHRIST'S RETURN (24:32–35)

See Mark 13:28–31; Luke 21:29–33. As leaves on a fig tree show summer is near, so the fulfillment of "all these things" (see 24:4–28) reveals that Christ's return is near. Jesus promises that "this generation" (likely referring to the generation of the Twelve) would not pass away until all these things have happened. Jesus is not promising to return during the lifetime of the Twelve, only that they would experience what he has been describing, which they did. Jesus could return at any time!

The need to be prepared for Christ's sudden return (24:36–25:46)

ONLY THE FATHER KNOWS THE TIME OF CHRIST'S RETURN (24:36)

See Mark 13:32. No one knows the time of Jesus's return, including the angels in heaven and the Son himself. In choosing to become human, Jesus accepted limitations on his divine knowledge.

ILLUSTRATIONS OF THE SUDDENNESS OF JESUS'S RETURN (24:37–41)

See Luke 17:26–35. In the days of Noah, people were going about everyday life when the flood came and "took them all away" (the wicked people were "taken"). That is how it will be at the coming of the Son of Man. Two men in a field or two women grinding with a hand mill will be separated. The wicked will be taken in judgment, while the righteous will be gathered to the Lord.

THEREFORE, STAY ALERT! (24:42)

Throughout the Olivet Discourse, Jesus warns us to be watchful, or to "keep watch" (24:4, 42, 43; 25:13). In other words, we should be prepared and ready for his return by staying faithful to Jesus.

PARABLES ON WATCHFULNESS (24:43–25:30)

See Mark 13:33–37; Luke 12:35–48; 19:11–27. Jesus gives four parables to teach disciples how to be ready for his return. The story of the homeowner and the thief (24:43–44) underscores that Jesus's return will be unexpected, like a thief in the night. The parable of the two kinds of servants (24:45–51) demonstrates that a faithful servant will be doing what he had been told to do when the master returns. The faithful servant will be rewarded, while the unfaithful servant will be judged. The parable of the ten bridesmaids (25:1–13) also stresses the need to be prepared and highlights the responsibility of every individual. The parable of the talents (25:14–30) instructs disciples to be faithful in using all their resources to honor and please Christ as they await his return.

✚ Jesus's return will be public, visible, loud, and obvious to all. Since we can't miss it, we shouldn't be fooled by false teachers who claim it has already occurred.

The Olivet Discourse concludes with an illustration about what will happen on judgment day. When King Jesus returns, he will separate the righteous (sheep) from the wicked (goats). He will reward the righteous with his presence forever and banish the wicked to everlasting punishment. In this illustration, a person's destiny is directly connected to whether they did or did not do "for one of the least of these brothers of mine" (25:40, 45). The term "brother(s)" in Matthew's Gospel either refers to biological relatives or to spiritual relatives (i.e., to other followers of Jesus). The word "least" is a form of "little one" that Matthew consistently uses to describe Christians (10:42; 18:6, 10, 14). Because Christ is mysteriously but powerfully connected to his people, especially his needy people, blessing or condemnation is tied to how people identify with Christ by relating to his followers.

If we pull together Jesus's commands or instructions in the Olivet Discourse, we see clearly what God is saying to us:

1. We should not be deceived by false teachers or false reports or false messiahs, even though they perform signs and wonders and deceive the masses. Rather, we should stay firmly anchored to Jesus and his teachings.

Sheep and goats often mix together.

2. We should not be alarmed by chaotic world events such as wars, famines, and earthquakes. These things are going to happen throughout history and do not necessarily signal the end of time.
3. We should be prepared to suffer for the cause of Christ and his kingdom. We should not be surprised if the world hates us because of our relationship with Jesus ("because of me" in 24:9).
4. We can be certain that Jesus will return.
5. The time of his return is uncertain. Jesus's return is always "near" or imminent, meaning that it could happen at any time. We should avoid the temptation to engage in useless speculation about when he will return.
6. We should be alert and prepared for his return. This is the central command repeated throughout the Olivet Discourse.
7. We stay prepared by doing what God has told us to do. Good and faithful servants use their abilities, gifts, and resources for kingdom purposes. It's all about being faithful.

Jesus's Crucifixion, Resurrection, and Great Commission (26:1–28:20)

In this climactic section of Matthew's Gospel, Jesus is betrayed, denied, rejected by the Jewish leaders and the Roman authorities, and executed on a cruel cross. But death does not have the final word. Jesus, the Messiah, is miraculously raised from the dead and commissions his followers to make disciples of all nations.

The plot to kill Jesus (26:1–5)

See Mark 14:1–2; Luke 22:1–2. We read here the fourth of Jesus's passion predictions (see Matt. 16:21; 17:22–23; 20:17–19). In just two days the Jewish Passover will occur, a fitting time for the Son of Man to be betrayed and crucified. The Jewish leaders plot to arrest and kill Jesus, but this is all part of God's plan.

Jesus anointed for burial (26:6–13)

See Mark 14:3–9; John 12:1–8.

Judas sells out for thirty pieces of silver (26:14–16)

See Mark 14:10–11; Luke 22:3–6; John 13:2. Judas makes a deal with the Jewish leaders to "hand over" or betray Jesus for "thirty silver coins"

(26:14–15; 27:9–10). That sum was the equivalent to about 120 days' wages for the average worker. We are not told why Judas decides to betray Jesus.

The Last Supper and the Lord's Supper (26:17–30)

See Mark 14:12–26; Luke 22:7–23; John 13:30. Jesus and his disciples prepare to celebrate the Passover in their final meal together (26:17–20). As they are eating, Jesus announces that one of the Twelve will betray him and confirms that it is indeed Judas (26:25). Just as the Passover meal celebrates God's powerful deliverance of his people from slavery through the exodus event, so this Last Supper will come to symbolize Jesus's deliverance of his people from sin through his death and resurrection. The Last Supper becomes the Lord's Supper. The bread and the cup represent Jesus's body and blood, broken and poured out "for many for the forgiveness of sins" (26:28). Jesus's sacrificial death on the cross makes forgiveness and a new relationship with God possible. Jesus concludes by saying he will not participate in the Supper again until he celebrates with his disciples in "my Father's kingdom," almost certainly a reference to the messianic banquet in the new heaven and new earth. After singing a hymn, they leave the upper room for the Mount of Olives.

Unleavened bread similar to that used by Jesus and the disciples at the Last Supper.

Jesus predicts Peter's denials (26:31–35)

See Mark 14:27–31; Luke 22:31–34; John 13:36–38.

Jesus's agonizing prayer in Gethsemane (26:36–46)

See Mark 14:32–42; Luke 22:39–46; John 18:1.

Arrested by enemies, deserted by disciples (26:47–56)

See Mark 14:43–52; Luke 22:47–53; John 18:2–12. Judas and an armed crowd sent from the Jewish leaders approach Jesus in Gethsemane after his time of prayer. Judas betrays him with a kiss, the typical greeting shared by genuine friends. Jesus replies, "Friend, do what you came for" (26:50), providing another indication that Jesus is in control of this whole sequence of

✚ By saying he would celebrate again with his disciples in the future (Matt. 26:29), Jesus alludes to the future messianic banquet (Isa. 25:6; Luke 14:15; Rev. 19:7–9).

The Trial(s) of Jesus

Bruce Corley

The New Testament documents and other contemporary sources attest to a two-stage judicial proceeding against Jesus, namely, after a religious trial before the Sanhedrin that found him guilty of blasphemy, the Jewish leaders brought a charge of sedition before Pilate who conducted a political trial and had Jesus crucified.

The trial and death of Jesus is better attested and supported with a wider array of evidence than any other comparable event known to us from the ancient world. The historians Josephus and Tacitus provide brief notices of the trial. Although the Jewish documents are sketchy, a number of late rabbinic texts maintain a common tradition about Jesus: he was executed as a dangerous teacher, a seducer, who led Israel astray. The evidence outside the New Testament supports three facts: (1) Jesus was crucified by Roman authority under the sentence of Pontius Pilate (Josephus, Tacitus); (2) the Jewish leaders made a formal accusation against Jesus and participated decisively in the events leading to his execution (Josephus); and (3) Jewish involvement in the trial was explained as a proper undertaking against a heretic or seducer who led Israel astray (Talmud).

Our best sources of information are the accounts of the Passion Story in the four Gospels, where the documents exhibit their highest degree of similarity. The Gospel writers narrate a unified story of some twenty episodes, beginning with a plot that converges on the arrest of Jesus. The decision recounted in John 11:47–57—an arrest warrant issued after the raising of Lazarus—marked the beginning of the legal process and, in effect, made Jesus a fugitive from Jewish law.

The Synoptic time note, "after two days was the feast of Passover" (Mark 14:1; par. Matt. 26:2; Luke 22:1), refers to a subsequent meeting of the council at the palace of Caiaphas. Here the discussion centered on a covert plan, as Luke puts it, "the how" (22:2) of getting rid of Jesus without causing an uproar during the feast (cf. Matt. 26:4; Mark 14:2). The question was how to implement the resolution already passed (John 11:53, 57). The arrest in Gethsemane was instigated by agents of the Jewish court in collaboration with the Roman authorities.

The Jewish Trial. The Gospels report that swiftly following the arrest, probably before midnight, the Jewish leaders began an interrogation and trial of Jesus, arguing the case throughout the night and returning a death verdict at daybreak. The Gospel accounts bring together four graphic scenes. First, according to John 18:24, Jesus was initially interrogated by Annas, a former high priest (AD 6–15) and father-in-law to his successor, Joseph Caiaphas (AD 18–36). It is likely that Annas and Caiaphas were in wings of the same residence somewhere in the upper city. Second, while Jesus was inside the high priest's residence until about 3 a.m. (the time of cockcrow for Jerusalem in April), Peter was outside in the courtyard below denying that he even knew Jesus (Matt. 26:69; John 18:16). Third, there was a nighttime trial before Caiaphas (Matt. 26:59–68; Mark 14:55–65). A false charge was contrived that Jesus had threatened to destroy the temple and rebuild it in three days (Matt. 26:61; Mark 14:58; cf. John 2:19). Then the high priest himself, driven by Jesus's unwillingness to answer the charge, pressed

events. When Peter cuts off the ear of the high priest's servant (John 18:10), Jesus tells him to put away his sword because those who sow violence tend to reap violence (26:52). He then reminds Peter that he could ask his Father to send seventy-two thousand angels to deal with this armed mob, but that would prevent the Scriptures from being fulfilled (26:53–54). God's way is

for an admission of guilt, "Are you the Christ, the Son of the Blessed?" (Mark 14:61; par. Matt. 26:63, "Son of God"). In Mark the explicit reply "I am" followed by the future "Son of Man" saying (Mark 14:62; cf. Matt. 26:64; Luke 22:69) linked Jesus's identity to three elevated titles—Messiah, Son of God, and Son of Man. This claim constituted blasphemy in the eyes of the court, and "they all condemned him as worthy of death" (Mark 14:64; par. Matt. 26:66). The blasphemy charge had three components: messianic claims, threats against the temple, and false prophecy, any one of which could carry a death warrant. Finally, Luke records the morning session of the Sanhedrin for the purposes of formulating the charges against Jesus (Luke 22:66).

The Roman Trial. The narratives of the trial before Pilate depict a separate prosecution aimed to secure a death sentence under terms of Roman law. The Sanhedrin, knowing well that blasphemy was not a capital offense in the eyes of Rome, urged the governor that Jesus had committed treason against the state. The reason why the Jews came to the Roman authority is made clear by John: "It is not lawful for us to put anyone to death" (John 18:31 ESV). Pilate did not simply ratify the Jewish decision but made a new investigation of the case, asking for the charges against Jesus: "What accusation do you bring against this man?" (John 18:29 ESV; cf. Matt. 27:12; Mark 15:3; Luke 23:2). Luke gives the precise wording in a threefold form: leading astray the nation, forbidding payment of taxes to Caesar, and claiming to be the Messiah, a king (Luke 23:2; cf. 23:5, stirring up the people; 23:14, inciting the people to rebel). The obvious political overtones of this accusation explain Pilate's first and uppermost question, "Are you the king of the Jews?" (Matt. 27:11; Mark 15:2; Luke 23:3; John 18:33). Fast upon Pilate's two failed maneuvers to avoid responsibility for Jesus—his transfer of Jesus to the jurisdiction of Herod Antipas and his release of Barabbas instead of Jesus (Matt. 27:15–26; Mark 15:6–15; Luke 23:6–25; John 18:39–40)—Jesus was sentenced to death by crucifixion (Matt. 27:26; Mark 15:15; Luke 23:24–25).

At a place called the *Lithostroton* ("stone pavement," John 19:13), the formal sentence of death was spoken from the judgment seat (*bema*) where Roman law required the magistrate to pronounce a capital sentence. The issue of kingship in Pilate's court raised the alarm of sedition (John 19:12), an act deserving crucifixion. Sedition, or inciting people to rebel, came under the treason crimes headed "offense against majesty" (*laesa maiestatis*), which were applied to all sorts of "misconduct." During the principate, especially under Tiberius, trials for lèse-majesté were exploited as a convenient means to dispose of enemies. The nature of the alleged crime and its penalty would have been obvious to Pilate, even while he harbored doubts about the guilt of Jesus.

Scourging and mockery were integral to Pilate's decision and emphasize the role of the Roman soldiers who carried out the order: "Then the governor's soldiers took Jesus into the Praetorium. . . . They led him away to crucify him" (Matt. 27:27, 31; par. Mark 15:16, 20). That Pilate attempted to end the trial by having Jesus flogged conforms to Roman practice. Scourging could be inflicted as the first stage of capital punishment or, as it is in the Gospels (Luke 23:16, 22; John 19:10), an independent penalty followed by release or imprisonment (cf. Acts 16:23; 22:24). The details of the Gospel narratives are, on the whole, in remarkable accord and are fully intelligible in light of the legal situation in Roman Palestine.

the way of the cross. Although he taught openly in the temple, the leaders hesitate to arrest him in a public place because they are cowards. Again, Matthew notes that things have happened this way to fulfill what the prophets have written. Sadly, this episode closes with these painful words: "Then all the disciples deserted him and fled" (26:56). Would we have done the same?

Jesus examined by the Jewish leaders (26:57–68)

See Mark 14:53–65; Luke 22:54–71; John 18:13–28. The Jewish leaders examine Jesus, looking for evidence they could use to get a Roman death sentence. They hear testimony that Jesus claimed to be able to destroy the temple and rebuild it in three days (26:61; see what Jesus actually said in John 2:19). When Caiaphas, the high priest, challenges Jesus to defend himself, he remains silent. Both the Jews and the Romans would take seriously threats against the temple. Well aware of the close connection between the Messiah and the restoration of Jerusalem, the high priest now says to Jesus: "I charge you under oath by the living God: Tell us if you are the Christ [Messiah], the Son of God" (26:63). Jesus now answers, "Yes, it is as you say" (26:64). Then Jesus makes a very provocative statement drawn from Daniel 7:13 and Psalm 110:1: "In the future you will see the Son of Man sitting at the right hand of the Mighty One and coming on the clouds of heaven" (26:64). Jesus is claiming to be the heavenly Son of Man who works at God's side as the divine judge. The high priest tears his clothes and accuses Jesus of blasphemy, a religious crime worthy of death in their view (26:65–66). The Jewish leaders then insult him by spitting in his face, physically abusing him, and mocking him: "Prophesy to us, Christ. Who hit you?" (26:68).

Peter denies Jesus (26:69–75)

See Mark 14:66–72; Luke 22:56–62; John 18:25–27.

Jesus's sentence and Judas's suicide (27:1–10)

See Luke 23:1; John 18:28. Early in the morning, the entire Jewish Sanhedrin meets to render an official verdict regarding Jesus (see Mark 15:1). After they decide he is worthy of death, they hand him over to Pilate, the Roman governor. Meanwhile, Judas begins to feel guilty for his betrayal, but it's too late to reverse the consequences of his actions. He returns the blood money to the Jewish leaders along with a confession, but they want nothing to do with him. Judas has been used and discarded by the false shepherds of Israel! After throwing the thirty coins into the temple, Judas hangs himself. Ironically, the chief priests insist on keeping their purity laws regarding the blood money, although they have just broken the greatest commandment by condemning the Son of God to death. They use the money to buy a field in which to bury strangers, a field that in Matthew's day was appropriately called the "Field of Blood" (27:8). Matthew notes how this whole scene fulfills Scripture (most likely Jer. 19:1–13; cf. Zech. 11:12–13).

Jesus on trial before Pilate (27:11–26)

See Mark 15:2–15; Luke 23:2–25; John 18:39–40. Before Pilate, the Roman governor, Jesus admits to being "the king of the Jews" (27:11) but doesn't respond to the other accusations made by the Jewish leaders (27:12–14). The governor's custom at the Passover Feast was to release one prisoner in order to pacify the crowds. Pilate tries to release Jesus because of his innocence and offers the crowd their choice of either Jesus or Barabbas. The Jewish leaders stir up the crowd to choose Barabbas (whose name ironically means "son of the father") so that Jesus, the Son of God the Father, is condemned to die. While sitting on the judgment seat, Pilate receives a message from his wife urging him not to condemn Jesus because she has had a frightening dream about his innocence. The people cry out for Jesus's crucifixion. In fact, they now believe that they are standing up for God against a false messiah. "Let his blood be on us and on our children," they shout (27:25). Pilate literally washes his hands as a public

The Antonio Fortress with its four towers was connected to the temple complex. This is the traditional location of Jesus's interrogation.

✚ A short time later on the cross, Jesus will pray for his enemies—likely referring to both Jewish and Roman enemies.

The Crucifixion of Jesus

Dan Wilson

Crucifixion was effective as an instrument of cruelty and shame, of military and political retribution, and of intimidation and fear, used by ancient Near Eastern rulers to control their subjects, especially the conquered and lower-class peoples. It was a standard form of execution in the ancient world predating the Roman period. The Persians and the Carthaginians particularly relished tormenting condemned criminals and enemies of the state.

As early as 519 BC the Persian Darius I crucified three thousand of the leading citizens of Babylon (Herodotus). The Greeks did not use crucifixion as extensively as others, but in 332 BC Alexander the Great crucified two thousand survivors of his invasion of Tyre. Although Jews viewed crucifixion as especially abhorrent, likely because of the curse expressed in Deuteronomy 21:23, the Hasmonean king, Alexander Jannaeus, crucified eight hundred Pharisees during the Jewish period of Hellenistic influence. The Carthaginians likely introduced crucifixion to the Romans, and, by the New Testament period, the Romans were regularly using crucifixion, particularly for the execution of noncitizens and slaves. In 73 BC the Roman general Marcus Licinius Crassus put down a slave revolt led by Spartacus and crucified along the Appian Way over six thousand gladiator and slave rebels on six thousand crosses. Vespasian and Titus also used the crucifixion of thirty-six hundred Jews related to the seige of Jerusalem in AD 70 as a deterrent to further revolt.

Although there were certainly variations based on the specific crime of the condemned and even based on the whims of the soldiers who carried out the deed, the pattern of events surrounding a Roman crucifixion was rather typical. This included the flogging of the criminal, not so much as a means of torture but as a means of forcing submission and of reducing resistance. The loss of blood and excruciating pain from the flogging would weaken even the most strong-willed person. The condemned criminal customarily carried to the place of execution at least the crossbeam upon which he would die, further weakening and decreasing the ability to resist. Public shame was central to Roman crucifixion. The Romans designated crucifixion sites near major thoroughfares into prominent cities, so as to create a public spectacle, removing the possibility of a hidden or private execution. This made crucifixion a deterrent, a warning about the consequence of a particular crime, identified by a sign hung on the cross or

demonstration of his innocence in the matter, but he releases Barabbas and has Jesus flogged in preparation for crucifixion. Flogging or scourging was a torturous (and often fatal) beating with a whip containing bone or metal fragments designed to rip open the victim's back. What Pilate finally demonstrates is that he is a pure pragmatist who avoids his responsibility to stand for justice.

Jesus the Messiah is crucified (27:27–44)

See Mark 15:16–32; Luke 23:26–43; John 19:2–3, 17–27. After being flogged, beaten, and ridiculed, Jesus is led away to be crucified. The soldiers force Simon of Cyrene to carry Jesus's cross to Golgotha, "the Place of the

around the neck of the condemned. Upon reaching the place of execution, the offender was placed on the cross and the cross uprighted. The hands were either tied or nailed to the crossbeam, and the feet were attached to the upright by a single nail through both feet. Typically the condemned straddled a small board that would support at least his partial weight. Breathing was extremely difficult in such a position, but in many cases a person might survive for several days. It was not unusual for the body of the crucified to be left on the cross, not only until death, but until the body was devoured by wild animals, which would eliminate the necessity of burial.

The crucifixion of Jesus as recorded in the New Testament is consistent with what is known about crucifixion from extrabiblical sources. These accounts, part of the more extended Passion Narratives, give the reader the framework for Roman crucifixion, but with little of the morbid detail; the Gospel writers simply say, "They crucified him." The four Gospels provide very similar versions of Jesus's crucifixion in Matthew 27:27–56, Mark 15:16–41, Luke 23:26–49, and John 19:16–30. All four accounts include a preceding scourging; the carrying of Jesus's cross by Simon the Cyrene; the placement of an inscription on the cross; the crucifixion at Golgotha (the Place of the Skull); the nailing of Jesus's body to the cross; the mockery by soldiers, religious leaders, and onlookers; and a relatively quick death, followed by

the removal of the body from the cross *before* the beginning of Sabbath.

The noun "cross" is used twenty-seven times in the New Testament, twenty-two of which point directly to the cross upon which Jesus died or in a broader sense to the cross event at the end of Jesus's passion. Five times the word is in Jesus's mouth related to followers "taking up the cross" (Matt. 10:38; 16:24; Mark 8:34; Luke 9:23; 14:27). The verb "crucify" is used fifty-three times, forty-eight of which refer directly to the crucifixion of Jesus or of the thieves crucified at Jesus's side; three of the other five are used of believers (Rom. 6:6; Gal. 2:20; 5:24).

The "foolishness" of the cross mentioned in 1 Corinthians 1:18 is related to the offensive and shameful nature of crucifixion in all of the cultures in which it was utilized as a means of execution. The cross is "foolish" in the ironic sense that an event so atrocious could have spiritual significance and could exhibit the power and the wisdom of God himself (1 Cor. 1:23). Paul is determined to know nothing among the Corinthians "except Jesus Christ and him crucified" (1 Cor. 2:2) and sees no reason for boasting apart from the "cross of our Lord Jesus Christ" (Gal. 6:14). He further sees Jesus's death on the cross as the ultimate act of obedience, followed by exaltation to the Father's right hand (Phil. 2:8–11).

Skull" (27:33). Our familiar word "Calvary" is the Latin term for skull. Crucifixion was a painful, shameful, horrific way to die, as the victim slowly became too weak to even breathe. Roman citizens were not subjected to crucifixion because of its barbaric reputation. Jesus is stripped and nailed to the cross. He refuses the drugged wine in order to bear the full weight of suffering. They gamble for his clothes, his only possessions. The sign above his head reads, "This is Jesus, the king of the Jews" (27:37). Death by crucifixion was reserved for the worst of criminals, like the two dying on either side of him. Those passing by ridicule and taunt Jesus for claiming the ability to destroy and rebuild the temple. "Come down from the cross, if you are the Son of God," they say as they shake their heads in disgust (27:39–40). Ironically,

Jesus, the true Son of God, by his very death will create a new temple, the people of God. The ridicule reaches its climax in the hostile words of the Jewish leaders recorded in 27:41–43. Little do they know that in just a few days Jesus will be vindicated as the King of Israel and the Son of God. Jesus even bears insults from the thieves being crucified beside him (27:44).

The death of Jesus the Messiah (27:45–50)

See Mark 15:33–37.

Events immediately following Jesus's death (27:51–56)

See Mark 15:38–41; Luke 23:47–49. The resurrection of Jesus seems to have supernatural effects. When Jesus gives up his spirit, the curtain of the temple is ripped in half from top to bottom, likely signifying that a new access to God for both gentiles and Jews has been opened up by the death of Jesus as well as God's judgment on the temple. Matthew next reports an earthquake as God opens up the tombs and "many holy people [or saints] who had died were raised to life" and appear to many in Jerusalem (27:52–53). This points to the beginning of a new age of salvation where Christ's resurrection guarantees the future resurrection of God's people. The Roman centurion also bears witness to Jesus's death with his exclamation, "Surely he was the Son of God!" (27:54). The final group of observers is a group of women watching from a distance (27:55–56). They have followed Jesus from Galilee and cared for him (Luke 8:2–3). Aside from John (John 19:26–27), these are the only faithful followers present at the cross.

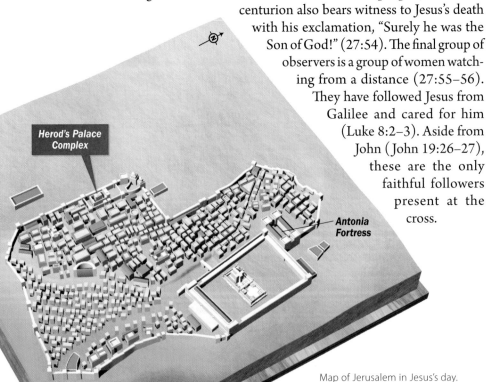

Herod's Palace Complex

Antonia Fortress

Map of Jerusalem in Jesus's day.

✚ At the resurrection of Jesus, some believers are temporarily raised from the dead much like Lazarus had been earlier (John 11).

Jesus is buried (27:57–66)

See Mark 15:42–47; Luke 23:50–56; John 19:38–42. Joseph of Arimathea, a rich member of the Jewish Sanhedrin who had become a follower of Jesus, asks Pilate for Jesus's body in order to provide a decent burial. Joseph prepares Jesus's body for burial, places it in a new tomb (perhaps the one he planned to use himself one day), and rolls a huge stone in front of the entrance. Mary Magdalene and the other Mary had apparently followed Joseph from the cross to the grave. The chief priests and Pharisees recall how Jesus had predicted that he would rise from the dead after three days (27:63). They ask Pilate for permission to make the tomb secure in order to prevent the disciples from stealing the body and then claiming that Jesus had risen. Pilate consents, and the Jewish leaders seal the tomb and post guards. Little good that would do.

Jesus is raised from the dead (28:1–15)

See Mark 16:1–8; Luke 24:1–12; John 20:1–18. The women disciples return to the tomb on Sunday morning to finish preparing Jesus's body for proper burial. But a violent earthquake interrupts their plans as an angel of the Lord descends from heaven and rolls away the stone. His appearance was like lightning and his clothes were as white as snow. The guards were terrified and became like dead men. But it's the angel's words to the women that announce the event that has changed history: "Do not be afraid, for I know that you are looking for Jesus, who was crucified. He is not here; he has risen, just as he said" (28:5–6). The angel invites them to see the empty tomb for themselves and then instructs them to go quickly and tell the disciples "he has risen from the dead and is going ahead of you into Galilee. There you will see him" (28:7). The women leave the tomb filled with a strange emotional mixture of both fear and great joy (28:8). They don't get far before the risen Jesus suddenly appears to them and greets them. They immediately fall at his feet, cling to him, and worship him (28:9). He calms their fears and also instructs them to "go and tell my brothers to go to Galilee; there they will see me" (28:10). Jesus lovingly uses the term "brothers" for those who have been less than loyal over the past few days. Grace turns our hearts back to God like nothing else. Meanwhile, the guards had regained their composure and reported everything that had happened to the Jewish leaders (28:11). The leaders devise a plan to limit their damages (28:12–15). They bribe the guards with a huge sum of money and devise a story—Jesus's disciples stole the body while the guards were sleeping. The leaders promise to protect the guards from Pilate should he hear the true story and keep them from being

✚ In 1 Corinthians 15 Paul describes the basis of Christian hope—Jesus's resurrection, which guarantees our future resurrection from the dead.

punished. In contrast to the worship of the women and restoration of the disciples stands the bribery, deceit, and corruption of the Jewish leadership.

Jesus's Great Commission (28:16–20)

A short time later Jesus meets the eleven disciples (minus Judas of course) in Galilee on a mountain. When they see him, some worship him right away while others aren't sure how to react (the term "doubted" in 28:17 probably indicates hesitation rather than unbelief). Jesus then gives the disciples marching orders for a worldwide mission. Actually, because Jesus joins us in the mission, it's commonly called the "Great Commission." Since all authority in heaven and on earth has been given to Jesus by the Father, he has the right to tell his followers what to do (28:18). The supporting command ("go") is essential for carrying out the main command ("make disciples"). To disciple the nations, we must go to the nations. To "make disciples" of Jesus involves (1) inviting people to enter a relationship with Jesus, and (2) helping them grow in that relationship. We are to make disciples of all "nations" or all peoples, excluding no one. The two actions that follow explain how we are to carry out this central command. To "baptize" refers to the one-time, public initiation into the Christian community. Baptism represents the birth phase of the new life in Christ. And it is baptism "in the name" (singular) of the "Father, Son, and Spirit" (one God in three persons). To "teach" speaks of the lifelong process of helping people grow as a Christian. In other words, evangelism alone does not fulfill the Great Commission. This kind of teaching involves more than discussion or debate. Jesus does not say "teaching them to know," but rather "teaching them to obey." Discipleship is education that results in life-changing obedience. The commission concludes with Jesus's promise to be present with us as we fulfill the commission. The fulfillment of this promise begins at Pentecost (Acts 2) when the Holy Spirit comes to live in believers (cf. John 14:16–17).

So What? Applying Matthew's Gospel Today

The Gospel of Matthew applies to our lives in many ways. Matthew emphasizes that Jesus is the Messiah or Deliverer who came to rescue us from sin. Two thousand years later and we still struggle with sin. Jesus came to set us free. He came first to the Jews in fulfillment of the prophetic Scriptures. And since Jesus fulfilled God's original promise to Abraham (Gen. 12:1–3), all the nations receive the blessings. As gentiles, we too have been given a Savior.

Matthew also emphasizes Jesus's teachings. The five discourses highlight what it means to be a Christ follower today. God expects us to live a certain

✦ Jesus's mission was initially to the lost sheep of Israel but ultimately it was a mission to all people (Matt. 28:18–20; Acts 1:8; Isa. 42:6).

way (5–7), to be mission-driven (10), to be kingdom-centered (13), to relate to one another with humility and forgiveness (18), and to be faithful as we wait for Jesus to return (24–25). If you're looking for direction and structure in your walk with God, these five discourses have much to offer.

We are reminded in Matthew that Jesus is powerful and authoritative. He casts out demons, heals people, calms the stormy sea, controls his own destiny, and will one day return as the Judge of the universe. Matthew reminds us that Jesus is the divine Messiah and King. Sometimes we forget that Jesus is powerful and that he can actually change our lives. Rather than trusting in our own ingenuity and abilities, we should submit to the King and trust him to work. In addition, Matthew stresses Jesus's compassion. Again and again, he is motivated to do his mighty work because he is the compassionate Shepherd. Jesus cares deeply about every aspect of your life.

Matthew is the only Gospel to mention the "church" (16:18; 18:17). Jesus has a lot to say about how Christians treat one another. Our faith should first work in our own family and community before we try to export it to the world. We need to have the attitude of a humble servant, and we need large doses of forgiveness to be able to maintain healthy relationships within the family of God. That's not always easy, but that is what God expects of his children.

Our Favorite Verse in Matthew

Then Jesus came to them and said, "All authority in heaven and on earth has been given to me. Therefore go and make disciples of all nations, baptizing them in the name of the Father and of the Son and of the Holy Spirit, and teaching them to obey everything I have commanded you. And surely I am with you always, to the very end of the age." (28:18–20)

The Garden of Gethsemane on the Mount of Olives.

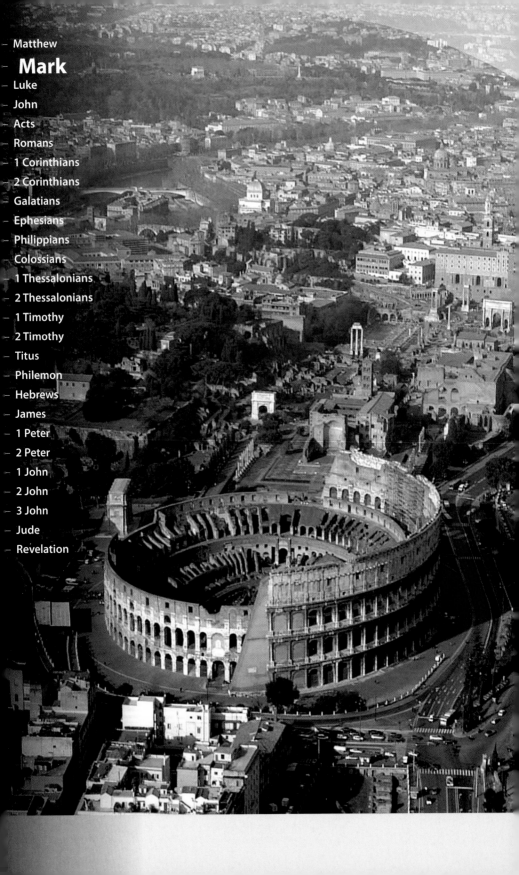

The Gospel of
Mark

Following Jesus, the Suffering Son of God

When our kids were young, I [Scott] wanted to be a responsible Christian father and read the Bible to them. I chose the Gospel of Mark. Right off the bat, however, we encountered an exorcism, then another one, and my young daughters were asking, "Daddy, what's a demon?" and "Daddy, are there demons under our bed?" After only a few chapters I switched to the Gospel of John. Why? Because Mark reads like a soldier's diary from the combat zone. Mark is full of exorcisms and confrontation and rebuke and warning and ultimately the violent death of its hero. But if you had been a Christian living in Rome in the late AD 60s, the Gospel of Mark would have been medicine to your soul. And for contemporary Christians trying to follow Jesus rather than be swept along by the prevailing culture, Mark will be just what we need to hear.

Who Wrote Mark?

Although Mark is technically anonymous, from a very early stage the title "Gospel according to Mark" was attached to it. The early Christian leader Papias, who served as bishop of Hieropolis in Asia Minor until about AD 130, made an important statement about Mark:

> And the Elder used to say: Mark, in his capacity as Peter's interpreter, wrote down accurately as many things as he [Peter?] recalled from memory—though not in an ordered form—of the things either said or done by the Lord. For he [Mark] neither heard the Lord nor accompanied him, but later, as I said, [he heard and accompanied] Peter.*

This provides clear and early evidence that Mark wrote the second Gospel, relying on the preaching of Simon Peter as his primary source. Other early Christian writers also affirm this connection between Peter and Mark (e.g., Justin Martyr, Irenaeus, Tertullian, Clement of Alexandria). The statement by Papias packs even more punch when we realize that the "Elder" he mentions is probably the apostle John himself. In a real sense, then, the Gospel of Mark is Simon Peter's Gospel.

There is the strong possibility that Mark is the same John Mark mentioned in other parts of the New Testament. His mother was prominent in the early Jerusalem church (Acts 12:12), and he accompanied his cousin Barnabas and Paul on the first missionary journey for a time before leaving the team (Acts 12:25; 13:5, 13; 15:37). He later reconciled with Paul and even ministered to him in prison (Col. 4:10; 2 Tim. 4:11). Mark was in Rome with Peter, who warmly referred to Mark as "my son" (1 Pet. 5:13).

Who Is Mark's Audience?

Early Christian tradition favors Rome as the place where Mark wrote his Gospel. He is likely in Rome with Peter during the 60s when the church is facing intense persecution under Emperor Nero (see 1 Pet. 3:13–17; 4:12–19; 5:13). In AD 64, after a major fire destroys much of Rome, Nero shifts the blame from himself to Christians, resulting in trouble for the church. Many believe that both Peter and Paul are martyred during this time. Meanwhile back in Judea, a Jewish revolt against Rome is under way that will result in the destruction of Jerusalem and its temple in AD 69–70 (see Mark 13). In light of these two cataclysmic world events, the church certainly needed the wisdom communicated in Mark's Gospel.

Mark writes for a target audience of gentile Christians in and around Rome, although the message certainly finds a much wider readership soon

* Eusebius, *Hist. eccl.* 3.39.15, as translated by Richard Bauckham, *Jesus and the Eyewitnesses* (Grand Rapids: Eerdmans, 2006), 203.

✛ Paul encourages Christians to submit to governing authorities (Romans 13). At that time, Nero would have been the Roman emperor. Ironically, he is also the emperor many believe would later sentence Paul to death.

after it is written. For his gentile audience, Mark explains Jewish customs (7:3–4; 15:42), translates Aramaic expressions (3:17; 5:41; 7:34; 14:36; 15:34), and even explains Greek expressions using Latin equivalents (12:42; 15:16). Interestingly, Mark 15:21 refers to Rufus and Alexander as sons of Simon of Cyrene, the man who carried Jesus's cross. Perhaps this is the same Rufus that Paul mentions in Romans 16:13 as a member of the church in Rome.

What Is at the Heart of Mark's Gospel?

Mark's main concern is to show that Jesus, the powerful Messiah and Son of God, is also the Suffering Servant. Notice how Mark's aim of showing Jesus as the suffering Son of God encloses the entire Gospel (emphasis added):

Mark 1:1—"The beginning of the gospel about Jesus Christ, the *Son of God*."

Mark 15:39—"And when the [Roman] centurion, who stood there in front of Jesus, heard his cry and saw how he died, he said, 'Surely this man was the *Son of God!*'"

The synagogue at Capernaum (light stone). It dates after the time of Christ but rests on the remains of a synagogue dating to the first century (dark stone).

Between these two bookends Jesus shows what it means that he is the Son of God and Messiah (see especially Mark 8:28–29; 10:45). Mark then connects who Jesus is (Christology) to what it means to follow Jesus (discipleship). We learn that following Jesus means going the way of the cross, that the path to glory leads through suffering—not only for the Lord, but also for those who follow him. Mark's first readers, who were navigating the turbulent waters of persecution, needed this message.

The basic outline below reflects how Mark's purposes flow through the entire Gospel:

- Introduction: Jesus, the Suffering Son of God, Prepares for Public Ministry (1:1–13)
- Jesus Begins His Ministry in Galilee: Teaching and Healing (1:14–45)
- Jesus Ministers with Divine Power, but Is Rejected by the Religious Leaders (2:1–3:6)
- Jesus Ministers with Divine Power, but Is Rejected by His Own People (3:7–6:6)
- Jesus Ministers beyond Galilee (6:6–8:21)
- Jesus, the Messiah, Journeys to Jerusalem (8:22–10:52)
- Jesus, the Messiah, Confronts Jerusalem (11:1–13:37)
- The Suffering, Death, and Resurrection of Jesus, the Son of God (14:1–16:8)

What Makes Mark Interesting and Unique?

- Jesus, the Son of God and Messiah, demonstrates his power over Satan, demons, sin, disease, death, and false religion.
- The book is a fast-moving, action-packed story (Mark uses the word "immediately" more than forty times, unfortunately not always translated by the NIV).
- Mark focuses on Jesus's actions, especially his miracles (more on miracles per page than any other Gospel).
- People often react in amazement at Jesus's authority revealed in his teaching and miracles (e.g., 1:22, 27; 2:12; 4:41; 5:20; 6:2, 51; 7:37; 11:18).
- Jesus often demands that those he interacts with should keep quiet about him (1:34, 43–44; 3:11–12; 5:43; 7:36; 8:26, 30).

The Jordan River.

- Whereas Mark always portrays Jesus as the positive example to follow, he often portrays the disciples as negative examples of what the reader should avoid.

- Mark features an apocalyptic point of view, meaning that the world is seen as a battleground between God and Satan, good and evil. Jesus is intervening to liberate the world from the domain of evil and usher in the kingdom of God.

- The story of Jesus's passion (his suffering and death) is quite lengthy (about 19 percent of Mark compared to 15 percent of Matthew and Luke).

- Mark stresses the cross of Christ and the demands of discipleship (e.g., 8:34–38; 9:35–37; 10:42–45).

- Mark includes several series of three (e.g., three predictions of Jesus's death, three boat scenes, three times he finds the disciples sleeping in Gethsemane, three times Peter denies him).

- Mark sometimes "sandwiches" two events together to make sure that the reader will connect the two stories and understand them in light of each other: (1) 3:20–21, 22–30, 31–35; (2) 5:21–24, 25–34, 35–43; (3) 6:7–13, 14–29, 30–44; (4) 11:12–14, 15–19, 20–25; (5) 14:1–2, 3–9, 10–11; (6) 14:53–65, 66–72; 15:1–15; (7) 15:6–15, 16–20, 21–32.

- The resurrection story (16:1–8) is comparatively short. The oldest and most reliable manuscripts do not include 16:9–20, and it seems likely that Mark's original ending has been lost. Another explanation is that Mark intentionally ends the story abruptly at 16:8 to make a theological point—this is only the "beginning of the gospel" (1:1). The gospel story continues past the last pages of Mark into the lives of its readers and beyond.

What Is Mark's Message?

Introduction: Jesus, the Suffering Son of God, Prepares for Public Ministry (1:1–13)

Unlike Matthew and Luke, which begin with Jesus's birth, the Gospel of Mark jumps right to the public ministry of Jesus. The good news of Jesus Christ, the Son of God, begins with the ministry of John the Baptizer followed by the baptism and temptation of Jesus.

The start of something new (1:1)

Mark's opening line—"The beginning of the gospel about Jesus Christ, the Son of God"—tells us what to expect from the whole book: "good news." Specifically the news will feature Jesus, the "Christ" or Messiah (8:29; 9:41; 12:35; 13:21; 14:61; 15:32). He is the much-anticipated king and ruler sent by God to bring salvation. But Jesus is more than your average human hero. He is the unique "Son of God" who defeats Satan, forgives sins, proclaims liberating truth, heals diseases, raises the dead, and introduces God's kingdom. While ancient inscriptions have been discovered that claim the Roman emperor to be "Son of God," Jesus is clearly portrayed in Mark as the true Son of God. Interestingly, the term "gospel"—used seven times in Mark (1:1, 14, 15; 8:35; 10:29; 13:10; 14:9)—was used in that day to refer to celebrations connected with the Roman emperor (e.g., his birthday). Mark's very first words show how Jesus stands in total contrast to evil emperors such as Nero. Although the Jesus way isn't easy, in the end it is the way of life rather than death. Definitely good news!

The opening act (1:2–8)

See Matthew 3:1–12; Luke 3:1–18; John 1:19–28. Mark begins his Gospel with the prophetic ministry of John the Baptizer. In fact, God's good news begins much earlier with the Old Testament prophets. In verses 2–3 Mark combines Old Testament quotes from Exodus 23:20, Isaiah 40:3, and Malachi 3:1 to show that Jesus fulfills Isaiah's promise of future salvation. Dressed similarly to Elijah of old (2 Kings 1:8), John prepares the way for Jesus, the Stronger One, who will baptize people not with water for repentance (as John is doing) but with God's Spirit.

The arrival of the suffering Son of God (1:9–11)

See Matthew 3:13–17; Luke 3:21–22; John 1:29–34. Jesus comes from the sticks of Nazareth in Galilee to be baptized by John in the Jordan River

✦ The Jordan River, where Jesus himself is baptized, is often connected with pivotal events in the Bible, such as the crossing of Israel into the Promised Land.

Healings

Healing Peter's mother-in-law	Mark 1:29-31; Matt. 8:14-17; Luke 4:38-39
Man with leprosy	Mark 1:40-45; Matt. 8:1-4; Luke 5:12-15
Paralyzed man	Mark 2:1-12; Matt. 9:1-8; Luke 5:17-26
Man with withered hand	Mark 3:1-6; Matt. 12:9-14; Luke 6:6-11
Bleeding woman	Mark 5:25-29; Matt. 9:20-22; Luke 8:43-48
Deaf mute	Mark 7:31-37
Blind man	Mark 8:22-26
Blind Bartimaeus	Mark 10:46-52; Matt. 20:29-34; Luke 19:35-43
Centurion's servant	Matt. 8:5-13; Luke 7:1-10
Two blind men	Matt. 9:27-31
Woman crippled for 18 years	Luke 13:10-17
Man with dropsy	Luke 14:1-6
Ten men with leprosy	Luke 17:11-19
Royal official's son at Cana	John 4:46-54
Paralytic at Bethesda	John 5:1-18
Man born blind	John 9:1-41
High priest's servant	Luke 22:49-51; John 18:10-11

Raising the Dead

Raising of Jairus's daughter	Mark 5:22-24, 35-43; Matt. 9:18-26; Luke 8:41-42, 49-56
Raising widow's son at Nain	Luke 7:11-16
Raising of Lazarus	John 11:1-45

Exorcisms

Possessed man in synagogue	Mark 1:23-27; Luke 4:33-36
Gadarene demoniac(s)	Mark 5:1-20; Matt. 8:28-34; Luke 8:26-39
Daughter of Canaanite woman	Mark 7:24-30; Matt. 15:21-28
Demon-possessed boy	Mark 9:14-29; Matt. 17:14-20; Luke 9:37-43
Blind, mute possessed man	Matt. 12:22; Luke 11:14
Mute possessed man	Matt. 9:32-34

Nature Miracles

Calming the storm	Mark 4:35-41; Matt. 8:22-25; Luke 8:22-25
Feeding of 5,000	Mark 6:35-44; Matt. 14:15-21; Luke 9:12-17; John 6:5-15
Walking on water	Mark 6:45-52; Matt. 14:22-33; John 6:16-21
Feeding of 4,000	Mark 8:1-9; Matt. 15:32-39
Fig tree withering	Mark 11:12-14, 20-25; Matt. 21:17-22
Coin in fish's mouth	Matt. 17:24-27
First catch of fish	Luke 5:1-11
Turning water into wine	John 2:1-11
Second catch of fish	John 21:1-14

somewhere east of Jerusalem, perhaps near Jericho. At his baptism God "tears open" the heavens, and the Spirit descends on Jesus. Later when Jesus dies, God again "rips open" the temple curtain secluding the Most Holy Place to show that all people can now come into God's presence through Jesus (Mark 15:38; Heb. 10:19–20). God also speaks from the Old Testament at the baptism to reveal more about Jesus. "You are my Son," from Psalm 2:7 (a royal Psalm), says that Jesus is the Son of God and King. The words "whom I love," perhaps from Genesis 22:2 where Abraham is asked to sacrifice his only son Isaac, point to Jesus as the perfect sacrifice, the Lamb of God. "With you I am well pleased," reflecting Isaiah 42:1 (a Servant Song), says that Jesus came as the Servant foretold. Putting all three together, we see that Jesus, the Son of God and King, will suffer as the Servant in order to save his people.

The battle begins (1:12–13)

See Matthew 4:1–11; Luke 4:1–13. "At once" ("immediately") the Spirit drives Jesus into the wilderness to face spiritual and physical enemies (only Mark mentions the "wild animals," perhaps as an encouragement to persecuted Christians in Rome). Throughout Mark, Jesus engages Satan and the powers of darkness, but here we read few details about Jesus's temptations. What matters most is that Jesus, unlike the people of Israel before him, faithfully endures forty days of wilderness testing and successfully crosses the Jordan into the land to fulfill God's plan.

Jesus Begins His Ministry in Galilee: Teaching and Healing (1:14–45)

Right off, Jesus announces, "The kingdom of God has come near." To demonstrate that God is at work to establish his kingdom, Jesus begins to create a new community, he teaches with authority, and he performs mighty miracles. The people are amazed.

The time is now! (1:14–15)

See Matthew 4:12–17; Luke 4:14–15. Jesus's ministry officially takes off as John's ministry comes to a close. After John's arrest, Jesus moves north into Galilee with the message: "The time has come. . . . The kingdom of God is near" (1:15). The "kingdom of God" refers to God's reign that is invading this world in the person of Jesus. In the distant future, God's kingdom will also include a place or a realm. The references to "good news" (gospel) in

✦ At his baptism, the voice of the Father combines three key Old Testament texts to describe Jesus and his mission: Genesis 22:2; Psalm 2:7; and Isaiah 42:1.

The Synagogue

Jeff Cate

The synagogue served as the religious, cultural, and social center for the Jewish community in Israel and beyond. Current knowledge of ancient synagogues comes from literary references and archaeological excavations.

The Greek term *synagoge* refers to the building or the people who gathered for such a meeting. In the Old Testament, especially the Torah, the term refers to the "congregation" of national Israel, but never to a building or local gathering. Therefore, the origins of the synagogue as an institution are debated. Traditionally, many Jews traced the synagogue back to Moses (Acts 15:21), even though evidence is lacking. More likely, the synagogue arose outside of Palestine at a much later time, possibly during the Babylonian exile or later in the Jewish dispersion when Jews lived far from Jerusalem. Ancient synagogues are known to have existed in Babylon and the Mediterranean world, and over a hundred synagogues have been excavated in Israel alone.

At the earliest stages, private homes or sometimes outdoor locations served as Jewish gathering places for prayer and Torah reading. Only later were buildings specifically erected as synagogues. Many bigger cities had more than one synagogue, sometimes as many as a dozen.

Synagogue floor plans varied, especially since some utilized buildings originally constructed for other purposes. Synagogues typically were oriented so that congregants would pray facing Jerusalem. The central item was a portable ark of scrolls or a permanent Torah shrine. A raised podium is where Scriptures were read, lessons taught, and benedictions led. The gatherers typically sat on stone benches lining the interior walls.

Synagogues also served as local centers for education and study. Religious instruction, including reading the Scriptures and discussing the law, served as the basic education for Jewish youths. Since the synagogue tended to be a large building, it often also functioned as a place for public meetings and political gatherings.

The synagogue's presiding officer was the "ruler of the synagogue" or "head of the assembly" (Mark 5:22; Luke 13:14; Acts 13:15; 18:8, 17) who maintained order, selected worship leaders, invited speakers, and represented the assembly to the outside world. Synagogues also utilized assistants to administer prayers, recitations, and other duties.

The Gospels describe Jesus teaching and healing in synagogues of Galilee. According to Acts, Paul's strategy for spreading Christianity was to start first in the Jewish synagogues. The earliest followers of Jesus continued to meet in synagogues until they eventually were excluded in the mid- to late first century. It is not surprising, then, that James 2:2 refers to a Christian assembly as a "synagogue" rather than a "church" (Greek: *ekklesia*). Most likely, Jewish synagogues served as a formative template for early Christian worship practices.

1:14–15 form a sandwich around "kingdom," clarifying that the good news *is* the coming of God's kingdom in Jesus.

Jesus begins to create a community (1:16–20)

See Matthew 4:18–22; John 1:35–51. Early in his ministry Jesus calls disciples as the first step in creating a new community of followers. Unlike the discipleship model of the Jewish rabbis where students enlisted teachers, Jesus takes the initiative to call his disciples. In addition, their primary allegiance will be to him rather than to a set of rules or traditions. He first calls four fishermen (two sets of brothers) to follow him, promising to equip them to fish for people (1:17). These ordinary guys respond in an extraordinary way by leaving their families and vocations to follow Jesus (1:18, 20).

A new, powerful teaching (1:21–28)

See Luke 4:31–37. Jesus bases his Galilean ministry in Capernaum, a town on the northwest shore of the Sea of Galilee. His teaching differs dramatically from the "teachers of the law" (scribes) who merely cite outside authorities. Jesus teaches with genuine power from God (1:22, 27). On one Sabbath while Jesus is teaching in the synagogue, a man with an unclean spirit cries out to Jesus. Although the demon appears to admit defeat before the "Holy One of God," it is actually trying to control Jesus by naming him (a common warfare strategy according to ancient magic books). Jesus simply tells the demon(s) to shut up and leave the man. The people are amazed that Jesus's teaching has power over the forces of darkness, and the good news spreads rapidly throughout Galilee.

A miracle for Simon's mother–in–law and others (1:29–34)

See Matthew 8:14–17; Luke 4:38–41. Simon Peter and his brother Andrew have a home in Capernaum just a short distance from the synagogue. Simon's mother-in-law, who now lives with him and his wife, is in bed with a fever.

Jesus walks from the synagogue to the home, where he heals her completely, as her immediate response of service indicates. This is the first recorded healing miracle of Jesus's ministry, but certainly not the last. After the Sabbath ends at sunset, the sick and demon-possessed line up to meet Jesus. Mark distinguishes between the physically ill and the demonized (1:32, 34; 6:13). With Capernaum's population at between one thousand and fifteen hundred, Jesus must have ministered late into the night (1:33, 35).

An ancient oil lamp.

Prayer brings perspective (1:35–39)

See Luke 4:42–44. While it is still dark and after very little (if any) sleep, Jesus leaves the crowded house to find a solitary place of prayer.

✝ The creation of a new community of twelve would have signaled to many the renewal of Israel with its twelve tribes.

Most likely he walks up into the hills surrounding the Sea of Galilee to the west. He draws strength and perspective from his conversation with the Father. When his disciples track him down, he announces they will now be taking the good news beyond the comfortable confines of Capernaum for all to hear.

Touching an untouchable (1:40–45)

See Matthew 8:1–4; Luke 5:12–16. Jesus encounters a man with leprosy, a repulsive skin disease that made a person ritually unclean. According to Leviticus 13–14, a leper had to be quarantined from the rest of the community and only the priest could pronounce him fit to reenter society. Normally touching a leper would make a person unclean, but Jesus's miraculous touch instantly heals the man (1:41–42). Jesus strongly warns the man to keep quiet and go show himself to the priest as a "testimony to them" (likely referring to the priests, who need to hear about God's actions through Jesus). Rather than doing as Jesus instructed, however, the man tells the world about his healing, and Jesus becomes even more popular.

Jesus Ministers with Divine Power, but Is Rejected by the Religious Leaders (2:1–3:6)

The kingdom of God arrives with Jesus, but will the people receive him? Many do, but ironically the religious leaders oppose him. It's an issue of "Who's in charge?" In the five conflict stories of Mark 2:1–3:6, Jesus links himself with God, ministers with authority, and faces growing opposition from the Jewish leaders.

Only God can heal and forgive (2:1–12)

See Matthew 9:1–8; Luke 5:17–26. You've heard of faith that moves mountains. How about faith that digs through dried-mud roofs? Jesus responds to the faith of these four men by healing their paralyzed friend. But surprisingly Jesus first tells the man, "Your sins are forgiven." The teachers of the law (scribes) are outraged and conclude: "Only God can forgive sins. This guy Jesus is claiming to be

Animal skins used to hold water or wine.

✦ Jesus's healing of the leper is a good example of how Jesus fulfills the Old Testament law rather than abolishing it or becoming enslaved to traditions surrounding it.

The Gospel of Mark 567

Son of Man

Rodney Reeves

Jesus often referred to himself in the third person (about one-fifth of the time in Mark's Gospel). Surprisingly, he didn't call himself "Christ" or "Son of God," two titles favored by Christians. A couple of times he referred to himself as "prophet" (Mark 6:4; John 4:44) and "teacher" (Luke 22:11; John 13:14). His favorite self-designation, however, was "Son of Man," a rather vague title that could mean a variety of things. Perhaps Jesus called himself the Son of Man in order to identify with humanity. In other words, Jesus was claiming that he was as much a son of Adam (in Hebrew "Adam" means "man" or "humankind") as any other person. Some think Jesus used the title as a proper means of referring to himself in public, similar to the English "one" (as in "one would think..."). In this way, Jesus was making no special claim; he was merely avoiding first-person reference in public to be modest. The weaknesses of these interpretations are apparent: (1) none of Jesus's contemporaries would have doubted he was human (they were offended when he made claims of divinity), so there would be no reason for him to emphasize his humanity; and (2) Jesus was not reticent at all to talk about himself in the first person, so why would he feel obliged occasionally to employ social graces? (Besides, scholars have determined third-person reference wasn't a common practice in Jesus's day.) Therefore, most scholars argue that Jesus *was* making a special claim when he called himself the Son of Man.

The few times "son of man" appears in the Old Testament, it refers primarily to the frailty of humanity. Sometimes when God or an angel addressed the prophet, he is called a "son of man" (many times in Ezekiel, e.g., 2:1; also Dan. 8:17)—obviously contrasting the divine message delivered to a human messenger. In a few places in Psalms, Job, and Isaiah, "son of man" refers to humanity in general (Job 35:8; Ps. 8:4), to Israel in particular (Ps. 80:17; Isa. 56:2), or to the vulnerability of all humans (Isa. 51:12). In all of these instances, "son of man" is used to emphasize the finiteness of humans compared to the majesty of God. The only place where "son of man" refers to a heavenly being is in Daniel's vision of the Ancient of Days (Dan. 7:13). In that vision, one "like a Son of Man" (note the simile) receives from God an eternal kingdom on earth. This is probably the association Jesus was trying to make when he repeatedly called himself the Son of Man. He believed he was the inaugurator of a heavenly kingdom on earth (Matt. 4:17). As the Son of Man he had the authority to forgive sins (Mark 2:10) and rule on Sabbath obedience (Mark 2:28). Jesus even quoted Daniel 7:13 twice to support his claim: for his disciples (Mark 13:26) and during his trial (14:62). The surprise, however, was that Jesus insisted that the Son of Man—this heavenly ruler—would have to suffer and die to make Daniel's prophecy come true (10:33).

God." Glad they get the point. Isn't sin the root cause of human problems? Since Jesus cares about the man's heart as well as his body, he heals him relationally before healing him physically. Jesus also sends a clear message to the scribes—"the Son of Man [Jesus] has authority [right now] on earth [right here] to forgive sins [something only God can do]" (2:10). Amazing! (2:12).

The soul doctor (2:13–17)

See Matthew 9:9–13; Luke 5:27–32. Healthy people don't need a doctor; sick people do. That's the point Jesus makes when he calls Levi to be his disciple ("Matthew" in Matt. 9:9). Don't think for a minute that Levi was different from all the other tax collectors. They were seen as corrupt traitors who worked for the Romans and regularly cheated their own people. Matthew and his sinner friends are "the sick" in Jesus's analogy. Like a compassionate physician, Jesus places their healing above his own reputation (real righteousness above pretend righteousness). To heal them, however, he must relate to them by joining them in table fellowship—a sign of genuine friendship. Yet Jesus doesn't minister alone (the sinners were eating with "him and his disciples" in v. 15), and he never condones their sin. In contrast, it never crosses the minds of the "self-righteous" (v. 17) that they might need a soul doctor.

The bridegroom (2:18–22)

See Matthew 9:14–17; Luke 5:33–39. Timing is everything, especially when it comes to fasting or feasting. While the bridegroom is present, the guests should feast rather than fast. Who is the "bridegroom"? In the Old Testament, God is the bridegroom (Isa. 61:10; 62:5; Jer. 2:2, 32). Now Jesus is the bridegroom, a clear identification of Jesus with God. Before Jesus is "taken from them" (a veiled reference to his death), his disciples should celebrate. Jesus adds two illustrations using items commonly found at weddings to make his point—one about old and new cloth and another about old and new wine and wineskins. The old (traditional Judaism) and the new (Jesus) simply don't mix. Through Jesus, God is making all things new.

A field of mustard plants.

✚ Throughout the Gospels, Jesus claims rights and privileges attributed to God alone (e.g., forgiving sin, healing disease, claiming to be Lord of the Sabbath).

The Gospel of Mark   569

Lord of the Sabbath (2:23–28)

See Matthew 12:1–8; Luke 6:1–5. Jesus and his disciples are walking through a grain field. It happens to be on a Sabbath. They happen to pick and eat some of the grain. Evidently a group of Pharisees was following them around. They accuse Jesus's disciples of breaking the Sabbath law. Jesus always seems to be in trouble with these religious leaders for breaking food laws or Sabbath laws. He responds with a story from 1 Samuel 21 about David eating the sacred bread to validate his decision to place basic human needs above food and Sabbath rules. The Pharisees need to change their priorities. Also, by speaking as "Lord of the Sabbath" (v. 28), Jesus again links himself with God (cf. 2:7–10, 19).

Silent killers (3:1–6)

See Matthew 12:9–14; Luke 6:6–11. As Jesus goes into a synagogue, he sees a man with a deformed hand. But the religious leaders in the audience don't so much as notice the man, since they are preoccupied with putting Jesus under a microscope. The Pharisees' motive is to accuse Jesus and destroy his ministry. "Will Jesus break our law by healing this man on the Sabbath? If he does, he's guilty and we'll have him!" But Jesus goes on the offensive by asking the man to stand up in front of everybody. Now they'll notice him (3:3). Jesus's question in verse 4 targets the Pharisees, and they respond . . . with dead silence. While full of compassion for the man, Jesus is angrily grieving the Pharisees' hard hearts (3:5). Sometimes compassion and anger go together in the same righteous heart. Jesus heals the man instantly. The Pharisees are fed up and begin plotting with the Herodians, their political rivals, about how to kill Jesus.

Jesus Ministers with Divine Power, but Is Rejected by His Own People (3:7–6:6)

As Jesus's popularity skyrockets, he chooses twelve to extend his ministry. He is forming a new community in spite of misunderstanding from his own family and rejection from the Jewish authorities. Jesus teaches about the kingdom in parables and continues to work miracles to demonstrate his divine power, but sadly the Son of God is not welcome in his own hometown.

Desperate crowds and talkative demons (3:7–12)

See Matthew 4:24–25; 12:15–21; Luke 6:17–19. With the Pharisees plotting to kill him, Jesus tries to pull away with his disciples. But he can't escape the crowds. They come from everywhere it seems (3:8), in hopes of getting rid of their diseases and demons. While the crowds threaten to

✝ Jesus redefines family so that faith takes priority over heredity.

The Family of Jesus

Bobby Kelly

A study of the family of Jesus highlights Jesus's genuine humanity and gives insight into a number of the most significant leaders in the development of Jewish Christianity.

The New Testament presents Mary as Jesus's mother and Joseph, the carpenter, his father. To embrace the virginal conception (Matt 1:18; Luke 1:26–28), however, one should qualify Joseph as adoptive father. The use of such an adjective explains Joseph's relative lack of mention either in the New Testament, notwithstanding Matthew's birth narrative (Matthew 1–2), or in church tradition. Mary, on the other hand, is a different story. While Mary is not mentioned by name in Paul's writings, he does declare that Jesus was born of a woman (Gal. 4:4), establishing Jesus's very human birth. Mary dominates Luke's birth narrative (Luke 1–2) and appears in numerous other passages in the Gospels. Although Mary is typically cast as lacking insight into the nature of Jesus's mission (Mark 3:20–21; John 2:1–12), Luke names her as one of the 120 followers of Jesus who gather in Jerusalem after Jesus's ascension (Acts 1:13–14).

Paul offers the earliest references to the presence of bodily brothers of Jesus (1 Cor. 9:5), specifically naming James the Lord's brother as a leader of the Jerusalem church in the mid-first century (Gal. 1:19; 2:9). The Synoptic Gospels provide more detail. Mark 6:3 (cf. Matt. 13:56) mentions four brothers of Jesus: James, Joses (the abbreviated form of Joseph, the name given by Matthew), Judas (abbreviated Jude and the likely author of the New Testament letter bearing that name), and Simon, as well as at least two sisters. Extracanonical sources identify the sisters as Mary or Anna, and Salome.

As early as the second century (Tertullian), the apparent clarity of the terms "brother" (*adelphos*) and "sister" (*adelphe*) led to the belief that these were actually "blood" brothers and sisters born to Mary and Joseph after the birth of Jesus. This position, commonly referred to as the Helvidian view after its fourth-century proponent, has been challenged by at least two streams of tradition. One of these, identified with Epiphanius, the fourth-century bishop of Salamis, contended that the "brothers" and "sisters" were actually children born to Joseph by a previous marriage. Jerome popularized the other competing theory, arguing that the names listed in Mark 6:3 were in fact cousins of Jesus born to Mary's sister, Mary of Clopas. Both challenges appear to be an attempt to defend the developing tradition of Mary's perpetual virginity. While it is true that the term "brother" in Greek can be applied to masculine relatives however distant, or even figuratively to anyone devoted to Jesus, there is no reason apart from ecclesial or confessional needs to think the named persons in these texts were anything other than full brothers and sisters of Jesus.

Unfortunately, any further statements about Jesus's family must rest on speculation drawn from fragmentary and legendary extracanonical sources. Finally, it should be noted that Jesus's true family consists of those who do the will of God (Mark 3:35).

The freshwater lake known as the Sea of Galilee (or Sea of Gennesaret).

crush him, the demons attempt to control him by naming him as "the Son of God" (3:11). And while their "confession" is true, the source is diabolical and the timing is wrong. He orders them to keep quiet.

The dirty dozen or the terrific twelve? (3:13–19)

See Matthew 10:1–4; Luke 6:12–16; 9:1–5; 10:3. Jesus now goes up on a mountainside (historically a place of revelation). From the disciples who accompany him he chooses twelve to be "apostles" so that they may (1) be with him (fellowship), (2) go out to preach (witness), and (3) have authority to drive out demons (ministry). Why twelve? Because the Jews anticipated a time when God would restore Israel by restoring the twelve tribes and establish his kingdom on earth. Jesus is now forming the new Israel, and the kingdom of God is coming. What an interesting group of men. Among them were four fishermen (Peter, Andrew, James, and John), two "sons of thunder" (James and John), a despised tax collector (Matthew/Levi), a super patriot (Simon the Zealot), and one who would become a traitor (Judas Iscariot).

Deranged and demon possessed? (3:20–35)

See Matthew 7:16–20; 9:32–34; 12:22–27, 46–50; Luke 6:43–45; 8:19–21; 11:14–32; 12:10. Here Mark sandwiches together two stories—the reaction of Jesus's physical family (3:20–21, 31–35) and the accusation of scribes (3:22–30). Jesus's family is probably trying to guard their reputation and honor by restraining him. They think he's lost his mind. When accused by the experts from Jerusalem of being demon possessed, Jesus uses powerful logic to refute their claim: it makes no sense for Satan to drive out Satan, since that would be self-defeating. The only one stronger than Satan is God, and he is acting through Jesus. The scribes, however, are in danger of blaspheming the Spirit (an unforgivable sin) by deliberately attributing the work of God through Jesus to the work of Satan (3:30). At the end, Jesus redefines family in spiritual rather than physical terms.

To reveal and to conceal (4:1–34)

See Matthew 5:15; 7:1–5; 13:1–35; Luke 6:37–42; 8:4–18; 10:23–24; 11:33; 13:18–21. For the first time in this Gospel, Mark gives us a sample of Jesus's actual teaching. A parable (a term meaning "to throw alongside") is a short story with two levels of meaning, where certain details in the story represent something else. Jesus's parables in Mark 4 include the parable of the sower (4:1–9) and its interpretation (4:13–20), along with the parable of the lamp (4:21–23), the measure (4:24–25), the seed growing secretly (4:26–29), and the mustard seed (4:30–32). Very often, Jesus's parables

✚ The timing of Jesus's revelation of himself as Son of God is important, especially in Mark. He slowly reveals that his messiahship would involve suffering as well as glory.

A first-century fishing boat discovered buried in the Sea of Galilee in the 1980s.

reveal some aspect of the kingdom of God (e.g., "the kingdom of God is like . . ."). They also conceal spiritual truth from outsiders whose hearts are unreceptive (see 4:10–12, 25, 33–34). For this reason, those who have ears should use them to listen to what Jesus is saying (4:9, 23).

Who is this? (4:35–41)

See Matthew 8:23–27; Luke 8:22–25. Following the five parables, Mark has four miracle stories that illustrate Jesus's power over nature (4:35–41), over demons (5:1–20), over disease, and over death (5:21–43). "Who is this?" they ask (4:41). Answer: he is the Son of God! But tragically, when Jesus returns to his hometown and to his own relatives, they are offended by him (6:1–6). In this first story, Jesus and the disciples are sailing from the west side (Jewish territory) to the east side (gentile territory) of the Sea of Galilee, a lake in a depression surrounded by hills and prone to sudden storms. Jesus is asleep when the sea (a symbol of evil for the Jews) turns violent. The disciples, including some veteran fishermen, panic and wake Jesus for help. He first rebukes the sea (same word used for rebuking a demon in 1:25) and then rebukes his disciples for having fear but no faith (4:40). They now know he is more than a "teacher" since even the sea obeys him (4:41).

Unclean spirits, unclean animals, and a clean man (5:1–20)

See Matthew 8:28–34; Luke 8:26–39. This second miracle story in the series shows Jesus's power over evil spirits. In gentile territory Jesus is confronted by a man who has been massively demonized and reduced to living like a dangerous and self-destructive animal among the tombs. The legion of demons begs Jesus to cast them into a herd of pigs. Ironically, Jesus allows unclean spirits to destroy unclean animals by driving them into a symbolically unclean place (the sea). Perhaps Jesus wants to show that one human life is worth more than a whole herd of animals or to demonstrate God's power to conquer armies of demons. The reaction is mixed. The pig farmers want him to leave since he is bad for business. The people are awed by his sheer spiritual power. The man wants to go with Jesus, but obeys Jesus's instructions to tell his own people what God has done (5:18–20). In this gentile region where Jesus is less likely to be misunderstood, he does not hesitate to admit to being "Lord" (5:19).

The tale of two daughters (5:21–43)

See Matthew 9:18–26; Luke 8:40–56. The third and fourth miracles in this series are sandwiched together to dramatize Jesus's power over disease and death. Just as the influential synagogue ruler Jairus cares deeply about his twelve-year-old daughter, so Jesus cares deeply about his "daughter" (5:34) who has been sick and socially isolated for twelve years. Jairus hopes Jesus will bring a healing touch to his daughter, while the poor, bleeding woman merely wants to touch Jesus's cloak. The woman's faith brings healing, while Jairus is challenged to have faith rather than fear when he learns his daughter has died. On his own timetable, Jesus goes to the little girl and gives her new life. He orders the few witnesses to tell no one about the miracle, but to give the child something to eat. She's been through a lot.

Kursi (or Gergesa), on the east side of the Sea of Galilee. Jesus likely healed the demoniac here.

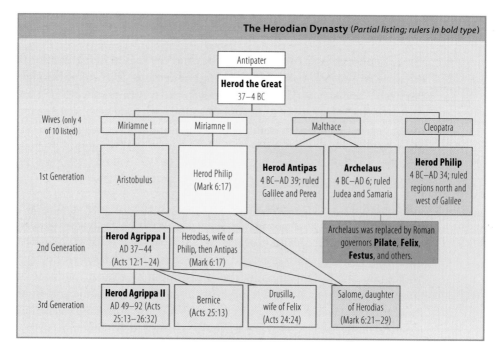

The Herodian Dynasty (*Partial listing; rulers in bold type*)

		Antipater		
		Herod the Great 37–4 BC		
Wives (only 4 of 10 listed)	Miriamne I	Miriamne II	Malthace	Cleopatra
1st Generation	Aristobulus	Herod Philip (Mark 6:17)	**Herod Antipas** 4 BC–AD 39; ruled Galilee and Perea · **Archelaus** 4 BC–AD 6; ruled Judea and Samaria	**Herod Philip** 4 BC–AD 34; ruled regions north and west of Galilee
2nd Generation	**Herod Agrippa I** AD 37–44 (Acts 12:1–24)	Herodias, wife of Philip, then Antipas (Mark 6:17)	Archelaus was replaced by Roman governors **Pilate, Felix, Festus,** and others.	
3rd Generation	**Herod Agrippa II** AD 49–92 (Acts 25:13–26:32)	Bernice (Acts 25:13)	Drusilla, wife of Felix (Acts 24:24) · Salome, daughter of Herodias (Mark 6:21–29)	

Familiarity breeds contempt (6:1–6a)

See Matthew 13:53–58; Luke 4:16–30. Jesus returns to Nazareth and begins to teach in the synagogue. This hick town probably has a population of only about one hundred people. The baggage Jesus grew up with continues to weigh him down here. Their comments show they are trying to force Jesus back into the familiar box of his childhood. "This construction worker can't possibly be as wise and powerful as it seems," they reason. Labeling him "Mary's son" probably shows they still haven't forgotten the controversy surrounding his birth. Jesus can calm the sea, cast out a legion of demons, heal a serious illness, and even raise a dead girl to life, but he can't work in the hard, stubborn hearts of those who think they know him best. This time it is Jesus who is amazed . . . at their lack of faith.

Jesus Ministers beyond Galilee (6:6–8:21)

Often the major sections in Mark open with a scene related to the disciples (1:16–20; 3:13–19; 6:6–13) and close with Jesus being rejected (3:1–6; 6:1–6). As Jesus's influence and ministry expands, the opposition grows even more intense.

Jesus's ministry multiplied through the Twelve (6:6–13)

See Matthew 9:35–38; 10:1, 7–16, 40; 11:20–24; Luke 8:1; 9:1–6; 10:1–16. Having been rejected by his own hometown, Jesus and his disciples now go on a preaching tour beyond the region of Galilee. Jesus extends his ministry of preaching, driving out demons, and healing through the twelve apostles, whom he sends out in pairs. Although we hear a lot about the disciples' lack of understanding and faith (and we haven't heard the last of that), here is an example of them doing something positive (cf. Mark 6:30).

The martyrdom of John the Baptizer (6:14–29)

See Matthew 14:1–12; Luke 3:19–20; 9:7–9. Righteous people are sometimes persecuted by the powerful people of this world. Such was the case when wicked Herod Antipas executed John the Baptizer. What happened to John will soon happen to Jesus and could also happen to Jesus's followers. Mark undoubtedly feels an urgent need to remind his Roman audience of these sober realities. When Herod hears about the successful mission of Jesus and the Twelve (6:14), his guilt-ridden conscience concludes that Jesus is actually John who has come back from the dead to haunt him (6:16). Here Mark provides a flashback of the grisly banquet scene where Herod is pressured into beheading John (6:17–29).

Five thousand object lessons (6:30–44)

See Matthew 14:13–21; Luke 9:10–17; John 6:1–15. The apostles report back to Jesus on the success of their mission (6:30). In spite of tragedies like the death of John, nothing can stop God's kingdom from expanding. Mark contrasts the wicked banquet in 6:17–29, where self-appointed King Herod destroys life, to the present feast, where King Jesus gives life to his people. Jesus involves the disciples in every phase of this shepherding experience. After their mission, Jesus calls them away to a quiet place for some rest, but the crowds race ahead of them to the resting spot. The disciples know the people need to eat, and Jesus challenges them to provide the food. Looking only to their own resources to solve the problem, they balk

✚ The early Christians in Rome needed to know that even persecution like the death of John the Baptizer could not stop God's kingdom from growing stronger.

John the Baptist

Preben Vang

According to Luke 3:1–2, John began his ministry around AD 28. His nickname, "The Baptizer," must have stuck early, since Matthew's first reference to John takes for granted that his readers recognize it (3:1). As the son of Zechariah and Elizabeth, John was of priestly origin, but unlike his father who ministered in the temple, John gathered a group of disciples to minister with him in the Judean desert close to the river Jordan. He came to reignite Israel's devotion to God in order to prepare them to accept and recognize God's visitation of his people through Christ.

The Gospels' description of John is laden with Old Testament references. By underscoring his birth to aging parents, the Gospel writers remind readers of God's covenant with Abraham, thereby placing John as the bridge between God's first and second covenant promises (Gen. 18:11; Luke 1:7). John's wilderness setting, and its description as the place for repentance and preparation before the coming of the kingdom, parallels the preparatory experience of Israel before the entrance into the Promised Land. The detailed description of John's dress (Mark 1:6), which goes beyond merely portraying him as a bedouin, draws a direct parallel to the Old Testament prophetic tradition (2 Kings 1:8; cf. Zech. 13:4) and makes John the prophet God will use to reawaken his people (Luke 7:26). To emphasize this covenantal prophetic connection even further, John understands himself and his mission in light of Isaiah 40:3 (Luke 3:4) as the one God chose to prepare the way for the coming of the kingdom—the arrival of the promised new covenant of the Spirit (Ezek. 36:27–28; Mark 1:8). Since the arrival of God's kingdom is clearly connected to the fulfillment of God's end-time promises, John's message, like the prophets' of old, underscores the need for a thoroughgoing repentance to avoid God's end-time judgment (Matt. 3:7–10).

Opposite the Pharisees and other contemporary groups, John did not consider ritual cleansings significant; rather, in a prophetic manner, he called for mercy and faithfulness (Luke 3:11–14; cf. Hosea 6:6). Those who with new devotion repented of their dispassionate ways and (re)turned to God were baptized. This baptism was not exclusive to a narrow group of his followers; rather every truly repentant person could participate. It was a baptism of repentance (Mark 1:4), not to convert people into a disciple of John but to call them to preparedness for God's coming kingdom (Mark 1:8).

John's uncompromising message cost him his life. When he called on King Herod to repent of his promiscuous lifestyle, John was imprisoned and shortly thereafter beheaded (Matt. 14:1–12). The force of his message, however, gave him status as an Old Testament prophet, and the belief even grew that he would return from the dead (Matt. 14:2; 16:14).

On top of this tel is the fortress of Machaerus, where Herod Antipas had John the Baptist executed.

An ancient Jewish ritual bath, or mikveh.

at the cost of providing food. Then Jesus miraculously feeds more than five thousand people from one sack lunch, using the disciples to organize the people, distribute the food, and pick up the leftovers. Each apostle has a basket of bread and fish as a reminder that Jesus has supernatural ability to provide.

God is passing by (6:45–52)

See Matthew 14:22–33; John 6:16–21. Following the disciples' mission and their participation in the feeding of the five thousand, it's back to the sea for a test (see also 4:35–41). Jesus tells them to take the boat to Bethsaida while he prays a while longer. In the middle of the night, as they are rowing hard into a headwind, Jesus passes their way. They panic, thinking he is a ghost. He calms their fears, climbs into the boat, and all is well. In this experience, Jesus again presents himself as God. He has fed the people in the wilderness; now he is crossing the sea, about to "pass them by" (v. 48), which is suggestive of God's passing by Moses (Exod. 33:19, 22; cf. Gen. 32:31–32). Jesus answers their cries much like God answered Moses at the burning bush—"It is I" or "I am" (Exod. 3:14). But they still don't get it, Mark says, "for they had not understood about the loaves; their hearts were hardened" (6:52).

The healing touch (6:53–56)

See Matthew 14:34–36. Gennesaret is a district on the northwest side of the Sea of Galilee. Jesus's popularity as a divine healer continues to escalate throughout the entire region. Hopefully the disciples are paying attention.

Obeying God's commands rather than hiding behind human traditions (7:1–23)

See Matthew 15:1–20; 23:4–36; Luke 11:37–41. Pharisees and scribes from Jerusalem accuse Jesus of being a lousy mentor, unable to teach his disciples to uphold the "tradition of the elders" (7:5). In this case, the traditions relate to ceremonial washings (7:3–4). Doesn't Jesus care about purity? Yes, he cares about purity, but what does real purity involve? Jesus tells the crowd that it's not food but the condition of a person's heart that defines purity (7:14–15). Later he tells his disciples that evils coming out of the heart make a person unclean (see Jesus's list of examples in 7:21–22). He charges

✦ Jesus often presents himself to his disciples using Old Testament images and terms they were familiar with.

the religious leaders with hypocrisy (7:6–7). They ignore the clear commands of God (e.g., honoring one's parents; 7:9–10) and create self-serving loopholes (e.g., refusing to support parents, claiming instead that the money has been "dedicated" to God; 7:11–12). We shouldn't hide behind human religious traditions in order to avoid God's commands. Purity is a matter of the heart.

The faith of a foreigner (7:24–30)

See Matthew 15:21–28. Following the purity debate in 7:1–23, where Jesus declares all foods clean (7:19), the next three episodes focus on Jesus ministering to non-Jews. In the gentile region of Tyre, Jesus is confronted by a Greek woman who asks him to drive a demon out of her daughter. Jesus insists that his ministry is focused on Israel (the "children"), but the woman humbly replies that even the "dogs" can eat what the children spill on the floor. Jesus then heals the woman's daughter.

Hands-on ministry (7:31–37)

See Matthew 15:29–31. Jesus moves from one gentile region (Tyre and Sidon) to another (the Decapolis), where he heals a deaf mute. In

Christ (Messiah)

Joseph R. Dodson

The word "Christ" means "anointed one." In the Old Testament, it refers primarily to Israel's kings (cf. Isa. 45:1), though in other cases, it is ascribed to the Lord's high priests. Occasionally, Israel evoked this title as an appeal for Yahweh to rescue them and their Davidic king, whom the Lord had anointed. In time, the term "messiah" progressed from a mere title for a current king to that of an end-time figure, full of everlasting promise, such as the future son of David in Isaiah 9:6–7:

> For to us a child is born. . . .
> And he will be called
> Wonderful Counselor, Mighty God,
> Everlasting Father, Prince of Peace. . . .
> He will reign on David's throne
> and over his kingdom . . .
> from that time on and forever.

Also in Isaiah, it is foretold that this king will receive the anointing of God's Spirit (Isa. 11:2) and that he will become a figure of hope for *all* nations (11:10).

Along with these associations, expectations for an anointed high priest and a "prophet like Moses" also began to arise during the intertestamental period, and the term became connected with other titles, such as "the son of man" and "the chosen one of God" (e.g., *1 Enoch* 48–52). Nevertheless, messianic understandings remained quite variegated. In actuality, much of the Jewish literature ignored the theme altogether—until the New Testament.

In the New Testament, the Messiah is no longer a vague idea: he *is* Jesus of Nazareth—the Son of Man, Son of God; the chosen and anointed one; the prophet like Moses, the priest from Melchizedek, and the everlasting king of David. One cannot overemphasize the importance the New Testament writers place on Jesus as *the Christ*: it is the question his opponents asked—"Are you the Christ, the Son of the Blessed One?" (Mark 14:61)—and the answer that Peter confessed—"You are the Christ, the Son of the living God" (Matt. 16:16); the title by which the angels announced him and demons addressed

hands-on fashion, Jesus touches the man's ears and tongue and sighs a prayer toward heaven ("Be opened"). He commands those involved not to tell anyone since he doesn't want his miracles replacing his kingdom message. But the man and his friends can't help but shout for joy (cf. Isa. 35:6). Much like God's good work in creation, Jesus does all things well (cf. Gen. 1:31).

Hungry gentiles (8:1–10)

See Matthew 15:32–39. Once again Jesus miraculously multiplies what little food can be found to feed thousands. The crowd in the Decapolis would have been predominantly gentile. They have been with Jesus in a remote place for several days and need food. Like before, the disciples can only imagine a human solution. Out of compassion, Jesus miraculously feeds this crowd also, repeating the faith lesson for his disciples.

✚ Jesus's compassion for the poor and hungry demonstrates God's concern for the poor emphasized in much of the Old Testament (e.g., Deut. 10:18; Prov. 19:17; Isa. 10:1–2).

him (Mark 1:34); the capstone by which Matthew concluded his genealogy (1:16); and the credential by which authors began their epistles (e.g., Rom. 1:1; 1 Pet. 1:1; Jude 1:1).

Moreover, John the Baptist did not fail to confess that he himself was *not* the Christ (John 1:20), but the first thing his disciple Andrew said to Peter was, "We have found the Christ" (John 1:41). Even the Samaritan woman said she knew the Messiah was coming, to which Jesus responded, "I who speak to you am he" (John 4:25–26). In Acts, "*Jesus is the Christ*" comprised the message announced by Peter (2:36), preached by Phillip (8:5), proved by Apollos (18:28), and explained by Paul (9:22; 17:2–3).

In fact, Jesus's identity as the Messiah was so important to Paul that he used the term some 70 percent of all of its uses in the New Testament, and he included Christ as part of Jesus's name. Paul professed that he fully proclaimed "the gospel of Christ" from Jerusalem all the way to Illyricum, and that he made it his ambition to preach wherever "Christ was not known" (Rom. 15:19–20). Ultimately, Paul understood that saving faith came by hearing, and hearing by the word of Christ (Rom. 10:17).

The message Paul considered most important was "that Christ was killed . . . was buried . . . was raised . . . and that he appeared . . ." (1 Cor. 15:3–4). Yet the idea of a suffering Messiah—especially a crucified one—presented a paradox unacceptable to many Jews (e.g., 1 Cor. 1:23). Regardless, compelled by the love of Christ, Paul continued on as an ambassador for Christ pleading that the world be reconciled on behalf of Christ (2 Cor. 5:15–21). So captivated was the apostle by the Messiah that he claimed no longer to live, saying instead, "But Christ lives in me" (Gal. 2:20).

Similarly, Paul often refers to believers as "the body of Christ," those who "belong to Christ," and those who are "in Christ." To the Galatians, Paul says he will not rest until "Christ is formed in you" (Gal. 4:19), and to the Colossians, "your life is now hidden with Christ" (Col. 3:3). Paul was not the only one to associate the believers closely with Christ. Although probably first meant as a derogatory remark, Christ's disciples became known as *Christians*—a name that Peter proclaims should lead to praise rather than to shame (1 Pet. 4:16).

Hard-hearted Pharisees and thick-headed disciples (8:11–21)

See Matthew 12:38–42; 16:1–12; Luke 11:16, 29–32; 12:1, 54–56. Jesus can multiply a few loaves to feed thousands, but it's not enough for the Pharisees who want a "sign from heaven" (8:11). Jesus reacts in a deeply emotional way to their hard-hearted refusal to believe that God is already at work through the many miracles (cf. Mark 1:41). As Jesus and the disciples are crossing the sea, Jesus warns them against the yeast of the Pharisees and Herod. Because they had forgotten to put any bread in the boat, they start blaming each other for the oversight. Yet again the disciples are thinking in purely physical terms. They have seen Jesus feed five thousand with five loaves and four thousand with seven loaves, and yet they've missed the spiritual point of it all. Jesus rebukes them with seven rapid-fire questions, ending with, "Do you still not understand?" (8:17–21).

Jesus, the Messiah, Journeys to Jerusalem (8:22–10:52)

This central section of Mark begins and ends with Jesus healing a blind man. The first healing is in Bethsaida on the northern coast of the Sea of Galilee, and the last one is in Jericho as Jesus nears Jerusalem. Between these two sight miracles, Jesus begins to unveil his true identity and mission to his disciples. The turning point is Peter's confession of Jesus as the Messiah, followed by three predictions of Jesus's death, three wrong responses from the disciples, and three teachings on what it means to follow the suffering Son of God.

Healing of a blind man at Bethsaida (8:22–26)

This healing (only recorded in Mark) introduces the central section of this Gospel and contrasts sharply with the spiritual blindness of the disciples displayed in the last scene. Jesus heals this man in stages, a process that parallels how the disciples are gaining their spiritual sight (first recognizing Jesus as Messiah and later seeing him as the suffering Messiah). As in many other cases, Jesus tells the healed man to keep a low profile (8:26).

Following the suffering Messiah #1 (8:27–9:1)

See Matthew 16:13–28; Luke 9:18–27; John 6:66–71. At a crucial moment in the mission, Jesus leads his disciples to Caesarea Philippi to the north. Far from Jerusalem and in a place best known for pagan worship (including the worship of Caesar as Lord), Jesus asks

Caesarea Philippi, where Peter confesses Jesus as the Messiah and Jesus begins to reveal that he will suffer.

✚ Jesus's predictions of his own sacrificial death remind us of the role of the Servant of the Lord in Isaiah 53–53, who suffers for the sins of the nation.

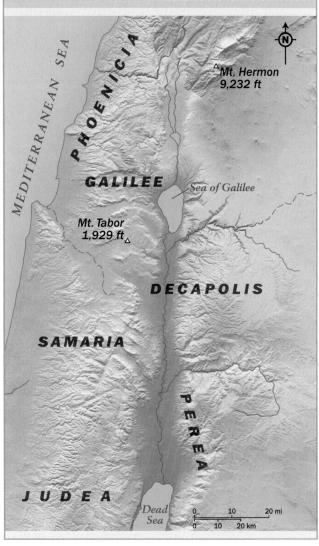

his disciples a hard question: "Who do you guys say I am?" Peter gives the right answer, "You are the Christ" (Messiah). Jesus then starts to teach them that he must suffer and die before rising again. (This is the first of three passion predictions in the central part of Mark.) Peter strongly objects to a suffering and dying Messiah, but Jesus holds fast to his God-given mission and resists the temptation from Satan (now verbalized by Peter) to avoid the cross. He calls together the whole crowd to explain that following him includes giving up control over their lives, being willing to experience shame and rejection, and devoting themselves to Jesus's teachings (8:34). The paradox is that those who want to save their lives will end up losing them, and those who lose their lives for Jesus will actually save them. How a person responds to Jesus in this life will determine how Jesus responds to that person on the day of judgment. The section closes with Jesus's promise that some of those standing in the crowd would see the kingdom of God come with power.

Glory on the mountain (9:2–13)

See Matthew 17:1–13; Luke 9:28–36. About a week later, Jesus fulfills the promise he made in 9:1. The unusual time reference in 9:2 tells us to understand Peter's confession and Jesus's transfiguration together. Jesus now takes Peter, James, and John up on a high mountain (likely Mount Hermon, but traditionally Mount Tabor) and is transfigured before them. They see a preview of the glory of the Son of God. While Peter is proposing to build shelters for Moses, Elijah, and Jesus, he is interrupted by God. The cloud of God's glorious presence falls upon them, and the divine voice speaks, for only the second time in Mark's Gospel, with a very similar message to the first occasion:

- Mark 1:11 (Jesus's baptism)—"You are my Son, whom I love; with you I am well pleased."
- Mark 9:7 (Jesus's transfiguration)—"This is my Son, whom I love. Listen to him!"

God is telling the disciples that Jesus is indeed a Messiah who will suffer and die and they should "listen to him!" (Deut. 18:15). The cross is God's plan. After the experience, Jesus tells them not to tell anyone what they had seen until he has "risen from the dead," a phrase they fail to grasp. Finally, Jesus explains to them that Elijah has already come, alluding to John the Baptizer (see Matt. 17:11–13).

Trouble in the valley (9:14–29)

See Matthew 17:14–21; Luke 9:37–43. Jesus and his inner circle walk down from the mountain of glory to find the other nine disciples struggling to drive out demons and squabbling with the Jewish leaders. They lack spiritual power and wisdom. Jesus seems to be experiencing a lonely frustration with the whole bunch, perhaps especially with his disciples (9:19). A boy's father confesses a feeble faith in Jesus's ability, perhaps because his disciples were unsuccessful, and asks for help to overcome his unbelief (9:23–24). Jesus drives out the demon with a single rebuke and restores the boy. The disciples may have taken for granted their ability to minister like Jesus, but apart from him they are powerless (9:28–29).

✚ The presence of Moses and Elijah at Jesus's transfiguration clearly communicates that Jesus is fulfilling the Old Testament promises. Peter's attempt to put Jesus on the same level as these Old Testament figures simply won't do. Jesus is the unique Son of God.

Following the suffering Messiah #2 (9:30–50)

See Matthew 5:13; 10:42; 17:22–23; 18:1–9; Luke 9:43–45; 10:16; 14:34–35; 17:1–2; John 13:20. For the second time, Jesus predicts his upcoming suffering and death (9:30–31). Yet again, the disciples fail to understand but are too afraid to ask for clarification. They do, however, have a heated argument about which of them is the greatest (9:34). It must have been extremely painful for Jesus to watch his followers go the wrong direction spiritually at the exact time he is pouring out his soul to them. They are expecting a military messiah who will overthrow the Romans and establish earthly political power. Jesus has much bigger things in mind, but his plans include a cross. Using a small child as an object lesson, Jesus patiently teaches them that true greatness in God's kingdom involves humility and service (9:35–37). He prohibits them from setting up barriers to keep out rivals who are also doing compassionate ministry (9:38–40). Jesus promises a reward to those who minister in his name (9:41) and issues a strong warning to anyone who hinders discipleship by tolerating sin (9:42–48). Disciples should live at peace with one another rather than be consumed with selfish competition (9:49–50).

Relational responsibilities of a Christ follower (10:1–31)

See Matthew 19:1–30; Luke 16:18; 18:15–30. Jesus's journey to Jerusalem takes a major leap forward beginning in 10:1 as he moves into the region of Judea. The three episodes of Mark 10:1–31 share the common theme of relationships, especially family relationships. In 10:1–12 Jesus faces a test from the Pharisees related to divorce. He shifts the focus from what Moses permitted to what God originally intended for marriage (quoting Gen. 1:27; 2:24)—one man and one woman together permanently. Jesus later explains to his disciples that remarriage to another person after a divorce constitutes adultery (10:11–12). In the second episode, when the disciples rebuke people for bringing their small kids to Jesus, he in turn rebukes the

Mount Hermon, the possible location of Jesus's transfiguration.

Jesus the Servant

Rodney Reeves

Jesus never called himself a servant or a slave. He did, however, imply he was a servant when he taught his disciples about his mission, giving them an example of service they should follow (Mark 10:43–45; John 13:12–17). In both cases, Jesus emphasized the humility that comes with being a servant (not the obedience of the servant, his relationship with the Master, or the tasks to be performed). And, in both cases, Jesus illustrated the lesson on humility by his self-sacrifice, offered for the good of others. After James and John asked for honorable positions in his kingdom, Jesus contrasted the way "rulers of the Gentiles" use their positions of power with the way the disciples will serve one another. The great men of the gentiles gain power to "lord it over" their subjects; Jesus's disciples will become great by giving power away. The moral is anchored by the example of Jesus: even the Son of Man (who should be served by lesser men) came to serve by giving "his life as a ransom for many" (Mark 10:43–45). Of course, the timing of this conversation is significant: it happened just before Jesus and his disciples entered Jerusalem, where he was crucified and the "blood of the covenant [was] poured out for many" (14:24).

There is no "Lord's Supper" memorial in John's Gospel. Instead, a story is told how Jesus performed the menial task of a household servant by washing the disciples' feet, despite the objection of Peter (John 13:1–11). Jesus even looked the part. He "took off his outer clothing" and wrapped a towel between his legs and around his waist, looking like a slave. After he finished, Jesus returned to the table fully clothed and asked the disciples whether they understood the lesson modeled for them. They rightfully called him "Teacher," yet he humbled himself and washed their feet like a slave. Therefore, they should do the same for one another, because "no servant is greater than his master" (v. 16). The way of Christ is humble service.

In light of these stories, it is somewhat surprising that the early church did not emphasize how Jesus fulfilled the role of the "humble" servant of the Lord prophesied in Isaiah (42:1–9; 49:1–7; 52:13–53:12). Matthew claims Jesus fulfilled the prophecy, but it had more to do with the withdrawal of Jesus from the crowds than with his humiliating death on a cross (Matt. 12:15–21). Luke comes closer to making the association when he records the sermon of Peter and the prayers of the first Christians: they referred to Jesus as God's servant who suffered at the hands of Pilate and Herod (Acts 3:13; 4:27). The clearest example comes from an early Christian hymn quoted by Paul: Jesus humbled himself when he became a man—like a slave he was "obedient to the point of death, even death on a cross" (Phil. 2:7–8). Despite the reticence of the New Testament to speak of Christ as a servant, Christians over the ages have featured the servant role of Jesus in many poems, liturgies, songs, sermons, and devotional materials.

disciples and welcomes the children with open arms (10:13–16). The kingdom belongs to people who are able to "receive" it "like a little child" (v. 15). In contrast to children who gladly receive gifts, the third episode describes a rich man who holds on tightly to his possessions (10:17–31). He asks Jesus what it takes to inherit eternal life. Although he has kept the commandments, Jesus says he lacks one thing. He must sell all he owns, give the money to the poor, and follow Jesus. The man walks away depressed, because he can't let go of his stuff. Rich people have a hard time entering the kingdom, Jesus warns, but all things are possible with God, so there is hope. Peter asserts, "We have left everything to follow you!" (v. 28). Jesus reassures him that those who have left everything will receive plenty of present rewards and in the future, eternal life.

Following the suffering Messiah #3 (10:32–45)

See Matthew 20:17–28; Luke 18:31–34; 22:24–30. Jesus leads the way to Jerusalem. The crowds are astonished, while the disciples are afraid. Something big is about to happen. For the third time Jesus announces his approaching passion. He will be betrayed, condemned by the Jewish leaders, and tortured and killed by the gentiles, but three days later he will rise (10:33–34). What happens next makes us drop our jaws in disbelief. Not only do the disciples not get it, James and John have the gall to ask for the seats of honor when Jesus sets up his kingdom (10:35–37). Jesus flatly tells them that they don't know what they are asking, since they have omitted suffering (symbolized by "the cup" and "the baptism") from their glorious request (10:38–40). Their boasting in verse 39 reminds us of Peter's later boast that he would never fail Jesus. The other ten disciples are furious at the two brothers, and Jesus follows up with a clear teaching about discipleship and leadership (10:41–45). Whereas pagan leaders "lord it over" people, kingdom leaders are to be servant leaders who pattern their lives after Jesus who "did not come to be served, but to serve, and to give his life as a ransom for many" (10:45; cf. Isaiah 53; Phil. 2:5–11). For good reason, many consider verse 45 to be the key verse in Mark's Gospel.

Healing of a blind man at Jericho (10:46–52)

See Matthew 9:27–31; 20:29–34; Luke 18:35–43. In strong contrast to the apparent blindness of the Twelve in the previous episode, blind Bartimaeus can see Jesus for who he is and twice confesses him as the "Son of David." He abandons his beggar's cloak (in contrast to the rich man of 10:17–31) and rushes to Jesus, who asks, "What do you want me to do for you?" (cf. the same question to James and John in 10:36). He

An ancient millstone used to crush olives (Mark 9:42).

✝ Within the early Christian community, social status was made secondary to equality established by a spiritual status in Christ (see 1 Cor. 12:25; Gal. 3:28; James 2:1–13).

replies, "Rabbi ['my master'], I want to see," and Jesus gives him sight in the last healing miracle in Mark. When told he could "go," Bartimaeus follows Jesus along the road to Jerusalem, an example of a true disciple.

Jesus, the Messiah, Confronts Jerusalem (11:1–13:37)

This section of Mark describes what happens on Sunday through Tuesday of Passion Week (the week of suffering). His "triumphal entry" into the city marks the beginning of the week that includes the cursing of the fig tree and condemning of the temple, debates with religious leaders, teaching in the temple area, and the extended teaching on the Mount of Olives.

The King's humble entry (11:1–11)

See Matthew 21:1–9; Luke 19:28–40; John 12:12–19. During Passover week in Jerusalem, the population grows significantly and messianic expectations run high. Jesus enters the city in dramatic fashion, moving from the Mount of Olives down into the city. It was believed that the Messiah would appear on this "mountain" in the last days (Zech. 14:4–5). Jesus has made arrangements to ride a donkey into the city, fulfilling the prophecy of Zechariah 9:9. The secret is now out, as Jesus openly announces himself to the world. He is the long-awaited Messiah, the King of the Jews. But he rides a humble donkey rather than a mighty stallion, symbolizing that he will conquer through suffering and sacrifice rather than with military power. As Jesus descends into Jerusalem, some in the crowd spread cloaks and palm branches before him, shouting praises and acknowledging Jesus as Messiah. He goes to the temple and inspects the situation before returning to Bethany.

The Mount of Olives viewed from the temple mount.

✦ Jesus fulfills the Old Testament expectation that the Messiah would appear on Mount Zion in the last days.

Herod's Temple

Jonathan M. Lunde

Among Herod the Great's most extraordinary building projects was his reconstruction of the temple and the expansion of its courtyard. This replaced the relatively unimpressive temple built after the exile under Zerubbabel's supervision (516/15 BC). Although Zerubbabel's structure was completely supplanted, Herod's temple is not considered to be the Third Temple, since sacrifices continued throughout the period of its construction. The work began in 20/19 BC and continued until AD 63, though most of the work was completed within a decade. It was subsequently destroyed by the Romans in AD 70.

In accordance with its predecessor, Herod's temple was divided into three main portions. The Vestibule served as the temple's entrance hall. Through its veiled back wall, access was given into the Sanctuary, where the seven-branched Menorah, the Showbread Table, and the incense altar each stood. Two thick veils separated this space from the Holy of Holies further in. Occupied by the ark of the covenant in Solomon's temple, this space was empty in Herod's temple—save for the protrusion of the hill's bedrock through the floor. The building's dazzling exterior was entirely white wherever it was not covered with gold plating.

The temple itself faced east, situated at the highest level within the Temple Mount. Each successive courtyard was lower in elevation. Surrounding the temple was a high wall, which had three gates on each of its northern and southern sides. Within this wall to the east side laid a courtyard where the great altar stood (Matt. 23:35). Beyond this, the courtyard was divided into two parts—the inner strip was the Priests' Court, while the outer strip was the Court of Israel, open only to Jewish men (Matt. 5:23–24; Luke 18:10–13; 24:53). These courts were set off from another court on the east by a wall and another gate. Known as the Court of Women, both Jewish men and women were permitted access here (Luke 2:37).

Surrounding all of this laid the large outer court, the area of which was doubled by Herod (approximately thirty football fields). But this space was also divided—a square area closest to the temple was reserved solely for Jews, set off from the Court of the Gentiles by a low balustrade. Entrances through this barrier were marked by engraved slabs warning gentiles of their ensuing deaths should they presume to enter (cf. Acts 21:27–29).

This outer courtyard was surrounded on all sides by roofed colonnades, the southern one of which was Herod's magnificent Royal Portico (Matt. 21:23; Luke 2:46;). Jesus likely expelled the moneychangers and sacrifice sellers from this area and the nearby courtyard (Matt. 21:12–16 and parallels). At the northwest corner of the courtyard stood the Antonia, a fortress Herod built to guard the Temple Mount. Its southern staircase descended to the courtyard for quick access (Acts 21:31–32).

Cursing a tree and condemning a temple (11:12–26)

See Matthew 21:10–22; Luke 19:45–48. Mark sandwiches together the stories about Jesus cursing the fig tree (11:12–14, 20–25) and condemning the temple (11:15–19) so that we will know they are making the same point. Rather than Jesus cleansing or reforming the temple, he is judging both the tree and the temple. On the way from Bethany to Jerusalem (just a few miles), Jesus curses an unfruitful fig tree that falsely advertises (through its many leaves) that it has fruit to offer. He will soon do the same thing to the temple for leaving the false impression that people can truly meet God there. The temple stands at the center of Jerusalem and serves as the economic, political, and religious heart of Judaism. The Court of the Gentiles becomes the place where people exchange money (for a fee) to pay the temple tax. By interrupting the moneychangers, Jesus symbolically condemns the temple. Rather than representing God's presence, the temple now stands under God's judgment. It is no longer a place of prayer for all nations (Isa. 56:7) and instead has become the religious hideout of those whose hearts are corrupt (Jer. 7:11; cf. Mark 7:1–23). As before, the crowds are amazed by Jesus's teaching, and the chief priests and scribes want to assassinate him (11:18). The next morning Peter points out the withered fig tree. We then learn that the new way of faith, prayer, and forgiveness in Jesus totally replaces the old way of the temple with its corrupt business practices, its hypocritical priesthood, and its useless sacrificial system. God now meets us in Jesus (11:22–25).

Debating and teaching in the temple courts (11:27–12:44)

See Matthew 21:23–27, 33–46; 22:15–46; 23:1–36; Luke 6:39; 10:25–28; 11:39–44, 46–52; 20:1–47; 21:1–4. This section features a series of intense exchanges between Jesus and the Jewish leaders related to Jesus's authority. The section closes with the contrasting example of a widow engaged in true worship. The parable in the middle becomes a very significant summary of the Jewish leaders' response to Jesus.

DEBATE ABOUT AUTHORITY AND JOHN THE BAPTIZER (11:27–33)

When they ask Jesus about the source of his authority, Jesus answers with a question about the source of John's baptism—heaven or human? They don't answer, so neither does Jesus.

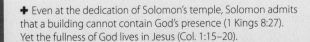

PARABLE OF THE WICKED TENANT FARMERS (12:1–12)

In this parable the man who owns the vineyard represents God. The wicked farmers represent the Jewish religious leadership, the servants represent God's various servants (e.g., the prophets), and the son "whom he loved" (v. 6) represents Jesus. The message is crystal clear—the vineyard owner will judge the wicked farmers and give the vineyard to others.

DEBATE ABOUT PAYING TAXES TO CAESAR (12:13–17)

The Jewish leaders try to trap Jesus by asking him if it's right to pay taxes to Caesar. Jesus gives a both/and (rather than either/or) answer. Give to God what he owns (all things, including human beings who bear his image) and give to Caesar his taxes.

DEBATE ABOUT THE RESURRECTION (12:18–27)

The Sadducees, who don't believe in the resurrection, try to show that it's a ridiculous belief using a hypothetical example of a woman who has been married seven times. Jesus rebukes them for not knowing how to interpret Scripture and for not understanding God's power. The resurrection is real, Jesus contends, because God is the God of the living, not the dead.

WHAT'S MOST IMPORTANT? (12:28–34)

When asked to name the most important commandment, Jesus names two—love God (Deut. 6:4–5) and love

A watchtower allowed tenants to guard olive groves or vineyards.

✦ The parable of the wicked tenant farmers in Mark 12 summarizes the story of God's dealings with Israel (cf. Isa. 5:1–2).

people (Lev. 19:18). No other commandment is greater than these. At this point no one dares to ask Jesus any more questions.

DEBATE ABOUT DAVID'S SON (12:35–37)

Jesus asks the teachers of the law (scribes) this question: why do the scribes say the Christ is David's son when David calls him "Lord"? Jesus isn't denying that Messiah is the Son of David, but he is adding that Messiah is more than that. In the line, "The LORD (*Yahweh*) says to my lord (*adonai*)" in Psalm 110:1, the first "LORD" refers to God and the second originally referred to the king of Israel. At the king's coronation, God was charging the king to become his assistant ruler. Later, when the monarchy ceased to exist, the rights and responsibilities of the king were transferred to the Messiah. As a divine figure, the Messiah's kingdom would endure forever.

JESUS REBUKES THE SCRIBES (12:38–40)

The scribes who love religious garb, pious greetings, and the most important seats are also the ones who devour widows' houses and pray for show. Hypocrites! Their punishment will be severe.

THE WIDOW'S OFFERING (12:41–44)

This poor Jewish widow stands in contrast to the Jewish religious leaders. Her tiny offering amounts to more than all the others, because she gives "everything—all she had to live on." Jesus points to her sacrificial giving as an example of what true worship is all about.

In AD 70 the Romans threw these temple stones down onto a first-century street.

✦ Psalm 110 is the psalm most frequently quoted and alluded to in the entire New Testament.

The Destruction of Jerusalem in AD 70

Paul Jackson

Throughout its history Jerusalem has seen its share of heartache and horror. In 586 BC, Nebuchadnezzar razed the city, its walls, and Solomon's temple. In AD 134, Jerusalem was destroyed after the Bar Kochba revolt, which led to the wholesale banishment of all Jews from the city. Israel's failure to repent of its moral shortcomings pointed out by several of God's prophets and even his own Son resulted in the dismantling of Jerusalem.

The destruction of Jerusalem in AD 70 marks the second of three times the holy city of David fell. The oncoming atrocities actually began in AD 66 when Cestius Gallus marched south from Syria with his legions to squelch a problem in Judea. But they had to withdraw, and in their retreat suffered heavy casualties at the hands of Jewish insurgents. This may have caused the inhabitants of Jerusalem to feel like they were reliving the glory days of Judas Maccabeus. Once troubles in Rome were quelled, however, a new general, Vespasian, returned to begin a systematic subjugation of all the areas surrounding Jerusalem. Eventually, he committed the final task of crushing this current Jewish revolt to Titus, the military commander in Judea.

The siege of Jerusalem began in April, 70. Although the defenders resisted desperately, by the end of September all attempts to withstand Titus failed. All that was left was the mopping-up operations of destroying three remaining strongholds, one of those being the practically impregnable Masada.

Interestingly, Jesus cryptically predicted the destruction of Jerusalem in Luke 23:28–31. As Jesus was led away to Golgotha, he addressed some mourning females with a chilling and sad note. The key to his message is connected to his reference to "green" and "dry" wood in verse 31. If men would exact this kind of punishment on him when the wood is green, what will they do when it is dry? Dry wood burns better. The contrast is driven deeper between the wood on which Jesus was crucified and the wood of Jerusalem. Jesus was basically giving them a warning that there were worse things on the horizon. The crucifixion of Jesus is one thing, but the destruction of Jerusalem will be another.

While one must read Josephus's full account to understand the total horror, one excerpt will sufficiently reflect the brutality:

> They were scourged and subjected to torture of every description, before being killed, and then crucified opposite the walls. Titus indeed commiserated their fate, five hundred or sometimes more being captured daily . . . but his main reason for not stopping the crucifixions was the hope that the spectacle might perhaps induce the Jews to surrender; for fear that continued resistance would involve them in a similar fate. The soldiers out of rage and hatred amused themselves by nailing their prisoners in different positions; and so great was their number, that space could not be found for the crosses nor crosses for the bodies. (Josephus, *Jewish War* 5.449–51)

The Olivet Discourse (13:1–37)

See Matthew 24:1–51; Luke 12:35–48; 17:20–37; 21:5–36. As Jesus and the disciples are leaving the temple, one of them comments on the massive stones and magnificent buildings. Jesus shocks them by announcing that "not one stone here will be left on another; every one will be thrown down" (13:2). Later, on the Mount of Olives, he explains more about when the temple would be destroyed. Jesus connects two important events: (1) the destruction of Jerusalem and its temple by the Romans in AD 70, and (2) his return at the end of the age. Some of what Jesus says is fulfilled in the first century (near future) and some is fulfilled at the end of the age (far future). Jesus warns the disciples to expect false messiahs, wars and rumors of wars, earthquakes and famines, persecutions, and betrayals (13:5–12), but those who endure to the end will be saved (13:13). Jesus seems to continue to describe the dreadful days when the temple is destroyed in 13:14–23, although the extent of the suffering seems to stretch beyond that event. What matters most is Jesus's reminder in verses 21–22 not to be deceived by false messiahs and false prophets. Beginning in 13:24, there is little doubt that Jesus begins describing events related to his return at the end of the age. The coming of the Son of Man with great power and glory is certain (v. 26), but its timing is uncertain (vv. 32–35). Therefore, followers of Christ should "be alert" and prepared for his unexpected return.

The Suffering, Death, and Resurrection of Jesus, the Son of God (14:1–16:8)

The story comes to a climax in the second half of Passion Week (Wednesday through Sunday), recorded in Mark 14–16. The Jewish leaders move forward with their plot to kill Jesus, assisted by Judas's betrayal. The disciples' faith faces a severe test. Jesus loves his friends to the end, submits to the Father's plan, endures unjust suffering and brutal torture, and gives himself through death as a ransom for many. But the final chapter of the story is resurrection!

The leaders' dilemma (14:1–2)

See Matthew 26:1–5; Luke 22:1–2. Jesus has condemned their temple and rebuked their hypocrisy. Now the Jewish religious leaders want to repay him with death, but they fear a negative reaction from the people during feast time because of Jesus's popularity. In the end, their desire to kill Jesus overcomes their fear.

A beautiful act of worship (14:3–9)

See Matthew 26:6–13; John 12:1–8. Between the leaders' plot to kill Jesus and Judas's plan to betray him (vv. 10–11), we read about an intimate act of worship. Jesus remains in his refuge at Bethany on the Wednesday of Passion Week. At a dinner that night at the home of Simon the Leper, Mary anoints Jesus for burial with a jar of very expensive perfume. When some (John 12:4

✦ The woman's sacrificial act of service to Jesus is placed between the religious leaders' evil plotting and Judas's betrayal.

says Judas) object that she has wasted a lot of money, Jesus defends her actions as a beautiful act of worship—she has anointed Jesus's body for burial.

Judas sells out (14:10–11)

See Matthew 26:14–16; Luke 22:3–6; John 13:2. As an insider or "one of the Twelve," Judas goes to the Jewish leaders and offers to deliver Jesus to them. This opportunity delights the leaders, and they promise money in return. Judas then looks for the best opportunity to perform his treacherous betrayal.

One final meal (14:12–26)

See Matthew 26:17–30; Luke 22:7–23; John 13:30. Jesus's final meal with his disciples is a Passover meal. He gives Peter and John the task of making the arrangements. They go into the city, meet a man carrying a jar of water, follow him to the room, and prepare the Passover meal (14:12–16). When evening comes (around 6:00 p.m., or sundown), Jesus gathers with his disciples in the upper room. While they are eating, Jesus announces that one of the Twelve will betray him and identifies the betrayer (14:17–21). The Passover celebrates God's mighty act of delivering his people from slavery during the exodus event. As the host of the meal, Jesus now gives the elements of the meal new meaning based on his upcoming death and resurrection (14:22–24). As the Lamb of God, Jesus's sacrificial death will bring deliverance from sin. Jesus promises to abstain from the meal until God's kingdom comes in full and he participates in the messianic banquet. After singing a hymn (traditionally from Psalm 113–118), they go to the Mount of Olives and the Garden of Gethsemane.

First-century perfume bottles shaped like dates, grapes, a pine cone, an acorn, and a seashell.

✦ The greatest saving act of God is the cross of Christ. The celebration of that act is the Lord's Supper. The cross and the Lord's Supper parallel the exodus and the Passover in the Old Testament.

Desertion and denials (14:27–31)

See Matthew 26:31–35; Luke 22:31–34; John 13:36–38. Jesus predicts that all the disciples will fall away (quoting Zech. 13:7), but reassures them that he will rise from the dead and meet them again in Galilee. Peter overestimates his strength and underestimates the power of evil. He boasts of his ability to stand with Jesus even if all the rest fail. Jesus specifically predicts that Peter will disown him three times that very night, but Peter continues to passionately boast that he will never, ever disown Jesus. And all the other disciples make the same claim.

Raw honesty and total submission (14:32–42)

See Matthew 26:36–46; Luke 22:39–46; John 18:1. Jesus and his disciples come to Gethsemane (meaning "oil press"), an olive orchard on the slopes of the Mount of Olives. He asks his disciples to wait for him while he struggles in prayer. Jesus then takes Peter, James, and John with him farther into the garden where he confesses to them the enormous weight he feels pressing down on him (14:34). He asks them to keep watch for him as he moves deeper into the garden and falls to the ground in prayer. He prays first that, if possible, this hour of suffering might pass him by (14:35–36). In raw honesty, Jesus expresses his deepest thoughts and feelings to the Father. Then Jesus moves past honesty to total submission to the Father: "yet not what I will, but what you will" (14:36). As Jesus struggles in prayer, his disciples sleep. Three times he returns to Peter, James, and John only to find them asleep. Although they boasted of their willingness to die for Jesus, they can't even stay awake with him. Finally Jesus tells them, "Rise! Let us go! Here comes my betrayer!" (14:42).

A kiss of death (14:43–52)

See Matthew 26:47–56; Luke 22:47–53; John 18:2–12. Judas arrives with an armed crowd sent by the Jewish leaders. He pinpoints the location of Jesus and his disciples at a time when a quiet arrest can be made. In the dark of the garden, Judas identifies Jesus with a treacherous kiss of betrayal. They grab Jesus and arrest him. Peter reacts by drawing his sword and taking a swipe at the slave of the high priest (John 18:10). Jesus tells Peter to put away his sword and then heals the slave's ear. Jesus asks them why they didn't arrest him when he was teaching in the temple area, insinuating that they are cowards and hypocrites. As Jesus predicted, all the disciples abandoned him. Only Mark includes the interesting detail of the young man (perhaps young John Mark himself or the key eyewitness to these events) who was seized, but left behind his garment and ran away naked.

✚ While the religious leaders plot, Judas schemes, and the disciples sleep, Jesus wrestles with doing the will of God in a lonely garden.

The Jewish trial (14:53–65)

See Matthew 26:57–68; Luke 22:54–55, 63–71; John 18:13–24. Jesus is led away to be interrogated by the Jewish leaders. Peter follows the procession to the courtyard of the high priest where he warms himself by the fire. The Sanhedrin (Jewish council) unsuccessfully tries to trump up charges against Jesus (14:55–59). Being a majority Sadducean group, they are particularly sensitive to Jesus's threat to the temple. To move things along, the high priest asks a key question: "Are you the Christ, the Son of the Blessed One?" Jesus clearly answers, "I am." Then Jesus adds a statement combining two Old Testament texts: Psalm 110:1 ("you will see the Son of Man sitting at the right hand of the Mighty One") and Daniel 7:13 ("coming

A Roman soldier with a flogging whip.

on the clouds of heaven"). He is now claiming divine status and authority to judge. The Jewish leaders are actually the ones on trial. The high priest tears his clothes and accuses Jesus of blasphemy. They condemn him and begin to punish him violently.

A dark night for a disciple (14:66–72)

See Matthew 26:69–75; Luke 22:56–62; John 18:15–18, 25–27. As Jesus remains faithful before the most powerful figures in Judaism, Peter fails to acknowledge Jesus when questioned by a bunch of servants. Peter is recognized by two different servant girls as one who was with Jesus (see Matt. 26:71). Both times he flatly denies it. Later when identified by others in the high priest's courtyard as being a Galilean and one of the disciples, he calls down a curse upon himself and swears, "I don't know the man" (v. 71). Peter then hears the rooster announce for a second time the rising of the sun. He remembers Jesus's prediction, and his own dark night begins as he collapses in tears over his unfaithfulness.

The Roman trial (15:1–15)

See Matthew 27:1–26; Luke 23:1–25; John 18:29–40; 19:16. The full Sanhedrin assembles after dawn to make their nighttime decision official (15:1). They want Jesus dead, and they want it to be a public, shameful death; but only the Romans can carry out a death sentence by crucifixion. When Jesus admits to being "the Christ" (a political figure), the Jewish leaders have

what they need to take him to Pilate. Before Pilate, Jesus admits to being "the king of the Jews" (15:2), but he remains silent as the chief priests pepper him with accusations. Pilate seems to want to flog Jesus for causing trouble and then set him free using the custom of turning back one prisoner to the people during the feast time (15:6–9). Throughout the Roman trial, the Jewish leaders stir up the crowd against Jesus (15:3, 11), while the crowd itself is easily manipulated to the point of violently demanding Jesus's crucifixion (15:11, 13–15). Above all, Pilate wants to appease the crowd, so he hands over Jesus to be flogged and crucified. Meanwhile Barabbas goes free.

Jesus, the suffering Son of God (15:16–47)

See Matthew 27:27–66; Luke 23:26–56; John 19:1–42.

MOCKED BY SOLDIERS (15:16–20)

The soldiers mock Jesus by dressing him in a purple robe (the color of royalty), crowning him with thorns, and shouting, "Hail, king of the Jews." They beat him in the head with sticks, spit on him, and bow (ironically) in mock worship. Then they strip him of the robe, put his clothes back on, and lead him away to be crucified.

"Skull hill" near the garden tomb.

✝ Much of what happens to Jesus was predicted by Isaiah the prophet (see Isa. 52:13–53:12).

ASSISTED BY SIMON OF CYRENE (15:21–22)

Jesus was apparently too weak from his flogging to carry the crosspiece. Simon of Cyrene (modern Libya) is forced to carry the cross to Golgotha (Aramaic for "the place of the skull"—either a place shaped like a skull or a place famous for executions). The names of his sons are included probably because they are known to Mark's audience in Rome.

CRUCIFIED (15:23–27)

Jesus refused the drugged wine and suffered without any painkillers. Crucifixion brought an extremely painful and slow death caused by loss of blood, exhaustion, and especially asphyxiation when the person no longer has strength to breathe. In addition, the Romans ordinarily stripped their victims naked to achieve an even more shameful death. Jesus is crucified between two thieves for rebelling against the government (treason) as the inscription indicates: "The King of the Jews." Behind this political charge stands the Jews' religious accusation of blasphemy.

INSULTED (15:29–32)

Jesus is insulted and verbally abused by the passersby, the Jewish religious leaders, and even those crucified with him. Ironically, much of what they say is true—the temple of his body will indeed be destroyed and rebuilt; to save others, he cannot save himself; and he *is* the Christ, the King of Israel.

DEATH (15:33–39)

The darkness of judgment (cf. Amos 8:9–10) falls on the land between noon and 3 p.m., the usual time for the afternoon sacrifice in the temple. Jesus then cries out Psalm 22:1 (the Psalm of the righteous sufferer): "My God, My God, why have you forsaken me?" This is the only of Jesus's seven last words from the cross recorded in Mark. Some think he is crying for Elijah, so they stand back to see if Elijah will deliver him. But Jesus, with his suffering finished, gives a loud cry and breathes his last. The temple curtain is ripped in two from top to bottom, signifying that his work has now opened access to God (cf. Mark 1:10). The Roman centurion witnessing these events concludes: "Surely this man was the Son of God!" (v. 39; cf. Mark 1:1). This gentile confession must have deeply stirred the emotions of Mark's readers in Rome who also confessed Jesus as the Son of God.

WOMEN WITNESSES (15:40–41)

Mark notes the presence of many women witnesses to the crucifixion, specifically three named women. He also notes that these women had followed Jesus in Galilee and cared for his needs.

✚ Ironically, although Jesus resisted promoting himself as a political messiah during his ministry, he is eventually crucified as a political messiah: "The King of the Jews" (Mark 15:26).

Preparation day is the Friday before the Saturday Sabbath. Joseph, a member of the Jewish Sanhedrin and a Jesus sympathizer (see John 19:38), secures permission to take Jesus's body. Pilate is surprised to hear that Jesus died so quickly, but the centurion verifies that Jesus has died. Joseph wraps Jesus's body in linen cloth and places it in a new "rolling-stone tomb." Two women witness the burial.

The resurrection of the Son of God (16:1–8)

See Matthew 28:1–8; Luke 24:1–12; John 20:1–13. The three women named in 15:40 as witnesses to the crucifixion come just after sunrise to the tomb on the first day of the week. They bring spices to anoint Jesus's body properly, but they are concerned with moving the heavy stone. They arrive to see that someone has already rolled away the stone. When they enter the tomb, they encounter an angel—the young man in white (v. 5). He calms their fears and then announces, "You are looking for Jesus the Nazarene, who was crucified. He has risen! He is not here. See the place where they laid him" (v. 6). Although Mark does not spend much time elaborating, there is no doubt that he clearly declares the resurrection of Jesus Christ. The women are told to go "tell his disciples and Peter" (perhaps stressing that Peter's failure is not fatal) to go to Galilee where Jesus will meet them. Trembling with fear, the women run from the tomb, presumably to find the other disciples.

So What? Applying Mark's Gospel Today

The Gospel of Mark stresses that Jesus is the Suffering Servant. To be sure, Jesus is the Son of God and reigns supreme over every evil power, but the greatest demonstration of his power comes at the cross, where he gives his life as a ransom for many (10:45). If the Son of God used his power to serve people, how much more should we use our God-given power to serve? The pagans use power to control people, but this Gospel reminds us to use power the way Jesus did, to love and serve people. We are occasionally tempted to do God's will the world's way. Mark reminds us that God's will should be done Jesus's way, the way of the Suffering Servant. With our family and friends, at work or play, in solitude or in community, we should focus on using our gifts and influence and authority to benefit and edify other people.

As you might recall, Mark's Gospel was originally written to believers who were facing persecution. Mark places enormous emphasis on the demands of discipleship. Following Jesus is costly, especially in an atmosphere of

✚ Throughout the passion experience, only the female followers of Jesus remain faithful.

opposition. We sometimes expect everyone to accept us and like us and praise us, but that is not the typical experience for Jesus's followers. To be sure, we must avoid persecution simply because of our annoying personality or insensitive behavior. But when we are ridiculed or slighted or excluded because of our connection to Jesus, we should realize this as an essentially normal part of Christian discipleship.

Mark's Gospel also reminds us that the Christian life consists of actions and not merely words. As the apostle Paul says in 1 Corinthians 4:20: "The kingdom of God is not a matter of talk but of power." While Jesus's teachings are certainly important, Mark points to his actions. In our culture where "Christian" words are plentiful and sometimes lose their power, a consistent Christian lifestyle always speaks loudly. May God give us the grace to keep our words and our actions tied closely together, for his glory!

Our Favorite Verse in Mark

For even the Son of Man did not come to be served, but to serve, and to give his life as a ransom for many. (10:45)

A tomb with a rolling stone.

The Gospel of
Luke

Jesus, the Savior for All People

Do you ever need reassurance as a follower of Jesus? We certainly do. Life gets tough. You may experience rejection or opposition because of your faith in Jesus Christ. Perhaps your new Christian friends are radically different from your old friends and, at times, you don't feel that you fit in. It's great to know that there is a Gospel written specifically to reassure believers. Both Luke and the sequel, Acts, are dedicated to Theophilus, so that he (and others like him) might "know the certainty of the things you have been taught" (1:4). Theophilus is probably a new believer who is trying to fit into this new community of Jesus followers. He needs reassurance. If you are facing increasing pressure to distance yourself from Jesus in order to fit in, take heart! What you are about to read will encourage and strengthen you. Jesus calls you to persevere and to stand strong. He wants you to know that you do fit into God's amazing plan. And you do belong to God's new community, the church. Things aren't perfect now, but God is faithful and is working. Trust him and continue in the way of Jesus.

Who Wrote Luke?

The early church evidence all points to Luke as the author of Luke–Acts, a single book in two volumes. Luke was a well-educated gentile, a physician, and a missionary co-worker of the apostle Paul (Col. 4:14; Philem. 24). Ironically, Luke the gentile wrote more of the New Testament than any other author, including Paul. Apparently he was not an eyewitness of the life of Jesus, but he did careful research and interviewed a number of eyewitnesses (Luke 1:1–4). He was a skilled linguist, and Luke–Acts exhibits excellent literary Greek. In sections of Acts the story shifts from the third to the first person (the "we" sections) to indicate the likelihood that Luke accompanied Paul on some of his missionary journeys (Acts 16:10–17; 20:5–21:8; 27:1–28:16). Luke is with Paul at the very end of his ministry (2 Tim. 4:11).

Who Is Luke's Audience?

Luke actually names his recipient—"most excellent Theophilus" (Luke 1:3; Acts 1:1). His name means "beloved by God" and his title ("most excellent") indicates a person of position and wealth. Quite possibly he financed the copying of the Luke–Acts scrolls for wider distribution. In addition, what Luke says in 1:1–4 makes it likely that Theophilus is a follower of Christ. Luke speaks of the events "that have been fulfilled among *us*" (1:1) and of the previous instruction that Theophilus had received (1:4). But the Gospel of Luke was also intended for a wider audience. Many scholars believe that Luke targets gentile Christians, perhaps even the churches planted by Paul. He is careful to explain Jewish customs (e.g., Luke 22:1, 7) and emphasizes the universal or comprehensive work of God

Statue of Caesar Augustus, the Roman emperor at the birth of Jesus Christ.

✝ What Jesus begins to do in the Gospel of Luke he continues to do in the book of Acts as the Holy Spirit works through his followers.

(e.g., tracing Jesus's ancestry back beyond the Jewish patriarchs to Adam). In terms of date, the Gospel was probably published around the same time as Acts, and the earliest possible date for Acts was around AD 62 when Paul was imprisoned in Rome (Acts 28:30). Since Luke makes use of other sources (possibly Mark or Matthew), the Gospel was probably written in the early to mid-60s.

What Is at the Heart of Luke's Gospel?

Luke's purpose in his Gospel connects directly to his purpose in Acts. In this two-volume work he explains the grand plan of God through Jesus Christ and his church (Luke 1:20; 4:21; 9:31; 21:22, 24; 24:44–47). He writes to instruct Theophilus and others like him so that they may know the certainty of the things they have been taught (Luke 1:4). In other words, Luke–Acts provides a discipleship manual for new believers coming from a pagan background and living in a culture that is either indifferent or hostile to the Christian faith. Luke wants his readers to know that their faith rests on the facts of history reflected in eyewitness testimony. The Christian faith was not invented by a community far removed from the events. God really did step into history in the person of Jesus and offer salvation to all people. The outline below reflects the primary theme of Jesus as the Savior of the whole world.

- The Birth of Jesus, the Savior (1:1–2:52)
- The Savior's Preparation for Public Ministry (3:1–4:13)
- The Savior's Galilean Ministry (4:14–9:50)
- The Savior's Journey to Jerusalem (9:51–19:44)
- The Savior's Ministry in Jerusalem (19:45–21:38)
- The Savior Is Betrayed, Tried, and Crucified (22:1–23:56)
- The Resurrection and Ascension of Jesus, the Savior for All People (24:1–53)

What Makes Luke Interesting and Unique?

- Luke is the first volume of a two-volume work: Luke–Acts.
- The middle section of Luke (9:51–19:44) features Jesus's journey to Jerusalem, while Acts stresses the church's journey away from Jerusalem on the mission to the whole world (Acts 1:7–8).
- Luke is the Gospel for all people, including social outcasts (18:9–14; 19:1–10), gentiles and Samaritans (2:32; 4:25–27; 10:29–37),

women (8:1–3; 10:38–42; 21:1–4; 23:27–31; 23:55–24:11), the poor (14:12–14; 16:19–31), the sick (4:18; 13:10–17; 17:11–19), and "sinners" (7:36–50).

- Only Luke and Matthew include birth stories of Jesus, and Luke includes a bit more about his early life.
- Luke's birth stories feature four famous "hymns"—the *Magnificat* (1:46–55), the *Benedictus* (1:68–79), *Gloria in Excelsis* (2:14), and the *Nunc Dimittis* (2:29–32).
- The needs and concerns of women are highlighted in this Gospel (e.g., 8:1–3).
- Luke provides more of Jesus's parables than any other Gospel, and contains many of Jesus's best-known parables (e.g., the Good Samaritan, the prodigal son).
- Luke stresses the importance of the Holy Spirit, prayer, and joy.
- Luke's Gospel is the longest single book in the New Testament in terms of verses.
- Luke is the only Gospel that names its recipient—"most excellent Theophilus" (Luke 1:3; cf. Acts 1:1).

What Is Luke's Message?

The Birth of Jesus, the Savior (1:1–2:52)

Luke tells the story of Jesus's birth by switching back and forth between John and Jesus. Luke shows that Jesus is superior to John, but that John plays an important role of preparing the way for the Savior. Much of what we read in these first two chapters is only found in Luke's Gospel.

The preface (1:1–4)

In this opening paragraph, Luke formally sets forth the stages of the development of the Gospels: the events themselves (1:1), the time when the stories about Jesus and his teachings were preached and handed down orally (1:2), the many written accounts (1:1), and Luke's own Gospel (1:3). Luke has done his historical homework carefully, and he opens his Gospel by stating his method, his audience, and his purpose in writing.

A gold coin featuring the portrait of Caesar Augustus.

✦ Both Matthew and Luke contain accounts of Jesus's birth.

Announcing the birth of John the Baptizer (1:5–25)

John's father, Zechariah, is a priest, and his mother is a descendant of Aaron, so John's religious ancestry was quite honorable (1:5). Both his parents are righteous and blameless, but they have not been blessed with children (1:6–7). Zechariah receives a rare opportunity to minister in the Holy Place in the temple. As he is burning the incense, the angel Gabriel appears to Zechariah and announces that God has answered his prayer—they will have a son, and he is to name him John. Not only will John be "a joy and delight" to his parents, but he will also play a special role in God's saving plan (1:14–16). Filled with the Holy Spirit while still in his mother's womb, John will go forth in the spirit and power of the prophet Elijah to prepare the people for their Savior (1:15–17). Zechariah is temporarily silenced for doubting Gabriel's announcement (1:18–20). When he emerges from the temple unable to speak, the people realize he has seen a vision (1:21–22). After Zechariah returns home, Elizabeth becomes pregnant and praises God for his favor (1:23–25).

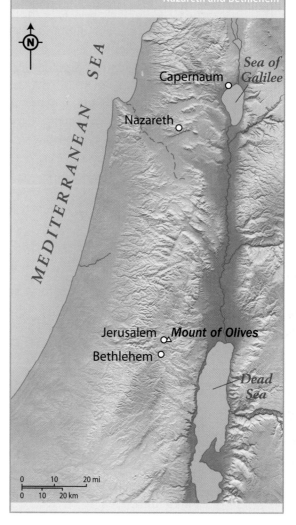

Nazareth and Bethlehem

Announcing the birth of Jesus the Savior (1:26–38)

Mary also receives a visit from the angel Gabriel (1:26–28). Although just a teenage girl from small-town Nazareth, Mary is nevertheless "highly favored" or graced by God (1:28, 30). She has been chosen to give birth to Jesus, "the Son of the Most High" (1:32–33). Not surprisingly, Mary asks how this is possible, since she is a virgin and is betrothed, but not yet

✚ Luke shows how the arrival of Jesus fulfills God's promise to bring salvation to Israel.

The Gospel of Luke   607

married, to Joseph. Gabriel explains that the Holy Spirit will "come upon you" and "the power of the Most High will overshadow you" so that the one born will be called "the Son of God" (1:35). Mary conceived by the supernatural influence of the Holy Spirit without any form of human intercourse (see Matt. 1:18, 20, 25; Mark 6:3; Luke 1:35; 3:23; John 8:41). The virginal conception of Jesus reminds us salvation is a gift from God and not a matter of human achievement. Mary is also given a sign that "nothing is impossible with God," the pregnancy of her relative Elizabeth (1:36–37). Mary humbly accepts her privileged but difficult role in light of her social situation: "I am the Lord's servant. May it be to me as you have said" (1:38).

Mary visits Elizabeth (1:39–56)

We read here of the meeting between the mothers of John and Jesus. As Mary greets Elizabeth, John "leaps for joy" inside Elizabeth's womb (1:41, 44; see also 1:15). Elizabeth, filled with the Holy Spirit, blesses Mary and praises God (1:41–45). The rest of this section contains Mary's beautiful song known as the *Magnificat*, receiving its name from the first word of the Latin version. Mary praises God for graciously allowing her to participate in this momentous event (1:46–49) and for his mighty deeds throughout the history of Israel (1:50–55). Her song reminds us of Psalms of old, especially the song of Hannah in 1 Samuel 2:1–10. Mary stays with Elizabeth for several months and then returns to Nazareth (1:56).

The birth and growth of John (1:57–80)

Elizabeth gives birth and announces that the baby will be called John ("the Lord is gracious"). Zechariah, still unable to speak since his traumatic temple experience, confirms that his name will be John. Immediately Zechariah is able to speak again and praises God. The awesome news

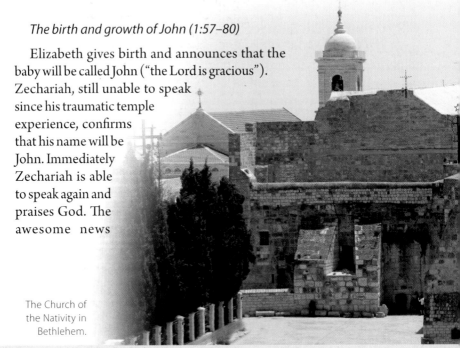

The Church of the Nativity in Bethlehem.

The Virgin Birth

Preben Vang

The birth of Christ by a virgin describes the method God chose for the incarnation. The scriptural emphasis is that Mary conceived a child due to the supernatural influence of God's Holy Spirit without human intercourse. This means the Son she birthed was *willed* by God rather than caused by humans.

The biblical evidence for virgin conception seems rather scarce at first. Only Matthew and Luke tell the story, and their stories relate different details. Mark and John seem uninterested in Jesus's special birth, and the letters seem occupied with Jesus's ministry. Does this mean that the virgin conception proves insignificant for Christian faith? Not at all! Although only Matthew and Luke give "full accounts" of Mary's virginity at the time of Jesus's conception, all of the New Testament affirms it when touching on the issue (cf. Mark 6:3 to Matt. 13:55). The true significance of the virgin conception concerns the very nature of Jesus. God could have chosen to bring Jesus to earth through a special creation similar to the way he created the first Adam. However, Matthew's and Luke's portrayal of *how* God connected eternity with history places Christ's eternal nature at the very core of the Christian faith. John's Gospel exposes this most clearly with his opening statement about Jesus's preexistence before his historical birth in Bethlehem.

Put differently, the virgin conception joins or unites the preexistent (or eternal) nature of Christ with his historical (or temporal) existence in a way that preserves both natures as coexistent. Without the virginal conception, there must have been a point of adoption, a specific historical time when Jesus became "Son of God." The problem with the idea of adoption is that it ultimately makes Jesus 100 percent man and 0 percent God. Adoption changes belonging, not being!

Some scholars have tried to connect Jesus's sinlessness to his virgin conception. Such efforts, however, misread the biblical material and make sin an issue of inheritance and chromosomes. Furthermore, it seems to suggest that Mary was sinless simply because she was a virgin. It proves more helpful to say that because Jesus was 100 percent human (born of a woman), he could have sinned; but, because he was 100 percent God (born of the Spirit), he also had the option *not* to sin. Opposite the first Adam who also had the option not to sin, the second Adam, Jesus, remained sinless and restored what the first Adam destroyed (Rom. 5:19; Heb. 4:15). That Jesus was born of a woman secures that he can relate 100 percent to the human situation. That he was born of God's Spirit secures that the salvation he offers is eternal, from God. The virginal conception remains significant to the Christian faith.

of the events surrounding John's birth spread, and people marvel at what God is up to. Now Zechariah, filled with the Holy Spirit himself, praises God for mercifully providing salvation (1:68–75) and for John's role in preparing people for Jesus the Savior (1:76–79). John grows and becomes spiritually strong as he lives in the wilderness preparing for his public ministry (1:80).

The birth of Jesus (2:1–20)

See Matthew 1:18–25; 2:1–12. Because Joseph belongs to the house and royal line of King David, he goes to Bethlehem, the town of David, to register for the census. Jesus is born around 6–5 BC, about six months after John was born (1:26). There is no room for the couple in the "inn," likely a guest room in a regular house (Luke 22:11). Because that room is occupied, Mary gives birth in the place where the animals stayed and lays the baby Jesus in a "manger" or feeding trough. Could God the Son have entered the world in a more humble way? Nearby, an angel of the Lord appears to ordinary shepherds with the announcement, "Do not be afraid. I bring you good news of great joy that will be for all the people. Today in the town of David a Savior has been born to you; he is Christ the Lord" (2:10–11). The heavens erupt with joy and celebration and praise to God for the birth of the Savior (2:13–14). God receives glory, and those who follow God experience peace (2:14). Meanwhile, the shepherds travel to see Jesus and leave praising God and telling the world about all the amazing things they have witnessed (2:17–18, 20). This whole experience is probably overwhelming for Mary, who "treasured up all these things and pondered them in her heart" (2:19).

Jesus presented in the temple (2:21–40)

See Matthew 2:22–23. Because Joseph and Mary are faithful Jews, they have Jesus circumcised on the eighth day, name him "Jesus" (God saves), and follow the proper purification laws prescribed in Leviticus 12:2–4. The fact that they offer two birds probably indicates that they are a working poor family. While at the temple they meet Simeon, a righteous and Spirit-filled man, who recognizes Jesus as Messiah and praises God for sending a Savior for all people (2:29–32). Simeon also adds that Jesus's mission to bring

A stone manger (Luke 2:7).

✚ Simeon predicts that Jesus will not only be a glorious Messiah but also a suffering Messiah (Luke 2:34–35).

salvation will involve suffering and pain (2:34–35). They also meet Anna, a pious, elderly woman, who thanks God for his provision and confirms Jesus's identity (2:36–38). The family returns to Nazareth where Jesus grows in strength, wisdom, and God's grace (2:39–40).

Jesus's boyhood visit to the temple and continued growth (2:41–52)

This is the only picture we have of Jesus between his infancy and adult life. The "silence" of our four Gospels about Jesus's younger years probably speaks volumes about the essentially normal life Jesus had as a boy and young man. At age twelve he goes up to Jerusalem with his family for the Passover Feast. As the clan starts home, Jesus stays behind in the temple discussing theology with the Jewish teachers. He amazes the religious experts with his understanding. When his parents return and gently rebuke him, Jesus replies, "Didn't you know I had to be in my Father's house?" (2:49). They don't understand. Even at an early age Jesus reveals his unique relationship with the Father and his divine mission. Jesus returns to his small hometown where he lives obediently, growing in wisdom and stature and favor with God and people (2:52). Again, Mary "treasured all these things in her heart" (2:51).

The Savior's Preparation for Public Ministry (3:1–4:13)

The prophet John prepares the way for Jesus, the Savior. The more powerful One is coming! Jesus enters public ministry by submitting to John's baptism. His credentials as the Savior for all humanity are traced back to Adam. When Satan confronts the Son of God in the wilderness in an attempt to derail the entire project, Jesus proves faithful.

The ministry of John the Baptizer (3:1–20)

See Matthew 3:1–12; 14:3–4; Mark 1:1–8; 6:17–18; John 1:19–28. Luke locates the ministry of John the Baptizer within world history rather than just local history (3:1–2). The "word of God came to John" the prophet to preach a "baptism of repentance for the forgiveness of sins" (3:2–3). This kind of language introduces the prophets of the Old Testament and identifies John as a continuation of their prophetic ministry. Luke cites Scripture from Isaiah to show that "all mankind together will see" God's salvation (Isa. 40:3–5). We are reminded that Jesus is the Savior for the whole world! When John confronts the crowds with the urgent need to "produce fruit in keeping with repentance" (3:8), they ask in response, "What should we do then?" (3:10). Genuine, fruit-bearing repentance will be demonstrated in concrete, ethical actions. John gives three examples: (1) rich people will

✚ The Old Testament prophet Isaiah had predicted that the Messiah would possess wisdom from God, and Luke highlights Jesus's growth in wisdom (Luke 2:40, 52).

The Gospel of Luke   611

give generously; (2) tax collectors will become honest; and (3) soldiers will refrain from violence and deceit and instead be content with their military pay (3:11–14). As the people wonder if John might be the Messiah, he sets the record straight. He's not even worthy of untying Jesus's sandals (a task too demeaning for even a slave), and his baptism pales in comparison to Jesus's baptism with the Holy Spirit and fire. No, John is not the Messiah, but the Messiah is coming . . . soon! John's prophetic integrity and boldness lands him in prison and ultimately costs him his life (3:19–20; see also Mark 6:14–29).

The baptism of Jesus (3:21–22)

See Matthew 3:13–17; Mark 1:9–11; John 1:19–34.

The genealogy of Jesus (3:23–38)

See Matthew 1:2–17. Genealogies were important in the ancient world to establish a ruler's legitimacy. Matthew's genealogy confirms Jesus as the Jewish Messiah by showing his connection to King David and Abraham, the Father of the Jewish nation. Luke, on the other hand, traces Jesus's ancestry all the way back to Adam, emphasizing his importance for all humanity.

The temptation of Jesus (4:1–13)

See Matthew 4:1–11; Mark 1:12–13. Luke's account of Jesus's temptations in the wilderness is very similar to Matthew's, except that the second and third temptations occur in a different order. Ancient writers often rearranged events in thematic or, in this case, theological order. Most likely Luke places the temptation involving the temple last because Jesus's journey to Jerusalem is such a significant theme in Luke. Also, don't miss the connection Luke makes to the genealogy. The last line in the previous section is ". . . the son of Adam, the son of God." Now Satan addresses Jesus as "Son of God." Jesus is the unique Son of God who, because of his faithfulness, provides salvation for the rest of humanity.

The Savior's Galilean Ministry (4:14–9:50)

Jesus begins his saving ministry of preaching the kingdom of God, healing diseases, casting out demons, and calling disciples in Galilee. While he is rejected in his own hometown, he reaches beyond the confines of typical Jews to a leper, a paralytic, a tax collector, and a gentile soldier, among others. He is judged by a Pharisee but supported by a group of faithful women

✦ Luke emphasizes how God's salvation will be available to gentiles as well as Jews by quoting Isaiah 40:5 in addition to what is quoted in Matthew and Mark.

disciples and anointed by a sinful woman. He conveys kingdom truths in parables for those willing to listen, and performs miracles to demonstrate his power over all other powers. The repeated question, "Who is this?" is finally answered by Peter who confesses Jesus as "the Christ." But Jesus makes it clear that he came to be a suffering Savior. Although rejected by the world, the Son's glory is previewed at the transfiguration.

A summary of his ministry in Galilee (4:14–15)

See Matthew 4:12–17; Mark 1:14–15. Luke emphasizes that Jesus returns to Galilee "in the power of the Spirit," ministers in Galilee, and everyone praises him.

Jesus preaches in Nazareth (4:16–30)

See Matthew 13:53–58; Mark 6:1–6. Jesus returns to his hometown, Nazareth, and teaches in the synagogue. When asked to read from the prophets, Jesus chooses passages from Isaiah 61:1–2 and 58:6 that reveal his Spirit-anointed role as Savior and Messiah (4:18–19). As was customary, Jesus then sits down to begin his exposition of the passage. "Today this scripture is fulfilled in your hearing," he says, and everyone is amazed at his gracious words (4:20–22). Then Jesus challenges their intentions by predicting they will demand even more miracles (4:23). "No prophet is accepted in his hometown," Jesus concludes (4:24), and he gives two examples from their

Remains from a synagogue at Chorazin.

history. Both Elijah and Elisha were sent to and welcomed by those outside the nation of Israel while they were rejected by Israel (4:25–27). Now the hometown crowd reacts with anger and rage as they drag him out of town to throw him down the cliff. But his time of suffering has not yet arrived, so he walks away unharmed (cf. Luke 22:53; John 7:30). This is the first, but not the last, time that Jesus will face rejection from the people of Israel in Luke's Gospel.

Jesus's ministry in Capernaum (4:31–44)

See Matthew 4:23; 8:14–17; Mark 1:21–39. Jesus's ministry includes teaching and healing in the synagogue at Capernaum, healing Simon Peter's mother-in-law, and healing many sick people late into the night. As he casts demons out of many people, the demons attempt to control Jesus by naming him: "You are the Son of God!" (4:41). But Jesus rebukes them and prevents them from speaking because they know he is "the Christ" or Messiah (4:41). Jesus wants to be confessed as Messiah by faithful followers, not by demonic spirits. As the sun rises, Jesus withdraws and plans to take the good news of the kingdom to other towns as well.

Catching fish and calling disciples (5:1–11)

See Matthew 4:18–22; Mark 1:16–20; cf. John 1:35–42. Luke reports Jesus's call of the first four disciples in the context of a miraculous catch of fish. After teaching the crowds from a fishing boat, Jesus instructs Peter to take the boat to the deep water and let down the nets. Peter complains that they have fished all night without success, but trusts Jesus enough to lower the nets anyway. Miraculously they haul in a huge number of fish that begin to sink their boats. As an experienced fisherman, Peter knows this is no accident, and he falls at Jesus's feet saying, "Go away from me, Lord; I am a sinful man!" (5:8). Jesus's miracle points to a deeper spiritual reality as he says to Peter, "Don't be afraid; from now on you will catch men" (5:10). As Peter becomes aware of who he is (a sinful man) in relation to Jesus (the powerful Lord), he submits to Jesus. God will use those who depend upon him to bring people into his kingdom. The two sets of brothers leave everything and follow Jesus (5:11).

Jesus cleanses a leper (5:12–16)

See Matthew 8:1–4; Mark 1:40–45. Luke adds that Jesus "often withdrew to lonely places and prayed" (5:16). Jesus's balance of ministry among people with solitude and prayer offers us an important example to imitate.

✦ Luke emphasizes Jesus's prayer life and records nine of his prayers (3:21; 5:16; 6:12; 9:18, 28; 11:1; 22:32; 23:34, 46).

Jesus heals a paralyzed man (5:17–26)

See Matthew 9:1–8; Mark 2:1–12. Luke points out that Jewish leaders from "every village of Galilee and from Judea and Jerusalem" had come to hear Jesus teach, indicating how Jesus's popularity and influence is growing (5:17). Interestingly, Luke also notes that "the power of the Lord was present for him to heal the sick" that day (5:17). If the Son of God depended on the Spirit of God during his earthly ministry, how much more do we need to depend upon the Spirit?

The call of Levi/Matthew (5:27–32)

See Matthew 9:9–13; Mark 2:13–17.

A question about fasting (5:33–39)

See Matthew 9:14–17; Mark 2:18–22. Luke adds a third illustration to the two in common with Matthew and Mark: "And no one after drinking old wine wants the new, for he says, 'The old is better'" (v. 39). Jesus seems to be admitting that many who hear his new teaching will prefer the old, more comfortable teaching instead and will reject him.

Controversial works on the Sabbath (6:1–11)

See Matthew 12:1–14; Mark 2:23–28; 3:1–6.

Peter's home in Capernaum near the synagogue. The house is now covered by a modern structure with a glass floor.

The choosing of the twelve disciples (6:12–16)

See Matthew 10:1–4; Mark 3:13–19. Luke observes that before Jesus chose twelve disciples and designated them as "apostles," he went to a mountainside to pray and spent the whole night in prayer to the Father (6:12).

Jesus continues his powerful ministry (6:17–19)

See Matthew 4:24–25; 12:15–21; Mark 3:7–12. Before teaching his disciples and the crowds how to relate to God and to other people in the Sermon on the Plain, Jesus continues to heal the sick and cast out demons. His fame continues to spread.

Jesus's Sermon on the Plain (6:20–49)

See Matthew 5:1–7:29. Luke notes earlier (6:17) that Jesus taught on a "level" place or plateau. There are many level places on the hills surrounding the Sea of Galilee, and this is not inconsistent with the mountain setting in Matthew. Virtually all of Luke's Sermon on the Plain can be found in Matthew's Sermon on the Mount. The only difference is that after the Beatitudes in 6:20–23, Luke includes a list of "woes" in 6:24–26. Luke has more of a physical, social focus indicating that Jesus cares about our physical needs as well as our spiritual needs. Those who are poor, hungry, sorrowful, hated, excluded, insulted, and rejected now because of their relationship to Jesus are blessed, for they are identifying with the true prophets of old (6:20–23). But those who are rich, well fed, haughty, and universally praised stand under the curse of God, for they are casting their lot with the false prophets (6:24–26).

Healing of the centurion's servant (7:1–10)

See Matthew 8:5–13. A Roman centurion commanded as many as one hundred troops. Interestingly, this gentile soldier sends a group of local Jewish leaders to ask Jesus to come heal his servant (7:3). Although the centurion was not a full convert to Judaism, he was sympathetic to the Jewish people and their worship practices (7:4–5). As Jesus is traveling to the village, he receives a message from the man—"Lord, don't trouble yourself, for I do not deserve to have you come under my roof" (7:6). The man doesn't even consider himself worthy of approaching Jesus. He trusts Jesus to heal his servant from a distance, which Jesus does (7:7, 10). Jesus commends the profound faith of this "pagan" (gentile) military man (7:9).

Healing a widow's son (7:11–17)

As Jesus and his disciples approach the small town of Nain, they are met by a funeral procession. A widow has lost her only son, leaving her without family and therefore any means of supporting herself in that society. Jesus's "heart went out to her" as he comforted her (7:13). Rather than becoming unclean by touching the dead body, Jesus heals the young man and gives him back to his mother (7:14–15). This is one of many occasions where Jesus's healing is not based on the person's faith but solely on his sovereign choice. Also, Jesus's main concern here is for the needy woman. The awestruck witnesses praise God for the "great prophet" among them (cf. 1 Kings 17:7–24; 2 Kings 4:32–37) as evidence that "God has come to help his people" (7:16). Jesus's fame continues to spread throughout the land of the Jews (7:17).

Jesus and John the Baptizer (7:18–35)

See Matthew 11:1–19. Luke is very similar to Matthew in this episode, except he adds a comment in 7:29–30: "All the people, even the tax collectors, when they heard Jesus' words, acknowledged that God's way was right, because they had been baptized by John. But the Pharisees and experts in the law rejected God's purpose for themselves, because they had not been baptized by John." In this way Luke directly targets the Jewish leaders as the ones who deserve a rebuke.

A sinful woman anoints Jesus at the Pharisee's house (7:36–50)

Compare similar but different events in Matthew 26:6–13; Mark 14:3–9; John 11:55–12:11. In Matthew and Mark the anointing occurs in a leper's house, which a Pharisee would never visit. As a result, we know this is a separate, but similar, incident. Jesus regularly associated with sinful people. This episode begins by Jesus accepting an invitation to have dinner with Simon, a Pharisee (7:36). We should take note that although Jesus criticizes the Pharisees for their hypocrisy, he still reaches out to individual Pharisees. During the meal a sinful woman approaches Jesus and anoints his feet with her tears, dries them with her long hair (a sign of promiscuity), kisses

A silver denarius depicting Caesar Augustus.

✦ Following Jesus's sermon on the plain, Luke shows how various people respond to Jesus: a Roman soldier, a grieving mother, John the Baptizer and his disciples, the Pharisees, and a sinful woman.

The Gospel of Luke   617

A 1695 depiction of a violent storm on the Sea of Galilee by Ludolf Backhuysen.

them, and anoints them with expensive perfume (7:37–38). The Pharisee immediately judges Jesus for allowing the act, which prompts Jesus to tell a story (7:39–40). In the parable two men owe money, one a huge amount and the other a much smaller amount. The moneylender cancels both of their debts. Jesus asks, "Which of them will love him more?" Simon correctly answers, "The one who had the bigger debt canceled" (7:42–43). Then Jesus applies the story to the immediate situation and concludes, "Therefore, I tell you, her many sins have been forgiven—for she loved much. But he who has been forgiven little loves little" (7:47). The woman knows her guilt and shame, whereas Simon feels confident in his own righteousness. They both need forgiveness, but only the woman recognizes her need. Jesus then pronounces her forgiven and saved by her faith and sends her out in peace (7:48, 50). The other guests ask that reoccurring question, "Who is this?" (7:49).

The women who minister to Jesus (8:1–3)

Luke emphasizes the role of women in the kingdom mission (1:5–39; 2:36–38; 7:11–17, 36–50; 10:38–42; 13:10–17; 15:8–10; 18:1–8). Here we learn of a group of women disciples who had benefited from Jesus's ministry and who travel with him lending their financial support. Three are named: Mary Magdalene, who had been delivered from demon possession; Joanna, the wife of Herod's household manager; and Susanna. Women play an important role throughout Jesus's ministry and in the life of the early church (Acts 1:14).

The parable of the sower (8:4–8)

See Matthew 13:1–9; Mark 4:1–9.

✦ People are constantly asking about Jesus's identity—Luke 7:19; 8:25; 9:9. Jesus answers these questions by pointing to his redemptive works—Luke 7:22 (cf. 4:18; Isa 29:18–19; 35:5–6; 61:1–2).

Women Followers of Jesus

Bobby Kelly

The Gospels present women as central figures in the ministry of Jesus. The fact that Jesus included women in such vital and varied roles marked a stark contrast to the status of Jewish, Greek, and to a large extent, Roman women. While one must be careful not to overstate the situation in the first century, it is safe to say that women had limited opportunities outside of domestic roles and had little control over their own lives. When viewed in this context, the revolutionary implications of Jesus's proclamation for women come more fully into view.

Mary, the mother and future follower of Jesus, dominates Luke's account of Jesus's birth. Mary's song (Luke 1:46–55) is the ultimate celebration of the "birth" of a revolution that will turn the current structures upside down, or perhaps more appropriately, right-side up (Luke 1:46–55). In this revolution the proud and wealthy are brought low and go hungry, while the humble and poor are elevated and filled. The song also infers that women, like Mary, will stand alongside men in the revolution. The presence of Elizabeth (Luke 1:5–7, 24–25, 39–45, 57–60) and Anna the prophet (Luke 2:36–38) provides confirmation. Men and women will participate equally in God's coming reign.

The Gospels present women as models of faithful discipleship, some of long-standing nature who support the mission financially (Luke 8:1–3) and who often succeed when the male disciples fail miserably. The list of such women would include Mary Magdalene, Mary the mother of James and Jesus, Salome, Mary the wife of Clopas, Joanna, Susanna, Mary and Martha of Bethany, and a number of unnamed women. While the Gospels depict these women as faithful followers of Jesus, nowhere is it more evident than during Passion Week. It is the women who remain with Jesus to the end. The unnamed woman who anoints Jesus "beforehand for burial" emerges as one of the few, if not the only one, who seems to understand Jesus's prediction that he will die but on the third day arise. Thus she anoints him on Tuesday since his body will be gone on Sunday. The Twelve remain completely in the dark. Furthermore, it is the "daughters of Jerusalem" who weep for Jesus as he is led away to crucifixion (Luke 23:27–31). In the Synoptics, while it is true that men stand alongside women as witnesses of the crucifixion, the emphasis is clearly on the women who "were watching from a distance" (Mark 15:40; par. Matt. 27:55–56; Luke 23:49). John highlights the women along with the Beloved Disciple standing by the cross (John 19:25–27). Similarly, the women alone observe the place where Jesus was buried (Matt. 27:60–61; Mark 15:47; Luke 23:55–56). While each Gospel highlights the women a bit differently at the empty tomb, it is clear that women are the chief witnesses, the first to be commissioned "go and tell," and in general display faith in strong contrast with the confused disciples (Matt. 28:1–10; Mark 16:1–8; Luke 24:1–12; John 20:1–18).

Modern interpreters should resist the urge to make Jesus a thoroughgoing egalitarian. Jesus made little if any effort to overturn traditional domestic expectations of women in the first century. While women did constitute part of the outer circle of Jesus's followers, he did not include a woman among the Twelve. Jesus does, however, work within the structures of the day in order to elevate the status of women both in the larger society and certainly in the coming rule of God.

Why parables? (8:9–10)

See Matthew 13:10–15; Mark 4:10–12.

The parable of the sower interpreted (8:11–15)

See Matthew 13:18–23; Mark 4:13–20.

The importance of listening to Jesus (8:16–18)

See Matthew 5:14–16; Mark 4:21–22. In the ancient world, oil lamps belonged in a place where their light could benefit the people in the house, not under a jar or a bed. In the same way, people should listen carefully to Jesus's words, the equivalent of spiritual light, so that they may benefit.

Jesus's true family (8:19–21)

See Matthew 12:46–50; Mark 3:31–35.

The calming of the storm (8:22–25)

See Matthew 8:23–27; Mark 4:35–41. This episode begins a series of four miracles to show Jesus's power over nature (8:22–25), over the demonic (8:26–39), over disease (8:43–48), and over death (8:40–42, 49–56). Following that demonstration of power, Jesus sends out the Twelve to do the very same things. His saving ministry is extended through the Twelve.

Jesus casts out a legion of demons (8:26–39)

See Matthew 8:28–34; Mark 5:1–20.

Jairus's daughter and the bleeding woman (8:40–56)

See Matthew 9:18–26; Mark 5:21–43.

The desolate and dangerous road linking Jerusalem and Jericho.

The House of Herod

Larry R. Helyer

The Herodian dynasty significantly shaped the Jewish world of Jesus and the apostles, playing a leading role in the political and cultural life of the Second Temple period for four generations.

The Roman senate appointed Herod the Great (born around 73 BC) "King of the Jews" in 40 BC. At the height of his political power, he exercised tyrannical control over his kingdom. Although most of his Jewish subjects detested him, there were some, the Herodians, who supported his dynasty (Mark 3:6; 12:13). He transformed his modest realm into a showpiece of Greco-Roman culture, the Jerusalem temple being one of the wonders of the Roman world (Mark 13:1).

Herod the Great is the villain in the story of the Magi (Matt. 2:1–18). Paranoid at being overthrown by rivals, he lashes out at numerous opponents, even putting members of his family to death on suspicion of treason. The massacre of the innocents at Bethlehem is consistent with this troubled period of his life. Herod's death in 4 BC provides the latest possible date for Jesus's birth.

Herod the Great's son Archelaus is mentioned once in the New Testament in connection with the holy family's return from Egypt. Fearful of living under his jurisdiction, Joseph returns to Nazareth in Galilee (Matt. 2:22). Augustus Caesar banished Archelaus in AD 6 for ineptitude and oppression.

Herod Antipas, another son of Herod the Great, became tetrarch of Galilee (Luke 3:1) and is the one who imprisoned and executed John the Baptist (Mark 6:14–29). When Jesus's fame as a preacher and healer spreads, Antipas is perplexed (Luke 9:7) and wonders if John the Baptist has been raised from the dead (Matt. 14:1–2). Jesus calls him "that fox" (Luke 13:32). Antipas plays a role in the trial of Jesus, egging him on to perform a sign and mocking him (Luke 23:7–12). Following his ill-advised attempt to gain the title "king," the emperor Caligula banished him in AD 39.

The territory of Herod Philip (Luke 3:1), a third son of Herod the Great, is the venue for Peter's confession (Mark 8:27–30) and the transfiguration (Mark 9:2–9). Philip married Salome, who danced before Herod Antipas and requested the head of John the Baptist (Mark 6:22–28). Philip died childless in AD 34.

Agrippa I, grandson of Herod the Great, persecuted the early church. He executed the apostle James and imprisoned the apostle Peter (Acts 12:1–4). Luke claims an angel of the Lord struck him down (Acts 12:19–23).

Agrippa II, a great grandson, appears in the New Testament, along with his sister Bernice, in connection with Paul's incarceration and defense before the Roman governor Festus (Acts 25:13–26:32). Agrippa tried unsuccessfully to stem the rush to rebellion in AD 66 and aided the Romans in crushing the revolt (AD 66–73). He died around AD 100, the last Herod to exercise rule over a portion of Palestine.

Jesus sends out the Twelve (9:1–6)

See Matthew 9:35; 10:1–16; Mark 6:6–13. They are to preach the kingdom (equivalent of preaching the gospel as v. 6 shows) and minister to people through driving out demons and healing diseases. In this way, the truthful word and the miraculous deed validate one another and reflect Jesus's power and authority.

Who is Jesus? (9:7–9)

See Matthew 14:1–2; Mark 6:14–16. When Herod hears about all that Jesus is doing, he is perplexed by the various explanations (John the Baptizer raised from the dead, Elijah appearing, or one of the prophets resurrected). Luke emphasizes Herod's question, "Who is this?" throughout this central section of his Gospel (e.g., 4:36; 5:21; 7:49; 8:25; 9:18–20). Peter will give the correct answer in his confession of Jesus as "the Christ of God" (9:20).

The feeding of the multitude (9:10–17)

See Matthew 14:13–21; Mark 6:30–44; John 6:1–15.

Peter's confession (9:18–21)

See Matthew 16:13–20; Mark 8:27–30; John 6:66–71.

The cost of following the suffering Savior (9:22–27)

See Matthew 16:21–28; Mark 8:31–9:1; John 12:25.

Jesus's transfiguration (9:28–36)

See Matthew 17:1–9; Mark 9:2–10. Jesus takes Peter, John, and James up onto a mountain to pray, and during his prayer he is transfigured (9:28–29). Jesus speaks with Moses and Elijah "about his departure" (or exodus), which he will accomplish in Jerusalem (9:31). The three disciples are half asleep when Jesus's glory makes them wide awake (9:32). In Luke's Gospel the voice from heaven says, "This is my Son, *whom I have chosen*; listen to him" (9:35, emphasis added; cf. Isa. 42:1; 49:7; Luke 23:35), expressing the Son's special role in the Father's saving plan.

Jesus succeeds where the disciples fail (9:37–43)

See Matthew 17:14–20; Mark 9:14–29.

More on following the suffering Savior (9:43–50)

See Matthew 10:42; 17:22–18:5; Mark 9:30–41. As the crowds marvel at Jesus, he warns his disciples that the Son of Man will be betrayed, but they don't understand (9:43–45). Not only are they slow to grasp Jesus's identity and mission, they are preoccupied with which one is the greatest. Jesus welcomes a little child to make the spiritual point that the least will be the greatest (9:46–48). Among Jesus's followers, power and rank should take a backseat to childlike humility. In spite of Peter's inspired confession,

✦ Peter clearly identifies who Jesus is by confessing him as "the Christ [or Messiah] of God" (Luke 9:20).

the disciples continue to stumble. They are powerless to cast out a demon, they argue over who is the greatest, and now they try to stop someone from driving out demons in Jesus's name because he's not part of their group. "Do not stop him," Jesus says, "for whoever is not against you is for you" (9:49–50). What timely words for competitive disciples!

The Savior's Journey to Jerusalem (9:51–19:44)

Jesus's journey to Jerusalem lies at the heart of Luke's Gospel, but the journey doesn't take a straight path to the holy city. For example, in Luke 10:38–42 he is in Bethany, just a short distance from Jerusalem, while in Luke 17:11 he passes between Samaria and Galilee in the northern part of the country. Although he travels in a roundabout way, Jesus's ultimate goal is Jerusalem, where he will fulfill God's plan as the suffering Savior. It is a journey of divine destiny. The Father has just told the disciples to "listen to him" (Luke 9:35). "Listening to Jesus" (allowing him to define what it means to follow him) serves as an important theme throughout this journey section.

Hill near Bethsaida in Galilee, a possible location of the feeding of the 5,000.

✚ The entire central section of Luke's Gospel presents Jesus's "journey to Jerusalem." In the book of Acts, Jesus's followers will journey away from Jerusalem with good news for the world.

The Gospel of Luke

Pharisees in the New Testament

Joseph R. Dodson

The New Testament presents the Pharisees in an unfavorable light. Jesus accuses them of being sons of hell (Matt. 23:15), lovers of money (Luke 16:14), and a brood of vipers (Matt. 23:33). Probably beginning around the time of the Maccabean revolt (168–164 BC), this group arose because of their desire to preserve Torah in the face of encroaching religious and political pollution; still, despite these noble intentions, the Gospels—especially Matthew—present Pharisaism as a foil for true righteousness (e.g., Matt. 5:20; Luke 18:10–14). Therefore, in contrast to those who will inherit the kingdom of God (Matt. 21:41–45; 23:13), Jesus vilifies the Pharisees—they are the blind leading the blind (Matt. 15:14; cf. John 9:40), a wicked generation demanding to see signs (Matt. 12:38–39; 16:4), greedy hypocrites swallowing camels but straining out gnats (Matt. 23:24), and whitewashed tombs concealing the corpses therein (Matt. 23:27). Finally, because of their sin, Jesus states that they will not escape the sentence of hell (Matt. 15:12–13; 23:13).

The Pharisees, however, also denigrate Jesus and plot against him for his seemingly impure acts of associating with sinners (e.g., Matt. 9:11–14; Mark 2:16–17; Luke 15:2); for his disregard for certain traditions of Israel, especially those regarding the Sabbath (Matt. 15:1–14; Mark 2:23–24; 7:1–5; Luke 6:2; 11:37–38); and for his claim to be God (e.g., Luke 5:17–21). They belittle Jesus by calling him a drunkard and a glutton, even going so far as to liken him to demons (Matt. 12:24; Luke 7:34). Furthermore, in John 12:42–43, the writer stresses the significant influence of the Pharisees, which hindered many from confessing their faith in the Christ.

Despite this mutual defamation in the Gospels, there were Pharisees, such as Nicodemus, who served as exceptions that proved the rule (see John 3:1–21; 7:50; 19:39–40). Some of these even took part in the Jerusalem council of Acts 15. Of course, the most notable of these exceptions is Paul, who at times uses both his Pharisaical status and some of his former Pharisaical theology to his advantage (see Acts 23:6; 26:5). Thus similarities in thought—such as belief in the resurrection of the dead, eternal rewards and judgment, as well as a high view of divine providence without excluding human responsibility—should not come as a surprise. Although Paul regards his Pharisaical status as an achievement, he comes to consider it rubbish compared to the surpassing value of knowing Christ (Phil. 3:4–8).

What does it mean to follow Jesus? (9:51–10:24)

See Matthew 8:18–22; 9:37–38; 10:7–16, 40; 11:20–27; 13:16–17; John 4:35; 13:20. As Jesus and his disciples encounter hostility in Samaria, James and John want to duplicate the miracle of Elijah and call down fire from heaven (1 Kings 18:38). But following Jesus means that we do not retaliate against those who reject us. Genuine disciples should be prepared to serve and suffer for Jesus (9:57–62). He then sends out the seventy-two (or seventy depending on the original text) to do what he had earlier commissioned the Twelve to do (Luke 9:1–6): travel lightly, depend on hospitality, heal the sick, and proclaim the kingdom. The "harvest is plentiful," Jesus tells them, "but the workers are few" (10:2).

The solution is to pray for more people to share Jesus's mission. There is so much to be done in this broken world. The disciples go out "like lambs among wolves," indicating that the mission may be dangerous (10:3). Those who listen to the disciples will be listening to Jesus and the Father (10:16). The seventy-two return with joy over a successful mission, especially their power over demons (10:17). Jesus delights that their mission has resulted in the downfall of Satan and his influence, but spiritual warfare should not be their primary focus (10:18–19). Instead, they should rejoice most of all that they have an eternal relationship with God (10:20). Full of joy through the Holy Spirit, Jesus praises the Father for his master plan and pronounces a blessing on the disciples (10:21–24).

Relating to people, to Jesus, and to the Father (10:25–11:13)

See Matthew 6:9–13; 7:7–11; 22:34–40; Mark 12:28–34. This section focuses on relationships. A lawyer tests Jesus with a question about how to gain eternal life. Jesus draws out the proper answer: love God and love people (Lev. 19:18; Deut. 6:5). Wanting to "justify himself," the lawyer asks Jesus to define "neighbor" (10:29). In response, Jesus gives the parable of the Good Samaritan, in which we see the principle that love for another person should transcend all human barriers such as race, religion, or economic status (10:30–37). The next episode occurs in Bethany just outside Jerusalem, where Martha is preparing an elaborate meal for Jesus and his disciples. Jesus grieves over Martha's fretfulness and commends Mary for listening to him. Doing good things for God can sometimes distract us from our relationship with God. Next, Jesus teaches his disciples how to communicate with the Father through prayer. Instruction about prayer (11:1–4) is followed by a short parable on prayer (11:5–8) and an exhortation to pray (11:9–13). Followers of Jesus should be loving neighbors to people in need, should not allow service to God to eclipse our time with God, and should cultivate our relationship with God through prayer.

A replica of the idol Pan, worshiped at Caesarea Philippi.

✦ Luke regularly shows how Jesus came to minister to outcasts, as the parable of the Good Samaritan illustrates (Luke 10:29–37).

The Gospel of Luke

Controversies related to Jesus's ministry (11:14–54)

See Matthew 5:15; 6:22–23; 9:32–34; 12:22–30, 38–45; 15:1–9; 16:1–4; 23:1–36; Mark 3:22–27; 4:21; 7:1–9; 8:11–12. While Jesus amazes the crowds with his miracles, some accuse him of getting his power from Satan (11:14–23). This can't be the case, since Jesus is reversing the works of Satan. Jesus drives out demons "by the finger of God," referring to God's power displayed at the exodus (11:20; see Exod. 8:19). We see the arrival of the kingdom of God when we see Jesus undo the damaging deeds of Satan. Jesus is stronger than Satan (11:21–23). Those who have been delivered from the clutches of the devil have a responsibility to fill that void with a new allegiance to Jesus (11:24–26). At that point a woman in the crowd blesses Jesus's mother for giving birth to him, but Jesus responds with a blessing for those who "hear the word of God and obey it" (11:27–28). As the curious crowds increase, Jesus rebukes them as a wicked generation for seeking a miraculous sign (11:29–32). The only signs they will receive are Jonah's preaching and the wisdom of Solomon. But this generation has been visited by the Son of Man, and they have failed to listen. Jesus again illustrates the importance of listening with the analogy of the lamp (see Luke 8:16–18). Jesus then goes to have dinner with a Pharisee, but he fails to perform the proper ceremonial washings before the meal (11:37–38). When the Pharisee is shocked by Jesus's lack of serious piety, Jesus responds with a series of rebukes. The Pharisees have unclean hearts, neglect justice and love, are consumed with pride, and lack integrity (11:39–44). When one of the lawyers (or scribes) insists that Jesus is insulting them too, he proceeds to rebuke them as well (11:45–54). The experts in religious law burden people but do nothing to help them, stand in the tradition of those who have rejected God's prophets, and have robbed people of God's truth. As you can imagine, the Pharisees and teachers of the law now begin to oppose Jesus fiercely.

Warnings about coming judgment (12:1–13:9)

See Matthew 5:21–26; 6:19–21, 25–34; 10:17–22, 26–36; 12:31–32; 16:2–3, 5–6; 24:42–51; 25:1–13; Mark 3:28–30; 8:14–15; 13:11, 33–37. As Jesus's popularity soars, he talks more about the need to be ready to face God's judgment (12:1). Much of what Jesus says in this section relates to righteousness and faithfulness before God. Beware of the hypocritical influence ("yeast") of the Pharisees, Jesus says, since one day everything will be revealed for all to see (12:2–3). As a result, disciples should fear the Lord, who cares deeply about them (12:4–7). If we acknowledge Jesus before people, he will acknowledge us before the Father at the last judgment. If we disown him now, he will disown us then (12:8–9). And confessing

✚ Jesus was not out to please everyone or avoid conflict at all costs. He courageously contended for God's truth, but he did so in love.

Jesus means submitting to the Holy Spirit, who will empower us to witness before a hostile audience (12:11–12). Jesus gives the parable of the rich fool to illustrate what he has just said (12:13–21). The rich man is selfish (notice the repetition of "I") and foolishly places his trust in possessions rather than God. But what about those who give generously? Who will take care of them? Jesus assures his disciples that their heavenly Father will care for their needs (12:22–34). There is no need to worry; rather, they should seek God's kingdom first and continue to invest in heavenly treasure. Instead of trusting in possessions or worrying about basic needs, Jesus's followers should be faithful as they anticipate his return (12:35–48). Jesus will return at a time we do not expect him (12:40, 46). Consequently, faithfulness should be our focus (12:43). Those who know God's will and fail to do it can expect severe judgment (12:45–47). Those who do not know God's will and are not prepared for his coming can expect a less severe judgment (12:48). We will be judged according to knowledge of God's will (12:48). Jesus brings a hard message to which people will respond differently, even resulting in divided families (12:49–53). Jesus's "baptism" (his death by crucifixion) will not only bring salvation but judgment as well ("fire on the earth"). Jesus criticizes the crowds for knowing how to discern the weather but not knowing how to discern spiritual matters (12:54–59). Jesus then mentions two recent tragedies to debunk the myth that tragedy only falls on serious sinners (13:1–4). All are sinners, Jesus declares, and death is inevitable. People need to repent and enter a right relationship with God (13:5). Jesus then tells a story about an unproductive fig tree to illustrate Israel's failure to have a fruit-bearing relationship with God (13:6–9). Time is running out—judgment is coming.

Jesus reminds his followers that just as God clothes the field with flowers, he will supply their basic needs.

✦ Jesus did not hesitate to speak about the coming judgment of God.

Who will enter the kingdom? (13:10–14:24)

See Matthew 7:13–14, 21–23; 8:11–12; 13:31–33; 19:30; 22:1–14; 23:37–39; Mark 4:30–32; 10:31.

In this section, two Sabbath miracles are followed by short illustrations and parables, then by extended teaching on how a person enters the kingdom of God. In the very middle, Jesus reaffirms his goal of dying in Jerusalem. He heals a crippled woman in a synagogue and a man with dropsy in the home of a prominent Pharisee, both on the Sabbath (13:10–17; 14:1–4). The Jewish leadership remains obstinate. In the illustrations and parables that follow the healings, Jesus speaks about the kingdom (13:18–30; 14:5–24). As the kingdom of God grows, people (Jewish leaders included) should seek to enter it. This calls for humility (14:11), and there will be many surprise attendees at the heavenly banquet (13:28–30; 14:13–14, 21–24). Many in Israel, however, who claim to know God but are rejecting Jesus, will be excluded from the heavenly banquet (13:28–30; 14:15–20). In the central "Jerusalem" section (13:31–35), the Pharisees warn Jesus that Herod is out to kill him (13:31). Jesus isn't intimidated. "Today and tomorrow" he will continue his miraculous ministry, but "on the third day" he will accomplish his goal of dying in Jerusalem (13:32–33). Jesus then laments over Jerusalem (and the entire nation of Israel) for rejecting God's messengers. As a result, they are also rejecting God, who longs to protect and care for them. Now they face God's judgment instead (13:35a; cf. 1 Kings 9:7–8; Ps. 69:25; Jer. 12:7; 22:5). Israel will not see Jesus again until he returns, but then it will be too late (13:35b; cf. Ps. 118:26).

Counting the cost of discipleship (14:25–35)

See Matthew 5:13; 10:37–39; Mark 9:49–50. Those who desire to follow Jesus must count the cost. Anyone who loves family more than Jesus cannot be his disciple (14:26). (We know from Matt. 10:37 that Luke's rhetorical term "hate" means to "love less.") Also, anyone who wants to avoid suffering and rejection cannot be Jesus's disciple (14:27). Jesus then illustrates the demands of disciples. First, a man plans to build a tower but doesn't plan properly and runs out of materials. The tower is never finished (14:28–30). Second, a king considers going to war with another king who has a bigger army. He decides that making peace is better than suffering a loss (14:31–32). In the same way, it's better to make peace with God than to oppose him. And making peace with God involves a willingness to give up everything (14:33). In any culture where becoming a follower of Christ is reduced to its bare minimum ("all you have to do is _____"), Jesus's words hit hard, as they should. Discipleship is costly, and people deserve to know up front what they are

✦ Jesus regularly made people more important than religious rules and traditions.

committing to, even if the number of converts doesn't meet a quota.

God pursues sinners (15:1–32)

See Matthew 18:10–14. Although the cost of following Jesus is high, God diligently and lovingly pursues sinners, as these three parables illustrate. In each case, something has been lost—a lost sheep, a lost coin, and two lost sons. These stories give us a clear picture of God's heart. When the one sheep (representing a lost person) strays, the shepherd (representing God) searches until he finds it. When he finds it, he rejoices and asks others to join the celebration. Jesus concludes: "There will be more rejoicing in heaven over one sinner who repents

The Return of the Prodigal Son by Rembrandt.

than over ninety-nine righteous persons who do not need to repent" (15:7). In other words, God loves to reclaim lost people! In the second story, a woman (representing God) searches carefully until she finds a lost coin (representing a lost person). She then rejoices and calls her friends to join her. Again Jesus concludes, "There is rejoicing in the presence of the angels of God over one sinner who repents" (15:10). The final parable is one of Jesus's most famous—the parable of the prodigal son. Because we typically find a main principle for each main character in Jesus's parables, this story teaches three main truths. First, the younger son (representing tax collectors and sinners) reminds us that our sin can never exhaust the grace of God. He will always welcome home rebellious children once they repent. Second, the older son (representing the Jewish leaders) reminds us that we should never presume upon God's grace or be resentful when he offers grace to undeserving people. We are all undeserving! Finally, the father (representing God) reminds us that God pursues both unrighteous sinners and self-righteous sinners. God runs to meet the younger son (15:20), and he leaves the party to find the older son (15:28). He pursues the lost, whatever their condition.

How to use money and possessions (16:1–31)

See Matthew 5:17–20, 31–32; 6:24; 11:12–13; 19:3–12; Mark 10:2–12. Often Jesus discusses the use of possessions in connection with discipleship.

✚ The three "lost parables" in Luke 15 seem to be directed to the two groups specifically mentioned in 15:1–2: "tax collectors and sinners" and "Pharisees and teachers of the law."

Jesus and the Kingdom of God

Preben Vang

Jesus's main message was that the kingdom of God has come near (Mark 1:15; cf. Luke 4:43). The other themes of Jesus's teaching, like, for example, love for enemies (Matt. 5:44) and salvation by grace rather than works (Matt. 22:1–10; Luke 23:43), are to be understood in light of his teaching on the kingdom. They expound on the quality of life in, and the character of, God's kingdom.

Jesus's claim that God's kingdom had come near proved so radical that not only did the protectors of first-century Judaism (Pharisees, Sadducees, etc.) quickly recognize that his message contradicted theirs, but even Jesus's own followers struggled to understand. Because of this, much of Jesus's teaching on the kingdom comes through replies to questions and in parabolic illustrations (e.g., Mark 4). Even John the Baptist got confused and asked about Jesus's mission. Jesus replied by pointing to the effects of the kingdom's presence: "The blind receive sight, the lame walk, those who have leprosy are cured, the deaf hear, the dead are raised, and the good news is preached to the poor" (Luke 7:22).

When Jesus used the phrase "kingdom of God/heaven," he did not refer to a political area or realm but to the reality of God's renewed presence among people. For Jesus, God's kingdom had nothing to do with Israel's borders; nor did it refer to the restoration of a Davidic kingdom in the geographical and political sense of that term. Rather, Jesus used the phrase to explain that God had stepped into history to make his presence known for the purpose of redeeming all his creation from the consequences of the fall. Put differently, in Jesus's teaching, the kingdom of God is the sphere where God rules and shows his glory.

According to Jesus, the kingdom of God is already here. Jesus inaugurated it! The "age to come" has broken into the "present age." God is making his presence felt now. At the same time, present experience clearly evidences that the kingdom of God is not here in full. Evil still exists; the "old age" is still here. Presently, God does not "fill all in all" (1 Cor. 15:28). We live "between the times," so to speak—in the tension of the already/not fully. The promised "age to come" has already begun, but is not here in full.

He opens with the puzzling parable of the shrewd manager (16:1–13). When a manager is faced with losing his job, he decides to act shrewdly by reducing what people owed his boss, perhaps by removing his own commission. In the end, both the boss and the manager gain honor, an important consideration in a culture that values honor and despises shame. Jesus doesn't commend anything unethical here, but he does pay tribute to the manager's clever shrewdness (16:8). Jesus then encourages disciples to use wealth to enhance relationships (16:9). How we handle small things is the best indicator as to how we will handle big things (16:10–12). In addition, we can't serve both God and material possessions, so we had best love God above all and use money wisely (16:13). The Pharisees, who love money, snub Jesus for his comments. He reminds them that God knows our hearts and that the world's value system is detestable to God (16:14–15). In the midst of this discussion about possessions, Jesus reassures his listeners that his message is completely in line with God's earlier revelation (16:16–17), including its ethical demands (16:18).

In the parable of the rich man and Lazarus that follows (16:19–31), the rich man has lived in opulent luxury in this life while the poor man has suffered horribly. After death, everything is turned upside down. The rich man suffers torment in hell, while the poor beggar enjoys the presence of God (16:22–23). The rich man begs in vain for relief from his punishment because the chasm between heaven and hell cannot be bridged (16:24–26). The rich man pleads for someone to warn his family lest they too experience torment, but he is told that they have "Moses and the Prophets; let them listen to them" (16:29). The rich man persists and asks that someone from the dead should appear to them and warn them (16:30). The truth is that those who have not listened to God's revelation through the Old Testament will not be convinced even if someone (i.e., Jesus) "rises from the dead" (16:31). Those who claim to follow Christ should show compassion for those in need by being generous with their money and possessions.

Inside a typical Galilean home.

What does real faith look like? (17:1–19)

See Matthew 17:19–21; 18:6–7, 15, 21–22; Mark 9:28–29, 42. Real faith begins with a concern for community members (17:1–3). To cause another follower of Christ to stumble warrants a terrible punishment, so we need to watch ourselves. Real faith also includes a willingness to confront fellow believers and forgive them when they repent (17:3–4). Jesus's disciples ask for more faith, but Jesus says that applying our faith is more important than increasing its quantity (17:5–6). Next Jesus gives the parable of the dutiful servant to illustrate the proper attitude corresponding to genuine faith (17:7–10). When the servant has done all he was told to do, he should still consider himself an "unworthy servant" before God. Authentic faith

✚ A true mark of a follower of Jesus is generosity. We see this throughout Luke's Gospel (e.g., 16:19–31) as well as in the book of Acts as the early Christians generously share with one another (Acts 2:44–45; 4:32–37).

reserves no place for boasting or entitlement, only humility. He is God, and we are servants. The only proper response to the undeserved grace of God is gratitude, illustrated by the story of Jesus cleansing ten lepers (17:11–19). When he heals ten men with leprosy, the highly contagious and socially detrimental disease, only one returns to say "thank you." The one who comes back to express gratitude happens to be a Samaritan, whereas the nine Jewish lepers fail to confess God's unique work through Jesus. Gratitude is a virtue difficult to counterfeit, and sometimes those outside the religious tradition are more appropriately grateful for God's miraculous deliverance.

When will the kingdom of God appear? (17:20–18:8)

See Matthew 24:17–18, 23–28, 37–41; Mark 13:14–16, 19–23. Most Jews expected God's kingdom to come in dramatic fashion and bring immediate political victory over their enemies. Jesus insists that God's kingdom is now "within you" (17:21). We tend to think of God's kingdom within our hearts, but the better translation for "within you" is "among you" or "in your midst." Jesus is claiming that the kingdom of God has now arrived in his very person and ministry! And yet the kingdom has not yet arrived in all its final glory. That will occur when Jesus returns, but first he must suffer and be rejected (17:25). Jesus discusses his second coming in more detail (17:22–37; cf. Matthew 24–25; Mark 13). His return will be public, spectacular, and unmistakable (17:24). People will be going about their business and be surprised by his coming (17:26–30). At his return, the righteous will be separated from the wicked, and the wicked will face condemnation (17:31–37). Jesus's coming is certain, but the time of his coming is uncertain. In the interim, followers of Jesus will face opposition and

✛ Jesus teaches that the kingdom of God has already arrived with his coming but has not been fully consummated, something that will happen at his second coming.

experience injustice. Jesus tells the parable of the unjust judge in 18:1–8 to encourage people to pray and persevere (18:1). A judge who neither fears God nor cares about people refuses to grant a widow justice. She persistently badgers him for relief, and he finally consents, lest she wear him out. Jesus concludes that if a corrupt judge can be moved to grant justice, how much more will a caring and compassionate God "bring about justice for his chosen ones, who cry out to him day and night" (18:7). God will certainly vindicate his people, but when Jesus returns, "will he find faith on the earth?" (18:8).

True righteousness (18:9–30)

See Matthew 19:13–30; Mark 10:13–31. The previous section ended with a question: when Jesus returns, will he find faith on the earth? Now we get a clear picture of the kind of faith or righteousness Jesus is looking for. He tells the parable of the Pharisee and tax collector for the benefit of those who are confident of their own righteousness and look down on others (18:9–14). The story is a contrast between the prideful Pharisee who boasts about his exemplary piety and the heartbroken tax collector who can only beg for God's mercy. In a surprise ending, the tax collector, rather than the Pharisee, goes home justified before God. True righteousness cannot be separated from genuine humility. Jesus then encourages the small children to come to him for a blessing. He declares that anyone who wants to enter the kingdom must do so "like a little child" (18:15–17). True righteousness includes childlike dependence on and trust in God. The story of the rich ruler concludes this section (18:18–30). Jesus tells this rich man that he must sell everything, give it to the poor, and follow Jesus—that is true righteousness. Observing how much is required, the disciples question the possibility of anyone being saved. But as the follow-up conversation makes clear, what is impossible with us is possible with God (18:27). Only God can enable people to live out saving righteousness.

Jesus arrives at Jerusalem (18:31–19:44)

See Matthew 9:27–31; 20:17–19, 29–34; 21:1–9; 25:14–30; Mark 10:32–34, 46–52; 11:1–10; 13:34; John 12:12–19. As Jesus nears Jerusalem, he once again predicts his coming death. When he explains to his disciples that they are going to Jerusalem where he will suffer, die, and rise again, they can't comprehend how the Messiah and Savior can possibly go down in defeat. The

Ancient weaving needle.

✚ When Jesus arrives in Jerusalem, he weeps over the city in anticipation of his coming rejection (Luke 19:41–44).

disciples' lack of spiritual understanding stands in contrast to what follows. Passing through Jericho, Jesus is met by a blind beggar who asks for mercy from the "Son of David" (18:35–43). When Jesus heals the man, he immediately follows Jesus, and both he and the crowd praise God (18:43). Jesus then encounters Zacchaeus, a wealthy chief tax collector who climbs a tree to get a glimpse of Jesus (19:1–10). Jesus graces the despised "sinner" with his presence at a meal, and Zacchaeus repents, as evidenced by his willingness to let go of his money. Jesus announces, "Today salvation has come to this house, because this man, too, is a son of Abraham. For the Son of Man came to seek and to save what was lost" (19:9–10). While the disciples struggle to follow Jesus on his terms, a blind man truly sees who Jesus is and a rich man gets into the kingdom, both sure signs that the Savior is at work.

As they approach Jerusalem, the people expect the kingdom of God to appear at once (19:11). Jesus tells the parable of the pounds to correct these false expectations (19:11–27). In the story, a nobleman goes to a distant country to be appointed king before returning (19:12). (Jesus will ascend to the Father to be exalted as Lord of Lords before returning to finalize the kingdom.) The nobleman gives ten servants ten minas (one mina = three months' wages), with instructions to put the money to work (19:13). When the man returns as king, he gets a report from three servants (19:14–15). Two put the money to good use and are rewarded with more responsibility (19:16–19), but because the third servant has earned nothing, even his one mina is taken away (19:20–26). This servant displays both a wrong view of the master and an unfaithful heart. Those who don't want the nobleman (or Jesus) to be king face certain judgment (19:14, 27). The first disciples needed to adjust their expectations about when Jesus would be appointed King. As we await Jesus's return as the anointed King, we need to faithfully use what he has given us. Finally, Jesus the Savior enters Jerusalem (19:28–44). Luke notes how the loud celebration and praise of the crowds trouble some of the Pharisees (19:37–39). But Jesus refuses to rebuke his followers for their praise, rebuking the Pharisees instead: "If they keep quiet, the stones will cry out" (19:40). Even the rocks recognize what the Pharisees fail to see. Jesus becomes quite emotional and weeps over the city (19:41). What a tragedy that God has paid a visit to the city and wasn't even acknowledged (19:42–44). Jesus's prediction of judgment matches the Roman destruction of Jerusalem in AD 70.

The Savior's Ministry in Jerusalem (19:45–21:38)

Prior to Passion Week, Jesus spends time in Jerusalem teaching in the temple area. He is in constant conflict with the Jewish leaders who want to

Walking with Jesus through the Holy (Passion) Week

Adapted from Michael J. Wilkins, *Matthew*, NIVAC (Grand Rapids: Zondervan, 2003).

Modern Calendar Days	Event of the Holy Week
Friday	• Arrival in Bethany (John 12:1)
Saturday	• Evening celebration, Mary anoints Jesus (John 12:2–8; cf. Matt. 26:6–13)
Sunday	• Triumphal Entry into Jerusalem (Matt. 21:1–11; Mark 11:1–10; John 12:12–18) • Jesus surveys the temple area (Mark 11:11) • Return to Bethany (Matt. 21:17; Mark 11:11)
Monday	• Cursing the fig tree on the way to Jerusalem (Matt. 21:18–22; cf. Mark 11:12–14) • Condemning the temple (Matt. 21:12–13; Mark 11:15–17) • Miracles and challenges in the temple (Matt. 21:14–16; Mark 1:18) • Return to Bethany (Mark 11:19)
Tuesday	• Reaction to cursing the fig tree on the way back to Jerusalem (Matt. 21:20–22; Mark 11:20–21) • Debates with religious leaders in Jerusalem and teaching in the temple (Matt. 21:23–23:39; Mark 11:27–12:44) • Olivet (Eschatological) Discourse on the Mount of Olives on the return to Bethany (Matt. 24:1–25:46; Mark 13:1–37)
Wednesday	• "Silent Wednesday"—Jesus and disciples remain in Bethany for last time of fellowship • Judas returns alone to Jerusalem to make arrangements for the betrayal (Matt. 26:14–16; Mark 14:10–11)
Thursday	• Preparations for Passover (Matt. 26:17–19; Mark 14:12–16) *After sundown:* • Passover meal and Last Supper (Matt. 26:20–35; Mark 14:17–26) • Upper room discourses (John 13–17) • Prayers in the Garden of Gethsemane (Matt. 26:36–46; Mark 14:32–42)
Friday	*Sometime perhaps after midnight:* • Betrayal and arrest (Matt. 26:47–56; Mark 14:43–52) • Jewish trial—Jesus appears in three phases in front of: —Annas (John 18:13–24) —Caiaphas and partial Sanhedrin (Matt. 26:57–75; Mark 14:53–65) —Sanhedrin fully assembled (*perhaps after sunrise*) (Matt. 27:1–2; Mark 15:1) • Roman trial—Jesus appears in three phases before: —Pilate (Matt. 27:2–14; Mark 15:2–5) —Herod Antipas (Luke 23:6–12) —Pilate (Matt. 27:15–26; Mark 15:6–15) • Crucifixion (*approx. 9:00 a.m. to 3:00 p.m.*) (Matt. 27:27–66; Mark 15:16–39)
Saturday	Jesus's body in the tomb
Sunday	• Jesus's resurrection • Resurrection witnesses (Matt. 28:1–8; Mark 16:1–8; Luke 24:1–12) • Resurrection appearances (Matt. 28:9–20; Luke 24:13–53; John 20–21)

kill him, but they are stumped by his wisdom and are fearful of the crowds. In contrast to the hypocritical leaders, Jesus draws attention to the pure, sacrificial worship of a poor widow. She does what the leaders are supposed to be doing. Jesus spends a good bit of time teaching his followers about his return and events leading up to that momentous event.

Jesus enters the temple area (19:45–48)

See Matthew 21:10–19; Mark 11:15–19. Jesus enters the temple area and drives out the moneychangers. They have turned the place of prayer into a hideout for hypocrites. As Jesus teaches daily in the temple area, the Jewish leaders search for a way to kill him but are prevented from doing so because of his popularity with the people.

Jesus's authority questioned (20:1–8)

See Matthew 21:23–27; Mark 11:27–33.

Parable of the wicked tenants (20:9–19)

See Matthew 21:33–46; Mark 12:1–12.

Paying taxes to Caesar (20:20–26)

See Matthew 22:15–22; Mark 12:13–17. Because the Jewish leaders are afraid of the people (20:19), they act deceitfully and send spies to trap Jesus in what he says (20:20). They attempt to catch him on the issue of the tribute paid to Rome, but he wisely avoids the trap. The coin has Caesar's stamp and should be given to Caesar, while a human life has the stamp of God's likeness and should be devoted to God. Unable to trap Jesus, his opponents are silenced.

Jerusalem as viewed from the Mount of Olives.

✚ Jesus responds with righteous anger when he sees the place of prayer for all nations serving as a hideout for hypocritical leaders.

The Sanhedrin

Larry R. Helyer

The word "Sanhedrin" usually refers to the supreme Jewish council in Jerusalem. However, in Matthew 5:22, 10:17, and Mark 13:9, it refers to local courts, and in Luke 22:66 (NASB) and Acts 4:15, it probably refers to the chamber in which the Sanhedrin met.

According to Jewish tradition, the Sanhedrin began with the seventy elders Moses summoned to assist in adjudicating disputes (cf. Num. 11:16). The actual origin, however, probably goes back to Persian times when it was called the "council of elders." During the period of the Roman procurators, the Jerusalem Sanhedrin exercised its greatest power.

The Jerusalem Sanhedrin was composed of aristocratic, high priestly members belonging to the Sadducees, and was presided over by the high priest. By New Testament times, representatives of the Pharisees were also admitted to membership (John 11:47; Acts 5:34; 23:6).

After the raising of Lazarus, the Sanhedrin determined to put Jesus to death (John 11:47–53). Following Jesus's arrest, a preliminary hearing takes place in the home of Annas, the former high priest (John 18:12–18). Jesus is then sent to Caiaphas, the current high priest (John 18:24). At daybreak, the entire Sanhedrin convened (Luke 22:66). Witnesses testify that Jesus spoke against the temple, but their testimonies conflict (Matt. 26:59–61; Mark 14:53–65). The high priest puts Jesus under oath and demands that he say whether he is the Messiah. Jesus's answer implies an affirmative answer. On this basis, the Sanhedrin charges him with blasphemy (Matt. 26:63–66; Mark 14:60–64). Since this was insufficient to merit capital punishment, the Sanhedrin turns Jesus over to Pontius Pilate on the charge of treason, since messianic claims carry nationalistic implications (Matt. 27:11–14; Mark 15:1–5; Luke 23:1–5).

Later the Sanhedrin admonishes the apostles to stop preaching in Jesus's name and has them flogged (Acts 4:5–21; 5:21–41). The martyrdom of Stephen follows his spirited defense before the Sanhedrin and his stinging attack on their leadership (Acts 6:12–8:1).

The apostle Paul stood before the Sanhedrin accused of violating the sanctity of the temple (Acts 21:27–30). He shrewdly bases his defense on the doctrine of bodily resurrection, a conviction shared with the Pharisaic members of the Sanhedrin but rejected by the Sadducees. This results in a "hung jury," as the Pharisees rally to Paul's defense (Acts 23:6–10). Some Jews, with complicit approval by the chief priests and elders, seek to convene another meeting of the Sanhedrin in order to assassinate Paul (Acts 23:12–15). Providentially, the plot is discovered and thwarted (Acts 23:16–35).

In the aftermath of the First Jewish Revolt (AD 66–73), the Roman government dissolved the Sanhedrin. A new "Sanhedrin" was constituted at Jamnia (ca. AD 68–80), quite different from its predecessor, composed of rabbinic scholars (successors to the Pharisees) and concerned only with matters of religious law. Its authority lay in voluntary compliance by observant Jews.

A question about the resurrection (20:27–40)

See Matthew 22:23–33; Mark 12:18–27. The Sadducees, who do not hold to a belief in the resurrection, try to trap Jesus with a question about the resurrection. They appeal to the law of levirate marriage, which is explained in Deuteronomy 25:5–6. In the Sadducees' ridiculous example, seven brothers marry the same woman, and they want to know which one will be her real husband at the resurrection. Jesus rebukes them for failing to understand the nature of life after the resurrection. Those who are resurrected for life in the new age will neither marry nor die; they are like angels, Jesus says (20:35–36). The Jewish leaders are impressed, and no one dares to ask him another question.

Jesus questions the Jewish leaders (20:41–44)

See Matthew 22:41–46; Mark 12:35–37.

Beware of the teachers of the law (20:45–47)

See Matthew 23:1–36; Mark 12:38–40.

The poor widow's offering (21:1–4)

See Mark 12:41–44. In contrast to the hypocrisy of the Jewish leaders stands the pure worship of a poor widow. Her two copper coins (*lepta*) were the smallest coins in use and worth very little. But her offering was worth more than all the others because she gave out of her poverty "all she had to live on" (21:4). It's not what we give so much as what we have left over afterward that shows the level of sacrifice.

The Olivet Discourse (21:5–36)

PREDICTION OF THE TEMPLE'S DESTRUCTION (21:5–6)

See Matthew 24:1–2; Mark 13:1–2.

SIGNS BEFORE THE END (21:7–11)

See Matthew 24:3–8; Mark 13:3–8.

COMING PERSECUTIONS FOR DISCIPLES (27:12–19)

The lepton of Alexander Jannaeus is sometimes called the "widow's mite."

See Matthew 24:9–14; Mark 13:9–13. Before all these initial events (the "birth pains"), disciples should expect to suffer for Jesus's sake. The persecution will afford an opportunity to bear witness, and the Lord will provide the needed words and wisdom at the appropriate time. The persecution will be especially painful because betrayal will come from friends and family. Some will even be put to death because of their loyalty to Jesus. Although disciples will experience persecution or tribulation, none will ever experience God's condemning wrath (i.e., none will perish).

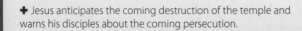

✚ Jesus anticipates the coming destruction of the temple and warns his disciples about the coming persecution.

Jesus's Seven Last Words from the Cross

1. "Father, forgive them; for they do not know what they are doing" (Luke 23:34).

   This prayer that the Father would forgive his enemies and executioners was actually answered by his own death, which made forgiveness possible.

2. "Truly I tell you, today you will be with me in Paradise" (Luke 23:43)

   This promise offers paradise—a place of life, rest, peace, and fellowship with God—to the repentant criminal being crucified beside Jesus.

3. "Woman, here is your son"… "Here is your mother" (John 19:26–27).

   Since Joseph had presumably already died by this time, Jesus as the oldest son is now responsible to care for his mother. He does so by entrusting her to "the disciple whom he loved."

4. "My God, my God, why have you forsaken me?" (Matt. 27:46; Mark 15:34; cf. Psalm 22:1)

   Jesus quotes Psalm 22:1, a prayer of King David who was suffering unjustly.

   As the ultimate righteous sufferer, Jesus also confesses his feelings of abandonment by God.

5. "I am thirsty" (John 19:28; cf. Pss. 22:14–15; 69:21).

   Jesus likely requested a drink in order to speak the final few words as well as to fulfill Scripture. Here he alludes to Psalm 22:14–15 and Psalm 69:21.

6. "It is finished" (John 19:30; cf. Ps. 22:31).

   The word "it" refers to his redemptive work, "finished" means to be "paid in full," and the verb tense indicates an action that has been completed but has ongoing results. The Son's work stands accomplished—now and forever!

7. "Father, into your hands I commit my spirit" (Luke 23:46; cf. Ps. 31:4–5).

   The backdrop is Psalm 31:4–5. Jesus anticipates restored fellowship with the Father and entrusts himself to the Father's care.

By enduring to the end we will gain life. We should expect persecution until Jesus returns. Are we prepared to suffer for Christ?

THE DESOLATION OF JERUSALEM (21:20–24)

See Matthew 24:15–22; Mark 13:14–20.

THE RETURN OF THE SON OF MAN (21:25–28)

See Matthew 24:29–31; Mark 13:24–27. Believers should be encouraged when they think about Christ's return. Jesus says to "stand up and lift up your heads, because your redemption is drawing near" (21:28). We have been saved and are being saved, but at Christ's return our salvation will be fully and completely realized.

✚ Luke explicitly identifies the "abomination of desolation" mentioned in Matthew 24:15 and Mark 13:14 (cf. Dan. 9:27; 11:31; 12:11) with the destruction of Jerusalem by the Romans in AD 70 (see Luke 21:20–21).

The Resurrection of Jesus

Darrell L. Bock

The Background and Importance of the Resurrection. The resurrection of Jesus represents a variation on the Jewish expectation of a bodily resurrection at the end of history. Jews hoped for a resurrection that was followed by a judgment and the vindication of the righteous (Dan. 12:1–4). The variation that Jesus's resurrection introduced was a resurrection in the midst of time with no judgment attached to it. The resurrection produced Jesus's exaltation by God, something Jesus predicted at his examination by the Jewish leadership when he said that the Son of Man (Jesus) would be seated at God's right hand, despite the crucifixion the leadership was contemplating (Mark 14:53–72). In effect, Jesus was saying that God would show who the chosen one was by vindicating him over death.

This point is precisely why the resurrection is so important. Most people think the resurrection is important because it points to life after death. This certainly is a key point of its teaching. As Paul says in 1 Corinthians 15:20–28, Jesus is the first born from the dead (the precedent maker in conquering death). However, more significant is what the resurrection says about Jesus. This is why Paul in the same passage goes on to discuss the exalted role Jesus has because of the resurrection. Jesus's position at God's right hand as a result of resurrection frees him to distribute the blessings of the new era, something Acts 2:30–36 describes.

The Presentation of the Resurrection. Interestingly, nowhere in the New Testament is the resurrection described. Rather, the New Testament records the effects of resurrection as seen in the empty tomb and the appearances. No one witnessed the resurrection; the texts simply testify to the impact of its having taken place. Skeptics often like to claim the early church fabricated these accounts. But what Scripture presents regarding the resurrection works against this claim. First, women were the first witnesses to the empty tomb and receive the first announcement of resurrection. Now women did not have a legal right to be witnesses in the first century. So if you were making up a story to introduce a controversial idea (gentiles did not believe in resurrection and neither did Sadducees), would you pick nonwitnesses to begin your case? That is very unlikely. The women open the story because it happened that the women were the first to hear the announcement. Second, if you were creating the story to give it credibility, would you have your chief leaders be so unbelieving upon first hearing the news? When the women report the resurrection to the disciples, the disciples think

THE PARABLE OF THE FIG TREE (21:29–33)

See Matthew 24:32–36; Mark 13:28–32.

WATCH AND PRAY! (21:34–36)

See Mark 13:33–37. Here we have specific instructions about what it means to watch and pray as we anticipate Jesus's return. We are to avoid being weighed down with "dissipation [carousing], drunkenness and the anxieties of life," so the day of his return doesn't catch us unprepared. We are to watch and pray so we can endure all that is going to happen and stand unashamed before the Son of Man.

the women's story is nonsense (Luke 24:11). Only Peter and John go to check to see what took place (Luke 24:12; John 20:3). This unbelief does not put the disciples in a good light in terms of their faith. Yet that is their response. Third, the early church could have made up a simpler story that fit Jewish expectations, if they had created it. They simply could have argued that Jesus would be raised at the end, in line with Jewish expectation, and that he would lead the judgment. But what was expected is not what happened. Something created the third-day precedent of a resurrection *within* history. Such features in the presentation show that it is very unlikely this account was made up.

Other More Skeptical Tales on Resurrection. Some like to suggest that the resurrection was really only a visionary experience. Usually it is seen to have been grief induced. But this cannot explain the meals Jesus is said to have taken (Luke 24:36–43), nor the group appearances, such as the one to five hundred recorded in 1 Corinthians 15:6. Still others argue that the earliest traditions were empty-tomb traditions, which do not require a resurrected body, and might allow for the removal of the body to create an impression of resurrection. The major problem with this theory, which Matthew 28:13 notes, is the disciples were persecuted for and were willing to die for this belief in resurrection. Those who took the body would have had to be able to do so successfully in the face of the tomb being guarded and then convince others about the resurrection. They would have had to be willing to go to the grave with their secret. This also cannot explain the starting point of the announcement with women, a point that, again, does not look created. In sum, the best explanation for the resurrection is that it happened.

How Far Back Can We Trace Resurrection Hope in the Church? The question here is a historical one. A biblical answer is that we see the resurrection being preached almost immediately after the resurrection, as the book of Acts shows. A historical answer (i.e., a case to be made to one who does not regard the Bible in any special theological way) is that we know resurrection is being preached within a few years of the events. Paul's (Saul's) conversion shows this. When Jesus comes and appears to this persecutor of the church (Acts 9), Saul needs to have heard messages about the raised Jesus in order to recognize the raised Jesus appearing to him. This tells us that both a raised and exalted Jesus was in place by the time Paul converted within a few years of Jesus's death.

The Centrality of Resurrection. 1 Corinthians 15 says clearly the resurrection is a core event of the Christian faith. It points to an exalted Jesus at God's right hand. It shows there is life after death. This is why the church commemorates this event each year and preaches it so regularly from its pulpits.

Jesus's ministry in Jerusalem (21:37–38)

Luke summarizes Jesus's ministry in Jerusalem. Each day he taught in the temple area, and each night he retreated to the Mount of Olives nearby. Although the Jewish leadership consistently opposes him, for a time he is popular with the crowds. All of that is about to change.

The Savior Is Betrayed, Tried, and Crucified (22:1–23:56)

All along Jesus has been saying that he "must" go to Jerusalem to suffer, die, and rise again. This is his divine destiny. The long journey concludes with his prediction coming true. Following a brief period of contentious ministry in the temple area, Jesus is finally betrayed by one of his own disciples. In order to save the people from their sins, the Savior must die and rise again. The hour of darkness has arrived, but it will not have the last word.

The plot to kill Jesus (22:1–2)

See Matthew 26:1–5; Mark 14:1–2.

Judas betrays his Savior (22:3–6)

See Matthew 26:14–16; Mark 14:10–11; John 13:2. Satan enters Judas Iscariot, one of the Twelve, and he decides to betray Jesus when no crowd is present. The Jewish leaders are delighted to cut a deal with Judas for a modest amount of money (see Matt. 26:15). Now nothing stands in the way of their putting Jesus to death.

The Last Supper (22:7–23)

See Matthew 26:17–30; Mark 14:12–26; John 13:1–30. Jesus prepares to eat his final meal with his disciples, a Passover meal celebrating God's miraculous rescue of his people from slavery in Egypt. He tells Peter and John to go ahead and make preparations. They go into the city, meet a man carrying a jar of water, and follow him to the large upper room where they prepare for the meal (22:7–14). They would have sat around several low tables or couches that formed the shape of a U. Everyone reclined on their left side, with their feet pointing outward, and used their right hand to eat (22:14). Most likely the host (in this case Jesus) would have been seated near the base of the tables with the honored guests on either side. Ironically, Judas may have occupied the place of an honored guest, right next to Jesus. Jesus transforms this last supper or Passover meal into the Lord's Supper through his words and

Very old olive trees on the Mount of Olives.

✝ Jesus teaches that the sacrifice of his life on the cross will establish the new covenant predicted by Jeremiah (see Luke 22:20; Jer. 31:31–34).

Jesus's Postresurrection Appearances

Darrell L. Bock

Some Key Appearance Texts. 1 Corinthians 15:5–8 contains a listing of key appearances by Jesus, outside of the initial appearance to the women in the Gospels. It reads, "He appeared to Peter, and then to the Twelve. After that, he appeared to more than five hundred of the brothers at the same time, most of whom are still living, though some have fallen asleep. Then he appeared to James, then to all the apostles, and last of all he appeared to me also." One of the more informative of the appearances comes to the pair of men walking to Emmaus in Luke 24:13–35. Here they expressed their hope that Jesus might be the promised Messiah, but were as of yet uncertain about the claims of an empty tomb. Jesus eventually opens up the Scripture for them and reveals himself to them. John 20:10–18 shares details of an appearance to Mary Magdalene. The physical nature of Jesus's body is evident when she clings to him. Jesus tells her to let him go, because he must go to the Father. The appearance to Thomas in John 20:24–29 is significant because Jesus appeared to one who doubted and invites him to touch him to see it is really him. This invokes a confession from Thomas of "My Lord and my God," a high point in John's Gospel and a call to believe without having to see a raised Jesus.

Some Observations about the Appearances. First, interestingly, no detail of any private appearance to Peter is recorded. Skeptics like to suggest the church invented these appearance accounts, but this seems very unlikely given there is no "created" private Peter appearance. Nor is there a detailed appearance for James. It is hard to imagine, if the claim to make up such accounts took place, that these appearances would lack details. The failure to have such appearances points to the care of the church in presenting this material. Second, other skeptics like to claim these appearances are the product of hope in the church in the midst of grief, as if these are grief-induced events. But claims about Jesus appearing to five hundred at once stand against such notions of emotional suggestion, especially when Paul notes that many of these folk are still alive. Third, some attempt to distinguish empty tomb accounts from appearance accounts, but this is an artificial distinction made by skeptics who argue that the idea of a physical resurrection is a later development. Finally, there are appearances where Jesus has a meal with the disciples (Luke 24:36–43). These accounts are designed to show the resurrection was physical (i.e., bodily) in nature and counter the suggestion that these appearances were the result of visions or dreams.

actions recorded in 22:15–20. Jesus gives them the broken bread, saying, "This is my body given for you" (22:19). Later he takes the cup, saying, "This cup is the new covenant in my blood, which is poured out for you" (22:20). The bread and the cup represent Jesus's giving of himself for the forgiveness of sins. He promises not to eat the meal again "until the kingdom of God comes" in all its fullness (22:16, 18). Now is the time of suffering; later will come the time of celebration. During the meal, Jesus predicts that one of the disciples will soon betray him (22:21–23).

On greatness in the kingdom (22:24–30)

See Matthew 19:28; 20:24–28; Mark 10:41–45. At the very time when Jesus is baring his soul and teaching them about the significance of his coming death, the disciples are arguing about which one is the greatest. He is talking about sacrificial suffering, and they are concerned about rank and privilege. Jesus reminds them that among his followers, leaders are to be servants. He himself sets the example of the leader doing the serving (22:27). The Twelve (less Judas) are not without their rewards, however, since they will receive Jesus's kingdom and important leadership responsibilities within that kingdom (22:28–30).

Jesus predicts Peter's denials (22:31–34)

See Matthew 26:31–35; Mark 14:27–31; John 13:36–38. Satan demands to sift the disciples like wheat, but Jesus prays for them, and especially for Peter, their spokesman. Although Peter boasts about his willingness to die with Jesus, he will in fact soon deny that he even knows him. Jesus prays that Peter's faith may not fail, and that once he turns back to God, he will strengthen other believers. Peter's experience will play out just as Jesus has prayed.

The two swords (22:35–38)

In their earlier missions, the disciples traveled lightly and depended on the hospitality of strangers (see Luke 9–10). Now the atmosphere has changed from hospitality to opposition. They

The Church of Saint Peter in Gallicantu (meaning "crowing of the cock") was built to commemorate Peter's denial of Jesus in the courtyard of the high priest. It is unlikely that this is actually Caiaphas's house.

✦ Jesus's message about sending out his disciples on a mission (Luke 22:35–37) may have later encouraged these same disciples to become involved in the mission work described in the book of Acts.

will need to take their own provisions, even a sword for protection (22:36). Jesus probably uses the term "sword" as a symbol for the need of spiritual armament in the days to come. This new situation will certainly affect Jesus as he goes to the cross, fulfilling the Scriptures (22:37; see Isa. 53:12). The disciples completely misunderstand Jesus and report that they have collected two swords. It's one of those times that Jesus can't seem to endure their ignorance any longer and therefore simply changes the subject (22:38).

Jesus's prayer in Gethsemane (22:39–46)

See Matthew 26:36–46; Mark 14:32–42; John 18:1. Twice Jesus tells his disciples to pray that they "will not fall into temptation" (22:40, 46). Prayerlessness makes us especially vulnerable to temptation. In Luke's version of the events, some early manuscripts don't include verses 43 and 44 about the angelic intervention and Jesus's sweat becoming like drops of blood. If they are original, we see the depth of Jesus's struggle with the cross. In any case, Jesus didn't sweat drops of blood. Rather, his sweat "was *like* drops of blood" (22:44).

Jesus betrayed and arrested (22:47–53)

See Matthew 26:47–56; Mark 14:43–52; John 18:2–12. The account of Jesus's arrest is spelled out in greater detail in the other Gospels. Luke alone notes that Jesus heals the servant's right ear (22:51), a detail we might expect a physician to include. This also shows Jesus's compassion on those who seek to destroy him. The hour of darkness has arrived (23:53).

Jesus's Jewish trial and Peter's denials (22:54–71)

See Matthew 26:57–75; Mark 14:53–72; John 18:13–27.

Jesus on trial before Pilate and Herod (23:1–25)

See Matthew 27:1–2, 11–26; Mark 15:1–15; John 18:28–40; 19:16. The Jewish leaders bring Jesus to Pilate in order to obtain the death sentence. They accuse Jesus of subverting the nation, opposing the payment of taxes to Caesar, and claiming to be Christ, a king (23:2). Although Jesus does admit to being the "king of the Jews" (23:3), three times Pilate declares Jesus innocent (23:4, 14–15, 22). The Jewish leaders continue to insist that Jesus stirs up the people throughout the region by his teachings. Pilate sends Jesus to Herod Antipas for more questioning (23:6–7). Herod wants Jesus to entertain him with a miraculous sign, which Jesus refuses to do (23:8–10). Jesus is further ridiculed by Herod and his soldiers and finally sent back to Pilate (23:11–12). Pilate again declares Jesus to be innocent of the trumped up charges and plans to have Jesus flogged and released (23:13–16). But the people begin to call for the release of Barabbas. They cry out for Jesus's crucifixion, and Pilate finally caves in (23:18–25).

Jesus the Savior is crucified (23:26–49)

See Matthew 27:31–56; Mark 15:20–41; John 19:17–30. As Jesus is led to Golgotha to be crucified, he is accompanied by a large crowd, including a group of women mourners (23:26–31). Jesus tells them not to mourn for him but for themselves and their children. A time of judgment for Israel is fast approaching (see Hosea 10:8). If God has allowed his beloved Son to suffer (the green tree), how much more will he judge the nation (the dry, unfruitful tree)? Two criminals are also led out to be crucified at this time. As Jesus is being crucified, Luke records his first of seven last words or statements from the cross: "Father, forgive them, for they do not know what they are doing" (23:34).

Ironically, his prayer for God to forgive both his enemies and his executioners is made possible by his death. Sadly, Jesus faces continuous mocking during his crucifixion (23:35–38). Luke records a debate between the two criminals crucified on either side of Jesus (23:39–43). At first both thieves ridicule Jesus (Matt. 27:44; Mark 15:32), but near the end, one has a change of heart. He asks Jesus to remember him when he comes into his kingdom, implying that Jesus and his kingdom cannot be conquered by death. Jesus assures the man that "today you will be with me in paradise" (23:43 is the second "word" from the cross). This man's last-minute confession is sufficient to secure him a heavenly home. Darkness descends on the scene from noon until 3 p.m. The temple curtain is ripped in two, and Jesus utters his seventh and final word: "Father, into your hands I commit my spirit" (23:46). The Roman soldier standing nearby praises God and confesses Jesus's righteousness (23:47). The heartbroken witnesses slowly leave the scene, but those who had known him, including the women disciples from Galilee, stand at a distance in silence (23:48–49).

Jesus's burial (23:50–56)

See Matthew 27:57–66; Mark 15:42–47; John 19:38–42.

The Resurrection and Ascension of Jesus, the Savior for All People (24:1–53)

On the third day, Jesus is raised from the dead! God's plan included suffering as the path to glory. After being raised, Jesus appears to many disciples,

✦ As a friend of sinners, Jesus is now crucified between two criminals.

proving to them he is actually alive and explaining what has happened. He commissions them to bear witness to all nations and promises them power from on high for their task. He ascends to heaven, but his ministry on earth will continue through his Spirit-empowered church. The book of Acts continues the Savior's amazing story.

The resurrection of Jesus (24:1–12)

See Matthew 28:1–10; Mark 16:1–8; John 20:1–18. On the first day of the week (Sunday), some women disciples return to the tomb to finish anointing Jesus's body for burial. They are surprised when they find the stone already rolled away, so they enter the tomb but don't find the body. Suddenly, two men (angels) appear in brilliantly white clothes and ask the women why they are looking for the living among the dead. "He is not here; he has risen!" they announce as they remind the women that Jesus had previously spoken about his coming betrayal, crucifixion, and resurrection (24:6–7). The women report to the eleven apostles what they have just seen, but the men don't believe them at first. Peter, however, runs to the tomb, looks inside, and finds grave clothes but no body.

Jesus's postresurrection appearances (24:13–43)

See John 20:19–23. After the resurrection, Jesus appears to many different people in different places. On one occasion, he appears to two disciples who are traveling to Emmaus, a small village a few miles from Jerusalem. Cleopas and the other disciple are discussing all that has recently happened when Jesus suddenly comes up beside them. They don't recognize him and wonder why this man seems totally unaware of the momentous events related to Jesus of Nazareth. Jesus was a "prophet, powerful in word and deed before God and all the people," they say (24:19). They had hoped he would be the deliverer (or Messiah) of Israel, but the Jewish leaders killed him. Since his crucifixion, these two disciples have heard strange but reliable reports of an empty tomb (24:21–24). Jesus then rebukes these two for being slow to accept that the Christ must suffer before being glorified and explains to them what the Scriptures say about the Messiah (24:25–27). That night as Jesus takes bread, gives thanks, and breaks it, their eyes are opened and they recognize him. He immediately disappears. They ask each other, "Were not our hearts burning

A Roman nail piercing the heel bone of a person who had been crucified.

within us while he talked with us on the road and opened the Scriptures to us?" (24:32). They return immediately to Jerusalem to report to the disciples what has happened and there learn that Jesus has appeared to Simon Peter as well (24:33–35). While they are still talking, Jesus appears among them (24:36). He calms his frightened followers and invites them to get rid of any doubts by looking at his nail-pierced hands and feet (24:37–40). Ghosts don't carry crucifixion wounds. Jesus now has a resurrection body! To affirm their faith even more, he eats a piece of broiled fish in their presence (24:41–43).

Jesus's farewell promise, commission, and ascension (24:44–53)

Jesus reminds his disciples that his death and resurrection had to happen to fulfill the Scriptures. He helps them understand how God's plan includes both the crucifixion and resurrection of the Messiah. Now "repentance and forgiveness of sins will be preached in his name to all nations, beginning at Jerusalem" (24:47). Jesus promises to empower the disciples as eyewitnesses. They must stay in Jerusalem, however, until they are "clothed with power from on high" (24:49; cf. Acts 1:4–5, 8). The story of Acts begins in Jerusalem and moves out to all nations in fulfillment of Jesus's commission. While Jesus is blessing the gathering of disciples near Bethany, he ascends into heaven (24:50–51; cf. Acts 1:9–10). The disciples return to the city with great joy and continually praise God in the temple as they wait to be empowered for their mission.

So What? Applying Luke's Gospel Today

The Gospel of Luke speaks to us about who Jesus is and how we should live as his disciples. Luke gives a thorough report of Jesus's birth and childhood to make sure we know that Jesus is God's unique Son. Through his mighty miracles and powerful teaching, Jesus brings God's salvation to the whole world. He is the Savior for all people—Jew and gentile, rich and poor, men and women, religious and pagan. No one is beyond God's gracious reach if they will simply turn to him in repentance and faith. Jesus came to "seek and to save what was lost," and that includes all human beings (19:10). Whether it is forgiving a sinful woman, welcoming home a prodigal son, healing a sick gentile, or honoring a poor widow, Jesus reaches out to all people in hopes of transforming their lives. The same is true today. No one is beyond the grace of God!

Jesus also calls his followers to live radically different lives. We should count the cost of following Jesus. Discipleship is more than a mere religious add-on. Jesus demands our full allegiance. He calls us to make people a priority. We

✛ Jesus instructs the disciples to wait for "power from on high," a promise that is fulfilled when the Holy Spirit comes at Pentecost in Acts 2.

learn from Jesus to be especially compassionate toward the poor and those our society pushes aside. So often in the ministry of Jesus, he reaches out to the underdogs who are being ignored by the powerful. Jesus emphasizes the importance of prayer and joy and gratitude. He also tells us that we can't live the Christian life in our own strength; we must depend on the power of the Holy Spirit. Like Jesus's necessary journey to Jerusalem, our path as his followers includes both a willingness to suffer as well as the hope of glory. Jesus *moved toward* Jerusalem to suffer for the sins of the world, and he empowers us to *move away* from Jerusalem with the best news ever—the world has a Savior!

Possible locations of Emmaus

Our Favorite Verse in Luke

But the angel said to them, "Do not be afraid. I bring you good news of great joy that will be for all the people. Today in the town of David a Savior has been born to you; he is Christ the Lord." (2:10–11)

In the model of first-century Jerusalem, the traditional location of Golgotha was outside the second wall of the city.

The Gospel of Luke   649

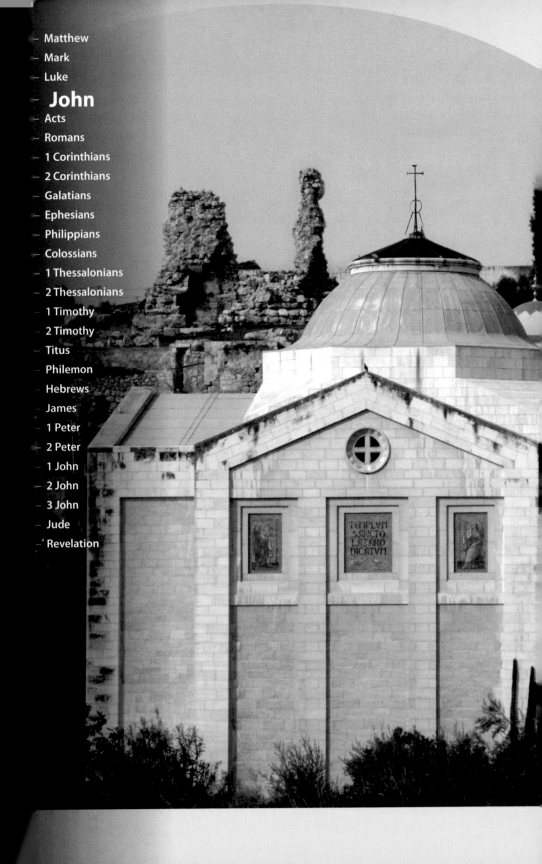

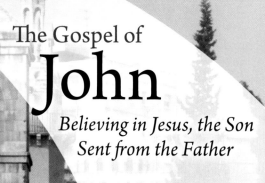

The Gospel of
John

*Believing in Jesus, the Son
Sent from the Father*

I f you have read through the Gospels lately, you
have probably noticed that John is different.
In fact, about 90 percent of John's Gospel is
not found in Matthew, Mark, or Luke (the Synoptic Gospels). The early church leader Clement
of Alexandria noticed the same thing about John:

> But, last of all, John, perceiving that the external
> facts had been made plain in the Gospel, being
> urged by his friends, and inspired by the Spirit,
> composed a spiritual Gospel. (Eusebius, *Hist. eccl.*
> 6.14.7)

A "spiritual Gospel" indeed. The vocabulary of John
is not technical. The language is plain, but the meaning is profound. The church father Augustine is often
quoted as saying, "The Gospel of John is deep enough
for an elephant to swim and shallow enough for a child
not to drown." We give a copy of John to children and new
converts, yet scholars continue to wrestle with its theological message. John is a unique and refreshing companion
to the Synoptics. Enjoy!

Who Wrote John?

Early church tradition points to John, the son of Zebedee and one of the Twelve, as the author of this Gospel (e.g., Irenaeus, Tertullian, Clement of Alexandria). Irenaeus was taught by Polycarp, who was a disciple of John himself. According to Irenaeus, John lived in Ephesus toward the end of his life and wrote his Gospel from there (*Against Heresies* 3.1.1). John refers to himself as "the disciple whom Jesus loved" (13:23; 19:26; 20:2; 21:7, 20). He makes it clear that he is an eyewitness of the life and ministry of Jesus (1:14; 19:35; 21:24–25). John was a Jew and, along with Peter and James, was one of Jesus's inner circle. From the cross, Jesus entrusts his mother, Mary, to John's care (19:26–27).

Who Is John's Audience?

As an eyewitness and one of Jesus's apostles, John becomes a leader of the church in the region of Ephesus. At this time, the church is facing increasing opposition from Judaism. We see hints of this setting within the Gospel. The phrase "the Jews" occurs more than seventy times to describe Jesus's opponents, and a sharp line is drawn between the church and "the world." John also notes several instances of people being put out of the synagogue (9:22; 12:42; 16:2). Many scholars believe that John is writing in the late first century (from the mid-60s to mid-90s), primarily for Christians who had pulled away from the Jewish synagogue. Along with encouraging them to continue trusting Jesus in the midst of difficult circumstances, he also writes to call others to faith in Christ.

What Is at the Heart of John's Gospel?

John states his purpose for writing in 20:31: "But these are written that you may believe that Jesus is the Christ, the Son of God, and that by believing you may have life in his name." Many books could have been written about Jesus, but John wrote his Gospel so that people's faith in Jesus might grow stronger. We begin and continue the Christian life by faith. By entrusting ourselves to Jesus, the Messiah and Son of God, we experience life, and John wants his readers to experience life!

The Gospel opens by identifying Jesus as the Word who was with God and who was God, but who has now become a human being to bring us life (John 1:1–18). The central section of the Gospel divides into two books.

✚ Polycarp, a disciple of John, was a leader of the church in Smyrna, one of the seven churches mentioned in Revelation 2–3.

The Book of Signs (1:19–12:50) features seven miracles or signs that Jesus performs to identify himself and call people to faith. The Book of Glory (13:1–20:31) focuses on the last week of Jesus's life. Passion Week is often described in John as Jesus's glorification (7:39; 12:16, 23, 28; 13:31–32; 17:1, 4; 21:19). The epilogue (21:1–25) describes Jesus's appearances to his disciples after the resurrection, Jesus's restoration of Peter, and a word about the author of the Gospel. The outline is simple, yet profound:

- Prologue (1:1–18)
- The Book of Signs (1:19–12:50)
- The Book of Glory (13:1–20:31)
- Epilogue (21:1–25)

What Makes John Interesting and Unique?

- John omits many sayings and stories found in Matthew, Mark, and Luke (e.g., Jesus's baptism, the transfiguration, parables, exorcisms) but includes others not found in the Synoptics (e.g., changing the water to wine, raising Lazarus, washing the disciples' feet).
- John uses simple, understandable words that often carry deep theological meaning (e.g., "The Word became flesh and made his dwelling among us" in 1:14 or "I am the bread of life" in 6:35).

Archaeological excavations at Bethsaida (John 1:44).

- Jesus is clearly presented as both human and divine (1:1–18).
- There are seven "I am" sayings and seven important miracles or signs that point to Jesus as the unique Son of God.
- Jesus claims a unique relationship with the Father (e.g., 5:17–18; 8:42; 10:30; 14:9–10).
- Almost half of this Gospel (13–21) deals with the last week of Jesus's life—Passion Week.
- Eternal life is both a present reality (e.g., 3:15–16, 36; 5:24–25; 6:47; 11:23–26) and a future hope (e.g., 5:28–29; 6:39; 11:25).
- John includes many of Jesus's teachings about the Holy Spirit as our Helper or Advocate (see John 14–16).
- John uses many spiritual symbols or metaphors (e.g., word, bread, light, door, shepherd, water).
- John features a strong dualism (e.g., light vs. darkness, belonging to God vs. belonging to the world).
- Irony runs throughout John, such as when the chief priests reject Jesus as the king and tell Pilate, "We have no king but Caesar" (19:15).
- Many of Jesus's teachings occur in the form of lengthy conversations (e.g., with Nicodemus or the Samaritan woman), heated debates (e.g., with the Jews in John 7), and private teaching (e.g., the Farewell Discourse in John 13–17).

What Is John's Message?

Prologue (1:1–18)

John's Gospel doesn't include a birth story, at least not a conventional one like Matthew and Luke. John provides instead a theological introduction to Jesus. He identifies Jesus as the "Word" (*logos*) who existed before creation with God and is himself God (1:1). In Greek philosophy the "word" was the principle of reason that governed all things. In Jewish history, the "word" was often associated with God's wisdom (see Proverbs 8–9), but even more directly with God's personal self-expression. Notice how much John 1:1 sounds like Gen. 1:1:

Ancient stone containers like these protected their contents from ritual impurities.

✚ In the Old Testament, God carries out his will through his word (e.g., Genesis 1–2; Deut. 8:3; Ps. 33:6; Isa. 55:11).

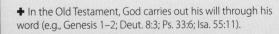

Incarnation

Preben Vang

Incarnation means "infleshed" (Latin: *in carne*) and should not be confused with the similar sounding term, reincarnation. Biblically speaking, "incarnation" is a term used to express what happened when Jesus, who had been with God for all eternity, stepped onto the historical scene as a human being. The significance of incarnation, therefore, goes beyond the specific circumstances surrounding Jesus's birth (1 Tim. 3:16). John, for example, claims those who reject incarnation prove themselves to be anti-Christ (1 John 4:2; 2 John 7). Similarly, Paul interprets Jesus's work on the cross in light of the incarnation (Col. 1:22), and considers incarnation the reason Christ could accomplish what the law of Moses could not (Rom. 8:3; Eph. 2:15).

The biblical emphasis on incarnation moves faith from the realm of mythology to the realm of history. God is not "out there in the unknown," but chose to step into history and reveal himself in a personal manner. Christ's incarnation protects Christian faith from turning into aloof speculations on the eternal; it secures the connection between God and the issues of the human situation. It follows that Christian faith cannot be indifferent to historical issues of faith. Different from Gnostic writings, for example, where God merely sends lofty, indefinite, timeless propositions for inner meditation (e.g., *The Gospel of Thomas*), Christian faith recognizes and responds to God's "real-life" actions on the human scene.

At the heart of the Christian doctrine on incarnation lies a statement about Christ's being. The New Testament story of incarnation shuts down any notion that Jesus was merely a pious person/prophet that God adopted. Rather, he was 100 percent God and 100 percent man. Not "just" man, not "just" God, nor 50 percent of each. One way to think about this is to recognize that everything Jesus said, did, and thought was exactly what God would have said, done, and thought. To say that Jesus is 100 percent God does not mean that he equals the Father, but that his being is the same as the Father's. Everything about Jesus is an exact expression of God, yet Jesus is not the Father.

Opposite the early Christians, who knew Jesus as a human being and struggled to understand his divinity (John 10:25–30; 14:9–10, 28), Christians today struggle to understand the significance of Jesus's humanity and find it easier to make him 100 percent God and 0 percent human. Being 100 percent God means he is the true Savior—not just one who can point to a saving God. That he is 100 percent human means he is fully acquainted with human experience. The incarnation calls followers of Christ to live lives that actively proclaim that God's love is not long-distance love, but a present and personal love (Heb. 2:18; 4:15).

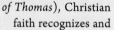

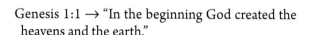

Genesis 1:1 → "In the beginning God created the heavens and the earth."

John 1:1–3 → "In the beginning was the Word, and the Word was with God, and the Word was God. He was with God in the beginning. Through him all things were made."

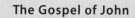

In Genesis 1 God creates through his personal word or speech ("and God said . . ."). That is how God expresses himself. Notice the many parallel themes in Genesis 1 and John 1 (e.g., creation, darkness, light, life). We see throughout the Old Testament that God's word has a personal quality to it (e.g., Ps. 19:1–4; Isa. 55:10–11). Now, John says, this personal "Word" of God has appeared in the person of Jesus of Nazareth (John 1:1; Rev. 19:13). Jesus is the perfect expression of God. Jesus is not only our Creator (1:1–2); he is also our Savior (1:3–5). He brings life and light into a dark world, and the world cannot overcome him. Throughout the early chapters of the Gospel, John the Baptizer bears witness to Jesus (1:6–9, 15, 19–34; 3:22–36). John consistently denies that he is the Christ and points to Jesus as the true light (1:6–9), the preexistent one (1:15), the Lamb of God (1:29), the Son of God (1:34), the Christ (3:28), and the bridegroom (3:29). Those disciples of John the Baptizer living in the region of Ephesus near the end of the first century should not be confused about which one is greater. In spite of who Jesus is, the world rejects him (1:10). Sadly, he is even rejected by his own people, the Jewish people, but all who accept him become children of God (1:11–13). The Word became "flesh" (1:14). John could have put it more respectably by saying that Jesus became a "man" (*anthropos*) or took on a body (*soma*), but instead he uses a tangible, almost crude term— "flesh" (*sarx*). Jesus completely and fully entered into our human situation in all its weakness and frailty. The technical term for God becoming man is "incarnation," a word that means "being in flesh." The phrase "made his dwelling" in verse 14 is important, especially in connection with the word "glory." During the wilderness wanderings of Israel, God chose to "dwell among them" and made his presence known in a temporary tent called a tabernacle (Exod. 25:8–9). God filled that tent with his presence and his glory (Exod. 40:34–35). Now God has "tabernacled" among us in the person of Jesus, and we can now behold God's glorious presence. Moses gave us the law, but Jesus brings grace and truth; we need both! The prologue to John's Gospel clearly teaches that Jesus is both fully human (1:10, 11, 14, 18) and fully divine (1:1–5, 9, 10, 14, 18). We can't see God, but "God the One and Only, who is at the Father's side, has made him known" (1:18). The word for "made known" means "to exegete" or "to lead out." Jesus reveals the character and nature of the invisible God. If you want to know what God is like, look at Jesus!

The Book of Signs (1:19–12:50)

The first half of John centers on Jesus's miraculous signs that reveal his identity as the One sent from the Father, who calls people to faith. All this

✦ In the Old Testament God revealed his presence through the tabernacle and temple, but now he "tabernacles" among us in Jesus.

occurs before the hour of glorification arrives.

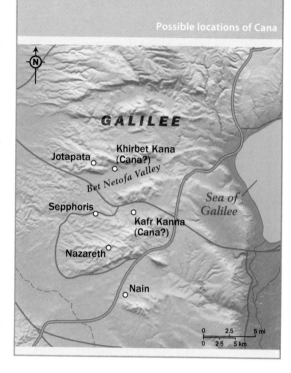

Possible locations of Cana

*The testimony of John the Bap-
tizer (1:19–34)*

See Matthew 3:1–17; Mark
1:2–11; Luke 3:1–22. When the
Jewish leaders inquire about John's
identity, he readily confesses that
he is not the Christ or Elijah or the
Prophet (1:19–21). John instead
plays a more minor role. He is a
voice in the wilderness preparing
the way for the Lord (1:22–23; cf.
Isa. 40:3). His job is to bear witness to Jesus. When Jesus appears,
John declares, "Look, the Lamb of
God who takes away the sin of the
world" (1:29). Unlike the Passover
lambs, Jesus's self-sacrifice really will be able to remove sins. John is inferior
to Jesus not only because Jesus will die for the sins of the people, but also
because Jesus will baptize people with the Holy Spirit (1:32–33). John's
testimony is that Jesus is truly the Son of God (1:34).

The testimony of the first disciples (1:35–51)

See Matthew 4:18–22; Mark 1:16–20. John the Baptizer plays his part
faithfully and points his own disciples to Jesus (1:35–37). Andrew and
another disciple follow Jesus initially (1:37–40). Then Andrew brings his
brother Simon to meet Jesus the Messiah (1:40–42), who promptly gives
Simon a new name—"Cephas" (Aramaic) or "Peter" (Greek), meaning
"rock" (1:42). Peter's life would never be the same! The next day Jesus calls
Philip to follow him, and Philip tells Nathaniel (1:43–45). Nathaniel honestly
wants to know if anything good can come out of the tiny, backwater town
of Nazareth, and Philip challenges him to "come and see" (1:46). Jesus sees
Nathaniel approaching and pays him a sincere compliment: "Here is a true
Israelite, in whom there is nothing false" (1:47). Nathaniel wonders how
Jesus even knows him, but when Jesus says that he saw Nathaniel under the
fig tree before Philip talked with him (1:48), Nathaniel confesses Jesus is
"the Son of God" and "the King of Israel" (1:49). Jesus then tells everyone
they will soon see greater things, perhaps alluding to the miraculous signs

✦ Nathaniel calls Jesus the "Lamb of God," alluding to the Passover lamb
of Exodus 12 and indicating the sacrificial nature of Jesus's mission.

to follow. Using the image of Jacob's ladder from Genesis 28, Jesus, the Son of Man, will now be the place of God's revelation of himself (1:51).

Sign #1—Jesus turns water into wine (2:1–12)

Weddings were important social events in the Jewish culture, and the extended celebration often reminded everyone of the rejoicing that would occur at the end-time messianic banquet. Jesus and his family are attending a wedding in Cana when the hosts run out of wine, a major social catastrophe (2:1–3). Mary implores Jesus to do something, but he reminds her the time has not come for him to reveal who he is (2:4). Nevertheless, Jesus miraculously changes the water to wine, and good wine at that (2:5–10). The bridegroom is honored instead of shamed. This is the first of Jesus's "miraculous signs" that he performs to reveal his glory and bolster faith (1:11). In dramatic fashion, Jesus announces the messianic age has now arrived.

Jesus clears the temple (2:13–25)

John's Gospel mentions the temple cleansing a lot earlier in Jesus's ministry than Matthew, Mark, and Luke. Quite possibly there were two temple cleansings. Jesus is observing the Passover in Jerusalem when he decides to chase out the moneychangers and their animals from the temple court. He accuses them of turning his Father's house into a marketplace (2:13–16). While Jesus's zeal reminds the disciples of Psalm 69:9, the Jews demand a miraculous sign to prove his authority (2:17–18). Jesus replies, "Destroy this temple, and I will raise it again in three days" (2:19). They think he is speaking about the physical temple, but he is referring to his coming death and resurrection, the ultimate sign (2:19–22). Jesus performs other signs during this time, and people believe (*pisteuo*) in him (2:23). But Jesus wisely does not "entrust [*pisteuo*] himself to them," for he knows how fickle human beings can be (2:24–25). Jesus knows that God alone should be the foundation of one's faith.

Jesus's conversation with Nicodemus (3:1–21)

Nicodemus, a Pharisee and member of the powerful Sanhedrin, approaches Jesus privately. He expresses an interest in Jesus but represents the Jewish leadership and displays a profound spiritual ignorance (3:4, 10). Jesus tells him straightforwardly that to enter God's kingdom a person must be "born again" (or "born from above"). Nicodemus fails to understand because he

Silver shekels from the city of Tyre were the main coin used to pay the temple tax in Judea.

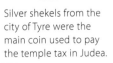

✦ When Jesus changed the water into wine at Cana, he signaled that he was bringing God's end-time salvation, complete with a messianic banquet (see Isa. 25:6).

Jewish Marriage and Wedding Customs
Craig S. Keener

Even more than many of their Mediterranean contemporaries, Jewish people highly valued marriage and childbearing. Later rabbis treated procreation as a sacred duty, avoidance of which was sinful; they required divorce for infertility. While a few Jewish sages considered marriage a distraction from Torah study, most considered it instead a relief from temptation (hence from distraction). Some Jews, however, differed from this cultural mainstream; for example, many ancient sources suggest that some Essenes remained celibate.

Virtually all religious Jews, however, morally confined sexual intercourse to marriage, and expected those who were married to normally engage in sexual relations. Monogamy was the norm. Though polygamy was legal for those who could afford it, there were very few cases (the most obvious being Herod the Great). The two schools of Pharisees (Shammaites and Hillelites) differed on grounds for which husbands could divorce wives: the former restricted it to a wife's infidelity, but the latter allowed it for virtually any cause. (Jesus apparently sided with Shammaites.) Following Greek custom, wealthier women also could divorce husbands, though this was probably not the norm for most Judeans or Galileans.

The age of marriage tended to be younger in antiquity than today; Jewish girls could legally marry once they entered puberty, and most probably married in their teens, and Judean men often by twenty. Because Jews rejected the discarding of female infants (apparently practiced by some Greeks), husbands tended to be closer in age to wives than among Greeks (where husbands averaged perhaps twelve years older than wives). Betrothal was an economic agreement between families more binding than modern engagement; it could be ended only by either divorce or the death of one of the parties.

The wedding (sometimes after a year of betrothal) ideally could last seven days, though many guests outside the main party and family would attend only some of those days. The first night was probably most important, and first intercourse would normally be attempted then. Wedding banquets provided much food and wine, hence tended to be costly; people invited as many guests as possible, sometimes even the entire village. Weddings and funerals represented the epitome of joy and sorrow respectively, and joining either kind of procession was a community obligation.

Judean women had more freedom to go in public than classical Athenian women did. Nevertheless, pietists frowned on men speaking with women other than their wives or relatives. Once married, Jewish women customarily covered their hair in public, reserving it for their husbands' view. Ideally the husband's specified duties included providing financially for the wife at the standard of living to which her upbringing had accustomed her, and intercourse. The wife's specified duties included grinding flour, cooking, nursing, and spinning. Wives were also expected to obey their husbands in this culture (an expectation emphasized even more among Hellenistic Jewish writers).

takes Jesus literally, but Jesus explains a person must be "born of water and the Spirit" (3:4–8). Most likely, the image of water refers not to Christian baptism or to natural birth, but to a spiritual birth connected with new life in the Spirit (see Isa. 44:3–5; Ezek. 36:25–27). Nicodemus still doesn't understand (3:9), and Jesus rebukes him for being a "spiritual leader" who fails to understand the

Eternal Life

Nicholas Perrin

In the Old Testament the concept of "life" was largely limited to life in the present (Deut. 30:19). Life was recognized as a creative act and the gift of God. The blessings of life (including security, health, and prosperity) were also a divine gift. To participate in the fullness of life was in some sense to participate in God himself, because God was the source of all life.

In its vision of the resurrection, Daniel 12 marks a pronounced shift from a this-world focus to life as a never-ending, postmortem reality: "Multitudes who sleep in the dust of the earth will awake: some to everlasting life, others to shame and everlasting contempt" (Dan. 12:2). Here the words "eternal life" (the only Old Testament occurrence of the phrase) are closely connected with the resurrected state. Since the Jewish literature closer to Jesus's day continued to preserve this association (*Pss. Sol.* 3.16; *1 Enoch* 37.4; *Test. Asher* 5.2), his language of "eternal life" must also entail the notion of resurrection.

In their respective emphases, John and the Synoptic Gospels treat eternal life differently. When compared to the Gospel of John, the Synoptic Gospels show only sparing use of the phrase. By contrast, John refers to "life" or "eternal life"—the two are virtually exchangeable—some three dozen times. Indeed, the prospect of his readers' obtaining eternal life is John's very reason for writing (John 20:31). Where "eternal life" does occur in the Synoptic Gospels, it consistently refers to the resurrected age to come (Matt. 25:46; Mark 10:17, 30; Luke 10:25). While John also sees eternal life as a future hope (John 3:36; 5:39), unlike the Synoptic witness, he emphasizes this life as something that can be possessed in the present (5:24; 10:10).

Some have suggested that John's emphasis on the "present-ness" of eternal life reflects the influence of Greek Platonic philosophy. Although the evangelist no doubt uses terms that would have been appreciated by readers familiar with Greek philosophy, the substance of his thought derives from a Jewish framework. In certain Greek philosophical texts, for example in *Poimandres*, eternal life is obtained by individual self-betterment and an impersonal intuition of reality. By contrast, John sees eternal life as a gift (John 5:25; 6:51), received by faith (3:15; 5:24), and co-identical with a personal knowledge of God the Father and the Son (17:3). And since Jesus is both the mediator and source of divine self-revelation, he is also the mediator (6:32–33; 10:10) and source (4:13–14; 11:25; 14:6) of eternal life. Until eternal life comes to full flower in the general resurrection, it remains an active agent in transforming individual lives and empowering for corporate mission.

work of the Spirit (3:10) and rejects the testimony of Jesus and his followers (3:11–12). Jesus, the Son of Man, has come from heaven and will be lifted up on the cross so that "everyone who believes in him may have eternal life" (3:13–15). Now comes the famous John 3:16: "For God so loved the world that he gave his one and only Son, that whoever believes in him shall not perish but have eternal life." Although God sent his Son to save the world rather than condemn it, everything hinges on how people respond (3:17). They will either experience salvation or condemnation. Whoever believes in Jesus will never be condemned (see Rom. 8:1), but those who reject Jesus stand condemned (3:18). John repeats the message using images of light and darkness (3:19–21). Jesus, the Light, has come into the world. Some love darkness and hate light, fearing that their evil deeds will be exposed, while others live by the truth and embrace the light so that their God-honoring deeds may be revealed.

More testimony from John the Baptizer (3:22–36)

As John continues his ministry as the forerunner to the Messiah, some of his disciples become envious of Jesus's growing popularity (3:22–26). John takes the opportunity to honor Jesus once again. He casts Jesus as the "bridegroom" and himself as the best man (3:27–29). John joyfully announces to all that Jesus must become greater and he must become

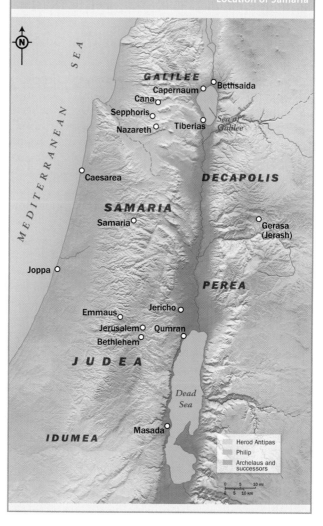

Location of Samaria

less (3:30). John's contentment with his God-given ministry challenges us to be content and grateful as well. Jesus is superior to John because he comes from heaven with a heavenly message, but not all accept his testimony (3:31–33). Truth is ultimately connected to divine revelation, which Jesus provides (3:34). The Father has given his Spirit and all authority to the Son (3:34–35). Once again, our response to Jesus determines our fate—either eternal life or God's condemning wrath (3:36).

Jesus's conversation with the Samaritan woman (4:1–42)

Jesus returns north to Galilee and passes through Samaria for a divine appointment (4:1–6). When a Samaritan woman comes to draw water at

✚ There are many contrasts in John's Gospel, such as light versus darkness, life versus condemnation, belief versus unbelief, the truth versus a lie, and "from above" versus "from the world."

The Samaritans

Jonathan M. Lunde

The origin of the Samaritans is historically murky, with competing views espoused by different groups. The Jews contend that the Samaritans' ancestors were the foreigners transplanted into Palestine by Assyria (2 Kings 17:24–41), who embraced the Jewish faith while retaining their pagan religions. The Jews argue this same group was rebuffed by the returning exiles in their offer to help rebuild the temple (Ezra 4:1–4).

Alternatively, the Samaritans maintain that they derive from a faithful remnant of Israelites who rejected the defilement of the Israelite faith when the place of worship was moved from Shechem to Shiloh and eventually to Jerusalem. Accordingly, they claim to have preserved the legitimate place of worship on Mount Gerizim and the true priesthood. Josephus complements this perspective, recounting the expulsion of a priest from Jerusalem, whose father-in-law (Sanballat) built him a sanctuary on Mount Gerizim.

Recent scholarship has rejected the links between the Samaritans and 2 Kings 17 or Ezra 4, since these passages most likely function with a political and geographical reference. Rather, the Samaritans have been associated with nonexiled, northern Israelites, who migrated to Shechem following Alexander the Great's violent suppression of a revolt in 331 BC. These were either joined or even preceded by priests who were expelled from Jerusalem during the stringent reforms in the wake of Ezra and Nehemiah. At some point in the fourth century BC they built a temple on Mount Gerizim, making explicit their rejection of the Jerusalem temple and its traditions (cf. John 4:19–24).

Over time, tensions developed between the Samaritans and the Jews on matters of priesthood legitimacy, temple location, and traditional interpretations. These tensions boiled over in 128 BC, when the Hasmonean John Hyrcanus conquered Shechem and destroyed the Samaritan temple. This antipathy expressed itself later in the scattering of bones by Samaritans in the temple precincts during Passover between AD 6 and 7 and in the massacre of Galilean pilgrims to Jerusalem in AD 52. Noteworthy also are Jesus's instructions not to enter Samaritan towns during his disciples' missionary journeys (Matt. 10:5) and the rejection of Jesus by a Samaritan village (Luke 9:51–53; cf. also John 8:48).

The Samaritans are best understood as a conservative form of Judaism, adhering solely to their own recension of the Law—the Samaritan Pentateuch. In general, the Samaritans believed in one God who communicated his law to his people through Moses. Jesus's provocative casting of the Samaritan as the one who truly loved his neighbor implies a positive view of Samaritan law observance (Luke 10:30–35). Samaritans also anticipated the end-time coming of a prophet like Moses. The Samaritan woman's reference to Messiah's coming may be John's paraphrase of her actual reference to the coming of this "prophet" (John 4:25).

a well outside of town, Jesus surprises her by asking for a drink. It was extremely unusual for a Jewish teacher to speak with such a woman, but Jesus engages her in a lengthy conversation (4:9). He begins with a spiritual analogy ("living water" in 4:10). She misunderstands him by taking him literally, much like Nicodemus had done earlier (4:11–12, 15). Jesus explains more about "living water" before revealing prophetic insight into the woman's personal history (4:16–19). When she tries to change the subject from her own life to religion, Jesus explains that true worshipers of God (whether

Jew or Samaritan) will worship God "in spirit and truth" (4:20–24). When the woman tries to delay the whole matter until the time when Messiah will come, Jesus declares that he is the Messiah (4:25–26). When the disciples return, they are shocked to see Jesus talking with the woman, but they don't say anything (4:27). Perhaps out of excitement, she leaves her water jar at the well and rushes back into town with the news that she has met a man who could be the Messiah (4:28–30). Meanwhile, the disciples urge Jesus to eat, but he insists that his food is to do the will of the Father and finish his work (4:31–34). Using a farming proverb, Jesus says the fields are now ready to harvest (4:35; cf. Matt. 9:37–38; Luke 10:2). God has been at work, and now the disciples get to reap the benefits of that labor (4:36–38). Many of the Samaritans from that town believe in Jesus because of the woman's testimony and confess that Jesus really is "the Savior of the world" (4:39–42).

Sign #2—Jesus heals the official's son (4:43–54)

Jesus returns to Cana in Galilee, where he had performed the first sign of turning water into wine (4:43–46). A royal official, whose son was deathly sick in Capernaum, came to beg Jesus to come heal his son (4:46–47). Although Jesus has a general rebuke for people who seek signs and wonders rather than believe, Jesus compassionately heals the man's son from a distance (4:48–53). The man takes Jesus at his word and returns home to find a healthy son. At that point, he and his entire household believe in Jesus (4:53). This was Jesus's second miraculous sign (4:54).

Sign #3—Jesus heals the man at the Pool of Bethesda (5:1–47)

While attending a Jewish festival in Jerusalem, Jesus heals a man who has been an invalid for thirty-eight years. The man is lying beside the Pool of Bethesda in hopes of getting to the healing waters after they are stirred. Jesus ignores the local tradition associated with the waters and heals the man instantly (5:5–9).

A water well from the Middle East.

✚ Jesus speaks not only with Nicodemus, a member of the religious leadership in Israel, but also with the Samaritan woman, a social outcast.

The Gospel of John   663

Seven Signs in John's Gospel

Matthew C. Williams

The word "sign" (*semeion* in Greek) appears seventeen times in John's Gospel, always in chapters 2–12, with the exception of 20:30. Though Jesus performed many signs (2:23; 20:30), John chose ones that would best inspire belief in Jesus, so that those who believe might find life (20:30–31). Signs *signify* something more glorious than the miracles themselves. It is sometimes difficult, however, to fully understand the veiled meaning behind the signs. They hint at the true nature of Jesus's messianic identity and his mission as the Son who was sent by the Father to bring life. Signs show us that the loving God is active and interested in his creation.

When a sign is seen correctly, it leads to faith in Jesus as God's agent of salvation. They do not, however, coerce faith. After the raising of Lazarus from the dead, for example, many believed in Jesus (11:45), but the Jewish leaders plotted to kill him (11:53). Although sign-based faith was insufficient (2:23–24), it was better than no faith at all, and often served as a

step toward true belief and salvation. One of John's goals was that people would believe even when they had not seen a sign, unlike Thomas (20:29).

It is often said the Gospel of John records seven signs. John, though, explicitly used the term "sign" for only four of Jesus's actions:

1. The changing of the water to wine (2:1–11) *signifies* that by changing the water used for Jewish ceremonial cleansing into the expected wine (Amos 9:11–14), Jesus was renewing Israel and launching the new covenant, which was superior to the old covenant (2:10; cf. Heb. 8:6–12).

2. The healing of the official's son (4:46–54) *signifies* that Jesus is the bringer of life. The son was on the verge of death, but Jesus healed him and gave him life.

3. The feeding of the five thousand (6:1–15) *signifies* that only Jesus can truly satisfy spiritual

Naturally, the man picks up his mat and walks, but the Jews condemn him for breaking the Sabbath law by carrying his mat (5:9–10). Later Jesus meets the man again and tells him he has been healed for good and he should sin no more (5:14). Certainly not all suffering is a direct result of sin, but in this case perhaps it was. Jesus deals with the whole person, body and spirit. The Jews begin to persecute Jesus for healing on the Sabbath (5:16). Jesus's response gets him into even more trouble. He claims that God is his Father, that God works on the Sabbath, and that he too works on the Sabbath (5:17). The Jews consider Jesus's claim to be blasphemous and try even harder to kill him (5:18). Jesus, the Son, is uniquely related to the Father; they are coworkers (5:19–20). Jesus has the ability to raise the dead (5:21, 25–26) and judge (5:22, 27, 30). How we treat Jesus is how we treat the Father (5:23). As a result, whoever embraces Jesus and the Father will not experience condemnation or spiritual death, but eternal life (5:24, 28–29). Jesus next points to three witnesses outside of himself who support his claims: John the Baptizer

hunger. Just as bread is a necessary element of the Mediterranean diet for physical survival, the full ingestion of Jesus—complete faith in him—is necessary for spiritual life.

4. The raising of Lazarus from the dead (11:38–44; 12:18) memorably *signifies* that Jesus came to give life to those who believe in him: "I am the resurrection and the life." It also foreshadows Jesus's own resurrection from the dead—the sacrificing of his own life in order to give life to others.

John indirectly refers to two other miraculous actions of Jesus as a "sign":

5. The healing of the invalid (5:1–9; see 7:31) *signifies* that the kingdom of God is now here, when "the lame leap like a deer" (Isa. 35:6). Jesus the Son makes himself equal to God the Father (5:18) by working to heal the needy in order to give life, even on the Sabbath (5:21, 24–26).
6. The giving of sight to the blind man (9:1–7; see 9:16) *signifies* that just as Jesus is able to heal physical sight, he is able to heal spiritual sight/blindness. In the Old Testament, blindness was evidence of the curse of disobedience (Deuteronomy 28). Now, in Jesus, there is a reversal of God's curse: light, or salvation, is given to those who respond to him (9:38); but blindness or condemnation follows for those who reject Jesus (9:40–41).

Most scholars, though, do not like having six signs, since the number six signifies imperfection in Judaism. Thus, they seek a seventh sign, a number that indicates perfection or wholeness. There is little agreement, however, on the identification of the seventh sign. Proposals include the cleansing of the temple (2:13–22), Jesus walking on water (6:16–21), the resurrection of Jesus, and the miraculous catch of fish (21:1–11). We need to remember, though, that John does not clearly enumerate seven signs, nor does he ever use the number seven in his Gospel. Perhaps John is less interested in the precise number of signs as he is in their goal: faith and life in Jesus.

(5:33–35), the signs the Father has given him to perform (5:36–38), and the Scriptures (5:39–40). Next Jesus turns the tables on his opponents and accuses them of loving the praise connected with religious life but failing to love God (5:41–44). They take pride in knowing what Moses has written, but now Moses's words accuse them because they are rejecting Jesus (5:45–47).

Sign #4—Jesus feeds the five thousand (6:1–15)

See Matthew 14:13–21; Mark 6:30–44; Luke 9:10–17. The feeding of the five thousand, walking on water, and the teaching on bread from heaven all occur during the Jewish Passover and connect to how God once delivered his people through the waters and provided manna for them in the wilderness. In these last days, God is once again delivering and providing for his people through Jesus. The miracle of multiplying the loaves causes the people to try to make Jesus king by force, but he withdraws until his appointed hour (6:14–15).

✦ John 6 carries several Old Testament Passover and exodus themes: feeding the multitudes, deliverance through the water, and bread from heaven.

"I Am" Sayings of Jesus

Matthew C. Williams

John uses the expression "I am" (*ego eimi* in Greek) much more frequently than the Synoptic Gospel. John uniquely uses seven "I am" constructions with a predicate. These explain different aspects of Jesus's mission as the One sent by God to fulfill Israel's promises by bringing life:

1. "I am the bread of life" (6:35, 41, 48, 51) who not only meets physical, but also spiritual needs.
2. "I am the light of the world" (8:12; 9:5), the one who fulfills the Feast of Tabernacles' light ceremony and reveals how to find life and freedom from darkness.
3. "I am the door of the sheep" (10:7, 9) who intimately knows, protects, and provides for the sheep. Jesus is the *only* way to enter the fold and be "saved" (10:9).
4. "I am the good shepherd" (10:11, 14) who comes to rescue the injured and the strays, in contrast to the bad "shepherds," the blind Jewish leaders (Ezek. 34; John 9:40–41).
5. "I am the resurrection and the life" (11:25) who overthrows the permanence of death.
6. "I am the way and the truth and the life" (14:6) who provides the *only* way to the Father.
7. "I am the true vine" (15:1, 5) in fulfillment of Israel, who was called "the vine" in the Old Testament. In contrast to Israel's lack of fruit (Jer. 2:21), Jesus obediently follows the Father, as do his followers who stay connected to the vine.

At other times, though, "I am" is used without a predicate (sometimes appearing in the English translations as "I am he"). Some think this use comes from a Hellenistic background because "I am" can be found in various religious and magical texts of antiquity. To date, though, not a single parallel to the Gospels' usage of "I am" has been found.

Sign #5—Jesus walks on water (6:16–21)

See Matthew 14:22–33; Mark 6:45–52. Just as God demonstrated his power over the sea during the exodus event, so also Jesus demonstrates his power over nature. After the disciples had rowed for hours against a strong wind and rough waters, Jesus comes to them walking on the water. They are terrified, but Jesus says to them, "It is I" ("I am" in Greek), reminding the Jewish disciples of God's "I am" statement to Moses (Exod. 3:14). Jesus is God incarnate, as the additional "I am" sayings throughout the rest of John will affirm. The crowds pursue Jesus to Capernaum.

Jesus is the bread of life (6:22–71)

When the crowds locate Jesus, he chides them for wanting more bread and missing the spiritual significance of the sign (6:25–26). Instead, they ought to consume food provided by the Son of Man that leads to eternal life (6:27). There is only one work that God requires, and that is to believe in Jesus (6:28–29). Ironically, the people who had observed the feeding of

It is more helpful to search for an Old Testament background. When Moses asked God for his name, he replied, "I am who I am" and told Moses to say, "I am has sent me to you" (Exod. 3:13–14). It is clear that the Septuagint (the Greek translation of the Old Testament) consistently used "I am" as a title for God, especially in the book of Isaiah: "so that you may know and believe me and understand that *I am*. Before me no god was formed, nor will there be one after me. I, even I, am the Lord" (43:10–11); "*I am, I am*, the one who blots out your transgressions" (43:25).

Jesus uses "I am" as a title to identify himself with the Sovereign God of the Old Testament. Job tells us God alone walks on the water (9:8). As Jesus walks on the water, the disciples are terrified. Jesus responds, "Take courage! *I am*! Don't be afraid" (Mark 6:45–50). At Jesus's trial the high priest asks him if he is the Christ, the Son of God. Jesus responds, "*I am*," signifying that he is indeed God's Son.

This absolute use of "I am" is more frequent in John. The most important are found in John 4:26, "*I* who speak to you *am* he"; 8:24, "If you do not believe that *I am* . . . you will indeed die in your sins"; 8:28, "When you have lifted up the Son of Man, then you will know that *I am*"; 8:58, "Before Abraham was born, *I am*"; and 13:19, "I am telling you now before it happens, so that when it does happen you will believe that *I am*." When the mob comes to arrest Jesus, saying they are looking for Jesus of Nazareth, "Jesus answered, '*I am*.' When Jesus said '*I am*,' they drew back and fell to the ground" (John 18:4–6). The soldiers acted like men who were in the presence of deity, falling to the ground prostrate before Jesus.

Jesus not only is the One who comes *in* the name of the Father, but he comes *with* the name of the Father—Jesus is not just human, he is the *divine* "I am." We can understand why the Jewish leaders did not understand. Monotheistic Judaism had no room for a divine Messiah. Thomas, though, got it right when he exclaimed: "My Lord and my God!" (John 20:28).

the five thousand now demand of Jesus a miraculous sign, claiming that God supplied their forefathers with manna in the wilderness (6:30–31). Jesus reminds them that Moses was not the source of the manna. Rather, God is the one who gives true bread from heaven (6:32–33). When the crowd demands this heavenly bread, Jesus boldly proclaims, "I am the bread of life" (6:33–35). The problem is that the crowds have seen Jesus, the bread of life, but still do not believe (6:36, 41–42). On the other hand, some do believe in Jesus, and those the Father draws to the Son will be protected and raised to eternal life on the last day (6:37, 39–40, 44). Jesus reiterates he has come from heaven to reveal the Father and do his will (6:38, 45–46). Those who ate manna in the wilderness died, but those who believe in Jesus, the bread from heaven, will never die (6:47–50). Interestingly, we are told of their "grumbling" in verses 41 and 43, perhaps connecting them with their ancestors who grumbled against Moses in spite of receiving manna. Jesus's disciples also grumble in 6:61. Jesus then invites the crowds to eat the heavenly bread, which he says is his flesh (i.e., his own bodily life) that will be given (on the cross) for the world (6:51). The Jews are stunned and shocked by this offensive image of eating Jesus's flesh (6:52). But Jesus pushes the image much further, inviting his hearers to eat his flesh and drink his blood (6:53–57). This means that we must receive Jesus in a deeply personal and intimate way. Eating flesh and drinking blood is a symbol for assimilating, absorbing, and receiving God's revelation in Jesus and entering into a relationship with him. There is perhaps a secondary reference to the Lord's Supper, which Jesus will institute near the end of his earthly ministry. Jesus repeats the main idea in verse 58: the one who feeds on the bread from heaven will live forever. There was nothing in their Jewish heritage to prepare the people for Jesus's graphic and offensive words. As a result, many stop following him at that point (6:60–61, 64–66). If they are offended by his sacrificial death, Jesus says, they will be even more offended by his resurrection and ascension (6:61–62). Jesus clarifies that his words are not meant to be taken literally ("the flesh counts for nothing" in v. 63). Rather, he is speaking Spirit-inspired and life-giving words (6:63). Then Jesus asks the Twelve if they too want to abandon him. Peter speaks for the group: "Lord, to whom shall we go? You have the words of eternal life. We believe and know that you are the Holy One of God" (6:68–69). Yet one of the Twelve is a traitor (6:70–71).

Excavations at Tiberias.

✦ Jesus's statements about eating his flesh and drinking his blood are clarified later when he institutes the Lord's Supper.

Jesus goes to the Feast of Tabernacles in Jerusalem (7:1–13)

The Feast of Tabernacles (or Booths) was one of the three great festivals on the Jewish calendar, along with Passover and Pentecost. Tabernacles celebrated the fall harvest and served as a reminder of God's provision for his people during their wilderness wanderings (Lev. 23:33–43).

At this time, Jesus's own brothers do not believe in him. Instead, they mock him as a wonder-worker and advise him to improve his public relations campaign by going up to Jerusalem (7:1–5). Jesus insists his time has not yet come, but later goes to Jerusalem privately (7:6–10). The crowds are divided in their reaction to Jesus (7:11–13).

Jesus teaches at the Feast (7:14–36)

As Jesus teaches in the temple courts, the crowds' reactions are mixed. In 7:16–19, Jesus repeats what he said in John 5 about being sent by the Father. In 7:21–24, Jesus defends his miracle of healing the invalid on the Sabbath (John 5:1–15). If it's permissible to circumcise a baby on the Sabbath, why should he not heal the whole man on the Sabbath? In 7:28–29, Jesus admits his human origins but insists he is more than a prophet from Nazareth. He claims once again to come from the Father. In 7:33–34, Jesus announces he will soon return to his Father, and the world will not be able to follow. The rest of this section consists of various reactions to Jesus. At points, his teaching is misunderstood because they take it literally (7:35–36). Some are amazed at his profound knowledge (7:15). The Jewish leaders plot to kill him (7:19–20, 25, 32), but they are hesitant to confront him during the Feast (7:25–26). Others are just confused (7:27). Finally, some "put their faith in him," concluding that the Messiah can't possibly do more miraculous signs than Jesus (7:31).

Jesus offers living water (7:37–52)

During the Feast of Tabernacles, the priests would draw water from the Pool of Siloam and lead a procession to the temple, where they would pour out the water at the base of the altar as a means of thanking God for his provision. Also, they would read from the Prophets (e.g., Ezekiel 47; Zechariah 14), which mention living water flowing from the temple. On the final day of the Feast, Jesus publicly invites the thirsty to come to him and permanently satisfy their thirst (7:37). Jesus will provide living water, a promise fulfilled later when he is glorified and sends the Holy Spirit (7:38–39). Again, the people's response is mixed (7:40–44). The temple guards who had been assigned to arrest Jesus are captivated by his words and return to the Jewish leaders empty-handed (7:45–47). The nervous leaders begin to react negatively toward Jesus, even to the point of neglecting wisdom and justice (7:48–52).

✛ Facing unbelief from his own family and opposition from the religious leaders, Jesus carries out his mission with wisdom, avoiding direct confrontation until the hour of his death arrives.

Jerusalem in the Time of Jesus

Nicholas Perrin

Ancient Jerusalem reached its peak size shortly before the time of the First Jewish Revolt (AD 66–70), after Agrippa I's decision to incorporate the northern outlying suburbs by building what is called the "third wall." The Jerusalem of Jesus's time, being marked out only by the "first wall" and "second wall," was considerably smaller: not even a half square mile in area.

The first wall was both the most ancient and the most extensive. It ran westward from the southwest corner of the temple (which itself was situated on the eastern hill at the far northeast corner of the city) all the way to Herod's Palace (the Praetorium) on the northwest corner. It is undoubtedly because the north side of Jerusalem was the only side without the natural protection of the hills that Herod the Great (37–4 BC) chose this spot—on the north edge but away from the temple—for building not only his base of operations but also three impressive towers: Hippicus, Phasael, and Mariamne. From here the wall plunged south for roughly a half mile, running along the brow of the western hill overlooking the Hinnom Valley (which Jesus refers to as Gehenna). By the point where the wall met the Gate of the Essenes, so-called because of a nearby "Essene quarter" and road leading out to Qumran, it veered eastward. Enclosing certain important water sources, including the Pool of Siloam (John 9:7), the city wall then shifted northward back toward the temple, hugging the eastern hill of the city overlooking the Kidron Valley to the east.

While the course of the second wall, built during the second century BC as an extension of the city's north side, cannot be firmly determined, we can be fairly sure that it began at the Garden Gate (which was probably about halfway across the northern edge of the first wall), shot up a quarter mile toward the north, and then eventually came back down to Fortress Antonia, which sat along the northwest corner of the temple grounds. These same walls in Jesus's day served to protect a base population of some forty thousand to fifty thousand people.

The city of Jerusalem was very economically diverse. On the one extreme was the wealthy high-priest class who lived in expansive and luxurious homes outside of Herod's Palace. On the other extreme were "the poor," a landless peasant class who fled from the countryside into the city in some hopes of eking out an existence through begging or unskilled day labor. In between were merchants, artisans, and tradesmen—most of whom depended on the temple and temple-related business. Relationships between the social-economic classes were often tense: economic resentment brewing in Jesus's time would have at least partly explained the emergence of the Zealots and the subsequent Jewish uprising a generation after Jesus's death. Jesus's recurring warnings against greed were a continuation of John the Baptist's preaching on this theme (Luke 3:10–14), which also happened to be largely directed against Jerusalemites (Mark 1:5).

The city was equally mixed on a sociocultural level. Jewish pilgrims from Galilee and from far abroad would make regular pilgrimages to the Holy City, causing its population to swell during

The woman caught in adultery (7:53–8:11)

This story is absent from the oldest and most reliable Greek manuscripts. As a result, most scholars agree that it was not part of the original Gospel of John. Nevertheless, there are hints in the historical record that this story reflects an actual event in the life of Jesus. The Jewish leaders

festival times. Given the highly politicized nature of these festivals, and the highly politicized nature of the temple itself, the Romans were also sure to make their military and cultural presence felt. It was a presence that was simultaneously feared and resented. Finally, due to its status as a world-class tourist spot (which had as much to do with Herod's political renown as with his improvements on the temple), the city attracted visitors from all reaches of the known world. The swirling cultural maelstrom within Jerusalem's walls virtually guaranteed that any strident political claim, including Jesus's implicit claims of messiahship, would go neither undetected nor uncontested. The cultural and political mix of Jerusalem, together with the watchful Roman eye on anyone liable to upset the status quo, certainly influenced the style, content, and timing of Jesus's public communications.

It is first and foremost the Gospel of John that focuses on Jesus's ministry in Jerusalem. In John 5, for example, we read of the lame man who frequented the pool by the Sheep Gate, just north of the temple grounds. Through this same Sheep Gate, herders would usher in the sacrificial flocks; it is a location that may well have set the stage for Jesus's parable of the sheep and the sheep gate (John 10:1–18). Elsewhere, when Jesus declares himself to be the "light of the world" (John 8:12) or associates himself with "living water" (John 7:37–38), he is probably using images drawn from temple rituals taking place at the concurrent festivals. In John especially, Jerusalem and its temple become a primary fund of images for Jesus's teaching.

Both John and the Synoptic Gospels give detailed accounts of Jesus's last week in Jerusalem. There is almost certainly symbolic significance

to Jesus's entering Jerusalem from the east, that is, across the Mount of Olives (Mark 11:1–11; cf. Zech. 14:4). Over the next few days, Jesus and his disciples spend the nights at nearby Bethany, but carry out their daytime activities in or right around the temple (Mark 11–13). After partaking of the Last Supper, which early tradition locates on Mount Zion (the south end of the western hill of the city), Jesus and his disciples proceed east, past the temple, and across the Kidron Valley to Gethsemane (John 18:1), on the lower slope of the Mount of Olives. After being arrested, Jesus was then led back and forth between Caiaphas's home near Herod's Palace and Pilate's base at Fortress Antonia (Luke 22:47–23:25; John 18). The best evidence suggests that Jesus was crucified due west from here, outside the city walls, at a location marked today by the Church of the Holy Sepulcher. After being raised, Jesus appears to the disciples over the course of forty days, and then finally ascends from the Mount of Olives (Acts 1:12). What this implies about Jerusalem in terms of Jesus's return is a matter debated among scholars.

It is clear, at any rate, that this small area that comprised first-century Jerusalem far outstripped any other area in terms of significance—both for first-century Judaism as a whole and for Jesus. Jerusalem was the focal point of Judaism's eschatological hopes; it was also the final stage for Jesus's ministry and calling. Given the complexities of the city's social and economic life, which constituted a microcosm of the Roman world as a whole, Jesus's turning his face to Jerusalem allowed not only the fulfillment of Scripture but also the confrontation of dark realities that have haunted individuals of all times and places.

bring to Jesus a woman caught in the act of adultery and remind him that the Mosaic law calls for death by stoning for such an offense. They are trying to trap Jesus. After some reflection, Jesus responds, "If any one of you is without sin, let him be the first to throw a stone at her" (8:7). Her accusers walk away one by one, leaving only Jesus and the woman.

Jesus does not condemn her but sets her free with the warning to leave her life of sin (8:11).

Jesus is the light of the world (8:12–30)

Torches lit during the Feast of Tabernacles remind the pilgrims of God's presence in the wilderness through the pillar of fire (Exodus 13–14). Jesus now claims to be "the light of the world," the true source of God's presence (8:12). The Pharisees try to discredit his testimony, but Jesus again appeals to his heavenly origin and unique relationship with the Father (8:13–19). He continues to teach in the temple area without being arrested because his "time had not yet come" (8:20). Jesus bluntly tells the Jewish leaders they cannot go where he is going (8:21), they will die in their sins (8:21, 24), and they are worldly (8:23), all because they do not accept him (8:24). As a result, they can expect to face judgment (8:25–26). Jesus's true identity will become evident to all when he, the Son of Man, is "lifted up" (8:28–29). The three references in John to this lifting up probably refer both to Jesus's crucifixion and his resurrection/exaltation (3:14; 8:28; 12:32–34). Jesus will soon demonstrate who he claims to be. In spite of opposition, however, many are putting their faith in Jesus (8:30).

Jesus is "I Am" (8:31–59)

Jesus now challenges the depth of the faith of those mentioned in 8:30. It appears that they claim to believe, but their actions don't support their claim. True disciples will embrace Jesus's word, which reveals the truth and liberates people from sin (8:31–32). Jesus is the truth and has the power to set people free from their bondage to sin (8:33–36). Many demonstrate their refusal to accept Jesus's word by trying to kill him (8:37). Jesus now accuses them of behaving like their father, whom he will later identify as the devil (8:38, 41, 44). The heated exchange continues as the Jews claim Abraham as their spiritual father (8:39). Jesus responds that their actions disprove that Abraham is their true father (8:39–41). They deny they are "illegitimate children," perhaps a cutting accusation about Jesus's own heritage (8:41). They insist, "The only Father we have is God himself" (8:41). Jesus replies that if God were their Father, they would love and accept him, but they refuse because the devil, not God, is their spiritual father (8:42–47). Jesus makes it crystal clear that those who don't accept him don't belong to God (8:47). The Jews now accuse Jesus of being a demon-possessed foreigner (8:48). Jesus denies he is demon possessed and instead claims that those who keep his word will never die (8:49–51). They react negatively to his claim to prevent death since even Abraham and the prophets eventually

✚ Jesus fulfills many of the Jewish traditions associated with the Feast of Tabernacles: he is "living water" (7:37–39) and the "light of the world" (8:12).

died. Does Jesus think he is greater than father Abraham? (8:52–53). Jesus again claims a special relationship to the Father, concluding that Abraham rejoiced at the thought of seeing Jesus appear (8:54–56). They object that Jesus is less than fifty years old and has never seen Abraham (8:57). At this point in the debate, Jesus makes his most dramatic claim yet concerning his relation to God—"I tell you the truth, before Abraham was born, I am!" (8:58). Jesus not only predates Abraham, he also shares the divine name, "I Am" (Exod. 3:14). Jesus is one with God! No wonder the Jews look for rocks to stone him to death for blasphemy (8:59). But his time has not yet come, and he slips away.

Sign #6—Jesus heals a man born blind (9:1–41)

Jesus encounters a man blind from birth, and his disciples wonder whose sin caused the blindness (9:1–2). Jesus says the man's blindness provides an opportunity for God to do his illuminating work (9:3). As the "light of the world" (8:12–30), Jesus restores the man's sight. He mixes his saliva with dirt and places the mud on the man's eyes with instructions to go wash in the Pool of Siloam (9:4–7). Once again, Jesus violates the Sabbath law in order to heal a person.

The modern remains of the Pool of Siloam.

+ Jesus not only claims to be greater than Abraham (the father of Israel) but also claims to be equal to God by assuming the divine name "I am" (John 8:58; Exod. 3:14).

Deity and Humanity of Christ

Thomas H. McCall

Orthodox Christians believe Jesus Christ is a person who is both human and divine. Existing as one person, he nonetheless possesses two "natures," and, in the words of the venerable Chalcedonian Formula (451), he has these natures "without confusion, without change, without division, without separation; the distinction of natures being in no way annulled by the union." This belief, which is at the very heart of the Christian faith, is grounded in the Bible's witness both to the humanity and the divinity of Jesus Christ.

The humanity of Jesus is attested to in several ways. The genealogies of Jesus (Matt. 1:1–17 and Luke 3:23–38) bear witness to the fact that he was the descendant of particular human ancestors. The New Testament says that he was born in "human form" or nature (Phil. 2:7), that he developed (Luke 1:80; 2:40, 52) and became a tradesman (Matt. 13:55; Mark 6:3). The Gospels are unembarrassed about the fact that Jesus was hungry (Matt. 4:2; 21:18) and thirsty (Matt. 25:35; John 19:28), as well as exhausted on many occasions (e.g., Matt. 8:24). The very full and vibrant emotional life of Jesus is on full display in the Gospel portrayals of his life: he exhibits anger and wrath (e.g., Mark 3:5; 11:15–19), he shows deep compassion (e.g., Matt. 9:36; 14:14; 15:32; Luke 13:34; John 11:35), he shows great sorrow over those who reject the love of God (e.g., Matt. 23:37), and he openly "wept over the city" of Jerusalem (Luke 19:41). His knowledge (at least as human) is plainly shown to be limited (Mark 5:30–33; 13:32; Luke 2:52), and he exhibits great stress and agony in the Garden of Gethsemane where his "sweat was like drops of blood" (Luke 22:42–44)—"my soul is overwhelmed with sorrow to the point of death" (Matt. 26:37–38). And most notably, Jesus died from the crucifixion. John 1:14 clearly says that the eternal Word "became" flesh, and this testimony to the full and complete humanity of Jesus is echoed in 1 John 1:1: "That which was from the beginning, which we have heard, which we have seen with our eyes, which we have looked at and our hands have touched—this we proclaim concerning the Word of life."

The deity of Christ is also well attested in Scripture. Jesus is worshiped by the earliest Christians, and this shows evidence that his first followers understood he was more than merely human (e.g., John 18:6; 1 Cor. 16:22; Heb. 1:6; Rev. 22:20). These followers understood Jesus Christ to be preexistent (John 1:1–2; 1 Cor. 8:6; Phil. 2:5–11; Col. 1:15–16; Heb. 1:5–6; Rev. 1:17; 2:8; 22:13). And they thought this for very good reason: Jesus himself claims preexistence and deity (John 8:58; 13:19). The New Testament goes further, for it makes strong claims that Jesus should be understood as performing works only God is able to do. Jesus Christ is the Creator, for "through him all things were made; without him nothing was made that has been made" (John 1:3; cf. Col. 1:16; Heb. 1:10). Jesus is the one who sustains the cosmos; he is the one who has defeated death (2 Tim. 1:10) and whose Lordship is eternal (Heb. 1:8). He takes upon himself the authority to pronounce forgiveness of sins (e.g., Mark 2:5–11; Luke 5:24; Rom. 10:9, 13), and he makes the astounding claim that he will be the final judge who holds the final destiny of all in his hands (e.g., Matt. 25:31–46; Rom. 2:16; 2 Thess. 1:7–8). Indeed, the exalted status of the man Jesus is portrayed as nothing less than complete unity and equality with the Father, for the Son is the "exact imprint" of God's being (Heb. 1:3 ESV), and he claims to be "one" with God (John 10:30; 17:22) as in him the "whole fullness of deity dwells bodily" (Col. 2:9). It is no wonder, then, that the titles of Christ testify to his divinity. Notably, the Pauline uses of "Lord" with reference to Jesus are loaded with implications of divinity: when we read that "every knee will bow . . . and every tongue confess that Jesus Christ is Lord, to the glory of God the Father" (Phil. 2:10–11), it is clear that Paul is including the self-emptying servant in a powerful statement of monotheism drawn from the Old Testament (Isa. 45:23). Similarly, when Paul says that "there is but one God, the Father, from whom all things came and for whom we live; and there is but one Lord, Jesus Christ, through whom all things came and through whom we live" (1 Cor. 8:6), he is doing nothing less than including Jesus in the Shema (Deut. 6:4). Finally, the New Testament does not shrink from referring to Jesus directly as God (John 1:1, 18; 20:28; Rom. 9:5; Titus 2:13; Heb. 1:8–9; 2 Pet. 1:1).

The humanity of Christ is so well attested that attempts to avoid or deny it (Docetism, from *dokeo*, which means "to seem," or "to appear") have generally been both less common and more susceptible to quick and decisive repudiation. The biblical witness to the humanity of Jesus is very clear and overwhelming evidence against Docetism.

The deity of Christ, on the other hand, has often been either misunderstood or rejected. Adoptionism (the view that Jesus Christ is a mere human who was adopted by God and given special status) is an extreme and outright rejection of the deity of Christ; but again the Scriptural witness to the preexistence and exalted status of Christ provides a very strong case against it. Arianism, on the other hand, is a much more subtle and sophisticated alternative. Seizing upon every biblical indication of ignorance, weakness, or subordination of the Son to the Father, the Arians argued that the Son indeed enjoyed preexistence and was "divine"—but only as a created and lower-ranked god. In response, the defenders of emerging orthodoxy argued that the multifaceted biblical witness to the full divinity of Jesus demanded much more than Arianism could affirm, that anything less than the full ontological equality of Jesus with his Father threatened genuine knowledge of God and even salvation (for if Jesus Christ were not divine, then we could not trust his revelation as a revelation *of God*, and he could not make atonement for our sins), and that Arianism would entail the abandonment of monotheism. Similarly, Apollinarianism (which taught that *part* of the human nature was replaced by the divine Logos), Nestorianism (which was understood to emphasize the distinctiveness of the two natures to the point that the unity of the person was endangered), and the various versions of Monophysitism (which emphasized the unity of the person to the point that the two natures were melded into one nature) were all rejected on the grounds that they could not account for the full biblical witness to the humanity and divinity of Christ, and because if any of these were true then we would not be joined to God in Christ—and thus would not be saved.

The scriptural witness both to the divinity and humanity of Christ ultimately led to the conclusions of the Niceno-Constantinopolitan Creed and the Chalcedonian Formula. Christians continue to marvel at the mystery of the incarnation while wrestling with fascinating questions: What kind of human nature was assumed? What is the best way to make sense of the *communicatio idiomatum*—how are the properties of the natures related to the person and to one another? Is the God-man Jesus Christ a whole composed of parts? But as Christians do so, they affirm the full, undiminished humanity as well as the complete equality and full divinity of the incarnate Son of God.

Throughout the Scriptures, only God has been able to heal the blind, and now he does so through Jesus (9:32–33). The follow-up discussion involves several parties. The neighbors are divided about whether this is the same man and finally bring him to the Pharisees to get their advice (9:8–13). Faced with an obvious miracle, the Pharisees too are split on their opinion of Jesus (9:14–17). They seem more concerned with the Sabbath issue than anything else. Next, the Jews question the man's parents (9:18–23). The parents admit he is their son, confess their ignorance as to how he can now see, and direct further questions back to their son for fear of being expelled from the synagogue. Finally, the Pharisees question the formerly blind man himself (9:24–29). Ironically, throughout the story, the man receives both physical sight and spiritual light, while the Jewish leaders slide further into spiritual darkness and blindness. Notice the progression of the man's statements about Jesus:

> 9:11 → "The man they call Jesus [healed me]."
> 9:17 → "He is a prophet."
> 9:25 → "Whether he is a sinner or not, I don't know. One thing I do know. I was blind but now I see!"
> 9:33 → "If this man were not from God, he could do nothing."
> 9:38 → "Then the man said, 'Lord, I believe,' and he worshiped him."

In contrast, the Pharisees doubt Jesus is from God because he breaks the Sabbath laws (9:16); they view Jesus as a sinner (9:24); they question Jesus's origins (9:29); and they reject Jesus's miraculous works (9:34). Jesus sums up the entire episode: "For judgment I have come into this world, so that the blind will see and those who see will become blind" (9:39). The Pharisees respond, "What? Are we blind too?" and Jesus basically says, "Absolutely!" (9:40–41).

Jesus, the good shepherd (10:1–21)

In the previous episode, the Jewish leaders treat the blind man with contempt. The present section shows how Jesus stands in sharp contrast to these leaders. He is the "gate for the sheep" (10:7) and the "good shepherd" (10:11), whereas the Jewish leaders are "hired hands" (10:12–13) or even "thieves and robbers" (10:1, 8). As the true spiritual leader, Jesus knows his people, offers them security and spiritual nourishment, and, above all, lays down his life for them (10:3–4, 9–11, 14–15, 17–18). Jesus is fully devoted to his followers and willingly sacrifices his life so they may have life in all its fullness. The Jewish leaders, on the other hand, are unloving, selfish

✚ The story of Jesus healing the man born blind drips with irony as the blind man begins to see and the religious leaders become blind.

Mary, Martha, and Lazarus

Matthew C. Williams

Mary, Martha, and Lazarus appear together only in John 11–12. We do not know very much about them: they lived in Bethany, cared for one another deeply (as seen in their grief when the brother, Lazarus, died), and loved Jesus.

Luke 10:38–42 records that Martha opened her home to Jesus and served him, while her sister Mary sat at Jesus's feet and listened. Martha and Mary also had great faith in Jesus. Both knew that if Jesus "had been here, my brother would not have died." Martha's declaration of faith in Jesus is perhaps the climax of John's Gospel: "I believe that you are the Christ, the Son of God, who was to come into the world" (John 11:27; cf. 20:30–31). After Lazarus is raised, Martha again serves Jesus at a dinner given in his honor, at which Mary extravagantly worships Jesus by anointing his feet with expensive perfume (John 12:1–3).

We know Jesus loved this family (John 11:5) and apparently visited their home often. When Lazarus became sick, the sisters sent word to Jesus, trusting he would help. Despite death threats in Judea, Jesus, the good shepherd who lays down his life for his sheep (John 10:11), returned to Judea to help Lazarus (whose name in Hebrew means "God has helped"). Jesus purposefully waited two days before going to Lazarus so that when he finally arrived, four days had passed since Lazarus's death. This was an impossible situation in the Jewish context because of their belief that the spirit of a dead person deserted the body after three days. Since four days had passed, there was apparently no hope. Even Martha thought that Jesus could not do anything (11:24, 39). In this impossible situation, Jesus raised Lazarus from the dead, a powerful display of God's glory. Jesus came to give life to those who believe in him. While this raising led many Jews to believe in him (11:45), it also led the Jewish leaders to plot Jesus's death (11:46–53).

Some deny the miracle's historicity because the name Lazarus is used in a parable (Luke 16:19–31). Lazarus, though, was the third most common name for Palestinian Jews of that time period. Other skeptics note that the Synoptic Gospels do not record this miracle. But the Synoptics emphasize miracles that took place in Galilee, not near Jerusalem; and they do record two other raisings (the widow's son, Luke 7, and Jairus's daughter, Mark 5).

Others suggest Lazarus is the "one whom Jesus loved," the author of the fourth Gospel (based on 11:3, 5, 36). But it makes little sense that Lazarus is called by name here and later referred to with a cryptic designation of the "one whom Jesus loved."

A sheepfold made out of stone.

✚ Jesus portrays himself as the Good Shepherd in contrast to the false shepherds of Ezekiel 34:2–10.

pretenders who will only harm their followers. The response to Jesus is again divided between those who think he is demon possessed and crazy and those who are amazed by Jesus's unique ability to heal a blind man (10:19–21).

"I and the Father are one" (10:22–42)

The Feast of Dedication (or Hanukkah) celebrated the purification of the temple after it had been desecrated by Antiochus Epiphanes in 167 BC (1 Macc. 4:36–61). The Jewish leaders confront Jesus about whether he is the Christ (10:24). Jesus points them to his words and his miracles, but doesn't expect them to believe him because they are not his followers (10:25–26). Jesus's "sheep" follow him and receive eternal life. No one can remove them from Jesus's hand or the Father's hand, since Jesus and the Father are one (10:27–30). This statement doesn't mean that Jesus and the Father are the same person, but that they possess equal authority and total unity in their purpose and will. The Jews prepare to stone Jesus for claiming to be God, which they considered blasphemy (10:31–33). Jesus quotes from Psalm 82 in his defense. If the Scriptures can use the term "gods" for someone other than God, isn't it appropriate that the term "Son" should be used for the unique Son? Jesus's claim to be God's Son is not blasphemous; it is true! (10:34–36). Jesus challenges the leaders to believe his miraculous signs, even though they won't believe his words, so that they can understand his special relationship to the Father (10:37–38). Again, they try to seize him, but he escapes. Jesus moves across the Jordan to where John had been baptizing, and many from that region believe in him (10:39–42).

Sign #7—Jesus raises Lazarus from the dead (11:1–54)

Jesus was very close to Lazarus and his two sisters, Martha and Mary (11:5). When he hears that Lazarus is sick, Jesus declares that this sickness will not end in death but will serve to glorify God and his Son (11:1–4). In spite of the fearful protests of his disciples, Jesus returns to the vicinity of Jerusalem, but after a two-day delay, so that the coming miracle will encourage their faith even more (11:7–16). His time of earthly ministry is drawing to a close (11:9–10), yet Jesus is in control and knows what he must do before his hour arrives. When Jesus gets to Bethany four days after Lazarus has died, both sisters meet him—first Martha and later Mary—with the same lament: "If you had been here, my brother would not have died" (11:21, 32). Jesus tells Martha that Lazarus will rise again, and he's talking about something more than the final resurrection of the righteous (11:23–24). Jesus boldly proclaims, "I am the resurrection and the life. He who believes in me will live, even though he dies; and whoever lives and believes in me will never die" (11:25–26). When

✦ The last and most dramatic of the seven signs in John's Gospel is the raising of Lazarus from the dead.

he asks if Martha believes this, she confesses him as "Lord," "the Christ," and "the Son of God" (11:27). When Mary and the others come to Jesus crying their hearts out, he is "deeply moved [better: 'angered'] in spirit and troubled" (11:33, 38). Jesus is "grieving mad" at death and the devastation it causes. All around him people are doubled over in emotional agony, and in response, Jesus weeps! If the Son of God wept, we too have permission to weep when we experience the pain that death causes (11:35–36). Jesus moves to the tomb still furious at death (11:38). He takes control and issues commands that will reverse the curse of death:

Traditional tomb of Lazarus in Bethany.

> 11:39—"Take away the stone."
> 11:40—"Did I not tell you that if you believed, you would see the glory of God?"
> 11:43—"Lazarus, come out!"

The Father answers the Son's prayer for a sign that will strengthen faith (11:41–42). Lazarus's resuscitation is a preview of what Jesus will do with death on the last day (see 1 Cor. 15:51–58).

The people's reaction to the miracle is mixed as usual. Many Jews put their faith in Jesus, while others report to their religious leaders (11:45–46). The Jewish leaders call a special meeting to discuss their dilemma. If they let Jesus continue to perform miraculous signs, everyone will believe in him and the Romans will take away their temple and nation (11:47–48). Ironically, they choose not to let Jesus continue, and the Romans still destroy Jerusalem. Also full of irony is Caiaphas's statement that it is better for one man to die for the nation than for the whole nation to perish (11:49–50). Caiaphas, the high priest, prophesied more than he knew, since Jesus would die for the whole nation and create an entirely new family of God, including both Jews and gentiles (11:51–52; cf. John 10:16). But from a human perspective, raising Lazarus seals Jesus's death warrant, so he withdraws to Ephraim with his disciples (11:53–54).

✚ From the time that Jesus raised Lazarus, the religious leaders began plotting to put Jesus to death (John 11:53).

Jesus anointed at Bethany (11:55–12:11)

See Matthew 26:6–13; Mark 14:3–9. Jesus again goes up to Jerusalem for the Passover (see John 2:13; 6:4). Everyone wants to see him, especially since the raising of Lazarus (11:55–56). The Jewish leaders want to find him in order to arrest him (11:57). He goes to Bethany and attends a dinner in his honor (12:1–2). While there, Mary anoints Jesus's head and feet for burial with some very expensive perfume (12:3). (This is likely the same event reported in Matthew and Mark.) Judas Iscariot, a thieving hypocrite, objects to the wasteful anointing, but Jesus defends Mary's actions as a precious act of devotion (12:4–8). The crowds arrive not only to see Jesus but also to see Lazarus, whom he had raised (12:9). The Jewish leaders now plot to kill Lazarus as well, since many Jews are believing in Jesus on account of him (12:10–11).

The triumphal entry into Jerusalem (12:12–19)

See Matthew 21:1–9; Mark 11:1–10; Luke 19:28–40. As Jesus humbly enters Jerusalem, the crowd praises him as "the King of Israel" (12:13). There is much the disciples don't understand until after the cross and resurrection (12:16). Jesus's popularity escalates because of the raising of Lazarus (12:17–18), and the frustrated Pharisees conclude, "Look how the whole world has gone after him!" (12:19).

The hour of Jesus's glorification has arrived (12:20–50)

The group of God-fearing gentiles searches for Jesus at the Feast (12:20–22), and this prompts him to speak about his work of salvation for the whole world. Jesus now plainly says, "The hour has come for the Son of Man to be glorified" (12:23). Up until now, Jesus's "hour" or "time" had always been in the future (2:4; 7:30; 8:20), but now his glorification (i.e., his death, resurrection, and exaltation) is at hand. Jesus's death will result in life for many (12:24). Those who give up or lose their life in service to Jesus will find eternal life and a heavenly home (12:25–26; cf. Matt. 16:24; Mark 8:34; Luke 9:23). As Jesus faces the "hour," his heart is troubled. Although he is honest about the upcoming suffering of the cross, he submits to the Father's glorious plan (12:27–28). The Father affirms the Son with a word from heaven that the crowd fails to understand (12:27–30). One thing is for sure—the lifting up of the Son on the cross will

Jewish coin with palm branches.

✚ Bethany, a small village a little under two miles from Jerusalem, became a refuge for Jesus. The home of Martha, Mary, and Lazarus was as close to a home as Jesus had on this earth.

defeat the prince of this world (12:31–33). While the crowd is curious about Jesus's work, he challenges them to respond to the light they have (12:34–36). Our response to Jesus is more important than satisfying our curiosity. Even after all the signs Jesus has performed, most people still do not believe, and this fulfills Isaiah 6:10 and 53:1 (John 12:37–40). In his vision of God on his throne (Isaiah 6), the prophet had actually seen Jesus's glory (John 12:41). The good news is that some do believe, even among the Jewish leaders, yet their faith remains feeble (12:42–43). When we accept Jesus, we also accept the Father and move out of darkness into the light (12:44–46). But those who refuse to believe will face judgment from the Father and from Jesus's words, which come from the Father (12:47–50).

The Book of Glory (13:1–20:31)

The second half of John's Gospel focuses on Jesus's final week and culminates in his glorification—the "hour" of his crucifixion, resurrection, and exaltation. Whereas the Book of Signs (John 2–12) was directed to all who would listen, often with a mixed reaction, the Book of Glory is addressed primarily to those who believe. John 13–20 doesn't read like a cold, distant lecture but like final, personal words from a dear friend.

Date palm trees grow in the area of Jerusalem and often served as a symbol of righteousness (Ps. 92:12).

Jesus washes his disciples' feet (13:1–17)

Jesus knows his "time" has come to return to the Father, so he loves his followers faithfully to the end of his life (13:1). As the host of the Passover meal, Jesus does something shocking. He assumes the role of a servant and does something even Jewish slaves weren't expected to do—he washes his disciples' feet (13:2–5). To love means to serve. Peter objects because the deed is beneath Jesus's dignity, but Jesus insists that part of being a disciple is allowing God to love you (13:6–10). After he washes their feet, Jesus explains what he has done. If Jesus as the "Teacher and Lord" humbles himself to serve the disciples, how much more should the disciples serve one another (13:12–14)? Jesus's act of humble

service becomes an example for us. We are not greater than our Master; if he served, we too should serve (13:15–16). Knowing is good, but doing brings blessing (13:17).

Jesus predicts Judas's betrayal (13:18–30)

See Matthew 26:21–25; Mark 14:18–21; Luke 22:21–23. Jesus had already said one of the disciples was not "clean" (13:10–11), and now he explains further. Jesus predicts one of the Twelve will betray him (13:18–21), fulfilling Psalm 41:9. We need to imagine how this unexpected announcement would have shocked the disciples emotionally (13:22). Peter motions to John ("the disciple whom Jesus loved"), who is reclining near Jesus, to ask him which disciple he is talking about (13:23–25). Jesus tells John that the one to whom he gives the bread is the one (13:26). Ironically, by dipping the bread in the dish and giving it to Judas, Jesus is honoring the one who would soon deliver him to be crucified. When Judas receives the bread, Satan enters into him (13:27). Jesus tells him to do his deed quickly, and only later do the rest of the disciples understand what has happened (13:27–29). As soon as Judas leaves the room, darkness descends (13:30; cf. Luke 22:53).

Jesus's Farewell Discourse (13:31–17:26)

A NEW COMMANDMENT (13:31–35)

Both Jesus and the Father will be glorified by what will soon happen (13:31–32). Meanwhile, Jesus prepares the disciples for his going away by giving them a new command: "Love one another . . . as I have loved you" (13:33–34). Although loving one another is not new, Jesus's own love for us becomes the model and standard of our love. Also, this love among believers will announce to all that we are followers of Jesus (13:35).

JESUS PREDICTS PETER'S DENIAL (13:36–38)

See Matthew 26:31–35; Mark 14:27–31; Luke 22:31–34. Peter doesn't hear the love command because he's thinking about Jesus's leaving. When Jesus tells Peter he can't follow him now, Peter boasts that he will lay down his life for Jesus (13:36–37). Jesus then predicts that before the rooster crows, Peter will disown him three times (13:38).

JESUS IS THE WAY TO THE FATHER (14:1–14)

It has been an emotional evening for the disciples, and Jesus urges them to stop being troubled. He calls for faith to replace their fears (14:1). Jesus is leaving to prepare a place for them and will return one day to bring them home (14:2–3). This could refer to Jesus's preparation of a heavenly home for his followers or to his sending of the Holy Spirit to live within his followers. Thomas objects that they don't know the way (14:5), and Jesus replies: "I am the way and the truth and the life" (14:6). All who come to the Father come through Jesus, and to know Jesus is to know the Father (14:6–7). As if he had heard nothing of what Jesus just said, Philip asks to see the Father (14:8). Jesus repeats again his close connection with the Father, reflected in both his inspired words and his miraculous signs (14:9–11). Jesus assures his disciples they will duplicate his works and do even greater works (14:12). This is possible because Jesus will ascend to the Father and send his Spirit, and because Jesus will answer prayers offered in line with his character and for the Father's glory (14:13–14).

OUR RELATIONSHIP TO JESUS—OBEDIENCE AND THE HOLY SPIRIT (14:15–26)

Jesus promises not to leave his followers as orphans (14:18). Because of his resurrection, the disciples too will be raised one day (14:19). The spiritual reality is that Jesus is in the Father, the disciples are in Jesus, and Jesus is in them (14:20). To make sure they experience this reality, Jesus promises the Holy Spirit ("another Helper" of the same kind as Jesus), who will be with them and in them forever (14:16–17, 26). The Spirit will indwell only followers of Jesus (14:17), and as the Spirit of truth, he will remind them of what Jesus taught (14:17, 26). If they love Jesus, they will obey his commands (14:15, 21, 23–24).

JESUS PROMISES HIS PEACE (14:27–31)

Jesus leaves his disciples with peace, an unwavering assurance that God is in control and that they are rightly related to the Father through the Son. The world cannot offer such peace. As a result, the disciples have no reason to despair or to let fear rule their lives (14:27). Jesus says again he is returning to the Father. His leaving is part of God's plan and does not signal a victory for Satan in any way (14:30–31). For this reason, the disciples' faith should actually grow stronger because of Jesus's departure (14:28–29).

A vineyard in Judah clarifies Jesus's analogy of the vine and the branches.

JESUS IS THE TRUE VINE (15:1–17)

Jesus offers an extended metaphor of the vine and the branches. Although Israel was often portrayed as the vine of God (e.g., Isa. 5:7), Jesus now presents himself as the true vine (15:1). In fact, Jesus consistently presents himself as the faithful replacement of

✦ Notice how selfless Jesus is on this final night, taking care of his followers by promising them the Holy Spirit, his peace, a future heavenly home, joy, and answers to their prayers.

the unfaithful nation (e.g., when he condemns the temple). The two categories of branches (alive or dead) correspond to the two types of people: believers or unbelievers. The dead, unfruitful branches are cut off (15:2, 6), while the living, fruitful branches are pruned so that they may bear even more fruit (15:2–5). Just as branches must remain in the vine in order to bear fruit, so disciples must stay vitally connected to Jesus by keeping his word (15:4–5, 9–10). Those who abide in Jesus will experience answered prayer and bear fruit to the glory of God (15:7–8). The basis for our relationship is Jesus's love, and the appropriate response is obedience, which in turn produces enormous joy (15:9–11). Again, Jesus commands us to love each other as he has loved us by laying down his life for us (15:12–13). Jesus's disciples are now trusted "friends" to whom he will reveal the Father (15:14–15). We have been chosen and appointed by Jesus to bear lasting fruit, as we call on the Father in prayer and love one another (15:16–17).

JESUS WARNS OF THE WORLD'S HATRED (15:18–16:4)

In John's Gospel the term "world" often refers to people who oppose God. Jesus warns his disciples the world will hate them because it first hated him (15:18–19). If disciples belonged to the world, the world would love them. But Jesus has chosen them out of the world, and they should expect to be treated like Jesus was treated (15:19–21). The world is guilty because Jesus entered the world and revealed the Father through his words and miracles

The Kidron Valley separates the Mount of Olives and the Temple Mount.

✚ As in the other Gospels, Jesus warns his followers that they will face persecution in this world.

(15:22, 24). But the world rejected both the Son and the Father, thus fulfilling the Scriptures (15:23–25; Pss. 35:19; 69:4). The disciples do not face the world's hostility alone. The Holy Spirit, the Counselor or Helper, will be with them and will testify alongside the disciples (15:26–27). To summarize, the disciples should expect to be persecuted by people who think they are serving God (16:2). (We are reminded here that at times the "world" includes religious opposition to Jesus.) Because the world does not truly know Jesus or the Father, they will persecute Jesus's followers (16:3). But Jesus has warned his followers about coming persecutions so that they can be prepared (16:1, 4).

THE WORK OF THE HOLY SPIRIT (16:5–15)

The disciples continue to grieve at the news of Jesus's departure (16:5–6). He comforts them with a reminder that his leaving means the Holy Spirit will come to them (16:7). The Spirit will continue Christ's work by convicting the world with regard to sin, righteousness, and judgment (16:8–11). The disciples can't absorb all Jesus wants to tell them now, but when the Spirit of truth comes, he will guide them into all truth (16:12–13). The Spirit will glorify Jesus by reminding the disciples of his teachings and preparing them for the future (16:13–15).

SORROW WILL TURN TO JOY (16:16–22)

The disciples are confused by Jesus's statement that "in a little while" they will not see him, and then "after a little while" they will see him again (16:16–19). He is referring to his upcoming crucifixion that will cause them to grieve deeply, followed by his resurrection, which will turn their grief to joy (16:19–20). Their experience can be compared to the anguish of labor pains followed by the joy of childbirth (16:21). Though they grieve now, later they will rejoice, and no one will take away their joy (16:22).

ASKING IN JESUS'S NAME (16:23–28)

After Jesus's ascension and the coming of the Spirit, the disciples will be able to ask the Father for anything in Jesus's name and receive their request (16:23–24). The qualifier "in Jesus's name" means anything that is in line with Jesus's character and for his glory. Their faith in Jesus, the One sent from the Father, gives them a direct relationship with the Father himself (16:25–28).

JESUS HAS OVERCOME THE WORLD (16:29–33)

The disciples now believe they understand everything clearly and even confess that Jesus has come from God (16:29–30). But Jesus knows their faith is fragile; in a matter of hours Peter will deny him, and the entire group will abandon him (16:31–32). He knows they will face trouble (or tribulation) in this world, but they should not lose heart. The cross and resurrection of Jesus will demonstrate he has overcome the world. For this reason, those who have a relationship with Jesus will be guarded by his peace (16:33).

THE LORD'S PRAYER (17:1–26)

In what is sometimes referred to as the "real" Lord's Prayer, Jesus prays for himself (17:1–5), for his original disciples (17:6–19), and for all future disciples (17:20–26). Since his hour has now arrived, Jesus asks the Father to glorify him so that he may glorify the Father (17:1). As Jesus obediently endures the cross and the Father raises him from the dead, the divine plan will be implemented and result in glory for both the Father and the Son. The Son has authority to give eternal life, defined here as a living, personal relationship with the only true God as revealed by Jesus Christ (17:2–3). Jesus has glorified the Father by completing his assigned work on earth. He now asks the Father to restore the glory he enjoyed before creation and prior to the humiliating incarnation (17:4–5; Phil. 2:5–11). Jesus now prays for his original disciples, who will become the foundation stones of the church (17:6–19). He has revealed the Father to them, and they have accepted this revelation (17:6–8, 10). Now Jesus prays for them because he is returning to the Father and they are remaining in the world (17:9, 11). He prays for their spiritual protection so that they may be unified. Such unity results in abundant joy (17:11–13). Next, he prays not for escape from the world but for protection from the evil one as they endure the world's hatred (17:14–16). Finally, he prays they would grow in holiness and truth in order that their mission in this world will succeed (17:17–19). You might be surprised to learn that Jesus also prays for you and me—all future disciples (17:20–26). He prays that we will be one, just as the Father and Son are one (17:20–21). This unity will provide a powerful witness to the world concerning God's saving plan (17:22–23). Jesus also prays that we will see his future glory, indicating that the story does not end until we join Jesus in the new heaven and new earth (17:24). In the meantime, we should hold on to Jesus, to his revelation of the Father, and to the Father's love for us (17:25–26). How amazing is it that we get to experience the very love the Father has for the Son? One aspect of Jesus's prayer is answered when we let God love us.

Jesus's arrest (18:1–12)

See Matthew 26:47–56; Mark 14:43–52; Luke 22:47–53. After the Farewell Discourse, Jesus leads his disciples across the Kidron Valley to an olive grove, named in the other Gospels as Gethsemane. When the arresting party arrives, Jesus boldly confronts them using the divine name: "I am"

✦ In his prayer for his followers, Jesus asks chiefly for spiritual protection and unity.

(18:5, 8). The group draws back and falls to the ground, much like people do throughout the Scriptures when they encounter God face-to-face (18:6; cf. Isa. 6:5; Ezek. 1:28; Acts 9:4; Rev. 1:17). Like the Good Shepherd that he is, Jesus repeatedly protects his disciples, fulfilling John 6:39 (18:4–5, 7–8). When Peter cuts off Malchus's ear, Jesus commands him to put away the sword. Jesus will drink the cup of suffering given him by the Father (18:10–11).

The Pontius Pilate inscription found in Caesarea in 1961 identifies him as "prefect of Judea."

Jesus before Annas, and Peter's denials (18:13–27)

See Matthew 26:57–75; Mark 14:53–72; Luke 22:54–71. After Jesus is arrested, they bring him to Annas, the father-in-law of Caiaphas, for a preliminary hearing (18:12–14). He asks Jesus about his disciples and his teachings, but little new information comes to light. Jesus says he has taught openly among the Jews, and the high priest can gather evidence from those who heard him teach. This response earns Jesus an unexpected blow to the face from a nearby official (18:22–23). Annas then sends Jesus to Caiaphas (18:24). In the meantime, Simon Peter and another disciple who was known to the high priest gain access to the courtyard of the house where Jesus is being interrogated (18:15–16). Twice Peter is asked if he is a disciple of Jesus, and once he is asked to admit he was with Jesus in the olive grove (18:17, 25, 26). All three times, Peter denies a connection to Jesus, and after the third time a rooster crows just as Jesus had predicted (18:27).

Jesus before Pilate (18:28–19:16)

See Matthew 27:1–2, 11–26; Mark 15:1–15; Luke 23:1–25. Jesus's trial before Pilate is filled with irony. To begin with, the Jews bring Jesus to Pilate to obtain an execution order, but they refuse to enter the Roman palace because it would make them ceremonially unclean and prevent them from eating the Passover (18:28). The Jewish leaders need Pilate (and Rome) to condemn Jesus to death (18:31–32). Pilate asks Jesus whether he is "the king of the Jews" (18:33). Jesus eventually admits to being a king but states plainly that his kingdom is not of this world (18:36–37). Everyone on the side of truth listens to Jesus, but Pilate's cynical question, "What is truth?" reveals his own heart (18:37–38). Pilate then declares no basis for charging Jesus with a crime and asks the Jews if he should release Jesus, the "king of the Jews" (18:38–39). They cry out for Barabbas instead, one who is actually guilty of leading a rebellion (18:40). Pilate has Jesus flogged and mockingly dressed as a king before presenting him again for a possible release (19:1–5). But the Jewish leaders show no sympathy and continue to demand that Jesus be crucified (19:6). The Jews insist that their law demands death for one who claims to be "the Son of God" (19:7), and the fun and games are over for Pilate, who is now afraid (19:7–8). He questions Jesus further under threat of force, but Jesus responds, "You would have no power over me if it were not given to you from above. Therefore the one who handed me over to you is guilty of a greater sin" (19:11). Pilate now tries to free Jesus, but the cause has gathered too much momentum. With the utmost irony, the Jewish leaders (who claim to follow only God as king) make two statements that drive Pilate to have Jesus crucified:

> 19:12—"From then on, Pilate tried to set Jesus free, but the Jews kept shouting, 'If you let this man go, you are no friend of Caesar. Anyone who claims to be a king opposes Caesar.'"
>
> 19:15—"But they shouted, 'Take him away! Take him away! Crucify him!' 'Shall I crucify your king?' Pilate asked. 'We have no king but Caesar,' the chief priests answered."

✦ Jesus repeatedly demonstrates that he is in control of his destiny and submits willingly to the coming death on the cross (e.g., John 18:4–9, 36; 19:11).

The crucifixion and death of Jesus (19:17–30)

See Matthew 27:31–56; Mark 15:20–41; Luke 23:26–49. Jesus carries his cross at least part of the way to the place of the Skull (Golgotha), where he is crucified (19:16–18). Much to the dismay of the Jewish leaders, Pilate places a notice on the cross that reads, "Jesus of Nazareth, the King of the Jews" (19:19–22). Psalm 22:18 is fulfilled when the soldiers divide his clothes into four shares and cast lots for the seamless undergarment (19:23–24). When Jesus sees his mother standing nearby, he speaks the third word from the cross, entrusting his mother to John's care (19:25–27). Not even the cross causes him to neglect the practical obligations of love.

Shortly before his death, Jesus utters the fifth word from the cross: "I am thirsty," thus fulfilling Scripture (19:28; Pss. 22:14–15; 69:21). He accepts the wine vinegar from the soldiers and speaks the sixth word from the cross, "It is finished" (19:30; Ps. 22:31). In three short words, Jesus declares that his redemptive work is now complete and will forever stand complete! He then bows his head and gives up his spirit (19:30). He dies on a tree, bearing the curse of God's wrath for the sins of the world (Deut. 21:23; Gal. 3:13).

Jesus is pierced and buried (19:31–42)

See Matthew 27:57–66; Mark 15:42–47; Luke 23:50–56. Because the next day (Saturday) would be a special Sabbath, the Jews don't want bodies left on the crosses. They ask Pilate to have the victims' legs broken to quicken death. When they come to Jesus, he is already dead so they don't break his legs (19:31–33, 36; Exod. 12:46; Num. 9:12; Ps. 34:20). But one of the soldiers does thrust his spear into Jesus's side, causing blood and water to flow out (19:34). This act confirms the certainty of Jesus's death and again fulfills Scripture (19:36–37; Zech. 12:10). The disciple whom Jesus loved (John) is the one who personally witnessed this event and offers this true testimony so that many may believe in Jesus (19:35). Joseph of Arimathea, accompanied by Nicodemus, takes Jesus's body and prepares it for burial (19:38–40). They place the body in a new garden tomb near the place where he was crucified (19:41–42). Jesus has died. Jesus has been buried. Jesus will rise again.

The Church of the Holy Sepulchre, Jerusalem, the traditional site of Jesus's death.

✚ Three of Jesus's seven last words from the cross are recorded in John (see article on p. 639).

Two kokhim from a first-century tomb inside the Church of the Holy Sepulchre.

The resurrected Son appears to his disciples (20:1–29)

See Matthew 28:1–10; Mark 16:1–8; Luke 24:1–12, 36–43. All the Gospels record that the first witnesses to Jesus's resurrection were women. In John 20:1–2, Mary Magdalene, likely accompanied by other women, discovers that the tomb is empty and runs to tell Peter and the disciple whom Jesus loved. In John 20:3–9, we learn that Peter and John immediately run to the tomb. John arrives first but only looks in, while Peter barges right into the tomb upon arrival. They discover grave clothes but no body. At this point John "saw and believed," although the disciples still did not fully understand that Jesus had to rise from the dead (20:8–9). In John 20:10–18, we read about Jesus's appearance to Mary Magdalene. Mary mourns deeply (twice she is asked, "Woman, why are you crying?"), and when she encounters the two angels and the one she believes to be the gardener, she pleads for more information about where they have put the body. When Jesus ("the gardener") calls her by name, she immediately recognizes him. She cries out to him, "Teacher," and grabs hold of him. Jesus tells her to let him go so that he can ascend to "my Father and your Father, to my God and your God" (20:17). Mary returns to the disciples with the amazing news, "I have seen the Lord" (20:18). In 20:19–23, Jesus appears to the disciples (minus Thomas), who are hiding in fear, and greets them with his peace. He shows them his hands and side, and the disciples are overjoyed to see their risen Lord. Next, Jesus commissions them and breathes on them the Holy Spirit, likely a temporary provision until Pentecost. Part of their mission will include pronouncing forgiveness or judgment, depending on the response of those who hear the message about Jesus. In John 20:24–29, Jesus appears again to the disciples a week later, and this time Thomas is present. When Jesus appears, he again greets them with peace before turning to Thomas with the invitation to touch his hands and side, something Thomas had insisted that he must do before he would believe that Jesus had risen from the dead. Jesus urges Thomas to "stop doubting and believe," and Thomas doesn't even need to touch him in order to believe; he confesses Jesus as "my Lord and my God." Jesus then pronounces a blessing on those who believe without seeing the resurrected Lord in person.

✝ In a manner similar to Acts 1–2, John records Jesus commissioning his disciples and empowering them with the Holy Spirit.

The purpose of John's Gospel (20:30–31)

John's Gospel has presented some, but not all, of Jesus's miraculous signs. If John had tried to record everything, "the whole world would not have room for the books that would be written" (21:25). But John wrote his Gospel so people might believe in Jesus as the Messiah and Son of God and, as a result, experience life in his name (20:31). Thus, John has in mind not just the initial belief or conversion but the whole experience of the life that comes from a relationship with Jesus.

Epilogue (21:1–25)

This final section of John ties up loose ends related to the main characters of the story and describes the upcoming mission of the church in a symbolic fashion. First, in 21:1–14 we read about Jesus appearing a third time to his disciples and miraculously enabling them to catch a large number of fish. At first they don't recognize this stranger on the shore who tells them to put down their nets on the right side of the boat (21:4–6). After their nets are filled with fish, however, John recognizes the man as "the Lord," and Peter immediately puts on his clothes and swims to shore (21:6–8). Many have speculated about the significance of the 153 fish without much success, but the larger point is that the net is full, just as the mission of the church will be full or successful. Also, when Jesus gives his disciples the bread and fish (21:13), this echoes his miraculous feeding of the multitudes (John 6). The same symbolism of the church's mission comes through in the next section when Jesus commands Peter to feed his sheep (21:15–23). The "charcoal fire" (*anthrakia*) is only mentioned in John in 18:18 (in the courtyard of the high priest where Peter denies Christ) and in 21:9 (the beach where Jesus will restore Peter). Isn't it just like Jesus to consider the sights and smells of denial when creating the setting for restoration? The chart below captures the conversation between Jesus and Peter.

	Three Questions from Jesus	Three Answers from Peter	Three Commands from Jesus
21:15 →	"Simon son of John, do you truly love [*agape*] me more than these?"	"Yes, Lord," he said, "you know that I love [*phileo*] you."	"Feed my lambs."
21:16 →	"Simon son of John, do you truly love [*agape*] me?"	"Yes, Lord, you know that I love [*phileo*] you."	"Take care of my sheep."
21:17 →	"Simon son of John, do you love [*phileo*] me?"	"Lord, you know all things; you know that I love [*phileo*] you."	"Feed my sheep."

Pilgrims walk the Via Dolorosa (the way of suffering) in Jerusalem, the traditional path Jesus took to the place of crucifixion.

Some have suggested that *agape* refers to God's kind of love, while *phileo* refers to human love, but this distinction doesn't hold true in the New Testament. In this context, both verbs are used interchangeably to simply mean "love." For stylistic reasons, John also uses different words for "know," "feed/take care," and "lambs/sheep." What is truly significant is the number three. Three times Peter stood by a fire and denied his Lord. Now he stands by a fire again, and three times affirms his love for Jesus. Restoration replaces failure. Grace is powerful! Jesus now gives Peter an important job to do—to lead and care for God's people. Ironically, Peter initially boasted that he was willing to die for Jesus, and now Jesus predicts that Peter will in fact die a martyr's death (21:18–19). Finally, Jesus redirects Peter's focus to the present: "Follow me!" (21:19). Peter wants to know what will happen to the disciple whom Jesus loves, but Jesus warns Peter not to compare (21:20–23). Comparison between disciples can be spiritually deadly! Jesus reminds Peter again of his priority—"You must follow me" (21:22). The testimony of this Gospel comes from the disciple whom Jesus loves (John), and the believing community knows that his testimony is true! (21:24).

So What? Applying John's Gospel Today

The first thing we notice about the Gospel of John is how it presents its message: profound theology in simple language. John's pattern of deep substance in plain words challenges us to avoid both overly technical Christian

✦ Although Peter had failed Jesus miserably, he has now been restored and will soon be used by God in a powerful way (see Acts 2–4).

terminology and superficial, religious foolishness when communicating the story of Jesus.

In addition, this Gospel calls for a correct understanding of Jesus Christ. To believe in Jesus means first and foremost to believe in Jesus as he has been revealed by the Scriptures. Since the day sin entered this world, human beings have been trying to remake God in our image. John's Gospel offers us a balanced, comprehensive portrait of Jesus. He is fully divine and one with the Father, while at the same time being fully human (1:1–18). Jesus entered this world to reveal the Father. When we begin to lose sight of who God is and what he is like, we need to look afresh at Jesus as revealed in the Gospels. Jesus is not merely one of the world's great religious leaders; he is God incarnate.

The Gospel of John was written so that people might believe in Jesus and experience eternal life. In John 17:3, eternal life is defined as knowing God relationally through Jesus Christ. This helps us understand that believing in Jesus is much more than intellectual assent. True belief includes whole-hearted discipleship.

In John, there is a strong contrast between good and evil, light and darkness, the disciples and the world, truth and falsehood, believing in the Son and rejecting the Son, and so on. John's "either-or" Gospel cuts against the grain of our pluralistic, politically correct culture and reminds us that following Jesus sometimes calls for taking a clear and courageous stand.

There is a lot of talk of "glory" these days in Christian circles, and these discussions would be helped by a careful reading of John's Gospel. In John, glory is repeatedly connected with Jesus's crucifixion, resurrection, and ascension. The glory of Christ is not just his willingness to receive praise from dutiful disciples, but can be seen most clearly in his willingness to humble himself by dying on the cross. From a biblical perspective, glory is not just about God reigning in power over all, but about God descending to the depths of human sin and suffering in order to bring life.

Our Favorite Verses in John

For God so loved the world that he gave his one and only Son, that whoever believes in him shall not perish but have eternal life. For God did not send his Son into the world to condemn the world, but to save the world through him. (John 3:16–17)

The Book of Acts
and Letters of Paul

The "Acts of the Apostles," or more accurately, the "Acts of the Holy Spirit through the Apostles and other Christians," tells the story of the birth and growth of the early church from about AD 30 to the early 60s. While we have four accounts of the life of Jesus in Matthew, Mark, Luke, and John, we have only one account of the life of the early church (although we do have New Testament letters that also provide a great deal of information about the early church). Luke, the gentile co-worker of the apostle Paul, wrote both Luke and Acts as a single work in two volumes (see Luke 1:1–4; Acts 1:1–2). Jesus now continues (through his Spirit and the church) the work he began during his earthly ministry. Acts 1:8 summarizes how the entire book is organized: "But you will receive power when the Holy Spirit comes on you; and you will be my witnesses in Jerusalem, and in all Judea and Samaria, and to the ends of the earth." In the Gospel of Luke, Jesus journeys to Jerusalem for the cross and resurrection, while in the book of Acts, the church moves out from Jerusalem to take the gospel of Jesus's death and resurrection to the nations. The central character in the first half of Acts (1–12) is Simon Peter, whereas Paul takes center stage in the second half of the book (13–28). Throughout Acts, the gospel marches triumphantly from Jerusalem, the holy city and birthplace of Christianity, to Rome, the epicenter of the Roman Empire.

Most of Paul's thirteen letters can be integrated with some confidence into the chronology of the book of Acts. His "early" letters include Galatians and 1–2 Thessalonians. His "major" letters include Romans and 1–2 Corinthians. The "prison" letters include Ephesians, Philippians, Colossians, and Philemon, while the "pastoral" letters include 1–2 Timothy and Titus. The arrangement in the English Bible is not chronological, but based on the book's length.

An Overview of Paul's Life and Letters

Event Date	Letter Date	Event	Acts Ref.	Letter (Location)
30/33		Jesus's death and resurrection	1:3–11	
31–34		Paul's conversion	9:1–30; 22:3–21; 26:2–23	
46–47		Barnabas and Paul take famine relief to Jerusalem	11:30	
47–49		First missionary journey	13–14	
	49			Galatians (Antioch)?
49		Jerusalem Council	15	
50–52		Second missionary journey	15:36–18:22	
	51–52			1–2 Thessalonians (Corinth)
53–57		Third missionary journey	18:23–21:16	
	53			Galatians (Ephesus)?
	54			1 Corinthians (Ephesus)
	56			2 Corinthians (Macedonia)
	57			Romans (Corinth)
57–59		Arrest in Jerusalem	21:26–33	
		Two-year imprisonment in Caesarea	24–26	
59		Journey to Rome	27:1–28:14	
60–62		Two-year house arrest in Rome	28:30	
	60–62			Prison Letters: Philemon, Colossians, Ephesians, Philippians

Event Date	Letter Date	Event	Acts Ref.	Letter (Location)
63		Release from prison and further missionary work?		
	63–67			Pastoral Letters: 1 Timothy, Titus, 2 Timothy
64–67		Second Roman imprisonment followed by martyrdom		

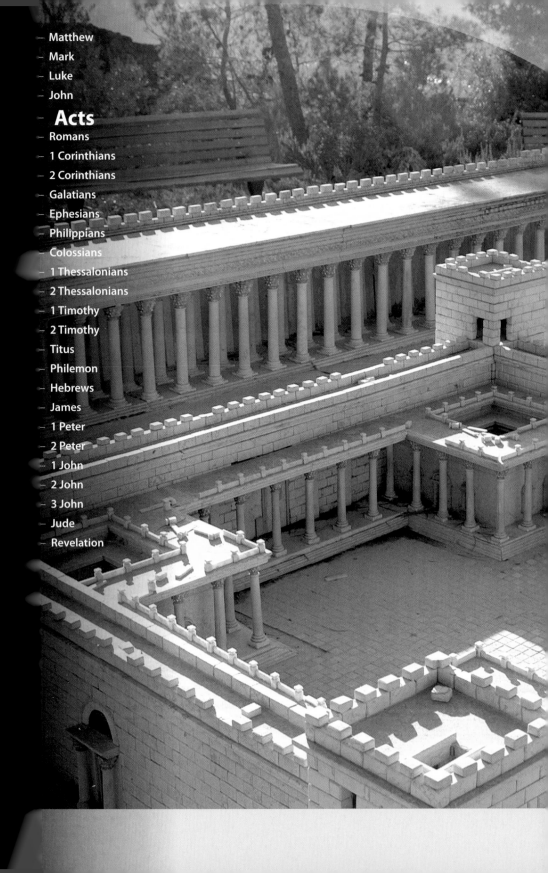

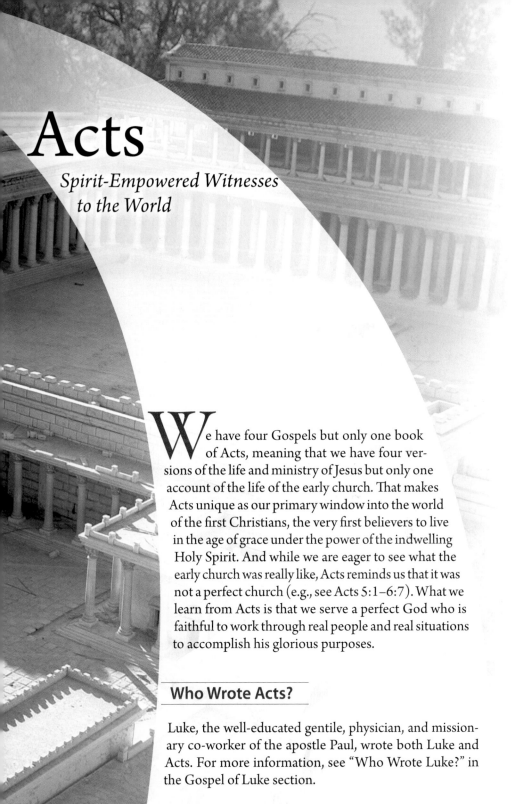

Acts

*Spirit-Empowered Witnesses
to the World*

We have four Gospels but only one book of Acts, meaning that we have four versions of the life and ministry of Jesus but only one account of the life of the early church. That makes Acts unique as our primary window into the world of the first Christians, the very first believers to live in the age of grace under the power of the indwelling Holy Spirit. And while we are eager to see what the early church was really like, Acts reminds us that it was not a perfect church (e.g., see Acts 5:1–6:7). What we learn from Acts is that we serve a perfect God who is faithful to work through real people and real situations to accomplish his glorious purposes.

Who Wrote Acts?

Luke, the well-educated gentile, physician, and missionary co-worker of the apostle Paul, wrote both Luke and Acts. For more information, see "Who Wrote Luke?" in the Gospel of Luke section.

Who Is Luke's Audience?

Both Luke and Acts are addressed to the same recipient: "most excellent Theophilus," a recent convert who needed to be instructed and encouraged in his faith (Luke 1:3; Acts 1:1). See "Who Is Luke's Audience?" in the Gospel of Luke section for more details. The book of Acts was also intended for Christian communities in the first century and for the entire church.

Regarding the dating of Acts, most scholars date the book between AD 70 and 90. Traditionally, evangelicals have dated the book to about AD 62–64, concluding that Luke finished the book while Paul was still in prison awaiting the outcome of his appeal to Caesar. Whenever it was written, the abrupt ending of the book reflects Luke's literary purpose of showing Paul's arrival in Rome.

What Is at the Heart of Acts?

Luke's purpose in Acts coincides with his purpose in the Gospel of Luke. In this two-volume work, he explains how God has continued to work out his redemptive purposes through the church. What Jesus started, the Spirit continues through his people (Acts 1:1–2). More specifically, Luke provides in Acts a "theological history" of the early church. Luke has assured his readers he has a keen interest in writing a carefully investigated, orderly history (Luke 1:1–4). Yet anyone who writes history must select events and experiences to include and others to exclude because of space restrictions. Luke's account is accurate, but selective. For example, Luke doesn't dedicate as much space to telling us about Paul's eighteen-month stay in Corinth (Acts 18:1–18) as he does to reporting Paul's much shorter stay in Philippi (probably several months; see Acts 16:12–40) or Athens (probably several weeks; see Acts 17:16–34). Luke makes these decisions based on his purpose of presenting an accurate account of what God is doing through the early church. Luke gives his readers typical or representative experiences that serve to advance God's purpose. For this reason, we can say Luke is writing "theological history"—an accurate record of events and words that demonstrates what God has been doing in and through his people. Here is how Acts unfolds:

- Preparation for Pentecost (1:1–26)
- Pentecost: The Coming of the Holy Spirit (2:1–47)
- The Holy Spirit Works through the Apostles (3:1–4:37)

✚ Luke presents not only reliable history but also profound theology in the book of Acts.

What Makes Acts Interesting and Unique?

- Acts is the second volume of a two-volume work: Luke–Acts.
- Acts describes the first Christian generation—the period between Jesus's crucifixion (about AD 30) and the end of Paul's ministry (mid-AD 60s).

✚ The first half of Acts features Peter as the primary
character, while the second half features Paul.

- The two main human characters in Acts are Peter (Acts 1–12) and Paul (Acts 13–28). Peter ministers mostly in a Jewish setting, while Paul ministers predominantly in a gentile setting.
- The "speeches" of Peter, Paul, and others make up nearly one-third of the book. Most of the time Luke provides an accurate summary of what was said rather than a full transcript (e.g., Peter's speech in the temple square began at about 3:00 p.m. and lasted until sundown, but Luke describes Peter's sermon in only seventeen verses; see Acts 3:1; 4:3).
- Luke wrote approximately 28 percent of the New Testament.
- Acts 1:8 describes a geographical expansion of the gospel that helps us understand the entire book: Jerusalem and Judea (Acts 1–7), out from Jerusalem (8–12), and to the ends of the earth (13–28).
- Luke includes six progress reports throughout Acts that move the story along: 6:7; 9:31; 12:24; 16:5; 19:20; 28:31.

Christians visit the upper floor of the Jerusalem Crusader Church of Saint Mary's to remember the location and events of Pentecost (Acts 2:1–2).

Pentecost

Preben Vang

Luke wrote the book of Acts to show that the church continued the ministry of Jesus. The enabling power for such ministry was granted to every follower of Christ through the outpouring of the Holy Spirit at Pentecost (Acts 2:1–4). The work of the early Christians went far beyond a mere conviction of the mind and the retelling of former experiences with their rabbi (Jesus). Rather than beginning their ministry immediately after Jesus's ascension, the disciples waited for God's Spirit to enable them to speak God's words and do God's deeds. Empowered by the Spirit, they would now, like Jesus, proclaim the presence of God's kingdom, demonstrate its presence through miracles, and fulfill Israel's original charge (Isa. 42:6) to bring people of all races and nations into a new relationship with God.

Pentecost fulfilled Old Testament prophetic promises that God would make a new covenant of the Spirit. In this new covenant, God would write his law on human hearts and guide them by his Spirit—in effect turning everyone into a prophet (Jer. 31:31; Ezek. 36:24; Joel 2:28–32). Pentecost, then, was the event that instituted the church Jesus had constituted earlier.

To the Jews, Pentecost was a yearly celebration connected with both the harvest and the covenant. As a harvest celebration, it was a thanksgiving banquet celebrating God's providence. As a covenant celebration, it was a celebration of the giving of the law at Sinai. Pentecost's origin in the Exodus account (Exod. 23:16) gave the event of Acts 2 an immediate context of presence, provision, and historical purpose (Deut. 16:9–12). God's people had come to Jerusalem from far away to celebrate their deliverance from captivity and God's dwelling among them (Deut. 16:11). That the traditional Jewish celebration of Pentecost became the event where God chose to pour out his Spirit afresh speaks volumes to its meaning. The fresh outpouring of God's Spirit upon the disciples was not an extraordinary phenomenon happening to a few people in a corner of Jerusalem, but evidence that God was making a new covenant in which his presence would be directly available to all who would trust what he had done through his Son, Jesus Christ.

Acts 2 describes how a group of 120 disciples were assembled in a house ten days after Jesus's ascension when suddenly they heard a sound as of a mighty wind—a sound that reminded them of Old Testament theophanies (1 Kings 19:11–12; 2 Kings 2:11) and of the law-giving at Sinai (Exod. 19:16–19). The new Pentecost event turned the frightened and hiding Jesus followers into bold evangelists who spoke fearlessly to large crowds in the streets of Jerusalem. More than three thousand people became believers after the first sermon by the apostle Peter.

What Is the Message of Acts?

Preparation for Pentecost (1:1–26)

Many of the important themes of the entire book are introduced in the very first chapter (e.g., mission of the church, power of the Holy Spirit, importance of prayer). Luke notes that his first volume records "all that Jesus began to do and to teach until the day he was taken up to heaven" (1:1–2). The implication, therefore, is that Acts records what Jesus continued to do

✛ God's promise to pour out his Spirit on his people is fulfilled at Pentecost (see Isa. 44:3; Jer. 31:31–34; Ezek. 36:24–27; Joel 2:28–29).

The Holy Spirit in the New Testament

Craig S. Keener

John the Baptist prophesied that the mighty one would baptize in the Holy Spirit and fire (Matt. 3:11; Luke 3:16). Because only God could pour out his own Spirit, John probably recognized the coming one as divine; he would baptize the wicked with fire (cf. Matt. 3:10, 12; Luke 3:9, 17) but the repentant, by contrast, with the Holy Spirit. This baptism probably encompassed the entire sphere of the Spirit's work (including salvation and empowerment). The Old Testament (and some Jewish groups like the Essenes) sometimes associated the Spirit with spiritual purification (Ezek. 36:25–27); most often the Old Testament and Judaism associated the Spirit with power like the biblical prophets had.

Not only John, but Scripture had also prophesied that the Spirit would be poured out in the time of God's people's promised restoration (Isa. 44:3; 59:21; Ezek. 36:24–28; 37:14; 39:29; Joel 2:28–29). Because of this, Jesus could speak of the kingdom active through his works by the Spirit (Matt. 12:28; cf. Luke 11:20). Likewise, Paul could envision the

Spirit as the "down payment" (2 Cor. 1:22; 5:5; Eph. 1:13–14), "first fruits" (Rom. 8:23), or foretaste of Christians' future (1 Cor. 2:9–10; cf. also Heb. 6:4–5).

Paul shows that everything in believers' lives depends on the Spirit. The Spirit produces in believers the fruit of God's own character, in contrast to merely human righteousness (Gal. 5:16–25; Rom. 8:2–17). Likewise, every believer is invited to minister to others by ministries or grace-"gifts" energized by the Spirit (1 Cor. 12:1–31; cf. Eph. 4:11–13). All God's gifts are, by definition, good; different believers are given different gifts for serving others (although in 1 Cor. 12:31 and 14:1 believers can apparently also seek some gifts to edify others).

Luke tends to emphasize the prophetic empowerment dimension of the Spirit (Acts 2:17–18). Although Luke surely agrees with other New Testament writers that the Spirit is involved in conversion (cf. Luke 3:16; Acts 2:38–39), he emphasizes especially the Spirit's inspiring power for witness (Acts 1:8).

and to teach through his Spirit after his ascension. Following his crucifixion and resurrection, the risen Jesus appears to his apostles over a period of forty days, speaking about the kingdom and instructing them not to leave Jerusalem until they receive "the gift my Father promised . . . the Holy Spirit" (1:2–5). In one of those postresurrection gatherings, they ask Jesus, "Lord, are you at this time going to restore the kingdom to Israel?" (1:6). Their responsibility, he tells them, is not to speculate about "times or dates" (1:7). They should focus on receiving power from the Spirit and serving as Jesus's witnesses, first in Jerusalem and then outward to the rest of the world (1:8). In 1:9–11, Luke records Jesus's ascension to heaven, which also implies his exaltation to God's right hand (Eph. 1:20–21; Phil. 2:9; Heb. 1:3; 2:9). The apostles, the women, and Jesus's mother and brothers gather regularly in the upper room in Jerusalem for prayer (1:12–14). (The resurrection had apparently convinced Jesus's brothers that he was the Messiah.) In 1:15–26, Luke reports on the replacement of Judas Iscariot. The vacancy among the Twelve

✦ Power precedes witness in God's plan.

Whereas other writers articulate principles about the Spirit, only Acts depicts the experience of the church. Here Luke shows that, though in principle believers receive the Spirit at conversion and might experience the empowerment dimension at conversion (10:44–45), sometimes they experienced this dimension afterward (8:14–17), and could do so on multiple occasions (4:8, 31; 13:9). Luke might choose to record incidents of prayer in other tongues at three of the initial receptions of the Spirit (2:4; 10:45–46; 19:6) because of his book's emphasis (Acts 1:8): this gift serves as a potent symbol that the Spirit has empowered the larger church to speak for God across cultural barriers.

John's Gospel sometimes associates the Spirit with the water of life (cf. John 7:37–39). In so doing, it reveals Jesus's gift as greater than Jewish water rituals such as John's baptism (John 1:31–33), ritual purity (2:6), proselyte baptism (3:5), the Samaritans' well (4:12–14), a supposed healing shrine (5:6–8), and so forth. Based on Zechariah 14 and Ezekiel 47, Jewish people expected rivers of living water from Jerusalem's temple at the time of the end; Jesus, the foundation stone of a spiritual temple, claims to be the true giver of such water in John 7:37–39.

Jesus's farewell discourse announces that the Spirit will come as a *parakletos* (John 14:16, 26; 15:26; 16:7), variously translated "helper," "intercessor," "counselor," and "advocate." The Spirit, coming to dwell in believers after Jesus's resurrection (20:22), will ensure that believers are continually in God's presence, as his dwelling place (14:16–17, 23). Thus even after Jesus's ascension, the Spirit would continue to reveal Jesus and make him present (16:13–15 with 15:15). Nevertheless, his revelation would always maintain continuity with the real, historical Jesus (14:26; 16:14–15; 1 John 4:2–3). He would also continue Jesus's ministry to the world, perhaps through believers' witness (John 15:26–27; 16:7–11).

John's description of the *parakletos* in John 14–16, as well as some trinitarian passages (most obviously Matt. 28:19), show that the Spirit is also a person, like the Father and the Son. The primary focus in the New Testament, though, is on what the Spirit does: revealing the Son, transforming believers into his likeness, and empowering believers to experience Christ and share his eschatological life and kingdom ministry with others.

was created by Judas's wicked decision and his subsequent suicide (1:15–20). Judas's betrayal of Jesus must have been especially painful to the other apostles since he had shared in their ministry. So the Scripture would be fulfilled (Pss. 69:25; 109:8), Peter leads the group to find Judas's replacement (1:21–26). They propose two men who are equally qualified. After prayer, they cast lots and the lot falls to Matthias, who is then added to the eleven. While on the surface the decision-making process seems to rely on chance, the church had prayed and narrowed the list to two equally qualified candidates before seeking God's sovereign direction (note their prayer in 1:24).

The Tower of Ascension on the Mount of Olives.

✛ In Isaiah 49:16 the Servant of the Lord is commissioned to be a "light for the Gentiles, that you may bring my salvation to the ends of the earth." Now Jesus commissions his disciples to take the gospel to the ends of the earth (Acts 1:8).

Pentecost: The Coming of the Holy Spirit (2:1–47)

After all the disciples' praying and waiting, the promised Holy Spirit finally arrives in a mighty way (2:1–13). The Jewish pilgrimage festival of Pentecost (also called the Feast of Weeks or Firstfruits) was observed fifty days after the Passover to celebrate the grain harvest. The 120 believers were together in one place when the miracle of Pentecost occured (2:1).

This event represents a major step in God's redemptive program, a time when the Holy Spirit would live permanently in individual believers. There is a sound like a violent wind coming from heaven and filling the house (2:2), tongues of fire rest on each person (2:3), and all are filled with the Holy Spirit and speak in other languages (2:4). This powerful outpouring of God's personal presence attracts God-fearing Jews from many nations who hear the Spirit-filled Galileans speaking in their native language (2:5–11). Amazed and perplexed, they wonder what it all means, but some of the crowd mock the believers as drunkards (2:13).

In 2:14–41, Peter explains from the Scriptures what has just happened. These believers aren't drunk since it is only nine in the morning. Rather, what Joel predicted has come to pass (2:14–21; Joel 2:28–32). The last days have arrived, and God has poured out his Spirit on all believers. Peter then uses more Scripture to demonstrate that Jesus is the Messiah. He first speaks about Jesus's death and resurrection (2:22–28; Ps. 16:8–11) before describing his exaltation (2:29–35; Ps. 110:1). His conclusion is that "God has made this

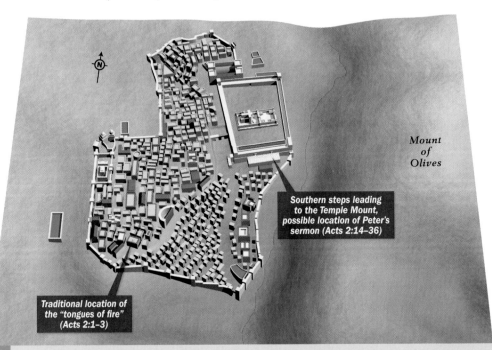

Mount of Olives

Southern steps leading to the Temple Mount, possible location of Peter's sermon (Acts 2:14–36)

Traditional location of the "tongues of fire" (Acts 2:1–3)

✦ In the Old Testament the Spirit of God came on select individuals to empower them for specific tasks. Now, at Pentecost, the Spirit comes on all believers to equip them to carry out the mission of the church.

Luke's Use of *Koinonia*

Scott Jackson

In Acts 2:42, Luke uses the word *koinonia* as one of his key terms for describing the vitality of life in the early church. Considering that Luke wrote almost one-third of the New Testament, it is significant that the word *koinonia* appears only here in his writings. It seems that Luke carefully and strategically chose this word to assist his readers in understanding what had taken place in the Jerusalem church. So, what exactly happened and what did Luke mean by the term?

The immediate context of the early chapters of Acts helps one to answer these questions (Acts 2:42–47). The context reveals that the early believers were participating together in worship activities such as listening to the apostles' teaching, partaking of the Lord's Supper, praying regularly, and experiencing praiseful worship. Additionally, they were sharing their possessions with each other, which included selling land and giving the money to the apostles to distribute to those in need, extending hospitality by hosting people in their homes, and sharing food through common meals. These common participations resulted in the early church experiencing miracles, salvation, and unity. All these events and experiences seem to be illustrating Luke's *koinonia*.

Also, *koinonia* was a familiar word in Greco-Roman society. It was a word often used in religious, familial, and social contexts. It was a word that Greco-Roman writers used to reflect some of their society's highest ideals of intimacy, sharing, interconnectedness, friendship, and unity. Thus Luke appears to borrow this word from Greco-Roman culture and society in order to explain and illustrate the special relationships that had developed within the early church—relationships that actually achieved the highest ideals of the Greco-Romans.

The word *koinonia* comes from the Greek root word *koinos*, which means "common." Based on this root and that Luke illustrates his *koinonia* by describing very specific common participations modeled by the early church, it seems best to define his *koinonia* as "participating together in life led by the Spirit" (i.e., sharing in the Spirit's common life). Based on the testimony of the early church, this life promotes ethnic and social equality. It is a life that is abundant, miraculous, hopeful, and joyful. It is a life among friends in the family of God. It is a life in which people overcome hardships together. It is a life of faith. It is the best life possible. It is life in the Spirit. May God's church today continue to seek, embrace, and experience this life of *koinonia*.

Jesus, whom you crucified, both Lord and Christ" (2:36). The listeners are "cut to the heart" and ask how they should respond (2:37). Peter calls them to repentance and public confession of faith through baptism, at which point they will receive the gift of the promised Holy Spirit (2:38–39). Amazingly, about three thousand people become followers of Jesus (2:40–41).

Luke paints a portrait of the community life of the church in 2:42–47. The new believers devote themselves to four practices: apostolic teaching, fellowship or sharing, observing the Lord's Supper (likely as a part of a community meal), and prayer (2:42). The community also experiences a sense of awe at what God is doing, shares their possessions with those

✚ Throughout Acts, the apostles "witness" to the crucifixion and resurrection of Jesus (see Acts 1:22; 2:32; 3:15; 5:32; 10:39, 41; 13:31; 22:15).

The House Church

Scott Jackson

After Jesus's ascension to heaven, the believers followed his instructions and went back to Jerusalem and waited for the promised gift of the Holy Spirit (Acts 1:4). In Jerusalem, they stayed in a house with a large upper room and joined together constantly in prayer (Acts 1:12–14). This passage foreshadows the significant role that houses would play in the life and mission of the early church.

Shortly after this prayer gathering, the promised Spirit came upon the believers, who again were all together in a house (Acts 2:1). The outcome of this event was the bold witness of the disciples throughout Jerusalem. This bold witness produced a great spiritual harvest with over three thousand people being saved in one day, while new believers continued to be added to the church each additional day (Acts 2:47).

How would the church take care of these new believers? How would they teach them? Where would they meet for their worship and prayer gatherings? How would they identify and meet one another's needs? These questions must have been at the forefront of issues for the apostles after the birth of Christ's church. And according to Acts, the answer to these questions was not to build large church buildings. (This did not occur until the fourth century when Constantine began erecting Christian basilicas.) Rather, it was to break the large group of believers into smaller groups. In addition to meeting in the temple courts, they regularly met in homes for teaching, prayer, worship, caregiving, meals, and the Lord's Supper (Acts 2:46). Thus coinciding with the birth of the church was the birth of the house church.

It is presumed that most of these churches consisted of large homes owned by upper-class Christians (archaeologists have discovered first-century homes of the wealthy in Jerusalem that could hold over one hundred people). Examples of these home owners include John Mark's mother, Mary (Acts 12:12), Lydia (Acts 16:15), Nympha (Col. 4:15), Philemon (Philem. 2), and Priscilla and Aquila (Rom. 16:3–5; 1 Cor. 16:19). In the first century, home ownership was a clear sign of wealth, and the early church utilized these wealthy believers as benefactors who would open their homes as Christian gathering places and undoubtedly provide ample hospitality of food and other material care. It is also noteworthy that many of these house-church hosts were women.

These house churches were ideal for the early church. They met a practical need of providing a gathering place that was relatively inconspicuous during a time when persecution was a constant threat. They could easily be multiplied as the church grew. They enabled the church to serve common meals and the Lord's Supper, two important aspects of early Christian worship. And ultimately, the house church provided a great context for discipleship, intimacy, and for experiencing Christian *koinonia*.

in need, spends time together in corporate worship, and welcomes more converts (2:43–47).

The Holy Spirit Works through the Apostles (3:1–4:37)

Empowered by the Spirit, the church begins to witness in Jerusalem. As Jewish Christians, these first believers continue to go to the temple for prayer. On one occasion, Peter and John encounter a crippled beggar at the Beautiful

Gate (3:1–4). To the man's request for money, Peter responds, "Silver or gold I do not have, but what I have I give you. In the name of Jesus Christ of Nazareth, walk" (3:6). The man is healed instantly and begins walking and jumping and praising God in the temple courts (3:7–8). The people respond in wonder and amazement (3:9–10).

As the crowd gathers in Solomon's Colonnade, Peter preaches a second sermon (3:11–26). Peter first makes a connection between the beggar's healing and the Christian message of Jesus crucified and resurrected (3:12–16). The apostles are quick to defer to Jesus's power as the source of the healing, rather than their own character or abilities (3:12, 16).

Because Jesus is the source of the healing, Peter uses the Scriptures to challenge the Jewish crowd to repent and accept Jesus as God's Messiah, the one Abraham and Moses predicted (3:17–26).

The man's healing and the apostles' message prompt the priests and the temple guard to arrest Peter and John for interrogation before the Jewish Sanhedrin (4:1–22). Theologically, they are disturbed that the apostles are proclaiming in Jesus the resurrection of the dead, a doctrine the Sadducees denied (4:1–2). Politically, they are deeply concerned that the man's healing is pointing many people to faith in Jesus (4:4, 9, 16–17, 21–22). Peter boldly proclaims that the crucified and resurrected Jesus is responsible for the man's healing, and that salvation is found in Jesus alone (4:12). The Sanhedrin warns them to speak no more in Jesus's name in hopes of hindering the Christian movement (4:17–18). But Peter and John declare they must obey God rather than men and vow to continue speaking about what they have seen and heard (4:19–20).

The southern steps of the Temple Mount, a possible location of Peter's sermon (Acts 2:14–41).

After their release, Peter and John report all that had happened to the other believers, who respond in prayer (4:23–31). They praise God for being the Sovereign Lord and Creator who is not at all surprised by the opposition to his people (4:24–27; Ps. 2:1–2). They ask for boldness in speaking his word and that he would continue to perform miraculous signs and wonders through Jesus's name (4:29–30). (Notice that they *didn't* pray for the opposition to cease.) In answer to their prayer, the meeting place is shaken, they are all filled anew with the Holy Spirit, and they speak the word of God with boldness (4:31).

✚ Peter, a Jew speaking to Jews in the vicinity of the temple, attributes the healing of the crippled beggar to the "God of Abraham, Isaac, and Jacob, the God of our fathers" who "has glorified his servant Jesus" (Acts 3:13).

Luke again describes the community's life together in 4:32–37, focusing here on their sharing of material possessions (cf. Acts 2:42–47). As the apostles continue to witness to Jesus's resurrection, the people voluntarily sell private property and give generously to meet the needs of those within the community. The contribution of Barnabas stands in contrast to the main characters of the next episode.

Threats to the Church (5:1–6:7)

Although God is at work and the community is thriving, serious threats to the church are beginning to emerge. In contrast to Barnabas's integrity and generosity (4:36–37) stands the greedy, hypocritical, deceptive actions of Ananias and Sapphira (5:1–11). This married couple didn't have to give to the church, but they sold property and appeared to give all the money while secretly keeping part of the proceeds for themselves. For lying to the Spirit and deceiving the community, they are put to death. Luke doesn't say they were eternally condemned, only that they experienced God's judgment of immediate physical death. (God's immediate judgment in this case is not repeated throughout the New Testament as a pattern, but these are critical days for the infant church, and God takes dramatic action at this point.) As a result, "great fear seized the whole church and all who heard about these events" (5:11).

Luke reports in 5:12–16 that the people continued to gather consistently in Solomon's Colonnade and the Lord added more and more people to the group of believers. The apostles performed many miraculous signs and wonders such as healing the sick and demon possessed. Jesus is indeed continuing to do through his Spirit and his apostles what he did during his earthly ministry.

The main road through the town of Samaria, also known as Sebaste.

✦ The generosity of the early Christians (Acts 2:42–47; 4:32–35) was threatened by the greed of people like Ananias and Sapphira (Acts 5:1–11).

Martyrdom in the New Testament

Douglas S. Huffman

Martyrdom, being put to death for one's faith, is the extreme of religious persecution. The English term "martyr" is a loan word from the Greek term for the broader idea of "witness" (*martys* and cognates). Paul's note of Jesus "testifying" (*martyreo*) before Pilate (1 Tim. 6:13) links testimony with eventual death. Likewise, Jesus is referred to as "the faithful witness, the firstborn from the dead" (Rev. 1:5; cf. 3:14). Jesus warned that persecution, including death, would come to his followers because of their testimony (*martyrion*; see Matt. 10:17–25; 24:9–14; Mark 13:9–13; Luke 21:12–19; cf. John 16:1–4). His instructions that every follower "take up his cross" is a clear reference to potential death for one's faith (Matt. 10:38; 16:24–27; Mark 8:34–38; Luke 9:23–26; 14:27). Revelation (2:13; 6:9–11; 12:11; 17:6) also makes a connection between death and being a witness (*martys*) or giving testimony (*martyria*). Nevertheless, it was not until the late second or mid-third century that "martyr" became a technical term for one who died for religious faith (e.g., *Martyr. Poly.* 1–2; Irenaeus, *Haer.* 5.9.2; Clement of Alexandria, *Strom.* 4.4–5, 21); the term "confessor" was used for one who gave testimony before authorities but was not killed (cf. Eusebius, *Hist. eccl.* 5.2.1–4). To die for one's faith was seen as admirable, and martyrs came to be honored heroes of Christianity (cf. Rev. 2:10). While some Christians were eager for martyrdom (e.g., Ignatius of Antioch in his *Eph.* 1.2; *Trall.* 4.2; 10; *Rom.* 1.1–8.3), the church soon decided that intentional martyrdom was not honorable (e.g., Clement of Alexandria, *Strom.* 4.10; *Mart. Pol.* 4.1; Justin Martyr, *Apol.* 2.4; Council of Elvira canon 60). The New Testament mentions Old Testament saints (and perhaps faithful Jews of the Maccabean period) who were killed for their faith and preaching (Matt. 23:27–36; Luke 11:44–51; Acts 7:51–53; Heb. 11:32–40). John the Baptist was imprisoned and killed for opposing the ungodliness of Herod Antipas (Matt. 14:1–12; Mark 6:14–29; Luke 3:19–20; 9:7–9). Jesus was persecuted and killed for his faithfulness to God (John 5:2–18; Acts 7:51–53). Stephen is considered the first specifically Christian martyr, one who died for his faith in the risen Lord Jesus Christ (Acts 6:8–8:2). Paul's testimony in Acts 22:20 is an important occurrence of the word *martys* in a context of Stephen dying as a "witness" for Christ. James the apostle was killed by Herod Agrippa I (Acts 12:1–2). And Paul indicates a readiness to be martyred (Acts 20:22–24; 21:13; Rom. 8:35–39; Phil. 1:12–21; 2:17; 2 Tim. 4:6–8). Extrabiblical sources describe the martyrdoms of the apostles—all except John, who is said to have died a natural death at Ephesus.

Just as healing the crippled beggar prompted the first arrest and interrogation (4:1–22), so the additional miracles result in a second arrest and appearance before the Sanhedrin (5:17–42). The miracles are signs pointing to Jesus as Lord and Messiah and calling people to faith. After being arrested and imprisoned, the apostles are rescued by an angel so they may go on speaking boldly about new life in Christ (5:18–21). When they are discovered in the temple courts teaching the people, they are rearrested (5:21–26). When asked why they have not stopped teaching in Jesus's name, Peter replies, "We must obey God rather than men" (5:27–29). Peter again recounts what God

✚ Although the New Testament clearly teaches submission to the state when it's doing its job of promoting justice and restraining evil, believers are obligated to obey God above all human authorities (see Peter's statement in Acts 5:29).

The forum of the city of Samaria. Peter and John traveled to this city to pray for the new Samaritan converts (Acts 8:14).

has done through Jesus and the apostles' role as Spirit-empowered witnesses to these historical events (5:30–32).

A Pharisee named Gamaliel persuades a furious Sanhedrin not to kill the apostles, but to release them in hopes of the movement dying out (5:33–39). After being flogged, the apostles are released with a warning not to speak any more in Jesus's name (5:40). The apostles now rejoice that they had been considered worthy to suffer for "the Name," and "day after day, in the temple courts and from house to house, they never stopped teaching and proclaiming the good news that Jesus is the Christ" (5:41–42).

Along with hypocrisy from within and persecution from without, the church faces the challenge of properly caring for an increasing number of disciples and the threat of division (6:1–7). The problem is some of the widows are being overlooked in the daily distribution of food (6:1–2). The proposed solution would allow the Twelve to focus on prayer and the ministry of the Word of God, while seven newly chosen men full of the Spirit and wisdom would oversee the distribution (6:3–4). All seven names mentioned in 6:5 are Greek, indicating that the overlooked widows will now have representation. Two of the seven, Stephen and Philip, will play important roles in the next few chapters of Acts. Luke concludes this section with a positive progress report on the Christian mission (6:7).

Stephen, the First Martyr (6:8–8:3)

The story of Stephen's martyrdom is also the story of how Christianity differs from Judaism. Luke gives extra space to Stephen's speech because of its importance for the Christian mission beyond Jerusalem and its temple. Stephen is described as "a man full of God's grace and power" who "did great wonders and miraculous signs among the people," as well as a man full of wisdom and the Spirit in public debate (6:8–10). Stephen is framed for blasphemy and arrested for speaking against the temple and the law

(6:11–15). He defends himself before the Sanhedrin in a lengthy speech in 7:1–53. Stephen tells the redemptive story from Abraham to David, making several important points: (1) God can't be restricted to one place or land (i.e., the temple in Jerusalem), (2) true worship is not confined to the temple, and (3) the Jews have rejected God's messengers in the past and most recently rejected God's Messiah, Jesus. After his closing words of accusation in 7:51–53, the members of the Sanhedrin are furious with rage (7:54). Stephen looks to heaven and sees Jesus the Son of Man exalted to God's right hand, and this drives the Jewish leaders over the edge (7:55–56). They drag him out of the city and stone

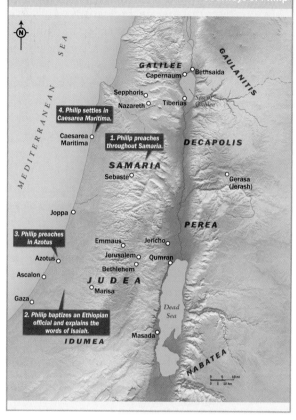

Journeys of Philip

him to death as the young man named Saul looks on approvingly (7:57–58; 8:1). Stephen responds just as Jesus responded on the cross: "Lord Jesus receive my spirit. . . . Lord, do not hold this sin against them" (7:59–60). From that day a great persecution arose against the church in Jerusalem, forcing everyone except the apostles to scatter throughout Judea and Samaria (8:1; cf. Acts 1:8). Luke also notes that Saul began to persecute the church intensely (8:3).

Philip the Evangelist (8:4–40)

The church's witness in all Judea and Samaria begins in 8:4. Philip, another one of the seven appointed in Acts 6:1–7, goes to a town in Samaria and proclaims Christ, casts out demons, and heals the sick, bringing great joy to the people (8:4–8). Many people believe and are baptized, including Simon the magician who had quite a following in the city (8:9–13). When the apostles in Jerusalem hear Samaria has accepted the Word of God, they send Peter and John to investigate (8:14). When they arrive, they pray for

✚ Stephen summarizes the Old Testament story in his speech in Acts 7 and dies in a manner that imitates Jesus's death (e.g., by forgiving his executioners).

them that they might receive the Holy Spirit (8:15–17). As the gospel moves across racial boundaries (Jews, Samaritans, gentiles), the apostles confirm the experience and play a significant role in the giving of the Spirit. This ensures unity within the multicultural body of Christ. When Simon connects the giving of the Spirit with the laying on of hands by the apostles, he offers Peter and John money for that same ability (8:18–19). Peter rebukes him severely for trying to buy the power of God and calls him to repentance (8:20–24). Peter and John return to Jerusalem preaching the gospel in many Samaritan villages (8:25).

The scene now shifts back to Philip. God directs Philip to take the desert road that runs southwest out of Jerusalem to Gaza (8:26). Philip encounters an Ethiopian finance minister who had been to Jerusalem to worship (he was probably a God-fearer or convert to Judaism) but is now sitting in his chariot reading the book of Isaiah (8:27–28). Led by the Spirit, Philip approaches the chariot and engages the man in a conversation about what he is reading (8:29–30). When the man asks for help understanding a section of Isaiah 53, Philip explains to him the good news about Jesus (8:31–35). After baptizing the official, Philip is taken away by the Spirit and he travels through various towns preaching the gospel, while the Ethiopian continues on his way rejoicing in his new faith (8:36–40).

The Conversion of Paul (9:1–31)

Now we read about the radical conversion of the man who will take the gospel to the gentiles, the apostle Paul. Luke reports on his conversion three times because of its great importance: 9:1–30; 22:3–21; and 26:2–23. On his way to Damascus to persecute those who belonged to the Way (an early name for Christians), Paul is thrown to the ground and blinded by a heavenly light (9:1–3). By persecuting Jesus's followers, Paul has actually been persecuting Jesus (9:4–5). Jesus tells the blinded persecutor to enter Damascus and await further instructions (9:6–9). The chief enemy of the church is being transformed into a leading witness for Christ. Meanwhile, the Lord gives a vision to both Ananias, a disciple from Damascus, and Paul about what happens next (9:10–12). Ananias at first objects because of Paul's notorious reputation, but the Lord responds, "Go! This man is my chosen instrument to carry my name before the Gentiles and their kings and before the people of Israel" (9:13–16). Ananias then goes to meet Paul so he may regain his sight and be filled with the Spirit (9:17–19). Almost immediately Paul begins to preach Jesus as the Son of God in the synagogues of Damascus, baffling those who knew of him only as an opponent of Christ (9:19–22). When the Jews conspire to kill him, friends lower him in a basket outside the city wall, and he escapes (9:23–25). Paul returns to Jerusalem and tries to join the disciples, but they are terrified of him (9:26). Barnabas takes the initiative to connect Paul, the newly transformed believer, with the cautious Christians in Jerusalem (9:27). Paul is then able to speak boldly about Christ in Jerusalem until the Grecian Jews attempt to kill him. At that point, the believers send Paul down to Caesarea and off to Tarsus (9:28–30). Luke concludes this dramatic conversion story with his second progress report: "Then the church throughout Judea, Galilee and Samaria enjoyed a time of peace. It was strengthened; and encouraged by the Holy Spirit, it grew in numbers, living in the fear of the Lord" (9:31).

A photo of Straight Street in Damascus taken around 1900 (Acts 9:11).

The Ministry of Peter beyond Jerusalem (9:32–11:18)

Peter has been involved with the mission to the Samaritans (8:14–25). Now he will join in the mission to Judea (9:32–43) and even to the gentiles (10:1–48). As Peter travels through the coastal towns of Judea, he is involved with two miracles of note. First, the healing of a paralytic in Lydda named Aeneas causes those who live in the area to turn to the Lord (9:32–35). Second, God uses Peter to raise a disciple named Tabitha (or "Dorcas" in Greek), who was always doing good and serving the poor (9:36–43).

After she dies, Peter is summoned from Lydda to Joppa. When he arrives, he observes the clothing Dorcas had made, sends the mourners out of the room, prays, and then speaks the command, "Tabitha, get up." Dorcas is raised from the dead, causing many people to believe in the Lord (9:42). Peter then stays in Joppa for some time, one step closer to Caesarea where a gentile named Cornelius lives.

Cornelius's conversion represents a major step forward in the Christian mission (10:1–11:18). The gospel is breaking out of its Jewish beginning to include the gentiles as well. The story begins with a Roman centurion named Cornelius having a vision from the Lord, telling him his prayers have been answered and instructing him to send for Peter in Joppa (10:1–8).

✚ Paul, once a fierce persecutor of the church (Acts 8:1–3), would soon suffer persecution himself as part of his mission as apostle to the gentiles (Acts 9:15–16).

Roman Soldiers

Joseph R. Dodson

In the New Testament, Roman soldiers play four primary roles: they serve as agents of government, as examples of gentile faith, as protectors of Paul, and as metaphors for Christian disciples. As agents of government, soldiers execute orders to flog and crucify Jesus, during which time they also mock the Messiah and gamble for his garment (e.g., Matt. 27:26–31; Luke 23:36; John 19:23–24, 32–34). Later, soldiers obey orders to guard Jesus's tomb (Matt. 27:65), and after his resurrection from that very tomb, they—following instructions from the Jewish leaders—endorse the lie that the disciples stole Jesus's body (Matt. 28:12). Soldiers also act as agents of government in Acts, where they are charged with guarding Peter and Paul in prison (e.g., Acts 12:4–18; 24:23; 28:16).

Second, Roman soldiers in the New Testament serve as examples of gentile faith and inclusion into the Christian community. For instance, the centurion in Matt. 8:5–13 amazes Jesus with his faith (cf. Luke 7:2–9); consequently, Jesus presents this soldier as an example of many other gentiles from all over the world who will participate with the patriarchs in the kingdom of heaven. Similarly, in Acts 10:1–48, God uses another soldier, Cornelius, to demonstrate to Peter that the Lord does not show partiality to the Jews, but that God accepts even gentiles who fear him and who work righteousness (vv. 34–35). Another possible act of faith could include the centurion in Matt. 27:54 who, upon witnessing the crucifixion, professes that Jesus was indeed the Son of God (cf. Luke 23:47). (In contrast to the positive examples of these centurions, John sees a vision in Rev. 6:15–17 of military captains cowering before the wrath of the Lamb and in Rev. 19:17–21 of their carcasses being gorged by birds at the final judgment.)

Third, God uses soldiers to protect Paul from hostile opponents so the apostle can make it to Rome; more than once the soldiers save Paul from the violent mob (Acts 21:30–35; 22:22–24) as well as from would-be assassins (Acts 23:11–35; but cf. 27:41–42).

Finally, New Testament writers draw on the commitment and calling of Roman soldiers to illustrate Christian discipleship. For instance, Epaphroditus and Archippus are referred to as Paul's fellow-soldiers (Phil. 2:25; Philem. 2). Moreover, Paul admonishes Timothy to fight the good fight (1 Tim. 1:18), to share in suffering as a good soldier of Christ (2 Tim. 2:3), and to avoid entanglement in "civilian affairs" so that his enlisting officer may be pleased (2 Tim. 2:4). Similarly, Paul compares Christian leaders to soldiers in order to argue that these leaders, too, are worthy of payment (1 Cor. 9:7). From this brief survey, one can see that Roman soldiers play vast and varied roles in the New Testament.

Cornelius's vision is repeated four times throughout the story (10:3–6, 22, 30–32; 11:13–14). Next, Peter has a corresponding vision, giving him permission to kill and eat unclean animals provided from heaven, with the order not to "call anything impure that God has made clean" (10:15). As has happened before in Peter's life, he hears the same instructions three times before the vision ends (10:9–16). These two visions result in Peter traveling to Cornelius's home in Caesarea (10:17–23). An angel told Cornelius to send three men to Joppa to find Peter, and the Spirit told Peter to accompany them.

✛ As the gospel moved beyond the Jews to the Samaritans and the gentiles, the apostles were sent to new converts in conjunction with them receiving the Holy Spirit (Acts 8:14–17; 10:34–46). This fostered unity in the church.

When Peter arrives, he enters Cornelius's house, although it is unlawful for Jews to associate with gentiles. The two men share the visions the Lord has given them (10:24–33). Peter then begins to speak to the people (10:34–43). He knows now God does not show favoritism, but accepts people from every nation who fear him and do what is right. He explains how God has revealed himself in Jesus of Nazareth, how the Jewish leaders crucified him, how God raised him from the dead, and how he appeared to many of his disciples. Peter and the other disciples were appointed as witnesses to proclaim that "everyone who believes in him receives forgiveness of sins through his name" (10:43).

But Peter's sermon is interrupted by the Holy Spirit who comes on all the gentiles listening to the message (10:44–48). The Jewish Christians who are traveling with Peter are astounded that the gift of the Spirit has now been poured out on gentiles. After receiving the Spirit, they are baptized in the name of Jesus Christ.

The final scene occurs back in Jerusalem, where Peter answers criticism from the Jewish Christians for entering a gentile's house (11:1–3). Peter defends his actions by summarizing everything that has happened (11:4–16). He concludes, "So if God gave them the same gift as he gave us, who believed in the Lord Jesus Christ, who was I to think that I could oppose God?" (11:17). The account persuades the Jewish believers. They offer no further objections, but praise God for granting "even the Gentiles repentance unto life" (11:18).

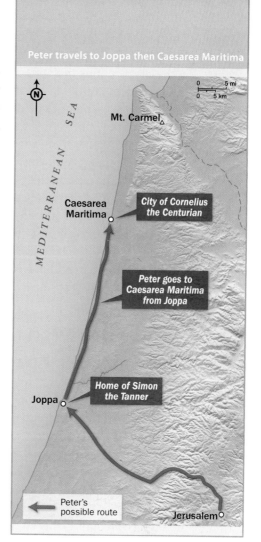

Peter travels to Joppa then Caesarea Maritima

Christianity Comes to Antioch (11:19–30)

Antioch in Syria was the third largest city in the Roman Empire, behind Rome and Alexandria. Anonymous Christians from Cyprus and Cyrene go to Antioch and share the good news of Jesus Christ with the gentiles in the city, resulting in a large number of conversions (11:19–21). When the Jerusalem church hears about what is happening in Antioch, they send Barnabas, who finds evidence of a genuine work of God. This good man, full of the Spirit and faith, encourages them to stay true to the Lord (11:22–24). As the work expands in Antioch, Barnabas goes to Tarsus to find Paul. They return to Antioch and carry on a teaching ministry for a year there. Luke reports that "the disciples were called Christians first at Antioch" (11:25–26). During this time a Christian prophet named Agabus came from Jerusalem and predicted a severe famine (11:27–28). Luke notes this happened during the reign of Emperor Cladius (AD 41–54). The church in Antioch collects money for the famine victims and sends it back to Jerusalem with Barnabas and Paul (11:29–30). They probably took the money to Jerusalem in about AD 46.

The Gospel Spreads in Spite of Obstacles (12:1–25)

Just as Herod the Great tried to kill the baby Jesus, so his grandson Herod Agrippa I now attempts to destroy the young church (12:1). The apostles become targets of persecution under Agrippa. He has James, the brother of John and one of the Twelve, put to death, and has Peter arrested and put in prison (12:2–4). As the church prays earnestly for Peter, God works to deliver Peter (12:5). First, an angel miraculously delivers Peter from prison, leading him out of his chains, past two sets of guards, and through an open gate to freedom (12:6–11). When Peter realizes it wasn't a dream, he goes to the house of John Mark's mother, where people had gathered to pray (12:12). He knocks on the door, and a servant girl named Rhoda answers (12:13). Almost comically, she recognizes Peter's voice but runs back to the group without opening the door (12:14). At first they don't believe her, but Peter continues to knock until they finally let him in (12:15–16). He explains how God delivered him and instructs them to tell James and the other believers (12:17). James is the younger brother of Jesus who became the leader of the Jerusalem church (Acts 15:13–21; 21:18). In the morning when guards discover Peter has escaped, Herod orders an all-out search and has the guards executed (12:18–19). Luke then recounts the story of Herod's arrogance and subsequent death under the judgment of God (12:19–23). The third progress report in Acts occurs in 12:24: "But the word of God continued to increase and spread." When Barnabas and Paul finish their mission to Jerusalem, they return to Antioch with John Mark to prepare for the first missionary journey to the gentiles (12:25). From this point

✦ Barnabas was very influential in Paul's life. He first vouched for Paul to the Jerusalem church when they questioned his conversion and later recruited him for an extended teaching ministry in Antioch (Acts 9:26–27; 11:25–26).

Roman Names

E. Randolph Richards

Roman citizens were required to have a tripartite name: a given name (*praenomen*), a clan/ancestral name (*nomen*), and a family/tribe name (*cognomen*). Somewhat the reverse of American culture, Romans often used only their family name in letters. *Nomen* (clan names) were not typically used alone in letters (see *T. Vind.* 291). Given names were so limited and common, they were often just written as an initial. Thus the famous orator M. (Marcus) Tullius Cicero referred to himself as Cicero. The *nomen*, clan name—for lack of a better term—came from the *gens*, referring to the ancestral founder of the family (or the one granting citizenship). Roman culture had great aristocratic families, including the Julius, Brutus, Aemilius, Vettenius, and Sergius clans.

Acts 13:7 tells of the proconsul Sergius Paulus, perhaps L. (Lucius) Sergius Paulus, brother of Q. (Quintus) Sergius Paulus. Perhaps they had a family connection with the aristocratic Sergius clan, but more likely when an ancestor of the Paulus family received his citizenship, he took the *nomen* of Sergius. Freedmen then used their given name for their new family name. Thus Marcus Tullius Cicero freed his secretary-slave, Tiro, who then became Marcus Tullius Tiro. He did not adopt the Cicero family name.

So what about "Saul, also called Paul" (Acts 13:9)? It is unlikely the apostle changed his name; he simply began using a different part of it. His name was perhaps Saul(us) Paul(us) or Paul(us) Saul(us). We are not given his full name. No Roman citizen in the New Testament is given all three names, but Greeks, Egyptians, Jews, and Christians were less likely than Romans to use all three names anyway (e.g., Apion was called Antonius Maximus). Acts places Paul's name switch precisely at the point of meeting Sergius Paulus. Paul subsequently visits Pisidian Antioch where the Pauli had connections. Some suggest Saul's family was freed (manumitted) by a Paulus (Acts 22:28). If so, his name was perhaps Paul Saul, but it seems less likely "Paul" was his clan name, since he uses it alone in his letters. It is not impossible the apostle was distantly related to the Paulus family, thus Saul Paul.

From inscriptions, ostraca (inscriptions on pottery), and Josephus, we know the name Saul was common in Palestine, but not in the Diaspora. Yet King Saul was the most famous person in Paul's tribe, Benjamin (Phil. 3:5), making "Saul" a great family/tribal name. In any event, why switch from Saul to Paul? Only Jews would be familiar with a Hebrew king named Saul from a thousand years earlier, making it a great given name or nickname in Jerusalem. Most Greeks had never heard of someone named Saul. They would assume it was a nickname. They only knew the adjective "saulos" (meaning the provocative way prostitutes walked). Also, as Saul moved into regions where the Paulus family was well known, a connection to them became an asset rather than a liability, while the name "Saul" became the reverse.

on in Acts, the focus shifts from Jerusalem and the apostles to Paul and the gentile mission.

Paul's First Missionary Journey (13:1–14:28)

The Christian mission to the gentiles formally begins with a commissioning from the church in Antioch (13:1–3). As they are worshiping, the Spirit

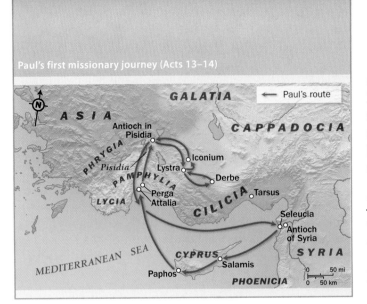

GALATIA

← Paul's route

ASIA

CAPPADOCIA

Antioch in Pisidia

PHRYGIA

Pisidia

Iconium

Lystra

PAMPHYLIA

Derbe

Perga

CILICIA

Tarsus

Attalia

LYCIA

Seleucia

Antioch of Syria

MEDITERRANEAN SEA

CYPRUS

SYRIA

Salamis

Paphos

PHOENICIA

0   50 mi

0   50 km

calls them to set apart Barnabas and Saul for the work. They fast and pray and lay hands on them before sending them off.

Accompanied by John Mark, Barnabas and Paul leave Antioch and sail to Cyprus, where they proclaim the gospel first in the Jewish synagogues (13:4–5).

When they reach Paphos on the other end of the island, Elymas, a Jewish sorcerer, tries to stop them from sharing the good news with Sergius Paulus, the proconsul (13:6–8). But Paul rebukes him and pronounces a word of judgment on him (13:9–11). When Sergius Paulus observes the power of Paul's teaching about the Lord, he believes (13:12). Incidentally, Paul's name changes here from "Saul" to "Paul," not because of his conversion, but because he has entered a new sphere of ministry where "Paul" is the more appropriate name for reasons explained in the sidebar "Roman Names" (page 719).

The team sails from Cyprus to the mainland at Perga in Pamphylia. There, for some unknown reason (homesickness, discomfort with the mission to the gentiles, exhaustion from the rough journey over the mountains to Antioch, Paul's leadership over his cousin Barnabas), John Mark leaves the missionary team to return to Jerusalem (13:13; cf. 15:38–39). Paul and Barnabas make the rugged hundred-mile journey inland to Pisidian Antioch, where Luke details one of Paul's sermons in the synagogue (13:14–52). Paul traces the Old Testament story to recount God's promises to his people (13:16–25). Then he shows how God's promises to Israel have been fulfilled in Christ (13:26–37). He concludes with an invitation to accept the forgiveness available in Jesus and a warning against rejecting God's offer (13:38–41). The people seem interested in what they have to say and agree to talk more (13:42–43).

The reception on the following Sabbath is not nearly so warm and friendly. When the Jews see the large crowds that have gathered to hear Paul, they begin to oppose the missionary team out of jealousy (13:44–45). Having fulfilled their obligation to speak the word of God first to the Jews, who apparently do not consider themselves worthy of receiving eternal life, Paul and Barnabas turn to the gentiles (13:46–47). While many of the gentiles believe, the Jews incite opposition from the leading citizens of the city (13:48–50).

✛ The church in Antioch was a "sending church." All three of Paul's missionary journeys began in Antioch (Acts 13:1–3; 15:35–36; 18:23).

Roman Prisons

Brian M. Rapske

Luke devotes almost as much space in Acts to describing the apostle Paul's ministry experiences while in Roman custody as he does to telling his readers of his free-ranging missionary exploits. Moreover, five of the thirteen letters of Paul are prison epistles. Some knowledge of Roman prisons, prison culture, and the ancient Roman process of the assignment of persons to custody can, therefore, be very helpful to creating a better understanding of these texts.

Roman incarceration served a number of purposes in antiquity. An accused might be confined for protection or to prevent his flight. Prison could also be a place to await sentence or execution and might even serve as the place of execution. Magistrates also used imprisonment as a means of coercion. It was not formally recognized in Roman law as a punishment in itself, but conscious magisterial delay in giving prisoners due process effectively made it such.

The range of Roman custodial possibilities from most to least severe were: prison, military custody, entrustment to civilian sureties, and freedom on one's own recognizance. There was further variability within each of these arrangements. Prisons and their relative appointments could be better or much worse. The keeping could be relaxed or very close. Chains and stocks might be applied or not. Chains might be light in weight, or so heavy that they severely chafed and even crippled the wearer over time.

Whether one was incarcerated and the severity of the conditions were a function not only of the seriousness of the crime alleged, but also of the known relative status of the accused and plaintiff (Ulpian, *Digest* 48.3.1). So, for example, when accused by Romans in a Roman court of law in Philippi, Paul and Silas could not affirm their Roman citizenship without, by implication, also denying their Jewishness (= Christianity). Consequently, the apostles suffered the humiliation of a severe public beating and imprisonment, treatment normally reserved for low-status malefactors (Acts 16). Alternatively, in Acts wherever Paul's citizenship became known to the Roman authorities, the conditions of his keeping were significantly improved (in the centurions' barracks in Jerusalem, the governor's residence in Caesarea, and his own rented apartment in Rome).

The apostles Paul and Peter are memorialized in a chapel in Rome's oldest state prison, the *Carcer*. It consisted of a barrel-vaulted upper structure and a subterranean death cell called the *Tullianum*. Whether Paul and Peter were actually kept there cannot be certainly determined. There were other prisons in Rome: the quarry prison, the prison of the Hundred, the prison built upon the site of the Theater of Marcellus, and the prison cells of Rome's regional fire stations.

Paul's final letter, 2 Timothy, is a prison epistle that bears witness to another significant dynamic. Greco-Roman culture was driven by issues of honor and shame; within that framework, one of the social consequences of imprisonment and chains was dishonor and shame for the prisoner (Acts 16:37; 1 Thess. 2:2). Feeding, clothing, and otherwise helping prisoners took great courage, because helpers had to act against the urge to protect themselves from the risk of being "infected" by association with one so publicly disgraced (2 Tim. 1:8–12; cf. Heb. 10:34). Paul celebrates Onesiphorus and his household for standing alongside of and helping him during his imprisonment in Rome (2 Tim. 1:16–18). Sadly, however, the apostle also recalls others who abandoned him in his time of need (2 Tim. 4:9–10, 16).

As a result, Paul and Barnabas leave Pisidian Antioch for Iconium, full of joy and the Holy Spirit (13:51–52).

At Iconium, they go as usual to the Jewish synagogue to share the good news of Christ. They speak boldly for the Lord, who confirms the message with signs and wonders (14:3). The reaction is mixed, but they are forced to leave the city when they learn of a plot to persecute and even stone them (14:4–7).

In Lystra, God uses Paul to heal a crippled man, which stirs the crowd to attempt to worship Barnabas and Paul as the gods Zeus and Hermes (14:8–13). They strongly resist, protesting that they are only human beings who come as messengers from the living God, creator of heaven and earth (14:14–18). Some Jews from Antioch and Iconium arrive and persuade the crowd that Paul is their enemy. They stone Paul and drag him outside the city thinking he is dead (14:19). The disciples gather around him, he gets up, and goes back into the city before leaving the next day for Derbe, where they preach the good news and win a large number of converts (14:20–21).

The team returns to Lystra, Iconium, Pisidian Antioch, Perga, Attalia, and finally back to Syrian Antioch. They remind the disciples that following Jesus often involves hardships, and they encourage them to remain true to the faith (14:22). In addition, they appoint elders in each church and entrust them to the Lord (14:23). They finally return to Antioch where they were originally commissioned. They gather the church and report "all that God had done through them and how he had opened a door of faith to the Gentiles" (14:27). They remained in Antioch a long time with the disciples (14:28).

The Jerusalem Council (15:1–35)

Acts 1:8 sets the stage for how the whole book of Acts unfolds. The Christian mission begins first in Jerusalem (Acts 1–7), then spreads through Judea and Samaria (Acts 8–9) and into gentile territory (Acts 10–12). The major venture outside Palestine on Paul's missionary journey was a success (Acts 13–14). Before the gentile mission can continue as a unified effort, the church needs to agree on how that mission should be conducted. That question is addressed at the Jerusalem Council in Acts 15, an event that probably takes place in about AD 49.

The occasion was some men from Judea coming to Antioch and teaching that gentiles must be circumcised in order to be saved (15:1). Paul and Barnabas sharply disagreed with these legalists, and the church appoints them to go to Jerusalem and discuss the issue with the apostles and elders (15:2). They arrive and report all God has done through them to bring salvation to the gentiles (15:3–4). They debate the issue in 15:5–21; believers belonging to the party of the Pharisees argue that gentiles must be circumcised and required to obey the

The Jerusalem Council

Paul Jackson

Although the first-century church's inclusion of the gentiles was remarkable in Acts 8–12, the most serious ingathering occurred during Paul's first mission trip recorded in Acts 13–14. Up to that point the stream of gentile entrance into the church had been merely a trickle. But the trickle turned to torrent. It is, therefore, no wonder the highly conservative circumcision-minded Jews from Jerusalem arrived in Syrian Antioch to demand these new "gentile Christians" become Jews first. After engaging them in serious argument and debate (15:2), Paul and Barnabas made their way south to attend what is known as the Jerusalem Council in order to settle the issue, probably in AD 49.

"What constitutes the people of God?" Without a favorable conclusion, future outreach efforts to the gentiles would be compromised, and the church would have functioned as a subset of Judaism. After much preliminary debate, Peter relayed the events of Acts 10, including a synopsis of his "second" Pentecost sermon, which concluded with the Spirit coming upon the gentiles as he had come upon the Jews. Then Barnabas and Paul recounted the wonders of the Spirit's power amid the gentiles (15:12). Lastly, James, the pastor of the church, weighed in using some deft pastoral skills to solidify the previous testimony. Ironically, he ensured the right outcome by building a bridge to the church's Jewish population. First, by referring to Peter's Hebrew name, Simeon,

he reminded them of their common heritage and he affirmed Peter's strong commitment to God's plan. Perhaps James intended to convey that if Simeon, a Jewish Christian, reached out to the gentiles, the rest of the church should too. Weighing heaviest though was James's quoting of two Old Testament Hebrew prophets who in the eighth century BC echoed God's favor toward the gentiles (Isa. 45:21; Amos 9:11–12).

We see the result in the most important verse in the chapter. James's judgment upheld the truth of the gospel—the only requirement for salvation amongst the gentiles was faith in Jesus Christ (15:19). With equal footing established between Jew and gentile, however, James knew gentile Christians would inevitably come into more open contact with Jewish Christians, so it was important to include some rules for common fellowship (vv. 20–21). This so-called Jerusalem Quadrilateral would serve to help the new Christians avoid giving unnecessary offense. Having reached a consensus, council members drafted an official letter to be sent and read to the church at Antioch (vv. 22–29). Judas and Silas, two prophets from the church, not only delivered the letter, but also remained for some time encouraging and strengthening the brothers with many additional words. The Jerusalem Council, therefore, built an important bridge between Paul's maiden mission trip and the rest of the gentile mission.

When traveling from Paphos to Pisidian Antioch, the missionary team would have faced the imposing Taurus Mountains. This is when John Mark turned back for Jerusalem.

✚ Paul was stoned and left for dead at Lystra (Acts 14:19–20). Ironically, Paul's faithful co-worker Timothy is from Lystra. From a place of great suffering comes a lifelong friend.

The Cult of Artemis

Mark W. Wilson

Artemis, known as Diana to the Romans, was a popular Greek deity. She was the daughter of Zeus and Leto, whose twin brother was Apollo. In art and literature she is portrayed as the wandering huntress and chaste virgin. Within the context of Asia Minor she also seems to have acquired characteristics of a mother goddess. Near Ephesus was a grove called Ortygia, which the Ephesians identified as the birthplace of Artemis. The celebration of her birthday each year was one of Ephesus's largest religious celebrations and attracted thousands of pilgrims. A second popular festival was the Artemesia, during which young men and women traditionally chose their marriage partners.

The temple of Artemis standing in the first century was actually the fifth temple on the site. This Temple E was built in the fourth century BC after Temple D, built by the Lydian king Croesus (560 BC), was burned to the ground by an arsonist. The new Temple E was the largest religious building in the Hellenistic world, measuring 230 feet by 427 feet and containing 127 columns. It was numbered among the Seven Wonders of the Ancient World. The cult image associated with this period is the many-breasted Artemis depicted on coins and statues. Two such statues were discovered by Austrian archaeologists and are now on display in the Ephesus Museum. Whether the appendages are to be identified as eggs, bull testicles, or breasts remains unresolved. Their interpretation depends, in part, on whether Artemis is viewed as a goddess of fertility and orgiastic behavior or as a protector of virgins and families. Two other temples to Artemis were located in the province of Asia—at Sardis and at Magnesia on the Meander.

Besides its religious function, the temple of Artemis served three other functions in Ephesus: (1) economic, as the banking center; (2) civic, as the repository of governmental inscriptions; and (3) social, as an asylum offering protection and aid to debtors and the indigent. The special covenant relationship between the city and Artemis's patron deity is evidenced by the cry raised by the silversmiths and the crowd: "Great is Artemis of the Ephesians" (Acts 19:28, 34). The city clerk quieted them by recalling that everyone knew Ephesus was the temple keeper (*neokoros*) of Artemis and of her image fallen from heaven (19:35). This neocorate relationship was depicted on some Ephesian coins, which portrayed a woman holding a temple in her outstretched hands.

In the apocryphal *Acts of John* 42 the apostle John is portrayed as having a role in the destruction of the Artemis temple. The truth is the final Temple E was destroyed by the Goths in about AD 262. In the fifth century AD the temple remains were turned into a church.

law of Moses (15:5), and Peter, James, Paul, and Barnabas argue that gentiles should not be burdened with either (15:6–21). The bottom line is God has accepted the gentiles by grace through faith as evidenced by the giving of his Spirit (15:8). The council concludes with James declaring that Jewish Christians should not make it difficult for gentile Christians who are turning to God (15:19). They send word back to the gentile believers in Antioch and elsewhere through Paul, Barnabas, Judas (Barsabbas), and Silas that gentiles are not required to add circumcision and obedience to the law to their faith in Christ

(15:22–35). They do, however, ask gentile Christians to avoid four things: food sacrificed to idols, meat from strangled animals, blood, and sexual immorality (15:20, 29). By abstaining from these particularly offensive practices, gentiles and Jews could have unhindered table fellowship, an important aspect of life together in the early church.

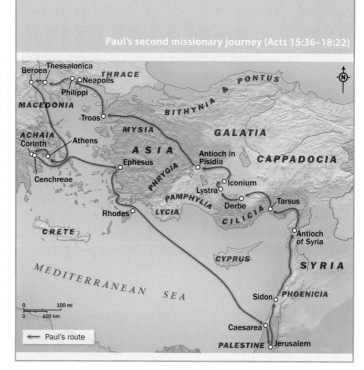

Paul's second missionary journey (Acts 15:36–18:22)

Paul's Second Missionary Journey (15:36–18:22)

The second missionary journey also launches from Antioch (15:36), but not before a dispute between Paul and Barnabas. Barnabas wants to take John Mark with them, but Paul disagrees because John Mark had deserted the team on the first journey (15:37–38). So Barnabas takes Mark and sails to Cyprus, while Paul takes Silas and heads for Syria and Cilicia (15:38–41). Barnabas shows faith in Mark when others saw him as a lost cause. Interestingly, earlier Barnabas showed faith in Paul when he introduced him to the apostles in Jerusalem just after his conversion (Acts 9:26–28). Eventually Paul is reconciled with Mark and reaffirms his effectiveness in ministry (Col. 4:10; Philem. 24; 2 Tim. 4:11).

Paul and Silas go to Derbe and then to Lystra, where Paul had earlier been stoned and left for dead (14:19–20). Upon returning to a place of great suffering, Paul discovers a disciple named Timothy, a young man who would become Paul's most beloved co-worker (16:1–5). Since by Jewish law Timothy is an Israelite, Paul has Timothy circumcised before taking him along on the missionary team. Clearly this decision is motivated by Paul's (and Timothy's) desire to avoid unnecessary offense to the Jews they will minister to. Paul makes it clear elsewhere that he has no regard for circumcision—it adds nothing to the work of Christ in salvation (Rom. 2:25–29; 1 Cor. 7:19; Gal. 5:6; 6:15; cf. Col. 2:11). They continue westward, announcing the encouraging decision reached at the Jerusalem Council and strengthening the churches.

✦ At the Jerusalem Council we see the early Christians wrestling with how to live out the same faith in different cultural situations.

Paul and the others continue through South Galatia and Phrygia, but the Spirit of Jesus prevents them from going north into Asia or Bithynia (16:6–7). They come to Troas, a coastal town on the Aegean Sea where Paul has his famous Macedonian vision (16:8–9). He leaves at once to preach the gospel in Macedonia (16:10). Arriving in Philippi, they speak with Lydia, a businesswoman and a God-fearer, on the Sabbath at a river outside the city. She and her household respond to the gospel and are baptized (16:11–15). On another occasion, Paul is pestered by an annoying slave girl who is possessed by a fortune-telling spirit (16:16–17). When he casts out the spirit, the girl's owners blame Paul and Silas for their lost profits, and they drag them before the city magistrates who order them stripped, severely flogged, and thrown into prison (16:18–24). As Paul and Silas sing praises to God at midnight in their prison cell, a mighty earthquake opens the prison doors and releases the captives from their chains (16:25–26). The guard is about to commit suicide when Paul stops him, explaining that all the prisoners are still accounted for (16:27–28). Because of the response of Paul and Silas and their witness to Christ, the guard and his household come to faith in Christ (16:29–34). The next day when the magistrates release them, Paul demands a public escort out of town since they are Roman citizens who have been punished without a trial

Paul was brought before the proconsul Gallio at the bema (or judgment) seat in Corinth (Acts 18:12–17).

(16:35–39). After their release and before leaving town, they met with the believers at Lydia's house, perhaps including Luke, who was thought to be a native of Philippi (16:40).

The missionary team continues on to Thessalonica, where they preach Christ in a synagogue, see a number of converts (especially among the God-fearing Greeks), and face opposition from the Jews for claiming that Jesus (not Caesar) is Lord (17:1–9). They quickly leave for nearby Berea, where they receive a better response (17:10–12). Soon, Jews from Thessalonica come to Berea to stir up opposition against the Christian missionaries. Paul therefore heads south to Athens, while Silas and Timothy remain in Berea (17:13–15).

Paul's arrival in Athens brings him intense emotional distress over the city's idolatry (17:16). He speaks with people about Christ in both the synagogue and the marketplace or agora (17:17). On one occasion, a group of philosophers takes Paul (the "babbler" as they call him) to the Areopagus (Mars Hill) to address a meeting of the Areopagus council (17:18–21). In his address to the group, Paul first establishes a point of contact with his audience (the altar to the unknown god in 17:22–23) before presenting the Creator God as the one worthy of true worship (17:24–25). Next, he reveals how a person may turn from the ignorance of idolatry and have a relationship with the true God through the resurrected Jesus (17:26–31). The response to Paul's speech is mixed (17:32–34).

Paul moves on to Corinth, where he meets the Jewish Christian couple Aquila and Priscilla, who had been expelled from Rome along with other Jews by Emperor Claudius in about AD 49 (18:1–2). He spends most of his time reasoning in the synagogue and testifying to Jesus as Messiah until the opposition drives him to focus more on the gentiles (18:3–6). Nevertheless, God continues to work as Crispus the synagogue ruler, his household, and many Corinthians become believers (18:7–8). Paul is encouraged to persevere in ministry through a vision from the Lord, so he continues teaching the Word of God for a year and a half in Corinth (18:9–11). Paul is never far from opposition, however, as the Jews renew their attack on Paul, charging him with causing people to worship God in ways contrary to the law (18:12–13). The proconsul Gallio is quick to recognize this as a matter of Jewish law rather than Roman law, and he throws them out of court, at which time they vent their anger on Sosthenes, their own synagogue ruler (18:14–17). Following this significant ruling from a Roman proconsul, Paul's ministry in Corinth continues unhindered for some time (18:18). He finally travels back to the sending church in Antioch, stopping along the way to leave Aquila and Priscilla in Ephesus (18:18–22).

✦ Paul's missionary pattern is to first speak about Jesus in the local Jewish synagogue when possible.

Roman Citizenship

Lynn H. Cohick

Roman citizens possessed several specific rights and privileges. Among them was that of *conubium*, the right to enter a licit Roman marriage, which gave their offspring the rank of Roman citizens and claim to their father's estate. Roman citizens had the right both to own and sell property outright, the *jus commercii*, and to access the Roman courts. While both women and men enjoyed these privileges, the latter benefited from the additional rights of voting, joining the Roman legion, and holding public office.

These basic rights of citizenship did not change over time; what changed was the criteria for inclusion on the citizen registry. Initially, the city of Rome granted all privileges of citizenship to male Patricians, wealthy, free-born landowners. Free-born men who belonged to the lower class of the Plebeians, and women in both categories, also enjoyed the rights of *conubium* and *commercium*.

For most of the history of the Roman Republic, only Roman citizens could serve in the legions. As Rome's influence stretched across Italy and Latin tribes were given the franchise (often as a group), the need for more troops grew. As a result, first Italians and then free men from free cities within the provinces were admitted to the legions, after first being given Roman citizenship. Julius Caesar began an aggressive program of offering Roman citizenship status to certain regions within the growing boundaries of Rome's influence. Augustus and subsequent emperors continued this trend in varying degrees. Those in the auxiliary forces were granted citizenship after completing their obligation of twenty-five years of service. Under the emperor Claudius, the grant was extended to the soldier's wife, children, and descendants retroactively.

A slave, male or female, owned by a Roman citizen was usually granted citizenship upon his or her manumission. Once freed, these new citizens could form licit marriages and their children were recognized as citizens. If either the mother or the father was a Roman citizen, but the other was not, then the marriage was not considered licit under Roman civil law, and the child followed the mother's status (Roman or non-Roman, slave or free). This general practice was qualified with the *lex Minicia* (ca. 90 BC), which restricted a foreign man (*peregrinus*) who married a Roman woman from having children with Roman citizenship. In this case, the children followed the father's status, even though the marriage was not licit by civil law.

A registry of citizens' names was kept in Rome and updated approximately every five years, coordinated with the census. The names of freed slaves would be recorded in the local registry with copies sent to Rome. Similarly, a child born to a citizen would be registered within thirty days of birth, and a personal copy could be kept at their home. The official document was held in the city's public archives and perhaps in Rome as well.

There is a final way citizenship could be gained—by paying for it. Such is the situation of Claudius Lysias, the tribune who supervised Paul's arrest recorded in Acts 22:26–29; 23:26. The tribune states he paid a large sum for his citizenship, which, as his name suggests, he seems to have received under the emperor Claudius.

In the early decades of the first century AD, a Roman citizen was numbered among a distinctive few who had access to resources and privileges. By AD 212, this distinction evaporated, when the emperor Caracalla extended Roman citizenship to all the inhabitants of the empire.

Paul's Third Missionary Journey (18:23–21:16)

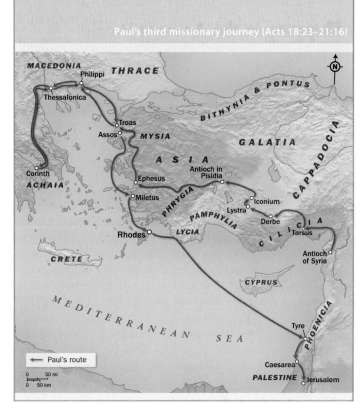

Paul's third missionary journey focuses on Ephesus, the dominant commercial city in Asia and guardian city of the goddess Artemis. Luke notes Paul traveled again through Galatia and Phrygia, strengthening the disciples before arriving at Ephesus (18:23; 19:1). (The journey from Antioch to Ephesus was about five hundred miles.) In 18:24–28, we get an update on the ministry of Aquila and Priscilla, who had remained at Ephesus when Paul returned to Antioch (18:19). Of note is their role in explaining "the way of God more accurately" to Apollos, a gifted teacher who eventually moved to Corinth to carry on an effective ministry there (1 Cor. 1:12; 3:4–6, 22; 4:6).

Acts 19 gives us a brief glimpse into Paul's nearly three-year ministry in Ephesus. When he arrives, he meets twelve disciples of John the Baptist who have not heard about Pentecost. Although they believe in God, they do not have the Holy Spirit and thus are not Christians. After Paul speaks to them about Jesus, they are baptized and receive the Spirit (19:1–7).

Paul preached Christ for three months in the Jewish synagogue, before being rejected and moving to the lecture hall of Tyrannus (19:8–9). There he taught for two more years so that "all the Jews and Greeks who lived in the province of Asia heard the word of the Lord" (19:10). Again, God confirmed the message through miraculous works (19:11–12).

Ephesus was known to be a center for the practice of magic and false religion, ranging from Jewish magicians to the worship of Artemis. In 19:13–16, we read about the seven sons of Sceva, a Jewish priest, who were trying to cast out demons using the name of Jesus as part of their magical formula.

✚ The husband and wife team of Aquila and Priscilla explained the faith to Apollos (Acts 18:24–26). Many scholars believe that Apollos may be the author of the New Testament letter of Hebrews.

Shipping in the Ancient World

Brian M. Rapske

Following his rise to power through the chaos and disruption of civil war, Augustus gave attention to establishing a Roman Empire free of the fear of invasion and piracy, adequately networked with roads and open seaways for ease of transportation and communication, and serviced by a reliable coinage. The effect of these measures was a significant increase in trade and travel. The timing of these arrangements could not have been better for the geographical spread of the gospel, as obedient believers and apostles became a part of that traffic (Acts 1:8). The particular interest of this article is shipboard travel.

Mediterranean ships varied considerably in size and configuration depending on their function. Merchant galleys were small, oared craft. While not dependent on the winds, they were slow, worked a more local trade, and stayed quite close to the shoreline. The average sailing vessel was a coasting craft with a single mast rig. With favoring winds, such craft made its destinations speedily and boasted an extended trade range. The ships taken by the apostle Paul and his colleagues from Philippi to Patara (Acts 20:6–21:1) and Caesarea to Myra (Acts 27:1–5) were coasters. Apostolic opportunities in gospel proclamation and stops for congregational encouragement often coincided with the time taken to load and off-load cargo in various ports along the way. Finally, it was left to much larger, multimasted ships like the famed Egyptian grain carrier *Isis* (it had three masts and an approximate 114-foot keel length and 1,228-ton carrying capacity) to risk the open waters of the Mediterranean individually or in fleets. Paul also traveled on such larger vessels (Acts 27:6; 28:11).

Ships carried a great variety of cargoes: foodstuffs like wine and olive oil, building materials, metals, various kinds of exotica, and that commodity most critical to the health and welfare of the empire and especially Rome: grain. The Egyptian portion of Rome's grain supply was strategic. The province of Egypt and its grain production were closely controlled by the emperor, and there were rich official inducements for free-merchants and investment cooperatives to ensure Rome's regular supply, even if that meant traveling during the dangerous season.

Mediterranean shipping was generally subject to seasonal weather patterns. Ancient sources indicate a safe season from early May to mid-September. The periods from early March to the end of April and from mid-September to early November were more risky. The most dangerous time was from early November to early March. Inclement weather could obliterate a view of the sun, moon, and stars, by which mariners navigated, and render well-known coastlines unfamiliar. Violent Mediterranean storms claimed countless ancient vessels. Luke's account of the wreck of the Alexandrian carrier on which Paul was a passenger (Acts 27)—not the first but the fourth shipwreck of Paul (2 Cor. 11:25)—reads with great accuracy to meteorological conditions in the dangerous season, the ship's appointments, and the attempts of crew and passengers to preserve the ship and its cargo. The account also redounds to the faith of Paul and the faithfulness of God (Acts 27:21–44).

The evil spirit failed to recognize their connection to Jesus, and it beat and stripped them so that they fled the encounter naked. This episode causes the name of Jesus to be held in greater honor, resulting in Christians deciding to make a complete break with their pagan past by burning their magic books (19:17–20). The great value of the scrolls (worth about 50,000 days' wages or about 137 years' worth of annual salary) shows how deep the problem was among believers.

Paul now plans to go to Macedonia and Achaia before returning to Jerusalem (19:21–22). In 19:23–41, Luke records an episode of violent opposition to Paul's ministry. Apparently Paul's preaching against idolatry leads many to renounce their allegiance to Artemis, resulting in declining sales of silver statues of the goddess. A silversmith named Demetrius stirs up the craftsmen of Ephesus, and the whole city is thrown into an uproar over the issue. The mob seizes two of Paul's traveling companions as the riot moves into the 25,000-seat theater, where they shout for two hours, "Great is Artemis of the Ephesians." The city clerk ultimately disperses the crowd, but the experience signals for Paul that it is time to leave (20:1).

Paul now travels through Macedonia (i.e., Philippi, Thessalonica, Berea) to Achaia (i.e., Corinth), where he spends three months (20:1–3). He probably writes the book of Romans during this winter in Corinth. Instead of sailing for Syria and Jerusalem, Paul travels by land back through Macedonia to Troas (20:3–6).

The night before he leaves Troas, Paul teaches late into the night (20:7). A young man named Eutychus (meaning "fortunate"), who was seated in the window, drifts asleep and falls from the third-story window to his death (20:7–9). Paul rushes downstairs, and God uses him to raise this young man from the dead (20:10–12). The group continues back upstairs where they share a meal (probably featuring the Lord's Supper) and listen to Paul until daylight, when it is time for him to leave.

The group travels down the coast of Asia, sailing past Ephesus in order to reach Jerusalem by Pentecost (20:13–16). They

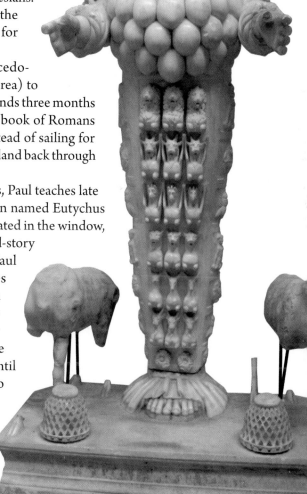

A statue of the goddess Artemis.

✚ If you make a trip to Ephesus today, you can still see the large theater where the people were rioting (Acts 19:28–31).

stop in nearby Miletus so that Paul can spend time with the elders of the church in Ephesus (20:17). Paul's farewell speech to those church leaders in Acts 20:18–38 is one of the most moving accounts in all of Scripture.

Paul begins by recounting his faithfulness to the cause of Christ in spite of much opposition from the Jews (20:18–21). Now he feels compelled to return to Jerusalem, although he expects to experience hardships there (20:22–23). He confesses, "I consider my life worth nothing to me, if only I may finish the race and complete the task the Lord Jesus has given me—the task of testifying to the gospel of God's grace" (20:24). Paul saddens them greatly by announcing they will probably never see his face again (20:25, 38). He has proclaimed the whole will of God to them, and his conscience is clear (20:26–27). He then exhorts them to keep watch over the flock of God, of which the Spirit has made them overseers (20:28). Savage wolves will come in among the church leadership and distort the truth, but they must be on guard and follow Paul's example of diligence and faithfulness (20:29–31). He then commits them to God and his grace (20:32). He has set an example of integrity, discipline, and generosity in life and ministry (20:33–35). They kneel down together and pray for one another before embracing and saying their emotional good-byes (20:36–38).

Paul and his traveling companions sail to Tyre and then to Caesarea before arriving in Jerusalem just in time for Pentecost in the spring of AD 57. Along the way, fellow believers warn Paul that he will suffer in Jerusalem (21:4, 10–12). Paul responds, "Why are you weeping and breaking my heart? I am ready not only to be bound, but also to die in Jerusalem for the name of the Lord Jesus" (21:13).

Paul's Witness in Jerusalem (21:17–23:35)

Paul receives a warm welcome from the believers in Jerusalem (21:17). He meets with James and the other elders to report all God has done among the gentiles (21:18–19). The elders express concern that many Jewish Christians are misunderstanding Paul's ministry, so they advise him to take a Nazarite vow along with four other men, which he agrees to do (21:20–26; Num. 6:2–21). But in the process, some Jews from Asia (probably Ephesus, see v. 29) spot Paul in the temple area and accuse him of teaching against the temple and the law (21:27–29). In the resulting riot, Paul is dragged out into the court of the gentiles and is about to be beaten to death when Roman soldiers break it up (21:30–32). They arrest and chain Paul and take him to the army barracks to protect him from the angry mob (21:33–36).

As the soldiers are leading him into the barracks, Paul gets permission from the commander to speak to his persecutors (21:37–40). He addresses the

✚ In his farewell to the Ephesian elders, Paul predicts that false teachers will emerge from the church leadership (Acts 20:29–30). This is exactly the problem Paul addresses in 1 Timothy (e.g., 1 Tim. 1:3–7).

crowd in Aramaic, the mother-tongue of Jews living in the area (21:40–22:2). Now he has their attention. In 22:3–21, Paul tells the story of his conversion for a second time, including his former life in Judaism, his encounter with Christ on the Damascus road, and his restoration by Ananias (22:3–16). The mob listens calmly until he tells them of his temple vision where God sends him on a mission to the gentiles (22:17–21). The crowd immediately begins calling for Paul's death (22:22). When the Roman commander orders Paul to be flogged, Paul reminds him that he is a Roman citizen by birth who has not been found guilty, a fact that alarms the commander (22:24–29).

The next day Paul makes his defense before the Jewish Sanhedrin (22:30). When he opens with a claim of innocence, the high priest orders him to be struck in the mouth (23:1–2). Paul responds with prophetic judgment against the high priest for his hypocrisy: "God will strike you, you whitewashed wall!" (23:3). When told he had just insulted the high priest, Paul changes his tone, perhaps with a hint of irony (23:4–5). Paul, a former Pharisee, then claims he is on trial for his hope in the resurrection of the dead, a doctrine accepted by Pharisees but rejected by Sadducees (23:6). His claim splits the group, causing a violent argument that effectively ends the trial (23:7–10). The following night the Lord appears to Paul to encourage him and assure him he must testify about Jesus in Rome also (23:11).

Meanwhile, forty Jewish men take an oath not to eat or drink anything until they have killed Paul (23:12–14). They enlist the help of the chief priests and the elders in plotting the ambush, but Paul's nephew learns of the plot and warns him (23:15–16). Paul relays the information to the Roman commander, who devises a way to protect him (23:17–22).

Under an escort of 470 soldiers, Paul is transferred from Jerusalem to Caesarea, where he is kept under guard in Herod's palace until Felix, the Roman governor of Judea, can hear his case (23:23–35).

The Roman road to Assos, the city where the missionary team took Paul on board (Acts 20:13–14).

✝ Paul gives his conversion testimony in Acts 9; 22; and 26.

Acts

Paul's Witness in Caesarea (24:1–26:32)

When Paul's Jewish accusers arrive in Caesarea, Felix hears the case (24:1–4). The Jewish lawyer Tertullus accuses Paul of being a troublemaker who stirs up riots among the Jews all over the world (24:5). He labels Paul the "ringleader of the Nazarene" heresy who was caught trying to desecrate the temple (24:5–9). Paul makes his own defense, first claiming they cannot prove any of these charges (24:10–13). Second, he argues that Christianity is the true fulfillment of Judaism, since it accepts Jesus as God's Messiah (24:14–16). He explains that recently he returned to Jerusalem to bring a monetary gift for the poor (i.e., the collection from the gentile churches). He did nothing to cause trouble (except perhaps shout his belief in the resurrection of the dead), but was unjustly accused by some Jews from Asia (24:17–21). Felix, who was well acquainted with Christianity, postpones his decision but keeps Paul in prison, although with some freedom (24:22–23).

A few days later Paul meets privately with Felix and his wife, Drusilla, a Jewess and one of three daughters of Herod Agrippa I (24:24; see Acts 12:19–23). Paul speaks about his faith in Christ, including righteousness and the future judgment, when suddenly Felix has had enough and concludes the meeting (24:25–26). For the next two years, Paul remains in prison in Caesarea (24:27).

When Festus takes over for Felix as Roman procurator, Paul's trial once again becomes a hot topic. The Jewish leaders request Paul be transferred back to Jerusalem with the plan to ambush and kill him along the way (25:1–3). Festus tells the Jews to come to Caesarea and he will hear their accusations against Paul there (25:4–5). Soon after arriving in Caesarea, Festus listens to the Jews present serious charges against Paul, all of which they cannot prove (25:6–7). Paul claims he has done nothing against the Jewish law, the temple, or against Caesar (25:8). When Festus entertains the option of changing the trial venue back to Jerusalem, Paul appeals to Caesar (25:9–12). Every Roman citizen had the right to have his case heard before the emperor in Rome. Rather than risk ambush on the journey or an unfair trial in Jerusalem, Paul opts to stand trial before Emperor Nero (in about AD 59).

When King Agrippa II and his sister Bernice arrive in Caesarea, Festus tells them about this odd prisoner named Paul, and they express interest in hearing him (25:13–22).

The next day, Festus provides Agrippa and Bernice with a bit of context before allowing Paul to speak (25:23–27). In short, Festus is not sure what to say to the emperor regarding the charges against Paul. For the third time in Acts, Paul tells the story of his former life in Judaism, his zeal in persecuting Christians, his Damascus road conversion, and his commission from Christ

✦ As the story of Acts is compressed due to space limitations, we often forget about the delays in real life. For instance, Paul stayed in prison in Caesarea for two years (Acts 24–26).

Map labels: Rome, Puteoli, ITALY, Rhegium, Syracuse, MALTA, Storm, MEDITERRANEAN SEA, MACEDONIA, THRACE, BLACK SEA, ACHAIA, ASIA, GALATIA, CAPPADOCIA, Cnidus, Myra, CRETE, Fair Havens, Salmone, Lasea, Sidon, Caesarea, Jerusalem

Paul's route — 0 100 200 mi — 0 100 200 km

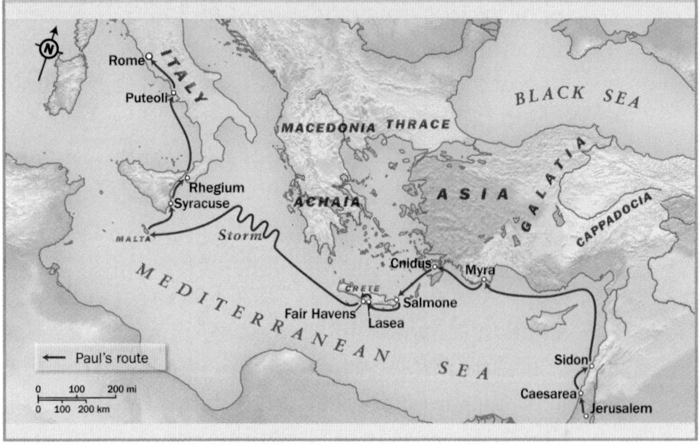

(26:1–18). Then Paul appeals to Agrippa, telling him how he has been obedient to the heavenly vision in preaching Jesus and his resurrection, and about the need for people to respond in repentance (26:19–23). Festus interrupts to say that Paul's great learning is driving him insane (26:24), but Paul counters that everything he is saying is true and reasonable (26:25). Paul bears faithful witness to Agrippa in an attempt to persuade him to become a Christian (26:26–29). After the hearing, Agrippa concludes Paul has done nothing deserving death or imprisonment and that he could have been set free if he had not appealed to Caesar (26:30–32). But God has appointed Paul to witness in Rome, and the journey to Rome begins.

Paul's Journey to and Witness in Rome (27:1–28:31)

Paul and the other prisoners are loaded onto a ship bound for Rome (27:1). Luke and Aristarchus also accompany Paul on the journey, as the "we" references in this section of Acts indicate. They sail up the coast from Caesarea and land at Sidon, where some of Paul's friends supply his needs (27:2–3). They sail west, finally landing at Myra in Lycia, where they board an Alexandrian ship bound for Italy (27:4–6). They sail farther west to Cnidus and then southwest to the island of Crete and the harbor of Fair Havens (27:7–8). It was now past "the Fast" or the Jewish Day of Atonement, which was in early October of AD 59—a dangerous time to sail the open seas (27:9). Paul warns the Roman centurion Julius, who was guarding them, of the danger of proceeding, but he fails to listen (27:10–11). They sail on, hoping to reach Phoenix, a more suitable harbor on Crete for wintering a ship (27:12).

After leaving Fair Havens, they sail slowly along the shore of Crete until a hurricane-force wind called a "northeaster" drives them out to sea (27:13–15). When they pass by a small island about twenty-three miles south of Crete, they secure the lifeboat, undergird the hull of the ship with ropes, lower the sea anchor, and throw cargo overboard (27:16–19). The ship is caught

✛ Paul travels to Rome to have his case heard by the Roman emperor Nero, the same emperor many believe sentenced both Peter and Paul to death.

in the violent storm for many days (27:20). When all hope seems lost, Paul has another vision from the Lord, assuring him he must stand trial before Caesar and that God will spare the lives of everyone on the ship (27:21–26).

After fourteen days and nights in a raging sea, the sailors sense they are quickly nearing land, so they lower more anchors (27:27–29). Some attempt to escape using the lifeboat, but Paul warns them to stay on the ship if they want to survive (27:30–32). Before dawn Paul urges everyone to eat (27:33–34). He takes some bread, gives thanks to God, and begins to eat in front of everyone (27:35). This act encourages the other 275 people on board this Alexandrian grain ship to eat (27:36–38). At daylight, they decide to run the ship aground in a bay with a sandy beach, but the ship strikes a sandbar and begins to break up (27:39–41). The soldiers want to kill the prisoners to prevent their escape, but the Roman centurion wants to spare Paul's life so he prohibits the slaughter (27:42–43). Instead, he orders everyone to swim to shore, and everyone reaches land safely as Paul has assured them (27:43–44).

They had landed on the island of Malta. Since Malta is a tiny island, only about seventeen miles long and nine miles wide, God's sovereign protection of Paul becomes evident. It would have been extremely easy for the ship to miss the island altogether. On this cold and rainy November morning, the islanders show unusual kindness by building a huge fire to keep everyone warm (28:1–2). As Paul is putting a pile of wood on the fire, a poisonous snake bites him. At

Saint Paul's Bay in Malta.

first, the islanders think he is a murderer who has finally met with justice, but when he suffers no ill effects, they declare him to be a god (28:3–6).

Publius, the chief official on the island, welcomes the small group of Christians into his home for three days (28:7). While there, Paul prays for and lays hands on Publius's sick father, who is then healed (28:8). As a result, the rest of the sick people on the island come to visit Paul and are healed (28:9). The Maltese honor the believers in many ways during their three-month stay and supply their needs when they are ready to sail (28:10–11).

Leaving Malta, they sail north to Syracuse, the main city of Sicily, then to Rhegium, then to Puteoli on the mainland of Italy (28:11–13). There they find some Christians with whom they spend a week, before going to Rome (28:14). The believers in Rome hear the good news of Paul's arrival and many travel as far as the Forum of Appius and the Three Taverns along the Via Appia—over fifty miles—to provide an encouraging welcome (28:15). When Paul arrives in Rome, he is allowed to live by himself with a soldier to guard him (28:16).

Within a few days of arriving in Rome, Paul meets with the Jewish leaders to explain his past actions and his message (28:17–20). They claim they have not heard anything bad about him from Judea, but they want to hear his views, since people everywhere are talking against the Christian sect (28:21–22). They arrange a time when Paul can explain from the Scriptures his understanding of the kingdom of God and Jesus as Messiah (28:23). Some were convinced, but others refused to believe, fulfilling the prophecy of Isaiah 6:9–10 (28:24–27). Paul then declares that God has offered his salvation to the gentiles who will listen (28:28).

Paul spends two unnerving years awaiting his trial before Nero, who is becoming more and more unstable mentally. Paul rents a modest house and, though constantly chained to a Roman soldier, welcomes friends and co-workers (28:30). The final verse of Acts reminds us that the focus is on the message, not the messengers. Like other witnesses through this amazing book, Paul has suffered greatly for the cause of Christ. Even now, he remains a faithful witness, although in chains. But the Word of God is not bound. The message has moved triumphantly from Jerusalem to Rome. In the Greek text, the word we translate "without hindrance" is actually the last word in the book. Paul may be in prison, but the gospel of Jesus Christ marches on "unhindered" (28:31)!

So What? Applying Acts Today

Applying Acts begins with knowing how to interpret Acts. We obviously don't want to duplicate every early church pattern we find in Acts (e.g., casting lots

✦ When Paul arrives in Rome, he finds a thriving church there. The church in Rome was most likely started by anonymous Christian missionaries or by Jewish Christians who had been in Jerusalem for Pentecost and returned to Rome.

Acts   737

or experiencing the judgment of Ananias and Sapphira). But we do want to embrace everything in Acts that should be normative for Christians today. The best way to determine what is normative is to find those themes in the book that are repeated.

To begin with, Acts calls us to follow the Holy Spirit. The Spirit is the main character throughout the entire book, empowering, guiding, unifying, and commissioning God's people. Closely related to the Spirit's role is the theme of God's sovereignty. Throughout Acts, God is in control, even when it seems everything is coming apart. God works primarily through the church to accomplish his will. As people worship God, care for each other, grow spiritually, and join in the worldwide mission, God is glorified. Prayer is another major theme in Acts. We find God's people are praying for protection, for guidance, for needs to be met, for healing, for missionaries, and so on. In almost every chapter in Acts, believers are praying. Luke also makes it clear that to be a follower of Jesus Christ means being a faithful witness. In Acts believers don't just share their personal stories, they witness to what God has done in history through the death and resurrection of Jesus. Because God has invaded this world in the person of Jesus, we have the opportunity to tell others the good news. Acts reminds us of the price paid by the early Christians to share this witness.

They suffered imprisonment, beatings, and rejection; they faced angry mobs, violent storms, persecution, and even death. Suffering is an essential part of the mission to the gentiles. Trials are worth enduring because all people need the good news, gentiles included.

As a result of considering repeated themes in Acts, we learn to follow the Spirit, trust in God's sovereignty, join with God's people, pray, give witness to what God has done in Christ, and be willing to suffer in order to take the message to all people.

Our Favorite Verses in Acts

So when they met together, they asked him, "Lord, are you at this time going to restore the kingdom to Israel?" He said to them: "It is not for you to know the times or dates the Father has set by his own authority. But you will receive power when the Holy Spirit comes on you; and you will be my witnesses in Jerusalem, and in all Judea and Samaria, and to the ends of the earth." (Acts 1:6–8)

The Colosseum in Rome.

Romans

*The Good News
of God's Righteousness*

Paul's letter to the Romans is probably the clearest and most powerful statement of the gospel in all the New Testament. Rather than affirming human potential or innate goodness apart from God, the gospel begins with bad news: humans are thoroughly sinful and guilty and without hope. But God has come to our rescue in Jesus Christ. He has done something for us we could never do for ourselves. He offers us forgiveness and membership in his covenant community, and promises never to condemn us or stop loving us. The four Gospels tell the story of Jesus's life, ministry, death, and resurrection, but Romans explains the theological and practical significance of that story. Throughout history, Romans has changed the lives of famous believers (e.g., Augustine, Martin Luther, John Wesley, Karl Barth) and many who are much less famous. One thing is for sure, reading, studying, and meditating on Romans will change our lives!

Who Wrote Romans?

Paul claims to have written Romans (1:1), and there is nearly universal agreement among New Testament scholars that he is indeed the author. For this letter, Tertius served as Paul's secretary or scribe (16:22).

Who Is Paul's Audience?

Romans is addressed to "all in Rome who are loved by God and called to be saints" (1:7), yet Paul did not plant the church and had apparently not even visited the church (1:8–15; 15:22–29). By the time Paul wrote, the church had been around for some time (1:8).

Most likely, the church in Rome originated either from converts on the day of Pentecost who then carried the gospel to Rome (Acts 2:10) or from anonymous Christian missionaries. In any case, many of the first Christians in Rome were Jewish Christians. Early on, Jewish Christians dominated the church in Rome. But in AD 49, Emperor Claudius expelled the Jews from Rome, and many Jewish Christians had to leave the city as well (e.g., Acts 18:1–3).

When the Jewish Christians left, the gentile Christians had to assume leadership responsibilities in the church. When Emperor Claudius died in AD 54 and the Jewish Christians were finally allowed to return to the city, things were not as they had left them. The church in Rome now had a gentile majority and gentile Christian leaders.

Most likely the church in Rome was organized into a number of smaller house churches (notice the greetings in Romans 16). These house churches were probably split along social lines (Jewish Christians and gentile Christians). These two groups had different—but equally valid—ways of expressing their faith in Jesus Christ. In Romans then, Paul is writing to a group of house churches with a gentile Christian majority and Jewish Christian minority. One of his main purposes in the letter is to encourage unity within the church in Rome.

We believe that Paul wrote Romans in about AD 57 from Corinth near the end of his third missionary journey (see Acts 20:2–3). Gaius is identified as his Corinthian host in Romans 16:23, and the greeting from Erastus, "the city's director of public works" (Rom. 16:23), coincides with the note in 2 Timothy 4:20 that Erastus lived in Corinth. In addition, Phoebe probably carried the letter to Rome, and she is connected with the church in "Cenchrea," a seaport city near Corinth (Rom. 16:1–2).

✚ The early church met in homes to learn, worship, share meals (including the Lord's Supper), and meet each other's needs.

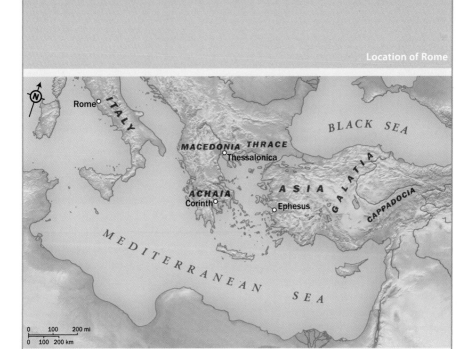

What Is at the Heart of Romans?

Paul's purpose in writing connects with (1) the situation of the church in Rome, and (2) his own circumstances and ministry plans. He seems to have not one, but several reasons for writing Romans.

One reason Paul writes this letter is to unify the different house churches. Notice the theme of "peace" that runs through the entire letter (Rom. 1:7; 2:10; 3:17; 5:1; 8:6; 14:17, 19; 15:13, 33; 16:20). Paul's attempt to heal this division is most apparent in his discussion of the "weak" and the "strong" in Romans 14:1–15:13. On the one hand, the "weak" Jewish Christians were probably condemning gentile Christians for failing to observe certain food laws or keep particular holy days. They believed strongly in the importance of religious rituals in the Christian life. On the other hand, the "strong" gentile Christians probably looked down on the Jewish Christians for not taking their freedom in Christ seriously enough. Paul rebukes both groups for placing their own personal convictions above the gospel itself. Paul can understand both worlds quite well as a Jew (see 9:1–5) who has also been commissioned to serve as the "apostle to the Gentiles" (1:5; 11:13; 15:16). He hopes this clear and comprehensive explanation of the gospel of Jesus Christ will refocus both groups on what is most important and, as a result, unify the church in Rome.

Paul's own circumstances also lead him to write the letter. He plans to take the collection from the gentile churches back to the poor Jewish

✚ Paul also discusses issues related to "strong" and "weak" in 1 Corinthians 8:1–11:1.

The City of Rome

Lynn H. Cohick

Known as the Eternal City, Rome captured the imaginations and terrified the hearts of many from its rise to power in the fifth century BC to its fall in the fifth century AD. Rome's origins reach back into myth and legend. The Latins who settled Rome trace their ancestry to Aeneas, son of the goddess Venus and defender of Troy, whose adventures are recounted by Vergil in *The Aeneid* (first century BC). Among Aeneas's descendants were twin boys, Remus and Romulus, who are credited with founding Rome in 753 BC. Legend asserts that as infants the twins were left to die near the banks of the Tiber River, but were suckled by a she-wolf, Lupa Capitolina, who came to represent Rome itself (Livy, *History of Rome* 1.4). Julius Caesar and his adopted son Octavian (later Emperor Augustus) traced their ancestry back to Aeneas and Venus.

Rome sits on the western side of the Italian peninsula, positioned at the northern border of the Latium region. The Estruscans were their neighbors to the north, and Campania lay south of Latium. The region enjoyed sufficient rainfall and fertile soil to support a large population center. The earliest settlers lived on the hills, which rose on the eastern shores of the Tiber River. The seven hills of Rome (Aventine, Caelian, Capitoline, Esquiline, Palatine, Quirinal, Viminal) became an identity marker for the city, so that when John in Revelation makes reference to the "seven hills" (17:9), his audience understands he is alluding to the "great city" (17:18). Near the Capitoline hill, an island in the Tiber disrupted the fast flowing river, making a natural fjord at this point. The Tiber's currents facilitated trade, as they were navigable by barges and small boats for quite a distance inland. Approximately sixteen miles from Rome, the Tiber emptied into the Mediterranean Sea at the port of Ostia.

In the seventh and sixth centuries BC, a marshy area between the Capitoline, Palatine, and Esquiline hills was drained, the Roman forum was built upon the resulting field, and temples to Vulcan and Vesta (the god and goddess of fire, hearth, and family) were erected. On the Capitoline hill, a large temple to Jupiter was constructed. When the seventh and final king of Rome was overthrown in about 510 BC, Rome established itself as a Republic, and in about 500 BC, the temple of Saturn was constructed in the Forum; it served as Rome's treasury and repository of the Senate's decrees. What would become the Circus Maximus was at this early stage a dirt racetrack located in the valley between the Palatine and Aventine hills. Legend places the Rape of the Sabines here. By Augustus's time (ruled 27 BC–AD 14), 150,000 spectators watched chariot races from bleachers extending around three-quarters of the oval track.

In 390 BC the Gauls attacked and burned Rome to the ground. Undaunted by this defeat, Romans chose to rebuild the city quickly without central planning, which explains why it does not follow the typical grid pattern (Livy, *History of Rome* 5.55). They restored and expanded their city walls, encompassing approximately seven hundred acres. They also built aqueducts, at first underground; then under Emperor Claudius (AD 41–54), an elevated aqueduct forty-three miles long brought water into the city. In 312 BC the foundations were laid for the famous road, the Via Appia. Approximately 350 miles

Christians in Jerusalem (15:25–27). Then he hopes to visit Rome on his way to Spain (15:22–29). He wants to encourage and strengthen the church in Rome (1:8–15), but he's also counting on their financial

✚ In following Jesus's command to take the gospel to the "ends of the earth," Paul planned a mission trip to Spain (Rom. 15:22–29).

long at its completion fifty years later, it was one of the oldest and most well-known roads, going south to Capua and then stretching southeast to the Adriatic Sea. Along this road many tombs of wealthy Romans have been uncovered, including the elaborate first-century-AD tomb of Cecilia Metella.

Having control of most of the Italian peninsula, Rome turned its attention to the powerful city of Carthage in North Africa. In 241 BC, Rome bested Carthage in the first Punic War; within twenty years, however, the Carthaginian general, Hannibal, marched across the Alps and approached Rome. While preparing to attack the city, Hannibal was called back to Carthage, which was besieged by Scipio Africanus (who defeated it in 202 BC). Wealth poured into Rome. By the end of the third century BC, Rome was the largest city in Italy, rivaling contemporary Alexandria, Egypt, and Antioch in Syria. Wealthy politicians and later the emperors built their residences mainly on the Palatine hill, and the Forum became a place of grand public buildings (*basilicae*). Through the center ran the Via Sacra, the parade route for victorious generals and later emperors.

During the first century BC, Rome was consumed with civil wars. In the late 50s BC Julius Caesar enlarged the Roman Forum to the northeast, which Augustus and later emperors expanded. Caesar's murder plunged the city into another bloody civil war, with most Romans longing for peace. The subsequent rise to power of his adopted son, Octavian, signaled the end of the Republic and the beginning of Imperial Rome. The new emperor (Augustus ruled from 28 BC–AD 14) recorded his accomplishments in the *Res Gestae*, wherein he declares he built or refurbished eighty-two temples in Rome, often using marble instead of brick in construction. For example, the Pantheon was constructed to honor all gods; it was refurbished by Hadrian in the early second century

AD. To honor Augustus's victories in Spain, the Senate commissioned the *Ara Pacis*, a monumental altar to Peace completed in 9 BC. The altar was enclosed by a marble screen decorated with reliefs portraying the imperial family and mythological scenes of Romulus and Remus, as well as Aeneas's adventures.

In AD 64 a great fire burned for six days and seven nights, consuming roughly 70 percent of the city. According to the historian Tacitus (*Annals* 15.38), it began at the Circus and quickly spread through the overcrowded wooden structures, creating havoc and destruction. The people blamed Nero, who deflected their accusations on to Christians, brutally killing many. Nero's suicide in AD 68 threw the city into disarray, but within a year the great general Vespasian became emperor (ruled AD 69–79). His son, Titus, quelled the Jewish rebellion in the Roman province of Palestine and sacked Jerusalem (including the temple) in AD 70; an arch commemorating that victory was commissioned by the Senate in AD 81 after his death. The monument includes a relief of Roman soldiers carrying away pillaged treasures from the Jerusalem temple. The Colosseum, perhaps the best-known building today in Rome, was commissioned by Vespasian to house gladiatorial games. The fifty thousand-seat amphitheater was built in no small part by Jewish slaves using plunder taken after the Jewish War. The Colosseum, finished by Titus in AD 80, was built over the private, artificial lake created by Nero, the external walls were covered with marble, and statues graced the many niches.

Outside the city walls can be found catacombs, burial tunnels used by Jews residing in Rome beginning in the first century BC. Inscriptions indicate there were at least thirteen synagogues within Rome. In the second century AD, Christians also used catacombs as burial sites, though these did not overlap with Jewish catacombs.

support for his mission trip farther west (the term for "assist" in 15:24 often refers to financial assistance). The heart of Romans may be summarized in this way:

The gospel → unity in the church → mission of the church

With his forceful and comprehensive account of the good news (gospel) of a righteousness from God (Rom. 1:17), Paul attempts to persuade the gentile and Jewish Christians in Rome to unite. A church unified around the gospel of Jesus Christ is a church on mission. The outline of Romans reflects this purpose:

- Introduction (1:1–17)
- Our Problem: All Are Sinful and Guilty (1:18–3:20)
- God's Solution: Righteousness (3:21–5:21)
- The Result: Our Participation with Christ (6:1–8:39)
- An Important Concern: God Has Been Faithful to Keep His Promises (9:1–11:36)
- Practical Implications: Relational Righteousness (12:1–15:13)
- Conclusion (15:14–16:27)

What Makes Romans Interesting and Unique?

- Paul did not plant the church in Rome and had never visited the church when he wrote this letter (1:8–15; 15:22–29).
- Paul greets close to thirty people at the close of this letter, an unusually long greeting list.
- Romans is the longest and most theologically profound of Paul's letters.
- The letter contains extensive treatments of very significant biblical themes: human sinfulness, justification by faith, life in the Spirit, God's relationship to Israel, and ethical obligations of Christians.

Emperor Claudius (ruled from AD 41 to 54), who expelled the Jews from Rome (Acts 18:1–2).

- Romans emphasizes the gospel or "good news" of God, at the beginning (1:1, 2, 9, 15–17), in the middle (2:16; 10:15, 16; 11:28), and at the end (15:16, 19, 20; 16:25).
- The doctrine of justification by faith that sparked the Protestant Reformation is clearly set forth in this letter.

What Is the Message of Romans?

Introduction (1:1–17)

Paul begins by identifying the sender and recipients of the letter, followed by a greeting (1:1–7). After giving thanks for the Roman Christians and explaining his own ministry plans (1:8–15), he concludes with the thesis paragraph (1:16–17).

Sender, recipients, and greeting (1:1–7)

Paul begins in typical fashion by identifying himself (1:1–6), naming the recipients, and offering a greeting (1:7). What is unusual here is how much space Paul gives to introducing himself, his gospel, and his apostolic ministry, perhaps because he had never visited the church in Rome and because of the situation in that church. There is nothing like the gospel of Jesus Christ crucified and resurrected to unify a divided church. He greets *all* the Christians in Rome, both Jewish and gentile, with God's grace and peace (1:7).

Thanksgiving, prayer, and ministry plans (1:8–15)

Paul thanks God for *all* the believers in Rome due to their reported faith. He prays regularly for them and seems eager for God to open a way for him to visit (1:8–10). He longs to "impart some spiritual gift" to these believers (1:11–12). The "gift" mentioned here probably connects more to the overall purpose of the letter than to any one particular gift. When the Roman Christians understand fully God's grand plan of uniting Jews and gentiles in Christ, their faith will become strong and mutually edifying. Such a unified faith will also do more to advance the good news of Jesus among the gentiles, the very thing Paul has been called to do (1:13–15).

Thesis of the letter (1:16–17)

Paul is eager to preach the gospel in Rome because he is not ashamed of the gospel—the "power of God for the salvation of everyone who believes:

✚ In his thesis statement of Romans 1:16–17, Paul might be alluding to the transformative "power" of the Spirit, which he will explain more fully in Romans 8.

first for the Jew, then for the Gentile" (1:16). He is not ashamed because he knows this message can totally change a person's life. In 1:17 Paul specifies that the gospel reveals God's righteousness. The important phrase "righteousness of God" (*dikaisyne theou*) probably includes one or more of the following ideas:

- God's character—God is righteous and just
- God's activity—God's faithfulness to keep his covenant promises, including making things right with the world
- God's gift—God's gift to individuals of a right relationship and right standing with him, including forgiveness of sins

Faith is what allows us to experience God's righteousness (1:17; Hab. 2:4).

Our Problem: All Are Sinful and Guilty (1:18–3:20)

After introducing God's good news to save people, Paul shocks us by switching to the topic of God's wrath against all sin and evil. The good news actually begins with some "bad news"—God absolutely hates evil. For people to acknowledge their need for a Savior, they need to admit they have a sin problem, and this is Paul's focus in 1:18–3:20.

The unrighteous are guilty (1:18–32)

Although God will certainly condemn evil at the last judgment, Paul announces God's wrath is now being revealed against sin (1:18–20). As people suppress the truth about God that is made known through general revelation, they make sinful choices and suffer the consequences: God gives them over to degrading passions (1:24, 26–27), to worshiping created idols rather than the Creator (1:25), and to depraved thinking that leads to all kinds of sinful behavior (1:28–31). The unrighteous (chiefly gentiles in the original context) not only practice wickedness, but also encourage others to do so (1:32). They rightly incur the wrath of God.

The self-righteous are guilty (2:1–16)

Paul begins to address Jewish believers in this section, although gentile moralists cannot be

✚ In Romans 1:17 Paul quotes Habakkuk 2:4 to show that faith is an essential element in true righteousness (see also Gal. 3:11; Heb. 10:38).

completely excluded. Just like the pagans, the moralists are "without excuse" before God. Their judgment of the "unrighteous" is hypocritical, since they themselves have committed many sins (e.g., envy, deceit, gossip, slander). This reveals a human tendency to be critical of others while excusing one's own sin. But God does not show favoritism when judging sin (2:2–3). Because of his kindness, we should be led to repentance rather than to presumption (2:4–5). Each person, whether Jew or gentile (2:10), will be judged by God according to what he or she has done (2:6, 11). Eternal life awaits those who seek God and persist in doing good, while condemnation ("trouble and distress") awaits those who are self-seeking, reject the truth, and follow evil. The Jews should not trust in the law to take away their sin, since only those who completely obey the law are righteous. The Jews sin "under the law," while the gentiles sin "apart from law," but in the end, the result is the same—all are guilty before God (2:12–16).

Self-righteous Jews in particular are guilty (2:17–3:8)

Paul now explicitly mentions Jews as his target audience (2:17). Although the Jews have the advantage of receiving God's special revelation (3:2), merely possessing the law (God's revelation—2:17–24) and circumcision (the sign of God's covenant—2:25–29) won't protect them from judgment. In contrast, a "true Jew" is one who has been transformed inwardly by the Spirit (2:28–29). Judging his own people for their sin does not make God unrighteous (i.e., unable to keep his covenant promises). In fact, in spite of their unfaithfulness and failure to bring his light to the gentiles, God's faithfulness even to unfaithful people (3:4–6) will accentuate his trustworthiness and bring him more glory. In spite of God's ability and willingness to turn a desperate situation around for good, humans are not exempt from judgment (3:5, 7) and certainly do not have license to do whatever they want (3:8), for God's reputation among the nations has been ruined by the sinful behavior of his covenant people (2:24). Now, to be true to his promises, God needs a people who will do what Israel failed to do, who will be faithful and bring his word to the gentiles. At the end of Romans 3, we see that God has found such a people. Praise be to God!

Arch of Titus in Rome.

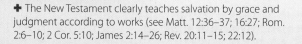

✚ The New Testament clearly teaches salvation by grace and judgment according to works (see Matt. 12:36–37; 16:27; Rom. 2:6–10; 2 Cor. 5:10; James 2:14–26; Rev. 20:11–15; 22:12).

Justification by Faith

Mark A. Seifrid

The confession that "faith alone" makes a person right with God became a central element of the Reformation and continues to distinguish Protestant Christianity from Roman Catholicism. According to the Catholic faith, justification is the movement of the heart by grace away from sin and toward God, a movement in which faith, hope, and love are infused by God, increase in good works, and in the best case issue in eternal life at the final judgment.

Paul's teaching on this matter—which appears prominently in Galatians and Romans, but also elsewhere in his letters—may be found in brief form in his summary assertion that "one is justified by faith, apart from the works of the law" (Rom. 3:28 ESV). The background to Paul's statement lies in the contention between God and the human being, who in idolatry and unbelief rejects the good Creator and declares him a liar, and in so doing becomes a liar (Rom. 1:18–32; 3:1–8). The holy, good, and gracious law of God was given to Israel in order to increase sin and thus to manifest the truth that we all are under the power of sin (Rom. 5:20; 7:1–25;

2 Cor. 3:4–11; Gal. 3:19–22). In this way the law points us to Christ (Rom. 3:19–21).

Paul's Jewish-Christian opponents and many other Jews imagined, however, that the law was given in order to further God's grace to them and so improve them (Rom. 2:17–29; Gal. 1:6–9; 5:1–12). Paul's assertion, that justification takes place "by faith apart from works of the law," constitutes an attack on that view. "Faith" for Paul is not an abstract quality, but rather exists only in relation to the proclamation of the incarnate, crucified, and risen Christ, in whom all God's unconditional promises have come to fulfillment. Therefore, when Paul says we are "justified by faith," he is saying we are justified by Christ, by whom God creates faith in the fallen human heart (Rom. 3:21–26; Gal. 3:23–29; Phil. 3:2–11).

Justification is the act of God's saving judgment—an extraordinary righteousness that transcends guilt and recompense—that took place in the cross and resurrection of Jesus and is distributed through the preaching of the gospel (Rom. 1:16–17; 3:21–26; Gal. 2:15–21). As an act of

Conclusion: Everyone is sinful and guilty before God (3:9–20)

Paul now draws a conclusion based on everything he has said in 1:18–3:8. All people, Jews and gentiles alike, are "under sin," portrayed here as a sinister power that captures and imprisons people (3:9). To support this conclusion, in 3:10–18 Paul strings together a list of quotations from the Old Testament. All these quotations point to an important truth (3:19)—before God, the righteous Judge, no one can say anything in his or her own defense ("every mouth is silenced"). There are no more excuses, nothing left to say. Everyone is speechless as we wait for God to announce the verdict of "Guilty!" In 3:20 we learn that not even Jews can be "declared righteous" by "observing the law" (i.e., by "works of law"—see Rom. 3:28; Gal. 2:16; 3:2, 5, 10). By trying to obey God's good law, they realize that they are sinners who don't measure up to God's standards. The whole world is sinful and guilty before God—immoral gentiles, moralizing Jews and gentiles, and even self-righteous Jews. All are guilty!

✚ In Romans 3:9–20 Paul quotes extensively from the Old Testament book of Psalms to demonstrate that human beings are sinful and guilty before God.

God, it is simultaneously a declaration and a deed, both a word and a work of God, in which the fallen human being is both forgiven and created anew (Rom. 6:1–11; 1 Cor. 6:11; 2 Cor. 5:17–21; Gal. 2:19–21). Our righteousness remains "located" in the crucified and risen Lord, to whom we are bound by faith (Rom. 10:4; 1 Cor. 1:30; Phil. 3:6–11). In this way, the fallen and idolatrous human being is restored to faith in the Creator, the right relation to God in which we were made to live (Gen. 3:1–13; 15:6). God counts this faith as righteousness, just as he did with Abraham, through whom he promised to bring blessing to all nations (Rom. 4:1–9; Gal. 3:6–9). This justifying work of God in the gospel is the fulfillment of God's promise to reveal his saving righteousness before all nations in an act of "ruling and judging" in which the Creator of the world conquers the powers of chaos and evil and establishes righteousness, just as he did in the original act of creation (Pss. 89:5–18; 98:1–9; Isa. 51:9–11; 59:9–11). "God's righteousness" is thus distinct from "God's faithfulness" in that it presupposes the context of battle and contention over righteousness.

Similarly, justification and sanctification are different dimensions of the one saving act of God in Christ, and not distinct events that may be placed in a logical order (1 Cor. 1:30; 6:11). Justification differs from "sanctification" in that justification bears a distinctly verbal (and thus forensic) dimension, bringing human beings to confess the wonder of God's righteousness in the face of our sin and rebellion. As the entrance of the new creation into the present, fallen world (2 Cor. 5:17–21), God's justifying work in Christ stands in closest proximity to Jesus's announcement of the kingdom of God as it appears in the Gospels (Matt. 5:6, 20; 6:33; cf. Rom. 14:17). Since in God's work of justification we already share in the age to come by faith in Jesus Christ, in Christ God shall yet bring us through final judgment to salvation (Rom. 5:9–10, 15–21). The works by which we shall stand at the final judgment are precisely the fruit of the Spirit and the age to come already at work in us (Gal. 5:1–6, 22–26; 6:14–16). Since God's justifying work in Christ is nothing other than the final judgment brought into the present, it becomes clear that Paul and James complement each other (Rom. 3:21–31; 4:1–25; James 2:18–26). To be justified is to have Jesus Christ as Lord and to live in the assurance that he has conquered our sin and our death in order that we might live forever with him in his kingdom.

God's Solution: Righteousness (3:21–5:21)

After hearing about sin for almost three chapters, we're ready for some good news. Beginning with the "but now" in 3:21, Paul begins describing God's solution to the human problem of sin. God's righteousness has now been graciously made available through faith in Jesus Christ and his atoning death on the cross.

The righteousness of God (3:21–31)

The theme of the gospel of God's righteousness (1:16–17) resurfaces again in 3:21:

1:17—"For in the gospel a righteousness from God is revealed."

3:21—"But now a righteousness from God, apart from law, has been made known."

This paragraph is packed with important theological realities, including righteousness, faith, sin, justification, grace, redemption, the atoning work of Christ, and the justice of God. It's true that no one will be declared righteous by works of law (3:20), but that is not the end of the story. Now God's righteousness has been made known apart from the law, and even the Law and the Prophets testify to this righteousness (3:21). We see now a new phase in God's plan of salvation (cf. Gal. 4:4–5). God's righteousness comes to those who acknowledge their sinfulness and believe in Jesus, the one who has been faithful unto death (3:22–24, 26). God has demonstrated his holy and righteous character by presenting Jesus as the atoning sacrifice, thereby averting God's wrath against sin and removing our guilt (3:25–26; cf. 1 John 4:10). God can now accept guilty sinners without violating his righteous character (Mark 10:45; Eph. 1:7; Col. 1:14; Titus 2:14; 1 Pet. 1:18–19). God's gracious gift, which comes by faith rather than works of law, leaves no room for boasting (3:27–28; Eph. 2:8–9). We can add nothing to the perfect atoning sacrifice of Christ. There is only one God, and he justifies Jews and gentiles in one way—by faith in Christ (3:29–30). But don't think that faith destroys the law or leads to lawlessness. No, faith actually upholds the law (3:31), since, as we will learn later, those who walk by the Spirit actually fulfill the law (8:4; 13:8, 10; Gal. 5–6).

Abraham: Old Testament illustration (4:1–25)

To show that the gospel is not a recent invention, Paul introduces Abraham, the faithful patriarch of all Jews, and David, Israel's greatest king. Abraham wasn't justified by works but trusted God, who credited his faith as righteousness (4:1–5; Gen. 15:6). Although we can never earn God's

✦ Before God gave the Law to Moses, he had already justified Abraham on the basis of his faith in God's promises.

righteousness like we earn a wage, we can receive it by faith as a free gift. Paul also cites David as an example of someone who is counted righteous before God apart from works (4:6–8). In 4:9–12, Paul announces the blessing of righteousness is available to all people, both Jews and gentiles (4:9). God counted Abraham righteous on the basis of faith *before* he was circumcised (4:10). Consequently, Abraham, whose righteousness came through faith rather than the law, is the father of all who believe—whether circumcised or uncircumcised, Jew or gentile (4:11–15). Since the promise comes by faith rather than through the law, both Jews and gentiles can join together as one people of God (4:16–17). In essence, Abraham's faith consisted of his belief that God would keep his promises (4:18–22). Just as God credited Abraham's faith as righteousness, he also credits our faith as righteousness (4:23–24). As Abraham trusted God's ability to "give life to the dead" (4:17), so we too believe that God has "raised Jesus our Lord from the dead" (4:24; cf. Rom. 8:11; 10:9). Jesus was "delivered over to death for our sins" and "raised to life for our justification" (4:25).

The blessings of justification (5:1–11)

Paul next spells out the blessings of being declared righteous by God—"since we have been justified by faith, we have . . ." (5:1). The first blessing is "peace with God through our Lord Jesus Christ" (5:1). Justification means that God forgives us *and* he accepts us into his covenant community. The second blessing is access to "grace in which we now stand" (5:2). Like an adopted child coming to live with his or her new parents, we enter into the state of grace and continue there forever. The third blessing is the privilege of rejoicing in "the hope of the glory of God" (5:2). While we see glimpses of God's glory now, one day we will experience his glory in all its fullness. The fourth blessing is the ability to rejoice in our sufferings, because we know God uses trials to reinforce hope (5:3–4). Our hope is more than wishful thinking because it is based on God's love and poured into our lives by the Spirit (5:5–8). The fifth blessing is we shall be saved from God's wrath—his holy opposition to and hatred of sin and evil (5:9–10). If God has already forgiven us and brought us into his family, he will certainly spare us from his future wrath. The sixth blessing deals with boasting. While we should never boast in our religious accomplishments (2:23; 3:27; 4:2), we are allowed to boast in what God has done for us in Christ (5:11).

Adam or Christ, death or life? (5:12–21)

In the second half of Romans 5, Paul compares Adam and Christ, the two figureheads or representatives of humanity. The disobedience of the

✦ From the beginning when God made a covenant with Abraham, God planned for his covenant community to include people of all races and nationalities (Gen. 12:3; 17:5; Rom. 4:16–17).

first Adam resulted in sin, death, and condemnation for all (5:12, 16–19). The obedience of Christ, the "second Adam," resulted in an abundance of grace, the gift of righteousness, and life for all who turn to him in faith (5:15–19). While the sin of the first brings a curse, the faithfulness of the second reverses the curse and reconciles people to God. From Adam until Moses there was no law, and there could therefore be no "transgression" or breaking of a law. Yet sin was still in the world and, as a result, death continued to reign during this time (5:13–14). Rather than solving the sin problem, the law reveals God's expectations with greater clarity and, as a result, transgressions actually increase (Rom. 3:20; 4:15; 5:13; 7:7–8, 13). But "where sin increased, grace increased all the more" (5:20). While sin reigns in death, grace reigns with even more authority and power "through righteousness to bring eternal life through Jesus Christ our Lord" (5:21).

The Result: Our Participation with Christ (6:1–8:39)

In Romans 1–5 we learn that human beings have a sin problem and that God has provided a solution through Jesus Christ. In Romans 6–8 we see how our participation with Christ reshapes the way we now live. Once we were enslaved to sin, but now we are servants of God. We're no longer under the law but are free to walk in the new way of the Spirit. We have been given new life, a new family, and a glorious future. Nothing can separate us from God's love.

Dead to sin, but alive to God (6:1–14)

Some might conclude from 5:20 that believers should sin even more so that God will show even more grace (6:1). Paul says,

Statue of Paul in the Basilica of St. Paul Outside the Walls in Rome.

✝ God's grace does not give us permission to sin even more (Rom. 6:1). Rather, his grace has brought us into a new relationship with Christ, and we are to offer ourselves to him in obedience (Rom. 6:11–14). Grace changes everything!

Law and Grace in Paul's Letters

Mark A. Seifrid

Although the law is the good and holy gift of God to Israel (Rom. 7:12), its fundamental purpose is to increase sin and transgression (Gal. 3:19–22). Through the law, we fallen human beings come to know the tragic and wretched experience of sinning (Rom. 7:7–13). We thereby come to know ourselves as sinners, who are accountable for our deeds and yet entirely and inescapably under the power of sin (Rom. 3:9–20; 7:14–25). The law thus furthers God's wrath (Rom. 4:15). Its ministry and purpose is to work our death (2 Cor. 3:6–11). The law works in this way because it comes to us fallen human beings as a sanction and demand to which life and death are attached: "Do this and you shall live!" (see Rom. 10:5; Gal. 3:12). For this reason, Paul speaks of the law as "written code" (Rom. 2:25–29; 7:6; 2 Cor. 3:6). While we are able to conform with many—or even all—of its outward demands (Phil. 3:6), no one can remove coveting from their heart. No one fears, loves, and trusts in God above all things. No one loves his neighbor as himself. The law thus works our particular and concrete condemnation (Rom. 7:7–13). It is weak "through the flesh," that is, through our bondage to sin (Rom. 8:3).

In the wonder of God's grace, God's saving righteousness has been revealed "apart from law" in the gospel (Rom. 3:21–26). In Jesus Christ alone, God has spoken and acted decisively on our behalf (Rom. 5:1–3, 15–21; 7:25; Gal. 1:6; 2:21; 5:4). In Christ and his resurrection, the law's righteous offer of life has come to its final and decisive fulfillment (Rom. 8:3–4). In the hand of God, then, the law works in a strange and backward way to further God's final purpose: God gives life only to those whom he has first put to death, justifies only those whom the law condemns, and makes saints only out of those whom the law declares sinners (Rom. 3:9–31; 4:1–25; 5:11–8:39; 2 Cor. 3:4–18;). In this way, the law serves the larger saving purpose of God. The law was given long after God gave Abraham his unconditional promise of blessing (Gal. 3:15–18). The law comes to its goal in Jesus Christ, in whom the age to come has entered the present (Rom. 10:4). As the good but limited gift of God to Israel, the law anticipates God's greater gift of himself to us in his crucified and risen Son (Rom. 10:5–13). Paul thus takes up the language of Jeremiah 31:31–34 and characterizes the law and its demands as "the old covenant" (2 Cor. 3:14). It has been overcome and transcended by the new covenant fulfilled in Jesus Christ, in whom God's Spirit and grace are found (Rom. 7:6; 1 Cor. 11:25; 2 Cor. 3:6).

"Absolutely not!" (6:2). We should not continue to sin, because at conversion we were "baptized into Christ Jesus" (6:3) and therefore now mysteriously participate in his death and resurrection (6:3–5, 8–10). Our "old self" (our whole self prior to conversion) has been crucified with Christ, and we have therefore died to sin (6:2, 6–7). Though we will still be tempted and sometimes sin, we should no longer allow sin to control us because it no longer has power over us. Yet we are not only "dead to sin" but also "alive to God in Christ Jesus" (6:11), because just as we died with Christ, so also we will one day be raised to new life (6:8). The certainty of future resurrection changes our lives right now. Instead of giving our bodies to sin as instruments of wickedness, we are to give ourselves (bodies and all) to God as tools of righteousness (6:12–13). While the law ironically seems to increase sin (5:20), living in grace actually prohibits sin.

Once servants of sin, now servants of God (6:15–23)

Paul anticipates and answers yet another objection—"shall we sin because we are not under law but under grace?" (6:15). Again he answers, "Absolutely not!" Paul reminds us of the principle of slavery: when we offer ourselves to a particular master, we become enslaved to that master (6:16). We choose our master, but our master determines the outcome, whether sin, leading to death, or obedience to God, leading to righteousness and life (6:16, 21–22). Thanks be to God we have made the right choice by responding to the core of Christian doctrinal and ethical teaching given by Jesus and handed down by the apostles (6:17–18; 1 Cor. 15:3; 2 Tim. 1:13; 1 Thess. 4:1). At conversion, we changed masters. We were slaves to sin and destined for death, but we've been set free from sin and enslaved to God, leading to holiness and eternal life (6:20–22). Sin pays the wage of death, but God offers the gift of life (6:23). What God has done for us in Christ makes our obedience possible, but it does not make it automatic (6:19). We must still give ourselves to our new master (God) with the same passion and fervor that we gave ourselves to our old master (sin).

Freedom from the law (7:1–25)

Romans 7 describes the Christian's freedom from the Mosaic law. In 7:1–6, Paul uses a marriage illustration to show that the law has authority over a person until their death, at which point the law loses its authority. Christians have "died to the law" and now belong to Christ (7:4). Although we were once controlled by sinful passions aroused by the law, we have now been released from the law so that "we serve in the new way of the Spirit" (7:6). In 7:7–13, Paul describes his former life in Judaism to demonstrate that the law itself is holy, righteous, and good (7:7, 12) and that the real culprit is sin, which takes advantage of the law to produce its disastrous results (7:7–9). Although the law was intended to bring life, its exposure of sin actually leads to death (7:10–11). In 7:14–25, Paul explains that sin does its work because human beings are enslaved to it (7:14). Interpreters are divided over whether the "I" in this section refers to Paul prior to his conversion or Paul as a Christian. Either way, the main point stands: the law cannot rescue a person from spiritual death. Again, the problem is not God's good law, but sin. Nevertheless, the law has no power to deal with sin.

✦ There is no mention of the Holy Spirit in Romans 7:14–25, but Paul mentions the Spirit almost twenty times in Romans 8.

Although Paul delighted in God's law, he couldn't obey it. Paul concludes in 7:24–25: "What a wretched man I am! Who will rescue me from this body of death? Thanks be to God—through Jesus Christ our Lord!" (see also Rom. 8:3–4).

New life through the Spirit (8:1–13)

Paul explains in 8:1–13 the "new way of the Spirit" mentioned in 7:6. To begin with, those who are in Christ will never be condemned (i.e., experience God's wrath) because the Spirit has set them free from sin and death (8:1–2). What the law could not do because of sin, God did through Jesus, who gave himself for our sins (8:3). Those who live according to the Spirit (i.e., Christians) fulfill the righteous requirement of God's law (8:4; cf. 13:8–10; Gal. 5:14). In 8:5–8, Paul contrasts the "sinful nature" (or "flesh") with the Spirit. When we are converted, we move from being "according to the flesh" to being "according to the Spirit" (cf. Col. 1:13). Everyone is under one power or the other, one realm or the other—either flesh or Spirit—and the power we belong to deeply influences our whole way of thinking. The fleshly mind-set is hostile to God, cannot please God, and leads to death, while the Spirit-filled mind-set leads to life and peace. Those who belong to God have the Spirit and are therefore not controlled by the flesh (8:9–11). Those who don't have

Paul reminds his readers that they are no longer slaves but children of God.

✚ At conversion, believers are transferred from the realm of "flesh" to the realm of the Spirit (Col. 1:13).

the Spirit don't belong to Christ (8:9). Although we must still die physically because of sin, the Holy Spirit's presence assures us that one day we will be raised from the dead just as Jesus was raised (8:10–11). In 8:12–13, Paul reminds us of how to live in light of all that God has done for us. Our obligation is not to the flesh but to the Spirit. If by listening to and obeying the Spirit we "put to death the misdeeds of the body" (the uses of our body to serve self rather than God and others), then we will live (8:13).

The Chi-Rho, a Christian symbol since the time of Constantine. The symbol combines the first two letters of the Greek word for "Christ."

Adoption and inheritance through the Spirit (8:14–17)

Not only has the Spirit given us new life (8:1–13), the Father has also adopted us into his family (8:14–17). God's children are those who are "led by the Spirit" (i.e., have their overall direction in life shaped by the Spirit). The Spirit does not lead us back into slavery to fear, but rather allows us to call God "Father"—the same word Jesus uses in his Gethsemane prayer (8:15; Mark 14:36). Because God has put his very Spirit within us, we can come to God with freedom rather than fear, with confidence rather than cowardice, and in full assurance that we belong to God (8:16). Since adopted children have all the legal rights of natural children, we can also expect to receive an inheritance, provided we are also willing to suffer (8:17).

Assurance of future glory (8:18–30)

Believers' present sufferings simply don't stack up to their future glory (8:18; 2 Cor. 4:17). Even creation itself waits eagerly for the children of God to be revealed in glory (8:19–21). Creation is broken. But when God's people are finally and gloriously restored, God's creation will also be fully restored (cf. Rev. 21:5). Until then, creation groans "as in the pains of childbirth" (8:22). Christians also yearn for things to be the way they are supposed to be. We experience God's presence now (i.e., the "firstfruits of the Spirit"), but we also wait patiently for the redemption of our bodies (8:23; 2 Cor. 1:21–22; 5:1–5; Eph. 1:14). We are not what we once were, but we are not what we will be one day. Thankfully, we wait in hope, looking forward with confidence to what God is going to do (8:24–25). In the meantime, God provides resources to help us wait patiently. The Spirit helps us in our weakness by praying for us (8:26–27), and we have God's promise to work for our good in all things (8:28). God's purpose is further defined in 8:29–30. God

✦ In the Old Testament people were discouraged from even pronouncing the divine name. Now, because believers have received the Spirit of God and have been adopted into God's family, they are able to cry out "Abba, Father" (Rom. 8:15).

The Relationship between Israel and the Church

C. Marvin Pate

That there is some sort of relationship between Israel and the church in the Bible is established in that the New Testament word for "church," *ekklesia*, occurs in the Septuagint almost always as a translation of the Hebrew word *qahal*. *Qahal* denotes Israel's sacred meetings as the people of God. Thus both *ekklesia* and *qahal* refer to the New Testament and Old Testament people of God, respectively. That is to say, Israel and the church form the one people of God.

But to speak of the one people of God transcending the eras of the Old Testament and New Testament necessarily raises the question of the relationship between the church and Israel. Modern interpreters prefer not to polarize the matter into an either/or issue. Rather, they talk about the church and Israel in terms of there being *both* continuity and discontinuity between them.

Continuity between the Church and Israel. Two ideas establish that the church and Israel are portrayed in the Bible as being in a continuous relationship. First, the church was present in some sense in Israel in the Old Testament. Acts 7:38 makes this connection explicit when, alluding to Deuteronomy 9:10, it speaks of the church (*ekklesia*) in the wilderness. The same idea is probably to be inferred from the intimate association (as noted earlier) existing between the words *ekklesia* and *qahal*, especially when the latter is qualified by the phrase "of God."

Furthermore, if the church is viewed in some New Testament passages as preexistent, then one finds therein the prototype of the creation of Israel (see Exod. 25:40; Acts 7:44; Gal. 4:26; Heb. 12:22; Rev. 21:11; cf. Eph. 1:3–14).

Second, Israel in some sense is present in the church in the New Testament. The many Old Testament names for Israel applied to the church in the New Testament establish that fact. Some of those are: "Israel" (Gal. 6:15–16; Eph. 2:12; Heb. 8:8–10; Rev. 2:14); "a chosen people" (1 Pet. 2:9); "the true circumcision" (Rom. 2:28–29; Phil. 3:3; Col. 2:11); "Abraham's seed" (Rom. 4:16; Gal. 3:29); "the remnant" (Rom. 9:27; 11:5–7); "the elect" (Rom. 11:28; Eph. 1:4); "the flock" (Acts 20:28; Heb. 13:20; 1 Pet. 5:2); and the "priesthood" (1 Pet. 2:9; Rev. 1:6; 5:10).

Discontinuity between the Church and Israel. The church, however, is not totally identical with Israel; discontinuity also characterizes the relationship. The church, according to the New Testament, is the eschatological (end-time) Israel incorporated in Jesus Christ, and, as such, is a progression beyond historical Israel (1 Cor. 10:11; 2 Cor. 5:14–21). However, a caveat must be issued at this point. Although the church is a progression beyond Israel, it does not seem to be the permanent replacement of Israel (see Romans 9–11, especially 11:25–27).

decided ahead of time to enter into a relationship with us (foreknowledge). Those who respond to his invitation through the gospel (the call) will be conformed to the likeness of Christ, justified (forgiven, accepted into God's family, and never condemned), and glorified.

Nothing can separate us from God's love (8:31–39)

To conclude this magnificent chapter, Paul asks a series of rhetorical questions to challenge anyone who wishes to deny these spiritual realities

God himself has established. There are no answers to these questions because no power or person or event or experience can challenge what God has done for us in Christ.

Question 1—"What, then, shall we say in response to this [these things]?" (8:31). The only appropriate response to 8:18–30 is to rejoice and live with renewed confidence that our relationship with God is secure and our future is certain.

Question 2—"If God is for us, who can be against us?" (8:31). Christians do face enemies (e.g., sin, the devil, the world), but none of these opponents will ultimately overcome us. We may lose a few minor skirmishes along the way, but we will never lose the war.

Question 3—"He who did not spare his own Son, but gave him up for us all—how will he not also, along with him, graciously give us all things?" (8:32). Since God has given us the greatest gift, he will not hesitate to give us the lesser gifts (see also Rom. 5:8–10).

Questions 4–5—"Who will bring any charge against those whom God has chosen? It is God who justifies. Who is he that condemns? Christ Jesus, who died—more than that, who was raised to life—is at the right hand of God and is also interceding for us" (8:33–34). God has chosen us to be his children. No one can bring a charge against us that will stand up in God's court of justice. There can be no lasting condemnation from our own hearts, from human enemies, or from demonic accusers. God the righteous Judge has already decided for us. Case closed (cf. Isa. 50:8–9)!

Questions 6–7—"Who shall separate us from the love of Christ? Shall trouble or hardship or persecution or famine or nakedness or danger or sword?" (8:35). Our standing with God is not just a legal matter, but also a relational one. We are not just the beneficiaries of a positive verdict; we are also the recipients of a perfect love. God is not only our Judge; he is also our Father, and nothing can separate us from his love. Nothing! Paul lists seven possible "separators" in 8:35, most of which he has endured himself (2 Cor. 11:23–27; 12:10). But the truth is that "in all these things we are more than conquerors [or "overcomers"] through him who loved us" (8:37). Paul concludes by listing additional "separators" that cannot actually tear us apart from God's love for us in Christ (8:38–39). We are never promised immunity from temptation or trials, but we should know beyond any doubt that God will never stop loving us.

✦ Romans 8:31–39 is perhaps the greatest affirmation of our security in Christ in the entire Bible.

An Important Concern: God Has Been Faithful to Keep His Promises (9:1–11:36)

In Romans 9–11 Paul is addressing two important matters: (1) the unbelief of Israel, and (2) how this unbelief affects God's faithfulness to his covenant promises. Israel's unbelief seems to call into question God's ability to keep his promises, an important aspect of God's righteousness. Paul addresses these matters by retelling Israel's story in order to show God has actually been faithful all along.

Paul's sorrow over Israel's unbelief (9:1–5)

Paul confesses his "great sorrow and unceasing anguish" that most of his fellow Jews ("those of my own race" in v. 3) have not accepted Jesus as the Messiah (9:1–2). Paul says he would be willing to be cursed and cut off from Christ for the sake of his fellow Jews (9:3). Israel had been granted many privileges—sonship, glory, the covenants, the law, temple worship, the promises, the patriarchs, and the Messiah (9:4–5).

But those who had been given so much have failed to acknowledge Jesus Christ, "who is God over all, forever praised!" (9:5).

God's faithfulness revealed in the story of Israel (9:6–29)

We learn in 9:6–13 that God has not failed to keep his covenant promises with Israel because "not all who are descended from Israel are Israel" (9:6). Not all physical descendants of Abraham are actually Abraham's children (9:7). The term "Israel" has two meanings (9:6, 8): physical Israel ("natural children") and true Israel ("children of promise"). Paul mentions two Old Testament situations that prove his point, one dealing with Abraham's sons and another with Isaac's sons (9:9–13). In 9:14–18, Paul explains God is not unjust to have mercy and compassion on sinful human beings. After all, salvation does not depend on human effort but on divine mercy (9:15–16). God has been merciful to Israel so that salvation may spread to the entire world (9:17–18). Having talked about the patriarchs and the exodus, Paul now moves on to the prophets and the exile in retelling the story

A potter forming the clay on a potter's wheel.

✝ To show that God has been faithful to his promises all along, Paul retells the story of Israel in Romans 9–11.

of Israel. His main point in 9:19–24 is that God's patience leads to salvation. To begin with, sinful creatures have as much right to question their sovereign Creator as a lump of clay has to question the potter (9:20–21). God has displayed great patience with his sinful people, people deserving of condemnation, in order to "make the riches of his glory known to the objects of his mercy" (9:22–23). To deal with sin and create a new covenant community, God has withheld judgment so that salvation may come to the whole world, including Jews and gentiles (9:24). As the Scriptures indicate, God's promise to Abraham is fulfilled in the saving of the remnant (9:25–29). This serves God's larger purpose of bringing salvation to the gentiles (9:25–26). The remnant includes that small number of Abraham's descendants ("children of promise") whom God preserved in order to keep his promise (9:29).

God's righteousness for everyone who believes (9:30–10:21)

Israel has failed to secure God's righteousness because they pursued it by works of law rather than by faith (9:30–32). While Israel has "tripped" or "stumbled" over Jesus, the "stumbling stone," those who trust in Jesus the Messiah "will never be put to shame" or condemned at the final judgment (9:32–33; 10:11; Isa. 8:14; 28:16; 50:7–8). Israel has stumbled because their zeal for God is not grounded in knowledge and truth (10:1–4). Instead of accepting the righteousness provided by Christ, they have attempted to

A model of the Jerusalem temple.

✦ Paul tells about the patriarchs, the exodus, the prophets, and the exile to show how God has brought salvation to the world through the Messiah.

construct their own righteousness through works of law. Paul continues to pray they will turn to Christ (10:1). In 10:5–13, Paul makes it clear God's righteousness comes by faith. Righteousness based on law comes by "doing" (10:5; Lev. 18:5; Gal. 3:12), while "righteousness that is by faith" looks to Christ (10:6), to his incarnation (10:6), his resurrection (10:7), and his gospel (10:8). Everyone—whether Jew or gentile—who confesses "Jesus is Lord" and believes God raised him from the dead will experience God's saving righteousness (10:9–10, 12–13; Joel 2:32). In 10:14–21 Paul demonstrates how Israel has rejected the good news. He first explains (using a series of questions) what comes before salvation: (1) preachers are sent out with a "timely" (sometimes translated "beautiful") task of proclaiming the good news, (2) people hear the message; and (3) people believe what they hear (10:14–15; Isa. 52:7). He then applies this sequence to Israel (10:16–21). Israel clearly heard and understood the good news of Jesus, but only a few Israelites accepted the message (9:6; 10:16–21; Deut. 32:21; Ps. 19:4; Isa. 53:1; 65:1–2).

God has not rejected Israel (11:1–10)

In Romans 11 Paul continues to insist Israel's unbelief does not nullify God's faithfulness to keep his covenant promises. God hasn't rejected his own people, since Paul and other Jews have believed in Jesus (11:1). But this remnant didn't manage to earn God's approval through works of law. Rather, the remnant was "chosen by grace" (11:2–6). In 11:7–10, Paul divides "Israel" into two groups: (1) the believing remnant and (2) the unbelieving others. Those within Israel who remain stubborn and refuse to trust God are hardened, just as the Scriptures said would happen (Deut. 29:4; Ps. 69:22–23; Isa. 29:10).

God's salvation of "all Israel" (11:11–32)

Israel has not fallen beyond recovery, but their rejection of the gospel means salvation has come to the gentiles (11:11–12). Paul hopes this rich harvest among the gentiles will make the Jewish people jealous and cause more of them to turn to Christ (11:13–14). When they do, that will certainly be a day to rejoice and celebrate, almost like a resurrection (11:15). Since the parts can often sanctify the whole (11:16), Paul hopes even more Jews will turn to Christ. In 11:17–24 Paul introduces an extended analogy of the olive tree. The "natural branches" that have been broken off are Jews. The "wild olive shoot" that has been "grafted in" represents the gentiles. The natural branches were broken off because of their unbelief so that the wild branches could be grafted in by faith.

✚ The "Romans Road" evangelistic plan uses the following verses from Romans to show a person how to become a follower of Christ: 5:8; 3:23; 6:23; 10:9–10, 13.

But this blessing that has come to gentiles as a result of the rejection of the Jews leaves no room for boasting or arrogance on the part of gentiles. Rather, they should continue in God's grace and kindness. If the Jews "do not persist in unbelief" but put their faith in Christ, God is easily able to graft these natural branches back into their own olive tree.

Whereas the remnant within Israel followed God, the rest of Israel who rejected Jesus is experiencing a "hardening" until the gentile mission is fulfilled (9:14–24; 11:7, 25). The much debated 11:26 comes at this point.

> NIV: "And so all Israel will be saved, as is written . . ."
>
> NIV (2010): "And in this way all Israel will be saved. As it is written . . ."

Traditionally, this verse is understood to mean that, immediately before or at the second coming of Christ, the final generation of Jews will suddenly turn to Christ. However, another interpretation is quite possible (e.g., N. T. Wright). The phrase "and so" at the beginning of verse 26 should probably be translated "in this way," speaking of how something is done, not when.

Ancient olive trees on the Mount of Olives.

Paul has been redefining "Israel" to refer to all who trust in Jesus, whether Jews or gentiles (see Rom. 2:28–29; 4:16; 9:6–8; Gal. 3:28–29; 6:15–16; Phil. 3:3–4). As a result, 11:26 would refer to what Paul has just said in 11:25 about the partial hardening of Israel leading to the salvation of the gentiles. In other words, God's plan of narrowing the chosen nation down to the crucified Messiah is his way of saving all people, both Jews and gentiles (i.e., "all Israel") who put their faith in Christ. The quotations from Isaiah and Jeremiah in 11:26–27 refer to God dealing with the sins of his people, not the second coming of Christ. Unbelieving Jews reject the gospel of Jesus Christ and are enemies of the church, but God has not written them off completely (11:28). God gave his word to Abraham, and his word has not failed (9:6). God's "gifts and his call are irrevocable" (11:29). In the past, the gentiles who were once disobedient to God have now received mercy because the Jews crucified Jesus the Messiah (11:30). In the present, the Jews are also now receiving mercy from God through the gospel of Jesus Christ (11:31). God has demonstrated that all people, Jews and gentiles alike, are guilty sinners in order that God may have mercy on all (11:32).

Praise be to God! (11:33–36)

Paul concludes his survey of salvation history in Romans 9–11 with an exclamation of praise. God is praised for his rich wisdom and knowledge, for his unsearchable judgments, and for his untraceable ways (11:33). No one has ever become God's counselor or put God in debt (11:34–35). God is the source, sustainer, and goal of all things and is totally deserving of all praise, glory, and honor (11:36).

Practical Implications: Relational Righteousness (12:1–15:13)

Paul now sets forth practical implications of the gospel of God's righteousness. Douglas Moo wisely says, "All theology is practical, and all practice, if it is truly Christian, is theological. Paul's gospel is deeply theological, but it is also eminently practical. The good news of Jesus Christ is intended to transform a person's life."*

Relating to God (12:1–2)

In light of all God has done for us in Christ ("God's mercy" detailed in Romans 1–11), we are to offer ourselves to him as living, holy, and pleasing

---

* Douglas J. Moo, *Romans*, NIV Application Commentary (Grand Rapids: Zondervan, 2000), 393. The "relational" outline of Romans 12–16 that follows is adapted from John Stott, *Romans: God's Good News for the World* (Downers Grove, IL: InterVarsity, 1994).

✠ Several of Paul's letters have a theological section followed by a more practical section (e.g, Romans 1–11; 12–16; Ephesians 1–3; 4–6; Galatians 1–4; 5–6).

sacrifices (12:1). This bodily response to God is our "spiritual" or "reasonable" (*logikos*—appropriate or fitting the circumstances) act of worship. Rather than being shaped by the world's priorities and values, we are to be transformed by the renewing of our minds. As a result, we will endorse through our behavior God's good, pleasing, and perfect will (12:2).

Relating to ourselves (12:3–8)

A right relationship to God leads to a right perspective about ourselves. The key quality is humility—not thinking too highly of ourselves, but thinking with sober judgment (12:3). To "think" in this context refers to an attitude or disposition or a way of viewing ourselves. We are to estimate ourselves "in accordance with the measure of faith," referring to the standard of the Christian faith shared by all believers. In 12:4–8 Paul shows how humility is best cultivated in community. We are one body in Christ, and each member belongs to and contributes to the entire body through her or his gifts. We think rightly about ourselves when we see our place in community.

Relating to others (12:9–21)

Above all, our relationships with others should be characterized by sincere love, a love without hypocrisy or pretense (12:9). Such love hates evil and holds tightly to what is good (12:9). In the rest of this section, Paul gives instructions for relating to both Christians (12:10–13, 15–16) and non-Christians (12:14, 17–21). When relating to other believers, Paul cites a circumstance or situation and then the appropriate response:

- When it comes to love, be devoted to one another.
- When it comes to honor, put others first.
- When it comes to zeal, don't be lazy.
- Be set on fire by the Spirit; serve the Lord.
- In your hope, rejoice.
- In your afflictions, persevere or endure.
- In your prayer, persist or stay faithful.
- Share with God's people in need and look for ways to show hospitality.

Occasions to rejoice or mourn offer additional chances to demonstrate love (12:15). Verse 16 reminds us of the importance of thinking rightly as an element of love (using the word *phroneo* that is used in 12:3 when defining humility):

- "Live in harmony" = think the same thing (common attitude)

- "Do not be proud" = do not think highly of yourself
- "Do not be conceited" = do not become wise (thoughtful) in your own eyes

When relating to non-Christians, the occasion is sometimes one of persecution or conflict. Paul offers four negative commands matched by four positive commands. Instead of cursing, we should bless (12:14). Instead of repaying evil with evil, we should do what is right and, if possible, live at peace with everyone (12:17–18). We should not avenge ourselves, but leave room for God to avenge (12:19; Deut. 32:35). We should not be overcome by evil, but overcome evil with good (12:21). It is crucial that we distinguish our responsibility from God's responsibility. God punishes and retaliates; we do not! In this context, heaping burning coals on our enemy (12:20; Prov. 25:21–22) probably refers to how our good actions can sometimes lead our enemy to feel shame to the point of repentance.

Relating to the state (13:1–7)

The state has been established by God with a dual role: rewarding good and punishing evil (13:1–4). Believers are to submit to the authority of the state when appropriate (e.g., the paying of taxes mentioned in 13:6–7). Paul actually describes the role of the state as that of a servant or minister (*diakonos*) in 13:4, and thus believers who are called to government occupations can see their task as a divine calling. The authority of the state, however, is derived from God and should never be used to justify evil. As John Stott put it, "If the state commands what God forbids, or forbids what God commands, then our plain Christian duty is to resist, not to submit, to disobey the state in order to obey God."*

Relating to the law (13:8–10)

The only debt we owe to fellow believers is the continuing debt to love one another (13:8). The commandments are summed up in the one rule to "love your neighbor as yourself" (Lev. 19:18). We cannot keep the law by trying to obey it perfectly, but when the Spirit empowers us to love one another, that love actually fulfills the law (13:8–10; Gal. 5:13–24).

---

* John Stott, *The Message of Romans* (Downers Grove, IL: InterVarsity, 1994), 42.

Roman coins often featured the face of a Roman emperor.

✚ Humility is thinking rightly about ourselves—not too much but also not too little of ourselves.

Relating to the day of the Lord (13:11–14)

We should focus on loving one another because the time of Christ's return is near (13:11–12). In the New Testament, salvation has past, present, and future-tense dimensions—we have been saved, are being saved, and will be saved. Romans 13:11 captures this idea in a nutshell: "The hour has come for you to wake up from your slumber [present], because our salvation is nearer now [future] than when we first believed [past]." Since the day of Christ's return is always near or imminent, we should behave like we are children of light rather than children of darkness, like people who are about to see the Lord (13:12–14).

Relating to the weak (14:1–15:13)

As we mentioned in the introduction, the house churches in Rome were likely divided on the basis of the relationship between Jews and gentiles. The division between the "weak" and the "strong" described here provides additional details about that division. Most likely the "weak" are Jewish Christians who abstain from certain foods and observe certain days out of loyalty to the Mosaic law. They don't believe they have to keep the law in order to be saved, but they prefer to abide by the law as a part of their Christian growth. In any case, Paul writes to heal the division within the church, and his major theme is mutual acceptance ("accept one another" in 14:1; 15:7). Love for fellow believers should limit our freedom. Specifically, the strong believer should not put a "stumbling block or obstacle" in the way of the weak believer (14:13). The context suggests something much deeper than doing things that might offend a legalistic believer. When the strong do things they feel free to do and that puts pressure on the weak to do those same things, which they might consider to be sinful, then the strong believer has caused the weak believer to stumble into sin by violating their own conscience. Throughout the passage, Paul argues that Christ died to save us and accept us, and we should accept one another (14:1–3). Christ then rose to be our Lord, and we are accountable to him (14:6–9). Christ is coming to be our judge (14:10–12). Paul might conclude: Christ has died! Christ is risen! Christ will come again! Accept one another!

After all, "the kingdom of God is not a matter of eating and drinking, but of righteousness, peace, and joy in the Holy Spirit" (14:17).

Conclusion (15:14–16:27)

Here Paul reflects on his own ministry, shares his travel plans, asks for prayer, sends greetings, and concludes with a powerful word of praise to God.

The Strong and the Weak

Jeannine K. Brown

Paul discusses the relationship between "weak" and "strong" Christians in 1 Corinthians 8:1–11:1 and Romans 14:1–15:6. To determine whether Paul addresses the same issues in both passages, we will first need to read each passage *discreetly*, avoiding the tendency to conflate the two texts where there is potential overlap. We must also read each passage *contextually*, attending to the distinct historical settings and the flow of Paul's argument in each. In 1 Corinthians 8:1–10:22, Paul admonishes those who eat idol meat in the dining area of a pagan temple (although not calling them the "strong" at any point; cf. 10:22). He argues that doing so is an act of idolatry (10:1–22) and a cause of stumbling to the "weak" (8:1–13). It is only after his extended argument against this behavior that Paul addresses the "gray area" of eating idol meat sold in the marketplace (10:23–11:1). Paul is convinced the Corinthians who are eating idol meat within a temple are courting idolatry (10:14–22). To eat idol meat in homes, however, is allowable, as long as a weaker Christian's conscience is not compromised (10:27–30). The "weak" are those (likely gentile) believers in Jesus whose former worship of idols makes it impossible to disassociate the act of eating in pagan temples from the act of idol worship itself (8:7, 10). The actions of those thinking themselves strong enough to eat at temples are dangerous to weaker believers (8:11) who have a less robust understanding of monotheism.

The "weak" in Romans 14:1–15:6 are those who abstain from meat and wine (14:2, 21) and deem "one day more sacred than another" (14:5), while the strong (15:1) are those who eat everything and consider all days alike (14:2, 5). Paul is not addressing eating idol meat in pagan temples, but eating meat more generally (with possible associations to idol meat sold in the marketplace). In this way, Romans 14:1–15:6 is more close in context and message to 1 Corinthians 10:23–11:1 than Paul's prohibition of idolatrous behavior in 1 Corinthians 8:1–10:22.

In the Romans passage, the weak are likely Jewish Christians and likeminded gentiles who follow conscience in observance of the law and additional strictures that help them avoid all possible contamination with meat and wine offered to idols. Like Daniel of the Old Testament, these Jewish Christians restricted their diet beyond the stipulations of the Torah to ensure no compromising of their loyalty to God. The strong—primarily gentiles (cf. 15:7–13; though Paul includes himself among the "strong" in 15:1)—feel free to eat meat in their common meals. The problem is this behavior distresses the weak Christians, causing them to stumble (14:14–15). Paul exhorts the strong to bear with the weak (Rom. 15:1) and avoid eating these offensive foods if they cause their brother or sister to stumble (14:19–21).

So, although Paul refers to the "weak" in both Romans and 1 Corinthians, the groups defined as such are not identical in each passage, and his message in each has distinctive contours.

Looking back on Paul's ministry (15:14–21)

Paul has written to the church in Rome with boldness to remind them of the foundational truths of the gospel and to fulfill his own ministry as apostle to the gentiles (15:15–16). Yet he remains confident that they know and live out the faith (15:14). He can only glorify God for what Christ has accomplished

✚ Romans 13 (submission to the state as a God-given authority) must be balanced by Revelation 13 (obeying God rather than the state when the state becomes an agent of evil).

Paul the Letter Writer

E. Randolph Richards

We Christians love reading other people's mail. What Paul wrote to others like the Philippians interests us. My grandmother called it "snooping," but scholars often call this "exegesis." While Philippians wasn't written to us, most of us believe God still speaks through that old letter. The more we know about how letters were written, the better we can read them now.

We often speak of "Paul's letters"; yet the letters themselves indicate Paul often had cowriters. "Paul . . . and our brother Sosthenes" wrote to Corinth (1 Cor. 1:1–2). While some argue Paul merely includes Sosthenes in the letter address as a courtesy, a study of first-century letters shows ancient letter writers did not do this. Courtesy comments were saved for the *end* of the letter. Why is Timothy mentioned as a sender in Philippians 1:1 and Colossians 1:1 but in the final greetings in Romans 16:21? Was Paul being less courteous to Timothy? No, Timothy was a cowriter of some letters but not others.

Christians often imagine Paul wrote letters like we did before email. For example, I sat down at a desk in a quiet place with pen and paper. After some thought, I composed as I wrote. I then signed it and mailed it off. Ancient letter writing was different in nearly every aspect. The lack of desks was the smallest difference. Modern Westerners value the individual. Paul always had a team. When he lost his first team partner, he did not journey again until he had another (Acts 15:36–41). It would not have occurred to a first-century Mediterranean to try anything solo. Scholars call this a "dyadic personality." Paul did not lock himself away in a private room to write. (It would have been too dark anyway.) Paul with trusted team members sat in an open atrium or an upstairs balconied apartment and talked of the letter they needed to send to Corinth.

Today, paper and pen are so inexpensive as to be negligible. In antiquity, this was not so. The entire process of writing his letter to the Romans probably cost Paul (in today's dollars) over $2,000, not including the traveling costs for whoever carried it to Rome (Phoebe?). Ancient letter writers, even literate ones, used secretaries (Rom. 16:22). This often surprises us. Yet, just a few decades ago, those in business often used secretaries to prepare letters. Why? Because many people didn't know how to type. In Paul's day, literacy meant the ability to *read*, not the ability to write. Aren't those the same? Actually, no. The ability to write is a matter of practice. When I write with my opposite hand, it is slow with large, clumsy letters, not because I am illiterate, but because I rarely write with my left hand. Most ancient people

through him in leading the gentiles to faith (15:17–18). Empowered by the Spirit and authenticated by signs and wonders, Paul has pursued his life calling of proclaiming Christ to those who have never heard (15:19–21).

Looking ahead to ministry in Jerusalem, Rome, and Spain (15:22–29)

Paul has not been able to visit Rome due to other missionary work, but he now looks to the future and shares these plans (15:22–24). First, he will be traveling from Corinth (his current location as he writes Romans) back to Jerusalem to deliver the collection from the gentile churches (15:25–27). Next, he plans to visit Rome and enjoy their company for a while before

✦ Throughout the New Testament, salvation has a past, present, and future dimension—we have been saved, are being saved, and will be saved.

rarely practiced writing. Paul makes a similar comment: "See what large letters I use as I write to you with my own hand" (Gal. 6:11).

Writing slowly was not the larger problem. Writing down a letter was considered a specialized skill. A secretary needed to know how to cut and glue papyrus, cut and sharpen pens, mix ink, and prick and line the sheets. A letter to a church, to be read publicly as Paul intended (Col. 4:16), could not be scratched messily across some sheet. Ancients had a sense of propriety. Important letters should be prepared neatly on good quality papyrus (Cicero, *Att.* 13.25; 13.21). The quickly scrawled first draft was not suitable for sending to a church. What would Corinth think of Paul if he cared so little for them as to send such a rag? Appearance was not the only reason a first draft was not appropriate. Careful thought and composition were essential. Ancient writers thoughtfully pondered their drafts, weighing each phrase. Cicero (*Att.* 7.3) debated over which preposition was best to use. Paul's letters were not carelessly written. Ancients expected a letter to use an appropriate structure and standardized phrases.

When Paul decided to send a letter to Corinth, he contracted a secretary. It would have taken more than the usual haggling. A typical letter of that time was about the length of 3 John. Paul's letters were extraordinarily long. Paul's opponents ridiculed his letters as "weighty" (2 Cor. 10:10). The secretary would bring a stack of wax tablets. In a typical scenario, as Paul speaks, the secretary scratches furiously on the tablets. Sosthenes interjects at times. Paul ponders and perhaps rephrases. Team members wander through the room at times, pausing to listen, offering suggestions. After several hours, the secretary leaves to prepare a rough draft of that portion. When the secretary returns a few days later, Paul listens to the draft, making corrections and additions. He then adds more to the letter. This process continues over the next few weeks until the letter is 100 percent precisely the way Paul wanted it, because as the primary sender, he is responsible for every word. The secretary brings the final draft to Paul (on nice papyrus and in good handwriting). As authentication (2 Thess. 3:17), Paul adds some closing remarks in his own handwriting, sometimes several verses (Gal. 6:11–18), sometimes just a line or two (1 Cor. 16:21; Col. 4:18; 2 Thess. 3:17–18), and sometimes just a final phrase ("Grace be with you" 2 Tim. 4:22). The letter is then rolled. A string is tied around it and clay pressed over the knot to seal it.

We today, of course, cannot know exactly the procedure Paul used or how long each letter took. We should not, though, make Paul write in *our* image. We should not imagine Paul locked away in a room one evening scribbling out his letter to the Corinthians. A better understanding of ancient letter writing helps us to see how truly "weighty" Paul's letters were. He invested much time and effort in writing them. We should do the same in reading them.

---

moving on to Spain (15:23–24, 28–29). He hopes the church in Rome will assist him on his mission to Spain (15:24). The gospel brings unity, and unity promotes the mission to bring the gospel to all.

Prayer for future ministry (15:30–33)

Paul is quite anxious about his trip to Jerusalem and asks the believers in Rome to struggle in prayer for him—that God would protect him from unbelievers in Judea and make his service in Jerusalem acceptable to the Christians there. He looks forward to the refreshing fellowship he hopes to experience with the church in Rome and prays God's peace upon them.

Commendation and greetings (16:1–16)

Paul now commends Phoebe, a servant (or deaconess) of the church in Cenchrea, and perhaps the one who carries Paul's letter to Rome (16:1–2). He then sends extensive greetings to many Christians in Rome. The greeting section is interesting for several reasons. First, Paul may have met some of these believers in places like Corinth and Ephesus before they returned to Rome (e.g., Priscilla and Aquila in Acts 18). Second, he greets at least three (perhaps as many as five) house churches. Third, about one-third of the persons named are women, indicating an important role for women in the early church. Fourth, "Andronicus and Junias" are described as "outstanding among the apostles," likely meaning this husband and wife team did an excellent job as commissioned missionaries. Fifth, a closer study of the names reveals the early church was both racially and economically diverse.

Warning, assurance, promise, and prayer (16:17–20)

Paul warns the Christians in Rome to watch out for and avoid those who "cause divisions" and "put obstacles" (stumbling blocks) in the way through

The road to the harbor in Cenchrea.

✛ Paul's message to the "strong" and the "weak" in the Roman churches: Christ has died! Christ is risen! Christ will come again! Accept one another!

Paul's Co-workers

David B. Capes

The apostle Paul succeeds in his gentile mission due in large part to a network of Christian brothers and sisters he began to establish shortly after his call to be an apostle (Galatians 1–2). Depending on how broadly the term is defined, eighty to ninety people are described as Paul's co-workers in Acts and the New Testament letters attributed to him. Some appear to relate to Paul as equals (e.g., Barnabas, Apollos, Priscilla and Aquila), and others as subordinates (e.g., Timothy, Titus, Tychicus). Some work closely with Paul (e.g., Timothy, Luke, Silas); others independently (e.g., Apollos, Priscilla and Aquila, Barnabas). Some carry out their work primarily in a local setting (e.g., Philemon, Euodia), and others travel with Paul or serve as his delegates when he cannot travel (Luke, Timothy, Titus).

In his letters, Paul refers to these associates by a variety of terms, including "co-worker" (*sunergos*), "apostle" (*apostolos*), "brother" (*adelphos*), "minister" (*diakonos*), "fellow servant" (*sundoulos*), "fellow soldier" (*sustratiotes*), and "fellow prisoner" (*sunaichmalotos*). The types of services these associates provide Paul and his congregations depend primarily on the gifts given to each (e.g., Rom. 12:6–8; 1 Cor. 12:4–11). Co-workers assist Paul in his travels, in his preaching and teaching ministry, in hosting church gatherings, in repairing problems in the churches, in meeting his needs while he is in prison, and in writing letters. When Paul establishes a church, he identifies and trains local leaders to work in cooperation with him. He instructs leaders and congregations in person when present and by letter when absent.

We should likely distinguish between "apostles of Jesus Christ" and "apostles of the churches." The phrase "apostles of Jesus Christ" refers to individuals who have seen the risen Jesus (1 Cor. 9:1) and have been commissioned directly by him. While the term "apostle" may be used narrowly to refer to "the Twelve" (e.g., Acts 4:35–37), Paul uses it more broadly to refer to others including himself, Apollos, and Barnabas. The phrase "apostles of the churches" extends the usage further by referring to individuals chosen and commissioned by local congregations (e.g., Epaphroditus [Phil. 2:25] and Andronicus and Junia [Rom. 16:7]).

Remarkably, given women's social status at the time, Paul designates a number of women as "co-workers," "ministers," and "apostles." Phoebe, Euodia, Syntyche, Apphia, Priscilla (= Prisca), and Junia exercise leadership locally and serve as traveling missionaries. These women assist Paul in a variety of ways. The more affluent serve as benefactors, providing hospitality by opening their homes for lodging and for gatherings of the local churches. Women gifted otherwise are involved in ministries of preaching and teaching.

Some of Paul's co-workers contribute to the letters he writes. Eight of the thirteen letters attributed to Paul name cosenders. As "apostle of Jesus Christ," Paul's name and titles appear first, followed by the names of others, including Sosthenes, Silvanus (= Silas), Timothy, and Titus. The extent of their contribution is unclear, but it is likely that they have some role in composing the letter. Likewise, most of Paul's letters bear the distinct marks of secretarial influence. The secretary's role may vary from letter to letter or section to section within a single letter. At times a secretary may take dictation from the author; at others he may take on more of an authorial role. The only named secretary in Paul's letters is Tertius (Rom. 16:22). His greeting "in the Lord" demonstrates he is not a hired pen but a co-worker in the mission. In the final analysis, Paul's letters are not products of a single mind. Properly understood, his letters are a collaborative enterprise, an interchange of ideas and traditions between Paul, his secretaries, and his cosenders.

✦ Paul's greetings in Romans 16 indicate that women played a prominent role in the early church.

Romans 773

false teaching (16:17). They are serving themselves rather than Christ, and they use smooth talk and flattery to deceive people (16:18). He then assures the believers in Rome and encourages them to be "wise about what is good, and innocent about what is evil" (16:19). Paul promises these believers the ever-present grace of the Lord Jesus and spiritual victory over Satan (16:20).

More greetings from Paul's co-workers (16:21–23)

Paul sends greetings from some of the co-workers who are with him in Corinth. The loyal associate Timothy is listed as a cosender in six of Paul's other letters. Jason is probably the person who welcomed Paul in Thessalonica (Acts 17:5–9). Sosipater is likely Sopater of Berea, named in Acts 20:4. Tertius is Paul's amanuensis or scribe, the one who physically "wrote down this letter." Gaius is probably the one mentioned in 1 Corinthians 1:14. Erastus, a prominent city official, is also a believer (cf. Acts 19:21–22; 2 Tim. 4:20).

Concluding doxology (16:25–27)

Paul closes his magnificent letter with a doxology. In the letter's thesis statement in 1:16–17, Paul describes the gospel as the power of God for salvation. Now in 16:25 he again links the gospel and God's power, this time "to establish you." God uses the good news of Jesus Christ to bring spiritual life and growth to believers. The Scriptures can attest that God's plan all along has been that "all nations might believe and obey him" (16:26), thus fulfilling his original promise to Abraham (Gen. 12:1–3). God is righteous and keeps his word! Finally, when all is said and done, to God alone be the glory through our Lord Jesus Christ (16:27).

So What? Applying Romans Today

Where do we begin? Almost every aspect of the Christian life is touched on in this amazing letter. Romans tells us about God's story and how we can become a part of that great story. Romans tells us how life was meant to be lived. To begin with, we have to admit our sinfulness. We have to give up hope of ever finding life on our own, apart from God. Today we emphasize God's grace and love, but they have become overly familiar, and therefore some of their depth and richness of meaning have been lost on us. Romans begins with our sin and guilt, and just before we are driven to despair and hopelessness, we read that phrase "But God" in 3:21. Just before we drown in the dark waters of sin and shame, we break the surface and gasp for

✦ The entire Old Testament points forward to Christ as the revelation of God's righteousness (Rom. 16:25–26; cf. Rom. 1:2; 3:21).

air—"But God." Now the grace of God has power and substance. Now we actually know that we need God's grace. We cling to grace because we have considered what it means to face God's condemning wrath. Paul explains this amazing grace in the central part of the letter, a grace that provides not only forgiveness but acceptance as well. We have not only received a gift; we have also mysteriously participated with the person of Jesus in his death and resurrection. This changes how we think and live every day, no longer as slaves to sin but now as free followers of Christ. The view widens in Romans 9–11 as Paul explains how God has been keeping his covenant promises all along. In the final section, we see the practical implications of this grace life. Theology is meant to be practical, after all. The letter concludes with an eloquent crescendo of praise to God, who deserves all the glory.

Our Favorite Verses in Romans

Therefore, there is now no condemnation for those who are in Christ Jesus, because through Christ Jesus the law of the Spirit of life set me free from the law of sin and death. (8:1–2)

This inscription honors Erastus (Rom. 16:23), who was the director of public works in Corinth.

1 Corinthians
Dealing with Church Issues

2 Corinthians
Defending a God-Given Ministry

In these two letters we see the heart of a missionary-pastor for a local congregation, warts and all. In 1 Corinthians, Paul wrestles with major problems in a believing community that is still struggling to separate from its pagan culture. In 2 Corinthians, he engages the congregation in light of rebellious opponents who are trying to drive a wedge between the church and their father in the faith. These letters are all about church, raw and unedited. Buckle your seat belts for a crazy ride through the Corinthian correspondence.

Who Wrote Corinthians?

Paul is identified in both letters as the author, along with Sosthenes in 1 Corinthians 1:1 and Timothy in 2 Corinthians 1:1. Most contemporary scholars conclude Paul did indeed write both letters, although some see 2 Corinthians 1–9 and 10–13 as separate letters because of the abrupt change in tone. Good arguments can be made for the unity of 2 Corinthians, especially since it was likely he wrote the letter over a period of time in which he learned of new developments in the church.

Who Is Paul's Audience?

Paul started the church in Corinth on his second missionary journey (Acts 18:1–18). The city of Corinth was a wealthy melting pot of cultures, philosophies, lifestyles, and religions, and it was especially well known for its sexual immorality (e.g., "to Corinthianize" meant to "play the prostitute"). In this pluralistic setting, Paul planted what would turn out to be his most challenging church. He wrote both letters while on his third missionary journey. He wrote 1 Corinthians from Ephesus in about AD 54 and 2 Corinthians from Macedonia in about AD 56.

Bust of Marcus Antonius Polemon, an ancient Greek Sophist.

What Is at the Heart of Corinthians?

The church at Corinth was wracked by problems caused by faulty beliefs, arrogance, and immaturity. The members' pagan past certainly didn't help (see 1 Cor. 6:9–11; 8:7; 12:1–3). The main problem in both letters seems to revolve around the issue of what it means to be truly "spiritual." They seem to have embraced a "spirituality" that included intellectual pride and emphasized exciting experiences (see, e.g., 1 Cor. 1:5; 8:1, 7, 10, 11; 12:8; 13:2). Some felt they had already arrived spiritually, and this overly triumphant attitude explains, for example, why they divided into rival factions (e.g., 1 Cor. 1:11–12) and why they prided themselves in displaying the more spectacular gifts of the Spirit (e.g., 1 Cor. 4:8; 13:1). Such an immature understanding of true spirituality led to a variety of problems within the church. In 1 Corinthians Paul deals with these local church issues.

1 Corinthians
- Greeting and Thanksgiving (1:1–9)
- Paul Responds to Reports about the Church (1:10–6:20)

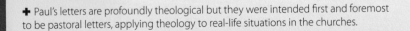
✝ Paul's letters are profoundly theological but they were intended first and foremost to be pastoral letters, applying theology to real-life situations in the churches.

An Overview of the Life and Letters of Paul

- Paul Responds to the Letter from the Corinthians (7:1–16:4)
- Concluding Matters (16:5–24)

After Paul wrote 1 Corinthians, his relationship with the church deteriorated. Apparently, Paul's opponents had been able to turn a portion of the church against their apostle. Because the church is now divided about the legitimacy of Paul's apostleship, he must defend his apostolic authority, which he does in 2 Corinthians. Paul's goal in defending himself and the message he preaches is to defend and strengthen the Corinthians' faith.

2 Corinthians
- Greeting and Thanksgiving (1:1–11)
- Paul's Apostolic Conduct and Ministry (1:12–7:1)
- Paul's Joy Related to Reconciliation and Giving (7:2–9:15)
- Paul's Response to the Rebellious (10:1–13:10)
- Conclusion (13:11–14)

The City of Corinth

Robbie Fox Castleman

Corinth is located about fifty miles west of Athens, Greece, on the northern side of the Peloponnesus. Corinth is situated on a four-and-a-half-mile-long isthmus between two harbors and is an international crossroads between the western Mediterranean and Asia. The ancient site of "Old Corinth" is situated a little over three miles from the center of the modern commercial city, which was partially destroyed by an earthquake in 1858. Excavations begun after the quake have uncovered a wall that runs six miles around the site of the ancient city.

Corinth was a Greek city-state before the fifth century BC and a leading center of commerce before its conquest by Rome in 146 BC. The city was not rebuilt for a century, but it was eventually repopulated by ambitious and competitive freedmen from Rome, whose social status was just above that of a Roman slave. In the first century BC, during the reign of Julius Caesar, the city made a significant shift toward its development as a Roman colony. Excavations have revealed the use of Latin coins dating from 44 BC, and the practice of civil religion no longer focused on the Greek gods but on the emerging emperor worship of the Romans.

A century later, when Paul lived in Corinth for eighteen months, Greek was still the official language, but the inscriptions and names of those in the city were predominantly Latin. Eight of the seventeen Corinthian Christians named by Paul in the New Testament have Roman names. Indeed, slaves outnumbered free citizens within the city two to one, and this also is an indication of the new wealth that was created in Rome's new Corinthian colony.

The aristocracy of the "new" Corinth reflected the ambition and independence of the "newly rich." The elite of the city identified with Rome, but Greek influence still prevailed in much of the city's culture. Corinth was the host city for the Panhellenic games, athletic events second only to the Olympics of Athens' fame.

However, like any urban city today, there was a wide disparity between the haves and have-nots, and the turmoil this often creates is clearly reflected in Paul's concern regarding the unity of the church and its witness to the city at large. Most Corinthian Christians were not wealthy (1 Cor. 1:26) and many were slaves (1 Cor. 7:20–24), but social conflict over status does appear to have been an issue in the Corinthian church. The independent, competitive spirit that had rebuilt the city was alive and well in the Christian faith community. It is evident in Paul's letters that Corinthian Christians would compete over anything, even which spiritual gift was superior to another!

The church of Corinth also reflected similar conflicts and problems that are still common today in any large harbor city with a culturally and socially diverse population and booming business. Corinth was a cauldron in which a broad religious pluralism mixed with crime, sexual promiscuity, and a variety of entertainment options. Five years before Paul founded the church during his second missionary

What Makes 1–2 Corinthians Interesting and Unique?

- Overall, Paul wrote more words to the Corinthian church than to any other.
- Paul uses the adjective "spiritual" in 1 Corinthians 2:13, 15; 3:1; 9:11; 10:3, 4; 12:1; 14:1; 15:44, 46, and the adverb "spiritually" in

journey, a 14,000-seat theater was renovated. And although the official practice of the empire's civil religion didn't require belief in any particular god, there were at least twenty-six sacred places and sanctuaries. The most popular sites were sanctuaries devoted to Asclepius, Athena, and Aphrodite.

Scholars differ on the extent of Corinth's reputation as a place for all sorts of sexual practices and pleasures. It is known that the temple of Aphrodite used many temple slaves as prostitutes. Ancient writers commented on the sexually promiscuous atmosphere of Corinth, some with a tone of condemnation and some with a measure of appreciation, promotion, and even humor. Prostitution was viewed as part of the city's trade and commerce. The sexual behavior of male gentiles would obviously come into conflict with the standards of monogamous purity mandated by Judaism. The influx of Jews from Rome to Corinth just before the founding of the church would certainly have heightened religious and social tensions within the city. This same tension and conflict within the church community seems to be a significant concern to Paul.

The apostle Paul stayed in Corinth for a year and a half (Acts 18:11) and was joined by a Jewish Christian couple who were exiles from Rome, Aquila and Priscilla (Acts 18:2). To say the least, Corinth was a challenging place for church planting. Not only did the pagan nature of the city make discipleship particularly difficult, but the Jewish population of the city notably resisted the establishment of the church, which they saw as an aberrant sect of Judaism. The volatile temperament of the city and its citizens is reflected clearly in Luke's account of Paul's appearance before the legal tribunal (Acts 18:12–17).

Two archaeological discoveries in the excavation of old Corinth are of notable interest to readers of the New Testament. The first is the discovery of the *bema* as the sight of the tribunal mentioned above. Situated in the marketplace, the *bema* was the place where Roman officials stood to make public appearances, including the rendering of legal judgments. The second archaeological find underscores the strong connection between the cities and Christians of both Corinth and Rome.

Paul wrote his letter to the Romans while staying in Corinth, and in the conclusion of that epistle the apostle includes a list of his own greetings to Roman Christians and greetings from Corinthian Christians who are acquainted with believers in Rome (Rom. 16:1–24). Erastus, the city treasurer (16:23), is one Corinthian Christian included in this section of Paul's letter to the Romans. On April 15, 1929, a stone was excavated at the northeast corner of the theater in Corinth. Studies have concluded the pavement surrounding the stone was laid in about AD 50, just before the time of Paul's visit and the founding of the Corinthian church. The Latin inscription on the stone translates as "Erastus in return for his aedileship laid [the pavement] at his own expense." In the Roman Empire an aedile was a person associated in some way with buildings, roads, sanitation, public games, and the like. The Greek word Paul uses to identify Erastus as the "city treasurer" is an appropriate word to describe this Roman official. In addition, the likelihood that the Erastus in Paul's letter is the Erastus carved into the stone is heightened in that the name is very uncommon and is not found in any Corinthian records other than in this stone and in Romans 16:23.

1 Corinthians 2:14 and 14:37. In his other letters combined, he uses both the adjective and the adverb only nine times.

- In the midst of the most comprehensive discussion of spiritual gifts in the New Testament (1 Corinthians 12–14) stands the famous "love chapter" (1 Corinthians 13).

✚ Ironically, the primary problem with the church at Corinth was spiritual immaturity, even though this church claimed to be extremely mature and spiritual.

- 1 Corinthians 15 gives more detail on the resurrection of the dead than any other place in the Bible.
- 1 Corinthians contains the longest discussion of human sexuality in all of Paul's letters (chapters 6–7).
- 2 Corinthians is probably the most personal of all of Paul's letters.
- 2 Corinthians 8–9 is perhaps the primary New Testament passage related to financial giving.
- The tone of 2 Corinthians 1–9 differs remarkably from 10–13, leading some scholars to conclude these are two separate letters.
- 2 Corinthians reminds us that reconciliation can be personally painful, disruptive to present ministry plans, and dependent on other people's response—but it is worth pursuing.

What Is the Message of 1 Corinthians?

The Lechaion Road, a major passageway through the ancient city, would have been lined with colonnades and shops.

Paul had received disturbing verbal reports from Chloe's household (1:11) and a letter from the Corinthians expressing a number of concerns (7:1; perhaps carried by the men mentioned in 16:17). In response to the reports and the letter, Paul writes 1 Corinthians.

Greeting and Thanksgiving (1 Cor. 1:1–9)

Paul the apostle and Sosthenes greet the church in Corinth, along with believers everywhere, with grace and peace from God our Father and the Lord Jesus (1:1–3). Often in the thanksgiving section Paul signals some of the main topics of the letter. Here he thanks God for sufficiently gifting the Corinthians. They have been enriched in their speaking and knowledge and "do not lack any spiritual gift" as they wait for Christ's return (1:4–7). He reassures them God is faithful and will keep them strong to the end so they will be blameless on the day of the Lord (1:8–9).

Paul Responds to Reports about the Church (1 Cor. 1:10–6:20)

Certain people from Chloe's household in Corinth brought Paul news about problems in the church. (It's possible that the three men mentioned in 16:17 formed part of this group.) Paul responds to four particular issues: factions (1–4), incest (5), lawsuits (6:1–11), and sexual immorality (6:12–20).

Divisions in the church (1:10–4:21)

PROBLEM: DIVISION OVER CHURCH LEADERS (1:10–17)

The first problem Paul addresses deals with rival factions within the church (1:11). He exhorts them to unity (1:10). They were arguing about which Christian teacher was the best (1:12). Elevating Christian leaders too highly has always proved to be a divisive disaster. Christ is not divided, and Christ's body should not be divided (1:13). These leaders weren't crucified for the Corinthians, and these believers weren't baptized into the name of a leader (1:13). Paul was called to preach the gospel, not with rhetorical polish, lest the power of the cross of Christ be undermined (1:17). He is grateful he baptized only a few people, since they seem to be idolizing the leaders who baptized them (1:14–16). In the section that follows (1:18–4:21), Paul provides an in-depth solution to this problem of division.

SOLUTION: UNITY UNDER THE LEADERSHIP OF CHRIST (1:18–4:21)

In 1:18–2:5, Paul starts to solve the problem of rival factions by pointing beyond the messengers to the message of the cross. The message of Christ crucified is foolishness to those perishing, but constitutes the power of God to those who are being saved (1:18–19; Isa. 29:14). The wisdom of this world, represented by the educational elite, can't bring people to know God (1:20–21). But God has revealed his wisdom through a crucified Messiah, something the Greeks consider absurd and the Jews regard as scandalous

✚ Paul considers disunity and division within the church as big a problem as sexual immorality.

(1:22–24). God's "foolishness" is far superior to man's wisdom and strength (1:25). The Corinthians' own experience testifies to the truth of the cross-centered message (1:26–31). God called many of the Corinthians from the lower social classes to shame the "wise," "noble," and "strong." But Jesus becomes for them righteousness, holiness, redemption, and wisdom. As a result, if people want to boast, they should not boast in Christian leaders; they should only boast in the Lord (1:29, 31)! Paul's own ministry among the Corinthians makes the same point: he came to them in the Spirit's power with the simple message of Jesus Christ and him crucified rather than with persuasive words or worldly wisdom (2:1–5).

In 2:6–16, Paul explains more about God's kind of wisdom, a wisdom that will enable the Corinthians to move beyond their divisiveness. God's wisdom is time-tested and reserved for those who love him (2:6–9). His wisdom is revealed by his Spirit, who indwells believers (2:10–12). While those without the Spirit (i.e., unbelievers) do not understand or accept the things of God (2:12–14), the person in whom God's Spirit lives understands the things of God; he or she has the "mind of Christ" (2:15–16).

Paul discusses the nature of the church and ministry in 3:1–23, as he continues to deal with the problem of divisions within the congregation. Although they have the Spirit, Paul can't address them as "spiritual"; he addresses them, but as worldly (i.e., as spiritual babies) because of the jealousy and quarreling (3:1–4). Fighting over leaders ignores the various roles leaders should play (3:5–9). One leader plants, another waters, but only God can cause the growth. Leaders are fellow workers with multiple roles that are complementary. "Different" does not mean "better." Paul briefly describes his own role as an "expert builder" who specializes in laying the one sure foundation, Jesus Christ (3:10–11). People need to be careful how they build on that foundation, since the quality of each person's work will be tested at the final judgment (3:11–13). Those who use high-quality materials will receive a reward, while those who use cheap materials will see their work burned up, although they themselves will be saved (3:14–15). The church is not just any building; it is God's sacred temple indwelt by God's Holy Spirit, and those who (through divisiveness?) seek to destroy the church can expect to be destroyed or condemned by God (3:16–17). Paul reminds them in 3:18–23 there should be no more boasting about men, because God's wisdom is infinitely greater than the world's wisdom. Believers have everything they need in Jesus, so there is no need to pursue such rivalries.

To conclude his appeal to unity, Paul explains the role of apostolic leaders and how the Corinthians should treat them (4:1–21). The apostles are first of all servants of Christ, entrusted with the secret things (or "mysteries") of God, that is, the gospel (4:1). As trustees, their primary responsibility is to

✦ God's dwelling place is no longer the temple in Jerusalem but the temple of his church, people indwelt by the Spirit of God (1 Cor. 3:16).

prove faithful (4:2). Human opinion about their status matters little, since they are subject to God's assessment when Jesus returns (4:3–5). Paul urges the Corinthians to stick to biblical principles (i.e., "Do not go beyond what is written"), and the Scriptures clearly prohibit boasting in human leaders (4:6–7). Paul now uses irony to contrast the Corinthian believers (rich, kings, wise, strong, honored) with the apostles, who have suffered unjustly as weak, dishonored, homeless, persecuted scum of the earth (4:8–13). The super-spiritual among the Corinthians take notice of what a fool for Christ really looks like. Paul's desire is not to shame them but to warn them about arrogance (4:14). He is the founding father of the church in Corinth, and his way of life in Christ is worthy of imitation (4:15–16). Timothy can demonstrate Paul's way of life until Paul arrives, and when he does, it will not be with cheap talk but in the power of the Spirit (4:17–20). Their attitude will determine Paul's response, either in love with gentleness or as a firm disciplinarian (4:21).

The case of incest and the lack of church discipline (5:1–13)

PROBLEM: A SEXUALLY IMMORAL BROTHER AND A PROUD CHURCH (5:1–2)

While the first church problem was disunity (1:11), the second relates to sexual immorality within the church, the kind even pagans do not tolerate

Corinth.

✝ Paul reminds the Corinthians that the kingdom of God centers on powerful actions rather than empty rhetoric (1 Cor. 4:20).

(5:1). Actually there are two problems, and both are related to spiritual arrogance: (1) a man is having sexual intercourse with his mother or stepmother, and (2) the church is tolerating the behavior of this person of high status rather than grieving over it and exercising church discipline (5:1–2).

SOLUTION: CHURCH DISCIPLINE FOR THE GOOD OF BOTH (5:3–13)

Paul pronounces judgment on the offending man (5:3), and orders the Corinthian congregation to exclude the man from the protective sphere of the community in order that his old way of life may be destroyed but his spirit saved (5:4–5; perhaps the same man mentioned in 2 Cor. 2:5–11; 7:8–13). The purpose of church discipline is remedial! Paul explains why the disciplinary action is necessary: a little bit of serious sin in the church can spoil the whole church (5:6–7). The sacrifice of Christ, our Passover Lamb, calls us to moral purity (5:7–8). In 5:9–13, Paul corrects a previous misunderstanding. In an earlier letter, he had advised them not to associate with sexually immoral people, but he was talking about Christians who are blatantly sinful, not unbelievers who have no reason to live otherwise. God does expect his people to judge those inside the fellowship, and the Corinthians should exercise that responsibility.

Lawsuits between believers before unbelieving judges (6:1–11)

PROBLEM: BELIEVERS GOING BEFORE PAGAN JUDGES (6:1)

Some in the congregation are taking their civil disputes to pagan judges rather than to their own Christian community. These secular judges often showed great partiality and were open to bribes.

The harbor in Cenchrea.

✚ Jesus mentions the issue of church discipline in one of the two places in the Gospels where he uses the term "church" (see Matt. 18:15–20).

Paul chides the Corinthians for handing over disputes between Christians to unbelievers. Do they not know that believers will judge the unbelieving world, both people and angels (6:2–3)? Is there no one wise enough in the fellowship to settle a simple dispute (6:4–6)? That lawsuits are common in the fellowship points to a deeper problem: these believers are overly concerned with demanding their own rights. Rather than treating others unjustly or defrauding them, it would be better to give up a few rights and absorb the wrong in order to preserve unity and protect the fellowship (6:7–8). Reflecting on these problems leads Paul to offer a list of vices that features selfishness and greed (6:9–10). No one whose life is characterized by such things will inherit God's kingdom. He reminds the Corinthians that some of them used to practice such things but were washed, sanctified, and justified in the name of Jesus and by the power of the Spirit (6:11). They need to act like the people they now are!

Sexual immorality in general (6:12–20)

PROBLEM: SEX OUTSIDE OF MARRIAGE (6:12–13)

Now Paul confronts the problem of sexual immorality in general, and prostitution in particular. Prostitution was a major problem in the city of Corinth, and most likely some of the Corinthian Christians used to participate in that lifestyle (6:9–11). Paul quotes some slogans (probably coming from the Corinthians) and gives them credence in certain contexts but not unlimited endorsement. "Everything is permissible," for example, does not apply to the area of sexual ethics (6:12). The body is not meant to be used for mere pleasure (as if sex is simply a physical need like eating—"food for the stomach and the stomach for food"), but rather is accountable to, and to be used for, the Lord (6:13).

SOLUTION: THE BELIEVER'S BODY IS A TEMPLE (6:14–20)

God raised Jesus, and he will also raise us—both being bodily resurrections (6:14). A believer's body is a member of Christ himself (6:15) and one with Christ in Spirit (6:17). Believers should never take their bodies, which are members of Christ, and unite them to a prostitute, because whoever unites with a prostitute becomes one body with her (6:15–16; Gen. 2:24). The solution is to "flee from sexual immorality," since this particular sin uniquely violates our physical bodies, which are temples of the Holy Spirit and belong to God (6:18–19). The body of every Christian is a temple of the Holy Spirit (6:19). We don't own ourselves. Rather, we have been purchased out of slavery to sin by God at the price of the blood of Jesus Christ, and we should therefore honor God with our bodies (6:19–20).

✚ The New Testament frequently calls believers to give up their rights in order to love and serve others (Matt. 5:39–42; 1 Cor. 6:7–8; Phil. 2:1–8).

Paul Responds to the Letter from the Corinthians (1 Cor. 7:1–16:4)

Paul now begins to address the issues the Corinthians had written him about, including marriage (7), food sacrificed to idols (8–10), public worship (11–14), the resurrection from the dead (15), and the collection for the Jerusalem church (16:1–4). The church included people with little self-control who indulged in worldly pleasures, as well as people who avoided legitimate gifts from God. Both hedonism and asceticism fail to solve life's problems.

Concerning marriage (7:1–40)

TO THE MARRIED OR THOSE PREVIOUSLY MARRIED (7:1–16)

Another Corinthian slogan is presented in 7:1: "It is good for a man not to have sexual relations with a woman" (NIV footnote). Some believers are suggesting it is better for married people not to have sexual relations. But Paul recommends marriage, in which marriage partners fulfill their marital obligations to have sex with each other (7:2–3). Their bodies belong to their marriage partner, and they shouldn't deprive one another lest they be tempted by Satan, except for a short time when they need to focus on prayer (7:4–5). Even this exception is a concession on Paul's part, not a command (7:6). Paul wishes everyone could enjoy being single, but he realizes God has not gifted everyone for singleness (7:7). In 7:8–9, Paul advises the widowers ("unmarried") and the widows to remain unmarried unless they can't control themselves, and then they should get married. It's better to marry than to burn with passion. In 7:10–11, Paul tells the married (based on the teachings of Jesus) that divorce is not a viable option for two believers. To the rest (apparently those in mixed marriages of believers and unbelievers), Paul permits divorce when the unbelieving partner leaves the believing partner (7:15–16). When possible, the believing partner should stay with an unbelieving partner who is willing to stay in the marriage, because the believer's presence will have a godly influence on the whole family (7:12–14).

PRINCIPLE: CALLING AND CONTENTMENT (7:17–24)

Paul now offers a general life principle to help them deal with the various situations: each person should "retain the place in life that the Lord assigned to him" and "remain in the situation which he was in when God called him" (7:17, 20, 24). In other words, when people become Christians, they should not try to radically change their life circumstances but allow God to work in their situation. He illustrates this principle in 7:18–19 with the issue of circumcision and in 7:21–23 with the issue of slavery.

✚ Paul seems to derive his views on marriage from Jesus's teachings (see Mark 10:11–12).

Contextualizing the Message

Jeannine K. Brown

The first task of contextualizing the Corinthian letters is to hear Paul's message well in its original context. Attention to the first-century setting is important for topics foreign to most modern readers (like eating idol food) and for more familiar topics (like marriage; 1 Cor. 7). In both cases, there will be situational factors particular to the original context that differ from contemporary facets of similar issues. Also critical for bringing the Corinthian letters into our own setting is asking *recontextualization* questions: How well do the proposed situations (then and now) align? If they are closely analogous, how does Paul's message to that original situation "translate" to contemporary ones? If it doesn't, what other situations might Paul's message inform? How might we recontextualize Paul's message for analogous (or partially analogous) contemporary situations? For instance, the message of Paul in 1 Corinthians 1–4 confronts a situation of hero worship and power leveraging in the Corinthian church. Paul has heard of divisions based on the personalities and speaking capacities of leaders, like Paul himself and Apollos (1:10–12; 3:4; 4:6–7). This picture fits the Greek setting of the Corinthian church, in which wealthy persons would provide material support for the best orators and would gain prestige through that relationship. A competition would then ensue, with the elite claiming something like, "My orator is better than yours." Addressing this situation, Paul denies his preaching came with eloquence; rather, his message and mode center on the cross of Christ (1:17).

Is there an analogous type of situation within the contemporary church when we treat human messengers of the gospel as heroes instead of as servants of God? Do we attempt to gain prestige by following the trendiest preacher or teaching type in the Christian circuit? If so, Paul's message re-contextualized confronts us: boasting in our favorite leader must give way to boasting in the Lord (1:28–31; 3:21).

A Corinthian issue that might seem less relevant to Western, contemporary Christians is that of eating idol meat (8:1–11:1). Yet a careful reading of this passage in its historical context yields two analogous situations. Paul's concluding exhortation (10:23–11:1) allows for eating meat that has been offered to an idol if it is purchased in the market (not eaten in a pagan temple) and if doing so does not disturb a weak Christian's conscience. Contemporary analogous situations would include *adiaphora* (actions neither commanded nor prohibited in Scripture) that are matters of Christian conscience.

Yet for most of his argument (8:1–10:22), Paul strongly warns the Corinthians against eating sacrificial meat *at temple meals* because of idolatrous connections and a devastating effect on the "weak" (e.g., 8:10; 10:14–22). To recontextualize this warning, we would need to address contemporary temptations toward allegiances that compete with our loyalty to the true God. In Western contexts, we might explore the pull of consumerism that is regularly at cross-purposes with our loyalty to God in Christ. By living as if we can serve two masters, we might actually provoke our Lord to jealousy (10:22).

TO THOSE NEVER MARRIED OR THOSE THINKING ABOUT MARRIAGE (7:25–40)

Historical evidence indicates there were food shortages in Corinth during this time, leading to a general anxiety about the basic necessities of life. The threat of famine was real, which probably explains the "present crisis" (7:26) and the shortness of time (7:29–31). Paul advises the "virgins" (a term referring to people who are the appropriate age to be married) to stay unmarried in light of the crisis (7:26). This is his judgment, not the Lord's command, so they don't sin if they do get married (7:25–28). In 7:32–35, Paul urges them to choose a path that leads to undivided devotion to the Lord. Married people are consumed with meeting the needs of their spouse and children, while unmarried people have fewer family obligations and can devote more time to minister to others. But Paul is quick to add that his recommendation is meant to bring more freedom, not add a load of guilt. In 7:36–38, Paul tells those who are engaged to be married that it's acceptable to get married, or, if they choose, it's acceptable not to get married. In 7:39–40, Paul affirms the permanence of Christian marriage and tells Christian widows (and presumably Christian widowers) that it's fine to remarry so long as they marry another believer. As one who has the Spirit (just as much as the spiritual ones in Corinth), Paul believes these people will be happier in the current situation staying single.

Concerning food sacrificed to idols (8:1–11:1)

PRINCIPLE: LOVE FOR FELLOW CHRISTIANS LIMITS FREEDOM (8:1–13)

The second issue Paul addresses is food sacrificed to idols. In the ancient world, most meat sold in the marketplace came from animals that had been sacrificed in pagan rituals. Were Christians free to eat such meat? Could they eat the meat when they attended a social gathering such as a wedding at a pagan temple? Although "we all possess knowledge" (another Corinthian slogan), and knowledge brings freedom, love trumps knowledge (8:1–3). An idol (or "so-called god") is nothing, and there is only one God and one Lord, Jesus Christ (8:4–6). But not every believer knows this like they should, and eating this meat defiles their weak consciences (8:7–8). Therefore, love for fellow believers should limit the freedom to eat, lest those with knowledge become a stumbling block to the weak for whom Christ died (8:9). If the weak violate their own consciences (a sinful act) by eating the meat, then those with knowledge have caused their brothers to sin, and this constitutes a sin against Christ (8:10–12). Paul concludes, "if what I eat causes my brother to fall into sin, I will never eat meat again, so that I will not cause him to fall" (8:13). The freedom that knowledge brings should be limited by love.

PAUL'S PERSONAL EXAMPLE: FORFEITING HIS RIGHT TO CHARGE (9:1–18)

Paul now illustrates from his own life the principle that freedom should be limited by love. Some of the Corinthians apparently doubt the legitimacy of Paul's apostleship because he doesn't charge a fee like other traveling religious

✚ The issue of eating food sacrificed to idols appears in 1 Corinthians 8:1–11:1 and Romans 14:1–15:6, although the two contexts are not identical.

teachers. But this would put him in the debt of the wealthy members, something he wants to avoid. In 9:1–12, Paul describes his rights as an apostle, including his right to charge for his ministry. In 9:12–18, he explains why he has voluntarily forfeited that right. He wants to be able to preach voluntarily as a response to God's calling (9:17) and offer the gos-

A bronze statue depicting a Greek "thermae boxer" (third to second century BC).

pel free of charge (9:18). He doesn't want to do anything that hinders the gospel (9:12). Love limits what he is free to do.

UNDERLYING MOTIVE: TO SAVE AS MANY AS POSSIBLE (9:19–27)

Although Paul is not under obligation to anyone, he has chosen to use his freedom to serve a wide range of people (e.g., Jews, gentiles, the "weak"). His motive is to draw them to Christ (9:19–22). He has become all things to all people so that some might be saved (9:22). Again, he limits his freedom for the sake of the gospel (9:23). Paul's missionary adaptability and innovation require a great deal of spiritual discipline. Paul must train intensely (like a runner or a boxer), so that once he has preached to others, he himself might not be disqualified for the prize (9:24–27).

EXAMPLES OF THE DANGERS OF UNLIMITED "FREEDOM" (10:1–22)

Paul uses the example of the Israelites in their wilderness wanderings to warn the Corinthians of the dangers of unlimited freedom. The Israelites were delivered, guided, and sustained by God, but they failed to please God (10:1–5). Although a privileged people, they committed idolatry and sexual immorality, tested the Lord, and grumbled, and God judged them severely (10:7–10). The Corinthians should learn from the Israelites' negative example and heed the warning (10:6, 11). To avoid imitating the Israelites, the Corinthians need to admit they too are spiritually vulnerable (10:12). Even so, God will provide a way to survive the temptation for those who trust him (10:13). Paul commands the Corinthians to "flee from idolatry" (10:14), meaning they should never participate in worship rituals in pagan temples. Christians have their own sacred meal—the Lord's Supper (10:16–17). While idols are nothing (10:19–20; 8:4), pagan worship involves demonic

✦ In 1 Corinthians 10:1–13 Paul mentions how God blessed Israel during the wilderness wanderings and how they rebelled against God as a way of warning the Corinthians about participating in idol feasts.

1 Corinthians 791

activity, idolatry, and sexual immorality. Christians should never think they are free to participate in such pagan worship experiences (10:18–22).

SUMMARY: FREEDOM LIMITED BY LOVE (10:23–11:1)

Paul wraps up the whole discussion that began in 8:1. He repeats the slogan "everything is permissible" and adds, "but not everything is beneficial" or "constructive" (10:23). Freedom, yes, but not unlimited freedom. Christians should "seek the good of others" rather than their own good (10:24). Believers are free to eat meat sold in the marketplace without worrying about it, for the "earth is the Lord's, and everything in it" (10:25; Ps. 24:1). They are also free to eat meat in a private home without worrying about it, unless a "weaker" person raises concerns. In that case they shouldn't eat for the sake of that person's conscience (10:27–30). Paul summarizes the entire discussion in 10:31–11:1. The general principle is to do everything "for the glory of God" (10:31). Paul doesn't want to cause anyone to stumble, so he behaves in a way that even more people might be saved (10:32–33). The Corinthians have an example worth following in Paul, since he follows the example of Christ (11:1).

Concerning behavior in public worship (11:2–14:40)

THE IMPORTANCE OF PERSONAL APPEARANCE (11:2–16)

In 1 Corinthians 11–14, Paul answers questions about public worship. This first issue relates to personal appearance, specifically to what people should wear on their heads. There are several debated issues in this passage. The use of "man" and "woman" could refer to "husband" and "wife." The word "head" has traditionally been understood to refer to "authority over," but it could refer to "source." And head coverings could refer to hair length or to a veil of some sort. Paul first praises the Corinthians for holding to the teachings he passed on to them (11:2). The gospel brought new freedom for women, but Paul says

A bust from Corinth showing one example of hair styles.

Women in Ancient Corinth

Robbie Fox Castleman

Women in ancient Corinth, to a great extent, generally reflected the social, cultural, religious, and familial circumstances of women in the Greco-Roman world. Socially, with rare exception, women in Greek-leaning cities, like Corinth, didn't often leave home even with their husbands. Women in cities with greater Roman influence did accompany their husbands outside the home more often, but most women lived relatively secluded lives tending to their homes and families. The social and cultural situation in Corinth in the middle of the first century may have been a bit more complicated due to the significant influx of a great number of Jewish families from Rome during the reign of the emperor Claudius, who in AD 49 had expelled all Jews from the capital city. The predominant Grecian atmosphere of Corinth, as well as its predominant gentile population, would have been challenged and eventually modified by the influence of these new inhabitants, including that of the newly founded Christian communities in the city.

However, women in the Corinthian church, whether Jewish or gentile, would have a life similar to women throughout the Roman Empire. Greco-Roman men, both Jewish and gentile, typically married women ten to fifteen years younger than themselves. It was the usual practice to arrange marriages based on social class, the needs of friends or families, or political and religious favor. Often, girls just past early pubescence would enter into marriage with men well over thirty years of age. Paul's advice in 1 Corinthians 7:36–38 regarding marriage as optional or delayed beyond custom was unusual for its time. This would have been much like Paul's countercultural comments regarding slaves within the church (e.g., Philemon).

Women would have been almost solely responsible for the nurture and education of their children for the first four or five years. After the fifth year of a child's life, fathers, tutors, and other social mentors became increasingly involved, especially in the lives of male children. Because more female infants than male infants were abandoned, there tended to be fewer women considered eligible to marry and beget legitimate children. Female infants weren't rescued just by Christians; it was common for owners of inns and taverns to claim them to be raised as brothel prostitutes. Prostitution was legal and subject to tax revenues throughout the empire.

Generally all women in the empire, not just Jewish or gentile women, were expected to be silent in any sort of social situation, especially when men to whom they were not related were present. A woman was expected to be submissive to the authority of her husband and to share his religious practices. Jesus included women in his ministry and mission, allowing them to learn and be discipled. Paul notably recognized women as disciples and included them in the practice of their gifts within the church with the same accountability to elders expected of men. This challenged Christian men and women to determine new patterns of relating to one another in the fellowship of the church as well as in family and society.

this freedom should not undermine the order of creation or obscure the differences between men and women (11:3). Christians should honor those distinctions by their personal appearance in worship (11:4–6). The cultural norm was short hair for men and long hair for women. Roman law prescribed that a woman who committed adultery and so disgraced her husband would have her head shaved. The lines of authority created

Spiritual Gifts

Kenneth A. Berding

Although in the Bible the Holy Spirit himself is sometimes described as a "gift" (e.g., Acts 2:38), normally when we speak of "spiritual gifts" we are referring not to the Holy Spirit but to particular activities that are given by the Holy Spirit to build up the "body of Christ." In particular, the "spiritual gifts" are those items listed by the apostle Paul in his four ministry lists. They include (by passage and in the forms in which Paul lists them):

- Rom. 12:6–8: prophecy, service/serving, one who teaches/teaching, one who encourages/encouragement, one who gives, one who leads, one who shows mercy
- 1 Cor. 12:8–10: a word of wisdom, a word of knowledge, faith, healings, workings of miracles, prophecy, distinguishing of spirits, speaking in different kinds of tongues, interpretation of tongues
- 1 Cor. 12:28–30: apostles, prophets, teachers, workers of miracles, those with gifts of healing, those able to help others, those with gifts of administration, those speaking in different kinds of tongues, [those who] interpret [tongues]
- Eph. 4:11: apostles, prophets, evangelists, pastor-teachers (or pastors and teachers)
- (Note also 1 Pet. 4:11: whoever speaks . . . whoever serves)

Some interpreters consider the items found in these lists to be comprehensive of all gifts of the Spirit, though most recent interpreters have viewed them as representative. The more significant question is what these lists are lists *of*. Throughout the twentieth century and into the present, it has been popular to view these listed items primarily in the category of special *abilities* that one must *discover* and *use* in ministry. This continues to be a prevalent view. But others have argued that it is more appropriate to view these items primarily in the category of Spirit-given *ministry assignments*.

The current issue most often discussed regarding spiritual gifts is whether the miraculous activities included in these lists—particularly those items clustered in 1 Corinthians 12:8–10, including healings, prophecy, and tongues—can and should be a regular part of contemporary Christian community life. "Cessationists" believe such miraculous activities ceased at the end of the apostolic age, since they were given by God as signs to confirm the message of the apostles (2 Cor. 12:12; Heb. 2:3–4). "Continuationists" agree that miracles confirmed the message in the first century, but ask whether there is no need for confirmation now, particularly since nowhere is it written in the Bible that miracles will cease. (Unlike earlier generations, many recent cessationists and continuationists agree that 1 Corinthians 13:10 does not speak to this issue because the second coming of Christ is in view; cf. 13:12.)

by God should govern public appearance in worship for men/husbands and women/wives (11:7–10, 13–15), although in the Lord there is mutual dependence rather than independence (11:11–12). Those who want to be contentious about Paul's teachings need to take note of the practice among all the other churches (11:16). In summary, Paul is calling the Corinthians to act in culturally appropriate ways so as to honor God's design for relationships and to promote the gospel.

Celebration of the Lord's Supper in conjunction with a corporate meal was a regular part of worship in the early church, but the Corinthian gatherings were full of problems (11:17). The wealthy members with more leisure time would gather early. They would eat the best food and drink too much wine, leaving nothing for the other believers. As a result, some got drunk, while others went hungry, and Paul certainly cannot praise them for despising the church of God in this way (11:18–22). In 11:23–26, Paul provides a summary of the essential Christian tradition related to the Lord's Supper. Consequently, the Corinthians need to make some changes. Whoever participates in the Lord's Supper "in an unworthy manner," that is, by indulging his or her own needs and ignoring the needs of fellow believers, will be guilty of sinning against the Lord (11:27). This calls for spiritual sensitivity to the "body of the Lord" so as to avoid God's judgment (11:28–32). When they gather, the believers should wait for others before beginning the meal (11:33). Those wealthy members who are hungry can eat at home before they gather so as not to incur judgment (11:34).

EXERCISING THE GIFTS OF THE SPIRIT (12:1-14:40)

Public worship also involves how people use their gifts, the topic of chapters 12–14. Paul begins by discussing the nature of unity and diversity within the body in 12:1–31. The Corinthians first need to know that ministry that is truly from the Holy Spirit will confess and honor Jesus Christ as Lord (12:1–3). From the one Spirit, Lord, and God come a diversity of gifts, ministries, and workings or activities (12:4–6). Paul lists a few of the many gifts in 12:7–11 (e.g., message of wisdom, faith, healing, tongues), emphasizing that they all come from the one Spirit, who empowers each person as he sees fit. In 12:12–26, Paul explains the nature of the body of Christ using the analogy of the human body. There is one body with many parts, and the individual body members were created to need one another. God in his sovereignty arranged the individual members to prevent division and enhance mutual care. In 12:27–31, Paul provides another sampling of gifts (e.g., apostles, prophets, teachers, miracle workers, administrators) to make the point that these gifts are distributed among the body. No one believer has all the gifts, and no one gift is given to all believers.

For Paul, the central concern in the passages in which he discusses spiritual gifts is that everything should be done with the aim of building up the "body of Christ" (= the community of believers). Paul's metaphor of the "body of Christ" is found in the immediate contexts of all four of his lists (Eph. 4:4, 12, 16; Rom. 12:4–5; 1 Cor. 12:12–27; cf. Col. 1:18; 2:19). This metaphor

✚ Along with the bride of Christ, the temple of the Spirit, and the household/family of God, the "body of Christ" stands as one of the major images of the church in the New Testament (Rom. 12:4–5; 1 Cor. 12:12–2; Eph. 3:6; 5:23; Col. 1:18–24; 2:19; 3:15).

emphasizes that although there is diversity in the "body," each member is important and needs to serve others with the aim of building up that body. Notably, Paul tends to move in the direction of love in each of these discussions (Eph. 4:15–16; Rom. 12:9–10; 1 Cor. 13). The fruit of the Spirit, of which love is first (cf. Gal. 5:22–23), should be distinguished from the gifts of the Spirit because no individual exercises all the gifts (1 Cor. 12:29–30), whereas everyone should exercise the fruit of the Spirit, especially love.

In 13:1–13, Paul declares that love as "the most excellent way" (12:31) should take priority over the gifts. If people speak with angelic tongues or understand all mysteries or move mountains with their faith or give up their bodies to benefit the poor, but fail to love, their gifts are worthless (13:1–3). In one of the most loved passages in all the New Testament, Paul defines biblical love (13:4–7). He uses fifteen verbs (seven positive and eight negative) to stress that love is primarily an action (e.g., "love is patient" is more like "love acts with patience"). All the gifts are temporary (13:8–9), for when Jesus returns, the gifts will fade away and leave only faith, hope, and love, and the greatest of these is love (13:10–13). This section reminds the Corinthians (and all who are overly fascinated with spiritual gifts) that biblical love should be their focus.

In 14:1–25, Paul encourages the Corinthians to follow the way of love and eagerly desire spiritual gifts. The gift of tongues is certainly legitimate, but in public worship the gift of prophecy should be preferred because it strengthens, encourages, and edifies the whole church (14:1–5). The problem with tongues in public worship is that other people can't understand what the speaker is saying. As a result, the gift of tongues fails to edify the church (14:6–12). One solution is for someone to interpret for the one who speaks in tongues. Even so, Paul thanks God for the gift of tongues, but his clear preference in the church is for intelligible speech (14:13–19). He prefers prophecy (the proclamation of God's word) in the church because it edifies believers and offers unbelievers a chance to understand the good news of Christ and respond in faith, thus avoiding God's judgment (14:20–25). If an unbeliever hears people

Ancient silver mirror from Pompeii.

✚ Interestingly, Paul puts the famous love chapter (1 Corinthians 13) right between two chapters on spiritual gifts.

only speaking in tongues, it will be a sign of judgment for him, meaning that he won't understand the gospel and will be lost in his sins.

In 14:26–40, Paul explains the importance of order in public worship. Everyone has a contribution to make, but all must be done to strengthen the church (14:26). This calls for order and self-control rather than confusion and self-promotion (14:27–28, 30–31). Also, prophecy must be properly evaluated (14:29). God is a God of order and peace, and he wants his community to reflect his character (14:32–33). Paul prohibits women (or "wives," as in 11:2–16) from participating in the evaluation of prophecy, normally the task of the church leaders (14:34–38). The command for women to be silent (14:34) should not be taken as a universal command in light of Paul's other teachings in the same letter (11:5, 13). As a general rule, women had fewer educational opportunities in the ancient world, and Paul prohibits women/wives from evaluating the prophecy publicly, which probably included interrogating the prophet and thus disrupting worship in an unedifying way. He summarizes the discussion about public worship in 14:39–40: be eager to prophesy without forbidding people from speaking in tongues, but above all, let everything be done "in a fitting and orderly way."

Concerning the resurrection of the dead (15:1–58)

THE FOUNDATION: JESUS'S BODILY RESURRECTION (15:1–11)

The Corinthians came to Christ out of paganism, in which the common view was the immortality of the soul rather than the resurrection of the body. This pagan doctrine had obvious implications for how people lived: "Let us eat and drink, for tomorrow we die" (15:32). In 1 Corinthians 15, Paul makes a solid case for the bodily resurrection of Christians and its ethical implications. In this section, Paul spells out the basis for the resurrection of believers; the bodily resurrection of Christ himself. Jesus's resurrection stands at the heart of the gospel (15:1–2, 11). The early Christian belief centered on Jesus's atoning death, his bodily resurrection, and his postresurrection appearances (15:3–8). As one arriving late on the scene, Paul was dramatically transformed by God's grace from a persecutor of the church into an apostle, causing him to respond with wholehearted devotion to Christ (15:9–11).

THE CERTAINTY OF OUR BODILY RESURRECTION (15:12–34)

In 15:12–19, Paul argues that if there is no future bodily resurrection of Christians, then Christ himself has not been raised, and the consequences are disastrous. The apostolic preaching is false and useless, the faith of believers is futile, those who have died are lost, and those who have lived for Christ should be pitied because they gave up so much for the cause. But,

Jerusalem Offering

E. Randolph Richards

Paul's letters discuss a "collection (*logeia*) for the saints . . . your gift (*charis*) to Jerusalem" (1 Cor. 16:1–4; also 2 Cor. 8–9; Rom. 15:25–29). The recipients are clear from Paul's explanation to the Romans (15:26): "the poor among the saints in Jerusalem." But what type of collection was it? Since Karl Holl, a few scholars have attempted to argue *logeia* was a tax and "saints" was a technical (religious) term referring to all members of the Jerusalem church. Thus the mother church was imposing a tax on all daughter churches. Yet *logeia* often meant a special levy. Paul's other descriptions—"gift" (*charis*, 1 Cor. 16:3; see 2 Cor. 8:4); "contribution" (*koinonia*, Rom. 15:26; see 2 Cor. 8:4); "service" (*diakonia*, Rom. 15:31; 2 Cor. 8:4; 9:1); and "generous gift" (*eulogia*, 2 Cor. 9:5)—indicate this was a freewill offering. Calling it *logeia* assures them it was a unique offering, not a recurring one.

What was Paul hoping to accomplish by collecting an offering from gentile Christians for Jewish Christians in Jerusalem? According to Paul's testimony, his ministry to gentiles included the exhortation to remember the poor (Gal. 2:10). Yet this offering seems more than merely implementing the Galatian mandate, since Paul (according to Acts 18:22–23) had returned to Jerusalem at least once without an offering. Ancient gifts always had strings attached.

The ancient honor system required the recipient of a gift to reciprocate in some way. Perhaps Paul was seeking to have his gentile churches accepted by the mother church in Jerusalem as a response to their gracious gift (2 Cor. 9:13; Rom. 15:31).

Was Paul's offering successful? Both Paul's later letters and the book of Acts are strangely silent. Acts seems aware of the gift (24:17) yet gives no indication the gift was accepted. Modern readers often assume it was: "Who turns down a free gift?" But the Jerusalem church could not accept the gift while rejecting the givers, all the more because the gift was delivered by the givers (1 Cor. 16:3; 2 Cor. 8:23–24). When Paul arrives in Jerusalem (Acts 21), James recounts the mandate of Acts 15, which does not include the exhortation to remember the poor (Gal. 2:10). Does James avoid accepting the gift by redirecting it to a temple offering (Acts 21:24)? We just do not know what happened to the Jerusalem offering.

Paul's principles for giving (1 Cor. 16:1–2: regularly, systematically, proportionately, freely) remain timeless, as does the Christian practice of giving (Phil. 4:15–20), even though Paul's experiences may remind us not every offering is used as well as we might wish.

thankfully, Christ has indeed been raised from the dead, guaranteeing the bodily resurrection of all believers (15:20–23). After Jesus has destroyed all powers and defeated death, the last enemy, he will hand over the kingdom to God the Father (15:24–28). In 15:29–34, Paul again argues against those who deny the resurrection of the dead. If the dead are not raised, why are people baptized for the dead (either proxy baptism for loved ones who had died or Christian baptism of those "spiritually dead"), and why do faithful believers suffer persecution (15:29–32)? Rather, if there is no tomorrow, they should simply live for the pleasures of the day (15:32). Paul urges the

Corinthians to reject this corruptive teaching, to return to their senses, and to stop sinning (15:33–34).

THE NATURE OF OUR RESURRECTION BODY (15:35–58)

In this section, Paul seeks to answer the questions raised in 15:35 about the resurrection body. Just like a seed grows into a plant that is totally new but still related to the seed, and just as heavenly bodies differ from earthly bodies, so the resurrection body will be a transformed natural body—imperishable, glorious, powerful, and spiritual or "supernatural" (15:36–44). Just as believers share in Adam's likeness (living, natural, from dust of the earth), so they will also share in Christ's likeness, including a resurrection body (15:44–49). Such a transformation is necessary because "flesh and blood cannot inherit the kingdom of God, nor does the perishable inherit the imperishable" (15:50). Not all believers will die before Christ returns, but when he returns *all* will be changed (15:51). When Christ returns, believers will be raised from the dead and their bodies transformed into imperishable, immortal bodies (15:52–53). What the prophets predicted will come true—the total defeat of the last enemy, death (15:54–55; Isa. 25:8; Hosea 13:14). Sin brought death, and the law makes people aware of sin, but thanks be to God that Jesus's death and resurrection brought victory (15:56–57). The reality of the resurrection has enormous implications for believers (15:58). Rather than being drawn into sin (15:32–34), believers need to stand firm in God's truth and give themselves fully to the Lord's work, knowing what they do in the body right now will carry over into eternity.

Bust of the second-century Greek Sophist Herod Atticus.

Concerning the collection for Jerusalem (16:1–4)

Many Jewish Christians in Jerusalem were poor. On his third missionary journey, Paul makes

✚ The New Testament emphasizes the importance of the resurrection of the body at the return of Christ, which promises much more than just going to heaven when we die.

it a priority to collect money from the gentile churches for the Jerusalem church (Rom. 15:26). The collection has the potential to further unify Jewish and gentile churches, showing unbelievers the gospel's power to break down barriers and bring reconciliation. Paul gives clear instructions about how to take up the collection (16:1–2). When he arrives in Corinth, he will give letters of introduction to people chosen by the Corinthians to carry the gift, and if necessary, Paul will accompany them to Jerusalem (16:3–4).

Concluding Matters (1 Cor. 16:5–24)

Paul discusses his travel plans in 16:5–12. He hopes to arrive at Corinth, where he can stay awhile. He will stay in Ephesus until Pentecost because a great opportunity for ministry has opened up, and (ironically) there are many who oppose him. He cautions them not to intimidate Timothy, but to accept him as one who does the Lord's work and to send him back to Paul in peace. Regarding Apollos, Paul encouraged him to travel to Corinth, but he was unwilling until the time was right. The apostle gives additional instructions in 16:13–18. The Corinthians should be on their guard, stand firm in the faith, be courageous and strong, and do everything in love. Paul endorses the household of Stephanas as Christian examples worthy of respect, and he expresses thanks for the visitors from Corinth. In 16:19–24, Paul closes the letter. He offers greetings from the churches in Asia and the believers with him as well as from Aquila and Priscilla and the church that meets in their house. He encourages the Corinthians to greet one another as the people of God should. Paul greets them in his own handwriting to indicate authenticity. All who do not love the Lord will be cursed, while those who do love him pray for his quick return. He closes with a benediction of grace from Jesus and love from their founding father, Paul himself.

What Is the Message of 2 Corinthians?

After Paul writes 1 Corinthians, his relationship with the church deteriorates significantly, thanks to some stubborn opponents. Paul probably made a short visit to Corinth from Ephesus (the "painful" visit of 2 Cor. 2:1) and followed up with another letter (the "tearful" letter of 2 Cor. 2:4; 7:8–9; 12:14; 13:1). This means that 2 Corinthians is actually Paul's fourth letter written to this difficult church.

At the time of writing, some Corinthians who had previously questioned Paul's apostleship appear to have repented and now support Paul (2:5, 8–9; 5:12; 7:2–16). A minority within the church still question whether Paul

✛ We read about what happened to Paul when he returned to Jerusalem in Acts 21–23. Although he was pleasantly received by the believers, he ran into a great deal of trouble when Jews from Asia stirred up trouble against him.

Paul's Contact with the Corinthian Church

The following reconstruction of Paul's relationship to the church in Corinth helps to explain how his visits to the church relate to his letters to the church.

50–51 VISIT 1 Evangelizes Corinth on Second Journey (Acts 18:1–18)

He was there a year and a half, had Jewish opposition, but many Jews and gentiles were converted. Paul then leaves Corinth and goes through Ephesus on his way back to Caesarea (Acts 18:18–22).

54 LETTER 1 "Previous" letter now lost (1 Cor. 5:9); perhaps a follow-up letter to his first visit

Paul returns to Ephesus (Acts 19:1) and stays for three years (Acts 20:31). In Ephesus he receives a visit from someone from Chloe's household (1 Cor. 1:11) reporting factions in the church, and he receives a letter from Corinth asking for advice and guidance (1 Cor. 7:1, 25; 8:1; 11:2; 12:1; 15:1; 16:1). Paul then writes 1 Corinthians in response (1 Cor. 16:8–9).

54 LETTER 2 1 CORINTHIANS (Ephesus); Third Journey

Paul sends Timothy to Corinth on a special mission (1 Cor. 4:17; 16:10). A powerful opponent in Corinth attacks Paul, and Timothy is unable to deal with it (2 Cor. 2:5–11). Timothy returns to report this to Paul, who then goes to deal with the situation himself.

55 VISIT 2 "Painful" visit (2 Cor. 2:1) from Ephesus to Corinth and back

55 LETTER 3 "Tearful" letter (2 Cor. 2:4, 9; 7:8–9; 12:14; 13:1)

Paul probably writes this letter from Ephesus after a painful visit. It is carried by Titus. Afterward, Paul goes to Troas, hoping to meet Titus with the report about Corinth (2 Cor. 2:12–13). Unable to find Titus, Paul travels to Macedonia. There, in 56, Paul finds Titus, who gives a good report about the church (2 Cor. 7:5–8).

56 LETTER 4 2 CORINTHIANS (Macedonia); Third Journey

This letter is carried by Titus to Corinth. Paul continues to defend himself against a rebellious minority in the church (especially in 2 Cor. 10–13) but there is a renewed joy and gentleness because most of the church has repented.

57 VISIT 3 Paul joins Titus in Corinth (Acts 20:2–3), spends the winter there, and writes Romans. After an intense period of conflict followed by reconciliation, this surely was a enjoyable time with the church.

The western end of the ancient ship trackway across the Isthmus of Corinth.

is a legitimate apostle (perhaps addressed in chapters 10–13). In addition, there are some false apostles who have arrived in Corinth who must be countered (11:1–15). In a deeply personal and emotional letter, Paul defends his authority as a genuine apostle of Jesus Christ as well as his way of life and ministry. He is forced to defend himself because the gospel and the spiritual life of the Corinthians are at stake.

Greeting and Thanksgiving (2 Cor. 1:1–11)

To the church that is questioning his apostleship, Paul opens with a clear statement that he is indeed "an apostle of Christ Jesus by the will of God" (1:1). To God's church in Corinth and throughout Achaia, he sends his usual greeting of "grace and peace" from the Father and the Son (1:1–2). Paul then praises God as the Father of "compassion" and the God of all "comfort," a concept that he mentions ten times in 1:3–7. Just as believers share Christ's sufferings, they also experience God's comfort in the midst of troubles, enabling them to comfort others also (1:4–5). This is the case with Paul's relationship to the Corinthians. Whether Paul suffers or experiences comfort, the result is good for the Corinthians: comfort, salvation, and endurance (1:6). Paul's hope for these believers is firm because they share in his sufferings and comfort, indicating their genuine faith (1:7). Paul now details his own sufferings in Asia (1:8). Although he suffered even to the point of despair, he learned through it all not to rely on himself but on God, who raises the dead (1:9). Paul's hope rests on God's ability to deliver him through such trials, yet he remains extremely thankful for the prayers of God's people for such deliverance (1:10–11).

Paul's Apostolic Conduct and Ministry (2 Cor. 1:12–7:1)

Paul's track record with the Corinthians (1:12–2:11)

After asserting the integrity of his apostolic ministry (1:12–14) and explaining why he changed his travel plans (1:15–2:4), Paul challenges the

✦ Paul begins his most personal and emotional letter by speaking of God as the "Father of compassion and the God of all comfort" (2 Cor. 1:3).

Corinthians to act with the same compassion and integrity toward an "offender" (2:5–11).

THE INTEGRITY OF PAUL'S MINISTRY AMONG THE CORINTHIANS (1:12–14)

Paul's boast or confidence is that God's grace has allowed him (and his co-workers) to conduct their ministry "in holiness and sincerity" rather than according to "worldly wisdom" (1:12). He has always communicated with the Corinthians clearly and with integrity, and he hopes they will come to a full understanding of the situation so that on the day of the Lord both can rejoice in what God has done through the other (1:13–14).

PAUL'S INTEGRITY REFLECTS GOD'S FAITHFULNESS (1:15–22)

Some in Corinth were criticizing Paul's legitimacy as an apostle because he changed his travel plans. But Paul didn't change his plans as part of an elaborate scheme to defraud the Corinthians. He's a person of his word, and he had good reasons for altering his plans. Just as God is faithful and the gospel is not contradictory (both "Yes" and "No" at the same time), so Paul's actions reflect God's character. God's promises are "Yes" in Christ, and he has "put his Spirit in our hearts as a deposit, guaranteeing what is to come" (1:22). As an apostle and a preacher, Paul's integrity reflects God's faithfulness.

A REASONABLE CHANGE OF PLANS (1:23–2:4)

Paul's second visit to Corinth had been a "painful visit" because of the conflict with those who were rejecting his apostolic authority. In the meantime, Paul decided not to make another such visit (2:1). Although he failed to make the return visit he had promised, his change of plans was reasonable and merciful (1:23–24). If the conflict had escalated, he feared his relationship with the church would have been permanently damaged (2:2). He writes them a "tearful" letter instead, hoping not to grieve them further but to express the depth of his love for them (2:4). Above all, Paul wants their relationship to be restored so that all will rejoice (2:3).

THE CORINTHIANS SHOULD ALSO ACT WITH COMPASSION AND INTEGRITY (2:5–11)

Paul doesn't mention the specific action of the offender alluded to here. The offense probably involved accusations against Paul, his apostleship, and his relationship to the Corinthian church. He was a person of influence, and many initially supported him. After Paul's "tearful" letter, the majority repented (2:4; 7:8–13). They then punished the offender (2:6). Just as Paul had been led by the Spirit to change his travel plans, now he urges the Corinthian majority to be willing to change their attitude toward the offender.

✚ Throughout the Bible, God is sometimes called as a witness either for or against human behavior (2 Cor. 1:23; cf. Gen. 31:44; 1 Sam. 12:5–6; 20:42; Isa. 43:10; Jer. 42:5).

The stone carvings inside the Arch of Titus in Rome depict captives from Jerusalem being led in procession.

True, he grieved the entire church (2:5), but his punishment has been sufficient (2:6). Now they should "forgive and comfort him, so that he will not be overwhelmed by excessive sorrow" (2:7). As they reaffirm their love for him and forgive him, Paul also forgives him (2:8–10). The restoration is essential to prevent Satan from using the situation to damage the church (2:11).

Paul's apostolic ministry (2:12–7:1)

After Paul made his "painful visit" to Corinth, he returned to Ephesus and wrote the "tearful" letter that he sent with Titus. The plan was to meet Titus in Troas to find out about the Corinthians (2:12–13), but his meeting with Titus is not mentioned until the end of this section (7:5–16). Between 2:12–13 and 7:5, Paul goes into great detail about the nature of his new covenant ministry and how God has been faithful to sustain him through a variety of circumstances.

AN OPEN DOOR FOR MINISTRY, BUT NO PEACE OF MIND (2:12–13)

When Paul came to Troas, the Lord opened a door for him to preach the gospel, but Paul didn't find Titus, and he was still deeply troubled about what was going on in Corinth. So he continued on his way to meet Titus by heading for Macedonia. Sometimes new opportunities for ministry must take a back seat to present concerns about reconciliation with other believers.

THANKS BE TO GOD, WHO LEADS US IN TRIUMPHAL PROCESSION IN CHRIST (2:14–17)

This paragraph is all about victory through suffering and sacrifice. In the illustration, Paul is not leading the procession but is being led. In some sense Paul has been conquered by Christ, and now he follows in support. But God is using Paul's sufferings, the "aroma of Christ," to bring life through the gospel (2:14–16). Unlike false apostles, Paul does not peddle the word of God for profit (2:17).

✦ When Paul arrived in Troas and had an open door for the gospel, he couldn't continue the ministry there because he needed to hear from Titus about the situation in Corinth (2 Cor. 2:12–23).

Triumphal Procession

George H. Guthrie

The Triumphal Procession was an elaborate parade granted by the Roman senate, celebrating a momentous victory by a Roman general who was the focus of the celebration. Such a parade was seen as the epitome of military glory, the zenith of a general's accomplishment. Writers of ancient Greco-Roman literature record over three hundred such processions, and depictions of the celebration occur in plays and paintings, as well as on coins, statues, cups, arches, medallions, and columns of the era. Thus such parades were part of the cultural fabric of the time and would have been readily recognized by Paul's readers.

The general, referred to as the "triumphator," entered the city standing on a two-wheeled chariot called the *currus triumphalis*. The chariot, pulled by four horses, was decorated at times with bells, whips, and laurel branches, and a phallus was attached to its underside, symbolizing the general's power and manhood. The triumphator wore richly embroidered, purple garments, ornamented at some stages in the parade's development with gold stars and palm branches. The general also wore the *corona triumphalis*, a crown symbolizing the victory, given to the triumphator by his army. The crown took various forms, the most prestigious being made of laurel or bay leaves. At other times the crown was made of gold and jewels, and being too massive to wear, was held over the head of the triumphator by a public officer, while the officer whispered in the general's ear, "Remember that you are just mortal."

The Triumphal Procession served to portray the general's victory to the crowds lining the streets of Rome. Spoils of war, such as weapons, jewelry, and other gold and silver treasures, were carried in the parade. Also displayed were large paintings of battle scenes or conquered cities. In the procession there were white oxen, which would be sacrificed on their arrival at Jupiter's temple. Trumpet blasts filled the air, as did the smell of burning incense, carried in bowls along the parade route. Chained prisoners, often the defeated leaders of the opposing army, marched in front of the general's chariot. At times these prisoners were killed in the dungeon of Jupiter's temple, just before the oxen were sacrificed. Others in the parade included members of the senate, the triumphator's own children, and Romans who had been slaves in the foreign land before being liberated by the general's victory. His army brought up the rear, singing bawdy songs deriding the general, meant to keep him humble.

In 2 Corinthians 2:14–16, Paul uses the image of the Triumphal Procession to portray the nature of authentic Christian ministry. In Paul's word-picture, Christ is the triumphator, Paul is an incense bearer and the gospel the incense, the lost are those being led to death, and the liberated those being led to life.

PAUL'S LETTER OF RECOMMENDATION FOR MINISTRY (3:1–3)

Paul's ministry is also legitimized by the Corinthian Christians themselves. As the result of his Christ-centered, Spirit-empowered, God-given ministry, they are the proof that Paul's ministry is authentic.

MINISTERS OF A NEW COVENANT (3:4–6)

Paul can carry out such a task (2:17) only by the power that God supplies (3:4–5). Through Christ, God has made Paul competent to carry out the new covenant ministry. Under the old covenant, the law was chiseled into stone tablets and proved powerless to transform the human heart (3:3, 6). But with the new covenant, the Holy Spirit works within the human heart to bring life (3:2, 6).

THE GLORY OF THE NEW COVENANT MINISTRY (3:7–18)

The old covenant ministry came with a degree of glory, fading though it was, but resulted in death and condemnation (3:7, 9–11). In contrast, the new covenant ministry of the Spirit, with its all-surpassing and lasting glory, brings righteousness (3:8–11). Paul and his co-workers, who have this hope coming from the new covenant, can be bold in ministry (3:12). They are not like Moses, who had to veil his face to prevent people from seeing the glory fade (3:13). Those who reject the new covenant still have their minds and hearts covered by a veil (3:14–15). When people turn to the Lord, however, the veil is removed (3:16). The Lord is the Spirit, and his presence brings freedom (3:17)! Those with unveiled faces now reflect the Lord's glory and are being transformed into his likeness by the power of the Spirit (3:18).

The bema (or judgment) seat in Corinth, where Paul appeared before the proconsul Gallio (Acts 18:12–17).

✚ The goal of the Christian life is to become like Christ (see 2 Cor. 3:18; cf. Rom. 8:29; 12:1–2; 2 Cor. 4:16; Gal. 4:19).

Because Paul has been entrusted with the new covenant ministry, he does not "lose heart" (4:1, 16). The word translated "lose heart" (NIV) can mean to "become discouraged," but in this context probably means to "act cowardly or timidly." To "not lose heart" would therefore mean to have courage and confidence and boldness in ministry (cf. 3:12). Such boldness means he doesn't have to use deception or distort God's word (4:2). Instead, he states the truth plainly with a clear conscience before God (4:2). Not all accept Paul's message, however, because the "god of this age" (Satan) has blinded their minds to prevent them from seeing the gospel of Christ's glory (4:3–4). Since the gospel is all about Christ and since Paul has experienced the glory of Christ, he preaches Christ as Lord and himself as a servant (4:5–6). But the power comes from God, not from the messengers, who are compared to fragile clay pots (4:7–9). Messengers like Paul are often exposed to death in order that the life of Jesus may be revealed (4:10–12). Sustained by faith in the midst of suffering, they continue to preach, knowing that the one who raised Jesus from the dead will also raise them (4:13–15; Ps. 116:10). Paul's confidence remains strong (4:16). Although his body is wearing out, inwardly he is being renewed daily, knowing that these "light and momentary troubles" are giving way to an "eternal glory that far outweighs them all" (4:16–17). As a result, ministers of the new covenant may fix their focus on what is unseen and eternal rather than on what is temporary (4:18). Believers who endure tremendous trials for the sake of Christ will be sustained by a sure and certain hope.

PAUL'S ULTIMATE HOPE (5:1–10)

Because Paul's focus is on what is unseen and eternal (4:18), he longs for his future resurrection (5:1–5). When Paul's "earthly tent" (present body) is destroyed (dies), he knows that he has in store a "building from God," an "eternal house in heaven"—a resurrection body (5:1). Right now he groans, longing to be clothed with this heavenly dwelling or resurrection body (5:2). When he gets this new body, he will not be found "naked" or ashamed before God at the judgment (5:3). But right now in his present body ("this tent"), he groans and is burdened because he desires to be clothed with his heavenly dwelling, his resurrection body (5:4). He longs for the mortal to be swallowed up by resurrection life (5:4; cf. 1 Cor. 15:50–58). God created us for a resurrection body, and the Spirit is God's deposit or down payment, guaranteeing we will receive one (5:5). Paul remains confident in his situation—at home in the present body, but not yet with a resurrection body in the Lord's presence—for he lives by faith, not by sight (5:6–7). He certainly prefers to be present with the Lord in his resurrection body (5:8), but either

✦ The Holy Spirit is God's guarantee that he will finish what he started (2 Cor. 1:21–22; 5:5; Eph. 1:13–14; 4:30).

way his goal is to please the Lord (5:9). Paul's ambition to please the Lord is based on the fact that all believers must appear before the judgment seat (*bema*) of Christ, who will give to each person their due for what they have done in this life, whether good or bad (5:10).

PAUL'S MINISTRY OF RECONCILIATION (5:11–6:2)

Because Paul is expecting to stand before the judgment seat of Christ (5:10), he is motivated to persuade people of the truth of the gospel (5:11). He explains his motives in ministry, not to promote himself but to enable the loyal Corinthians to answer Paul's opponents in the church (5:12). Although he sometimes uses unintelligible speech in private worship (i.e., "out of our mind"), he speaks plainly to the Corinthians (5:13). Paul is not only motivated by a healthy fear of the Lord, he is also compelled by the love of Christ, who died and rose again for all (5:14–15). As a consequence, Paul sees things differently now (5:16). Everyone who is "in Christ" is completely new (5:17). All this was made possible when God reconciled the world to himself in Christ and committed to Paul and others like him the ministry of reconciliation (5:18–19). As Christ's ambassadors or messengers, they announce to the world: "Be reconciled to God!" (5:20). A great exchange has occurred: the sinless Christ became a sin offering for the guilty sinner, so that the sinner might become the righteousness of God (5:21). As God's fellow worker, Paul pleads with the Corinthians not to receive God's grace in vain by rejecting the gospel or him as their father in the faith (6:1–2).

Bedouin tent.

The gospel of reconciliation depends, to some degree, on the integrity of those who proclaim it. Paul now commends himself as a true minister of God (6:3–4). The hardships he has endured (6:4–5) and the spiritual integrity of his lifestyle (6:6–7) validate his ministry. He has acted like the true servant of God that he is through everything life has thrown at him, whether good or bad (6:8–10). With his actions supporting his verbal claims to legitimacy, Paul now reminds the Corinthians he has opened his heart wide to them and not withheld any affection. Many of them, however, are not responding to him like the apostle that he is (6:11–12). Paul now speaks as a father to his children: "open wide your hearts also" (6:13).

In this closing section to 2:12–7:1, Paul specifies the implications of his new covenant ministry for the current situation in the church. He opens with a clear command: "do not be yoked together with unbelievers" (6:14). Paul now characterizes his opponents in Corinth as "unbelievers" and calls true believers to separate from them. In 6:14–16, Paul asks a series of questions aimed at supporting the command. The answer to all the questions is that true believers have no spiritual partnership with unbelievers! The church as the temple of the living God belongs to God alone. Then, in 6:16–18, Paul adds a series of pointed Old Testament quotations to strengthen the original command further. Finally, in 7:1 Paul restates the command: "Since we have these promises, dear friends, let us purify ourselves from everything that contaminates body and spirit, perfecting holiness out of reverence for God." The genuine believers at Corinth should reject the opponents and accept Paul because his apostleship and ministry genuinely represent the gospel of Jesus Christ.

Paul's Joy Related to Reconciliation and Giving (2 Cor. 7:2–9:15)

The previous section (2:12–7:1) contains Paul's defense of his apostolic ministry, while this section carries the feel of challenges from a loving pastor. Paul seems to be speaking to those in the church who had repented and are ready to get on with life and ministry. After expressing his joy at their reconciliation (7:2–16), Paul encourages them to renew their commitment to the collection for the church in Jerusalem (8:1–9:15).

Paul's joy at reconciliation (7:2–16)

Although the reconciliation has already taken place, Paul reaffirms the need for full reconciliation on the part of the Corinthians: "make room for us in your hearts" (7:2). Paul hasn't wronged or taken advantage of anyone. In fact, Paul has a large place in his heart for these believers, who are his pride and joy (7:3–4). In 7:5 Paul picks up the story from 2:12–13:

- 2:12–13: "Now when I went to Troas to preach the gospel of Christ and found that the Lord had opened a door for me, I still had no peace of mind, because I did not find my brother Titus there. So I said good-by to them and went on to Macedonia."
- Long digression in 2:14–7:4
- 7:5–7: "For when we came into Macedonia, this body of ours had no rest, but we were harassed at every turn—conflicts on the outside, fears within. But God, who comforts the downcast, comforted us by the coming of Titus, and not only by his coming but also by the comfort you had given him. He told us about your longing for me, your deep sorrow, your ardent concern for me, so that my joy was greater than ever."

Paul encouraged the believers in Corinth to give generously to those in need.

Reconciliation at last! Titus carried the "tearful" (sometimes called "severe") letter to Corinth following Paul's "painful" visit. Now Paul gets word that the church has repented, and he sees this as God's gentle hand of comfort (7:8–13). Although he was initially sorry to have to write such a letter, he now rejoices that it led to genuine repentance and reconciliation. Being sorry for our sins is not the same thing as godly sorrow that leads to repentance, and repentance is essential to reconciliation. Paul is also beside himself with delight because Titus was deeply encouraged by the outcome (7:13–15). Now Paul can have complete confidence in the Corinthians (7:16).

Paul expects the Corinthians to give generously (8:1–15)

Now Paul turns his attention to a matter close to his heart: the collection for the poor believers in Jerusalem (1 Cor. 16:1–4; Rom. 15:25–33). To motivate the Corinthians, Paul mentions the powerful example of the Macedonians, who gave "beyond their ability" in spite of a "most severe trial" and "extreme poverty" (8:1–5). The Macedonians pleaded with Paul for the "privilege of sharing in this service to the saints" (8:4). Paul urges the Corinthians to follow suit by keeping their commitment to give (8:6, 8). He challenges them to excel in generous giving just as they excel in faith, speech, knowledge, earnestness, and love (8:7). He also mentions the example of Christ, who humbled himself and became poor through his incarnation in order that others might benefit (8:9; cf. Phil. 2:5–11). Last year the Corinthians began to give, and now they need to finish the job (8:10–11). They don't have to give beyond their means for the gift to be acceptable (8:12). Paul is not interested in depriving the Corinthians, but in promoting equality among believers, so that those with plenty share with those in need (8:13–15; cf. Exod. 16:18).

Commendation of the delegation (8:16–24)

Paul makes it a priority to commend to the Corinthians the three co-workers who will be responsible for carrying and administering the offering: Titus (8:16–17, 23), a brother who is "praised by all the churches for his service to the gospel" (8:18–19), and a third man with proven zeal and a "great confidence" in the Corinthians (8:22). Paul takes pains to "avoid any criticism of the way we administer this liberal gift" that is meant to honor the Lord and help people (8:19–20). Paul feels accountable not only to God but also to the church (8:21). He asks the Corinthians to receive this delegation in love (8:24).

The need for the Corinthians to be prepared (9:1–5)

Paul acknowledges the Corinthians have been eager to give for some time (9:1–2; 1 Cor. 16:1–4). He is sending the delegation to make sure they have the offering ready when Paul arrives (9:3). He doesn't want them to be ashamed if he arrives and they are not prepared, and he doesn't want to have to badger them either (9:4–5). Poor planning often hurts people.

Principles of generous giving (9:6–15)

Unlike some pastors and missionaries, Paul thinks theologically and conducts practical ministry according to theological principles. He now provides the theological basis for the collection by offering several principles of generous giving. There is the principle of the echo: what goes around comes around (9:6). Then the principle of the deliberate decision: each one should give "what he has decided in his heart to give, not reluctantly or under compulsion, for God loves a cheerful giver" (9:7). Next, there is the principle of sufficiency: God is able to make his grace abound for those who give so that their needs will be met and they may continue to abound

✛ When Paul met James, Peter, and John in Jerusalem, they affirmed his ministry to the gentiles (Gal. 2:9). They did ask him to "remember the poor," and Paul is doing that very thing in 2 Corinthians 8–9.

in good works (9:8–10; Ps. 112:9). The principle of result says that generous giving not only meets the needs of people but also results in an abundance of thanksgiving and praise to God (9:11–14). Last of all, generous giving is but a reflection of the ultimate sacrifice of Jesus, God's "indescribable gift" (9:15).

Paul's Response to the Rebellious (2 Cor. 10:1–13:10)

The tone of 2 Corinthians 10–13 is noticeably harsher than that of chapters 1–9, as Paul responds to the rebellious minority that continues to oppose him. In preparation for his third visit to Corinth, Paul defends himself and his apostolic ministry and turns the tables on his opponents with a vigorous attack.

Paul's apostolic authority (10:1–18)

Paul's opponents accuse him of being "timid" in person and "bold" in his letters (10:1, 10). In reality, Paul doesn't fight as the world fights (10:3). Instead, he uses weapons that have divine power to demolish spiritual strongholds, destroy arguments raised against the knowledge of God, and take thoughts captive to Christ (10:4–5). He will come in unbridled boldness, prepared to "punish every act of disobedience" (10:6), but it would be better for everyone if he didn't have to arrive with such force (10:2). The Corinthians need to realize that Paul too belongs to Christ and that he is not ashamed to use his apostolic authority to encourage believers rather than tear them down or frighten them (10:7–9). But Paul has a warning for his opponents: he is quite capable of meeting them face-to-face and taking strong action against them (10:11). In 10:12–18, Paul contends that his boast or claim to apostolic authority is valid, while his opponents' claim is invalid. In other words, the key question concerns the legitimate basis for claiming apostolic authority over the Corinthians. Paul's opponents commend themselves, a false basis for true apostleship (10:12). In contrast to their self-commendation, Paul's commendation comes from the Lord (10:13–18). Paul boasts about only what God himself has done in and through his life to carry the gospel to the mission field, which includes the Corinthians. Those who commend themselves are not approved by the Lord, but only the one whom the Lord commends (10:18).

Paul's foolish boasting (11:1–12:13)

After clarifying that only God can give proper praise, Paul resorts to a little foolishness in order to defend himself against the slander of his opponents

Honor and Shame

David B. Capes

Honor and shame serve as primary motivational factors in keeping order and perpetuating the ideals of a society. Honor is the recognition or attribution of respect, worth, and approval by one's peers. Shame is the removal of respect or disapproval by one's peers based on community-recognized standards. Since human beings are by nature communal, the pursuit of honor and the avoidance of shame shape behavior in powerful ways.

Honor in first-century Greco-Roman culture could be based on a number of factors, including family, wealth, education, skill, social connection, and accomplishments. These, of course, were not monolithic. A person might not be born to an honorable family, but they could always be adopted into a more prestigious line. Likewise, people may gain honor by increasing their education, expanding their social circles, or doing something honorable.

Shame would result from some sort of action deemed undesirable by the broader society. Adultery, disrespecting one's elders, fleeing from battle, or being defeated by an enemy led to shame and disgrace. A shamed person could expect to be insulted, ostracized, and, in extreme cases, faced with violence. These actions did more than punish the dishonored; they also provided an example of what could happen if others violated community standards. Further, groups might anticipate that those they had shamed would change their ways, reenter the group, and thereby reinforce the community values.

In Mediterranean cultures honor could be won or lost, so individuals were always on guard against challengers. An "honor challenge" was an attempt by an opponent to gain honor at the expense of another.

Two responses were typical. First, if the challenge was perceived as insignificant, a person could ignore the challenge altogether and effectively dishonor the challenger. Second, if the challenge was perceived as a threat, a person could act to defend his/her honor (*riposte*), win the challenge, and either maintain or gain greater honor. The outcome of any honor challenge was in the hands of the group. This is likely the social situation behind the Pharisees' frequent public challenges to Jesus (e.g., Mark 7:1–16; Luke 13:10–17).

"Boasting" of one's pedigree, training, and experience could be employed to either answer challenges or dissuade opponents from attacking one's honor in the first place. Leaders were expected to remind others of their claim to honor in order to maintain order and preserve the honor of the group. Paul's frequent habit of boasting (e.g., 2 Cor. 11–12) is best explained as his response to theological opponents who have attacked his credentials and criticized his ministry.

To a significant degree, one's sex played a role in matters of honor and shame. Culturally, men occupied more public, civic functions, while women took care of private, domestic affairs. When these boundaries were crossed, it created disorder and shame resulted. Some of Paul's teachings on husband–wife relationships may reflect these social realities. For example, Paul urges wives not to pray or prophesy with heads uncovered so as not to disgrace their husbands (1 Cor. 11:2–16). Likewise, he limits wives from speaking publicly in the churches while encouraging private conversations between husbands and wives (1 Cor. 14:34–36; cf. 1 Tim. 2:9–15).

(11:1). Using the rhetorical strategy of foolish boasting, he hopes to show his opponents for what they truly are—false-teaching fools empowered by Satan. He simply cannot allow them to lead the church in Corinth astray.

Paul betrothed the Corinthians to Christ, and he plans to jealously guard that relationship (11:2). He is concerned that false apostles who preach a different Jesus and a different gospel and come with a different Spirit will deceive the church (11:3–4). But although these so-called super-apostles might be trained in professional rhetoric, they don't hold a candle to Paul's knowledge of the Lord and the gospel (11:5–6).

In 11:7–11, Paul defends his practice of supporting himself as an apostle so that he can preach the gospel free of charge. He has never burdened anyone at Corinth, and he doesn't plan to change that policy (11:8–10). He refuses to charge ministry fees, not because he doesn't love the Corinthians, but because he wants to show his opponents for what they are—false apostles in love with money (11:11–12). They are deceitful workmen, masquerading as apostles of Christ when they are actually servants of Satan headed for judgment (11:13–15).

Paul resumes his "foolish boasting" from 11:1, since the Corinthians are so prone to put up with fools (11:16–19). They seem to be attracted to false teachers who want to enslave, exploit, take advantage of, abuse, and insult them (11:20). To his shame, Paul admits that he was "too weak" for such belittling authoritarianism (11:21).

While many societies today still operate with a strong sense of honor and shame, Western societies now seem more motivated by material concerns. Still, for the world of the Bible, honor and shame were powerful factors in shaping societies. In the last half of the twentieth century, scholars began

Ruins of the Temple to Apollo in Corinth.

✦ Paul used wisdom in taking money from churches. For example, he received money from the Philippian church (Phil. 4:10–19) but didn't accept money from the Corinthians (2 Cor. 11:7–10).

God's Power in Weakness

George H. Guthrie

In Greco-Roman culture, self-aggrandizement—the gaining of honor, position, and prestige via one's communication abilities—was highly valued. Paul's opponents, who probably were from the Sophist tradition, were elitists who despised the various manifestations of weakness in Paul and his mission. For the Sophists, preaching was an opportunity to showcase one's superior abilities and, perhaps, grow in position and influence. Thus Paul's "weaknesses"—his constant afflictions (2 Cor. 4:7–11; 6:4–10; 11:23–33), his lack of charging for his services, and his unimpressive public speaking—would suggest the apostle was unfit for leadership according to the value system of his opponents.

Yet Paul makes clear that weakness, properly understood, stands as a vital prerequisite for power in an authentically Christian ministry. First, weaknesses force a minister to depend on Christ's power rather than the minister's own power. In 2 Corinthians 1:8–9, for instance, Paul records the despair he and his co-workers experienced under severe persecution in Asia. Completely overwhelmed, taxed beyond their own power, and despairing of life, they were taught to hope in Christ who raises the dead.

Second, weakness in the minister manifests the power of God. At 2 Corinthians 4:7, again in a context dealing with persecution, Paul uses a striking word picture, proclaiming that the treasure of the gospel is delivered in "clay pots," earthen vessels that could crack or break, so that the power surrounding his ministry could be seen as clearly from God and not originating with the minister. This is what Paul means when he comments on the Lord's words at 12:9, "But He said to me, 'My grace is sufficient for you, for my power is made perfect in weakness.'" In the midst of Paul's weaknesses, including his thorn in the flesh from which he asked deliverance, God's power was brought to an apex. This is why Paul boasted in his weaknesses (11:30; 12:5, 9) and could say that he was pleased in his weaknesses (12:10). His weaknesses manifested the power of God in and through his ministry (12:10).

to explore these social dynamics as part of the overall context of biblical interpretation.

Paul first boasts about his Jewish pedigree and then about his service to Christ, supported by a catalog of hardships that seems almost beyond belief (11:21–29). Paul suffered persecution: being imprisoned, flogged, exposed to death, beaten with rods, stoned, and in constant danger from unbelievers. He suffered trials: being shipwrecked, stranded in the open sea, on the move, without food or water or sleep or clothing. On top of all of that, he worked extremely hard and handled the daily pressure of concern for all the churches and their problems. He is boasting about his weaknesses, as his secret exit from Damascus as a new believer illustrates (11:30–33). Even from the beginning of his life as a believer, Paul's weakness has been his strength in the Lord.

Paul also boasts about his visions and revelations in the Lord (12:1). He speaks in the third person of a vision he had fourteen years ago (about AD 42) when he was caught up to the third heaven or paradise. There he heard "inexpressible things" which he cannot repeat (12:2–4). Although Paul has had these kinds of private supernatural experiences, he doesn't boast about them regularly so as not to draw unnecessary attention to himself (12:5–6). But God gave him a thorn in the flesh, a messenger of Satan to keep Paul from becoming conceited (12:7). God is completely sovereign over Satan and permits him to act in ways that ultimately serve God's purposes. Paul responded by asking God to remove this tormenting thorn, but God said "[No,] my grace is sufficient for you, for my power is made perfect in weakness" (12:8–9). Knowing God's answer, Paul decides to boast about and delight in his weaknesses—insults, hardships, persecutions, and difficulties—so that Christ's power may rest on him; for when he is weak, then he is strong in the Lord (12:9–10).

For Paul, therefore, weakness was not an end in itself. The key to his perspective may be found in his final statement on power and weakness in the book, 2 Cor. 13:4: "In fact, [Jesus] was crucified in weakness, but He lives by God's power. For we also are weak in Him, yet toward you we will live with Him by God's power" (HCSB). Paul simply understood his ministry as following the pattern laid down by the ministry of his Lord. In a ministry from God, weakness and vulnerability open the way for the manifestation of resurrection power and life.

The Corinthians have forced Paul into such foolish boasting by failing to commend him properly as an apostle. He is not, after all, inferior to the so-called super-apostles in any way, even though he is "nothing" (12:11). God performed, through Paul, "signs, wonders and miracles" among the Corinthians with great perseverance, so they have witnessed his apostolic authority (12:12). He never deprived the Corinthians, except he failed to charge them for his ministry among them. Now he sarcastically asks them to forgive him this wrong (12:13).

Carvings of menorahs from an ancient Jewish synagogue in Corinth.

✠ Paul had learned that heritage and accomplishments and possessions are worth nothing compared to the value of knowing Christ (Phil. 3:3–11). In his weakness he had learned to rely on God's strength and power.

Paul's final appeal in preparation for a third visit (12:14–21)

As he prepares to visit them for a third time, Paul assures the Corinthians that he will not burden them; he doesn't want their money (12:14). He comes as a parent responsible for caring for the children, willing to spend his money and expend himself for their benefit (12:14–15). Will his sacrificial love cause them to love him less (12:15)? His strategy of supporting himself is indeed a "tricky one" (12:16). But the opponents have misrepresented Paul's financial policy and have accused him of being weak or deceitful or both. They probably charged him with planning to use the Jerusalem collection for himself, so Paul insists again that Titus and the two brothers have acted with complete integrity (12:17–18). Paul has been responding in this way not just to defend himself, but also to strengthen the Corinthians by protecting them from the false apostles (12:19). He fears, however, that their reunion will not be a pleasant one. He anticipates that many have refused to repent and are still living in blatant immorality (12:21). They probably won't like how Paul will confront them about their sin and the unhealthy conflict that results (12:20). The Corinthians' response to Paul will reveal their relationship to the Lord.

Paul's final warning to the rebellious (13:1–10)

When Paul arrives, he will abide by the legal requirement that every matter must be established by two or more witnesses (13:1; Deut. 19:15; Matt. 18:16; 1 Tim. 5:19). In other words, everything will be out in the open to be verified by the community. He has warned them before and now warns them again that he will not spare the rebellious (13:2). The proof that Christ is powerfully at work in him will be his exercise of judgment against the rebellious (13:3–4). They should examine their hearts to determine whether they truly believe. If they pass the test and realize that Christ Jesus is in them, one indication will be that they will also admit that Paul is a true apostle (13:5–6). His primary concern is not the Corinthians' opinion of him, but their spiritual welfare (13:7). He is glad to be considered weak if it means the genuine strengthening of the Corinthians (13:9). Regardless, he and his co-workers are committed to the truth of the gospel (13:8). He has taken the trouble to write this complex, deeply personal letter so that when he arrives he may use his apostolic authority to build them up rather than tear them down (13:10).

Conclusion (2 Cor. 13:11–14)

The conclusion is short and to the point, beginning with, "Finally, brothers, good-bye" (13:11). Four commands follow: "aim for perfection [or

✚ Both Jesus and Paul taught that religious authority should be used for building up others rather than tearing them down or using them in any way (see Mark 10:42–45; 2 Cor. 13:10).

2 Corinthians   817

work for restoration], listen to my appeal, be of one mind, live in peace" (13:11). Each command focuses on relational healing and reconciliation, either between Paul and the Corinthians or between the various factions at Corinth. Paul assures them the "God of love and peace" will be with them (13:11). After encouraging them to greet one another and sending greetings from other believers (13:12–13), Paul closes with a powerful trinitarian benediction: "May the grace of the Lord Jesus Christ, and the love of God, and the fellowship of the Holy Spirit be with you all" (13:14).

So What? Applying 1–2 Corinthians Today

First and 2 Corinthians applies to our contemporary situation as much as any two books in the New Testament. Here are just a few ways to live out these significant letters. From 1 Corinthians we learn that there is no room for personality cults in the local church. Worshiping charismatic leaders leads to division and draws praise away from the Lord. We also learn that God expects his people to be holy, as a glance at all the issues in Corinth reveals: factions (1–4), incest (5), lawsuits (6:1–11), and sexual immorality (6:12–20). In dealing with these matters and others, Paul often employs a "yes, but..." strategy, meaning that he grants the truth of the opposing view or unbalanced theology, but seeks to bring balance with a holistic view of the situation from God's perspective. We see too in 1 Corinthians that our

Ruins of the odeon (ancient musical theater) in Corinth.

freedom as believers should be limited by our love for other believers. We are part of a community and not free to act in a way that destroys the faith of family members. When he discusses corporate worship, Paul helps us to see that love should have priority over the gifts and that our corporate worship should seek to combine order and freedom. Lastly, we should move away from our typical folk-religion view of heaven and return to the biblical doctrine of the bodily resurrection of all believers at the return of Christ. Our hope as believers is not death, and not even rapture, but resurrection from the dead!

In 2 Corinthians we are reminded that sometimes ministry doesn't go the way we expect it to go. People cast doubt on our motives, misconstrue our actions, and turn other believers against us. How should we respond? Although we are not apostles, Paul's way of struggling through this ministerial mess provides a model for us. He repeatedly says he doesn't want to respond in an authoritarian way and that he embraces weakness and suffering as legitimate badges of authentic ministry, but he is also willing to defend himself when important things are at stake (e.g., the gospel and the spiritual well-being of believers). We have to tread cautiously here, but there are times when conflict is essential to long-term healthy relationships within the body of Christ. Reconciliation is our goal. Our focus, however, should be on the integrity of our beliefs and our actions.

Our Favorite Verses in 1–2 Corinthians

Love is patient, love is kind. It does not envy, it does not boast, it is not proud. It is not rude, it is not self-seeking, it is not easily angered, it keeps no record of wrongs. Love does not delight in evil but rejoices with the truth. It always protects, always trusts, always hopes, always perseveres. Love never fails. (1 Cor. 13:4–8)

But he said to me, "My grace is sufficient for you, for my power is made perfect in weakness." Therefore I will boast all the more gladly about my weaknesses, so that Christ's power may rest on me. That is why, for Christ's sake, I delight in weaknesses, in insults, in hardships, in persecutions, in difficulties. For when I am weak, then I am strong. (2 Cor. 12:9–10)

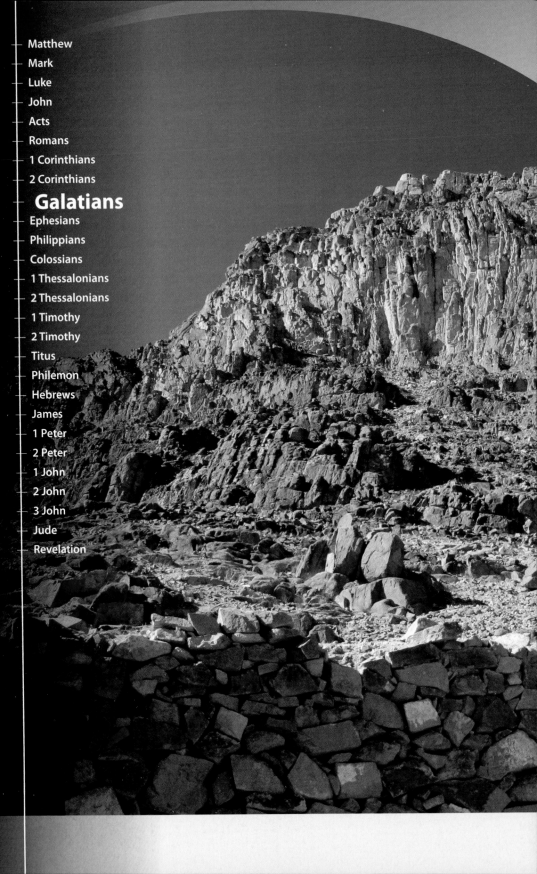

Galatians

Liberated to Love!

Galatians is all about what makes a person truly and fully Christian. In this letter, the apostle Paul provides one of the clearest explanations of the gospel of Jesus Christ found anywhere in the New Testament. For this reason, Martin Luther, one of the great leaders of the Protestant Reformation, affectionately said about Galatians: "I have betrothed myself to it; it is my wife." When we are tempted to focus on religious rules rather than a living relationship with God, Galatians will sink deep into our souls and remind us that Jesus has set us free. We shouldn't squander our freedom in selfishness; rather, we have been liberated to love!

Who Wrote Galatians?

Almost all scholars agree that the apostle Paul is the author of Galatians (Gal. 1:1; 5:2).

Who Is Paul's Audience?

The letter is addressed to "the churches of Galatia" (1:2). Paul also refers to the recipients as "foolish Galatians" (3:1). The Galatians were gentile Christians (4:8–9), but there is some debate about where they lived. The term "Galatia" could refer to the region in northern Asia Minor where the ethnic Gauls lived, but it probably refers to the southern Roman province of Galatia that included the cities of Antioch (Pisidian), Iconium, Lystra, and Derbe. Paul visited these cities on his first missionary journey (Acts 13–14), and later again to strengthen these churches (Acts 16:6; 18:23).

When did Paul write Galatians? The letter itself mentions two of Paul's visits to Jerusalem: 1:18–20 and 2:1–10. The book of Acts mentions five such visits: 9:26–30; 11:30; 15:1–30; 18:22; 21:15–17. Of the many attempts to match the visits described in Galatians with those recorded in Acts, the following two are the most popular.

- Galatians 2 = Acts 11 (early date)—Paul wrote Galatians from Syrian Antioch soon after his first missionary journey (see Acts 14:21–28) in about AD 48–49. The first two visits in Galatians match the first two visits in Acts, and Galatians was written prior to the Jerusalem Council (Acts 15).
- Galatians 2 = Acts 15 (late date)—Paul wrote Galatians during his third missionary journey, between AD 53 and 58. The second Jerusalem visit mentioned in Galatians matches the third visit recorded in Acts and puts Galatians after the Jerusalem Council.

Our preference is that Paul wrote to the Christians living in the Roman province of Galatia in about AD 48–49. This would make Galatians the earliest of Paul's letters.

What Is at the Heart of Galatians?

The situation or crisis in the Galatian churches involves three key players: the apostle Paul, the false teachers, and the Galatian Christians. When Paul first preached the gospel of Christ crucified to the Galatians, they not only accepted him (4:13–15) but also believed his message and received the Holy Spirit, a sign of God's blessing (3:1–5; 4:6–7). But soon after Paul planted the churches in Galatia, false teachers arrived and began to demand that these new gentile Christians observe the Jewish law in order to receive the full blessing of God. These agitators taught that the Galatians must submit to

✚ An important question in early Christianity was how gentile Christians were supposed to relate to the law. Galatians helps to answer that question.

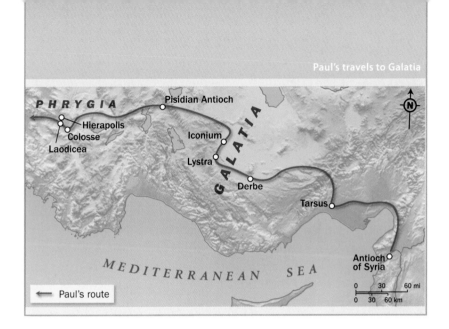

PHRYGIA

Pisidian Antioch

GALATIA

Hierapolis
Colosse
Laodicea

Iconium

Lystra

Derbe

Tarsus

Antioch
of Syria

MEDITERRANEAN SEA

0   30   60 mi
0 30 60 km

Paul's route

circumcision (5:2–4; 6:12–13) and other religious requirements (4:9–10) for full Christian status. The false teachers probably appealed to the example of Abraham as well as to the authority of the Jerusalem apostles. Many scholars refer to this movement as "Judaizing."

It is not completely clear who these "agitators" or opponents were, but Paul's letter does indicate some of their activities. They are twisting the true gospel into a false gospel out of selfish motives (1:7–9; 4:17; 5:4, 8–9; 6:12–13). They are disturbing and troubling the Galatian Christians by hindering their obedience of the truth (1:7; 3:1; 5:7, 10, 12). They are advocating observance of the law and circumcision for Christians, although they fail to keep the law themselves (2:4, 12; 4:9–10; 5:2; 6:12–13). Finally, they are driving a wedge between Paul and the Galatian Christians (4:16–17; 6:17).

We should remember Paul is primarily in dialogue with the Galatian Christians rather than with his opponents. The false teachers' persuasive message must have been very attractive to the Galatians, who were beginning to believe that if they added works of law to their new faith in Christ, then they could live a more "spiritual" life. The childlike dependence on Christ with which they had begun the Christian life was being replaced by attempts to keep the law (3:3). This shift in focus was causing divisions in their churches (5:15), and was pushing them away from their father in the faith (4:16).

These gentile Christians were being told that to be fully Christian, they had to live like Jews. Paul tries to deal with this crisis by treating the underlying theological issue—what makes a person fully Christian? Paul considers the message of the false teachers to be a gospel "different" (1:6–9) from the one he had originally preached and the Galatians had originally received. He must first defend his apostleship and authority (1:1–2:14) because the integrity of the gospel is connected to the integrity of the preacher. Next, Paul moves to clarify the true gospel (2:15–4:11). He argues that real righteousness—and the freedom that comes with it—is available only through faith in Christ, the faithful One. Paul then calls the Galatians to a decision (4:12–6:10). He urges them to depend on the Spirit who will empower them to love—the deepest demonstration of true spirituality. Finally, Paul closes by contrasting the true gospel with the false gospel of his opponents. Paul writes to persuade the Galatians to halt their compromise and decide once and for all in favor of the way of the cross (6:11–18). The outline below gives a clear picture of Paul's persuasive argument:

- Letter Opening: Paul's Authority and Message (1:1–5)
- The Occasion: Faltering Galatians, False Teachers, and a Faithful Apostle (1:6–10)
- The Divine Origin of Paul's Apostleship and Gospel (1:11–2:14)
- Righteousness by Faith in Christ, the Faithful One (2:15–21)
- Arguments Supporting Righteousness by Faith (3:1–4:11)
- Personal Appeal: "Become Like Me" (4:12–20)
- Scriptural Appeal: Children of the Free Woman (4:21–31)
- Identity-Performance Appeal: Two Contrasting Options (5:1–12)
- Performance Commanded and Illustrated: Spirit-Empowered Love (5:13–24)
- Performance Specified: Individual and Corporate Responsibilities (5:25–6:10)
- Letter Closing: Compromise or the Cross? (6:11–18)

What Makes Galatians Interesting and Unique?

- Galatians is perhaps Paul's earliest letter.
- The letter reminds us that the integrity of the gospel and the integrity of Christian leaders are closely connected.
- You find here the "works of the flesh" and "fruit of the Spirit" lists (5:19–23).
- Paul discusses the relationship between law and grace.

✛ The integrity of the gospel message is often tied to the integrity of the messenger.

- Paul demonstrates how to deal with false teachers and the theological dangers they introduce into local churches.
- The important doctrine of justification by faith is explained in 2:15–21.
- Galatians emphasizes that Spirit-empowered love fulfills the law.

What Is the Message of Galatians?

Letter Opening: Paul's Authority and Message (1:1–5)

Paul stresses he is a legitimate apostle of Jesus Christ and preaches the one true gospel (1:1). The blessing of this gospel is "grace and peace," the source of the gospel is God the Father, and the heart of the gospel is the death of Jesus Christ, who "gave himself for our sins to rescue us from the present evil age" (1:4).

The Occasion: Faltering Galatians, False Teachers, and a Faithful Apostle (1:6–10)

Paul shockingly omits his usual thanksgiving or prayer from this letter, and quickly moves to confront the Galatians about their dangerous

The theater at Pisidian Antioch, a city in the Roman province of Galatia.

spiritual behavior. What stuns Paul is that the Galatians are so quickly deserting the true gospel for a "different gospel" (1:6–7). He invokes a condemning curse on anyone who preaches a false gospel (1:7–9). His willingness to speak the truth bluntly proves he is more concerned with obeying Christ than pleasing people (1:10).

The Divine Origin of Paul's Apostleship and Gospel (1:11–2:14)

Paul's conversion (1:11–17)

Paul received his gospel neither by invention nor from tradition but from Christ (1:11–12). This God-given gospel completely transformed Paul's life. He used to zealously persecute Christians even as he pursued his devotion to the Jewish tradition (1:13–14). But by the grace of God he was converted and commissioned as an

Relief showing comedy masks worn by actors. Paul accused Peter of hypocrisy, of wearing a spiritual mask. A "hypocrite" was a Greek actor.

apostle of Jesus Christ (1:15–16). As a result, he didn't confer with human authorities or consult with Jerusalem apostles but retreated for a time of preparation and ministry (1:16–17).

Paul's visits to Jerusalem (1:18–2:10)

When Paul finally met the other apostles, their brief meeting was filled with praise to God that the former persecutor was now preaching the Christian faith (1:18–24). His second visit to Jerusalem some fourteen years later likely coincides with the visit mentioned in Acts 11:27–30 (2:1–2). The apostles endorsed Paul's ministry of preaching the gospel to the gentiles and added nothing to his gospel (2:3–10). They decided that Titus the Greek, who was traveling with Paul, did not need to be circumcised (2:3–5). In the end, the gathering agreed to a common gospel with different spheres

✦ In addition to the three reports of Paul's conversion in Acts (chapters 9; 22; and 26), Paul refers to his own conversion here in Galatians 1.

of ministry but both strongly united in ministering to the poor (2:7–10).

Paul responds to Peter's hypocrisy (2:11–14)

Peter held to the conviction that Jews and gentiles could unite around the gospel of grace. When he visited the church in Antioch, he used to have table fellowship with gentile Christians, at least until "certain men came from James" (2:12). When they arrived, however, Peter separated himself out of fear. Paul confronted Peter about his hypocritical behavior and its deadly influence (2:13–14). It takes courage to confront fellow believers about the core aspects of the gospel, but sometimes it is necessary.

Righteousness by Faith in Christ, the Faithful One (2:15–21)

This crucial paragraph presents the thesis of the letter: right standing with God and adoption into God's family (righteousness) come by faith in Christ rather than by works of law. No one (Jewish Christians included) is made right with God by observing the law, but only by trusting in Christ (2:15–16). In 2:17–20, Paul deals with some objections to justification by faith. He refuses to accept the conclusion that Christ promotes sin by allowing people to eat with gentile "sinners" because it is not sinful for Jews to eat with gentiles (2:17). If the law is reinstated to govern the Christian life, then Paul (and other Christians) will be seen as lawbreakers (2:18). When we come to Christ, we cease to be under the direct supervision of the law. By faith we now have a direct relationship with God through Christ (2:19–20). If, however, righteousness could be gained through the law, then Christ died for nothing (2:21)!

Arguments Supporting Righteousness by Faith (3:1–4:11)

Argument from the Galatians' personal experience (3:1–5)

The Galatian Christians are being bewitched or enslaved (3:1). Paul asks them a series of questions designed to shake them out of their spiritual slumber:

- Did you receive the Spirit by keeping the law or by believing the gospel? (3:2)
- After beginning by the Spirit, are you now trying to attain your goal by human effort? (3:3)
- Has your suffering for the cause of Christ been for nothing? (3:4; cf. Acts 14:1–20)
- Does God give his Spirit and work miracles among you because you keep the law or because you believe the gospel? (3:5)

Argument from Scripture: Abraham and Christ (3:6–14)

The Galatians should consider that Abraham was justified by faith and should imitate his experience (3:6–9; Gen. 12:3; 15:6). On the contrary, those who rely on keeping the law are under a curse (3:10; Deut. 27:26). Trying to keep the law and trusting Christ are two incompatible ways of seeking God's acceptance (3:11–12; Lev. 18:5; Hab. 2:4). The good news is that by dying on the cross, Christ became a curse for us and set us free from the curse of the law (3:13; Deut. 21:23). Through faith in Christ, we can now experience the blessing promised to Abraham (3:14).

Argument from the past: The promise and the law (3:15–25)

Paul explains that the promises made to Abraham and to "his seed" (i.e., to Christ) came 430 years before the law was given to Moses. God's original covenant promise to Abraham was not nullified by the giving of the law (3:15–18). The law was given to reveal God's will and human sinfulness, rather than give life or salvation (3:19–22). No one can obey the law perfectly. As people become more conscious of their sin, they become more desperate for a Savior. The law prepared people for the coming of Christ (3:23–24). But now that "faith has come, we are no longer under the supervision of the law" (3:25).

Argument from the present: From slavery to members of God's family (3:26–4:7)

The Galatian Christians should look in the mirror to realize the power of the gospel. They now have a new relationship to God through Christ (3:26–27). They have a new relationship to one another in Christ (3:28). They also have a new relationship to Abraham as heirs of God's promise (3:29). Finally, in 4:1–7, Paul explains that they now have a new spiritual status—from slaves to family members! When Christ came, he liberated those under the law and adopted them into his family. Those whom God adopts as children are given the very Spirit of his Son. By faith, we are now children and heirs.

✛ Paul demonstrates that righteousness comes by faith rather than by keeping the law by showing how God's promise came to Abraham hundreds of years before the law was given to Moses.

The Sign of Circumcision

Justin K. Hardin

The Jewish practice of male circumcision can be traced back to the Abraham story in Genesis 17. God instructs Abraham to circumcise every male person in his household as a sign of God's covenant with him. God also announces that circumcision is to be practiced in subsequent generations by having all male infants circumcised on the eighth day. Indeed, circumcision became the quintessential mark of being Jewish. Even when Antiochus IV "Epiphanes" (ca. 168 BC) made it a capital crime for Jewish people to practice circumcision, the people continued to do so (1 Macc. 1:48–63).

This covenant sign, however, was always meant to be coupled with a heart of obedience to God (cf. Genesis 17). As Moses prepares the people to go into the land of Canaan, he thus commands them to circumcise their hearts; that is, they were to love God and walk in obedience to him (Deut. 10:16). Jeremiah's prophetic rebuke harked back to these original instructions, exclaiming that God will punish all those who are circumcised in the flesh but not in the heart (Jer. 9:25–26). The apostle Paul similarly argues that physical circumcision always requires spiritual obedience (Rom. 2:25–29; 1 Cor. 7:19; Gal. 5:6; 6:15).

Unfortunately, God's people did not consistently combine the practice of circumcision with a loving obedience to him. But despite their disobedient inclinations, Moses assures the people that God will ultimately restore them and will circumcise their hearts and the hearts of their children so that they will love him wholeheartedly (Deut. 30:6–10). Again, the prophetic message hinges on this promise of future restoration when God writes his laws on their hearts and gives them his Spirit so that they can keep his laws (Jer. 31:31–34; Ezek. 36:24–27).

According to the New Testament authors, the prophetic promise—that God would circumcise the hearts of his people—was fulfilled in Jesus the Messiah. Although Jewish believers in Jesus naturally continued to practice circumcision, gentiles did not need to be circumcised because the Holy Spirit had been poured out on Jew and gentile alike through faith in the Messiah. In Acts 15, for example, we read that the church in Jerusalem held a council on the question of gentile circumcision and concluded gentiles did not need to be circumcised to be saved. Paul thus explains to the churches of Galatia that gentiles need not be circumcised for inclusion into God's people, lest they be severed from the Messiah (Gal. 5:2–6). In Romans 4, Paul also explains that Abraham's faith was credited to him as righteousness before he was circumcised. In this way, Abraham became the father of both Jew and gentile through faith (Rom. 4:10–12).

On this understanding, it therefore comes as no surprise that Paul would not circumcise Titus (Gal. 2:1–5), but he was nevertheless happy to circumcise Timothy, who had a Jewish mother (Acts 16:1–4). In Acts 21:17–26, we also read that Paul went to great lengths to correct a *false* rumor that he had been instructing Jewish people not to circumcise their children. Although the early church understood that Jewish people would continue to practice circumcision, the church recognized that both Jews and gentiles were adopted as God's children through faith in Jesus the Messiah.

Application: Paul's concern for the Galatians (4:8–11)

Once the Galatians were enslaved to false gods, but now they have a genuine relationship with the true God (4:8). Why are they forsaking freedom and returning to spiritual slavery (4:9)? Do they think they are growing in the faith by adding religious rules? Paul says by doing so, they are actually returning to paganism (4:10). He is deeply concerned for them and fears that his missionary work in Galatia might have been in vain (4:11).

Personal Appeal: "Become Like Me" (4:12–20)

Instead of following the false teachers, the Galatian Christians should imitate Paul (4:12). This will draw them back to Christ. Paul ministered sacrificially to them, and they initially received him and his gospel with joy (4:13–14). But, sadly, things have changed. Their original love for Paul has been replaced by suspicion and separation (4:15–16). The false teachers have crept in, but their motives are selfish (4:17–18). Paul is deeply troubled as he seeks to guide these vulnerable believers into mature spiritual formation (4:19–20). As we help others become more like Christ, we too can expect our journey to include painful moments.

Scriptural Appeal: Children of the Free Woman (4:21–31)

Paul once again uses Scripture to counter the false gospel and persuade the Galatians. He applies the story of Abraham and his two wives, Hagar and Sarah, typologically or "figuratively" to make a spiritual point (4:24). The two women represent two covenants. The Jews were physical descendants of Sarah, while the gentiles were physical descendants of Hagar. But Paul shows how spiritual realities have reversed the story. Hagar, the slave woman, symbolizes Mount Sinai and Jerusalem (i.e., those who rely on keeping the law for salvation). In contrast, Sarah, the free woman, symbolizes the promise, the heavenly Jerusalem, and the power of the Spirit (i.e., everyone who responds to the gospel, including gentiles). Paul concludes with an exhortation to "get rid of the slave woman and her son," meaning the Galatians should get rid of the false teachers (4:30–31).

Identity-Performance Appeal: Two Contrasting Options (5:1–12)

Paul now contrasts two opposing spiritual identities: slavery and freedom. Those who strive for spiritual maturity by keeping the law (e.g., submitting to circumcision) will fall into spiritual slavery (5:2–4). Christ will be of no benefit to them, since they will be turning away from the grace he offers. In contrast, those who trust Christ and express their faith through love will be empowered by the Spirit and have the hope of salvation (5:5–6). Christ has set us free and we should stand firm in that freedom (5:1). The Galatian

✛ In Paul's theology, our identity in Christ established by God's grace always serves as the foundation or basis of our response of obedience.

Christians got off to a good start, but lately they have stumbled (5:7). The false teachers are poisoning the entire church with their dangerous theology, and they will pay the price (5:8–10, 12). Bad theology ultimately hurts people! But Paul remains confident that the Galatians will come around (5:10). Authentic gospel ministry includes the preaching of the cross and a willingness to suffer persecution for Christ (5:11).

Performance Commanded and Illustrated: Spirit-Empowered Love (5:13–24)

An icon portraying the ancient rite of circumcision.

Now Paul addresses the Galatians' behavior directly. Christ has set them free (5:1, 13), but they are not free to indulge the "sinful nature" (or "flesh"). Rather, they have been liberated to love (5:13–14)! Why is love so important? Love fulfills the law! But if they go the way of the flesh, they will destroy their community (5:15). How are believers supposed to love? The Holy Spirit empowers love, which fulfills the law (5:16–18, 25). When believers are led by the Spirit, they will not gratify the desires of the flesh, since the Spirit and the flesh oppose each other (5:16–18). To illustrate the two different life choices (Spirit-life vs. flesh-life), Paul provides two lists—the works of the flesh in 5:19–21, and the fruit of the Spirit in 5:22–23. Those who belong to Christ have already made a firm commitment not to try to do life apart from God—the way of the "flesh" (5:24).

✚ Those who live by the Spirit will never, ever, under any circumstances, gratify the desires of the flesh—a rock-solid promise (Gal. 5:16).

Performance Specified: Individual and Corporate Responsibilities (5:25–6:10)

Now Paul spells out specific responsibilities for the Galatian Christians (and for us). Those who get life from the Spirit should also "keep in step with the Spirit" (5:25–26). This military expression portrays soldiers marching in a straight line behind a leader. Keeping in step with the Spirit involves: restoring those who are caught in a sin (6:1); carrying each other's burdens (6:2); evaluating our own actions (6:3–5); sharing with our Christian teachers (6:6); seeking to please the Spirit rather than pleasing ourselves (6:7–8); and persevering in doing good, especially to fellow believers (6:9–10).

In our walk with Christ, the harvest is directly connected to what is planted by our decisions (Gal. 6:7–9).

Letter Closing: Compromise or the Cross? (6:11–18)

Paul likely takes up the pen from his secretary at this point and adds his personal greeting (6:11). He contrasts false teachers with true teachers. False teachers avoid persecution for the cross of Christ and attempt to use people for their own selfish purposes (6:12–13). In contrast, true teachers rely completely on the work of Christ and the new life he gives (6:14–15). Paul closes the letter by pronouncing a blessing on "the Israel of God" (i.e., the true people of God, whether Jew or gentile), issuing a final warning to the false teachers, mentioning his own sufferings, and offering a final benediction of grace (6:16–18).

So What? Applying Galatians Today

Galatians reminds us that there is one true gospel that centers upon the atoning death of Jesus Christ, and that false gospels should be rejected. To say it again, bad theology ultimately hurts people! Salvation is a free gift graciously

✦ Following the Spirit results in practical, concrete acts of love for other people, especially for fellow believers (Gal. 6:1–10).

given by God and is meant to be accepted by faith. Christ has set us free. There is nothing we can do to add to the work of Christ. We become children of God not by performing works of religious law, but by trusting Christ personally. God then gives us his Holy Spirit, who empowers us to please the Lord. We are reminded in this letter that we continue the Christian life the same way we began the Christian life—by depending on God's grace to transform us. It's not that Jesus saves us and then we have to perfect ourselves by moral effort. From beginning to end, we depend on the Lord in faith. We're now free to follow the Spirit who will transform us and empower us to love people. If you're worried about meeting God's holy standard, remember that love fulfills the law.

The German monk and reformer Martin Luther was deeply influenced by the message of Galatians.

Our Favorite Verse in Galatians

You, my brothers, were called to be free. But do not use your freedom to indulge the sinful nature; rather, serve one another in love. (5:13)

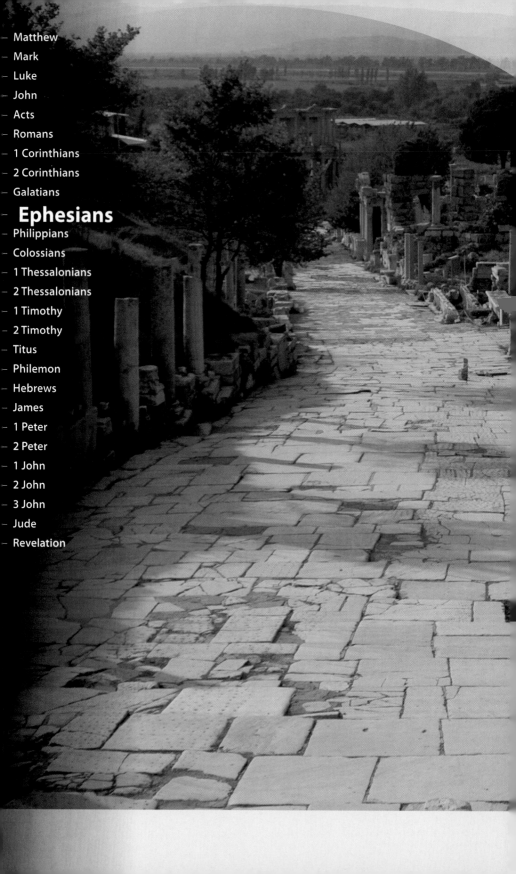

Ephesians

New Life and New Community in Christ

E phesians declares God's magnificent plan
to give new life and create a new community in Christ. Rising above the ordinary routine
of church life, Paul pens a majestic letter calling
Christians to remember what God has done for
them in Christ and to walk worthy of that calling.
Ephesians stands as an extremely significant and
intensely practical book for today's church.

Who Wrote Ephesians?

Paul claims to be the author of Ephesians (1:1–2;
3:1), and its authenticity as one of his genuine letters
is well attested in the early church. A good portion of
Ephesians is presented in the first person (see 1:15–18;
3:1–3, 7–8, 13–17; 4:1, 17; 5:32; 6:19–22), including
information related to his prayers, apostolic ministry, call
to unity and holiness, as well as comments about the letter carrier, Tychicus. Also, Ephesians seems to have been
quoted by many of the apostolic fathers and is included in
early lists of New Testament books. Since the nineteenth
century, however, Pauline authorship of Ephesians has
been doubted by some because of the different language

and style, its parallels with Colossians, its unusual theological emphases, and the author's lack of familiarity with his audience. While the arguments against Pauline authorship should be taken seriously, the traditional view that Paul wrote Ephesians remains the preferred option. The explicit statements within the text, the unanimous support of the early church, the likely use of a secretary, the absence of any looming crisis, the movement from theology to ethics, and the overall purpose of the letter offer good reasons why we can believe with confidence that Paul wrote Ephesians.

Who Is Paul's Audience?

Ephesians was written while Paul was a prisoner (see Eph. 3:1; 4:1; 6:20), but he was imprisoned on more than one occasion and in more than one location. The three leading options are Rome, Ephesus, and Caesarea. The traditional view that Paul wrote this letter (along with the other Prison Letters: Colossians, Philemon, and Philippians) from Rome while under house arrest remains the most persuasive, in our opinion. Since Tychicus carried both Ephesians and Colossians (and likely Philemon) to their respective readers, all three letters must have been written from the same place (Eph. 6:21–22; Col. 4:7–9). Acts reports that Paul was held captive in Rome for two years (28:30–31), but retained limited freedom to meet with people and minister (Eph. 6:19–20; Col. 4:3–4; Phil. 1:12–13). Luke's use of "we" in Acts 28 indicates he was with Paul in Rome during Paul's imprisonment (see also Philem. 24; Col. 4:14). Also, Aristarchus, who traveled with Paul to Rome (Acts 27:2), is mentioned in two Prison Letters (Philem. 24; Col. 4:10).

An ancient seal. Paul uses this image in Eph. 1:13 to illustrate a believer's security in Christ.

If the place of origin is Rome, then Paul would have written Ephesians during his first Roman imprisonment in about AD 60–62. Most likely Paul wrote Ephesians about the same time he wrote Colossians and Philemon, in the early or middle part of that imprisonment.

Although the letter has traditionally been connected to Ephesus, the phrase "in Ephesus" in 1:1 is absent from some of the earliest and best Greek manuscripts. The letter itself even suggests that Paul may have intended Ephesians for a wider readership (e.g., 1:15; 3:2; 6:21–24). Perhaps this general letter was intended to circulate among several churches

✚ The early church thrived in major cities of the Roman Empire such as Ephesus, the leading city in the Roman province of Asia.

The City of Ephesus
Mark W. Wilson

Ephesus, situated on the Aegean Sea near the mouth of the Cayster River, was an important city in early Christianity. Its name is probably the Hellenized form of the Hittite word *Apaša*. According to the city's founding myth, Androclus established an Ionian settlement at the foot of Mount Pion in the thirteenth century BC. After the Lydian king Croesus captured the city, it was moved to the foot of Mount Ayasoluk near the temple of Artemis. Cyrus's defeat of Croesus in 546 BC brought the city under Persian control for over two centuries. Alexander's defeat of the Persians brought the city once again under Greek hegemony. When his successor, Lysimachus, gained control of Ephesus around 294 BC, he moved the city to a valley between Mount Coressus and Mount Pion. The city was then governed alternately by the Seleucids and Ptolemies until 188 BC when the Attalids took control. In 133 BC Attalus III bequeathed his kingdom to the Romans, who then made Ephesus an important administrative center and later the provincial capital. During the first century AD, Ephesus was the fourth largest city of the Roman Empire with an estimated population of over 200,000 residents. The city was a judicial center, and the Greek term for courts (*agoraioi*) in Acts 19:38 refers to this activity. Although a temple to the goddess Roma and the deified Julius Caesar was built in 29 BC for Roman citizens, a temple for the imperial cult was not built until AD 89/90 during Domitian's reign.

Ephesus was a center of spiritual activity, and tension was high among the many religiously diverse communities. Ephesus was known as the temple keeper (*neokoros*; Acts 19:35) of the goddess Artemis. Thousands made pilgrimages to Ephesus each spring for the annual Artemisia festival. The Artemis cult remained an opponent of Christianity until the temple's destruction by the Goths in about AD 262.

The worship of at least seventeen other deities has been documented in the city. Ephesus also had a large Jewish community. Paul spoke in the synagogue for three months after his arrival (Acts 19:8). Acts mentions seven sons of a Jewish priest who practiced exorcism in the city (19:13–16). When the Ephesian Jews attempted to mollify the crowd assembled in the theater against Paul, their representative, Alexander, was shouted down when the crowd realized he was a Jew (19:34). This reaction underscores the underlying tensions between the monotheistic Jews and the pagan Greeks of the city. The city was also renowned as a center for magical practices. Foremost among these were the so-called Ephesian letters. These were written magical spells thought to contain apotropaic power to ward off evil spirits. Acts 19:19 describes how a number of new Christians renounced their involvement with sorcery by burning their scrolls.

Near the end of his second journey Paul stopped briefly in Ephesus, leaving Priscilla and Aquila there (Acts 18:19–21). On his third journey Paul ministered for more than two years in Ephesus (Acts 19), which served as a base for reaching the entire province of Asia. After the riot provoked by Demetrius and the silversmiths, Paul left Ephesus. During his first imprisonment, Paul wrote a letter traditionally called Ephesians, although "in Ephesus" is missing in 1:1 of the earliest manuscripts. After his release, Paul apparently returned to Ephesus to deal with problems in the church, leaving Timothy there (1 Tim. 1:3). Later Paul sent Tychicus to Ephesus to relieve Timothy so he might join Paul in Rome (2 Tim. 4:12–13). Tradition holds that John relocated to Ephesus before the fall of Jerusalem in AD 70. Ephesus is the first of the seven churches addressed by John in Revelation (Rev. 1:11; 2:1–7). The traditional provenance of John's Gospel and three letters is Ephesus.

in Asia Minor, with each church "filling in the blank" in the greeting as the letter is read publicly. The letter became associated more permanently with Ephesus because it was the leading city in the region. It is also possible that this is the "letter from Laodicea" mentioned in Colossians 4:16, especially if Tychicus left the letter first in the major seaport city of Ephesus with instructions that it later be sent to Laodicea and then to Colossae.

What Is at the Heart of Ephesians?

Paul didn't write Ephesians to solve a major problem or deal with any particular emergency. Instead, he wrote a general (yet majestic) letter to house churches in the city and the region to help them stay strong in their faith. He had spent almost three years teaching and caring for some of these people, and he wanted to make sure they continued to follow Jesus. Specifically, Paul wanted believers to have a deeper understanding and experience of three realities:

1. The new life we have in Christ.
2. The new community we are connected to in Christ.
3. The new walk our community is called to by Christ.

In this letter Paul focuses on Jesus Christ (*new life*). The expression "in Christ" (and parallel phrases like "in the Lord" or "in him") are found almost forty times in Ephesians. God will unite and restore all of creation under one Lord: Christ (1:10). Paul also stresses unity (*new community*) through words like "unity," "one," "with/together with," and concepts such as church, body, temple, and bride. When we are connected to Christ, we are also connected to a new community. This new community is maintained and preserved as we live in a way that pleases Christ (*new walk*). This new lifestyle is characterized by love for God and love for people. The outline of Ephesians reflects these three realities:

- Letter Opening (1:1–2)
- Praise for Spiritual Blessings in Christ (1:3–14)
- Prayer for Spiritual Understanding (1:15–23)
- New Life in Christ (2:1–10)
- New Community in Christ (2:11–22)
- Paul's Unique Role in God's Plan (3:1–13)
- Paul's Prayer for the New Community (3:14–21)
- New Walk in Christ (4:1–6:20)
- Letter Closing (6:21–24)

✝ In Ephesians Paul sets forth God's grand purposes for all of humanity. Everything centers in Christ.

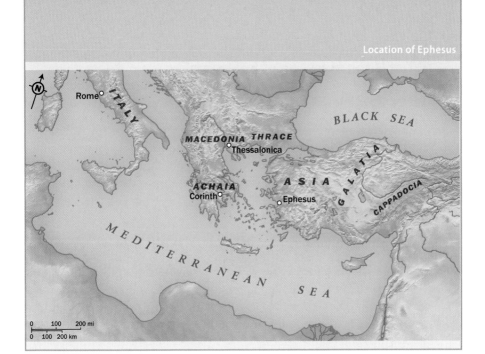

What Makes Ephesians Interesting and Unique?

- Ephesians presents God's grand, sweeping purpose for all humanity as achieved through Christ and demonstrated in the life of the church.
- Paul stresses our identity in Christ and our unity in Christ with expressions such as "in Christ," "in him," and "in whom" occurring almost forty times.
- More than the cross of Christ, Ephesians highlights Christ's resurrection and exaltation (e.g., 1:20–23; 2:1–10).
- Ephesians regularly recognizes the three persons of the Trinity (1:4–14, 17; 2:18, 22; 3:4–5, 14–17; 4:4–6; 5:18–20).
- The letter emphasizes the universal nature of the church (see 1:22; 3:10, 14–15, 21; 5:23–25, 27, 29, 32, as well as images like body, building, temple, and new humanity).
- Paul draws attention to how hostile groups (such as Jews and gentiles in the first century) can be reconciled in Christ (2:11–22).
- Ephesians shares many themes in common with Colossians (e.g., compare Col. 3:18–4:1 with Eph. 5:22–6:9).
- Paul tells us how the Christian faith should be lived out in the household (5:21–6:9).
- Paul teaches believers how to engage in spiritual warfare (6:10–20; see Acts 19:18–19).

What Is the Message of Ephesians?

Letter Opening (1:1–2)

The letter opens in typical fashion: Paul, an "apostle of Christ Jesus by the will of God," writes to God's people in Ephesus and surrounding cities. The recipients are identified as "saints" (simply another word for "Christians" in the New Testament). Paul then greets his readers with "grace and peace" from the Lord.

Praise for Spiritual Blessings in Christ (1:3–14)

Most of Paul's letters begin with thanksgiving and a prayer, but Ephesians explodes in adoration and praise. We praise God for choosing us in Christ (1:4–6), for redeeming us and giving us wisdom to understand his plan (1:7–12), and for sealing us with the Holy Spirit (1:13–14). In other words, the Father came up with a plan to rescue people from sin and Satan, the Son carried out the plan through his life, death, and resurrection, and the Holy Spirit now makes the plan a personal reality for those who respond to God's gracious offer. Each section ends with a similar phrase: "to the praise of his glory," showing that God is worthy of our highest praise (1:6, 12, 14).

Prayer for Spiritual Understanding (1:15–23)

After praising God for his blessings, Paul now asks for spiritual wisdom to comprehend those blessings. He prays that the Spirit would help believers understand and live out what God has done for them in Christ. As the Spirit enlightens their hearts, they come to know the hope of God's calling, the glory of God's inheritance, and the greatness of God's power (1:18–19). God supremely displayed his power in Jesus when he raised him from the dead, exalted him to the place of honor and authority, subjected all powers to his reign, and gave him as head over all things to the church (1:20–23).

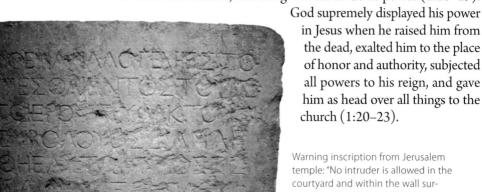

Warning inscription from Jerusalem temple: "No intruder is allowed in the courtyard and within the wall surrounding the temple. Whoever enters will invite death for himself." Christ destroyed such dividing walls (Eph. 2:14).

✚ Some of the most majestic prayers in the entire Bible can be found in Ephesians 1 and 3.

New Life in Christ (2:1–10)

Paul now turns his attention to the new life available in Christ. First, he offers a lengthy description of a person's spiritual state without Christ (2:1–3). Second, he explains God's plan to rescue such helpless and hopeless people. Moved by his love and mercy, God "made us alive with Christ," "raised us up with Christ," and "seated us with him in the heavenly realms" (2:4–6). Believers now share (mysteriously) in Christ's resurrection, ascension, and exaltation. God's purpose in saving people was to demonstrate the "incomparable riches of his grace" expressed to us in Jesus (1:7). Believers are trophies of God's grace. The Christian message is summarized beautifully in 2:8–10: the basis of salvation is God's grace, the means of receiving salvation is faith, and the result of salvation is good works.

New Community in Christ (2:11–22)

God has not only given new life to individuals in Christ but he has also created a new community, composed of both Jews and gentiles. Ephesians 2:11–22 is perhaps the most significant "church" (ecclesiological) passage in all the New Testament. As gentiles, the Ephesians' condition outside of Christ was desperate: no Messiah, no connection to God's people, no promise of salvation, no hope, and no relationship to God (2:11–12).

But now, these gentiles who were once alienated from God have been brought near through Christ (2:13). In Christ, Jews and gentiles now form "one new man" as the former hostility has now been replaced by peace. They have not only been reconciled to God, but they have also been reconciled to one another in a new spiritual community (2:14–18). These gentile Christians are now full-fledged members of God's family. They are even part of God's holy temple, built upon the foundation of the apostles and prophets, with Jesus as the cornerstone (2:19–22).

Paul's Unique Role in God's Plan (3:1–13)

Paul begins to pray for these believers (3:1), but he interrupts his own prayer to explain more about God's plan (the "mystery") and his own role in that plan. Not until the coming of Jesus the Messiah and the Holy Spirit at Pentecost would Jews and gentiles be united into one body in Christ. This plan is brand new (3:4–6). And God chose Paul, self-described as "less than the least of all God's people," to make known God's marvelous mystery. Only the grace and power of God could transform a persecutor of the church into one of the church's great leaders (3:2–9). Now God is using

✚ In Ephesians, Paul uses four major images for the church: body of Christ (3:6; 5:23), bride of Christ (5:25, 27, 31–32), temple of the Spirit (2:21–22), and household/family of God (2:19; 3:15).

his multicultural church to announce his manifold wisdom to the heavenly powers (3:10–11). Since God is using Paul to fulfill his amazing plan, no one should get discouraged by Paul's sufferings (3:12–13).

Paul's Prayer for the New Community (3:14–21)

Now Paul resumes the prayer he began in 3:1. He prays that God would strengthen believers by the Holy Spirit in their inner being according to his glorious riches (3:16). Believers will know the prayer has been answered when Christ feels at home in their hearts and they experience his indescribable love more and more. The final purpose of the prayer is that they be filled with the "fullness of God" or become like Christ (3:17–19; cf. 4:13). While it may seem that Paul has asked for too much, the doxology in 3:20–21 affirms that God "is able to do immeasurably more than all we ask or imagine."

New Walk in Christ (4:1–6:20)

God's magnificent plan to give new life and create a new community in Christ (Ephesians 1–3) results in a new walk for the believer (Ephesians 4–6). The important word "then" (or "therefore") in 4:1 marks a transition from the calling, blessings, and privileges of believers (1–3) to the conduct and responsibilities of believers (4–6).

Walk in unity (4:1–16)

Believers are urged to live (or walk) worthy of their calling (4:1), and this worthy walk begins by maintaining the unity of the Spirit (4:3). The word "one" is used seven times in 4:4–6 to illustrate how the Triune God perfectly exemplifies a diverse unity. Next, Paul illustrates how diversity within the body of Christ actually enriches unity (4:7–13). Following Christ's descent to earth (the incarnation) and his resurrection/exaltation, the Holy Spirit was given to God's people, including the gifts of the Spirit. All members are gifted, but they are gifted in different ways so as to benefit the body. God has given gifted leadership to the body so that all may grow together in unity. The goal of unity is full maturity in Christ that results in discernment, truth, edification, and love (4:14–16).

Walk in holiness (4:17–32)

Rather than living like people who do not know God (4:17–19), believers should remember they have put off the old self or former way of life and have put on "the new self, created to be like God in true righteousness and

✚ In Ephesians 4–6 the Christian life is portrayed as a "walk" or way of life, recalling the expression "the Way" used in the book of Acts to describe the early church (Acts 9:2; 19:9, 23; 24:14, 22).

Household Codes

Karen H. Jobes

Three passages in the New Testament are commonly referred to as household codes: Ephesians 5:21–6:9, Colossians 3:18–4:1, and 1 Peter 2:18–3:7. Each passage contains apostolic instruction for how Christians are to live in society's most basic unit, the family household. Martin Luther was the first to refer to these passages with the name "household table" (German: *Haustafel*) in his German translation of the Bible. The form of these New Testament passages is striking, addressing paired relationships within the first-century household of master-slave, husband-wife, and father-children, though not consistently in this order or with equal treatment of each pair.

While the instructions in the New Testament household codes are distinctively Christian, the form is widely found among the writings of the Greek moral philosophers from Plato (427–348/347 BC) to Aristotle (384–322 BC), to Plutarch (ca. 46–120 AD) and Seneca (ca. 4 BC–65 AD). Although these writers had very different views on how the head of the household was to relate to his wife, children, and slaves, all shared the belief that orderly relationships in the household in which each member knew and occupied his or her place was necessary for the well-being of society. No religion or philosophy entering the moral world of Greco-Roman culture could fail to address order in the household, and new movements would be evaluated largely on their ideas about this culturally important topic. It is therefore not surprising that when the apostles Peter and Paul write to destinations holding a Greco-Roman worldview, such as Ephesus, Colossae, and the northern provinces of Asia Minor, they needed to provide instruction for Christians whose conversion to Christ raised social problems within their household relationships.

The specific function of household codes in the New Testament is debated. Some argue they were included in response to social unrest among women and slaves in the church. Still others see the household codes as apologetic, both upholding and critiquing the social status quo, to allow for effective evangelization. Still others see them primarily as the apostolic response to criticism about what effect Christianity might have on the household, and therefore on society at large. From an apologetic perspective, the household codes defend the Christian way of life as nonthreatening to order in the greater society.

Each New Testament household code has a somewhat different purpose within its immediate context, but all redefine the nature of household relationships by grounding them in a relationship with Christ rather than in Greco-Roman moral philosophy. All three of the New Testament household codes uphold, but at the same time subvert, the first-century social status quo by a redefinition of terms in comparison to the instruction found in the secular writers. Based on the example of Jesus Christ, obedience is redefined for the slave; submission is redefined for the wife; and love is redefined for the husband.

---

holiness" (4:20–24). Believers need to live like the new people they actually are in Christ. Paul offers five specific exhortations in 4:25–32 to show what it means to walk in holiness. Each exhortation has a negative command, a positive command, and a reason for the positive command. Truth, self-control, diligence, edifying talk, compassion, and forgiveness are character qualities of a holy lifestyle.

Relief featuring a soldier's armor.

Walk in love (5:1–6)

Along with walking in unity and holiness, believers are called to walk in love. Positively, this means imitating the Father and loving sacrificially like the Son (5:1–2). Negatively, this includes refusing to indulge in selfish sensuality (5:3–6). Walking in love, then, involves both a "yes" to God and a "no" to evil. Paul closes with a stern warning that immoral, impure, greedy, idolatrous people will inherit God's wrath rather than God's kingdom.

Walk in light (5:7–14)

Believers who once lived in darkness are now light in the Lord, and should walk as children of light (5:7–8). Darkness symbolizes evil, while light represents God's character and such things as "goodness, righteousness, and truth" (5:9). Since believers have been transferred from darkness to light (Col. 1:13), they are to discern what pleases the Lord and reject the useless deeds of darkness (5:10–11). Instead of participating in the darkness, they are to expose and transform the darkness (5:11–14).

Walk carefully (5:15–6:9)

Paul cautions believers to walk carefully using three contrasts: not as unwise, but as wise (5:15); not as foolish, but with understanding (5:17); and not getting drunk, but being filled with the Spirit (5:18). He further explains this third contrast. At conversion, Christians are sealed with the Spirit (a one-time event explained in 1:13–14) but throughout life are encouraged to be filled with the Spirit (a repeated experience). Three results of being filled with the Spirit are mentioned in 5:19–21: worship, gratitude, and mutual submission. These are distinguishing characteristics of the people of God. In 5:22–6:9, Paul explains how this final characteristic (mutual submission) is applied within the Christian household.

Walk in the Lord's strength (6:10–20)

Paul concludes the practical section of his letter with instructions about walking in the Lord's strength. Christ has already conquered the powers

✦ Christians receive the Holy Spirit at conversion (Eph. 1:13–14) but should be filled with the Spirit repeatedly (Eph. 5:15–21).

of evil, so there is no need to live in fear or despair, but believers should expect continued attacks. Their job is to stand firm using God's armor of truth, righteousness, the gospel of peace, faith, salvation, and the word of God (1 Thess. 5:8). We need prayer to make use of the armor of God. Paul began the letter by praying for his readers (1:15–23). Now, he asks them to pray that he will fearlessly declare the mystery of the gospel.

Letter Closing (6:21–24)

Paul concludes with a commendation of Tychicus, the letter carrier and co-worker, and a benediction of peace, love, and grace from God the Father and the Lord Jesus Christ.

So What? Applying Ephesians Today

This rich letter from Paul applies especially well in our contemporary world. Ephesians reminds us that God's grace is what transforms us (2:1–10). We accept this life-changing gift by faith. So many religions and religious agendas in our world are based on human effort and performance, that is, what we can do for God. But without Christ, we are helpless and hopeless. We need someone outside our sinful predicament to rescue us, and Jesus Christ has done that very thing. We never grow too old or too "spiritual" for God's amazing grace. Ephesians also makes it clear that people who do not get along, even people who are bitter enemies, can be reconciled to one another when they are reconciled to God (2:11–22). There is one body of Christ with many members. God not only rescues us from sin, he brings us into a new community. Lastly, Ephesians speaks volumes about how we should live as believers in the daily grind of life. The second half of the letter leaves little doubt about how God expects us to live. Because of all he has done for us, we should live a life worthy of what we have received. In Christ we experience new life, new community, and a new walk.

Our Favorite Verses in Ephesians

For it is by grace you have been saved, through faith—and this not from yourselves, it is the gift of God—not by works, so that no one can boast. For we are God's workmanship, created in Christ Jesus to do good works, which God prepared in advance for us to do. (2:8–10)

Philippians

A Joyful Thank-You Letter

Many believers would say that Philippians is their favorite letter from Paul. This personal correspondence to a group of close friends touches our hearts in many ways. We find ourselves dealing with giving generously, living courageously, maintaining unity, being content, seeking humility, serving sacrificially, rejoicing instead of worrying, making peace instead of grumbling, and trusting in Christ's righteousness rather than seeking to develop our own. At every turn, this letter speaks to us in powerful ways.

Who Wrote Philippians?

There is little disagreement that the apostle Paul wrote Philippians. Early church leaders such as Irenaeus, Clement of Alexandria, Tertullian, and even Polycarp believe that Paul wrote this letter, and most contemporary scholars agree.

Who Is Paul's Audience?

Paul founded the church at Philippi on his second missionary journey (Acts 16:12–40). This church supported him financially like no other (see Phil. 4:10–19 and the references to the "Macedonians" in 2 Cor. 8:1–5; 11:8–9). They remained loyal to Paul through the most difficult times of his ministry (Acts 16:19–24, 35–40; Phil. 1:29–30). Even recently, the Philippian church sent Epaphroditus (along with a monetary gift; 4:18) to minister to Paul when they heard he was in prison (2:25). While visiting Paul, Epaphroditus became gravely ill and almost died (2:26–27, 30). After he recovered, Paul sent him back to the Philippians (2:26, 28–30) and took this opportunity to say "thank you" to the Philippians through this pastoral letter. We prefer the traditional view that Paul was in prison in Rome when he wrote Philippians (AD 60–62). Because of communications between the church and Paul while he was in prison (probably taking no more than one year), he may have written Philippians near the end of his Roman imprisonment.

What Is at the Heart of Philippians?

In this joyful thank-you letter, Paul seeks to accomplish several things. He wants to thank the church for being so generous in supporting his ministry (1:5; 4:10–19). He updates them on his circumstances (1:12–26; 4:10–19) and

The Via Egnatia, which passed through Philippi.

✚ Paul first came to Philippi when his plans to go north into Bithynia were changed by a God-given vision of a man from Macedonia calling him to come west (see Acts 16:6–10).

prepares them for an upcoming visit from Timothy (2:19–24). He exhorts the congregation to unity (2:1–11; 4:2–5) and warns them against false teachers (3:1–4, 18–19). The outline of Philippians below reflects these various pastoral concerns:

- Letter Opening (1:1–2)
- Thanksgiving and Prayer (1:3–11)
- Paul's Circumstances and Attitude (1:12–26)
- Live in a Manner Worthy of the Gospel (1:27–30)
- Appeal to Unity with the Fellowship (2:1–4)
- Imitate Christ's Humility (2:5–11)
- Continue to Work Out Your Salvation (2:12–18)
- Two Examples of Unity: Timothy and Epaphroditus (2:19–30)
- Warning against False Teachers (3:1–6)
- A Righteousness from God (3:7–11)
- Press On toward the Goal (3:12–4:1)
- Concluding Exhortations (4:2–9)
- Letter Closing (4:10–23)

What Makes Philippians Interesting and Unique?

- In one of the most eloquent and powerful passages in the entire New Testament, Philippians 2:5–11 describes the humiliation and exaltation of Jesus Christ.
- The first convert in Philippi was Lydia, the wealthy businesswoman whose house became the first meeting place of the church in Philippi (Acts 16:14–15, 40).
- The tone of Philippians is warm and familiar, like one would expect in a friendship letter.
- Paul draws on the city's special privileges as a Roman colony to emphasize the importance of our heavenly citizenship (1:27 [ESV note]; 3:20).
- The theme of joy appears throughout the letter ("joy" in 1:4, 25; 2:2, 29; 4:1; "rejoice" or "rejoice with" in 1:18; 2:17–18, 28 [ESV]; 3:1; 4:4, 10).
- The letter stresses the return of the Lord (1:6, 10; 2:9–11, 16; 3:20–21; 4:5).
- As in several of his letters, Paul confronts false teachers who are demanding that gentiles keep the Jewish law (3:1–6).

✚ While Paul refused to accept monetary support from the Corinthian church, he gladly received such support from churches in Macedonia (see 2 Cor. 8:1–7; 11:8–9; Phil. 4:10–19).

What Is the Message of Philippians?

Letter Opening (1:1–2)

Paul and Timothy, both "servants of Christ Jesus," greet all the believers in Philippi along with the "overseers and deacons" with grace and peace from God. Most believe these particular church leaders are mentioned because they are chiefly responsible for raising the financial gift sent to Paul or because they are involved in the problems of disunity.

Thanksgiving and Prayer (1:3–11)

When Paul thinks about the believers in Philippi, he thanks the Lord (1:3). He is grateful for their "partnership in the gospel" (1:5) and remains confident (as we should also) that God will continue to work in their lives until Jesus returns (1:6). Paul's strong emotional attachment to the Philippians stems from their gracious support of him, even during his imprisonment (1:7). They are truly partners in the ministry of the gospel, and his feelings for them run deep (1:8). He prays with joy (1:4) that their love and knowledge may go together and allow them to discern the things that matter most and to be morally pure and righteous to the glory and praise of God (1:9–11). Often when love lacks knowledge (superficial zeal) or when knowledge fails to love (religious arrogance), there is very little discernment and righteousness. God intends love and knowledge to go together.

Paul's Circumstances and Attitude (1:12–26)

Paul reassures the Philippians that the gospel has not suffered a setback because of his imprisonment; his tough circumstances have even served to advance the gospel (1:12). Now everyone, including the whole palace guard, knows about Paul's faith, and other believers have been encouraged to speak more courageously (1:13–14). But not everything is rosy for Paul; he still has his enemies (1:15–17). Suffering for Christ normally mixes the bitter with the sweet. Paul's Spirit-led attitude about life is what enables him to thrive in affliction (1:18–26). He can rejoice that Christ is preached, even if the motives of some preachers are ungodly (1:18). Through the Philippians' prayers and the help given by the Spirit of Jesus, Paul knows his circumstances will turn out for his salvation and he will be faithful to the end (1:19–20). Whether Paul lives and continues a fruitful ministry or dies and goes into the presence of Christ, his ambition is to please the

Lord (1:21–24). He seems confident he will be released from prison and will continue his ministry among the Philippians (1:25). It appears that joy is sometimes affected by circumstances (1:26).

Live in a Manner Worthy of the Gospel (1:27–30)

Now Paul tells the Philippians to "conduct yourselves in a manner worthy of the gospel of Christ," using a word that means to live like a model citizen (1:27; cf. 3:20). As citizens of a Roman colony, they should take even more seriously their higher calling to live as a citizen of God's kingdom. They should stand as one for the gospel, not fearing those who oppose them (1:27–28). After all, it is a privilege not only to believe in Christ but also to suffer for him (1:29–30).

Appeal to Unity with the Fellowship (2:1–4)

Paul now encourages the church to make his joy complete by being unified (2:2). The basis or foundation of this unity comes from what they have already experienced in their relationship with Christ—encouragement, comfort, fellowship, affection, and compassion (2:1). This unity entails being like-minded by having the same love and being joined in soul (2:2). This unity means avoiding selfishness and empty conceit (2:3) and embracing humility that leads to sacrificial service (2:3–4).

✚ As in many other places in the New Testament, believers are encouraged to count suffering for Christ as a privilege (Phil. 1:29–30; cf. Matt. 5:10–12; Acts 5:41; 2 Tim. 1:8; 1 Pet. 4:12–16).

Imitate Christ's Humility (2:5–11)

Paul's exhortation to unity through humility (2:1–4) is linked by 2:5 to Jesus as the supreme example of humility (2:6–11). More commentary has been written about 2:6–11 than about the rest of Philippians combined. This section is probably an early Christian hymn, either originally written by Paul (our preference) or used by Paul because it expresses his convictions. In either case, 2:6–11 is one of the most profound paragraphs about Christ in the entire New Testament. Although Jesus is God, he did not consider equality with God to consist of grasping or hoarding or seizing (2:6). That is, Jesus demonstrates that God is essentially self-giving rather than selfish. Notice how Jesus steps down the ladder in the process of self-giving: he became a human being, a human being who died, and a human being who died a shameful, humiliating death on a cross (2:7–8). From reigning as Lord of heaven to dying as a cursed criminal—that demonstrates humility! In 2:9–11 we see that the Father highly exalted the Son. God gave him the "name that is above every name." Most likely this "name" to which every knee will bow and which every tongue will confess is given in 2:11: Jesus Christ is "Lord" (*kurios*, the term used by the Greek Old Testament to translate the personal name for the God of Israel, Yahweh). The Philippians should take note: God exalts those who humble themselves.

Continue to Work Out Your Salvation (2:12–18)

Now Paul applies the example of Christ's humility and obedience to the Philippian church ("therefore" in 2:12). Just as they have always obeyed, and because God is at work within them, they should continue to work out their salvation with fear and trembling (2:12–13; cf. 1:6). Salvation includes our wholehearted response to the grace of God. Part of working out our salvation relates to unity within the fellowship. As they avoid "complaining or arguing" (i.e., when they maintain unity), their witness to a watching world will be much more effective (2:14–16). All believers, Paul and the Philippians included, look forward to standing before the Lord at his return with a confidence that they have been faithful to their calling, even if it included suffering (2:16–17). Working toward this end with other believers produces a deep, unshakable joy (2:17–18).

Two Examples of Unity: Timothy and Epaphroditus (2:19–30)

Why would Paul insert here news about two co-workers? It seems out of place until we remember Paul's line of thinking. The Philippians are to live a

✦ Philippians 2:6–11 is one of the most important passages in the Bible on the topic of Christ's incarnation.

Early Christian Hymns

David B. Capes

The first generation of Christ followers gathered regularly in house churches for instruction, encouragement, and worship. A central part of these gatherings was the chanting and singing of hymns. Explicit reference to the use of hymns in the Christian church is found in Paul's admonition to sing psalms (*psalmoi*), hymns (*humnoi*), and spiritual songs (*ode*) with gratitude to God (Col. 3:16; cf. Eph. 5:19–20). These three terms likely refer to the practice of using the biblical Psalter along with distinctly Christian compositions. The worship of God with hymns had its immediate background in Jewish synagogue practices. Early believers used psalms, particularly messianic psalms, to express uniquely Christian perspectives on God's recent actions in the world. Likewise, Ephesians 1:3–14 is constructed on a Jewish hymn-pattern known as the *berakah* ("blessed is . . ."). While the pattern is clearly Jewish, the author used it in a way that is explicitly Christian. Gentile believers would have also been accustomed to hymn-singing in the ethos of Greco-Roman religion.

Scholars have detected hymns and hymn fragments throughout the Gospels, Acts, letters, and Revelation utilizing various criteria, including introductory phrases (e.g., "therefore it says," Eph. 4:8), poetic parallelism, special uses of relative pronouns and participles, the presence of unusual vocabulary and rhyming features, and disruptions to the context. Although not all scholars agree, there is a general consensus that the following passages represent early Christian hymns: Romans 11:33–36; Philippians 2:6–11; Colossians 1:15–20; 1 Timothy 3:16; Hebrews 1:3–4; 1 Peter 2:21–24; and Revelation 4:8–11, 19:1–4. These hymns may have been preformed traditions quoted or alluded to by a writer or spontaneous compositions understood to be Spirit-inspired. Some hymns are so clear and self-contained that later generations of Christians have named them (e.g., the Magnificat = Luke 1:46–55; the Benedictus = Luke 1:68–79). The New Testament contains both hymns to Christ and to God the Father, demonstrating a binitarian shape to early Christian devotion. Furthermore, the content of early Christian hymns is directed to soteriological themes such as creation, incarnation, and redemption. For early Christ believers, hymnic praise was essentially a response to God's saving actions in Christ.

Though not all agree, many scholars think the earliest extant Christian hymn is the hymn to Christ found in Philippians 2:6–11. The hymn consists of two parts. The first narrates the descent and humiliation of the preexistent Jesus to become a man and to suffer a merciless death on the cross. The second describes the ascent and exaltation of the crucified Jesus by God to receive the adoration of every creature and the confession "Jesus Christ is Lord." This hymn functioned to recall the essential story and therefore had a didactic purpose. Paul utilized it further to make Jesus the lordly example of humility and service (cf. 1 Pet. 2:21–24).

By its nature, poetic or hymnic language appears to affect in significant ways those who use it. Whether it was chanted or accompanied with musical instruments, hymns were easier to memorize and recall than other forms of instruction. Therefore, it seems that early Christians used New Testament hymns for several purposes: (1) to instruct; (2) to express praise and thanks to God; (3) to confess faith; (4) to form communal identity; and (5) to provide an example for proper behavior.

---

life worthy of the gospel (1:27) by imitating the example of Paul (1:12–26) and Christ (2:5–11). Along with announcing his travel plans, Paul offers Timothy and Epaphroditus as two more examples of humility and service worthy of imitation. Timothy "takes a genuine interest in your welfare" rather than looking out for his own interests (2:19–20). He has also proved faithful in the work of the gospel (2:22). Epaphroditus "longs for all of you" and "almost died for the work of Christ" (2:26, 30). Their examples of humble service to others and obedience to Christ speaks volumes to the Philippians.

Warning against False Teachers (3:1–6)

In contrast to the positive examples mentioned above, Paul reminds the Philippians to watch out for "those dogs, those men who do evil, those mutilators of the flesh" (3:2). Certain false teachers were seeking to promote their message, that Christians must keep the Jewish law in order to truly belong to God. But those who truly belong to God are those who worship by the Spirit of God, glory in Christ Jesus, and put no confidence in the flesh (3:3). Before he met Christ, Paul put his confidence in the flesh and climbed much higher up the ladder of legalistic righteousness than any of the false teachers (3:4–6).

A Righteousness from God (3:7–11)

When Paul met Christ, he realized that his former trust in the flesh was totally worthless compared to knowing Christ personally (3:7–8). His spiritual eyes were opened to see that what mattered most was having a "righteousness that comes from God" through faith in Christ, rather than

The stadium in Aphrodisius, Turkey, was built in the first century for athletic contests. It was eventually used for gladitorial combat. The stadium is 270 meters long and would seat up to 30,000 people.

✚ Paul believed that the Jewish rite of circumcision was of no value for gentile Christians (Rom. 2:25–29; Phil. 3:1–6; 1 Cor. 7:19; Gal. 5:6; 6;15; Col. 2:11).

a righteousness of his own that comes from works of the law (3:9). The gift of God's righteousness moved Paul to want to know Christ in a deeper way, even to the point of experiencing Christ's sufferings in hopes of also experiencing Christ's resurrection (3:10–11).

Press On toward the Goal (3:12–4:1)

Paul doesn't want people to mistakenly conclude he has already attained spiritual perfection. He certainly hasn't arrived, but he continues to grow in Christ-likeness (3:12). His growth strategy is to forget the past and run hard in the present toward the future (3:13). The finish line means resurrection life in the presence of Christ (3:14). The Philippians too should adopt this strategy and imitate Paul's example (3:15–17). Paul knew that legalism often leads people to compare their accomplishments with others. The "winners" are sometimes tempted to adopt an attitude of "super spirituality" with two components: (1) a sense of having arrived, at least in comparison to others, and (2) hypocrisy caused by a hidden life of sin. This helps to explain how the false teachers could influence the Philippians and perhaps reveals more of the underlying problems with disunity. Sadly, believers will have enemies. But Paul reminds the Philippians that their "citizenship is in heaven" and that believers eagerly await the return of Christ (3:20). At that time Jesus will "transform our lowly bodies so that they will be like his glorious body" (3:21; see 1 Cor. 15:51–58). Because this is true, believers should "stand firm in the Lord" (4:1)!

✝ Since Philippi was a Roman colony, meaning the Philippians were Roman citizens, they would have listened carefully when Paul reminded them of their heavenly "citizenship" in Philippians 3:20 (cf. 1:27 where he uses the verb "conduct yourselves").

A relief of Nike, the godess of victory.

Concluding Exhortations (4:2–9)

In these concluding admonitions, Paul first emphasizes unity. Euodia and Syntyche, a couple of Paul's trusted co-workers who are having trouble getting along, need to reconcile (4:2–3). The Philippians are to replace anxiety with rejoicing and prayer and trust that God's peace will be able to guard their hearts and minds (4:4–7). They are to focus their thinking on eight excellent virtues and imitate Paul's teaching and conduct (4:8–9). Again, God will give his peace, no matter how difficult the situation.

Letter Closing (4:10–23)

Paul closes the letter by saying "thank you" once again for the Philippians' support (4:10, cf. "partnership" in 1:5). As an apostle to the gentiles, Paul has to balance his need for support with his desire not to become too dependent on anyone (e.g., 1 Cor. 9:1–18; 1 Thess. 2:9). As a result, he exercises caution when expressing gratitude (4:11, 17). Through God's faithfulness, Paul has learned to be content in every situation, whether having plenty or being in need (4:11–13). He is grateful for their consistent support and doesn't say this merely to get even more money (4:14–17). Rather, he knows God must be pleased by their generous hearts (4:18). The Philippians too can trust God to meet their needs (4:19). He closes the letter by greeting all the believers, especially "those who belong to Caesar's household," along with a benediction of grace from the Lord Jesus Christ (4:21–23).

✝ The exhortation to unity based on the example of Christ's humility in Philippians 2 may have been aimed at resolving a conflict between the two women named in Philippians 4:2.

So What? Applying Philippians Today

There are numerous ways that Philippians applies to us. We see the importance of supporting missionaries financially. This continues to be an important way to partner in the work of the gospel. Paul models how to be content in difficult circumstances. He is writing from prison, uncertain of the outcome. He has enemies who are trying to mislead the churches. (The gospel of grace warns consistently against the dangers of legalism.) We learn from Paul to stay faithful in such situations and to rejoice that God is bringing good out of the situation. One central application of the letter is the importance of maintaining unity within the fellowship. Unity is cultivated as people adopt an attitude of humility and serve one another. Of course, the supreme example is Jesus (2:6–11). Lastly, the letter reminds us that we haven't arrived in the Christian life. Our past should not enslave us. Rather, we should obey in the present, knowing that God is always working in us and that he has a wonderful future in store.

Our Favorite Verses in Philippians

Do nothing out of selfish ambition or vain conceit, but in humility consider others better than yourselves. Each of you should look not only to your own interests, but also to the interests of others. Your attitude should be the same as that of Christ Jesus. (2:3–5)

Colossians

The Supremacy and Sufficiency of Christ

T he way we think about Christ and the Christian faith will ultimately affect how we live. In other words, theology affects practice in monumental ways. The believers in Colossae were confronted with a new teaching that promised a deeper experience with God, a new and mysterious freedom, a protection from evil powers, and a more intense form of spiritual formation. This new teaching, however, demoted Jesus Christ and eventually produced spiritual arrogance and division in the body. Paul's answer is simple: Jesus Christ is the supreme revelation of God, and he is sufficient for the deepest experience of life with God.

Who Wrote Colossians?

Colossians shares many of the same authorship issues with Ephesians (see "Who Wrote Ephesians?" for more detail). In spite of the doubts of some scholars, most evangelicals continue to affirm the apostle Paul as the author of both letters.

Who Is Paul's Audience?

Most likely, both Colossians and Ephesians were written by Paul while he was a prisoner in Rome in the early AD 60s (see the "Who Is Paul's Audience?" section of Ephesians). Colossae was a small town located about a hundred miles east of Ephesus, near Laodicea and Hierapolis. Epaphras probably planted the church in Colossae (1:7; 4:12–13) and later visited Paul in Rome with a report on the Colossian church (Philem. 23). Although Epaphras has many positive things to report (Col. 1:8; 2:5), he also raises serious concerns about a false teaching that is threatening the church. Paul never explicitly defines this "heresy" or "philosophy," but his response in the letter leads us to conclude that it emphasized "fine-sounding arguments" (2:4, 8), private visions and special knowledge (2:18, 23), mystical experience (2:8, 18), and strict rules and regulations, even ascetic practices (2:16–17, 21–23). Paul labels the false teaching a "hollow and deceptive philosophy, which depends on human tradition and the basic principles of this world rather than on Christ" (2:8).

The false teachers at Colossae probably blended Jewish beliefs, pagan ideas, folk religion, magic, astrology, and elements of Christianity to convey the idea that Jesus was one among many gods who needed to be appeased. Paul writes Colossians to counter this false teaching.

What Is at the Heart of Colossians?

The dangerous "philosophy" gives Christ "a place" but not "the place." In Colossians, Paul emphasizes that Christ is supreme over all other spiritual powers and is sufficient for the Colossian Christians. A false knowledge of Christ must be countered by a full knowledge of Christ. The many qualities of Christ described in 1:15–22; 2:3, 8–10, 15, 17; and 3:1 stand in contrast to particular aspects of the false philosophy. The outline below shows how Paul goes about refuting the false teaching:

- Letter Opening (1:1–2)
- Thanksgiving and Prayer (1:3–14)
- The Supremacy of Christ (1:15–23)
- Paul's Mission and Concern for the Colossians (1:24–2:5)
- The Solution to False Teaching: Fullness in Christ (2:6–23)
- The Christian's New Life in Christ (3:1–17)
- The Christian Household (3:18–4:1)
- Further Instructions (4:2–6)
- Letter Closing (4:7–18)

✦ There are many parallels between Ephesians and Colossians, suggesting that they were written close the same time.

Stoicheia ("Elements") in the New Testament

William W. Klein

English versions render the seven uses of *stoicheia* in the New Testament (Gal. 4:3, 9; Col. 2:8, 20; Heb. 5:12; 2 Pet. 3:10, 12) in a dizzying variety of ways. The word has three fundamental senses: (1) natural *substances*; (2) supernatural *powers*; or (3) basic *principles*. No one of these meanings fits all six New Testament uses, but we must seek within the context of each verse (and epistle) the meaning that best captures the author's intention.

In all but one of his four uses, Paul qualifies *stoicheia* with the phrase "of the world." Were the Galatians (Gal. 4:3, 9) formerly enslaved to powers or principles of the world (the sense that natural substances cannot fit)? Paul includes both Torah observance (4:5, 10) and the readers' prior religious practices (4:3–4, 8–9) within this former bondage, so it's unlikely that *stoicheia* refers to spiritual beings (the demonic world). Thus any principle or religious teaching—whether the preparatory way of the law or any human religion that steers people away from embracing Christ alone—is weak and worthless (4:9) and must be abandoned.

Were the Colossian readers (Col. 2:8, 20) in danger of captivity to dangerous powers (spirit beings) or aberrant principles? In Colossians Paul exalts the role of Christ, suggesting that a philosophy or tradition (2:8) that elevated alternative "elements" (whether spirits or teachings) above Christ lay at the heart of the Colossian heresy. Were these *stoicheia* rival deities (celestial beings)? Paul's refutation includes a reminder that Jesus "disarmed the powers and authorities . . . triumphing over them by the cross" (2:15). Perhaps Paul's mention of "worship of angels" (2:18)—whether it means angels as objects of worship or some celestial worship that angels celebrate—suggests *stoicheia* are spiritual beings. Alternatively, any *stoicheia* ("principle" or tradition) that promotes such worship—even though it alleges to produce a form of spirituality through its ascetic practices (2:16, 18, 20–22)—fails utterly to secure a true internal transformation (2:23) and the salvation (2:11–15) found in Jesus alone. Besides, in Jesus dwells all God's fullness (1:19; 2:9). Why settle for lesser (alleged) gods or a teaching that subscribes to this view?

The situation in Hebrews (5:12) is straightforward. The readers' progress in the Christian faith was stunted; they ought to have been farther along the road toward maturity. The author laments that they require *stoicheia*, basic teaching, the simple truths or elementary Christian principles based on the oracles or utterances of God.

Finally, 2 Peter speaks of the conflagration that dissolves the *stoicheia* on the day of the Lord (3:10, 12). This denotes "natural substances." *Stoicheia* are the world's basic elements, that is, the literal elements that make up the world. Some scholars suggest that *stoicheia* are celestial bodies (stars), though that would make redundant the reference to "heavens" and "stars"—since heavens includes the stars.

What Makes Colossians Interesting and Unique?

- Paul writes to a church he had never visited (Col. 2:1).
- Colossians includes more about the person of Jesus Christ than most of Paul's letters because the supremacy of Christ is the main theme.
- This letter has much in common with Ephesians (e.g., compare Col. 3:18–4:1 with Eph. 5:22–6:9).

- Paul includes a section on how Christians should live in the household (3:18–4:1).
- While Colossians applies generally to all Christians, much of the letter is focused on a particular false teaching with many contemporary parallels.

What Is the Message of Colossians?

Letter Opening (1:1–2)

The apostle Paul and his co-worker Timothy write to the Colossians, "the holy and faithful" followers of Christ (1:2). In a subtle way, Paul begins to encourage the Colossians to be who they are. He greets them with grace (God's loving provision of life through Christ) and peace (the well-being and wholeness that come from a relationship with Christ).

Thanksgiving and Prayer (1:3–14)

Paul now includes a thanksgiving (1:3–8) and a prayer (1:9–14) in which he introduces some of the letter's main themes. He thanks God for the Colossians' faith and love that spring from a heavenly hope they received when they responded to the "word of truth, the gospel" (1:3–5). Paul assures the Colossians of their connection to this world-changing gospel—they heard it, understood it (from Epaphras), and accepted it, as demonstrated by their "love in the Spirit" (1:6–8). Now Paul prays that God will fill them with "the knowledge of his will through all spiritual wisdom and understanding" (1:9). He prays this so that they may live a worthy life, pleasing to God (1:10). This worthy life is defined in 1:10–14: bearing fruit in good works, increasing in their knowledge of God, being strengthened with spiritual power, and joyfully giving thanks for all God has done for them. He rescued them from the domain of darkness and brought them into the kingdom of Jesus, redeemed them, forgave them, and gave them an inheritance (1:12–14). When we stop to think about what God has done for us, joyful gratitude is the only proper response.

The Supremacy of Christ (1:15–23)

This is the central paragraph of the entire letter. In 1:15–17, Christ is praised as the Lord of all creation. Jesus perfectly reveals the invisible God and reigns supreme over all creation, including all thrones, powers, rulers,

✚ Many of the false teachings faced by the early Christians consisted of a blending of many beliefs. The early church, however, insisted on the uniqueness of Jesus Christ as the one and only Lord.

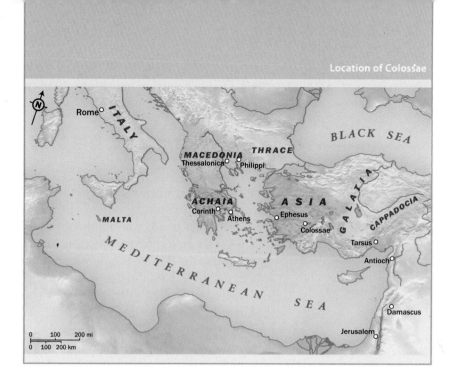

and authorities (1:15–16). He existed before creation, and creation holds together in him (1:17). Jesus Christ is also praised as Lord over the church (1:18–20). All the fullness of God lives in Jesus. Through his death and resurrection, he has made reconciliation possible and has supremacy in everything. Now Paul reminds the Colossians of how Jesus's lordship over creation and the church applies to them (1:21–23). Once alienated from God, they have now been reconciled to God through Christ (1:21–22). They now stand before God "holy in his sight, without blemish and free from accusation" (1:22). They must now persevere and endure, holding on to the hope provided by the gospel (1:23). False teaching produces doubt and uncertainty, while the gospel brings hope and assurance.

Paul's Mission and Concern for the Colossians (1:24–2:5)

As a servant of the gospel (1:23), Paul's mission is to bring the word of God to the gentiles, including the Colossians. Suffering goes hand in hand with fulfilling his calling to announce God's "mystery" to the nations (1:24–27). The heart of this good news is "Christ in you, the hope of glory" (1:27). He labors and struggles with the energy God provides to proclaim Christ and teach everyone how to grow in Christ (1:28–29). Paul struggles also for the believers at Colossae and Laodicea who have never met him (2:1). He wants to encourage and unite them in a deeper understanding of their faith in Christ, so that no one may deceive them with "fine-sounding arguments" (2:2–4). Nevertheless, he is delighted to hear of the stability of their faith in Christ (2:5).

The Solution to False Teaching: Fullness in Christ (2:6–23)

Now the Colossians are urged to continue in the way of Christ (2:6–7). They should not allow anyone to enslave them through "hollow and deceptive philosophy, which depends on human tradition and the basic principles of this world rather than on Christ" (2:8). Evil powers often use legalism to imprison people. In 2:9–15, Paul details what Christ has done and how the Colossians relate to him. In Christ, "all the fullness of the Deity lives in bodily form, and you have been given fullness in Christ, who is the head over every power and authority" (2:9–10). In Christ they have put off the sinful nature ("flesh"), have been buried with him, and have been raised with him through faith (2:11–12). God gave them life, forgave their sins, and nailed their debt to the cross (2:13–14). He also disarmed the powers and authorities, triumphing over them by the cross (2:15). Now Paul applies what he has just said about fullness in Christ to the problem in Colossae (2:16–23). The Colossians should resist the false teachers and their legalistic, pseudospiritual ideas. The false philosophy is nothing more than religious shadow, while Christ is the reality (2:17). These ideas are temporary human commands that do not come from God and have no power to produce genuine spiritual transformation. The false teachers are disconnected from Christ, the Head of the body (2:18–19).

Bust of the ancient Greek philosopher Epicurus.

✝ While Ephesians focuses on the church as the body of Christ, Colossians focuses on Christ as the head of the church.

The Christian's New Life in Christ (3:1–17)

After condemning the false teaching, Paul reminds the Colossians about their new life in Christ. Colossians 3:1–4 serves as the theological foundation for the more practical instructions that follow. Because they have participated with Christ in his death and resurrection, and since their past, present, and future have been determined by Christ, they should focus on these heavenly realities (3:1–4). When their thinking changes, so will their behavior. In 3:5–11, Paul warns them to "put to death" and "rid themselves" of evil thoughts and actions. In 3:12–17, he exhorts them to put on Christlike virtues such as compassion, humility, patience, forgiveness, gratitude, worship, and love. Everything in life (both words and actions) should be done in a way that honors Christ.

The Christian Household (3:18–4:1)

As in Ephesians 5:22–6:9, this section deals with relationships within the Christian household. Paul identifies three sets of relationships: wives and husbands, children and fathers (or parents), and slaves and masters. (In the ancient world, slaves were part of the household.) The repetition of "the Lord" throughout the passage emphasizes the importance of living out the faith in family relationships and at work. In comparison with other ancient household codes, Paul's inspired instructions give both parties added dignity and responsibility. Paul's extended advice to Christian slaves applies generally to Christian workers today (3:22–25).

Further Instructions (4:2–6)

Paul encourages the Colossians to be prayerful and thankful (4:2), and to pray especially that Paul will continue to proclaim the mystery of Christ clearly (4:3–4). He advises them to be wise in relating to non-Christians, especially in choosing their opportunities and engaging in conversation (4:5–6).

Letter Closing (4:7–18)

Paul explains how he plans to keep in touch with the Colossian Christians, largely through Tychicus and Onesimus (4:7–9). He gives extended greetings from fellow believers (4:10–17). There is a special note about Epaphras, their father in the faith, who "is always wrestling in prayer for you, that you may stand firm in all the will of God, mature and fully assured"

✦ Paul discusses the Christian household in Colossians 3:18–4:1 and Ephesians 5:21–6:9, while in 1 Peter 3:1–7 Peter focuses on a situation where a believing wife is married to an unbelieving husband.

(4:12). After this letter is read to the church in Colossae, he tells them to send it to the church in Laodicea (4:16). Paul takes up the pen and asks for prayer before closing with a greeting of grace (4:18).

So What? Applying Colossians Today

Colossians applies extremely well to believers and churches who are threatened by false teaching, a very common occurrence in our day. Some Christians today are heavily influenced by folk religion or pagan ideas (e.g., magic or astrology). If the horoscope predicts bad events, they live in fear. They are more concerned with fate, fortune cookies, luck, and superstition than they are with the words of Christ. Perhaps even more believers are in bondage to religious rules and regulations, human commands that have no power to encourage true spirituality. Legalism continues to plague the church. We

live in a syncretistic age, in which various ideas blend together to provide false teachers with plenty of material for their deceptive acts. Colossians states truly and boldly that Christ is supreme over all so-called gods and powers, and he is sufficient for every believer! In Christ all the fullness of God lives in bodily form, and even in a postmodern culture, Christians have been given spiritual fullness in Christ. There is no need to search for a spiritual supplement.

Our Favorite Verses in Colossians

For in Christ all the fullness of the Deity lives in bodily form, and you have been given fullness in Christ, who is the head over every power and authority. (2:9–10)

The theater at Hierapolis, a city in Asia Minor only a short distance from Colossae (Col. 4:13).

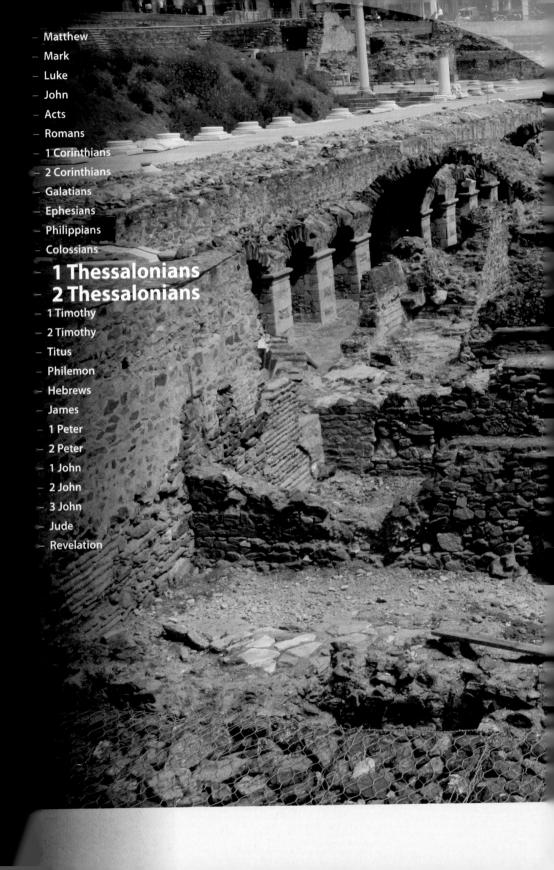

1–2 Thessalonians

Living in Light of Christ's Coming

I n these two letters we see the heart of a pastor for a local congregation. These new believers are struggling against external pressure and wrestling with internal issues. Paul emphasizes repeatedly the hope we have in Christ that will be displayed at his second coming. He invites Christians to understand the nature of our hope and to live accordingly in light of that hope.

Who Wrote Thessalonians?

Both letters come from "Paul, Silas, and Timothy," but the content of the letters and the use of "I" (1 Thess. 2:18; 3:5; 5:27; 2 Thess. 2:5; 3:17) indicate that Paul is probably the lead author. Both letters were affirmed by early church tradition as Pauline, and much of contemporary scholarship agrees, at least in regard to 1 Thessalonians. Some scholars doubt that Paul also wrote 2 Thessalonians, primarily because the two letters are very similar, the tone is less personal, and the topics have been narrowed significantly. But the circumstances call for exactly the kind of follow up letter we see in 2 Thessalonians. We affirm Pauline authorship of both letters.

Who Is Paul's Audience?

Acts 17:1–10 tells the story of Paul and Silas founding the church in Thessalonica. They leave after a brief stay because of violent opposition from the Jews (Acts 17:5–10). The young, fragile church now faces strong external pressure without their founding fathers (e.g., 1 Thess. 1:6; 2:2, 14; 3:3–5, 7; 2 Thess. 1:4–7; 3:2). Paul fears for their spiritual well-being. After leaving Thessalonica, the missionary team travels to Berea, Athens, and finally to Corinth (Acts 17:10, 15; 18:1). Paul tries numerous times (unsuccessfully) to return to Thessalonica (1 Thess. 2:18) but resorts to sending Timothy instead (3:1–5). Timothy finally arrives in Corinth himself with good news: the believers in Thessalonica are staying strong in their faith, but they need encouragement and additional instruction. Paul writes these two letters from Corinth in the early AD 50s for the purpose of encouraging and instructing.

What Is at the Heart of Thessalonians?

Both letters are devoted to encouragement and instruction about how to live in light of the return (or *parousia*) of the Lord Jesus. Paul mentions Christ's return near the end of every chapter in the first letter (1:10; 2:19; 3:13; 4:13–18; 5:23), and almost 40 percent of the second letter deals with this topic. The outline reflects this central concern:

1 Thessalonians
- Letter Opening (1:1)
- Thanksgiving (1:2–10)
- Paul's Faithful Ministry among the Thessalonians (2:1–16)
- Paul's Ongoing Concern for the Thessalonians (2:17–3:13)

Statue of Zeus, the king of the ancient Greek gods.

✦ Much of what Paul writes about the second coming of Jesus comes from Jesus's own teachings about this topic (see Matthew 24–25; Mark 13).

- Instructions about Pleasing the Lord (4:1–12)
- Questions about Christ's Return (4:13–5:11)
- Final Instructions about Church Life (5:12–22)
- Letter Closing (5:23–28)

2 Thessalonians
- Letter Opening (1:1–2)
- Thanksgiving and Prayer (1:3–12)
- Instructions about Events Leading up to Christ's Return (2:1–12)
- Reassurance and Prayer for Believers (2:13–3:5)
- Warning against Disruptive Behavior (3:6–15)
- Letter Closing (3:16–18)

What Makes Thessalonians Interesting and Unique?

- These may be Paul's earliest letters in the New Testament (AD 51), depending on when we date Galatians.
- These letters are addressed to new believers who are facing trials. The key question is, "Will their faith survive?"
- Paul mentions several hot topics related to the second coming of Jesus, such as "rapture" (NIV "caught up" in 1 Thess. 4:17) and the "man of lawlessness" (2 Thess. 2:3).
- Many of the first converts in Thessalonica came from the God-fearing Greeks, including a number of prominent women (Acts 17:4).

What Is the Message of 1 Thessalonians?

Letter Opening (1 Thess. 1:1)

The letter opens as Paul, Silas, and Timothy greet the "church of the Thessalonians in God the Father and the Lord Jesus Christ" with grace and peace.

Thanksgiving (1 Thess. 1:2–10)

Paul begins with thanksgiving for the believers' labor and endurance motivated by their faith, love, and hope (1:2–3). He then encourages them by reminding them how the gospel came to them with the power of the Spirit and deep conviction (1:4–5). They welcomed the message with joy in spite of severe suffering (1:6). Their faith became known everywhere, and they even became models to other believers (1:7–8). Their conversion was evident as they turned from idols to serve the true and living God and to "wait for his Son from heaven" (1:9–10). They have transferred their allegiance to the God who loves them and has chosen them (1:4).

Paul's Faithful Ministry among the Thessalonians (1 Thess. 2:1–16)

Because Paul wisely left Thessalonica when the opposition grew much worse, he was accused by some of being a charlatan, of peddling the gospel for personal profit. Paul denies that he came to them out of error or impure motives and insists he was not trying to trick them (2:3). He then defends the truth of the gospel and the validity of his apostleship through a series of arguments. First, he is willing to suffer for the gospel (2:1–2). Second, he is not concerned with pleasing people as a cover for greed (2:4–6). Third, he maintains financial integrity, working constantly so as not to be a burden (2:6–9). Fourth, he relates to the Thessalonians in both holiness and love (2:10–12). And finally, the Thessalonians' own reception of the message as the true word of God and their willingness to suffer persecution for the gospel (2:13–16) defends Paul's message and ministry.

Paul's Ongoing Concern for the Thessalonians (1 Thess. 2:17–3:13)

Paul had attempted to return to Thessalonica again and again, but those attempts had been hindered by Satan (2:18). Paul saw these believers as his hope and joy and crown in whom he will "glory in the presence of our Lord Jesus when he comes" (2:17–20). He sent Timothy to Thessalonica in his place to strengthen and encourage them in their trials and to see how their faith was holding up (3:1–5). Timothy's positive report (3:6–8) leads Paul to pray for them once again (3:9–13). He asks God to make a reunion possible (3:11), and he prays that their love will increase and for spiritual strength so that they may endure faithfully until the return of Christ (3:12–13).

Instructions about Pleasing the Lord (1 Thess. 4:1–12)

Paul urges these believers to continue to please the Lord (4:1–2). In the rest of this section, he highlights three specific areas. First, it is God's will that they avoid sexual immorality and learn to control their own bodies in a way that is holy and honorable (4:3–8). Second, instead of lust, believers should make it a priority to love one another (4:9–10). Third, he challenges them to live productive lives so as not to become dependent on anyone and to win the respect of outsiders (4:11–12).

✦ Both 1 Corinthians 15 and 1 Thessalonians 4:13–5:11 clearly present the bodily resurrection of believers at the return of Christ as a significant Christian doctrine.

Questions about Christ's Return (1 Thess. 4:13–5:11)

The church has questions about those who die prior to the return of Christ, so Paul instructs them in this matter. First, Christians should not grieve at the death of fellow believers like unbelievers grieve. Christians grieve, but they grieve in hope (4:13). The believer's hope is based on the resurrection of Jesus, who promises to raise those who have "fallen asleep" (died) in him (4:14). Believers who are alive at Christ's return will not have an advantage over those who have already died (4:15). At Christ's return, which will be public and visible (a loud command, voice of the archangel, and trumpet of God), the dead in Christ will rise first (no disadvantage). Then those who are alive at his return will be gathered to the Lord to meet him in the air. And all God's people will be with the Lord forever (4:16–17). These words of instruction are meant to encourage Christians (4:18). No one can predict the time of Christ's return, and for some this event will be as unexpected as a thief's intrusion during the night (5:1–3). But believers, who are children of light, should be alert and self-controlled so as not to be surprised (5:4–8). God did not appoint his children to suffer wrath (condemnation) but to experience salvation and live forever with him (5:9–11).

Final Instructions about Church Life (1 Thess. 5:12–22)

Paul concludes the body of the letter with a series of miscellaneous commands that encourage community health, including respect for leaders, industry, maintaining peace, patience, kindness rather than revenge, joy, prayer, thanksgiving, attentiveness to the Spirit, doing good, and avoiding every kind of evil.

Letter Closing (1 Thess. 5:23–28)

Paul closes the letter with a prayer that the believers would be thoroughly sanctified and kept blameless until

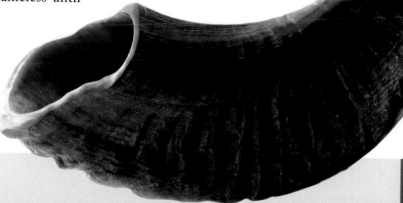

The last trumpet would have reminded the first readers of a shofar, a musical instrument made from an animal horn.

the coming of Christ. God's faithfulness makes this possible (5:23–24). He requests prayer, encourages them to greet one another as family, and charges them to have the letter read to everyone in the church (5:25–27). Finally, he pronounces a benediction of the "grace of our Lord Jesus Christ" (5:28).

What Is the Message of 2 Thessalonians?

Between the two letters it appears that external pressure had grown stronger (1:3–10), and some of Paul's teachings have been misunderstood, particularly those concerning Christ's return. Someone was confusing the Thessalonians by teaching that the "day of the Lord" had actually arrived (2:1–2). This must have been an attractive thought for people wanting to be delivered from persecution and may explain why some of them were disrupting the community (3:6–15). Paul writes 2 Thessalonians to correct the false teaching about the Lord's return and to encourage the Christians to persevere in holy living.

Letter Opening (2 Thess. 1:1–2)

The opening is the same as that of the first letter, except for an additional reference to God the Father and the Lord Jesus Christ.

Thanksgiving and Prayer (2 Thess. 1:3–12)

Paul thanks God for their growing faith and increasing love in the midst of persecutions and trials (1:3–4). Their lives of faith and love serve as affirmation that they are indeed citizens of God's kingdom, for which they are suffering (1:5). God is just, and he will judge those causing them trouble and bring relief to those who are suffering when Jesus returns in blazing fire with his holy angels (1:6–7). Jesus will punish those who don't know God and don't obey the gospel of Jesus, a punishment of everlasting destruction and exclusion from God's glorious presence (1:8–10). Paul prays that God may count them worthy of their calling and empower them to live faithfully (1:11). He prays this so that the name of our Lord Jesus may be glorified (1:12).

Instructions about Events Leading up to Christ's Return (2 Thess. 2:1–12)

In this central section of the letter, Paul attempts to correct the church's recent misunderstanding about Christ's return. He first tells them not to

✦ Between the letters, someone had confused these believers by teaching that the "day of the Lord" had already arrived. Since the Lord's return was supposed to bring relief from suffering, Paul has to clarify his teaching on the subject.

The Restrainer?

Todd Still

Second Peter 3:16 contends that there are some things in Paul's letters that are hard to understand. Second Thessalonians 2:1–12 lends support to this assessment. Indeed, a slew of complex interpretive questions confront students of this passage. What had caused the eschatological confusion in the Thessalonian congregation? What was the origin of this deception? What apostasy or rebellion did the apostle anticipate prior to the "day of the Lord"? Did Paul fashion the sinister figure he refers to as the "man of lawlessness"/"son of perdition" on a historical personage like Antiochus Epiphanes, Pompey, or Caligula? Did Paul have a literal temple in mind wherein this lawless one would take his seat and play God? To be sure, this text is chock-full of confounding comments.

No piece of the puzzle that is 2 Thessalonians 2:1–12 has perplexed Pauline interpreters more, however, than the identity of the "restraining force"/"restrainer" mentioned in vv. 6–7. Having been duly instructed regarding "the day," the Thessalonians knew "what is restraining (or holding back)" (*to katechon*) the "man of lawlessness" (2:6). Correlatively, they were fully apprised regarding "he who restrains (or holds back)" (*ho katechon*) the revelation of the lawless one. If they were "in the know," we are "in the dark." At least we are not alone in our confoundedness. In commenting on 2 Thess. 2:6, Augustine of Hippo (AD 354–430) remarked, "We who do not have their [i.e., the Thessalonians'] knowledge wish and are not able even with pains to understand what the apostle referred to." In addition, Augustine maintains that verse 6 is "made still more obscure by what [Paul] adds [in v. 7]." After citing 2:7, Augustine admits, "I frankly confess I do not know what he means" (*City of God* 20.19). As Augustine rightly notes, the difficulty of interpreting 2:6–7 is compounded in that whereas "what is restraining (or holding back)" (*to katechon*) in verse 6 is neuter, "he who restrains (or holds back)" (*ho katechon*) in verse 7 is masculine.

If Augustine was taken aback by the "audacious conjectures" of his contemporaries regarding the identity of the "restraining power"/"restrainer," then one can but imagine how bemused he would be at the proliferation of subsequent proposals. Exegetes have long suggested that in 2 Thessalonians 2:6–7 Paul had in mind the Roman Empire (*to katechon* [neuter]) on the one hand, and the person of the emperor (*ho katechon* [masculine]) on the other. A variation on this interpretation is that "the principle of order" is the "restraining power" and the "restrainer" is the personification of the same. Other views regarding *to katechon*/*ho katechon* include the Jewish state, Satan, a force and person hostile to God, God and his power, the Holy Spirit, an angelic figure, and the gospel as proclaimed by the apostle Paul. Beyond eliminating those views that construe the "restraining power"/"restrainer" as sinister (why would evil seek to restrain or hold back evil?), it is perhaps most prudent to leave this befuddling interpretive question open, as the title of this essay suggests.

become unsettled or alarmed by the teaching (falsely rumored to come from Paul) that the day of the Lord has already come (2:1–2). Paul teaches that Christ will not return until certain events take place: "the rebellion" must occur and the "man of lawlessness" must be revealed, and these things have not yet happened (2:3). The "rebellion" (*apostasia*) refers to a falling away from God. This man of lawlessness will exalt himself and claim to be God, and that description generally corresponds to other New Testament accounts of an end-time enemy of God ("antichrist" in 1 John 2:18 and "beast of the sea" in Rev. 13:1). Satan's empowerment of this rival messiah, along with the use of counterfeit signs and wonders, also fits the description (2:9). Because Paul had instructed the Thessalonians about these things (2:5), they know "what is holding him back" (2:6) and "the one who now holds it back" (2:7). The identity of this restraining influence/person, however, remains a mystery to us. What is clear is that when it/he is removed, the lawless one will be revealed only to be defeated and destroyed by the Lord Jesus at his coming (2:3, 8; Rev. 19:11–21).

Unbelievers will be deceived by the man of lawlessness and condemned by God because they have rejected God's truth and delighted in wickedness rather than giving themselves to God's truth (2:3, 9–12).

Reassurance and Prayer for Believers (2 Thess. 2:13–3:5)

After speaking about the judgment coming on unbelievers (2:8–12), Paul reassures the believers that God has chosen and called them to experience salvation through the work of the Spirit and belief in the truth (2:13–14). He urges them to stand firm and hold fast to the teachings they had previously received from Paul and his co-workers (2:15). He prays that God, whose love and grace they have experienced, will encourage and strengthen their hearts (2:16–17). Paul asks these believers to pray that the Lord's message would spread and that God would deliver the missionaries from wicked people (3:1–2). Paul affirms God's faithfulness and protection against the evil one, along with his confidence that the Thessalonians will continue to obey the apostolic teachings (3:3–4). Finally, he prays once again that the Lord would direct their hearts into God's love and Christ's perseverance (3:5).

Warning against Disruptive Behavior (2 Thess. 3:6–15)

Paul takes on an authoritative tone as he confronts a persistent problem within the church (e.g., issuing commands "in the name of the Lord Jesus Christ" in 3:6, 12). He first commands the church to keep away from people who are "idle" (perhaps better understood as "disruptive" or busy doing the wrong kind of work) and rebellious (3:6). He reminds them of his example and teaching (3:7–10). He worked hard in ways that benefited the community rather than draining it. Responsibility and privilege should go together. But there are some in Thessalonica who are busy doing selfish and divisive things that damage the community (3:11). Paul now commands

✦ Both Jesus in the Olivet Discourse and Paul here in 2 Thessalonians remind believers that responsible obedience in the present is the best way to prepare for the future.

Work and the Thessalonian Christians

Todd Still

Although Paul indicates that his initial ministry in Thessalonica was fruitful for the work of the gospel (see, e.g., 1 Thess. 1:5, 9; 2:13; 3:6; 4:1; cf. 2 Thess. 1:3; 2:13), he does not suggest that the founding and forming of the fellowship was easy. On the contrary, as he reflects on his first visit to the city, he depicts it as fraught with hardship. Not only did he and his fellow missionaries experience opposition from unbelieving outsiders (note 1 Thess. 1:6; 2:2, 14–15; 3:3–4), but they also engaged in toilsome labor during their stay. Paul puts it this way in 1 Thessalonians 2:9: "For you remember, brothers and sisters, our labor and toil; we worked night and day, so that we might not be a [fiscal] burden to any of you, while we preached to you the gospel of God" (ESV; cf. 2 Thess. 3:7–8). Despite having the right to make a living from the gospel (see 1 Thess. 2:6; 2 Thess. 3:10; 1 Cor. 9:12), it was Paul's missionary *modus operandi* to ply his trade as a tentmaker (note Acts 18:3) so that he could preach the gospel free of charge (see 1 Cor. 9:18; 2 Cor. 11:7).

In addition to serving as an example for the Thessalonians relative to work (1 Thess. 2:10; 2 Thess. 3:9), the apostle also offered the Thessalonian congregation instructions regarding work both in person and by letter. In 1 Thessalonians 4:11 Paul admonishes the assembly "to work with your hands, just as we [previously] told you" (cf. 2 Thess. 3:10). He also exhorts the church near the close of the letter to "warn those who are idle" (1 Thess. 5:14). In 2 Thessalonians 3:6–13, there is an explicit link between the disorderly or unruly on the one hand, and work on the other. Seemingly, some of the Thessalonian congregation were living unruly lives precisely due to their unwillingness to work (2 Thess. 3:11). That they were sponging off of the assembly stood in stark contrast to the example of their founders and threatened the stability of the fledgling fellowship.

Whatever the root of this brewing congregational crisis (an aversion to work in general, an errant eschatology in particular, or both?), Paul wants to "nip it in the bud." He seeks to do so by commanding the congregation to "steer clear" of the work-shy (2 Thess. 3:6), by reminding the assembly of his conduct and instruction (2 Thess. 3:7–10), and by appealing directly to the unruly to work in quietness and eat their own bread (2 Thess. 3:12). In the event that the disorderly fail to respond positively to the instructions given, then they are to be shunned so that they might be ashamed (and subsequently restored) (2 Thess. 3:14–15). Regardless, the Thessalonian believers are to "never tire of doing what is right" (2 Thess. 3:13) lest the labor of Paul and his co-workers be all for naught (1 Thess. 3:5).

such people to "settle down and earn the bread they eat" (3:12), while the rest of the church should never tire in doing what is right (3:13). Paul spells out the harsh consequences in store for those who reject his teachings on the matter (3:14–15). Sometimes love has to be tough.

Letter Closing (2 Thess. 3:16–18)

Paul closes with a benediction of peace (3:16) and grace (3:18), along with a greeting in his own hand to authenticate this letter (3:17).

So What? Applying Thessalonians Today

Perhaps above all, we find here wisdom and balance on the issue of the second coming of Christ. While some Christians are consumed with all things eschatological, others seem to forget that Jesus promised to return. Paul reminds us here that Jesus is indeed coming back. Those who die prior to that event will not be disadvantaged. They will be first in line for a resurrection body. We grieve, but not without hope. When Jesus returns, he will gather his children to himself, and we will be with the Lord forever. This hope should comfort and strengthen our hearts. We are also reminded that our priority should be to live faithfully right now as we anticipate Christ's return. Paul provides plenty of pastoral instruction about holy living, perseverance, reassurance, personal responsibility, and hope. New believers

Remains from the marketplace in Thessalonica.

who are under pressure because of their faith will find plenty of wisdom and encouragement in these letters. In addition, they offer some of the most profound intercessory prayers in the New Testament.

Our Favorite Verses in Thessalonians

For the Lord himself will come down from heaven, with a loud command, with the voice of the archangel and with the trumpet call of God, and the dead in Christ will rise first. After that, we who are still alive and are left will be caught up together with them in the clouds to meet the Lord in the air. And so we will be with the Lord forever. Therefore encourage each other with these words. (1 Thess. 4:16–18)

1 Timothy

Teach the Truth

Titus

Devote Yourself to Doing Good

2 Timothy

A Final Word to a Faithful Friend

First and 2 Timothy and Titus are known as the Pastoral Letters because they are addressed to two pastors. Timothy accompanied Paul on his second and third missionary journeys and is listed as co-sender in five of his letters. He was serving as pastor of the church in Ephesus at the time of these letters. Titus, a gentile believer and one of Paul's closest companions in ministry, was serving as pastor on the island of Crete. To these trusted and dearly loved partners in ministry, Paul writes three very significant letters for life in the local church. We will look at the letters in the order in which they were written by Paul.

Who Wrote the Pastoral Epistles?

All three Pastoral Letters claim Paul as their author, but his authorship has been questioned by many contemporary scholars because their literary style and doctrinal emphases vary from Paul's other letters and because there is no place in the book of Acts where the Pastorals seem to fit. For these reasons many conclude they were written years later by a disciple of Paul. Nevertheless, solid arguments remain in favor of Pauline authorship of the Pastorals. Since the letters were likely written after the story told in Acts concludes, there is no need to harmonize the chronologies. In addition, the different subject matter, purposes, and circumstances (e.g., written to individual pastors rather than to churches) accounts for many of the differences. Lastly, because of the similarities between the Pastorals and Luke–Acts, it is quite possible that Luke served as Paul's trusted secretary and was given added freedom to compose the letters (see Paul's statement in 2 Tim. 4:11 that "only Luke is with me").

Who Is Paul's Audience?

When the book of Acts closes, Paul is still under house arrest in Rome awaiting his trial before Caesar (Acts 28:30–31). We are not told how things turned out for Paul, but early church tradition says that Paul was released from prison, continued his ministry for a time, was imprisoned again in Rome, and was eventually martyred (see Eusebius, *Hist. eccl.* 2.22.2, 5). The following reconstruction of the historical setting is one way of making sense of the scriptural evidence:

- First Roman imprisonment in about AD 60–62
- Released from first Roman imprisonment (not recorded in Acts)
- Traveled to the "limits of the West" (perhaps made it to Spain; Rom. 15:24, 28)

A bust of Emperor Nero, the Roman emperor when Paul wrote the Pastoral Letters.

✝ Timothy and Titus were among Paul's many co-workers who played a significant role in the mission to the gentiles.

- Went to Crete, left Titus (Titus 1:5)
- Went to Miletus (2 Tim. 4:20)
- Went to Ephesus, left Timothy (1 Tim. 1:3)
- Went to Macedonia (1 Tim. 1:3; Phil. 2:24) and Nicopolis (Titus 3:12)
- Arrested on the way to Ephesus (possibly at Troas; 2 Tim. 4:13)
- Imprisoned a second time in Rome and martyred during persecution of Nero in about AD 67–68 (2 Tim. 1:16–17; 2:9; 4:6–8, 13, 20–21)

Sometime between AD 63 and 67, Paul wrote letters to Timothy (in Ephesus) and Titus (in Crete), instructing them about local church ministry and encouraging them to persevere. After he was imprisoned a second time, he wrote Timothy one final letter, a farewell to his faithful friend.

What Is at the Heart of the Pastoral Letters?

Paul had earlier warned the Ephesian elders that false teachers from their own group would distort the truth and lead people astray (Acts 20:30). According to 1 Timothy 1:3–7, that is exactly what happened. The problem in Ephesus was false teaching (1 Tim. 1:3, 7; 6:3–5), and the elders were responsible for teaching (1 Tim. 3:1–7; 5:17–25). In other words, the church in Ephesus was being threatened by some of its own leaders. Paul writes 1 Timothy to stop the false teaching and to teach the church how to conduct itself.

1 Timothy
- Letter Opening (1:1–2)
- Charge to Timothy: Teach the Truth (1:3–20)
- Instructions about Church Worship and Leadership (2:1–3:16)
- Pursue Godliness and Avoid False Teachings (4:1–16)
- Instructions for Groups within the Church (5:1–6:2)
- Concluding Warnings (6:3–21)

Paul left Titus on Crete to appoint leaders in the various house churches (Titus 1:5). The people of Crete had a reputation for dishonesty, gluttony, and laziness (1:12), so it's no surprise that Paul's focus in the letter to Titus is on how God's people should live in the midst of a pagan society. Christians should devote themselves to doing what is good, and this is the main theme of the letter (Titus 1:8, 16; 2:7, 14; 3:1–8, 14).

✚ The Pastoral Letters offer insight into how the early church was organized for ministry.

False Teachers

Ray Van Neste

False teachers are found throughout the story of the Bible (see 2 Tim. 3:8). Their emphases may vary, but they are essentially those who teach something different from the truth ("deposit") entrusted to us by Christ through the apostles (see 1 Tim. 1:3; 2 Tim. 1:14). The verb translated "teach false doctrines" in 1 Timothy 1:3 literally means "to teach something strange or different." In the New Testament, some false teachers are too strict, requiring things God does not require (e.g., Gal. 6:12; 1 Tim. 4:1–5), while others are too lax, failing to uphold God's requirements (Titus 1:10–11; 2 Tim. 3:1–9). In the Pastoral Epistles (as in the rest of the New Testament), improper teaching is closely linked with improper behavior (2 Tim. 3:1–9; 1 Tim. 1:3–7; 6:3–10). False teaching is not simply an intellectual or academic issue; it's always a moral issue as well.

Similarly, moral error is linked with doctrinal trouble. The true, apostolic gospel produces godliness in its adherents (Titus 2:11–12).

False teachers are to be rebuked and silenced (1 Tim. 1:3; Titus 1:11–13). Paul does not take false teaching lightly. Such error will upset whole families (Titus 1:11), "destroy the faith of some" (2 Tim. 2:18), "spread like gangrene" (2 Tim. 2:17), and deceive people into thinking they are right with God when they are not (Titus 1:16). Doctrinal error jeopardizes souls and, therefore, must be dealt with firmly and clearly. Hope is held out that false teachers and their followers will repent (2 Tim. 2:24–26), in which case they will be received by the church. However, those who persist in teaching false doctrine must be put out of the church (Titus 3:10–11).

Titus
- Letter Opening (1:1–4)
- Instructions for Groups within the Church (1:5–2:15)
- Devote Yourselves to Doing Good (3:1–11)
- Letter Closing (3:12–15)

Whereas Paul's first Roman imprisonment was a house arrest, his second imprisonment seems more severe—in a cold, damp, hard-to-find place (2 Tim. 1:17; 4:13), deserted by some (2 Tim. 1:15; 4:10), opposed by others (2 Tim. 2:17–18; 4:14), with a sense that death is at hand (2 Tim. 4:6–8, 18). Second Timothy is Paul's intensely personal farewell to his life-long co-worker, a kind of last will and testament. Paul exhorts Timothy to stay faithful, proclaims the victory of the gospel of Jesus Christ, and calls Timothy to his side.

2 Timothy
- Letter Opening (1:1–2)
- Encouragement to Stay Faithful (1:3–18)
- Be Strong in God's Grace and Endure Hardship (2:1–13)

✚ Paul had once put believers in prison (Acts 8:3; 9:4–5; 22:4, 19; 26:10). Ironically, as a believer he himself was put in prison on several occasions (2 Cor. 6:5; 11:23; Acts 16:23–40; Phil. 1:13–14; 2 Tim. 1:16; 2:9; Philemon 10, 13).

- A Workman Who Correctly Handles the Word (2:14–26)
- Persevering in Difficult Times (3:1–17)
- Paul's Final Words to Timothy (4:1–18)
- Letter Closing (4:19–22)

What Makes the Pastoral Epistles Interesting and Unique?

- Paul changes his normal pattern of writing to entire churches and writes these letters to two co-workers who are leading churches: Timothy and Titus.
- He presents qualifications and instructions for church leaders (elders and deacons) in 1 Timothy 3:1–13; 5:17–25; and Titus 1:6–9.
- First Timothy 2:11–15 offers a significant (and much debated) passage on the role of women in the church.
- First Timothy 6 contains wise advice about how Christians should use money.
- Second Timothy is most likely Paul's final letter, written a short time before he was martyred (see 2 Tim. 4:16–18).
- Paul's letter to Titus repeatedly stresses good works as the normal expression of a genuine Christian faith (e.g., Titus 2:7, 14; 3:1, 8, 14).
- Second Timothy 3:16–17 offers an extremely important affirmation of the inspiration of Scripture.

What Is the Message of 1 Timothy?

Letter Opening (1 Tim. 1:1–2)

Paul writes as an apostle of Jesus Christ to Timothy, his "true son in the faith" (1:1). To the normal greeting of grace and peace, Paul adds "mercy" from God the Father and Christ Jesus our Lord (1:2).

A Roman coin with Nero's portrait.

Charge to Timothy: Teach the Truth (1 Tim. 1:3–20)

Paul first charges Timothy to command certain men in the church to stop teaching false doctrines, which encourage controversies and even apostasy rather than God's work (1:3–7). Those who claim to be experts in

✦ Paul had predicted that the church in Ephesus would struggle with false teachers within its leadership (Acts 20:28–31).

the law fail to realize the proper approach to the law, which Paul explains in 1:8–11. Paul offers a thanksgiving in 1:12–14 for God's abundant grace that transformed him from a persecutor of the church to an apostle. In 1:15–17, we read the first of five "trustworthy sayings" in the Pastorals (1 Tim. 1:15; 3:1; 4:9; 2 Tim. 2:11; Titus 3:8). The core of this saying is that Christ came into the world to save sinners, and this display of unlimited patience will result in honor and glory to God.

Closing out the section, Paul again encourages Timothy to stay strong in the faith (1:18–20).

Instructions about Church Worship and Leadership (1 Tim. 2:1–3:16)

Prayer should be a priority in worship, so that believers might live peaceful and quiet lives in godliness and so that people will come to a saving knowledge of the truth revealed in our mediator and redeemer, Jesus Christ (2:1–7). In 2:8–15, Paul instructs men (or husbands) to pray without arguing and women (or wives) to dress appropriately, to learn with a respectful spirit, and to refrain from teaching or having authority over a man (most likely referring to a single function: the role of elder). Paul grounds these commands in the order of creation. In 3:1–13, which includes a second trustworthy saying, Paul provides qualifications and responsibilities of church leaders, first for the elders (3:1–7), then for deacons (3:8–13). Overseers are to live godly lives, be faithful and responsible in relationships, have a good reputation with outsiders, and be able to teach. The criteria for deacons are much the same, except the teaching responsibilities are omitted. Paul reminds Timothy (and the entire church) that his written instructions substitute for his personal presence, and he concludes with a confession of faith concerning Jesus Christ (3:14–16).

Pursue Godliness and Avoid False Teachings (1 Tim. 4:1–16)

According to 4:1–5, the false teaching at Ephesus includes a strong element of asceticism (i.e., forbidding gifts from God such as marriage and certain foods). Such teachings come from hypocritical liars and have their origin in the demonic. God's gifts are to be received with thanksgiving. Timothy's role as a good minister of Christ Jesus is to point out the falsehoods, avoid them himself, and pursue godliness (4:6–8). The third trustworthy saying highlights the living God as the Savior of those who believe (4:9–10). Paul then encourages Timothy to be diligent, to set an example of godliness, and to teach others to do the same (4:11–16).

✦ Paul provides insight about the qualifications and responsibilities of church leaders in 1 Timothy 3.

Church Leaders

Ray Van Neste

The Pastoral Epistles contain the most detailed discussion in the New Testament about the office of church leaders. Three main terms are used for church leaders: elders, overseers, and deacons. "Elder" occurs most commonly in the New Testament (Acts 11:30; 14:23; 15:2, 4, 6, 22–23; 16:4; 20:17; 21:18; 1 Tim. 4:14; 5:17, 19; Titus 1:5; 1 Pet. 5:1–5). "Overseer" is the term used in the list of qualifications in 1 Timothy 3:1–7 (see also Phil. 1:1). In the list of qualifications in Titus 1:5–9, the terms "elder" and "overseer" occur together (as in Acts 20:28). Because of the use of "elder" and "overseer" together (and the use of the verb form "oversee" as a duty of "elders" in 1 Pet. 5:1–5), scholars commonly agree that they refer to the same office. Even those who do not agree still group them together in distinction from "deacons." There are then two main offices of church leaders: overseers/elders and deacons.

Qualifications. The primary texts on qualifications for these church leaders are 1 Timothy 3 and Titus 1:5–9. Overseers/elders are addressed in 1 Timothy 3:1–7 and Titus 1:5–9. Deacons are addressed in 1 Timothy 3:8–13 (also see Acts 6). These qualifications focus more on Christian character than on ability or duties. Church leaders are to be those whose lives are shaped by the gospel. They are to embody the message both personally and in their home life.

Duties. Overseers must be able to teach sound doctrine and to refute false teachers (1 Tim. 3:2; Titus 1:9). First Timothy 5:17 says special honor should be given to those who "labor in preaching and teaching" (ESV). The repeated exhortations throughout the Pastoral Epistles for faithful, sound teaching also demonstrate the importance of the teaching duty of church leaders (e.g., 1 Tim. 1:18; 4:6, 11; 6:2–3; 2 Tim. 2:14; 4:1–2; Titus 2:1; 3:8). There is also a significant degree of authority in this teaching (e.g., Titus 2:15), though it is to be used in gentleness (2 Tim. 2:24–26).

Deacons are not required to be able to teach. This is a key distinction in the offices. There is no explicit mention of the duty of deacons in the Pastoral Epistles. They would appear to assist the overseers. If Acts 6 refers to the first deacons (which seems likely), deacons assisted elders by attending to specific needs in the congregation and in that way guarded the unity of the church.

In addition to teaching, overseers are to lead the church and oversee the members. Teaching, guiding, and living holy lives are ways in which elders guard and shepherd the souls of their flock (Acts 20; 1 Tim. 4:16; Heb. 13:17).

Instructions for Groups within the Church (1 Tim. 5:1–6:2)

False teaching eventually damages relationships within the church, and Paul now offers corrective instructions for several groups. He first calls for respect for all ages, including the young and the old (5:1–2), before addressing the situation regarding widows (5:3–16).

Widows with supporting families should be cared for by those families (5:4), while the godly widows older than sixty without family support should be cared for by the church (5:3, 5–9). Those family members who fail to support

✚ The terms "elders," "overseers," and "shepherds/pastors" seem to be interchangeable in the New Testament (see Acts 20:17, 28; 1 Tim. 3:1–7; 5:17–19; Titus 1:5–9; 1 Pet. 5:1–4).

widows in their families are worse than unbelievers (5:8, 16). He counsels the younger widows to remarry and focus on their family responsibilities as a way of living out their faith (5:11–15). In 5:17–25, Paul encourages financial support for those elders who direct the affairs of the church, especially those who preach and teach (Deut. 25:4; Luke 10:7). Any accusation against an elder should be brought by several witnesses, but those elders who are sinning should be reproved before everyone as a warning to all. Paul reminds Timothy not to show favoritism and not to ordain anyone too quickly to the office of elder, although it's not always easy to tell a person's character. Timothy should keep himself pure, but this does not prohibit taking a little wine for his health instead of only water. In 6:1–2, Paul reminds slaves to respect their masters so that God's name may be honored rather than slandered. Slaves with Christian masters should not slough off just because they are serving fellow believers, but should instead serve them even more diligently.

Concluding Warnings (1 Tim. 6:3–21)

Timothy should continue to teach the truth, and those who teach otherwise or disagree with the teachings of Jesus are conceited, ignorant troublemakers bent on using the faith for personal profit (6:3–5). Godliness with contentment is spiritually profitable, but those who want to get rich fall into temptation themselves that often results in ruin and destruction (6:6–9). Since "the love of money is a root of all kinds of evil," many who pursue that love suffer spiritual bankruptcy (6:10). Paul warns Timothy as a man of God to run away from such temptations and pursue "righteousness, godliness, faith, love, endurance and gentleness" (6:11). He must fight the good fight of faith and stay true to his confession until the return of Christ, which God, who is worthy of all honor and praise, will bring about in his own time (6:12–16). Paul also commands wealthy believers not to be arrogant or to put their hope in riches but to put their hope in God, to be rich in good deeds, and to share generously (6:17–18). In this way, they will be laying up treasure for the coming age (6:19). Once again, Paul charges Timothy to stay faithful, turning away from the false teaching that leads people away from the true faith (6:20). He closes the letter with a prayer that God's grace be with them (6:21).

What Is the Message of Titus?

Letter Opening (Titus 1:1–4)

Paul writes as a "servant of God and an apostle of Jesus Christ" (1:1) to Titus, his "true son" in the "common faith," with his usual greeting of "grace and peace from God the Father and Christ Jesus our Savior" (1:4). But Paul expands the purpose of his apostleship with rich references to faith, knowledge, godliness, eternal life, God's faithfulness, and his calling (1:1–3).

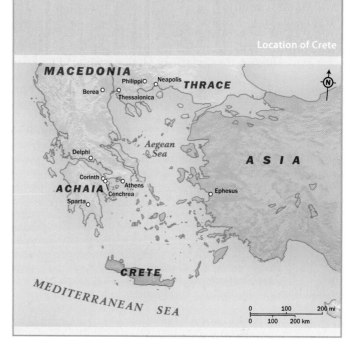

Location of Crete

Instructions for Groups within the Church (Titus 1:5–2:15)

Titus was left in Crete to appoint elders or overseers in the various house churches (1:5, 7). In 1:6–9, Paul details the criteria for this leadership position, including personal godliness, an exemplary home life, an absence of ethical vices, and an abundance of Christian virtues, especially a firm grasp of the faith, so that he could encourage believers and refute false teachers. Paul addresses the false teaching in 1:10–16. It has a distinctively Jewish element (1:10, 14), generally reflects Cretan society (1:12), and adds an ascetic twist (1:15). Paul labels the false teachers as greedy, rebellious, deceptive, corrupt, disobedient, and unfit for doing anything good. He commands Titus to rebuke the false teachers and steer the churches away from their harmful influence. Next, Paul has special instructions for Titus regarding teaching older people (2:1–3) and younger people (2:4–8). He encourages the older believers to live lives worthy of imitation by the younger believers and to teach the truth faithfully so that outsiders will have no grounds for criticizing the church (2:5, 8). Titus himself should set the example for all (2:7–8). Paul then instructs slaves to respect their masters and demonstrate their trustworthiness so as to make the gospel attractive to them (2:9–10). Paul offers a theological conclusion to his behavioral instructions (2:11–15). The "grace of God that brings salvation" has appeared to all (2:11). This grace teaches us to say "no" to ungodliness and "yes" to righteousness (2:12) while we wait for "the blessed hope": the return of "our great God and Savior, Jesus Christ" (2:13). Jesus (clearly affirmed here as God) gave himself to redeem us from our sins and purify us as his people eager to do what is good (2:14). Again, Titus is charged with teaching these truths and allowing no one to despise him (2:15).

✦ Whereas Paul discourages Christians from pursuing "works of law" (Rom. 3:21–4:25; Gal. 3:1–4:7; 5:1–12), he encourages Christians to demonstrate "good works" that flow out of faith (e.g., Titus 2:7, 14; 3:1, 8, 14).

Devote Yourselves to Doing Good (Titus 3:1–11)

As part of devoting themselves to doing what is good, the Christians on Crete need to submit to civil authorities and display a humble, peaceable, considerate attitude (3:1–2). This will stand in stark contrast to their previous way of life that was full of things like foolishness, disobedience, and hatred (3:3). Paul then provides another "trustworthy saying" in 3:4–7. When God's kindness and love appeared in Christ, he saved people, not on the basis of their good works but on the basis of his mercy through the renewing power of the Holy Spirit. As a result of this justification by grace, believers now become heirs of eternal life. People who have been saved on the basis of God's grace will devote themselves to doing what is good (4:8). As he has stated previously in 1:10–16, Paul again warns Titus about the false teachers and recommends a process of church discipline in 3:9–11.

Letter Closing (Titus 3:12–15)

Paul closes with personal greetings from other co-workers and instructions for Titus related to Paul's travel plans (3:12–13). Paul adds one final exhortation about doing what is good, this time related especially to living productive lives in order to provide for daily needs (3:14). The letter closes with the additional greetings and a benediction of grace to all (3:15).

What Is the Message of 2 Timothy?

Letter Opening (2 Tim. 1:1–2)

In his final letter, Paul writes as an apostle of Christ Jesus by God's will, adding "according to the promise of life that is in Christ Jesus" (1:1). So close to death, Paul holds fast to the hope of eternal life. He greets Timothy, his "dear son," with "grace, mercy, and peace" from the Father and the Son (1:2).

The harbor at Fair Havens on the Island of Crete.

Encouragement to Stay Faithful (2 Tim. 1:3–18)

Paul's emotional thanksgiving that begins in 1:3 includes his memories, longings, and challenges to Timothy. As he prays, he remembers their close relationship and Timothy's sincere faith that was passed down from his grandmother and

The Mamertine Prison in Rome, where Paul may have been imprisoned when he wrote 2 Timothy.

mother (1:4–5). He reminds Timothy to serve boldly, lovingly, and diligently according to his God-given gifts (1:6–7). Rather than being ashamed of the Lord or of Paul, Timothy should join in suffering for the gospel as God empowers him (1:8), for God has provided salvation and calls believers to holiness, not based on their actions but rather on his purpose and grace (1:9). This grace has been revealed in Jesus Christ, who destroyed death and provided life through the gospel, of which Paul is a minister (1:9–11). Although Paul now faces imminent death, he doesn't pull back in shame but trusts Jesus's faithfulness to finish what he started (1:12; Phil. 1:6). Timothy should imitate Paul by holding on to the "sound teaching" with faith and love and "guarding the good deposit" (i.e., the gospel) with the help of the Spirit (1:13–14). Paul provides negative models for Timothy to avoid (1:15) and positive models for him to emulate (1:16–18). During times of suffering, faithful friends are gifts from God!

Be Strong in God's Grace and Endure Hardship (2 Tim. 2:1–13)

Paul urges Timothy to "be strong in the grace that is in Christ Jesus" and to continue passing on the true faith to reliable people who are qualified to teach others (2:1–2). To fulfill his responsibilities, Timothy will need to endure hardship, stay focused, and work hard (much like a soldier, athlete, and farmer), knowing that there will be an eternal reward (2:3–7). Paul once again reminds Timothy of the gospel of Christ crucified and resurrected, which cannot be imprisoned even when its messengers are put in chains (2:8–9). Enduring such hardship is worth it when it results in salvation for others (2:10). Another "trustworthy saying" in 3:11–13 reaffirms basic truths about our relationship to Christ.

✦ Like a faithful father speaking his final words to a loyal son, 2 Timothy offers us a glimpse into Paul's deep love and affection for Timothy, his son in the faith.

2 Timothy   891

A Workman Who Correctly Handles the Word (2 Tim. 2:14–26)

Timothy is to remind believers of the true faith and warn them about useless and harmful word battles that deny the gospel and destroy people spiritually (2:14, 16–18, 23). Timothy should focus on offering himself to God as a "workman who does not need to be ashamed and who correctly handles the word of truth" (2:15). Responsible interpretation and application of the Scriptures remains at the heart of pastoral ministry. God knows his children and will protect them, but believers are responsible for rejecting false teaching (2:19). Paul challenges those attracted to the false teaching to cleanse themselves and return to their Lord, who can purify them and use them for every good work (2:20–21). For his part, Timothy should run away from the false teaching, run after righteousness, faith, love, and peace, and run with those who call on the Lord from a pure heart (2:22). Rather than being quarrelsome, the Lord's servant (minister) should be kind and gently instruct those who oppose him in hopes that God will grant them repentance and an escape from the devil's trap (2:25–26).

Persevering in Difficult Times (2 Tim. 3:1–17)

Timothy should be aware that there will be "terrible times in the last days," meaning the time between the first and second comings of Christ (3:1). Paul uses nearly twenty negative qualities in describing what many people will become, and he warns Timothy to have nothing to do with such people (3:2–5). Next, Paul unmasks the deceptive tactics of these false teachers, noting their use of religion to prey on vulnerable women (3:6–7). These men, like the men who opposed Moses, have depraved minds and reject the truth (3:8), but God has rejected them and will soon show them for the spiritual fools they are (3:9). In contrast, Timothy has a point of reference in Paul's way of life and teachings and sufferings (3:10–11). As a result, Timothy pursues godliness and can expect persecution (3:12), whereas impostors will continue down their wicked path (3:13). Paul urges Timothy to persevere in the faith, knowing both the role models that taught him and the Scriptures that were taught (3:14–15). After all, the Scriptures are "God-breathed," and their inspiration makes them useful for equipping people to live godly lives and carry out their God-given ministry (3:15–16).

Paul's Final Words to Timothy (2 Tim. 4:1–18)

Paul's final words to Timothy are packed with emotion. First, he charges Timothy in the presence of God to "preach the Word," being always ready to "correct, rebuke and encourage" with patience and careful teaching (4:1–2). The time will come, Paul warns, when people won't put up with sound doctrine but will surround themselves with teachers who say only what the people want to hear (4:3–4). Timothy must keep his composure in all situations, endure hardship, spread the gospel, and fulfill his ministry (4:5). Sadly, Paul's "departure" (death) is at hand (4:6). Indeed, he has fought the fight, finished the race, and kept the faith, and the Lord will reward him (and all who long for Jesus's return) on that day (4:7–8). Paul pleads with Timothy to come to him quickly, for some have deserted him, others are on assignment, and only Luke remains by his side (4:9–11). When he comes, Timothy should bring Mark (who earlier deserted the mission team but is now helpful), Paul's cloak for warmth in the cold, damp prison cell, and his parchment scrolls or his "Bible" (4:11–13). On his trip, Timothy should beware of Alexander the metalworker, who strongly opposes the faith (4:14–15). At his first defense, everyone deserted Paul, but he prays in effect, "Father, forgive them" (4:16). But the Lord was with him and enabled him to proclaim the good news in the very heart of the gentile empire, Rome itself (4:17). One wonders if Paul had the chance to proclaim Jesus to Emperor Nero. Paul knows the Lord will rescue him from every evil attack and bring him safely into his heavenly kingdom (i.e., protect him spiritually through death to resurrection)—to God be the glory (4:18).

The starting line used for the Pythian games at Delphi, Greece.

✝ As Paul awaits the outcome of his trial, he hopes to see Timothy one last time before the shipping lanes close for the winter.

2 Timothy 893

Letter Closing (2 Tim. 4:19–22)

While exchanging final greetings, Paul says to Timothy, "Do your best to get here before winter" (4:19–21). If Timothy doesn't get on a ship bound for Rome before the shipping lanes shut down for the winter, he won't get to see his beloved mentor before his death.

With this one passionate plea, Paul reveals his deep love for his faithful friend. After praying that Timothy would know God's presence, he closes the letter, his final letter, with the expression that characterizes his life perhaps more than any other: "Grace be with you" (4:22).

So What? Applying the Pastoral Epistles Today

The Pastoral letters continue to speak in meaningful ways about life and ministry in the local church. The theme of godliness runs throughout the Pastorals. In a culture in which church leaders are commonly caught in scandalous sins, Paul's demand that a leader set a godly example remains just as relevant today. Paul also highlights (especially in Titus) the importance of doing what is good. We are saved by grace and not by good works, but true believers will devote themselves to doing good works as a demonstration of the genuineness of their faith. Paul also spells out various qualifications and responsibilities of church leaders (1 Tim. 3:1–13; Titus 1:5–9). Today, we should pay attention to all the items on these lists rather than being selective about which ones to apply. Serving as a spiritual leader for a congregation remains a serious calling. Along with setting a godly example, certain leaders are charged with teaching the Scriptures faithfully and accurately. Since false teaching continues to threaten the church by steering people away from Christ, it is the leader's job to lovingly shepherd the flock away from danger and back toward truth. In addition, God's people should not be surprised when they encounter opposition, for "everyone who wants to live a godly life in Christ Jesus will be persecuted" (2 Tim. 3:12). Along with a willingness to suffer, we should prepare for a long-distance race. The Christian life is a life of endurance and perseverance rather than a short sprint. May God help us remain faithful to the end as we hold on to our ultimate hope of enjoying his presence forever.

Our Favorite Verses in the Pastoral Epistles

Command those who are rich in this present world not to be arrogant nor to put their hope in wealth, which is so uncertain, but to put their hope in God,

✦ The Pastoral Letters remind us that the Christian life is to be lived in community rather than in isolation and that this life is more like an endurance race than a short sprint.

who richly provides us with everything for our enjoyment. Command them to do good, to be rich in good deeds, and to be generous and willing to share. In this way they will lay up treasure for themselves as a firm foundation for the coming age, so that they may take hold of the life that is truly life. (1 Tim. 6:17–19)

All Scripture is God-breathed and is useful for teaching, rebuking, correcting and training in righteousness. (2 Tim. 3:16)

For the grace of God that brings salvation has appeared to all men. It teaches us to say "No" to ungodliness and worldly passions, and to live self-controlled, upright and godly lives in this present age, while we wait for the blessed hope—the glorious appearing of our great God and Savior, Jesus Christ, who gave himself for us to redeem us from all wickedness and to purify for himself a people that are his very own, eager to do what is good. (Titus 2:11–14)

A papyrus scroll. In 2 Tim. 4:13, Paul instructs Timothy to bring his "scrolls, especially the parchments."

Philemon

Equality in Christ

What do a Jewish Christian apostle, a wealthy gentile slave owner, and a runaway slave have in common? Nothing, unless they are united as brothers in Christ. This short letter tells the story of how our relationship to Christ changes all of our other relationships.

Who Wrote Philemon?

Paul wrote the letter, most likely when he was a prisoner in Rome in the early AD 60s, about the same time he wrote Ephesians and Colossians.

Who Is Paul's Audience?

Besides Paul, there are two main characters in this drama. Philemon is the slave owner who became a believer in Colossae through the ministry of Paul (19). Onesimus is the runaway slave who may have stolen from his master (18), came in contact with Paul in Rome, and subsequently became a Christian (10).

What Is at the Heart of Philemon?

Paul writes to persuade Philemon (1) to receive Onesimus as he would receive Paul himself (17), without punishing him or putting him to death (the usual treatment for runaway slaves under Roman law); (2) to welcome Onesimus as a "dear brother" (16); and perhaps (3) to set Onesimus free to serve in the cause of Christ (21). The phrase "even more" in verse 21 is likely a hint that Paul wanted Philemon to free Onesimus and send him back to assist Paul in mission service. The one-chapter book may be outlined as follows:

- Letter Opening (1–3)
- Thanksgiving and Prayer (4–7)
- Paul's Plea for Onesimus (8–21)
- Paul's Personal Request (22)
- Letter Closing (23–25)

What Makes Philemon Interesting and Unique?

- Paul makes heavy use of rhetoric (the art of persuasion) in this letter.
- Rather than call directly for the overthrow of the institution of slavery, Paul preaches a gospel of freedom and equality in Christ, and this gospel eventually destroys the institution.
- The important phrases "in Christ" (6, 8, 20, 23) and "in the Lord" (16, 20) appear throughout the letter to illustrate the main theme.

What Is the Message of Philemon?

Letter Opening (1–3)

This is the only time Paul identifies himself as a "prisoner of Christ Jesus" (1, 9), perhaps to lower his own status and identify with Onesimus in the eyes of Philemon. Paul and Timothy send greetings of grace and peace from the Father and the Son to Philemon, "our dear friend and fellow worker," to Apphia and Archippus (perhaps Philemon's wife and son), and to the entire church. This list of character witnesses adds positive accountability for Paul's forthcoming request.

Thanksgiving and Prayer (4–7)

Paul thanks God for Philemon's faith in Jesus and love for other believers (4–5). He next prays for Philemon, not that he might become a great

✝ The beauty and power of the gospel of Jesus Christ lies in its ability to overcome all social obstacles in order to unite people in community.

Slavery in the New Testament

Jeff Cate

The word "slave" (Greek, *doulos*) is used 126 times in the New Testament and at least once in all but six of the New Testament books. This frequency should not be surprising since virtually all cultures of the first-century Mediterranean world practiced slavery.

Even though slavery was widespread, the conditions varied from place to place. The Greek and Roman economies were slave-based, since such a large percentage of their populations was indentured. Estimates indicate that roughly one-fifth of the people in Rome were slaves, and in other large cities maybe as many as one-third. In Palestine, however, slavery was not nearly as common, and the Qumran community near the Dead Sea was one of the few ancient groups to forbid slavery.

Slavery of the first-century world needs to be distinguished from slavery of the New World in the eighteenth and nineteenth centuries. Most important, slavery of the Greco-Roman world was not race-based. Slaves could not be identified by nationality because slavery was not limited to certain ethnic groups. Instead, the Greco-Roman slave system was populated variously by prisoners of war, litigants found liable in the courts, financial debtors, freeborn children who were abandoned or sold, or most commonly by children born to women who were slaves.

Perspectives on slavery varied as well. Some Greek writers spoke of their slaves as "living tools."

Based on the Torah, however, Jewish slaves were granted important privileges such as a weekly Sabbath, restrictions from certain abuses, and circumcision in order to share in community worship.

Due to their status in the Greco-Roman world, slaves did not have personal rights regarding work or travel, but slaves could own personal property and hold their own beliefs. Unlike the New World slaves, first-century slaves had freedom to assemble, and slavery was not considered a lifelong indenturement. An elderly slave was a rare exception in the Greco-Roman world, since most slaves gained their freedom by their thirties or forties.

New Testament writers frequently mention slavery, sometimes literally but often metaphorically. Slaves were called to render their service obediently and cheerfully, and masters were instructed to be fair and considerate (Eph. 6:5–9; Col. 3:22–4:1; 1 Pet. 2:18–20). In an egalitarian spirit, Paul envisioned the new people of God as being neither "slave" nor "free" (1 Cor. 7:21–24; Gal. 3:28; Philem. 16). Metaphorically, Paul often referred to himself as a *doulos* ("slave") of Christ Jesus, which was an appropriate analogy since Jesus was his *kurios* ("Lord" or "master" or "owner"; see Col. 4:1; Eph. 6:9). Furthermore, Paul's concept of redemption seems to be largely based on the manumission of slaves.

evangelist (NIV: "sharing your faith"), but that he might grow in the "fellowship" (*koinonia*) of his faith so as to understand what belongs to believers in Christ (6). In other words, he prays that Philemon would have a better grasp of what true fellowship really means, including his relationship to Onesimus. Paul mentions again how Philemon's love has brought great joy and encouragement by refreshing the hearts of the saints. There is a powerful word play using the word "heart" in verses 7, 12, and 20. Philemon has refreshed the hearts of other believers (7). Paul is sending Onesimus, his heart, back to Philemon (12). Now Paul wants Philemon to refresh his own heart by accepting Onesimus without punishment (20). Philemon's present character becomes the basis for his future decisions.

Paul's Plea for Onesimus (8–21)

In the body of the letter we see Paul's plea for Onesimus. Although Paul could use his positional authority as an apostle, he prefers to use personal authority and appeals on the basis of love (8–9). As an "old man" and a "prisoner" he appeals for his "son Onesimus" (9–10). Onesimus apparently became a Christian when he met Paul in prison (10). Now Paul makes another word play, showing how Onesimus (whose name means "useless") has now become "useful" (11). Philemon has refreshed the hearts of others; now Paul is sending his "very heart" (Onesimus) back to him (12). In speaking of the help Philemon might have given (13), and in equating Philemon and Onesimus as brothers (16), Paul is putting slave owner and slave on the same level. Paul encourages Philemon to respond in a godly manner as a spontaneous act rather than a forced favor (14). He then gives Philemon eternal perspective—Philemon's loss is the kingdom's gain (15–16).

The Philemon–Onesimus relationship needs to be like the Philemon–Paul relationship (17). Paul promises to repay anything Onesimus owes Philemon, but he mentions in passing that Philemon owes Paul his very life (18–19). Paul hopes to have some benefit from Philemon in the Lord, using a term for "benefit" (*oninamai*) that sounds a lot like Onesimus's name, and he asks Philemon to refresh his "heart" in Christ (20; cf. vv. 7, 12). Lastly,

✛ Although he did not directly call for the abolishment of slavery in the Roman Empire, Paul lived and taught a gospel that undermines and destroys human slavery.

Paul issues a subtle but powerful command that uses future expectations to motivate a certain action in the present (21).

Paul's Personal Request (22)

In preparation for his upcoming visit, Paul asks Philemon to prepare a guest room for him. Such a visit would add personal accountability to Paul's request.

Letter Closing (23–25)

Paul sends greetings from Epaphras, his fellow prisoner, as well as Mark, Aristarchus, Demas, and Luke (23–24). He closes with a benediction of grace from the Lord Jesus Christ (25).

So What? Applying Philemon Today

Above all, the letter reminds us that being in Christ changes how we treat other people, especially people of different social, racial, and economic situations (Gal. 3:28). As brothers and sisters in Christ, we should respond differently to one another (e.g., forgiving, accepting, interceding, returning). Philemon reminds us that a new relationship with God should result in new relationships with God's people.

Our Favorite Verses in Philemon

Perhaps the reason he was separated from you for a little while was that you might have him back for good—no longer as a slave, but better than a slave, as a dear brother. (15–16)

The cast of a corpse of a slave (as indicated by the manacles on his ankles) recovered from the ruins of Pompeii.

The General Letters

The "General Letters" (also known as the "catholic" or universal letters) include Hebrews, James, 1–2 Peter, 1–3 John, and Jude. In contrast to Paul's letters, which are addressed to more specific groups like the Colossians or the Corinthians, the General Letters take their titles from their authors rather than from the recipients of the letters. Because Hebrews does take its name from the audience rather than the author (like Paul's letters), some do not include Hebrews with the General Letters.

The General Letters

Letter	Approximate Date	Author
James	Late 40s	James, the half-brother of Jesus and leader of the Jerusalem church
Jude	Early 60s	Judas, the half-brother of Jesus
1 Peter	Early to mid 60s	The apostle Peter
2 Peter	Mid 60s	The apostle Peter
Hebrews	Mid 60s	Author unknown, perhaps Apollos
1–3 John	70s to 90s	The apostle John

✦ As a subcategory, 1–3 John are commonly referred to as the Johannine Letters.

Hebrews

God Has Spoken to Us in His Son Jesus

Faith is easy until it's tested. The letter of Hebrews is more like a sermon, delivered to a group of people who are thinking about giving up on the Christian faith. Here we find a compassionate and capable preacher explaining and exhorting these believers with all his might in hopes of drawing them back to spiritual safety. The book establishes Jesus's credentials: he is preexistent and sovereign; he demonstrates God's faithfulness to his promises; he is the only sufficient sacrifice; and he understands our weaknesses and speaks in our defense. Even in the darkest of times, our confidence can be in the one who willingly endured this same darkness in order to reconcile us to the Father. *This* is the Christ in whom we put our faith and hope, and he will never let us down. With rhetorical power and theological depth, the book of Hebrews calls us to stay strong in the faith, fixing our eyes on Jesus, God's ultimate word to us.

Who Wrote Hebrews?

A number of people have been suggested as the author of Hebrews: Paul, Barnabas, Luke, Apollos, Silvanus, and Philip, just to name a few. Whereas Paul always identifies himself as the author in his letters, the author of Hebrews does not identify himself (i.e., he writes anonymously). He does not appear to have been an apostle or eyewitness of the life of Jesus (Heb. 2:3). He was highly educated because of his polished Greek style, persuasive rhetorical arguments, and extensive knowledge of the Old Testament. He was also a powerful preacher and a committed follower of Jesus Christ. This description fits Apollos perhaps better than any of the others, but we must remain cautious. According to Acts 18:24–28, Apollos was a Jewish Christian from Alexandria who was "a learned man" with a "thorough knowledge of the Scriptures." He had the ability to speak "with great fervor" and engage in public debate, "proving from the Scriptures that Jesus was the Christ." After discussing who wrote the book of Hebrews, Origen, a Christian leader in the third century, concluded: "But who wrote the epistle, in truth, God knows" (Eusebius, *Hist. eccl.* 6.25.14). In spite of our uncertainty about who wrote Hebrews, God continues to speak powerfully through this book.

The interior of the Colosseum in Rome and what lies beneath the stadium floor.

✚ Hebrews reminds us that the inspiration of Scripture does not nullify its persuasive complexity and power. God worked through the personalities and experiences and abilities of the biblical writers to give us his word.

Who Is the Audience?

The audience is likely a Christian house church or group of house churches composed of believers with a background in the Jewish synagogue (i.e., likely Jews but possibly gentile converts to Judaism). They probably lived somewhere near Rome and had been Christians for a while (5:11–6:3; 13:24). They had faced persecution for their faith but had not yet suffered martyrdom (10:32–34; 12:4). In addition to references to suffering, we are given a hint of the historical situation in 10:25: "Let us not give up meeting together, as some are in the habit of doing, but let us encourage one another—and all the more as you see the Day approaching." Apparently one or more house churches had begun to pull away from the main body of believers in the city and was considering a return to Judaism in order to avoid persecution. (As an ancient religion, Judaism received a degree of protection from persecution.) These discouraged believers were not growing spiritually and were in danger of drifting away from the true faith. A date in the AD mid-60s, at the beginning of Nero's persecution of the church in and around Rome, seems reasonable.

What Is at the Heart of Hebrews?

This letter is more specifically called a "word of exhortation" or a sermon (13:22; Acts 13:15). It was written to challenge a group of fragile believers to persevere in their commitment to Christ rather than drift away in unbelief. The author of Hebrews, or "the preacher," focuses on a central theme: God's final word is Jesus! He constantly points out how Jesus as the supreme revelation of God is "superior to" the previous revelation. Consequently, the listeners cannot ignore or dismiss Jesus if they want to relate properly to God. To persuade the listeners to take the proper course of action, the preacher combines words of warning (2:1–4; 3:7–19; 4:12–13; 6:4–8; 10:26–31; 12:25–29) with words of assurance (6:9–12, 19–20; 7:25; 10:14, 32–39). For this reason, the book of Hebrews carries a tension between the danger of failing to persevere in faith and God's promises for those who do endure. The book may be outlined as follows:

- Jesus, God's Final Word (1:1–4)
- Jesus, the Provider of Salvation, Is Superior to the Angels (1:5–2:18)
- Jesus's Faithfulness Calls Us to Faithfulness (3:1–4:13)
- The Superiority of Jesus's Priesthood and Ministry (4:14–10:25)

✦ It is surprising that Hebrews may have been originally written to a house church or small group of house churches, meaning dozens rather than hundreds of people. Over time, of course, this powerful sermon has ministered to millions.

- Call to Persevere in the Journey of Faith (10:26–12:29)
- Practical Exhortations (13:1–19)
- Closing (13:20–25)

What Makes Hebrews Interesting and Unique?

- We're not sure who actually wrote the book of Hebrews.
- The book appeals to an original audience with a fairly advanced understanding of the Old Testament.
- The letter goes into great detail about Jewish worship practices, including the role of the high priest and the function of the tabernacle.
- While Hebrews does say that the new covenant displaces the old covenant, the author points to many Old Testament believers as faithful examples for Christians to imitate (see Hebrews 11).
- The letter presents both the fear of God (warning) and the grace of God (comfort) as important spiritual realities. Neither one should be neglected.
- The body of the letter shifts back and forth between teaching about Christ (exposition) and commands to live out that teaching (exhortation).
- We find in Hebrews a clear and strong emphasis on Jesus's full humanity and full deity.

What Is the Message of Hebrews?

Jesus, God's Final Word (1:1–4)

While God spoke to his people in the past at many times and in various ways, he has now spoken an ultimate word by his Son, Jesus Christ (1:1–2). Jesus, through whom the world was created, is the "radiance of God's glory and the exact representation of his being" (1:2–3). The entire universe holds together by Jesus's word (1:3). After he provided purification for our sins through the cross, he was exalted to the right hand of God (1:3–4).

Jesus, the Provider of Salvation, Is Superior to the Angels (1:5–2:18)

As creator and sustainer of the universe, Christ is above the angels, but he made himself lower than the angels in order to provide salvation through his atoning death.

✦ Hebrews points to Jesus as the culmination and fulfillment of God's revelation of himself to his people.

Angels and Demons

William W. Klein

Angels and demons constitute an order of celestial spirit beings created by God to serve God. The Greek word *aggelos* and the corresponding Hebrew term *mal'ak* mean "messenger," though their tasks are broader than that. They represent God and the celestial world to his creation. As spirit beings they can navigate between the heavenly and earthly realms, even appearing in human form at times (Gen. 19:1–2; Judg. 13:15–21; Acts 12:7–11). The Bible divides angels into two groups: "good angels" and "bad angels." Created with free will, angels decided whether to serve God faithfully or to rebel.

The faithful angels, called "holy angels" or "angels of God" (or "of the Lord"), also have titles such as "heavenly beings," "holy ones," or "hosts." The Bible names only two, the archangel Michael (Dan. 10:13, 21; Jude 9; Rev. 12:7–8) and Gabriel (Dan. 8:16; 9:21; Luke 1:19, 26). Angels function chiefly as God's messengers in the Old Testament (Gen. 16:7–12; 1 Kings 19:5–8), sometimes even identified with the Lord himself (Judg. 6:11–18). Angels appear at the significant events of Jesus's life: birth (Matt. 1:20; Luke 1:26–27), temptation (Mark 1:13), resurrection (Matt. 28:2, 5), and his return as judge of the world (Matt. 24:31; 25:31; Mark 8:38). Angels aided the expansion of the church in a variety of ways (Acts 5:19; 8:26; 10:22; 12:7; 27:23). The writer of Hebrews captures their essential ministry to God's people: "Are not all angels ministering spirits sent to serve those who will inherit salvation?" (Heb. 1:14).

In Revelation angels feature prominently. They lead worship around God's throne (5:11; 7:11), they transmit God's message (1:1; 14:6), and they carry out judgments on the earth and its inhabitants (8:8; 14:15; 15:1).

A large number of angels rebelled against God, and their leader, Satan (also called the devil, the ancient serpent, Beelzebul), instigated Adam and Eve to sin. Satan and his angels—also called demons or unclean spirits—provoke evil, injure, destroy, and seek to thwart God's purposes. Their destiny is the lake of fire (Matt. 25:41; Rev. 19:20; 20:10). The Greek Old Testament uses the word "demon" to refer to pagan deities (Deut. 32:17; Ps. 106:37; cf. 1 Cor. 10:20–21; Rev. 9:20) or worthless idols (Ps. 96:5), perhaps implying that Satan energizes all false gods. In the New Testament, most references to demonic activity occur in the Gospels in connection with Jesus's ministry. The New Testament writers considered the demons to be personal agents who could take up residence within people (Luke 4:33; Acts 16:16)—and could be cast out. Jesus's healings often involve exorcising demons (Matt. 9:23; Mark 1:23–28; 6:13; Luke 8:2), and he passed on to his disciples this authority (Matt. 10:8; Acts 5:16; 16:18). Paul warned his churches against the powers of the fallen spirit world—rulers, authorities, powers, lordships, and thrones (Rom. 8:38; Eph. 1:21; 6:12; Col. 1:16). Only in Christ can Christians achieve victory over these demonic forces of evil.

The unique Son is superior to angels (1:5–14)

Hebrews argues for Jesus's superiority to the angels using a string of seven Old Testament quotations. Both Psalm 2:7 and 2 Samuel 7:14 assert that Jesus, the Son, has a unique relationship to the Father (1:5). The second pair (Deut. 32:43; Ps. 104:4) describes how the angels serve the Son in their ministry (1:6–7). Psalms 45:6–7 and 102:25–27 reflect on Jesus eternal reign (1:8–12).

In conclusion, the preacher cites Psalm 110:1 to point to Jesus's exalted status as Messiah or Christ (1:13; cf. Mark 12:35–37). The Son is superior to the angels, who play an important but subservient role in God's kingdom (1:14).

Warning #1—the danger of rejecting the salvation provided by the Son (2:1–4)

In light of Christ's superiority to the angels, the preacher warns the listeners to pay attention to the Christian message so they will not drift away (2:1). If those who rejected the older revelation spoken through angels were punished, then those who reject God's salvation provided in Jesus and confirmed by the Holy Spirit cannot possibly escape judgment (2:2–4).

The Son's humiliation (2:5–9)

Jesus, the superior Son, was made lower than the angels for a time at his incarnation. The preacher quotes Psalm 8:4–6 to show that Jesus became a human being to accomplish salvation through his death before being crowned with glory and honor at his exaltation. Jesus's humble descent into our world is what accomplished our salvation and enabled the Son to identify with humanity (cf. Phil. 2:5–11).

Jesus, the author of salvation, made perfect through suffering (2:10–18)

Through his suffering, Jesus identifies with humanity, those he is not ashamed to call brothers and sisters (2:10–13). The divine Son shared in our flesh and blood (the incarnation) in order to die for our sins. Through his death, he destroyed the power of death, the devil's major weapon, and liberated human beings, who were enslaved by the fear of death (2:14–16). For this reason, Jesus was made like us in every way in order to become a "merciful and faithful high priest" and to "make atonement for the sins of the people" (2:17). Because Jesus experienced full humanity and "suffered when he was tempted," he knows how to help those who are being tempted (2:18).

Jesus's Faithfulness Calls Us to Faithfulness (3:1–4:13)

Jesus, the faithful Son, is superior to Moses, and those who believe in the Son will enter God's promised rest.

A faithful servant versus a faithful Son (3:1–6)

Moses has been faithful to God as a servant within his house, but Christ is the faithful Son who built or created the house (likely referring to the

✦ The author of Hebrews repeatedly shows how God's revelation of himself in Jesus is superior to earlier forms of revelation (e.g., angels, Moses, the Levitical priesthood, the sacrificial system).

people of God). Therefore, Christians should give utmost honor and obedience to Jesus (3:1, 6).

A double-edged sword.

Warning against faithlessness (3:7–19)

The preacher quotes Psalm 95:7–11 and then uses that passage to challenge the listeners to faithfulness. The people Moses led out of Egypt proved unfaithful to the Lord. They displayed hard, rebellious hearts and were not allowed to enter God's rest (3:7–11, 15–19). The preacher warns against sinful, unbelieving hearts that turn away from God (3:12), and he urges his listeners to encourage one another daily in order to persevere in faith and avoid the deceitfulness of sin (3:13–14).

Promised rest for the faithful (4:1–10)

While the people led by Moses failed to enter God's rest because of their unbelief, there remains a rest for the new people of God. Those who have believed in Jesus have entered that rest, and the listeners need to make sure they are among the faithful (4:1–3). In 4:3–11, the preacher develops the concept of rest. God himself rested on the seventh day of creation (4:3–4; Gen. 2:2). David also suggests in Psalm 95 that while those who followed Moses did not enter God's rest, the time for entering that rest is "today" (4:5–9). Therefore, "God's rest" refers to something more than entering the Promised Land; it is a spiritual reality in which we cease depending on our own work and begin to rely on God's work on our behalf (4:9–10).

Warning to enter God's rest (4:11–13)

Those who have heard the gospel and responded in faith have entered God's rest (4:3). But the preacher is concerned that some "have fallen short of it" (4:1), and he exhorts them to "make every effort to enter that rest" by holding fast to their confession of faith (4:11). At least three times in this section the listeners have heard the expression, "Today, if you hear his voice" (Ps. 95:7), and now the preacher issues a strong warning about the living, active, penetrating, judging, word or voice of God (4:12). Nothing is hidden from God, "to whom we must give account" (4:13).

The Superiority of Jesus's Priesthood and Ministry (4:14–10:25)

In contrast to the Levitical priests who are sinful and limited, Jesus, a high priest according to the order of Melchizedek, has a permanent, eternal

✦ In addition to words of comfort and encouragement, Hebrews is full of words of warning and challenge.

ministry of delivering people from sin. His priesthood and ministry are superior to the priests and ministry of the old covenant. Therefore, we should draw near to Jesus and persevere in faith.

Drawing near to Jesus, our great high priest (4:14–16)

Here the entire sermon is summarized. Because Jesus, our great high priest, has been exalted, we should hold firmly to our faith in him (4:14). Also, because he became a human being, he can sympathize with our weaknesses, having been tempted as we are, yet remaining without sin (4:15). In other words, Jesus understands our human situation, but he has risen above it to reign on the throne of grace. Therefore, we may draw near to his throne with confidence "so that we may receive mercy and find grace to help us in our time of need" (4:16).

Christ's qualifications for the high priesthood (5:1–10)

High priests such as Aaron are appointed by God to represent the people before God and to offer sacrifices for sins (5:1, 4). Since the high priests themselves are subject to weakness, they can deal compassionately with people, but they must also offer sacrifices for their own sins (5:2–3). In 5:5–6, 10 we learn that Jesus was appointed by the Father as a permanent high priest, not according to the order of Aaron but according to the order of Melchizedek (Pss. 2:7; 110:4; see Heb. 7:1–28 for more detail on Melchizedek). His appointment involved the incarnation, during which he suffered greatly (e.g., his agony in Gethsemane and death on the cross) and came to understand what obedience involved (5:7–8). With his resurrection from the dead and exaltation (what the author means by "once made perfect"), he became the source of eternal salvation for all who follow him (5:9).

The problem of spiritual immaturity (5:11–6:3)

As happens so often in Hebrews, the preacher switches from explanation about God's plan of salvation in Christ to exhortation directed at the listeners. Now he admonishes the listeners for being slow to learn, seemingly stuck on the basics of the Christian faith (5:11–12). They are spiritual babies, needing milk rather than solid food (5:12–14). In 6:1–3, the preacher challenges them to move beyond the basics (e.g., repentance, faith, baptism, laying on of hands, resurrection of the dead, eternal judgment)—all elements that Christianity shared with Judaism—and build on this foundation what is distinctively Christian.

✦ We are able now to draw near to God because Jesus's priesthood on our behalf is eternal.

Warning Passages in Hebrews

George H. Guthrie

Throughout the book, Hebrews has two very distinct types of literature: exposition and exhortation. These alternate back and forth, weaving a tapestry of concepts and rhetorical tools used to call the reader of Hebrews to endure in following Christ. The expositional material focuses on the person and work of Christ, while the exhortation material uses various means to motivate readers of the book to respond positively to God's Word. Among the various tools the author uses to exhort his readers (e.g., promises and warnings, positive and negative examples), the warnings play a striking role, confronting readers with noticeably harsh language, calling them to turn away from a path that leads to the judgment of God.

There are five main warning passages in Hebrews: 2:1–4; 4:12–13; 6:4–8; 10:26–31; and 12:25–29. Each build on the broader theological teachings in the book, and each concerns the Word of God and God's judgment on those who do not respond well to God's Word. Three of these warnings (2:1–4; 10:26–31; and 12:25–29) are built around arguments "from lesser to greater" (called *a fortiori* arguments), which reason that if something is true in a lesser situation, it certainly is true in a greater situation and has greater implications. For instance, in 2:1–4 the "lesser" situation is the receiving of the Word of God, through angels, under the old covenant, and the "greater" situation is the hearing of the word of the gospel. The author reasons, if under the old covenant those who rejected God's Word delivered through angels were punished, how much greater punishment is deserved by those who reject the word of the gospel given by God's superior Son?

Although we often read Hebrews 4:12–13 positively as a melodious reflection on the power of God's Word, this warning functions to echo the treatment of Psalm 95, quoted in Hebrews 3:7–11. Those who do not listen to God's voice experience God's Word as a word of judgment.

Throughout the history of the church, Hebrews 6:4–8 has prompted the spilling of much ink in discussion of the theological issue of apostasy. Here the author uses "wilderness wandering" language (6:4–6), language of crucifixion (6:6), and agricultural imagery (6:7–8) to describe those in his own era who have turned their backs on Christ and the church. Similarly harsh language occurs in 10:26–31, where, again using an argument from lesser to greater, the author describes those who reject Christ as having trampled him underfoot, as treating his blood as unworthy of sacrifice, and as having insulted the Spirit of grace. Finally, in 12:25–29, the author again warns that God, who speaks from heaven, must not be rejected, for, as prophesied in Haggai 2:6, the day is coming when God will shake the heavens and the earth. In other words, a day of reckoning approaches.

With these five warning passages of Hebrews, the author does much more than instruct; he seeks to motivate, to challenge his audience to endure in following Jesus.

Warning against falling away and encouragement to endure (6:4–12)

Here we come to one of the most controversial sections in the book of Hebrews, but it must be read in context. In 6:4–8, the preacher issues a strong warning meant to strike fear in the hearts of the listeners. Those who appear to be genuine believers (i.e., enlightened, tasted of the heavenly gift, shared in the Holy Spirit, tasted of God's word and power) and then renounce

A stone anchor.

Christ willfully and finally ("fall away" or apostatize) cannot be brought back again because they have rejected Christ, the only provider of salvation. Some say this refers to loss of reward, but its opposite is "salvation" in 6:9. Others claim this refers to loss of salvation, and perhaps so, but it is a once-for-all loss with no possibility of repentance. Some prefer to see this as a hypothetical warning, but its urgency argues for more. Perhaps it is best to opt for a divine-human perspective on the issue. We know our own hearts imperfectly and must demonstrate our profession outwardly through perseverance under pressure. God knows our hearts perfectly, and he promises to keep and protect his own to eternity (John 6:39–40; 10:27–29; Rom. 11:29; Phil. 1:6; 1 Pet. 1:5; 1 John 2:1). True believers will persevere, and perseverance serves as evidence of a genuine Christian faith. Warnings play the important role of shaking believers out of their apathy and presumption and putting them back on track. But we also need encouragement and assurance, and the preacher provides such in 6:9–12. He is confident that 6:4–8 does not apply to his listeners (6:9). God knows how their lives of love have demonstrated their faith (6:10). The preacher encourages them to remain diligent—not to become lazy but to imitate those who endured to the end in order to make their hope sure (6:11–12). Believers need both warning and assurance, both confrontation and comfort in order to persevere faithfully.

God's promise is the basis of our hope (6:13–20)

The preacher now begins moving back toward a fuller explanation that Christ is a high priest forever in the order of Melchizedek (6:20; 7:1–28). In this transition, he reminds his listeners that God made his promise to Abraham and his heirs contingent on God's own character and unchanging nature (6:13–18). As a result, this hope anchors our souls, which can rest firm and secure in God's faithfulness as revealed in the work of Jesus, our high priest forever (6:18–20).

✝ God's unchanging character and his faithful Word make our hope solid and secure.

The superior order of Melchizedek's priesthood (7:1–10)

Now the preacher returns to the topic of Melchizedek's priesthood that he first introduced in 5:1–10. All we know about this mysterious figure can be found in Genesis 14:17–20.

The preacher's main point is that Melchizedek's priesthood is superior to the Levitical priesthood, represented by Aaron. We know this because Genesis 14 tells us Melchizedek received a tenth of what Abraham had won in battle and then blessed Abraham in return (6:4–10). The "lesser" (Abraham) was blessed by the "greater" (Melchizedek). In addition, Melchizedek's priesthood is superior because it is eternal (6:1–3). So Christ's priestly line (founded by Melchizedek) is superior to the priesthood of the Levites (founded by Abraham).

The superiority of Jesus's priesthood (7:11–28)

The preacher notes the imperfections of the Levitical priesthood and how the better hope rooted in Jesus's eternal priesthood replaces the former regulations that were weak and useless (7:11–19). Jesus, who became a priest with an oath from God, guarantees a better covenant (7:20–22; Ps. 110:4). And what's more, Jesus's priesthood is permanent because he lives forever, and can save people completely because he always lives to intercede for them (7:23–25). This is the kind of high priest we need: one who is holy, sinless, and exalted, and who doesn't need to atone for his own sins (7:26–27). Whereas other high priests are ultimately helpless to deliver people from sin, Jesus's obedience, atoning death, and glorious resurrection/exaltation into God's presence (7:28) have made him forever perfect for his role as high priest.

The superior ministry of Jesus, our heavenly high priest (8:1–6)

Jesus has been exalted to the throne of God and now serves as high priest in the true tabernacle, the very presence of God (8:1–2). Earthly high priests served in the tabernacle built by Moses, but Jesus has a superior ministry of a superior covenant, serving as our heavenly high priest.

The superiority of the new covenant (8:7–13)

If the first covenant was sufficient, there would be no need for a "new" covenant. But, as Jeremiah 31:31–34 attests (8:7–12), God established a new covenant with his people that made the first covenant obsolete (8:7, 13).

Old covenant worship (9:1–10)

In order to contrast Christ's sacrifice with worship under the old covenant, the old system must be properly explained. In 9:1–5, the preacher

The Jewish High Priest

George H. Guthrie

Hebrews makes much of "high priest" imagery (Heb. 2:17; 3:1; 4:14–15; 5:1, 5, 10; 6:20; 7:26–8:1; 8:3; 9:7, 11, 25; 13:11) and is the only New Testament book to speak of Christ as "high priest."

In the Old Testament, the high priest is referred to variously as "the priest" (Exod. 31:10), the "chief priest" (2 Chron. 26:20), the "anointed priest" (Lev. 4:3), or "the high priest" (Lev. 21:10). Aaron was the first high priest, and his descendants were to serve as his successors (Exod. 29:29–30). The high priest was to be especially holy, as shown by his consecration to his position and his special garments, which included a turban inscribed with "Holy to the Lord" (Exod. 28:36), a blue, richly embroidered robe, and an ephod with its jewel-adorned breastplate (Exod. 29:1–37; Lev. 6:19–22; 8:5–35). The twelve jewels of the breastplate represented the twelve tribes, symbolizing the high priest as the representative of the people of God.

Hebrews capitalizes on the image of high priest in a number of ways. The author summarizes the role of the high priest in 5:1–4, and this lays the foundation for the author's reflections on Jesus as high priest. First, the high priest, taken from "among men," had a special solidarity with people (5:1). Exodus 28:1 says Aaron was brought to Moses "from among the Israelites," and the author of Hebrews might have this passage in mind. So too Jesus is a merciful high priest who sympathizes with people (Heb. 2:17; 4:15).

Second, although the high priest had certain responsibilities in common with priests in general (Heb. 5:1), the high priest alone offered the sacrifice on the Day of Atonement (Exod. 29:1–46; Lev. 16:1–25), and he alone could go into the Holy of Holies to offer that sacrifice. The Day of Atonement sacrifice involved two goats and a ram. One of the goats was offered as a sin offering; the other was the "scapegoat," which the high priest sent into the desert, having laid hands on its head and confessing the sins of the people (Lev. 16:15, 20–22). This backdrop points to the main way Hebrews appropriates the high priest imagery. Yet Christ's sacrifice is superior in three ways: his blood was shed, rather than the blood of animals; Jesus entered the heavenly holy place rather than the earthly tabernacle; and Jesus's sacrifice, rather than being made annually, was made once for all time (Heb. 9:1–10:18).

Third, on the Day of Atonement the high priest also had to offer a sacrifice for himself and his household prior to offering the sacrifice for the people (5:3; Lev. 16:11). This sacrifice dealt with the high priest's own weakness (5:2), weakness that enabled him to "deal gently with those who are ignorant and are going astray" (5:2). By contrast, Christ needs no such sacrifice, since he is without sin (Heb. 4:15; 7:26–28).

A fourth general principle of high priesthood in Hebrews 5:1–4 concerns how one becomes a high priest. High priests didn't enlist, but rather were appointed by God (5:1, 4; Exod. 28:1; Lev. 8:1; Num. 16:5). Thus the foundation for the position of high priest rests in the authority of God. This is true of Jesus (5:4–6), but Jesus's appointment was based not on heredity (he was not from the tribe of Levi), but rather on God's oath, found in Psalms 110:4: "You are a priest forever according to the order of Melchizedek." Also, because of his indestructible life, Jesus serves as a high priest eternally (Heb. 7:11–25).

briefly introduces how the earthly sanctuary was set up for worship. Then in 9:6–10, he explains how the priests would carry out the worship rituals in that sanctuary. Regularly they would offer sacrifices for sins, but once a year the high priest would enter the Most Holy Place with a blood sacrifice for

✛ Jesus's sacrifice on which the new covenant is based is superior to the old covenant sacrifices because he spilled his own blood, because he entered into the heavenly temple, and because it lasts forever.

his own sins and those of the people (9:6–7). But those gifts and sacrifices were not able to "clear the conscience of the worshiper," being only external regulations in place until the time of the new order (9:8–10).

The superiority of Jesus's offering for sin (9:11–28)

Now the preacher shows how the Son's sacrifice is superior to the sacrifices offered by the priests under the old covenant. Christ appeared first to die on the cross for our sins (9:12), then in heaven to intercede for us in God's presence (9:24), and he will appear again to bring salvation to those who long for his return (9:28). Jesus's once-for-all sacrifice for sin is superior to the old covenant sacrifices in several ways. First, Jesus used his own blood rather than animal blood for the sacrifice (9:11–22). He gave his own life (i.e., shed his own blood) to provide cleansing for our consciences and forgiveness of our sins (9:14–15). Both covenants were established through the shedding of blood, since "without the shedding of blood there is no forgiveness" (9:22). The wages of sin means our death, and the price of forgiveness called for his life. The second reason Jesus's sacrifice is superior is that his sacrifice led him beyond the earthly tabernacle into the very presence of God himself, the heavenly holy of holies (9:23–24). Third, Jesus's sacrifice is superior because it lasts forever (9:25–28). Whereas the high priest would enter the Most Holy Place every year to make atonement, Christ sacrificed himself once for all in order to take away sins.

Christ's perfect sacrifice (10:1–18)

The law and the sacrificial system it provides for relating to God are limited and ineffective in dealing with sin (10:1–2). It is impossible for the blood of animals to take away sins and cleanse the human heart

A model of the tabernacle described in the Old Testament.

(10:3–4). The preacher then quotes Psalm 40:6–8 to explain that Christ came to obey the Father and offer himself as the ultimate sacrifice for sin (10:5–10). As a result, Christ's perfect sacrifice has displaced the old sacrificial system. Whereas the priests would daily offer sacrifices that could never remove sins, the once-for-all sacrifice of Christ "made perfect forever those who are being made holy" (10:4, 11). Now, Jesus has sat down at the right hand of God, waiting for his enemies to be made his footstool (10:12–13). Quoting Jeremiah 31:33–34, the preacher reminds the listeners that God had predicted a new covenant, when he would put his laws in our hearts and write them on our minds, when he would remember our sins no more (10:15–17). Now that Christ, the perfect high priest, has offered the perfect sacrifice that brings full and complete forgiveness, there is no need for any additional sacrifice for sin (10:18). Praise be to God!

We have a great high priest (10:19–25)

Since 4:14–16, the preacher has been explaining Jesus's priesthood and perfect ministry. Now in 10:19–25, he draws everything together and prepares for the strong exhortations that follow. The present section sums up what Christ has accomplished in 10:19–21: the sacrifice of Christ, our great high priest, has opened a way for us to approach God. As a result, we should (1) "draw near to God" with confident faith and a clean heart (10:22); (2) "hold unswervingly to the hope we profess" because of God's faithfulness (10:23); (3) consider "how we may spur one another on toward love and good deeds" (10:24); and (4) "not give up meeting together, . . . but encourage one another" (10:25).

Call to Persevere in the Journey of Faith (10:26–12:29)

Following the masterful explanation of Christ's person and work, the preacher challenges the listeners to persevere by issuing warnings, offering examples to imitate, providing helpful analogies, and calling for a response of obedience and worship.

Warning against deliberate rejection of the gospel (10:26–39)

The preacher sternly warns his readers that if they deliberately and repeatedly reject the gospel of Jesus Christ, then no other sacrifice for sins remains (10:26). With no place left to turn, all that is left is a fearful expectation of God's terrifying judgment (10:27). If those who rejected the old covenant were judged, how much more severely will God judge those who trample his Son, dismiss his sacrifice on the cross, and insult the Spirit of

✚ Our obedience and perseverance are always in response to the finished work of Christ.

grace (10:28–29)? For the intentionally rebellious, it will be a "dreadful thing to fall into the hands of the living God" (10:30–31). As he did after the harsh warning in 6:4–8, the preacher now reminds the listeners of their past faithfulness (10:32–34) before encouraging them to stay the course (10:35–39). They gained confidence by enduring persecutions in the past. Now they need to persevere, knowing that God will reward their faithfulness in the end. The preacher assures them that he believes they are among those "who believe and are saved" (10:39).

Imitate the faith of the faithful (11:1–40)

The starting blocks and the arena for foot races in Delphi, Greece.

After warning and encouraging the listeners, the preacher provides an extensive list of examples for them to follow in their faith journey. "Faith," a word repeated throughout the passage, is the firm confidence (NIV: "being sure") about things hoped for and the certainty of what is unseen (11:1). Faith holds on to God's promises, even when they are out of sight or far into the future. Throughout this famous "hall of faith" chapter, the author follows a similar pattern: the expression "by faith," the name of the example, what they did to demonstrate faith, and the positive result. He names people from God's creation of the world to the time of Joshua, focusing especially on Abraham, Sarah, and Moses as worthy examples (11:2–31). He pauses briefly in 11:13–16 to highlight that the faithful don't always receive what is promised in this life. The faithful are "aliens and strangers on earth" (11:13). They don't belong in this world. They are on a journey to the heavenly country, where they are registered as full-fledged citizens. The preacher then adds a second set of examples, moving from the period of the judges toward the first century AD (11:32–38). Here he focuses on the unbelievable accomplishments and trials experienced by

✦ The original readers were encouraged to look to the great multitude of witnesses mentioned in Hebrews 11 as examples of people who trusted God even in the face of persecution.

people of faith. "The world was not worthy" of such people, he observes (11:38). Verses 39–40 connect the situation of these ancient believers with the present situation, which the preacher focuses on in Hebrews 12.

The call to endure (12:1–17)

Because of all the examples of faith mentioned in the previous chapter ("cloud of witnesses" meaning we look to them as witnesses to God's faithfulness, rather than them peering down on us from heaven), believers should get rid of every unnecessary hindrance and run the endurance race set before them (12:1). The Christian life is more like a marathon than a sprint. We should fix our eyes on Jesus, the pioneer and perfecter of our faith, as our ultimate example of perseverance (12:2). He endured the shame of the cross because of his firm confidence in the joy of future resurrection and exaltation. As these listeners considered the example of Jesus, they would also be reminded that they had not yet persevered to the point of martyrdom (12:3–4). In 12:5–11, the metaphor of a distance runner gives way to the analogy of a parent disciplining a child. Commenting on Proverbs 3:11–12, the preacher reminds believers that the Lord disciplines his children because he loves them. They should endure hardship in submission to the Lord's discipline, knowing that what is painful and unpleasant in the short run will ultimately produce a harvest of righteousness and peace. In 12:14–17, believers are admonished to live peacefully in community, be holy, rely on the grace of God (in contrast to the example of Esau), let go of bitterness, and avoid sexual immorality. Some of these problems may have been caused by the Christian community's response to people who had abandoned the faith and community.

The proper response of obedience and worship (12:18–29)

Mount Sinai represents the old covenant with its fire, darkness, gloom, and fear of God's judgment (12:18–21). In contrast stands Mount Zion, which represents the new covenant with its angelic worship, community of the faithful (whether on earth or in heaven), the God of justice, and Jesus, the mediator of the new covenant by his shed blood (12:22–24). Therefore, believers should listen to and obey the voice of God (12:25). Since those who rejected God's warnings from Mount Sinai were not spared judgment, those who reject God's heavenly warning will certainly not escape judgment (12:25–27). God will shake the entire cosmos, and only those who belong to the unshakable kingdom of God will survive (12:27–28). Our response to our holy, all-consuming God should be gratitude, reverence, and awe (12:28–29).

✦ Worship is linked to listening to and obeying the Word of God.

Practical Exhortations (13:1–19)

The preacher concludes his sermon with a practical teaching about how believers should live. First, he exhorts them to love one another, exercise hospitality, minister to those in prison and to those who have been mistreated, honor marriage, avoid sexual immorality, steer clear of the love of money, and be content with the Lord's provision (13:1–6). Second, he urges them to obey, respect, and imitate their leaders, especially the unchanging Lord Jesus, whom they serve (13:7–8, 17). Third, he challenges them to reject false teaching, which attempts to replace the sacrifice of Christ, and instead to offer the proper Christian sacrifices of gratitude, praise, service, and generosity (13:9–16). And finally, he asks for prayer (13:18–19).

A statue of an athlete tying a victor's ribbon around his head.

Closing (13:20–25)

The "word of exhortation" or sermon (13:22) closes with a prayer that the God of peace, who raised Jesus from the dead, would equip believers to do his will and would work in their lives (13:20–21). The preacher includes a few personal remarks and greetings (13:23–24) before closing with a pronouncement of grace (13:25).

So What? Applying Hebrews Today

Jesus's particular claim to be the divine-human Savior of the world will always draw opposition. Christians are, by definition, people who follow Jesus Christ. This means Christians will encounter persecution and may be tempted to lapse into a

✚ Hebrews reminds us that the Christian life is like a long-distance race with plenty of obstacles along the way. As Jesus himself said, "No servant is greater than his master. If they persecuted me, they will persecute you also" (John 15:20).

safer form of religion in order to avoid trouble. Hebrews warns us not to go down that path. Those who turn their back on Jesus have no hope of salvation. This sermon both warns and encourages. For the presumptuous and untested who are drifting toward an easier option, the warnings in Hebrews should shake them awake from their spiritual lethargy. For the conscientious believers who are struggling to run the distance race, the encouragement and comfort should bring renewed hope. Throughout the book, the preacher reminds believers to listen to and heed God's word. Are we opening the Scriptures on a consistent basis to listen to the Lord? It is very difficult for believers to mature in their faith apart from a consistent habit of taking in the Word of God. In addition, Hebrews reminds us that previous obedience does not guarantee present and future obedience. While we may have experienced spiritual victories in the past, our race is a marathon, not a sprint, and we are called to persevere. We persevere by fixing our eyes on Jesus, by imitating godly examples, by listening to God's Word, by staying connected to the body of Christ, and by allowing the Spirit of God to lead us down the long road. But take courage, we are journeying toward a heavenly city, whose architect and builder is God (11:10, 16; 13:14).

Our Favorite Verses in Hebrews

Therefore, since we are surrounded by such a great cloud of witnesses, let us throw off everything that hinders and the sin that so easily entangles, and let us run with perseverance the race marked out for us. Let us fix our eyes on Jesus, the author and perfecter of our faith, who for the joy set before him endured the cross, scorning its shame, and sat down at the right hand of the throne of God. Consider him who endured such opposition from sinful men, so that you will not grow weary and lose heart. (12:1–3)

In the model of first-century Jerusalem, the traditional location of Golgotha was outside the second wall of the city.

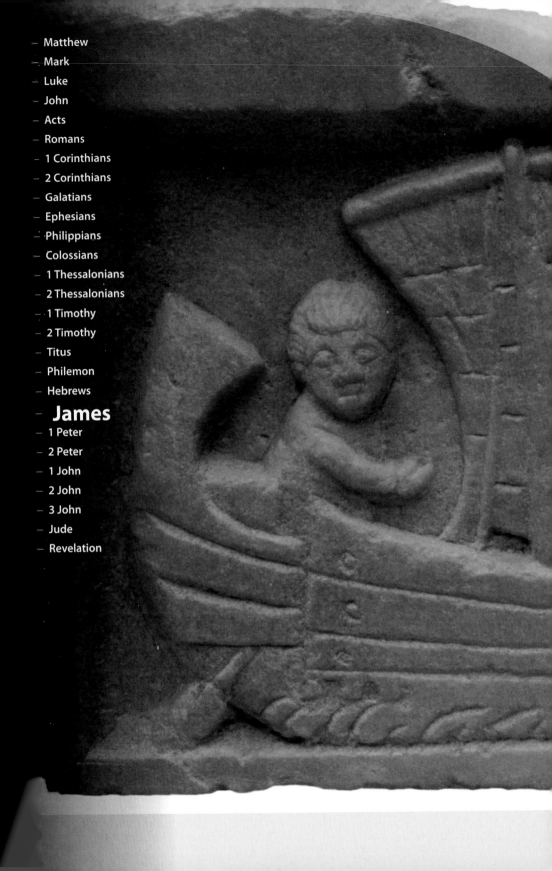

James

True Faith Works

Many lives have been profoundly changed through an encounter with the biblical doctrine of justification by faith, usually explained in one of Paul's letters. As crucial as this important truth is to the Christian faith, James calls our attention to another important dimension of the faith: the good works that flow out of genuine faith. Saving faith will eventually result in a life changed in tangible ways, such as how we spend money, what we say about other people, and how we face trials.

Who Wrote James?

The author identifies himself as "James, a servant of God and of the Lord Jesus Christ" (1:1). There are four men named James mentioned in the New Testament. James the apostle, the brother of John and son of Zebedee (Mark 1:19; 5:37; 9:2; 10:35), was put to death by Herod Agrippa I in about AD 44 (Acts 12:2). The early date of his martyrdom argues against identifying him as the author. Then there is James, the son of Alphaeus and one of the twelve (Mark 3:18), and James, the father of

Judas (Luke 6:16; Acts 1:13), both considered too obscure to have written the letter. Early church tradition strongly suggests the letter was written by James, the half-brother of Jesus and leader in the Jerusalem church (Matt. 13:55; Mark 6:3; Acts 1:14; 12:17; 15:13–21; 21:18; 1 Cor. 9:5; 15:7; Gal. 1:19; 2:9). He became a believer after the resurrection of Jesus and was visited individually by the risen Lord (1 Cor. 15:7). The historian Josephus tells us James was stoned to death for his commitment to Christ in AD 62 (Josephus, *Ant.* 20.9.1).

Who Is James's Audience?

The letter is addressed to the "twelve tribes scattered among the nations" (1:1). Most likely this refers to Jewish Christians living outside Palestine but still in an agricultural setting (5:1–7). Some (or most) of these Christians may have come from the church in Jerusalem that was scattered after the persecution associated with Stephen's death (Acts 8:1; 11:19).

The letter must have been written prior to James's death in AD 62, and many scholars believe it to have been written in the late 40s AD, prior to the Jerusalem Council in AD 49, and before Paul's letters had circulated widely. If this is the case, James is the earliest New Testament letter.

What Is at the Heart of James?

James offers practical advice for living out the Christian faith in everyday life. He is extremely concerned with three key themes: trials and temptations, wisdom (especially as it relates to our speech), and riches and poverty.*

- Greetings (1:1)
- Three Key Themes (1:2–11)
- Three Themes Repeated (1:12–27)
- Three Themes Explained (2:1–5:18)
- Letter Closing (5:19–20)

* The outline that follows is adapted from the commentary on James by Peter Davids and modified by Craig Blomberg in *From Pentecost to Patmos: An Introduction to Acts through Revelation* (Nashville: B&H, 2006), 392.

✝ James is likely the earliest New Testament letter and draws heavily on the teachings of Jesus, especially those contained in his Sermon on the Mount.

What Makes James Interesting and Unique?

- There are many parallels between James and the teachings of Jesus, especially the Sermon on the Mount (Matthew 5–7).
- James was most likely written by the half-brother of Jesus, who became a believer after Jesus's resurrection.
- Although James and Paul appear to contradict each other on the issue of faith and works (see James 2:24 and Gal. 2:15–16), further study reveals that they are addressing different issues. (See sidebar on this topic below.)
- James is fond of commands. In the 108 verses of James, we find more than fifty commands.

What Is the Message of James?

Greetings (1:1)

James identifies himself not as an apostle but as a "servant" (or slave) of God and of the Lord Jesus Christ. He sends greetings to the "twelve tribes scattered among the nations."

Three Key Themes (1:2–11)

Encountering trials (1:2–4)

James urges his readers to "consider it pure joy" when they encounter various kinds of trials, perhaps especially economic and social difficulties (1:2). They can respond with joy or deep contentment (versus an emotional happiness) because they know God is using the trials to produce endurance and, over time, to make them mature and complete (1:3–4).

Ancient mirrors.

✝ Although Paul faced constant opposition from the Jews in his gentile mission, there were many Jewish Christians who were faithful to the Lord Jesus.

James   927

James	Matthew
1:2	5:11–12
1:4	5:48
1:5	7:7
1:17	7:11
1:20	5:22
1:22	7:24
1:23	7:26
2:5	5:3, 5
2:10	5:19
2:11	5:21–22
2:13	5:7
2:15	6:24
3:12	7:16
3:18	5:9
4:2	7:7
4:3	7:7–8
4:4	6:24
4:11–12	7:1
4:13–14	6:34
5:2	6:19–20
5:9	5:22; 7:1
5:10	5:11–12
5:12	5:34–37

Wisdom (1:5–8)

If we need wisdom (perhaps to handle various trials), we should ask God, trusting in his kind and generous character, and he will give us wisdom (1:5). If we doubt, however, we can be compared to a storm-tossed wave of the sea (1:6). Such an unstable, "double-minded" (lit. "double-souled") person shouldn't expect to receive anything from the Lord (1:7–8). The key to godly wisdom has always been a healthy fear of or trust in the Lord (cf. Prov. 9:10).

Riches and poverty (1:9–11)

Believers who find themselves in humble or humiliating financial circumstances can always put their confidence in their high standing with the Lord (1:9). The wealthy believer should remember the fleeting nature of his wealth and put his confidence in his relationship with God (1:10–11).

Three Themes Repeated (1:12–27)

Trials and temptations (1:12–18)

The Greek word for "trial" (*peirasmos*) can also mean "temptation." Those who persevere under trials will be blessed by God with the promised "crown of life," which is eternal life (1:12). Although God allows trials, he cannot be tempted by evil and doesn't tempt anyone (1:13). When put under pressure by trials, some people persevere in faith, while others turn to sinful solutions in an attempt to cope. But sinful remedies never make things better; they make things only worse as desire leads to sin, which in turn results in spiritual death (1:14–15). Ultimately, people are accountable for how they respond in trying times. In any case, we can't blame God, who consistently gives good and perfect gifts to his children (1:16–18).

Wisdom in our speech (1:19–26)

Wisdom leads believers to be "quick to listen, slow to speak and slow to become angry" (1:19). Human anger doesn't produce the kind of life God desires (1:20). A righteous life comes about as people take in the saving gospel ("the word planted in you") and rid their lives of moral filth and evil

✦ Over and over James emphasizes speech as a true indicator of the condition of a person's heart (James 1:19–26; 2:12; 3:1–12; 4:11–12, 13–17; 5:9, 12, 16).

(1:21). Being "quick to listen" involves more than physical hearing; it also includes obedience to the "perfect law that gives freedom," that is, the gospel (1:22–25). Being "slow to speak" involves keeping a "tight rein on [one's] tongue" and demonstrates the validity of a person's religion (1:26).

The proper use of possessions (1:27)

Along with keeping ourselves morally pure, believers should use their possessions to take care of the needy (e.g., orphans and widows). The Bible connects two important realities that are often separated: paying close attention to our own spiritual formation and meeting people's basic needs.

Three Themes Explained (2:1–5:18)

Riches and poverty (2:1–26)

James condemns the favoritism some believers are showing toward the rich while discriminating against the poor (2:1–4). He condemns favoritism because many who are rich in faith and who love the Lord come from the lower classes (2:5). These believers should not be despised or defrauded by the wealthy, the very ones who overpower them in court and slander the name of Christ (2:6–7). In addition, the law condemns favoritism, and those who show favoritism are actually lawbreakers (2:8–11). Believers should speak and act as those who will be judged by "the law that gives freedom" (i.e., the Old Testament as filtered through the teachings of Jesus and the apostles). Those who show mercy to the poor will be shown mercy at the judgment, for "mercy triumphs over judgment" (2:12–13). How should one show mercy to the poor? By giving generously to meet their needs, as James explains in 2:14–26. He condemns a "faith" that has no works or deeds— for example, that does not lead to generous giving to meet basic needs (2:14–17). These "believers"

✚ Although the Christian faith removed social obstacles to fellowship such as wealth, believers continued to struggle with showing favoritism to the wealthy and neglecting the poor (e.g., James 1:9–11; 2:1–26; 4:1–3; 5:1–6).

Faith and Works in James 2:24 and Galatians 2:15–16

On the surface, these two passages seem to contradict one another:

> James 2:24—"You see that a person is justified by what he does and not by faith alone."

> Galatians 2:15–16—"We who are Jews by birth and not 'Gentile sinners' know that a man is not justified by observing the law, but by faith in Jesus Christ. So we, too, have put our faith in Christ Jesus that we may be justified by faith in Christ and not by observing the law, because by observing the law no one will be justified."

We begin to resolve the apparent contradiction by understanding the situation addressed by the two authors. James and Paul are fighting different problems. James is fighting a "head-knowledge-only" view of faith that neglects works. As a result, he needs to stress the importance of doing works. Paul, however, is fighting against the teaching that works of law are necessary to be a true member of the people of God. Paul needs to emphasize the truth that people are justified by grace through faith in Jesus Christ.

Next, we should notice how James and Paul define faith. James attacks a "faith" that is dead (James 2:17, 26), demonic (2:19), and useless (2:20). His main point is that true faith is more than mere intellectual assent; true faith works! Paul certainly does not teach that "faith" is only verbal profession (cf. Rom. 1:5; Eph. 2:8–10). Notice also that both Paul and James use the same person—Abraham—to illustrate what they mean by true faith (Gal. 3:6–29; James 2:21–24).

We should also look closely at the two passages in question. In Galatians 2, Paul is referring to "works" that precede conversion. No one can earn salvation; it is a gift of grace. In contrast, James is referring to works that follow conversion. One who is truly saved will act like it. This sounds a lot like Paul's emphasis in his letter to Titus.

The two passages are not really contradictory, but only apparently contradictory. Paul and James are like soldiers in the same army standing back to back fighting a common enemy coming from different directions. The one true gospel is given by God's grace *and* results in our good works. When we tamper with either grace or works, we tamper with the one true gospel.

---

claim to have faith, but they refuse to help a fellow believer who needs food and clothing. James concludes that such "faith" is dead (2:17). Some may object, "Can't we have faith without works?" James emphatically says, "No" (2:18). A "workless faith" is also demonic (2:19) and useless (2:20). Both Abraham and Rahab demonstrated their faith (and their righteous standing before God) through their works (2:21–25). As the human body without the spirit is dead, so faith without actions is dead (2:26).

Wisdom demonstrated through actions (3:1–4:17)

This central section of the letter deals with wisdom, specifically how wisdom is demonstrated through our speech (or the "tongue"). James warns

✚ Both Paul and James use Abraham as an example of a person who lived by genuine faith in God's promises.

people against presuming to be teachers, since that role relates directly to speech and carries both great responsibility and additional accountability (3:1–2). In 3:3–6, James provides three illustrations of the power of the tongue: bits that control horses, rudders that control ships, and sparks that start forest fires. Our speech has great potential for bringing good or causing evil. Unlike the animal kingdom, our speech is untamable (3:7–8), and unlike nature, our speech is often inconsistent, as we praise God one minute and curse people made in his image the next (3:9–12). Wisdom is demonstrated through actions (3:13).

Worldly wisdom, as portrayed in 3:14–16, is contrasted with heavenly wisdom, described in 3:17–18. Worldly wisdom with its envy and selfishness leads to fights and quarrels within the church (4:1–2). Such friendship with the world is hatred toward God because God's Spirit longs to have a strong and healthy relationship with his children (4:4–5). God's people need to communicate with him in prayer, asking him to meet their needs but asking with right motives (4:2–3). More than anything, true prayer involves a genuine turning away from sin and a sincere and humble submission to God, who promises to come near to us and give us grace (4:6–10). As we humble ourselves before God, the only true Lawgiver and Judge, we will see the evil of slandering one another—that we are judging rather than loving our neighbor (4:11–12). One final example of wisdom relates to planning. Worldly wisdom boasts about future plans that leave no room for God's will, while godly wisdom makes tentative plans with an openness to the Lord changing our plans at any time (4:13–17).

Trials and temptations (5:1–18)

The rich people who have brought hardship and trials upon innocent, hardworking poor people will be severely judged by God (5:1–6). Believers who are being put through such trials shouldn't turn on one another in anger (certainly a tempting reaction) but should stand firm and wait patiently on the Lord's return (5:7–9). There are plenty of encouraging examples of patience in the face of suffering, such as Job and the prophets (5:10–11). The Lord is faithful, and they can count on him to respond with compassion and mercy (5:11). In any case, they shouldn't try to talk their way out of the trial by swearing an oath (5:12). In 5:13–18, James instructs those who are facing trials related to physical sickness to pray (notice how often words for prayer are repeated). Prayer is to be a community affair (e.g., calling the elders, confessing sins to one another) and is sometimes connected not only to healing but also to repentance and forgiveness (5:15–16). James reminds his readers that the prayer of a righteous person is "powerful and effective" (5:16) and should be the Christian's primary response to trials.

✚ Rather than preparing people to be removed from persecution and suffering, early Christian leaders prepared believers to endure suffering faithfully (e.g., James 1:2–8, 12; 5:7–11).

Letter Closing (5:19–20)

In a letter dealing with trials and temptations, worldly versus godly wisdom, and poverty and riches, no doubt some members of the congregation had wandered from the truth and needed help. James commends those who do the painstaking work of restoring a fellow believer to spiritual health. As Proverbs 10:12 says, "love covers over all wrongs" (5:20; 1 Pet. 4:8).

So What? Applying James Today

Life is not always fair. Many of the trials mentioned by James were caused by rich, powerful people oppressing poor, vulnerable people. While condemning the favoritism and calling for justice, James also encourages us to face trials with the right attitude—a peaceful confidence that God can use trials to make us more like Jesus. He warns us not to look for relief from sinful painkillers; they lead only to spiritual death. James calls us to reject worldly wisdom and exercise godly wisdom, especially in how we speak.

An ancient decorated horse bit.

Our speech has tremendous potential for good or evil, for tearing down or building up. Being "quick to listen" and "slow to speak" gives us time to consider which purpose our words will serve. James reminds us that biblical faith involves more than assenting to certain doctrines; genuine faith also expresses itself in actions or deeds. In other words, true faith works! One of the main ways our faith should work is by using our possessions to meet the practical needs of others. How dare we claim to have biblical, saving faith and refuse to help fellow believers who are in need? A living faith is one that attends to our own spiritual formation and helps the needy in practical ways, all in the name of Jesus.

Our Favorite Verses in James

Consider it pure joy, my brothers, whenever you face trials of many kinds, because you know that the testing of your faith develops perseverance. Perseverance must finish its work so that you may be mature and complete, not lacking anything. (1:2–4)

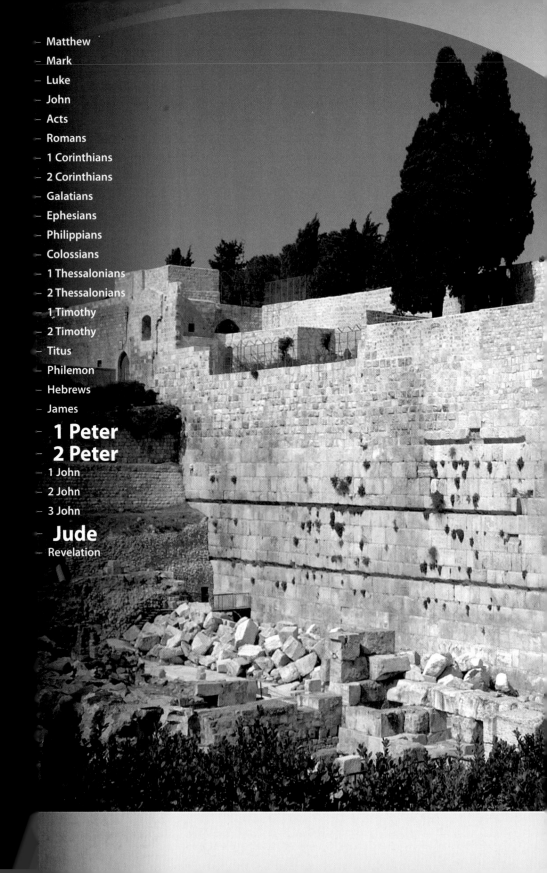

1 Peter

Stand Firm in the Face of Suffering

2 Peter

Grow in the Knowledge of Christ

Jude

Contend for the Faith

The early church struggled with threats from both the outside (persecution) and the inside (false teaching). First Peter was written to help Christians respond to the first, while 2 Peter and Jude target the second.

Who Wrote 1–2 Peter and Jude?

Both 1 and 2 Peter claim to have been written by Peter, an apostle of Jesus Christ (1 Pet. 1:1; 2 Pet. 1:1). In the first letter, he writes with the help of "Silas" (or Silvanus) from Rome (5:12–13). He also writes as a fellow elder who has witnessed Christ's sufferings (5:1). In addition, early Christian tradition unanimously supports Simon Peter as

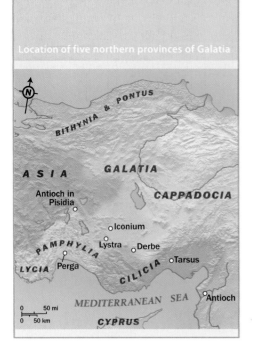

the author of 1 Peter. Because of stylistic differences from the first letter, the authorship of 2 Peter has been debated since ancient times. The author claims to have been on the mount of transfiguration with Jesus (2 Pet. 1:16–18), to have written a previous letter (3:1), refers to Paul as "our dear brother" (3:15), and expects to die soon (1:14). Some have suggested the contribution of a different secretary accounts for the language and style differences, while others believe the letter was completed after Peter's death by faithful friends as a kind of last testament to Peter.

Regarding Jude, the author describes himself as a "servant of Jesus Christ and a brother of James" (1). Christian tradition identifies Jude as the half-brother of Jesus (Matt. 13:55; Mark 6:3). His brother James wrote the New Testament letter of James.

Who Is the Audience?

Peter says he is writing from "Babylon," most likely a veiled reference to Rome (1 Pet. 5:13; cf. Rev. 14:8; 16:19; 17:4–6, 9, 18). He writes to believers scattered in five Roman provinces of Asia Minor (1 Pet. 1:1) who are experiencing a degree of persecution for their faith (e.g., 2:11–12, 19–21; 3:14, 17; 4:1, 12–16; 5:9–10). Church tradition reports that Peter was martyred when Nero began persecuting Christians in AD 64. Consequently, 1 Peter was probably written in about AD 63–64.

If the letter mentioned in 2 Pet. 3:1 is indeed 1 Peter, then we may assume both letters were intended for the same audience. The problems addressed in 2 Peter relate more to false teaching than to persecution. The primary heresy involved is a denial of Christ's return, which leads to a rejection of Scriptural truth, to immoral living, and to a denial of any future judgment. Second Peter is written shortly before Peter's death (1:14–15), sometime between AD 64 and 68.

Second Peter and Jude have a lot in common, and one may have borrowed from the other. Most scholars assume that Jude was written prior to (but close to the same time as) 2 Peter. Jude also writes to refute false teaching, which is mentioned throughout his letter: 4, 7, 8, 10–12, 16, 19.

✝ The early church not only faced threats from the outside (persecution addressed by 1 Peter) but also from within (false teaching addressed by 2 Peter and Jude).

What Is at the Heart of 1–2 Peter and Jude?

When the threat is from persecution as in 1 Peter, the solution is to stand firm in the grace of God (5:12). God's grace will allow believers to continue living a holy life even in the midst of suffering.

1 Peter
- Greeting (1:1–2)
- Praise to God for Providing Salvation (1:3–12)
- A Call to Holy Living (1:13–2:3)
- A Community Belonging to God (2:4–10)
- Living Godly Lives before Outsiders (2:11–3:12)
- Suffering Unjustly for the Name of the Lord (3:13–4:19)
- Final Exhortations (5:1–11)
- Closing (5:12–14)

In 2 Peter and Jude the threat is more from the inside (false teaching) than the outside (persecution). Second Peter calls on believers to "grow in the grace and knowledge of our Lord and Savior Jesus Christ" (2 Pet. 3:18), and Jude urges believers to "contend for the faith that was once for all entrusted to the saints" (v. 3).

2 Peter
- Greeting (1:1–2)
- Growing in Our Knowledge of God (1:3–11)
- A Personal Appeal (1:12–15)
- A Reminder of the Lord's Return (1:16–3:10)
- Closing Remarks (3:11–18)

Jude
- Greeting (1–2)
- Occasion and Purpose of the Letter (3–4)
- Resisting False Teachers (5–19)
- Contending for the Faith (20–23)
- Doxology (24–25)

What Makes 1–2 Peter and Jude Interesting and Unique?

- First Peter speaks volumes about how Christians should understand and face suffering for the cause of Christ. It places a strong emphasis on the eternal nature of what they hope in—in contrast to what they are temporarily experiencing—in order to encourage them to persevere and to convince them that it is worth it (1:2, 4, 6–7, 17–18, 20, 23–25).

- One motivation for living godly in this world is the impact it will have on outsiders. This stands out as an important topic in 1 Peter.
- First Peter 2 contains a fascinating metaphor for the church: living stones being built into a spiritual house or temple for God.
- First Peter contains several powerful Christ-centered confessions (1:19–21; 2:21–25; 3:18–22).
- Second Peter has a lot to say about the return of Christ and why God has delayed his return.
- Jude is one of two letters in the New Testament that is believed to have been written by a half-brother of Jesus (James being the other).

What Is the Message of 1 Peter?

Greeting (1 Pet. 1:1–2)

The apostle Peter sends greetings to believers (belonging to God but strangers in this world) who are scattered throughout Asia Minor (1:1). Peter sends "grace and peace" to those who have a relationship with the Father who chose them, the Spirit who sanctifies them, and the Son who died for them (1:2). As in Exodus 24, where the sprinkling of the blood of animals was part of establishing the Mosaic covenant, so now the new covenant is established by the blood (or sacrificial death) of Jesus Christ.

Praise to God for Providing Salvation (1 Pet. 1:3–12)

Peter now praises God for providing salvation through the death and resurrection of Jesus Christ (1:3). This living hope and imperishable inheritance is currently protected by God's power and our faith, and will one day be revealed (1:4–5). Believers take great joy in this salvation, although they now "suffer grief in all kinds of trials" that

Bronze coins depicting Nero celebrating his military and civic achievements.

serve to refine their faith (1:6–7). When he appears, their faith will achieve its ultimate purpose: the salvation of their souls (1:8–9). Peter reminds his audience that the prophets of old predicted this coming salvation, which his readers have been graciously allowed to experience through accepting the gospel (1:10–12).

A Call to Holy Living (1 Pet. 1:13–2:3)

To live out this amazing salvation in the midst of suffering, believers need to prepare their minds for action, exercise self-control, fix their hope on what God has promised, resist conforming to the world, and live holy lives, because God is holy (1:13–16; Lev. 19:2). Holiness is called for because God will judge our work impartially and because we have been redeemed with the precious blood of Christ (1:17–21). As in other New Testament letters (e.g., 1 John), obedience to God and love for one another are closely connected (1:22). Again, our motivation comes from the eternal nature of God's truth (1:23–25). Loving one another deeply necessitates getting rid of sins that destroy community, such as malice, deceit, envy, and slander (2:1), and replacing such vices with healthy spiritual growth that strengthens community (2:2–3).

A Community Belonging to God (1 Pet. 2:4–10)

When believers enter into a relationship with Jesus ("the living Stone"), they become "living stones" which are being built into a "spiritual house" (2:4–5). God's temple is now his people, built upon Jesus, the "capstone" (or "cornerstone"), a rock rejected by human builders but precious to God (2:6–7). While those who disobey the gospel stumble over Jesus, those who receive Jesus become "a chosen people, a royal priesthood, a holy nation, a people belonging to God" (2:8–9). Now the multicultural church, composed of both Jews and gentiles, has become the people of God, a description once reserved only for Israel (2:9–10).

Living Godly Lives before Outsiders (1 Pet. 2:11–3:12)

As "aliens and strangers in the world," Peter urges believers not to give in to sinful desires, but to live good lives among the pagans in order to minimize negative reactions and encourage positive responses to the Lord (2:11–12). Outsiders will notice their good lives as they display a submissive attitude and behavior.

✦ Many Old Testament themes come together in 1 Peter 2 as Peter describes the church as a spiritual temple of living stones (2:4–5), as well as a "chosen people, royal priesthood, and holy nation" (2:9).

Citizens and governing authorities (2:13–17)

Although Christians owe ultimate loyalty to the Lord (e.g., Peter's response in Acts 4–5), believers should normally submit to political authorities, who are charged with punishing evil and rewarding good (2:13–14). As believers "fear God" and "honor the king" through a life of good works, they will make proper use of their freedom, draw outsiders to the Lord, and please God (2:15–17).

Slaves and masters (2:18–25)

Peter exhorts slaves to submit to their earthly masters even when they are treated harshly and unjustly (2:18–19). God is honored not when slaves suffer for wrongdoing, but when they endure suffering as innocent victims, following the example of Jesus (2:20–21). Peter inserts at this point a Christ-centered confession, which highlights Jesus's role as the righteous sufferer (2:21–25; Isa. 53:9).

Husbands and wives (3:1–7)

In contrast to Paul's rules for a Christian household (Eph. 5:22–33; Col. 3:18–19), Peter focuses on a situation involving a believing wife and an unbelieving husband. He encourages the wives to consider how their exemplary lives and respectful behavior can play an evangelistic role within their marriage (3:1–2). If they follow the example of other godly women such as Sarah, and prioritize inner beauty rather than outward adornment, they will certainly please the Lord (3:3–6). For those husbands who were believers, Peter advises them to be considerate and understanding toward their wives, so that their own relationship with God would not be hindered (3:7).

✤ The household codes of 1 Peter 3 differ from those found in Ephesians 5 and Colossians 3 in that Peter focuses on a mixed marriage—that is, a marriage where one partner is a believer and the other an unbeliever.

Live in harmony with one another (3:8–12)

One final way to maintain a positive witness to outsiders is to live in harmony with other believers (3:8). Instead of seeking revenge, believers should respond with a blessing (3:9). In both speech and actions, we should refrain from evil and seek out opportunities to make peace and do good (3:10–11). God blesses this kind of godly response, but sets himself against those who promote evil (3:12).

Suffering Unjustly for the Name of the Lord (1 Pet. 3:13–4:19)

Peter now encourages his readers to embrace suffering in the name of the Lord by being prepared to respond properly, following the example of Jesus, living urgently in light of Christ's return, and counting it a privilege to suffer.

Be prepared to give an answer (3:13–17)

Peter doesn't think it likely that these believers will suffer persecution as long as they continue to do good (3:13). Nevertheless, it could happen, and believers shouldn't be overwhelmed with fear (3:14). Rather, they should be prepared to explain their Christian hope with gentleness and respect, always making sure their actions support their words (3:15–17).

Jesus's example of suffering (3:18–22)

In this third christological confession, Peter highlights how Jesus's example of suffering results in something good: salvation. He will apply this truth later in 4:1–6. The paragraph notes Christ's substitutionary death, his resurrection, and his exaltation to God's right hand above all powers and authorities. We are also told Christ "preached to the spirits in prison," likely meaning that he proclaimed victory to the demonic spirits (rather than offering salvation to dead human beings) either between

Roman woman with braided hair (likely Julia Domina, wife of Emperor Severus).

✚ As with other biblical writers, Peter prepares his audience to respond to suffering appropriately.

1 Peter   941

his death and resurrection or at his ascension. Just as God conquered the wicked powers and saved the righteous during Noah's day (2 Pet. 2:4–5; Jude 6), he will also rescue those who have been cleansed by the death and resurrection of Christ (symbolized by water baptism).

Our suffering can also lead to good (4:1–6)

Just as the sufferings of Christ led to salvation, so believers' sufferings can also lead to good. The one who "has suffered in [the] body is done with sin" (4:1). Suffering purifies our lives and directs our affections away from evil human desires and toward the will of God (4:2). Peter reminds his readers of their sinful past (4:3). Naturally, their pagan friends will ridicule them for giving up the fun life to follow God, but these same people will have to face God's judgment (4:4–5). Thankfully, the gospel was preached to people (though they are now dead) so that they may experience eternal life from God, even though the world will judge them foolish (4:6).

Live in light of Christ's return (4:7–11)

Because Christ's return is near, believers should live for God with a sense of urgency. This includes being intentional about prayer, loving one another deeply, offering hospitality without grumbling, and using our spiritual gifts faithfully, all to the glory of God.

The privilege of suffering for Christ (4:12–19)

Believers shouldn't be surprised when the world rejects them (4:12). Instead, believers should rejoice that they can participate in the sufferings of Christ (4:13). Actually, it is a blessing to suffer insult and ridicule for the name of Christ, because it reminds us that God's Spirit does indeed rest upon us (4:14). There is no glory, however, in suffering for wrongdoing on our part (4:15), but we should count it a great privilege to suffer as a Christian (4:16). Our decisions matter because of the coming judgment. If God begins by judging his own people, those without a relationship with God have no hope (4:17–18; cf. Prov. 11:31). Even in times of trials, believers should focus on trusting God and doing good (4:19).

Final Exhortations (1 Pet. 5:1–11)

When churches go through times of suffering, they need wise and effective leaders to guide them. Peter now addresses the elders or overseers, who are charged with shepherding God's flock under their care (5:1–2). They should

Persecution in the Early Church

Douglas S. Huffman

Targeted by hatred and hostility because of their relationship to Jesus (Matt. 10:22; Mark 13:13; Luke 21:17; John 15:18–25; Rev. 1:9; 12:17), the early church could suffer verbal (e.g., Matt. 5:10–11), social (e.g., John 9:22), and economic (e.g., Heb. 10:32–34) persecution. Most often, however, persecution in the New Testament includes some kind of physical harm in opposition to someone's faith (e.g., Acts 16:19–24). Persecution reaches its zenith in death.

Source of Persecution. While persecutors might have political (e.g., Acts 12:1–3), social (e.g., Acts 17:5), and/or economic (e.g., Acts 19:23–34) influence, persecution in the New Testament stems primarily from those with religious influence, often from people of the same general faith. For example, the Jews persecuted Jesus much like the Israelites had treated their own prophets (Acts 7:51–53). With religious authority, Paul persecuted Christians as if they were enemies of God (Acts 9:1–2; 22:3–8; 26:1–15; cf. John 16:2). After coming to faith, Paul's message that Jesus is God's Messiah was often met with opposition and persecution from the Jews (e.g., Acts 9:23–25; 20:3, 19; 21:27–36; 23:12–22). Thus Christians suffered persecution from adherents of Judaism (e.g., Acts 5:17–42; 6:8–8:1), sometimes in complicity with gentiles (e.g., Acts 13:45–52; 14:1–7, 19–20; 17:1–15; 18:5–17; 28:16–20). The New Testament also describes persecution of Christians due to gentile instigation (Acts 16:19–24; 19:23–41). Prior to AD 250 various Roman emperors are known to have supported (while not necessarily initiating) persecution of Christians: Nero, Domitian, Trajan, Hadrian, and Marcus Aurelius. Finally, persecution of Christians is even evidenced as coming from other Jesus followers (e.g., Phil. 1:15–17).

Value of Persecution. The New Testament indicates persecution has greater purposes for believers. Persecuted believers share in the sufferings of Christ (Rom. 8:14–17; 2 Cor. 1:3–7; Phil. 3:10–11; 1 Pet. 4:13). With salvation accomplished only by Christ's suffering (Heb. 9:24–10:23), persecution serves an identification purpose, showing connectedness to Christ and his people (Mark 10:28–31; Acts 5:40–41; 1 Thess. 2:14; 2 Thess. 1:3–12; 2 Tim. 1:8–12; Heb. 11:24–27; 1 Pet. 5:9) and following Christ's example (1 Pet. 2:19–25). Thus Jesus counts persecution of believers as persecution against himself (Acts 9:4–5; 22:7–8; 26:14–15). Persecution services evangelism. What is "lacking in Christ's suffering" and "filled up" by believers' suffering (Col. 1:24) is the spread of the gospel (Col. 1:25). Christ suffered to accomplish salvation; believers suffer in spreading that message (Matt. 10:16–20; Mark 13:9–11; Luke 21:12–15; 2 Tim. 2:1–10; e.g., Acts 8:1–4; 11:19–21). Persecution strengthens faith, demonstrating God's power and keeping him the focus of hope (2 Cor. 1:8–11; 4:7–15; 6:1–10; 12:7–10). Persecution clears away false believers (Matt. 13:18–23; Mark 4:13–20; Luke 8:11–15) and helps render temptation less effective in true believers (1 Pet. 4:1–5).

carry out their responsibilities (1) not under compulsion but willingly, (2) not out of greed but out of a heart of service, and (3) not in an authoritarian manner but leading the way as an example (5:2–3). They will be rewarded when Jesus, the Chief Shepherd, returns (5:4). The younger men (the ones most likely to rebel?) should submit to their leaders, and everyone should put on humility, for "God opposes the proud but gives grace to the humble"

(5:5; Prov. 3:34; James 4:6). A big part of humbling oneself includes casting all our anxieties or cares upon the Lord, rather than trying to live life in our own strength (5:6–7). In addition, believers should be self-controlled and alert to the devil's tactics (5:8). The appropriate warfare strategy in regard to Satan involves resistance and perseverance, being encouraged in that other believers are going through the same things with us (5:9). After we have suffered for a little while, the God of all grace and power who called us will himself restore us and make us "strong, firm and steadfast" (5:10).

Closing (1 Pet. 5:12–14)

Peter has written with the help of Silas (or Silvanus) to bring encouragement and to testify about the grace of God (5:12). Now the readers are called to "stand fast in" God's grace (5:12), the theme of the entire letter. Following closing greetings from those in Rome, including Mark, along with an encouragement to greet one another, Peter pronounces peace to all who are in Christ (5:13–14).

What Is the Message of 2 Peter?

Greeting (2 Pet. 1:1–2)

To those who have received a precious faith through the righteousness of Jesus Christ, both Savior and God, Peter sends his greeting of grace and peace. In line with the overall purpose of the letter, he adds that grace and peace come in abundance "through the knowledge of God and of Jesus our Lord" (1:2).

Growing in Our Knowledge of God (2 Pet. 1:3–11)

Peter assures his readers they have everything they need for life and godliness through their knowledge of God (1:3). Through God's calling and promises, believers may grow more like Christ and escape the corruption promoted in the world by evil desires (1:4). To "participate in the divine nature" is defined in this context as a synonym for godliness or spiritual growth rather than an affirmation that humans will one day become gods. In 1:5–8, Peter mentions godly qualities in which believers should grow in order to be effective and productive in their knowledge of the Lord. Believers who are not growing fail to see and remember all that God has done for them (1:9). As in 1 John, a believer's own spiritual growth brings assurance of his or her calling, election, and future place in God's eternal kingdom (1:10).

✚ Peter's list of godly qualities in 2 Peter 1:5–8 looks a lot like Paul's fruit of the Spirit list in Galatians 5:22–23.

A Personal Appeal (2 Pet. 1:12–15)

Peter is keenly aware that his death is near (1:14–15). He also feels a heavy responsibility to remind his readers of the basic truths of the faith, things they already know but need to live out consistently (1:12–13, 15).

A Reminder of the Lord's Return (2 Pet. 1:16–3:10)

The certainty of Jesus's return (1:16–21)

The false teachers seem to be denying that Christ will return (3:3–4). Peter reminds his readers that he personally witnessed Jesus's transfiguration, an event that previewed Jesus's final return in glory (1:16–18). Just as the transfiguration was not a cleverly invented story but a historical event, so also the return of Christ will be a historical event. The Holy Spirit inspired the prophets, and much of what they predicted has already been fulfilled in the coming of Jesus the Messiah (1:19–21). Therefore, believers should expect the rest of the prophecies, such as the return of Christ, to be fulfilled as well (1:19–21).

A denial of Jesus's return brings judgment (2:1–22)

In this lengthy section Peter describes the actions of the false teachers and their fate. These false prophets introduce harmful heresies, such as denying the sovereign Lord and his return (2:1). Because there is no place for accountability in their invented stories, they live shamefully, disgrace the truth (2:2), and seek to exploit believers in the process (2:3). But their destruction

The shrine built above the traditional tomb of the apostle Peter in Rome.

✦ Along with 2 Timothy 3:16–17, Peter affirms the full trustworthiness and inspiration of God's Word (see 2 Pet. 1:20–21).

is certain (2:1, 3). If God didn't spare angels when they rebelled (2:4), didn't spare ungodly people in ancient times (2:5), and condemned Sodom and Gomorrah (2:6), then he knows how to punish the unrighteous (2:9–10). If God protected Noah and his family (2:5) and rescued Lot from Sodom and Gomorrah (2:6–8), then he knows how to rescue godly people (2:9). In 2:10–22, Peter describes the false prophets in greater detail. In their arrogance, they slander and blaspheme spiritual matters they don't understand (2:10–12). They revel in worldly pleasures such as adultery, seduction, and greed (2:13–16). They are slaves of moral depravity and lustful desires, who nevertheless promise spiritual freedom (2:17–19). They either were genuine believers who renounced Christ and his salvation or they were never truly believers (2:20–21). The two proverbs quoted in 2:22 tend to support the latter option. In any case, the apostle makes it very clear these false prophets are destined for judgment (2:12, 13, 17, 20).

Why God is delaying (3:1–10)

In both letters, Peter has encouraged his readers to "wholesome thinking" by reminding them of the words of the Old Testament prophets and the words of Jesus set forth by his apostles (3:1–2). Since nothing has changed for a long time, the false teachers scoff, "Where is this 'coming' he promised?" (3:3–4). But they forget God's power demonstrated through his creation of the world and the great flood (3:5–6). Just as God created the world by his word, by that same word "the present heavens and earth are reserved for fire, being kept for the day of judgment and destruction of ungodly men" (3:7). The Lord is neither unable to keep his promises nor late in keeping them. No, he is patient, not wanting people to perish but desiring everyone to repent (3:9). God sees time very differently than we do (3:8). But when the day of the Lord does arrive, it will come suddenly and surprisingly, like a thief in the night (3:10). The present earth and heavens will be destroyed by fire, making way for the creation of the new heavens and the new earth (3:10, 12–13; Isa. 65:17; Heb. 12:26–27; Rev. 21:1).

Closing Remarks (2 Pet. 3:11–18)

The day of the Lord is coming, when the present universe will be destroyed in preparation for the new heavens and new earth (3:11–13). Believers should look forward to the day of the Lord and can even speed its coming (3:12). The Lord's patience means salvation for more people, as the apostle Paul wrote about in his letters (3:15–16). In the meantime, God's people should not be carried away by theological errors (3:17), but should live "holy and

✦ The "day of the Lord" from the Old Testament is here associated with Christ's second coming, an event that will bring judgment on the rebellious and salvation to the faithful.

godly lives" (3:11) so that they may be found "spotless, blameless, and at peace with him" (3:14). In summary, believers should "grow in the grace and knowledge of our Lord and Savior Jesus Christ," to whom be the glory (3:18).

What Is the Message of Jude?

Greeting (Jude 1–2)

Jude, a servant (and likely half-brother) of Jesus and brother of James, writes to the called, who are loved by God and kept by Jesus (1). He offers the following greeting/prayer: "mercy, peace and love be yours in abundance" (2).

Occasion and Purpose of the Letter (Jude 3–4)

It seems that Jude wanted to focus more on the salvation God has provided, but he feels compelled to deal with the situation related to the false teaching. He encourages his readers to "contend for the faith that was once for all entrusted to the saints" (3). Godless men have secretly slipped into the church and are not only denying the Lord but are twisting God's grace into a license for godless living (4).

Resisting False Teachers (Jude 5–19)

Jude denounces the false teachers throughout the central section of his letter. Just as the Lord delivered his people during the exodus but later

Sodom.

destroyed unbelievers (5), and as he imprisoned rebellious angels for the day of judgment (6), so he will punish those who are committed to immorality (7). Along with being perverted, the false teachers are also blasphemous. They reject authority and slander spiritual beings as if all the power belonged to them (8–10). Jude quotes a Jewish work in verse 9 (*Assumption of Moses*) to make the point that all judgment, even the judgment of Satan, belongs to the Lord. Using negative examples from the Old Testament (Cain, Balaam, Korah), Jude criticizes the selfish leadership of the false teachers. They are like "shepherds who feed only themselves" (11–12). Their behavior is unnatural, like unnatural phenomena in the natural world (12–13). Jude quotes the Jewish apocalyptic work of 1 Enoch as a prophecy against the false teachers: the Lord is coming with a large company of angels to judge everyone and to convict the ungodly (14–15). In addition, the false teachers are complainers, faultfinders, boastful, and selfish (16). The Lord's own apostles also predicted that such false teachers would appear in the last days, worldly men who do not have the Spirit (unbelievers) but who sneak their way into churches to create chaos (17–19; cf. Acts 20:29–31; 1 Tim. 4:1–3; 2 Tim. 3:1–9).

Contending for the Faith (Jude 20–23)

After launching into an impassioned attack on the false teachers, Jude addresses the faithful believers about how to contend for the faith. They should grow in their knowledge of scriptural truth, pray in the Spirit, live in God's love, stay hopeful about Christ's return, and serve others through ministries of restoration and evangelism.

Doxology (Jude 24–25)

Jude closes the letter with a poetic and powerful word of praise to God, who is able to protect his children and bring them into his glorious presence with great joy and without fault (24). The only God our Savior through Jesus Christ our Lord deserves all "glory, majesty, power and authority," from eternity past into the present and on into eternity future (25).

So What? Applying 1–2 Peter and Jude Today

Persecution takes various forms for Western Christians: ridicule, slander, ostracism, and economic discrimination, to name a few. First Peter provides much-needed perspective and encouragement for those who are suffering unjustly. We are reminded of who we are as members of God's people, of the

✚ Jude quotes not only from the Old Testament but also from extra-biblical literature to drive home his case against the false teachers.

rock-solid nature of our hope in Christ, and of the need to live a holy life. We should think about how best to respond to persecution, knowing that Jesus himself suffered and that suffering can also lead to good. To face unjust suffering in a godly manner, we need a fresh reminder of God's grace, and 1 Peter provides that very thing. In addition to persecution, believers sometimes face a different kind of threat: false teaching. Second Peter reminds us that knowledge is important in the Christian life. For instance, every few years some group sets a date when they claim Christ will return. Those who know the Scriptures won't be misled by such teaching because Jesus clearly taught that date-setting was not our job. Specifically, 2 Peter explains why the return of Christ is being delayed: so that even more people may be brought to Christ. Jude makes the point that there are times when false teachers need to be confronted as a matter of contending for the historic Christian faith. Not all conflict is unhealthy, and it may be necessary when others are being steered away from the true gospel. Paul himself does this very thing in 2 Corinthians.

Our Favorite Verses in 1–2 Peter and Jude

And the God of all grace, who called you to his eternal glory in Christ, after you have suffered a little while, will himself restore you and make you strong, firm and steadfast. (1 Pet. 5:10)

But do not forget this one thing, dear friends: With the Lord a day is like a thousand years, and a thousand years are like a day. The Lord is not slow in keeping his promise, as some understand slowness. He is patient with you, not wanting anyone to perish, but everyone to come to repentance. (2 Pet. 3:8–9)

To him who is able to keep you from falling and to present you before his glorious presence without fault and with great joy—to the only God our Savior be glory, majesty, power and authority, through Jesus Christ our Lord, before all ages, now and forevermore! Amen. (Jude 24–25)

Sinai.

✚ Both Peter and Jude encourage Christians to grow in grace and knowledge—two essentials for believers who want to become mature in their faith.

1 John

True Christian Belief and Behavior

2 John

Walk in Love and Truth

3 John

Imitate What Is Good

At a time when the traditional teaching about Jesus Christ and the Christian faith were being challenged, John offered a theological plumb line for his struggling churches. In 1 John he set forth three marks of true Christianity: a correct view of Jesus, the need to obey God, and the importance of loving one another. These are applied to specific situations in 2–3 John. Because our context is remarkably similar to the original context, we will discover in John's letters plenty of wisdom and encouragement to assist us in lining up with the historic Christian faith.

Who Wrote John's Letters?

Although the author never identifies himself, the traditional view is that John—the apostle, the disciple whom Jesus loved, and the author of the fourth Gospel—also wrote these three letters. In addition, similarities of content and style between the Gospel of John and John's letters suggest the same author. In 2 John 1 and 3 John 1, the author is described as "the elder," but this designation probably applies to the apostle John, who also served as an elder in his local church. Early traditions (e.g., Irenaeus, Polycarp, Polycrates) indicate that John moved to Ephesus in the latter part of the first century and planted churches in that area.

Who Is John's Audience?

John wrote to Christians in the region of Ephesus near the end of the first century (in the AD 70–90s). The churches were being threatened by a false teaching that blended elements from several heresies. The false teaching suggested that knowledge, rather than grace, provides the way to God and that the human body is evil (an early form of gnosticism). The emphasis on "special knowledge" led to an arrogance and lack of love. Their ideas about the body led some to treat their bodies harshly (asceticism) and others to indulge their bodily desires (licentiousness). In addition, some were denying Jesus's full humanity and deity. Jesus could not have taken a real human body, they said, because matter is evil. Either Jesus only seemed to be human (Docetism), or the "divine Christ" who joined the "human Jesus" at the baptism left him before his death (Cerinthianism). To complicate matters, those falling for this false teaching are pulling away from the fellowship (1 John 2:19), claiming they have arrived at a state of sinless perfection (1 John 1:8, 10; 3:9–10).

What Is at the Heart of John's Letters?

John writes to encourage the faithful by reminding them of what true Christians believe and how they should behave. There are two purpose statements in 1 John: (1) to warn believers about the false teaching (2:26), and (2) to help believers know they have eternal life (5:13). As the table shows, John repeatedly emphasizes the marks of a true believer and how these counter the false teaching.*

Theme	Obey God	Love One Another	Correct Christology
False Teaching	Licentiousness	Arrogance	Body Is Evil
	1:5–2:6	2:7–17	2:18–27
	2:28–3:10	3:11–24	4:1–6
	5:16–21	4:7–21	5:1–15

* Table is adapted from John Stott, *Epistles of John* (Downers Grove, IL: InterVarsity, 2009) and Craig Blomberg, *From Pentecost to Patmos: An Introduction to Acts through Revelation* (Nashville: B&H, 2006).

✚ Both 1 John and the Gospel of John begin with an emphasis on Jesus becoming a genuine human being (incarnation).

The outline for 1 John also demonstrates these three themes of obedience, love, and correct Christology.

1 John
- Prologue (1:1–4)
- Obeying God #1 (1:5–2:6)
- Loving One Another #1 (2:7–17)
- Correct Christology #1 (2:18–27)
- Obeying God #2 (2:28–3:10)
- Loving One Another #2 (3:11–24)
- Correct Christology #2 (4:1–6)
- Loving One Another #3 (4:7–21)
- Correct Christology #3 (5:1–15)
- Obeying God #3 (5:16–21)

Second John is addressed to "the chosen lady and her children" (1:1), which could be an individual Christian woman and her family or a figurative description of a local church. Because the "you" in 2 John 8, 10, and 12 is plural, because no family names are mentioned in 2 John 1 or 13, and because the "woman" is beloved by *all* who know the truth (1), it seems that John is writing to a church. He warns about false teachers, encourages believers to love one other, and instructs them to use discernment in welcoming and supporting traveling teachers.

Ancient Byzantine baptismal font at the Church of Saint John near Ephesus.

2 John
- Opening (1–3)
- Love (5–6)
- Truth (4, 7–11)
- Closing (12–13)

The context of 3 John seems to be a dispute between church members. An authoritarian leader in one of the churches has rejected traveling teachers sent out by John. John writes to correct the problem by urging believers not to imitate what is evil but to imitate what is good.

3 John

- Opening (1)
- Commendation of Gaius (2–8)
- Rebuke for Diotrephes (9–11)
- Praise for Demetrius (12)
- Closing (13–14)

What Makes John's Letters Interesting and Unique?

- Of the twelve apostles of Jesus, John probably lived the longest. The early church leader Irenaeus says John lived until at least AD 98 (*Haer.* 2.22.5; cf. John 21:18–23).
- There are many parallels and connections between the Gospel of John and 1 John (e.g., eternal life, light, belief, Jesus as God's Son, the Holy Spirit, truth, abiding, new commandment of love).
- The term "antichrist" is used only four times in the Bible, all in the letters of John (1 John 2:18, 22; 4:3; 2 John 7).
- While 2 and 3 John read like traditional letters, 1 John looks more like a sermon or a treatise intended for several congregations.
- Second John is the shortest book in the New Testament.
- As Christians traveled, they relied on the hospitality of other believers for lodging and food. Third John speaks directly to the important practice of Christian hospitality.

What Is the Message of 1 John?

Prologue (1 John 1:1–4)

As with the prologue to John's Gospel, this prologue stresses that Jesus existed with the Father before creation and that he entered this world as a real human being who could be seen, heard, and touched. Jesus, the "Word of life" and "the eternal life," came to bring people into fellowship with God, and with those who love him. Writing about these things brings great joy for John and his audience.

Obeying God #1 (1 John 1:5–2:6)

John's message is that "God is light" (1:5) and that those who have fellowship with him walk in the light—in obedience to his word (1:5; 2:3–6).

✚ As with James and other New Testament letters, 1 John makes it clear that our love for the Lord and our love for other believers are closely tied together.

God as Light and Love

Joel Williams

First John contains two direct affirmations about the character of God: "God is light" (1:5) and "God is love" (4:8). What is significant about these aspects of God's character for the interpretation of 1 John is that they correspond with the major themes in the letter concerning what can be expected of those who know God: obedience and love. The first half of 1 John emphasizes that true children of God obey his commands, while the second half of 1 John emphasizes that true children of God love those who belong to God's family.

God is light without any hint of darkness. He shines forth perfect holiness. Therefore, those who know God walk in the light, with the result that they are continuing to be made clean from their sin through the blood of Jesus (1:6–7). To walk in the light involves learning and following God's ways. Anyone who claims to know God but refuses to obey God is lying and walking in the darkness (2:4; cf. 2:9–11). Those who make it the pattern of their lives to disobey God and to continue in sin have never really been born of God (3:7–10). Instead, those who know and love God make it the pattern of their lives to obey his commands (2:3). They see the light and walk in it.

God is also love. Loving relationship and sacrificial giving belong to the very nature of God. He revealed his love by sending his Son to die for us so that we might have life through him (4:9–10; cf. 3:16). God poured out his love toward us by making us his children (3:1). Since God is love, all those who know God and have experienced his love naturally live with love as well (4:7–11). We love because he first loved us (4:19). Our love for others in God's family serves as evidence that we have in reality moved out of death into life (3:14). It is impossible to know and love God and yet hate the children of God, and anyone who claims to love God while hating his brother is lying (4:20–21). If he does not love his brother whom he has seen, how can he love God whom he has not seen? In the context of 1 John, love involves laying down one's life for others and giving with compassion to those in need (3:16–17). In this way, our love is grounded in the love that we have received in Jesus, who first laid down his life for us in our time of need. Therefore, through faithful obedience and sacrificial love, our lives reflect the God who is both light and love.

Ironically, the false teachers were claiming to be without sin (1:8, 10). Because those who strive to obey God still fall into sin, obedience also includes confessing our sins and relying on Jesus's sacrifice and faithfulness to cleanse and purify us (1:7, 9; 2:1–2). Those who claim to know God but walk in the darkness are liars, and the truth of God is not in them (1:6; 2:4).

Loving One Another #1 (1 John 2:7–17)

Obeying God is connected to God's greatest command to love, which is both an old and a new command (2:7–8; Lev. 19:18; Deut. 6:4–5; Mark 12:29–31). Those who claim to be in the light but hate other believers are

The end of 2 Peter and the beginning of 1 John in Codex Alexandrinus, an important early manuscript of the New Testament.

still in the darkness (2:9, 11). Only those who love fellow believers actually live in God's light (2:10). John writes to the entire community of genuine believers, encouraging them to remember God's forgiveness, their knowledge of God, and their victory over the evil one (2:12–14). In this unusual section, John addresses three groups twice and repeats some of what he says the first time. Since "dear children" comes first (rather than "fathers"), it probably refers to the entire Christian community. Then John addresses two groups—the more mature ("fathers") and the younger Christians ("young men" or "young people")—with more specific instructions. The love command does not involve loving the world and its temporary pleasures: the lust of the flesh, the lust of the eyes, and the pride of life (2:15–16). The world and its desires are fading away, but the one who loves God lives forever (2:17).

Correct Christology #1 (1 John 2:18–27)

John writes to warn believers about the false teachers (2:26), whom he labels "antichrists" (2:18). In pulling away from the Christian community, they demonstrate they didn't truly belong to that community (2:19). They promote falsehood by denying Jesus is the Christ (2:22). John makes it very clear that the one who denies the Son also denies the Father, but whoever acknowledges the Son has the Father (2:23). These believers should remain faithful to the one true gospel, since it guards their relationship with God and brings assurance of eternal life (2:24–25). In addition to the truth of the Scriptures, they have "the anointing" (i.e., the Holy Spirit) from Jesus who will guide them into truth (2:20–21, 27). They don't need to follow

✦ John encourages Christians to acknowledge that they sin and to confess their sins, expecting forgiveness and cleansing because of the character of God (1 John 1:9).

"super spiritual" leaders who claim to have all the answers; they can trust the Scriptures and the Spirit.

Obeying God #2 (1 John 2:28–3:10)

John commands his fellow believers to "continue in him" (i.e., to obey Jesus) so that they may be confident and unashamed when Christ returns (2:28). According to John, the righteous are those who have accepted the Father's love and respond by doing what is right. Although rejected by the world, they have been accepted into God's family (2:29–3:1). The children of God continue to purify themselves because of their hope that they will be like Christ when he appears (3:2–3). John then explains how to detect false believers—they "keep on sinning" (3:6) and "continue to sin" (3:9). That is, unbelievers are characterized by a lifestyle of sin. John's readers should not be deceived, for a person's obedience reflects his or her true identity (3:7–10). Those who are born of God will reflect God's character in their obedience and their love, while those who are of the devil will continue in their rebellious and sinful lifestyle.

Loving One Another #2 (1 John 3:11–24)

From the beginning (in contrast to the false teaching), the Christian message has emphasized the importance of love (3:11). The negative example of Cain demonstrates the deadly effects of hatred (3:12–15), while Christ's sacrifice offers the supreme example of love (3:16). Believers should expect rejection from the world (3:13), but this shouldn't stop them from following Christ's example and laying down their lives for fellow believers (3:16). More specifically, love should move beyond mere talk to specific actions, such as sharing material possessions (3:16–18). When we are tempted to doubt that we believe in Jesus, these specific acts of love for fellow believers can assure our hearts and bring us confidence in our relationship with God, especially as it relates to our prayer life (3:19–22). The most important thing is to believe in Jesus Christ, the Son of God, and to love one another (3:23). Our obedience and the presence of the Holy Spirit work together to offer assurance of a genuine relationship with Christ (3:24).

Correct Christology #2 (1 John 4:1–6)

Not every prophet who is popular in this world is actually empowered by the Holy Spirit (4:1, 5). Prophets who are in line with the Spirit will acknowledge that Jesus Christ is fully divine and fully human (i.e., "that Jesus

✚ To believe in Jesus and to love one another (1 John 3:23) recalls Jesus's words about the greatest commandments (Matt. 22:37–40; cf. Lev. 19:18; Deut. 6:5).

Christ has come in the flesh"). Those who fail this test are not from God but from the antichrist (4:2–3). Believers must test the spirits to see whether they are from God (4:1, 6). In the process, we need not fear popular false prophets because "the one who is in you [the Holy Spirit] is greater than the one who is in the world" (4:4).

Loving One Another #3 (1 John 4:7–21)

For the third time, John emphasizes love as a mark of a true Christian. Love is from God and those who love demonstrate the genuineness of their relationship with God (4:7–8). God himself defined love by sending his one and only Son into the world as an atoning sacrifice for our sins (4:9–10). Since we have experienced this magnificent love of God, we should also love one another (4:11–12). We receive assurance of our salvation from the presence of the Spirit (4:13) and by our confession that the Father sent Jesus, the Son of God, to be the Savior of the world (4:14–16). But assurance also comes as we love one another (4:16). The presence of love in our lives gives us confidence for the day of judgment by driving out any fear that God will condemn us (4:17–18). God is love and his love enables believers to love one another (4:16, 19). It all comes down to this: if people claim to love God but hate other believers, they are liars (4:20). Whoever claims to love God must love other believers as well (4:21).

Correct Christology #3 (1 John 5:1–15)

Along with correct Christology, the other two key themes are mentioned here as well (i.e., obeying God and loving one another). "Everyone who believes that Jesus is the Christ is born of God" (5:1). There is certainly a connection between believing in Jesus, obeying God, and loving other believers (5:2–3). Everyone born of God overcomes the world because they have faith that Jesus is the Son of God (5:4–5). Jesus Christ came "by water and blood," likely referring to his baptism and to the cross (5:6). The Spirit testifies to the truth about Jesus, since he was with the Son throughout his entire ministry (versus false teaching; 5:6–8). We should accept what God says about his Son—that eternal life is in the Son and whoever has the Son has life (5:9–12). John now states his purpose for writing: to help Christians know they have eternal life (5:13). False prophets have a way of destabilizing a church, and John brings a strong word of assurance. In addition, believers should also have confidence that God will answer their prayers according to his will (5:14–15).

✚ 1 John reminds us that beliefs are as important as behavior in following Jesus.

Obeying God #3 (1 John 5:16–21)

Obeying God involves dealing with sin. We should definitely pray for fellow believers who commit a sin that does not lead to death (perhaps sinful acts by conscientious Christians), and God will give them life (5:16). John doesn't discuss (but neither does he prohibit) praying for people whose sin leads to death (5:16). Perhaps John has in mind a state of willful and intentional rejection of Christ much like the blasphemy of the Spirit mentioned by Jesus (Luke 12:10). All wrongdoing is sin, but some sin does not prevent our repentance and restoration (5:17). John concludes the letter with three "we know" statements (5:18, 19, 20) and a final warning (5:21). We know that genuine believers do not maintain a sinful lifestyle but are kept spiritually safe against the attacks of the evil one (5:18). We know that believers belong to God while the whole world belongs to the evil one (5:19). And we know that Jesus came so that people may know the one true God and experience eternal life (5:20). Finally, John warns believers to keep themselves from idols: anything that could substitute for God (5:21).

This replica of a first-century house reminds us of how much John likes to compare the Christian community to a family.

✚ John relates eternal life directly to knowing Jesus (1 John 1:2; 2:24–25; 5:11–13, 20; cf. John 3:15–16, 36; 5:24; 6:40; 10:27–28; 11:25; 17:2–3).

What Is the Message of 2 John?

Whereas 1 John may have been read to all the house churches, 2 John may have been intended for a particular congregation. All three marks of the true believer are stressed again in 2 John.

Opening (2 John 1–3)

John, now identified as "the elder," writes to the "chosen lady and her children," likely a house church in Ephesus (1). Along with a greeting of "grace, mercy and peace" from "God the Father and from Jesus Christ, the Father's Son," John introduces two important spiritual realities that form the theme of the book: love and truth (2–3).

Love (2 John 5–6)

He reminds his readers of the love command they have had from the beginning (5). More specifically, love for one another and obedience to the Lord are connected (6).

Truth (2 John 4, 7–11)

Love and truth are not enemies but friends. John takes joy in seeing his spiritual children walk in the truth (4). False teachers (the deceivers and antichrists) fail to acknowledge that Jesus Christ has come in the flesh (7). Those who follow the false teachers will suffer great spiritual loss (8). Believers must continue in the teaching of Christ or they will demonstrate that they do not belong to God (9). John warns this congregation not to welcome the false teachers or give them a platform for their wicked work (10–11).

Closing (2 John 12–13)

John closes the letter with much left to say, but he would rather say it in person in hopes that both his joy and theirs will be made complete (12). The members of a sister church send greetings (13).

What Is the Message of 3 John?

The context of 3 John seems to be a dispute between church members. An authoritarian leader in one of the churches has rejected traveling teachers sent out by John. John writes to attempt to correct the problem. John calls for believers not to imitate what is evil, but to imitate what is good (11).

✦ The term *antichrist* is only used four times in the Bible (1 John 2:18, 22; 4:3; 2 John 7).

Hospitality

Joel Williams

The letter of 3 John commends a man by the name of Gaius for showing hospitality to traveling missionaries, even though they were strangers to him when they arrived. The letter also encourages Gaius to continue responding in the same way when other opportunities arise (3 John 5–8). Such hospitality would have included providing the travelers with food and a place to sleep, and therefore with public recognition as people worthy of honor and support. In addition, John considered it appropriate "to send them on their way in a manner worthy of God" (3 John 6). In other words, John was calling on Gaius to provide them with sufficient food and financial support to enable them to reach the next stop in their journey. Paul used the same expression in his letter to Titus, asking that Zenas and Apollos might be sent on their way and might therefore have everything they need (Titus 3:13; cf. Rom. 15:24; 1 Cor. 16:6, 11; 2 Cor. 1:16). Such support could be offered at various levels, and John called for a provision that erred on the side of generosity, since it was directed toward those who worked for God.

Who were these recipients of Gaius's hospitality? They were apparently missionaries who left their homes for the sake of Jesus's name in order to bring the message of truth to unbelievers. They had no intention of receiving any financial help from those they hoped to reach with the message of Christ (3 John 7). Therefore, they were dependent solely on other Christians for support. Believers like Gaius who showed them hospitality joined with them in their ministry and by doing so became fellow-workers for the truth (3 John 8).

The letter of 3 John also criticizes a man named Diotrephes for failing to welcome these traveling Christian workers. His refusal to show hospitality grew out of his desire to have all the attention in the church directed toward him (3 John 9–10). The letter of 2 John touches on another problem related to hospitality, although in a different direction. In that letter, John found it necessary to warn a congregation not to welcome false teachers to stay in their homes and not to offer them support (2 John 10–11). Such hospitality would serve only to spread the destructive work of false teachers who were insisting that Jesus Christ was not fully human (2 John 7). Shortly after the time of the New Testament, an early Christian document shows that church leaders also found it necessary to warn congregations not to take in and support charlatans who were seeking to take advantage of believers (*Didache* 11–12). Hospitality calls for a balance of generosity and wisdom.

Opening (3 John 1)

John greets his good friend Gaius, whom he loves in the truth.

Commendation of Gaius (3 John 2–8)

John begins by praying that Gaius's physical health may match his spiritual health (2). John's joy is multiplied when he hears about the obedience of fellow believers and he expresses gratitude for Gaius's faithfulness to the truth (3–4). He specifically commends Gaius for his ministry of showing hospitality to traveling teachers (5). These teachers went out "for the sake of the Name [of Jesus]," have depended on the hospitality of Christians, and report about the love and support of Gaius (6–8).

Rebuke for Diotrephes (3 John 9–11)

John now rebukes a troublemaker named Diotrephes, who rejects John's leadership, refuses to welcome the traveling teachers, and expels from the church those who want to show Christian hospitality (9–10). John warns this congregation in verse 11 not to imitate evil (i.e., the selfish ambition of Diotrephes) but to imitate what is good (i.e., the ministry of Gaius). Those who do what is good are from God while those who do evil haven't experienced God (11).

Praise for Demetrius (3 John 12)

John offers another example of godliness in Demetrius, whom everyone speaks well of (12).

Closing (3 John 13–14)

Again, John has much to say but prefers to say it in person (13–14). He exchanges greetings and pronounces peace on his fellow believers (14).

So What? Applying John's Letters Today

The three marks of a true believer serve as our application points for 1 John. The biblical view of Jesus is that he is fully God and fully man. Any teaching that deviates from this by denying his deity or humanity (or a virtual denial by an overemphasis on one or the other) is not from God. In our contemporary pluralistic context, we need to guard our Christology. What we believe about Jesus ultimately determines how we relate to God and to God's people. John also makes it clear that obedience to God is of utmost importance for the believer. We're quite familiar with rationalizing our sin, but John also warns against the lure of perfectionism (changing our definition of "sin," then claiming we have not

Ruins from ancient Ephesus, the leading city where many of John's readers lived.

✦ John challenges believers to discern which teachers and ministries deserve support and then to be generous in supporting them.

sinned). John says that anyone who claims they can go extended periods of time without sinning is a liar. Instead of excusing our sin or redefining sin, we must earnestly confess our sin to the Lord. When we do, we find he is faithful (willing) and just (able) to forgive us and cleanse us (1 John 1:9). Finally, John highlights the importance of love. We cannot claim to love God and at the same time hate fellow believers; that makes us a liar. Love and truth are friends rather than enemies. As John said in his Gospel, "grace and truth came through Jesus Christ" (John 1:17). In our defense of truth, we must never lose love, and in our efforts to love, we must never neglect the truth. When false teachers suggest we are missing out on something, we can assure our hearts before God by a correct view of Jesus and our submission to God's Word, including the love we show to other believers.

Taken together, 2 and 3 John offer a balanced approach to supporting Christian ministries. On the one hand, 2 John teaches us to use discernment and good judgment. We should check out their message before we invest in their ministry. On the other hand, 3 John teaches us not to allow our love to grow cold toward all ministries just because some of them are misleading and deceptive. We should have discerning hearts to separate the true from the false, and loving hearts to support in practical ways those involved in genuine Christian ministry.

Our Favorite Verses in John's Letters

If we confess our sins, he is faithful and just and will forgive us our sins and purify us from all unrighteousness. (1 John 1:9)

We love because he first loved us. (1 John 4:19)

Anyone who runs ahead and does not continue in the teaching of Christ does not have God; whoever continues in the teaching has both the Father and the Son. (2 John 9)

I have no greater joy than to hear that my children are walking in the truth. (3 John 4)

Apocalyptic Literature

The book of Revelation takes its name from its opening words: "The revelation (*apocalypsis*) of Jesus Christ" (Rev. 1:1). The word *apocalypsis* refers to an "unveiling" or a "revelation." Jesus Christ is the center of this revelation, either as the main topic of discussion throughout the book or as the one responsible for unveiling God's plans for the world, or perhaps some of both. In any case, the book was intended to let believers know more about God's sovereign control of human history.

Revelation is the primary New Testament example of a type of literature known as "apocalyptic" literature. We find other examples of this kind of literature in both the Old Testament (e.g., Daniel, Zechariah, Isa. 24–27; 56–66; Ezek. 38–39) and the New Testament (e.g., Matt. 24–25; Mark 13). Apocalyptic literature was very popular during the intertestamental period (e.g., *1–2 Enoch, Jubilees, 2–3 Baruch, 4 Ezra*).

In apocalyptic literature, there is a divine revelation through a heavenly being to a well-known figure, in which God promises to step into human history for the purpose of defeating evil and establishing his kingdom. This kind of literature often contains strange visions and bizarre images. Brent Sandy notes twelve prominent themes of New Testament apocalyptic literature:*

---

* D. Brent Sandy, *Plowshares and Pruning Hooks: Rethinking the Language of Biblical Prophecy and Apocalyptic* (Downers Grove, IL: IVP Academic, 2002), 169–89.

✚ Probably the closest parallel we have today to apocalyptic literature would be fantasy literature, such as C. S. Lewis's *Chronicles of Narnia*.

Twelve Themes of New Testament Apocalyptic Literature

Striking presentation of the transcendent Lord	Horrors experienced by the animal world
Unprecedented turmoil in the world	Preservation of God's elect (the remnant)
The end of history is near	Coming of a new society for the righteous
God's terrifying judgment of evil	Rewards for the righteous
Horrors in the heavens	Satanic forces attack God's people
Horrors on earth	Backlash of evil experienced by saints

Apocalyptic literature such as the book of Revelation assumes a crisis of faith—why are the evil powers having their way if God is truly in control? Revelation offers a vivid and dramatic reminder that God is sovereign and

that he will defeat evil, vindicate his people, and establish his eternal kingdom. Jesus is Lord and God is still on his throne! The book creates a symbolic world for the reader to enter, where their perspective is realigned with what is spiritually real, although temporarily unseen. The readers are then empowered to see things from a heavenly perspective. They see the final future and God's ultimate victory over the forces of darkness. As a transforming vision, the main message of Revelation is "God wins, so remain faithful to Jesus no matter what!"

Revelation

The Transforming Vision

In powerful language and vivid imagery, Revelation presents the final chapter in God's story of salvation in which he defeats evil, reverses the curse of sin, restores creation, and lives forever among his people. The closing book of the Bible is known by its opening line: "The revelation of Jesus Christ" (1:1). Although the details are often difficult to understand, the main idea of Revelation is clear—God is in control and will successfully accomplish his purposes. In the end, God wins! Revelation invites those who hear its message to take in the heavenly perspective so that they may persevere faithfully in this fallen world until Jesus returns.

Who Wrote Revelation?

The author of Revelation identifies himself as John, the servant of Jesus Christ (1:1, 4). He also shares in "the suffering and kingdom and patient endurance" with other believers and has been banished to the island of Patmos for proclaiming the message about Jesus (1:9). In addition, John is the recipient of the heavenly vision, a fellow servant, and a true prophet of God (22:8). The author doesn't explicitly identify himself as John the apostle, and some think this is another John. But many, though not all, of the early church fathers identified the author as the apostle John (Justin Martyr, Irenaeus, Tertullian, Clement of Alexandria). Church tradition says a group of Christians moved from Judea to Asia in about AD 66 when the Jews began to revolt against Rome. Supposedly John the apostle was among that group and settled in Ephesus. On the whole, the conclusion that John the apostle wrote the book of Revelation still makes the best sense.

Who Is John's Audience?

John is writing primarily to Christians in the seven churches of Asia Minor mentioned in Revelation 2–3. They are beginning to suffer for their faith with the real possibility that these trials could get much worse. John has already been exiled because of his witness for Jesus (1:9). Antipas, a Christian in Pergamum, has been put to death for his faith (2:13). In his message to the church at Smyrna, Jesus indicates they should not fear what they are about to suffer (2:10). The book also includes several references to Christians being put to death (6:10; 16:6; 17:6; 18:24; 19:2).

There are two main possibilities for when Revelation was written: (1) a time shortly after the death of Nero (AD 68–69), or (2) a date near the end of Domitian's reign (AD 95). Although there is solid evidence for both dates, we prefer the date during the reign of Domitian, when persecution threatened to spread across the Roman Empire. The Imperial Cult (i.e., the worship of the Roman emperor) was a powerful force to be reckoned with primarily because it united religious, political, social, and economic elements into a single force. Domitian wanted people to address him as *dominus et deus noster* ("Our Lord and God"). But the earliest and most basic Christian confession was "Jesus is Lord." When Christians refused to confess "Caesar is Lord," they were considered disloyal to the state and were subject to persecution.

A coin bearing the image of Emperor Domitian.

But not all Christians in the area were standing firm in their faith. When faced with the possibility of suffering, some were tempted to compromise. The messages to the seven churches are filled with warnings for those who are compromising with the world system. Ephesus has forsaken her first love (2:4). Some in Pergamum and Thyatira are following false teachers (2:14–15, 20). Sardis has a reputation of being alive, but it is dead (3:1). And then there is lukewarm Laodicea, which the Lord is about to spit out of his mouth (3:16). Revelation

✦ John writes to comfort those who are standing firm in the faith and warn those who are compromising with the world.

has a pointed message for those who are standing strong as well as those who are compromising, and this central message ties into the overall purpose of the book.

What Is at the Heart of Revelation?

The Siege and Destruction of Jerusalem by the Romans under the Command of Titus, AD 70 by David Roberts.

Revelation addresses a situation in which pagan political power has formed a partnership with false religion. Those who claim to follow Christ are facing mounting pressure to conform to this ungodly partnership at the expense of loyalty to Christ. The overall purpose of Revelation is to comfort those who are facing persecution and to warn those who are compromising with the world system.

During times of opposition, the righteous suffer and the wicked seem to prosper. This raises the question, "Who is Lord?" Revelation says Jesus is Lord in spite of how things appear, and he is returning soon to establish his eternal kingdom. Those facing persecution find hope through a renewed perspective, and those who are compromising are warned to repent. Revelation's goal is to transform the audience and enable them to follow Jesus faithfully.

To carry out this purpose, Revelation makes use of strange images and symbols. This picture language creates a symbolic world that the believers enter as they hear the book read aloud. Here they get a heavenly perspective on current events. They see reality differently. While it seems now that Caesar is Lord, they see in Revelation that God is in control of history and that Jesus truly is Lord! They see that God will win in the end. As a result, they are strongly encouraged to persevere in faithfulness to Jesus. The outline below shows how this transforming vision unfolds:

- Introduction (1:1–20)
- Messages to the Seven Churches (2:1–3:22)
- A Vision of the Heavenly Throne Room (4:1–5:14)
- The Opening of the Seven Seals (6:1–8:1)
- The Sounding of the Seven Trumpets (8:2–11:19)
- The People of God versus the Powers of Evil (12:1–14:20)

✦ The central message of Revelation is that Jesus is Lord!

- The Pouring Out of the Seven Bowls (15:1–16:21)
- The Judgment and Fall of Babylon (17:1–19:5)
- God's Ultimate Victory (19:6–22:5)
- Conclusion (22:6–21)

What Makes Revelation Interesting and Unique?

- Revelation features three literary types (genres): letter, prophetic, and apocalyptic. For this reason, it is a challenge to interpret.
- Revelation is the only place outside the Gospels and Acts where Jesus speaks directly, and the only place where he speaks from heaven.
- The book has much in common with Ezekiel, Daniel, and Zechariah, books in the Old Testament that contain similar apocalyptic elements.
- Together Genesis and Revelation serve as bookends to the entire Bible, with many of the beginning elements in Genesis matching the concluding elements in Revelation. (See the chart comparing Genesis and Revelation at the end of this book.)
- We should take Revelation seriously but not always literally, since it uses picture language to convey historical truth.
- Revelation assigns special significance to numbers.
- The Old Testament is alluded to in Revelation more than in any other New Testament book.

What Is the Message of Revelation?

Introduction (1:1–20)

Revelation 1 includes both a prologue (1:1–8) as well as John's vision and commission to write what he sees (1:9–20). John's vision focuses on the risen, glorified Christ and his continued presence among the seven churches.

This inscription at Pergamum uses divine titles for the Roman emperor.

Numbers in Revelation

Mark W. Wilson

Numbers play an important literary and structural role in Revelation. Whether the numbers are to be interpreted literally or symbolically is a much-debated hermeneutical problem. The meaning of some numbers is interpreted. For example, in 1:20 the seven stars and seven golden lampstands are identified as seven angels and seven churches. However, most numbers are not interpreted. Revelation's numerology draws on ancient Jewish cosmology in the Old Testament. The numbers four, seven, twelve, and their multiples have particular significance.

Four stands for cosmic completeness, and is the number of living creatures around the throne. Four angels restrain the four winds in the four corners of the earth from prematurely harming the earth before the saints can be sealed.

Seven is the most frequently used number and symbolizes perfection and completeness. The Holy Spirit is repeatedly called the "seven spirits" or "seven-fold Spirit." Seven is also used as a structuring device. Revelation is addressed to seven churches in Asia (1:11; 2:1–3:22). The three judgment cycles feature seven seals (6:1–8:1), seven trumpets (8:2–11:19), and seven bowls of seven plagues (15:1–16:21). The great prostitute sits on a beast with seven heads. The number's meaning here is polyvalent: the seven heads are interpreted both as Rome's seven hills and also as seven kings who ruled the empire in the first century (17:3, 9). The identity of these seven emperors is much debated by scholars.

Probably the best-known number in Revelation is 666. John exhorted his audience to calculate the number of the beast—a man—using this isopsephism, or gematria (13:18). In the Greek and Hebrew languages, letters were also used as numbers. The sum of the letters in a name could thus be converted to a number (see the article on Bible Codes). Throughout church history there has been much speculation about this individual's identity, and various antichrist figures have been associated with 666. Many scholars believe that 666 refers to the Hebrew gematria of the Emperor Nero, NERON KAISAR. Nero conducted the first general persecution of Christians after the fire in Rome in AD 64, and during his reign both Peter and Paul were martyred.

The number twelve likewise represents completeness as well as unity in diversity. Twelve doubled equals the twenty-four elders on twenty-four thrones around the heavenly throne (4:4). There are twelve gates in the heavenly city inscribed with the names of the twelve tribes of Israel. There are also twelve foundations; on them are the names of the twelve apostles (21:12, 14). The square of twelve is the thickness of the city, 144 cubits; twelve times one thousand is the size of the city cubed (21:16–17). Twelve squared times one thousand equals the number of God's servants from the twelve tribes of Israel, the 144,000 (7:4; 14:1, 3).

The prologue (1:1–8)

The book takes its title from the opening line: "The revelation (*apocalypsis*) of Jesus Christ" (1:1). This phrase could indicate a revelation *about* Jesus Christ (the main character) or a revelation *from* Jesus Christ (the one who gives the vision to John), or perhaps some of both. The chain of revelation appears as follows:

God → Jesus Christ → his angel → John → believers (1:1–3)

✦ Rather than providing a blueprint about future events, Revelation proclaims how God's people should live in their current situation.

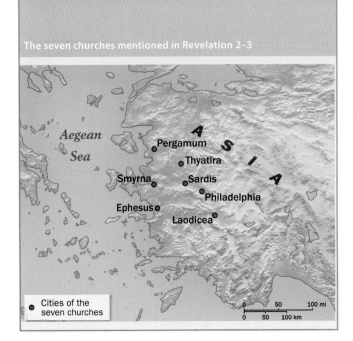

Aegean Sea

Pergamum

Thyatira

Smyrna

Sardis

Philadelphia

Ephesus

Laodicea

A S I A

● Cities of the seven churches

0   50   100 mi
0 50 100 km

The book also claims to be a prophecy and carries a blessing for the one who reads this book to the gathered church and for those who listen and obey (1:3; 22:7–8). The book also serves as a letter to the seven churches of Asia Minor (1:4). The greeting of grace and peace comes from the Father ("him who is, and who was, and who is to come"), the Spirit ("the seven spirits before his throne"), and the Son (1:4–5). Through his death, resurrection, and ascension, Jesus has made us to be "a kingdom and priests" to serve God (1:6–7). Jesus is returning soon, and all the nations of the earth will see him (1:7). The "Lord God" who is the "Alpha and the Omega, who is, and who was, and who is to come, the Almighty" is firmly in control of human history.

John's vision and commission (1:9–20)

Before Jesus speaks to the seven churches, he reveals himself in a vision to John, who is in exile on Patmos for being an obedient witness to Jesus (1:9). On the Lord's Day (Sunday) while John is "in the Spirit," he receives a vision of Jesus and a prophetic commission. He is told to write what he sees on a scroll and send it to the seven churches (1:10–11). What he sees is the glorified Christ—"one like a son of man" standing among the lampstands or churches (1:12–16, 20). Here Jesus is closely connected to the "Ancient of Days," a divine figure in Daniel 7 and 10. John falls down out of fear, but Jesus reassures him by revealing that he is both divine and sovereign (1:17–18, 20). John is instructed to write down the visions he receives from Jesus (1:19).

Messages to the Seven Churches (2:1–3:22)

Revelation 2–3 contains messages to seven churches of Asia Minor: Ephesus, Smyrna, Pergamum, Thyatira, Sardis, Philadelphia, and Laodicea. The messages come from the glorified Jesus who walks among these churches

✦ Revelation 1–3 introduces all the main characters: God, Jesus, John, and the churches.

Messages to the Seven Churches (Rev. 2:1–3:22)

Churches	Command to Write to an Angel of a Church	Description of Jesus	Commendation of Good Works	Accusation Related to Sin	Exhortation and Warning and/or Encouragement	Admonition to Listen	Promise to Overcomers
Ephesus	2:1	2:1	2:2–3, 6	2:4	2:5	2:7	2:7
Smyrna	2:8	2:8	2:9–10			2:11	2:11
Pergamum	2:12	2:12	2:13	2:14–15	2:16	2:17	2:17
Thyatira	2:18	2:18	2:19	2:20–23	2:24–25	2:29	2:26–28
Sardis	3:1	3:1	3:1, 4	3:1	3:2–3	3:6	3:5
Philadelphia	3:7	3:7	3:8–11			3:13	3:12
Laodicea	3:14	3:14		3:15–17	3:18–20	3:22	3:21

(1:12–13, 20). A map of the seven churches shows they are addressed in the order in which a letter carrier would have arrived, beginning with Ephesus and moving clockwise.

The seven messages follow a similar literary pattern: command to an angel to write; description of Jesus; a commendation of the church's good works; an accusation against the church; an exhortation followed by a warning and/or word of encouragement; an admonition to hear what the Spirit says; and a promise to those who overcome.

These messages reflect the twin dangers faced by the church—persecution and compromise. Every church except Smyrna and Philadelphia appear to have serious problems. While a few are proving faithful and are facing persecution as a result, many churches are in danger of losing their influence and identity because of compromise. Each church is challenged to "overcome," a prominent theme in Revelation. Jesus gives each church a difficult but clear choice: listen to his voice and persevere in obedience or cave in to the surrounding culture but face God's judgment.

Each letter closes with the prophetic admonition to "hear what the Spirit says to the churches."

A Vision of the Heavenly Throne Room (4:1–5:14)

In Revelation 4–5 the scene shifts to the heavenly throne room, where God reigns in majestic power. All of heaven worships the Creator and the Lion-Lamb (Jesus), who alone is qualified to open the scroll because of his sacrificial death.

✚ In addition to representing churches of every age (because of the number seven), these seven specific congregations have their own particular challenges. All seven wrestle with how to live faithfully in a world where Caesar claims to be lord.

God, the Creator, is on his throne (4:1–11)

In his vision, John is invited to come up to heaven for additional revelation (4:1). He is once again "in the Spirit" (see 1:10; 4:2; 17:3; 21:10), and arrives to see God in all his glory seated on the throne (4:2–3). In Revelation, the throne becomes a central symbol of the absolute power, majesty, and sovereignty of God (4:5–6). "Flashes of lightning, rumblings and peals of thunder" are reminiscent of the theophany on Mount Sinai and recur throughout the book as signs of God's presence. The twenty-four elders who surround the throne appear to be an exalted order of angels connected especially to the prayers of the saints and to worship (e.g., they fall down in worship in 4:10; 5:8, 14; 11:16; 19:4). The four living creatures, an even more exalted order of angels, also surround God's throne (4:6–8; cf. Ezek. 1; Isa. 6). The heavenly beings continuously worship God as the holy, powerful, and sovereign Creator (4:8–11).

Christ, the Lamb, is worthy to open the scroll (5:1–14)

God holds in his right hand a scroll, probably a symbol for his plan to judge evil and redeem his people. The scroll has writing on both sides and is secured with seven seals, likely an indication of the fullness of the divine plan (5:1). No creature is found worthy to break the seals and open the scroll, and John weeps in despair (5:3–4). But an angel announces that Jesus, the Lion and the Lamb who now stands in the center of the throne and possesses the sevenfold Spirit, is found worthy to open the scroll (5:5–6). When Jesus takes the scroll from the Father, all of creation explodes in worship of Jesus the Redeemer (5:7–14). God's plan will unfold!

A document closed with a seal (bulla).

✚ Revelation 4–5 provides one of the most glorious and overpowering worship scenes in the entire Bible. God is worshiped as Creator and Jesus as Redeemer.

The Opening of the Seven Seals (6:1–8:1)

The unveiling of God's ultimate victory formally begins here with the first of three judgment visions, each with seven elements: seals (6:1–8:1), trumpets (8:2–11:19), and bowls (15:1–16:21). Before the opening of the final seal, there is an interlude consisting of two visions (7:1–17). The seventh seal consists of silence in heaven (8:1).

The first six seals (6:1–17)

The first four seal judgments (commonly known as the "four horsemen of the Apocalypse") include military conquest, violent bloodshed, famine, and death (6:1–8; see Zech. 1:7–11). These judgments have operated throughout history as a result of human sinfulness (cf. the "birth pains" mentioned by Jesus in Mark 13:5–8; Matt. 24:6–8). The fifth seal reveals martyrs under the heavenly altar (6:9). They cry out for vindication: "How long, Sovereign Lord, holy and true, until you judge the inhabitants of the earth and avenge our blood?" (6:10). The phrase "inhabitants of the earth" is a synonym for "unbelievers" in Revelation (3:10; 8:13; 11:10; 13:8, 12, 14; 17:2, 8). God's people have suffered unjustly, and they cry out for justice. God assures the martyrs that he has heard their prayers, but they must wait a while longer for the answer (6:11). Additional persecution must occur. With the opening of the sixth seal, the martyrs' prayer is answered as the day of the Lord arrives. The entire cosmos is shaken by God's judgment, and the wicked have no place to hide (6:12–16). The wrath of God and the Lamb has come. The only remaining question is, "Who can stand?" meaning, "Who can survive or endure the wrath of God?" (6:17; cf. Joel 2:10–11). The interlude of Revelation 7:1–17 answers the question: only the "servants of God" who are protected from his wrath can survive. With the opening of the seventh seal, there is a dramatic pause that anticipates the next series of judgments (8:1).

Interlude: The 144,000 and the great multitude (7:1–8:1)

THE SEALING OF THE 144,000 (7:1–8)

The two visions of Revelation 7 signify the protection and victory of God's people during this time of judgment. In the first vision, 144,000 from all the tribes of Israel have the seal of God placed on their foreheads (7:3–4; 14:1–5). The 144,000 could represent a literal number of Jews, a group of Jewish Christian martyrs, or the whole people of God as the true Israel. Because the seal is given to all true believers (3:12; 7:3–5; 14:1; 22:4) and the use of numbers in Revelation tends to be symbolic, the final two

---

✦ The Bible makes a clear distinction between persecution/tribulation, which believers will endure, and God's wrath, which believers will never encounter.

Seals, Trumpets, and Bowls

Seals 6:1–8:1	Trumpets 8:2–11:19	Interlude—12:1–14:20	Bowls 15:1–16:21
1 White horse—military conquest	Hail and fire, mixed with blood, burn up one-third of earth		Sores on those with beast's mark
2 Red horse—violent bloodshed	Burning mountain causes one-third of sea to turn to blood and destroys one-third of creatures and ships		Sea turns to blood and everything in it dies
3 Black horse—famine	Blazing star (Wormwood) turns one-third of fresh water bitter, killing many people		Rivers and springs turn to blood
4 Pale horse—Death and Hades bring death to one-quarter of earth	One-third of sun, moon, and stars turn dark		Sun scorches people with fire and they curse God
5 Martyrs cry out to God for vindication and are told to wait	Fallen star opens Abyss, releasing locust-scorpions to harm those without seal of God for five months		Throne of beast cursed with darkness. Again, people in agony curse God
6 Shaking of entire cosmos followed by wicked attempting to hide from wrath of God and Lamb	Release of four angels bound at Euphrates who then raise an army of serpent-lions to kill one-third of people on earth		River Euphrates dries up as demonic forces gather kings of earth for battle at Armageddon
Interlude—7:1–17	Interlude—10:1–11:14		No interlude
7 Silence and seven trumpets	Christ's kingdom arrives as elders thank God for his judgment, rewarding of saints, and vindication of his people		Voice from temple says, "It is done," followed by storm-quake and destruction of Babylon by God. Islands and mountains disappear and huge hailstones fall on people who respond by cursing God
Storm-earthquake at 8:3–5	Storm-earthquake at 11:19		Storm-earthquake at 16:18

options are most likely. In any case, this group represents the righteous, who are sealed or protected from the coming wrath of God, in contrast to the wicked, who take the mark of the beast and experience God's judgment.

✝ It is quite possible that the Holy Spirit is God's seal on believers since he is presented as such in other parts of the New Testament (2 Cor. 1:22; Eph. 1:13; 4:30; cf. Ezekiel 9).

Now we move forward in time to the eternal state where victorious believers ("the great multitude") cry out praises to God and the Lamb (7:9–10). The heavenly creatures join them with a sevenfold praise (7:11–12). One of the elders identifies the great multitude as those who have come through the "great tribulation" by purifying themselves and trusting in the death of Christ (7:13–14). They serve God continually and experience God's presence ("his tent") and provision and comfort, along with the Lamb's shepherding care (7:15–17). As the seventh seal is broken and the scroll is opened, heaven becomes silent for a brief time, sobered by the next phase of God's plan (8:1).

The Sounding of the Seven Trumpets (8:2–11:19)

The trumpet judgments, drawing on the plagues of Egypt, reveal God's judgment on a wicked world. Again, between the sixth and seventh judgments, there is an interlude with two visions that instruct and encourage God's people (10:1–11 and 11:1–14).

The first six trumpet judgments (8:2–9:21)

In preparation for the seven trumpets, an angel offers incense and the prayers of the saints on the altar before the throne (8:2–4; cf. 6:9–11). As God hears the prayers of these believers for justice, fire from the altar is hurled to the earth and the seven angels prepare to sound the trumpets (8:5–6). Like the seals, the trumpets have a $4 + 2 + 1$ structure. The first four trumpets primarily affect the physical universe (8:7–12), the next two are directed against wicked humanity (8:13–9:21), and the final trumpet reveals the day when Christ returns (11:14–19). The last three trumpets are announced as "woes" (8:13). At the sound of the fifth trumpet (the first woe), demonic locusts are permitted to torment those who do not have God's seal (9:1–11). At the sound of the sixth trumpet (second woe), four angels of destruction lead a massive demonic army to attack wicked humanity (9:12–19). The sad result is that the surviving unbelievers still do not repent of their idolatry and immorality (9:20–21). Throughout these judgments, God uses the self-destructive power of evil to pour out his wrath (demons torment unbelievers). God's people are protected and will never experience God's wrath.

Interlude: The little scroll and the two witnesses (10:1–11:13)

The little scroll held by the mighty angel is likely the same scroll as in Revelation 5, although the focus here may be on the role of God's people in the

✚ The interludes in Revelation often provide the people of God with glimpses of the final future under God's rule and offer perspective on their current situation (cf. Rev. 7:1–8:1; 10:1–11:13; 12:1–14:20).

Revelation   979

redemptive plan (10:1–2). As the mighty angel shouts the seven thunders, John is told not to write them down (10:3–4). How long, O Lord? (6:10). The angel proclaims "no more delay" (10:6). With the seventh trumpet, the "mystery of God will be accomplished" (10:7), referring to the day of the Lord. John is then told to take the scroll and eat it (10:8–11). As he internalizes the message, it is both sweet in his mouth (symbolizing that God's plan will now be carried out) and sour in his stomach (symbolizing that God's plan will include suffering and persecution for believers).

THE TWO WITNESSES (11:1–13)

In the previous vision, the church is told it must suffer (sour) as God works out his master plan (sweet). This vision says much the same thing, with added details about the role God's people will play. The temple refers to the people of God, both Jew and gentile (11:1). John is told to measure the inner court but not measure the outer court (11:2). While God's people will be protected from spiritual harm (inner court), they will not be exempted from persecution (outer court). The theme of victory through sacrifice is repeated throughout Revelation. The two witnesses (the two olive trees and two lampstands; see Rev. 1:20) symbolize the witnessing church (11:3–4). Two witnesses were required for a valid testimony (Deut. 17:6; 19:15; Zech. 4), and they stand in contrast to the two beasts of Revelation 13. God uses his witnessing church to do spiritual battle, to perform miracles, and to call down God's judgment on a wicked world (11:5–6). They are temporarily defeated and even put to death by the powers of evil (11:7–10). In the end, however, God raises them from the dead and brings them into his presence as their terror-stricken enemies look on (11:11–13).

The seventh trumpet (11:14–19)

The perspective now shifts from earth to heaven as the heavenly choir announces God's victory (11:14–15). The elders fall down in worship of the Lord God Almighty for exercising his great power (11:16–17). Although the nations (unbelievers here) are angry at God and his people, God is righteous and will condemn evil and reward his servants (11:18). God's heavenly temple is opened and his presence revealed (11:19).

The People of God versus the Powers of Evil (12:1–14:20)

Revelation 12–14 serves as an interlude between the trumpet judgments and the bowl judgments. This interlude explains why God's people face hostility in this world, identifies the unholy trinity (the dragon and the two beasts), and reminds believers of the blessings God has in store for the righteous and the judgment he will execute against evil.

The woman and the dragon (12:1–17)

The chapter opens with a woman who is about to give birth to a male child (12:1–2, 5). The male child represents Jesus, and the woman most likely symbolizes the faithful community who gives birth to both the Messiah and the church. An enormous red dragon (Satan) is waiting to devour the child (12:3–4). As soon as the child is born, he is snatched up to God (referring to Jesus's resurrection and ascension), and the woman flees to a place of spiritual refuge for "1,260 days," the time of persecution between the ascension of Jesus and his return (12:5–6; cf. 11:2; 12:14; 13:5). The scene now shifts to heaven, where the archangel Michael and his angels fight against the dragon and his angels. After his defeat, the dragon and his angels are thrown down to the earth (12:7–9). The hymn of victory in 12:10–12 praises God for defeating Satan, explains how believers overcome the devil, and warns of Satan's ongoing rage. As a defeated foe who has had to forfeit his place in heaven, the dragon pursues the woman with a vengeance and makes war against the rest of her offspring—those who "obey God's commandments and hold to the testimony of Jesus" (12:13–17). This central chapter reminds us that God has defeated Satan through Jesus's death and resurrection and that the victory is certain; even so, God's people will continue to suffer persecution.

Remains of the Temple of Flavian Sebastoi (emperors of the Flavian family) in Ephesus.

✝ Revelation 12 serves as the center of the book and explains why God's people face trouble in this world—we are involved in a real spiritual battle!

The Imperial Cult

Mark W. Wilson

The imperial cult, or ruler-cult, was a religious and political institution in which the Roman emperor was worshiped as a divine being. It was widespread in the Roman Empire in the first three centuries AD, with its center being in the eastern Mediterranean, particularly Asia Minor. Offering divine honors to rulers was not native to the Romans but developed under Greek influence.

An antecedent of the cult was the worship of Alexander the Great, who was declared a god at Siwa in 331 BC. The Hellenistic rulers who succeeded him were likewise accorded divine honors. The erection of a statue of Antiochus IV in the temple of Jerusalem was one of the provocations for the Maccabean revolt in 167 BC. After his assassination in 42 BC, Julius Caesar was deified by the Roman senate. The Romans would give divine honors to their rulers only after death, while the Greeks would worship living emperors as gods.

In 29 BC Caesar's adopted son, Augustus, authorized the Greek provincial assemblies (*koina*) to construct the first imperial cult temples in Pergamum and Nicomedia, the provincial capitals. These temples, dedicated to Augustus and Roma, the patron goddess of Rome, were for the Greeks in Asia and Bithynia. For the Roman residents, Augustus granted Ephesus and Nicea the right to dedicate a sacred precinct to Divus Julius and Dea Roma. In AD 26 Tiberius chose Smyrna to become the temple keeper (*neokoros*) for Asia's second imperial cult temple. Smyrna was a long-time ally of Rome, having established the first temple in the east to Dea Roma in 195 BC (Polycarp, the bishop of Smyrna, was martyred in AD 156 for refusing to offer incense to the emperor).

Gaius Caligula (AD 12–41) was the first emperor to demand worship from his subjects while still living. The imperial cult sanctuary built for him in Miletus was closed by the Roman senate after his assassination in AD 41. Ephesus received its first neocorate (a rank granted by the Roman Senate for building a temple for emperor worship) in AD 89/90 when

The beast from the sea and the beast from the earth (13:1–18)

Chapter 13 introduces Satan's two agents for waging war against God's people—the beast out of the sea (13:1–10) and the beast out of the earth (13:11–18). The dragon and the two beasts constitute a satanic or unholy trinity resolute on seducing and destroying God's people. The first beast, commonly referred to as the antichrist, represents pagan political and military power allied with Satan (13:1–3). First-century readers would have identified the beast as the Roman Empire, personified in the emperor. The healing of the fatal wound (13:3) may refer to the *Nero redivivus* legend ("Nero revived") that said Nero had been resurrected and was in the east preparing an army to invade Rome and recapture his empire. This first beast receives power from Satan, blasphemes and slanders God, persecutes God's people, and forces the nations to worship him (13:4–7). Everyone who does not belong to God will worship this beast (13:8), and God's people should prepare to persevere faithfully, even if it means death (13:9–10). The beast

982 ✦ Although Revelation never uses the term "antichrist," many interpreters equate the beast out of the sea with the antichrist and the beast out of the earth with the false prophet. Together with Satan, they constitute the unholy trinity.

Domitian built the temple of the Sebastoi there. The refusal of Christians to worship the emperor appears to underline the tensions with the state depicted in Revelation 13. It was probably one of the reasons John was exiled to Patmos (Rev. 1:9).

The principal official of the provincial assembly (*koinon*) was the imperial cult's chief priest. This official, chosen annually, is regarded by most interpreters as the second beast out of the earth (Rev. 13:11–17). The identification of Pergamum as the throne of Satan (Rev. 2:13) probably refers to the city as a center of imperial cult activity. The woman seated on seven hills in Revelation 17:9 is the personification of Dea Roma.

The imperial cult existed in other biblical cities in the first century. Coins document the presence of a temple in Antioch on the Orontes. In AD 25 the assembly of Galatia authorized the construction of imperial cult temples in the capital Ancyra and at Pisidian Antioch. On the walls of the Greek-style temple in Ancyra is the bilingual Greek and Latin inscription of the *Res Gestae*, a biographical propaganda piece detailing the deeds of Augustus. Fragments of the same inscription were found in the entrance gate of the Roman-style temple at Pisidian Antioch. Imperial cult worship was likewise practiced in Greece and Macedonia, especially in Roman colonies such as Corinth and Philippi. Josephus reports that Augustus built three imperial cult temples in Judea: at Caesarea Maritima, at Sebaste in Samaria, and at Caesarea Philippi.

Statues of the emperor, which John calls the image of the beast (Rev. 13:14–15), were erected in the cult temples. Processions, sacrifices, and games were likewise held in the emperor's honor. It has been questioned whether the imperial cult met any religious needs of the people or was just a political institution. The cult seemingly contained genuine religious content as the worshipers expressed devotion to their ruler. The emperor as an incarnation of god was thought to bring order and stability to daily life, viewed generally as governed by capricious Fate. It is little wonder the early Christians came into sharp conflict with the imperial cult. Emperors were called such names as *divus* (divine), savior, lord, creator, and son of god—the same names that Christians used for Jesus Christ. Christians were to submit to the emperor (Rom. 13:1; 1 Pet. 2:13) but never to pray or sacrifice to him.

from the earth, commonly called the False Prophet, represents false religion that supports the first beast (13:11–12). In the first century, the imperial priesthood that fostered emperor worship played this role. The beast from the earth performs miraculous signs designed to deceive people, promotes worship of the image of the first beast, and forces everyone to take the mark of the beast (13:13–17). The number of the first beast is 666 (13:18). Of the many suggestions for solving this riddle, the best options point to the number representing a Roman emperor (Nero or Domitian). Satan uses pagan political and military power supported by false religion to oppose God and persecute God's people.

The Lamb and the 144,000 (14:1–5)

Revelation 14 gives the reader another glimpse of the future blessings God has in store for his people (the 144,000). Believers are described as pure, blameless followers of the Lamb who have been sealed by God. In spite of

✛ Some Greek manuscripts have the number 616 instead of 666 (omitting a final letter), yet both spell the same name: Nero Caesar.

the difficulties they face now, one day they will stand with the Lamb in the heavenly Jerusalem and sing a new song of redemption.

The three angels (14:6–13)

The three angels proclaim the eternal gospel and a final chance to repent (14:6–7), the fall of Babylon the Great (14:8), and the judgment reserved for those who follow the beast (14:9–11). God's people are called to "patient endurance," and the second of seven beatitudes in the book is announced (14:12–13; cf. 1:3; 16:15; 19:9; 20:6; 22:7, 14). Those who remain faithful to the end (i.e., they "die in the Lord") will experience eternal rest from their labor of endurance.

The harvest of the earth (14:14–20)

God's judgment is now portrayed in two visions using the harvest theme (cf. Joel 3:13). Both the grain harvest (14:14–16) and the grape harvest (14:17–20) could portray God's judgment on the wicked, or they could describe the gathering of the righteous (grain harvest) and the condemnation of the wicked (grape harvest), much like Jesus's parable of the wheat and the tares (Matt. 13:24–30; cf. John 4:35–38).

The Pouring Out of the Seven Bowls (15:1–16:21)

The seven golden bowls follow the trumpets and seals as the final series of seven judgments. As the bowls of God's wrath are poured out on an unrepentant world, the plagues are intense, devastating manifestations of God's wrath against sin and evil. In response, unbelievers not only refuse to repent; they also go so far as to curse God.

Preparation for the bowl judgments—seven angels with plagues (15:1–8)

Seven angels are given seven last plagues (15:1). The heavenly temple is opened, and the seven angels are prepared and commissioned to pour out the seven golden bowls filled with God's wrath (15:5–8). In 15:2–4, we hear the song of those who have been victorious over the beast. They sing the song of Moses (a connection to the exodus background) and the song of the Lamb as they praise the Lord God Almighty for his great and marvelous deeds.

✛ The bowl judgments are more intense than the seals and the trumpets, suggesting that God is bringing the final judgment on evil.

The bowl judgments (16:1–21)

The bowls, like the trumpets, draw on the plagues in Exodus to depict the pouring out of God's wrath on unbelievers. In contrast to the seals and trumpets, the bowl judgments contain no interlude between the sixth and seventh elements. While the seals and trumpets are both partial judgments, affecting one-quarter and one-third of the earth, respectively, the bowl judgments are universal. These are the final judgments of God's wrath. The bowls do contain three added features: (1) a song of praise for God's justice (16:5–7); (2) the evil trinity gathering the nations for war (16:13–14; 19:11–21); and (3) a warning from Jesus that he will return unexpectedly (16:15). As a result of the bowl judgments, unbelievers continue in rebellion and even curse God (16:9, 11, 21).

With the seventh bowl judgment, history comes to a close (16:17). God's decisive judgment of evil described in the seventh bowl is developed more fully in Revelation 17–19.

The Judgment and Fall of Babylon (17:1–19:5)

In this section we see a contrast between two cities: the earthly Babylon, the great mother of prostitutes destined for destruction, and the heavenly Jerusalem, the bride of Christ where God will live forever among his people. In the end God's people celebrate as he brings about justice by condemning Babylon.

The "mountain of Megiddo" in Israel becomes a symbol for the final battle between God and the forces of evil (i.e., Armageddon in Rev. 16:12–16).

✚ Babylon destroyed Jerusalem in 587/586 BC and came to epitomize the enemies of Israel. In Revelation "Babylon" represents ancient Rome (cf. 1 Pet. 5:13) and all future centers of power opposed to God and his kingdom.

A denarius featuring Emperor Domitian on one side and his infant son on the other.

The woman on the beast (17:1–18)

John is carried away "in the Spirit" to see the "great prostitute" who sits on a "scarlet beast" (17:1–3). The harlot symbolizes "Babylon the Great" or Rome in the first century and any subsequent power-center opposed to God (17:5, 15, 18). The beast was first introduced in chapter 13. The prostitute lives in luxury, engages in blatant immorality, and persecutes those who follow Jesus (17:4–6). The angel explains the vision in 17:7–14. The beast will ascend from the Abyss and deceive the "inhabitants of the earth" (unbelievers) through a counterfeit resurrection (17:8: "once was, now is not, and yet will come"). The "seven kings" likely represent Roman emperors (17:9–11), and the "ten horns" represent political rulers who join the beast to fight against the Lamb (17:12–13). But the Lamb will overcome them because he is "Lord of lords and King of kings," and with him will be his faithful followers (17:14). The self-destructive power of evil is demonstrated by the beast and the ten horns destroying the prostitute (17:16), all under the sovereign control of God (17:17).

The fall of Babylon (18:1–24)

The destruction of Babylon mentioned in 17:16 is now fully explained in chapter 18. Babylon's fall is announced and is due mainly to spiritual and economic adultery (18:1–3). The people of God are commanded to "come out of her" so that they will not share her sins or her punishment (18:4–5). She will experience a double portion of judgment from the Lord God (18:6–8). Those who profited from her offer a funeral lament (18:9–19), while the righteous rejoice that God is bringing about justice (18:20). God destroys Babylon for the sin of excessive materialism, for deceiving the nations, and for murdering the saints (18:21–24).

Hallelujah (19:1–5)

The funeral laments for the deceased Babylon in chapter 18 give way to a massive celebration that includes the heavenly multitude (19:1–3), the twenty-four elders and four living creatures (19:4), and all of God's servants (19:5). They sing mighty hymns of praise to God for his true and just judgments, for condemning the prostitute, and for avenging the blood of his servants (19:2).

✚ Babylon is guilty of three major types of sins: (1) living in wealth, luxury, and greed; (2) deceiving the nations; and (3) murdering the saints.

Millennialism

Three major interpretive views are related to the issue of the millennium. *Premillennialism* ("pre" meaning "before") is the view that Christ will return before establishing an earthly reign with his saints for a thousand years. This may or may not be a literal thousand-year period of time, but it will be a full and complete earthly reign. Many premillennialists understand the millennium to be the fulfillment of many Old Testament prophecies portraying the son of David ruling over a kingdom of righteousness and peace on earth. Premillennialists tend to take Revelation 19–21 as a sequence of events occurring at the end of the age. Christ will return (Revelation 19), Satan will be bound, and the saints resurrected to reign with Christ for a thousand years (Rev. 20:1–6). Then Satan will be released for a final rebellion before his ultimate defeat (Rev. 20:7–10). Then comes the last resurrection and the final judgment (Rev. 20:11–15), followed by the new heaven and new earth (Rev. 21).

Postmillennialism ("post" meaning "after") believes that Christ will return after the millennium. Postmillennialists maintain that the gospel of Christ will eventually triumph and bring about the millennial age (e.g., wars cease, peace and righteousness prevail, the conversion of most of humanity). This view is founded on the notion of progress, since it is the progress of the gospel rather than the return of Christ that ushers in the spiritual reign of Christ known as the millennium. The millennium will be followed by the return of Christ, a general resurrection and judgment, and the eternal kingdom.

Amillennialism ("a" meaning "no") contends that there will not be a visible, earthly millennial reign of Christ. This view stresses the symbolic nature of Revelation and interprets Revelation 20:4–6 either as symbolizing (1) the heavenly reign of Christ with Christians who have already died and are now with the Lord, or (2) the spiritual reign of Christ during the present age in the hearts of believers on earth. Satan has been bound by the gospel of Christ. At the end of history and as part of the transition to the eternal state there will be the return of Christ, a general resurrection, and a last judgment.

God's Ultimate Victory (19:6–22:5)

This climactic section describes God's ultimate victory over evil and the final reward for the people of God.

The return of the warrior Christ (19:6–21)

John hears the sound of a great multitude offering praise that the Lord God Almighty reigns, that the wedding of the Lamb has arrived, and that the bride now stands prepared, having been made ready by means of her righteous acts (19:6–8). John is told to record a blessing on those invited to the wedding supper of the Lamb (19:9). John attempts to worship the angel but is quickly corrected: worship is reserved for God alone (19:10)! In contrast to his "triumphal entry" into Jerusalem on a humble donkey,

Ways of Interpreting Revelation

There are five main theories about how Revelation should be interpreted: preterist, historicist, futurist, idealist, and eclectic. The *preterist* theory views Revelation as relating only to the time in which John lived rather than to any future period. John communicates to first-century readers how God plans to deliver them from the wickedness of the Roman Empire. The *historicist* theory argues that Revelation gives an overview of the major movements of church history from the first century until the return of Christ. The *futurist* theory claims that most of Revelation (usually chapters 4–22) deals with a future time just before the end of history. The *idealist* theory maintains that Revelation is a symbolic portrayal of the ongoing conflict between good and evil. Revelation offers timeless spiritual truths to encourage Christians of all ages. The *eclectic* theory combines the strengths of several of the other theories (e.g., a message to the original audience, a timeless spiritual message, and some future fulfillment), while avoiding their weaknesses.

Jesus now arrives from heaven on a white horse. He comes in power and great glory carrying a sharp sword to strike down the nations and execute God's justice. His name is "King of kings and Lord of lords" (19:14–16). The scavenger birds gather for the great supper of God, which will consist of God's enemies and stands in contrast to the wedding feast of the Lamb (19:17–18). The stage is set for the climactic battle between God and evil, but there is no battle to speak of. The warrior Christ simply appears, and the victory is won (19:19–20). He captures the beast and false prophet and throws them into the "fiery lake of burning sulfur," while their armies are killed by his sword (19:20–21).

The binding of Satan, the millennial reign, and the destruction of Satan (20:1–10)

This is probably the best-known and the most controversial section of the entire book. To begin with, Satan is seized, bound, and locked in the Abyss for a thousand years to prevent him from deceiving the nations (20:1–3). At the return of Christ and the beginning of the millennium, believers who have been loyal to Jesus to the point of death and have not followed the beast "came to life and reigned with Christ" (20:4). The second death has no power over those who participate in the first resurrection (20:5–6). Believers now reign with Christ for a thousand years (symbolic of an indefinite but complete period of time). Following the millennium, Satan is released from his prison and once again deceives the

✦ The millennial debates often hinge on the various interpretations of Revelation 20:1–6.

nations, who willingly join him and justify the judgment they are about to receive (20:8). Although they intend to destroy God's people, fire comes down from heaven and devours them (20:9). Finally, Satan joins the beast and false prophet in the lake of burning sulfur where the unholy trinity is eternally tormented (20:10).

The great white throne of judgment (20:11–15)

God, seated on the great white throne, judges the dead according to what they have done (20:11–13). Anyone whose name is not found in the book of life is thrown into the lake of fire (20:15). Death and Hades are also thrown into the lake of fire, as sin and evil are fully and finally destroyed (20:14). Having judged evil, God now ushers in the eternal state of glory.

The new heaven and new earth (21:1–22:5)

John describes the vision of the eternal state briefly in 21:1–8 and more thoroughly in 21:9–22:5. He sees a "new heaven and new earth" without any sea (a symbol of evil), along with the arrival of the Holy City, the new Jerusalem, prepared as a beautiful bride (21:1–2). The city and bride are symbols of God's people among whom he will live for eternity. This fulfills God's promise to live with his people and take away their pain and suffering (21:3–4). God is making all things new, completing his work, remaining in control, and providing the water of life (21:5–6). The overcomers will inherit God and his eternal blessings, while the wicked will be assigned to the lake of fire, the second death (21:7–8).

The angel now gives John a more detailed look at the bride-city in 21:9–27. God's plan all along has been to live among his multicultural people in all his glory (21:9–14). The city is shaped like a cube, reflecting the dimensions of the holy place of God's presence in the temple (21:15–17). But this city that is beautiful beyond words contains no temple "because the Lord God Almighty and the Lamb are its temple" (21:18–22). God's glory replaces the sun and moon as the source of light (21:23). Even the nations (gentiles) may enter this "temple" if their names are written in the book of life (21:24–27).

The image now shifts to a garden, a restored Eden, fulfilling God's master plan to bring human beings into fellowship with the divine community of Father, Son, and Spirit (22:1–5). The river of life flows from the throne, and people may now eat from the Tree of Life that heals the nations (22:1–2). Sin's curse has been removed, and redeemed humanity bears God's name, sees his face, serves him, and reigns forever in his glorious presence (22:3–5).

✚ The Bible consistently speaks of a "new heaven *and* a new earth" as the final home of the righteous (see Isa. 65:17; 66:22; Heb. 12:26–27; 2 Pet. 3:10–13; Rev. 21:1, 4–5).

Conclusion (22:6–21)

Revelation draws to a close with the angel's verification that God is the source of its message (22:6). Jesus is coming soon, and those who keep the words of this prophecy will be blessed (22:7). Again, prophecy often focuses more on proclamation than prediction. John, the recipient of the heavenly vision, is tempted to worship the angel but is told to worship only God (22:8–9). He is also instructed not to seal up this prophecy because the time is near (22:10). The wicked and the righteous should continue down their respective paths (22:11). Jesus is coming soon and will bring his reward with him, whether eternal life or condemning wrath (22:12). Now Jesus is identified with divine titles: "the Alpha and the Omega, the First and the Last, the Beginning and the End" (22:13, 16). Those who are allowed into the heavenly city will be blessed, while the wicked will be cast outside (22:14–15). There are pleas for Christ to return (22:17). A strong warning is given for anyone who adds to or subtracts from the words of this prophecy (22:18–19).

Jesus assures his people his return is imminent, and John responds with a prayer-statement that Christians of all times can make their own—"Come, Lord Jesus" (22:20). A grace benediction closes the book (22:21).

So What? Applying Revelation Today

Although Revelation has been a closed and confusing book to many, it carries a powerful message that can encourage and strengthen today's church. The key is to focus on the bigger picture and not get bogged down in all the details. First, the messages to the seven churches in chapters 2–3 remind us of what Jesus thinks of his church. We see the importance of things such as truth, holiness, and love. We hear again what Jesus expects of his church.

Second, Revelation reminds us that God is sovereign and that Jesus is Lord. No matter how things appear in our nation or in our world, God is still on his throne! God's people should not lose hope. Jesus will return again to set things right. In the end, God wins!

Third, the book makes it clear that God's people can expect to face opposition in this world. The notion that Christians will be exempt from tribulation is unbiblical and without historical support (John 16:33). Christians all around the world even now are being persecuted. Believers should be prepared to suffer for their faith. Our hope lies in God's ability to raise us from the dead, not to protect us from physical death. God will always protect us spiritually and we will never experience his wrath, but we should be

✦ Creation has come full circle, from the perfect Garden of Eden in Genesis 1–2 to the city-garden of the New Jerusalem in the new heaven and new earth of Revelation 21–22.

Genesis 1–11	Revelation 19–22	
Sinful people scattered	God's people unite to sing his praises	19:6–7
"Marriage" of Adam and Eve	Marriage of Last Adam and his bride, the church	19:7; 21:2, 9
God abandoned by sinful people	God's people (New Jerusalem, bride of Christ) made ready for God; marriage of Lamb	19:7–8; 21:2, 9–21
Exclusion from bounty of Eden	Invitation to marriage supper of Lamb	19:9
Satan introduces sin into world	Satan and sin are judged	19:11–21; 20:7–10
The Serpent deceives humanity	The ancient Serpent is bound "to keep him from deceiving the nations"	20:2–3
God gives humans dominion over the earth	God's people will reign with him forever	20:4, 6; 22:5
People rebel against the true God resulting in physical and spiritual death	God's people risk death to worship the true God and thus experience life	20:4–6
Sinful people sent away from life	God's people have their names written in the Book of Life	20:4–6, 15; 21:6, 27
Death enters the world	Death is put to death	20:14; 21:4
God creates first heaven and earth, eventually cursed by sin	God creates a new heaven and earth where sin is nowhere to be found	21:1
Water symbolizes unordered chaos	There is no longer any sea (symbol of evil)	21:1
Sin brings pain and tears	God comforts his people and removes crying and pain	21:4
Sinful humanity cursed with wandering (exile)	God's people given a permanent home	21:3
Community forfeited	Genuine community experienced	21:3, 7
Sinful people are banished from presence of God	God lives among his people	21:3, 7, 22; 22:4
Creation begins to grow old and die	All things are made new	21:5
Water used to destroy wicked humanity	God quenches thirst with water from spring of life	21:6; 22:1
"In the beginning God . . ."	"I am the Alpha and the Omega, the Beginning and the End"	21:6
Sinful humanity suffers a wandering exile in the land	God gives his children an inheritance	21:7
Sin enters the world	Sin banished from God's city	21:8, 27; 22:15
Sinful humanity separated from presence of holy God	God's people experience God's holiness (cubed city = Holy of Holies)	21:15–21
God creates light and separates it from darkness	No more night or natural light; God himself is the source of light	21:23; 22:5
Languages of sinful humanity confused	God's people is a multicultural people	21:24, 26; 22:2
Sinful people sent away from garden	New heaven/earth includes a garden	22:2
Sinful people forbidden to eat from tree of life	God's people may eat freely from the tree of life	22:2, 14
Sin results in spiritual sickness	God heals the nations	22:2
Sinful people cursed	The curse removed from redeemed humanity and they become a blessing	22:3
Sinful people refuse to serve/obey God	God's people serve him	22:3
Sinful people ashamed in God's presence	God's people will "see his face"	22:4

prepared to suffer. Anytime false religion forms a partnership with pagan political and military power, the result is usually not good for God's people.

Fourth, we are faced with the choice to compromise with the world system or to overcome out of loyalty to Jesus. The promises in Revelation are directed toward those who overcome. Believers overcome by depending on the gospel of Christ crucified even to the point of death (Rev. 12:11).

Fifth, Revelation reminds us our present sufferings are not worth comparing to the glorious future God has in store. What God planned in Genesis 1–2 is now being completed in Revelation 19–22. God's desire to live among his people in intimate fellowship will be realized. Most of what we sing and say about heaven falls short of what Revelation actually teaches. It will be a "new heaven and new earth," a perfect garden-city, without any evil, where we will live forever in the presence of God with people who love God. Forever! We too pray, "Come Lord Jesus!"

Our Favorite Verse in Revelation

> They overcame him
>> by the blood of the Lamb
>> and by the word of their testimony;
> they did not love their lives so much
>> as to shrink from death. (12:11)

PART II

How the Bible Came to Be

The Inspiration of the Bible

Mark L. Strauss

Introduction

At its most fundamental level, the doctrine of inspiration means that the Bible is not merely human reflections about God or meditations on religious themes. It is rather divine communication—God's message to human beings. "Inspired" does not mean merely inspiring or inspirational in the way that a great work of literature or a piece of art is inspiring. It means that God himself has spoken and has disclosed himself to his people.

The Scriptural Basis for Inspiration

Scripture attests to its own inspiration both directly and indirectly. The Old Testament law is to be obeyed because its imperatives come from God himself. On Mount Sinai Moses receives the word of the Lord and delivers it to the people. The Ten Commandments begin with the affirmation, "And God spoke all these words" (Exod. 20:1). Consider these statements from the great acrostic Psalm 119, a celebration of the precepts, commands, and statutes that God gave to his people:

119:4—"You have laid down precepts that are to be fully obeyed."

An Egyptian flask from the time of Moses (1550–1295 BC) in the shape of a scribe.

119:13—"With my lips I recount all the laws that come from your mouth."

119:86—"All your commands are trustworthy."

119:88—"I will obey the statutes of your mouth."

119:89—"Your word, O Lord, is eternal; it stands firm in the heavens."

119:138—"The statutes you have laid down are righteous; they are fully trustworthy."

119:152—"Long ago I learned from your statutes that you established them to last forever."

God's word is faithful and true because it comes from the mouth of the one who is "Faithful and True" (Rev. 19:11).

Scripture as God's own self-revelation is equally affirmed in the prophets, where God speaks through his human servants. The formula, "the word of the Lord came to . . ." appears throughout the prophetic corpus (Jer. 1:2; Hosea 1:1; Jon. 1:1; Mic. 1:1; Zeph. 1:1; Hag. 1:1; Zech. 1:1; cf. Luke 3:2). The first chapter of Isaiah illustrates well the multiplicity of expressions: "the Lord has spoken" (Isa. 1:2); "hear the word of the Lord" (1:10); "says the Lord" (1:11); "for the mouth of the Lord has spoken" (1:20); "the Lord, the Lord Almighty, the Mighty One of Israel, declares" (1:24). The prophets

Jebal Musa, a possible location of Mount Sinai, where Moses received the Ten Commandments.

confirm that inspiration is the convergence of the human and the divine. Jeremiah's prophecies are simultaneously "the words of Jeremiah son of Hilkiah" and "the word of the Lord" (Jer. 1:1–2). This convergence is especially clear in quotations of the Old Testament in the New. New Testament writers easily move back and forth referring to Scripture as the words of the human prophet ("this is what was spoken by the prophet Joel"; Acts 2:16, citing Joel 2:28–32) or a message given directly by the Holy Spirit ("So, as the Holy Spirit says"; Heb. 3:7, citing Ps. 95:7; see also Heb. 10:15–17, citing Jer. 31:33, 34). The prayer of the church in Acts 4 provides the fullest description: "You [God] spoke by the Holy Spirit through the mouth of your servant, our father David" (Acts 4:25; citing Ps. 2:1, 2). God spoke by means of the Spirit through his human agent.

Scripture's inspiration, affirmed implicitly in these passages, finds explicit expression in 2 Timothy 3:16–17:

> All Scripture is God-breathed and is useful for teaching, rebuking, correcting and training in righteousness, so that the man of God may be thoroughly equipped for every good work.

The Greek word translated "God-breathed" is *theopneustos*, a term possibly coined by Paul himself to express the nature of inspiration. The King James Version rendering, "inspired by God," finds it roots in the Latin Vulgate (*divinitus inspirata*). Unfortunately "*in*-spired" might suggest that God "breathed into" Scripture its authority, while *theopneustos* more likely means that God "breathed out" Scripture. Inspiration does not mean divine validation of a human work, but God's self-revelation of his own purpose and will. Second Timothy 3:16 further affirms that the purpose of inspiration is to enable God's people to live in right relationship with God ("training in righteousness") and with others ("equipped for every good work"). The Bible is not an icon to be worshiped or an oracle to be consulted. It is rather a living account of God's actions in human history and a practical guidebook for living as the people of God.

Second Peter 1:21 provides further insight into the process of inspiration: "For prophecy never had its origin in the human will, but prophets, though human, spoke from God as they were carried along by the Holy Spirit" (TNIV). While this passage again confirms the divine-human origin of Scripture, it expressly concerns the prophets, who often received oracles and visions directly from God, and so may not be a definitive expression of the manner and means of inspiration. What does it mean, for example, that the prophets were "carried along" by the Holy Spirit? While the precise mode of inspiration remains a mystery, the following clarifications can be made.

Clarifications Related to Inspiration

How can texts written by ordinary human beings in the context of common human experience be at the same time the eternal and unchanging Word of God? The following points seek to clarify the nature of inspiration.

Inspiration Is Not Dictation

Except in some specialized cases, inspiration does not mean dictation. God did not whisper into the ears of the biblical authors, but rather worked *through each author's own circumstances, thoughts, intentions, and personalities* to communicate his divine message. The exceptions would be in those cases where the author is told to write exactly what he is told (as in some prophetic texts) or where God himself inscribes the text (as in the Decalogue, inscribed on stone tablets "by the finger of God"; Exod. 31:18). Evidence that inspiration does not mean dictation is the differences among biblical authors in literary styles, including vocabulary choice, sentence structure, level of diction, and choice of genre. Mark's Gospel, for example, is written in a rather rough Semitic style, with a great deal of parataxis (parallel sentences linked by "and"), while Luke's has a more refined Hellenistic literary style.

Inspiration Concerns Contextually Located Utterances

The diversity of authorship goes beyond issues of literary style. The authors wrote from within their own historical and cultural contexts, and their writing reflects the boundaries and limitations of each of those contexts. The inspiration of Scripture therefore relates to its original genre, purpose, and occasion. For example, Isaiah's message of coming judgment against Israel at the hands of the Assyrians is an inspired and authoritative message from God *to the Israelites of the eighth century BC*. Its message must be understood within the language, culture, context, and literary conventions of that day. Furthermore, this message was intended for that audience in their particular situation. Application to other times and places must be determined carefully through sound principles of hermeneutics. In the same way, Paul's letters to the Corinthians, for example, were written to a specific group of first-century Christians living in the Greco-Roman city of Corinth and were intended to address their unique problems and concerns. Paul's instructions and exhortations must be understood first of all within this social, cultural, and ecclesiastical context before they can be applied to other church contexts. Inspiration does not negate the need for the hard work of interpretation (exegesis) or application (contextualization).

Contextual location also relates to the Bible's many genres and modes of expression. A poem, for example, is inspired as a poem, and so its truth and authority must be understood within the parameters of its literary form. Inspiration must take into account the use of figu-

Isaiah's message of judgment was to the Israelites of the eighth century BC. Depicted above is an Israelite family from Lachish being led away into exile after defeat by the Assyrians.

rative language ("the trees of the field will clap their hands"; Isa. 55:12), metaphor and simile ("the Lord is my rock"; 2 Sam. 22:2), phenomenological language ("the sun rose"; Gen. 32:31), irony ("Nazareth! Can anything good come from there?" John 1:46), sarcasm ("you are so wise!" 2 Cor. 11:19), approximations ("about eight days later"; Luke 9:28; cf. Mark 9:2: "six days"), and a host of other "nonliteral" literary forms. Narrative must be understood as a story, so that not every statement made is necessarily true. When the high priest says of Jesus, "He has spoken blasphemy" (Matt. 26:65), this is a false statement given by an unreliable character. The dragons and beasts of apocalyptic literature may be mythical and symbolic images meant to communicate spiritual truth.

Inspiration Does Not Negate the Use of Written and Oral Sources

A third clarification relates to the manner in which inspired Scripture was composed. The authors of Kings and Chronicles, for example, drew from a variety of sources, both canonical and noncanonical (1 Kings 11:41; 14:19, 29; 1 Chron. 29:29; 2 Chron. 9:29; 12:15; 20:34; 24:27; 26:22). Luke refers to written and oral accounts that preceded him and from which he likely borrowed (Luke 1:1–4). Most scholars assume both Matthew and Luke used Mark as one of their primary sources ("Markan priority"). The letter of Jude cites or alludes to various intertestamental works, including 1 Enoch (Jude 14) and the Assumption of Moses (Jude 9). Paul occasionally quotes from pagan poets and philosophers, including Menander (1 Cor. 15:33), Epimenides (Titus 1:12–13), and Aratus (Acts 17:28 [Luke quoting Paul]). It

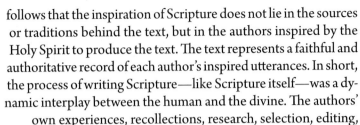

follows that the inspiration of Scripture does not lie in the sources or traditions behind the text, but in the authors inspired by the Holy Spirit to produce the text. The text represents a faithful and authoritative record of each author's inspired utterances. In short, the process of writing Scripture—like Scripture itself—was a dynamic interplay between the human and the divine. The authors' own experiences, recollections, research, selection, editing, and composition were together guided by the Holy Spirit so that the result was the Word of God.

Verbal and Plenary Inspiration

Two terms often used to describe inspiration are *plenary* and *verbal*. Plenary means "full" and indicates that all Scripture is inspired and authoritative (2 Tim. 3:16). Verbal means that the words themselves, not just the ideas, are inspired by God. Article VI of the Chicago Statement on Biblical Inerrancy (see discussion below) affirms "that the whole of Scripture and all its parts, down to the very words of the original, were given by divine inspiration." While verbal and plenary inspiration is an important doctrine, both terms must be carefully qualified. For example, while plenary means that *all* Scripture is inspired, authoritative, and useful, this does not negate the reality of the progress of revelation or of controlling texts and motifs. Old Testament affirmations of the efficacy of animal sacrifices must be understood as incomplete and preparatory statements qualified by the once-for-all sacrifice of Christ on the cross (Heb. 10:4, 14). The God who communicated partially and incompletely through the prophets has now revealed himself "in these last days" through his Son (Heb. 1:1–2). There are also controlling or paradigmatic texts. Jesus could subordinate the whole law under two commands: love for God and love for others (Matt. 22:35–40).

The doctrine of "verbal" inspiration must also be qualified. While the (Hebrew and Greek) *words* of Scripture are indeed inspired, words are symbols that indicate conceptual content. It is the *meaning* of these words—the message that they convey—that is ultimately inspired by God. And words do not carry meaning in isolation, but in dynamic interplay with other words, phrases, and clauses, and in historical, social, and cultural contexts. The ultimate goal of Scripture is not to place words on a page, but to communicate a message from one person to another. Any theory of inspiration that does not give priority to communication over verbal form will fall short, since it

Menander (342–291 BC), an Athenian poet and playwright whom Paul quotes in 1 Cor. 15:3.

misrepresents the nature and purpose of language. This has important implications for the task of Bible translation. An English translation of Scripture remains God's Word even though it changes all the words (from Hebrew/Greek to English) *if it accurately reproduces the meaning of the text.* "God's Word" ultimately means the conceptual content that the author intended to communicate through Hebrew, Greek, and Aramaic sentences.

Inspiration and Canonicity

The doctrine of inspiration is closely related to the question of the canon. The canon refers to those books that comprise the church's authoritative Scripture (see the following articles on the Old Testament and New Testament canons). The ultimate test of canonicity is not whether a book is confirmed by a church council, or written by a prophet or an apostle, or historically reliable, or that its doctrine is in agreement with the rest of Scripture (though these are all important *confirmations* of canonicity). The ultimate test is whether a book is inspired by the Holy Spirit: "all Scripture is inspired by God" (2 Tim. 3:16 NASB). As Bruce Metzger insightfully observes, the canon is not an authoritative collection of books, but a collection of authoritative books. It is not a church council's authority that makes them a part of Scripture. It is the inspiration and authority of the books themselves. The Holy Spirit is the ultimate test of truth. The apostle John affirms this when he tells his readers, "you have an anointing from the Holy One, and all of you know the truth" (1 John 2:20; cf. 2:27). The Holy Spirit indwelling, guiding, and empowering

The Hagia Sopia, first built in the fourth century AD, was an important church in Byzantium (now Istanbul, Turkey).

the people of God recognizes the Spirit-inspired books of Scripture. This is not a subjective test, as some might argue, since the Spirit is not a feeling or intuition, but a real Person who objectively confirms the truth for God's people: "But when he, the Spirit of truth, comes, he will guide you into all the truth" (John 16:13).

This understanding of inspiration also means that biblical interpretation should be a community activity. As the Spirit indwells the individual believer (1 Cor. 6:19), so he indwells the church as a body (1 Cor. 3:16), and together the Spirit-filled and Spirit-guided community provides essential checks and balances for an individual's own interpretation. This is true both presently—in local congregations and in the church worldwide—and historically—through the councils, creeds, and collective wisdom of the church through the ages.

Inspiration and Inerrancy

Closely related to the doctrine of inspiration is that of the *inerrancy* of Scripture. The debate over inerrancy arose especially in the context of concerns that the doctrine of inspiration was being undermined by claims of partial or limited authority. Some, for example, have argued that Scripture is authoritative when discussing ethical and theological issues, but not in matters of science or history. The term *infallibility* is sometimes used in this regard, limiting the scope of inspiration to matters of faith and practice. Others have argued that the Bible *contains* the Word of God but is not itself the Word of God. Still others claim that Scripture is not divine communication per se, but is a human record of God's actions in salvation history. Historical or other errors are of little consequence, since it is the God about whom the Bible testifies who is true, rather than the testimony itself.

In contrast to these views of partial inspiration, the doctrine of inerrancy claims that Scripture is wholly true in all that it affirms. The most definitive statement of inerrancy is the Chicago Statement on Biblical Inerrancy, produced in 1978 by the International Council on Biblical Inerrancy and signed by three hundred evangelical scholars. Article III of the Chicago Statement affirms "that the written Word in its entirety is revelation given by God," and denies "that the Bible is merely a witness to revelation, or only becomes revelation in encounter, or depends on the responses of men for its validity."

Inerrancy must be seen as a philosophical presupposition rather than an empirically verifiable fact. It is impossible, for example, to "prove" the reliability of every historical event in Scripture. There is simply not enough historical data. We can reason, however, that if God is perfect, his self-revelation must also be perfect. Inerrancy is a philosophical given based on the nature of God. Some have criticized the term "inerrancy," claiming that it is a recent innovation and that the concept is not found in Scripture. Others reject it because it is a negative term, telling us what the Bible is *not* rather than what it *is*. Both of these criticisms can be muted by using a more positive definition: inerrancy means that the Bible is *true* in all that it affirms. As noted above, statements about the truth of God's Word abound in Scripture, and throughout church history the people of God have affirmed the trustworthiness of God's self-revelation. Jesus repeatedly spoke about Scripture's authority and emphatically stated that it could not be broken (John 10:35; cf. Matt. 4:4, 7, 10; 5:17–19; etc.).

As with inspiration in general, the doctrine of inerrancy must be qualified in certain ways. Some of these have been mentioned above, including the use of nonliteral and phenomenological language, approximations, generalizations, and diverse literary forms. A parable is not in error if it recounts fictitious events, since this is the nature of parables. A genealogy is not in error when it skips generations for literary or structural reasons (cf. Matt. 1:1–16; Luke 3:23–38), since this was common practice in ancient genealogies. Scripture must be read and interpreted within its historical and literary context. The following are two other important qualifications for the doctrine of inerrancy.

Inerrancy Is Limited to the Original Autographs

Before the invention of the printing press, all documents were copied by hand (a handwritten copy is known as a "manuscript"), a process that inevitably resulted in errors. Of the thousands of biblical manuscripts that have survived, no two are exactly alike. Inerrancy, therefore, relates only to the "autograph" (the original copy penned by the author), none of which have survived. This, however, should not disturb students of Scripture. While it is true that we do not have exact copies of Scripture, the wealth of early and reliable Hebrew and Greek manuscripts, together

The Bodmer Papyrus dates to AD 175–225 and contains the Gospels of Luke and John.

with the finely developed discipline of *textual criticism*, means that we can reproduce the original text with a very high degree of accuracy. As Article X of the Chicago Statement reads,

> We affirm that inspiration, strictly speaking, applies only to the autographic text of Scripture, which in the providence of God can be ascertained from available manuscripts with great accuracy.

The Bible is without exception the best-preserved document from the ancient world, both in terms of age and number of manuscripts. Furthermore, despite some uncertainties on individual readings, no point of Christian doctrine is at stake because of a textually disputed passage. This is so because the great doctrines of the faith are confirmed not by one passage, but by the whole testimony of Scripture.

Inerrancy and the Limitations of Human Language

Another necessary qualification for the doctrine of inerrancy is that all language carries a measure of ambiguity and imprecision. Though the Holy Spirit who inspired Scripture may be perfect, the vehicle of transmission (human language) is subject to ambiguity and imprecision. Our comprehension of divine revelation is therefore always partial and incomplete (1 Cor. 13:12). While this is certainly true, common sense and human experience teach us that we can know *truly* even if we can't know *perfectly*. If this were not the case, no human communication would be successful. Those reading this paragraph, for example, cannot know with absolute precision the author's intention in every nuance of every word. (The author himself could probably not tell you that!) Yet the reader can discern enough to say, "I understand." Though the human element (languages and readers) inevitably results in less-than-perfect comprehension, the creative power of human language together with the illumination by the Holy Spirit means that the message comes through truly, even if not perfectly.

Inspiration and Authority

A natural implication of the inspiration of Scripture is its authority. If the Bible is God's Word, then it has authority over God's people in matters of faith and practice. The authority of the Bible encompasses experience, reason, and tradition. Authority over experience means that personal feelings or intuitions must not overrule the Bible's clear teaching. Of course, all interpretation is affected by one's life experiences and background, and it is impossible to approach the text completely free of bias. Yet the goal must always be to hear God's voice in Scripture rather than to impose one's feelings and agendas on the text.

Authority over reason does not mean that biblical truth is irrational or illogical. Rather, it means that we take the supernatural as a given, expecting that God can and does act above and beyond the natural world. It also means that apparent contradictions and historical problems do not negate biblical truth. Rather, we adopt a "wait-and-see" attitude, expecting Scripture's veracity to be vindicated. It also means that we develop an attitude of humility and open-mindedness, recognizing that Western standards of empirical truth may not always correspond with the enculturated nature of biblical revelation.

Finally, authority over tradition means that the church's historical councils and creeds represent truth inasmuch as they reflect the teaching of the Bible. The Bible stands in judgment over historical and systematic theology. Each generation of the church must therefore return to Scripture to examine, confirm, and even correct its beliefs and practices.

A modern Bible.

The Production and Shaping of the Old Testament Canon

Stephen Dempster

Introduction

The Old Testament canon consists of thirty-nine books in Protestantism, forty-six books in Roman Catholicism (adding Tobit, Judith, Baruch, Ben Sira, Wisdom, 1–2 Maccabees, with additions to Daniel and Esther), and forty-eight books in the Orthodox church (adding 1 Esdras, 3 Maccabees). The Jewish Bible, which is identical with the content of the Protestant Old Testament, consists of twenty-four books, but divided and arranged differently. Christian Old Testaments emphasize eschatology (the future) by placing the prophets at the end; Jewish Bibles highlight ethics by having their first five books (the Law of Moses) function as a structural center, around which the other main divisions (the Prophets and the Writings) are organized in concentric circles.

The Notion of Canon

The word "canon" is derived from a Hebrew word signifying "reed" (*qaneh*) and by extension "measuring stick." It enters into the Greek language as "canon" (*kanon*) with a wider semantic range signifying exemplary standards in relation to literary works, grammatical rules, and even certain human beings. The word was coined in the early church to indicate an absolutely authoritative, complete list of God-inspired books, which was the standard of truth (Athanasius, *39th Festal Letter*). Although such a list was considered closed, it is clear that the creation of the canon did not happen in an instant. It had a long and complex history before such closure occurred. The historian Josephus (AD 95) describes a closed list of inspired books that had been authoritative for all Jews for centuries (*Against Apion* 8).

Scholars frequently distinguish between two senses of canon: material and formal. "Material" refers to a collection of *authoritative* books that is in the process of formation—an evolving canon. Sometimes this is named Canon 1, or proto-canon. "Formal" signifies an *authoritative collection* of books, or Canon 2—a closed canon.

Scribes were highly venerated in Egypt. Often the pharaohs would have statues made of themselves pictured as scribes. The statue pictured above is of Pharaoh Horemheb (about 1300 BC).

Writing, Books, and Literacy

The Bible did not become a book in the modern sense until well into the first few centuries AD when the codex (the modern book) was invented. Before that time it was a collection of scrolls. Greek manuscripts from Christian sources in the fourth and fifth centuries AD were the first "books" to contain all the writings of the Old Testament (two of the most complete manuscripts are Codex Vaticanus and Codex Sinaiticus). In Judaism, the first attested Bible containing all the sacred writings is dated to the eleventh century AD (Codex Leningradensis).

The Bible first existed as oral proclamation, which was then made permanent through writing because of its importance. The Hebrew word used to indicate the activity of oral proclamation is the word "to call, to call out." Later Jewish tradition refers to the Bible as not that which is written but that which is called out. Thus the biblical literature was preeminently that which was read aloud, frequently in public gatherings.

Nevertheless, the Bible consisted of *writings*. In the ancient world, writing and reading were the prerogative of an elite group of scribes. Writing systems were complex and ponderous, requiring the memorization of hundreds of signs. Consequently only a small number of professionally trained scribes would be literate, employed in administrative tasks such as record keeping and accounting as well as political and cultural ones such as the production of royal propaganda, legal documents, and culturally significant texts. With the dawn of the alphabet at the turn of the second millennium BC, this changed. Due to the vast reduction of writing symbols down to a few dozen signs, literacy became democratized—at least in theory. Semitic alphabets start appearing in the land of the Bible in the second half of the second millennium BC (at sites such as Ugarit and Izbet Sartah). One has recently been found in Tel Zayit, dating to the tenth century BC. The beginnings of the Bible take place, then, in the midst of an epistemological and social revolution as well as a religious one—the God of the universe begins to make himself known in texts! The gods of all the other nations revealed themselves in images, but Israel found her God in the text. This provided a theological motivation for literacy (Deut. 6:9).

In ancient Israel, literacy probably expanded outside of the limited scribal circles. For example, in the book of Judges, a young man could write out the ancient version of a "hit list" when he was captured (Judg. 8:14); Isaiah could divide people into literate and illiterate classes (Isa. 29:11); a common soldier found it incredible that his superior officer considered him illiterate (*Lachish Letter #3*); an ordinary laborer could commemorate the completion of a building project in writing (Siloam Inscription). In addition, the ending of Ecclesiastes (12:12) assumes a great deal of literacy among its audience, not to mention that it was incumbent upon the head

Statue of a royal scribe in ancient Egypt (about 2500–2300 BC). Scribes were important officials in ancient Egypt.

of each Israelite household to write on the doorposts and gates of his homestead (Deut. 6:9).

The Old Testament as a Whole: Different Arrangements and Canons

The formation of the Old Testament occurred over a long period of time. The earliest writer to appear in its pages is Moses (Exod. 17:14) and the last is Ezra (8:1), a scribe patterned after the great Moses. Between these two Mosaic figures is a potpourri of writings spanning centuries that became part of the Old Testament: legal collections, poetry, narratives, prophecies, apocalypses, proverbs, lamentations, hymns, riddles, protests, curses, chronicles, lists, letters, and love songs. In the Hebrew Bible this diversity has been arranged in a story line that begins with creation (Genesis) and ends with Israel's return from exile (Ezra–Nehemiah, Chronicles). This order is different from our English translations of the Old Testament used in churches today. These translations are largely based on Greek Bibles of the early church in which the Prophets sometimes occur at the end. The Hebrew order is designated by the acronym *Tanak*, which refers to its three major divisions: *Torah* (Law, Instruction), *Nevi'im* (Prophets), and *Ketuvim* (Writings). The first division is identical with that of our English Bibles. The second division consists of eight books, later divided into four books of Former Prophets (Joshua, Judges, Samuel, and Kings) and four books of Latter Prophets (Jeremiah, Ezekiel, Isaiah, the Twelve [minor prophets]). The third (last) division consists of eleven books, but the sequence of the books is not as fixed. Probably the earliest order was as follows: Ruth, Psalms, Job, Proverbs, Ecclesiastes, Song of Songs, Lamentations, Daniel, Esther, Ezra–Nehemiah, and Chronicles.

In the early church there were lists of books and manuscripts that contained additional writings. As the church moved away from the geographical center of Judaism, there was some confusion about its canon, and some books that became popular made their way into various Christian lists and manuscript collections. In order to eliminate some of this confusion, Melito, a bishop from Sardis, made a journey to Palestine around AD 170 to determine the original order and number of the books of the "Old Covenant." Origen (AD 230) also indicates that he was aware of books that had been added. Later, individuals like Athanasius and particularly Jerome recognized the differences between the canon of Hebrew "truth" and other books. However, the force of tradition was so strong that it was not until the Reformation that there was a concerted attempt within the new Protestant Christian movement to return to the Hebrew canon. This was probably an influence of the Renaissance, which stressed the importance of cutting through the "logjam" of tradition to get back to the original sources. For obvious reasons, this path was not followed by the Roman Catholic and Orthodox churches. They kept some of these additional books that are often called "deutero-canonical" to indicate their distinction from the earlier "proto-canonical" books.

The Beginning of the Old Testament Canon

If there was an event that can be regarded as providing the impetus and nucleus for the canonical process, it was the Sinai covenant. The content of the covenant was largely the giving of the Ten Words (Commandments), which reflected the will of the Creator for Israel to embark on a divine mission to the world (Exod. 19:5–6; 20:1–17). In this public event, God spoke directly to Israel in the thunder of Sinai. This oral proclamation was then made permanent in stone tablets written by God.

The climax of the covenant at Sinai underlines the importance of the written word. The experience of being confronted with the unmediated presence of God traumatized the Israelites, causing them to plead for Moses to be a mediator (Exod. 20:18–20). Moses wrote the words of God in "a book of the covenant," which was an application of the Ten Words to the daily life of the people (Exod. 21–23). This "book," which was probably written on papyrus, became part of a sacrificial blood ritual in which the Israelites affirmed obedience to God (Exod. 24:1–8). They were consecrated and cleansed to accomplish a priestly mission to the world. The ritual of the word and blood led to communion: Moses, Aaron, and seventy elders ascended Sinai and experienced a unique encounter with God (Exod. 24:9–11). The basis of this fellowship was God's grace and the people's desire to obey the words written in the book.

A consequence of the Sinai covenant was the presence of God with the people, housed in a tent (the tabernacle) in the center of the Israelite camp (Exodus 25–31). In the heart of this tabernacle, God's invisible presence hovered above the ark of the covenant—a footstool for the divine throne. The ten words written on two stone tablets were placed in the ark, with the book of the covenant placed nearby. The idea of canon is thus inextricably related to covenant.* Unique content and conspicuous setting demarcate these writings and ensure their privileged authoritative status among a people with whom God has chosen to dwell.

---

* Meredith G. Kline, *The Structure of Biblical Authority* (Grand Rapids: Eerdmans, 1972), 90.

Canonical Expansion

Over time a gradual expansion of the canon occurred. Moses is depicted as writing other texts that would have been added to the nuclear canon: a memorial (Exod. 17:14), a travelogue (Numbers 33), and a poem (Deut. 31:22). After his death, provision is made for a prophetic institution that continued the oral proclamation of the will of God (Deut. 18:15–22). The authority of the members of this institution was authorized by their adherence to the nuclear canon and not to dramatic charismatic qualities (Deut. 13:1–6). This opened the way for the integration of future prophetic texts into the nuclear canon of Moses. At the end of the Pentateuch, Moses writes a copy of "this Torah," a form of the book of Deuteronomy, and places it beside the ark. It was to be read publically every sabbatical year (Deut. 31:9–13, 24–26).

Two other laws in Deuteronomy stressed the importance of this new text. First, each future ruler had to make a new copy of Deuteronomy from one in the possession of the Levites. The royal copy was to govern the thinking of the king, who was envisioned as literate (Deut. 17:14–21). Second, this type of Torah-thinking was to percolate down to the head of every Israelite household, who was to write down Torah words on his doorposts and gates. This suggests an ideal of functional literacy for many members of Israelite society, and not just royalty and the court (Deut. 6:4–9).

During the conquest, Joshua functioned like a good Israelite leader by writing part of the Torah written by Moses on a newly made altar on Mount Ebal (Josh. 8:30–35). There it was read in the presence of all Israel, including the blessings and the curses (cf. Deuteronomy 27). This was the "doorposts and gates" of the new, national house of Israel. After the conquest, Joshua renewed the covenant with Israel at Shechem, after which he wrote the words of the covenant down in "a book of the Law [Torah] of God" (Josh. 24:26), which was placed near a stone in a sanctuary. Later, immediately preceding

Mount Ebal, where Joshua built an altar and copied "the law of Moses" on the altar (Josh. 8:30–35).

the rise of kingship, Samuel wrote down the responsibilities of a king in a book, placing it in a sanctuary (1 Sam. 10:25). Other literature dealing with the history of the nation would have gradually been added to this collection.

Streams of Revelation

Other streams of revelation contributed to the growth of the canon besides Torah. Prophecy and wisdom also played a role (Jer. 18:18; Ezek. 7:26; cf. 1 Sam. 28:6). In the biblical tradition, the *Torah*, associated with Moses, was interpreted to the people by priests. Its locus was the sacred space of the sanctuary. The *word* was associated with prophets, and it was in harmony with the Torah and based upon it. Its locus was the prophet and his disciples who preserved and transmitted it (Isa. 8:16–20; Jeremiah 36). But *wisdom* was more of a human word from below—immanent revelation, the ability to discern through reason the divine will in nature and human experience. This type of revelation came to be associated with the sage (the wise person), who had the powers of observation and insight, the sage par excellence being Solomon. The locus for this writing would have probably been the royal court where scribes were responsible for preservation of texts and their transmission (Prov. 25:1).

The court or the sanctuary may also have been the locus for musical compositions, which reflected human address to God in prayer, protest, and praise: *the Psalms*. David and various musicians were associated with many of these, and later texts show that written materials provided the basis for such worship (e.g., 2 Chron. 29:30). The authority for such compositions would have been linked to the most venerable kings in Israel, David and Solomon, God's chosen instruments to lead his people.

Exile and Canon

The exile had a profound impact on the nation, calling its very existence into question. Although the temple was destroyed, the literature housed in it would have been saved, and literature from prophetic and wisdom sources, including psalms, would have been gathered. In the absence of sacred space, sacred texts became all the more important. A sustained effort was made to make sense of the exile in historical narrative, and the result was largely a four-volume work that used many older sources and that narrated Israel's history from the conquest to the middle of the exile. Combined with the Torah, the new story line would have extended from creation to the exile. The extension of the history (Joshua–2 Kings, excluding Ruth) represented the outworking of the predictions of the last book of the Torah, Deuteronomy—blessings for obedience and curses for disobedience—in the life of the nation. It began with a celebration of Passover in the land (Joshua 5) and ended with one during Josiah's reformation (2 Kings 23). The history was completed with the release of the exiled Davidic king, Jehoiachin, from a Babylonian prison (2 Kings 25:27–31).

Formulaic language characteristic of this history also appears in the titles of the major prophetic works, and there are crucial repetitions that link the Former and Latter Prophets (2 Kings 25 = Jeremiah 52; 2 Kings 18–20 = Isaiah 36–39). These works complemented one another as the history leading to the exile is matched by the unheeded prophetic words that predicted the doom of the nation. But the literature was not only gathered and edited to explain disaster; it also offered hope. In the Former Prophets there is a covenant with David, that he would have an everlasting dynasty (2 Samuel 7); Jehoiachin's release from prison shows that this promise is not dead. In the Latter Prophets there are also many announcements of future salvation that cluster around the resurrection of the Davidic house. The fact that the Twelve contain postexilic prophets (Haggai, Zechariah, Malachi) indicates that the last prophetic scroll was completed after the exile.

The apocryphal book of 1 Maccabees implies that prophecy has ceased (from Codex Sinaiticus).

Post Exile, Canonical Synthesis, and Closure: From Canon 1 to Canon 2

After the return of the exiles from Babylon to Judah, another reform occurred that was inspired by the written word. Reforms instituted by Ezra and Nehemiah culminated with a dramatic reading of the Torah before a large assembly of Jews (Nehemiah 8). In a public square of the city, a large wooden podium was erected upon which Ezra, the latter day Moses, stood to read this book. When he opened the scroll, his audience stood, and as he read in the Hebrew of the Torah, the priests helped the people understand it by paraphrasing it in Aramaic. The people learned about various issues and festivals, and were eager to obey. The Torah clearly consisted of Genesis–Deuteronomy, since the prayer of Nehemiah in the next chapter rehearses the history of Israel in sequence through the Pentateuch and beyond. The importance of the written word is symbolized not only by its physical elevation, but by its importance for governing the life of the people. During this time, there certainly would have been an archive in the temple for the sacred writings.

Jewish tradition indicates that sometime during the latest period in the Old Testament, canonical revelation came to an end. Prophecy was waning (Zech. 1:5; 7:7, 12). In the apocryphal Jewish history titled Maccabees, written in the second century BC, there is an awareness that prophecy has ceased (1 Macc. 4:46; 9:27; 14:41). Writing toward the end of the first century AD, the Jewish historian Josephus states categorically that the Jewish Bible has been a finished product since the Persian period because of "the failure of the exact succession of the prophets" (*Against Apion* 8). Later Jewish tradition confirms this picture. Moreover, any book that tried to present itself as "canonical" had to be written under the guise of an ancient biblical figure in order "to make the canonical cut" (e.g., Enoch, Joseph and Asenath, Baruch).

Since revelation ceased at the end of the biblical period, a decision was probably made to synthesize all the authoritative writings into an integrated unity, making collections of *authoritative* books into one *authoritative collection*. The various types of revelation were organized into three distinct sections: Torah, Prophets, and Wisdom. The latter category became more generic. If the threefold division is not in evidence in Ben-Sira as "Torah, Wisdom and Prophecy" (39:1), it is by the time of his grandson ("Torah, Prophets and the Rest of the Books"). It was not until the second century AD that the third division became known as "the Writings."

Probably during the latest period of the Old Testament under Ezra (the second Moses, so to speak), the literature was edited and synthesized into a complete whole. Much of the Torah and the Prophets (both Former and Latter) were substantially shaped, as were other documents outside these categories. A final redaction probably took place, which imparted to the material a definitive canonical stamp, its distinctive eschatological message, as well as the importance of study and meditation leading to wisdom. The focus was on becoming spiritually literate while waiting for God to act in the future.

Significant canonical seams stitch together the major divisions. At the end of the Torah, there is the recognition that Moses was a prophet that was unequalled (Deut. 34:10), which implicitly calls for wisdom in studying his revelation while waiting for a comparable prophet (Deut. 18:15–18). Joshua, the new leader, is the preeminent wise man, endowed with the Spirit of wisdom (Deut. 34:9). At the end of the Prophets, there is a coordination of Moses representing the Torah and Elijah representing the Prophets. The exhortation is to remember the Torah and anticipate Elijah, whose coming will usher in a new age (Mal. 4:4–6) and will be the precursor of the final Mosaic prophet.

At the beginning of the Torah, the word of God creates light that establishes the rhythm of the day and night (Gen. 1:3–5); at the beginning of the Prophets, there is a call for Joshua to meditate on the Torah day and night and thus prosper in his way (Josh. 1:8), and at the beginning of the Writings, there is an identical exhortation to each Israelite (Ps. 1:2–3). The great words of life that lit up the world can now light up one's life as one meditates on them day and night.

Lachish Ostracon #3, where the writer exclaims indignantly, "No one has ever had to call a scribe for me."

This editorial uniting of these major units into an integrated whole has a number of implications. The awareness that a great era of revelation has come to an end inspires believers to meditate on the Scriptures day and night while waiting for the next great revelation. Thus it is probably not an accident that many of the last books of the *Tanak* are wisdom books, and stress the importance of the sage, the student. Chronicles may well have been written as a way to close the entire sequence, as it is clearly a book of reflection and constantly reinforces through its stories the importance of obeying the divine word and prospering (2 Chron. 20:20; 31:21; 32:30). Its focus on the story of David indicates the main locus of biblical hope—the Davidic covenant.

External evidence for such a canonical process consists of a few clues. In 2 Maccabees, there is a reference to Nehemiah gathering books to form a library, which could represent books from the second and third divisions of the canon (2 Macc. 2:13–14). A later text dating to the end of the first century AD indicates that Ezra was involved in producing ninety-four books, twenty-four of which were to be used in public and seventy in private by the enlightened (2 Esdras 14:44–47). The first collection refers to canonical books and identifies Ezra as having had an important role in their production. Similar comments are made in later Jewish sources.

The New Testament Era and Beyond

One common reference to designate the Scriptures in the New Testament is the bipartite formula, "the Law and the Prophets" (Matt. 7:12; John 1:45;

Martin Luther, one of the central leaders of the Protestant Reformation. Protestant Christianity went back to Jewish sources to determine the canon of the Old Testament, but it arranged the books differently.

Rom. 3:21). However, in two texts Jesus refers to the vast canonical sweep of revelation either in promise or judgment implying the tripartite (three-part) division. In Luke 24 Jesus states that his death and resurrection fulfilled all the predictions in all of the Scriptures, which he calls not only "Moses and the prophets," but also "the Law of Moses, the Prophets and the Psalms" (Luke 24:27, 44). The "Psalms" may have been an abbreviated reference to the "Writings," the third part of the canon, which contained the book of Psalms. Moreover, in Luke 11:49–51, Jesus predicts the completeness of judgment that is going to come upon the present generation for rejecting him. He accuses religious leaders of belonging to a chain of murderers who killed prophets from Abel to Zechariah the priest, whose respective martyrdoms both called out for vengeance (Gen. 4:10; 2 Chron. 24:22). It is no coincidence that both figures are found in the first and last books of the *Tanak*. Thus Jesus is attacking the religious leaders for their scriptural piety—a piety that has killed the prophets, from the first book of the Bible to the last, and all those in between. This *completeness in judgment* is particularly effective if there is *completeness to the entire canonical range of Scripture.*

Shortly after this period, the Jewish historian, Josephus, writing in an apologetic tone to a Greek and Roman audience, indicates that Jewish history is superior to that of its contemporary gentile competitors because of the reliability and inspiration of its historical record, consisting of twenty-two books arranged in a tripartite category, which has been closed for a long period because of a break in the succession of prophets (*Against Apion* 8). If Josephus's claims are taken seriously—and there is no reason why they should not be—it means that the Old Testament canon had been well established for some time and was accepted by most of the various streams of Judaism. Although Josephus's arrangement of the canon was unique, it still respected the tripartite structure. His concern for history dictated that he move all the historical books from the third section into the second section after the five books of the Torah, and leave the wisdom and poetic books alone in the third division.

Another enumeration from the late first century testifies to an order of twenty-four books (2 Esdras 14:45). Later tradition (Origen, AD 230) suggested that twenty-two and twenty-four were alternate orders, with the smaller number resulting from books being combined with one another (Ruth with Judges and Lamentations with Jeremiah). The first explicit

Christian list claiming Jewish influence names twenty-one books and occurs at the end of the second century AD. Missing from this canon (Melito's) is Esther, which had been a controversial book in both Christianity and Judaism. Nevertheless, there is a remarkable continuity with the numbering of Josephus and 4 Ezra. Another source, dating from the Mishnaic period (AD 1–200), also presents a tripartite canon, beginning with Genesis and concluding with Chronicles (*Baba Bathra* 14b).

Conclusion: Text and Hermeneutics

After Christianity separated from Judaism because of the events surrounding the destruction of the temple and the influx of gentiles into the church, the Greek Bible (the Septuagint) was quickly adopted for use in the church. In fact Paul used it widely in the developing church of the first century as his citations from the Old Testament clearly indicate. As the rift between Judaism and Christianity widened, it was inevitable that there would be confusion within Christianity regarding the exact limit and contours of the Jewish Scriptures (the Old Testament). As the geographical distance increased between the church and the center of Judaism, Christian "canons" reflected this difference. Protestant Christianity emerging out of the Reformation returned to its Jewish sources for the Old Testament, but with a different arrangement and numbering system based on Christian antecedents.

Within Judaism, there is remarkable stability and continuity, not only in the numbering of the books but also in their texts. This suggests that an archetype produced in temple circles would have been preserved after the destruction of the temple to provide the basis for transmission for the next one thousand years. The scrupulous care this process demonstrates is enough to prove the practical authority of these books. The fact that shortly before the first century AD Greek translations of Hebrew texts were being revised to this particular archetype implies canonical authority.

The structure of the Hebrew Bible stresses the importance of internalizing the divine word, and meditating on it while waiting for a Davidic descendant. By closing with the Prophets, the Christian Old Testament emphasizes this eschatological aspect further. While both texts are in search of an ending, the New Testament begins joyfully and unequivocally with the announcement that the search is over in Jesus Christ, David's greater Son. He is the ultimate embodiment of the divine Word (John 1:14), the definitive exegesis and goal of the canon (John 1:18, 45), the decisive end of the Law and the Prophets (Matt. 17:1–8).

Writing, Copying, and Transmitting the New Testament Text

Daniel B. Wallace

he original twenty-seven books of the New Testament disappeared most likely within a few decades of their composition. We must rely on handwritten copies, or manuscripts (MSS, singular MS), to determine the wording of the original (or autographic) text. Because they are handwritten copies, no two MSS are exactly alike. Even the two closest early MSS have several differences per chapter. With over 250 chapters in the New Testament, one can easily see that wording variations among the MSS will be abundant.

The discipline known as textual criticism is concerned with these MSS. It is the study of the copies of any written document whose autograph (the original) is unknown or nonexistent for the primary purpose of determining the exact wording of the original. Textual criticism is necessary for virtually all ancient literature. The New Testament is no different in this regard. New Testament textual criticism (NTTC) is needed because of these two facts: disappearance of the originals and disagreements among the extant (remaining) MSS.

My limited objective in this chapter is to (1) discuss the history of the transmission of the New Testament text, (2) lay out the problems of NTTC, and (3) examine the practice of NTTC.

History of the Transmission of the Text of the New Testament

When an apostle wrote a letter to a congregation, it was only natural that that church would want to share that letter with other congregations. (Indeed, this was even mandated on occasion [Col. 4:16].) All such copies had to be made by hand. Differences would inevitably arise in these copies. For the most part, the changes introduced by scribes were unintentional—confusing letters or words, skipping or duplicating words or even whole lines, and the like.

As the early church grew, the demand for copies of the New Testament documents grew with it. When the Synoptic Gospels became known in various parts of the Roman Empire, scribes would notice the differences among them. And they would tend to harmonize the Gospels by "correcting" the wording in a MS of one Gospel so that it would conform to the wording in a parallel passage in another. Copyists also tended to smooth out the text grammatically and stylistically, add clarifying words and phrases, and substitute common forms for unusual forms. Scribes made such alterations most often because they thought that their exemplar was corrupt, but in so doing they often inadvertently changed the text from its original wording.

As the church branched out into regions where Greek was not the primary language, the need for translations of the New Testament became apparent. In the second and third centuries, the New Testament was translated into Latin, Syriac, and Coptic for people groups in Italy, North Africa, Syria, and Egypt. In later centuries, the New Testament was translated into Armenian, Gothic, Georgian, Arabic, and several other languages.

Greek, however, continued to be the major vehicle of the New Testament in most Mediterranean regions through the early centuries. The major churches in larger cities began to exercise an influence on the form of the text, so that "local

A copy of a Syriac translation of the New Testament dating to the sixth century AD.

texts" emerged. Two distinct text-forms from the earliest centuries have been detected: the Alexandrian and the so-called Western. The Alexandrian text was produced, as its name implies, in and around Alexandria, Egypt. Alexandria had a history of careful MS production long before Christianity existed. Christian scribes, influenced by this tradition, generated what is considered today as the most reliable text of the New Testament. The Western text, though not beginning in the West, found its way to Gaul, Italy, and North Africa. A much less accurate text-form (full of harmonizations, expansions, and theological alterations), the Western text nevertheless enjoyed wide influence, though most of the Western MSS extant today are in Latin. It is probable that the missionary impulse, rather than faithful copying practices, was responsible for many of the Western text's alterations of the original wording.

By the fourth century, a new text-form, the Byzantine, began to emerge. Largely based on the Alexandrian and Western, and, in time, heavily influenced by the church's liturgy, the Byzantine text became the dominant form in the East, especially after Constantine moved the capitol from Rome to Constantinople. This text-form was inferior due to its late date and dependence on the earlier text-forms. As Latin continued to spread throughout Western Europe, Greek was becoming increasingly restricted to the East. By the ninth century, the Byzantine became the predominant text-form in Greek, with the Alexandrian shrinking due to the Muslim conquest of Egypt and the Western being relegated mostly to Latin MSS. Thus, because Greek was increasingly restricted geographically, the Byzantine text not only became dominant among Greek MSS, but was also produced under tighter controls than the Latin MSS. In light of the historical situation concerning the production of these text-types, most scholars allot the greatest preference to the Alexandrian MSS and the least to the Byzantine.

The Problems of New Testament Textual Criticism

The problems of NTTC can be succinctly discussed under two broad labels: materials and methods.

The Materials

While scholars of other ancient literature suffer from a lack of data, those who work with New Testament MSS suffer from an embarrassment of riches. These witnesses to the text of the New Testament fall under three subcategories: Greek MSS, ancient translations (or versions), and quotations from the New Testament in the writings of the church fathers. Like great works of art, most are possessed by institutions and a few by individuals. Consequently, most are housed in libraries around the world.

Greek manuscripts

The Greek MSS are the principal documents used to determine the wording of the New Testament. They are broken down into four categories: papyri, majuscules, minuscules, and lectionaries.

The first group, papyri, are identified by the material the MS is made of. The second and third groups, majuscules and minuscules, refer to the writing style (either capital letters or cursive hand) of the MSS. And the last group, lectionaries, refers to MSS that are not continuous texts from the Gospels, Epistles, and so on, but are various portions of text that were assigned reading for particular days. Generally speaking, the papyri are the earliest of these four groups of MSS, and certainly the rarest (owing to the fragile writing material), while the majuscules are next, followed by the minuscules and lectionaries.

As of July 2009, the statistics on the Greek MSS of the New Testament were as follows:

Papyri	Majuscules	Minuscules	Lectionaries	Total
124	318	2895	2436	5773

These MSS date, for the most part, from the second to the sixteenth centuries. Some of the more important papyri are P^{45} (third century), P^{46} (ca. AD 200), P^{66} (ca. AD 200), and P^{75} (third century). These are early and substantial MSS that include large portions of the Gospels and Paul's letters.

By the fourth century, the great majuscule MSS were produced, including the earliest complete extant New Testment, Codex Sinaiticus. Codex Vaticanus, also from the fourth century, is nearly complete. Sinaiticus (aka A, or 01) and Vaticanus (aka B, or 03) both belong to the Alexandrian text-form. Their common ancestor

St. Catherine's Monastery, where Constantine von Tischendorf discovered Codex Sinaiticus in the mid-1800s.

must be quite ancient since they are relatively closely related and yet there are numerous and substantial differences between them. This suggests that there were several intermediary ancestors between the common archetype and these two majuscules. Indeed, when they agree, their common reading usually is from the early second century.

A few of the later MSS were copied from a much earlier source. For example, MS 1739, a tenth-century minuscule, was copied directly from a late fourth-century MS. Even some of the early MSS show compelling evidence of being copies of a much earlier source. Consider again Codex Vaticanus, whose text is very much like that of P[75] (B and P[75] are much closer to each other than either is to A). Yet the papyrus is at least a century older than Vaticanus. In several places, the wording of Vaticanus is certainly more primitive than that of P[75]. This means that P[75] is not the ancestor of B, but that both go back to a still earlier common ancestor, probably one that is deep in the second century.

Ancient translations (or versions)

The second most important kinds of witnesses to the New Testament text are known as versions (or early translations). The value of a version depends on its date, the translation technique and care, and the quality of the text from which it is translated. The versions are important for another reason: except in rare and controlled instances, once a version was completed it did not interact with the Greek MSS again. Thus when a particular version consistently has one reading in its extant copies, that reading usually reflected that version's original. The three most important versions are the Latin, Coptic, and Syriac. Other important versions are the Gothic and Armenian, followed by the Georgian and Ethiopic.

There are almost twice as many Latin MSS of the New Testament as there are Greek (over 10,000 compared to about 5,700). They date from the third to the sixteenth centuries, but their origins may go back into the second century. They are basically representatives of the Western text.

The Coptic MSS come from Egypt, with roots reaching back to the beginning of the third century. Perhaps thousands of Coptic MSS exist today, but only a few hundred have been cataloged. They are representatives of the Alexandrian text.

The New Testament was translated into Syriac no later than the early third century. The earliest form is a representative of the Western text. The surviving copies of Syriac New Testament MSS number in the hundreds, perhaps thousands.

Besides the Latin, Coptic, and Syriac, other ancient versions should be noted. The Gothic was translated originally in the fourth century, as was the Ethiopic, and the Armenian probably from the fifth. These three versions have a yield of well over two thousand MSS extant today.

All told, the ancient versions of the New Testament still in existence are probably between fifteen thousand and twenty thousand. Exact numbers are difficult to come by because not all the MSS have been cataloged.

Quotations by church fathers

Commentaries, homilies, and other writings by ancient church leaders known as church fathers are so plentiful that if all the Greek and versional witnesses were destroyed, the text of the New Testament could be virtually reconstructed just from the data in these patristic writings.

The quotations of the New Testament by the fathers number well over a million. The fathers write as early as the late first century, with a steady stream through the thirteenth, making their value for determining the wording of the New Testament text extraordinary.

There are problems in citing fathers, however. First, the fathers' writings are found only in copies, not originals. Second, some fathers are notorious for quoting the same passage in different ways.

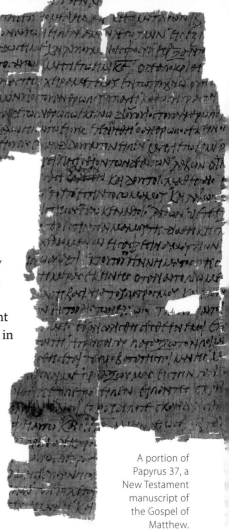

A portion of Papyrus 37, a New Testament manuscript of the Gospel of Matthew.

But there are means to determine on many occasions, with a great deal of certainty, what form of the New Testament text a particular father was quoting from. When carefully evaluated, patristic citations of the New Testament are quite valuable because the date and locale of the father can be pinpointed, and thus they can fill in many gaps in our knowledge of the transmission of the text.

Summary: An embarrassment of riches

The wealth of material that is available for determining the wording of the original New Testament is staggering: over 5,700 Greek New Testament MSS, as many as 20,000 versional MSS, and more than 1 million quotations by patristic writers. In comparison with the average ancient Greek author, the New Testament copies are well over a thousand times more plentiful.

These thousands of MSS, versions, and patristic quotations have produced hundreds of thousands of textual variants (the best estimates are about 400,000). These two considerations—the number of MSS and the number of variants—lead to our next consideration: How should scholars sift through all this material? What methods should they use to determine exactly the wording of the autographs?

Codex Vaticanus, one of the oldest and best Greek manuscripts.

The Methods

There are two broad databases of textual criticism: external evidence and internal evidence. External evidence has to do with the materials—the MSS, versions, and fathers. Internal evidence has to do with the wording of the text in these various witnesses and why it has undergone changes. In other words, external evidence looks at the variety of *witnesses*, while internal evidence looks at the variety of *variants*.

The predominant school of NTTC is called reasoned eclecticism. In essence, it treats both external and internal evidence equally, giving no mandatory preference to either aspect, no exclusive preference to any text-type or group of MSS. It regards both internal and external evidence as subjective in varying degrees, and views skillful wrestling with both considerations as the surest way to recover the wording of the original text.

The Practice of New Testament Textual Criticism

When the external and internal evidence point in the same direction, there is greater confidence that the wording of the autographs has been determined. Internal evidence is often in apparent conflict with external evidence, however, requiring more probing to determine the wording of the autographs.

Examination of the Internal Evidence

Internal evidence is an examination of the *wording* of the variants in order to determine which reading gave rise to the other(s) and is therefore most probably original. The basic guideline of internal criticism is: *choose the reading that best explains the rise of the other(s)*. Although judging internal evidence can appear to be a subjective exercise, scholars bring to bear sound and proven methods for analyzing the material: transcriptional probability and intrinsic probability.

Transcriptional probability

Transcriptional probability has to do with what a scribe would be likely to do. There are two types of changes to the text that scribes made—intentional and unintentional. Often scribes intended to alter the text—either for grammatical, theological, or explanatory reasons, as noted earlier. But due to problems of sight, hearing, fatigue, or judgment, scribes also often changed the text unwittingly. A common mistake of the scribes was to write once what should have been written twice (haplography). It especially occurred when a scribe's eye skipped a second word that ended the same way as the word before it; it also occurred when two lines ended the same way. Another error was when a scribe wrote twice what should have been written once (dittography).

Intrinsic probability

Intrinsic evidence examines what the biblical author was likely to have written. Two key issues are involved: context and style. Which variant best fits the context? Considerations of the flow of the argument generally reveal one reading to be superior to the other(s). Which variant better fits the author's style? Here the question concerns how an author normally expresses himself, what his motifs and language usually involve. One of the reasons that most scholars do not regard Mark 16:9–20 to be authentic, for example, is that the vocabulary and grammar are quite unlike the rest of the Gospel of Mark. When this observation is coupled with the strong likelihood that scribes could hardly resist letting Mark's Gospel end with verse 8, and with the fact that the earliest and best MSS lack these twelve verses, the evidence is overwhelmingly in favor of seeing Mark 16:9–20 as added later.

Once the internal evidence has been examined, one usually has a sense as to which reading likely gave rise to the other(s). To the degree that the intrinsic and transcriptional probabilities confirm each other, one can have relative confidence that that reading is most likely authentic.

Examination of the External Evidence

Three external criteria are used to judge which variant is more likely to be the wording of the original: date and character, genealogical solidarity, and geographical distribution.

Date and character

The preferred variant is one found in the earliest MSS. This is because there is less time between them and the originals and thus less time for intermediary copies. Also, the MSS that elsewhere prove themselves to be the most reliable are given preference (but it is not an absolute preference). A meticulous scribe working on a fifth-century MS may produce a more reliable text than a third-century scribe who is more interested in getting the job done quickly. Thus the date of the MS is a significant factor, as is the general character of the MS.

Genealogical solidarity

When almost all of the MSS of a certain text-type agree on a reading, the local ancestor of that text-type probably contained that reading; the reading is thus considered genealogically solid.

What exactly is a text-type? A text-type is a large group of MSS that share a pattern of readings. There are three major text-types: the Alexandrian, the Western, and the Byzantine. (See the previous discussion on origins and locations, "History of the Transmission of the Text of the New Testament.") When the better Alexandrian MSS have the same reading, for example, there is high probability that the Alexandrian local original had that reading. Thus by genealogical solidarity one can hypothesize the date of a reading *within* a text-type back to its local original. Since the Alexandrian and Western texts have roots that reach deep into the second century, when each has genealogical solidarity, their readings are probably second-century readings.

Codex Sinaiticus, the earliest complete surviving New Testament manuscript.

Geographical distribution

The variant found in geographically widespread locations in the first few centuries of the Christian era is more likely to be original than one that is found in only one location. This is due to the fact that collusion of witnesses is much less probable when these witnesses are distributed in Rome and Alexandria and Caesarea than when they are all located in just Jerusalem or Antioch. By this method, scholars legitimately "push back" the date of a reading behind the time of the witnesses that attest it.

In sum, date and character, genealogical solidarity, and geographical distribution are three ways of looking at the external data and deciding which reading is most likely earlier than the other(s). These need to be compared to one another with the objective of determining which reading is the earliest and thus which reading gives rise to the other(s). But external evidence is not the whole approach. In places where the early MSS disagree, where there is minimal geographical distribution, or where one of the readings is predictable (i.e., is the kind of wording a scribe would be likely to create), internal evidence may be far more important.

Conclusions

Once external evidence and internal evidence are compared, a conclusion as to which reading is the original can be finalized. The textual variant that has the greater claim to authenticity will be found in the earliest, best, and most geographically widespread witnesses; it will fit the context and author's style; and it will be the obvious originator of rival reading(s). For the vast majority of textual problems, this is a "no-brainer." And even of the relatively few that are difficult to resolve, a good portion of them can be decided with some confidence by a careful comparison of the external and internal evidence.

There are many occasions, however, in which the external evidence seems to point one way, while the internal evidence points another. How do scholars decide in such instances? If a particular variant is found only in non-Greek MSS, or is found only in a few late MSS, even if its internal credentials are excellent, it is almost always rejected. When there are many thousands of MSS, unpredictable accidents and unknowable motives may be the cause of a stray reading here or there that internally may have good credentials. On a rare occasion, however, the external evidence is very solidly on the side of one reading, but there are sufficiently important MSS for an alternate reading, and the internal evidence is completely on the side of the second reading. In such instances, the second reading is most likely original.

Although the issues are complex, the net result is that 99 percent of the autographic text is well established. And of the remainder, although the interpretation of hundreds of passages is at stake, no cardinal doctrine depends on textually dubious texts.

The Canon of the New Testament

M. James Sawyer

Introduction

Canon (Greek: *kanon*) originally designated a "reed" that was used for measuring. From this usage, the idea of measuring was derived. Ultimately the term came to be used to refer to a "rule" or "standard" and was applied to any set of books or rules that were normative in a particular discipline. Applied to the New Testament, it has reference to the books that are normative for the church's faith and practice.

Beneath the idea of *canon* lies the question of authority. Scholars recognize two different aspects to the concept of the New Testament canon: (1) material canon, and (2) formal canon. From the perspective of the *material canon*, each book of the New Testament is divinely inspired and was thus authoritative as soon as it was written. In this sense the New Testament is "a collection of authoritative books." The recognition of the New Testament as it is constituted today, however, took several centuries. The complete list of twenty-seven books was not firmly accepted until the fifth century AD, at which time the *formal canon* of the New Testament was generally recognized. That is, the church at large recognized these and only these books as having been given by divine inspiration, hence only these books comprised the formal canon. In this sense the canon is an "authoritative collection of books."

Canon in the Apostolic Era

Christ as Canon

For the early church, Christ, who had recognized and validated the Old Testament and its permanent status as Scripture, was himself the unquestioned authority. In the Gospels we find that while Jesus looked like any one of numerous rabbis, he taught in a manner that set him apart. The first-century rabbis' teaching was studded with references to traditional authorities. Jesus, however, taught "as one who had authority" (Mark 1:22; Matt. 5:21–22). Believers recognized this as the authority of one who was "both Lord and Messiah" (Acts 2:36), and they treasured his words.

Paul demonstrates that the sayings of the Lord were already in use as a final authoritative guide for behavior—in short, as an early Christian "canon." A "word of the Lord" was sufficient to settle matters of things like marriage and divorce (1 Cor. 7:10–11). Likewise, the controversy concerning the conduct of the Corinthians at the Lord's Supper was settled on the basis of the word of the Lord concerning its institution (1 Cor. 11:23–26).

These "sayings of the Lord" clearly had normative status in the early Christian community before the composition of the canonical Gospels. For example, the Last Supper narrative of 1 Corinthians 11 corresponds with Mark 14:22–25, which was written later. Likewise the teaching on marriage in 1 Corinthians 7:10 corresponds with Mark 10:9, and the declaration in support of missionaries (1 Cor. 9:14) corresponds with Matthew 10:10 and Luke 10:7. We do have one clear example of an unwritten saying, not found in the canonical Gospels, quoted authoritatively by Paul: "It is more blessed to give than to receive" (Acts 20:35).

Evidently, the "canonical" status of the words of the Lord produced the motivation to collect these utterances and required that the collection process be conducted with careful regulation. Were this not the case, someone might attempt to introduce some doubtful doctrine or practice by appeal to a new and theretofore unknown "Word of the Lord." Already by Luke's time "many" had undertaken the task of writing accounts (Luke 1:1). But apparently there were questions about the authenticity of some of the material circulating. This gave rise to the question of the basis upon which the churches could confidently receive material as authentic. It is in this context that we should understand Luke's preface to his Gospel. In it Luke tells Theophilus he wrote so that Theophilus might be certain that the things he had been taught were true (Luke 1:1–4).

Canon and the Apostles

Ephesians 2:20 declares the church had "been built on the foundation of the apostles and prophets, with Christ Jesus himself as the cornerstone." This adds another level of authority in the early church—that of the apostles.

Both the Gospels and the Epistles of Paul make it clear that the apostles held a unique place in the establishment of the church. They were personally chosen by Christ, and they accompanied him from the beginning of his ministry through the crucifixion and resurrection until his ascension. Also, Christ promised them that the Holy Spirit would come, bringing to mind all the things that he (Jesus) had said, and guiding them into all truth. The basis of their witness was their constant companionship with the Savior from the beginning. The special position of the apostles as the authority or standard by which all later teaching was measured became a critical factor in the formal establishment of the canon of Scripture.

The popular idea that a church hierarchy or council imposed the canon on the church does not fit the evidence. It is crucial to note that even the New Testament itself hints of canonical apostolic authority arising. Peter implicitly recognizes the "canonical" authority of Paul's writings, stating, "There are some things in them hard to understand, which ignorant, unsteadfast people twist to their own ruin, just as they do the rest of the scriptures" (2 Pet. 3:15–16).

Canon in the Postapostolic Church

Tradition and Authority

The apostolic fathers (the church leaders immediately following the apostles) recognized that the authority given to the apostles by Christ was unique and that in the most complete sense the apostles could have no successors. Thus the apostolic fathers recognized a definitive break in authority. Those leaders of the generation after the apostles, such as Ignatius, bishop of Antioch (ca. AD 50–107), acknowledged that the apostles belonged to a clearly marked and now completed stage between the Lord and the then-contemporary church.

Papias, bishop of Hierapolis (ca. AD 70–160), described the problem faced by the early generations of church leadership in determining which (oral) traditions of the Lord were authentic and which were spurious. His answer centered on apostolic authority: if a saying or interpretation can be clearly traced to an apostle, it could be accepted as genuine and authoritative.

The concept of an authoritative Christian tradition can be traced back into the New Testament itself. Paul speaks of the chain of receiving and delivering a body of teaching (e.g., 2 Tim. 2:2; 1 Cor. 11:23). It is therefore not surprising to see in this early period both written works and oral tradition existing side by side in some sort of authoritative fashion. Tradition was grounded in apostolic authority, which had its origin in the Lord himself. In the early decades of the church, apostolic tradition was an authoritative voice in the infant and early church.

In the immediate postapostolic period we find a great stress on apostolic tradition alongside apostolic writings that had not yet begun to be collected into any kind of formal New Testament canon. As the apostles died, this living stream of tradition grew fainter. The written documents became progressively more important to the ongoing life of the church.

The Collection of the Books

The earliest canonical list that we know of was composed by the radically anti-Jewish heretic Marcion (ca. AD 100–165), who accepted only a truncated version of the Gospel of Luke (he excised the infancy narratives) and ten of Paul's epistles (from which he purged all Jewish references). Two observations need to be made about Marcion's list. First, while Marcion's teaching would have been in large measure congruent with gnostic perspectives, his canon included only part of the works received by the church and did not include any "gnostic" works such as the Gospels of Thomas or Mary or the Acts of Peter or the like. Most likely these books had not yet been written, but if they did exist, they were not accepted because of their obvious recent origin. Thus his list, though incomplete, does testify to the authority of the books he included. Second, Marcion's canon acted as a goad to the church to publish a less eccentric and more complete list of its recognized books. At this time there were collections of the Gospels and of the Pauline Epistles that were circulating, but no formal lists had yet been published. Marcion's canon prompted the church to act.

In the latter half of the second century the Muratorian Canon was published. This list includes the four Gospels, Acts, Paul's thirteen letters, Jude, Revelation, 1 John, and at least either 2 John or 3 John or both. So before the end of the second century, at least twenty-one New Testament books were listed as authoritative. The author of the list also notes several other books that were circulating. He comments that these other books fall into three categories: (1) those books that were disputed—that is, accepted by some churches but rejected by others; (2) those that were edifying for use but not authoritative; and (3) those that were to be rejected as heretical. The

The *Shepherd of Hermas* was deemed to be edifying but not authoritative (canonical). Depicted above is the first page of this work, from Codex Sinaiticus.

A bust of the Roman emperor Diocletian, who launched a vicious persecution against the church in AD 303, especially targeting the sacred books of the church. Many Christians died protecting the books of the Bible.

author lists one disputed book (*The Apocalypse of Peter*) and one that is edifying but not authoritative (*The Shepherd of Hermas*), noting that it was of recent origin. He also lists several other books that were heretical and recent and therefore not to be read in the churches.

By the end of the second century there was a remarkably high degree of agreement concerning the vast majority of the New Testament. The twenty-one- or twenty-two-book core remained stable, though the fringe books of the New Testament canon remained unsettled for centuries. This high degree of unanimity concerning the greater part of the New Testament was attained independently among the very diverse and scattered congregations not only throughout the Mediterranean world but also over an area extending from Britain to Mesopotamia.

The development of the canon had reached a "status quo." While in some places certain books achieved local temporary canonical status, these aberrations were few and short-lived. In about AD 320 Eusebius presents a list that is nearly identical with that of the Muratorian Canon in the second century.

Persecution and Canonicity

During the first three centuries of its existence, the church came under repeated persecutions. In the third century the imperial strategy against Christianity shifted; instead of merely coercing individuals to recant their faith, now, in order to destroy the movement, the inquisitors targeted their apostolic books for destruction. This provided a renewed urgency in determining what was and was not inspired and authoritative. The bishops (generally the guardians of the Scriptures in the early church) needed confidence that the books they were willing to die for were indeed Scripture.

The Criteria of Canonicity

Apostolic Origin and Apostolic Doctrine (Orthodoxy)

Documents read in the early church worship services were to be doctrinally pure. This concern for true doctrine can be seen within the New Testament itself. First John identifies as "antichrist" those who deny the humanity of Christ. Paul warns the Ephesian elders in Acts 20 of the dangers of false teachers, as do both Jude and 2 Peter.

Similar concern is seen within the early church. Serapion, bishop of Antioch (ca. AD 200), rejected the *Gospel of Peter* since its teaching was nonapostolic, saying, "For we, brethren, receive both Peter and the other apostles as Christ; but we reject intelligently the writings falsely ascribed to them, knowing that such were not handed down to us."

Emphasis on the necessity of apostolic authorship (either directly or through an author's association with an apostle) was declared by Papias (ca. AD 130) who connected the Gospel of Mark to the authority of Peter. Likewise, it was acknowledged that Luke–Acts, while not written by a member of the inner apostolic circle, nonetheless preserved and propagated apostolic doctrines and had direct apostolic connection to Paul.

The question of the necessity of apostolic origin for a book to be considered canonical is demonstrated by the decades-long debate over the status of the book of Hebrews. In the Greek-speaking East the book was generally considered Pauline and accepted as canonical, whereas in the Latin-speaking West the book was not regarded as Pauline and thus was not initially considered canonical. While the acceptance of Hebrews into the canon was a longer process than the Pauline Epistles, it was ultimately recognized that the work could be traced to a Pauline mode of thought and had the "ring of truth" of apostolic doctrine.

We see here the image of a church fully engaged with verifying the authenticity of its roots. There was no simple credulity to accept even purported apostolic documents at face value. It evaluated those claims both on the basis of external historical evidence and internal consistency with the received apostolic tradition and the undisputed received works that were regarded as having divine authority.

Catholicity and Canonicity

Catholicity is related to the acceptance of a book by the majority of the churches. In the early fifth century Vincent of Lerins articulated the "Vincentian Canon" as a means for determining what was genuinely Christian as opposed to that which was sectarian, idiosyncratic, or heretical. Vincent's canon did not refer to the authoritative collection of Scripture but rather to that which has "always, everywhere, and by all Christians been believed [about God's self-disclosure]." The Vincentian Canon reflects the early church's underlying commitment to catholicity.

Back in the second century, some appealed to secret traditions (e.g., *The Secret Gospel of Thomas*) for practices and teachings. These largely gnostic works were uninterested in the historicity of the faith and in Jesus's death and resurrection. Instead they focused on his public sayings as well as his purported secret teachings that he had not entrusted to the masses, or even to all of the apostles. The appeal to catholicity challenged the new "gospels" that arose during the second and third centuries. The church leaders argued that these documents failed the test of catholicity as well as the test of apostolicity and were thus not authoritative.

Public Worship and Canonicity

The early church included from its birth the public reading of Scripture (at first the Old Testament) as part of its worship, a practice inherited from the synagogues. Paul also gave instructions for his epistles to be read publicly in the assembly. The Gospel of Mark gives us a hint (Mark 13:14, possibly addressed to the public reader) that Mark expected the same of his writing. About a century later Justin Martyr describes Christian worship as including the reading of "the memoirs of the apostles or the writings of the prophets." Thus the four Gospels had come to be regarded as Scripture (on the level of the Old Testament) certainly as early as the second century.

In such a context the public reading of a document was an implicit endorsement of its authority and its canonicity. Significantly, fewer than fifty years after Paul had written his epistles to the Corinthians, Clement of Rome urged his Corinthian readers to "take up the epistle of the blessed Paul the apostle." This indicates that both he and his readers viewed it as authoritative.

The Fourth-Century Consensus and Beyond

The first complete listing of our present canon of twenty-seven books comes from Athanasius in AD 367. He gave his rationale for this list in his opening paragraph. Here he decried those who had fabricated books bearing the names of the saints as authors and by so doing had led the "ignorant and simple . . . astray by evil thoughts concerning the right faith." Augustine, concurring with Athanasius's canonical list, gave his criteria for canonicity noting that he preferred "those [books] that are received by all the catholic churches to those which some do not receive." Neither Athanasius nor Augustine made appeal to any council, only to consensus. In the following decades numerous Latin fathers independently published their understanding of the limits of the New Testament canon. All agreed with the Council of Carthage (where the Gospels and the rest of the New Testament were finally canonized), Augustine, and Athanasius. This consensus effectively closed the canon in the West.

Contrary to what is widely assumed, no early church council ever produced an official definition of the canon of the New Testament, or even addressed the issue. The early church *never* reached a conscious and binding decision as to the extent of the canon. Proof of this fact can be seen in the canons of the various churches of the empire.

While the canon in the West proved to be relatively stable from the late fourth century AD, the canon in the Eastern churches varied, sometimes widely. The Syrian church at the beginning of the fifth century AD employed only the *Diatesseron* (in place of the four Gospels), Acts, and the Pauline Epistles. During the fifth century the Syriac *Peshitta* translation was produced and became the standard Syriac version. The *Diatesseron* was replaced by the four Gospels, 3 Corinthians was removed, and James, 1 Peter, and 1 John were included. The Apocalypse and the other Catholic epistles were excluded, making a twenty-two-book canon. The remaining books did not find their way into the Syrian canon until the late sixth century. While the Syrian church recognized an abbreviated canon for two centuries beyond the Western and the Greek speaking churches, the Ethiopic church recognized the twenty-seven books of the New Testament plus *The Shepherd of Hermas*, *1–2 Clement*, and eight books of the *Apostolic Constitutions*.

Even in the West the canon was not closed so tightly as to eliminate all discussion and questioning. A case in point is the apocryphal *Epistle to the Laodiceans*. In the tenth century, Alfric, the archbishop of Canterbury, lists the work as among the canonical Pauline Epistles. From the sixth century

onward *Laodiceans* occurs frequently in Latin manuscripts, including many that were prepared for church use. The epistle was so common in the medieval period that it was included in several vernacular translations, including the Bohemian Bible (as late as AD 1488). It also appeared in the Albigensian Version of Lyons, and while not translated by Wycliffe personally, it was added to several manuscripts of his translation of the New Testament.

On the eve of the Reformation, Martin Luther questioned the canonicity of James. Specific doubts about canon were also being expressed even by prominent figures in the Catholic hierarchy. Cardinal Cajetan, an opponent of Luther, expressed doubts concerning the canonicity of Hebrews, James, 2 and 3 John, and Jude. Erasmus likewise expressed doubts concerning Revelation as well as the apostolicity of James, Hebrews, and 2 Peter. As the Protestant Reformation progressed, it was Luther's willingness to excise books from the canon (especially Old Testament apocryphal books) that prompted the Roman Catholic hierarchy to formalize its consensus on the extent of the New Testament canon into a concilar pronouncement. Likewise, by the end of the Reformation the major Protestant traditions also included a list of canonical books in their confessional statements. Although both Protestant and Catholic leaders had raised questions about several books, in the end they both formalized the same list of New Testament books. On the extent of the New Testament, both the Protestant and Catholic traditions finally agreed officially, although in practice neither had ever questioned the four Gospels or the Epistles of Paul.

When all is said and done, there has never been a serious attempt to add a book to the canon nor has there been an effort to excise any of the books agreed to by the early consensus. In the final analysis it must be admitted that the church did not create the canon but discovered it. The books that were recognized attained canonical status because no individual or organization could stop them from becoming so. In other words these books possessed and continue to posses a self-authenticating quality by virtue of the testimony of the Holy Spirit as to their divine origin so that they individually and as a whole imposed themselves on the church as its final authority.

The Dead Sea Scrolls

C. Marvin Pate

Introduction

In the spring of 1947, three young Bedouin shepherds were in the area called Qumran, which is on the northwest side of the Dead Sea, apparently tending their flock. One of the young shepherds amused himself by throwing rocks at a cave opening in the cliffs to the west of the plateau at Qumran. One of the stones went into the cave and made a shattering noise. The Bedouin did not enter the cave that day, but when one of them did venture in two days later, he found ten clay jars. One of those jars held three ancient manuscripts. The rest of the containers were empty, but later four additional scrolls were found hidden in that cave. This initial find led to a scouring of the area, which revealed more caves and more manuscripts. The discovery of those ancient documents, appropriately called the Dead Sea Scrolls, is regarded by many as the most significant archaeological finding in the twentieth century and as nothing short of providential. This chapter surveys three points regarding the Dead Sea Scrolls: the literature comprising the Dead Sea Scrolls (hereafter DSS); the community producing the DSS; and the theology undergirding the DSS.

The Literature Comprising the DSS

The publication of the DSS stretched from 1947 to 1991, creating a storm of controversy along the way. Such an academic tempest stemmed from inadequate numbers to piece together and translate the scrolls, scholarly hoarding of the manuscripts, and, until late in the process, non-Jewish participation in the project. Keep in mind that the DSS are composed of over 900 separate manuscripts in over 25,000 pieces. Some of the scrolls were almost totally intact (like the Great Isaiah Scroll), but most of them had deteriorated into small fragments, many of them the size of postage stamps. So the task of organizing and putting the fragments back together was huge. Finally, however, all of the DSS were published in 1991. The scrolls themselves date from about 160 BC to AD 68. Four types of literature comprise the DSS: Old Testament books, apocryphal and pseudepigraphical literature, commentaries on the Prophets, and writings about the community.

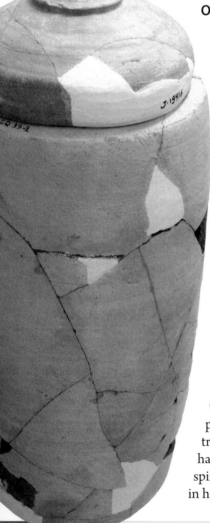

One of the clay jars that held the Dead Sea Scrolls.

Old Testament Books

Over two hundred Old Testament manuscripts have been found in the eleven caves associated with the DSS, representing every Old Testament book except Esther. The Pentateuch is the division most represented in the DSS. This stands to reason, for the community was extremely devoted to the Mosaic Law. The Prophets (especially Isaiah) receive the next highest distribution of manuscripts, undoubtedly because the community applied these prophecies to itself as well as appealed to them as the basis for its messianic expectation. Except for Psalms and Daniel, the Writings are not heavily drawn upon. The Psalms were utilized in the sect's worship, and Daniel's predictions were believed to be actualized in the group. Beyond these examples, the presence of the Writings is minimal.

Apocryphal and Pseudepigraphical Literature

By apocryphal or Deuterocanonical literature we mean those Jewish works written after the close of the Old Testament (400 BC). Although they most probably found a place in the Septuagint (the Greek translation of the Hebrew Old Testament), these books have never been considered by official Judaism to be inspired. Nevertheless, Jews have rightly held the apocrypha in high regard, both for its historical and ethical value. In fact, some Christian traditions (Roman Catholic and Eastern Orthodox) include them in their canon. Four apocryphal pieces were found in the DSS caves: Tobit, Sirach, Psalm 151, and the Epistle of Jeremiah.

In addition to apocryphal literature, pseudepigraphical works were discovered among the DSS. The pseudepigrapha are Jewish materials written in the last centuries BC and the first two centuries AD, and are not considered canonical by Jews or Christians. Nevertheless, they are valuable historically, ethically, and theologically in that they provide a window into the thought of early Judaism. Three especially are dear to the Qumran community that produced the DSS: 1 Enoch, Jubilees, and the Testament of the Twelve Patriarchs.

Commentaries on the Prophets

One of the fascinating discoveries that emerged in the DSS was the Qumran community's unique interpretation of the biblical prophets. Labeled *pesher* (derived from an Aramaic term meaning "interpretation"), this hermeneutical method contemporized Old Testament prophetic oracles by applying them to current events relative to the Qumran people. Two assumptions informed their approach: (1) they believed that the biblical prophets ultimately referred not to their own time in biblical history, but to the latter days of history; and (2) the Qumran readers also believed that they were living in the end-time and that therefore many of the biblical prophecies pertained to them. They also believed that spiritual insight for grasping the meaning of the text was given to the Qumran members by God. The method itself unfolds in the following steps: the biblical verse is quoted; the formulaic phrase occurs, "its interpretation concerns" (*pesher*); the application to the day of the Qumran expositor is supplied.

Writings about the Community

The fourth major type of literature in the DSS relates to writings concerning the Qumran community itself, which may be conveniently classified under four genres (literary styles): legal, eschatological, liturgical, and sapiential (wisdom).

1. The legal type of literature in the DSS is basically composed of four foundational documents that stress the utmost importance of the Mosaic law for the Qumran community: the Damascus Document, the Rule of the Community, the Temple Scroll, and *Some Works of the Torah*.

2. The eschatological (end-time) literature in the DSS reflects the community's apocalyptic self-understanding. That is to say, the Qumran sect

viewed itself to be the true Israel, the righteous remnant with whom God was establishing his new covenant in the last days (see, e.g., 1QS 1:1; CD 4:2). As the faithful of God, the people of the DSS equated their sufferings with the severe messianic woes that Judaism expected would test Israel before the advent of the Messiah (CD 1:5–11; 20:13–15; 1QH 3:7–10). The community's exile into the desert (Qumran) under the eventual leadership of the Teacher of Righteousness was understood to be the final preparation for the arrival of the messianic age.

Probably the sect's scrupulous observance of the Mosaic law was motivated by the belief that if Israel kept the Torah, the Messiah would come (cf. CD 4:1–17 with the following rabbinic literature [ca. AD 200–500]: Pirke' Abot 2:8; b. Sanh 97b; Sifre Deut 34). But by the same token, the period of trials to which the sect was exposed was predetermined by God (CD 1:5–11; 1 QM [War Scroll, Cave 1]). The DSS harbor the hope for the two Messiahs of Aaron and Israel (CD 20:1; 1QS 9:11–12). At that time the sons of light (the Qumran members) will wage war against the sons of darkness (everybody else) and will prevail, thus ushering in the kingdom of God (1 QM) and the New Jerusalem (4QFlor 1:11–12; New Jerusalem texts [5Q554–55]). In anticipation of that day, the Qumran sect observed a messianic meal (1QS 2:11–22), worked at overcoming the evil inclination within them by submitting to the law and the good inclination (the struggle between the two was expected to give way to the cosmic eschatological holy war; 1QS 3–4), and convened to worship God with the angels, which was a proleptic experience of the coming messianic age.

3. Besides the biblical Psalms, other DSS were utilized in a liturgical setting, notably the Thanksgiving Hymns (1QH = *Hodayot*) and the Angelic Liturgy (4QShirShabb; 4Q400–405; 11Q17). The former consists of some twenty-five psalms and takes its name from the verb that introduces these poems: *'odekah* ("Thank you [Lord]"). Form analysis of these hymns suggests they fall into two categories. The first group is written in the first person singular, quite possibly by the Teacher of Righteousness. These lament hymns recount the author's struggles with his enemies and petition God to vindicate his servant. The second group of hymns in the *Hodayot* seems to articulate the experiences of the community, which match those of their founder.

The lament form of the *Hodayot* suggests they served a liturgical purpose. This seems to be confirmed by the fact that they also express the notion that the congregation is united with heaven in a cultic setting to join the angels in worship.

The last mentioned theme is central to the Angelic Liturgy or Songs of Sabbath Sacrifice (4QShirShabb), a collection of poems designed to be read on the Sabbath. These psalms give instruction on how and when to praise

God, based on the solar calendar. One of their striking features is the correspondence of heavenly and earthly worship. These materials also borrow from the language of Ezekiel 1 and its presentation of the glorious throne of God. In doing so the Angelic Liturgy serves as an important witness to the pervasiveness of mysticism in early Judaism.

The great Isaiah Scroll, a particularly well-preserved text of Isaiah dating to 100 BC.

4. That wisdom is vitally important in the DSS is evident from the fact that they preserved the canonical wisdom books, fragments of the popular wisdom work *Sirach* (ca. 180 BC), and approximately fourteen other wisdom texts (e.g., 4Q184–185; 4Q413–419; 4Q424; 4Q521; 4Q525). Wisdom at Qumran was essentially the Essenes' (see below) reinterpretation of the Mosaic law.

The Community Producing the DSS

Though debate continues to rage over who wrote the DSS (Essenes, Zealots, Sadducees, Jewish military outpost, etc.), the majority view remains the Essene hypothesis. This understanding also assumes a connection between the DSS and the community revealed by the Qumran excavations. Four pieces of data seem to confirm that the Essenes at Qumran wrote the DSS. First, sociologically the DSS were written by a sectarian, marginalized group, which matches Pliny the Elder's description of the Essenes (*Natural History*, AD 77). Second, the archeological evidence connects the DSS with Khirbet Qumran, a site that fits Pliny the Elder's geographical description of the Essenes (see his *Natural History* 5.73). Indeed, Pliny's placement of the Essenes to the west of the Dead Sea, with En-gedi to the south, nicely fits Khirbet Qumran. This is all the more so since the area Pliny describes shows no archaeological evidence of having been inhabited by any other communal group besides the one at Qumran. Third, the paleographical evidence indicates that numerous duplicate copies of manuscripts as well as various styles of handwriting characterize the DSS. This strongly suggests that Qumran was the library or headquarters of a larger movement, which aligns well with Josephus's description of various branches within the Essene following (*Jewish War* 2.8.4 [124]; *Ant.* 18.1.5 [22]). Finally, historically, the period of Qumran existence, which ranged from the mid-second century BC to AD 68, is in agreement with the time frame mentioned by Josephus regarding the Essenes (*Ant.* 13.5.9 [171]; *Life* 1.2). Moreover, it is significant that the period when Qumran was not inhabited, 31–4 BC, correlates with the reign of Herod the Great. Josephus specifically states that the Essenes were highly respected by that ruler (*Ant.* 17.13.3), implying a relationship between the two (the lack of occupation of Qumran and Herod's approval of the Essenes). It is a reasonable conjecture that the Essenes, because they enjoyed a positive relationship with Herod, felt no need to live in the desert at that particular time.

The Theology Undergirding the DSS

Most likely, the theology driving the DSS is the familiar Old Testament theme of the story of Israel: sin-exile-restoration. Thus Israel broke the law of Moses; God sent Israel into exile as punishment; Israel will be restored to her land if she returns to the law of Moses. The DSS adhere to this story line, except that they reinterpret the law of Moses along the lines of their sectarian, strict perspective. This is clear from one of the DSS's earliest foundational documents: *Some Works of the Torah* (4QMMT). 4QMMT is a short text consisting of three parts: (1) a calendar, consisting of lines 1–20, (2) a section of laws extending from lines 21–92a, and (3) an epilogue composed of lines 92b–118.

The sin-exile-restoration pattern is evident in the epilogue: (1) Israel repeatedly sinned against the Lord from the time of Jeroboam to Zedekiah (lines 104–5); (2) consequently, God rained the Deuteronomic curses on the nation (the exile) (lines 97, 101, 130–36); (3) but true Israel, the Essene community, has repented of its sin (lines 101–2) by segregating itself from the rest of the people (lines 92–94). This has secured for the covenanters the Deuteronomic blessings (restoration) (lines 100, 103–4, 106–8).

Furthermore, the laws required to be followed in order to experience the Deuteronomic blessings are the community's *halakah*, which lines 1–92a are devoted to explaining. These consist of the covenanter's stringent reinterpretation of purity regulations and Sabbath-keeping. It is the sectaries' commitment to these rules that has caused them to separate from society (lines 92b–94). The Qumran community is thereby justified by God (line 117).

Space does not permit individual treatment of the other DSS. But that data can be summarized under the following categories: (1) wisdom as the sectaries' reinterpretation of the Mosaic law; (2) the realization of the eschatological Deuteronomic blessings in the Qumran community; and (3) the actualization of the Deuteronomic curses on nonsectarian Jews and gentiles.

It is transparent in all of this that the DSS operate under the assumption that the Torah (more strictly defined) must be kept in order to remain in the covenant, a relationship that excluded gentiles and non-Qumran Jews.

Conclusion

The DSS impact the Bible in two major ways. First, the DSS help to identify and confirm the text of the Hebrew Bible. Second, though there is no direct link between the DSS and the New Testament, the story of Israel as reinterpreted eschatologically by the DSS distinctively reminds one of the New Testament. The difference is, of course, that the latter portrays Jesus as the true Messiah who has brought an end to the law of Moses and that, therefore, salvation is by faith in Christ alone.

The ruins of one of the buildings at Qumran, the community that probably produced the Dead Sea Scrolls. Some scholars believe that the scrolls were copied in this very room, but it is difficult to be certain.

The Septuagint

KAREN H. JOBES

Introduction: What Is the Septuagint?

The term *Septuagint* refers broadly to the ancient Greek versions of the Old Testament originally produced for Greek-speaking Jewish communities and later adopted by the Christian church. The term comes into English through the Latin word for the numeral seventy, *septuaginta*, a reference to the number of translators who, according to the tradition preserved by Philo, were the first to translate the Hebrew Scriptures into Greek. Consequently, a common abbreviation for Septuagint is the Roman numeral seventy, LXX. This designation is first found in the phrase "from the seventy" included in scribal notes in the earliest Christian manuscripts of the Greek Old Testament.

How and When Was the Septuagint Produced?

The beginning of the ancient Greek version of the Hebrew Bible is believed to have been in Alexandria, Egypt, during the reign of the Hellenistic king Ptolemy Philadelphus (285–247 BC), when a translation of the first five books of the Hebrew Bible, the Pentateuch, was apparently produced. About AD 150, a document known as the *Letter of Aristeas* was written that describes the origin and production of this first translation as a defense of its authority and accuracy. Aristeas explains that King Ptolemy was gathering a copy of every book known at that time and commissioned a translation of the Hebrew Scriptures for his library in Alexandria. While the historical accuracy of the *Letter of Aristeas* is questionable, the extant Greek version of the Pentateuch does exhibit vocabulary that is consistent with an origin in third-century Alexandria. The motive for the translation certainly involved the needs of the Greek-speaking diaspora community of Jews (i.e., those Jews who had been scattered across Asia Minor and the Mediterranean world).

Aristeas claims that from Jerusalem six elders from each of the twelve tribes of Israel were chosen to produce the trans-

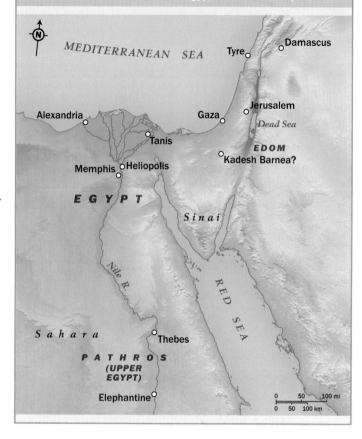

lation and were sent to Alexandria by the high priest Eleazer along with Hebrew scrolls from the temple. This tradition that seventy-two translators were originally involved in the work conflicts with Philo's later claim that seventy translators worked independently for seventy days and produced identical translations of the Pentateuch. In both cases, the number of translators is no doubt symbolic. The former, seventy-two, indicates that the translation was produced by representatives of all Israel, and therefore should be read by all Israel as its authorized version. The latter number, seventy, is likely an allusion to the number of elders who assisted Moses in the administration of the law (Exodus 24), expressing the view that subsequent translators of the law are also assisting Moses in its administration. The tradition preserved by Philo that the seventy worked independently and yet produced identical translations is his claim to the divine inspiration of the Septuagint, and therefore a defense of an authority for the Old Greek translation that is at least equal to or superior to that of the Hebrew Scriptures or to subsequent competing Greek versions.

Stela depicting Ptolemy II Philadelphus of Egypt. Aristeas claimed that the Greek translation of the Old Testament occurred during his reign.

The Greek translation of the Pentateuch probably does date from the third century BC in Alexandria, but it is unknown precisely when and where translations of the other books of the Hebrew Bible were produced. Nonetheless it is clear that over the next few centuries the remaining books of the Hebrew Bible were also translated into Greek. By the beginning of the New Testament era, the entire Hebrew Bible had been completed and was in widespread use. Keep in mind that this was a collection of scrolls (bound books, called *codices*, were not in use yet). The term Septuagint is usually used in reference to this collection of scrolls.

Over the next two hundred to three hundred years, however, additional Greek translations of the Hebrew Bible were also produced. These are referred to as "versions." The Christian scholar Origen (ca. AD 185 to ca. AD 254) knew of as many as six Greek versions for many of the books of the Old Testament. In addition to the original Septuagint/Old Greek version, Origen knew of three additional major versions by name—those of Aquila, Symmachus, and Theodotion. Moreover, for the book of Psalms and a few other Old Testament books, he also knew the versions now referred to as the Quinta, Sexta, and Septima. Because Aquila's version was produced to closely follow the Hebrew text that had become the standard text in the early second century, Jewish communities tended to adopt Aquila's version over the older Septuagint/Old Greek version, which continued to be used and preserved by Christians. Origen himself produced a revised version of the Septuagint for the Christian church that brought its text closer to the Hebrew text used at that time. Later, Lucian of Antioch (died AD 312) produced yet another version. One question of scholarly debate is whether these versions were produced by revision of an existing text or new translation of the Hebrew.

The modern edition of the Septuagint (Rahlfs-Hanhart, 2006), binds together the Greek version of each of the canonical Old Testament books along with a number of additional books commonly known as the Apocrypha or Deuterocanonical books, perhaps giving the appearance that the Septuagint is composed of a broader canon than the historic Protestant canon. The earliest Christian codices do include some of the apocryphal books bound together with the canonical books, but the apocryphal books as a corpus do not appear to have been accepted as canonical Scripture by either Second Temple Judaism or the Christian church.

The Septuagint and the Early Church

Though originally produced within Judaism, the Septuagint and other Greek versions are an important part of the heritage of the Christian church because the New Testament writers frequently quoted one of the Greek versions of the Old Testament. Therefore, the Septuagint and other Greek versions produced before Christ form the most direct literary and theological background for understanding the New Testament. Even though the Hebrew text of the Old Testament is the canonical text for the Protestant churches, methodologically sound exegesis of the New Testament writings must look to the Greek version of the Old Testament where it has been used in the New. As the early church expanded outside of Palestine, the vast majority of Christians could read the Old Testament only in a Greek translation, which, together with the Greek New Testament, stood as the Bible of the church for more than a thousand years. With the exception of a few individuals, such as Origen and Jerome, the church soon lost the ability to read the Hebrew Scriptures until the time of the Protestant Reformation in the sixteenth century, when the study of Hebrew was revived in the church. When the Roman Empire split in two at the end of the fourth century, the Eastern church continued to read the Greek versions as their Scripture, and the Greek Old Testament remains the canonical text in the Eastern Orthodox churches yet today.

Bible Translations and the English Bible

S ince the Bible was originally written in Hebrew and Greek (and a small portion in Aramaic), how did it come to be translated into English? Evangelicals believe that the Bible is entirely God's Word, but that God has worked through various human authors, including their personalities, circumstances, cultural contexts, and writing styles, so that what they wrote was the inspired Word of God. Paul reminds Timothy of the Bible's divine inspiration: "All Scripture is God-breathed and is useful for teaching, rebuking, correcting and training in righteousness" (2 Tim. 3:16). Up to this point the process looks like this:

Divine author → Human author → Original text of Scripture (Hebrew, Aramaic, Greek)

People then wanted to make copies of the original documents (the autographs), and copies were made from the copies, and so on. Although the autographs no longer exist (the case with all ancient documents), we do possess numerous copies of the books of the Bible. For example, there are almost six thousand Greek manuscripts (handwritten copies) of all or parts of the New Testament in existence today.

Before the invention of the printing press in the 1400s, all copies were made by hand, and scribes sometimes made mistakes (e.g., misspelling a word or reversing two letters or omitting a line of text). As a result, the copies we have don't look exactly the same, although they look remarkably similar, and no major doctrine of the Bible is in doubt because of the wealth of manuscripts.

Textual criticism (or analysis) is the scholarly discipline that compares the various copies of a biblical text in an effort to determine what was most likely the original text. The

work of the best textual analysts is presented in the modern critical editions of the biblical text. For the Old Testament, the standard critical text is the *Biblia Hebraica Stuttgartensia* (*BHS*). For the New Testament, it is reflected in the latest edition of the United Bible Societies' *Greek New Testament* (*GNT*) or Nestle-Aland's *Novum Testamentum Graece*. These critical editions form the basis for almost all modern English translations of the Bible. A translator or translation committee will use these critical editions to translate the Bible from Hebrew, Aramaic, or Greek into English for the benefit of English-speaking readers.

> Copies of the original text → Critical text → Translators
> → English translations → Readers

At this point in the process a translator (or usually a translation committee) will translate the Bible from the source languages (Hebrew or Aramaic or Greek) into the receptor language (in our case modern English). Here is where you enter the picture. As the reader, you pick up your English Bible and begin to read and interpret.

It's quite a process. God spoke through human authors who composed an original text. The originals were copied and recopied. Textual critics study all the various manuscripts and produce a modern critical edition of the Old and New Testament texts. Translators move the meaning of the ancient biblical text into English for our benefit.

Although the process of Bible translation may seem like a simple process, it's really fairly complex. No two languages are exactly alike, so there is no one-to-one correspondence between words in the ancient language and

English words. A very literal rendering of John 3:16 would read, "So for loved the God the world, so that the son the only begotten he gave, that the one believing into him might not be destroyed, but might have life age." Is this really the best translation of John 3:16? Could we even read an entire Bible "translated" in this way?

Since languages differ in many ways, making a translation is a complicated endeavor. A more literal translation is not necessarily a more accurate translation. Translation involves more than just stringing together words. Translating the Bible into English calls for reproducing the meaning of a biblical text (in Hebrew, Aramaic, or Greek) in English as fully as possible. There are difficult choices involved in the details of such a process and that explains why English translations differ so much. The translators wrestle with how best to move the meaning in the ancient text into English.

Approaches to Bible Translation

There are two main approaches to translation: the *formal* approach ("word-for-word") and the *functional* approach ("thought-for-thought"). Actually, no translation is completely formal or functional. All translations have a bit of both, but some are more formal and others more functional. The more formal translations—such as the New American Standard Bible, English Standard Version, and Holman Christian Standard Bible—try to preserve the structure and words of the ancient text as much as possible, but they run the risk of sacrificing meaning for the sake of form. The more functional translations—such as New Century Version, New Living Translation, Contemporary English Version, and God's Word Translation—focus on expressing the meaning of the original text in today's language, but they risk distorting the meaning of the text by moving too far from the form of biblical language. The following chart shows where many contemporary translations appear on the continuum of translation approaches.

More Formal (Word for Word)												More Functional (Thought for Thought)
ASV	NASB	RSV	NRSV	NAB	NIV	NJB	NLT	NCV	GW	GNB	CEV	Living	Message
KJV	NKJV	HCSB	NET		TNIV	REB							
	ESV												

The Living Bible on the right side of the continuum is actually a paraphrase rather than a translation. Instead of translating from the original biblical languages, a paraphrase will restate or explain an existing English translation with easier-to-understand English words and style. Paraphrases such as the Living Bible (1967–1971) or the Amplified Bible (1958–1965) should be viewed as commentaries on the Bible rather than translations of the Bible. But, as the following survey shows, there are many good English Bible translations from which to choose.

English Translations prior to 1611

John Wycliffe produced the first complete translation of the Bible into English in the 1380s. He translated the New Testament from Latin into English and was persecuted for his willingness to put the Bible into the language of ordinary people. John Purvey produced a revision of the Wycliffe Bible (1388), and this translation dominated until the time of William Tyndale. With the invention of the printing press in the mid-1400s, English Bible translation rapidly moved forward.

William Tyndale produced the first English New Testament (1526) based on the Greek text rather than the Latin. Tyndale was executed and his body burned in 1536 for his courageous commitment to Bible translation. In 1535, Miles Coverdale produced a translation of the entire Bible into English (Coverdale Bible). The Matthew Bible was completed two years later (1537) by John Rogers, an associate of Tyndale. Rogers also suffered martyrdom for his work as a translator. In 1539, Coverdale revised the Matthew Bible, a revision better known as the Great Bible because of its larger-than-normal pages. The Great Bible was very popular with the people and was the first English translation authorized to be read in the Church of England.

The 1534 New Testament Tyndale Bible enjoyed wider distribution because of the printing press.

From Geneva, Switzerland, Oxford scholar William Whittingham and others produced a revision known as the Geneva Bible (1560), which featured Calvinistic marginal notes. This Bible became extremely popular among groups such as the Puritans, but was not permitted to be read in English churches. The Bishops' Bible, a revision of the Great Bible,

was completed in 1568 for this purpose. The Roman Catholic Church also needed an English translation with marginal notes in support of its doctrine, and in 1593 it produced the Douai-Rheims Bible.

The Authorized Version of 1611

In 1604, King James I authorized a new translation of the whole Bible for use in the churches of England. The leading university scholars in England produced the Authorized Version of 1611, commonly known as the King James Version (KJV). The King James Version of 1611 also included the Apocrypha, a group of Jewish books recognized as canonical by Catholics but not by Protestants.

The goal of the KJV translators was to produce an English translation from the original languages that ordinary people could understand and that would be worthy of public reading in the churches. In spite of early criticisms, the KJV became one of the most widely used English translations. The KJV has been revised numerous times since 1611. It's a revision of the 1769 edition that is prominent today—an edition that differs significantly from the 1611 edition. For example, the original KJV contained the Old Testament Apocrypha, books traditionally accepted by Catholics and rejected by Protestants.

The 1583 edition of the Geneva Bible, an extremely popular early English Bible translation among Protestants.

In spite of the popularity of the KJV, translators have been motivated to continue producing new Bible translations for two reasons. First, the translators of the KJV used only about a half dozen, very late Greek manuscripts to translate the New Testament. Since that time, many older manuscripts have been discovered and most scholars contend that these are more likely to reflect the original text. Today, New Testament scholars are able to translate from a Greek text that draws on almost six thousand Greek manuscripts, some dating back to the second century. Sometimes the differences between the KJV and contemporary translations are due to differences in the underlying Greek text (e.g., Acts

How the Bible Came to Be

8:37; 1 John 5:7–8; Rev. 22:19). Second, the KJV's use of archaic English words and phrases such as "aforetime," "must needs," "howbeit," "holden," "peradventure," and "whereto" confuses contemporary readers. For other examples of outdated language in the KJV, see Exodus 19:18; 1 Samuel 5:12; Psalm 5:6; Luke 17:9; Acts 7:44–45; 2 Corinthians 8:1; James 2:3; 5:11. The KJV was a good translation for its day, but has been eclipsed by numerous contemporary translations.

English Translations Since 1611

The English Revised Version (ERV; 1881–1885) was the first major revision of the KJV, and the first English translation to make use of the modern discipline of textual criticism. American scholars produced their own revision of the ERV in 1901: the American Standard Version (ASV). Toward the middle of the twentieth century (1946–1952), the Revised Standard Version (RSV) appeared, still based on the KJV but with the goal of representing the best scholarship in language designed for public and private worship. The New American Standard Bible (1971) claimed to be a revision of the ASV, but should really be considered a new translation. The New King James Version (1979–1982) made an effort to update the language of the KJV while retaining the same underlying Greek text. The New Revised Standard Version, a thorough revision of the RSV, was completed in 1989 with the goal of being as literal as possible but as free as necessary (in order to accurately communicate the meaning).

There have been many other contemporary translations in recent years that are not tied to the KJV. The New American Bible (1941–1970) and the Jerusalem Bible (1966) are major Catholic translations of the Scriptures. The New Jerusalem Bible, a revision of the Jerusalem Bible, appeared in 1985. Both the New English Bible (1961–1970) and its revision, the Revised English Bible (1989), are translations into contemporary British idiom. The American Bible Society completed the Good News Bible in 1976 (also called Today's English Version) with the goal of expressing the meaning of the original text in conversational English.

The New International Version (NIV; 1973–1978, 1984) sought to produce a translation in international English offering a middle ground between a word-for-word approach and a thought-for-thought approach. Today's New International Version (TNIV; 2001) is an attempt to revise the NIV using the best of contemporary biblical scholarship and changes in the English language, especially as it relates to the issue of gender and language. The NIV was thoroughly revised in 2010. As a result, the NIV (1984) and the TNIV will eventually be discontinued. The issue of gender-inclusive language was brought to the fore by the publication of the TNIV. Bible translators will continually be challenged as to how best to translate the meaning of the biblical text into contemporary English in light of language changes such as those in the area of gender.

The New Century Version (1987) and the Contemporary English Version (1991–1995) are recent thought-for-thought translations. The New Living Translation (1996) is a fresh, thought-for-thought translation based on the popular paraphrase, the Living Bible (1967–1971). The New International Reader's Version (1996) was created to enable early readers to understand God's Word. Eugene Peterson's The Message (1993–2002) is an attempt to render the message of the Bible in the language of today's generation. The New English Translation, commonly referred to as the NET Bible (1998–2005), offers an electronic version of a modern translation for distribution over the Internet (complete with over sixty thousand explanatory notes by the translators). The English Standard Version (2001) is a word-for-word translation that uses the RSV as its starting point. The Holman Christian Standard Bible (1999–2004) also promotes a word-for-word approach unless clarity and readability demand a more idiomatic translation.

Translations for the World

Bryan Harmelink

Introduction

From the beginning of time, God has communicated with his creatures by translation of the divine word into human language. The multilingual character of society and the need for translation are evidenced in the pages of Scripture in the interplay of Hebrew, Aramaic, and Greek. The Gospels themselves are prime examples of translation, expressing in Greek what would have originally been spoken in Aramaic. This has led some scholars, such as Lamin Sanneh, to refer to Christianity as a "translating religion" that places God at the center of human culture. Scripture translation follows the paradigmatic event of Pentecost when God's Spirit made it possible for those present in Jerusalem to hear the wonders of God in their own languages.

Brief History

Scripture translation is one of the oldest activities of the people of God. The Septuagint, the Greek translation of the Hebrew Scriptures, and the other ancient versions in languages such as Syriac, Coptic, and Latin, are all early evidence of this essential activity that has gone hand in hand with the expansion of the church.

Missionary Era

By the year AD 1500, there had been Scripture translation in approximately twenty languages, but during the next three hundred years this number increased to eighty. Various historical factors such as the intellectual climate produced by the Renaissance, the changes set in motion by the Reformation, and increased exploration around the world contributed to this higher translation activity. These historical factors also set the stage for the missionary era of translation, which was characterized by a cross-cultural translator working within the larger context of other mission activity.

Translation Agency Era

The formation of the British and Foreign Bible Society in 1804 could be considered the early beginnings of a new era of focused attention on Bible translation through agencies that focused specifically on the translation and distribution of the Scriptures. This era witnessed an even greater increase in the numbers of translations around the world.

In the 1920s, William Cameron Townsend was working as a colporteur, distributing and selling Bibles in Guatemala. He encountered Cakchiquel speakers who were not able to read the Spanish Bibles he was selling. Their desire for God to speak their language prompted him to learn Cakchiquel and subsequently to begin the translation of the New Testament in that language. Townsend soon realized that translation was needed in many other languages in the world, and in 1934 he organized the first "Camp Wycliffe" to teach insights from the newly developing field of linguistics in order to train others to work in Bible translation. This set the stage for the eventual founding of the Summer Institute of Linguistics (SIL), an organization that would bring linguistics and other academic disciplines to

William Cameron Townsend (second from left) on his way to Guatemala in 1917.

bear on the analysis of numerous indigenous languages in diverse regions of the world. It was within this intellectual milieu that Eugene Nida, working with the American Bible Society, developed the model of translation known as Functional Equivalence. This theory provided important conceptual tools for many translators working on Bible

Dates of Incorporation of Bible Translation Agencies

New Tribes Mission	1942
Lutheran Bible Translators	1964
Institute for Bible Translation	1973
Pioneer Bible Translators	1976
Evangel Bible Translators	1976
Word for the World	1981

translation in very diverse linguistic and cultural settings around the world.

From the middle of the twentieth century onward, several agencies were founded with a specific focus on Bible translation. The work of the Bible societies, SIL, and these agencies contributed to the greatest increase in Scripture translation ever. As a point of reference, in the decade following 1810, translation work was undertaken in twenty-six languages, giving a total of 107 languages with at least some Bible translation. In the decade following 1910, 102 new languages were added to the list—almost as many were added in one decade as the cumulative total a century before. The trend continues: in 1910 the cumulative total was 722 languages, and in 2010 the total surpassed 2,500.

One of the common threads woven through the history of Bible translation is the desire to effectively and appropriately communicate the Word of God in another language. Nida was convinced that the best way to improve the quality of translations was to work directly with translators in the field and provide them with reference helps that addressed translation issues. He was also instrumental in the early stages of training for translation consultants who would become integral members of translation teams by providing additional expertise and periodic training for the translators. In addition to their role as advisers and trainers, consultants typically assist translators by checking their translations prior to publication. Indeed, providing training and consulting expertise is one of the continuing contributions of translation agencies in the twenty-first century.

Further developments in linguistic and communication theories during the final decades of the twentieth century continued to impact translation theory and practice, bringing about a reassessment of the Functional

The 100th New Testament translation completed by Wycliffe Translators (1979). In 2010 the total number of languages with some Bible translation surpassed 2,500.

Equivalence model as translators continued to work toward effective and appropriate communication of the Word of God in diverse linguistic and cultural contexts. One of the most significant changes was an increased awareness of the need to provide readers with background materials that assist them in their comprehension of Scripture.

Another influential intellectual current was the rapid growth of Translation Studies as a recognized discipline in the final quarter of the twentieth century. This has brought increasingly diverse fields of study—such as ethics, cultural studies, and postcolonial criticism—to bear on translation philosophy and practice. These fields of study provide Bible translators with important concepts for researching the cultural impact of translation in society, considering key ethical concerns in complex multicultural contexts, and developing a critical awareness of the role of the translator and the translation agency.

Global Translation Era

The final decades of the twentieth century and the beginning of the twenty-first also witnessed unprecedented growth of the global church. This growth is bringing about significant changes in the Bible translation movement as an increasing number of non-Westerners get involved in Bible translation. In many places this growth may itself be the result of prior translation work.

There is still considerable mission agency involvement in translation around the world, but the emphasis is on the training and participation of people in local communities and churches. This is a significant new era in the history of Bible translation, reflected, for example, by Samuel Escobar's statement in *The New Global Mission* that mission in the twenty-first century is the responsibility of a global church. In *Whose Religion Is Christianity?* Lamin Sanneh states that in the global church the representative believer is no longer a white Westerner, but rather someone from a Nigerian village or a Brazilian *favela*. The same changes are being seen in the global translation movement where the typical translator is no longer a Western missionary, but rather someone from the language community for whom the translation is being done. The ages-old desire of the church to hear and understand the Word of God is alive and well in the global church.

The Scope of the Remaining Task

According to 2008 statistics, 6,909 languages are spoken by the world's 6.5 billion people. Of these totals, there is still no Scripture translation for 2,393 languages, spoken by about 200 million people. There is, however, an unprecedented number of translation, linguistic, or literacy programs in progress in 1,998 languages, representing 1.2 billion people. These statistics make it clear that the remaining task is of global proportions and beyond the capacity of any translation agency. Significant progress toward providing Scripture for the remaining language communities will be possible only through the active participation of the global church. Scholars such as Andrew Walls, Lamin Sanneh, and Philip Jenkins have written volumes on the history and role of Scripture translation in the global Christian movement, but there are many chapters that have yet to be written.

Technology

Advances in information technology have directly impacted the Bible translation movement by providing electronic resources and data management tools specifically designed for translators. Having resources on digital media makes it possible for translators in even the most remote corners of the world to access substantial libraries of exegetical and translation help in a way not previously possible in the history of Bible translation.

One of the most significant ways in which software tools aid the translation process is by simplifying the process from draft to publication. The same digital files can quickly go from an editing session to being printed for trial copies with a few clicks. Most of the tools for prepublication checks on a new Scripture translation are built into the software, which has helped to streamline this phase of the translation process.

New Translation Strategies

Most Bible translation projects have traditionally been carried out in and for one particular language community. There are some situations, however, where certain factors lend themselves to different types of "cluster" approaches. One such approach involves using specialized computer tools that take direct user-input from linguists and translators to process a base

A translation team in Cameroon begins their day with devotions.

translation and produce one or more predrafts in other related languages. Another type of "cluster" approach is where translation teams come from different language communities but share a common Language of Wider Communication, which allows them to work together and take advantage of the expertise of the same translation adviser or consultant. The computer does not in any way replace the translator, but it can be an important tool for certain otherwise tedious text-processing tasks.

Scripture Engagement

The goal of Bible translation has never been about translation as an end in itself. Rather, it's about providing Scripture in the language people understand so they can use it and effectively engage with it. There has been an awareness of the need for Scripture engagement for many decades, but it has only recently become a primary focus of translation agencies. For some, the sufficiency of Scripture seems to have meant that providing an understandable Bible was enough, but effective engagement with a new translation does not necessarily follow from the translation and publication process. Typically, complex sociolinguistic and missiological factors affect the use of a translation, especially in the diverse multilingual contexts in which most Scripture translation is being done. In current translation projects, these factors are taken into consideration in early planning stages in order to develop strategies for effective engagement with Scripture.

New Distribution Strategies

New information technologies have not only impacted the translation process, but also the distribution of the translated Scriptures through web-based delivery. Digital media have opened up new frontiers for making the Scriptures available in ways never before imagined possible. The world is not equally "flat" everywhere, but access to digital media no longer requires costly computers with internet connections. Many less expensive mobile devices are becoming more available, thereby creating new and exciting avenues for Scripture distribution and engagement.

Digging
Deeper into
the Bible

PART III

How to Read, Interpret, and Apply the Bible

The Bible is the most influential book in human history. Believers have approached the Bible in various ways, depending on their individual circumstances and needs. While there are many helpful ways of listening to God's Word that are not mentioned below (e.g., Scripture memorization), three ways remain basic and essential for every believer. We need to read the Bible (appealing to our hearts), interpret the Bible (challenging our minds), and apply the Bible (transforming our lives). All three are important aspects of loving God with our whole being by listening faithfully to God's Word.

Reading the Bible

Sometimes we need to sit back and take in bigger sections of the Bible. We need to fly over the biblical terrain as well as walk through it. When reading the Scriptures in this way, we are not looking to analyze individual words or scrutinize sentence structure. It's not that we turn off our minds, but we read more with our hearts. We zoom out to get a feel for the big picture, to see how the larger story unfolds, to observe God's overarching plans for his creation. We are searching for wisdom more than information. We are synthesizing more than analyzing. This kind of wide-angle reading deserves an important place in the life of the church.

Reading through the whole Bible in a year or two can provide this kind of perspective. Here is a plan to read through the entire Bible in two years:

Month	Year 1	Year 2
January	Genesis	1 Chronicles, 1 Thessalonians–Titus
February	Exodus, Mark	2 Chronicles, Philemon, Hebrews
March	Leviticus, Matthew	Ezra, Nehemiah, Esther, Psalm 73–89
April	Psalm 1–41	Job, James
May	Numbers, Luke 1–9	Proverbs, Ecclesiastes, Song of Songs
June	Deuteronomy, Luke 10–24	Isaiah
July	Joshua, John	1 Peter–Jude, Psalm 90–106
August	Judges, Ruth, Acts	Jeremiah, Lamentations
September	1 Samuel, Romans	Ezekiel
October	2 Samuel, Psalm 42–72	Hosea–Malachi (excluding Zechariah)
November	1 Kings, 1–2 Corinthians	Psalm 107–150
December	2 Kings, Galatians–Colossians	Daniel, Zechariah, Revelation

For this type of reading, a thought-for-thought translation such as the New Living Translation often works best. Also, many people benefit from writing down their thoughts and insights as they watch the bigger picture unfold (e.g., how God repeatedly deals with his people or the qualities of a godly person in the story or how particular promises are fulfilled). Studying the details of the Bible is important (as we will see shortly), but so is reading larger sections of text. We need both!

Interpreting the Bible

Along with reading through the whole Bible in order to see the big picture, we will also benefit from studying smaller sections of Scripture. (For more information on interpreting the Bible, see our books *Grasping God's Word* and *Journey into God's Word*.) When we study details such as words, sentences, and paragraphs in this way, we will, of necessity, also be interpreting. It's impossible to read and understand and apply the Bible without interpreting the Bible. Interpretation is not an option. The only question is whether we will interpret the Bible accurately and responsibly.

Responsible Bible interpretation begins with the question: "What did this text mean to the biblical audience?" We can't know what it means for us without knowing what it meant for them. To answer this question properly, we need to consider two matters: *context* (both historical-cultural and literary) and *content*.

Context

In order to know what a biblical text meant for an ancient audience, we must know the context. There are two types of context to consider: literary context and historical-cultural context. *Literary context* includes the literary form of the passage you are studying (e.g., narrative, law, prophecy, gospel, letter, apocalyptic) and the surrounding context (i.e., what comes before and after your passage). For example, if you are studying Hebrews 12:1–3, you would first identify the form of the passage as part of a New Testament letter, and you would approach the passage using rules of interpretation designed for New Testament letters. Then you would consider the surrounding context. Hebrews 11 lists the "cloud of witnesses" or heroes of faith spoken of in 12:1. As we look to them, we are encouraged to endure in faith as they did. Hebrews 12:4–13 describes hardship as God's discipline. We endure God's loving discipline, knowing he allows these circumstances for our good, in order that we may share in his holiness (12:10). The literary context helps us know that 12:1–3 will probably have something to do with faithfully enduring difficult circumstances.

The second type of context is *historical-cultural context* or background context. Here we are moving outside of the text to background information we need in order to make sense of the passage. We want to know about the author of the book, about his relationship with the audience, and why he is writing. We want to know more about the biblical audience and their situation at the time. We also could benefit from knowing more about any specific background issues alluded to in the passage that might help us understand its meaning.

In the case of Hebrews, we are not sure who the author is, but we do know something about why he is writing. The audience is likely a house church in or near Rome that is thinking about leaving Christianity and returning to Judaism in order to avoid persecution (10:25). Hebrews was written to warn these believers about the dangers of drifting away from the true faith and to encourage them to persevere in their commitment to Christ. Within 12:1–3, the author uses the image of a long-distance race to encourage believers to endure. The more we know about ancient runners, the better we will understand some of the details of the passage (e.g., "let us throw off everything that hinders" or "the race marked out for us"). We need to study the historical-cultural context because God chose to speak first to ancient peoples living in cultures that are radically different from our own. As we recapture that original context, we will be able to understand the meaning of the passage and apply that meaning to our lives.

Content

As we continue to answer the question, "What did this text mean to the biblical audience?" we need to look more closely at the content of the passage. There are several important steps involved in this phase of interpretation.

First, compare different translations of your passage. This exercise will often pinpoint key issues and can also often clarify the meaning of the passage.

Second, read your passage over and over, looking for repeated words, contrasts, comparisons, lists, results or consequences, figures of speech, important conjunctions, key nouns and verbs, answers to questions, purpose statements, conditional clauses, commands, the tone of the passage, and so on. Take time to look closely at the details of your passage. You also might want to raise questions that you can find help with later in the process. Here are a few observations about the first part of Hebrews 12:1–3:

- "Therefore" refers back to Hebrews 11 and the "great cloud of witnesses."
- In what sense do these witnesses "surround" us?
- Figure of speech—the image of a long-distance race.
- We are supposed to throw off "everything that hinders" and "the sin that entangles." Is the author referring to the same thing or to two different things?
- Running is qualified by perseverance.
- Throwing off precedes running with perseverance.
- What does it mean that the race is "marked out for us"?

- "Let us" is repeated three times in verses 1–2.
- Jesus is described as "the author and perfecter of our faith." What do these words mean?

The list could go on. Don't underestimate the importance of looking closely at what your passage actually says.

Third, consult the experts in order to discover the meaning of key words, to better understand all the connections within the passage, and to find answers to your questions. Reliable Bible commentaries provide valuable information on just about every aspect of a passage. It's wise to consult several commentaries on your passage rather than just one. Here are a few reliable commentary series:

- Baker Exegetical Commentary (Baker Academic)
- Bible Speaks Today (InterVarsity)
- Expositor's Bible Commentary (Zondervan)
- IVP New Testament Commentary (InterVarsity)
- New American Commentary (Broadman & Holman)
- New International Commentary on the New Testament (Eerdmans)
- New International Commentary on the Old Testament (Eerdmans)
- NIV Application Commentary (Zondervan)
- Pillar New Testament Commentaries (Eerdmans)
- Preaching the Word (Crossway)
- Tyndale New Testament Commentaries (InterVarsity)
- Tyndale Old Testament Commentaries (InterVarsity)

The Circus Maximus in Rome, where many Christians were martyred.

Don't forget, you're still trying to answer the question, "What did this text mean to the biblical audience?" Having studied the contexts and the content, now is the time to attempt an answer to that question. In light of all that you have learned, write a past-tense statement that summarizes the meaning of the passage for the biblical audience. Here is one possible statement for Hebrews 12:1–3:

> The author of Hebrews used the image of a long-distance race to challenge his audience to persevere in their commitment to Christ in spite of opposition. Rather than drifting away from Christ and reverting to Judaism, they needed to run the race of the Christian life with endurance, drawing inspiration from saints who have already endured and focusing on Jesus, the ultimate example of perseverance under pressure.

Applying the Bible

People often get frustrated when preachers and teachers fail to move beyond the meaning of the ancient text. Interpreting the Bible deals with what it meant to its orginial audience. Applying the Bible, however, deals with how that meaning connects to us today. The original meaning is the same for all Christians, whereas how that meaning applies will vary widely among believers.

We cross over from the ancient world to our contemporary world in two ways. First, it is important to identify how our situation is different from and similar to that of the biblical audience. We are separated from the ancient audience by many things, including language, time, culture, situation, and sometimes covenant. At times the gap is fairly wide (e.g., in some parts of the Old Testament), while at other times the gap is narrow. When it comes to Hebrews 12, we are probably not tempted to revert back to Judaism to avoid persecution, but we still may be tempted to move away from Christ and toward some more acceptable form of religion in order to minimize ridicule and opposition. Many other elements of the Hebrews 12 passage are the same for us today (e.g., our culture also includes long-distance races).

Second, we cross into our world by identifying the timeless theological message(s) or principle(s) of the biblical text. Write out a present-tense statement that reflects what the text means for all Christians. You may have several such statements for each passage. Once you have written a statement, ask yourself the following questions to make sure it is a valid statement: Does the statement accurately reflect the biblical text? Does the statement apply equally well to both the ancient and the modern audiences? Here are a few possibilities for Hebrews 12:1–3:

- The believers who have persevered and are now with the Lord give us valuable examples of endurance. We should look to them for inspiration and encouragement.
- The Christian life is like a difficult long-distance race, which requires both effort and endurance.
- To run the race successfully (faithfully), we need to reject things that hinder our progress, and, most important, focus on Jesus and his perfect example of perseverance in the face of hardships.

Take the second theological statement mentioned above as an example. People who are facing rejection because of their faith in Christ need to be reminded that the Christian life is more like a marathon than a sprint. Being a faithful Christian takes both effort and endurance. So the passage is meant to encourage (and even warn) Christians who are tempted to take an easier route or even quit. Have you ever experienced a situation where you were tempted to move away from your commitment to Christ in order to reduce the ridicule, shame, or rejection coming your way? It is in that kind of situation, one that parallels the ancient situation faced by the house church in Rome, that the truth of Hebrews 12:1–3 speaks most deeply.

The application could be made even more specific, depending on the situation. This might include defining what "effort" and "endurance" would look like in a specific setting, such as staying faithful to Christ at work where you are in a distinct religious minority, or holding firm to your faith in Christ in a college classroom where the professor and most of the students are openly hostile to Christians. The wisdom of the Holy Spirit and the community of faith work together in helping us know how to apply the meaning of the Bible in specific ways.

The Unity and Diversity of the Bible

One of the most amazing things about the Bible is that it is both incredibly complex and yet, at the same time, simple and easy to grasp. Brilliant scholars can spend their entire lives studying very specific aspects of the Bible, engaging with other learned scholars in heated debates and disagreements that are built on complex arguments, often deriving from the grammar and syntax of ancient Greek and Hebrew. Yet five-year-old children can understand the basic essential message, truly accept the Lord, and find salvation. What an incredible book! It is complicated enough that scholars can struggle with it for fifty years and never grasp all of its depth and richness, yet it is simple enough that young children can "get it."

This combination of simplicity and complexity in the Bible is closely related to the issue of its unity and diversity. The Bible has unity in that it is all inspired by God and it all combines together to tell one basic story about how God relates to people (a story of sin, exile/separation, and then restoration). See the article titled "The Grand Story of the Bible" in part 1 for a summary of this central story of the Bible. This grand overarching story ties all of the Bible together from Genesis to Revelation. It starts in a garden (Genesis 1–3), takes a long detour, and then ends up back in a garden (Revelation 20–22). At the center of this story is Jesus Christ.

Yet while the main outline of the story is simple, the details and the manner in which the story is presented can be complex. The story itself gives the Bible unity, while the complex manner in which it unfolds can present us with diversity, but a diversity that still stays within the overarching theological unity of the story.

In What Ways Does the Bible Reflect Unity?

The central story running throughout the Bible unites the many diverse parts into a coherent, unified whole. The story is introduced in Genesis 1–12 (creation, sin, salvation, consummation). In the rest of the Old Testament the nation of Israel lives out this cycle, but the Old Testament ends with Israel (and the nations) still short of ultimate salvation and consummation, and still looking forward to the Messiah who will come to provide a spectacular time of salvation and restoration, both for Israel and for the nations of the world. Thus when one turns the page from Malachi (the last book of the Old Testament) to Matthew (the first book of the New Testament) there is no disruption to the story. Jesus comes as the fulfillment of the promise expressed clearly by the Prophets, but a promise that started way back in Genesis 12. Theologically, the major break in the Bible does not come between Malachi and Matthew, but between Genesis 11 and Genesis 12. Genesis 3–11 presents the problem of sin. Genesis 12 to Revelation 22 presents God's solution to that problem.

Likewise, the character of God is a constant throughout the Bible. Those who say that the Old Testament God is different than the New Testament God are not reading carefully. For example, some people note the severe judgment of God on the Canaanites at Jericho (the entire city was destroyed) in the Old Testament (Joshua 1–7), and they see tension between this and the New Testament picture of gentle, loving Jesus with children in his lap. But this is a distorted reading. The Old Testament

The Good Shepherd (third–fourth century AD). The image of God as the shepherd who cares for his people runs throughout both the Old Testament and the New Testament.

is filled with texts stressing the love and gentleness of God (Hosea 1–3, for example). Likewise, the New Testament does not shy away from speaking about the wrath and judgment of God. In Revelation 9:15 one-third of all people on earth are killed in one verse, making the destruction at Jericho look insignificant in comparison. The truth is that both the Old Testament and the New Testament present a God who is characterized by both love and righteousness, salvation and judgment. On the one hand, the Old Testament focuses more on the problem of sin; thus it contains many, many passages that underscore the terrible consequences of unrepentant sin (judgment). Yet the love of God and his promise of deliverance and restoration are always present as well. The New Testament, on the other hand, focuses on salvation and restoration. Yet the consequences of rejecting Jesus Christ the Messiah are serious and severe and hover throughout the New Testament as well.

Related to the character of God are numerous important theological themes that are very similar in both testaments. The tension between the law and grace, for example, discussed by Paul at great lengths in Romans and Galatians, is already readily apparent in the Old Testament Prophets. Paul will explain this tension by discussing the Mosaic covenant (law) in relation to the Abrahamic covenant (grace), a relationship already reflected in the Old Testament Historical Books and the Old Testament Prophets.

In What Ways Is the Bible Diverse?

God uses a wide variety of literary styles in the Bible to convey his story to us. Thus as we read the Bible we will encounter narrative in the Gospels, letter-like exposition in Paul's letters, strange apocalyptic imagery in Revelation, and Hebrew poetry in Psalms. The Bible contains songs, stories, royal decrees, parables, visions, speeches, trials, laments, genealogies, history, polemics, and proverbs. These various types of literature function differently in how they communicate God's truth to us. Poetry, for example, just works differently in how it communicates God's truth to us than do expositional letters (like the book of Romans). So is Psalms different than Romans? Absolutely—in style and in the way the author communicates with us as readers. Psalms also deals with different topics than Romans does and has a much different historical context than Romans. But does the book of Psalms reflect a different understanding of God than Romans does? Certainly not.

Another difference we will notice as we read both the New Testament and the Old Testament carefully is the realization that the Old Testament presents the introduction and early part of the story while the New Testament presents the climax and consummation of the story. Related to this is the fact that Jesus Christ advances by leaps and bounds the entire revelation of God to mankind. So the New Testament, on numerous points, is a clearer and more complete revelation to us than the Old Testament. This doesn't mean that the Old Testament was wrong or in conflict with the New Testament, but just that in regard to some truths the Old Testament is limited or incomplete in its viewpoint. Scholars call this development from the Old Testament to the New Testament "progressive revelation."

For example, the Old Testament is limited and incomplete in its teaching about the Trinity. It just does not give us much clear teaching on this subject. After we read the New Testament, however, and see the Trinity clearly from the New Testament pespective, we can then go back into the Old Testament and see it there (still rather fuzzily). But without the New Testament it would be difficult to perceive the Trinity in the Old Testament. Once again the nature of God presented in the Old Testament is not incorrect, just incomplete. The interaction between the Father, Son, and Spirit is revealed much more clearly in the New Testament, as the revelation "progresses" due to the incarnation of Christ.

The Old Testament often connects blessings for God's people with life here and now in the Promised Land (i.e., in the literal, physical land of Israel). The land is a central theme throughout most of the Old Testament. The New Testament, however, drops the land theme like a hot potato, and focuses instead on the kingdom of God. Likewise, as the Old Testament tends to focus on rewards here and now (again, physical blessings in the Promised Land during the Israelites' lifetime), the New Testament looks more to spiritual blessings and the future afterlife, focusing primarily on the believers' resurrection from the dead. The Old Testament presents a very brief and sketchy doctrine of the afterlife (heaven, resurrection). The New Testament "progresses" this teaching and, indeed, stresses the hope of resurrection.

Conclusion

So while the Bible is rich, complex, and inexhaustibly deep, it is also consistent and unified, with a central and ongoing story that is easy to grasp and believe. Scholars like us will continue to study and argue, slowly moving our understanding of this incredibly complex book forward. And five-year-olds, totally ignorant of New Testament Greek or biblical Hebrew, will continue to grasp the most important truth of all human existence, and find salvation in Jesus.

The Use of the Old Testament in the New Testament

GARY MANNING

It would be hard to overemphasize the influence of the Old Testament (OT in this chapter) on the writings of the New Testament (NT in this chapter). For NT authors, "the Scriptures" *were* the OT. Words, phrases, sentences, and ideas from the OT fill every page of the NT. Even when NT authors use no quotes or allusions, the theology of the OT is the assumed starting place. New Testament authors develop their ideas about God, his people, his covenants, and his plan of redemption from the OT Scriptures.

There are several types of references to the OT in the NT: direct quotes with introduction formulae ("as it is written"); quotes without introduction formulae (Rom. 2:6/Ps. 62:12); and allusions, in which the NT author recalls OT events, people, or ideas by the use of names or distinctive phrases (John 1:51/Gen. 28:12).

Quoting the Old Testament

In many cases, the wording of the OT quotation diverges from the OT passage with which modern readers are familiar. In some cases, the NT author appears to be citing loosely, perhaps from memory. The quotation may combine elements from two or more OT passages, or it may loosely resemble several similar OT verses. The NT author sometimes adds explanatory phrases into the middle of the quote, or changes pronouns to make the quotation make sense in his own discourse. Quotations and allusions are also complicated by the form of the OT that the NT author uses. Most NT quotations are based on the Septuagint (LXX, the Greek translation of the OT), since it was the most commonly used version of the OT in the first century. Sometimes the quotations reflect the author's own translation from Hebrew to Greek, and a few quotations are perhaps influenced by the targumim (early Aramaic translations of the OT with explanatory comments). To further complicate matters, NT authors may quote from OT texts with a different textual history from the LXX or the Masoretic Text (the Hebrew text used for modern translations).

What Is the Point of Quoting the Old Testament?

A quotation or allusion to the OT can be pictured as an hourglass: the upper chamber of the hourglass is the context of the OT reference; the neck of the hourglass is the quotation or allusion; and the lower chamber of the hourglass is the context of the NT quote. The NT's brief reference to the OT is often a way of showing connections between the theology of an entire OT passage and the theology of the entire NT passage. In many cases, references to the OT that at first appear strained make sense when the connections between the theology of the OT and NT passages are observed. For example, the five OT references in Matthew's birth narratives (Matt. 1:23/Isa. 7:14; Matt. 2:6/Mic. 5:1–3; Matt. 2:15/Hosea 11:1; Matt. 2:18/Jer. 31:15; Matt. 2:23/Isa. 11:1) are troublesome because some of the usages appear to ignore the meaning of the OT passage. However, a careful reading of the context of the OT passages reveals a common theme: the desperate plight of God's people and their promised rescue. Matthew is showing a connection between God's OT promises of rescue and the NT birth of the rescuer. In addition, four of these OT quotes make salvation-history connections between the locations of OT and NT events (Bethlehem, the tomb of Rachel, Egypt, and Nazareth).

Since references to the OT often involve the full contexts of both OT and NT passages, any analysis of an OT reference must include careful attention to both contexts. Since NT authors normally refer to the OT in order to make ethical and theological claims, it is important to look for ethical or theological ties between the contexts of the OT and NT passages. It is not enough to observe that a quotation or allusion exists; one must determine how the NT author uses the OT reference (and its context) to advance his own message. For example, Jesus's proclamation that "they will all be taught by God" (John 6:45/Isa. 54:13) evokes Isaiah's promise of the coming new covenant and implies that God's teaching will draw people to Jesus, who inaugurates the new covenant.

There are a variety of reasons for a NT author to make use of OT material. It is important to understand first what the NT author is *not* doing. The NT author is rarely engaging in exposition of the OT text; that is, he is not trying to merely explain what the OT author meant in the fashion of a commentary or expository sermon. The NT author has his own message, and he refers to the OT to advance that message. This is not to say that the NT author is disinterested in what the OT author meant; rather, he is interested in the theology of the OT passage and how it can be used to advance his NT message.

The ways in which the NT authors use the OT reveal two sources of authority: the OT Scriptures themselves, and the formational events of the new covenant. The NT authors use the OT precisely because they regard the OT as the words of God, but the NT actions of God, such as raising the Messiah from the dead and giving the Spirit, carry equal authority. The tensions between the original meaning of the OT and the NT authors' appropriation of that meaning are caused by the interaction between these two sources of authority. In a sense, NT authors always conform their OT references to the NT message. In some cases, there is only a slight modification, as when OT commands are now obeyed by those who belong to Christ and are empowered by the Holy Spirit (Gal. 5:16–24). In other cases, the transformation is more thorough, as when the NT redefines the people of God or revokes specific requirements of the OT.

Citing the Old Testament Law and Wisdom Books

New Testament authors often use OT quotations for moral and ethical purposes. Usually these are straightforward quotations of law or wisdom passages from the OT, and their use signifies the author's belief in the ongoing validity of OT moral commands. In some cases, the NT author may use an OT command as support for a different NT command. For example, Paul uses the OT command to allow oxen to eat while working as support for providing pay for ministers (1 Cor. 9:9–10; 1 Tim. 5:18/Deut. 25:4). New Testament authors sometimes advance their moral/ethical purposes by citing moral exemplars from the OT. Rather than citing a particular command from the OT, the NT author calls his audience to imitate the model of faith or practice found in OT heroes (Gal. 3:6–10; James 2:21–26). Such references may be tied to a particular OT event or invite the reader to consider the entire recorded life of the OT exemplar.

New Tesatment authors at times appear to correct or overturn OT laws (Matt. 5:31–39; 1 Cor. 7:19). Jesus's corrections to the law call the listeners to a "greater righteousness" that includes an inner obedience to the principle of the OT law; in some cases, his emendations correct contemporary abuses of the law. Paul, while in general upholding the ethical commands of the OT, overturns commands related to circumcision, food laws, and the observance of holy days. The combination of these two types of references to the law (authoritative citation and emendation/revocation) suggests that NT authors believed that OT law was not completely abolished, but that the arrival of the new covenant somehow transformed the law's applicability for God's people. For NT authors, the death and resurrection of Christ, the giving of the Spirit, and the formation of the church required a rethinking of the law and its purpose.

Citing Old Testament Prophecies

Many NT references to the OT are designed to show that NT people or events fulfill prophetic hopes of the OT. Some OT prophecies look forward to the blessings of a new age: a new anointed king from the line of David, peace and prosperity for Israel, reformed worship in the temple, gentiles submitting to Israel and worshiping Israel's God, the giving of the Spirit on all God's people, and a new ability to obey and know God. New Testament authors teach that these prophecies are fulfilled in Jesus Christ, in the founding of the church, in the giving of the Spirit, and in the second coming of Christ. In some cases, this fulfillment is relatively straightforward; for example, Matthew points out Jesus was born in Bethlehem, in fulfillment of the OT expectation that the anointed king would be born in David's town (Matt. 2:6/Mic. 5:2).

However, in many cases the NT author's citation of OT prophecy creates difficulties, because the NT author appears to significantly alter the meaning of the OT prophecy. For example, Matthew explains Jesus's ministry in Galilee as a fulfillment of Isaiah's prophecy of "great light" to Galilee (Matt. 4:13–16/Isa. 9:1–2). However, Isaiah 9 originally promised Galilee's deliverance from Assyria, a promise long since fulfilled. New Testament scholars take several approaches to such phenomena. One solution is to interpret the OT passage in such a way that it matches the NT author's apparent interpretation. This requires re-examining the OT passage to find a way that ordinary rules of interpretation will lead to the interpretation found in the NT. Another solution is to claim that the NT author has unlocked a fuller meaning (*sensus plenior*) of the OT passage that was not apparent to the author or original readers of the OT. In this view, the NT author is able to discern a meaning that was intended by God in the OT, even if the OT author was not aware of it (perhaps because the NT author functions as an inspired interpreter). New Testament authors often cite the royal Psalms (Psalms 2, 45, 110, and others) as prophecies about the Messiah. However, the royal Psalms were originally sung in honor of Israel's righteous kings, such as David and Josiah. *Sensus plenior* may explain how these psalms can apply to the Messiah: these royal Psalms ultimately apply more to Jesus, the Son of David and King of Israel, than to any earlier king.

Another solution (which can be consistent with the second solution of *sensus plenior*) is to identify such NT passages as typological rather than prophecy-fulfillment; that is, the NT author saw the NT event as a recapitulation of an OT event rather than as the literal fulfillment of prophecy. In this approach, Matthew quotes Isaiah (Matt. 4:13–16/Isa. 9:1–2) to claim that Jesus's ministry in Galilee was *like* Galilee's earlier deliverance from Assyria. Typology may be defined as the NT author's explanation of theological connections between entities in the OT (called "types") and entities in the NT age (called "antitypes"). The terms are derived from Greek terms (*typos* and *antitypos*) used in two typological passages (Rom. 5:14; 1 Pet. 3:21) and can be translated as "model" and "copy." The NT author, believing that God acts in a consistent fashion, sees correlations between God's work in the OT (the type or model) and God's work in the new age (the antitype or copy). In some cases, the antitype may far surpass the type in significance, as in Paul's typological comparison of Adam and Jesus (Rom. 5:12–19/Genesis 3). Thus typology can be viewed as something similar to using illustrations from the OT to explain NT events.

Unusual Uses of the Old Testament in the New Testament

Some of the unusual uses of the OT in the NT may also derive from the NT authors' use of interpretational methods common to their time, although the extent of such use is debated. New Testament authors used methods common among rabbis and the writers of the Dead Sea Scrolls, such as connecting different passages that share key words or phrases, and using lesser-to-greater arguments (Heb. 9:13–14/Lev. 16:15–16). New Testament authors also often seem to agree with Jewish traditions not explicitly found in the OT, such as the idea that angels were involved in the giving of the law (Gal. 3:19; Heb. 2:2).

How to Interpret and Apply the Old Testament Law

Introduction

One of the most challenging sections of the Bible to interpret and apply to our lives today is the Old Testament law. Within the Pentateuch (the first five books of the Bible) large sections in Exodus, Leviticus, Numbers, and especially Deuteronomy are filled with legal material (laws). All in all, there are over six hundred individual laws in these books. That is a lot of laws! How do we interpret these Old Testament laws? They seem to be very important, but many of them just don't connect with us very well, and to be honest, some of them are rather strange. For example, Exodus 34:26 states, "Do not cook a young goat in his mother's milk." What is that about? At least we don't have to worry about breaking that one! Or what about Leviticus 19:19, "Do not wear clothing woven of two kinds of material"? What is wrong with blending two kinds of material together? Is it sinful to wear a shirt that is not 100 percent cotton? I suspect that most of us break this one with some regularity. Or what about Deuteronomy 22:5, "A woman must not wear men's clothing, nor a man wear woman's clothing"? Ladies, are you obeying that one? Or Leviticus 19:28: "Do not . . . put tattoo marks on yourselves"? Or Deuteronomy 14:8: "The pig is also unclean; although it has a split hoof, it does not chew the cud. You are not to eat their meat or touch their carcasses." Obviously there are lots of very devout Christians violating these laws regularly.

In general most Christians tend to ignore most of the laws mentioned above. Yet there are other Old Testament laws that we strive to obey rigorously, placing them right at the center of Christian moral behavior. In contrast to the ones we ignore, these verses we try hard to obey. They include such statements as: "Love your neighbor as yourself" (Lev. 19:18); "You shall not murder" (Exod. 20:13); "You shall not commit adultery" (Deut. 5:18). Why do we obey some and not others?

The Willy-Nilly Approach

When it comes to interpreting the Old Testament, and especially the Old Testament law, most people inadvertently employ the good ol' standby method we call the "willy-nilly" approach. In this interpretive approach one simply skims along through the verses of the Old Testament making quick verse-by-verse assessments: "Hmm . . . this verse can't apply, all about sacrifices . . . this one doesn't make sense . . . here's one about farm animals . . . this one is just too weird . . . more sacrifices . . . priests and things," and so on. And then we come upon one that looks like it might apply to us, and suddenly we underline it and claim it as our "promise" for the day! So we have skipped over six or seven laws as totally irrelevant and then grabbed on to one and made it a law to live by. Surely this willy-nilly approach to interpreting the Old Testament law is inadequate. The very inconsistency of it should make us suspicious. But what method should we use?

The Classification Approach

One method that many people have found helpful involves classifying the laws into different categories, and using these categories as guidelines for determining which laws apply to us and which don't. The three main categories of this approach are *moral laws*, *civil laws*, and *ceremonial laws*.

Those laws that present universal timeless truths regarding God's intention for human behavior are classified as moral laws. "Love your neighbor as yourself" is a good example of a moral law. Moral laws still apply directly to us.

Laws dealing with ancient Israel's basic legal system (i.e., the courts, economics, land, crimes, and punishment) are classified as civil laws. Deuteronomy 15:1 is an example: "At the end of every seven years you must cancel debts." Likewise, those laws that cover sacrifices, festivals, and priestly activities are classified as ceremonial laws. A good example would be Deuteronomy 16:13, which instructs the Israelites to "celebrate the Feast of Tabernacles for seven days after you have gathered the produce of your threshing floor and your winepress." Under the classification approach, neither the civil laws nor the ceremonial laws have relevance or application for Christians today.

Under this approach, however, the process of classifying the laws into the categories of moral, civil, and ceremonial is a vitally important step because the classification will determine which laws apply to us today and which don't. On the one hand, in the classification approach moral laws are universal and timeless, and thus still apply to Christian believers today *as law*. On the other hand, the civil and ceremonial laws apply only to ancient Israel and not to believers today. Thus they can be for the most part ignored.

This approach has a long history, going back at least as far as the influential Reformer John Calvin (sixteenth century AD). Many Christians through the years have found it to be beneficial, providing them with a methodology whereby verses such as "Love your neighbor as yourself" can still be claimed as law for Christians today, while passages describing sacrifices and punishments can be relegated to the category of historical interest only.

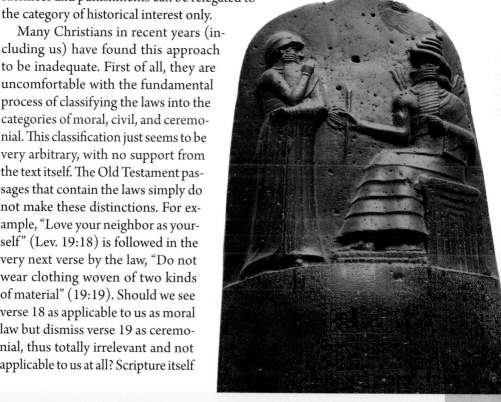

This stele contains the Law Code of the Babylonian king Hammurabi (1792–1750 BC) and addresses a wide range of civil laws (agricultural, domestic, commercial, etc.).

Many Christians in recent years (including us) have found this approach to be inadequate. First of all, they are uncomfortable with the fundamental process of classifying the laws into the categories of moral, civil, and ceremonial. This classification just seems to be very arbitrary, with no support from the text itself. The Old Testament passages that contain the laws simply do not make these distinctions. For example, "Love your neighbor as yourself" (Lev. 19:18) is followed in the very next verse by the law, "Do not wear clothing woven of two kinds of material" (19:19). Should we see verse 18 as applicable to us as moral law but dismiss verse 19 as ceremonial, thus totally irrelevant and not applicable to us at all? Scripture itself gives no indication whatsoever that any kind of interpretive shift has taken place between Leviticus 19:18 and 19:19.

Another problem with the classification approach is that it is often difficult to decide into which category a law should be classified. Because the essence of the law was defining the covenant relationship between God and Israel, the law as a whole, by nature, was *theological*. Thus *all* of the law had some kind of theological content. The difficult question that emerges out of this observation is, "Can a law be a *theological law* but not a *moral law*?"

This problem surfaces repeatedly in the book of Leviticus. Most of the laws in Leviticus deal with some aspect of Israel's worship system, so on the surface it would appear that most of these laws could simply be classified as ceremonial and thus dismissed. But we will miss out on a lot if we do this. One of the primary theological themes running throughout Leviticus is the holiness of God. A basic component of this theme is the understanding of the importance of "separation." That is, *holy* things must be kept separate from *profane* or *common* things. This is the underlying principle behind Leviticus 19:19, for example, which states: "Do not plant your field with two kinds of seed. Do not wear clothing woven of two kinds of material." It is true that we probably do not understand all the historical context and nuances of this prohibition against mixing things together, but we can be assured that it does relate back to the holiness of God.

So how should we classify Leviticus 19:19? Civil? Unlikely. It is unrelated to the legal, judicial needs of society. Ceremonial? On the surface this would be the logical choice, but in reality this law does not really deal with ceremonies or sacrifices. It deals with agriculture and cloth production (mundane field and home activities). God wanted the Israelites' *entire* way of life to be dominated by the consciousness of the holiness of God, who was dwelling right among them in the tabernacle or temple. The holiness of God in their midst demanded that holy things and profane things be kept separate. One of the things that was to help the Israelites keep this "worldview" before them constantly was that as they obeyed the law, their day-to-day life would be dominated by the concept of holiness and separation. Many items in their daily activities had to be kept separate. Thus even how the Israelites planted their seeds and wove their cloth would remind them of the holiness of God. These activities had *theological* significance to them. How can these laws *not* be classified as moral laws? If we classify them as ceremonial laws, thus dismissing them as having no relevance to us today, will we not be missing out on an important theological teaching?

It seems to us that the traditional classification into moral, civil, or ceremonial laws is too ambiguous and too inconsistent to be a valid approach to interpreting Scripture. The Scriptures themselves just do not make this distinction. Furthermore, the imprecision and ambiguity in the critical step of classifying each law makes us uncomfortable with this approach. The traditional classification approach also regularly dismisses the many so-called civil and ceremonial laws as not being applicable. Yet we read in the New Testament that *all* Scripture (and this verse especially includes the Old Testament) is applicable to the New Testament believer (2 Tim. 3:16–17).

The Principle Approach

So, how should we interpret the Old Testament law? First of all, we should have a method that can be used consistently with all of the legal texts. Second, it needs to be a method that does not make arbitrary *nontextual* distinctions between verses. A proven approach that meets both requirements is the "principle" approach.

With this approach we first recognize that all the laws are given in a narrative context and are also tightly interconnected to the Mosaic covenant that dominates much of the narrative from Exodus to Deuteronomy. So we will interpret the laws as part of the narrative and in light of the covenant. Then we will seek to develop universal principles from that narrative-driven interpretation that can be applied universally to Christians today.

Law: The Narrative Context

There is a continuous narrative story that runs from Genesis 12 to 2 Kings 25. The laws presented in Exodus, Leviticus, Numbers, and Deuteronomy are presented within the context of this big story. That is, the Old Testament laws do not just appear by themselves in isolation or without context, as if they were some sort of timeless universal code for all people of all time. The Old Testament law is firmly embedded into the story of Israel's theological history that describes how God brought Israel up out of Egypt, established his Presence among them, and then moved them into the land he had graciously given them. Thus we should approach the Old Testament law in the same manner as we approach Old Testament narrative, for the law is contextually part of the narrative.

Law: The Covenant Context

The covenant dominates the story in Exodus to Deuteronomy and, in fact, God introduces the law as part of that covenant, stating clearly, "Now if you obey me fully and keep my covenant, then out of all nations you will be my treasured possession" (Exod. 19:5). A critical component of the covenant was God's promise to dwell in Israel's midst, a theme that is stressed over and over in the latter half of Exodus (Exod. 25:8; 29:45; 33:14–17; 40:34–38). If God is going to dwell in their midst, then he needs a place to stay, so it is no surprise that the latter chapters of Exodus contain instructions for constructing the ark and the tabernacle, God's new dwelling place (Exodus 25–31; 35–40). The book of Leviticus follows the latter half of Exodus quite naturally, for Leviticus defines how the nation of Israel is to live now that the holy, awesome God dwells right there among them.

The book of Numbers continues the narrative story. In Numbers, Israel refuses to obey God and to enter the Promised Land (Numbers 13–14), so God sends them back into the desert for thirty-eight more years, during which time that disobedient generation grows old and dies. But before God takes the next generation back to the Promised Land, he renews the covenant with them, calling on them once again to commit to covenant obedience. In essence, God reinstates the Mosaic covenant that he originally made with their parents back in Exodus. Most of the book of Deuteronomy is related to this renewed call to covenant obedience that God makes with Israel just before they enter into the land. In Deuteronomy God is even more explicit than he was in Exodus, elaborating and providing more details about the covenant and how they were to behave in the Promised Land. It is important to grasp the narrative significance of Deuteronomy, for this book describes in detail the terms by which Israel would be able to live in the Promised Land successfully and be blessed by God.

We can see, therefore, that the Mosaic covenant and the Old Testament law are inextricably interconnected. That is, the law is providing the terms of the covenant that Israel is expected to keep. Our understanding of the law and our attempts to apply the law must keep this tight connection in mind. Because of this tight relationship between the law and the Mosaic covenant, several important observations about the covenant need to be noted.

1. *The Mosaic covenant is closely associated with Israel's conquest and occupation of the Promised Land.* The covenant defined the terms by which Israel could successfully occupy the land and live there prosperously with God in their midst. The inseparable connection between the covenant and the land is evident everywhere in Deuteronomy.
2. *The blessings from the Mosaic covenant are conditional.* This is a very important observation. Throughout Deuteronomy, God and Moses continually warn Israel of the consequences of ignoring the laws of the covenant, explaining repeatedly to Israel that obedience to the covenant will bring blessing and disobedience to the covenant will

bring punishment and curses. Deuteronomy 28 sums up the contrasting consequences of blessings and curses, dependent on Israel's obedience.

3. *The Mosaic covenant is no longer a functional covenant.* If the laws in the Pentateuch are tightly interconnected to the Mosaic covenant, then this point is critical to how we apply them. The New Testament is quite clear in stating that we as New Testament believers are no longer under the old, Mosaic covenant. This is the main point of Hebrews 8–9. Jesus came as the mediator of a *new* covenant that replaced the *old* covenant. "By calling this covenant 'new,' he has made the first one obsolete" (Heb. 8:13). Remember that the Old Testament law comprises the terms of the agreement by which Israel could live prosperously in the Promised Land under the old (Mosaic) covenant. If the New Testament declares the old covenant as no longer valid, then the laws that made up that covenant cannot continue to function in the same manner as they did before.

4. *The Old Testament law as part of the Mosaic covenant is no longer applicable over us as law.* The New Testament is not ambiguous about this. Paul stresses that Jesus has removed Christians out from under the Old Testament law, stating, "We . . . know that a man is not justified by observing the law, but by faith in Jesus Christ" (Gal. 2:15–16). Similarly in Romans 7:4 Paul explains, "you also died to the law through the body of Christ." Galatians 3:25 continues this theme: "Now that faith has come, we are no longer under the supervision of the law." The apostle Paul states repeatedly that Christians should not try to keep the Old Testament law in the same manner as Israel had done. As we seek to apply the Old Testament law in our lives, it is critical that we pay attention to Paul's admonition. As Christians we are now freed from the law through Jesus Christ; we cannot allow our interpretive approach to the law to put Christians back under the law.

5. *We must interpret the law through the grid of New Testament teaching.* The law is still Scripture, and 2 Timothy 3:16 declares that "all Scripture is God-breathed and is useful for teaching, rebuking, correcting and training in righteousness." The Old Testament law is certainly included in the category of "all Scripture." This passage indicates to us that we cannot simply jettison the Old Testament law because we are under the new covenant. As part of God's Word, there are teachings to be found in the Old Testament law that are eternal and beneficial to us. Thus we need to continue to study and to try to apply all of Scripture, even the unusual laws. However, it is critical to remember that the law no longer functions as the terms of the covenant for us. That is, the

Old Testament law *no longer applies as direct literal law for us*. Jesus Christ changed that forever. But like the wonderful narratives of the Old Testament, the legal material also reflects rich *principles* and *lessons* for living that are still relevant to us, so long as we interpret them through New Testament teaching.

Steps in the Principle Approach

In light of the discussion above, we suggest the following steps in interpreting and applying any of the Old Testament laws.

Step 1: Determine what the law meant to the biblical audience.

The first step involves placing the law into the context of the larger narrative story. That is, read and study it as you would a narrative text. Where are the Israelites when this law is given? What is the purpose of this particular law in the life of Israel at this particular moment? Has this law been given as a response to a specific situation, or is it describing the requirements for Israel after they move into the land? Which other laws are in the immediate context? Are there any connections between these laws? How did this law relate to the Mosaic covenant? Does it teach how the people were to approach God, or does it deal with how they should treat one another? Try to specify exactly what this law meant for the Old Testament audience.

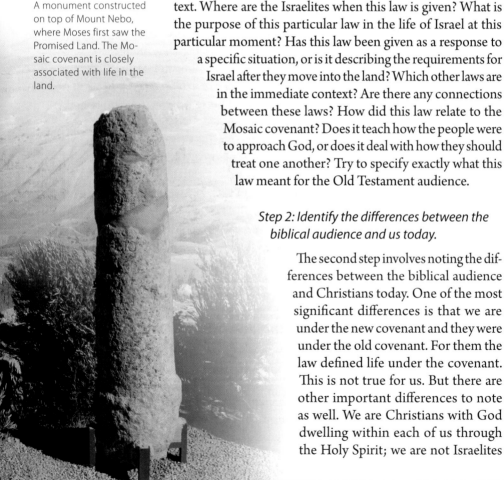

A monument constructed on top of Mount Nebo, where Moses first saw the Promised Land. The Mosaic covenant is closely associated with life in the land.

Step 2: Identify the differences between the biblical audience and us today.

The second step involves noting the differences between the biblical audience and Christians today. One of the most significant differences is that we are under the new covenant and they were under the old covenant. For them the law defined life under the covenant. This is not true for us. But there are other important differences to note as well. We are Christians with God dwelling within each of us through the Holy Spirit; we are not Israelites entering the Promised Land with God dwelling in the tabernacle. Likewise, we approach God through faith in the sacrifice of Jesus Christ and not through the sacrifice of animals. We do not face theological and social pressure from the Canaanites and their pagan religions, but we do face pressure from non-Christian worldviews and philosophies. The Israelites lived under a theocratic government, while most of us live under a secular democracy. What other differences can you identify?

Step 3: Determine the theological principle in the text.

The Old Testament laws define specific, concrete actions and behavior for the Israelites. This action and behavior was usually closely interconnected to the Mosaic covenant relationship they had with God. But this specific, concrete expression of the law was usually based on a broader universal truth. That is, behind each of the specific laws there was a universal truth about God or human behavior. Usually this truth is also applicable to all of God's people, regardless of when they live and which covenant they live under. Our application today will take a different form, but it will reflect the same principle. In this step we ask the question, "What is the theological principle that is reflected in this specific law? What is the broad principle that God has behind this text that allows for this specific ancient application?" Behind the Levitical laws regarding separation (grass seeds, cloth, etc.), for example, we will see the universal principle that God's holiness demands a separation between clean, holy things, and unclean, defiled things. But now, for us, the New Testament will define the shape this separation will take.

Determining the universal principle is not always easy. The following guidelines can help:

- The principle should be reflected in the text.
- The principle should be timeless.
- The principle should correspond to the broad theology of the rest of Scripture.
- The principle should not be culturally tied.
- The principle should be relevant to both Old Testament and current New Testament audiences.

In many of the Old Testament laws, we will discover that the principles emerging out of the law using this criterion will often be directly related to the character of God and his holiness, the nature of sin, or concern for other people.

Step 4: Determine if the New Testament addresses this law or the principle emerging out of the law. Use the New Testament perspective to refine and narrow the universal principle into a specific and concrete directive that New Testament believers can apply today.

In this step we take the principle we found behind the Old Testament law and we filter it through the New Testament. For example, if we are dealing with Exodus 20:14, "You shall not commit adultery," the universal theological principle emerging out of this law will relate to the sanctity of marriage and the requirement of faithfulness in marriage. When we turn to the New Testament to engage with its teaching, we note that in Matthew 5:28 Jesus states, "But I tell you that anyone who looks at a woman lustfully has already committed adultery with her in his heart." So Jesus has actually expanded the range of the principle behind this law, for he says it applies not only to *acts* of adultery but also to *thoughts* of adultery. So as we seek to apply the principle today, we must note that it applies to thoughts and not just deeds.

Step 5: Prayerfully apply the principle as modified by the New Testament.

It doesn't do any good to go through this entire academic process if we do not obey the Scripture and actually apply the principle that we develop. So in Step 5 we will take the expression that we developed in Step 4 and apply it to specific situations that we as *individual* Christians encounter today.

How to Interpret Parables

Jesus was a master communicator and one of his favorite tools of the trade was the parable. Approximately one-third of Jesus's teaching can be found in parables. Even people who are unfamiliar with the Bible have usually heard of the parable of the prodigal son or the parable of the good Samaritan. A *parable* (the term meaning "to throw alongside") is a short story with two levels of meaning, where certain details in the story represent something else. In the parable of the prodigal son, for example, the father represents God. In the story of the good Samaritan, the priest and the Levite represent religious leaders who use their religious status as an excuse not to love others. We may find it difficult at times to know how many details in these stories should stand for other things.

Throughout church history many Christians have taken great liberty with the parables by saying that almost every detail in these stories should represent something. For instance, notice how the early church leader Augustine allegorized the parable of the good Samaritan found in Luke 10:30–37.*

The wounded man	=	Adam
Jerusalem	=	The heavenly city from which Adam fell
Jericho	=	The moon (signifying Adam's mortality)
The robbers	=	The devil and his angels
Stripping him	=	Taking away his immortality

---

* See Robert H. Stein, *An Introduction to the Parables of Jesus* (Louisville: Westminster John Knox, 1981), 46.

Beating him	=	Persuading him to sin
Leaving him half dead	=	Due to sin, he was dead spiritually (half dead)
The priest and Levite	=	The priesthood (Law) and ministry (Prophets) of the Old Testament
The Samaritan	=	Christ himself
Binding of the wounds	=	Binding the restraint of sin
Wine	=	Exhortation to work with fervent spirit
Beast	=	The body of Christ himself
The inn	=	The church
Two denarii	=	Promise of this life and life to come
The innkeeper	=	The apostle Paul
Return of the Samaritan	=	Resurrection of Christ

Since the late nineteenth century, however, many New Testament scholars began to insist that every parable makes essentially one point. This was a welcome corrective to the allegorical method used by Augustine and others. But does the "one-point rule" restrict meaning more than Jesus would have intended? Do we have to choose between the two extremes of a parable making dozens of points or making only one point?

Take the parable of the prodigal son in Luke 15 as an example. What is the one point? Does the point that comes to your mind deal with the rebellious son, the resentful brother, or the forgiving father? Do you really want to pick just one and say that Jesus did not intend to make a point about the other two? The one-point approach appears to be inadequate. After all, not many stories of any kind make only one point.

The road from Jericho to Jerusalem went up and through these desolate mountains.

Recently a balanced approach to interpreting the parables has been offered by the evangelical scholar Craig Blomberg. Jesus's parables are not to be allegorized down to the last detail, but neither are they to be limited to just one point. Blomberg suggests that we look for one main point for each main character (or group of characters). Most parables will make one, perhaps two, but usually not more than three main points. All the other details are there to enhance the story. Look at how this guideline helps us to identify three main points in the parable from Luke 15:11–32:

- Younger brother → sinners may confess their sins and turn to God in repentance
- Older brother → those who claim to be God's people should not be resentful when God extends his grace to the undeserving; rather, they should rejoice
- Forgiving father → God offers forgiveness to undeserving people

Because it is difficult to know whether to count proverbs, riddles, metaphors, and short sayings as parables, the lists of parables found in study Bibles and other reference books vary. Below you will find a list of the main parables arranged according to the number of points they make:*

One-Point Parables

- Mustard seed and leaven (Matt. 13:31–33; Mark 4:30–32; Luke 13:18–21)
- Hidden treasure and pearl of great price (Matt. 13:44–46)
- Tower builder and warring king (Luke 14:28–33)

Two-Point Parables

- Secretly growing seed (Mark 4:26–29)
- Wise and foolish builders (Matt. 7:24–27; Luke 6:47–49)
- Householder and the thief (Matt. 24:42–44; Luke 12:35–40)
- Friend at midnight (Luke 11:5–8)
- Rich fool (Luke 12:16–21)
- Barren fig tree (Luke 13:6–9)
- Lowest seat at the feast (Luke 14:7–11)
- Unprofitable servant (Luke 17:7–10)
- Unjust judge (Luke 18:1–8)

---

* See Craig Blomberg, *Interpreting the Parables* (Downers Grove, IL: InterVarsity, 1990), chaps. 6–8.

Three-Point Parables

- Children in the marketplace (Matt. 11:16–19; Luke 7:31–35)
- Sower and the seed (Matt. 13:1–9, 18–23; Mark 4:1–9, 13–20; Luke 8:5–8, 11–15)
- The wheat and the tares (Matt. 13:24–30, 36–43)
- The dragnet (Matt. 13:47–50)
- The unforgiving servant (Matt. 18:23–35)
- Laborers in the vineyard (Matt. 20:1–16)
- Two sons (Matt. 21:28–32)
- Wicked tenants (Matt. 21:33–46; Mark 12:1–12; Luke 20:9–18)
- Wedding feast (Matt. 22:1–14)
- Faithful and unfaithful servants (Matt. 24:45–51; Luke 12:42–48)
- Ten maidens (Matt. 25:1–13)
- Talents (Matt. 25:14–30; Luke 19:12–27)
- Sheep and goats (Matt. 25:31–46)
- Two debtors (Luke 7:41–43)
- Good Samaritan (Luke 10:25–37)
- Great banquet (Luke 14:15–24)
- Lost sheep and lost coin (Luke 15:4–10)
- Lost (prodigal) son (Luke 15:11–32)
- Unjust steward (Luke 16:1–13)
- Rich man and Lazarus (Luke 16:19–31)
- Pharisee and the tax collector (Luke 18:9–14)

As you follow this "one-point-per-main-character" rule for interpreting parables, there are still other factors to keep in mind when trying to read parables responsibly.* First, we should seek to understand the stories as Jesus's first-century audience would have understood them. This may require some background studies on our part to become familiar with their original context. Second, we need to make sure our interpretation of the parable can be validated elsewhere by the nonparabolic teachings of Jesus. If it cannot be validated in this way, we have probably interpreted the parable incorrectly. Third, we need to interpret what is presented in the story, not what is left out of the story. We shouldn't focus on what is left out of the story to

* Many of these insights have been adapted from Klyne Snodgrass, *Stories with Intent: A Comprehensive Guide to the Parables of Jesus* (Grand Rapids: Eerdmans, 2008), 24–31.

the neglect of what the story actually includes. For example, in the parable of the Prodigal Son we shouldn't focus on the gory details of the younger son's sins in a gentile country since we can only speculate about what those might have been. Fourth, we need to know when to stop interpreting. There are limits to every analogy and the same is true with parables. Even parables we love and treasure cannot be made to say everything we want them to say. Fifth, we should pay special attention to what comes at the end of the parable. Often the ironic twist or the surprise or the theological clincher occurs at the end of the story.

Jesus's parables provide some of the most fascinating and engaging reading in the entire Bible. He uses the stuff of ordinary life—such as family relationships, business practices, weddings, feasts, agriculture, and politics—to teach us about God and his kingdom and how life should work in that kingdom. These stories are not just frilly decoration to the real teachings of Jesus. In many ways, the parables represent the very core of his teachings. As Jesus himself said, "Whoever has ears to hear had better listen."

How to Interpret and Enjoy Figures of Speech in the Bible

Figures of speech have sometimes been called the spice of language. That is, an effective use of figurative language can add interest, color, emotion, humor, or power to both the spoken word and the written word. Figures of speech also often create visual images, and these images can contribute in powerful ways to communication. So we are not surprised to see that those who speak in the Bible and those who wrote down the words of the Bible use figurative language frequently and effectively. Jesus himself was a very dynamic and colorful speaker, and in his hands figures of speech were powerful rhetorical tools to be wielded with skill, creating interest in his audience and making a powerful impact on them. Some of the many, many figures of speech Jesus uses include: "You are the salt of the earth" (Matt. 5:13); "You are the light of the world" (Matt. 5:14); "If anyone would come after me, he must deny himself and *take up his cross daily* and follow me" (Luke 9:23); and "I am the bread of life" (John 6:35). Paul also employs figures of speech in his letters (e.g., Rom. 11:17–21). In the Old Testament books that contain poetry (especially Psalms, Job, Song of Songs, the prophetic books), figures of speech are extremely common, occurring in nearly every verse. In fact, one of the basic characteristics of Old Testament poetry is the extensive use of figures of speech.

Figures of Speech in Everyday English

As with many languages, English is rich with figures of speech, and most of us use figures of speech *all the time*. Note that the preceding phrase *all the time* is itself a figure of speech, falling into the category of hyperbole (intentional exaggeration for effect). So as English speakers we are familiar with figurative language. Sometimes we are so familiar with it that we don't even notice it when we use it. Consider the silly monologue below as a student explodes and unloads on a friend after a particularly tough chemistry test:

> That chemistry professor is an absolute psycho. He just gave us the hardest test ever in the entire world. He asked the most stupid and ridiculous questions that have ever been written. I studied forever for that test, yet I really bombed on it. I had no idea what he was asking. Nobody knows the answers to some of those questions. He must have dreamed them up. It was absolutely the most ridiculous thing in the world. Everybody in the class bombed on it. Is he from outer space or what? I could strangle him. He expects us to study chemistry twenty-four hours a day. I do have a life, you know. But if I get a "D" in chemistry my GPA will drop right through the floor. Mom and Dad will be mad as hornets. And all because of a psycho professor.*

Figures of speech occur in practically every sentence above. Can you identify all of them? Some figures of speech are rather simple

_____
* See our *Grasping God's Word*, 2nd ed. (Grand Rapids: Zondervan, 2005), 352–53.

An orchard of pruned olive trees. In Romans 11 Paul compares Israel and the church to an olive tree.

(comparing Mom and Dad to mad hornets), but in other cases the figures of speech can be extremely complex, especially if we try to analyze them and seek to understand how they work. For example, what does the student mean by the phrase, "I do have a life"? Most of us understand everything the student is trying to convey and thus for us the use of figurative language works very effectively. If we were from another country, however, and we were not familiar with American-English idioms and figures of speech, we might be very confused by what the student said, especially if we tried to interpret everything literally. To truly understand the student we would need to recognize the student's use of figurative language, and we would need to interpret those figures of speech in accordance with the student's intended meaning.

We are in a similar situation with the biblical authors. They, like the student above, are conveying real thoughts, events, and emotions to us—that is, *literal* truth—but they often choose to express this truth figuratively. Our job as readers is to grapple with the figures of speech and to strive to understand the reality and the emotion the authors are conveying by their figurative language.

Types of Figures of Speech

Most of the time we can recognize and understand the figures of speech in the Bible if we just stop and think about them for a moment. Many of the figures of speech in the Bible are relatively simple and straightforward. However, some of the figures of speech occurring in the Bible can be rather complex and sometimes extremely subtle, requiring more thought and reflection on our part. Usually it is well worth the extra effort, for as we reflect on the figurative imagery used in the Bible and as we struggle to grasp the image conveyed by the figure of speech, we will understand the Scriptures better, which is one of our overarching goals as we read God's Word.

Figures of speech are a lot like poetry or art. By their very nature they resist categorization. Nonetheless, definitions and categories can be helpful, so long as we keep in mind that by nature figurative language is artistic and thus a little slippery. Most figures of speech in the Bible can be placed into one of two major categories: figures involving *analogy* and figures involving *substitution*. Occasionally, however, we will encounter figures of speech that do not really fit into either of these categories. For lack of something better, we will place these other figures of speech into a broad third category called *miscellaneous figures of speech*.

Figures of Speech Involving Analogy

Many figures of speech simply draw analogies between two different things. That is, the author wants to comment on or describe one item by comparing it to an aspect of a different item. The analogy provides a window for looking at something by using the attributes of something else that is normally quite different. In our example above, the student exclaimed, "Mom and Dad will be mad as hornets." This is an analogy, comparing the angry, buzzing attack mode of disturbed hornets to the expected reaction of the student's parents over the outcome of the test. This type of figure of speech works best if the reader (or hearer) can visualize the imagery being conveyed. In this case the reader needs to visualize angry hornets descending on the student as she runs for her life. With this image in mind the hearer/reader now needs to pull the parents into focus and try to catch the agitated upset reaction that the student anticipates.

Analogies can be used in many creative ways, so it is helpful to place them into several subcategories. We discover a wide range of analogies among the figures of speech in the Bible. The most common analogies we encounter are *simile, metaphor, indirect analogy, hyperbole,* and *personification/anthropomorphism/zoomorphism.*

Simile

A simile draws the analogy between two different things by using the words *like* or *as* to explicitly state that one thing resembles another. The chemistry student's statement that "Mom and Dad will be mad *as* hornets" is a simile. We use similes regularly in speech, and they are very common in the Bible as well. Some biblical examples are:

Jesus declares, "I am the vine and my Father is the gardener" (John 15:1).

Matthew 23:27—"You are *like* whitewashed tombs."
Proverbs 12:18—"Reckless words pierce *like* a sword."
1 Peter 5:8—"Your enemy the devil prowls around *like* a roaring lion looking for someone to devour."
Isaiah 40:15—"Surely the nations are *like* a drop in a bucket."

Metaphor

This figure of speech makes an analogy between two items, but doesn't use *like* or *as*. It just makes a direct statement. For example:

John 15:1—"I am the true vine and my Father is the gardener."
Psalm 18:2—"The Lord is my rock."

1 Corinthians 12:27—"Now you are the body of Christ."

Psalm 23:1—"The Lord is my shepherd."

Indirect Analogy

An "indirect" analogy is made in the sense that a comparison or analogy is made without directly stating it. That is, a declaration is made that implies a comparison rather than stating it outright. For example, suppose that the biblical writer wanted to compare the wrath of the Lord to a storm. He could use a simile and write, "The wrath of the Lord is like a storm." Or he could express the analogy with a metaphor, stating, "The wrath of the Lord is a storm." But if he opts to use indirect analogy, he would skip the words that make the analogy explicit and imply the comparison by declaring, as Jeremiah does, "the storm of the Lord will burst out in wrath, a driving wind swirling down on the heads of the wicked" (Jer. 30:23). Other examples include:

> Psalm 22:16—"Dogs have surrounded me." David is comparing his enemies to dogs.
>
> Matthew 16:6—"Be on your guard against the yeast of the Pharisees and Sadducees." Jesus is comparing the teaching of the Pharisees and Sadducees to yeast.
>
> Jeremiah 4:7—"A lion has come out of his lair." Jeremiah is comparing the Babylonian king Nebuchadnezzar to a lion.

Hyperbole

Hyperbole can be defined as "conscious exaggeration for the sake of effect." This figure of speech "advertises its lack of literal truth" and makes no pretense at all of being factual.* It intentionally exaggerates as an expression of strong feeling. Hyperbole is used repeatedly in the chemistry student's monologue above: "He gave us the *hardest* test in the world.... I studied *forever*.... It was the *most ridiculous* thing in the world.... *Everybody* bombed on it." The chemistry student intentionally exaggerates, overstating the case, in order to express strong feelings. The speaker's intention is not to be understood literally, and such exaggerated statements certainly do not reflect on the speaker's honesty.

The biblical speakers and writers use hyperbole quite often. As they express deep emotion and strong feelings, or as they seek to stress an important point, they frequently consciously exaggerate and overstate the situation. For example, consider the following:

---

* Leland Ryken, *How to Read the Bible as Literature* (Grand Rapids: Zondervan, 1985), 99.

Matthew 5:29—"If your right eye causes you to sin, gouge it out and throw it away."

Psalm 42:3—"My tears have been my food day and night."

Luke 14:26—"If anyone comes to me and does not hate his father and mother, his wife and children, his brothers and sisters—yes, even his own life—he cannot be my disciple."

In each of the examples above the speaker consciously overstates or exaggerates his point in order to underscore deep emotion or the extreme seriousness of the point being made.

Personification/Anthropomorphism/Zoomorphism

These three figures of speech are related, and they work in similar fashion. They speak of one entity by using the characteristics of a totally different kind of entity. *Personification* involves attributing human features or human characteristics to nonhuman entities. This figure of speech occurs often in Psalms and in the Prophets. For example,

Psalm 66:1 declares, "Shout with joy to God, all the earth!" as if the earth could shout like people.

Isaiah states, "Burst into song, you mountains, you forests and all your trees" (44:23), as if mountains and forests could sing.

Anthropomorphism typically speaks of God by using human features or human characteristics. This is very common in Psalms and in the Prophets, but it also occurs in the New Testament. In the Bible, God is described as having hands, arms, feet, a nose, breath, a voice, and ears. He walks, sits, hears, looks down, comes down, thinks, talks, remembers, plans, gets angry, shouts, lives in a palace, prepares tables, anoints heads, builds houses, and pitches "tents." He has a rod, staff, scepter, banner, garment, tent, throne, footstool, vineyard, field, chariot, shield, and sword. He is called a father, husband, king, and shepherd. All of these actions and articles are things that are normally used literally of people. When used of God, they are being used figuratively. A few examples are as follows: "Let the light of your *face* shine upon us, O Lord" (Ps. 4:6). "My cry came before him, into his *ears*" (Ps. 18:6). "Your *hands* shaped me and made me" (Job 10:8).

Zoomorphism is a figure of speech in which nonhuman, animal images are used to refer to God. For example, the psalmist declares, "He will cover you with his *feathers*, and under his *wings* you will find refuge" (Ps. 91:4).

Psalm 44:6 uses the bow and sword to represent military strength. Depicted above are Assyrian bowmen.

For obvious reasons, *zoo-morphism* is not as common as *personification* or *anthropomorphism*.

Figures of Speech Involving Substitution

Figures of speech involving substitution are a lot more complicated than those involving analogy. Basically there are two major ways that substitution works: stating *effects* when *causes* are meant, and *representing* part of an item when the whole item is actually being referred to.

Effects and Causes

In *effects and causes* the writer or speaker states the effect of something when what he really wants to point to is the cause that produces that effect. For example, suppose you are at a baseball game in the ninth inning and your team is up by one run. The other team is at bat, the bases are loaded, and there are two outs. Their best hitter is at the plate. In your nervousness and enthusiasm you shout out to your pitcher, "Please make me happy! Make me happy! Make me happy!" You would be using a figure of speech, stating the effect (Make me happy!) instead of the actual event that will produce the effect you are hoping for (Strike out the batter so we will win the game!). Thus you substitute the *effect* (your happiness) for the *cause* (striking out the batter).

The writers and speakers of the Bible use substitution-type figures of speech frequently. David, for example, declares in Psalm 51:8, "Let me hear joy and gladness." What David figuratively asks for here is the effect. What he is really asking for is forgiveness for his sin with Bathsheba. This forgiveness will be the cause that produces joy and gladness in his life (the effect). So David has used a figure of speech, substituting the effect for the cause. Another good example is seen in Jeremiah 14:17, where the prophet declares, "Let my eyes overflow with tears." What Jeremiah is really talking about is the coming Babylonian invasion (the cause), but what he describes is the effect the invasion will have on him (weeping).

Representation

The other major figure of speech that uses substitution is called *representation*. This figure of speech works by citing a representative part of an entity to refer figuratively to the entire entity. For example, the Old Testament writers and speakers will often use capital cities and/or individual tribes to represent entire nations. Ephraim (the name for the largest northern tribe) is often used figuratively to refer to the entire northern kingdom of Israel. The Old Testament writers will also use Samaria (the capital city of Israel) to represent Israel. Likewise, the capital city of Jerusalem is often used representatively to refer to the entire southern kingdom of Judah.

Yet numerous other representational figures of speech occur throughout the Bible, especially in Old Testament poetry. The terms *bow* and *sword* are used representatively when speaking of armies and military weapons of war in general, as in Psalm 44:6, "I do not trust in my *bow*, my *sword* does not bring me victory." Likewise armies and military power can be inferred from the figurative use of other terms like *chariots* and *horses*. "Some trust in *chariots* and some in *horses*, but we trust in the name of the Lord our God" (Ps. 20:7). Mentioning one or two weapons used by armies implies the rest of the army; this is how the representational figure of speech works. Other examples are plentiful. *Feet* are often used in the Old Testament to represent the entire person (Pss. 40:2; 44:18; 122:2). The term *bones* is also used to represent the entire person, but is usually used in contexts of pain or suffering (Pss. 6:2; 31:10; 32:3; 42:10). Likewise, the biblical writers use *lips* or *the tongue* as a frequent figurative substitute for ones' speech (Pss. 12:2; 17:1; 31:18; 63:3; James 3:5–9).

Miscellaneous Figures of Speech

It is difficult to place all figures of speech into a few nice neat categories, so we include a miscellaneous category to catch two of the primary remaining figures of speech: *apostrophe* and *irony*.

Apostrophe

Apostrophe is the figure of speech being used when a speaker or writer addresses a person or entity as if they were present, when in reality the one being addressed is not actually there. Often this is done to express strong feelings or to give special emphasis to a particular point. Writers can employ apostrophe without any prior warning, turning to address someone who seems to instantly appear. This figure of speech is sometimes interconnected with personification, for often the writers will address inanimate objects such as heavens, earth, or gates. For example, the psalmist uses apostrophe (addressing someone who is not there) combined with personification (treating an inanimate object as if it were human) when he declares, "Lift up your heads, O you gates; be lifted up, you ancient doors" (Ps. 24:7). Another instance of apostrophe is when a biblical writer turns aside to address himself or his soul as if it were a separate person: "Why are you downcast, O my soul?" (Ps. 43:5); "Praise the Lord, O my soul" (Ps. 103:1).

Irony

Irony is the figure of speech that is working when an author or speaker intentionally says the exact opposite of what he really means. When something bad happens to us, for example, we might say sarcastically, "Oh, that is really great!" The truth is, the situation is not great, but exactly the opposite. This is irony.

We often use irony hand in hand with sarcasm, which implies a certain tone in our voice. The biblical writers and speakers also often combine irony with sarcasm. God himself employs this figure of speech, using irony with a touch of sarcasm when he chides Job for questioning divine justice and wisdom. "Have you comprehended the vast expanses of the earth? Tell me, if you know all this. . . . Surely you know, for you were already born! You have lived so many years!" (Job 38:18–21).

How to Interpret Figures of Speech

As we read the Bible it is important for us to notice figures of speech when they occur. If we miss the figure of speech and try to interpret the verse literally, we will be trying to force a meaning on the text the biblical author did not intend. Yet we must keep in mind there are literal realities behind the figures of speech, so we also cannot just dismiss the verse as merely figurative and not reflective of truth. God is certainly not equivalent to a literal lion, but when Amos declares, "the Lord roars from Zion," he is communicating a very literal reality (God is quite angry and dangerous) by using a figure of speech.

So when you encounter a figure of speech, try to classify it into one of the categories above, and then spend some time reflecting on just how the figure of speech is working. Try to determine exactly what the writer is seeking to convey with the figure of speech.

Another helpful step is to try to visualize the figure of speech. In general, figures of speech are colorful images writers create in our heads for powerful effect. Pause and try to visualize the actual image being painted. If God is being compared to a roaring, dangerous lion, then ponder for a moment what it meant for those in the ancient world to be on foot in the dark (without rifles or lights) when a hungry lion roars nearby. If we can visualize the image, it will help us to feel the entire range of emotional and intellectual impact the writer is trying to make on us.

Once we have visualized the image conveyed by the figure of speech and reflected on how the figure of speech is working, then we can place it back into its context and use our understanding of the figure of speech to assist us in understanding the rest of the passage.

"Lift up your heads, O you gates; be lifted up, you ancient doors" (Ps. 24:7). Depicted below are the ruins of the city gates to Megiddo.

Literary Features in the Bible

D. Brent Sandy

The Bible is the richest, deepest, most engaging book ever written. It topped the bestseller lists before there were such lists. It is, after all, the Word of God. The King of all kings inspired the Book of all books.

But the Bible stands out for another reason: the skill of the human authors. Under inspiration, the authors selected the most appropriate literary forms and figures of speech for communicating the revelation from God. When you have something important to say and you say it in a profound way, the message has the best chance of getting through to its listeners. (The original audiences of the Bible generally did not read the Bible; they listened to it being read. Even when people in the audience were literate, they probably did not have their own personal copies of the Scriptures.)

If we desire to be good listeners, if we want to know the whole counsel of God, there is much to learn about God's Word. No matter how deeply we may believe and love the Bible, poor listening can lead to misconstruing divine truth, even resulting in disobedience. As Walt Whitman noted, "To have great poets, there must be great audiences." The Bible becomes a message of increasing power and impact when we are good audiences.

The Bible as Literature

We generally think of biblical authors as shepherds, fishermen, and the like, seemingly run-of-the-mill, ordinary people who could have been our next-door neighbors. But they were much more. When they received inspiration from the Spirit, they didn't just grab a quill pen, some lampblack ink, and a piece of papyrus and—in machine-like fashion—put into writing what God revealed.

While we do not understand many things about the process of inspiration, we stand in awe when we look at the product. It is God-breathed Scripture, the result of humans being carried along by the Holy Spirit (2 Tim. 3:16; 2 Pet. 1:21). But it is also great literature, rivaling the best the world has ever known.

Though theological in nature, the Bible is literary in form. It uses human experience to communicate God's values. It doesn't report only what *happened*; it gives insight into what *happens*. When Jesus wanted to explain who a neighbor was, he could have composed a very good definition or even written a detailed encyclopedia article. Instead, he told the story of the good Samaritan. Few people will forget his story of human experience; few people would have remembered the details of an encyclopedia article. Second, the compendium of stories, history, poetry, parables, letters, and visionary writing in the Bible comprise an impressive collection of literary forms. Literature is marked by the conscious use of various forms. The Bible as an anthology, however, is unique: it is unified around an all-encompassing story of conflict and resolution—of sin and redemption—from Genesis to Revelation. Third, the Bible is a treasury of artistry: master storytelling, spectacular dramas, creative figures of speech, brilliant poetry. "Joseph and His Amazing Technicolor Dreamcoat," along with other plays, music, movies, and works of art, confirms the enduring value of the Bible's art forms. However, the artistic qualities of the Bible were not simply for art's sake. This was art for God's sake.

> Just as God created the world with spectacular beauty, so he likewise placed artistic beauty in the Scriptures.

There is much to admire in the literary qualities of the books of the Bible, but we need to do more than admire. Literary features and meaning are interrelated. We will not comprehend the message from God looking only at words. We must pay close attention to how an author used words. Written compositions begin with three basic components: what someone wants to say, what impact they want to have, and how they are going to say it. The first is meaning; the second, function; and the third, form. We will not adequately understand one without the other two. Every state of the union speech, every inaugural address, every battlefield oration—like every portion of the Bible—needs to be understood in light of how meaning, function, and form work together in an act of communication.

God's attributes include beauty, and he calls us to image his beauty in our lives and relationships. So whether we are representing God as light in the darkness—or presenting God in written and oral forms—we seek to be beautiful as he is beautiful. The authors of the Bible crafted their words in the most beautiful ways, in the most impacting ways, to communicate the divine message.

Literary Forms in the Bible

The most significant advancement of the twentieth century for understanding Scripture centered on the literary forms biblical authors used. The technical term is *genre*. Most of us tend to take genres for granted, often without even thinking about their differences.

Suppose you have an antique wardrobe to sell, and you decide to submit a question to a newspaper columnist to inquire about its value. You might begin, "My great-grandfather purchased a cherry wardrobe just after the Great Depression. It doesn't have a scratch on it. How do I determine its value?" But if you're advertising the wardrobe in the classified section of a local newspaper, you would write something very different: "Antique wardrobe. In same family for 80 years. Mint condition. $1800 obo." (People who regularly read classifieds will immediately know that *obo* is shorthand for "or best offer.") If thieves break into your home and steal the wardrobe, however, the police report might state, "Furniture piece, family heirloom valued at $2,000 stolen." Each of these is a valid way to describe the wardrobe, but they are not interchangeable. You would not find this statement in a classified ad or a police report: "My great-grandfather purchased a cherry wardrobe just after the Great Depression."

Or suppose you are composing a eulogy for a funeral service. If you are the minister, you would likely comment on the deceased's place of birth, date of marriage, involvement in the church, and so forth. The eulogy may read like an obituary in the newspaper, almost like an encyclopedia article. A minister may also elect to turn a eulogy into a sermon and use the deceased as an example for how other people should live. But if you are a granddaughter of the deceased and you are doing the eulogy, you are more likely to choose from a different set of options. Will you write a poem? Will you tell stories about making cookies with your grandmother? Will you include humor? The different forms a eulogy may take are examples of genre distinctions.

Prose and poetry are two obvious genres in the Bible. It may be surprising that more than one-third of the Bible consists of poetry. From Job through the Song of Songs there are 243 chapters of poetry. From the prophet Isaiah to the prophet Malachi, there are 250 more chapters, most of it poetic. In addition we find poems included in prose. But poetry and prose need to be subdivided into more discrete genres. The poetry of the Psalms consists of three formal categories: laments, songs of thanks, and hymns. The genre of prophecy can be subdivided into pronouncements of judgment, promises of blessing, and apocalyptic. The prose of the Old Testament includes narrative, history, and law. The genres of the New Testament include gospels, parables, speeches, history, letters, and apocalyptic. Sometimes it is necessary to subdivide genres even further.

For each genre, there is a reciprocal understanding between author and audience. An author must speak in ways listeners can understand, and listeners must take into account the ways an author is speaking. For communication to achieve its intended objective, an author and an audience need a common understanding of genre. If an author uses irony and we fail to see it, we will think the author meant the opposite of what he intended (see, for example, Amos 4:4). A universal rule for interpreting Scripture says we must read it in context. Genres are an important part of that context. We risk violating God's inspired Word if we ignore such an important aspect of his revelation.

Poetry in the Bible

Many readers expect the Bible to manage its thoughts very closely, to be a storehouse of information, to speak clearly and logically to the left side of the brain. Our post-Enlightenment culture encourages this notion. We are programmed to think in scientific, rational, detailed ways. We like specific information that quickly and easily addresses issues and problems.

Poetry, however, does not fit such a one-sided idea. It speaks to both sides of the brain. Poetry is characterized by human experience, by the language of emotion, by figures of speech that grip our emotions. Poets may exaggerate to make a point: "The voice of the Lord twists the oaks and strips the forests bare" (Ps. 29:9). We call that hyperbole. Poets may use numerous figures of speech in imaginative ways to heighten their message: "If I rise on the wings of the dawn, if I settle on the far side of the sea, even there your hand will guide me, your right hand will hold me fast" (Ps. 139:9–10).

If we fail to appreciate how poetry communicates, on the one hand, insisting on reading at a surface level, we may read more into poetry than was intended. On the other hand, if we are only interested in feelings, intuition, and generalities, then we may miss the truths underscored in poetry. These are two extremes we must avoid.

When we read in Psalm 103:3 that he "heals all your diseases," does that mean we should decline any form of medical assistance, because we can count on God to heal us? When the psalmist says, "He [the Lord] protects all his [the righteous person's] bones, not one of them will be broken" (Ps. 34:20), is that evidence that a broken bone is a sign of sin in someone's life? Does God really "forget" our sins when he forgives them? (See Pss. 25:7; 51:1, 8–9; Isa. 43:25; Jer. 31:34.) Since Psalm 22 begins, "My God, my God, why have you forsaken me?" and 22:14 says, "all my bones are out of joint," should we conclude that Jesus's bones were *all* dislocated as he hung on the cross? If we fail to understand how poetry functions, these kinds of statements may mislead us, as they have many people.

A biblical poet went about his craft something like this. Though it is a mystery to us, the Holy Spirit and the human author worked hand in hand, and there is a sense in which we can refer to both of them in the singular as "the author." The biblical poets, especially in the Old Testament, usually conveyed their ideas or truths two poetic lines at a time. That is, they would use different, but parallel words and imagery in two consecutive lines of text to emphasize the same basic point. The second line, fashioned to balance the first, takes the thought of the first and adds something to it, advancing it or qualifying it in some way. We refer to the repetition as poetic parallelism.

"If I rise on the wings of the dawn, if I settle on the far side of the sea, even there your hand will guide me, your right hand will hold me fast" (Ps. 139:9–10).

Terseness is a mark of both lines, compressing as much meaning as possible into as few words as possible (this is especially evident in the Hebrew language). In some cases the parallelism will go on for several verses. For example, in Psalm 19, the psalmist focuses on the revelation of God's greatness in creation, and he expresses the same thought in four different lines.

> The heavens declare the glory of God;
>> the skies proclaim the work of his hands.
> Day after day they pour forth speech;
>> night after night they display knowledge. (Ps. 19:1–2)

If we fail to recognize the poet's technique, we might look for specific information about the skies or the night. But that would miss his point. He's using creative imagery to restate a truth in multiple ways. His parallelism and figures of speech add emphasis to the greatness of God revealed in creation.

In Psalm 139 the poet enhances the idea of a personal creator with a crescendo of imagery, again with each line expressing the same basic concept.

> You created my inmost being;
>> you knit me together in my mother's womb. . . .
> My frame was not hidden from you
>> when I was made in the secret place.
>> When I was woven together in the depths of the earth, your eyes
> saw my unformed body. (Ps. 139:13, 15)

We are not good listeners of poetry if we think the statement *woven together in the depths of the earth* informs us about the precise nature of human origins. The line exists not as a theological statement but as poetic parallelism, illustrating a psalmist's freedom to express ideas in creative and figurative ways.

Poetry reaches inside us and tugs at our heartstrings. It seeks to transform us into worshiping creatures. But the primary objective is not to inform us. While poetry is rooted in important facts and truths, its objective is less about revealing truth and more about bringing truth to life.

If you compare Exodus 14 and 15—one a prose description of the Egyptian armies drowning in the Red Sea, and the other a poetic description of the same event—you will gain a new appreciation for the power of God displayed in the exodus. Moses and Miriam became poets and turned a historical event into a command performance.

Psalm 114 is also a description of the exodus:

> The sea looked and fled,
>> the Jordan turned back;
> the mountains skipped like rams,
>> the hills like lambs.
> Why was it, O sea, that you fled,
>> O Jordan, that you turned back,
> you mountains, that you skipped like rams,
>> you hills, like lambs? (Ps. 114:3–5)

The psalmist's description of mountains skipping like lambs leads to a principle for interpreting poetry: we need to look *through* a poet's words to see his point, not *at* the words as if each one is a point in and of itself. We must ponder the power of the images as a whole, not look for separate significance in each figure of speech or line of poetry. The psalmists want us to feel, to be affected, to be emotionally moved by their poetry. Taking a gourmet entrée into a laboratory and using centrifuges and spectrometers to identify each ingredient will destroy the chef's creation. Diners do not need to know about each ingredient and its proportions to be nourished and to appreciate the quality of the eating experience.

Stories in the Bible

Even as poetry is transforming, so are stories. They mesmerize, refresh, and even free us. Their suspense holds our attention; the twists in plot catch us off guard; the mystery keeps us guessing. From nursery rhymes to *Chicken Soup for the Soul*, stories shape lives. Becoming absorbed in a story allows us to live beyond ourselves, to ponder what we would do if we were in another's shoes.

Stories motivate us to think differently about real-life situations, to do something we had not thought of, to become a person we didn't realize we needed to be. Reading about the lives of others helps us to make sense of the relationships, feelings, impulses, and yearnings of our own stories.

A focus on biblical stories and how they function was another advancement of the twentieth century. The technical term is narrative. Authors are referred to as narrators. The central component of narrative is plot. Protagonists are generally close to God and act on his behalf, while antagonists work against God's plans.

Contrary to what we might expect, the Bible contains an almost unlimited number of stories about humans. It's a fascinating concept: God chose human narrative in which to reveal divine truth. While a story's function is sermonic, it doesn't look like a sermon. Even as God became incarnate in the person of his Son—bringing to earth the answer to the human condition—so the Bible is incarnational. God knows all about us from beginning to end, including what is good and bad for us. He incarnated those insights into the stories of humans. What was outside this planet in the possession of God came into this planet embodied in humans.

Narratives in the Bible were shaped by three principles. The first was *history*. Biblical authors had true events to report—past, present, and future. So they told stories about their experiences and others' experiences.

These events and experiences were especially important because God was involved, sometimes working behind the scenes and sometimes in front, in either case demonstrating the interaction between divine and human spheres.

Second, while biblical authors were recording historical incidents, the history was not raw events and details. It was *aesthetic history*, eloquent stories. The Bible's stories are beautiful in their own right. God superintended the authors as they constructed narratives with consummate skill. This was not fancy writing just to be fancy: the authors were communicating important concepts, and they recognized the importance of writing well.

Third, biblical authors knew they were bearers of a message from God and about God. They had been commissioned by God to speak on his behalf (see Isa. 6:8–13; Ezek. 2:1–3:27). So their narratives are *theological history*. The authors would not be satisfied if we only appreciated their storytelling skill and did not open our hearts to the truths embedded in the stories. Biblical narrative manifests the character of God. As we make the Bible's stories our own, they define us, helping us see ourselves as God sees us.

Rarely is the point of a biblical narrative explained in the text. Narratives draw readers into stories, raise questions, leave gaps, and encourage contemplation. We must choose sides, enter into decision-making processes, and interpret the experiences of characters. It is an unexpected strategy for a revelation from God. But like parents raising teens and giving them increasing opportunity to find themselves and make their own decisions, God empowers readers to develop values under his guidance, which they can then apply to their own life experiences.

Some commentators seek to reduce a story's meaning to one specific moral or application. But that approach is under the influence of the Enlightenment and left-brained thinking. It's reductionistic to insist on a single, clearly defined point for every story. Narrative illustrates ideas rather than announcing them. Stories take up residence in our minds and send off implications in various directions. It's the power of a story's suggestion.

To counterbalance this point, it would be wrong to conclude that anyone can freely manufacture individual interpretations and applications of biblical narratives. Even as Scripture was not revealed by human imagination or impulse (2 Pet. 1:20–21), it's wrong to invent a meaning that would be a surprise to the biblical author.

An Egyptian chariot. Exodus 15 is a song celebrating the destruction of the Egyptian chariots in the Red Sea. "The Lord is a warrior. . . . Pharaoh's chariots and his army he has hurled into the sea. . . . They sank to the depths like a stone" (Exod. 15:3–5).

Since narrators could tell stories in any number of ways, using a variety of techniques, we must pay attention to the specific ways the stories were crafted in order to fully understand what the authors were communicating. But their techniques may not be self-evident.

- In Genesis 11:1–9 the narrator uses a literary feature known as chiasm. By beginning and ending the story with similar elements (a form of bracketing), and inside those brackets using a series of similar elements that move toward the center of the story, the author underscores a central idea in the narrative.
- In Joshua 2–7 the author paints a vivid contrast between Rahab and Achan: an outsider comes under God's grace because of her obedience, while an insider comes under God's judgment because of his disobedience. The narrator's contrast is easily overlooked because of all the intervening details regarding the fall of Jericho.
- The characterization of Saul and David is remarkable in 1 Samuel 15–31, emphasizing the ineptitude of Saul as king and the versatility of David to succeed him. Patterns of repetition occur often, such as David sparing King Saul (chap. 24), David sparing Nabal (chap. 25), and David sparing King Saul again (chap. 26).
- Irony is evident in the description of Solomon's grandeur as king (1 Kings 4–11): his supposed greatness is his undoing.
- Jesus's healing of a blind man in stages (Mark 8:22–26) makes sense only when the connections are noted with the preceding and following episodes. The disciples were experiencing stages of awareness of who Jesus was.
- In the book of Acts the literary technique of interchange is evident as the narrator switches back and forth between the lives of Peter and Paul, demonstrating that they were equally empowered by God and both important in the growth of the early church.

These are only a few examples of the breadth of narrative technique.

Conclusion

The Bible is great literature. It is God's revealed truth. Thankfully, it was not coded in some language from outer space. That gives us the privilege of listening to it, and the *responsibility* of understanding it.

Archaeology and the Bible

Steven M. Ortiz

Introduction

The relationship between archaeology and the Bible has a long history. Today, the term *biblical archaeology* can refer to any of three different approaches to the intersection of archaeology and the Bible. The first is an approach in which the goal is apologetic, where archaeology is used to try to "prove" the Bible. This is the view commonly portrayed in the media or popular accounts. It is usually practiced by untrained individuals and includes the search for places or "finds" mentioned in the Bible.

The second approach, popular throughout the second half of the twentieth century, views archaeology as a "handmaiden of biblical studies." Archaeology is one of many methods used by biblical scholars to study the Bible. Textbooks on biblical interpretation list it alongside grammatical, cultural, and theological approaches. But this approach tends to subordinate archaeology to the needs and the agenda of biblical studies.

The third approach views biblical archaeology as separate from the discipline of biblical studies, but not unrelated. From this viewpoint biblical archaeology is considered part of the larger discipline of archaeology of the ancient Near East or, more specifically, the archaeology of the southern Levant (Israel/Palestine/Jordan, etc.). Even more specifically, biblical archaeology is a subset of Syro-Palestinian archaeology. This third view is the approach favored in this chapter.

Archaeology is the multidisciplinary systematic recovery and analysis of the surviving material objects of human society and the environmental context of human activity. Biblical archaeology is the use of archaeological enterprise to clarify and illuminate the biblical text and the historical context of the text. Thus archaeology is a separate discipline from biblical studies, but one that can inform and be very helpful to biblical studies. Yet archaeology has its own research agenda, methods, and theoretical foundations. The point of intersection is that both archaeology and biblical studies attempt to reconstruct the past. The archaeologist is focused on cultural history, while the biblical studies scholar is focused on biblical history. A secular biblical archaeologist cannot discount the biblical text since it contains much data concerning cultural history; a biblical scholar cannot discount the archaeological data because it contains much data for reconstructing biblical history. This essay will focus solely on the discipline of archaeology.

The Archaeological Process

Archaeology is multidisciplinary. It is considered to be a scientific discipline, a historical discipline, and especially a subset of anthropology. There is a debate among theorists about whether it is a discipline that belongs to the hard sciences or the humanities. Archaeologists work at reconstructing the past using the material remnants of past human behavior. Thus the archaeological enterprise addresses and uses methods and theories from the social sciences.

History of the Discipline

Archaeology was first viewed as cultural-historical with the emphasis on reconstructing historical periods. In the 1960s a theoretical program called the "new archaeology" (processual archaeology) began to dominate the discipline. This new focus of research was to view culture as a system with various processes. The main process viewed culture as adapting to its external environment. Archaeological theory attempted to define general laws of human behavior in contrast to the historical particularism of the cultural-historical approach. Underlying this process-oriented (processual) archaeology was a strict scientific approach to archaeological data and an underlying evolutionary model. In reaction to this processual model, the 1980s produced a "post-processual" critique. The main critique was that processual archaeology deemphasized the human actor as a rational participant. Related to this was the recognition of the inability of archaeologists to develop general laws of human behavior. Theoretical shifts included: (1) viewing archaeology as long-term history; (2) studying ideology and how it influences human behavior; (3) developing structures of meaning as evidenced in material culture; and (4) self-critiquing the relationship between the interpretation of data and the interpreter. The result is that archaeologists need to study each archaeological data within its context (geographical, chronological, cultural, etc.) and place the individual back into the analysis of the past.

Today, archaeological method and theory operates within the tension of the processual and post-processual approaches. Theorists acknowledge the following: (1) the environment and ecology are constraining rather than causing change; (2) archaeologists must address historical as well as anthropological questions; (3) the archaeological record results from the cumulative behaviors of individuals as well as societies; (4) both the cognitive and physical domains of human behavior pattern the record; and (5) contextual interpretations rather than predictive models and covering laws should be emphasized.

Classic biblical archaeology was grounded in the cultural-historical approach. The birth of biblical archaeology started in the nineteenth century with the early explorations of the Holy Land. In the twentieth century, considered the formative years, biblical archaeologists excavated *tels* (human-made mounds), realizing they were the accumulated remains of ancient cities. (See the sidebar "The *Tels* of Biblical

Cuneiform tablet describing the activities of the Assyrian king Tiglath-Pileser III. Historical annals like these help to correlate archaeological data.

Archaeology.") The principles of stratigraphy (analyzing different layers of a site) and ceramic seriation (using the historical development of pottery types to date excavation levels) were developed. The "golden age" of biblical archaeology started after World War I. The discipline of biblical archaeology developed into a serious academic discipline under William Foxwell Albright. Albright was instrumental in (1) advances in stratigraphy and ceramic seriation, (2) wedding the results of archaeology to biblical hermeneutics, and (3) legitimizing biblical archaeology as a subset of biblical studies. As part of this, he created programs and schools, and trained a generation of students. The Albright school became the dominant paradigm for most of biblical archaeology for much of the early twentieth century. One of Albright's students, G. Ernest Wright, attempted to merge archaeology and theology, an endeavor often labeled as the Biblical Theology Movement (1950s to 1960s).

During the 1970s and 1980s biblical archaeology adopted the "new archaeology" into its research goals and methodology. This view was championed by William G. Dever, a student of Wright's. Biblical archaeology adopted the new paradigm prevalent in the larger field of worldwide archaeology. Biblical archaeology matured by (1) becoming a separate discipline from biblical studies, and (2) emphasizing the broader field of Syro-Palestinian archaeology.

Today there is a contextual paradigm as both historical and anthropological models are used for archaeological and textual data. The archaeological and textual data are equally valuable to reconstruct the past, the only difference being that each discipline uses different hermeneutical methods. Yet within this framework, biblical archaeologists still continue to address issues coming from biblical studies.

Domains of Archaeological Inquiry

The primary research questions of archaeologists today can be grouped into three categories: pots, people, and processes. These categories correspond to three major domains of inquiry: material culture studies, history, and anthropology.

The first domain is material culture studies. Since material culture is the basis for what is left in the archaeological record, it makes sense that archaeologists will emphasize research on material culture (e.g., pottery, weapons, architecture, etc.). Pottery plays a primary role in the study of material culture by biblical archaeologists. Pottery was made by all cultures; it is durable and survives in the archaeological record. It is invaluable for determining the date of the various strata uncovered during an excavation. In addition to classifying the material culture, archaeologists study the origin, production, and distribution of the material culture.

A second domain of inquiry is historical reconstruction, where inferences and connections are made between historical texts (when available) and archaeology. The main emphasis of biblical archaeology in the past has been on correlating the history of ancient Israel with its broader context (e.g., Egypt and Assyria). In general this connection between archaeology and history has focused on political history and the activities of kings and rulers. A current trend, however, is to go beyond the political history and reconstruct the "unwritten" history of those in society not found in major literary texts, such as peasants and women. More and more frequently, archaeologists are asking questions that deal with the daily life of the people, rather than just focusing on kings and conquests.

The third domain is the study of processes. This research domain asks broader questions about human society. Such inquiries focus on the rise and collapse of states, plant and animal domestication, social stratification, and the nature of ruralism and urbanism. No longer are archaeologists solely focused on proving or defining events of the Bible such as the exodus, conquest, and so on, but on defining processes such as state formation, urbanization, tribalism, and ethnicity.

The Archaeological Record

The archaeological record is always fragmentary and incomplete. This is due to two factors: (1) the nature of cultural encoding on material objects, and (2) the formation processes that affect the archaeological record. A majority of human behavior is not encoded on material culture (religious beliefs, social customs, worldviews), and those that are encoded (e.g., clothing, writing, art) usually do not survive for us to analyze. And then those that do survive are usually ambiguous. For example, archaeologists may uncover a clay figurine, but they might not know whether that figurine is a toy, a decoration, a goddess, or something else. Archaeologists must make inferences based on historical texts, comparison with living cultures (e.g., ethnoarchaeology), and the context of the object within its broader archaeological context (e.g., was the object found in a temple or in a sacred corner of a house?).

Formation processes refer to all the effects that act on the archaeological record. The first type is cultural transforms—those processes that are caused by human activity. A majority of the archaeological record is garbage—what society throws away or abandons because no one wants it anymore. Archaeologists are fortunate when an event such as a quick destruction—whether natural or human-caused—seals a site with all of its possessions. This provides a better picture of how people lived as opposed to a site that has been abandoned and most of the possessions taken with the people who abandoned it.

In addition to cultural transforms, there are natural transforms. These are post-depositional variables, such as natural decomposition and erosion, both by wind and by water.

Archaeological Dating

At the core of any archaeological interpretation is dating. Four methods or principles are used to determine the date of a specific strata at a site: (1) material culture, specifically, pottery sequencing; (2) relative stratigraphy; (3) historical collaboration; and (4) the use of scientific dating methods (i.e., carbon 14).

Ceramic analysis (pottery) is the basic mode of inquiry of biblical archaeology because pottery is present at all archaeological sites. While other material remains of ancient society are also key to documenting chronological change (e.g., metal artifacts, figurines, architecture), none is as plentiful and durable in the archaeological record as pottery. Therefore the most basic analysis of the archaeological data is the development of ceramic typologies that correlate pottery types with specific time eras.

Historical correlations can provide absolute dates for the archaeological record. Most of these correlations involve military campaigns of Egyptian and Assyrian kings that are recorded in the historical annals of those nations. Important historical correlations for biblical archaeology are the Egyptian campaigns of the kings of the New Kingdom (Thutmose III, Rameses II, and Merneptah) as well as the tenth-century Shishak campaign. In addition to the Egyptian invasions, there were several Assyrian and Babylonian campaigns that also provide historical correlations. While military campaigns might provide absolute dates, other helpful historical correlations are also occasionally available. These include events and descriptions in the biblical text (e.g., battles between the Israelites and their neighbors such as the Philistines and the Transjordan kingdoms, boundary lists, specific deeds of Israelite and Judean kings, etc.).

Other attempts at historical correlations are based on artifacts that can be associated with a person, usually a

A jar stamped with the term *lamelek* ("belonging to the king") was found in the Jerusalem area.

ruler. Examples include hundreds of Egyptian cartouches, scarabs, and seals that contain the name of a pharaoh or a high-ranking Egyptian official. Some of the best examples are the jars stamped *lamelek* ("belonging to the king") associated with Hezekiah, king of Judah.

Recently, carbon 14 has also been used as a means to obtain absolute dates without having to rely on biblical or extra-biblical data. Most of the carbon 14 dating comes from sites currently being excavated in the northern regions of Israel. The use of scientific dating provides a range of absolute dates.

Archaeological Excavation: Methods and Theory

Popular media accounts of archaeologists as treasure hunters portray a very inaccurate picture. The archaeological endeavor is a long, slow process of research and labor. The two basic methods of accumulating archaeological data are the excavation and the survey. The two basic principles of excavation are (1) stratigraphic analysis, along with the fundamental assumption that material culture is patterned by human behavior (e.g., elite and poor, ethnic markers, rural and urban, religious beliefs); and (2) that material culture changes over time and we can compare artifacts from one site or region with another site or region to determine relative chronology and relationship.

At the core of the archaeological process is the excavation and survey. Four major processes are involved: (1) development of a research design for the excavation; (2) actual excavation; (3) postseason analysis; and (4) comprehensive analysis and publication.

In the early days of biblical archaeology, a single individual could carry out an expedition. Today, an archaeological expedition usually involves several scholars and other individuals, as well as institutions, combined into a team. Most projects are led by a principal investigator with one or two codirectors. They are responsible for raising funds and research design. In addition, most countries in which excavation projects take place have government agencies that supervise and protect their archaeological sites, which are usually considered as irreplaceable national property belonging to the citizens of that country. Thus the principal investigator and the codirectors must work closely with the appropriate agency in coordinating the project and in following the national guidelines for archaeological excavations in that country.

There is a hierarchy of field staff consisting of field archaeologists and area supervisors who are responsible for directing student volunteers and/ or paid workers. If the project is using student volunteers, it is usually run as a field school and there are various labs, lectures, and teaching practicum throughout the day. In addition to the supervision of workers, the field staff is responsible for the recording of all data and supervising the removal of materials. In addition to the field staff, a host of other specialists—such as architects, conservators, archaeobotanists, zooarchaeologists, physical anthropologists, geologists, and photographers—assist in the analysis of the special finds.

The average excavation associated with a field school will spend about a month in the field, usually in the summer, for five to ten excavation seasons. Most of the archaeological work, however, takes place in the off-season (postseason), sometimes away from the site. The postseason analysis can be very labor intensive, involving several researchers. For every month of excavation, it takes at least ten months to process the data from the excavation. Sometimes this can take even longer, because most archaeologists are also full-time professors. They normally "dig" in the summer and then spend the school year analyzing and processing the results of the dig. Often the demands of teaching limit the time they can spend on their archaeological research, thus expanding the time required for postseason analysis of the summer's work. Sometimes it can take from five to fifteen years after the last season of excavation to produce the final formal publication of the site results, depending on the size of the project.

Overview of Archaeological Periods

Archaeologists who work in the southern Levant have classified the world history of this area into archaeological periods. This classification is based on (1) historical correlations, and (2) major changes in the material culture. The major periods that relate to biblical archaeology are Prehistory (Neolithic and Chalcolithic), Bronze Age (Early, Middle, Late), Iron Age, Persian, Hellenistic, and Roman.

Prehistoric

The Neolithic period (ca. 8500–4300 BC) represents an agricultural revolution where human society shifts from food gathering to food production. Concurrent is the domestication of animals (e.g., sheep, goats, cattle). An important technological innovation during this period was the development of pottery. We see an active religious life reflected in burials and the arts, and we find new social organizations in villages with public structures, social differentiation, and craft specialization.

The Chalcolithic period (4300–3300 BC) follows next. This period reflects a complex and stratified society divided into professional groups and social classes. One of the regional characteristics of this period was the

The *Tels* of Biblical Archaeology

Many of the ancient cities of the southern Levant (Israel/Palestine/Jordan) are over five thousand years old. Usually the people who first built the city chose the location wisely, based on things like water supply, trade routes, or agricultural lands. Thus when the city would get destroyed by some invading army (as happened in this area with regularity), usually it would be rebuilt on the same site. People would reuse much of the stones and debris of the destroyed city in their reconstruction, but some of the destroyed material would get covered up. Since the new city construction was on top of the old destroyed buildings, houses, and roads, it would usually be a little higher than the previous city. Before too long, however, the new city would also be destroyed, adding its burned level of destruction on top of the earlier city. Then people would rebuild on top of that city and so forth throughout history. Examples of ancient cities that were destroyed and rebuilt numerous times like this are Megiddo and Hazor. As time went by, the cities grew higher and higher in elevation, forming hills out of the earlier destruction levels, and using the growing hill to assist in the defense of each new city. The remains of these ancient city sites today form distinctive looking hills called *tels*. Indeed, *tel* is the Hebrew (and Arabic) word for hill. These *tels* can be distinguished from natural hills by their distinctive slope and by their shape, for most of the *tels* are square-shaped, in contrast to natural hills, which are usually round. Another indication that a hill-like mound might be a *tel* containing the ruins of an ancient city is the presence of broken pottery, usually even on the surface of the ground, but certainly easily found by minor excavation. The amazing thing to remember about *tels* is that while they look like hills, they are entirely human-made. Apart from a little dust, nothing in the *tel* is natural; everything on the mound (every rock and piece of pottery) was carried there by somebody.

prevalence of unwalled villages. Copper was first used during this period, which was a major technological development. This period is marked by the emergence of craft specialization and metallurgy.

Early Bronze Age

The Early Bronze Age (3300–2000 BC) is the first urban revolution in the Levant, and during this period cities become the basic social and political unit of society. The towns of the Chalcolithic period develop into walled towns in the Early Bronze Age. Most Early Bronze Age towns become urbanized cities, erecting extensive fortifications and public buildings. We see the development of urban planning, accompanied by social stratification. The Mediterranean trade economy starts, and the ox-drawn cart is introduced. The rich and powerful city-states of the Early Bronze Age become affluent, partially due to trade, mostly with Egypt. Although no written records within

Palestine have been found for this period, numerous written records have been discovered from this era in Egypt and Mesopotamia.

The Early Bronze Age period is subdivided into four shorter periods: EBI, 3300–3000 BC; EBII, 3000–2700 BC; EBIII, 2700–2300 BC; and EBIV, 2300–2000 BC. Other archaeological regions (especially Egypt and Mesopotamia) have their own period classifications for this time era. The Early Bronze Age of the Levant corresponds with the Early Dynastic, Old Akkadian, Gutian, and Sumerian periods in Mesopotamia as well as the Narmer and Old Kingdom (Pyramids) periods of Egypt (Dynasties I–VI).

Middle Bronze Age

The Middle Bronze Age (2000–1550 BC) has traditionally been associated with the patriarchal period of the Bible (i.e., the age of Abraham, Isaac, and Jacob). This period is characterized by the presence of numerous powerful semi-independent city-states, a kind of urban golden age that is accompanied by secondary state formation. The material culture reflects influence of Syrian and other northern Levantine cultural patterns. Some cuneiform texts from this period have been found at Palestinian sites, but not the amount of writing as found at such places as the Mari and Nuzi Archives to the north or Egyptian texts of the Middle Kingdom to the south.

During the Middle Bronze Age a radical shift in the distribution, size, and character of the settlements results in both an increase in area and density of the settlements and their fortifications. There is an increasing hierarchy of sophistication found on the sites, running from villages and hamlets to medium-sized towns to large urban centers. Most noticeable are the massive fortifications of the large

A round altar from the Early Bronze Age (3300–2000 BC) at the city of Megiddo.

urban centers, composed of thick walls, extra strengthening at the base of the walls called "glacis," and elaborate gate systems. The complexity and immense scale of such fortifications reflects a highly centralized system of planning and deployment of men and material and an efficient socioeconomic organization that includes surpluses, as well as a bureaucracy that can control and enforce public policy. These cities reflect a planned, functional layout with administrative buildings, temples, commercial and judicial areas, domestic housing, streets, courtyards, water and food storage facilities, stables, and industrial operations.

Late Bronze Age

During this period (1550–1200 BC) the region was often under Egyptian dominance, both militarily and culturally. The material culture found at excavated sites from this time period demonstrates it was part of the Egyptian Empire (province). There were numerous Egyptian military campaigns into Palestine (Canaan) and the surrounding areas, led by Pharaohs Thutmose III, Rameses II, Merneptah, and Seti I. From this period we have the Amarna Letters, a collection of over 350 cuneiform tablets that reflect administrative correspondences between Egypt and the Canaanite city-states. In addition to Canaanite city-states, Egyptian administrative centers are constructed. This is a cosmopolitan period, characterized by many import products and a high degree of internationalism. The Late Bronze is a continuation of Middle Bronze culture, especially in regard to urban development, but most cities in this period are unfortified, and settlement population decreases to about 25 percent of the early Middle Bronze Age period.

Iron Age I

Iron Age I (1200–1000 BC) is the period usually associated with the Israelite settlement and conquest of the Promised Land. During this period there was a shift from the urban city-states of the Bronze Age to village and town life. In the hill country of Palestine nearly three hundred new highland villages appeared, and along the coast numerous Philistine settlements developed. During the early part of this period (Iron I) the balance of power between Egypt to the south and the Hittites to the north, a balance that developed in the Late Bronze Age, collapsed and led to the decline of the entire eastern Mediterranean area. The geopolitical nature of the Levant changed as the region became a staging ground for smaller states to try and flex their military power into the political vacuum. International trade was likewise disrupted, evidenced by the complete cessation of imports. The southern Levant was characterized by the collapse and destruction of the major city-states and a shift in settlement patterns. Iron Age I material culture represents remnants of Canaanite Bronze Age cultures that were overlapped by new cultures. Palestine entered a phase of regionalism that would eventually develop into the small states that characterize the next period (Iron Age II). These regions include the western highlands (hill country), the southern coastal plain (Philistia), the Jezreel valley, the Phoenician coast, and the Transjordan. Iron Age I is associated with the biblical period of Joshua and the judges. Hill country settlements comprise small villages and towns. One of the characteristic features of this period was that a traditional house style dominated the domestic architecture, the "four-room house."

Iron Age II

The Iron Age II period (1000–586 BC) was that in which the Israelite monarchy developed. Thus there was a transition from the regionalization of the Iron Age I (tribal and chiefdoms) to the territorial state. This state level of society is seen in the monumental buildings of the period and the development of a centralized government. This phenomenon of secondary state formation was found throughout the southern Levant during this period. New innovations and technological advances included the broad spread of literacy, the development of a common international and cultural market with the Phoenician merchants playing the middle man, and continued nation building with a trend toward centralization and state initiative. The cities and towns of Iron Age II exhibit well-developed urban planning with complex fortification systems, as well as advanced hydrological development. Several small nations and ethnic groups can be defined in the archaeological record, including the Israelites, Philistines, Arameans, Edomites, Moabites, and Ammonites. While the pottery from this period exhibits strong tendencies toward standardization, imports are also common. From Mesopotamia, this period corresponds with the Neo-Assyrian and Babylonian empires, and historical and chronological correlations abound. Written texts, inscriptions, seals, and amulets are common in the archaeological record. Likewise from this period comes our earliest surviving written biblical text (the Priestly Benediction of Numbers 6:24–26, written on two thin strips of silver, discovered in a tomb near Jerusalem).

The Persian and Hellenistic Periods

The Persian period (539–333 BC) and the Hellenistic period (333–64 BC) were periods of large empire building. While the southern Levant exhibited some regionalism, culturally and archaeologically it mirrored the material culture of the larger Mediterranean Basin. During these two periods, ancient Palestine became a province of these empires, and evidence of these two cultures appears frequently in the archaeological record: hippodrome city plans; imports in pottery; and the manner of construction of temples, public buildings, and estates. In addition, this period has produced several inscriptions that are bilingual (Greek and Aramaic). Toward the end of the Hellenistic period in Palestine, a short period called the Maccabean period is well documented in the archaeological record.

Early Roman/Herodian

This period ran from 64 BC to AD 135. After the Maccabean period, King Herod the Great continued local Jewish rule over Palestine while also building cities in the tradition of Hellenistic (Greek) cities, called *polis*. He left his mark on the archaeological record with numerous building projects throughout the region. From this time period, in addition to the large administrative urban centers, archaeologists are now starting to excavate the numerous small villages and synagogues that dotted the Jewish countryside, thus providing us with a picture of the life of Jesus and his disciples.

An aqueduct built during the early Roman/Herodian period to carry water to Caesarea.

Biblical Archaeology and Faith

As mentioned above, biblical archaeology is a subset of the archaeology of the ancient Near East. While its original emphasis was to use archaeological finds to prove the Bible, it is now a multinational and multifaith discipline that seeks to reconstruct history using both archaeological and biblical data. The Bible is an edited work, and its focus is on the mighty acts of God. The Bible uses historical events to make theological statements, and its focus is not on writing a secular history, but on recording salvation history. Thus the biblical text is selective and does not provide data on all events of history. Likewise, the archaeological record is ambiguous and does not provide evidence for every event mentioned in the Bible. Hence there can never be a direct one-to-one correlation between text and artifact. Nonetheless, modern biblical archaeology has developed a wealth of information that can be used beneficially to provide helpful background for biblical studies.

What does archaeology have to do with faith? Archaeology helps to provide the historical and cultural context often needed for the proper interpretation of Scripture. Since the revelation of God's Word occurred in a particular time, place, and culture, a better understanding of that context will help us to gain a deeper knowledge of God's Word. The Bible is an Eastern, not a Western document—hence the roots of our faith are found in the soil and history of ancient Palestine. In addition, the Christian faith is based on historical events, and not mere philosophical or theological statements; therefore archaeology is a discipline that supports faith statements and helps to provide a fascinating and colorful historical background for the Scriptures that give us these faith statements.

A volunteer at the excavation of Gezer carefully brushes away the dirt from a significant piece of pottery. The analysis of pottery plays a central role in the archeological study of ancient cultures.

Are There Hidden Codes in the Bible?

For hundreds of years both Jews and Christians have been intrigued with the idea that the Bible might have some mysterious hidden code divinely implanted in the text, just waiting for the readers with the right insight to uncover it. Through the centuries numerous individuals and groups have claimed to have found hidden "codes" in the Bible. At the close of the twentieth century and into the beginning of the twenty-first, new code systems were supposedly "discovered" through the use of computer analysis. What are these codes about and do they have any validity?

Although numerous "code" systems have been proposed throughout the years, in general they can be synthesized down into three basic code systems: an Old Testament-era system (*atbash*), a New Testament-era system (*gematria*), and a modern, computer-era system (*equidistant letter sequencing*).

Atbash—an Alphabet Cryptogram

How the Atbash Code Works

Some people may have used the atbash code back in grade school without even knowing it. Atbash is a simple alphabetic cryptogram in which one uses the first letter of the alphabet to represent the last letter, the second

A lion from the "Procession Street" in ancient Babylon. Twice Jeremiah uses the Atbash Sheshach to refer to Babylon (25:26; 51:41).

letter to represent the next to the last letter, and so forth. In English, one would use *A* to represent *Z*, *B* to represent *Y*, *C* to represent *X*, and so on.

Biblical Examples of Atbash?

There is little doubt that Jeremiah uses atbash at least three times (25:26; 51:1; and 51:41). In Jeremiah 25:26 and 51:41, the prophet uses the term Sheshach in a context that clearly refers to Babel. Applying atbash to the Hebrew alphabet, the letter *shin* (sh), next to last in the alphabet, represents the letter *bet* (b), which is second in the alphabet, and so forth. Thus Sheshach as an atbash represents Babel. Another example is in Jeremiah 51:1, where the prophet proclaims judgment on Leb Kamai, an unknown place if interpreted literally, but if seen as an atbash it refers to Chaldea, another name for Babylonia.

Is the Atbash Code Valid?

Evidence of atbash being used in the ancient world goes back as early as 1200 BC. Most of the time when it occurs in the nonbiblical literature it is associated with children's or other students' educational exercises. Within the context of Jeremiah there is little doubt that the words Sheshach and Leb Kamai are references to Babylon and Chaldea, so we can be fairly certain that Jeremiah is using the atbash code. What is not clear is why. First of all, this code is so simple that it wouldn't have actually fooled anyone. So Jeremiah's motive cannot be to keep his prophecies secret from the Babylonians in order to keep safe. Furthermore, the book of Jeremiah is filled with prophecies against Babylon. In a book where he mentions Babylon frequently and openly, what is the point of coding or hiding three references? So why does Jeremiah use the atbash cryptogram? In all probability Jeremiah is being a little bit sarcastic. As the Israelites go into exile, they do probably enter a time where they had to be very cautious about saying anything against the conquering Babylonians. Perhaps they used "code" words when they spoke negatively against Babylon. Jeremiah, who openly proclaims the end of Babylon, probably uses these rather silly code words for Babylon with a touch of sarcasm. His message is probably something along the lines of "This great power Babylon—which frightened you so much that you used secret code words to speak against her—will be destroyed by God completely."

The use of atbash in the Bible is rare, and there is little convincing evidence that atbash is used in the Bible anywhere else than in the three texts mentioned above.

Gematria—a Numbers Cryptogram

How Gematria Works

The Hebrew language can use the letters of the alphabet to represent sounds in the spelling of words (i.e., the normal use of alphabet letters), but it can also use the letters to represent numbers. For example, *aleph*, the first letter in the Hebrew alphabet, can be used as a letter in a word, or it can represent the number 1. Likewise, *beth*, the second letter of the alphabet, can also stand for 2, and so forth up to the number 9. The next consecutive letters in the alphabet are used to stand for 10, 20, 30, and so on, up to 90, followed by letters representing 100 to 900, and so forth.

What gematria does is to suggest that the interconnection between the letters and the number value they represent is much deeper than that suggested above. That is, using the numerical value of the letters in regular words and by applying basic math (addition, subtraction, multiplication, division), the proponents of gematria find all kinds of new and hidden meanings in the words. For example, the Hebrew word for *father* is composed of the two letters *aleph* and *beth*. *Aleph* stands for 1 and *beth* stands for 2, so the sum of the word is 3. *Mother* is comprised by the letters *aleph* (1) and *mem* (40), the sum of the word equaling 41. The word for *child* has three letters—*yod* (10), *lamed* (30), and *dalet* (4), which equals 44. So *father* (3) plus *mother* (41) equals *child* (44). This is an example of a very simple use of gematria. In advanced discussions, it can be very complex and mystical (which is often the intention).

Biblical Examples of Gematria?

Gematria is used as an important interpretive approach to the Hebrew Bible (Old Testament) within certain Jewish mystical movements, primarily the movement known as Kabbalah. However, although using individual Hebrew letters to represent numbers was probably widespread by the first century AD, there is no firm evidence that the individual letters of the Hebrew alphabet were used to represent numbers during the time when the Old

Caesar Nero depicted on a Roman coin.

Testament was written. The conceptual system underlying gematria (that the writers would use individual letters to represent numbers) is not attested until well after the close of the Old Testament canon. Thus the many complex examples of gematria in the Old Testament proposed in the Kabbalah and rabbinic literature are highly unlikely.

Ironically, it is in the New Testament that we find the most likely candidate for gematria. It is well established that by the New Testament era, number cryptogram systems similar to gematria were in use throughout the Mediterranean world. Thus it was a literary tool that was readily available to the writers of the New Testament and it was a feature that readers in the first century would probably have recognized. Some New Testament scholars think that gematria provides our best interpretive approach to understanding Revelation 13:18, which reads: "This calls for wisdom. If anyone has insight, let him calculate the number of the beast, for it is man's number. His number is 666." These scholars note that the letters in the Hebrew equivalent of the name Nero Caesar add up to 666. But there is no consensus among scholars on this.

Is the Gematria Code Valid?

There is no doubt that gematria was being used by writers in the ancient world by the time of the New Testament (first century AD). So it is certainly plausible that John could use it as he wrote the book of Revelation. However, numbers in general play a significant symbolic role in the apocalyptic literary style of Revelation, so it is difficult to establish with certainty whether John is using gematria for the number 666 in Revelation 13:18 or just using standard apocalyptic symbolism. For the Old Testament, as mentioned above, it cannot be established that writers were even using individual letters to represent numbers in the Old Testament era, so it is doubtful that gematria was used by any of the authors in the Old Testament.

Equidistant Letter Sequencing: A Modern Bible Code

How the Equidistant Letter Sequencing (ELS) Code Works

This so-called Bible code works on the premise that there are names and predictions hidden in the biblical text. What "hides" them is that each letter of the name is separated from the next letter by a large number of other "spacer" letters (sometimes thousands of letters). Each letter of the name is equidistantly spaced by the same number of letters. Often one of the letters also intersects some regular word that helps to make the prediction.

This code was "discovered" at the end of the twentieth century through the use of computers. Usually the procedure is as follows. The operators take a certain portion of the Old Testament Hebrew text, usually the Pentateuch. Then they remove all spaces between words, creating a continuous stream of consecutive letters. Then they instruct the computer to search for a name or other word. First the computer looks at every other letter. Then it looks at every third letter, every fourth letter, every fifth letter, and so forth until it is looking at letters spaced thousands of letters apart. The computer then analyzes the new word possibilities that the equidistant letters can create and tries to find a "hit" or match against one of the words the operators are looking for.

A simple example might help to clarify how this works. Let's take a short three-letter word like *cat* and search through a small portion of text (Num. 4:3), looking for an equidistant letter spacing for *cat*. Does Numbers 4:3 contain the hidden word cat? Here is the text:

Cats were important in Egypt, both as pets and as symbols of deities. But there is not a hidden code reference to cats in Num. 4:3.

> Count all the men from thirty to fifty years of age who come to serve in the work in the Tent of Meeting. (Num. 4:3)

The first step is to remove all of the spaces between the words. Thus we have:

> Countallthemenfromthirtytofiftyyearsofagewhocometoser veintheworkinthetentofmeeting

Next we want to look at every other letter, then every third letter, fourth letter, and so on, until we find *cat*. If we persist long enough, we can indeed find the word *cat,* with each letter in *cat* separated from the next by a 32-letter spacing! We have shown the results below with the *cat* letters in bold. Starting with the *c* in *count*, skip over 32 letters and arrive at *a* in *years*, followed by a 32-letter skip to *t* in *the*.

> **C**ountallthemenfromthirtytofiftyye**A**rsofagewhocometoservein theworkin**T**hetentofmeeting.

Obviously three-letter words are easy to find and we could find "cat" in hundreds, if not thousands of locations in the Old Testament. Longer words are much more difficult to find. However, if one has enough text and a computer program to carry out the search, often even very long names can be found.

Biblical Examples of the ELS Bible Code?

One of the more famous examples that was used to popularize this Bible code at the end of the twentieth century centered on the name of a former Israeli Prime Minister, Yitzhak Rabin, who had been assassinated. The ELS advocates tried to prove that the Bible had predicted (in hidden code) the assassination of Yitzhak Rabin thousands of years in advance. Here is what they did. They had their computer search throughout the Pentateuch until it located the twelve-letter name of Yitzhak Rabin and with an equidistant spacing for each of the twelve letters. The sequence started in Deuteronomy 2:33, with the first letter of Yitzhak Rabin. The computer then skipped the next 4,722 letters to find the next letter in his name in Deuteronomy 4:42, followed by another skip of 4,722 letters to Deuteronomy 7:20, and so forth, skipping 4,722 letters each time until reaching the last letter in Deuteronomy 24:16. Those who were arguing for the validity of this approach pointed out that the second letter of Yitzhak Rabin's name is part of Deuteronomy 4:42. This verse, it was claimed, contains the phrase "the assassin will assassinate" (although this translation is rather puzzling; most English translations do not translate the verse in this manner). According to the proponents of this code, the intersection of the name Yitzhak Rabin with the verse about "assassination" was a prediction of the assassination of the prime minister thousands of years before it happened. Many ELS proponents claimed that the ELS code also contained predictions of dozens of other significant modern people and events, including President Clinton, Watergate, the 1929 stock market crash, the Apollo moon landings, Adolph Hitler, Thomas Edison, the Wright brothers, and numerous others.

Is the ELS Bible Code Valid?

Bible scholars and statisticians alike have overwhelmingly rejected the validity of the ELS Bible code. Bible scholars point out that the actual number of letters in the Hebrew Bible was constantly changing as grammar and spelling changed over the years. If one is searching for hidden words with letters separated by thousands of other letters, the insertion of one different letter in a spelling variation will throw off the sequence. The spelling of *Jerusalem*, for example, varies in the Old Testament and apparently underwent some spelling variations over time. So which spelling contains the hidden ELS codes? Also, newer editions of the Hebrew Bible that reflect the findings of the Dead Sea Scrolls differ in numerous small ways from editions of the Hebrew Bible that were printed at the beginning of the twentieth century. The differences are largely insignificant as far as meaning goes, but they are highly significant if one is counting letter spacings across spans of thousands of letters. Most of the "spectacular" ELS results that were paraded out as proof of the method were taken from computer analysis of a Hebrew Bible that was being printed in the early twentieth century and not the Hebrew Bible that scholars read and study today. The Yitzhak Rabin example cited above works only on that one particular edition of the Hebrew Bible; it doesn't work on older manuscripts, nor does it work on modern editions.

Even though the proponents of the ELS Bible code argue to the contrary, numerous books and review articles have pointed out that the ELS code fails statistically as well. The sheer number (hundreds of thousands) of letters in the Hebrew Bible (and even in the Pentateuch), along with the numerous variations in which ELS searches and counts, makes it a high statistical probability that even twelve-letter names like Yitzhak Rabin will be found and will also intersect a context that can be loosely connected in one way or the other into some sort of "prediction." One set of scholars ran ELS tests in English on the novel *Moby Dick*. They also found numerous hidden "names" and "predictions" of assassinations and the like. This is very strong evidence that the ELS Bible code is not at all a code placed in the Bible by God, but rather a statistical oddity, fueled by a modern infatuation with computers and hidden knowledge.

Responding to Contemporary Challenges to the Gospels

Darrell L. Bock

The Gospels are often under attack by skeptics as not reflecting histori-cal reality. These challenges take many forms. Here we tackle five such prominent issues. We do not take them in any prioritized order. Each area is important in its own way.

Authorship Issues

It is often suggested that the Gospels are not written by the people whose names are traditionally attached to them. Now it is true that none of the Gospels names its author internally. Unlike Paul's letters, where the apostle identifies himself, these works are anonymous. So the question becomes whether the tradition of the church in the first few centuries can be trusted with identifications of the authors they set forth. These issues are much discussed among scholars; some are comfortable with the traditional authors, and others question the tradition at this point. Determining authorship for these works involves a discussion between internal features pointing to a specific author versus what tradition says about authorship. I am going to discuss as examples the two books that are not connected to apostles—Mark and Luke. It is important to remember that the common argument of those who question these identifications is that the church selected (creatively identified) an author to increase the credibility of a work and cause it to be accepted. They did this by attributing the work to an apostle or one close to an apostle. Does such an argument work?

Let's start with Luke. The basis for identifying Luke is tied to the "we" sections in Acts (16:10–17; 20:5–15; 21:8–18; 27:1–28:16). If these identify someone present with Paul at certain points (something the early church accepted), then we know the author was a sometime companion of Paul. It is important to note that these units are rather randomly distributed throughout Acts. If they were created to give the impression of the author being present at some events (as some skeptics claim), then why do they not appear at many of the key events of the book (something that might be expected if they were made up for the mere purpose of enhancing credibility)? Their randomness has the appearance of real notes about presence, not to make an apologetic point. All that the "we" tells us is that the person was sometimes with Paul. The list of possible candidates here is long: Barnabas, Timothy, Titus, Apollos, Mark, Silas, and Epaphras, among others. So just knowing the "we" does not give us a specific author. Yet the tradition we have unanimously identifies Luke as this figure. Luke is noted rather briefly in Colossians 4:14, 2 Timothy 4:11, and Philemon 24. These references show that Luke is not the first Pauline companion to leap to mind in making a prominent association with Paul. So why is the tradition so uniform? If the goal were to create a credible link for the book to enhance its reputation, Luke is not the name one would select out of the Pauline hat! Yet there he is, stubbornly and consistently present. The best explanation for this evidence is that Luke was in the tradition because the church knew the identity of this otherwise somewhat obscure figure. If Luke is the author, he tells us he did not directly experience some of what he reports. He relied on the tradition of the church and the reports of others he knew (Luke 1:1–12).

What about Mark? The tradition of the early centuries consistently portrays Mark as having taken Peter's reports about Jesus and placed them in his gospel. Two things about this are interesting. First, the church, despite the association with Peter, never called this gospel the Gospel of Peter. This seems to indicate the church was careful about who it identified as an author in the tradition. If giving a work credibility was the point, then Peter would have become the author to tie this gospel to, but it never happened. Second, Mark hardly qualifies as a prominent and respected figure to name in this gospel-enhancing role. Here is what tradition tells us about Mark. He went home after failing to persevere during Paul and Barnabas's first missionary journey (Acts 15:37–38). The following verses in Acts 15:39–40 also note that Mark caused a disagreement and split between Barnabas and Paul, because Paul did not want to take him along a second time after he left them the first time. This is hardly a great set of credentials to enhance a gospel. And yet, there is Mark, consistently said to be the author of the second Gospel. Why is the tradition so stubborn here as well? The likely explanation is the church knew something about this authorship. Our tradition tied to these identifications reaches back to a figure named Papias and what he taught in the late first century, even though his testimony comes to us through the early fourth-century church historian Eusebius.

These examples show us there is reason to regard the tradition with respect on the issue of the identification of these authors. If the authors of these works are apostles or those who worked closely with them, then we are in touch with the living voice of those who walked with Jesus, people able to give us a direct glimpse of him and his teaching.

Oral Tradition

The Jesus stories originally circulated orally. Often this is portrayed as allowing a great deal of freedom for how the material came to be developed. The picture is of the "telephone game," where a story or joke starts at the front of a line of people and is passed on one person at a time until at the end the final story or joke differs from what began the chain. This illustration has a variety of problems in serving as an analogy for what happened in the church. First, we do not live in an oral culture that is used to passing on stories in an oral manner. We write or record our stories. Second, this model ignores the role of the apostles in carrying the tradition. Luke 1:1–2 notes how those who orally passed on these accounts were both eyewitnesses and ministers of the Word. Judaism had a way of passing on material. Third, our own Gospels are a deposit of this oral process in written form. They show that the gist of these stories remains consistent. There are slight variations (and we shall discuss these shortly), but the core story is consistent, so we see an oral process that has some fluidity but that also has a stable core.

When I discuss this topic with people, I like to let my grandson make the point for me. My grandson is four years old. He lives in an oral world. He does not yet read or write. So all that he processes, he does orally. As his grandfather, I get to read to him (or watch his mother and father do it). There is a phenomenon I observe when I play around and change the story he is familiar with; he complains that this is not the story! So my point is that there are kinds of orality, and that the controls and natural instincts of popular oral accounts lead to a more conservative kind of orality than the free-flow view suggests.

Differences between Accounts and Wording of Utterances

It does not take long to read the Gospels and see that events appear in different order, often with slightly different wording, and with different details added by each author. My book *Jesus according to Scripture* covers these differences in some detail. Here are some things to keep in mind about these differences.

1. Jesus had an itinerant ministry, so he traveled around and taught. This means he surely taught the same kinds of things in different locales, possibly with minor differences. I travel and teach as well. I often have given the same message a dozen times. I change it up now and again, in part to keep it fresh. So some differences are the result of different versions of the same kind of teaching, perhaps including even distinct traditions with the same kind of teaching.
2. The Gospel writers have different concerns for different audiences. For example, Matthew is writing to a Jewish audience that differs from the more gentile audience of Mark and Luke. So when Matthew presents the Sermon on the Mount, he presents detailed treatments of issues tied to the oral tradition and the law that Luke lacks in his Sermon on the Plain. Such issues would be irrelevant to Luke's audience, so he omits them.
3. Different wording of sayings often appears. Usually the gist of these sayings is the same, but the expression differs slightly. This even happens in parallel points in the same event, showing that inspiration has room for such flexibility. For example, in Mark and Luke the voice from heaven says to Jesus, "You are my Beloved Son in whom I am well pleased," while Matthew has "This is my Beloved Son, with him I am well pleased." It is likely here that Matthew has presented the significance of this utterance made directly to Jesus. This has been called the difference between the *ipsissima verba* (the very words) of an utterance and the *ipsissima vox* (the very voice) of an utterance. Interestingly, we often see similar kinds of wording differences in the way the Old Testament is cited in the New Testament. So utterances are not the only area where Scripture often paraphrases itself.

4. Sometimes a Gospel writer will collapse details and simplify the story. For example, in the healing of the centurion's slave, Matthew has the centurion speak directly to Jesus, while Luke has the details that Jewish emissaries spoke to Jesus on the centurion's behalf. Matthew has likely simplified the account. In the healing of Jairus's daughter, the daughter dies in the middle of the account in Luke, while Matthew introduces the daughter as dead at the account's start. Again Matthew is simplifying the story. Both accounts share the point that Jesus raised a girl who was dead when he got there. Sometimes people complain about doing such "harmonizing," but these differences show there was no collusion in telling these stories, and doing this kind of reconciling is something that is often done when accounts differ in details. We often try to do this today, too. Just sit on a jury sometime and watch people try to make sense out of differing testimony about the same event.

5. Sometimes events are arranged topically, not chronologically. Mark 2:1–3:6 has five controversies, one after another. Matthew 8–12 has these same controversies spread across four chapters. Mark's grouping is surely topical. Luke 4:16–30 (Jesus in the synagogue in Nazareth) is likely thrown forward by Luke from its real location, since it appears in the middle of Mark and Matthew (Mark 6 and Matthew 13). Luke did this because this event typifies the Galilean ministry he is now describing. A second clue of a relocation (besides the relative location in each Gospel) is that the crowd asks Jesus to perform miracles like those he did in Capernaum, when Jesus has not yet been to Capernaum in Luke's Gospel.

6. Sometimes an evangelist fills in a detail left unaddressed in another Gospel. For example, in Mark's version of the crucifixion Jesus cries out twice, once citing Psalm 22:1 and the second time with no specific utterance. In Luke, at the very location of the second outcry Luke notes Jesus uttered a word from Psalm 31:5.

These kinds of differences are valuable to keep an eye out for in Bible study. They are not surprises or causes for concern in reading about the events. They are indications that we are dealing with live traditions where there is multiple input and thus variations at points.

All Those Miracles

It is sometimes claimed that the miracles Jesus performed reflect nothing but a work written in a premodern age where miracles were commonplace.

Now sometimes this objection is an outright rejection that miracles happen. Anyone with a naturalistic worldview will have trouble with the miracles of the Bible, not only those of Jesus but of other biblical figures as well. They will try to present naturalistic explanations for the stories we see. Such objections involve people's worldview and are suppositional. There is little one can do with such a view other than to challenge it as being closed to God's possible work in the world.

However there is another, more substantive and subtle challenge to miracles. If we accept miracles from Jesus, it is argued, then we need to accept such claims from others in the ancient world. This view oversimplifies the record we have. First, although it is true such miracles are claimed for others, part of what makes Jesus unusual is the scope of the miracles he performed. Vespasian is said to have healed someone. Caesar is said to have calmed a storm. Jewish wise men performed a miracle here and there. None of them did the range of miracles Jesus is said to have performed. The only exception here is a Greek hero known as Aesclypius, but the dates tied to traditions associated with him are later than the time of Jesus, so he is not really a parallel to Jesus. Second, the way Jesus heals is different. The Jewish wise man who calms the storm prays for God to calm the storm, and God is said to have responded. Jesus calms the storm by addressing it directly. Jesus's authority to perform miracles differs from the use of magic formulas or prayers that other miracle workers use.

Third, even Josephus, a Jewish historian of the first century, noted that Jesus performed "unusual" works (*Ant.* 18.63–64). This is important, because Josephus represents the "opposition" tradition to Jesus and they do not claim he did not do such works. In fact, our writings from the Bible through the church father Justin Martyr, to the rabbis' own Talmud, show that Jews attributed the power Jesus had to demons, meaning ironically enough that they recognized Jesus did do unusual things, they just attributed them to a different source. These factors should lead us to take the claims of miracles tied to Jesus seriously.

Those Other Gospels

Often one hears about a host of other gospels that tell us other stuff about Jesus. Most of these works come from the second or third century. Often they are associated with the significant finds of text that surfaced from Nag Hammadi, Egypt, in 1946. Most of these gospels are too late to put us in touch with the living voice of those who knew Jesus or to be written by the authors they claim as their writers. Many of these works belong to an approach to

Christianity that emerged in the second century known as gnostic Christianity. This form of theology tried to combine Christian symbolism with Neo-Platonic dualism, a Greek philosophical movement that claimed (1) matter was evil and only the spirit was good, and (2) as a result, creation was flawed from the beginning, and God did not create the creation but underling gods did. We can see this story of creation in a work like the *Apocalypse of John*. Sometimes the claim is also made that these gospels are newly known. However, this claim is exaggerated. When the texts of Nag Hammadi were discovered, as scholars read the *Apocalypse of John* they recognized the story of creation there because Irenaeus in the late second century told us this story when he described gnostic Christian theology. So we have known about this kind of teaching and even the content of some of the key works for about 1,800 years. We know that these views of creation and evil cannot be traced back to Jesus. This is because Jesus and the disciples held to the views of the Hebrew Scripture (what we call the Old Testament). The Hebrew Scripture taught in Genesis and the Psalms that God was the Creator (not underling gods) and that this creation was good at the start. So many of these new gospels tell us about these newly emerging movements of the second and third century but do not go back to the first-century time of Jesus.

The most prominent of these new gospels is called *The Gospel of Thomas*. In fact, this work is not a gospel at all in the sense we think of it. It is simply a collection of 114 alleged sayings of Jesus. Its date is debated. Some like to put it as early as the mid-first century, but this is a decidedly minority position. Most place it in the early second century. Still others have made a case for its origin in the late second century. What makes for this debate is that the sayings give indications of a variety of origins. Some (about a quarter of the whole) read like material in our four Gospels. Another quarter of the material reads like something close to our Gospels. The remaining half is material distinct from our Gospels. So it appears that *Thomas* has a hybrid and varied set of sources. This is why this gospel has generated so much discussion. It is not as gnostic as other works I noted, lacking a creation story. Yet there are some sayings that appear gnostic. The work seems to have material that has some roots in the traditions that fed our four Gospels, but more important, it also gives evidence of accepting material from sources the church rejected. Origen reports that *Thomas* was not read in the churches, a sign of its rejection in the early third century.

So for all the fascination these other gospels have generated, there is nothing in them that shows us they reflect as a whole the theology of the earliest disciples. Much of what they show indicates they are the product of views that developed long after the time of Jesus, with views that Jesus and his followers, as good Jews, would never have held. The exception to this is

Thomas. However, even in its case the book gives evidence of a theology not reflective of Jesus's teaching. For example, in a famous saying (114), Jesus says symbolically the only way females can enter into heaven is if Jesus makes them male. Interpreters who defend this reading argue it is only a way of picturing reconciliation in the end that gives us all equal status, but it does so only by eliminating one of the genders God was said in Genesis to have created as a reflection of the divine image. The incongruence shows *Thomas* is not a part of a theology that embraced a positive view of the creation, something the earliest Christians would have believed.

Conclusion

We have only briefly been able to survey some of the contemporary challenges to the Gospels. The Gospels have solid roots in the living voice of the earliest Christian generation. They can be trusted to give us solid access to Jesus and his teaching. For other issues and details involving specific passages, the use of a solid commentary on the Gospels that respects the apostolic roots of the Bible can be helpful. Commentary series like the Baker Exegetical Commentary on the New Testament and the Pillar New Testament Commentary are accessible to people without technical background.

About the Photos, Illustrations, Maps, and Artwork

Unless otherwise indicated, photos, illustrations, and maps are copyright © Baker Photo Archive.

Additional Baker Photo Archive Permissions

Photos on pages 46, 48, 94, 98, 115, 120, 132, 150, 166, 177, 181, 190, 191, 195, 199, 206, 222, 226, 233, 234, 242, 246, 249, 256, 258, 274, 276, 282, 287, 288, 289, 290, 298, 299, 304, 306, 307, 311, 312, 316, 319, 320, 321, 322, 324, 327, 328, 331, 343, 365, 367, 369, 374, 378, 995, and 999 are copyright © Baker Photo Archive. The British Museum, London, England.

Photos on pages 67, 1008, and 1111 are copyright © Baker Photo Archive. The Cairo Museum, Egyptian Ministry of Antiquities.

Photos on pages 86, 186, 229, 237, 240, 266, 291, 342, 350, 354, 434, and 1081 are copyright © Baker Photo Archive. Musée du Louvre; Autorisation de photographer et de filmer—LOUVRE, Paris, France.

Photo on page 111 is copyright © Baker Photo Archive. The Skirball Museum, Hebrew Union College—Jewish Institute of Religion, 13 King David Street, Jerusalem 94101.

Photos on pages 152 and 153 are copyright © Baker Photo Archive. Archaeological Museum of Hatzor, Israel.

Photos on pages 205, 219, 294, and 1032 are copyright © Baker Photo Archive. The Archaeological Museum of Istanbul, Turkish Ministry of Antiquities.

Photos on pages 313 and 319 are copyright © Baker Photo Archive. Eretz Israel Museum, Tel Aviv, Israel.

Photo on page 341 is copyright © Baker Photo Archive. The Oriental Institute of the University of Chicago.

Photo on page 1000 is copyright © Baker Photo Archive. The Archaeological Museum of Selçuk, Turkish Ministry of Antiquities.

Photos on pages 1019, 1049, 1051, and 1052 are copyright © Baker Photo Archive. Sola Scriptura—the Van Kampen Collection, on display at the Holy Land Experience, Orlando, Florida.

Photo on page 1131 is copyright © Baker Photo Archive. The Ismailia Museum, Egyptian Ministry of Antiquities.

Photo on page 1038 is copyright © Baker Photo Archive. The Amman Archaeological Museum, Jordanian Minstry of Antiquities.

Additional Image Permissions

Image on pages 41–42 is copyright © BigStockPhoto/David5962.

Photo on page 43 is copyright © Radoslaw Drożdżewski.

Image on page 45 is copyright © Cameraphoto Arte, Venice/Art Resource, NY.

Images on pages 53 and 76 are copyright © Bildarchiv Preussischer Kulturbesitz/Art Resource, NY.

Image on page 55 is copyright © Scala/Art Resource, NY.

Photos on pages 93, 107, 193, 267, 348, 457, 615, 1015, and 1041 are copyright © Dr. James C. Martin. Collection of the Israel Museum, Jerusalem, and courtesy of the Israel Antiquities Authority, exhibited at the Israel Museum, Jerusalem.

Images on pages 116 and 346 are copyright © Erich Lessing/Art Resource, NY.

Image on page 174 is copyright © Réunion des Musées Nationaux/Art Resource, NY.

Images on pages 228 and 368 are copyright © Werner Forman/Art Resource, NY.

Image on page 244 is copyright © SEF/Art Resource, NY.

Photo on page 257 is copyright © Ziemor/pl.wikimedia.

Photo on page 259 is copyright © Sascha Wenninger.

Photo on page 261 is copyright © Direct Design.

Image on page 323 is copyright © National Trust Photo Library/Art Resource, NY.

Image on page 359 is copyright © The Trustees of the British Museum/Art Resource, NY.

Photo on page 368 is copyright © Dynamosquito/Flickr.

Image on page 379 is copyright © The Metropolitan Museum of Art/Art Resource, NY.

Image on page 445 appears courtesy of Ken Ramsey.

Image on page 534 is copyright © 2008 Karbel Multimedia, Logos Bible Software.

Photos on page 611 are copyright © Classical Numismatic Group, Inc.

Photo on page 681 is copyright © Marion Doss/Wikimedia.

Photo on page 686 is copyright © Zehnfinger/de.wikimedia.

Photo on page 774 is copyright © by Dantadd/Wikimedia.

Photo on page 783 is copyright © Marie-Lan Nguyen/Wikimedia.

Photo on page 787 is copyright © Claus Ableiter/Wikimedia.

Photo on page 798 is copyright © Dan Diffendale/Wikimedia.

Photo on page 866 is copyright © Nevit Dilmen/Wikimedia.

Photo on page 889 is copyright © David Monniaux/Wikimedia.

Photo on page 928 is copyright © Ealdgyth/Wikimedia.

Photos on page 982 are copyright © Classical Numismatic Group, Inc.